LITTLE, BROWN AND COMPANY

Law School Casebook Series

Federal Income Taxation: Cases, Problems, Notes. WILLIAM D. ANDREWS, Professor of law, Harvard University

Antitrust Analysis: Problems, Text, Cases. PHILLIP AREEDA, Professor of Law, Harvard University

Land Transfer and Finance. ALLAN AXELROD, Professor of Law, Rutgers University, CURTIS J. BERGER, Professor of Law, Columbia University, and QUINTIN JOHNSTONE, Justus S. Hotchkiss Professor of Law, Yale University

Land Ownership and Use: Cases, Statutes, and Other Materials. CURTIS J. BERGER, Professor of Law, Columbia University

International Law: Cases and Materials. Third Edition. WILLIAM W. BISHOP, JR., Edwin M. Dickinson Professor of Law, University of Michigan

Federal Income, Estate and Gift Taxation. Fourth Edition. BORIS I. BITTKER, Southmayd Professor of Law, Yale University, and LAWRENCE M. STONE, Professor of Law, University of California at Berkeley

Materials on Reorganization, Recapitalization and Insolvency. WALTER J. BLUM, Professor of Law, University of Chicago, and STANLEY A. KAPLAN, Professor of Law, University of Chicago

Civil Procedure: Cases and Comments on the Process of Adjudication. PAUL D. CARRINGTON, Professor of Law, University of Michigan

Estate Planning. Third Edition. A. JAMES CASNER, Weld Professor of Law, Harvard University

Cases and Text on Property. Second Edition. A. JAMES CASNER, Weld Professor of Law, Harvard University, and W. BARTON LEACH, Story Professor of Law, Emeritus, Harvard University

International Legal Process. ABRAM CHAYES, Professor of Law, Harvard University, THOMAS EHRLICH, Professor of Law, Stanford University, and ANDREAS F. LOWENFELD, Professor of Law, New York University

Cases and Materials on Debtor and Creditor. VERN COUNTRYMAN, Professor of Law, Harvard University

The Lawyer in Modern Society. VERN COUNTRYMAN, Professor of Law, Harvard University, and TED FINMAN, Professor of Law, University of Wisconsin

Commercial Law: Cases and Materials. VERN COUNTRYMAN, Professor of Law, Harvard University, and ANDREW L. KAUFMAN, Professor of Law, Harvard University

Law, Medicine and Forensic Science. WILLIAM J. CURRAN, Frances Glessner Lee Professor of Legal Medicine, Harvard Medical School, Harvard School of Public Health, and E. DONALD SHAPIRO, Adjunct Professor of Law, New York University

Family Wealth Transactions. JESSE DUKEMINIER, Professor of Law, University of California at Los Angeles, and STANLEY M. JOHANSON, Professor of Law, University of Texas

Political and Civil Rights in the United States. Third Edition. THOMAS I. EMERSON, Lines Professor of Law, Yale University, DAVID HABER, Professor of Law, Rutgers University, and NORMAN DORSEN, Professor of Law and Director, Arthur Garfield Hays Civil Liberties Program, New York University

Cases and Materials on Family Law. CALEB FOOTE, Professor of Law and Criminology, University of California at Berkeley, ROBERT J. LEVY, Professor of Law, University of Minnesota, and FRANK E. A. SANDER, Professor of Law, Harvard University

Constitutional Law: Cases and Other Problems. Third Edition. PAUL A. FREUND, Carl M. Loeb University Professor, Harvard University, ARTHUR E. SUTHERLAND, Bussey Professor of Law, Emeritus, Harvard University, MARK DE WOLFE HOWE, late Charles Warren Professor of American Legal History, Harvard University, and ERNEST J. BROWN, Langdell Professor of Law, Harvard University

Cases and Materials on Corporations. ALEXANDER H. FREY, Algernon Sidney Biddle Professor of Law, Emeritus, University of Pennsylvania, C. ROBERT MORRIS, JR., Professor of Law, University of Minnesota, and JESSE CHOPER, Professor of Law, University of California at Berkeley

Cases and Materials on Torts. Second Edition. CHARLES O. GREGORY, John B. Minor Professor of Law, Emeritus, University of Virginia, and HARRY KALVEN, JR., Professor of Law, University of Chicago

Land-Use Planning: A Casebook on the Use, Misuse, and Re-use of Urban Land. Second Edition. CHARLES M. HAAR, Professor of Law, Harvard University

Administrative Law: Cases and Materials. Third Edition. LOUIS L. JAFFE, Byrne Professor of Administrative Law, Harvard University, and NATHANIEL L. NATHANSON, Frederic P. Vose Professor of Law, Northwestern University

Criminal Law and Its Processes: Cases and Materials. Second Edition. SANFORD H. KADISH, Professor of Law, University of California at Berkeley, and MONRAD G. PAULSEN, Dean and John B. Minor Professor of Law, University of Virginia

Constitutional Law: Cases and Materials. Fourth Edition. PAUL G. KAUPER, Henry M. Butzel Professor of Law, University of Michigan

Contracts: Cases and Materials. Second Edition. FRIEDRICH KESSLER, Professor of Law, University of California at Berkeley, and GRANT GILMORE, Harry A. Bigelow Professor of Law, University of Chicago

Basic Business Associations: Cases, Text and Problems. ELVIN R. LATTY, Dean Emeritus and William R. Perkins Professor of Law, Duke University, and GEORGE T. FRAMPTON, Professor of Law and Vice-Chancellor for Campus Affairs, University of Illinois

Cases and Text on the Law of Wills. Second Edition, 1960 Revision. W. BARTON LEACH, Story Professor of Law, Emeritus, Harvard University

Labor Law: Cases, Materials, and Problems. BERNARD D. MELTZER, Professor of Law, University of Chicago

Commercial Transactions: Cases and Materials. SOIA MENTSCHIKOFF, Professor of Law, University of Chicago

Family Law: Cases and Materials. Second Edition. MORRIS PLOSCOWE, Adjunct Professor of Law, New York University, and HENRY H. FOSTER, JR., Professor of Law, New York University and DORIS JONAS FREED, of the New York and Maryland Bars

State and Local Government Law. SHO SATO, Professor of Law, University of California at Berkeley, and ARVO VAN ALSTYNE, Professor of Law, University of Utah

Problems and Materials on Decedents' Estates and Trusts. EUGENE F. SCOLES, Dean and Professor of Law, University of Oregon, and EDWARD C. HALBACH, JR., Dean and Professor of Law, University of California at Berkeley

Cases and Other Materials on Civil Procedure. AUSTIN WAKEMAN SCOTT, Dane Professor of Law, Emeritus, Harvard University, and ROBERT B. KENT, Professor of Law, Boston University

Select Cases and Other Authorities on the Law of Trusts. AUSTIN WAKEMAN SCOTT, Dane Professor of Law, Emeritus, Harvard University, and AUSTIN WAKEMAN SCOTT, JR., late Professor of Law, University of Colorado

The Civil Law System: Cases and Materials for the Comparative Study of Law. ARTHUR TAYLOR VON MEHREN, Professor of Law, Harvard University

The Law of Multistate Problems: Cases and Materials on Conflict of Laws. ARTHUR TAYLOR VON MEHREN, Professor of Law, Harvard University, and DONALD THEODORE TRAUTMAN, Professor of Law, Harvard University

Labor Relations and the Law. Third Edition. THE LABOR LAW GROUP TRUST Under the Editorship of JERRE WILLIAMS, Rex G. and Edna Heflin Baker Professor of Constitutional Law, University of Texas, and Others

Federal Income Taxation of Business Enterprise. BERNARD WOLFMAN, Dean and Professor of Law, University of Pennsylvania

Law School Textbook Series

Public Law Perspectives on a Private Law Problem: Auto Compensation Plans. WALTER J. BLUM, Professor of Law, University of Chicago, and HARRY KALVEN, JR., Professor of Law, University of Chicago

American Civil Procedure. WILLIAM WIRT BLUME, Professor of Law, University of California, Hastings College of Law

Readings in Jurisprudence and Legal Philosophy. MORRIS R. COHEN, late Professor of Law, City College of New York, and FELIX S. COHEN, late Visiting Professor of Law, City College of New York, and Visiting Lecturer, Yale University

Handbook of Modern Equity. Second Edition. WILLIAM Q. DE FUNIAK, Visiting Professor of Law, McGeorge School of Law, University of the Pacific

The Fundamentals of Legal Drafting. F. REED DICKERSON, Professor of Law, University of Indiana (Bloomington)

The Growth of American Law: The Law Makers. JAMES WILLARD HURST, Vilas Professor of Law, University of Wisconsin

Judicial Control of Administrative Action. Abridged Student Edition. LOUIS L. JAFFE, Byrne Professor of Administrative Law, Harvard University

Civil Procedure. FLEMING JAMES, JR., Sterling Professor of Law, Yale University

Trial Tactics and Methods. ROBERT E. KEETON, Professor of Law, Harvard University

Securities Regulation. Student Edition. LOUIS LOSS, William Nelson Cromwell Professor of Law, Harvard University

A Concise History of the Common Law. Fifth Edition. THEODORE F. T. PLUCKNETT, Late Professor of Legal History in the University of London

Effective Legal Research. Third Edition. MILES O. PRICE, late Professor of Law and Law Librarian, Columbia University, and HARRY BITNER, Professor of Law and Law Librarian, Cornell University

Scott's Abridgment of The Law of Trusts. AUSTIN WAKEMAN SCOTT, Dane Professor of Law, Emeritus, Harvard University

Handbook of Law Study. FERDINAND FAIRFAX STONE, W. R. Irby Professor of Law and Director of Institute of Comparative Law, Tulane University

FAMILY WEALTH TRANSACTIONS: WILLS, TRUSTS, FUTURE INTERESTS, AND ESTATE PLANNING

Cases and Materials

JESSE DUKEMINIER, JR.

PROFESSOR OF LAW
UNIVERSITY OF CALIFORNIA, LOS ANGELES

STANLEY M. JOHANSON

PROFESSOR OF LAW
UNIVERSITY OF TEXAS

LAW SCHOOL CASEBOOK SERIES

LITTLE, BROWN AND COMPANY
BOSTON · TORONTO
1972

LIBRARY OF CONGRESS CATALOG CARD NO. 70–183982

S7-Y-I

FOURTH PRINTING, 1976

Acknowledgment of permission to reprint previously published material appears on pages xii–xv.

Published simultaneously in Canada by Little, Brown & Company (Canada) Limited

PRINTED IN THE UNITED STATES OF AMERICA

Preface

The field of wills, trusts, future interests, and estate planning is an enormous one — much too large for any one book or any one course to cover in depth. Yet there is a large measure of agreement that the field should be integrated, that the traditional dividing lines no longer make much sense, and that fewer curricular hours should be devoted to this area than have been traditionally allotted. The dilemma is: What should be excluded and what included?

We have chosen to reduce the breadth of coverage which the old courses had in order to enable us to penetrate some subjects in depth. We think the students would be short-changed intellectually by a survey course in this area, which did not from time to time require the student to dissect a problem painstakingly. Although we provide the student with basic information about practices, doctrines, and institutions relevant to the estates practitioner, we have tried to gather material that challenges the student's analytical and linguistic skills. We are trying to produce lawyers, as distinguished from persons who know rules of law. For the student who wants to learn more about the various areas that we touch upon, there are good modern treatises in this field which we frequently cite and which we hope students will read from time to time.

In order to produce a basic book in the field within manageable proportions and without too great a sacrifice in depth, we have deliberately excluded an intensive treatment of tax planning of family wealth and of trust administration. As for the former, this is an area for the specialist, which should be dealt with in a separate course covering income tax planning as well as estate tax planning. In this area there are already excellent books available. Our reasons for exclusion of trust administration are several. First, the law of trust administration is generally quite rational, and apart from tax and accounting problems is easier to learn from reading a text than most of the other law in the area of wealth transmission. We opted in favor of eliminating the easier material. Second, the general practitioner in the estates area is largely concerned with planning and drafting problems and estate administration, and not with trust administration. Third, we think a separate trust administration course, offering intensive training in modern income tax problems and principal and income problems, along with the traditional material on investments and trustee's duties, should be provided for the prospective specialist.

This book can be taught in its entirety in ninety classroom hours. However, both of us now teach sixty-hour courses. This has required each of us to eliminate certain topics from classroom coverage. Needless to say, we differ — as would any other two teachers in the country — as to which material should be eliminated. Indeed, in some years each of us has taught portions of the book not covered in the preceding year and skipped portions previously taught. We think the students suffered not a bit. Professor Herbert Schwartz of U.C.L.A. has taught Chapters 11 and 13 before Chapter 6 (on taxation) as he wanted his students to be familiar with the conceptual apparatus of estates before discussing taxation. In Chapter 9, on protection of the family, the teacher in a common law state may wish to skip or treat selectively the section on protection of the surviving spouse in community property states.

From our experience we believe the book has considerable flexibility as a teaching tool. We think it can fit into the curricular arrangements of most law schools, and we hope it will satisfy the needs of instructors to organize and teach materials in their own individual ways.

We find this area of the law intellectually exciting as well as dynamically developing. Because it is rooted in history, few areas of the law offer so splendid an opportunity to teach how rules grow and die, how doctrines are avoided by the invention of evasive techniques, how changes in society require concomitant changes in law — in short, to teach the process of legal change. With the swift changes in American society, with the astonishing increase in individual wealth in the last two decades, and with the development of new forms of wealth such as pension plans must come changes in the law of wealth transmission. This used to be law for the rich; now it is law for the common man.

On the horizon is another force which will bring changes in this law as well as possibly in the structure of the legal profession itself. In Heyer v. Flaig, 70 Cal. 2d 223, 74 Cal. Rptr. 225, 449 P.2d 161 (1969), a lawyer was held liable to the bereft intended beneficiaries for negligence in drafting a will, with the statute of limitations beginning to run from the date of the testator's death. This case is MacPherson v. Buick in the will-drafting field. Although its implications are far from clear, it almost certainly will trigger significant pressure from the bar to clean out the unexpected, the booby-traps, the irrational — which have long plagued wealth transmission.

In this book we deal with people, the quick as well as the dead. There is nothing like the death of a moneyed member of the family to show persons as they really are, virtuous or conniving, generous or grasping. Many a family has been torn apart by a botched-up will. Each case is a drama in human relationships — and the lawyer, as counselor, draftsman, or advocate, is an important figure in the dramatis personae. This is one reason the estates practitioner enjoys his work, and why we enjoy ours.

Jesse Dukeminier, Jr.
Stanley M. Johanson

June 1, 1972

Acknowledgments

I was blessed with four superb teachers in this field who were, in order of impact, W. Barton Leach, Ashbel G. Gulliver, Elias Clark, and Myres S. McDougal. One cannot be taught by giants — particularly by giants whose ideas clash and strike fire — and escape unmarked. Much that is good in this book is attributable to the influence of these remarkable men.

Several other persons have had a hand in the book and deserve acknowledgment. For four years Marjorie Johnson typed and retyped portions of the manuscript with skill and utmost devotion. I wish to thank her and her successor, Eleanor Pierce, for their excellent work. I also want to thank Fanny Rogers Gratz, a cherished friend whose ideas and subtle perceptions of reality have contributed much to my own way of thinking, and Dr. David Sanders, from whom I have profited immoderately in our many conversations about problems in this book.

Finally, I must acknowledge my great indebtedness to my mother and, were he alive, my father, to whom my work on this book is dedicated.

JESSE DUKEMINIER, JR.

I owe a debt of gratitude to a number of people who have contributed, in one way or another, to my collaboration in this endeavor. To Robert L. Fletcher, who sparked my interest in this area of the law. To John Richards, who made an inconspicuous but immeasurable contribution to my decision to enter law teaching.

To W. Barton Leach and A. James Casner, who made this field come alive for me, and from whom I find myself still learning. To Bill Gibson, who tested the book in the classroom and made criticisms and suggestions that strengthened the final product. To Page Keeton, under whose deanship at the University of Texas there has developed an atmosphere among faculty and students that is conducive to effective and enjoyable law teaching and writing.

The secretarial staff at the University of Texas, and Miss Gayle McCuiston in particular, have put in long hours on the manuscript, and I was materially aided by several research assistants, most notably Gordon Wise and Bill Allen.

Finally there is my wife, Gerrie, whose devotion and support have sustained me through this project, as well as through everything else I have done over the past fifteen years. To the extent that words can express my appreciation, I wish to dedicate my work on this book to Gerrie.

STANLEY M. JOHANSON

We wish to acknowledge the courteous permission extended by the following publishers, journals and authors, as indicated, to reprint excerpts from their works:

Albany Law Review: Rights to Stock Accretion Which Occur Prior to Testator's Death, 36:182 (1971).

Arno Press Inc.: Commercial Banks and their Trust Activities, Introduction by A. A. Berle, Arno Press edition 1969.

American Bar Association: Real Property, Probate and Trust Journal; Minimum Fee Schedules — Development and Utilization, a publication of the American Bar Association's Standing Committee on Economics of Law Practice; Wellman, Selected Aspects of Uniform Probate Code, 3:206-207 (1968); from vol. 5, Further Trends in Perpetuities, 333, 334-335, 342-345, Estate Distributions to Minors, 491-492, and Variation in Probate Practices and Their Effects on Fees, 506; American Bar Association Journal, Gerhart, A New Look at Estate Planning: The General Practitioner and Mr. Average, 50:1043 (1969).

American Journal of Comparative Law: Griffin, The About Turn: Soviet Law of Inheritance, 10:431 (1961).

The Bobbs-Merrill Company Inc.: The Modern Rule Against Perpetuities, by Robert Lynn, copyright 1966, by the Bobbs-Merrill Company Inc. Reprinted by permission all rights reserved.

Boston University Law Review 47:303 (1967), Mistake and Fraud in Wills — Part I: A Comparative Analysis of Existing Law, by James A. Henderson, Jr.

California Law Review and Fred B. Rothman & Co.: Stare Decisis and Rules of Construction in Wills and Trusts, by Edward C. Halbach, 52 California Law Review 921 (1964). Copyright ©, 1964, California Law Review, Inc., Reprinted by Permission.

Case Western Reserve Law Review, Downing, Duration and Indestructibility of Private Trusts, 16:350-391 *passim* (1965).

Charles Scribner's Sons: My United States, by Frederic Stimson.

Columbia Law Review: Trusts: Modification of Irrevocable Trusts Through Appointment of a Guardian for Unborn Heirs — Repudiation of Worthier Title Doctrine, 66:1552 (1966) and, Compulsory Removal of Cadaver Organs, 69:693 (1969).

Connecticut Law Review: Clark, The Recapture of Testamentary Substitutes to Preserve the Spouse's Elective Share: An Appraisal of Recent Statutory Reforms, 2:513, 543-545 (1970); Wellman, The Uniform Probate Code: Blueprint for Reform in the 70's, 2:453 (1970).

John Creedon, Some Uses of Life Insurance in Estate Planning, paper presented at Southwestern Legal Foundation Institute on Wills and Probate, May 1968, pp. 7-8.

Duke Law Journal: Cook, American Land Law Reform: Legal Co-ownership, Dower and Curtesy. Copyright 1960 Duke Law Journal. Reprinted by permission of the copyright holder and author. Original citation 1960 Duke Law Journal 485.

The Dunellen Company, Inc.: Death, Property and Lawyers, by Thomas L. Shaffer, 1970.

James F. Farr, An Estate Planner's Handbook, third edition, Little, Brown and Company, 1966, pp. 39, 40, 42-43.

Farrar, Straus & Giroux, Inc.: Masochism in Modern Man, by Theodor Reik, copyright © 1941.

Fireman's Fund American Insurance Companies and The Surety Association of America: Fidelity and Surety Rate Manual.

Foundation Press, Inc., and the authors: Leach and Logan, Cases and Text on Future Interests and Estate Planning, 1961.

Harcourt Brace Jovanovich, Inc.: "The Lawyers Know Too Much" from Smoke and Steel, copyright, 1920, by Harcourt Brace Jovanovich, Inc.; renewed, 1948, by Carl Sandburg. Reprinted by permission of the publishers. Excerpts from The American Economic Republic, © 1963 by Adolf A. Berle. Reprinted by permission of Harcourt Brace Jovanovich, Inc.

Harvard Law Review: Note, Ademption and the Testator's Intent, 74:741 (1961); Kales, General Powers and the Rule Against Perpetuities, 26:64 (1912); McDougal, Future Interests Restated: Tradition Versus Clarification and Reform, 55:1077 (1942). Copyright 1961 [1912, 1942, 1955] by The Harvard Law Review Association: Laufer, Flexible Restraints on Testamentary Freedom — A Report on Decedents' Family Maintenance Legislation, 69:277 (1955).

Illinois State Bar Association: Estates of Decedents, Minimum Fee Schedule, September 13, 1968.

Iowa Law Review: Fratcher, Powers and Duties of Guardians of Property, 45 Iowa L. Rev. 264 (1960); Note, Guardians Ad Litem, 45 Iowa L. Rev. 376 (1960).

Kansas Law Review: Haviland, Shall We Rebuild Our House of Probate? The Uniform Probate Code, 19:575 (1971).

Lawyers Co-operative Publishing Co.: 19 American Law Report 3d, 575, 1968.

Matthew Bender: Powell, Real Property. Copyright © 1970 by Matthew

Bender & Company, Inc., and reprinted with permission from Powell on Real Property.

Michigan Law Review: Browder, Construction, Reformation, and the Rule Against Perpetuities, 62:1-32 (Nov. 1963).

Minnesota Law Review: Dukeminier, Contingent Remainders and Executory Interest: A Requiem for the Distinction, 43:13 (1958).

The Mutual Life Insurance Company of New York: settlement option tables, Best's Settlement Option Manual, 1971.

National Bureau of Economic Research: Robert Lampman, The Share of Top Wealth-Holders in National Wealth, 1922-1956, p. 23.

New England Journal of Medicine: Anthropophagy: Swift Reprisal, 279:413 (1968).

New York Law Journal: Midonick & Bush, The Surrogate's Court As a Family Protector, Nov. 4, 1971, p. 1.

The New York Times: Manhattan Surrogates' Court Is Focus of Political Disputes, July 5, 1966, p. 1, col. 8. © 1966 by The New York Times Company. Reprinted by permission.

Norman F. Dacey, How to Avoid Probate, advertisement copy and forms.

Outerbridge & Dienstfrey: Homosexual Oppression and Liberation, by Dennis Altman, 38 (1971).

Playboy, The New Yorker, and Punch for permission to reproduce cartoons.

Praeger Publishers, Inc.: Grzybowski and Gsovski, Government, Law and Courts in the Soviet Union and Eastern Europe (1959).

Russell Sage Foundation: The Family and Inheritance, by Marvin B. Sussman, Judith N. Cates, and David T. Smith, Russell Sage Foundation, Publishers, New York, 1970.

Stanford Law Review: Note, Testamentary Capacity in a Nutshell: A Psychiatric Re-evaluation, 18:1119, 1123-1143 (1966).

Sweet & Maxwell Limited: Morris and Leach, The Rule Against Perpetuities, published by Stevens & Sons, 2d ed., 1962; R. E. Megarry's comment on Lucas V. Ham, 81 Law Quarterly Review 428 (1965), published by Stevens & Sons.

Syracuse Law Review: Fetters, Future Interests, 19:419, 428 (1967). All rights reserved.

Tate Gallery, reproduction of Soest's portrait of Henry Howard, Sixth Duke of Norfolk.

Tax Law Review: Eisenstein, The Rise and Decline of the Estate Tax, 11:223 (1956).

Texas Law Review and Fred B. Rothman & Co.: Johanson, Revocable Trusts and Community Property, 47:537 (1969).

Trusts and Estates: Polasky et al., Estate Planning for the Migrating Client, 101:876 (1962); Robert D. Ferguson, Some Hints on How to Grow Trust Business, 103 Trusts & Estates, 1097 11/64; Copyright 1964 Fiduciary Publishers, Inc., 461 Eighth Avenue, New York, New York 10001.

University of California: Table of Consanguinity, California Decedent Estate

Administration, vol. I, p. 805, 1971. Copyright © Regents of the University of California.

University of Chicago Law Review: Blum and Kalven, The Uneasy Case for Progressive Taxation, 19:501-504 (1952); Dunham, The Method, Process and Frequency of Wealth Transmission at Death, 30:248-264 (1963).

University of Michigan Journal of Law Reform: Mulder, Intestate Succession Under the Uniform Probate Code, 3 Prospectus 321.

University of Michigan Law School: MacDonald, Fraud on the Widow's Share, 1960; Simes, Public Policy and the Dead Hand, 1955.

Washington Law Review: Fletcher, Washington's Non-Intervention Executor — Starting Point for Probate Simplification, 41:33 (1966).

West Publishing Company: Atkinson, Wills, 2d ed., 1953; Lowndes and Kramer, Federal Estate and Gift Taxes, 2d ed., 1962; Simes, Future Interests, 2d ed., 1966; Simes and Smith, The Law of Future Interests, 2d ed., 1956.

Wonderland Music Company, Inc.: "Supercalifragilisticexpialidocious," Music by Richard M. Sherman & Robert B. Sherman. © 1963 Wonderland Music Company, Inc., Glendale, California 91202. Used by permission.

Yale Law Journal: Gulliver and Tilson, Classification of Gratuitous Transfers. Reprinted by permission of The Yale Law Journal Company and Fred B. Rothman & Company from The Yale Law Journal, vol. 51, pp. 2-5, 14.

Yale University Press: Man Adapting, by René Dubos, 1965.

Table of Contents

3. Administration of Estates

4. Intestacy: An Estate Plan by Operation of Law

5. Life Insurance, Social Security and Employee Benefits

PART III. CONSTRUCTION OF THE ESTATE PLAN: THE LAW OF WILLS, TRUSTS AND FUTURE INTERESTS

7. Formalities of Transfer: Wills

9. Restrictions on the Power of Disposition: Protection of the Family

10. Restrictions on the Power of Disposition: the Transferor, the Survivors, and Social Policy

11. Future Interests

12. Securing the Transferor's Intent: Lessons in Amphibology

13. Building Flexibility into the Estate Plan: Powers of Appointment

14. Gifts to Charity

15. The Duration of Family Settlements: The Rule Against Perpetuities and Related Rules

Appendices

Table of Cases

Principal cases are set in italics, while cases cited in the text and in the editors' footnotes are set in roman type. An asterisk following the name of a principal case indicates that the case was noted in the law reviews, and that case note citations are given at the end of the opinion.

Table of Citations to Internal Revenue Code of 1954

Table of Citations to Treasury Regulations

Table of Secondary Authorities

(See also the list of reference books on page 6.)

CHAPTER 1. THE WEALTH TRANSMISSION PROCESS

Books

Berle, The American Economic Republic (1963)	39, 48
Grzybowski, Soviet Legal Institutions (1962)	52
Gsovski, Soviet Civil Law (1948)	53
——— & Grzybowski, Government, Law and Courts in the Soviet Union and Eastern Europe (1959)	53
Kolko, Wealth and Power in America (1962)	37
Lampman, The Share of Top Wealth-Holders in National Wealth 1922-1956 (1962)	32, 37
Plucknett, A Concise History of the Common Law (5th ed. 1956)	7
Roady & Andersen, Professional Negligence (1960)	20
Scurlock, Retroactive Legislation Affecting Interests in Land (1953)	45
Shaffer, Death, Property and Lawyers (1970)	49
Shultz, The Taxation of Inheritance (1926)	51
Sussman, Cates & Smith, The Family and Inheritance (1970)	30, 37, 49
Wedgwood, The Economics of Inheritance (1929)	47

Law Review Articles

Blum & Kalven, The Uneasy Case for Progressive Taxation, 19 U. Chi. L. Rev. 417 (1952)	55
Bordwell, The Statute Law of Wills, 14 Iowa L. Rev. 172 (1929)	47
Brimmer, Inflation and Income Distribution in the United States, 55 Rev. Econ. & Stat. 37 (1971)	38
Cairns, The Explanatory Process in the Field of Inheritance, 20 Iowa L. Rev. 266 (1935)	8
Chroust, Estate Planning in Hellenic Antiquity: Aristotle's Last Will and Testament, 45 Notre Dame Law. 629 (1970)	46
Dunham, The Method, Process and Frequency of Wealth Transmission at Death, 30 U. Chi. L. Rev. 241 (1963)	33

Law Review Comments, Notes

Chapter 2. An Estate Planning Problem

Books

Law Review Comments, Notes

Chapter 3. Administration of Estates

Books

Law Review Articles

Law Review Comments, Notes

Chapter 4. Intestacy: An Estate Plan by Operation of Law

Books

Law Review Articles

Law Review Comments, Notes

Chapter 5. Life Insurance, Social Security and Employee Benefits

Books

Law Review Articles

Law Review Comments, Notes

Chapter 6. The Federal Estate and Gift Taxes and State Succession Taxes

Books

Law Review Articles

Law Review Comments, Notes

Chapter 8. Formalities of Transfer: Trusts and Gifts

Books

Law Review Articles

Law Review Comments, Notes

Chapter 9. Restrictions on the Power of Disposition: Protection of the Family

Books

Law Review Articles

Law Review Comments, Notes

Chapter 10. Restrictions on the Power of Disposition: The Transferor, the Survivors, and Social Policy

Books

Law Review Articles

Law Review Comments, Notes

Chapter 11. Future Interests

Books

Law Review Articles

Law Review Comments, Notes

Chapter 12. Securing the Transferor's Intent: Lessons in Amphibology

Law Review Articles

Law Review Comments, Notes

Chapter 14. Gifts to Charity

Books

Law Review Articles

Law Review Comments, Notes

Chapter 15. The Duration of Family Settlements: The Rule Against Perpetuities and Related Rules

Books

Law Review Articles

Law Review Comments, Notes

FAMILY WEALTH TRANSACTIONS: WILLS, TRUSTS, FUTURE INTERESTS, AND ESTATE PLANNING

THE LAWYERS KNOW TOO MUCH*

The lawyers, Bob, know too much.
They are chums of the books of old John Marshall.
They know it all, what a dead hand wrote,
A stiff dead hand and its knuckles crumbling,
The bones of the fingers a thin white ash.
        The lawyers know
        a dead man's thoughts too well.

In the heels of the higgling lawyers, Bob,
Too many slippery ifs and buts and howevers,
Too much hereinbefore provided whereas,
Too many doors to go in and out of.

        When the lawyers are through
        What is there left, Bob?
        Can a mouse nibble at it
        And find enough to fasten a tooth in?

        Why is there always a secret singing
        When a lawyer cashes in?
        Why does a hearse horse snicker
        Hauling a lawyer away?

The work of a bricklayer goes to the blue.
The knack of a mason outlasts a moon.
The hand of a plasterer holds a room together.
The land of a farmer wishes him back again.
        Singers of songs and dreamers of plays
        Build a house no wind blows over.
The lawyers — tell me why a hearse horse snickers
        hauling a lawyer's bones.

— CARL SANDBURG

* From *Smoke and Steel*, copyright, 1920, by Harcourt Brace Jovanovich, Inc., renewed, 1948, by Carl Sandburg. Reprinted by permission of the publishers.

I. THE WEALTH TRANSMISSION PROCESS

1. The Wealth Transmission Process

SECTION A. Introduction

1. *What We're About*

These materials on family wealth transactions are intended to provide the basis for a foundation course in estate planning. The materials bring together problems that traditionally have been discussed under separate titles, and often in separate law school courses. The subject matter deals principally with what is conventionally known as the law of wills, gifts, future interests, trusts, estate administration, and estate and gift taxation. Practically all the legal doctrines and practices that are found under these rubrics are functionally related to the disposition of family wealth in two ways. First, the social process with which we are concerned is the allocation and transmission of wealth under conditions where the claimants have not given consideration that can be valued in money or money's worth. In most, but not all, cases these conditions arise where the claimants are members of the prior owner's family or where there is a donative transfer. For simplicity we may refer to this social process as the disposition of family wealth. The specific practices and doctrines by which family wealth is allocated among various claimants can be broken down, for convenient handling, into the law of wills, the law of trusts, and the law of future interests, and so forth. But from a functional viewpoint all this law interrelates as part of one wealth transmission process. The social values sought in this process give rise to community policies. The same community policies run (or ought to run) all through all this law.

The second way in which this law is functionally interrelated can easily be seen if we shift our perspective to that of the estate planner. A competent attorney must understand how this law functions as part of the social process; to give sound advice he must have insight into which doctrines are dying, which are growing, and which, from a policy perspective, are functional equivalents. His role requires much more than this, however. He must examine alternative methods for disposing of wealth to carry out his client's objectives. He must consider the advantages and disadvantages of various kinds of inter vivos dispositions and of various kinds of testamentary dispositions, and he must assess the tax implications of the alternatives. His problems cannot be compartmentalized as problems in wills or gifts or trusts. He must move in and out of all these areas of the law.

These materials place special emphasis on two ways of thinking which correspond with the ways in which this law is functionally interrelated. The first is "policy thinking"; the second is "alternative thinking." Policy thinking requires the clarification of community values; the examination of how or whether these values are served by specific practices, doctrines, and other conditions; the projection of future developments and trends; and the invention and evaluation of alternative policies. Alternative thinking requires the careful analysis of different methods of accomplishing one given objective. You should be concerned both with the ends and means of the social process as well as with the ends and means of clients.

Our focus on the lawyer's roles as social critic and as estate planner has governed both the organization and selection of materials. Parts I and II of this book set the stage for our examination of the substantive law. Part I (Chapter 1) provides important background information, and raises some basic policy questions about the wealth transmission process and about the lawyer's professional responsibility. In Part II we shift our focus to basic estate planning. Chapter 2 presents the estate planning problem of Adam Smith, a young family man of modest circumstances whose principal asset is life insurance. His family and asset situation represents one frequently encountered by practicing attorneys, and it is simple enough to be handled in a foundation course for the estate practice. The extensive scope of the law of wills, trusts, and future interests precludes treatment of the more complex problems faced, say, by a businessman whose assets include stock in a closely held family corporation, a partnership, and a large securities portfolio. In this latter situation, business planning and income, estate, and gift tax considerations would be major factors in the formulation of a suitable estate plan. Our objective, so far as federal estate and gift tax principles are concerned, is to provide basic information that will enable you to discern when tax considerations can safely be ignored, and when and how death taxes play a role in shaping an estate plan. Tax questions of substantial complexity we leave to advanced courses in Estate Planning, Estate and Gift Taxation, and Business Planning. At the same time the estate planner, whether he is representing a millionaire or an Adam Smith, must have a clear understanding of the law of wills and trusts, of the problems encountered in drafting dispositive language, and of the Rule against Perpetuities. These and other substantive problems, common to large estates and small ones, are the primary concern of this course.

In Part II we begin by considering why, or whether, Adam Smith needs a will at all. This requires an assessment of the functions, other than the disposition of property at death, that can be served by a will. Chapter 3 provides an overview of the estate administration process, an examination of the recent criticisms of our probate system, and a brief look at the organized bar's response to those criticisms — the Uniform Probate Code. In Chapter 4 we explore intestacy as an alternative to a will: If the inheritance laws of Smith's home state provide a suitable distributive plan, why should he go to the trouble and expense of writing a will?

In Chapter 5 we take up the role of life insurance, social security and employee benefits in estate planning. Life insurance proceeds are a major asset in the estates of most deceased persons; and, as we shall see, how Adam Smith decides to settle the proceeds of his life insurance policies will have a decided impact on the formulation of a plan for his remaining assets. We shall consider the advantages and disadvantages of settling life insurance by lump-sum payment, under policy settlement options, and in trust. In recent years social security and employee benefits have taken on an increasingly important role in providing economic security for the family of a deceased person. Although there is little for the attorney to do in planning for the settlement of these benefits, he must assess their value for two reasons. First, the amount of projected benefits will have an impact on the life insurance needs of the client. Second, the manner in which the benefits are to be paid out should be considered in formulating a plan for disposition of the client's other assets.

Chapter 6 gives an overview of the operation and scope of the federal estate and gift tax laws, and of state inheritance and estate tax systems. After studying these materials, we should be able to determine whether Adam Smith's estate will require "tax planning."

At this point the student will have been introduced to the various dispositive arrangements — outright transfers by will or gift, joint and survivor arrangements, life insurance settlement options, lifetime and testamentary trusts — that are available to Adam Smith for the settlement of his assets. He should then be able to sketch, in outline form, an estate plan for Smith. Part III of this book is devoted to the problems encountered in putting an estate plan into operation and in expressing the dispositive provisions of the plan in language that will effectuate the client's objectives. In short, Part III covers most of the substantive law of wills, trusts, and future interests (with the exception of trust administration). Chapter 7 treats the formalities of testamentary transfers: execution and revocation of wills, components of wills, and contracts to make wills. Chapter 8 deals with the creation and requisites of inter vivos and testamentary trusts, the requirements for an effective gift, and the various will substitutes that are currently growing both in variety and in extent of use. Also considered here are problems arising from integrating the will with lifetime transfers via "pour-over" arrangements. In Chapter 9 we consider the various doctrines and policies that are designed to protect the surviving spouse and children from disinheritance. In Chapter 10 we take up sundry restrictions on a transferor's ability to do with his property as he wishes: herein of legal capacity, undue influence and fraud; prohibited beneficiaries such as killers, aliens, and charities; disposition of the decedent's body; interference with the conduct of the beneficiary; and restraints on alienation. The recurring question in this chapter is: When must a transferor's freedom of disposition give way to some more important social interest? As we shall see, the relevant policies are refractory and controversial.

If an estate plan includes a trust that provides for the payment of income to one or more beneficiaries for life, it will be necessary to make further provision for distributions of principal at future points in time. That is, it will be necessary to create future interests. Chapter 11 surveys the evolution of the law of estates and future interests and their contemporary relevance. In part, our study of this subject has a positive function: Out of the array of future interests recognized at common law we must find the tools by which effective provision can be made for future distributions of property on various contingencies. In part, our study has a negative function: We must learn which future interests should *not* be employed because of the tax problems or other problems they raise; and we must be able to identify, so that we can sidestep, some of the technical traps of future interest law that have resulted from the American courts' adoption of the good along with the bad of the common law system of estates.

In Chapter 12 we are concerned with the problems encountered in drafting dispositive provisions for wills and trusts. If the will makes outright bequests to various beneficiaries, the possibility that a beneficiary may predecease the testator gives rise to the "lapse" problem, and the possibility that property specifically described in the will may not be owned by the testator at his death may invoke the doctrine of "ademption." Also considered are some of the problems of construction that are encountered when future interests are created. Among these are the requirement of survivorship, and the problems that arise when a gift is made to a class of persons, such as "children," or "issue," or "heirs." We hope that when you finish this chapter you will be able to spot, and avoid, the ambiguities that plague this field.

Chapter 13 deals with the means by which flexibility can be built into the estate plan, permitting future adjustments to meet contingencies that may arise, through the use of powers of appointment. The power may take the form of an invasion power held by the trustee or income beneficiary to permit distributions of principal if trust income should prove insufficient to support the beneficiary. Or, it may take the form of a special or general power of appointment, by which the distribution of future interests may be redirected if circumstances should warrant. The materials analyze the types of powers, their functions, and the problems attendant to their creation and exercise.

Since World War II, the amount of assets held in charitable trusts has greatly increased. This is largely the result of income and estate tax deductions allowed gifts to charity. New problems are arising as to what purposes are charitable, and, with swift social change rendering some charitable purposes obsolete, the courts increasingly are called upon to permit changes and deviations from the donor's original intent. These problems are the subject of Chapter 14.

If Adam Smith decides to create a trust, what is the legally permissible duration of the trust? In Chapter 15 we take a long look at the Rule against Perpetuities, the doctrine developed by the courts to check dead-hand control over the duration of family settlements. We will discover that the Rule's operation is not limited to instances in which the transferor has attempted to create a trust that might last for several generations: In nearly all the cases in which the Rule has been applied to invalidate a transfer, the draftsman has simply "fallen into the net which the Rule spreads for the unwary." [1] The manner in which the Rule has been applied by the courts makes it a point of major concern to the draftsman of any trust, and even to the draftsman of a will that does not create future interests. Thus Adam Smith, who has absolutely no intention of creating a "perpetuity," must contend with the Rule. In this chapter we also examine recent statutory and judicial reform measures designed to temper the "remorseless" common law Rule.

Although we have arranged the material so that it can be dealt with from a planner's perspective, it must be remembered that the lawyer's contact with this area of the law is not restricted to the planner's role alone. The lawyer may represent an interested party seeking a favorable interpretation of obscure language in a poorly drafted will, or a fiduciary who needs guidance because the will or trust makes no provision for a contingency that has occurred. He may represent a disappointed relative who seeks to set the transfer aside, or a creditor who wishes to reach estate assets or property settled in a trust, or a fiduciary charged with the duty of administering the trust or estate. Finally, as we said earlier, the attorney — and also the law student — should not limit his perspective to the resolution of the particular problems faced by a particular client. He should also be concerned about the social values underlying our society's wealth transmission process, and about the effectiveness with which these values are satisfied by existing doctrines and concepts. In order to provide a comprehensive understanding of the wealth transmission process, the materials include a large number of cases, text notes, and problems that are not directly related to the Adam Smith situation or to an estate planning perspective.

Nor will the more traditional ways of thinking be ignored. No teacher of wills, trusts, and future interests could happily avoid the marvelous opportunity this field presents for exposing two of the most persistent oddities of legal reasoning: (1) "thing-thinking," or reifying abstractions; and (2) "the fallacy of the transplanted category," [2] or trying to solve many different problems with one big ambiguous lump of a concept moved from problem to problem without re-examining the policies applicable to the problem. One of our objectives is to make you into a fallacy-hunter — for the rest of your life. But remember . . . though we may scoff at some of the law in this field, there is not an ounce of malice in our fun.

[1] Gray, The Rule against Perpetuities xi (4th ed. 1942). See Lucas v. Hamm, page 15, infra.

[Editors' Note: Throughout the book, footnotes to opinions and other quoted materials are numbered consecutively from the beginning of each chapter. Some footnotes in opinions and secondary authorities are omitted. Editors' footnotes to quoted materials are indicated by the abbreviation: — Eds.]

[2] For a dissection of this fallacy in another context, see Hancock, Fallacy of the Transplanted Category, 37 Can. B. Rev. 535 (1959).

2. A List of Reference Books

Students having problems to solve in the family wealth area sometimes do not know how to begin. We recommend that you consult one or more of the good, recent treatises for solutions to any specific problem that perplexes you. If the treatise doesn't answer the question, at least it will start you towards a solution. Here is a list of useful modern treatises in the family wealth field.

General

American Law of Property (Casner ed. 1952, with supplements). 8 volumes.
Powell, Real Property (1968 recompilation, with supplements). 6 volumes.
Powell and Rohan, Real Property (Abridged ed. 1968).

Wills

Atkinson, Wills (2d ed. 1953). Hornbook.
Page, Wills (Bowe–Parker rev. 1960). 9 volumes.

Trusts

Bogert, Trusts (4th ed. 1963). Hornbook.
Bogert & Bogert, Trusts and Trustees (2d ed. 1965, with supplements). 15 volumes.
Scott, Abridgment of the Law of Trusts (1960).
Scott, Trusts (3d ed. 1967, with supplements). 6 volumes.

Future Interests

Schwartz, Future Interests and Estate Planning (1965).
Simes, Future Interests (2d ed. 1966). Hornbook.
Simes & Smith, The Law of Future Interests (2d ed. 1956, with supplements). 4 volumes.

Estate Planning

Casner, Estate Planning (3d ed. 1961, with supplements). 2 volumes.
Lowndes & Kramer, Federal Estate and Gift Taxes (2d ed. 1962). Hornbook.
Prentice-Hall, eds., Successful Estate Planning — Ideas and Methods (1968, with supplements). Looseleaf.
Rice, Family Tax Planning (1960, with supplements).
Trachtman, Estate Planning (Revised ed. 1968).

Do not be discouraged by this formidable list of reference books. Many of them cover the same ground. Indeed, you should be grateful that so many of the problems in this field have been thoroughly discussed, although after reading some of these works you may think as Edgar Allan Poe did (in another context): "In one case out of a hundred a point is excessively discussed because it is obscure; in the ninety-nine remaining it is obscure because excessively discussed." [3]

[3] Quoted in Gulliver, Cases on Future Interests 13 (1959).

Although this list of reference books should not unnecessarily frighten you, you should *note well* that the course in family wealth transactions will not be easy. Estate planning is inherently complex because of the great difficulty, first, of foreseeing (and drafting instruments to cover) all possible events that might happen in the future and, second, of using language in dispositive instruments that will have the same meaning to all persons. These two difficult problems are enormously complicated by an abundance of highly technical legal rules filled with traps for the unsuspecting.

This field, as a result of a long and complicated history, is overgrown with an excessive number of rules, and hiding under this overgrowth of verbiage is a semantic quagmire of dimensions that cannot be believed by anyone who has not ventured into it. Although probably it will prove impossible for us to avoid all the great sucking mudholes of ambiguity, one of the objectives of this course is to teach you how to avoid most of them and how to get out if you are trapped. You also may need a pair of good hip boots.[4]

3. *A Brief Venture into History and Its Legacies*

History has had a greater impact upon the transmission of family wealth than upon any other field of law, and to understand modern concepts and terminology it is necessary to venture briefly into the ancient law of England.[5] Maitland wrote: "Such is the unity of all history that anyone who endeavours to tell a piece of it must feel that his first sentence tears a seamless web." [6] Yet we do not hesitate, for in this field tradition dictates tearing into the seamless web at the year 1066.[7] Prior to the time of William the Conqueror, we can come to few safe conclusions about how property passed upon death in England. Not only is the evidence fragmentary, but there were apparently many local customs and few ideas clear enough to be called "rules." During this Anglo-Saxon period the courts were not distinctively either secular or ecclesiastical. Clergymen, who were perhaps the only ones possessed of scholarly learning, sat in county courts with the full consent of the ruling princes. All this changed after the arrival of William the Conqueror in 1066. To consolidate his power over England, William imposed a far more systematic and effective feudal system than had theretofore been known. This system was built upon the

[4] Professor McDougal has used a more pungent metaphor in writing about the semantic confusion in this area. In reviewing Volume 3 of the Restatement of Property, which deals with future interests, he wrote: "To make a superb inventory of the Augean stables is not to cleanse them." McDougal, Future Interests Restated: Tradition Versus Clarification and Reform, 55 Harv. L. Rev. 1077, 1115 (1942).

[5] For detailed historical accounts see 2 Pollock & Maitland, History of English Law 237-361 (1895); Plucknett, A Concise History of the Common Law 675-746 (5th ed. 1956). Volumes 3, 4, 5 and 7 of Holdsworth, A History of English Law (1903), are a mine of information for that rare bird, the student of legal history.

[6] 1 Pollock & Maitland, id. at 1.

[7] Sellar & Yeatman, 1066 And All That (1956), a delightful "history" of England comprising only the parts people remember, concludes that only two historical dates are remembered — 55 B.C., when Julius Caesar landed in England, and A.D. 1066. "The Norman Conquest was a Good Thing, as from this time onwards England stopped being conquered and thus was able to become top nation." Id. at 17.

ownership of land. The person who owned land had to render to the king military services and, upon various occasions, money payments. Depending upon his position in the hierarchical feudal system, the landowner had wide or minimum public administrative power. A system of public order was built upon land ownership, and William created his own courts to supervise the system.

Thus began an historic division of court jurisdiction, which resulted in two entirely different sets of laws governing the disposition of property at death. The king's common law courts controlled succession to land; the ecclesiastical courts controlled succession to personal property. The policies which moved these courts were different. Charged with making the feudal system work, the king's courts invented rules to prevent the fracturing of land ownership which might result in the dissolution of the feudal structure. Examples of these were primogeniture (i.e., all the land descended to the eldest son)[8] and the preference for joint tenancies over tenancies in common. Feudal incidents, roughly equivalent to modern inheritance taxes, were collectible every time land descended. By design or by accident there grew up a number of rules that resulted in land "descending" more frequently, thus augmenting the revenues of the overlords. Among these were the Rule in Shelley's Case and the Doctrine of Worthier Title. Devises of land were also prohibited by the common law courts. Prohibiting devises increased the chances of escheat and prevented the church from acquiring land by death-bed gift from a man in fear of his soul. Moreover, since public office went along with ownership of certain land, there probably was some feeling that this land should not be freely transferable, just as today we would not like to think that a judge or a governor could transfer his office at death to whomever he chose. Only when property and public office became separated did property become freely alienable.

Inasmuch as the king's common law courts did not assert any jurisdiction over succession to chattels, personal property was distributed according to various unwritten customs if a man died without a will. Under the prevailing religious beliefs, however, it was unusual for a man to die intestate. Except in the case of sudden demise, a last confession was essential for the salvation of the soul after death and for burial in consecrated ground. When a dying man made his last confession it was quite natural at the same time to give the priest directions for the disposition of his property, including a portion for pious uses to wipe out past sins. A last confession and a will became so fused in the popular mind that it was assumed that if a man died intestate probably he also had died unconfessed, rejecting the ministry of the church.

Intestacy (re personal property) came to be regarded as a sin, very nearly a crime. People had a holy horror of it. In such a climate of opinion it is not surprising that the king, the feudal lords, and the bishops began to claim that an intestate, like a traitor or a felon, forfeited his chattels to them. Popular dissatisfaction with forfeiture upon intestacy resulted in a clause in Magna Carta providing that an

[8] Maitland concluded that primogeniture came into existence to make it easier for the feudal lords to secure military services due from their tenants. This explanation has been questioned, however, inasmuch as primogeniture has existed in many societies, advanced and primitive, where there were no lords and no services. See Cairns, The Explanatory Process in the Field of Inheritance, 20 Iowa L. Rev. 266 (1935); Maine, Ancient Law, c. 7 (Pollock ed. 1930).

intestate's goods should be distributed by his kin and friends per visum ecclesiae. And so it came about that the ecclesiastical officers supervised the distribution of chattels, regardless of whether the owner died testate or intestate.

The ecclesiastical courts were staffed by priests ("ordinaries"). They were not burdened with the duty of maintaining the feudal system, and the set of rules which they developed drew heavily upon Roman and canon law. In some ways their policies were directly opposed to those of the common law courts. For example, devises of land were not permitted in the common law courts (although, to be sure, devious ways of avoiding this prohibition grew up). This feudal aversion to wills finds expression in a maxim of construction we still hear today: "It takes specific words to disinherit an heir." The horror of intestacy led ecclesiastical courts to adopt the opposite policy, and with it the opposite maxim: "One who writes a will is presumed to intend to dispose of all his estate and not to die intestate as to any portion thereof."

Meanwhile a third force had grown into a very powerful court. Ever since the Norman Conquest every king had his chancellor, who had custody of the great seal and was the head of all the king's clerks. The chancellor was almost always an ecclesiastic, usually a bishop. He was also a member of the King's Council — indeed, the specially learned member. When relief was not forthcoming from the common law courts, petitioners asked the Council to interfere on behalf of the king for the love of God and in the way of charity. Because of the chancellor's acquaintance with Roman and canon law, the Council more and more referred petitions to him. Strictly speaking, the chancellor was not a judge, but an administrative officer; nonetheless, a Court of Chancery gradually began to exercise an equity jurisdiction.

While the common law courts were cumbrous and inflexible, prior to the fall of Cardinal Wolsey in 1529 (the last of the great ecclesiastical chancellors), equity was vigorous and developed flexible remedies that undercut the legal rules. For our purposes the most important was the development of the *use*. For many reasons it had become a common practice for a landowner (O) to convey his land to a friend (A) upon the understanding that although A had legal title to the property, O was to have all the benefits of ownership (the use of the land). This dodge was employed for a variety of purposes, including evading the Statute of Mortmain and the common law prohibition of devises of land.[9] According to the ideas of the time O in equity should be protected — and he was, by the chancellor. Although Parliament and the lawyers who practiced before the common law courts did not like the equitable jurisdiction of the chancellor, they, as well as other owners of land, found it highly beneficial to have land "in use."

About the time Henry VIII came to the throne the common law courts began to wage war on all rival courts. They soon rendered the ecclesiastical courts powerless. As a result grave abuses arose. The worst was that a wicked administrator could pay off the decedent's debts and appropriate to himself what remained of the decedent's chattels. The church courts could not compel the administrator to distribute because the common law courts had prohibited suing on the administrator's bond, and the common law courts declined to give the distributees a remedy. This scan-

9 See page 703, infra; Fratcher, Uses of Uses, 34 Mo. L. Rev. 39 (1969).

dalous state of affairs lasted more than a century, until in 1670 Parliament was moved to correct the matter by passing the Statute of Distributions. The primary purpose of this act was to strengthen the ecclesiastical courts, but the common law courts continued to impede the clergy's control of administration.

Also during the reign of Henry VIII, Parliament, in a political deal with the king, attempted to abolish the equitable use by turning it into a legal interest, thus abrogating a large part of the chancellor's jurisdiction (The Statute of Uses, 1536). But the chancellors — with few exceptions, lawyers from 1529 to the present day — would not admit defeat. A century after the Statute of Uses, the Court of Chancery effectively nullified it by recognizing in equity a use-on-a-use.[10] Equity came back into its own with the appointment of Lord Nottingham to the woolsack in 1673; he did more perhaps than his predecessors to develop uniform and rational rules.[11] Subsequent chancellors systematically developed the modern trust. With its flexible procedure and its power to enforce personal duties, Chancery also gradually took over the administration of estates. Ecclesiastical jurisdiction over decedents' estates was finally abolished in 1857, when a court of probate was established in Chancery. However, not until 1925, with the Administration of Estates Act, was one English court given sole jurisdiction over succession to real and personal property. Thus ended the historic division of court jurisdiction over decedents' estates which began with William the Conqueror some eight centuries before.

These rival court systems left us with a great abundance of divergent rules. "Hence it is," as Holdsworth said, "that the law of succession is historically one of the most variegated, and, therefore, one of the most complicated of all branches of English law." [12] When the American legislatures and courts came to establish statutes and rules respecting transmission of wealth, they had on almost all important points a choice of alternative rules. The resulting diverse peculiarities among the states may lead anyone wishing for a national rule to agree with Maitland:

> It is in the province of inheritance that our medieval law made its worst mistakes. They were natural mistakes. There was much to be said for the simple plan of giving all the land to the eldest son. There was much to be said for allowing the courts of the church to assume a jurisdiction, even an exclusive jurisdiction, in testamentary causes. We can hardly blame our ancestors for their dread of intestacy without attacking their religious beliefs. But the consequences have been evil. We rue them at the present day, and shall rue them so long as there is talk of real and personal property.[13]

A Legacy From History: Distinctions Between Real and Personal Property

One needlessly complicating factor in this field is that we have two legal vocabularies — one applicable to real property, one applicable to personal property.

[10] See 1 Scott, Trusts §71 (3d ed. 1967).

[11] For more on this important figure of the law, "the father of equity," see pages 959-962, infra.

[12] 3 Holdsworth, A History of English Law 534 (1903).

[13] 2 Pollock & Maitland, History of English Law 361 (1895).

Some, but not all, of the duplicative words are traceable to the historic division of court jurisdiction. Take *last will and testament.* A common belief is that this phrase arose because a *will* disposed of real property and a *testament* disposed of personal property; therefore one instrument disposing of both was a will and testament. The belief that "testament" referred to personal property is based on its Latin origin ("testamentum"). It is assumed that the Latin-trained ecclesiastical courts introduced "testament" into the language to refer to an instrument disposing of property over which they had jurisdiction. It is then assumed that "will," an old English word, was used by the common law courts and by a process of association came to relate to the type of property over which these courts had jurisdiction. The evidence does not support these assumptions. As far back as the records go, the words have been used interchangeably. To speak of a testament disposing of land, or of a will disposing of a cow, would not have sounded strange to the medieval ear. Professor Mellinkoff believes the phrase "last will and testament" is traceable to the law's habit of doubling Old English words with synonyms of Old French or Latin origin (e.g., had and received, mind and memory, free and clear), "helped along by a distinctive rhythm." [14] In any case the myth of will : land : : testament : chattels dies terribly, terribly slowly. Today it is perfectly proper to use the single word "will" to refer to an instrument disposing of both real and personal property.

A person who dies leaving a will is a *testator* if a man, or a *testatrix* if a woman. He or she is said to *devise* real property to *devisees* and to *bequeath* personal property to *legatees*. Using "devise" to refer to land and "bequest" to personalty became a lawyerly custom little more than a hundred years ago,[15] although the distinction, like that between "will" and "testament," is sometimes erroneously thought to have had more ancient roots in the different courts handling the dead man's property. Although these linguistic distinctions still have currency, there are signs that synonymous usage is returning in respectable circles. The Restatement of Property applies "devise" to both realty and personalty.[16] In drafting wills, "I give" is an excellent substitute for "I devise," "I bequeath," and "I give, devise, and bequeath." "I give" will effectively transfer any kind of property, and no fly-specking lawyer can ever fault you for using the wrong verb.

When intestacy occurs we use different words to describe what happens to the intestate's real property and what happens to his personal property. We say his real property *descends* to his *heirs,* his personal property is *distributed* to his *next-of-kin.* At common law heirs and next-of-kin were not necessarily the same. For example, when primogeniture, which applied only to land, was in effect, real property descended to the eldest son, but personal property was distributed equally among all the children. Today in almost all states a single *statute of descent and distribution* governs intestacy.[17] The same persons are named as intestate successors to both real

14 Mellinkoff, The Language of the Law 331 (1963).

15 Cf. Shakespeare, King John I, 1, 109:

> "Upon his death-bed he by will bequeath'd
> His lands to me . . ."

16 1 Restatement of Property §12 (1936).

17 Delaware, Tennessee, and Texas are among the jurisdictions that have separate schemes

and personal property. Thus today the word "heirs" usually means those persons designated by the applicable statute to take a decedent's intestate property, real and personal. "Next-of-kin" usually means exactly the same thing.

At common law a spouse was not an heir; he or she had only curtesy or dower rights. Today in all states the statutes of descent and distribution name the spouse as an intestate successor, and a spouse thus may be an heir.

In the eyes of the law no living person has heirs; to use the Latin phrase, nemo est haeres viventis. The persons who would be the heirs of A, a living person, if A died within the next hour, are not the heirs of A but the *heirs apparent*. They have a mere *expectancy*. This expectancy can be destroyed by A's deed or will. It is not a legal "interest" at all.[18] Not being an interest, an expectancy cannot be transferred (though a purported transfer of an expectancy, for a fair consideration, may be enforceable in equity as a contract to transfer). An expectancy is merely a factual possibility or hope of inheriting property.

(*Parenthesis: A Biblical diversion.* Undoubtedly the most famous sale of an expectancy was the sale of Esau's birthright to Jacob. Esau and Jacob were twin sons of Isaac (who, you will recall, was the son born to Sarah when she was ninety years of age). Although Jacob was holding on to Esau's heel when they emerged from the womb, Esau was the first born. Therefore, Esau was entitled to a double portion of Isaac's estate. Of the subsequent sale of the birthright the Revised Standard Version says:

> Once when Jacob was boiling pottage, Esau came in from the field, and he was famished. And Esau said to Jacob, "Let me eat some of that red pottage, for I am famished!" (Therefore his name was called Edom.) Jacob said, "First sell me your birthright." Esau said, "I am about to die; of what use is a birthright to me?" Jacob said, "Swear to me first." So he swore to him, and sold his birthright to Jacob. Then Jacob gave Esau bread and pottage of lentils, and he ate and drank, and rose and went his way. Thus Esau despised his birthright. — Genesis 25:29-34.

This first recorded sale of an expectancy has been the subject of much debate among Biblical scholars. Was it enforceable? At one extreme is the position that the

---

for the descent of land and the distribution of personalty. Del. Code Ann. tit. 12 §§501 et seq. (1953, 1970 Supp.); Tenn. Code Ann. §§31-101, 31-201 (1955); Tex. Prob. Code Ann. §38(b) (1956).

[18] Why not? Suppose O transfers property to A for life, remainder as A shall appoint by deed or will, and in default of appointment to the heirs of A. Here the heirs of A are said to have an interest, called a contingent remainder. Can you give any reasons for treating this case in a different manner than the case in which A has a fee simple and A's heirs apparent have an expectancy?

Although the holder of an expectancy is protected against misrepresentations calculated to induce the ancestor to disinherit the heir (Restatement (Second) of Torts §774B (Tent. Draft 14, 1969)), and although an expectancy is an insurable interest in some jurisdictions (Home Ins. Co. v. Mendenhall, 164 Ill. 458, 45 N.E. 1078 (1897)), orthodox doctrine still declares the heirs apparent do not have an "interest" in property. 3 Restatement of Property §315, Comment a (1940).

sale of an expectancy would not have been enforceable under Hebrew law. "A message was sent from Palestine: If a first-born son had sold his share before the division of the estate took place, that sale is invalid. This shows that the first-born is not regarded as the legal possessor of his share before distribution had taken place." [19] At the other end of the spectrum of opinion is the position that the oath, which Jacob demanded, made the agreement absolutely binding. This position is based upon an assumption that the oath in Biblical times functioned much as the seal did during the medieval period.[20] Between these two positions are various views. The Talmudic scholars Sforno and Rashbam believed that the pottage was merely a down payment, and the actual price was not given in the Bible. Others believed that the agreement, in referring to Esau's birthright, did not refer to the inheritance of property but referred to "purely spiritual" privileges as head of the family. Although there is some evidence that Esau considered the sale of the birthright binding (Genesis 27:36), there is no evidence that Jacob sought specific performance. Nor is there evidence that Jacob did in fact receive Esau's share of their father's property. By deceit Jacob subsequently secured his blind father's blessing, which was the due of the firstborn, Esau. So far as Biblical history is concerned, the blessing, which made Jacob head of the family, was the important benefaction. For those interested in exploring this matter further, an excellent beginning is David Daube's Studies in Biblical Law 191-200 (1947).

Under modern American law, was Esau's promise enforceable? 3 American Law of Property §14.12 (Casner ed. 1952); 3 Powell, Real Property ¶383 (1970). *End Biblical diversion.*)

PROBLEM

H and W enter into a separation agreement whereby W is to have custody of their daughter, D, and H is to pay a stated monthly sum for support. H and W also agree upon a specified division of their property. In a separate instrument H assigns to D one-half of his expectancy in the estate of his father, F, who is then living, "for the consideration of one dollar and other valuable considerations received to my full satisfaction from my wife . . . on behalf of my daughter." W obtains a divorce and the decree incorporates the separation agreement but does not mention the assignment. F dies intestate survived by two children, of whom H is one. F's estate is worth $490,000. Is the assignment valid? Scott v. First National Bank of Baltimore, 224 Md. 462, 168 A.2d 349 (1961). Suppose that after the divorce H remarries, has three children by his second wife, and then F dies. Would your answer be the same? Would your answer to these two questions be the same regardless of whether F had notice of the assignment? Atkinson, Wills 729 (2d ed. 1953).

[19] The Babylonian Talmud, Nezikin IV, 524 (Epstein ed. 1935).
[20] Von Rad, Genesis 261 (Marks trans. 1961).

Another Legacy: The Strange Law of Future Interests

Over the centuries there developed a highly artificial system of analysis, complete with its own metalanguage, applicable to wealth transmission problems where future interests were created. The doctrines which grew out of this system fit together into a structure known as the law of future interests. Once you step into this Inner Sanctum of the Law, you will be struck by the strangeness of the verbiage that beats upon your ears. Here we practice a sort of black magic, and, like mediums at a seance, reading the minds of the dead, incant a mumbo-jumbo too intricate for easy understanding. It is this magic — this other-worldness — that makes practical future interests problems so intensely fascinating. It is also what makes them tough. The law of future interests is filled with words that have no meaning for the layman and no referents in ordinary experience: e.g., vested remainder, contingent remainder, executory interest, possibility of reverter, right of entry, reversion. These words are names for "future interests," which are thought of as things. They move about in accordance with certain rules. These rules permit these interests to accelerate, merge with another, divest (oust) another, be destroyed, be captured, and so on.[21] If you understand the terminology and can think straight or in circles or in hyperbolas, some portion of which lies in infinity, you will find that in a surprising number of problems you can come to one, and only one, answer. If you accept the premises on which it is constructed, the law of future interests may seem to you like a mathematical game. And, as in all mathematics, symbols (words) must be used precisely and not approximately. This will take some practice, some adjustment in what you think the mind is capable of,[22] and more precision in verbal analysis and in the use of words than you are accustomed to. Bertrand Russell once defined philosophy as "an unusually ingenious attempt to think fallaciously." [23] You may find that statement conveniently fits the law of future interests.

Nonetheless, you must not fool yourself into thinking that this "mathematical game" *describes* accurately why the court reached a decision, or that mastery of the system will, by itself, permit you to *predict* how a court will solve a problem. Many of the abstract terms conceal rather than solve the problem; too many of them are tautological or ambiguous. Thus even within the confines of traditional formulae there is ample room for courts (and students) to let their minds play over a number

[21] All this is explained in Chapter 11.

[22] You may find the advice of the White Queen sound:

"Now I'll give *you* something to believe. I'm just one hundred and one, five months and a day."

"I can't believe *that*!" said Alice.

"Can't you?" the Queen said in a pitying tone. "Try again: draw a long breath, and shut your eyes."

Alice laughed. "There's no use trying," she said: "one *can't* believe impossible things."

"I daresay you haven't had much practice," said the Queen. "When I was your age, I always did it for half-an-hour a day. Why sometimes I've believed as many as six impossible things before breakfast." — Carroll, Through the Looking-Glass, c. V.

[23] Russell, Philosophy's Ulterior Motives, in Unpopular Essays 45 (1950).

of alternatives, all of which can be rationalized doctrinally. Yet even if the doctrines laid down in England between 1066 and 1776 were all clear and rational, realistic prediction of judicial decisions could not be based wholly upon them. Law is a dynamic process. Any useful system of description must be open-ended; new variables are constantly discovered and old variables redefined. Because men do not live in, and courts do not operate in, a space-time void, the solution of contemporary problems cannot be found in a closed system of basic assumptions and deductions made originally to solve problems of an ancient age. At the present time the law of property is very clearly undergoing a change from a formalistic to a rationalistic system. Unfortunately we do not yet have an objective framework that will account for all the nondoctrinal, nonformalistic variables in the legal process. It is the task of the present generation to invent such a framework. In the meantime, until law completes the transition, it is necessary for you to learn the formal, doctrinal arguments as well as to analyze the other variables which move, or should move, judicial decisions.

SECTION B. Professional Responsibility

LUCAS v. HAMM

Supreme Court of California, 1961

56 Cal. 2d 583, 364 P.2d 685, 15 Cal. Rptr. 821

Gibson, C.J. Plaintiffs, who are some of the beneficiaries under the will of Eugene H. Emmick, deceased, brought this action for damages against defendant L. S. Hamm, an attorney at law, who had been engaged by the testator to prepare the will.[24] They have appealed from a judgment of dismissal entered after an order sustaining a general demurrer to the second amended complaint without leave to amend.

The allegations of the first and second causes of action are summarized as follows: Defendant agreed with the testator, for a consideration, to prepare a will and codicils thereto for him by which plaintiffs were to be designated as beneficiaries of a trust provided for by paragraph Eighth of the will and were to receive 15 per cent of the residue as specified in that paragraph. Defendant, in violation of instructions and in breach of his contract, negligently prepared testamentary instruments containing phraseology that was invalid by virtue of section 715.2 and former sections 715.1 and 716 of the Civil Code relating to restraints on alienation and the rule against perpetuities. Paragraph Eighth of these instruments "transmitted" the residual estate in trust and provided that the "trust shall cease and terminate at 12 o'clock noon on a day five years after the date upon which the order distributing the trust property to the trustee is made by the Court having jurisdiction over the pro-

[24] L. S. Hamm was admitted to the bar in 1915, and, according to the plaintiff's brief, had served as Emmick's attorney for thirty years when the latter died. The same source states that Hamm received more than $50,000 in fees as attorney for Emmick's estate. — Eds.

bation of this will." After the death of the testator the instruments were admitted to probate. Subsequently defendant, as draftsman of the instruments and as counsel of record for the executors, advised plaintiffs in writing that the residual trust provision was invalid and that plaintiffs would be deprived of the entire amount to which they would have been entitled if the provision had been valid unless they made a settlement with the blood relatives of the testator under which plaintiffs would receive a lesser amount than that provided for them by the testator. As the direct and proximate result of the negligence of defendant and his breach of contract in preparing the testamentary instruments and the written advice referred to above, plaintiffs were compelled to enter into a settlement under which they received a share of the estate amounting to $75,000 less than the sum which they would have received pursuant to testamentary instruments drafted in accordance with the directions of the testator.

. . .

It was held in Buckley v. Gray, 110 Cal. 339, 42 P. 900, 52 Am. St. Rep. 88, 31 L.R.A. 862, that an attorney who made a mistake in drafting a will was not liable for negligence or breach of contract to a person named in the will who was deprived of benefits as a result of the error. The court stated that an attorney is liable to his client alone with respect to actions based on negligence in the conduct of his professional duties, and it was reasoned that there could be no recovery for mere negligence where there was no privity by contract or otherwise between the defendant and the person injured. (110 Cal. at pp. 342-343.) The court further concluded that there could be no recovery on the theory of a contract for the benefit of a third person, because the contract with the attorney was not expressly for the plaintiff's benefit and the testatrix only remotely intended the plaintiff to be benefited as a result of the contract. (110 Cal. at pp. 346-347.) For the reasons hereinafter stated the case is overruled.

The reasoning underlying the denial of tort liability in the Buckley case, i.e., the stringent privity test, was rejected in Biakanja v. Irving, 49 Cal. 2d 647, 648-650, 320 P.2d 16, 65 A.L.R.2d 1358, where we held that a notary public who, although not authorized to practice law, prepared a will but negligently failed to direct proper attestation was liable in tort to an intended beneficiary who was damaged because of the invalidity of the instrument. It was pointed out that since 1895, when Buckley was decided, the rule that in the absence of privity there was no liability for negligence committed in the performance of a contract had been greatly liberalized. (49 Cal. 2d at p. 649.) In restating the rule it was said that the determination whether in a specific case the defendant will be held liable to a third person not in privity is a matter of policy and involves the balancing of various factors, among which are the extent to which the transaction was intended to affect the plaintiff, the foreseeability of harm to him, the degree of certainty that the plaintiff suffered injury, the closeness of the connection between the defendant's conduct and the injury, and the policy of preventing future harm. (49 Cal. 2d at p. 650.) The same general principle must be applied in determining whether a beneficiary is entitled to bring an action for negligence in the drafting of a will when the instrument is drafted by an attorney rather than by a person not authorized to practice law.

Many of the factors which led to the conclusion that the notary public involved in Biakanja was liable are equally applicable here. As in Biakanja, one of the main purposes which the transaction between defendant and the testator intended to accomplish was to provide for the transfer of property to plaintiffs; the damage to plaintiffs in the event of invalidity of the bequest was clearly foreseeable; it became certain, upon the death of the testator without change of the will, that plaintiffs would have received the intended benefits but for the asserted negligence of defendant; and if persons such as plaintiffs are not permitted to recover for the loss resulting from negligence of the draftsman, no one would be able to do so and the policy of preventing future harm would be impaired.

Since defendant was authorized to practice the profession of an attorney, we must consider an additional factor not present in Biakanja, namely, whether the recognition of liability to beneficiaries of wills negligently drawn by attorneys would impose an undue burden on the profession. Although in some situations liability could be large and unpredictable in amount, this is also true of an attorney's liability to his client. We are of the view that the extension of his liability to beneficiaries injured by a negligently drawn will does not place an undue burden on the profession, particularly when we take into consideration that a contrary conclusion would cause the innocent beneficiary to bear the loss. The fact that the notary public involved in Biakanja was guilty of unauthorized practice of the law was only a minor factor in determining that he was liable, and the absence of the factor in the present case does not justify reaching a different result.

It follows that the lack of privity between plaintiffs and defendant does not preclude plaintiffs from maintaining an action in tort against defendant.

Neither do we agree with the holding in Buckley that beneficiaries damaged by an error in the drafting of a will cannot recover from the draftsman on the theory that they are third-party beneficiaries of the contract between him and the testator. Obviously the main purpose of a contract for the drafting of a will is to accomplish the future transfer of the estate of the testator to the beneficiaries named in the will, and therefore it seems improper to hold, as was done in Buckley, that the testator intended only "remotely" to benefit those persons. It is true that under a contract for the benefit of a third person performance is usually to be rendered directly to the beneficiary, but this is not necessarily the case. (See Rest., Contracts, §133, comment d; 2 Williston on Contracts (3d ed. 1959) 829.) For example, where a life insurance policy lapsed because a bank failed to perform its agreement to pay the premiums out of the insured's bank account, it was held that after the insured's death the beneficiaries could recover against the bank as third-party beneficiaries. (Walker Bank & Trust Co. v. First Security Corp., 9 Utah 2d 215, 341 P.2d 944, 945 et seq.) Persons who had agreed to procure liability insurance for the protection of the promisees but did not do so were also held liable to injured persons who would have been covered by the insurance, the courts stating that all persons who might be injured were third-party beneficiaries of the contracts to procure insurance. (Johnson v. Holmes Tuttle Lincoln-Merc., 160 Cal. App. 2d 290, 296 et seq., 325 P.2d 193; James Stewart & Co. v. Law, 149 Tex. 392, 233 S.W.2d 558, 561-562, 22 A.L.R.2d 639.) Since, in a situation like those presented here and in the Buckley case, the main purpose of the testator in making his agreement with the attorney is to benefit the persons named in his will and this intent can be effectuated, in the event of a breach by the attorney, only by giving the beneficiaries a right of action, we should recognize, as a matter of policy, that they are entitled to recover as third-party beneficiaries. (See 2 Williston on Contracts (3d ed. 1959) pp. 843-844; 4 Corbin on Contracts (1951) pp. 8, 20.)

. . .

We conclude that intended beneficiaries of a will who lose their testamentary rights because of failure of the attorney who drew the will to properly fulfill his obligations under his contract with the testator may recover as third-party beneficiaries.

However, an attorney is not liable either to his client or to a beneficiary under a will for errors of the kind alleged in the first and second causes of action.

The general rule with respect to the liability of an attorney for failure to properly perform his duties to his client is that the attorney, by accepting employment to give legal advice or to render other legal services, impliedly agrees to use such skill, prudence, and diligence as lawyers of ordinary skill and capacity commonly possess and exercise in the performance of the tasks which they undertake. . . . The attorney is not liable for every mistake he may make in his practice; he is not, in the absence of an express agreement, an insurer of the soundness of his opinions or of the validity of an instrument that he is engaged to draft; and he is not liable for being in error as to a question of law on which reasonable doubt may be entertained by well-informed lawyers. . . . These principles are equally applicable whether the plaintiff's claim is based on tort or breach of contract.

The complaint, as we have seen, alleges that defendant drafted the will in such a manner that the trust was invalid because it violated the rules relating to perpetuities and restraints on alienation. These closely akin subjects have long perplexed the courts and the bar. Professor Gray, a leading authority in the field, stated: "There is something in the subject which seems to facilitate error. Perhaps it is because the mode of reasoning is unlike that with which lawyers are most familiar. . . . A long list might be formed of the demonstrable blunders with regard to its questions made by eminent men, blunders which they themselves have been sometimes the first to acknowledge; and there are few lawyers of any practice in drawing wills and settlements who have not at some time either fallen into the net which the Rule spreads for the unwary, or at least shuddered to think how narrowly they have escaped it." (Gray, The Rule Against Perpetuities (4th ed. 1942) p. xi; see also Leach, Perpetuities Legislation (1954) 67 Harv. L. Rev. 1349 [describing the rule as a "technicality-ridden legal nightmare" and a "dangerous instrumentality in the hands of most members of the bar"].) Of the California law on perpetuities and restraints it has been said that few, if any, areas of the law have been fraught with more confusion or concealed more traps for the unwary draftsman; that members of the bar, probate courts, and title insurance companies make errors in these matters; that the code provisions adopted in 1872 created a situation worse than if the matter had been left to the common law, and that the legislation adopted in 1951 (under which the will involved here was drawn), despite the best of intentions, added further complexities. (See 38 Cal. Jur. 2d 443; Coil, Perpetuities and Restraints; A Needed Reform (1955) 30 State Bar J. 87, 88-90.)

In view of the state of the law relating to perpetuities and restraints on alienation and the nature of the error, if any, assertedly made by defendant in preparing the instrument, it would not be proper to hold that defendant failed to use such skill, prudence, and diligence as lawyers of ordinary skill and capacity commonly exercise. The provision of the will quoted in the complaint, namely, that the trust was to terminate five years after the order of the probate court distributing the property to the trustee, could cause the trust to be invalid only because of the remote possibility that the order of distribution would be delayed for a period longer than a life in being at the creation of the interest plus 16 years (the 21-year statutory period less the five years specified in the will). Although it has been held that a possibility of this type could result in invalidity of a bequest (Estate of Johnston, 47 Cal. 2d 265, 269-270, 303 P.2d 1; Estate of Campbell, 28 Cal. App. 2d 102, 103, 82 P.2d 22), the possible occurrence of such a delay was so remote and unlikely that an attorney of ordinary skill acting under the same circumstances might well have "fallen into the net which the Rule spreads for the unwary" and failed to recognize the danger. We need not decide whether the trust provision of the will was actually invalid or whether, as defendant asserts, the complaint fails to allege facts necessary to enable such a determination, because we have concluded that in any event an error of the type relied on by plaintiffs does not show negligence or breach of contract on the part of defendant. It is apparent that plaintiffs have not stated and cannot state causes of action with respect to the first two counts, and the trial court did not abuse its discretion in denying leave to amend as to these counts.

. . .

The judgment is affirmed.

Traynor, J., Schauer, J., McComb, J., Peters, J., White, J., and Dooling, J., concurred.[25]

NOTES

1. Do you understand why the will provision allegedly violated the Rule against Perpetuities? See pages 979-987, infra.

2. What does this case say about the degree of competence required of attorneys who practice in this area of law? About the desirability of purchasing profes-

[25] Noted 4 Ariz. L. Rev. 100; 42 B.U.L. Rev. 256; 30 Fordham L. Rev. 369; 75 Harv. L. Rev. 620; 45 Marq. L. Rev. 459; 22 Md. L. Rev. 161; 34 Rocky Mt. L. Rev. 388; 16 Rutgers L. Rev. 475; 14 Stan. L. Rev. 580; 40 Texas L. Rev. 1046; 64 W. Va. L. Rev. 361. — Eds.

sional liability insurance? Should ignorance of the law be a good defense for *lawyers?*

3. Miller, Functions and Ethical Problems of the Lawyer in Drafting a Will, 1950 Ill. L. Forum 415, 423: "Indeed, it would be no exaggeration to say that of all the moral obligations of the lawyer who undertakes to prepare a will the obligation of competence is paramount. . . . No lawyer should prepare a will unless he considers himself competent to do so. He should approach this question with a realization that to the client the will is probably the most important document of his life. . . . The property may be the result of a lifetime of effort. Its disposition will have lasting and significant effect both upon those included as beneficiaries and upon those excluded who might naturally expect or hope to be included. . . . If the lawyer doubts his ability to produce the best possible will for the client, he should decline to prepare one."

4. On attorney's liability for malpractice see Roady & Andersen, Professional Negligence (1960); Hutcheson, Lawyers, How is Your Malpractice? 30 Ins. Counsel J. 423 (1963); Wade, The Attorney's Liability for Negligence, 12 Vand. L. Rev. 755 (1959); Wallach & Kelly, Attorney Malpractice in California: A Shaky Citadel, 10 Santa Clara Law. 257 (1970); Note, Attorney Malpractice, 63 Colum. L. Rev. 1292 (1963).

A leading authority on English property law, Megarry (now Mr. Justice Megarry), commented on Lucas v. Hamm thus (81 L.Q. Rev. 478, 481 (1965)): "An Englishman's comment on the decision must perforce observe a proper restraint. Doubtless the Supreme Court of California is the best judge of the standard of competence which is to be expected of California lawyers of ordinary skill and capacity. Let it be accepted that it is highly unlikely that it would take longer than the perpetuity period for the estate to be distributed. The question then becomes whether an ordinary lawyer who undertakes to draft a will should be expected to know that a gift will be void for perpetuity if there is any possibility, however unlikely, that the perpetuity period will be exceeded. This part of the rule is so fundamental, and so highly stressed by all the books and teachers, that he who does not know it must be expected to know little or nothing of the rest of the rule. The standard of competence in California thus seems to be that it is not negligent for lawyers to draft wills knowing little or nothing of the rule against perpetuities, and without consulting anyone skilled in the rule (a point mentioned by the Court of Appeal but ignored in the judgment of the Supreme Court). If the rule against perpetuities is in this category, what other fundamentals of the law are there of which the California attorney may be ignorant without culpability? How does California translate and apply spondet peritiam artis? [26] However bright the future of

[26] For those who do not have a Latin dictionary handy the maxim means "he promises to do the work in a skillful manner," and is applied to a paid agent or a workman for hire. See Williston, Contracts §1012C (3d ed. 1957); Restatement (Second) of Torts §299A (1959). — Eds.

Lucas v. Hamm may be in England on the score of privity, it is to be hoped that on the standard of professional competence it will prove to be a slur on the profession which, like the mule, will display neither pride of ancestry nor hope of posterity." [27]

HEYER v. FLAIG
Supreme Court of California, 1969
70 Cal. 2d 223, 449 P.2d 161, 74 Cal. Rptr. 225

TOBRINER, J. This case presents a single, basic question: When does the statute of limitations commence to run against an intended beneficiary of a will who, under the authority of Lucas v. Hamm (1961) 56 Cal. 2d 583, 15 Cal. Rptr. 821, 364 P.2d 685, acquires a right of action against an attorney for malpractice in negligently failing to fulfill the testamentary directions of his client? Under the alleged facts of this case, we conclude that the limitations period starts from the date that the cause of action accrues: namely, the incidence of the testatrix' death when the negligent failure to perfect the requested testamentary scheme becomes irremediable and the impact of the injury occurs. Accordingly, the trial court erroneously sustained a demurrer to plaintiff's complaint on the ground that the statute of limitations bars the present action brought later than two years[28] after the defendant drafted the will. Since the plaintiffs filed their complaint within two years of the testatrix' death, the cause avoids the statutory bar.

The plaintiffs' complaint sets forth inter alia the following allegations: In December 1962 Doris Kilburn, the testatrix, retained defendant Flaig[29] to prepare her will. She told defendant that she wished all of her estate to pass to her two daughters, plaintiffs in this action. She also told him that she intended to marry Glen Kilburn. On December 21, 1962, Doris Kilburn executed a will prepared by defendant. On December 31, 1962, she married Glen Kilburn.

The will purports to leave the entire estate of Doris Kilburn to the plaintiffs. The testament however, does not mention the testatrix' husband, except that it names him executor. On July 9, 1963, Doris Kilburn died; thereafter the Los Angeles County Superior Court admitted to probate the above-described document as her last will and testament. In these probate proceedings, Glen Kilburn claimed a portion of the estate as a post-testamentary spouse under Probate Code section 70.[30]

[27] With deference, we think Megarry's statement is also a slur on the mule. The phrase is attributed originally to nineteenth-century populist leader Ignatius Donnelly who said: "The Democratic party is like a mule — without pride of ancestry or hope of posterity." But few hybrids produced by man have been so economically valuable as the mule. See Savory, The Mule, Scientific American, Jan. 1971, p. 102. — EDS.

[28] The two-year limitations period of Code of Civil Procedure section 339, subdivision 1, governs legal malpractice actions.

[29] Joseph L. Flaig was admitted to the bar in 1958. 1 Martindale-Hubbell Law Directory 277 (1971). — EDS.

[30] "If a person marries after making a will, and the spouse survives the maker, the will is revoked as to the spouse, unless . . . the spouse is provided for in the will, or in such way men-

Plaintiffs allege that defendant negligently failed to advise Doris Kilburn of the consequences of a post-testamentary marriage, and negligently failed to include in the will any provision as to the intended marriage. Plaintiffs allege further that, subsequent to the marriage, and up until the date of testatrix' death, the defendant negligently failed to advise her of the legal consequences of omitting from the will any provision relative to her husband's claim to a share of her estate. Plaintiffs allege that this negligence caused them to suffer damages in the amount of $50,000. They also pray for $50,000 punitive damages on the ground that defendant proceeded maliciously, in wanton disregard of their rights.

Alleging uncertainty, ambiguity, unintelligibility, failure to state facts sufficient to constitute a cause of action, and failure to state a cause of action by reason of the bar of the statute of limitations, section 339, subdivision 1, of the Code of Civil Procedure, defendant demurred to the complaint. On the stated basis that the statute of limitations bars the action because plaintiffs filed the complaint later than two years after the commission of the "negligent act" (presumably the drafting of the will),[31] the trial court sustained the demurrer. Following plaintiffs' failure to take advantage of the court's leave to amend, the court granted defendant's motion to dismiss the action pursuant to section 581, subdivision 3, of the Code of Civil Procedure. From this dismissal plaintiffs appeal.

1. *An attorney who negligently fails to fulfill a client's testamentary directions incurs liability in tort for violating a duty of care owed directly to the intended beneficiaries.*

In the case of Lucas v. Hamm, supra, 56 Cal. 2d 583, we embraced the position that an attorney who erred in drafting a will could be held liable to a person named in the instrument who suffered deprivation of benefits as a result of the mistake. Although we stated that the harmed party could recover as an intended third-party beneficiary of the attorney-client agreement providing for legal services, we ruled that the third party could also recover on a theory of tort liability for a breach of duty owed directly to him. At the heart of our decision in Lucas v. Hamm lay this recognition of duty.

. . . [The third-party beneficiary contractual] theory of recovery, however, is conceptually superfluous since the crux of the action must lie in tort in any case; there can be no recovery without negligence. This reading of Lucas is reinforced by the following language recited with approval in the case of Eads v. Marks (1952) 39 Cal. 2d 807, 811, 249 P.2d 257: " 'It has been well established in this state that if the cause of action arises from a breach of a promise set forth in the contract, the action is ex contractu, but if it arises *from a breach of duty growing out of the contract* it is ex delicto. . . .' "

In the recent case of Connor v. Great Western Sav. & Loan Assn. (1968) 69

---

tioned therein as to show an intention not to make such provision; and no other evidence to rebut the presumption of revocation can be received."

[31] The trial judge relied upon the general rule for attorney malpractice actions that the statute of limitations "begins to run at the time of the negligent act, *not* at the time of discovery of the negligence. [Bustamante v. Haet (1963)] 222 CA 2d 414, 35 Cal. Rptr. 176."

Cal. 2d 850, 73 Cal. Rptr. 369, 447 P.2d 609, we held that a lending institution, which financed and "shared in the control" (69 Cal. 2d at p. 863) of a residential tract development, and "cooperated" with the developer in that undertaking (id.), incurred liability in tort to the buyers of improperly built houses. We said that the lending institution owed a duty to the purchasers "to exercise reasonable care to prevent the construction and sale of seriously defective homes" (69 Cal. 2d at p. 867). Connor, like the preceding cited cases, recognizes that liability may flow from relationships which are not expressed by contract between the parties, not in "privity" with each other, and that such duty could emanate from the policy considerations described in Biakanja v. Irving, 49 Cal. 2d 647, 320 P.2d 16. Indeed, the early common law posited "rights and duties upon the relationship of parties within the socio-economic system rather than upon factors, such as consensual agreement, dependent on the will of individual litigants" and such relationship concepts served as the major framework of the legal structure. (See Tobriner and Grodin, The Individual and the Public Service Enterprise in the New Industrial State (1967) 55 Cal. L. Rev. 1247, 1249-1250.) The Biakanja line of cases does no more than apply to the issues there involved these concepts of duties and rights based upon the relationship between the tortfeasor and the injured parties.

Turning to the present case we therefore concentrate on the tortious aspect of defendant's conduct. We inquire as to whether there was such a duty; the breach, if any; the possibility of the bar of the statute of limitations.

When an attorney undertakes to fulfill the testamentary instructions of his client, he realistically and in fact assumes a relationship not only with the client but also with the client's intended beneficiaries. The attorney's actions and omissions will affect the success of the client's testamentary scheme; and thus the possibility of thwarting the testator's wishes immediately becomes foreseeable. Equally foreseeable is the possibility of injury to an intended beneficiary. In some ways, the beneficiary's interests loom greater than those of the client. After the latter's death, a failure in his testamentary scheme works no practical effect except to deprive his intended beneficiaries of the intended bequests. Indeed, the executor of an estate has no standing to bring an action for the amount of the bequest against an attorney who negligently prepared the estate plan, since in the normal case the estate is not injured by such negligence except to the extent of the fees paid; only the beneficiaries suffer the real loss. We recognized in Lucas that unless the beneficiary could recover against the attorney in such a case, no one could do so and the social policy of preventing future harm would be frustrated.

The duty thus recognized in Lucas stems from the attorney's undertaking to perform legal services for the client but reaches out to protect the intended beneficiary. We impose this duty because of the relationship between the attorney and the intended beneficiary; public policy requires that the attorney exercise his position of trust and superior knowledge responsibly so as not to affect adversely persons whose rights and interests are certain and foreseeable.

Although the duty accrues directly in favor of the intended testamentary beneficiary, the scope of the duty is determined by reference to the attorney-client context. Out of the agreement to provide legal services to a client, the prospective testator, arises the duty to act with due care as to the interests of the intended beneficiary. We do not mean to say that the attorney-client contract for legal services serves as the fundamental touchstone to fix the scope of this direct tort duty to the third party. The actual circumstances under which the attorney undertakes to perform his legal services, however, will bear on a judicial assessment of the care with which he performs his services.

We turn now to the facts of the present case. The complaint alleges that defendant negligently prepared a will purporting to carry out the testatrix' testamentary intention, to give her entire estate to the plaintiffs. The defendant's alleged negligence consisted of his omitting from the will any language which would defeat the rights of the testatrix' husband who could claim a statutory share of the estate as a post-testamentary spouse under Probate Code section 70.

In rendering legal services, an attorney must perform in such manner as " 'lawyers of ordinary skill and capacity commonly possess and exercise' " (Estate of Kruger (1900) 130 Cal. 621, 626, 63 P. 31). A reasonably prudent attorney should appreciate the consequences of a post-testamentary marriage, advise the testator of such consequences, and use good judgment to avoid them if the testator so desires. In the present case, defendant allegedly knew that the testatrix wished to avoid such consequences. Despite his knowledge that the testatrix intended to marry following the execution of the will, the attorney drafted a will which arguably lacked adequate provision against such consequences (cf. Estate of Ryan (1923) 191 Cal. 307, 216 P. 366). Furthermore, the complaint alleges that defendant negligently failed to advise the testatrix that she should change her will after her marriage and continued this negligent omission until the time of her death. The complaint states a sufficient cause of action in tort under the doctrine of Lucas; we proceed, therefore, to determine when the cause of action accrued so as to commence the running of the statute of limitations.

2. *The statute of limitations does not commence to run until the testatrix' death, at which time the defendant's negligence becomes irremediable and before which time the plaintiffs possess no recognized legal interest in the testatrix' estate.*

The continuing nature of the defendant's conduct as alleged in the complaint prevents the running of the statute of limitations before the testatrix' death. The negligence involved in the original drafting of the will continued after that date in defendant's failure to advise the testatrix of the possible undesired consequences if she died without having changed her will.

As to the plaintiffs' interests, defendant's action in negligently drafting the will and his omission in negligently failing to correct his error before the testatrix' death caused equally damaging consequences. Defendant owed a duty of care to the plaintiffs to effectuate in a non-negligent manner the testamentary scheme of the testatrix. Such a duty may extend beyond the date of the original drafting of the will when the attorney's negligent acts created a defective estate plan upon which the client might rely until her death. The duty effectively to fulfill the desired testamentary scheme continued until the testatrix' death, when the testatrix' reliance became irrevocable. Because defendant owed plaintiffs this continuing duty the cause of action did not accrue nor the statute of limitations commence to run until the defendant's negligence became irremediable.

A second basic reason that bars the running of the statute until the testatrix' death lies in the fact that plaintiffs could not bring an action against defendant before that time. A statute of limitations does not commence to run until a cause of action accrues, and "a cause of action . . . invariably accrues when there is a remedy available." (Irvine v. Bossen (1944) 25 Cal. 2d 652, 658, 155 P.2d 9.)

An intended testamentary beneficiary acquires no recognized legal rights under a will until the testator dies, at which time his interest will vest or, indeed, possibly fail. (Cf. Estate of Harvey (1958) 164 Cal. App. 2d 330, 332, 330 P.2d 478.) Before her death, the testatrix in the present case could have altered her will at any time and for any reason. Furthermore, she could have changed her testamentary intention to conform to the actual disposition of her estate under the "defective" will; in such a case, the plaintiffs here would have suffered no actionable injury. Before the testatrix' death, the plaintiffs can state no cause of action because until that time there can be no injury.

To adopt a rule which would start the running of the statutory period from the date of some "original" negligence, we would be compelled to accept the absurd proposition that the only plaintiff who could recover under the doctrine of Lucas v. Hamm, supra, 56 Cal. 2d 583, would be one whose testator had died and who could file a complaint prior to two years after the drafting of the will or after the occurrence of some other original negligent act. Such a rule would vitiate the decision of Lucas by allowing the right to enforce the duty there recognized to turn on mere fortuity.

We cannot accept defendant's argument that the application to the instant case of the present rule with respect to legal malpractice actions, i.e., that the statutory period commences to run from the time of the negligent act, requires a different result here. . . . The defendant argues that, under this rule, even if the testatrix herself had filed a complaint on the date of the present action the statute would have barred it. If plaintiffs here are not also barred, says defendant, we violate the rule that a third-party beneficiary is as much subject to the statute of limitations as the promisee to the contract which creates the rights of the beneficiary. (Bogart v. George K. Porter Co. (1924) 193 Cal. 197, 223 P. 959, 31 A.L.R. 1045.)

This argument proceeds from the erroneous assumption that the rights of an intended testamentary beneficiary recognized in Lucas flow exclusively from the attorney-client agreement. As we discussed supra, the court in Lucas merely extended the principle of Biakanja v. Irving, supra, 49 Cal. 2d 647, to attorneys, holding that by reason of public policy a duty of care arises directly in favor of a third person. Our analysis of the decision in Lucas points to the conceptual superfluity of the third-party beneficiary rationale of that case: the right of action sounds in tort and enures by reason of our determination that public policy requires the recognition of a duty of care on the part of the attorney which accrues directly to the third party, the intended beneficiary. The rule of Bogart v. George K. Porter Co., supra,

193 Cal. 197, should not be rigidly applied to a case in which the policy behind the rule may be inappropriate.[32]

A rule placing the beneficiary in the same position as the testatrix as to the running of the statute of limitations would be viable only if an action by either were equally available and vindicated identical substantive rights. We have noted that the intended beneficiary of a will acquires no cause of action until his testator's death, whereas the prospective testator may sue immediately to recover the cost of drafting the will. Furthermore, the interests at stake in an action by the intended beneficiary and in an action by the testator differ. The former seeks to recover an intended bequest which has been denied him because of the attorney's negligence. The latter seeks to perfect his testamentary scheme, now defective because of the attorney's negligence. In the latter case, the plaintiff's damages will be slight and the consequences of finding a statutory bar will be mild since the testator can create a new and effective estate plan.[33]

The intended beneficiary, on the other hand, suffers a great and irrevocable loss: he has nowhere to turn but to the attorney for compensation. Indeed, Lucas recognizes that unless the beneficiary can recover from the attorney the beneficiary suffers a wrong without a compensating remedy. The duty which the attorney owes the beneficiary is separate and distinct from the duty owed the client; so, too, are the remedies for breaches of these duties. Hence, we violate no policy of Bogart in holding that the rights of the beneficiary may in some instances rise higher than those of his testator.[34]

In the present case we have determined that the plaintiffs' action would have been premature until the testatrix' death and that the defendant's negligence was continuing and incomplete until that time. Hence the statute of limitations does not commence to run until the testatrix' death and consequently the trial judge erroneously sustained defendant's general demurrer on the ground of the bar of the statute of limitations. . . .

[32] Even conceding the validity of alternative theories of recovery arising from the "alternative" rationalia of Lucas, we suggest defendant's argument must fail because of the rule that when a case sounds both in contract and in tort the plaintiff has an election as to which theory of recovery he will pursue. (Comunale v. Traders & General Ins. Co. (1958) 50 Cal. 2d 654, 663, 328 P.2d 198; Cason v. Glass Bottle Blowers Assn. (1951) 37 Cal. 2d 134, 142, 231 P.2d 6, 21 A.L.R.2d 1387.) An election to pursue the action strictly in tort would destroy an automatic application of the Bogart rule to the present case.

[33] After the testator's death, no one but the intended beneficiary has an interest in the defeated bequest. The estate could sue only for the attorney's fees expended since presumably there will have been no other diminution of the estate funds due to the error.

[34] Throughout this discussion we have assumed that if the testatrix had lived and filed suit on the date of the present action, her action would be barred by the statute of limitations under the rule that the statutory period commences to run from the negligent act and not from the date of discovery of the negligence. We note the contrasting rule as to medical malpractice cases: the period does not commence to run until the discovery of the negligence.

. . . The judicial rule against postponed accrual of the statute of limitations in legal malpractice actions rests upon a tenuous basis. . . . [In Neel v. Magana, Olney, Levy, Cathcart & Gelfand, — Cal. 3d —, 98 Cal. Rptr. 837, 491 P.2d 421 (1971), the court held that the statute of limitations begins to run in a legal malpractice action from the time when the client discovers the negligence or, in the exercise of reasonable diligence, should have done so. In an opinion worthy of Justice Cardozo, Justice Tobriner did not find it necessary to overrule a single California Supreme Court case in changing the law. — Eds.]

The judgment of dismissal is reversed with directions to the trial court to overrule the general demurrer and to rule on the points presented by the special demurrers.

Traynor, C.J., Peters, J., Burke, J., and Sullivan, J., concurred.

Mosk, J., concurred in the judgment.

McComb, J. I dissent. I would affirm the orders of dismissal for the reasons expressed by Mr. Justice Bishop in the opinion prepared by him for the Court of Appeal in Heyer v. Flaig (Cal. App.) 67 Cal. Rptr. 92.

NOTES AND PROBLEMS

1. In a state that has a statute similar to California's Probate Code §70, an attorney drafts a will for Mrs. Jones, a widow with two children. The will devises all the testatrix' property "to my children in equal shares." The attorney asks no questions about Mrs. Jones's future plans regarding possible remarriage, and Mrs. Jones offers no information — in fact she has no plans to remarry. Four months later Mrs. Jones meets the attorney at a social gathering and introduces him to "my fiancé, Jack Brown." The attorney offers his congratulations, and reminds Mrs. Jones that he wants to be invited to the wedding. One month later the attorney receives a wedding invitation in the mail and reads it, but he does not attend the wedding.

Two years later Mrs. Brown dies. She is survived by her two children and by her husband, who promptly claims his intestate share pursuant to the state's statute. The children sue the attorney, citing Heyer v. Flaig as authority. What arguments would you make for the children if you were representing them? What arguments would you make for the attorney? What analogy can you make to medical malpractice cases?

2. Prior to 1970 the "charitable remainder trust" was an estate planning device that was frequently used by the rich. H's will would settle a portion of his assets in a trust under which the income was to be paid to his wife, W, for life, and on her death the trust corpus was to be paid to a charity. H's estate received a substantial charitable deduction for the present, discounted value of the remainder interest that would ultimately pass to charity, thus leaving a larger fund from which to provide for W's income and support needs. Because of various abuses and difficulties in valuing the charitable remainder deduction if the trust included "invasion powers" in favor of the income beneficiary, the Tax Reform Act of 1969 made a wholesale revision of the charitable remainder rules. Under the 1969 law a charitable deduction is allowed only if the trust meets the specific and highly technical requirements for a "unitrust" or "annuity trust." (See page 237, infra.)

Suppose these facts. Between 1965 and 1968 A, an attorney, drafted several wills containing charitable remainder trust provisions that conformed to the old rules. One of A's clients dies after October 9, 1972 (the grace period allowed by the statute), without having revoked or modified his will. The client's estate is denied a charitable deduction since the trust created by his will is not a "unitrust" or "annuity trust." The consequence is that the deceased's federal estate tax is $25,000 higher than it would have been had the deduction been allowed. The decedent's executor sues A for negligence, citing Heyer v. Flaig and Lucas v. Hamm as authority. What result? ABA Code of Professional Responsibility, Canon 2, fn. 126 (1969).

3. On November 16, 1960, Henry Weber asked banker Harold Holmes to prepare a will for him leaving one-half of his estate to his wife and one-half to his niece Lillian Price. The banker drafted the will which Weber signed. Two witnesses attested Weber's signature, but he did not sign in their presence nor did they in his presence. Weber died on November 21, 1960, and five days later, on November 26, 1960, his will was offered for probate. Weber's widow contested the will on the ground that the will was not legally executed because Weber and the two witnesses were not all present at the time of execution and attestation. The probate court and the district court ordered the will probated. The widow appealed. On November 25, 1963, while the appeal was pending, Lillian Price died. On December 7, 1963, the Kansas Supreme Court held that the will was not entitled to probate. On February 3, 1964, Lillian Price's administrator was appointed; he filed suit against the banker-draftsman on June 4, 1965. The statute of limitations is three years. When did the cause of action against Holmes accrue?

The Kansas Supreme Court held that a cause of action in tort accrued on December 7, 1963, when that court held the will void. Prior to that time, the court said, the will had been upheld by two courts and Lillian Price had suffered no damage. On December 7, 1963, however, Lillian Price was dead, and no cause of action in tort survived her because she did not have one at death. On the other hand, the court held that the cause of action in contract accrued when the contract was breached. The court reasoned further that the statute of limitations was tolled during the period of the will contest (November 26, 1960, to December 7, 1963), since Lillian could not sue the draftsman until the will was declared void. Thus, regardless of whether the breach of contract occurred when the will was executed or when Weber died, the suit by Lillian's administrator for breach of contract was not barred by the statute of limitations. Price v. Holmes, 198 Kan. 100, 422 P.2d 976 (1967). On the general problem of when the statute of limitations should begin to run, see Note, The Commencement of the Statute of Limitations in Legal Malpractice Actions — The Need for Re-evaluation, 15 U.C.L.A.L. Rev. 230 (1967).

4. In a medical malpractice case, the Massachusetts Supreme Judicial Court held that an instruction incorporating the locality rule, which measures a physician's conduct by the standards of other doctors in similar communities, was incorrect as applied to an anesthesiologist practicing in New Bedford. The court thought that he should be held to the same standard of care as an anesthesiologist in Boston. Brune v. Belinkoff, 354 Mass. 102, 235 N.E.2d 793 (1968). See also Naccarato v. Grob, 384 Mich. 248, 180 N.W.2d 788 (1970): "The standard of care for a specialist should be that of a reasonable specialist practicing medicine in the light of present day scientific knowledge. Therefore, geographical conditions or circumstances control neither the standard of a specialist's care nor the competence of an expert's testimony."

A.B.A. SPECIAL COMMITTEE ON EVALUATION OF ETHICAL STANDARDS, CODE OF PROFESSIONAL RESPONSIBILITY

Disciplinary Rules

DR 2-105 Limitation of Practice.

(A) A lawyer shall not hold himself out publicly as a specialist or as limiting his practice, except as permitted under DR 2-102(A)(6) [35] or as follows:

(1) A lawyer admitted to practice before the United States Patent Office may use the designation Patent Attorney, Patent Lawyer, Trademark Attorney, or Trademark Lawyer, or any combination of those terms, on his letterhead and office sign, and a lawyer actively engaged in the admiralty practice may use the designation Admiralty or Admiralty Lawyer on his letterhead and office sign.

(2) A lawyer may permit his name to be listed in lawyer referral service offices according to the fields of law in which he will accept referrals.

(3) A lawyer available to act as a consultant to or as an associate of other lawyers in a particular branch of law or legal service may distribute to other lawyers and publish in legal journals a dignified announcement of such availability, but the announcement shall not contain a representation of special competence or experience. The announcement shall not be distributed to lawyers more frequently than once in a calendar year, but it may be published periodically in legal journals.

(4) A lawyer who is certified as a specialist in a particular field of law or law practice by the authority having jurisdiction under state law over the subject of specialization by lawyers may hold himself out as such specialist but only in accordance with the rules prescribed by that authority.

DR 6-101 Failing to Act Competently.

(A) A lawyer shall not:

(1) Handle a legal matter which he knows or should know that he is not competent to handle, without associating with him a lawyer who is competent to handle it.

(2) Handle a legal matter without preparation adequate in the circumstances.

(3) Neglect a legal matter entrusted to him.

DR 6-102 Limiting Liability to Client.

(A) A lawyer shall not attempt to exonerate himself from or limit his liability to his client for his personal malpractice.

[35] Disciplinary Rule 2-102(A)(6) permits listing of a specialty in a reputable legal directory if the specialty is authorized under DR 2-105(A)(4). — Eds.

SUSSMAN, CATES & SMITH, THE FAMILY AND INHERITANCE
[*A study of probate practice in Cuyahoga County, Ohio*] *294* (*1970*)

Probate work is a continuing process that begins with planning the estate; this is followed by making the will and then by settlement of the decedent's estate. In the will-making phase, the lawyer must develop and maintain a close relationship with his client and maximize the expression of testamentary freedom within constraints imposed by the law and culture. In administering the estate, the lawyer has a greater opportunity to exercise autonomy, namely, employing his skill and using his knowledge with a minimum of supervision. There are few criteria to judge his competence because the lawyer operates in an area of client ignorance.

Will making was not perceived as a highly professional task by the sample lawyers because of the competition from nonprofessionals, and in many instances it was a one-time relationship in which a standard form was used. In more complicated estates, however, there was a condition for a fiduciary relationship with the client. Over-all, will making was viewed as a necessary activity in order for the lawyer to gain entrance into the more lucrative area of estate administration.

Lawyers were very concerned about the competition they encountered from banks and to a lesser degree from insurance firms and other economic, religious, and social institutions involved in will making. This expressed anxiety and irritability referred more to a potential reduction in the number of administrable estates than to the professional competence of these competing organizational systems and their functionaries.

GERHART, A NEW LOOK AT ESTATE PLANNING: THE GENERAL PRACTITIONER AND MR. AVERAGE
50 Am. Bar Assn. J. 1043 (*1964*)

. . .

We can now draw these interesting statistical conclusions:

(1) 82 per cent of *all* estates filing returns in New York state in the fiscal year ended March 31, 1962, were under $60,000. Therefore, four out of five of all these New York estates presented *no* federal tax problem whatever.

(2) 89 per cent of *all* estates filing returns for the same period in New York state were under $100,000. Therefore, nine out of ten of these New York estates presented no *major* federal estate tax problem.

(3) 38.9 per cent of the estates in the United States filing federal returns for the year 1961 were under $100,000. So four out of ten estates required to file federal estate tax returns present no *major* estate tax problem.

(4) Only slightly over 2 per cent of federally taxed estates and just over 1 per cent of the New York taxed estates were over $1,000,000 for this period. Therefore, with 285,933 actively practicing lawyers in the United States in 1961 and with 1,503 gross estates over $1,000,000 that year, the average American lawyer had one chance

in 190 of representing a $1,000,000 estate. The New York state lawyer's chance was about one in 102 taxable estates.

The general practitioner is in no position to ignore the importance of estate planning and probate work because it produces a considerable part of his own professional income. . . . A recent survey showed that approximately 16 per cent of a Manhattan law firm's work is devoted to wills, trusts and estates. In upstate New York the percentage increased to 26 per cent.

"Outside Manhattan," the survey reported, "three types of law make up the most important sources of income for 80 per cent of all lawyers. These are, in order: first, negligence; second, wills, estate planning and probate; and third, real estate. Of the three, negligence and wills, estate planning and probate are the more lucrative, lawyers in these groups averaging in the $10,001 to $15,000 range." [36]

The subject of estate planning, therefore, is of substantial economic importance to all lawyers in general practice, both the city lawyer and his rural brother alike.

. . .

The general practitioner should not have an inferiority complex about his legal ability to handle the estate planning of his client of moderate means. He should wisely know when he is in over his head and seek the specialist's aid. But the general practitioner will also realize that outside his own field the specialist is just a layman. The expert's seat is not that of final judgment.

Someone said that war is too important to be left to generals. Lifetime property planning often requires the *expertise* of the specialist to be sure, but it also needs the earthy, work-a-day, common sense of the good old general practitioner. Like the traditional British solicitor, the family lawyer knows the client, his background, his faults, his dreams, the skeletons in his closet — and also his hopes and ambitions for those he loves. The family lawyer is surely wise enough not to let his client impoverish himself just to save taxes and thus put himself at the mercy of his children. It is a good policy to pay some taxes as a premium to insure independence in later life.

WELLMAN, SELECTED ASPECTS OF UNIFORM PROBATE CODE

3 Real Prop., Probate & Trust J. 199, 206-207 (1968)

People with small estates want and surely should have acceptable legal consequences for their estates. They are aware that existing laws are bad and that they should do something about their affairs. A questionnaire distributed recently at an annual meeting of a 35,000-member consumer organization in the Detroit area indicated that legal services concerning estate matters [were] second only to assistance in regard to garnishment matters as most generally desired by the members. Annual income of more than [eighty] per cent of the group was estimated to range between

[36] The New York State Bar Association 1961 Program on Economics Report 20 (Daniel J. Cantor and Company of Philadelphia).

$7,500 and $15,000. Other surveys have indicated rather convincingly that, although the average man knows he probably needs a will or at least advice about his affairs, he does not get to a law office until he reaches relatively senior age levels. In point of fact, the older a person gets, the less he may need a will, except where increasing age pushes his accumulation into the areas where split estate, marital deduction planning becomes advisable.

In view of these indicators, why do people not seek legal advice about estate matters more frequently? Part of the answer lies in the general inaccessibility of lawyers which recent studies and discussions focusing on Group Legal Services have pointed up. But I believe the problems in regard to estate counselling are even more serious than problems of adequate legal service in other areas of our profession. The difficulty is that all estate problems are complex. Everyone needs a will and we are not really ready or able to mass produce wills. The result is that the minimum complexity and cost of the lawyer's service in the estate area is too great a barrier to the average person who might seek legal advice if it were not such a "big deal."

The upshot is that lawyers are seriously impeded by cumbersome rules of law from giving service to most people who want it. Worse, circumstances push our estate specialists toward concentration on tax and other complexities attending big estate matters. In consequence, our inability as a profession to deal simply with simple matters involving the personal and financial affairs of the vast majority of the population is growing ever more severe.

The implications of this drift by the profession away from the problems of most people are many and very serious. At this point, I would observe that lawyers are caught in a trap which prevents them from taking advantage of a vast potential for small fees from many millions of potential clients. Also, they are driving the business they presently enjoy in this area of service into the arms of various service groups who are delighted to receive it.

SECTION C. Transmission of Private Wealth in the United States: The Statistical Setting

1. *The Estate*

Who owns what kind of property at death, and to whom is it transferred, with what objectives, under what conditions, and with what effects upon the survivors and upon society? These are not easy questions to answer; our public records are very incomplete. Two primary sources of information are available: federal estate tax returns and probate records. Estate tax returns need not be filed for decedents with a gross estate of less than $60,000. Before 1950, less than 2 percent of decedents' estates filed estate tax returns.[37] By 1969 that figure had jumped to 6.4 percent (123,000 estate tax returns).[38] One reason for this increase is that the $60,000 exemption, unchanged since 1942, becomes less and less significant as long-term infla-

[37] Lampman, The Share of Top Wealth-Holders in National Wealth 1922-1956 at 29 (1962).
[38] U.S. Statistical Abstract 47, 385 (1970).

tion continues and as stock and real estate values rise. Probate records provide information for a greater percentage of estates, but most decedents do not leave wealth to be distributed through probate court. Powell and Looker found that in 1929 probate was initiated for thirty percent of Kings County, New York, decedents.[39] Ward and Beuscher found that in 1941 47 percent of Dane County, Wisconsin, decedents left property to go through probate.[40] Yet in 1957 Dunham found that only 15 percent of the deaths in Cook County, Illinois, were followed by probate proceedings.[41]

Not only are there no probate records for a large percentage of decedents, but also the records do not describe fully the decedents' assets. A great many will substitutes are used to prevent property from passing (through probate court) by way of intestate or testate succession. These include inter vivos gifts, deathbed gifts, and inter vivos trusts. Particularly among the rich, the revocable inter vivos trust is a currently fashionable device to avoid probate and public disclosure of assets. Also, life insurance is not a probate asset, but is paid in accordance with the contract;[42] and jointly held assets — including joint tenancies in real property,[43] government bonds with a survivor beneficiary designation,[44] and joint bank accounts — pass to the survivor without going through probate. Moreover, in some states an executor's inventory can be waived by the decedent and hence may never be filed. Thus probate records offer very incomplete information about a particular decedent's wealth.

Nonetheless, despite the incompleteness of records, some useful data are available.

DUNHAM, THE METHOD, PROCESS AND FREQUENCY OF WEALTH TRANSMISSION AT DEATH

[*A study of Cook County, Illinois, probate court records in 1953 and 1957*], *30 U. Chi. L. Rev. 241, 248-264* (*1963*)

III. Why People Have Wills

A. *The Evidence as to Frequency of Wills*

These figures when compared with those in Table 2 for earlier years indicate a substantial change in the proportion of testate estates. While estimates for 1959 seem to indicate that a major trend toward testacy has developed, we should exam-

39 Powell & Looker, Decedents' Estates, 30 Colum. L. Rev. 919 (1930).

40 Ward & Beuscher, The Inheritance Process in Wisconsin, 1950 Wis. L. Rev. 393.

41 Dunham, The Method, Process and Frequency of Wealth Transmission at Death, 30 U. Chi. L. Rev. 241 (1963).

42 The Life Insurance Fact Book of 1970 reported that all types of life insurance in force totaled over $1.3 trillion. Id. at 5. At least one member of 86 percent of American households owned some type of life insurance. Id. at 10. The average size life insurance policy in force was around $6000. Id. at 24.

43 U.S. Statistical Abstract 686 (1970) estimated that about 64 percent of householders own their own homes, but what portion of these homes is held in joint tenancy is unknown.

44 In 1969, $77 billion in federal securities were owned by individuals, partnerships, and personal trusts. Id. at 393. What portion had a death designee is unknown.

ine what the probate office classifies as an "administratorship" in the earlier years before we conclude that a change in testacy has occurred. The sample does indicate that almost 60 per cent of the estates are testate. This gross statistic tells us nothing about why people leave wills and does not in itself permit us to conclude that this is a high or low percentage. The better than 40 per cent intestate estates may not in fact involve much wealth or even persons for whom a will would have been useful or important. Further breakdown of the will statistics is necessary.

B. *Frequency of Wills according to Age, Occupation and Sex of Decedents with Estates*

Tables 3, 4, and 5 summarize the tendency toward wills according to a number of factors such as sex and occupation. Among factors other than wealth, age would appear to be significant in the frequency of testacies just as it was significant in determining the frequency of estates in Table 1. In the group age eighty and over, where there was a high correlation between the percentage of estates and percentage of deaths, 100 per cent of the estates were testate. The age category seventy to seventy-nine was testate in 56 per cent of the cases. Where the estates are classified by the occupation of the deceased, proprietors appear most prone to have wills. Ten of the 11 estates, or 90.9 per cent, of proprietors in 1957 were testate. Of the groups that had a substantial number of estates such as skilled workers (classified as craftsmen, operators, sales workers and clericals) the percentage of testate estates was in each case less than 40 per cent, a proportion substantially less than the proportion of testacies in the sample as a whole.[45]

In Table 4, men were 53 per cent testate and women were 57 per cent testate. It would appear therefore that while the estates of men predominated in the sample, women are more likely to have a will than men.

As Table 5 indicates, whether the decedent is a widow or widower seems to be the only marital status that substantially affects the frequency of testate estates. Decedents with that status were testate in 59 per cent of the cases. . . .

The marital status does not seem a significant factor. The most significant factor again seems to be the fact that decedent was widowed. Women, for example, who were testate in only 30 per cent of the cases when survived by a spouse, became testate in almost three-fourths of the cases when no spouse survived. Although the difference was not as pronounced for men, widowed men with children were testate in three out of five cases, but in only one out of two cases if there was a surviving spouse. This suggests that a previous experience with death and its property problems in the immediate family tends to induce both men and women to have wills.

C. *Accumulated Wealth and the Use of Wills*

Tables 7 and 8 indicate the distribution of the estates among various brackets of wealth and also the significance of wealth in the frequency of testacy.

[45] The Wisconsin survey did not show that occupational differences significantly affected the use of wills; the average of all groups was approximately 47 percent. The Wisconsin Study at 411-12. [The Wisconsin Study is Ward & Beuscher, The Inheritance Process in Wisconsin, 1950 Wis. L. Rev. 393, a study of probate records in Dane County, Wisconsin. — Eds.]

TABLE 7
Distribution of Estates by Value of
Estate and Sex of Decedent*

Value of Estate	*Percentage of Estates*		
	Total	*Male*	*Female*
Below 5,000	44	48	37
5,000–9,999	18	17	19
10,000–24,999	22	20	27
25,000–49,999	8	7	9
50,000–99,999	5	5	5
100,000 and over	3	3	3
Total	100	100	100
(Number of cases)	(6683)	(4060)	(2623)

*1950 data.

TABLE 8
Percentage Testate of all Estates by Value of
Estate and Sex of Decedent*

Value of Estate	*Male*	*Female*	*Total*
Below 5,000	22	31	25
5,000–9,999	51	61	56
10,000–24,999	60	67	63
25,000–49,999	78	80	79
50,000–99,999	85	89	86
100,000 and over	98	94	96
Total	44	56	49

*1950 data.

Tables 7 and 8 taken from the last complete data for Cook County in 1950 indicate that while the largest percentage of estates is found in the lower valuation brackets, the largest percentage of testate estates is in the higher brackets. Table 8 reveals a steady progression from less than 50 per cent testacy in estates below \$10,000 to almost 100 per cent testacy in estates over \$100,000. The sharpest increase in percentage of testacy occurs with respect to female decedents, and it is not until the largest category of estates is reached that the percentage of male testacy exceeds that of the female. In the sample years a similar result is reached as to estates subject to estate taxes; 100 per cent of this type of estate is testate if the decedent is male but only 75 per cent if the decedent is female. From the estates in the sample years 1953 and 1957 as to which sufficient information was available to obtain a total of the values stated for probate, it would appear that 90 per cent of the wealth transmitted at death through probate was transmitted in testate estates. $4,031,458 was transmitted by will as against $441,680 by intestacy.[46] This conclusion, that the bulk of the wealth is transmitted by will even though only about 60 per cent of the estates are testate, is significant in evaluating the public relations efforts of the legal profession and corporate executors attempting to induce people to leave wills. While the ideal may be that 100 per cent of the wealth transmitted at death should be transmitted by will, nevertheless, if about 90 per cent of the wealth is now transmitted by will, it is questionable whether any substantial "return" would accrue from intensifying efforts to induce people to plan their estates. At least if an objective of the public relations campaign is to aid the economic status of the Bar, it is questionable whether an important increase in legal business would result from having 100 per cent of the decedents die with wills. Of course there may be important by-products to a campaign concerning wills and estate planning insofar as this attracts to the corporate trustee or lawyer persons who have business other than will drafting.

. . .

V. The Estate

A. *Size of Estates*

The study indicates that few persons die owning an accumulation of any sizable fortune. Taking the two years 1953 and 1957 together, 42.7 per cent of the estates that passed through the Probate Court had a stated value of less than $10,000.[47] 72.3 per cent had a stated value of less than $25,000. Of the estates in which the stated value was given, out of 159, 46 had a stated value of less than $5,000 and 22 had a stated value between $5,000 and $10,000. Ten, or 6.2 per cent, of the estates had a stated value of $100,000 or over.

In the sample the average stated value of worth on death for all testate estates probated was $41,885 and for intestate estates the average value was $7,920. In 1953 the mean testate estate was $15,000 and the mean intestate estate was $4,000. The 1957 figure was substantially higher for the testate estates where the mean figure was $22,000 compared with $5,000 for intestate estates.[48] In both years the modal size of estates, that is, the figure that had the largest number of estates in that category, was $1,000 for both testate and intestate estates.

[46] Stephenson, Trust Business in Hawaii, 100 Trusts & Estates 73 (1961) reports that in Hawaii in 1949 it was estimated that 85% of the total property transmitted at death passed under a will.

[47] The Wisconsin Study at 399, 401 indicated that 45.3% of people having an estate had a net worth on death of less than $5,000. Only 3.13% of the Wisconsin estates exceeded $50,000. These [1941] dollars are not the same as 1953 or 1957 dollars.

[48] The Wisconsin Study at 400-01 found an average net worth on death of all estates probated of $11,500. This study used figures obtained from the inheritance tax returns so as to include in the net worth figures the face value of all life insurance disclosed on the tax return.

Perhaps the most significant feature of this analysis may be recalled if it is noted that only 15 per cent of the adult deaths were deaths of people who seemed to have accumulated sufficient capital during their lifetimes to have an estate admitted to probate. But, when this is projected for the total adult deaths in Cook County, then 95 per cent of the adults in Chicago accumulate property worth less than $10,000 during their lifetimes.[49] Only 1 per cent accumulate property worth more than $100,000 during their lifetimes.

For a study of probate records in Cuyahoga County, Ohio, which came to conclusions similar to Dunham's, see Sussman, Cates & Smith, The Family and Inheritance (1970).

2. *The Distribution of Wealth in the United States*

In a study highly regarded by economists, The Share of Top Wealth-Holders in National Wealth 1922-1956 (1962), Professor Robert J. Lampman undertook to analyze the share of the national wealth owned by the top individual wealth-holders in this country.[50] He took basic data from federal estate tax returns for selected years between 1922 and 1956, and then employed the estate-multiplier method. This method calls for multiplying the number and property of decedents in each age-sex group by the inverse of the mortality rate for that age-sex group. This process yields an estimate of the number of living persons and the amount of estate in each age-sex group and in each estate size. Lampman recognized that persons may have income interests in trusts and equities in pension and retirement funds, which do not appear on the estate tax return; for these he attempted to make quantitative corrections in his estimates (pp. 62-83).

Lampman's findings include the following:

1. The total of all personally owned wealth in the United States in 1953 was estimated to be $1 trillion (p. 84).

2. In 1953 over 30 percent of the assets and equities of the personal sector of the economy was held by 1.6 percent of the total adult population (p. 23).

3. This group of 1.6 percent owned 82 percent of all corporate stock, almost all state and local (tax-exempt) bonds, 38 percent of government bonds, 88 percent of other bonds, 16 percent of real estate, 13 percent of life insurance reserves, and 6 percent of pension and retirement funds (pp. 191-192).

[49] The Wisconsin Study at 400 indicated that 77% of the people of Dane County accumulated property worth less than $5,000. [In an omitted portion of this article Dunham warned the reader to be skeptical of such conclusions because of the impossibility of securing meaningful statistics on the number of decedents who had wealth that did not pass through probate. A Survey of Financial Characteristics of Consumers, issued by the Board of Governors of the Federal Reserve System in 1966, found that in 1962, 39 per cent of consumer units had a net worth of more than $10,000 exclusive of life insurance and equities in annuities and retirement plans. — Eds.]

[50] See also Kolko, Wealth and Power in America (1962).

4. "From these and related facts of estate composition, this picture of changing preference emerges. As people get richer, they shift from purchase of consumer capital, including real estate and life insurance, to U.S. bonds and mortgages and notes. As they get still richer, they shift over to corporate stock and state, local and 'other' bonds. As people get older, they reduce their liabilities, 'cash out' of miscellaneous property (which includes interest in unincorporated business) and life insurance, and convert to larger holdings of cash, U.S. bonds, corporate stock, and mortgages and notes. As wealth moves into the hands of women, liabilities are reduced, life insurance falls as a percentage of estate and, consequently, all other types of property rise in relative importance" (p. 23).

5. The following table shows the percentage of national wealth-holdings for the top 1 percent of adult population for the indicated years (p. 204):

Year	*Percent*
1922	31.6
1929	36.3
1933	28.3
1939	30.6
1945	23.3
1949	20.8
1953	24.3
1954	24.0
1956	26.0

Lampman estimated that the share of capital wealth held by the top 2 percent of families fell from about 33 to 29 percent from 1922 to 1953, which is compatible with the general belief that there has been some lessening of inequality in the United States in recent decades.[51] However, Lampman also noted that the degree of inequality increased from 1949 to 1956 (p. 24).[52]

6. In 1951 the top 1.4 percent received 14.2 percent of all income though they held more than 28 percent of personally owned wealth (p. 234). The top 1 percent, though they held more than 25 percent of the wealth, were only able to save 15 percent of all savings (p. 244).

7. A much greater inequality of wealth exists in England and Wales than in the United States. In 1946-47 the top 1.5 percent of adults owned 53 percent of the total wealth in England and Wales, while in 1953 the top 1.5 percent of adults in the United States owned only 27 percent of the wealth. But the historical picture of

[51] Note that capital distribution appears to have changed less than *income* distribution during this period. The share of the top 5 percent in income dropped from 30 percent in 1929 to 20 percent in 1959 and during the 1960s dropped three more percentage points. Kuznets, Modern Economic Growth 211 (1966); Brimmer, Inflation and Income Distribution in the United States, 55 Rev. Econ. & Stat. 37, 41 (1971).

[52] Smith & Calvert, in a paper prepared for the American Statistical Association in 1965 entitled "Estimating the Wealth of Top Wealth-Holders from Estate Tax Returns," support the thesis that the concentration of wealth was slowly increasing between 1953 and 1958.

decline in the degree of inequality is similar in the two countries. In 1911-13 1 percent of the persons twenty-five and over in England and Wales owned 70 percent of the capital; by 1946-47 this figure had fallen to 50 percent (pp. 211-215).

Commenting on these findings by Lampman, Berle wrote: "There is, therefore, a steady force eroding this concentration. Probably this is chiefly accounted for by the incidence of income tax. I suggest that the American economic republic, though it has not socialized wealth, has gone a substantial distance toward socializing income." The American Economic Republic 221 (1963).

Another study of personal wealth based upon federal estate tax returns is U.S. Treasury Department, Internal Revenue Service, Statistics of Income . . . 1962, Supplemental Report (1967). This report concluded that there were 4.1 million individuals with gross assets of $60,000 or more in 1962, or about 3.7 percent of the adult population. These top wealth-holders had net assets totaling $669.3 billion. Individuals numbering 177,000 had net worths of $500,000 or more. Three-fifths of the top wealth-holders were men, two-fifths were women. The overall differences between the holdings of men and women were not very great except in three respects. Eighty-seven percent of the men owned life insurance versus 46 percent of the women. Fourteen percent of the men's assets were burdened with debts and mortgages compared with 7 percent of the women's. Three out of four powers of appointment were held by women. The report agreed with Lampman's analysis of the composition of estates (finding 4 above). There was a sharp decline in insurance holdings after top wealth-holders passed fifty years of age, which reflects both the reduced need for protection and the increase in other forms of wealth.

3. *Wealth Held in Trust*

Prior to the 1960s data on wealth held in personal trusts were very hard to come by. Banks were reluctant to reveal any information. In the 1960s some studies began to appear. Statistics of Income — 1965, Fiduciary, Gift and Estate Tax Returns, published by the Treasury Department in 1967, gives us a starting point. In 1965, 220,593 estates and 576,908 trusts filed fiduciary income tax returns reporting $8.5 billion total income. Of this amount $6.6 billion was attributable to trusts — $4.2 billion in ordinary income and $2.4 billion in capital gain (p. 22). The trust income was almost evenly divided between inter vivos and testamentary trusts (p. 21). $298 million of the trust income was distributed to charities (p. 27). The number of trusts grew from 360,617 in 1956 to 576,908 in 1965 (p. 39). These figures do not include "grantor trusts" (such as revocable trusts) where the income is taxable to the grantor rather than to some other beneficiary.

Wealth held in private trusts is concentrated in a few states, as is shown by the table on the next page.

How much wealth is held in personal trusts, and what portion is managed by corporate trustees? We can only estimate this. Capitalizing the reported trust income of $6.6 billion at 4 percent indicates total trust assets of $165 billion in 1965.

	Number of Estates and Trusts	Total Income (in millions)	Per Cent of Total Income
Total in All States	798,842	8,515	100.0
New York	126,779	1,571	18.4
Illinois	56,252	683	8.0
California	73,101	678	8.0
Pennsylvania	69,059	672	7.9
Delaware	5,182	488	5.7
Texas	39,322	477	5.6
Ohio	36,967	475	5.6
Massachusetts	39,470	472	5.5
New Jersey	27,806	271	3.2
Michigan	22,717	236	2.8
Florida	19,920	223	2.6
Connecticut	20,994	202	2.4
Top 12 States	537,569	6,448	75.7

Assuming the amount in trust increased 33 percent from 1965 to 1969 — as it did from 1962 to 1965 — $219 billion was held in personal trusts in 1969. What portion of this amount was managed by corporate trustees? A Congressional subcommittee has reported that as of December 31, 1967, the personal trust accounts of all insured commercial banks amounted to $126 billion.[53] A 1969 report by the Board of Governors of the Federal Reserve System stated that approximately $118 billion was held in personal trusts by insured commercial banks in 1969.[54] These figures indicate that somewhat more than 50 percent of personal trust assets are managed by commercial banks. Of course many of the trusts with corporate trustees have individual trustees as well. What advantages might there be in designating a member of the family, or a lawyer, as co-trustee with a bank?

FERGUSON, HOW TO GROW TRUST BUSINESS, 103 Trusts & Estates 1097 (1964): ". . . As estate taxes decimated family fortunes, our bank made a rough guess that our future lay in reaching for the medium-sized estates of first-generation property owners. This did not prove to be so. A study of estates in our county [(Pittsburgh) Allegheny County, Pa.] over an 11-year period showed that

[53] U.S. Congress, H.R. Committee on Banking and Currency, Subcommittee on Domestic Finance, Commercial Banks and Their Trust Activities: Emerging Influence on the American Economy 34 (1968). This report also states, at 34, that private trusts account for 49.8 percent of all trust assets held by commercial banks. The major sources of other trust assets held by commercial banks are employee pension and profit-sharing plans. See page 176, infra.

[54] Bd. of Gov. of Fed. Reserve System, Trusts Assets of Insured Commercial Banks — 1969 at 5 (1969). Sixty-five percent of the trust assets were invested in common stocks. The report also stated that the average size of a personal trust account was $35,500 in banks doing trust business of less than $10,000,000, and that the average size increased with the size of the trust department until, in banks with a trust department exceeding $1 billion, the average size trust reached $304,900. Id. at 7.

those under $100,000 had a 112% increase; $100,000 to $500,000, a 290% increase; $500,000 to $1 million a 278% increase; and over $1 million a 311% increase. At least in our market, the large, profitable estates are not a thing of the past."

Just as trust business controlled by banks is unevenly distributed throughout the country, within each state a few banks dominate. The twelve largest private trust departments in banks in the United States in 1967 were:[55]

	Amount (billions)	*Percentage of Total of Private Trust Business of Banks*
First National City Bank, New York	$ 4.1	3.3
Wilmington Trust Co., Wilmington	3.9	3.2
Morgan Guaranty Trust, New York[56]	3.2	2.6
U.S. Trust Co., New York	3.2	2.6
Mellon National Bank, Pittsburgh	3.1	2.5
Chase Manhattan Bank, New York	3.0	2.4
Manufacturers Hanover Trust Co., New York	2.9	2.3
Northern Trust Co., Chicago	2.6	2.1
Girard Trust Bank, Philadelphia	2.3	1.9
Cleveland Trust Co., Cleveland	2.3	1.9
Old Colony Trust Co., Boston	2.2	1.8
Bankers Trust Co., New York	2.2	1.8
	$35.0	28.4

Beginning around 1950, trusts managed by commercial banks began to grow rapidly. In addition to private trusts, banks began to manage mutual investment funds and pension trust funds. Most of these funds are heavily invested in common stocks. Taken together, the three sets of trust funds might contain stock sufficient to give trustee banks working control of large segments of American industry. This problem was investigated by the House of Representatives Committee on Banking

[55] H.R. Committee on Banking and Currency, Subcommittee on Domestic Finance, Commercial Banks and Their Trust Activities: Emerging Influence on the American Economy 35 (1968).

[56] In addition to $3.2 billion in private trusts, the Morgan Guaranty Trust Co. has employee benefit trust assets of $10 billion, giving it the largest trust department in the country. The Morgan Guaranty holds more trust assets than are found in all 36 banks exercising trust powers in the entire state of California. Id. at 60.

and Currency, Subcommittee on Domestic Finance, which published its findings in a report entitled Commercial Banks and Their Trust Activities: Emerging Influence on the American Economy (1968). Examination of this report reveals an intricate power structure giving rise to new questions of power, balance, and control.

BERLE, COMMERCIAL BANKS AND CONTROL OF AMERICAN INDUSTRY, introduction to Arno Press and N.Y. Times reprint (1969) of Commercial Banks and Their Trust Activities: "There is, however, a yet unfilled lacuna in our knowledge of the facts. Unquestionably it is true that if the institutional holdings are aggregated, the managers of these institutions can elect directors, can perhaps constitute or remove the managements of many industrial corporations. The unknown factor is the extent to which they use or combine with each other to use this latent power.[57] . . . It seems unlikely that so immense a latent power will continue to exist without being used. Temptation to use economic power is rarely resisted.

"This power does not exhaust the subject. There is another means by which economic power could be concentrated. Its potential is likewise great — we shall ask in a moment whether it has been realized. It arises from interlocking directorates.

"The big banks whose trust departments hold stock familiarly have as members of their own boards of directors executives or directors of other big financial or industrial corporations. The extent of these interlocks is reviewed by the report. Forty-six major industrial corporations have one of their own directors on the boards of one or more of the great trust companies, which are, of course, also holders of their stock.

. . .

"But if this is to be changed, the problem invariably arises: Where should it go? I do not see the possibility, now, of returning to a system of relatively small industrial corporations, or even of relatively small banks. The massive onslaught of technology seems to require large aggregates of capital, more extensive operations for plant building, mass marketing and mass servicing, and consequent greater capacity to gather capital and provide credit.

"If these are not to be broken up (I think they can not be) we must ask the second question: What do you want these great financial and commercial mechanisms to do? What criteria can be established for judging their results and the ability of their managements to produce these results? This is to change the subject. Instead of asking, Who shall choose managements and managers? we must ask the question, What results shall we expect from managers, and where shall power be located to guide and change them if the results are undesirable?"

[57] For the view that the money market does not control corporations, see Lintner, Financing of Corporations, in The Corporation in Modern Society 166 (Mason ed. 1960). — Eds.

HARRISS, ECONOMIC EFFECTS OF ESTATE AND GIFT TAXATION

Joint Committee on the Economic Report, Federal Tax Policy for Economic Growth and Stability 855 (1955)

One major economic effect of estate taxes results from the opportunity under the law to reduce the total tax over the years, reduce it substantially, by placing property in trust. Consequently, the use of trusts is stimulated by the taxes in their present form. Although there is no doubt about the tendency, no data for measuring it are available. Thus, knowing that over 25 percent of gifts reported on 1950 gift tax returns were of property in trust, we still cannot say how much of this use of trusts was due to the tax system. Certainly some, probably much! And the extent will grow as the tax-saving advantages of trusts are recognized more widely and as wills now being made come into effect.

What, then, is the economic significance of trusteeship of wealth? More cautious and conservative investment is one result. Although trusts made today generally permit investment beyond the restrictive limits of the past, the tendency is to stick to relatively "high quality" assets. Another, and related, is greater emphasis on rationality in making investment decisions; specialized, technically competent personnel generally guide the decision making. While the wisdom of trustees will vary widely, their influence will make the preservation of wealth more likely than if heirs were given greater responsibility and freedom for investment. The dissipation of inheritances that can come from foolish investment or reckless spending by heirs who are free to use their property is largely prevented by trusteeing wealth. The economy as a whole, as well as the particular families involved, will benefit from any such reduction of folly and waste.

On the other hand, the conservative and restricted nature of trusts removes wealth from markets where it might be available for more venturesome and risky investment. Fortunes in trust cannot, as a rule, be used for financing some of the most dynamic parts of the economy. Even the beneficiary of a trust seeking capital for his own business often cannot use assets which under a freer system would have been available to him. Yet it is the large concentration of wealth that can finance the scrutiny of new ventures and afford to take the extreme risks that are involved in true economic pioneering.[58] Of course, there is no way to determine how much, if any, of the wealth now in trust for rich families would in fact be used to finance dynamic ventures intelligently were it not for trustification. It is easy, perhaps, to romanticize a bit about the part existing fortunes would play in financing the expansion of economic frontiers, especially by new businesses. There can be no doubt,

[58] Giant corporations now perform some of the venturesome undertaking once left more to individuals; the giants seeking funds for expansion may at times get them by sale of new common stock to trusts. There is little basis for judging how adequately established firms do the job or what gaps they leave that might be filled by use of private fortunes. My own feeling, which may be largely prejudice, is that innumerable opportunities will not be developed by firms large enough to draw, directly or indirectly, on wealth in trust.

however, that much wealth now in trust cannot conceivably be used for such purposes; in addition there are assets which in fact will not be used for dynamic economic growth even though the trustees are not absolutely prohibited from doing so.

However, there develops a group — not large in relation to the whole population — receiving income (about $2 billion a year before income tax) from trusts whose capital assets they do not fully own or control and may not consume. Although the social and economic effects of such a development are not obvious, they will hardly assume the relative importance of those associated with rentier groups in some civilizations in the past.

SECTION D. Should Society Permit Inheritance?

JEFFERSON, 7 JEFFERSON'S WORKS 454 (Monticello ed.): "The earth belongs in usufruct to the living; the dead have neither powers nor rights over it. The portion occupied by any individual ceases to be his when he himself ceases to be, and reverts to society."

2 BLACKSTONE, COMMENTARIES
** 10-13*

The right of inheritance, or descent to the children and relations of the deceased, seems to have been allowed much earlier than the right of devising by testament. We are apt to conceive, at first view, that it has nature on its side; yet we often mistake for nature what we find established by long and inveterate custom. It is certainly a wise and effectual, but clearly a political, establishment; since the permanent right of property, vested in the ancestor himself, was no *natural*, but merely a *civil* right. . . . It is probable that [the right of inheritance arose] . . . from a plainer and more simple principle. A man's children or nearest relations are usually about him on his death-bed, and are the earliest witnesses of his decease. They become, therefore, generally the next immediate occupants, till at length, in process of time, this frequent usage ripened into general law. And therefore, also, in the earliest ages, on failure of children, a man's servants, born under his roof, were allowed to be his heirs; being immediately on the spot when he died. For we find the old patriarch Abraham expressly declaring that "since God had given him no seed, his steward Eliezer, one born in his house, was his heir." [59]

[59] Genesis XV, 3. [The words put in quotation marks are Blackstone's paraphrase of two verses of the Bible, which no one has yet translated from the original Hebrew to everyone's satisfaction. Blackstone's statement that servants took as heirs in the absence of children has been disputed by many scholars. "Israel does not know a general rule like this for regulating the inheritance." Von Rad, Genesis 178 (Marks trans. 1961). Cf. Neufeld, Ancient Hebrew Marriage Laws 262 (1944). Abraham's declaration was never put to the test for thereafter, when Abraham was 100 years old and his wife Sarah was ninety, Sarah gave birth to a son, Isaac. Genesis 17:15. — Eds.]

While property continued only for life, testaments were useless and unknown: and, when it became inheritable, the inheritance was long indefeasible, and the children or heirs at law were incapable of exclusion by will; till at length it was found, that so strict a rule of inheritance made heirs disobedient and headstrong, defrauded creditors of their just debts, and prevented many provident fathers from dividing or charging their estates as the exigencies of their families required. This introduced pretty generally the right of disposing of one's property, or a part of it, by *testament;* that is, by written or oral instructions properly *witnessed* and authenticated, according to the *pleasure* of the deceased, which we, therefore, emphatically style his *will.* This was established in some countries much later than in others. With us in England, till modern times, a man could only dispose of one-third of his movables from his wife and children; and in general, no will was permitted of lands till the reign of Henry VIII; and then only of a certain portion: for it was not till after the Restoration that the power of devising real property became so universal as at present.

Wills, therefore, and testaments, rights of inheritance and successions, are all of them creatures of the civil or municipal laws, and accordingly are in all respects regulated by them; every distinct country having different ceremonies and requisites to make a testament completely valid; neither does anything vary more than the right of inheritance under different national establishments.

IRVING TRUST CO. v. DAY, 314 U.S. 556, 562 (1942): "Rights of succession to the property of a deceased, whether by will or by intestacy, are of statutory creation, and the dead hand rules succession only by sufferance. Nothing in the Federal Constitution forbids the legislature of a state to limit, condition, or even abolish the power of testamentary disposition over property within its jurisdiction."

It is generally stated by courts and writers that the law of inheritance is entirely within the control of the legislature, subject only to the constitutional guarantees of equal protection and due process.[60] The only court in the United States to hold that legislative power over testamentary succession is not plenary is the Supreme Court of Wisconsin. In Nunnemacher v. State, 129 Wis. 190, 108 N.W. 627 (1906), the court asserted that the right to dispose of property by will was a natural right, protected by the Constitution. And, says Professor Powell, the Wisconsin court "is still struggling to escape the corollary tentacles of this unsupportable position." [61]

To support its position, the Wisconsin Court drew not only upon philosophy, but upon history. "The right to make a will is very ancient and considered as incidental to the right to acquire property, and, so, one of the inherent rights guaran-

60 These broad statements may not be wholly reliable inasmuch as the power of the legislature to abolish inheritance has never been directly tested. See Scurlock, Retroactive Legislation Affecting Interests in Land 90-105 (1953).

61 6 Powell, Real Property ¶940 (1956).

teed by the Constitution. Its recognition antedates common and civil law. It is as ancient as any sort of civilization. It has been held sacred in all nations and under all conditions." Cowie v. Strohmeyer, 150 Wis. 401, 136 N.W. 956, 973 (1912). However one may view the court's philosophy, the court either had not read its history or was rewriting history to fit its notions of what history ought to have been. In actual history, as Blackstone has reminded us, freedom of testation has been the exception, not the rule.[62]

In many early societies testation was never known. In classical Greece a man could make a will, but a jury could override it if the jury thought it unfair. And no testator could escape the limitations imposed by custom. Inasmuch as the individual was viewed as only a link in the chain of his family, if there were legitimate male descendants the testator could make only limited bequests.[63] In western civilization, the will did not evolve into its modern concept until the time of the Romans. The Roman ancestor of the modern will consisted at first of a formal public declaration before the Patrician Assembly designating an heir. The ceremony, which simulated a sale, irrevocably and immediately conveyed all the testator's property to the heir. The unattractive features of this ceremony were publication before death, irrevocability, and immediate vesting of title in the heir. These inconveniences were soon remedied by the Romans, and the will took on the characteristics by which we know it today.[64]

Up until the French Revolution, French law prohibited devising ancestral lands. In Scotland lands could not be devised prior to 1868, except in limited circumstances. In England freedom of disposition had an on-again-off-again history until the time of Henry VIII. When that wayward monarch ascended the throne devises of land were prohibited by the law courts, but the landed gentry had established a practical equivalent of a will of land by using a feoffee to uses. When uses were abolished in 1536, the landed class became aroused because this substitute for a will was no longer available. To mollify them the Statute of Wills was passed in 1540, making land devisable by will.

It should be added that the Statute of Wills did not establish freedom of testation for everyone in England. For centuries before and after the Statute a mar-

[62] See Page, Wills §§2.1 to 2.18 (Bowe-Parker rev. 1960); McMurray, Liberty of Testation and Some Modern Limitations Thereon, 14 Ill. L. Rev. 96 (1919).

[63] Chroust, Estate Planning in Hellenic Antiquity: Aristotle's Last Will and Testament, 45 Notre Dame Law. 629 (1970).

[64] For development of the Roman will see Maine, Ancient Law, cc. 6 and 7 (Pollock ed. 1930). Maine doubted that the will would ever have been invented had it not been for (a) a rule of intestate succession excluding decedent's emancipated sons and (b) the Roman theory of universal succession. Under Roman law every person who had legal rights or duties had two personalities, one natural and the other legal. The legal personality, which Maine analogized to a corporation sole, was vested with rights and duties. One of the remarkable things about the legal personality was that it existed after death, and every person with rights and duties must perforce have an heir to exercise them. The heir (or co-heirs) succeeded instantly to the entire legal position of the dead man. So completely were the heir's rights and duties identified with the decedent's that the creditors of an insolvent decedent could collect the debt from the heir's own assets. The only way the heir could escape the liabilities was to reject the succession. For analysis of the concept of universal succession, see Pelletier & Sonnenreich, A Comparative Analysis of Civil Law Succession, 11 Vill. L. Rev. 323 (1966).

ried woman had no right to make a will;[65] her incapacity continued in the United States until the end of the 19th century.[66]

PROBLEMS

1. The Fifth Amendment to the United States Constitution provides: ". . . nor shall private property be taken for public use, without just compensation." The Fourteenth Amendment to the United States Constitution provides: "No State shall . . . deprive any person of life, liberty, or property, without due process of law; nor deny to any person within its jurisdiction the equal protection of the laws." How would these Amendments apply, if at all, to an act of a state legislature providing that upon death a person's estate would pass to a public trustee to pay the income to the decedent's spouse for life, and then to pay the income to the decedent's minor children, if any, until they reach twenty-one, then to pay the principal to the state? Mapp, The 1969 Oregon Probate Code and Due Process, 49 Ore. L. Rev. 345 (1970).

2. Does the legislature have plenary power over inter vivos donative transfers as well as over testamentary dispositions?

3. It is generally conceded that a legislature may not deprive a landowner of *all* reasonable use of his land without paying him compensation therefor. Arverne Bay Construction Co. v. Thatcher, 278 N.Y. 222, 15 N.E.2d 587 (1938). Why can the legislature declare that all land escheats to the state at death of the owner, but during his life it cannot prohibit all use of the property without paying compensation?

The unequal distribution of wealth, which is seen as perpetuated by the institutions of inheritance, has led some to call for the abolition of inheritance. The arguments pro and con have usually been stated at a high level of generalization, and are here summarized. No one has yet produced a penetrating study of the economic and social impact of the abolition of inheritance.

Arguments Against Inheritance

1. A goal of a democratic society is equality of opportunity. Those who inherit — or whose parents inherit — wealth are given favorable, unequal treatment, unrelated to their abilities or performance.[67]

[65] When the ecclesiastical courts in the fourteenth century attempted to loosen slightly the hold of the husband on his wife's property by giving a married woman power to leave some property "for the good of her soul," the common law courts prevented this by allowing her husband to maintain an action against her executor for any property so disposed of.

[66] Bordwell, The Statute Law of Wills, 14 Iowa L. Rev. 172, 179 (1929).

[67] This argument is best spelled out in Wedgwood, The Economics of Inheritance (1929). Wedgwood proposed to abolish inheritance but not gifts during life. See also Sayre, Recent Ideologies in the Law of Succession to Property, 32 Ill. L. Rev. 691 (1938).

2. "[I]nherited economic power is as inconsistent with the ideals of this generation as inherited political power was inconsistent with the ideals of the generation which established our Government." [68]

3. Inheritance makes possible a class of idle rich, depriving society of the productive energies of the recipients. ["In the United States it does not do so. In the social norms of American life, leisure is no longer considered a creditable way of life. The real luxury, as Americans see it, is having an interesting job, preferably one which enjoys the regard and esteem of the community. The son of a multimillionaire could loaf his life away without economic difficulty; but those who do are disliked by the community, and perhaps because of that (as well as for other reasons) are desperately unhappy. He therefore seeks, according to his taste and capacity, a job as university instructor, or in the diplomatic service of the United States, or in a museum, or in a publishing house, or in politics, or running a country newspaper — unless he wishes to go into a business or a profession for the primary reason of achieving a financially unnecessary commercial or professional success. But because the American social system has, and does not hesitate to express, a low opinion of a leisure class in general, and men of leisure in particular, this does not mean that the possibility can be entirely discounted. There have been countries where, and periods in history when, leisure classes were not only tolerated, but esteemed — and when they turned in a substantial dividend intellectually and esthetically. . . . One can imagine without difficulty a civilization to come in which everyone's wants and comforts are provided — except adequate opportunity to participate in significant tasks. Then, the intriguing, the use of influence, the wangling, and the throat-cutting competition will be addressed toward getting and holding jobs which have and give this sense of participation. Wealth will seek such jobs. The 'lower class' will then be, not a class in poverty or want, but a class in meaningless comfort." [69]]

4. The costs of political campaigns are so great that the rich hold a great advantage in competing for high elective office and exercise a disproportionate influence in American politics.

Arguments for Inheritance

1. A person has a moral obligation to support his dependents after he is dead. [There are several difficulties with this argument. In the first place, most heirs — excluding the spouse — are not dependent, and receive their inheritance in their thirties or thereafter when their pattern of living has become more or less fixed. Second, statutes could be, and in some jurisdictions have been, enacted giving dependents the right to support from the decedent's estate. The general power of testation is not necessary to accomplish this goal. Third, this argument sustains only inheritance by dependents in the amount necessary for support, not inheritance generally.]

[68] Message to Congress from President Roosevelt, H.R. Rep. No. 1681, 74th Cong., 1st Sess. 2 (1935), 1939-1 Cum. Bull. (Part 2) 643.

[69] Berle, The American Economic Republic 50 (1963).

2. Inheritance leads to family stability and attention to the aged through the reciprocities of giving and receiving.[70] As Bentham observed, "when we recollect the infirmities of old age, we must be satisfied that it is necessary not to deprive it of this counterpoise of factitious attractions. In the rapid descent of life, every support on which man can lean should be left untouched, and it is well that interest serve as monitor to duty." [71]

3. By honoring expectations based upon reciprocities, society preserves confidence in the rectitude of the social order.

4. The ability to give at death provides psychological satisfaction to the donor in two ways. First, by treating property as an extension of his personality, the donor is able to achieve a measure of immortality.[72] Second, giving expresses love. "No system, no state, whether based on property or based on power, will ever prevent most parents from endeavoring to bequeath to their children some inheritance of use to them in this world or the next: a good name, a presumption in their favor by their father's friends, a kit of skills, economic tools. I know of no civilization ever maintained on a completely equalitarian basis. The Communist civilizations certainly have not done so. There the individual who has scored some advance in the bureaucratic pyramid takes the greatest care to pass on to his son such advantage as he can. A dissident Yugoslav Communist, Milovan Djilas, has written of this in The New Class." [73]

5. Inheritance of tangible personal property satisfies the need for a symbolic identification of the benefactor-heir relationship.

6. Inherited property "can be used — is now used — to provide resources for those activities which are not, or should not be, carried on commercially. Endowments for universities, schools, and hospitals and operating funds for philanthropic foundations are already large and growing. . . . Because there is danger in any purely statist system, nonstatist institutions must always be in existence to pace them, and to avoid the deadening hand of bureaucratic monopoly." [74]

7. The right to devise property is an incentive to work[75] and, by saving, the creation of capital. If a person could not devise property he would be tempted to turn it into a life annuity and spend it up before death.

8. Future growth in economic production is largely dependent upon present savings, and the level of savings is a function of, among other things, the inequality of wealth. Therefore, at least at present levels of production, some inequality of wealth is necessary for economic growth.[76]

9. The abolition of inheritance could be effective only if lifetime gifts were likewise abolished. But a gift, which is an economic transfer at no price, is necessary

[70] Sussman, Cates & Smith, The Family and Inheritance 1-11, 310-314 (1970).

[71] Bentham, The Theory of Legislation 184 (Ogden ed. 1950).

[72] See Mauss, The Gift (Cunnison transl. 1967); Shaffer, Death, Property and Lawyers 3-9 (1970).

[73] Berle, The American Economic Republic 52 (1963).

[74] Id. at 50.

[75] In a technological society an incentive to work may not be a value. See Ellul, The Technological Society (1964).

[76] Cf. Harriss, Estate Taxation and Needs for Capital, 110 Trusts & Estates 538 (1971); Tullock, Inheritance Justified, 14 J. Law & Econ. 465 (1971).

to the economic system.[77] Since it is impractical to abolish gifts, abolishing inheritance would be futile.

10. To be effective, the abolition of inheritance would also require the abolition of life estates, joint tenancies, joint and survivor annuities, life insurance and all other forms of property ownership where a person acquires an economic benefit upon the death of another.

CALIFORNIA LEGISLATURE, 1972 REGULAR SESSION, ASSEMBLY BILL NO. 333

Introduced by Assemblymen Burton, Brown, Miller, Waxman, Brathwaite, Bill Greene, Ralph and Vasconcellos (Coauthors: Senators Dymally and Roberti)

[Editors' note: Not enacted.]

The people of the State of California do enact as follows:

SECTION 1. Section 13444 is added to the Revenue and Taxation Code, to read:

13444. Notwithstanding any other provision of this article, if the value of property transferred to any transferee described in Sections 13307 to 13309, inclusive, has a value in excess of one million dollars ($1,000,000) after the taxes otherwise required by this part and the taxes required to be paid to the United States on the estate have been paid, the additional tax shall be in an amount equal to such excess.

This section shall have no application to a transfer to a surviving spouse.

SEC. 2. Section 17041.2 is added to the Revenue and Taxation Code, to read:

17041.2. (a) Notwithstanding any other provision of this part, under rules and regulations adopted by the Franchise Tax Board, a tax is hereby imposed upon the adjusted gross income of any individual in an amount equal to such income if —

(1) The individual owns property with a value, less any liens or encumbrances thereon, of two million five hundred thousand dollars ($2,500,000) or more on the last day of the taxable year;

(2) The individual and the spouse of the individual own property with a value, less any liens or encumbrances thereon, of five million dollars ($5,000,000) or more on the last day of the taxable year;

(3) The individual and the spouse of the individual having one dependent, as defined in Section 17056, own property with a value, less any liens and encumbrances thereon, of seven million five hundred thousand dollars ($7,500,000) or more on the last day of the taxable year; or

(4) The individual and the spouse of the individual, having two or more dependents, as defined in Section 17056, own property with a value, less any liens or encumbrances thereon of ten million dollars ($10,000,000) or more on the last day of the taxable year.

[77] Friedman, The Law of the Living, The Law of the Dead: Property, Succession, and Society, 1966 Wis. L. Rev. 340, 351-353.

(b) For purposes of subdivision (a), "property" means only property accumulated on and after January 1, 1973.

(c) The tax imposed by this section shall be in lieu of the tax imposed by Section 17041 or 17048.

Sec. 3. Section 1 of this act shall apply to transfers from decedents whose date of death occurs on and after January 1, 1974. Section 2 of this act shall apply to the computation of taxes for taxable years beginning on and after January 1, 1974.

Sec. 4. This act provides for a tax levy within the meaning of Article IV of the Constitution and shall go into immediate effect.

SHULTZ, THE TAXATION OF INHERITANCE 198 (1926): "One economic result of these proposals for the abolition of inheritance must be indicated. If all or the greater part of the accumulated wealth of decedents were to escheat to the State, it would supply a revenue greater than the combined total of all present taxes. It is doubtful if any credit or monetary system would enable this transfer to be made in monetary terms; the Government would have to accept the decedent's wealth in the form it appeared at his death — largely landed property and title to business enterprises and instruments of production. It would find itself forced, not merely to expend revenue, but to manage and administer these properties; it would find itself entering upon a career of State Socialism — a career narrow during the earlier years of the operation of such escheat, but steadily broadening as more and more of the accumulated capital wealth of the country passed into the possession of the State. . . . Any proposal for the abolition of inheritance must accept State Socialism in one form or another as a more or less inevitable accompaniment."

NOTE ON INHERITANCE IN THE SOVIET UNION

In 1918 the Soviet Bolsheviks, carrying out the teachings of Marx and Engels, abolished inheritance. The 1918 law, translated into English, reads: "Inheritance, testate and intestate, is abolished. Upon the death of the owner his property (movable and immovable) becomes the property of the R.S.F.S.R."

By a series of steps Soviet law has backed away from this original extreme position. In fact, it has backed so far that the question must be asked whether the Soviet law of inheritance today differs in essence from bourgeois or capitalist law of inheritance. The first step away from Marxism was to modify the 1918 decree to permit close dependent relatives of the decedent to receive from his estate whatever was needed for their support. Then in 1922 the decedent was given power to transfer by will property up to 10,000 rubles in value among a very limited class: spouse, issue, and persons dependent upon the decedent. In 1926 the 10,000 ruble maximum was abolished. Two years later, in 1928, the legitime was re-established for children under eighteen years of age. They were given forced shares, and the decedent could not cut them off by will. At the same time the class of eligible testamentary beneficiaries was broadened to include the communist party, the state, and public bodies. A decade after inheritance was abolished the Soviet picture was this: An intestate's property went to his dependent relatives and, if none, to the state. A decedent could by will transfer his property to his spouse, issue, dependents, the communist party, the state or any public body, except that his children under eighteen could not be deprived of certain fixed shares. "The re-institution of inheritance rights was seen, moreover, as a wise political manoeuvre. The existence of such rights was seen as of assistance in developing thrift and an incentive to work." [78]

During the 1930s the testamentary power was broadened by giving a decedent unrestricted testamentary power over certain types of property. These included stocks and bonds, insurance policies, and many types of investments in government banks, including money deposits. In a capitalist system these assets are the major forms of wealth, and by giving a decedent testamentary power over them the communist system in theory resembled the capitalist system of inheritance. Inheritance of land and tangible personal property often has been restricted in capitalist countries as well as in the Soviet Union, e.g., by American homestead laws.

In 1945 the Soviet law of inheritance underwent a complete overhaul. The resulting scheme is in effect today. The essential features of the present inheritance laws of the Soviet Union are as follows. If a person dies intestate his property passes: (1) to his spouse, issue, actual dependents, and parents incapable of earning a living; (2) if none of the above, to his able-bodied parents; (3) if none of the above, to his brothers and sisters; (4) if none of the above, to the state. Intestate succession by heirs more remote than brothers and sisters is not permitted, unless such persons are "actual dependents" of the decedent.

By will a person can devise his property to any persons falling within the first three classes above, except that minor children and "heirs who are unable to earn" cannot be deprived of their intestate shares.[79] He can also leave his property to "governmental agencies and public organizations." If no persons within the first three classes above survive decedent, he can devise his property to any person he pleases.[80]

Community farming property is handled in a unique way, which is somewhat analogous to an unseverable joint tenancy in Anglo-American law. The farmer has a right to share in the community use of the farm lands and chattels. He can transmit nothing at death. The surviving members of the farm community share the community property among themselves.

Two additional items of interest: (a) The inheritance tax, introduced in 1926, was abolished in 1943. (b) When inheritance was first permitted after the Bolshevik Revolution, illegitimate children succeeded to property in the same way as legit-

[78] Griffin, The About Turn: Soviet Law of Inheritance, 10 Am. J. Comp. Law 431, 435 (1961).

[79] The surviving spouse is protected by a system similar to community property. Property earned during marriage is "common property." When one party to the marriage dies the other party takes one-half of the common property. See Wallach, Comparative Legal Status of American and Soviet Women, 5 Valparaiso L. Rev. 439 (1971).

[80] Soviet authorities have proposed removing this restriction upon the power of testation. Grzybowski, Soviet Legal Institutions 154 (1962).

imate children. In the inheritance law overhaul of 1945 the Soviet Union returned to a strict bourgeois view of how illegitimates should be treated. Illegitimates born after 1945 inherit as heirs of the father only if they are legitimatized by a subsequent marriage.

"The outcome of the development of the Soviet law of inheritance strongly argues for inheritance as an indispensable legal institution of an organized society. The right of succession must be deeply rooted in the human mind to withstand, as it did, the challenge included in the original provisions of the Soviet laws and the teachings of the Soviet legislators and jurists." [81]

The dilemma that results from permitting inheritance while adhering to the Marxist principle that he who eats must work will have to be resolved in the future. "At the present time, private enterprise is practically barred in the Soviet Union; there is no 'capitalist private ownership' but 'socialist ownership of the means of production' and 'personal ownership' of articles of consumption and small housing. Therefore, the Soviet jurists argue that inheritance of property can no longer result in the resurrection of private enterprise and of capitalism. This, of course, is a matter of future development. It may be pointed out, however, that economic leveling is no longer attempted but is directly condemned in Soviet Russia. High wages for the executive and technical personnel in government, industry and commerce, and extra remunerations and bonuses given to the above as well as to inventors, scientists, writers and artists useful to the regime, permit very considerable accumulations of money and properties as compared to the meager earnings of ordinary laborers.[82] Such capital can be invested in government stocks and bonds and may bring winnings in government lotteries. Only the future will show what will happen with this capital if inherited and increased in the course of two or three generations. One thing is clear: the possibility of an unearned income for the coming generations is established under the Socialist regime of present day Russia. Thus, in this field, as in many others, the Soviet leaders have had to sacrifice many of their original Socialist principles in order to keep things going and to maintain the Communist Party in power." [83]

EISENSTEIN, THE RISE AND DECLINE OF THE ESTATE TAX

11 Tax L. Rev. 223, 252-259 (1956)

I have yet to examine the operation of the estate tax in terms of its social objective — the levelling of hereditary wealth. Here the critical question is not how

[81] 1 Gsovski, Soviet Civil Law 655-656 (1948).

[82] "Korney I. Chukovsky, 77, the Soviet poet who died Tuesday, left a fortune of more than $1,110,000, literary sources said Thursday. . . .

"Chukovsky was one of the country's few millionaires. The others also are writers. The maximum income tax in the Soviet Union is 13% of the gross income." Los Angeles Times, Oct. 31, 1969, pt. 1 at 27, col. 3. — Eds.

[83] Gsovski and Grzybowski, Government, Law and Courts in the Soviet Union and Eastern Europe 1173-1174 (1959).

much the tax should produce, but how much the heirs should keep. . . . It is generally agreed that the estate tax should, in the language of the Finance Committee, "prevent undue accumulation of wealth." [84] An "undue" accumulation, it seems, is an accumulation that is considered excessive for social reasons. Or, to state the obvious, a premeditated policy of levelling presupposes that if an estate left at death is too large, it should be made less large. But how large is too large? And how can we tell whether an estate which is overly ample had been adequately reduced? If we are to make an intelligent appraisal, we must have a discriminating standard which guides our appraisal. A word like "undue" may be convenient, but it is rarely instructive.

. . .

Finally, the estate tax should be made a true leveller of wealth beyond "a reasonable inheritance" for the "security" of the decedent's family. I need not rehearse the old and familiar arguments which sustain this conclusion.[85] It seems sufficient to say that an economic system which prides itself on equality of opportunity should level "unreasonable" estates without compunction.[86] Wedgwood has referred to three sources of economic inequality: unequal ability, unequal luck, and unequal inheritance.[87] Unequal luck seems bad enough without unequal inheritance.[88] The mere incident of birth is not a significant contribution to society.

Obviously, a system of private enterprise presupposes disparities in wealth; and inequality of property among parents engenders inequality of opportunity among children. To that extent we are committed to less than full equivalence of opportunity. But it does not follow that inequality justifies much more inequality. In other words, large differences in wealth do not inevitably imply the same large differences in inherited wealth. For that matter, inheritance of any kind is neither a necessary nor inherent attribute of private property. It is not impossible to have individual ownership without devolution by will or intestacy. However, I am not in the least inclined to argue for the abolition of inheritance. My position is a good deal milder. In my view, inheritance exhausts its useful purpose once it provides for the comfort of the surviving spouse and prepares the offspring to live by their own exertions.

Many years ago John Stuart Mill made a proposal which we would do well to borrow and revise. The estate tax should fix a limit on "what anyone may acquire by the mere favour of others without any exercise of his faculties." If "he desires any further accession of fortune, he shall work for it." [89] Or in Theodore Roosevelt's

[84] [S. Rep. No. 558, 73d Cong., 2d Sess. 1, 7 (1934), 1939-1 Cum. Bull. (Part 2), 591.]

[85] Many of them are stated with admirable brevity and clarity in Franklin D. Roosevelt's message of 1935. See H.R. Rep. No. 1681, 74th Cong., 1st Sess. 2 (1935), 1939-1 Cum. Bull. (Part 2) 643.

[86] Secretary Mellon argued differently. He thought that an estate tax frustrated equality of opportunity. See Mellon, Taxation: The People's Business 123 (1924).

[87] Wedgwood, The Economics of Inheritance 81 (Pelican ed. 1939).

[88] See Friedrich, The Economics of Inheritance in 1 Social Meaning of Legal Concepts 35 (Cahn ed. 1948). In 1930 Julius Rosenwald estimated that 95 per cent of the large fortunes were due to luck. See Myers, The Ending of Hereditary American Fortunes 236 n. 8 (1939).

[89] 1 Mill, [Principles of Political Economy, bk. 2, c. 2 (5th ed. 1894)], at §4. Mill would have controlled the size of bequests by a direct limitation.

exuberant language, he should "show the stuff that is in him when compared with his fellows." [90] When inheritance does much more, it gravely and inexcusably augments inequality of opportunity. It then becomes hereditary economic power, which is no more tenable than hereditary political power. As Roger Babson so succinctly put it, "I do not see why the control of ten or twenty thousand men should descend by inheritance through the death of some manufacturer, any more than the control of a city or a State should pass on to the son of a mayor or a governor." [91] If we genuinely believe in a substantial equality of opportunity, then we should cheerfully desire an estate tax which truly levels. We cannot have one unless we also have the other.

BLUM & KALVEN, THE UNEASY CASE FOR PROGRESSIVE TAXATION
19 U. Chi. L. Rev. 417, 501-504 (1952)

There is still another road leading to the problem of equality. Almost everybody professes to be in favor of one kind of equality — equality of opportunity. What remains to be investigated is the relationship between this kind of equality and economic equality.

Equality of opportunity might well have been discussed in connection with both the general welfare approach to equality and the arguments concerning rewards. While consideration of equality of opportunity has been isolated here as a matter of convenience, neither the previous discussion of general welfare nor that of rewards can be taken as complete without some reference to it. In terms of the justice of rewards, the point is that no race can be fair unless the contestants start from the same mark. Tawney said:

> If the rules of a game give a permanent advantage to some of the players, it does not become fair merely because they are scrupulously observed by all who take part in it. When the contrast between the circumstances of different social strata is so profound as today, the argument — if it deserves to be called an argument — which suggests that the income they receive bears a close relation to their personal qualities is obviously illusory.[92]

In general welfare terms, the relevance of inequalities of opportunity is that without equal opportunity for individuals to develop their talents society will be deprived of the full use of its potential human resources. In this sense equality of opportunity is viewed as a sufficient good in itself and not as a way of correcting for distortions in the allocation of rewards by the market. For all practical purposes it makes little

[90] 17 Works of Theodore Roosevelt 505 (Memorial ed. 1925). — Eds.

[91] Myers, op. cit. supra note [88], at 255.

[92] Equality 143-44 (1929). For a somewhat different point of view see Mellon, Taxation: The People's Business 12 (1924): "Any man of energy and initiative in this country can get what he wants out of life."

difference whether equality of opportunity is approached by one of these routes or the other. Whatever can be said about it will in the main be relevant under both approaches.

It might simplify matters somewhat to go directly to the heart of the problem — the children. While there is still a flickering interest in eugenics, the concern today is not with lessening hereditary inequalities. We now realize that so little is known about human heredity that we never get to the hard question whether we would be willing to put into practice our knowledge of heredity. Nor is the problem today one of removing explicit legal barriers; even in the area of racial discrimination these scarcely exist in our society. The important inequalities of opportunity are inequalities of environment, in its broadest sense, for the children. It is the inequalities in the worlds which the children inherit which count, and this inheritance is both economic and cultural.

The inheritance of wealth at death is of course an old and familiar topic in itself. The controversies over it need not be reviewed at length here. It need only be noted that the basic argument for levelling such inheritances is simply the case for equality of opportunity among the children, and today few dispute the force of the equalitarian case in this context. On the other hand the impairment of incentives to work and to accumulate and the disruption of the family standard of living are not without considerable force or familiarity as counterbalancing arguments against too severely limiting the inheritance of wealth.

For our purposes it can be safely concluded that the case for lessening inequalities in such inheritance is surely stronger than the case for lessening inequalities of income. The windfall aspect of inheritance clearly distinguishes the two cases. Moreover there is a tradition of favoring a progressive tax on inheritance but a proportionate tax on income. In any event the progressive income tax is certainly not a direct equivalent of a progressive inheritance tax.[93] An inheritance tax reaches accumulated wealth; an income tax, while it may retard further accumulations of wealth, can only reach the income from existing wealth and not the wealth itself. It thus performs the primary function of an inheritance tax only to the limited extent that it prevents disparities in wealth from growing.

But this interpretation of the role of the income tax misses the most suggestive part of the relationship between the case for a progressive inheritance tax and the case for a progressive income tax. Looking only at the inequality involved in some children inheriting wealth at the death of kin and other children inheriting no wealth ignores the more far-reaching instances of economic discriminations among children. These can most easily be pointed up where the parents survive until the children have reached adulthood. In such situations the critical economic inheritance occurs prior to the death of the parents and need not be related to the wealth, if any, which they pass on directly at death or by way of inter vivos gifts of wealth.

[93] The point is that a tax on annual income in the ordinary sense does not perform the same functions as a tax on transfers of wealth. It would be possible, as Simons urged, to treat inheritance and inter vivos transfers as income to the recipients under the regular income tax. Personal Income Taxation c. 6 (1938).

The critical economic inheritance consists of the day to day expenditures on the children; it is these expenditures which add up to money investments in the children's health, education and welfare which in the aggregate are, at least in our society, gravely disparate. No progressive inheritance tax, or combination of gift and inheritance taxes, can touch this source of economic inequalities among children. On the other hand a progressive income tax can, as one of its effects, help to minimize this form of unequal inheritance. It is income, not wealth, which is the important operative factor here, and by bringing incomes closer together the tax tends to bring money investments in children closer together.[94]

But the gravest source of inequality of opportunity in our society is not economic but rather what is called cultural inheritance for lack of a better term. Under modern conditions the opportunities for formal education, healthful diet and medical attention to some extent can be equalized by economic means without too greatly disrupting the family. However, it still remains true that even today much of the transmission of culture, in the narrow sense, occurs through the family, and no system of public education and training can completely neutralize this form of inheritance. Here it is the economic investment in the parents and the grandparents, irrevocably in the past, which produces differential opportunities for the children. Nor is this the end of the matter. It has long been recognized that the parents make the children in their own image, and modern psychology has served to underscore how early this process begins to operate and how decisive it may be. The more subtle and profound influences upon the child resulting from love, integrity and family morale form a kind of inheritance which cannot, at least for those above the minimum subsistence level, be significantly affected by economic measures, or possibly by any others. If these influences on the members of the next generation are to be equalized, nothing short of major changes in the institution of the family can possibly suffice.[95] At a minimum such changes would include socializing decisions not only about how children are to be raised but who is to raise them. And this in turn would call into question the very having of children.

[94] It might be noted that a tax on inheritance also serves to bring incomes closer together.

[95] "A human being, as a person and a member of society, has needs and rights which are ignored and flouted when he is taken economically as a datum. He has rights to be and to have which it is absurd and monstrous to take as defined and measured by his productive capacity, which is so largely beyond his control. Obviously, the family is much more real as a social-economic unit than is the literal, biological individual, and the problems center more in the family, and the various forms of inheritance, than in the relations between individuals." Knight, The Meaning of Freedom, 52 Ethics 86 (1940). See also Knight, The Ideal of Freedom: Conditions for Its Realization, in The Philosophy of American Democracy (Perry ed., 1943) 87, 115 et seq.

II. THE ELEMENTS OF ESTATE PLANNING

2. An Estate Planning Problem

SECTION A. The Client's Letter and Its Enclosures

September 15, 19—

Dear ———:[1]

For some time now, Jane and I have been considering the rewriting of our wills since we now have very simple wills giving all our property to each other in case of death, and then to our three children when the survivor of us dies. However, in this day of air crashes where Jane and I might die simultaneously, the problems of settling our estate might be complicated.

These, in general, would be the assets with which we are concerned:

Residence	$32,000 ($19,000 mtge.)
Lot, Lake Murray	5,000
Pontiac station wagon	2,500
Volkswagen	1,000
Household furniture, etc.	???
Checking account	$0 to $1,000
Savings account	$4,000 to $5,000
Stocks:	
Mutual funds	4,000
General Corp.	600
Union National Bank	7,500
Life insurance	30,000
Group life insurance	17,000

[1] This letter was received by a colleague of one of the editors a few years ago. The names of the parties have been changed, and the client's assets and family situation have been modified to provide a more suitable estate planning problem for this course.

It seems that our main objectives should be to avoid probate and eliminate as many inheritance taxes as possible. I am enclosing the following:

1. Copies of our present wills.
2. Copy of ad from the local Sunday newspaper.
3. Samples of forms from book, "How to Avoid Probate!"

These are some of the questions I would like your help on:

1. Since our assets are not very great, it may be that we do not need wills at all. Can we let our property pass by inheritance or by joint and survivor arrangements? (Our bank accounts and some of our stocks are set up to pass by a joint and survivor arrangement.)

2. As a sort of corollary to that first question, I have read in various places that it would be a good idea to use a living trust to pass our house, cars, etc. With the use of living trusts plus the joint and survivor arrangements, could we avoid the need for a will and probate entirely?

3. If you think we should have a will, are our present ones all right? If not, how should they be changed? Do you have any sample wills which might be helpful in our situation?

4. What is the difference between Trustee (I assume controller over the trust fund) and Executor? Should they be the same person?

5. Should we have separate but identical wills for each one of us, or should we use a joint will?

6. In case of simultaneous death most of our estate would be going to our three young children. Should we name a Trustee as well as a Guardian? What is the difference between the two?

Any advice you have for us will be appreciated. I will be expecting to hear from you in the near future.

Sincerely yours,
/s/ Adam
Adam Smith

[The enclosures to Adam Smith's letter are reproduced on pages 61 to 71.] [2]

[2] The advertisement copy on pages 65 to 67 and the forms on pages 67 to 71 are reproduced with the permission of Mr. Norman F. Dacey.

LAST WILL AND TESTAMENT
OF
ADAM SMITH

In the name of God, amen. I, Adam Smith, of the city of Arlington, County of ...., and state of ...., being over the age of twenty-one (21) years and of sound and disposing mind and memory, and realizing the necessity of making an orderly disposition of my affairs, do hereby make, ordain, publish and declare this to be my Last Will and Testament, hereby revoking any and all other wills and codicils thereto which I have heretofore made.

I.

I hereby direct that all of my just debts, funeral expenses, and expenses of administration of my estate be paid out of my estate as soon as may be practicable after my death.

II.

I name and appoint my beloved wife, Jane Smith, to be the executrix of this, my Last Will and Testament, and I direct that she not be required to give bond or other security.

III.

I give, devise and bequeath all of my property, both real and personal, of whatever kind and nature and description, and wherever located, including household furniture and equipment, and personal effects of which I now have or may die seised and possessed of or be entitled to, to my beloved wife, the aforesaid Jane Smith, should she survive me. Should she not survive me, I then give, devise and bequeath all of my property, as aforesaid, to my children.

IV.

I authorize and empower my said Executrix or anyone appointed to administer this my Last Will and Testament, to sell and convert into cash any and all of my personal property without a Court order, and to convey any such real estate by deed without the necessity of a Court order authorizing such conveyance or approving such deed.

V.

In the event that my beloved wife, the aforesaid Jane Smith, predeceases me, I name and appoint my beloved wife's sister, Barbara Preston Widman, of San Francisco, California as legal guardian of my children during their respective minorities.

IN TESTIMONY WHEREOF I have hereunto set my hand and seal this 27th day of November, 19—.

/s/ Adam Smith
Adam Smith

The above and foregoing instrument, consisting of two typewritten pages, of which this is the second, with paragraphs numbered from I to V, inclusive, was on the 27th day of November, 19—, signed by Adam Smith, in our presence, and he did then declare this to be his Last Will and Testament, and we at his request and in his presence and in the presence of each other, did sign this instrument as witnesses thereunto and as witnesses to his signature thereto.

WITNESSES: /s/ Orland Cunningham
/s/ Jerry J. Hanson

LAST WILL AND TESTAMENT
OF
JANE SMITH

IN THE NAME OF GOD, AMEN. I, Jane Smith, of the city of Arlington, County of ...., and state of ...., being over the age of twenty-one (21) years and of sound and disposing mind and memory, and realizing the necessity of making an orderly disposition of my affairs, do hereby make, ordain, publish and declare this to be my Last Will and Testament, hereby revoking any and all other wills and codicils thereto which I have heretofore made.

I.

I hereby direct that all of my just debts, funeral expenses, and expenses of administration of my estate be paid out of my estate as soon as may be practicable after my death.

II.

I name and appoint my beloved husband, Adam Smith, to be the executor of this, my Last Will and Testament, and I direct that he not be required to give bond or other security.

III.

I give, devise, and bequeath all of my property, both real and personal, of whatever kind and nature and description, and wherever located, including household furniture and equipment, and personal effects of which I now have or may die seised and possessed of or be entitled to, to my beloved husband, the aforesaid Adam Smith, should he survive me. Should he not survive me, I then give, devise and bequeath all of my property, as aforesaid, to my children.

IV.

I authorize and empower my said Executor or anyone appointed to administer this, my Last Will and Testament, to sell and convert into cash any and all of my personal property without a Court order, and to convey any such real estate by deed without the necessity of a Court order authorizing such conveyance or approving such deed.

V.

In the event that my beloved husband, the aforesaid Adam Smith, predeceases me, I name and appoint my beloved sister, Barbara Preston Widman, of San Francisco, California as legal guardian of my children during their respective minorities.

IN TESTIMONY WHEREOF I have hereunto set my hand and seal this 27th day of November, 19—.

/s/ Jane Smith
Jane Smith

The above and foregoing instrument, consisting of two typewritten pages, of which this is the second, with paragraphs numbered from I to V, inclusive, was on the 27th day of November, 19—, signed by Jane Smith in our presence, and she did then declare this to be her Last Will and Testament, and we at her request and in her presence and in the presence of each other, did sign this instrument as witnesses thereunto and as witnesses to her signature thereto.

WITNESSES:

/s/ Orland Cunningham

/s/ Jerry J. Hanson

DACEY, HOW TO AVOID PROBATE!

Copy from ad in local newspaper's Sunday Magazine, 1966

Americans work harder than any people on earth to make adequate financial provision for their families after they are gone — BUT much of their hard-earned money is *wasted*, siphoned off by a scandalous probate system *before* it ever reaches their loved ones.

WHY HAVEN'T YOU AND YOUR FAMILY BEEN TOLD THESE FACTS?

- On average, it takes one to five years to close out an estate. During that time your spouse can draw a pitifully-small "widow's allowance" but your children can't draw a cent.
- It costs three to ten times as much proportionately to settle a poor man's estate as that of a millionaire.
- Under the existing probate system, complete strangers may share your estate with your family.

But, in the next sixty seconds I will tell you of an astonishingly simple way to transfer absolutely everything you now own to your loved ones after your death without delay, without red tape and without the excessive probate costs which your estate may otherwise be called upon to bear.

If you don't take the steps I suggest, my advice to you is "Don't die," because complications will start the moment you do. Your estate will come under the jurisdiction of a special court. Sometimes called the "orphans," "chancery" or "surrogate" court, its most common name is "probate" court. If you've left no will, it will dictate one for you in accordance with your state's laws which won't necessarily read as *you* would wish. Now your children can start their long one-to-five-year wait to get what is left of their inheritance after the appraiser fees, executor or administrator fees and probate court costs are deducted.

THE UGLY SIDE OF PROBATE

Senator Robert F. Kennedy recently charged that courts handling probate are "shot through with scandal, scandal that has been documented over the years."

Fiorello LaGuardia called the probate system "the most expensive undertaking establishment in the world." The New York Herald-Tribune editorially denounced those "club-house lawyers" who "profit to the extent of one million dollars annually in fees, many taken, at a large percentage, from small guardianships where every dollar is needed." The Bridgeport Post called the probate system a "gravy train." An article in the Journal of the American Bar Association called the Connecticut probate system "one of the most viciously corrupt." . . .

THE MAGIC KEY TO AVOID PROBATE

How can you give your loved ones the very maximum estate in the very minimum time after you have gone? By *avoiding probate.* Yes, virtually everything you now own can be quickly and easily transferred to your heirs after your death — and exactly as you specify, without any red tape, without publicity, without strangers meddling in your affairs and draining off the financial security you worked so hard to build for your family.

You can achieve all this very simply by a method which few laymen know about called an "inter vivos" or "living" trust. Indeed, only a small proportion of lawyers fully understand its use — *the American Bar Association has just issued a training film to be shown to local bar associations to educate them on its advantages.*

It's amazingly simple: Let's assume that you own a piece of real estate which you wish to leave to your wife at your death. In a simple "declaration of trust" you say in part: "I declare that I am holding this property in trust for my wife. Upon my death my successor trustee is to turn the property over to the beneficiary and terminate this trust. I hereby appoint as successor trustee the beneficiary hereunder." Upon your death, your wife, acting in her capacity as successor trustee, simply turns the property over to herself as beneficiary. She is then immediately the complete and absolute owner of the property. That's all there is to it — no executor's fees, no appraiser's fees, no probate court cost. No one-to-five-year wait. No piece in the paper telling all your business. . . .

WHY THIS BOOK IS AMERICA'S NUMBER ONE BEST SELLER

I wrote this book to tell a few friends and their clients how to avoid probate. They told *their* friends . . . and now it has zoomed to the top of the best-seller list because Americans everywhere are discovering that it frees them from the bondage of the iniquitous probate system.

In it you will find an explanation of why it is vitally important to you and your family that you avoid probate. Next, you will find the *actual trust instruments* needed to exempt your home or other real estate, your savings or checking account, your stocks, your mutual fund shares, your small incorporated business, your close corporation . . . even your personal effects such as jewelry, antiques, paintings, etc.

With each instrument are instructions that even a school child can understand, and a picture of how the instrument should look when it is completed. All of the instruments are specially perforated for easy removal from the book and *actual use.*

In addition, you'll find precise advice on a wide range of family financial planning decisions which you are called upon to make on matters of life insurance, taxes, investments and the like . . . the very things you and I would talk about if we sat down in your own home to discuss your financial estate problems. . . .

[Advertisement continued on page 71]

Declaration of Trust

DT-13

WHEREAS, I,____of the

City/Town of____________________, County of____________________, State of____________________,

am the owner of certain shares of the capital stock of:

____

(Name of Corporation)

NOW, THEREFORE, KNOW ALL MEN BY THESE PRESENTS, that I do hereby acknowledge and declare that I hold and will hold said Shares and all right, title and interest in and to said Shares IN TRUST for the following uses and purposes:

1. To hold said Shares and all right, title and interest therein for the use and benefit of:

(Name)____, of

(Address)____

Number Street City State

Upon my death, unless the beneficiary shall predecease me or unless we shall die as a result of a common accident or disaster, my Successor Trustee is hereby directed forthwith to transfer said Shares and all right, title and interest in and to said Shares unto the beneficiary absolutely and thereby terminate this trust; *provided,* however, that if the beneficiary hereunder shall then be a minor, the Successor Trustee shall hold the trust assets in continuing trust until such beneficiary attains the age of twenty-one years. Prior to that date, the Successor Trustee may apply or expend any or all of the income or principal for the maintenance, education and support of the minor beneficiary without the intervention of any guardian and without application to any court. Such payments of income or principal may be made to the parents of such minor or to the person with whom the minor is living without any liability upon the Successor Trustee to see to the application thereof. If such minor survives me but dies before attaining the age of twenty-one years, at his or her death the Successor Trustee shall deliver, pay over, transfer and distribute the trust property to such minor's personal representatives, absolutely.

2. I reserve the right to register any shares held hereunder in the name of a nominee, which nominee may be myself as an individual. The right, power and authority is hereby conferred upon any Successor Trustee hereunder, at any time during the minority of the beneficiary, to invest and reinvest without limitation or restriction, to sell all or any part of the Shares being held, holding either Shares or the proceeds of the sale thereof until the minor beneficiary attains the age of twenty-one years.

3. This Trust is created upon the express understanding that the issuer or transfer agent of the Shares hereunder shall be under no liability whatsoever to see to its proper administration, and that upon the transfer of the right, title and interest in and to said Shares by any Trustee hereunder, said issuer or transfer agent shall conclusively treat the transferee as the sole owner of said Shares. In the event that any shares, cash or other property shall be distributable at any time under the terms of said Shares, the said issuer or transfer agent is fully authorized to pay, deliver and distribute the same to whosoever shall then be Trustee hereunder, and shall be under no liability to see to the proper application thereof. Until the issuer or transfer agent shall receive from some person interested in this Trust, written notice of any death or other event upon which the right to receive may depend, the issuer or transfer agent shall incur no liability for payments made in good faith to persons whose interests shall have been affected by such event. The issuer or transfer agent shall be protected in acting upon any notice or other instrument or document believed by it to be genuine and to have been signed or presented by the proper party or parties.

4. The death during my lifetime, or in a common accident or disaster with me, of the beneficiary designated hereunder shall revoke such designation, and in the former event I reserve the right to designate a new beneficiary. Should I for any reason fail to designate such new beneficiary and should no designated beneficiary be surviving, this Trust shall terminate upon my death and the trust property shall revert to my estate.

5. I hereby reserve unto myself the power and right at any time during my lifetime, before actual distribution to the beneficiary hereunder, to revoke in whole or in part or to amend the Trust hereby created without the necessity

of obtaining the consent of the beneficiary and without giving notice to the beneficiary. Any one of the following acts shall be conclusive evidence of such revocation of this Trust:

(a) The delivery to the issuer or transfer agent of the Shares by me of written notice that this Trust is revoked in whole or in part;

(b) The transfer by me of my right, title and interest in and to said Shares;

(c) The delivery by me to the issuer or transfer agent of the Shares of written notice of the death of the beneficiary hereunder.

I hereby reserve unto myself the right, upon the revocation or termination of this Trust, to create a new Trust for the benefit of any person whatsover.

6. In the case of my death or legal incapacity, I hereby nominate and appoint as Successor Trustee hereunder whosoever shall at that time be beneficiary unless he or she shall be a minor or otherwise legally incapacitated, in either of which events I hereby nominate and appoint as Successor Trustee:

(Name)____, of

(Address)____

Number Street City State

and upon his or her failure to act (or should I for any reason fail to designate the person intended to be nominated), then and in either event I nominate and appoint as such Successor Trustee whosoever shall qualify as Executor or Administrator of my estate, as the case may be.

7. This Declaration of Trust shall extend to and be binding upon the heirs, executors, administrators and assigns of the undersigned and upon the successors to the Trustee.

8. This Declaration of Trust shall be construed and enforced in accordance with the laws of the State of

________________________.

IN WITNESS WHEREOF, I have hereunto set my hand and seal this____________________day

of________________________, 19____.

(sign here)____________________________L.S.

Witness: (1)______________________________

Witness: (2)______________________________

STATE OF________________________ }
COUNTY OF________________________ } ss: ________________________

On the________________day of________, nineteen hundred and________________, before me came________________________, known to me to be the individual described in, and who executed the foregoing instrument, and________acknowledged that________executed the same; and in due form of law acknowledged the foregoing instrument to be________free act and deed and desired the same might be recorded as such.

WITNESS my hand and notarial seal the day and year aforesaid.

(Notary Seal) ____________________________

Notary Public

Declaration of Trust

DT-22

1. WHEREAS, I, ____,

of the City/Town of______________________________, County of______________________________

and State of______________________________, am the sole and undisputed owner of the following articles of personal property:

2. NOW, THEREFORE, KNOW ALL MEN BY THESE PRESENTS, that I do hereby acknowledge and declare that I hold and will hold said articles of personal property, and all right, title and interest in and to said articles IN TRUST for the use and benefit of:

(Name) ____, of

(Address) ____

Number Street City State

or, if such person does not survive me, for the use and benefit of:

(Name) ____, of

(Address) ____

Number Street City State

3. I reserve the right to deliver the trust property to the beneficiary during my lifetime or, in my discretion, to defer such delivery until my death.

4. Upon my death, if the above-described trust property has not theretofore been delivered to the beneficiary, my Successor Trustee is hereby directed forthwith to transfer such property and all right, title and interest in and to such property, unto the beneficiary, to be his (or hers) absolutely and forever.

5. I reserve unto myself the power and right at any time during my lifetime to amend or revoke in whole or in part the trust hereby created without the necessity of obtaining the consent of the beneficiaries and without giving notice to the beneficiaries. The sale or other disposition by me of the whole or any part of the trust property shall constitute as to such whole or part a revocation of this trust.

6. The death during my lifetime of both the primary and the contingent beneficiaries designated hereunder shall revoke such designation, and in such event, I reserve the right to designate new beneficiaries. Should I for any reason fail to designate such new beneficiaries, this trust shall terminate upon my death and the trust property shall revert to my estate.

7. In the event of my death or legal incapacity, I hereby nominate and appoint as Successor Trustee hereunder whosoever shall then be beneficiary hereunder, unless such beneficiary be a minor or legally incompetent, in which event I hereby nominate and appoint as Successor Trustee hereunder:

(Name) ______________________________, of

(Address) ______________________________

Number Street City State

8. This Declaration of Trust shall extend to and be binding upon the heirs, executors, administrators and assigns of the undersigned and upon the Successors to the Trustee.

9. The Trustee and his successors shall serve without bond.

10. This Declaration of Trust shall be construed and enforced in accordance with the laws of the State of

______________________.

IN WITNESS WHEREOF, I have hereunto set my hand and seal this______________day of

______________, 19____.

(sign here)______________________L.S.

Witness: (1)______________________

Witness: (2)______________________

STATE OF______________________ }
COUNTY OF______________________ } ss:______________________

On the______________day of______________, nineteen hundred

and______________, before me came______________________,

known to me to be the individual described in, and who executed the foregoing instrument, and______acknowledged

that______executed the same, and in due form of law acknowledged the foregoing instrument to be______free act

and deed and desired the same might be recorded as such.

(Notary Seal) ______________________
Notary Public

To my knowledge, there's never been a book like this before. It is truly a "do-it-yourself kit" which will enable any literate American to administer his own estate. If you came by your money easily and you don't much care who gets it when you're gone, the book isn't for you. But if you're a hard-working American and you want to decide for yourself, with a conscientious lawyer if you like, who is to get your estate when you're gone, and if you have no intention of bequeathing a chunk of it to the local probate court, this book was written for you. . . .

SECTION B. Some Preliminary Questions Raised by Smith's Letter

Although the tone of Adam Smith's letter indicates that he would just as soon draft his own will if we could provide him with a good sample form, we shall assume he has been persuaded that it might be helpful for him to have the assistance of an attorney. From time to time we will refer back to Smith's estate planning situation in the context of the substantive areas being considered. But before we embark on our studies, it may be profitable to reflect on some of the questions raised in — and by — Smith's letter.

1. Examine Smith's present will in the context of the asset and family situation described in his letter. Can you detect any problems that may be raised, or any contingencies that are not provided for, by the will provisions?

Clause I: What is the point of this "just debts" clause? Would it put the executor of Smith's estate under any duty he would not otherwise have?

What is the effect of this clause on the mortgage on Smith's home? See In re Estate of Miller, 127 F. Supp. 23 (D.D.C. 1955); In re Estate of Keil, 51 Del. 351, 145 A.2d 563 (1958). See also discussion at page 86, infra.

Would death taxes incurred at Smith's death be "just debts," making this a tax apportionment clause requiring payment of all taxes out of Smith's residuary estate? See Thompson v. Thompson, 230 S.W.2d 376, 380 (Tex. Civ. App. 1950); In re Doerfler's Estate, 348 Ill. App. 347, 109 N.E. 2d 230 (1952); Int. Rev. Code of 1954, §§2206, 2207.

Clauses II and IV: Has suitable provision been made to insure the appointment of an executrix? Will the executrix have sufficiently broad powers to enable her to administer the estate effectively? See pages 82 to 85, infra.

Clause III: Is the dispositive plan established by Smith's will a sound one? Should he make an outright distribution of his entire estate to Mrs. Smith, or should he consider making some other distribution? Have all contingencies that might arise been provided for?

Which of the assets listed in Smith's letter will be governed by his will, and which will pass "outside" the will as "non-probate assets"?

Clause V: If Mr. and Mrs. Smith both die before their children attain majority, a guardianship administration will be required. Is this desirable? See pages 125 to 129, infra.

The person named as guardian resides in another state. Does this raise any problems? See Comment, The Nonresident Testamentary Guardian, 43 Texas L. Rev. 541 (1965).

2. What do you think of Smith's stated planning objectives? Why should he want to "avoid probate"? Should this be one of "our main objectives" in formulating an estate plan for the Smiths? What functions does probate serve, and if probate is "avoided" how are these functions satisfied?

3. In view of Adam Smith's fairly straightforward asset and family situation, does he need a will? Will not the intestacy laws of his home state provide a satisfactory distributive scheme for his assets at his death? And if so, doesn't this dispense with the need for a will? Can a will serve any function other than designating the takers of one's property at death?

4. To what extent (and for what purposes) should Smith consider alternatives to a will or intestacy, such as joint and survivor arrangements and "living trusts" (are there others?), as a means of transferring his property at death?

Reread the two "Dacey trust" forms and the copy of the advertisement describing their purpose and operation. Be sure that you understand how this plan purports to "avoid probate" and pass title to the named successors at death. Does this really work? If so, should Adam Smith consider employing this or some similar "living trust" arrangement? Can you see any advantages or disadvantages in Smith's utilizing such a plan?

5. One can readily understand Smith's desire to eliminate "as many inheritance taxes as possible." But in view of the size of Smith's estate, to what extent (if at all) will tax considerations be a factor in drafting his will? In general, should tax savings be one of "our main objectives" in estate planning?

6. Perhaps it has occurred to you by now that we don't really know very much about the Smith family or the assets they own. What further information on what subjects should (must?) we obtain from the client before we can proceed further? [3]

SECTION C. Additional Data on Smith's Family and Asset Situation

Following receipt of the letter from Adam Smith asking for a review of the present wills of Mr. and Mrs. Smith, a conference was held with the client, and the following additional information was obtained.

[3] "Estate plans suffer for three main reasons: first, a wrong emphasis — the construction of a warped plan for a collateral reason, like the saving of taxes; second, a lack of understanding of the law — the construction of a plan which fails to provide needed powers and working provisions because of ignorance of their need or because of doubt or uncertainty as to how to phrase them; and third, a failure to get the facts at the outset and to study them thoroughly — the construction of a plan which fails to suit the circumstances of the case. Of these three faults, the last is the most serious, for a plan is worthless, no matter how beautifully or soundly constructed it may be, if it does not suit the family or business situation which it in fact will control." — Farr, An Estate Planner's Handbook 38 (3d ed. 1966).

On obtaining the necessary data from the client, see Wormser, The Planning and Administration of Estates 1, 300 (1961); Casey, Estate Planner's Kit 103 (Inst. for Bus. Planning 1966).

[Note: In reading the memorandum that follows, consider whether there may be other information that we should elicit from Smith before we can properly advise him.]

1. *Family Data*

Members of immediate family		*Age*	*Birth date*	*Health*	*Insurable?*
Husband	Adam Smith	36	7/12/ —	good	yes
Wife	Jane Smith	33	6/1/ —	"	yes
Child	David Adam	8	9/25/ —	"	
Child	Susan Jane	5	11/19/ —	"	
Child	Barbara Carolyn	2	8/22/ —	"	

None of the children has any special health or physical problem.
Mr. Smith stated that he and his wife do not intend to have any more children.

Residence

Home address: 2220 Casino Lane, Arlington. GR 7-5882
Business address: Tresco Machine Tool Company, 7318 Burnet Road, Arlington. GR 5-2200
Period of residence in this state: all of life (except for college, military service).
Note: No problems regarding domicile. Also, note that none of present assets acquired while residing in another state. Does not own property located in any other state.

Parents; other dependents; collateral relatives

Mr. Smith's father died of heart attack at age sixty. Mother, Mrs. Howell Smith, is sixty-three years old and is in good health. Lives in Arlington. Smith stated that his mother has a modest but comfortable income from property left by her husband and from social security. When I asked whether he would inherit property from his mother at her death, he indicated that any such inheritance would be modest in amount. Father's will left all property to mother outright; Smith has no interest under father's will.

Smith estimated that mother owns property worth about $60,000, of which $20,000 is represented by residence, which is owned outright. Smith is familiar with the terms of his mother's will; it provides for an equal distribution between himself and his brother and sister. Smith is named as executor under the will.

Mr. Smith is the oldest member of his family. A brother, Henry M. Smith, lives in Salem. He is married, has two children, and is an assistant cashier at the Salem First National Bank. A sister, Amanda Blake, is married to Robert Blake, a graduate student at Iowa State University. She has one child.

Jane Smith's parents (Robert Preston, aged fifty-seven, and Rachel Preston, aged fifty-five) are both still living. Mr. Smith stated that his father-in-law is a well-known doctor in Boston and is quite well off. When I asked "how well off," Smith said he is probably "worth" around $200,000. (Note: Probably a conservative estimate.) Mrs. Smith has a sister and two brothers, all younger than she is. From this it would appear that Mrs. Smith may acquire a substantial inheritance upon the death of her parents.

Mrs. Smith's collateral relatives: Sister, Barbara Preston Widman, lives in San Francisco, where her husband, Ross Widman, is a CPA with a national accounting firm. They have two children. Brother, Robert Preston, Jr., is married, has no children; is currently on active duty with the Army in South Carolina. Brother, John Preston, unmarried, is a sophomore at Harvard.

Special family problems: None.

2. *Assets*

The Smiths have lived in Arlington since they were married ten years ago. Since neither brought into the marriage any property of substantial value, there appears to be no problem in establishing their marital rights in the property they now own. All life insurance policies were taken out after the Smiths married.

Tangible personal property

Tangible personalty consists of the usual furnishings in a family residence; two automobiles; outboard motor boat; personal effects such as clothing and jewelry; and other miscellaneous items. No items of unusual value. Estimated value: $8,000

Real estate

(a) Family residence: The Smiths purchased their home at 2220 Casino Lane, Arlington, five years ago. Although the purchase price for the property was $25,000, Smith believes that it is now worth around $32,000. Present balance on mortgage loan (note held by Arlington National Bank) is $19,000. The deed shows that title to the property was taken by "Adam Smith and Jane Smith, husband and wife." $32,000

(b) Lot: Two years ago the Smiths purchased a lot on Lake Murray for $4000. Title to the land was taken in Adam Smith's name alone. Unimproved. Based on current values, Smith believes he could sell the lot for at least $5000. $5,000

Bank accounts

(a) Checking account, Arlington National Bank. The account balance fluctuates from around $500 to $1500 each month. Mr. and Mrs. Smith are both authorized to draw checks on the account. $1,000

(b) Savings account, First Federal Savings and Loan Association, Arlington. The account is in the name of "Adam Smith and Jane Smith, husband and wife, as joint tenants with right of survivorship and not as tenants in common." $4,000

Securities

(a) 200 shares, Varoom Mutual Fund. When Mr. Smith's father died four years ago, his mother gave each of her three children $3000. Smith used most of this money (the rest was spent) to purchase these 200 shares of the Varoom Fund at $9.25 per share, and 10 shares of General Corp. common stock. (See next item.) Present value of the Varoom Fund stock is $10 per share. The stock is registered in the name of Adam Smith as owner. $2,000

(b) 10 shares, General Corp. common stock. Purchased four years ago at $53 per share. Current price: $56 per share. Registered in the name of Adam Smith as owner. $560

(c) 190 shares, American Growth Fund stock. For the last three years the Smiths have invested $50 per month in the American Growth Fund, under some form of monthly investment plan. The first purchases were at $9.25 per share, and fell to as low as $7.75 per share two years ago. Smith says that he has kept records on the price of the stocks as purchased. Current price: $11.50 per share. Registered in the name of "Adam Smith and Jane Smith, as joint tenants with right of survivorship and not as tenants in common." $2,185

(d) 150 shares, Union National Bank common stock. Was given to Mrs. Smith by her parents two years ago. At the time of the gift the value of the stock was $55 per share; current market price is $50 per share. Registered in the name of Jane Smith as owner. $7,500

Life insurance

(a) Mutual of New York policy #624-05-91, ordinary life, participating, acquired nine years ago. Annual premium: $205. Cash surrender value this year $1160; CSV increasing at about $160/year. $10,000

(b) Mutual of New York policy #624-05-92T, five-year-renewable term, participating, guaranteed convertible, acquired nine years ago. Annual premium this year and next: $75. For the next five years, $95; for the next five years, $125. $10,000

(c) Metropolitan policy #2,313,505, ordinary life, participating, acquired six years ago. Annual premium: $230. Cash surrender value this year $710; CSV now increasing at about $185/year. $10,000

(d) Aetna Life Insurance Group policy, group term. Premiums paid by Smith's employer. Face value of policy determined by employee's salary, to a maximum of $25,000. $17,000

Note: Policies (a) and (b) contain double and triple indemnity provisions: Double indemnity in case of accidental death, and triple indemnity in case of accidental death while riding on public conveyance. Policy (c) contains double indemnity provision. All policies name Mrs. Smith as primary beneficiary; "the insured's children, in equal shares" as secondary beneficiaries.

Observe that the annual premiums on the three commercial policies total around $510 (less dividends of about $100 last year). With $50 being invested in mutual funds each month, Smith is investing around $1000 per year in insurance-investment program.

Employee benefits

In addition to the group life insurance mentioned above, Smith's employer provides Blue Cross/Blue Shield coverage, disability insurance, and a qualified pension plan. The plan is "contributory": Smith contributes 4 percent of his annual salary to the plan and his employer contributes 8 percent. The plan will provide substantial retirement benefits to Smith, under a formula based on his years of service and his average annual salary. Based on his present salary level, Smith would be able to retire at age sixty-five with an annuity of about $9600.

The pension plan is primarily designed to give retirement benefits; it does not have substantial death benefits. Upon Smith's death before retirement, his wife would receive a lump-sum payment representing Smith's contributions to the plan plus interest compounded annually. At the present time, the fund represented by Smith's contributions is about $4200. To give an idea of the rate of growth of this fund, if Smith were to stay at his present salary level, in six years (at age forty-two) this fund would grow to around $8600.

Mrs. Smith would have an option of (1) receiving the fund in a lump-sum payment or (2) settling it under an annuity. Because of the small size of the fund and Mrs. Smith's long life expectancy if Smith were to die in the next few years, it would probably be advisable for Mrs. Smith to select the lump-sum payment.

Stock options: None.

Business interests: None.

Other special facts: None.

Powers of appointment: None.

Annual income: Mr. Smith is an industrial design engineer for the Tresco Machine Tool Company in Arlington. He has been with this firm for the past six years, and he feels that he has a secure and responsible position with the firm. His current annual salary is $17,000.

Last year interest on the Smith savings account and dividends on the various securities owned by the Smiths returned about $500.

3. *Liabilities*

Real estate mortgages: $19,000 mortgage loan, Arlington National Bank. Loan not insured.

Other notes to banks, etc.: None.

Loans on insurance policies: None.
Accounts to others: "Usual" store, etc. accounts.
Other: None.

4. *Assets and Liabilities: Summary*

1. Estate of Mr. and Mrs. Adam Smith

Tangible personalty	$8,000
Realty:	
Residence (title in "Adam Smith and Jane Smith, husband and wife")	32,000
Lot, Lake Murray	5,000
Bank accounts:	
Checking (joint and survivor)	1,000
Savings (jtwros)	4,000
Securities:	
Varoom Fund (title in Adam Smith)	2,000*
General Corp. common (title in Adam Smith)	560*
American Growth Fund (jtwros)	2,185
Union Nat'l Bank common (title in Jane Smith)	7,500*
Life insurance	47,000
Tresco pension plan (Smith's contributions)	4,200
Total	$113,445

Note: Items marked by an asterisk were acquired by gift from their respective parents. All other assets are attributable to Adam Smith's earnings during their marriage.

2. Liabilities

Mortgage loan, Arlington National Bank: $19,000.

3. Other factors

If Smith dies by accidental means, policies (a), (b) and (c) pay double indemnity. Life insurance proceeds would total $77,000. If he dies by accidental means on a public conveyance, policies (a) and (b) pay triple indemnity, (c) pays double indemnity. Life insurance proceeds would total $97,000.

Probable inheritance by Smith of about $20,000 from mother. Probability of substantial inheritance by Mrs. Smith from her parents — but no knowledge of whether this would be outright or in some form of trust arrangement.

5. *Planning Objectives, Goals*

Copies of the Smiths' wills are in the file. Smith's will leaves all property outright to his wife if she survives; otherwise to the children. Her will contains reciprocal provisions. While there are weaknesses in the dispositive and administrative provisions of the wills, they are not critically deficient; hence no need to draft interim wills.

Smith stated that the dispositive provisions in his present will accurately reflect his desires as to how he would like his property to pass at his death. I did not have the opportunity to discuss this subject further, nor did I discuss with him any alternative plans that he might consider. We will take this up at our next conference.

3. Administration of Estates

SECTION A. The Functions of Administration

While the general pattern of administering decedents' estates is quite similar in all jurisdictions,[1] there are widespread variations in the procedural details. In each state the procedure is governed by a collection of statutes and court rules giving meticulous instructions for each step in the process. Happily, this precludes our being concerned about specific rules and procedures, and enables us to advise you that you can safely postpone any concern about the mechanics of probating a will and administering an estate until you can "learn by doing" when that first estate file comes across your desk.

At the same time, it is important that you have a general picture of the process before we embark on our study of family wealth transactions. Also, since Adam Smith has asked us whether he really needs a will, we must determine initially what functions, other than designating the takers of assets at death, can be served by a will. This text note is intended to provide the necessary background information.

When a person dies, the procedure for administering his estate is similar to the liquidation process that takes place when a corporation or partnership goes out of business. The first step is the appointment of a personal representative to oversee the winding up of the decedent's affairs. Much like the receiver of a defunct corporation, the principal duties of the personal representative are (1) to inventory and collect the assets of the decedent, (2) to manage the assets during administration, (3) to receive and pay the claims of creditors, and (4) to distribute the remaining assets to those entitled. The function of the estate administration process is to pro-

[1] Except Louisiana, which "has the civil law system of universal succession wherein the heir may step into the place of the ancestor at once with the latter's full rights and liabilities and the additional obligations of paying legacies according to the latter's will." Atkinson, Wills 562 (2d ed. 1953).

tect the respective rights of debtors, creditors, and beneficiaries of the decedent's estate.

1. *Appointment of the Personal Representative*

If the decedent dies testate and in his will names the person who is to execute (i.e. carry out the terms of) the will and administer the estate, such person is called an *executor*. When the person in charge of administering the estate is not named in the will he is called an *administrator*. There are various types of administrators:

a. *administrator* — person originally appointed when decedent dies intestate.

b. *administrator with the will annexed* (also known as administrator cum testamento annexo or administrator c.t.a.) — person originally appointed when the decedent dies testate but no executor is named in the will or the executor named in the will fails to qualify.

c. *administrator of goods not administered* (also known as administrator de bonis non or administrator d.b.n.) — person appointed to succeed an original administrator and complete the administration of the estate.

d. *administrator c.t.a.d.b.n.* — person appointed to succeed an executor or an administrator c.t.a. and complete the administration of the estate.

e. *special administrator* — person appointed to preserve the assets pending qualification of the regular executor or administrator — for example, when it is necessary to take immediate action that cannot await appointment of the regular personal representative, or when the assets must be administered pending the outcome of a will contest.

All of these persons are appointed by, under the control of, and accountable to a court, generally referred to as a probate court. The appellation and composition of the courts that exercise probate jurisdiction vary from state to state.[2] For example, in Pennsylvania probate matters are heard by an Orphans' Court. In some counties in New York the Surrogate's Court has probate jurisdiction; in counties having no Surrogate's Court, the county judge acts as Surrogate. In many states probate jurisdiction is exercised by the base line court of general jurisdiction. And in some states there is no requirement that the probate judge be a lawyer; indeed, the chief administrative officer of the county sometimes serves as probate judge.[3]

One of the advantages of writing a will is that the testator can designate the person (or corporate fiduciary) who is to administer his estate. The testator can name as executor anyone who is not disqualified by statute (usually minors, persons of unsound mind, and convicted felons).[4] If a person dies intestate or leaves a will that fails to name an executor who qualifies, the administrator is selected from a

[2] See Simes & Basye, The Organization of the Probate Court in America, 42 Mich. L. Rev. 965 and 43 id. 113 (1944).

[3] What problems might result where the probate judge is not a lawyer? See id. 42 Mich. L. Rev. 981, 992-993.

[4] In a number of states nonresident corporate fiduciaries cannot be appointed as executor, and in a few states this prohibition extends to nonresident individuals. Can you think of any function that this restriction serves, other than to preserve "the business" of estate administration for resident corporations and individuals?

statutory list of persons who are to be given preference, typically in the following order: surviving spouse, children, parents, siblings, creditors.

The person appointed as administrator must give bond, usually in an amount double the value of the personal property in the estate. In most states, if the will names an individual rather than a corporate fiduciary as executor, the executor also must give bond unless the will waives the bond requirement. Thus another reason for writing a will is that the requirement and expense of a fiduciary bond can be eliminated.[5]

PROBLEMS

1. T dies leaving a probate estate that includes personal property worth $30,000, consisting mainly of tangible personalty, securities, bank accounts and cash. T's will names his eldest son as executor; the will does not waive the executor's bond. The administration of T's estate runs for three years. Using the schedule in footnote 5, what is the total of fiduciary bond premiums that must be paid?

2. In drafting a will that names an individual as executor, would you recommend to the client that the bonding requirement be waived . . .

a. If the will names the client's spouse, who is also the primary beneficiary under the will, as executrix?

b. If the will names an adult child as executor?

c. If the will names a trusted friend or business associate as executor?

3. Why are corporate fiduciaries exempt from giving bond? Is this exemption itself a reason for appointing a corporate fiduciary as executor — to avoid the bonding expense?

2. *Collection of the Decedent's Assets*

Upon being appointed and giving bond (if required), the executor is granted *letters testamentary*, or the administrator is given *letters of administration*. These

[5] The annual premium rate schedule for fiduciary bonds issued by the National Surety Corporation (applicable in all states except California, New York, Ohio, Vermont, Virginia and West Virginia) is as follows:

Amount of bond	
Up to $2,000: for each $1,000	$10.00
$2,000 to $50,000: $20 plus for each add'l $1,000 above $2,000	5.00
$50,000 to $200,000: $260 plus for each add'l $1,000 above $50,000	4.00
$200,000 to $500,000: $860 plus for each add'l $1,000 above $200,000	3.00
$500,000 to $1,500,000: $1,760 plus for each add'l $1,000 above $500,000	2.00
Above $1,500,000: $3,760 plus for each add'l $1,000 above $1,500,000	1.00
Minimum $10.00	

The above scale of rates applies to original and renewal premiums for bonds equal to or less than double the value of the assets of the estate. Bonds double the value of assets are subject to a discount of 20%. Value of the assets means the value of the personal property of the estate. When bond is given on behalf of national or state bank or trust company as sole or joint principal, or on behalf of an individual as principal serving as cofiduciary with such bank, whether or not such bank is bonded, figure premium at above scale and discount by 33⅓%.

show his appointment and authority to act on behalf of the estate, and authorize him to receive full payment from an estate debtor and to discharge the obligation. One of the representative's first responsibilities is to make an inventory of the decedent's assets and to obtain an appraisal of their value. The inventory and appraisal show the location and value of all items of tangible personalty and realty owned by the decedent, and all intangibles such as securities, bank accounts, and accounts receivable. The representative collects the latter by showing his letters and by giving the debtor a receipt and release. If a debtor refuses to pay, the representative may bring suit to enforce collection. He also has authority to sue on tort actions that survive the decedent and, by statute in most states, to bring a wrongful death action on behalf of the decedent's dependents.

3. *Management of the Estate*

Traditionally, the personal representative's primary duty is regarded as being to collect, conserve, and distribute the estate assets, not to actively manage or invest them. Unlike a trust, which contemplates management and investment duties over a long period, an estate administration is seen as a short-term fiduciary arrangement in which the statutes place emphasis upon conservation of the assets pending distribution to the estate beneficiaries. While this is an area in which the rules vary widely from state to state, the representative's management powers are ordinarily quite limited and in many instances are exercisable only with court approval. Typically, he cannot invest estate funds in other than savings accounts or government obligations in the absence of a will provision authorizing other investments, or court approval upon a showing that the proposed investment is in the best interest of the estate. Similarly, except for such temporary operation as is necessary to keep a business in salable condition, he ordinarily has no authority to carry on a business owned by the decedent unless he is given this power by the will, by consent of all the interested parties, or by court authorization under a statute that permits such approval. If the representative makes improper investments, or if he carries on the decedent's business without authority, he is personally liable for all losses incurred.

Unless the will includes a power of sale, the personal representative ordinarily cannot sell estate realty or personalty without court approval. The Texas statute,[6] which is typical, shows what is involved in selling a parcel of real estate. First, the representative must file application for an order to sell the property. The application must describe the property, and must be accompanied by a notarized affidavit "showing fully and in detail the condition of the estate, the charges and claims that have been approved or established by suit, or that have been rejected and may yet be established, the amount of each such claim, the property of the estate remaining on hand liable for the payment of such claims, and any other such facts tending to show the necessity or advisability of such sale." The application also must show that the sale is for one of the limited purposes authorized by statute: for the payment of expenses of administration, funeral expenses, expenses of last sickness, or allowances

[6] Tex. Prob. Code Ann. §§341-356 (1956).

or claims against the estate. Second, a date for hearing the application is set, and notice is given to all persons interested in the estate, so they may be given an opportunity to object to the proposed sale. Third, a hearing is held and (if the application is granted) the court orders the sale to be made, the order specifying the terms of the sale and whether it is to be by public auction or private sale. (The statute details the permissible terms of sale and the procedures to be followed if the transaction is by private sale or public auction.) Fourth, the property is sold. Fifth, within thirty days the personal representative must report the sale to the court. Sixth, a hearing is held on the report of sale. Seventh and finally, the representative gives a deed conveying the property.

Observe. Four trips to the courthouse by the personal representative or his attorney: to file the application and set a date for the initial hearing; to obtain an order authorizing the sale; to file the report of the sale; and to obtain an order confirming the sale. Six documents to be prepared: the application for sale (calling for, in effect, a balance sheet accounting of the administration up to that point); the notice to interested parties; the order authorizing the sale; the report of the sale; the order confirming the sale; and the deed. This elaborate procedure must be complied with even though relations between the estate beneficiaries are harmonious and no possible objection to the sale is contemplated. The process is as expensive as it is complicated, calling as it does for numerous filing fees and substantial participation by the executor's attorney (and by the attorney's stenographer).

While the provisions governing sales of estate realty comprise the most elaborate component of the probate machinery, they reflect the general philosophy underlying the statutory procedures for administering estates. The emphasis is upon protection of the estate assets and close court scrutiny of any decision the personal representative wishes to make.

The lack of flexible fiduciary powers is not too serious a problem if the estate is an uncomplicated one and its administration can be completed in a short period of time. It is not uncommon, however, for the administration of even a medium-sized estate to run for two, three or more years, in which case the lack of flexible powers becomes critical. Several factors tend to prolong the administration of estates. First, creditors have a set period of time in which to file claims, usually six months or a year from the date notice to creditors is given. The prudent representative ordinarily will not close the administration and distribute all the assets until the time for filing creditors' claims has elapsed. Otherwise he may end up being forced to pay the creditors out of his own pocket. Second, the federal estate tax is due nine months after the decedent's death. The representative ordinarily waits until then to pay the tax to determine whether selection of the alternate valuation date results in a lower tax.[7] The return then must be audited and accepted by the Internal Revenue Service before the representative (who is responsible for seeing that the tax is paid) safely can make final distribution. In many parts of the country, the IRS is running

[7] For federal estate tax purposes, assets are valued either as of the date of decedent's death or the alternate valuation date, at the personal representative's option. The alternate valuation date is six months after the date of death except for assets which are sold within the six-month period, in which case it is the date of sale. Int. Rev. Code of 1954, §2032. See page 234, infra.

about a year behind schedule in its audit of estate tax returns. If there is disagreement over the valuation of estate assets, administrative or judicial review of an unfavorable IRS determination may lead to further delays. Third, the state tax agency often will postpone its audit of the inheritance tax return until the IRS completes its audit of the federal return—in part to rely on the same asset valuation figures and save administration costs, but chiefly because a portion of the state succession tax is determined by the amount of the federal tax.[8] These tax administration delays often will cause a three- or four-year estate administration.

Finally, if the estate includes income-producing assets, it may be to the estate beneficiaries' decided advantage to prolong the administration for as long as possible. The estate is a separate income tax entity with its own $600 exemption. To the extent that estate income is retained by the representative and is not distributed to the beneficiaries in any tax year, the income is taxed to the estate, not to the beneficiaries. Utilization of the estate as a separate tax entity can produce substantial income tax savings — to the point where it may be Uncle Sam, not the beneficiaries, who will be calling for a windup of the administration.[9]

One of the functions that can be served by a will is to broaden the executor's powers, to enable him to make better decisions on behalf of the estate more quickly, and to reduce the number of trips to the courthouse for routine approvals. Going back to the statutory procedure for selling estate realty, if the will had given the executor the power to sell estate assets at private sale without court approval, no trips to the courthouse would be necessary to complete the sale, and only one document would be required: the deed. Provided the choice of an executor is soundly made, it is generally advisable to give him as broad powers as are permitted in the jurisdiction, such as a power of sale, the power to make reasonable investments of estate assets, and the power to continue in operation or sell business interests of the decedent.[10]

In Texas and Washington, and in states that have enacted the Uniform Probate Code, statutory provision is made for the administration of estates without court supervision.[11] In these states the personal representative can be given broad administration powers that are exercisable without court approval or scrutiny. We shall take a closer look at these procedures in Section B of this chapter.

Several states, mainly east of the Mississippi River, follow the procedure formerly used by the English ecclesiastical courts in distinguishing between conten-

[8] See page 269, infra.

[9] If, for example, the principal beneficiary of the estate is in a 50 percent income tax bracket, it is to his advantage to have at least a portion of the estate's income taxed to the estate, to be distributed to him later as "principal" free of any further income tax burden. The first $600 of estate income is tax-free (producing an immediate tax saving of $300), and the remaining undistributed income is taxed in brackets that begin at 14 percent. The problems (and tax-saving possibilities) of taxing estate income can get complicated. See Ferguson, Freeland & Stephens, Federal Income Taxation of Estates and Beneficiaries (1970); Halbach, Post-Mortem Estate Planning, 1963 U. Ill. L.F. 212.

[10] See, e.g., In re Friedman's Estate, 251 Wis. 180, 28 N.W.2d 261 (1947); In re Wander's Will, 141 Misc. 584, 252 N.Y. Supp. 813 (1931).

[11] See page 118, infra.

tious and noncontentious probate proceedings. Under the English system, the executor had a choice of probating a will "in common form" or "in solemn form." Common form probate was an ex parte proceeding in which no notice or process was issued to any person. Due execution of the will was not proved by the testimony of the attesting witnesses, but simply was accepted by the court upon the executor's oath. The will was admitted to probate at once, letters testamentary were granted, and the executor began administration of the estate. If no one raised any questions or objections, this procedure sufficed. However, within thirty years an interested party could file a caveat, compelling probate of the will in solemn form. Here notice to interested parties was given by citation, due execution of the will was proved by the testimony of the attesting witnesses, and administration of the estate involved greater court participation. This procedure is recognized in several states, sometimes preserving the common form/solemn form terminology,[12] more often not.[13] In these states, the effectiveness of the ex parte proceeding as an alternative to a formal, court-supervised administration turns on the acceptance given the procedure by the state's courts, by practicing attorneys, and by title insurance companies and other groups concerned with the marketability of titles to real estate. Generally, its use is restricted to uncomplicated estates of modest size.

4. *Payment of Creditors' Claims*

Within a set period after his appointment, the personal representative must give notice to the decedent's creditors. Typically, the statute requires notice by service to secured creditors and notice by publication to general creditors. In all but a handful of states a nonclaim statute (that is, a special short statute of limitations) applies to creditors' claims against the estate of a decedent. A general creditor must file his claim within a given period (usually six months after the first notice by publication); otherwise his claim is barred notwithstanding that the general statute of limitations otherwise applicable to his claim has not run.[14]

The procedure for handling creditors' claims varies from state to state. In some jurisdictions the claims of general creditors are presented directly to the personal representative; in others they are filed with the court. The representative may be authorized to pay claims he determines to be valid without prior court approval; in some states court authorization is required. If the representative rejects the claim, or if he simply fails to pay within a certain period set by the statute, once again the creditor faces a limitations problem: he must bring suit within a certain time; otherwise his claim is barred.

[12] E.g., Ga. Code Ann. §§113-601, 113-602 and 113-605 (1959).

[13] E.g., Fla. Stat. Ann §§732.23, 732.29 (1964).

[14] In several states there is no special statute of limitations applicable to creditors' claims. For example, in Texas a statute requires presentment of claims within six months from the date of granting letters testamentary or of administration. However, the only penalty for failure to file a claim within that time is that the creditor falls to the bottom of the priorities list. If the estate is insolvent, he (and other creditors who failed to file) will be the last to be paid. Tex. Prob. Code Ann. §298 (1956, Supp. 1971). See also N.Y. Sur. Ct. Proc. Act §1802 (1967, Supp. 1970).

Typically, secured claims involve a double option on the part of the mortgagee and the personal representative. The mortgagee may present his claim during administration and compel its payment, notwithstanding that the principal obligation is not yet due. Alternatively, he can "let the claim ride"; that is, let it continue to stand on its original terms. If the mortgagee chooses the latter, the representative has a similar choice. He can pay the debt during administration; alternatively, he can let the claim ride.[15]

Among the creditors who must be satisfied during administration are the federal and state tax authorities. State succession taxes are of two types: inheritance tax and estate tax. An inheritance tax is a tax on the right to inherit, and is based on the amount passing to each beneficiary and on the relationship of the beneficiary to the decedent. Lower tax rates apply to property that passes to members of the deceased's immediate family. In most states the burden of the inheritance tax falls on each beneficiary unless the will provides otherwise. However, the personal representative is responsible for filing the tax return and seeing to it that the tax is paid. In jurisdictions having an estate tax, the amount of the tax is (as with the federal estate tax) determined by the value of the decedent's taxable estate, without regard to the degree of relationship of the estate beneficiaries to the decedent. Here the tax is a claim against the estate, and payment is made by the representative out of the residuary assets unless a will provision or an "apportionment statute" provides otherwise.

5. *Distribution of Assets to the Beneficiaries*

During the administration, the representative may make periodic accountings to the probate court. At the close of the administration he files a final accounting showing the items of property received at the commencement of and during the administration; the amounts paid to creditors and distributed to beneficiaries; the expenses of administration, including attorney's fees and the personal representative's compensation; and the balance of assets still in his hands. His final act is to obtain a decree of distribution and an order relieving him from his duties as personal representative and from any further liability. The decree of distribution lists the property on hand at the close of administration and the persons to whom the property is to be distributed. The representative then makes distribution pursuant to the decree.

[15] This assumes that the secured property has not been specifically devised, and is a part of the residuary estate. Most jurisdictions follow the common law rule regarding exoneration of liens, under which the devisee of specifically devised property can compel the executor to discharge the obligation out of the residuary estate, causing the property to pass to the devisee free of the encumbrance. Atkinson, Wills 764 (2d ed. 1953).

If the secured creditor does not present his claim for payment, ordinarily he will require the person who succeeds to the encumbered property to "assume the mortgage"; that is, to sign the secured note and assume personal liability for the obligation. If this is not done, the property passes to the beneficiary "subject to" the mortgage, in which case the beneficiary is not personally liable on the underlying obligation.

6. *The Title-Clearing Function of Probate*

One of the chief functions of the probate process is to provide judicial recognition of the ownership rights of the decedent's successors in interest. The decree of distribution and the probate file, all matters of public record, serve this function. Taking land as an example, suppose Adam Smith dies leaving a will that devises his entire estate to his wife, that Smith owned a tract of land on Lake Murray, and that the last recorded deed to the tract names Smith as grantee. Without probate of the will, Mrs. Smith probably would be able to continue to occupy the land — assuming no other heirs challenged her possession, and no creditors asserted claims against the land — but she would encounter difficulties if she attempted to sell the property. Since Adam Smith is record owner of the tract and there is nothing to indicate that Mrs. Smith has the authority to sell, there is a gap in the chain of title. Mrs. Smith could not convey marketable title. But after probate of the will and administration of the estate, the decree of distribution will show (either by itself describing the tract or by referring to the inventory which includes a legal description) that Adam Smith owned the tract, and that by reason of his will, which devised all of his property to his wife, Jane Smith, who survived him, title to the land is now vested in Mrs. Smith. Since the probate records will also show that the will was duly proved, that due notice was given to all creditors, that all creditors who made timely claims were paid, that all federal and state taxes were paid (releases will be in the probate files), and that the time for contesting the will has elapsed, any prospective purchaser of the land can be assured that Mrs. Smith can give good title, free of any incipient claims of creditors or frustrated heirs. In short, the probate records become a link in the chain of title, and show that Mrs. Smith has a marketable fee simple title to the land.

As a practical matter, the title-establishing function of probate is not essential for most items of tangible personal property, such as furniture or personal effects. Mrs. Smith would encounter no practical difficulties if she were simply to assume possession and ownership of these items. No prospective purchaser of a sofa or a suit of clothes is likely to inquire of Mrs. Smith, "Where's your title?" But for items of property for which ownership is evidenced by a document, such as an automobile certificate of title, a stock certificate, a deed to land, and perhaps also a bill of sale to a valuable art object or jewelry, Mrs. Smith would have to obtain some official recognition of her ownership rights before she could transfer those rights to others.

7. *The Effect of Passage of Title at Death*

The way title legally passes at death may affect the rights of the recipients of the property. By common law when a person dies intestate, title to real property passes directly to his heirs, without the intervention of an administrator. With personal property it is different: the administrator steps in and takes title to the personal property, and then distributes the property. The different routes that title follows at death were the result of — or the reason for (history does not tell us which) — the rule that land was not chargeable for the decedent's debts unless specially bound by deed, while personal property was so chargeable.[16] Today in all states real property may be taken to pay decedent's debts, although in some states a vestige of the common law immunity of land survives in the requirement that personal property be insufficient to satisfy creditors before real property can be taken. The question today is: Does it make any difference whether title passes (1) directly to the heirs or (2) to the administrator and then to the next-of-kin? Consider the following problems:

PROBLEMS

1. T dies in January. His will devises an eight-unit apartment house to A. Immediately after probate of T's will A gives notice to each tenant that A is the owner of the apartment house, and on February 1 each tenant begins paying rent to A. T's estate is insolvent. In October T's executor applies to the court for an order for sale of the apartment house to pay T's debts. At the same time the executor sues A to recover the rents collected by A; the rents will be used by the executor to pay T's creditors. Is A entitled to keep the rents? In re Boyle's Estate, 133 N.J. Eq. 149, 30 A.2d 827 (1943). Would the result be different if the first clause of T's will provided: "I direct that all my debts be paid as soon after my death as practicable"?

Assume that before T's executor applies for an order of sale and brings suit against A, A sells the apartment house to B, who has no personal notice of unpaid debts. The fair market value of the apartment house at the time of sale is $80,000. B pays A $50,000 for the apartment house. What are the rights of T's executor? 3 American Law of Property §§14.7, 14.33 (Casner ed. 1952).

2. George Hardenburgh dies intestate, leaving as his heirs his wife, his daughter, and his son (by a former marriage). Decedent's estate consists of real property worth $30,000 and personal property worth $290,000. The wife and the daughter, generous as well as rich in their own right, "renounce and reject" their intestate shares, resulting in distribution of the entire estate to the son. The Internal Revenue Code imposes a tax upon the transfer of property by gift. Section 2511 of the Code provides that the tax applies "whether the gift is direct or indirect." Have the wife and daughter made a taxable gift to the son? Hardenburgh v. Commissioner, 198 F.2d 63 (8th Cir. 1952), cert. denied, 344 U.S. 836 (1952); Treas. Reg. §25.2511-1(c) (1958); see N.C. Gen. Stat. §29-10 (1966).

Suppose, instead, that Hardenburgh died leaving a will that devised his entire estate to his wife, daughter and son in equal shares. If the wife and daughter were to renounce their testamentary gifts in favor of the son, would this result in a taxable gift? Brown v. Routzahn, 63 F.2d 914 (6th Cir. 1933).

3. In some jurisdictions the rules respecting devolution of title have been uni-

[16] 3 American Law of Property §14.6 (Casner ed. 1952). Prior to 1540 land could not be devised, and the administrator and executor were *personal* representatives only and had nothing to do with land.

fied by statute. In Maryland title to realty passes to the personal representative rather than directly to the heirs. Md. Ann. Code art. 93, §1-301 (1969). In California the opposite unification scheme has been adopted. Title to real and personal property passes to decedent's heirs or devisees and legatees. Cal. Prob. Code §300 (1956). Which unification scheme is preferable?

In Estate of Kalt, 16 Cal. 2d 807, 108 P.2d 401, 133 A.L.R. 1424 (1940), Ella Kalt bequeathed the residue of her estate to her two sons, Earl and Stanley. Shortly thereafter two actions on promissory notes were commenced against Stanley. Stanley then renounced all interest in the estate of Ella Kalt as heir, legatee, or devisee. Held: Stanley's creditors can reach his interest in his mother's estate. Since title passed to him at his mother's death, Stanley's renunciation was a transfer of title to another, and that transfer was in fraud of creditors.

8. *Must a Will Be Probated? Must a Decedent's Estate Be Formally Administered?*

The above questions are indirectly answered by a statistic. For every one hundred adult deaths in America each year, there are fewer than fifty testate or intestate administrations filed with the courts.[17] What this indicates is that in well over fifty percent of the cases either a conscious decision has been made not to formally administer the decedent's estate or, more likely, the need for a court administration has not occurred to any of the surviving family members. In these cases the functions served by a court administration apparently are satisfied without resort to the formal probate machinery. If the decedent's estate is a small one, so that the assets can be gathered together without relying on the authority of letters of administration, the claims of creditors can be satisfied informally, and the decedent's family can reach an amicable agreement on distribution of the assets, there is no reason to subject the family to the delays and expense of a formal administration. In cases that are handled in this manner, it is probably inappropriate to say that there has been no administration of the estate; what has occurred can be characterized as an informal administration by family settlement.

If the estate is a modest one, but it cannot be settled informally because an automobile certificate of title or a bank account is in the decedent's name, or because the family cannot agree on an appropriate distribution of the assets, it still may be possible to settle the estate without a full court-supervised administration. Every jurisdiction has at least some of the statutes described below, authorizing simplified procedures for handling modest estates.[18] Among them are statutes permitting collection of small bank accounts[19] or wage claims,[20] or transfer of an auto-

[17] See pages 34 to 37, supra.

[18] See Basye, Dispensing with Administration, 44 Mich. L. Rev. 329 (1945); Sullivan & Hack, Streamlining Probate — A Proposal to Expand Summary Settlement, 51 Marq. L. Rev. 150 (1968).

[19] E.g., Miss. Code Ann. §5205 (1942) ($1000 per bank); N.Y. Sur. Ct. Proc. Act §§1305-1306 (1967) ($3000 in the aggregate).

[20] E.g., Mich. Stat. Ann. §27.3178 (451) (1962, Supp. 1971); N.Y. Sur. Ct. Proc. Act §1310 (1967, Supp. 1971); Ohio Rev. Code Ann. §2113.04 (1968).

mobile certificate of title to the decedent's heirs,[21] upon affidavit by the heirs. For cases falling under these statutes, no court proceedings are necessary. By filling out the appropriate forms, the heir is able to collect the property from the decedent's debtor, or receives a new certificate of title.

Another group of statutes provides for simplified administration of "small estates." [22] While the figures defining a small estate are, at first blush, on the low side (ranging from the District of Columbia's $500 to Montana's $10,000), two factors operate to extend the reach of the statutes. First, the stated dollar amount ordinarily applies only to the value of the probate estate — meaning that the dollar limit does not include non-probate assets such as employee death benefits, life insurance proceeds, and bank accounts or other assets that pass by right of survivorship. Second, many of the statutes provide that the dollar limit is exclusive of homestead real property and exempt personal property, and of the amount set aside for a family allowance. If the state's homestead or family allowance laws are on the generous side,[23] it is quite possible for an estate of substantial dollar value to qualify as a "small estate" under the statute. This procedure has the advantage of providing a court determination of the beneficiaries' rights, and can be used when there is some need for an administration, but not much of a need.

Typically, the proceeding is instituted by a petition setting out the necessary facts: e.g., that thirty days have elapsed since the decedent's death; that no formal administration of his estate has been instituted; that the value of the probate estate of the decedent, exclusive of homestead or exempt property, is less than $2500; and that the petitioners are the heirs or devisees of the decedent. In some states the county clerk or registrar is authorized to issue an affidavit declaring that the affiants are entitled to the decedent's property. In other states a hearing is held on the petition, and the court grants an order or decree of distribution establishing the rights of the beneficiaries. Armed with the affidavit or order, the beneficiary can then collect assets from the decedent's debtors, or cause a stock transfer agent to issue a new stock certificate in his name. If the estate includes real property, the court order or affidavit serves as a muniment of title.

PROBLEMS

1. Aaron Jones died three weeks ago. His wife has come to your law firm with Jones's will in hand: the will devises Jones's entire estate "to my wife, Martha, if she survives me; otherwise to my children in equal shares." The will names Mrs. Jones as executrix. An interview with Mrs. Jones reveals that the Jones family consists of two adult sons and several grandchildren, and that Jones owned the following property:

[21] E.g., Iowa Code Ann. §321.47 (1966); Mich. Stat. Ann. §9.1936 (1968); N.C. Gen. Stat. Ann. §20-77(b) (1965, Supp. 1971); Tex. Penal Code art. 1436-1, §35 (1953, Supp. 1971).

[22] E.g., D.C. Code Encycl. Ann. §20-2101 (1967) ($500); Nev. Rev. Stat. §145.040 (1967) ($5000); Ohio Rev. Code Ann. §2113.03 (1968) ($3000); Pa. Stat. Ann. tit. 20, §320.202 (Purdon 1950, Supp. 1971) ($5000); Tex. Prob. Code Ann. §137 (1956, Supp. 1971) ($2500).

[23] See page 568, infra.

Furniture, furnishings, other items of tangible personal property (estimated value)	$ 5,000
Savings account naming as owners "Aaron or Martha Jones, or the survivor of them"	3,000
Checking account on which Mr. and Mrs. Jones were both authorized to write checks	1,500
Series "E" government bonds, payable to "Mr. or Mrs. Aaron Jones"	5,000
Cash	500
Ordinary life insurance policy naming Mrs. Jones as primary beneficiary	10,000

Jones owned no real property; he and his wife lived in a rented apartment. Jones's debts consisted of last month's utility bills ($40) plus the usual consumer charge accounts: Sears Roebuck ($300 balance), the local department store ($125), Humble Oil ($35). There is also a funeral bill ($825) and the cost of a cemetery lot ($300). Mrs. Jones wants your advice: What should she do with the will? Must it be offered for probate? Must there be an administration of her husband's estate?

2. Same facts, except that the state has statutes which declare:

> "Every executor having knowledge of his appointment shall, within thirty days next after the death of the testator, exhibit the will for probate to the court of probate of the district where the testator last dwelt; and every executor neglecting to do so shall be fined not more than one hundred dollars or imprisoned not more than thirty days or both." Conn. Gen. Stat. Ann. §45-163 (1960).
>
> "Any person having in his possession any will or codicil shall, forthwith, after he has knowledge of the death of the testator, deliver such will either to the executor or one of the executors thereof, or to the judge, clerk or assistant clerk of the court of probate which by law has jurisdiction of the estate of such deceased person, and, on his neglect to do so for the period of thirty days, he shall be fined not more than one thousand dollars or imprisoned not more than one year or both." Id. §45-164.

See Tator v. Valden, 124 Conn. 96, 198 A. 169, 117 A.L.R. 1243 (1938); In re Pendergrass' Will, 251 N.C. 737, 112 S.E.2d 562 (1960).

3. Same facts, except that Jones also owned a one-year-old Oldsmobile, the certificate of title to which is in Jones's name. Mrs. Jones wants to sell the car and buy a used Volkswagen. She has lined up a purchaser who is willing to pay her $2500 for the Oldsmobile.

4. Same facts, except that Jones died intestate, and the state's statute of descent and distribution provides that where a decedent is survived by a spouse and children, one-half of his real and personal property shall descend to the spouse, and the remaining one-half shall descend to the children.

5. Same facts as in Problem 1, except that the savings account is in Aaron Jones's name as sole owner. Mrs. Jones went to the bank and presented the manager with a certified copy of the death certificate, a xerox copy of the will, and an obituary notice from the local newspaper showing that "Mr. Jones was survived by his wife, Martha, and by two sons, John Jones and Marshall Jones." She also presented the manager with a notarized release and agreement to indemnify against loss, signed

by herself and by her two sons. Despite this impressive array of documentary evidence, the bank refuses to pay the account to Mrs. Jones. What should she do now? See Brobst v. Brobst, 190 Mich. 63, 155 N.W. 734 (1916).

6. Same facts as in Problem 1, except that Jones also owned a house and lot worth $25,000, and another lot worth $5000. The deeds to both tracts name Aaron Jones as grantee. The residential property is subject to a mortgage with a current balance of $12,000; title to the other lot is free of encumbrances. Must (should?) Jones's will be probated and his estate formally administered? See Tex. Prob. Code Ann. §§49, 89 (1956, Supp. 1971).

7. Let us look at Aaron Jones's problem from another perspective. Suppose Jones comes to you during his lifetime. He tells you that he does not have a will. He describes his family situation and the assets owned by him: the assets listed in Problem 1, the car described in Problem 3, but not the real estate described in Problem 6. His question: In view of his family situation and his modest estate, does he really need a will?

8. Suppose Adam Smith were to die survived by the present members of his family and owning the assets that he now owns (see pages 72 to 77). Would the probate of his will devising everything to his wife be necessary or desirable?

In re ESTATE OF HARPER

Supreme Court of Kansas, 1968
202 Kan. 150, 446 P.2d 738

FATZER, Justice. The appeal is from the district court's judgment that the order of the probate court admitting the last will and testament of Rosa C. Harper, deceased, to probate in Douglas County and appointing the Lawrence National Bank, Lawrence, Kansas, as executor, was not only proper, but required.

Rosa C. Harper duly executed her last will and testament in Douglas County on October 12, 1962, and named the Lawrence National Bank as her executor to serve without bond. She devised her estate, after payment of debts and other expenses, to her three daughters and two grandchildren, being children of a deceased daughter, who were all of age and who resided outside the state of Kansas.

On October 4, 1967, the testatrix died, leaving as her entire estate personal property of the estimated value of $150,000. The estate contained no real estate, and was free from debt.

On October 6, 1967, the decedent's three surviving daughters wrote the bank that they were cognizant of the will their mother executed on October 12, 1962, in which she named the bank as executor of her estate, and that: "We hereby request The Lawrence National Bank to retain Robert B. Oyler as attorney for the bank in the probating of the will and the handling of her estate."

Thereafter, on October 20, 1967, the bank's reply to their letter of October 6, 1967, requesting it retain Robert B. Oyler as attorney in the probating of their mother's estate reads in part as follows: "The policy of the Lawrence National Bank is to retain the attorney who prepared the will, which in this case is Forrest A. Jackson, Lawrence, Kansas."

On October 23, 1967, the bank filed its verified petition in the probate court to probate the will of Rosa C. Harper, deceased, and for its appointment as executor, and, among other things, alleged the following:

> "That the said Rosa C. Harper left surviving as her sole and only heirs at law the following:
>
> "Elizabeth Harper Hood, a daughter;
> "Margaret Harper Snow, a daughter;
> "Carolyn Harper McGuire, a daughter;
> "Karen Dooley Bower, a granddaughter; and,
> "Peter Chamberlin Dooley, a grandson.
>
> "That the decedent had no spouse or children or adopted children or issue of deceased children, natural or adopted, who survived her, other than the persons above named."

It further alleged that the decedent's original will was in the possession and custody of Robert B. Oyler, which necessitated attaching a copy thereof to its petition. The petition was set for hearing on November 16, 1967, at 10:00 A.M. and notice by publication and by mail was duly given.

On November 14, 1967, Mr. Oyler was served with a subpoena duces tecum in which he was commanded to appear before the probate court on November 16, 1967, with the decedent's original will. On that date, Mr. Oyler produced the will and it was filed in the probate court.

On November 10, 1967, all of the beneficiaries named in the decedent's will filed written defenses and objections to the bank's petition alleging, among other things, that they were the sole and only heirs at law of the decedent; that as her sole heirs at law each would take a share of her estate under the statutes of descent and distribution in exactly the same proportions as devised in the will; that there were no creditors of the estate and all bills owing had been paid; that as the beneficiaries and decedent's sole heirs at law, they had arrived at a full and complete family settlement agreement for the distribution of the estate; that the family agreement had been reduced to writing and signed by all the heirs, devisees and parties in interest; that the property of the estate consisted solely of personal property and there was no necessity or reason for probating or administering the estate; that all parties in interest had agreed that the estate should not be probated or administered and that the last will and testament of Rosa C. Harper, deceased, should not be admitted to probate. A copy of the family settlement agreement was attached to the pleading and made a part thereof, and it was further alleged all that was necessary as far as the decedent's estate was concerned was a finding of descent at the end of one year after her death. The prayer was that the court refuse probate of the decedent's will and dismiss the bank's petition for probate.

The instrument attached to the beneficiaries' defenses and objections to admitting the will to probate was entitled "Agreement" and reads:

. . . [Portions of the agreement, summarized in the preceding paragraph, have been omitted.]

> "Now, therefore, it is agreed as a family settlement by and between all of the heirs, devisees and legatees of Rosa C. Harper, deceased, as herein named, in consideration of the mutual agreement of the parties hereto and of the additional amount of several thousand dollars which will be available for distribution to them by reduction of the probate court costs and expenses of administration under the procedure hereinafter provided for, that the last will and testament shall not be probated in Douglas County, Kansas, or in any other county in the State of Kansas, or any other state; that the assets of Rosa C. Harper shall remain to accumulate for one year, and that after one year from the date of death of Rosa C. Harper, a determination of descent as provided by the laws of the State of Kansas shall be brought in Douglas County, Kansas, and all of her property, after payment of legal fees, court costs and taxes, shall be distributed as follows:
>
> "Elizabeth Harper Hood, an undivided one-fourth;
> "Margaret Harper Snow, an undivided one-fourth;
> "Carolyn Harper McGuire, an undivided one-fourth;
> "Karen Dooley Bower, an undivided one-eighth;
> "Peter Chamberlain [*sic*] Dooley, an undivided one-eighth.
>
> Parties hereto further agree that Robert B. Oyler be and he is hereby retained to assist in the making out of income tax returns for Rosa C. Harper from January 1, 1967 to October 4, 1967; to assist in making out income tax returns on the estate from October 4, 1967 to October 1, 1968; and that he also prepared the federal estate tax return and the Kansas state inheritance tax return; that he commence and complete a determination of descent proceeding in Douglas County, Kansas, which will be started one year from the date of death of Rosa C. Harper, and that he assist in the transferring and assigning of the property to the heirs of Rosa C. Harper as herein provided.
>
> "Parties hereto further agree that the said Robert B. Oyler be and he is hereby authorized to oppose and contest any effort made to probate the last will and testament of said decedent, and that he is hereby authorized and directed to retain any attorney in Lawrence, Kansas, to assist him in such a contest, provided that Robert B. Oyler pay out of his fee the fee for the services of such other attorney so retained."

The family settlement agreement was dated October 28, 1967, and was circulated for execution, which was completed between that date and November 6, 1967, being signed by all the beneficiaries and heirs at law and duly acknowledged by them in states other than the state of Kansas and in a province of Canada. The bank, as the named executor, did not sign the agreement to withhold the will from probate.

The bank filed its reply to the beneficiaries' defenses and objections and alleged that the decedent's three daughters made a written request to the bank to probate the decedent's will; that in keeping with its policy, the attorney who drew the will had been retained by the bank as the executor of the decedent's will; that the Harper family agreement, "is an Agreement for Suppression of Will, in violation of

Kansas law and against public policy and is null and void and unenforceable"; that the administration and conservation of the assets of the decedent's estate was necessary and proper; that all assets including stocks, bonds, money, savings and all other assets should be inventoried and appraised; that federal and state income tax returns should be made; that the Kansas inheritance taxes and federal estate taxes should be determined and paid; that there is a period of nine months within which claims may be filed against the estate following the first publication of notice of appointment; that it had not been determined who were all of the alleged interested parties in the decedent's estate, and that the testatrix had a right to direct the method of management and disposal of her property after her death, which the court cannot be compelled to disregard. The bank renewed its prayer for the probate of the will and its appointment as executor. . . .

Turning to the legal questions presented, the appellants contend that the family settlement agreement was valid and authorized the withholding of the decedent's will from probate and that proceedings for determination of descent in lieu of full probate is available, adequate and proper. They further contend that the bank's petition for probate of the decedent's will was based upon insufficient grounds since it was not shown the family settlement agreement constituted an illegal or improper withholding of the decedent's will from probate. In support of their contentions they argue that family settlement agreements are favorites of the law and may provide for distribution either in accordance with or contrary to the will and that such agreements may dispense with the probate of the will and that the assent of the executor named therein is not required. They cite and rely mainly upon In re Estate of Swanson, 239 Iowa 294, 31 N.W.2d 385. They argue there is a vital distinction between the suppression of a will in violation of K.S.A. 59-618 by any person who has possession or knowledge of such will and access to it and who knowingly withholds it from probate, and a family settlement agreement not to probate the will where it has been produced to the probate court and there is no element of deception as to the existence of the will.

The appellants further argue there is no criminal penalty under K.S.A. 59-618, and, in fact, the only penalty under the statute is that any person who knowingly withholds a will from probate for more than one year may not take thereunder, and that the appellants could not be so penalized since their share is the same either under testacy or intestacy; that there was no concealment or improper withholding of the will which was actually before the court on November 16, 1967, when the bank's petition was heard; that the appointment of an executor was not necessary for administration and conservation of the assets of the estate, or to enable creditors to file their claims within the prescribed period since there were no creditors by whom claims could be filed, as all obligations, including the funeral expenses, had been paid; that an executor was not necessary to determine and satisfy state and federal estate taxes since provision is made in Kansas for the determination of inheritance taxes without probate or administration and that 59-2251 relating to the determination of descent provides for a tax finding prior to a final descent; that the only duty devolving upon the executor was the preservation and distribution of fixed assets which could be performed by the administrator designated in the family settlement agreement and the bank could do nothing more than serve as a mere conduit to transmit to the beneficiaries those assets since the will created no trust, and that the bank as the named executor had no pecuniary interest in the estate other than that of administration.

. . . Upon this state of the record, was the Harper family settlement agreement a valid defense to the probate of the will? A majority of the court is of the opinion it was not.

The appellants concede the petition to probate the will was sufficient in form to comply with the requirements of K.S.A. 59-2220 (all references hereafter are to Kansas Statutes Annotated unless otherwise noted), and no claim is made that the bank as the named executor was not authorized to file a petition for probate of the will. In In re Estate of Smith, 168 Kan. 210, 212 P.2d 322, it was held that a person named as executor in a will is a "person interested in the estate" of the decedent and qualified under 59-2221 to petition for probate of the will or for administration. Moreover, under our own early decisions and various provisions of the probate code and cases construing them, it was the duty of the bank as the named executor in the will to present it for probate and endeavor to procure its admission. . . .

The law of Kansas gives to every person competent to do so, the right to make a will, and to select someone in whom he has confidence to execute it. It is easy to conceive of many valid wills which the parties directly interested might not care to have probated, but that appears to furnish no reason for suppressing or withholding from probate such an instrument. In this state no will shall be effectual to pass real or personal property unless it shall have been duly admitted to probate (59-616), and application for probate is required to be made within one year after the death of the testator. (59-617.) It is the policy of our law that all wills shall be delivered to the probate court having jurisdiction as soon after the death of the testator as is possible. Our statutes relating to the subject are 59-618, 59-620 and 59-621. The provisions of 59-618 bars [*sic*] any beneficiary from all rights under a will who has possession of it, or has knowledge of its existence and access to it for the purpose of probate, and knowingly withholds it from probate for more than one year. The bar prescribed by the statute does not arise by reason of the act of the testator as to whether it was executed in the manner prescribed by law, but because of the act of the beneficiary in failing to have it probated or offered for probate within the required time. . . . The provisions of 59-621 place the positive duty upon any person having custody of a will to deliver it to the court having jurisdiction to probate it (In re Estate of Morgans, 188 Kan. 50, 57, 360 P.2d 1069), and the court may compel a person having the custody of the will to produce it for the purpose of having it proved. These statutes express the legislative intent that the will of every person shall be offered for probate. They decree there is a clear public policy in the establishment of every legally executed will. That policy requires the probate of a will, not its suppression or to withhold it from probate.

In the instant case, the probate court ordered the person having custody of the decedent's will to produce it in court which was complied with, and the will was filed of record. The probate court did not order the will produced in court for inspection, but for the purpose of being proved. (Pee v. Carlyle, 120 Kan. 200, 243 P. 296; 2 Bartlett's Kansas Probate Law and Practice, §545, p. 47.) The privilege to make a will would be a barren privilege if it did not extend to probate, and when the will was produced by the custodian it was the duty of the probate court to notify the executor or others interested in the will and to proceed upon the bank's petition, irrespective of the attitude of the beneficiaries, to find if the will was freely executed by a competent person as her will and was duly witnessed. . . .

We agree with the appellants that family settlement agreements are favorites of the law and that beneficiaries under a will have a right to agree among themselves upon a distribution of the estate contrary to a disposition made under the will or to abrogate the will, and such an agreement containing the mutual promises of the contracting parties is based upon a sufficient consideration. The foregoing rule has been so frequently and forcefully stated that the marshalling of our many decisions on the point is unnecessary. . . .

There are at least two exceptions which limit the rule permitting family settlement agreements. First, that beneficiaries under a will cannot defeat a trust or specific restriction placed upon the property in the testator's will, and second, such an agreement may not deprive one not a party thereto of his interest in the estate or prejudice the rights of nonconsenting creditors. . . .

Neither of the foregoing exceptions is applicable in the case at bar. The will created no trust; all of the beneficiaries and heirs at law of the decedent are parties to the family agreement, and they alleged, which was not denied, there were no creditors. However, the foregoing rule is applicable only in testate estates after the will of the decedent has been duly proved and admitted to probate. As indicated, our statutes relating to probate of a will decree a clear public policy in the establishment of every legally executed will, and we hold that the probate court did not have the authority to determine the validity or approve the Harper family agreement at the time of hearing the bank's petition to admit the decedent's will to probate . . . and that such agreement to withhold the will from probate was not a valid or proper defense to that probate proceeding.

It is not contended the Harper family settlement agreement was invalid. In order to obtain a decree of final settlement and an assignment of the personal property in accordance with its provisions, it would be necessary to have the agreement submitted to and approved by the probate court. . . .

We note the appellee's contention that it was an interested party in the estate and since it did not sign the Harper family settlement agreement to withhold the will from probate, the agreement was ineffective and was not binding upon the executor named in the will. The point is not well taken. The nomination of an executor is a part of a decedent's will. (In re Estate of Grattan, 155 Kan. 839, 130 P.2d 580.) Unlike an heir at law, a devisee, a legatee, or a creditor of the decedent, the bank had no pecuniary interest in the distribution of the estate of which it was deprived by the family settlement agreement. The fact that it was nominated as executor and had the right and duty to petition for probate of the will, and would be compensated when appointed, gave it no such pecuniary interest. Its interest in the estate after appointment as executor, aside from its duty to faithfully serve as such fiduciary, was for reasonable compensation only in return for services rendered. . . .

We have fully considered the authorities and decisions from foreign jurisdictions cited by the appellants holding that beneficiaries under a will may enter into a family settlement agreement not to probate the will and have the estate distributed as intestate or in any manner they see fit (In re Estate of Swanson, supra; Henry v. Spurlin, 277 Ky. 114, 125 S.W.2d 992; In re Martin's Estate, 349 Pa. 255, 36 A.2d 786; In re Will of Pendergrass, 251 N.C. 737, 112 S.E.2d 562; 57 Am. Jur., Wills, §1013, p. 657; Anno., 117 A.L.R. 1252), but in view of what has been said and held, we are of the opinion that whatever the rule may be elsewhere, those authorities are not controlling in this jurisdiction, and it follows that the Harper family settlement agreement constituted no valid defense to the probate of the decedent's will.

The judgment is affirmed.

KAUL, Justice (dissenting).

I cannot agree that our statutes governing the probating of a will decree a public policy that every valid will must be admitted to probate nor do I concur in the conclusion based thereon that a family settlement agreement, valid in all respects, wherein all of the legatees and devisees of the will and heirs of the deceased agree to withhold the will from probate, does not constitute a legal defense to the petition of a named executor, the sole proponent of the will.

The favor with which this court has always viewed family settlements has been so frequently and so forceably stated that a listing of decisions and quotations therefrom is unnecessary. However, the question posed where the interests of the members of a family, who have agreed to withhold a will from probate, are in conflict with the interest of a named executor, who insists on the probation of a will, has not been considered by this court.

Our statutes relating to the subject are K.S.A. 59-618, 59-620 and 59-621. The statutes mentioned give probate courts power to compel the production of a will and prescribe penalties and impose liabilities for the concealment, or withholding by one who has custody or knowledge of a will or access to it. There is no direct obligation expressed in any of the statutes mentioned that the will be admitted to probate after it is delivered or produced. Considering the pertinent provisions of our probate code, together with the expressions of this court, that family settlement agreements are favored in the law, I am unable to find a declaration of public policy such as that announced in the majority opinion. This is the viewpoint taken in most jurisdictions where the question has arisen. (117 A.L.R., Anno., 1249; 95 C.J.S. Wills §325, p. 159; 57 Am. Jur., Wills, §1013, p. 657.)

From a reading of cases dealing with the subject, it appears that many of the jurisdictions referred to have probate code provisions quite similar to those of this state. What appears to be the majority rule is stated in 95 C.J.S. Wills §325:

> "It has been held that a compromise or settlement agreement, entered into for the purpose of avoiding the trouble and expense of a will contest, is not void as against public policy, where no persons or interests other than the persons and interests of the contracting parties are prejudicially affected thereby, unless it is entered into through connivance or fraud. . . ." (P. 162.)

A minority rule prevails in some jurisdictions, notably Wisconsin, (Graef v. Kanouse, 205 Wis. 597, 238 N.W. 377 [1931]), Connecticut (Tator v. Valden, 124 Conn. 96, 198 A. 169, 117 A.L.R. 1243) and North Carolina (In re Will of Pendergrass, 251 N.C. 737, 112 S.E.2d 562), wherein agreements have been declared to be invalid as contrary to public policy.

In New York a statute (Surrogate's Ct. Act, §144, subd. 2), similar to our previous code provision (R.S. 1935, 22-218, repealed in 1939), was held to compel the admission of a will to probate. (In re Cherkoff's Will, 9 A.D.2d 557, 189 N.Y.S.2d 530.)

. . .

More recently, the Supreme Court of Oregon was confronted with the identical conflict between a named executor and parties in interest who had entered into a written agreement to withhold a will from probate. In Dover v. Horger et al., 225 Or. 492, 358 P.2d 484, in adhering to the majority rule, the court considered the Oregon statutes and policy and in disposing of the matter stated:

> . . .
>
> "There was no reason to compel the expense of administration in this case. No creditor or other interested party was involved. The only interest plaintiff had was to collect his fee as executor. No statute or policy can be found which would require the court to grant administration where the only right that was involved was that of the person named as executor to receive his fee." (P. 494, 358 P.2d p. 484.)

. . .

The rationale of the majority rule is set out in 2 Page on Wills (Bowe-Parker Revision), §25.5, pp. 624, 625, and the cases in support thereof are catalogued. . . .

In their written objection to the probate of the will in this case, the members of the family do not ask the court to approve the settlement agreement or to determine the rights of the heirs-at-law entitled to the estate. They merely request the court to refuse probation of the will and to dismiss the petition. No other determination is necessary or appropriate at this stage of the proceedings. There was no contention made as to the validity of the agreement or any suggestion of the existence of any of the exceptions in the majority opinion to the rule permitting family settlement agreements. The agreement here provides for the disposition of the estate exactly in accord with the terms of the will and, also, with the statutes providing for intestate succession (K.S.A. 59-501 et seq.). The effect of a holding that a family settlement agreement is not a valid defense to an executor's petition for probation of a will deprives the members of a family of any choice as to the administration of their own inheritance and as a practical matter actually gives the option to a named executor.

I think it may be said in this case, but for insistence on the part of the named executor that the will be admitted to probate, the case would not be here. In my view the decision of the trial court should be reversed.

FONTRON and O'CONNOR, JJ., join in the foregoing dissent.[24]

NOTE

The Uniform Probate Code permits a will to be probated without the appointment of an executor by the court. Uniform Probate Code §§3-301, 3-401. What are the advantages of probate without administration? See Rheinstein, The Model Probate Code: A Critique, 48 Colum. L. Rev. 534, 537 (1948).

ROBBINS v. SIMMONS' ESTATE

Texas Court of Civil Appeals, 1952
252 S.W.2d 970

MONTEITH, Chief Justice. This is an appeal by Allyn W. Robbins and the National Bank of Commerce of Houston as executors named in one of the instruments alleged to be a will of Helene Simmons, deceased. The judgment appealed from is that of the 80th Judicial District Court of Harris County, Texas, entered in a probate proceeding in Harris County, Texas, denying probate of such will.

Mrs. Simmons died in Harris County, Texas, on May 3, 1950, leaving three alleged wills, each of which was in conflict with the others. All of the wills were offered for probate. Appellants in the appeal are the National Bank of Commerce of Houston and Allyn W. Robbins, a trust officer and agent of the bank. They were named in one, the will of Mrs. Simmons dated February 6, 1950, involved in the will contest.

At the death of Mrs. Helene Simmons the appellants offered for probate in the County Court of Harris County, Texas, as the last will and testament of Mrs. Simmons an instrument dated February 6, 1950, in which they were named as executors.

Appellee Clarence C. Booth and others presented for probate another instrument, wholly written by hand and dated February 8, 1950, which purported to revoke all other wills and codicils. Baylor University was not named as beneficiary in this instrument.

Frank A. Simmons, the surviving husband of the deceased, was omitted as a beneficiary in both of the other wills. He opposed the probate of both of the other two wills and offered for probate as the last will and testament of the deceased an instrument dated December 9, 1946, in which he was named as the principal beneficiary.

The provisions of the three named wills were in sharp conflict. Under the will dated February 6, 1950, Baylor University College of Medicine was bequeathed the

[24] Noted 9 Washburn L.J. 167. — EDS.

major portion of Mrs. Simmons' estate as a charitable donation, to be known as "The Crosby Estate Students' Loan Fund," to be used in assisting needy students to obtain medical education at said institution. Under the second will the parties who offered it for probate would have received the bulk of the estate. Under the third will Frank A. Simmons was named as the principal beneficiary. He was not provided for in the other two wills. Appellants were named as executors in the will dated February 6, 1950.

Appellee Clarence C. Booth is the brother of the deceased. Appellees Mrs. Maude Moore and Mrs. Florence Werminghaus are her sisters. Appellees Carlton Moore Jr., Eugene Werminghaus and Clarence Reginald Booth are her nephews. Donald Crosby, her son by adoption, predeceased her.

At the time of Mrs. Simmons' death she was in litigation with her husband, Frank A. Simmons, in the District Court of Harris County, Texas, and in the courts of California, he claiming to own one-half of all the property of the deceased by inter vivos gift, that he was interested in the estate as an heir and as beneficiary under the will he offered for probate. In his pleadings he contended that the other testamentary instruments were void for want of testamentary capacity in the deceased and because of undue influence.

While the case was pending in the Probate Court, Baylor University and the proponents of the instrument dated February 8, 1950, made an agreement under which they agreed to make an effort to defeat the claim of Frank A. Simmons in his various law suits.

After trial in the Probate Court, the instrument dated February 6, 1950, was admitted to probate. Frank A. Simmons appealed to the District Court of Harris County.

While the case was pending in the District Court, Baylor University and the proponents of the instrument dated February 8, 1950, above mentioned, reached a compromise settlement with Frank A. Simmons. Under the terms of this agreement Frank A. Simmons would be paid a consideration for a release of all of his claims to the estate, and that the parties who were named as specific legatees under the wills in controversy who were not parties to the agreement were to be paid the amount of the largest legacies provided for them by any of the wills, and after the payments of all debts and taxes, the balance of the estate would be divided in agreed proportions among the parties to the agreement.

In accordance with that agreement, Frank A. Simmons has been paid the amount of the consideration for his release and has released all of his claims.

All parties for whom specific legacies were provided by any of the controversial wills and who were not parties to the agreement have been paid the amount of the largest legacies provided for them in any of the wills and with the exception of K. D. Buddy McDuff, have all released their claims upon the estate. No party for whom any specific legacy was provided by any of the wills was an heir of the deceased.

The sum of $5,000 was tendered to K. D. Buddy McDuff, who is a cousin of the deceased. He refused to accept the $5,000 tendered until after it had been tendered into the registry of the court for him, and has since withdrawn it and has agreed to this judgment along with the other beneficiaries and heirs.

After the consummation of the agreement, an agreed judgment signed by the attorneys representing all of the appellees and giving effect to the agreement of the parties was presented to the judge of the 80th District Court of Harris County, Texas. The entry of said judgment was opposed by appellants. After an extended hearing of testimony and argument of counsel, the court entered said judgment, from which appellants appeal.

In the case of Wade v. Wade, 140 Tex. 339, 167 S.W.2d 1008, in which the facts are similar in all material respects to the facts in the instant case, the Supreme Court of this State held that the devisees and heirs of the deceased had a right to compromise their differences and to partition the property among themselves by mutual consent, subject to the rights of creditors and thus dispense with the necessity of probating the will. The Court, in its opinion, held that even if an administration in the estate had been pending in the probate court the effect would have been the same.

In the early case of Stringfellow v. Early, 15 Tex. Civ. App. 597, 40 S.W. 871, 874, it was held that an agreement among the heirs and beneficiaries to take the estate on terms different from those of the wills destroys the legal existence of the will. The trial court sustained a demurrer to the contest and such action was the subject of the appeal. It was held that, "Parties may make any contract with reference to their property rights that is not illegal, may adjust by compromise their differences and disputes concerning the same, and, as they bind themselves, so shall they be bound. It is difficult to understood why this cannot be effected by an agreement not to probate a will, or how it interferes with public policy. The power to litigate and to establish a right by appeal to the courts is as much the subject of contract as any other right in property. Such adjustments by contract are favored by the law and the courts, and are not deemed to be an unwarranted interference with the jurisdiction of the courts, or against public policy. On the contrary, public policy favors them." . . .

In the case of Fore v. McFadden, Tex. Civ. App., 276 S.W. 327, 329, in which the questions involved are similar in many respects to those in the instant case, it was held that, "It has been definitely decided by the courts of this state, and of many other states, that the beneficiaries under a will have a right to agree among themselves upon any distribution they see proper of the property bequeathed to them." The Court stated in its opinion that the property was theirs, that no one else is interested in its disposition, and they may, with propriety, make any distribution of it that suits them, so long as they do not invade the rights of other parties or infringe some rule of public policy.

The above decisions by the courts of this State are, we think, controlling in this appeal. They establish the fact that the devisees and heirs of an estate have a right to compromise their difficulties and to partition the property among themselves by mutual consent subject to the rights of creditors and to thus dispense with the necessity for probating a will.

Decisions from other jurisdictions dealing with a similar state of facts, with few exceptions, follow substantially the same line of reasoning as was adopted by our courts in the case of Wade v. Wade, supra. . . . [The court cites and discusses cases from Maryland, Missouri, Illinois, and Rhode Island.]

Appellees in the case at bar contend that appellants have no litigable interest in the subject matter and that this appeal should be dismissed for the further reason that any question which appellants might be able to raise is moot and entirely extinguished by the agreement of the parties for the reason that appellate courts will not review judgments if the controversy between the parties has terminated. State v. Society for Friendless Children, 130 Tex. 533, 111 S.W.2d 1075.

We have carefully considered all other points of error presented by appellants in their briefs and, finding no reversible errors therein, this appeal must be dismissed.

PROBLEMS

1. Who were the plaintiffs in the Robbins case, and why were they suing? Did they really want to probate the will of February 6, 1950?

2. Although the facts reported in the case do not indicate the amount of money involved, this was apparently a substantial estate — witness the number of parties interested in the outcome of the litigation. This would suggest that there was a need for an administration: assets to be collected from third persons, creditors to be paid, tax returns to be filed, and evidence of title to be furnished to Mrs. Simmons' successors in interest. Since there was no formal administration of Mrs. Simmons' estate, how could these functions be satisfied?

3. If any of the beneficiaries under either of the three wills or any of Mrs. Simmons' heirs had been minors, would the settlement arrangement agreed to by the parties have been possible?

4. Refer back to In re Estate of Harper. What decision would the Kansas court have reached in the case of Robbins v. Simmons' Estate? If your answer is that they would have required the probate of Mrs. Simmons' will, which of the three wills would they have admitted to probate?

Section 2053 of the Internal Revenue Code of 1954 allows a deduction against the federal estate tax for expenses incurred in the administration of an estate. If an estate is not formally administered because there are no debts or claims against the estate and the interested parties have agreed on a settlement of the assets, are attorney's fees and other expenses incurred in working out the settlement deductible under section 2053? Pitner v. United States, 388 F.2d 651 (5th Cir. 1967): "At first blush, the notion that administration expenses may be deducted when there is no administration seems too paradoxical for serious consideration. On reflection and after considering Texas law, and somewhat to our surprise, we find ourselves in agreement with the plaintiffs' theory of recovery. . . . [T]he policy of the Code is not to rely upon formal probated actions in determining permissible deductions. The Eighth Circuit has suggested the reason for this policy: Section 2053(a) is meant to apply anywhere in the world, *'even in countries where administration of estates is had otherwise than through courts,* if any such countries exist.' (Emphasis added.) Commissioner of Internal Revenue v. Bronson, 8 Cir. 1929, 32 F.2d 112, 114. Succession laws of Texas present us with just such a situation. Although Texas law establishes a formal court proceeding for the proving of wills . . . in some situations a will need not — indeed, may not — be administered through a formal court proceeding. The administration of a decedent's estate under the eye of a probate judge is a means to protect creditors, widows, and minor children. When no such protection is necessary Texas courts tend to reject petitions for formal court-supervised administration on the ground that such a proceeding would be a waste of time and money."

SECTION B. Criticisms of Probate and the Uniform Probate Code

Public dissatisfaction with our probate court system has increased in recent years. The reasons are complex and varied, but they include the expenses and delays incurred in estate administrations, objections to specific practices (such as the appointment of guardians ad litem), and doubts about the necessity for all the formalities attendant on the probate process. The Uniform Probate Code, promulgated in 1969, is the organized bar's answer to some of these criticisms.

1. *Executors' Commissions and Attorneys' Fees*

In most, but not all, states executors' and administrators' commissions are set by statute. In the remaining states the statutes either provide for reasonable compensation or make no provision with respect to compensation. In some states the specified rates set only the maximum fees. On the other hand, in most states additional compensation may be allowed for unusual or extraordinary services.

Among the states there is wide variation in statutory rates of executors' commissions. In New Jersey, where commissions are among the highest, the personal representative is entitled to six percent of the income and five percent of "all corpus that comes into the fiduciary's hands" not exceeding $100,000; and on the excess, such percentage not in excess of five percent as the court may determine, depending upon actual services rendered.[25] If there are two or more personal representatives, the court may allow additional commissions at a rate not exceeding one percent of the corpus for each additional fiduciary. Hence on an estate of $100,000, the personal representative is entitled to a $5000 fee. Jurisdictions with the lowest commis-

[25] N.J. Stat. Ann. §3A:10-2 (1953, Supp. 1971).

sions (about half the size of New Jersey's) include Iowa, Georgia, and Nevada.[26]

Unlike the commissions of the personal representative, fees of the attorney for the estate are rarely fixed by statute. Often, however, state or local bar associations publish a minimum fee schedule; these schedules are given varying weight where the legal fees are contested in court.

ILLINOIS STATE BAR ASSN.
MINIMUM FEE SCHEDULE
Sept. 13, 1968

ESTATES OF DECEDENTS

1. This schedule is to be used solely as a guide in determining the fees to be charged for legal services rendered to the personal representative of the decedent's estate including the preparation and filing of income, estate and Illinois inheritance tax returns:

Gross Value of Estate	Fee
to $5,000	$400
from $5,000 to $25,000	$400 plus 5% of the amount in excess of $5,000
from $25,000 to $50,000	$1,400 plus 4% of the amount in excess of $25,000
from $50,000 to $100,000	$2,400 plus 3% of the amount in excess of $50,000
from $100,000 to $500,000	$3,900 plus 2½% of the amount in excess of $100,000
from $500,000 to $1,000,000	$13,900 plus 2% of the amount in excess of $500,000
Over $1,000,000	Fee to be agreed upon in discussion with client

"Gross Value" consists of:

(a) Market value of personalty at date of death passing to the personal representative, plus

(b) Gross income from personalty and real estate collected by the personal representative, plus

(c) The market value of real estate required to be inventoried in the estate, less balance due on encumbrances and past due taxes.

2. Where inheritance or federal estate tax returns are filed which include real estate or personalty not included in "Gross Value" as defined in paragraph

26 See American College of Probate Counsel, Fees of Executors, Administrators and Testamentary Trustees (1969); Bauer, Watch Those Fees! 104 Trusts & Estates 1117 (1965); Bauer, Legal Fees in Probate, 105 id. at 850 (1966).

1, above, regardless of whether or not a probate estate is opened, it is suggested that the attorney is entitled to additional compensation. It is further suggested that a reasonable charge would be computed in accordance with paragraph 1, above, as to such property included in both returns by adding to "Gross Value" as above defined, 50% of the value of such property as included in the Illinois inheritance tax return, and, as to property included in only one such return by adding to "Gross Value" as above defined, $33\frac{1}{3}\%$ of the value of such property as included in such return. In any such case, it is suggested that the additional fee normally be charged against the property involved.

3. Where a fee is not otherwise charged with regard to property of a decedent, then if services of any nature whatsoever are rendered by an attorney with regard to said property, a fee may be charged for such services at the suggested minimum hourly rate.
4. Additional services, for which it is contemplated that additional charges may be made are those rendered:

   A. In a court other than the probate division,
   B. In a contested matter in the probate division,
   C. In connection with the audit, protest or contest of an income, gift, estate or inheritance tax return filed or liability incurred by the decedent or personal representative,
   D. In connection with the settlement of estate or inheritance taxes with respect to insurance not payable to the estate, joint tenancy property, gifts in contemplation of or to take effect on death, or general testamentary powers of appointment, whether or not exercised by the decedent, and any other services related to assets not included in the "Gross Value" of the estate,
   E. With respect to problems of valuation of property for estate and inheritance taxes or to the protest of such taxes,
   F. In connection with matters which are unusual or excessive for the size of the estate involved, and
   G. In connection with the performance of duties normally performable by the personal representative but which fall to the lawyer because of the personal representative's inexperience, lack of ability or absence from the place from which the assets of the estate must be managed.

5. The problems presented in the probate of the estate, the nature of the property included in estates and the degree of experience of the personal representative, cover such a wide range that the services required of the attorney in a particular estate may be greater or less than the average contemplated by the foregoing paragraphs, in which event the fees may be adjusted accordingly.
6. The attention of the attorney is directed to the Small Estates Act, Sections 324-328a, Chap. 3, Ill. Rev. Stat., on estates of less than five thousand dollars ($5,000) in which case the hourly charge is suggested.

A.B.A., MINIMUM FEE SCHEDULES — DEVELOPMENT AND UTILIZATION

Committee on Economics of Law Practice 1, 3-5 (1970)

The general purpose of a minimum fee schedule is to indicate, for the benefit of the bar and the public, an advisory schedule of minimum charges which have been recommended by the organized bar after consideration of the various factors anticipated in normal or usual circumstances. . . .

What a lawyer has to sell is his knowledge and skill in terms of time — time to research and acquire the knowledge to handle his client's affairs; time to gain the experience and skill necessary to solve his client's problems. These characteristics of the law practice make the determination of charges a particularly difficult problem. How much to charge for services constantly confronts the legal practitioner no matter how long he has been a member of the Bar. However, the time spent on a particular problem is seldom the sole criterion for fixing the fee. The younger lawyer must spend more time than the older lawyer in order to perform a certain task. He must deduct the time spent educating himself, and charge only for the hours taken to acquire the knowledge the average practitioner would not be expected to have. On the other hand, the seasoned lawyer, having gained experience and skill cannot be expected to charge less because he can do the job in less time than the average attorney would take.

Thus there are other factors in addition to the time expended that must be considered in fixing the fee. These factors include: (1) the benefit to the client; (2) the sum involved in the problem; (3) the certainty of compensation; (4) whether the lawyer has been precluded from other employment; (5) the novelty and difficulty of the problem; and (6) whether the employment is for a single matter or for an established client. Since no one factor is controlling and each varies in importance, there is often a wide range in the fee charged by different lawyers for a particular service. This has created confusion and misunderstanding for the lay public, who have often found it expedient to shop around for a lower price. Both the public and the bar are entitled to a reasonably uniform measure of charges for comparable services. For one person to pay $10.00 for a simple deed, and for his neighbor to pay $25.00 for the identical service is not only unfair to the public, but brings the bar into disrepute. This situation is undesirable for all concerned. A lawyer who cuts his fees, frequently renders cut-rate service in order to continue his practice. Competition among lawyers should be on the basis of services rendered, rather than in the fees charged.

Minimum fee schedules serve as one means of insuring quality legal service for a fair and adequate charge. The client is entitled to a better product than the inferior legal service that is frequently rendered by the lawyer who solicits business by "fee cutting."

A minimum fee schedule should not purport to be a mandatory statement of charges, for the final determination of fees must always be made in light of the relevant considerations prescribed by the Code of Professional Responsibility.

There are numerous advantages for both the public and the profession that follow from adoption of minimum fee schedules. For the public, the existence of a minimum fee schedule promotes an understanding of legal fees and helps allay fears that lawyers' charges are determined haphazardly without regard to ascertainable standards. Fee schedules encourage a broader understanding of the availability of reasonably priced legal services and help eliminate wide divergencies in fees between individual lawyers in the same or contiguous geographic areas. This reduces the client's fear of discrimination and tends to insure that the charge bears a sound relationship to the value of the service rendered. Minimum fee schedules also tend to discourage lawyer shopping by clients on the basis of cost of services rather than the quality of services rendered.

For the lawyer, minimum fee schedules base competition within the profession on skill and the quality of service rather than on the price charged. This tends to minimize inadequate service and discourage unethical practices. Furthermore, minimum fee schedules promote efficiency within the profession by encouraging all lawyers to critically evaluate their operations and revise or dispose of obsolete and inefficient procedures.

HAUPTFUHRER, VARIATION IN PROBATE PRACTICES AND THEIR EFFECTS ON FEES

5 Real Prop., Prob. & Trust J. 503, 506 (1970)

What kind of order can be made from all this hodge-podge? In spite of the earlier disclaimer, these reports do have value in highlighting reasonably accurately:

(1) The fact that great variations exist in the legal services rendered in connection with the settlement of estates, not only among practitioners in different states, but, perhaps even more importantly, among individual practitioners; and

(2) The probable failure of the bar in many instances to relate fees in probate matters to the amount and value of the services rendered and the responsibility assumed.

For these reasons our committee [ABA Section of Real Property, Probate and Trust Law, Committee on Administration Expenses] recommended that this Section should disapprove the practice of fixing fees in probate cases solely by applying a fee schedule to the amount of the estate, and that this Section should approve the policy that the amount of the fee of the attorney in probate matters be the reasonable value of the services rendered to the estate in accordance with the guidelines of the Code of Professional Responsibility.[27]

. . .

Recently, two well known lawyers spoke on the subject of minimum fee sched-

[27] The Committee subsequently prepared a Statement of Principles for the Council of the Section, which stated that minimum fee schedules should be one of several factors in determining the reasonableness of the fee. 6 Real Prop., Prob. & Trust J. 590 (1971). — Eds.

ules. They were defended by a speaker before the National Conference of Bar Presidents on the ground that such a schedule "tends to ensure that the charge bears a sound relationship to the value of the services rendered." That statement finds little support in our committee's investigation. On the other hand, ABA President Edward Wright suggested that minimum fee schedules in many instances do violence to the Code of Professional Responsibility. That statement is clearly supported by our committee's investigation. Accordingly, should we not make certain that minimum fee schedules are not followed slavishly, and that fees in probate matters bear a reasonable relationship to the value of the services actually rendered and the responsibilities actually assumed?

QUESTIONS

1. With respect to an estate in the $100,000 range, would you expect the attorney's and executor's fees to be different if (a) in one case the estate consisted almost entirely of securities listed on the New York Stock Exchange, United States Government bonds and cash; and (b) in another case the estate consisted mainly of a sheep ranch and a drugstore owned by the decedent and his partner, in which assets had to be sold or mortgaged to pay debts and expenses of administration, and extended negotiations were conducted with the taxing authorities on the proper valuation of estate assets?

2. Lawyer Jones is named executor of a will. He is a sole practitioner and does not employ a separate attorney. Is Jones entitled to collect executor's commissions or attorney's fees or both? Note, 65 A.L.R.2d 809 (1959). American College of Probate Counsel, Attorneys' Fees in Probate (1967), reports that many local bar associations in Massachusetts have minimum fee schedules charging six percent for acting as executor without attorney, four percent as attorney for an executor other than a bank, and two percent as attorney for a corporate executor.

3. Lawyer Cohen is named executor of a will. He employs as counsel the law firm of Smith, Cohen, and Macy, in which he is a partner. The jurisdiction does not allow extra compensation for legal services rendered by the executor. Is the law firm entitled to legal fees paid out of the estate? Estate of Parker, 200 Cal. 132, 251 P. 907 (1926); In re Hallenback's Estate, 122 F. Supp. 212 (D.D.C. 1954).

4. If the attorney prepares the estate tax return, is he entitled to extraordinary compensation for that service? Estate of Bray, 230 Cal. App. 2d 136, 40 Cal. Rptr. 750 (1964).

2. *Guardians ad Litem*

NOTE, GUARDIANS AD LITEM

45 Iowa L. Rev. 376, 381-384 (1960)

Woerner, in his work on guardianship, has stated that: "A judgment cannot properly be rendered against an infant who has no probate guardian or guardian ad litem, although his parents in fact represent him at the trial, and by the aid of counsel defend the action against him on his behalf." [28] It can safely be said that a guardian ad litem is necessary to the validity of a judgment against a minor or incompetent to the extent that a judgment obtained without such a representative will be subject to attack. The question then remains as to whether such a judgment is *void* or whether it is valid until some prejudice is shown by the disabled party to justify overturning the judgment.

Generally, judgments obtained against disabled parties in the absence of a guardian ad litem are voidable but not void. Under this rule, such a judgment is good against all but direct attack. If the judgment were deemed void and subject to collateral attack, the *appointment* of the guardian ad litem would assume a more jurisdictional than procedural status. The rule in Iowa apparently is that a judgment obtained without a guardian ad litem is voidable. However, language in one Iowa case strongly suggests a contrary rule. In Irwin v. Keokuk Sav. Bank & Trust,[29] a five-thousand dollar inheritance belonging to a minor was given to the minor's father. After reaching majority the minor challenged the decree of the probate court. The Iowa Supreme Court stated that "minors who are unable to act for themselves *may not be legally deprived* of legacies or the property of an estate to which they are heirs without representation in judicial proceedings by a legally appointed guardian or a guardian ad litem." [30] This strong language has led McCarty to state in his treatise on probate practice that the Iowa rule is that judgments obtained against infants without representation by a guardian ad litem are void.[31] The strong equities in favor of the plaintiff, who would have been deprived completely of his inheritance had the judgment been upheld, and the fact that the father as natural guardian for the infant did not possess the authority to receive the money[32] may well have been the justification for the use of such strong language. Since the Irwin case is the only Iowa decision suggesting that judgments obtained without a guardian ad litem are void, it seems unlikely that this case, in view of all its facts, states the Iowa rule on this point.

. . .

Statutory language may also bear upon the validity of a judgment obtained against a minor or incompetent without a guardian ad litem. A statute couched in permissive terms could be construed as leaving the necessity of an appointment to the discretion of the court. For example, the Federal Rules provide that: "The court shall appoint a guardian ad litem for an infant or incompetent person not otherwise represented in an action *or shall make such other order as it deems proper for the protection of the infant or incompetent person.*" [33] Although the majority of

[28] Woerner [Guardianship (1897)], §21.

[29] 218 Iowa 477, 255 N.W. 671 (1934).

[30] Id. at 480, 255 N.W. at 673. (Emphasis added.)

[31] McCarty, Iowa Probate Practice §§1627-28 (1942).

[32] The distribution legally could have been made only to a guardian of the property of the minor. 218 Iowa at 480, 255 N.W. at 673. See Fratcher, Powers and Duties of Guardians of Property, 45 Iowa L. Rev. 264 (1960) (this symposium).

[33] Fed. R. Civ. P. 17(c). (Emphasis added.) See 3 Moore, Federal Practice ¶1726, at

statutes are mandatory in terminology, permitting the appointment of a guardian ad litem to rest upon the discretion of the court would be desirable in that it would eliminate unnecessary appeals and uncertainty as to the precise effect of the judgment obtained without representation for the disabled party.

. . .

The majority of statutes state in substance that a regularly appointed representative such as a general guardian, if there be one, will be responsible for the representation of his ward in court. The Iowa Rules of Civil Procedure provide that: "an action of a minor or any person judicially adjudged incompetent shall be brought by his guardian." [34] It is further provided that "the regular guardian or the attorney appearing for a competent party" may defend for the minor or incompetent.[35] Thus, the important factor is that the party under disability have competent representation. Therefore, the question of the necessity of appointing a guardian ad litem will not arise unless there is either no guardian or personal representative for the disabled party, or, for some reason, the interests of such regularly appointed representatives are adverse.

NEW YORK TIMES, MANHATTAN SURROGATES' COURT IS FOCUS OF POLITICAL DISPUTES

July 5, 1966, p. 1, col. 8

Buried in files that spread over four floors of the gloomy Surrogates' Court building across Chambers Street from City Hall are documents detailing how the two Manhattan surrogates administer almost a billion dollars worth of estates each year.

The files include the wills, along with records of the legal work involved in carrying out the provisions of the wills, of those with assets in New York County who have died since 1662. They record the names of guardians, the lawyers appointed as guardians by the surrogates to protect the interests of minors and mental incompetents, and the fees collected by the guardians.[36] These fees are requested by

---

1421 (1948): "[T]he subdivision [rule 17(c)] does not make appointment of a guardian ad litem mandatory, if the court feels that the interests of the infant or incompetent can be as well protected without this action, and if the court has jurisdiction over the person under disability." For examples of other apparently permissive statutes, see Alaska Comp. Laws Ann. §55-3-4 (1949) ("It shall be *lawful* for the court to appoint guardian ad litem") (Emphasis added.); Ariz. R. Civ. P. 17(g) (similar to federal rule); Conn. Gen. Stat. §45-54 (1958) (court *may* appoint guardian ad litem). Compare D.C. Code Ann. §13-105 (1951) (in cases involving infants it *shall be duty* of court to appoint guardian ad litem), with D.C. Code Ann. §13-107 (1951) (court *may* appoint guardian ad litem for person non compos mentis).

[34] Iowa R. Civ. P. 12.

[35] Iowa R. Civ. P. 13.

[36] In New York guardians ad litem must be appointed to represent minors' interests at the various estate administration proceedings, including probate of the will, petitions for the sale of real property, intermediate accountings, and the final accounting. See Miller, A Practical Guide to the Administration of New York Estates (1969). In 1967 the legislature enacted a statute

the guardians, approved or amended by the surrogates and deducted from the estate.

. . .

Repeated attempts to interview Mr. Cox and Mr. DiFalco about the operation of their court were turned aside by aides in their offices. But an inspection of the records and interviews with persons familiar with the court showed the following:

A former law partner of Surrogate Cox is assigned all the legal work on estates valued in the millions, in which there are no heirs.

A former law partner of Surrogate DiFalco was assigned by him as a guardian for two children of John J. Shubert, of the theater family. The judge granted his ex-partner's application for a $15,000 fee after the children received $12,500 each and renounced their claim to a $15-million estate.

Twenty-one of Manhattan's 30,000 lawyers got 15 per cent of the appointments as guardians in 1959, the year before publication of guardians' names ceased.

. . .

An inspection of the records of cases in which prominent names were appointed as guardians showed that value of the estates ranged from "more than $500,000" to "an estimated $64-million."

Guardian reports were found in only one of the folders containing records of these major cases. In that case, two attorneys each received $10,000 for a month's work.

Critics of the Surrogates' Court system have contended over the years that guardians are appointed from lists supplied by political clubs of various persuasions. The charge has never been proved and if it were, there would be nothing illegal about such lists — the surrogates have the power to appoint any lawyer they wish to.

. . .

Mayor Fiorello H. LaGuardia called the Surrogates' Court "the most expensive undertaking establishment in the world" when, during his anti-Tammany administration, he found himself unable to cut off that source of patronage to Tammany lawyers. The politically well-connected also benefit on occasion from Supreme Court appointments as referees, but there is no single source of appointments in the state that approaches the magnitude of the Manhattan Surrogates' Court.

Manhattan has two surrogates and the city's other boroughs have one each. The two in Manhattan run far and away the busiest such court in the nation, since the borough is the nation's financial capital and many estates involve assets here. The Manhattan surrogates are elected to the $37,000-a-year posts for 14-year terms.

For the whole state in fiscal 1965, according to the State Department of Taxation and Finance, surrogates handled 30,615 taxable estates with gross value of $3.7-billion. Of this, the six city surrogates handled 12,775 with gross value of $1.8-billion. Surrogates Cox and DiFalco reported that in 1965 there were 4,432 estates filed in their court, with a total value of $941-million.

---

providing for virtual representation of minors under certain circumstances in Surrogates' Court proceedings. N.Y. Sur. Ct. Proc. Act §315 (1967). See Looker, Virtual Representation, 34 Brooklyn L. Rev. 395 (1968). — Eds.

NEW YORK SURROGATE'S COURT PROCEDURE ACT (1971)

§402. *Appearance for infant or incompetent*

1. An infant may appear by the guardian of his property and an incompetent by the committee of his property. The appointment of a guardian ad litem does not bar the guardian or committee from appearing as a party. The person so appearing and his attorney shall each file on or before the return day of process an affidavit showing

(a) that he is qualified to protect their rights,

(b) whether he is related to or connected in business with any party to the proceeding or the attorney for any party,

(c) whether he is entitled to share in the estate in which the infant or incompetent is interested or is in any way interested therein,

(d) whether he has any interest adverse to or in conflict with that of the infant or incompetent and

(e) such additional facts as may be required by the court.

2. A person under disability shall appear by a guardian ad litem where no appearance is made as provided in subdivision 1 or where the court so directs because of possible adversity or conflict of interest or for other cause.

§403. *Appointment of guardian ad litem*

1. By nomination. (a) An infant over the age of 14 years or his parent or guardian may petition the court on or before the return day of process for the appointment of a named attorney as his guardian ad litem. There shall be filed with the petition the affidavit of the attorney showing

(i) that he is qualified to protect the rights of the infant and has no interest adverse to him and

(ii) the circumstances which led to his nomination.

(b) When the infant is under the age of 18 years there shall also be filed with the petition the affidavit of the parent with whom the infant resides, or if not residing with a parent by the person having his legal custody or an adult person with whom he resides, showing that the affiant

(i) consents to the appointment of the nominated attorney,

(ii) has no interest adverse to that of the infant and if he has an adverse interest, whether he has influenced the infant in the nomination and

(iii) such additional facts as may be required by the court.

(c) The court may appoint the nominated attorney guardian ad litem unless because of adversity or conflict of interest or for other cause a different appointment is required.

2. By the court. A person under disability who does not appear by his guardian or committee pursuant to 402 shall except as otherwise expressly provided appear by a guardian ad litem appointed by the court on nomination or on its own initiative whenever such person is a necessary party or for other reason the court deems it necessary to appoint a guardian ad litem to protect the interests of such party.

§404. *Qualification and duties of guardian ad litem*

1. A guardian ad litem shall be an attorney admitted to practice in New York.

2. Before entering upon his duties he shall file a consent to act and unless he has previously done so, a statement of no interest adverse to or in conflict with the person under disability.

3. He shall file an appearance and take such steps with diligence as deemed necessary to represent and protect the person under disability and file a report of his activities together with his recommendation upon the termination of his duties or at such other time as directed by the court.

§405. *Compensation of guardian ad litem*

1. For services rendered a guardian ad litem shall receive reasonable compensation to be allowed by the court payable from the estate or from the interest of the person under disability or from both in such proportion as directed by the court.

2. The court may direct that the fixation of the amount of compensation be reserved for future determination.

3. If an infant or incompetent appears by his guardian or committee pursuant to 402 the court may allow the guardian or committee such sum as the court deems reasonable for his counsel fees and other expenses incurred in protection of the infant's or incompetent's interest subject to the same requirements in the case of a guardian ad litem of the provisions of the preceding subdivisions of this section.

Substantial changes in the law relating to guardians ad litem were recommended in 1965 by the New York Temporary State Commission on the Law of Estates. The Commission proposed that no guardian ad litem be appointed in the following cases: (1) In the discretion of the surrogate in an uncontested probate proceeding where (a) the will leaves the entire estate to the surviving spouse, if alive, and if not alive, to the testator's children and (b) the surviving spouse states under oath that the infant is the issue by birth or adoption of the spouse and testator. (2) In an uncontested probate proceeding where the person under disability is given by the will at least the amount of his intestate share. (3) In an accounting where the person under disability is entitled to a general bequest of a specified number of dollars and the executor states that it will be paid in full. (4) Where an alien nonresident under disability is represented by his consular representative. (5) Where a person under disability is cited on an application for letters of administration.

The Commission also proposed that guardians ad litem who seek fees in excess of $500 must file an affidavit of services, and that any interested party who objected to the fee could apply to the Appellate Division to review the amount of compensation allowed the guardian on the original papers and without the expense of printing the record. In addition, the Commission recommended (in the section that became Surrogate's Court Procedure Act §403(1)(c)) that the court *shall* (rather than *may*) appoint the attorney nominated by the child or his parent or guardian as the guardian ad litem. The Commission disapproved of a proposal to require publication in a newspaper of the names of guardians ad litem appointed. See N.Y.

Temporary State Commission on Estates, Report No. 7.12A, in 4th Report, Appendix 33 (1965).

Most of the Commission's proposals were rejected by the New York legislature.

MIDONICK[37] & BUSH, THE SURROGATE'S COURT AS A FAMILY PROTECTOR

New York Law Journal, Nov. 4, 1971, p. 1

Much debate about court-appointed guardians ad litem (formerly "special guardians") has appeared in recent years in the press and in popular journals. Criticism is often directed against the process of selection of such guardians, but no one seriously questions the need for the guardianship mechanism in some instances. Guardians most often play a real and important role in Surrogate's Court as a protector of the family.

. . .

There are, however, some desirable improvements in the rules governing when guardians are to be appointed, and how they are to function, that may, indirectly, suggest new answers to some of these important questions.

As a result of the work of the Bennett Commission on Estates, New York now has a form of virtual representation governing proceedings in the Surrogate's Court[;] section 315 of the Surrogate's Court Act, provides that: (1) where a remainder interest in an estate is bequeathed to a class of persons on the happening of a future event, such as income to A for life, remainder at A's death to A's issue, only those persons who would take if the event happened now, need be made parties to the proceeding; (2) where a remainder is bequeathed to A, or if A is dead, to his surviving issue, only A need be made a party; (3) where a remainder is bequeathed to A, or if A is dead, to B, only A need be named a party. These rules were substantially based upon similar rules already in effect in the Supreme Court respecting [inter vivos] trusts.

Same Interests

The rationale for permitting the initially-named taker of a remainder interest to represent those who take in substitution, is that their economic interests are substantially identical; what is good for one being probably good for the other. It would not require too much to extend the same approach to the class remainder cases. If the persons comprising the class "A's issue," to whom the remainder, at A's death, is limited, now consist of some adult persons and some minors, these adult persons logically can now represent the interests of their minor co-members of the class.

This is the position taken in the Uniform Trustees Accounting Act (1957), which has not, however, been adopted, as a Uniform Act, in New York. If this extension of the concept of virtual representation should be effected in this state, there would be no substantial weakening of the protection of the property interests

[37] Family Court Judge Millard L. Midonick was elected Surrogate of New York County on Nov. 2, 1971. — Eds.

of minors. At the same time, there would be no necessity, in such cases, for the appointment, and compensation, of a guardian ad litem.

Another step toward limiting the number of situations in which the appointment of a guardian ad litem is necessary, would be to apply in the Surrogate's Court the same rules respecting informal accountings as now obtain in the Supreme Court.

The grantor of an inter vivos trust is free, if he so chooses, to provide, in the trust agreement, that written approval of the trustee's accounts by all the adult [beneficiaries will be binding on all other persons?] beneficially interested in the trust, whether those others are minors or incompetents and whether the interests so bound are vested or contingent. Consequently, trustees of such inter vivos trusts may, if they desire, informally settle their accounts without the expense of judicial proceedings, including the appointment and compensation of guardians. Yet, a similar privilege is denied to testators.

Obviously, there is no coherent public policy against use of such a device if it is not violated by such an arrangement in connection with a living trust, but is impermissible in relation to a like provision in a will. If testators can validly dispense with the extra protection of a fiduciary bond, they should be able to authorize the informal settlement of accountings by adult beneficiaries. If contrary precedent of long standing now prevents a judicial change in the rule as to wills, then corrective legislation should follow.

The principal area, today, where guardians ad litem are needed to protect infant interests, is on the judicial accountings of executors and trustees. Experience in the Supreme Court has shown that, at times, even trustees of inter vivos trusts containing provisions for the informal settlement of their accounts, nevertheless, still prefer a judicial settlement, with the presence of a guardian ad litem representing the minors involved. A similar situation would undoubtedly obtain in the Surrogate's Court, as well.

IN RE MOUSSEAU'S WILL, 30 Minn. 202, 14 N.W. 887 (1883). "As respects proceedings for the probate of a will, our statute provides for notice, either by newspaper publication or by personal service on all parties interested, at the discretion of the judge of probate. Gen. St. 1878, c. 47, §14. No provision is made for or in reference to the appointment of a guardian ad litem for any minor interested in the estate. It follows that, as respects the matter of notice, the newspaper publication or personal service (as the case may be) gives the probate court complete jurisdiction to proceed in the premises. . . . No appointment of a guardian ad litem, as respects the proceedings to admit a will to probate, being required by statute, none is necessary, and a probate in other respects regular is valid as to all the world without any such appointment. It follows that in the case before us the probate (May 13, 1878) of the will of Fannie Mousseau, to which no objection is taken, except for the non-appointment of a guardian for the minor heir, Minnie Mousseau, is valid and effectual for all purposes."

3. *Appraisers' Fees*

MINNESOTA STATUTES ANNOTATED (1969): "§525.331. *Appraisal.* If the inventory lists no property other than moneys of the United States, no appraisal shall be required; otherwise, the property shall be appraised at its full and fair value as of the date of death, or in a guardianship as of the date of the appointment of the guardian, by two or more disinterested persons appointed by the court. Within two months after appointment unless a longer time has been granted by the court, the appraisers shall set down in figures opposite each item after deducting the encumbrances, liens, and charges, the net value thereof and show the total amount of each class, and of all classes, and forthwith deliver such inventory and appraisal certified by them, to the representative who shall immediately file the same. Such appraisers shall be allowed such reasonable fees, necessary disbursements, and expenses as may be fixed by the court and be paid by the representative as expenses of administration or guardianship."

CALIFORNIA PROBATE CODE (1971): "§605. (a) The appraisement shall be made by the executor or administrator and an inheritance tax referee as follows:

"(1) The executor or administrator shall appraise at fair market value moneys, currency, cash items, bank accounts and amounts on deposit with any financial institution, and the proceeds of life and accident insurance policies and retirement plans payable upon death in lump sum amounts, excepting therefrom such items whose fair market value is, in the opinion of the executor or administrator, an amount different from the ostensible value or specified amount. . . .

"(2) All assets other than those appraised by the executor or administrator pursuant to paragraph (1) shall be appraised by an inheritance tax referee appointed by the court or judge.

"§609. Each referee shall receive from each estate appraised by him as compensation for his services commissions upon the total value of the assets appraised by him as follows: For the first five hundred thousand dollars ($500,000), a fee of one-tenth of 1 percent thereof, but not less than a minimum fee of five dollars ($5); for all over five hundred thousand dollars ($500,000), a fee of one-twentieth of 1 percent. In addition to the fee herein provided each referee is entitled to receive his actual and necessary expenses to be allowed by the court. . . .

"The fee shall not apply to items appraised by the executor or administrator under the provisions of paragraph (1) of subdivision (a) of Section 605."

NOTES

1. In 1964 William M. Keck died a resident of California. His estate totalled $180 million. It largely consisted of Superior Oil Co. stock ($150 million) and other stocks traded on the New York and American stock exchanges. What is the ap-

praiser's fee under California Probate Code §609? After newspaper publicity was given the fee in this case, the appraiser agreed to accept a fee to be fixed by the court on the basis of the reasonable worth of the services involved. And what was the "reasonable worth"? $30,187.58.

2. Are court-appointed appraisers necessary? Desirable? Among the purposes for which appraisals may be needed are the valuation of assets for estate and inheritance tax purposes; the proper proration of estate taxes among the beneficiaries; the amount to be allocated to a spouse who elects to take against the will, and the sources from which her share is to be satisfied; the amounts distributable to legatees who are given a certain percentage of the estate; whether the value of a homestead exceeds the homestead exemption; whether a summary administration of small estates may be granted; whether the personal representative is liable for selling assets for less than a fair value; the amount of the executor's bond and of executor's commissions and attorney's fees.

If an appraiser is not appointed, how will these purposes be satisfied?

How likely is it that the appraisers who are appointed will have the expertise required to value assets without a readily ascertainable market value? That the appraisers' determinations of value will be accepted by the taxing authorities? See Smith, Appraisers and Appraisements Under the Texas Probate Code, 45 Texas L. Rev. 842 (1967).

3. Section 3-706 of the Uniform Probate Code provides that the personal representative shall prepare an inventory of property, indicating its fair market value, and either send the inventory to interested persons who request it or file the inventory in court. If the personal representative elects the former route, the inventory does not become part of the records of the probate court. Section 3-707 provides that the personal representative may employ a qualified and disinterested appraiser to assist in determining the fair market value of assets where there may be doubt as to such value. Prior to the Uniform Probate Code (1969) only a handful of jurisdictions — including Pennsylvania and New York — had no system of court-appointed appraisers. See Estate Administration: Current Practices and Proposed Uniform Probate Code, 3 Real Prop., Prob. & Trust J. 143, 149 (1968).

4. *The Uniform Probate Code: Non-Court Administrations of Decedents' Estates*

FLETCHER, WASHINGTON'S NON-INTERVENTION EXECUTOR — STARTING POINT FOR PROBATE SIMPLIFICATION
41 Wash. L. Rev. 33, 74-75 (1966)

. . . [T]he process of winding-up a decedent's affairs is mostly routine and usually friendly; it is neither complex nor litigious. Given the proper tools, an honest and modestly able person, with competent help, should be able to carry out the process pretty much on his own. The basic fallacy in the regular probate procedure is that it is designed primarily to handle problem situations — dishonest and incompetent personal representatives, scheming and dishonest relatives and creditors, will forgers, poorly drafted wills and insolvent estates. For the great bulk of situations — ordinary persons, straightforward wills, and solvent estates with ordinary assets — it provides only the most grudging relaxation of its elaborate precautions and formalities.

What is needed is a reversal in attitude. Rather than make all persons and all probates go through the elaborate machinery in order to be sure that all persons are protected, allow the mass of them to be wound up in a simple manner, providing, to be sure, machinery adequate to detect or prevent wrongdoing and adequate avenues by which the adjudicatory process and strong arm of the court can be invoked.

The advantages of such an approach are to be found in the elimination of much of the detail of reports and other filings with the court and in the saving of time and effort of lawyers, parties, witnesses, judges, and other court personnel engaged in court hearings when there really is no argument or issue to be resolved. Out-of-pocket expenses would incidentally be substantially reduced, for much of the publication of notices incident to the old procedures would be unnecessary, lawyers' time would be reduced (a ten-minute hearing in probate can take most of a morning, with the usual full calendar), and parties to the proceeding would not need to take time from their work or to travel substantial distances for needless court appearances.

Prior to 1970, in only two states was it possible to make testamentary provision for an estate administration virtually free of court supervision and control. Under Texas' "independent administration" statute[38] and Washington's "non-intervention will" procedure,[39] the executor's only mandatory contact with the probate court is to prove the will's due execution and to file an inventory, appraisal and list of claims against the estate. Once this is done, the executor administers the estate independent of the courts, collecting, investing and selling estate assets, paying creditors and distributing the estate — all without the accountings, petitions for court approval, hearings and judicial confirmations that comprise the typical court-supervised administration. In these two states, nearly every testate estate is administered under these streamlined probate procedures.

The Uniform Probate Code authorizes a procedure for independent estate ad-

[38] Tex. Prob. Code Ann. §145 (1956); Marschall, Independent Administration of Decedents' Estates, 33 Texas L. Rev. 95 (1954).

[39] Wash. Rev. Code Ann. §11.68.010 (1967, Supp. 1971). Arizona also has a statute authorizing independent administration, but apparently little use is made of the procedure in administering decedents' estates. Ariz. Rev. Stat. §14-502 (1956).

Independent administration has been used in England since 1925. Fratcher, Fiduciary Administration in England, 40 N.Y.U.L. Rev. 12 (1965).

ministration. These provisions of the Uniform Code have been the basis for probate reform in Idaho, Maryland, and Oregon.[40]

HAVILAND, SHALL WE REBUILD OUR HOUSE OF PROBATE? THE UNIFORM PROBATE CODE
19 Kan. L. Rev. 575, 579-585 (1971)

The Uniform Probate Code establishes three sets of tools for the probate of an estate: the informal proceeding, the formal proceeding, and the supervised administration. Informal proceedings are conducted before the registrar, usually require no notice, and, if filed within two years, are conclusive at the end of three years from date of death unless they have been vacated or superseded by formal procedings. Formal proceedings are hearings before the court after notice. Each formal proceeding is a separate entity to adjudicate a given question, although several matters may be embraced by one proceeding. Formal proceedings become final judgments of the matters they concern if not appealed. Supervised administration is essentially the procedure now used in Kansas requiring court approval of all acts of the personal representative. No proceeding, formal or informal, may be initiated less than five days nor more than three years from the date of death. . . .

Unless requested, notice is seldom required under the provisions of the Uniform Code. Required notice may be given in either of two ways: by registered or certified mail 14 days in advance of the hearing, or by personal service five days in advance. If the address or identity of any interested person is unknown and cannot be ascertained with reasonable diligence, a publication notice similar to that of Kan. Stat. Ann. §59-2209 (1964) is provided. Any person interested in an estate may file a request for notice at any time after death of the testator. If he does so, no proceeding, either formal or informal, may be had without notice to him. He may also deliver a request for notice to any other person, and the person receiving it must give notice. This provision is one of the chief safeguards of the Uniform Code. Since no will may be probated and no personal representative may be appointed until at least five days have elapsed from the death of the decedent, it supplies a means by which interested persons may allay their apprehensions concerning informal proceedings. Finally, waiver of notice is liberally allowed by the Uniform Code, even by a guardian ad litem.

A. *Informal Probate*

The mechanics of informal probate are simple indeed. The application under oath contains approximately the allegations of a petition to admit a will or appoint an administrator. It is presented to the registrar, who must approve it if the essential elements are present. The registrar issues a written statement of informal probate,

[40] Idaho Code Ann. §§15-1-101 et seq. (1948, Supp. 1971); Md. Ann. Code art. 93, §§5-101 et seq. (1969); Ore Rev. Stat. cc. 111, 113, 114 (1970).

and the matter becomes conclusive until superseded by a formal order. A registrar may presume due execution of a will that appears to be duly executed, or he may accept a sworn statement or affidavit of any person, whether or not that person was a witness to the will. Wills containing an attestation clause are admitted without further proof.

If the registrar believes that an application should be disallowed on any grounds other than failure to satisfy the statutory requirements for the sworn application, he may decline it with the approval of the judge. In the case of a will, the judge's approval must be in writing. . . .

If an application for appointment of a personal representative indicates the existence of an unrevoked testamentary instrument that is not being offered for probate, the registrar must refer the matter to the judge for approval. Approval is proper if all [devisees] of the decedent are competent and join in the written request that the estate be administered intestate. Since the Code definition of devisee would not include a personal representative, this section would change the sometimes troublesome rule of In re Estate of Harper.[41] Devisees could agree not to probate a will regardless of the wishes of a named executor.

B. *Formal Testacy Proceedings*

Formal testacy proceedings under the Uniform Probate Code may be used to determine whether a decedent left any valid will, which of several instruments is his valid will, or whether he may have died intestate as to part of his estate and testate as to the balance. They may be used as an original proceeding to probate a will, to corroborate a previous informal probate, to block a pending application for informal probate or prevent the filing of informal proceedings, to contradict a previous informal probate, or to secure a declaratory judgment of intestacy. A request for an adjudication of intestacy must include a request that the court determine the heirs. It may, but need not necessarily, also request the appointment of a personal representative.

Notice, in formal testacy proceedings, must include publication notice in addition to normal notice to heirs and devisees on the theory that unknown beneficiaries under possible unknown wills should have some degree of notice. Objections to the petition must be in writing, but if the petition is unopposed, the judge may enter the order on the strength of the pleadings without conducting a hearing. The affidavit of one subscribing witness is sufficient evidence to prove execution of a will. . . .

Supervised administration may be granted by the court if directed in the decedent's will or if the court finds it necessary under all of the circumstances. Even though the testator provides in his will that his estate be supervised, the court may deny supervision if it finds that circumstances bearing on the need for supervision have changed since the execution of the will or that there is no necessity for supervision. If the will directs unsupervised administration, the court may order it only

[41] Page 92, supra. — Eds.

upon finding that alternative remedies are inadequate to secure full performance by the personal representative. These provisions seem to be in accord with the general philosophy pervading the Uniform Probate Code. Consistently, those who survive are allowed to alter the wishes of the poor old testator. Whether this be good or bad is all a matter of policy.

As has already been observed, supervised administration is quite similar to our present system of probate administration and therefore needs no further comment.

D. *Personal Representatives*

A personal representative under the Uniform Probate Code has the broadest possible powers and, except in the case of supervised administration, is subject to very little supervision from the court unless an interested party petitions for court intervention. He submits to the jurisdiction of the court by filing his acceptance; thereafter, any required notice may be served upon him in person or by ordinary mail.

No bond is required unless bond is specified in the will, although a party with a substantial interest may ask the court to require bond. If bond is required, the registrar fixes the amount of bond on the basis of an estimate of the value of the estate supplied by the personal representative, but no hint as to total value appears in the ordinary petition. An interested party may secure an order restraining the personal representative from doing particular acts that he fears may harm his interest and may petition for the removal of the personal representative for fraud, disregard of a court order, or mismanagement of the estate.

Until termination of his powers, the personal representative expressly has the same power over the title to property of the estate as an absolute owner would have, in trust, however, for the benefit of creditors and others interested in the estate. Bona fide purchasers from him or his distributees are protected fully. The thrust of all this is that the court and registrar are not responsible for seeing that personal representatives perform as they should. The burden of coercing performance is placed squarely upon those who might be injured by nonperformance.

A personal representative may not be surcharged for acts or distributions that were authorized at the time they were made. An informally probated will is authority to distribute according to its terms, and an order appointing a personal representative is authority to distribute to the heirs. However, it does not follow from the fact that a personal representative may have distributed under authority that the distributees may not be liable to restore the property or values received if the assumption concerning testacy later is changed.

Within three months after his appointment, a personal representative is required to prepare an inventory in reasonable detail and indicate the fair market value of each item as of date of death. In his discretion he may employ appraisers, but he is not required to do so. He may either send a copy of the completed inventory and appraisal to all persons interested in the estate except creditors, or he may file it with the court and furnish a copy to any interested person who requests it. If he chooses the former method he avoids making the value of the estate a matter of public record. In his fiduciary capacity to creditors, he would, of course, be obligated to furnish copies to creditors who might request them.

. . .

Self-dealing is still prohibited under the Uniform Probate Code. The personal representative may not sell or encumber property to himself, his spouse, his agent, his attorney, or any corporation in which he has a substantial beneficial interest. Any transaction affected by a substantial conflict of interest on the part of the personal representative is voidable. However, if a will or binding contract of the decedent expressly authorizes the transaction, or if the transaction is approved by the court after notice to all interested parties, it is a valid transaction.

The broadest possible enumerated powers are given to a personal representative. Among these are: the right to pay written charitable pledges of the decedent, whether contractual or not; the right to employ agents to perform any acts of administration; almost unlimited powers to conduct the business of the estate as he sees fit; the right to fix and pay his own compensation; and the right to employ and pay attorneys, auditors, and investment advisors, among others, even if they are associated with him in business. He is, of course, required to act reasonably for the benefit of the interested persons, and, upon application, any fees he may have paid to himself or his agents may be reviewed by the court and refunds ordered.

G. *Closing*

Under the Uniform Probate Code a personal representative may petition to close an estate any time after six months have elapsed from the date of his appointment. Others may petition to close any time after a year from the date of the appointment. The hearing may determine testacy, consider or compel an accounting, construe a will, determine heirs, and adjudicate final distribution. It may also order discharge of the personal representative. It is final as soon as the appeal period has run.

Estates may also be closed by the filing of a sworn statement of the personal representative at any time after six months from the date of his appointment. The statement must assert that he has published notice to creditors, administered the estate, paid all claims, and sent a statement and accounting to all known distributees. At the end of one year from its filing, the statement becomes final and bars further action by heirs or distributees.

WELLMAN, THE UNIFORM PROBATE CODE: BLUEPRINT FOR REFORM IN THE 70's
2 Conn. L. Rev. 453, 496-498 (1970)

Is the Code defensible in regard to notices? The approved version imposes a duty on every personal representative to mail notice to every interested person, including heirs apparently disinherited by the will which provided the basis for his appointment.[42] Further, each personal representative is under a statutory duty to publish notice for creditors once each week for three weeks following his appointment.[43] Failure to advertise makes the personal representative personally liable to creditors who may prefer to reach him than to pursue distributed estates. No other notices are required unless some interested person seeks an adjudication in formal proceedings. Then, only those given notice in accordance with the Code's scheme for notice are bound.[44] If an adjudication of a decedent's testacy is sought, the Code requires mailed or delivered notices to all known persons having interests and a published notice for the benefit of possible unknown successors.[45] As previously noted, if property is distributed to devisees under an informally probated will which is later contested successfully in proceedings started before the three year limitation period runs, the personal representative is exonerated, but the persons who received the estate remain personally liable to restore what they have received or its value. Purchasers from the personal representative, or from distributees following an unadjudicated distribution, are protected from liability to the heirs in the case supposed.[46] The same pattern of relationships [applies] to an estate which is distributed prior to discovery and probate of a will in a case where there was no prior adjudication of intestacy.

Lawyers in states which presently require some form of notice to interested persons before issuance of letters tend to recoil from the idea that the wide power over estate assets given by the Code to a personal representative may be obtained without some form of advance notice to interested persons. There are, however, several justifications for the Code's position on this point. The most important is that the proposed system, featuring issuance of letters without notice and non-supervised administration, has been proved satisfactory by generations of use in Pennsylvania. Many other states also permit letters of administration to be obtained without advance notice,[47] and it is widely recognized that one with letters has full practical control of the decedent's liquid assets notwithstanding the degree of "supervision" exerted by the court following appointment. Thus, accumulated experience affirms that survivors do not avail themselves of the possible opportunity afforded by ability to get letters quickly and without notice to take advantage of fellow heirs.

---

[42] §3-705.
[43] §3-801.
[44] §3-106.
[45] §3-403.
[46] §§3-174, 3-190.
[47] In a recent ABA survey, respondents from eleven of twenty-three states contacted indicated that no notice, other than possibly by publication, is required in regard to an application for appointment of an administrator. The states so indicated as supporting the proposition that letters are available without notice are: Colorado, Florida, Illinois, Iowa, Maryland, Minnesota, North Carolina, Ohio, Pennsylvania, Texas and Vermont. See Estate Administration: Current Practices and Proposed Uniform Probate Code, 3 Real Property, Probate & Trust J. 2 (1968).

For a critique of the Uniform Probate Code see Zartman, An Illinois Critique of the Uniform Probate Code, 1970 U. Ill. L. Forum 413, and a reply by the chief draftsman, Wellman, A Reaction to the Chicago Commentary, id. at 536.

On the problems raised by the no-notice probate provisions of the Uniform Probate Code, see Mapp, The 1969 Oregon Probate Code and Due Process, 49 Ore. L. Rev. 345 (1970); Parker, No-Notice Probate and Non-Intervention Administration Under the Code, 2 Conn. L. Rev. 546 (1970).

Where the decedent owned property located in a state other than his domicile, ancillary probate in the second state may be necessary. On ancillary probate see Currie, The Multiple Personality of the Dead: Executors, Administrators, and the Conflict of Laws, 33 U. Chi. L. Rev. 429 (1966); Vestal, Multiple-State Estates Under the Uniform Probate Code, 27 Wash. & Lee L. Rev. 70 (1970).

SECTION C. Guardianship Administration of Minors' Property[48]

The laws governing guardianship of minors contemplate two kinds of guardians: A guardian of the person, charged with the custody and care of the minor and responsible for his maintenance and education; and a guardian of the estate, charged with the possession and management of the child's property. While the same person ordinarily serves in both capacities, it is possible to name one individual as guardian of the minor's person and another individual (or corporate fiduciary) as guardian of his estate. Also, circumstances may require the appointment of a guardian of a minor's estate but not of his person. So long as one parent of the child is living and competent, that parent is the natural guardian of the child's person, and is responsible for his custody and care. But if a child receives property requiring active management while one or both of his parents are alive, a guardian of his estate must be appointed to manage the assets. This could occur if the child received a gift or legacy from a grandparent, or if one parent died intestate and a portion of his estate passed to the child by inheritance.

One of the principal reasons a person with minor children should have a will is to take advantage of the opportunity to designate a guardian of the person for his children in the event he and his wife both die before the children attain majority. If he fails to make this selection, it will be made by the probate court from a list of available relatives. The statutes list the persons entitled to serve as guardian, usually in the following order of preference: (1) parents; (2) grandparents; (3) uncles and aunts; (4) other next of kin; (5) other persons. The list of priorities suggests the problems of selection faced by a court. Grandparents are rarely a satisfactory choice. First, they may not want to "raise another family." Second, because of their age and possibly also health problems, they may not live long enough to see the children attain majority. Third, because of their age, grandparents may not offer a lively,

[48] See generally Mackay, Guardianship Law (1948); Symposium: Guardianship, 45 Iowa L. Rev. 209-413 (1960).

stimulating, and flexible environment for young children. Finally, the statute does not say which grandparents, maternal or paternal, are to be selected. This may produce hand-to-hand combat in the courtroom, if both sides of the family want custody of the orphaned children. The problem is aggravated even further if the father and mother were of different religious faiths. One set of grandparents may, for example, have a strong moral conviction that the children must (or must not) be raised as Catholics.

Moving to the siblings of the deceased parents (the class from which most guardians are selected), once again the statute does not indicate which of the uncles or aunts, on which side of the family, shall be given preference.[49] If the parents die without having designated a guardian, the two families may agree among themselves which relative shall have custody of the children. Most parents, however, when presented with the problem, are not likely to want to leave this important decision to others. Deciding who should be the guardian of one's children is no easy task, but it is a decision best made by the parents.

If both parents die before the children attain majority, a guardian of the person, charged with the responsibility of raising the children, must be appointed. However, guardians of the children's estates will have to be appointed only if no other provision has been made for management of the children's property. This brings us to another reason why it is important for the person with minor children to write a will: To avoid the necessity of a court-supervised guardianship administration if his estate should pass to his minor children.

In all but three states (Idaho, Maryland, and Oregon have adopted most of the guardianship provisions of the Uniform Probate Code) the procedures governing guardianship administrations of minors' estates[50] are so restrictive, complicated, inefficient, and expensive that prudent and efficient management of the children's property is virtually impossible. "There are two basic problems with guardianship administrations. . . . First, the strict court supervision over virtually every action of the guardian is so burdensome and time-consuming that it hinders effective management of the estate, and the resulting court costs and attorney's fees constitute a substantial and often unnecessary expense of administration. Secondly, the investment power of the guardian is so restricted that it is impossible for the guardian to obtain a fair return on the money invested, or to protect the estate against inflation." [51] Our guardianship laws developed in the context of an agrarian society, where land was the principal source of wealth, and where the concern was for the protection and preservation of the minor's inheritance until he attained legal age. In modern times the primary concern should be that property devised to children by

[49] The problem of selection is aggravated by the fact that, in some jurisdictions, it is not possible to name a nonresident as guardian. See Cabiness, The Nonresident Testamentary Guardian, 43 Texas L. Rev. 541 (1965).

[50] With a few minor exceptions, the laws governing guardianships of incompetents' estates are the same as those governing children's estates. The estates of incompetents raise totally different estate planning considerations, however. See Zillgett, Planning for Incompetency, 37 S. Cal. L. Rev. 181 (1964); Comment, Effect of Guardianship on Estate Plans, 65 Mich. L. Rev. 1613 (1967).

[51] Davis, Problems of Guardianship Administration in Texas, 47 Texas L. Rev. 1124 (1969).

their parents is invested and managed in a manner that assures their suitable support and education during minority. Unfortunately — and incredibly — this objective is difficult to accomplish under existing guardianship laws.

Typically, the person appointed as guardian must give bond,[52] with the annual bond premium paid out of the income from the guardianship property. If there are two or more children, there must be a separate guardianship for each child. While the same person may be (and invariably is) appointed as guardian for all the children, he must keep separate books, file separate accountings and give separate bond for each guardianship. At the time of his appointment he is granted letters of guardianship, which serve the same function as letters of administration in a decedent's estate proceeding. As with the personal representative of a decedent's estate, he takes possession of the ward's property, files an inventory with the court, and makes periodic accountings (usually annually) thereafter.

A formal procedure is prescribed for handling creditors' claims. In many states the guardian cannot pay the claims of creditors arising during the guardianship without prior court approval. The guardian's investment powers are limited. Permissible investments are usually enumerated in a statute, and in a number of states they are restricted to first mortgages on land, bank savings accounts, and local, state, and federal bonds. The attitude towards corporate stock as an investment varies. In some jurisdictions stock is a permissible investment (usually up to a stated percentage of the ward's estate), but prior court approval of a specific investment action may be required. In other states the guardian may retain securities that were a part of the original estate, but he may not acquire others. In several states he must sell all corporate stocks that were a part of the original estate as soon as possible; stocks are forbidden investments. Professor Fratcher has written: "Frequent references in the statutes to the medieval concept of waste indicate that [the guardian's] primary duty has been deemed to be the preservation of the status quo. All property transactions except short leases have been treated as exceptional and made difficult or impossible. The traditional powers are not even sufficient to permit efficient management of an estate consisting of a small family farm. For the management of an estate consisting of a large portfolio of securities or an active business they are woefully inadequate. . . . If a guardian is really to manage his ward's property as a prudent man would manage his own, he must have every power which an owner has with respect to his own property. . . . The guardian's duty to be careful, prudent and loyal to his ward's interests, enforced by his personal liability and that of his surety are far more adequate protection to the ward than arbitrary restrictions which make prudent management impossible." [53]

In nearly every state prior court authorization is required for sales of personal property as well as for realty, with the sale conducted under the same strict proce-

[52] Unless the guardian was nominated in the parent's will and the requirement of a bond was waived. The cost of the bond is the same as that required of the personal representative of a decedent's estate. See footnote 5 supra.

[53] Fratcher, Powers and Duties of Guardians of Property, 45 Iowa L. Rev. 264, 335 (1960). Special rules govern the guardianship administration of funds received from the Veterans Administration and other federal agencies. Id. at 264.

dure as is required for the sale of realty in the administration of decedents' estates.[54] A sale is ordinarily authorized only for certain enumerated purposes, as for payment of the ward's debts, or for his maintenance when income is insufficient for this purpose. In making expenditures for the ward's care and maintenance, the guardian is typically limited to the net income from the ward's property, in the absence of a court order authorizing the sale or distribution of principal for this purpose. And "net income" is really net, for it means the income from those low-yield, fixed-dollar investments in savings accounts and government obligations, *less* the guardian's compensation, the annual fiduciary bond premium, and the attorney's fees, filing fees and court costs that are an inevitable, and substantial, component of the guardianship administration. In one study of fifty-three guardianship files,[55] seven showed accumulated expenses that equalled 5 to 9 percent of the original value of the ward's estate, nine cases showed costs of 10 to 14 percent, thirteen showed costs of 15 to 19 percent, eleven showed costs of 20 to 49 percent, and three showed accumulated expenses that were more than 50 percent of the value of the original estate.

In recent years increased attention has been given to the clear need for legislative reform of our guardianship laws,[56] but in the main the only reforms adopted have been of the patchwork variety. Until the situation changes, the only effective way to handle guardianship administrations is to avoid them.[57] For modest estates, when the parent intends to devise his entire estate to his wife if she survives him, the will could include a "contingent trust" — that is, a trust that is to become operative only if the testator's wife predeceases him and his estate passes to minor children.[58] The individual named in the will as guardian of the persons of the children might also be named the trustee, or the trustee could be some other person or a corporation. For example, an aunt of the children might be named guardian of the persons, while an uncle manages the property as trustee. Provision would also have

[54] See page 82, supra.

[55] Weissman, Guardianship, A Way of Fulfilling Public Responsibility for Children 131 (1949).

[56] See Simes, Model Probate Code 183 (1946); Uniform Probate Code art. 5 (1969).

The Uniform Probate Code gives the guardian broad management and investment powers that are exercisable without the need for application to, approval of, or ratification by a court. Among the powers: to lease, sell, mortgage or exchange assets, to borrow money, to pay creditors' claims, to disburse principal or income for the care, welfare and support of the ward. Investment powers and bonding and accounting requirements are also liberalized. Various other provisions of the Code are designed to minimize or avoid the necessity of guardianship. A "facility of payment" clause (§5-103) permits a person to pay up to $5000 per year directly to a minor if he is over eighteen or married, or to a minor's parent or grandparent or other adult with whom the minor resides, or by deposit in a bank account in the minor's name — thus avoiding the need for a guardianship in many cases.

As of 1971 three states have adopted most of the Code's guardianship provisions. Idaho Code Ann. §§15-5-101 et seq. (1948, Supp. 1971); Md. Ann. Code art. 93A (1969); Ore. Rev. Stat. c. 126 (1970).

[57] Several states provide by statute that a testamentary guardian's powers may be enlarged by specific will provision. E.g., Cal. Prob. Code §1484 (1956); N.D. Cent. Code §30-14-01 (1960); Pa. Stat. Ann. tit. 20, §320.1045 (Purdon 1950); Wyo. Stat. Ann. §3-12 (1957). Instead of redrafting the guardian's charter of administration, however, the more effective way to proceed is to designate a trustee for the children's estates. Even if the trustee's powers are not enumerated in the will, his statutory powers will be more substantial than those applicable to guardians.

[58] See page 423, infra; see also Appendix C, infra.

to be made for inclusion of non-probate assets (most notably, life insurance proceeds) in the trust. Under this arrangement the children's interests would be administered under the "prudent man" standards generally applicable to trustees, rather than the restrictive rules applicable to guardians. For more substantial estates, where planning and tax considerations point toward the use of a testamentary trust even if the testator's wife survives him, the trust provisions would insure that interests passing to minor children would be held in trust, rather than passing outright to the children and requiring guardianship administration. We will be taking a closer look at these planning arrangements at later points in the course.

4. Intestacy: An Estate Plan by Operation of Law

> Since our assets are not very great, it may be that we do not need wills at all. Can we let our property pass by inheritance or by joint and survivor arrangements?
>
> — ADAM SMITH

If Adam Smith were to die without a will, survived by the present members of his family and owning the assets he now owns, what distribution of his assets would be made under your state's inheritance laws? If the distribution given by the intestacy statutes is similar to the dispositive plan that Adam Smith has in mind, wouldn't this eliminate the need for his executing a will?

In order to answer these questions, we must take a look at the intestacy statutes, and at the patterns of distribution that they provide.

SECTION A. The Pattern of Intestate Distributions

When a person dies intestate the disposition of his property is governed by the statute of descent and distribution of one or more states. Generally speaking, the law of the state where the decedent was domiciled at death governs the disposition of his personal property, and the law of the state where the decedent's real property is located governs the disposition of such real property. Although it is a safe bet that the law of intestacy is not exactly the same in all details in any two states, most of the intestacy statutes are based upon the English Statute of Distribution (22 & 23 Charles II, c. 10), passed in 1670.

It is essential that you become familiar with the intestacy statutes of the state in which you intend to practice. It is quite impossible to answer any specific question as to who succeeds to property without looking at the statutes of a particular state. To discuss problems of intestacy in a meaningful way requires us to pick a state. Ohio is here chosen, as its statutory scheme is similar to the one found in a large number of states. It should be profitable for you to compare the Ohio provisions with those of your own state, as well as with the model provisions of the Uniform Probate Code,[1] portions of which are set out in the text and footnotes that follow.

OHIO REV. CODE ANN. (PAGE 1968)

§2105.06: When a person dies intestate having title or right to any personal property or to any real estate or inheritance in this state, such personal property shall be distributed and such real estate or inheritance shall descend and pass in parcenary, except as otherwise provided by law, in the following course:

(A) If there is no surviving spouse, to the children of such intestate or their lineal descendants, per stirpes;

(B) If there is a spouse and one child or its lineal descendants surviving, one half to the spouse and one half to such child or its lineal descendants, per stirpes;

(C) If there is a spouse and more than one child or their lineal descendants surviving, one third to the spouse and the remainder to the children equally, or to the lineal descendants of any deceased child, per stirpes;

(D) If there are no children or their lineal descendants, three fourths to the surviving spouse and one fourth to the parents of the intestate equally, or to the surviving parent; if there are no parents, then the whole to the surviving spouse;

(E) If there is no spouse and no children or their lineal descendants, to the parents of such intestate equally, or to the surviving parent;

(F) If there is no spouse, no children or their lineal descendants, and no parent surviving, to the brothers and sisters, whether of the whole or of the half blood of the intestate, or their lineal descendants, per stirpes;

(G) If there are no brothers or sisters or their lineal descendants, one half to the paternal grandparents of the intestate equally, or to the survivor of them, and one half to the maternal grandparents of the intestate equally, or to the survivor of them;

(H) If there is no paternal grandparents [*sic*] or no maternal grandparent, one half to the lineal descendants of such deceased grandparents, per stirpes; if there are no such lineal descendants, then to the surviving grandparents or their lineal descendants, per stirpes; if there are no surviving grandparents or their lineal descendants, then to the next of kin of the intestate, provided there shall be no representation among such next of kin;

[1] Nat'l Conference of Commissioners on Uniform State Laws, Uniform Probate Code (1969).

(I) If there are no next of kin, to stepchildren or their lineal descendants, per stirpes;

(J) If there are no stepchildren or their lineal descendants, escheat to the state.

§2105.11: When a person dies intestate leaving children and none of the children of such intestate have died leaving children or their lineal descendants, such estate shall descend to the children of such intestate, living at the time of his death, in equal proportions.

§2105.12: When all the descendants of an intestate, in a direct line of descent, are on an equal degree of consanguinity to the intestate, the estate shall pass to such persons in equal parts, however remote from the intestate such equal and common degree of consanguinity may be.

§2105.13: If some of the children of an intestate are living and others are dead, the estate shall descend to the children who are living and to the lineal descendants of such children as are dead, so that each child who is living will inherit the share to which he would have been entitled if all the children of the intestate were living, and the lineal descendants of the deceased child will inherit equal parts of that portion of the estate to which such deceased child would be entitled if he were living.

This section shall apply in all cases in which the descendants[2] of the intestate, not more remote than lineal descendants of grandparents, entitled to share in the estate, are of unequal degree of consanguinity to the intestate, so that those who are of the nearest degree of consanguinity will take the share to which they would have been entitled, had all the descendants in the same degree of consanguinity with them who died leaving issue, been living.

Surviving Spouse

The Ohio distributive scheme, of giving the spouse a one-half share if there is one child and a one-third share if there are two or more children, is the single most common statutory pattern. "Approximately a third of the jurisdictions fix the fraction (with minor variations) at a one-half share where the intestate leaves no more than one stirpes of descendants. . . . Approximately one-fourth of the jurisdictions fix the fraction at either one-third or one-half of the total assets without reference to the number of descendant stirpes. . . . A small group of states fix the share at either one-fourth of the assets or a child's share." [3]

If there are no children or other descendants, most states provide, as does

[2] The word "descendants" in this statute has been construed to include all those to whom an estate descends, including collateral heirs as well as lineal descendants. Oakley v. Davey, 49 Ohio App. 113, 195 N.E. 406 (1934). This construction is quite unusual; the term ordinarily is given its dictionary meaning of lineal relations in a later generation. 3 Powell, Real Property ¶360 (1970). — Eds.

[3] 6 Powell, Real Property ¶995 n. 9 (1970).

Ohio, that the spouse shares with the intestate's parents, if any; if no parents, the spouse takes all to the exclusion of collateral kin.

Are these the kinds of distributions a typical husband or wife with moderate wealth would make if he or she were to execute a will? All of the available evidence indicates that the answer to this question is no. "In ordinary circumstances, a man and wife with a modest estate will each make a will leaving everything outright to the other. Available information indicates that most testators prefer that their spouses receive all their property to the exclusion of others, including their own children. The clearest demonstration of this is found in the study made by Allison Dunham of 170 files in the probate court of Cook County, Illinois. In every one of the twenty-two testate estates where the deceased was survived by spouse and children, the surviving spouse received all the property." [4] Yet despite the strong evidence that the spouse is the preferred taker, in only a few states does the surviving spouse succeed entirely to a moderate estate.[5]

Children and Other Descendants

"The present law of intestate succession, as it affects descendants of an intestate, has changed greatly from the Canons of Descent, and considerably from the American colonial modifications thereof. Primogeniture early came under heavy attack. The English and continental reason for retaining it — the avoidance of the too rapid subdivision of agricultural lands — had little weight in a frontier country with literally millions of acres available for expansion. The double portion for the oldest son lasted in New Jersey until 1817, and in Vermont until 1821. Thus, the historic preference for males over females, and for the eldest over the others, succumbed to the rule of equality among children, which is now universally accepted." [6]

What happens when the intestate is survived by descendants of deceased children? The Ohio pattern, of providing a per stirpes distribution unless all of the

[4] Gibson, Inheritance of Community Property in Texas — A Need for Reform, 47 Texas L. Rev. 359, 364 (1969). This article analyzes a number of studies involving pension plan beneficiary designations and life insurance policies as well as wills, all of which show that the surviving spouse is the preferred taker in the overwhelming majority of cases. See also page 163, infra.

[5] The Uniform Probate Code (§2-102) provides:

"The intestate share of the surviving spouse is:

"(1) if there is no surviving issue or parent of the decedent, the entire intestate estate;

"(2) if there is no surviving issue but the decedent is survived by a parent or parents, the first $50,000, plus one-half of the balance of the intestate estate;

"(3) if there are surviving issue all of whom are issue of the surviving spouse also, the first $50,000, plus one-half of the balance of the intestate estate;

"(4) if there are surviving issue one or more of whom are not issue of the surviving spouse, one-half of the intestate estate."

The UPC's alternate provision for community property states (§2-102A) would give the same distribution for separate property but provides (as does Cal. Prob. Code §201) that all community property would pass to the surviving spouse whether or not the intestate was survived by descendants or parents.

[6] 6 Powell, Real Property ¶996 (1970).

intestate's children have predeceased, is a common one. The meaning of per stirpes is explored in the problems on page 137.

Parents, Collaterals

"In describing existing statutes with respect to the circumstances under which ascendants can become intestate distributees, it must be observed that (1) They do not ever take when the decedent is survived by descendants; (2) Where there are no descendants, the growing favor of the law for a surviving spouse excludes the ascendants in some jurisdictions completely, and in most jurisdictions to the extent of a half or more of the assets; . . . (4) The majority of American states direct that where the decedent left no descendants, the intestate assets (after satisfying the surviving spouse's claims) shall go to the parents in equal shares, or to the survivors of such parents; . . .

"The trends to minimize the claims of both parents and collaterals when they conflict with those of a surviving spouse and to grant priorities to parents over collaterals accord with modern circumstances. Descendants and the surviving spouse constitute the primary group needing, and deserving, maintenance and whatever more than maintenance becomes available. But increased longevity increases the number of persons likely to die with living parents, and these surviving parents are themselves likely to be, as of the decedent's death, of more advanced years and of less physical strength than in earlier decades. In contrast with brothers and sisters, often widely scattered and living separate and unrelated lives, parents are likely to be, in general, closer to the decedent and socially more deserving of subsidy than the siblings." [7]

If the intestate is not survived by a spouse, descendants or parents, his property passes to brothers, sisters, their descendants, or other collateral relatives. Section 2-103 of the Uniform Probate Code would eliminate inheritance by more remote relatives than grandparents and the issue of grandparents. The statutes of Maryland, New York, Oregon, Pennsylvania, and Wyoming contain similar restrictions,[8] but in the remaining states there is no limit placed on the remoteness of collateral relatives able to benefit by intestacy. (See, for example, Ohio Rev. Code Ann. §2105.06(H)).

If an estate is inherited by kin more remote than brothers or sisters or their descendants, how are the heirs determined? Most states follow the "civil law" method in determining degrees of relationship.[9] Under this method, to ascertain

[7] Id. ¶997.

[8] Md. Ann. Code art. 93, §3-104 (1969); N.Y. Estates, Powers & Trusts Law §4-1.1(8) (1967); Ore. Rev. Stat. §112.045 (1969); Pa. Stat. Ann. tit. 20, §1.3 (1950, Supp. 1971); Wyo. Stat. Ann. §2-37 (1959).

[9] Another method is the canon law method, which was developed originally to determine within what degrees intermarriage of relatives was prohibited. Blackstone misread history and erroneously assumed that the canon law method (renamed the common law method) was used by common law courts to govern descent of real property. 2 Blackstone, Commentaries *204. Under the canon law method you count (a) the degrees (steps) from the common ancestor down to the decedent, and then you make a separate count of (b) the degrees from the common

the relationship of A to B you count the steps (counting one for each generation) up from A to the nearest common ancestor of A and B, and then you count the steps down to B. The total number of steps is the degree of relationship.[10] See the Table of Consanguinity, page 136.

If the intestate leaves no kin, in all jurisdictions his property escheats to the state. Escheats of substantial estates are rare. Human nature being what it is, the general rule is that the larger the estate, the larger the number of "heirs" who step up to claim it.

PROBLEMS

1. Assume that Adam Smith dies intestate. After payment of debts, taxes, and expenses of administration, the assets of his estate include:

	Property Acquired from H's Earnings During Marriage[11]	*H's Property Acquired by Gift*[11]
Tangible personalty:	$ 8,000	
Real estate:		
Residence (title is in "Adam Smith and Jane Smith, husband and wife"); subject to mtge. of $19,000	32,000	
Lot, Lake Murray (title is in Adam Smith alone)	5,000	
Bank accounts:		
Checking (joint tenancy with wife)	1,000	
Savings (joint tenancy with wife)	4,000	
Securities:		
Varoom Mutual Fund (registered in Adam Smith's name alone)		$2,000
General Corp. common (registered in Adam Smith's name alone)		560
American Growth Fund (held in joint tenancy with wife)	2,185	
Life insurance:		
(wife is named primary beneficiary; "the insured's children in equal shares" are named secondary beneficiaries if Smith's wife does not survive him)	47,000	
	$99,185	$2,560

ancestor down to the surviving relative. Whichever of these two separate counts produces the greater number of degrees is taken to be the degree of kinship. This method is given limited application in a few states. Atkinson, Wills 45 (2d ed. 1953).

10 A common variant of the civil law method is a provision that if there are two or more collateral kindred in equal degree claiming through different ancestors, those claiming through the nearest ancestor shall be preferred to those claiming through an ancestor more remote. See e.g. Mass. Ann. Laws c. 190, §3(6) (1969).

11 The source of the property is irrelevant in common law property states; how title is held at death is controlling. In community property states, property acquired from H's earnings during marriage is community property, and at H's death passes under a different intestate scheme than separate property.

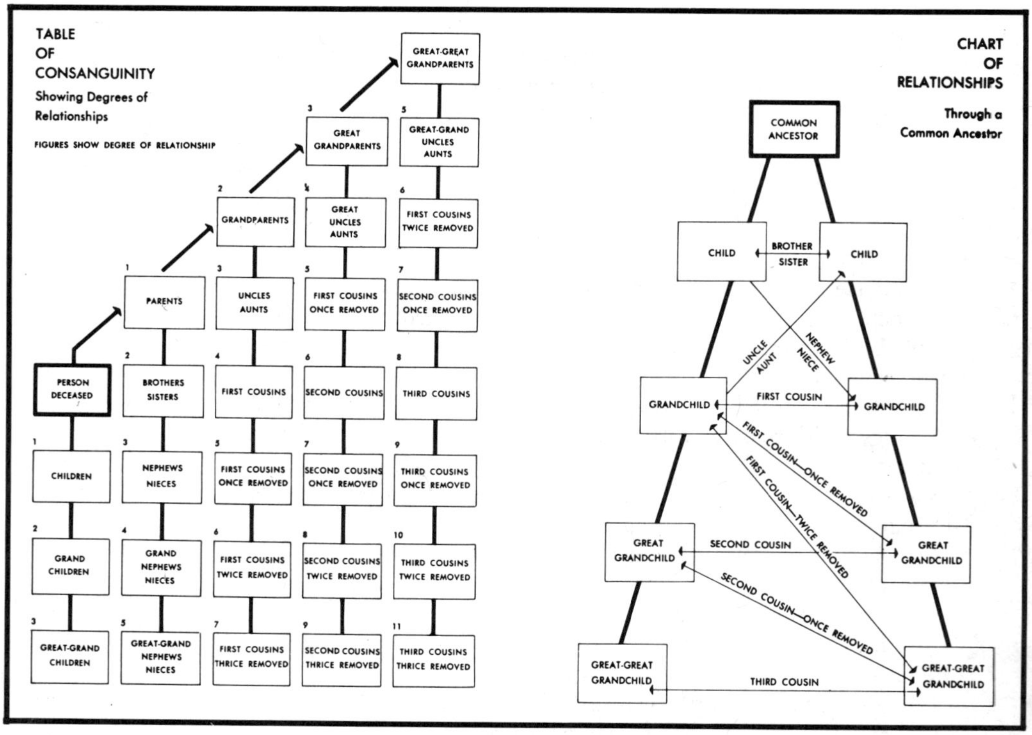
TABLE OF CONSANGUINITY
Showing Degrees of Relationships
FIGURES SHOW DEGREE OF RELATIONSHIP
PERSON DECEASED
PARENTS
GRANDPARENTS
GREAT GRANDPARENTS
GREAT-GREAT GRANDPARENTS
CHILDREN
GRAND CHILDREN
GREAT-GRAND CHILDREN
BROTHERS SISTERS
NEPHEWS NIECES
GRAND NEPHEWS NIECES
GREAT-GRAND NEPHEWS NIECES
UNCLES AUNTS
FIRST COUSINS
FIRST COUSINS ONCE REMOVED
FIRST COUSINS TWICE REMOVED
FIRST COUSINS THRICE REMOVED
GREAT UNCLES AUNTS
FIRST COUSINS ONCE REMOVED
SECOND COUSINS
SECOND COUSINS ONCE REMOVED
SECOND COUSINS TWICE REMOVED
SECOND COUSINS THRICE REMOVED
GREAT-GRAND UNCLES AUNTS
FIRST COUSINS TWICE REMOVED
SECOND COUSINS ONCE REMOVED
THIRD COUSINS
THIRD COUSINS ONCE REMOVED
THIRD COUSINS TWICE REMOVED
THIRD COUSINS THRICE REMOVED
CHART OF RELATIONSHIPS
Through a Common Ancestor
COMMON ANCESTOR
CHILD
BROTHER SISTER
CHILD
UNCLE AUNT
NEPHEW NIECE
GRANDCHILD
FIRST COUSIN
GRANDCHILD
FIRST COUSIN—ONCE REMOVED
FIRST COUSIN—TWICE REMOVED
GREAT GRANDCHILD
SECOND COUSIN
GREAT GRANDCHILD
SECOND COUSIN—ONCE REMOVED
GREAT-GREAT GRANDCHILD
THIRD COUSIN
GREAT-GREAT GRANDCHILD

Smith is survived by his wife and their three minor children. How is Smith's estate distributed under the Ohio statute? Under the intestacy statute of your state?

2. Based on the distribution that would result if Adam Smith were to die intestate, and in view of Smith's planning objectives, would you recommend that he should have a will?

In Problems 3, 4, 5, 6 and 7 immediately following, assume that Smith's wife predeceased him, leaving a will that bequeathed all of her property to Smith. Assume further that the items enumerated in Problem 1 are in his estate.

3. Two of Smith's three children predeceased him. One child, C-1, died before Smith, survived by a wife and one child, D. One child, C-2, died before Smith, survived by a wife and two children, E and F. Thus Smith is survived by one child (C-3), two daughters-in-law, and three grandchildren (D, E and F). How is Smith's estate distributed under the Ohio statute? Under the intestacy statute of your state? [12]

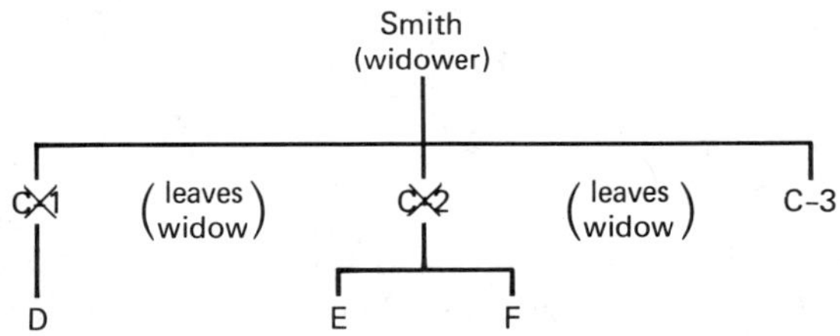

4. Same as Problem 3 except that all three of Smith's children predecease him. C-1 and C-2 were survived by their wives and children as given in Problem 3. C-3 was survived by his wife but not by any children. How is Smith's estate distributed under the Ohio statute? Under the intestacy statute of your state?

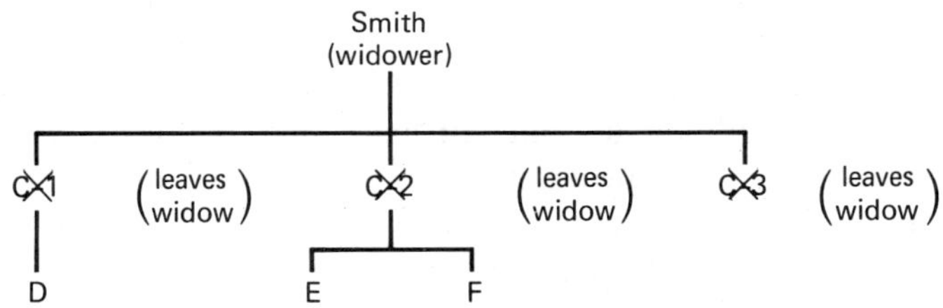

5. All three of Smith's children predeceased him. One child, C-1, died before Smith, survived by one child, D. One child, C-2, died before Smith, survived by two

[12] The North Carolina statute, which has been described as "a somewhat radical departure from the old law and . . . perhaps the most novel feature of the new Intestate Succession Act" (McCall, North Carolina's New Intestate Succession Act, 39 N.C.L. Rev. 1, 12 (1960)), provides for a per capita distribution to all persons in the same degree of relationship to the decedent. Thus in Problem 3, C-3 would take his one-third share; the two-thirds that would have passed to C-1 and C-2 had they been living would be divided *equally* among all the children of C-1 and C-2: Each of these grandchildren would take a two-ninths share. N.C. Gen. Stat. §29-16 (1966).

children, E and F. One child, C-3, died before Smith, survived by three children, G, H and J. However, J died before Smith, survived by two children, K and L. Thus Smith is survived by five grandchildren (D, E, F, G and H) and two great-grandchildren (K and L). How is Smith's estate distributed under the Ohio statute? Under the intestacy statute of your state? Under the North Carolina statute (see footnote 12 supra)? For different views as to the meaning of per stirpes, compare Balch v. Stone, 149 Mass. 39, 20 N.E. 322 (1889) (majority view) with Lombardi v. Blois, 230 Cal. App. 2d 191, 40 Cal. Rptr. 899 (1964) (minority view). See generally Page, Descent Per Stirpes and Per Capita, 1946 Wis. L. Rev. 3.

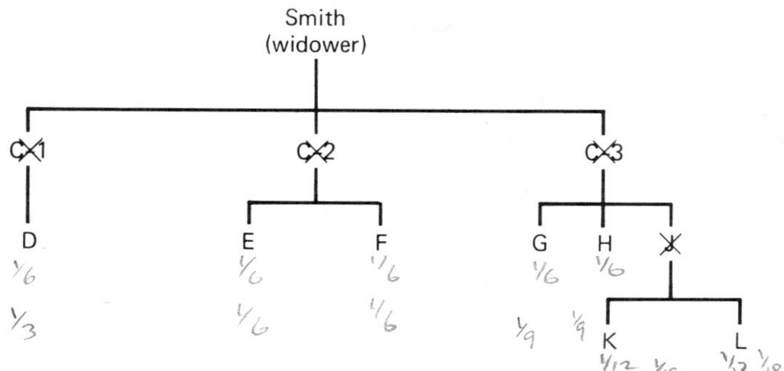

6. Smith never had any children. He is survived by his mother, his sister, and two nephews (children of a deceased brother). How is Smith's estate distributed under the Ohio statute? Under the intestacy statute of your state?

7. Smith never had any children. His parents predeceased him. He is not survived by any brother or sister or descendant of brother or sister. He is survived by an uncle of his mother (Q), the first cousin of his father (R), and the grand-nephew of his father (S). How is Smith's estate distributed under the Ohio statute? In re Estate of Kelly, 165 Ohio St. 259, 135 N.E.2d 378 (1956). Under the intestacy statute of your state? Under Mass. Ann. Laws c. 190, §3(6) (1969), referred to in footnote 10 supra?

8. Those interested in genealogy puzzles might like to try the one posed by the Rev. Charles L. Dodgson, an eminent mathematician better known as Lewis Carroll. The problem: The Governor of Kgovjni wants to give the very smallest dinner party possible, and at the same time invite his father's brother-in-law, his brother's father-in-law, his father-in-law's brother, and his brother-in-law's father. To do this, how many guests is it absolutely necessary to invite? The answer: One. If you cannot figure how this is done, using a genealogical tree of only fourteen people, see Carroll, The Complete Works of Lewis Carroll 1031 (Mod. Lib. ed.).

SECTION B. Subsidiary Rules Governing Intestacy

The scheme for distribution of an intestate's property outlined above is subject to a number of subsidiary rules.

1. *Simultaneous Death*

No person succeeds to property at the death of another unless he survives the decedent for an instant of time. With the airplane and automobile came an increase in accidents in which a person and his intestate successors or devisees die simultaneously or under circumstances which make it difficult or impossible to ascertain the order of death. To take care of this problem all but four states have enacted the Uniform Simultaneous Death Act or its equivalent. This Act provides that "where the title to property or the devolution thereof depends upon priority of death and there is no sufficient evidence that the persons have died otherwise than simultaneously, the property of each person shall be disposed of as if he had survived." The Act goes on to provide that if two joint tenants die simultaneously, one-half of the property is distributed as if one tenant survived and one-half as if the other tenant survived. With respect to life insurance, when the insured and the beneficiary die simultaneously the proceeds are distributed as if the insured survived the beneficiary. The decedent may, of course, provide for a different distribution in his will.

The purpose of the Simultaneous Death Act is to make sure that if A the property owner and B the beneficiary (whether by will, intestate succession, life insurance contract, etc.) die in the same accident, A's property will pass down *his* family line, rather than to B's distributees via B's will or by intestacy. The Act also operates to prevent double taxation and double estate administration of the same assets in quick succession.

PROBLEMS

1. By her will Anna Rowley bequeathed $15,000 to Eulah Cooper. Eulah was driving a Cadillac in which Anna was riding on the right side of the front seat. Eulah, driving north at 75 mph on a rain-slick highway, lost control of the car, which skidded broadside into the southbound lane. The Cadillac was struck by a Falcon going south. The Falcon hit the right side of the Cadillac and was a third of the way inside the Cadillac when the car came to rest. Both Eulah and Anna were crushed to death. Neither showed any sign of life when witnesses arrived. The coroner testified that Anna died 1/150,000th of a second before Eulah, computed as follows: "I took the highway patrolman's report of the speed of the Cadillac and the speed of the Falcon coming together, and made a rough guess at how much longer time it took the Falcon to push Mrs. Rowley over and kill Mrs. Cooper. That would be a rough mathematical guess." A medical witness testified that he too concluded that Anna must have died first because the Falcon hit the passenger side of the car first. Upon this evidence the trial court found that Anna's death preceded Eulah's "by an interval of time," and that Eulah was entitled to the $15,000 bequest. The jurisdiction has enacted the Uniform Simultaneous Death Act. Upon

appeal, what result? Estate of Rowley, 257 Cal. App. 2d 324, 65 Cal. Rptr. 139 (1967). How would you draft a will to avoid this problem? [13]

2. H and W die in an automobile-train collision. The first witnesses testify that they detected no signs of life in the husband. They further testify that the wife was decapitated, her head lying about ten feet from her body, which was gushing blood from the neck in spurts. Did W survive H? Gray v. Sawyer, 247 S.W.2d 496 (Ky. 1952).

3. Mark's sole heir apparent is his son Luke. On February 1 Mark suffers a brain concussion in an accident. The doctors say he cannot live long. On February 5 Mark is hooked up to a heart-lung machine which keeps his heart going. On February 7 he has a flat electroencephalogram (no brain activity). On February 8 Luke dies intestate, survived by his wife Rachel. On February 9 the physicians shut off the heart-lung machine attached to Mark's body, and there is no spontaneous breathing or circulation. Is Rachel entitled to any share of Mark's estate? Suppose an autopsy shows Mark's brain in an advanced stage of decomposition? See Smith v. Smith, 229 Ark. 579, 317 S.W.2d 275 (1958); A Definition of Irreversible Coma, 205 J.A.M.A. 337 (1968); Kusanovich, Medical Malpractice Liability and the Organ Transplant, 5 U. San Francisco L. Rev. 223, 238-256 (1971); Wasmuth, The Concept of Death, 30 Ohio St. L.J. 32 (1969).

Is the Kansas statute defining death sound? Kan. Stat. Ann. §77-202 (1969, Supp. 1971):

> A person will be considered medically and legally dead if, in the opinion of a physician, based on ordinary standards of medical practice, there is the absence of spontaneous respiratory and cardiac function and, because of the disease or condition which caused, directly or indirectly, these functions to cease, or because of the passage of time since these functions ceased, attempts at resuscitation are considered hopeless; and, in this event, death will have occurred at the time these functions ceased; or
>
> A person will be considered medically and legally dead if, in the opinion of a physician, based on ordinary standards of medical practice, there is the absence of spontaneous brain function; and if based on ordinary standards of medical practice, during reasonable attempts to either maintain or restore spontaneous circulatory or respiratory function in the absence of aforesaid brain function, it appears that further attempts at resuscitation or supportive maintenance will not succeed, death will have occurred at the time when these conditions first coincide. Death is to be pronounced before artificial means of supporting respiratory and circulatory function are terminated and before any vital organ is removed for purpose of transplantation.
>
> These alternative definitions of death are to be utilized for all purposes in this

[13] To meet this problem, Uniform Probate Code §§2.104 and 2.601 provide that an heir or devisee who fails to survive the decedent by 120 hours is deemed to have predeceased the decedent. A few states have comparable provisions. Md. Ann. Code art. 93, §§3-110, 4-401 (1969, Supp. 1971) (30 days' survival required); Ohio Rev. Code Ann. §2105.21 (Page 1968) (3 days' survival required).

state, including the trials of civil and criminal cases, any laws to the contrary notwithstanding.

See Kennedy, The Kansas Statute on Death — An Appraisal, 285 N. Eng. J. Med. 946 (1971).

2. *Posthumous Children*

Where, for purposes of inheritance or of determining property rights, it is to a child's advantage to be treated as in being from the time of conception rather than from the time of birth, he will be so treated.[14] Although an infant en ventre sa mere was treated as in being for many purposes before Reeve v. Long, 3 Lev. 408, 83 Eng. Rep. 754 (K.B. 1695), that case has given rise to a famous jingle which will help you remember the principle involved. In Reeve v. Long there was a conveyance to B for life, then to B's first son in fee simple. B had no son born during his lifetime, but at B's death his wife was pregnant. A son was born a few months later. The question was whether the remainder to the son was destroyed because there was no one in being to take seisin upon the death of B. The Court of Common Pleas held the remainder was destroyed because it did not vest before the preceding life estate terminated. The Court of King's Bench unanimously affirmed. The House of Lords reversed the decision, holding the gift to the son must be construed as an executory devise in order that testator's intention not be defeated. Because the decision of the House of Lords appeared inconsistent with the Rule of Purefoy v. Rogers, 2 Wms. Saund. 380, 85 Eng. Rep. 1181 (K.B. 1670),[15] the judges were "much dissatisfied" and "very much blamed Baron Turton for permitting it to be found specially where the Law was so clear and certain." After reading Reeve v. Long and the relevant passages in Charles Fearne's celebrated work on Contingent Remainders, a student in Professor Leach's Future Interests class at Harvard in 1938 reduced the matter to verse:

> Let's fill the cups to Baron Turton
> Who, though the law was clear and certain,
> Would rather help a little foetus
> Than round out Charlie Fearne's dull treatise.
>
> — Donald G. McNeil[16]

If a man died without children and his widow claimed to be pregnant, the person who would be the heir if there were no child could at common law obtain a

[14] Comment, When is Child En Ventre Sa Mere Regarded as in Being, 33 Mich. L. Rev. 414 (1935). The principle is an ancient one. See 1 Blackstone, Commentaries *130. A similar rule has been adopted in the Soviet Union. Edict of the Federal Presidium, Mar. 14, 1945, §418, note.

[15] The rule was: "No limitation capable of taking effect as a remainder shall be construed as an executory interest."

[16] The verse and how it came to be written are set forth in Leach, Langdell Lyrics of 1938 (1938).

writ de ventre inspiciendo for a jury to determine if the widow was in fact pregnant. "The writ directs that, in the presence of knights and women, the female tractari per uberem et ventrem, — the presumed necessity of the case dispensing at once with common decency and with respectful deference to sex." 1 Blackstone, Commentaries *456 n. 19. Courts have established a rebuttable presumption that the normal period of gestation is 280 days (ten lunar months). If the child claims his conception dated more than 280 days before birth, the burden of proof is usually upon him.[17]

3. *Adopted Children*

Adoption was known in ancient civilizations and was frequently used by the Romans for the purpose of creating an heir. It was unknown to the English common law, however, and was legalized in England only in 1926. Reflecting both the inherited reverence for heirs of the blood of the ancestor and the changing public attitudes toward adoption, American law on succession by adoptees is multifarious.[18] The statutes have been in a constant state of change for the past fifty years. Although the clear trend in the United States is to transplant completely an adopted child into the adoptive family, and to cut off all inheritance rights between the adopted child and his natural relatives, many states have not yet reached this goal. Two common patterns are reflected in the statutes set out below:

NORTH CAROLINA GENERAL STATUTES §29-17 (1966): "(a) A child, adopted in accordance with chapter 48 of the General Statutes or in accordance with the applicable law of any other jurisdiction, and the heirs of such child, are entitled by succession to any property by, through and from his adoptive parents and their heirs the same as if he were the natural legitimate child of the adoptive parents.

"(b) An adopted child is not entitled by succession to any property, by, through, or from his natural parents or their heirs, except as provided in subsection (e) of this section.

"(c) The adoptive parents and the heirs of the adoptive parents are entitled by succession to any property, by, through and from an adopted child the same as if the adopted child were the natural legitimate child of the adoptive parents.

"(d) The natural parents and the heirs of the natural parents are not entitled

[17] On supposed periods of gestation beyond 280 days, the modern record for a protracted pregnancy apparently belongs to a lady from North Carolina. In Byerly v. Tolbert, 250 N.C. 27, 108 S.E.2d 29 (1959), a child was born to the decedent's widow 322 days after his death. The child (through a guardian ad litem, of course) claimed an intestate share. The trial court held as a matter of law that the infant was not the decedent's child. *Reversed.* Although there is a presumption that a child born more than 280 days after death is not the decedent's child, the presumption is not irrebuttable, and the child was entitled to have the issue submitted to a jury. For older cases see Note, 7 A.L.R. 329 (1920).

[18] See Binavince, Adoption and the Law of Descent and Distribution: A Comparative Study and a Proposal for Model Legislation, 51 Cornell L.Q. 152 (1966); Comment, The Adopted Child's Inheritance from Intestate Natural Parents, 55 Iowa L. Rev. 739 (1970).

by succession to any property, by, through or from an adopted child, except as provided in subsection (e) of this section.

"(e) If a natural parent has previously married, is married to, or shall marry an adoptive parent, the adopted child is considered the child of such natural parent for all purposes of intestate succession."

TEXAS PROBATE CODE §40 (1956): "For purposes of inheritance under the laws of descent and distribution, an adopted child shall be regarded as the child of the parent or parents by adoption, such adopted child and its descendants inheriting from and through the parent or parents by adoption and their kin the same as if such child were the natural legitimate child of such parent or parents by adoption, and such parent or parents by adoption and their kin inheriting from and through such adopted child the same as if such child were the natural legitimate child of such parent or parents by adoption. The natural parent or parents of such child and their kin shall not inherit from or through said child, but said child shall inherit from and through its natural parent or parents. . . ."

PROBLEMS

M, a sixteen-year-old high school cheerleader, becomes pregnant by F, the school's star basketball player. M's wealthy and socially prominent parents ship her off to a Florence Crittenden Home for unwed mothers in another state. After the child (A) is born it is put out for adoption, and is adopted by H and W. M and F marry after graduating from high school.

(a) Many years down the road, H dies intestate. He is survived by W, A, and a natural child of his marriage to W. Is A entitled to a child's intestate share of H's estate under the North Carolina statute? Under the Texas statute? Under the intestacy laws of your state?

(b) Suppose, instead, that M dies intestate some years after inheriting the family fortune from her parents. M is survived by F, A, and a natural child of her marriage to F. Is A entitled to an intestate share of M's estate under the North Carolina statute? Under the Texas statute? Under the intestacy laws of your state?

(c) Suppose, instead, that it is A who dies intestate, unmarried and fabulously rich. He is survived by his adoptive parents (H and W) and a "sister" (a natural child of H and W), and by his natural parents (F and M) and a "brother" (a natural child of F and M). Who takes A's estate under the North Carolina statute? Under the Texas statute? Under the intestacy laws of your state?

Very few adoption or inheritance statutes draw any distinction between adoption of a minor and adoption of an adult. Occasionally, the adoption of an adult may be useful in preventing a will contest. The only persons who have standing to challenge the validity of a will are those persons who would take if the will were denied probate. If the testator adopts a child, his collateral relatives may not be able to contest his will since ordinarily they now can inherit nothing by intestacy. Hence, if an unmarried man wishes to leave his property to a friend, under some circumstances it might be wise to adopt the friend as his child. In Greene v. Fitzpatrick, 220 Ky. 590, 295 S.W. 896 (1927), a wealthy bachelor adopted a married woman who had been his secretary for many years and with whom, it was alleged, the bachelor had been living in sin. In Collamore v. Learned, 171 Mass. 99, 50 N.E. 518 (1898), a seventy-year-old man adopted three persons aged forty-three, thirty-nine and twenty-five. In both cases it was held that the adoptions could not be set aside by the persons who would have been the heirs but for the adoptions. In the second case Holmes, J., remarked that adoption for the purpose of preventing a will contest was "perfectly proper." [19]

PROBLEMS

On February 11, 1917, F. Roger Miller and his wife, Helen Topping Miller, brought into their home a baby boy and had him baptized in the local Episcopal Church, stating that they were his parents and that the child was born on January 1, 1917. They named the child Frederick. Thereafter he was reared in the home of the Millers. He considered the Millers his parents, and at all times they represented to the public that Frederick was their son. After he married they treated his children as their grandchildren. However, the formal procedures for adoption, then in existence, were never complied with. F. Roger Miller died, devising all his property to his wife. In 1960 Helen Topping Miller died intestate, survived by Frederick and several brothers and sisters. Does Frederick have any interest in the estate of Mrs. Miller? Barlow v. Barlow, 170 Colo. 465, 463 P.2d 305 (1969); compare Bank of Maryville v. Topping, 216 Tenn. 597, 393 S.W.2d 280 (1965).

(a) Suppose, instead, that one of Helen Topping Miller's sisters died intestate, not survived by spouse or descendants. Does Frederick have any interest in the estate of his "aunt"?

(b) Suppose, instead, that Frederick died intestate, unmarried and without children. He is survived by Helen Topping Miller. Does Mrs. Miller have any interest in the estate of her "son"? If not, who inherits from Frederick? [20]

4. *Illegitimates*

Innocent of any sin or crime, children of unmarried parents were given harsh and pitiless treatment by the common law. A child born out of wedlock was filius

[19] In a more recent case, a thirty-five-year-old WAC Army captain was adopted by a fifty-six-year-old WAC sergeant. In re Libertini, 244 Md. 542, 224 A.2d 443 (1966). See, generally, Wadlington, Adoption of Adults: A Family Law Anomaly, 54 Cornell L.Q. 566 (1969).

[20] Generally on the doctrine of "equitable adoption" or "adoption by estoppel," see Comment, Equitable Adoption: A Necessary Doctrine? 35 S. Cal. L. Rev. 491 (1962); Comment, Adoption by Estoppel: History and Effect, 15 Baylor L. Rev. 162 (1963).

nullius, the child of no one.[21] He could not inherit from or through his father or his mother. Only his spouse and issue could inherit from him. If he died intestate and left neither spouse nor issue, his property escheated to the king or other overlord. Even though the father married the mother after the birth of a bastard child, such child remained the child of no one and could inherit nothing from his parents. Such was the law of England until the Legitimacy Act of 1926. Only recently did the English abolish the Civil Service office devoted to "The Escheated Estates of Intestate Bastards." [22]

All of the American states have alleviated this harsh treatment of illegitimates to some extent, but the patterns vary. "Under presently existing statutes, intestate succession both by the mother from her child born out-of-wedlock, and by such child from its mother, is permitted without restriction, in all states except Louisiana. In some states there is no intestate succession between the child and its father, except where the child has been 'legitimated' by intermarriage of the parents and/or acknowledgement of paternity by the father. . . . At the very opposite extreme are states such as Arizona and Oregon, which authorize intestate succession between any child born out-of-wedlock and its father." [23]

UNIFORM PROBATE CODE §2-109 [24]

If, for purposes of intestate succession, a relationship of parent and child must be established to determine succession by, through, or from a person, . . .

(2) . . . a person born out of wedlock is a child of the mother. That person is also a child of the father, if:

(i) the natural parents participated in a marriage ceremony before or after the birth of the child, even though the attempted marriage is void; or

(ii) the paternity is established by an adjudication before the death of the father or established thereafter by clear and convincing proof, except that the paternity established under this subparagraph (ii) is ineffective to qualify the father or his kindred to inherit from or through the child unless the father has openly treated the child as his, and has not refused to support the child.

[21] For description of the legal position of the bastard at common law, see 1 Blackstone, Commentaries *454 ff.; 2 id. *247 ff. In the first book of Blackstone (1 id. *457) you may find out, if you care to, how a child could be "more than ordinarily legitimate."

[22] In 1969 the English law was changed to provide that an illegitimate child, and issue of such child, shall be entitled to the same interest in the child's father's and mother's estates as he would have taken if he were legitimate. Family Law Reform Act, 1969, §14(2). Where there is reference in a will to a "child" or "children" of a person, illegitimates are presumed to be included, but not where the reference is to the "heirs" of a person. Id. §15.

[23] 6 Powell, Real Property at ¶1003 (1970).

[24] See Comment, Uniform Probate Code — Inheritance and the Illegitimate: A Model for Probate Reform, 69 Mich. L. Rev. 112 (1970).

LABINE v. VINCENT

Supreme Court of the United States, 1971
401 U.S. 532

MR. JUSTICE BLACK delivered the opinion of the Court. In this appeal the guardian (tutrix) of an illegitimate minor child attacks the constitutionality of Louisiana's laws that bar an illegitimate child from sharing equally with legitimates in the estate of their father who had publicly acknowledged the child, but who died without a will. To understand appellant's constitutional arguments and our decision, it is necessary briefly to review the facts giving rise to this dispute. On March 15, 1962, a baby girl, Rita Vincent, was born to Lou Bertha Patterson (now Lou Bertha Labine) in Calcasieu Parish, Louisiana. On May 10, 1962, Lou Bertha Patterson and Ezra Vincent, as authorized by Louisiana law, jointly executed before a notary a Louisiana State Board of Health form acknowledging that Ezra Vincent was the "natural father" of Rita Vincent. This public acknowledgment of parentage did not, under Louisiana law, give the child a legal right to share equally with legitimate children in the parent's estate but it did give her a right to claim support from her parents or their heirs. The acknowledgment also gave the child the capacity under Louisiana law to be a limited beneficiary under her father's will in the event he left a will naming her, which he did not do here.

Ezra Vincent died intestate (that is, without a will) on September 16, 1968, in Rapides Parish, Louisiana, leaving substantial property within the State, but no will to direct its distribution. Appellant, as the guardian of Rita Vincent, petitioned in state court for the appointment of an administrator for the father's estate; for a declaration that Rita Vincent is the sole heir of Ezra Vincent; and for an order directing the administrator to pay support and maintenance for the child. In the alternative, appellant sought a declaration that the child was entitled to support and maintenance of $150 per month under a Louisiana child support law.[25]

The administrator of the succession of Ezra Vincent answered the petition claiming that Vincent's relatives were entitled to the whole estate. He relied for their claim upon two articles of the Louisiana Civil Code of 1870: Art. 206, which provides: "Illegitimate children, though duly acknowledged, can not claim the rights of legitimate children . . . ." and Art. 919, which provides: "Natural children are called to the inheritance of their natural father, who has duly acknowledged them, when he has left no descendants nor ascendants, nor collateral relations, nor surviving wife, and to the exclusion only of the State." The court ruled that the relatives of the father were his collateral relations and that under Louisiana's laws of intestate succession took his property to the exclusion of acknowledged, but not

[25] La Civ. Code Ann., Art. 240 provides: "Fathers and mothers owe alimony to their illegitimate children, when they are in need. . . ." Art. 241 provides: "Illegitimate children have a right to claim this alimony, not only from their father and mother, but even from their heirs after their death."

legitimated, illegitimate children. The court, therefore, dismissed with costs the guardian mother's petition to recognize the child as an heir. The court also ruled that in view of Social Security payments of $60 per month and Veterans Administration payments of $40 per month available for the support of the child, the guardian for the child was not entitled to support or maintenance from the succession of Ezra Vincent.[26] The Louisiana Court of Appeal, Third Circuit, affirmed and the Supreme Court of Louisiana denied a petition for writ of certiorari. The child's guardian appealed and we noted probable jurisdiction. 400 U.S. 817 (1970).

In this Court appellant argues that Louisiana's statutory scheme for intestate succession that bars this illegitimate child from sharing in her father's estate constitutes an invidious discrimination against illegitimate children that cannot stand under the Due Process and Equal Protection Clauses of the Constitution. Much reliance is placed upon the Court's decisions in Levy v. Louisiana, 391 U.S. 68 (1968), and Glona v. American Guaranty & Liability Insurance Co., 391 U.S. 73 (1968). For the reasons set out below, we find appellant's reliance on those cases misplaced, and we decline to extend the rationale of those cases where it does not apply. Accordingly, we affirm the decision below.

In Levy the Court held that Louisiana could not consistently with the Equal Protection Clause bar an illegitimate child from recovering for the wrongful death of its mother when such recoveries by legitimate children were authorized. The cause of action alleged in Levy was in tort. It was undisputed that Louisiana had created a statutory tort and had provided for the survival of the deceased's cause of action, so that a large class of persons injured by the tort could recover damages in compensation for their injury. Under those circumstances the Court held that the State could not totally exclude from the class of potential plaintiffs illegitimate children who were unquestionably injured by the tort that took their mother's life. Levy did not say and cannot fairly be read to say that a State can never treat an illegitimate child differently from legitimate offspring.[27]

The people of Louisiana, through their legislature have carefully regulated many of the property rights incident to family life. Louisiana law prescribes certain formalities requisite to the contracting of marriage. Once marriage is contracted

[26] Rita Vincent qualifies as Ezra Vincent's child for federal social security and veteran's benefits by virtue of his acknowledgment of paternity, 42 U.S.C. §416(h)(3)(A)(i)(I) (1964 ed., Supp. V) and 38 U.S.C. §101(4) (1964 ed., Supp. V). No question has been raised concerning the legality under federal law of reliance upon such benefits to relieve parents or their estates from the state-imposed obligations of child support. [In an additional statement of facts given in his dissenting opinion, Mr. Justice Brennan noted that "Mr. Vincent and Mrs. Patterson continued to live together and raise Rita Nell until Mr. Vincent died in 1968." 401 U.S. at 542. — Eds.]

[27] Nor is Glona v. American Guaranty & Liability Insurance Co., 391 U.S. 73 (1968), analogous to this case. In Glona the majority relied on Louisiana's "curious course" of sanctions against illegitimacy to demonstrate that there was no "rational basis" for prohibiting a mother from recovering for the wrongful death of her son. Id., at 74-75. Even if we were to apply the "rational basis" test to the Louisiana intestate succession statute, that statute clearly has a rational basis in view of Louisiana's interest in promoting family life and of directing the disposition of property left within the State.

there, husbands have obligations to their wives. Fathers have obligations to their children. Should the children prosper while the parents fall upon hard times, children have a statutory obligation to support their parents. To further strengthen and preserve family ties, Louisiana regulates the disposition of property upon the death of a family man. The surviving spouse is entitled to an interest in the deceased spouse's estate. Legitimate children have a right of forced heirship in their father's estate and can even retrieve property transferred by their father during his lifetime in reduction of their rightful interests.

Louisiana also has a complex set of rules regarding the rights of illegitimate children. Children born out of wedlock and who are never acknowledged by their parents apparently have no right to take property by intestate succession from their father's estate. In some instances, their father may not even bequeath property to them by will.[28] Illegitimate children acknowledged by their fathers are "natural children." Natural children can take from their father by intestate succession "to the exclusion only of the State." They may be bequeathed property by their father only to the extent of either one-third or one-fourth of his estate and then only if their father is not survived by legitimate children or their heirs. Finally, children born out of wedlock can be legitimated or adopted, in which case they may take by intestate succession or by will as any other child.

These rules for intestate succession may or may not reflect the intent of particular parents. Many will think that it is unfortunate that the rules are so rigid. Others will think differently. But the choices reflected by the intestate succession statute are choices which it is within the power of the State to make. The Federal Constitution does not give this Court the power to overturn the State's choice under the guise of constitutional interpretation because the Justices of this Court believe that they can provide better rules. Of course, it may be said that the rules adopted by the Louisiana Legislature "discriminate" against illegitimates. But the rules also discriminate against collateral relations, as opposed to ascendants, and against ascendants, as opposed to descendants. Other rules determining property rights based on family status also "discriminate" in favor of wives and against "concubines." [29] The dissent attempts to distinguish these other "discriminations" on the ground that they have a biological or social basis. There is no biological difference between a wife and a concubine, nor does the Constitution require that there be such a difference before the State may assert its power to protect the wife and her children against the claims of a concubine and her children. The social difference between a wife and a concubine is analogous to the difference between a legitimate and an illegitimate child. One set of relationships is socially sanctioned, legally

28 "Natural fathers and mothers can, in no case, dispose of property in favor of their adulterine or incestuous children, unless to the mere amount of what is necessary to their sustenance, or to procure them an occupation or profession by which to support themselves." La. Civ. Code Ann., Art. 1488 (1952).

29 "Those who have lived together in open concubinage are respectively incapable of making to each other, whether inter vivos or mortis causa, any donation of immovables; and if they make a donation of movables, it can not exceed one-tenth part of the whole value of their estate. Those who afterwards marry are excepted from this rule." La. Civ. Code Ann., Art. 1481 (1952).

recognized and gives rise to various rights and duties. The other set of relationships is illicit and beyond the recognition of the law. Similarly, the State does not need biological or social reasons for distinguishing between ascendants and descendants. Some of these discriminatory choices are perhaps more closely connected to our conceptions of social justice or the ways in which most dying men wish to dispose of their property than the Louisiana rules governing illegitimate children. It may be possible that some of these choices are more "rational" than the choices inherent in Louisiana's categories of illegitimates. But the power to make rules to establish, protect, and strengthen family life as well as to regulate the disposition of property left in Louisiana by a man dying there is committed by the Constitution of the United States and the people of Louisiana to the legislature of that State. Absent a specific constitutional guarantee, it is for that legislature, not the life-tenured judges of this Court, to select from among possible laws. We cannot say that Louisiana's policy provides a perfect or even a desirable solution or the one we would have provided for the problem of the property rights of illegitimate children.[30] Neither can we say that Louisiana does not have the power to make laws for distribution of property left within the State.

We emphasize that this is not a case, like Levy, where the State has created an insurmountable barrier to this illegitimate child. There is not the slightest suggestion in this case that Louisiana has barred this illegitimate from inheriting from her father. Ezra Vincent could have left one-third of his property to his illegitimate daughter had he bothered to follow the simple formalities of executing a will. He could, of course, have legitimated the child by marrying her mother in which case the child could have inherited his property either by intestate succession or by will as any other legitimate child. Finally, he could have awarded his child the benefit of Louisiana's intestate succession statute on the same terms as legitimate children simply by stating in his acknowledgment of paternity his desire to legitimate the little girl. See Bergeron v. Miller, 230 So. 2d 417 (La. App. 1970).

In short, we conclude that in the circumstances presented in this case, there is nothing in the vague generalities of the Equal Protection and Due Process Clauses which empowers this Court to nullify the deliberate choices of the elected representatives of the people of Louisiana.

Affirmed.

Mr. Justice Harlan, concurring. In joining the opinion of the Court, I wish to add a few words, prompted, I may say, by the dissenting opinion, which in my view evinces extravagant notions of what constitutes a denial of "equal protection" in the constitutional sense.

It is surely entirely reasonable for Louisiana to provide that a man who has entered into a marital relationship thereby undertakes obligations to any resulting offspring beyond those which he owes to the products of a casual liaison, and this whether or not he admits the fact of fatherhood in the latter case. With respect to a substantial portion of a man's estate, these greater obligations stemming from mar-

[30] See Krause, Bringing the Bastard into the Great Society, A Proposed Uniform Act on Legitimacy, 44 Tex. L. Rev. 829 (1966).

riage are imposed by the provision of Louisiana law making a man's legitimate children his forced heirs. For the remainder of his estate, these obligations are not absolute, but are conditional upon his not disposing of his property in other ways. With all respect to my dissenting Brethren, I deem little short of frivolous the contention that the Equal Protection Clause prohibits enforcement of marital obligations, in either the mandatory or the suppletive form. See H. M. Hart & A. Sacks, The Legal Process: Basic Materials on the Making and Application of Law 35-36, 251-256 (tent. ed. 1958).

In addition to imposing these obligations, Louisiana law prohibits testamentary dispositions to one's illegitimate children. Even were my dissenting Brethren prepared to hold this rule of law unconstitutional, to do so would not affect the outcome of this case. First, appellant is a "natural" rather than an "illegitimate" child; and second, if her father desired her to have his property after his death, he did not manifest that desire in the appropriate way.

Mr. Justice Brennan, with whom Mr. Justice Douglas, Mr. Justice White, and Mr. Justice Marshall join, dissenting. In my view, Louisiana's intestate succession laws, insofar as they treat illegitimate children whose fathers have publicly acknowledged them differently from legitimate children, plainly violate the Equal Protection Clause of the Fourteenth Amendment. The Court today effectively concedes this, and, to reach its result, resorts to the startling measure of simply excluding such illegitimate children from the protection of the Clause, in order to uphold the untenable and discredited moral prejudice of bygone centuries which vindictively punished not only the illegitimates' parents, but also the hapless, and innocent, children. Based upon such a premise, today's decision cannot even pretend to be a principled decision. This is surprising from Justices who have heretofore so vigorously decried decisionmaking rested upon personal predilections, to borrow the Court's words, of "life-tenured judges of this Court."

I respectfully dissent. . . .

II . . . Article 178 of the Louisiana Civil Code provides in full: "Children are either legitimate, illegitimate, or legitimated." Not all illegitimate children can be legitimated, however — only those whose parents do not have legitimate descendants or ascendants and could lawfully have married each other at the time of the child's conception, or those whose parents later marry can be legitimated. An illegitimate child who can be legitimated becomes a "natural" child when his father formally acknowledges him. However, Article 206 of the Louisiana Civil Code provides that, "[i]llegitimate children, though duly acknowledged, can not claim the rights of legitimate children." Thus, the primary consequence under Louisiana succession law that flows from acknowledgment is that the natural child may inherit under a will, and inherits if there is no will, only after the father's other descendants, ascendants, collateral relations, and surviving spouse, but before the estate escheats to the State. An illegitimate child whose parents could lawfully have married each other at the time of the child's conception, but who has not been publicly acknowledged, or an illegitimate child whose parents were not capable of marriage at the time of conception, may not inherit *at all*, either by will or intestate succession, "the law allowing them nothing more than a mere alimony." La. Civ. Code Ann., Art. 920 (1952).

III Under Louisiana law a legitimate child would have had an absolute right to inherit Mr. Vincent's estate; Mr. Vincent could not have totally disinherited such a child. This is a consequence of Louisiana's "forced heirship" law, in other words a consequence of a state decision, however contrary that might be to Mr. Vincent's own desires. Similarly in the present case, Mr. Vincent's illegitimate daughter, though duly acknowledged, is denied his intestate estate, not because he wished that result but because the State places her behind Mr. Vincent's collateral relations — indeed behind all his relations — in the line of succession.

The State's discrimination is clear and obvious.[31] Ordinarily, even in cases of economic regulation, this Court will inquire, under the Equal Protection Clause of the Fourteenth Amendment, whether there is some "reasonable basis" for a discrimination in a state statute, or whether the discrimination is invidious. E.g., Morey v. Doud, 354 U.S. 457 (1957); Williamson v. Lee Optical Co., 348 U.S. 483 (1955); Yick Wo v. Hopkins, 118 U.S. 356 (1886). Such an inquiry does not question the State's *power* to regulate; rather, it focuses exclusively on whether the State has legislated without the invidious discrimination that is forbidden by the Fourteenth Amendment.

For reasons not articulated, the Court refuses to consider in this case whether there is any reason at all, or any basis whatever, for the difference in treatment that Louisiana accords to publicly acknowledged illegitimates and to legitimate children. Rather, the Court simply asserts that "the power to make rules to establish, protect, and strengthen family life as well as to regulate the disposition of property left in Louisiana by a man dying there is committed by the Constitution of the United States and the people of Louisiana to the legislature of that State." . . . But no one questions Louisiana's power to pass inheritance laws. Surely the Court cannot be saying that the Fourteenth Amendment's Equal Protection Clause is inapplicable to subjects regulable by the States — that extraordinary proposition would reverse a century of constitutional adjudication under the Equal Protection and Due Process Clauses. It is precisely state action which is subjected by the Fourteenth Amendment to its restraints. It is, to say the least, bewildering that a court that for decades has wrestled with the nuances of the concept of "state action" in

[31] As Part II of this opinion makes clear, only parents of illegitimate children who could have married at the time of conception and who have no legitimate ascendants or descendants may legitimate those children by notarial act. . . . The Court relies on the fact that Mr. Vincent was within this narrow class of fathers of illegitimate children to suggest that Louisiana law allows fathers to decide whether or not their illegitimate children will inherit the father's estate. . . . Even as to this class, however, Louisiana law places the burden on the father of a publicly acknowledged illegitimate child to take affirmative action to *inherit* that child, while virtually disabling the same father from disinheriting a legitimate child, or, at least, placing a burden of affirmative action on the father in order to *disinherit* the legitimate child. Thus, even as to this small group, the discrimination imposed by the State is clear.

order to ascertain the reach of the Fourteenth Amendment, in this case holds that the state action here, because it is state action, is insulated from these restraints.

Putting aside the Court's repeated emphasis on Louisiana's power to regulate intestate succession — something not questioned and wholly irrelevant to the present constitutional issue — only two passages in the Court's opinion even attempt an argument in support of today's result. First, the Court tells us that Louisiana intestate succession law favors some classes of a deceased's relatives over other classes. That is certainly true, but the Court nowhere suggests what bearing these other discriminations have on the rationality of Louisiana's discrimination against the acknowledged illegitimate. It is a little like answering a complaint of Negro school children against separate lavatories for Negro and white students by arguing that the situation is no different from separate lavatories for boys and girls, or for elementary school children and high school students. These other discriminations may be rational or irrational. But their only relevance to the rationality and constitutionality of the specific challenged discrimination is the light they throw, if any, on the basis for that discrimination. The conclusion the Court appears to draw from its itemization of other discriminations among a deceased's relatives is that Louisiana needs *no* justification at all for any of the distinctions it draws. That reasoning flies in the face not only of the Equal Protection and Due Process Clauses of the Fourteenth Amendment, but also of the very notion of a rule of law.

The only other hint at an attempt to support today's result may appear in the purported distinction of Levy v. Louisiana, 391 U.S. 68 (1968): "We emphasize that this is not a case, like Levy, where the State has created an insurmountable barrier to this illegitimate child." . . . There may be two implications in this statement: (1) that in Levy, there was an insurmountable barrier to recovery; and (2) that any discrimination that falls short of an "insurmountable barrier" is, without need for further analysis, permissible. As to the first, Levy involved an unacknowledged illegitimate child. Louisiana permitted an illegitimate child to recover in tort for the death of the child's mother, under the State's wrongful death act, only if the illegitimate child had been acknowledged. There was no insurmountable barrier to the child's recovery; if the mother had formally acknowledged the child, recovery would have been permitted. My Brother Harlan's dissent emphasized this fact and argued that the State was entitled to rely on specified formalities. Plainly then Levy did not involve any "insurmountable barrier."

The Court's second implication — that any discrimination short of an "insurmountable barrier" is permissible — is one of those propositions the mere statement of which is its own refutation. Levy, as I have pointed out, holds squarely to the contrary specifically in the context of discrimination against illegitimate children. And numerous other cases in this Court establish the general proposition that discriminations that "merely" disadvantage a class of persons or businesses are as subject to the command of the Fourteenth Amendment as discriminations which are in some sense more absolute.

In short, the Court has not analyzed, or perhaps simply refuses to analyze, Louisiana's discrimination against acknowledged illegitimates in terms of the requirements of the Fourteenth Amendment.[32] Since I still believe that the Constitution does prohibit a State from denying any person the "equal protection of the laws," I must therefore undertake my own analysis to determine, at a minimum, whether there is any rational basis for the discrimination, or whether the classification bears any intelligible proper relationship to the consequences that flow from it.[33] See, e.g., Dandridge v. Williams, 397 U.S. 471 (1970); McLaughlin v. Florida, 379 U.S. 184, 190-191 (1964); Morey v. Doud, supra; Gulf, C. & S.F.R. Co. v. Ellis, 165 U.S. 150, 155 (1897).

Certainly, there is no biological basis for the State's distinction. Mr. Vincent's illegitimate daughter is related to him biologically in exactly the same way as a legitimate child would have been. Indeed, it is the identity of interest "in the biological and in the spiritual sense," Levy v. Louisiana, 391 U.S., at 72, and the identical "intimate, familial relationship," id., at 71, between both the legitimate and illegitimate child, and their father, which is the very basis for appellant's contention that the two must be treated alike.

Louisiana might be thought to have an interest in requiring people to go through certain formalities in order to eliminate complicated questions of proof and the opportunity for both error and fraud in determining paternity after the death of the father. This argument, of course, was the focal point of the dissent in Levy and Glona v. American Guarantee & Liability Insurance Co., 391 U.S. 73 (1968). I leave aside, for the moment, the fact that the holdings of those two cases indicate that this consideration is insufficient to justify a difference in treatment when there is no dispute over the fact of parentage. For my Brother Harlan's dissenting opinion in those cases explicitly recognized that the State's interest in this regard is fully satisfied by a formal public acknowledgment. 391 U.S., at 80. When a father has formally acknowledged his child or gone through any state authorized formality for declaring paternity, or when there has been a court judgment of paternity, there is no possible difficulty of proof, and no opportunity for fraud or error. This purported interest certainly can offer no justification for distinguishing between a formally acknowledged illegitimate child and a legitimate one.

It is also important not to obscure the fact that the formality of marriage primarily signifies a relationship between husband and wife, not between parent and

[32] In one sentence in a footnote, the Court says, "Even if we were to apply the 'rational basis' test to the Louisiana intestate succession statute, that statute clearly has a rational basis in view of Louisiana's interest in promoting family life and of directing the disposition of property left within the State." . . . I agree that Louisiana has an interest in promoting family life and in directing the disposition of property left within the State. I do not understand how either of these interests provides any basis for Louisiana's discrimination against the acknowledged illegitimate, and the Court does not explain the relevance of these state interests.

[33] In view of my conclusion that the present discrimination cannot stand even under the "some rational basis" standard, I need not reach the questions whether illegitimacy is a "suspect" classification which the State could not adopt in any circumstances without showing a compelling state interest, or whether fundamental rights are involved, which also would require a showing of a compelling state interest. See Levy v. Louisiana, 391 U.S. 68, 71 (1968); Harper v. Virginia Board of Elections, 383 U.S. 663 (1966); Skinner v. Oklahoma, 316 U.S. 535 (1942). This Court has generally treated as suspect a classification that discriminates against an individual on the basis of factors over which he has no control.

child. Analysis of the rationality of any state effort to impose obligations based upon the fact of marriage must, therefore, distinguish between those obligations that run between parties to the marriage and those that run to others. My Brother Harlan, unlike his colleagues in the majority, concedes that the Equal Protection Clause requires a justification for Louisiana's discrimination against illegitimates, and he attempts one; he argues that it is reasonable for a State to impose greater obligations on a man in respect to his wife and their children than in respect to other women and any other children of whom he may be the father. In other words, contrary to the Louisiana court below, he apparently believes that Louisiana's discrimination against illegitimates reflects a state policy that would discourage marriage by imposing special burdens, such as those of forced heirship, upon those who enter into it. However that may be, such force as his argument may have stems directly from its lack of specificity. Imposition by a State of reciprocal obligations upon husband and wife that are not imposed upon those who do not enter into a formalized marriage relationship is based upon the assumptions (1) that marriage may be promoted through pressure applied on or by the party seeking the benefit of obligations imposed by the married status, and (2) that in any event the choice is entirely within the control of the two individuals concerned. These elements are entirely lacking when we consider the relationship of a child vis-a-vis its parents. . . .

Intestate succession laws might seek to carry out a general intent of parents not to provide for publicly acknowledged illegitimate children. However, as the summary of Louisiana law I have made shows, one of the primary hallmarks of Louisiana's civil code is its detailed, extensive regulation of the family relationship. Its discrimination against the illegitimate in matters of inheritance and succession is official state policy, completely negating any argument that such discrimination merely represents a legislative judgment about the probable wishes of a deceased or the desires of most persons in similar situations. The opinion of the state court below itself eliminates that possibility. The Louisiana court affirmatively states that the disinheritance of acknowledged illegitimates is in furtherance of specific state policy goals — goals that are unrelated to parents' intentions. 229 So. 2d, at 452. Finally, viewing the general statutory treatment of illegitimates as a whole, particularly the facts that only a narrow class of fathers can legitimate their children by declaration, and that unacknowledged and "adulterous" illegitimates are prohibited from inheriting even by will, I think the conclusion is compelled that Louisiana's discrimination represents state policy, not an attempt to aid in the effectuation of private desires.

Even if Louisiana law could be read as being based on a legislative judgment about parents' intent, the present discrimination against illegitimates could not stand. In order to justify a discrimination on the ground that it reflects a legislative judgment about the desires of most persons in similar situations, there must be some rational basis for finding that the legislative classification does reflect those persons' desires or intentions as a general matter. The Court makes no argument that fathers who have publicly acknowledged their illegitimate children generally intend to disinherit them. No Louisiana court opinion or Louisiana legislative pronouncement that I can discover, or the Attorney General of Louisiana in this case, has ever argued that the Louisiana scheme reflects the general intentions of fathers of illegitimate children in that State. Indeed, the state court below justified the discrimination on the ground that "the denial of inheritance rights to illegitimates might reasonably be viewed as encouraging marriage and legitimation of children." 229 So. 2d, at 452. Such denial could encourage marriage only if fathers generally desire to leave their property to their illegitimate children; otherwise, disinheritance would not operate as a sanction to encourage marriage.

Moreover, logic and common experience also suggest that a father who has publicly acknowledged his illegitimate child will *not* generally intend to disinherit his child. A man who publicly announces that he has fathered a child out of wedlock has publicly claimed that child for his own. He has risked public opprobrium, or other sanctions, to make the public announcement. Surely, it does not follow that he will generally desire to disinherit that child and further discredit his reputation by refusing to contribute to his own child at death. All the writing cited to us, including a United Nations study report,[34] an English study commission,[35] the proposed Uniform Probate Code,[36] and a variety of law review commentary in this country,[37] suggest precisely the opposite conclusion. Moreover, Louisiana is the only State in the country that denies illegitimate children rights of inheritance from the mother equal to those of legitimate children,[38] and one of only four States that have expressly provided by statute that the illegitimate child may not inherit from his father.[39] The legislatures of 20 States by statute allow acknowledged illegitimate children to inherit equally from their fathers.[40] Three States grant equal rights of

34 Subcommission on Prevention of Discrimination and Protection of Minorities of the Commission on Human Rights, United Nations Economic and Social Council, Study of Discrimination against Persons Born Out of Wedlock: General Principles on Equality and Non-Discrimination in Respect of Persons Born out of Wedlock, U.N. Doc. E/CN. 4 Sub. 2/L 453 (Jan. 13, 1967).

35 Stone, Report of the Committee on the Law of Succession in Relation to Illegitimate Persons, 30 Mod. L. Rev. 552 (1967).

36 National Conference of Commissioners on Uniform State Laws, Uniform Probate Code §2-109 (official text 1969).

37 Note, Illegitimacy, 26 Brooklyn L. Rev. 45 (1959); Krause, Equal Protection for the Illegitimate, 65 Mich. L. Rev. 477 (1967); Krause, Bringing the Bastard into the Great Society — A Proposed Uniform Act on Legitimacy, 44 Tex. L. Rev. 829 (1966); Gray & Rudovsky, The Court Acknowledges the Illegitimate: Levy v. Louisiana and Glona v. American Guarantee & Liability Insurance Co., 118 U. Pa. L. Rev. 1 (1969); Note, The Rights of Illegitimates Under Federal Statutes, 76 Harv. L. Rev. 337 (1962).

38 See the table summarizing state statutes in Note, Illegitimacy, 26 Brooklyn L. Rev. 45, 76-79 (1959). In 1959, New York as well as Louisiana did not allow illegitimate children to inherit equally from their mothers. New York has since changed its law. N.Y. Est., Powers & Trusts Law §4-1.2(a)(1) (1967).

39 Hawaii Rev. Laws §577-14 (1968); Ky. Rev. Stat. §391.090 (1962); Pa. Stat. Ann., Tit. 20, §1.7 (1950).

40 Cal. Prob. Code §255 (Supp. 1971); Colo. Rev. Stat. Ann. §153-2-8 (1963); Fla. Stat. §731.29 (1965); Ga. Code Ann. §74-103 (1964); Idaho Code §14-104 (1947); Ind. Ann. Stat. §6-207 (1953) [adjudication of paternity required]; Iowa Code Ann. §633.222 (1971); Kan. Stat. Ann. §59-501 (1964); Mich. Stat. Ann. §27.3178 (153) (Supp. 1970); Minn. Stat. §525.172 (1967); Mont. Rev. Codes Ann. §91-404 (1964); Neb. Rev. Stat. §30-109 (1964); Nev. Rev. Stat. §134.170 (1967); N.M. Stat. Ann. §29-1-18 (1953); N.Y. Est., Powers & Trusts Law §4-1.2 (1967) [order of filiation required]; Okla. Stat. Ann., Tit. 84, §215 (1970); S.D. Compiled Laws Ann. §29-1-15 (1967); Utah Code Ann. §74-4-10 (1953); Wash. Rev. Code §11-04-081 (1967); Wis. Stat. Ann. §237.06 (Supp. 1970).

inheritance from the father regardless of acknowledgment.[41] The legislatures of the other 23 States have not passed upon the question.

The Court nowhere mentions the central reality of this case: Louisiana punishes illegitimate children for the misdeeds of their parents. The judges of the Third Circuit Court of Appeal of Louisiana, whose judgment the Court here reviews, upheld the present discrimination "[h]owever unfair it may be to punish innocent children for the fault of their parents. . . ." 229 So. 2d, at 452. It is certainly unusual in this country for a person to be legally disadvantaged on the basis of factors over which he never had any control. "Distinctions between citizens solely because of their ancestry are by their very nature odious to a free people whose institutions are founded upon the doctrine of equality." Hirabayashi v. United States, 320 U.S. 81, 100 (1943). The state court below explicitly upheld the statute on the ground that the punishment of the child might encourage the parents to marry.[42] If that is the State's objective, it can obviously be attained far more directly by focusing on the parents whose actions the State seeks to influence. Given the importance and nature of the decision to marry, cf. Boddie v. Connecticut, ante, p. 371 (1971), I think that disinheriting the illegitimate child must be held to "bear no intelligible proper relation to the consequences that are made to flow" from the State's classification. Glona v. American Guarantee & Liability Insurance Co., 391 U.S. 73, 81 (1968) (Harlan, J., dissenting).

In my judgment, only a moral prejudice, prevalent in 1825 when the Louisiana statutes under consideration were adopted, can support Louisiana's discrimination against illegitimate children. Since I can find no rational basis to justify the distinction Louisiana creates between an acknowledged illegitimate child and a legitimate one, that discrimination is clearly invidious. Morey v. Doud, 354 U.S. 457 (1957). I think the Supreme Court of North Dakota stated the correct principle in invalidating an analogous discrimination in that State's inheritance laws: "This statute, which punishes innocent children for their parents' transgressions, has no place in our system of government, which has as one of its basic tenets equal protection for all." In re Estate of Jensen, 162 N.W.2d 861, 878 (1968).[43]

NOTES AND QUESTIONS

1. How does the majority distinguish this case from Levy and Glona, the two wrongful death action cases which also involved Louisiana law? Is the court's dis-

---

[41] Ariz. Rev. Stat. Ann. §14-206 (1956); N.D. Cent. Code §56-01-05 (Supp. 1969); Ore. Rev. Stat. §§111.231; 109.060 (1957).

[42] The state court also argued that Louisiana's disinheritance of the illegitimate would serve the State's interest in the stability of land titles, by avoiding "the disruptions and uncertainties to result from unknown and not easily ascertained claims through averments of parentage. . . ." 229 So. 2d, at 452. This is simply a variation on the State's interest in relying on formalities, . . . which is completely served by public acknowledgment of parentage and simply does not apply to the case of acknowledged illegitimate children.

[43] Noted 38 Brooklyn L. Rev. 428; 22 Case W. Res. L. Rev. 793; 75 Dick. L. Rev. 377; 49 Texas L. Rev. 1132; 46 Tulane L. Rev. 167. — Eds.

tinction persuasive to you? For other cases distinguishing between wrongful death actions and inheritance, see Schmoll v. Creecy, 54 N.J. 194, 254 A.2d 525, 38 A.L.R.3d 605 (1969); Estate of Ortiz, 60 Misc. 2d 756, 303 N.Y.S.2d 806 (1969); Strahan v. Strahan, 304 F. Supp. 40 (D.C. La. 1969).

2. Levy and Glona were 6-3 decisions. Justice Douglas wrote the majority opinions, in which he was joined by Justices Brennan, White, Marshall, Warren and Fortas. Justice Harlan wrote the dissenting opinion, in which he was joined by Justices Black and Stewart. Labine v. Vincent was a 5-4 decision. Justices Black, Harlan, Stewart, Burger and Blackmun were in the majority. Justices Brennan, Douglas, White and Marshall were in the minority.

3. As indicated in the dissenting opinion, the North Dakota Supreme Court held unconstitutional that state's statute denying inheritance by illegitimate children from a legitimate child of a common mother. In re Estate of Jensen, 162 N.W.2d 861 (N.D. 1968). In its decision the North Dakota court relied heavily on the reasoning of the United States Supreme Court in Levy v. Louisiana. The North Dakota statute was immediately amended to conform to this decision. N.D. Cent. Code §56-01-05 (1960, Supp. 1971).

Other state court challenges of the constitutionality of intestacy statutes discriminating against illegitimates have not been successful. Pettiford v. Frazier, 226 Ga. 438, 175 S.E.2d 549 (1970); Burnett v. Camden, 254 N.E.2d 199 (Ind. 1970); In re Estate of Pakarinen, 287 Minn. 330, 178 N.W.2d 714 (1970).

4. Suppose a state statute gave the right of inheritance from an illegitimate child to the mother but not to the father. Would the father's claim of unconstitutional discrimination be valid? In Munn v. Munn, 168 Colo. 76, 450 P.2d 68 (1969), a child support case, the father of an illegitimate child claimed he was denied equal protection since his duty of support was fixed by a final jury verdict, thus making no allowance for possible future financial changes. The court found, on the basis of Glona, that it could not permit such discrimination against the father of an illegitimate child.

5. *Half-Bloods*

Suppose this fact situation. M has two children (A and B) by her first marriage. Her husband dies; she remarries and has two children (C and D) by her second marriage. Although A and B live in the home of their mother and stepfather, he does not adopt them. M and her second husband die; then D dies intestate, unmarried and without children. Who inherits D's property? Do A and B (D's half-brothers) share in the inheritance with C? If so, what are their shares?

If these facts sound a bit complex, maybe this diagram will help.

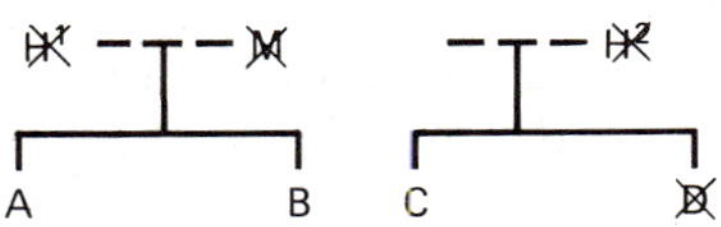

"In the rules applicable to collaterals of the half-blood, we again find divergence between the rules developed in the English land law and the rules evolved in the Church courts with respect to personalty. . . . [R]elatives of the half-blood were wholly excluded from those able to take land on intestate succession. Under the Church-evolved rules, applicable to personalty, the rule was the exact opposite — relatives of the half- and whole blood were treated identically. . . .

"The present American statutes fit some one of the patterns established prior to 1800. The District of Columbia and approximately one-sixth of the states have completely abolished the difference in treatment of kindred of the whole and half-blood. An equal number have taken the same position except in cases involving ancestral property. Several have followed the early lead of Virginia, by giving half-bloods half shares. A few have followed the early lead of Connecticut in allowing half-bloods to take only when whole blood relatives of the same degree are missing. . . .

"With due respect to the contrary opinions of Bentham and Atkinson, it seems unrewarding to continue different treatments for collateral relatives of the half- and whole blood." [44]

Thus in the District of Columbia, A, B and C would each take a one-third share of D's estate; in Virginia C would take a one-half share and A and B would take one-fourth shares; in Connecticut D's entire estate would pass to his full brother C.

Suppose, instead, that it was H-2 who died intestate, survived by his son C and by his stepsons, A and B. Are A and B entitled to inherit from their stepfather? The answer, in all states, is no. A and B were not related by blood to H-2, and he never adopted them. Unless they have a claim based on "equitable adoption" or "adoption by estoppel," [45] they cannot inherit.

We said that this is the answer in all states. Is the situation different in the District of Columbia?

ESTATE OF HUMPHREY

United States District Court, District of Columbia, 1966
254 F. Supp. 33

Holtzoff, District Judge. The question presented by this case is whether under the law of the District of Columbia a stepchild is entitled to inherit from a stepparent who died intestate. We answer this question in the affirmative.

William F. Humphrey, a domiciliary of the District of Columbia, died intestate. His wife, Hattie E. Humphrey, had predeceased him. William F. Humphrey left no natural or adopted children surviving him. However, he left a stepdaughter, Maxine L. Tolson, who was a natural daughter of Hattie Humphrey by a prior marriage. Unfortunately the record is very scanty. It was stated in open court at the argument, however, and was not disputed that at the time of her mother's marriage

[44] 6 Powell, Real Property at ¶1000 (1970).
[45] See note 20 supra.

to the deceased, Maxine Tolson was eight years old and was brought up and grew up in her stepfather's and mother's household.

The deceased was also survived by two brothers and by several nephews and nieces, who are the children of the decedent's deceased brothers. One of the nephews, Samuel Humphrey, filed a petition for letters of administration and was appointed administrator of his uncle's estate. The stepdaughter of the deceased, Maxine Tolson, then filed a cross-petition seeking a revocation of the letters of administration theretofore granted to Samuel Humphrey, and asking that she be appointed as administratrix. The administrator moves to dismiss the cross-petition.

The matter now comes before this Court on the motion to dismiss the cross-petition. Its determination depends on the question whether the stepdaughter is entitled to inherit in preference to the brothers and nephews and nieces of the deceased. The question is not free from doubt. There is a dearth of authorities on this point. There are no reported decisions in this jurisdiction discussing the effect of the local legislation on this subject.

It is undisputed that at common law a stepchild did not inherit from his stepparent. No doubt this rule originated from the fact that the common law of descent and distribution was based on feudal tenures. The ultimate query is whether local statutes have changed the law in this respect. A great deal of the American law of descent and distribution has gradually become statutory, pursuant to a tendency to modify some of the rigorous and inflexible doctrines of the common law.

The following are the pertinent provisions of the District of Columbia Code, 1961 Edition, Supp. V (1966):

> Section 19-306. When the intestate leaves children and no other descendants, the surplus is divided equally among them.
>
> Section 19-315. There is no distinction between the kindred of the whole- and the half-blood.

The problem becomes whether the abolition of the common law distinction between kindred of the whole- and half-blood enables stepchildren to inherit from stepparents. It will be observed that the statute is phrased in broad, sweeping terms and contains no limitations. It applies wherever a question arises as to relative rights of persons of the whole-blood or half-blood. The abrogation of any legal distinction between kindred of the whole- and half-blood, may arise in situations of various types. One that is analogous to that presented in the instant case is where the deceased marries a widow or divorcee with a child or children; a child or children are later born of the second marriage; the wife dies first; and then the deceased dies intestate. At common law only the children of the second marriage would have inherited from the father. The statute, however, provides that "There is no distinction between the kindred of the whole- and the half-blood." It would seem to follow that no distinction may be drawn between the children of the mother's two marriages, because the two groups of children are kindred of the half-blood to each other. The conclusion would seem to follow that they inherit equally from their mother's second husband. No reason is discernible why a different conclusion should be reached if the deceased leaves only a stepchild and had no natural child of his own.

It is argued, however, that a stepchild is not either of the whole-blood or of the half-blood of the stepparent and that the statutory provision abolishing the distinction between kindred of the whole and the half-blood, should be limited to collateral kindred. It is urged that consequently, for example, half brothers and half sisters may inherit equally with full-blood brothers and sisters from one of themselves but not from the stepparent, since the stepchildren are not of either the whole or half-blood of the stepparent, but of no blood at all as concerns the stepfather. The statute, however, contains no such limitation. It provides that there should be no distinction between kindred of the whole or half-blood. The provision is not restricted to particular types of situations. It governs whenever there arises a problem of reciprocal rights as between persons of the whole and half blood. Wherever such a situation is confronted irrespective of its form, no distinction may be made.

To confine the statute to collaterals when they inherit from each other would be too narrow a view. It would disregard the broad scope of the phraseology of the statute. It would put a more restricted interpretation on the Act of Congress than its phraseology warrants. There is no suggestion in the statute that it should be limited to distribution of decedent's property among his collateral kindred.

Counsel for the administrator relies principally on a decision of the Supreme Court of the State of Washington, In the matter of Smith's Estate, 49 Wash. 2d 229, 299 P.2d 550. That case, however, is distinguishable because it construes and applies a statute that is substantially different from the broad District of Columbia Act. The Washington statute is a limited recognition of kindred of the half-blood only in certain instances, and not for all purposes, as is true of the District of Columbia enactment. . . .

The Administrator's motion to dismiss the cross-petition is denied.

NOTES

1. The Humphrey case is noted in 35 Geo. Wash. L. Rev. 845 (1967); 51 Minn. L. Rev. 382 (1966); and 28 Montana L. Rev. 133 (1966). In all three notes the authors conclude that the case was incorrectly decided — the last note declaring that the Humphrey decision is "clearly erroneous in its legal analysis." Do you agree? Where is the "flaw" (if it be such) in Judge Holtzoff's reasoning?

2. The Humphrey case was appealed to the United States Court of Appeals. What result on appeal? Humphrey v. Tolson, 384 F.2d 987 (D.C. Cir. 1966).

6. *Advancements* [46]

If any child of the decedent wishes to share in the intestate distribution of his estate, the child must permit the administrator to include, in determining the total

[46] See Elbert, Advancements: I, 51 Mich. L. Rev. 665 (1953); Advancements: II, 52 id. 231 (1953); Advancements: III, 52 id. 535 (1954).

distributable assets, the value of any property which the decedent in his lifetime gave the child by way of *advancement*. At common law, any lifetime gift to a child was presumed to be an advancement — in effect, a prepayment — of the child's intestate share. The doctrine is based on the assumption that a parent would want an equal distribution of all his assets among his children, and that true equality can be reached only if lifetime transfers are taken into account in determining the equal shares. When a parent makes an advancement to a child and the child predeceases the parent, the amount of the advancement will be deducted from the share of such child's issue, if other children of the parent survive.

Largely because of problems of proof engendered by the doctrine (What do you do with large birthday or Christmas presents, or graduate school tuition fees expended on behalf of one child and not the other?) many states have reversed the common law presumption of advancement. In these states a lifetime gift is presumed *not* to be an advancement unless it is shown to have been intended as such. In other states, statutes declare that a gift is not an advancement unless it is declared such in a writing signed by the grantor or grantee. If the decedent leaves a will, the doctrine of advancements does not come into play even though there is a partial intestacy. (Why should this be so?)

UNIFORM PROBATE CODE §2-110: "If a person dies intestate as to all his estate, property which he gave in his lifetime to an heir is treated as an advancement against the latter's share of the estate only if declared in a contemporaneous writing by the decedent or acknowledged in writing by the heir to be an advancement. For this purpose the property advanced is valued as of the time the heir came into possession or enjoyment of the property or as of the time of death of the decedent, whichever first occurs. If the recipient of the property fails to survive the decedent, the property is not taken into account in computing the intestate share to be received by the recipient's issue, unless the declaration or acknowledgement provides otherwise."

If a gift is treated as an advancement, the donee must bring it "into hotchpot" if he wants to share in the decedent's estate. This is how hotchpot works: Assume decedent leaves no spouse, three children, and an estate worth $26,000. One child, A, received an advancement of $4000. To calculate the shares in the estate, the $4000 gift is added to the $26,000, and the total of $30,000 is divided by three. A has already received $4000 of his share; thus he receives only $6000 from his father's estate.

PROBLEMS

1. Suppose, in the example discussed above, A was given property worth $16,000 as an advancement. How would the father's $26,000 estate be distributed? Would A have to give back a portion of his $16,000?

2. F, a father, had five children: A, B, C, D and E. He died intestate leaving an

estate of $97,000. Prior to his death he gave checks of $3000 and $1000, respectively, to A and B. He wrote on A's check "present," and on B's check "birthday present." The date of the checks was not the birthday of either A or B or of F.

Fifteen years before F died, he gave his son, C, who was married and had nine children, $7000 to purchase a farm. F told C that his large brood would be better off living on a farm than in the city. Four years after the gift C sold the farm for $16,000.

Twelve years before F died, he gave his unmarried daughter, D, a farm of 80 acres valued at $11,000. D and F lived on this farm, and D kept house for her father.

Three years before F died, he gave his married daughter, E, a farm of twenty-one acres valued at $8000. At the time, E had ten children and a husband unable to work. F stated that E needed help, and that this was the reason he was giving her the farm.

All of these events take place in a jurisdiction that applies the common law doctrine of advancements, not modified by any statute. Which, if any, of the above gifts should be treated as advancements? See Miller v. Richardson, 85 S.W.2d 41 (Mo. 1935).

3. O has two children, S and D. S wants his share in O's estate paid during O's lifetime. For $25,000 S releases his interest in O's estate to O. O, a widower, then dies intestate with an estate of $80,000. Does S share in O's estate? Atkinson, Wills 727 (2d ed. 1953). Suppose that D had predeceased O without issue, and, except for S, O's closest kin are his collaterals. Does S share in O's estate? Pylant v. Burns, 153 Ga. 529, 112 S.E. 455, 28 A.L.R. 423 (1922). Suppose that D had survived O, but that S had predeceased O leaving issue. Do S's issue share in O's estate? Suppose that both D and S predecease O, and that both D and S leave issue. Do S's issue share in O's estate? 3 Restatement of Property §316 (1940).

SECTION C. Some Problems of Policy

What policies are involved in framing an intestacy statute? Do they carry out the expectations of the average decedent and of the recipients? How does one determine who is the "average decedent"?

As the above questions indicate, framing an intestacy statute to give effect to the probable intent of the decedent requires us to decide what persons who do not have wills would most likely want. Professor Dunham undertook to find this out in a study of probate court records in Cook County, Illinois.[47] Dunham hypothesized that the class of persons who make wills is the same as the class of persons who do not make wills; therefore, by examining wills, and discovering how they deviate from an intestate distribution, one can infer what persons who do not make wills

[47] Dunham, The Method, Process and Frequency of Wealth Transmission at Death, 30 U. Chi. L. Rev. 241 (1963).

want. How did the wills deviate from the distribution scheme of the intestacy statute? Where decedent was survived by a wife and children, Dunham found that in about 50 percent of the cases, largely in the smaller estates, the decedent preferred the surviving spouse to take everything. Where no children survived the decedent, the wills almost always gave the spouse everything, cutting out other heirs. Where a decedent was survived only by children, in about one-half of the cases the wills made unequal distribution among the children. Where neither spouse nor children survived decedent, in about one-half the cases the decedent left a will avoiding equality of distribution among brothers and sisters.

Professor Dunham concluded that, where a spouse survives, most testators with moderate estates, say $50,000 or less, would prefer the surviving spouse to take all. Where a spouse is not involved, Dunham concluded that the deviations from the intestacy scheme are so great and the variables so many that no pattern of preferences could be found which could be reduced to a statute.

A second study, by two sociologists and a law professor, was recently made of probate court records in Cuyahoga County (Cleveland), Ohio.[48] The study came to the same conclusion as did Dunham: the surviving spouse's intestate share is too small. Nearly 90 percent of the testators in the study gave their entire estate to the spouse when no issue or parent survived. When children and a spouse survived, 85 percent of the testators devised everything to the surviving spouse. And — here is an interesting bit of information — in 81 percent of the intestate distributions where spouse and issue survived, the issue voluntarily redistributed the property by giving the spouse all or a greater share.

In the Dunham study 42 percent of the estates that passed through probate court had a stated value of less than $10,000. Seventy-two percent had a stated value of less than $25,000. Only 6 percent had a stated value of more than $100,000. The average value of intestate estates was $7920; the average value of testate estates was $41,885. The Cleveland study reported similar figures. Persons with small estates are more likely to die intestate.

MULDER, INTESTATE SUCCESSION UNDER THE UNIFORM PROBATE CODE, 3 Prospectus 301, 321 (1970): "Under the [Uniform Probate] Code, as well as under most state intestate law, if a child of the decedent predeceases him, the child's spouse will not receive an inheritance. In the Cleveland study, Professor Sussman noted that the absence of close family members triggered gifts to spouses of those absent family members. Professor Dunham likewise recognized the tendency of testators to deviate from the Illinois intestate law by including the spouses of the children. This evidence suggests that the Code be revised to provide a share for the spouse of a deceased child provided that the spouse has not remarried. Moreover, where the issue of the decedent's children take by the right of representation, a share should not be given to both the surviving spouse of the

[48] Sussman, Cates & Smith, The Family and Inheritance (1970).

decedent's child and to the issue. Rather, the spouse should serve as a substitute for the children, taking the share her marriage partner would have taken had he survived the decedent."

SUSSMAN, CATES & SMITH, THE FAMILY AND INHERITANCE *138-139 (1970)*

Laughing Heirs

The term *laughing heir*, in the broad sense, signifies the "succession by one who is so loosely linked to his ancestor as to suffer no sense of bereavement at this loss." [49] David Cavers predicted over thirty years ago that ultimately the rules of succession would be revised to prevent these unintended windfalls.[50] Although some reformation has occurred, he was overly optimistic. Laughing heirs are still with us in the 1960's, but few obtain large windfalls. They receive the publicity because they have an aura of mystery and suggest, in addition, larceny in inheritance manipulating.

Several cases reported in a Cleveland daily newspaper indicate also that the locating of relatives may be a plum for the attorney. In one case involving a $22,000 estate, the attorney's fees were more than four times the suggested fee, and the administrator's were three times the suggested fee. In this particular case, the attorney and administrator failed to find the heirs. Two reporters found second cousins in Iowa after checking marriage records, newspaper death notices, deeds, land sales, tax records, wills, employment records, and old city directories. About six months after they were located, the cousins were able to claim their inheritance.

In another case of missing heirs, the same man acted as attorney and administrator and was awarded $7500 in fees out of a $25,000 estate for services that included a trip to Ireland to look for heirs. The reporters first checked the estate of the decedent's mother and thereby obtained a list of the decedent's siblings. Marriage records were then used. In three days, the reporters found three grandnieces.

Newspaper stories have been used for these extreme laughing-heir cases because there are relatively few such cases in which a decedent leaves no will and no known heirs. According to the newspaper, these cases average a little over a dozen within . . . [Cuyahoga County, Ohio] each year. In the majority of 23 such cases checked by the newspaper, the attorneys were paid extraordinary fees.

In other cases, professional heir hunters find the missing relatives probably through a search of public records similar to those undertaken by the reporters. These professionals usually take from one-third to one-half of the estate for their

[49] Cavers, Change in the American Family and the "Laughing Heir," 20 Iowa L. Rev. 203, 208 (1935).

[50] Ibid.

efforts.[51] A laughing heir may first be informed of his new wealth by a letter from such a tracing company.[52] One such letter read:

"We have been working on an estate matter and it appears from our investigation that you may be an heir to this estate. We should like to handle the matter for you on the following basis: in consideration of disclosing the name and location of the estate, preparing the necessary genealogical chart and obtaining necessary vital records, we are to receive an amount equal to one-third of what you recover."

There are three famous American cases in this century where hordes of fortune seekers appeared on death. These are the cases of Ella Wendel, Ida Wood, and Henrietta Garrett, all of whom died during the Great Depression.

Ella Wendel, a recluse, died in 1931, leaving a will devising most of her $40,000,000 estate to charity. The only persons who may contest a will are those persons who would take if the will is held invalid. Some 2303 fortune hunters strove to establish they were her next of kin, so that they might contest her will. Reams of evidence were fabricated, birth and death certificates altered, and tales of bastardy and incest spun. One man was sent to jail for fabricating evidence, and Surrogate Foley referred the activities of six others to the Grievance Committee of the Bar. Ultimately nine persons were established to be her cousins, and they settled out of court with the charities. Matter of Wendel, 143 Misc. 480, 257 N.Y.S. 87 (Sur. Ct. 1932); 146 Misc. 260, 262 N.Y.S. 41 (Sur. Ct. 1933); 159 Misc. 443, 287 N.Y.S. 893 (Sur. Ct. 1936).

Ida E. Mayfield Wood, the widow of a United States congressman from New York, died intestate in 1932. For more than twenty years she and her two sisters (who predeceased her) had barricaded themselves in a New York hotel room, into which no one was permitted to enter. During her life Ida had spun a web of deceit to hide who she really was. The evidence finally accepted by the court showed she had been born Ellen Walsh in Ireland, had moved with her parents to Boston, and had been her husband's mistress for ten years before he legalized her name. Once married, and propelled into high society, Ida drew a curtain across her past. She made up vague stories of having been born a Mayfield and brought up in New Orleans. Her mother, and some other members of her family, took the name Mayfield, and Ida carved "Mayfield" on their tombstones. Fearful of a depression, Ida kept $500,000 in cash tied around her waist. When she died, some 1100 persons claimed to be her next of kin — including a great many persons named Mayfield

[51] There are at least twenty-five full-time tracing firms in the United States. Allen Rankin, "Billions of Dollars Unclaimed!" Reader's Digest, May, 1964, p. 78.

[52] This approach can be used by disreputable firms as well as reputable ones. A California firm was branded by the Cleveland Better Business Bureau as a "get-rich-quick scheme." Their approach is to write to anyone named Davis or Nash or Perkins, or other common name, telling him of the existence of an unclaimed estate under the particular name and requesting the "marks" to send $4 to cover fees for the relevant documents. Cleveland Press, 10 May 1967. [This footnote has been moved by the editors from an omitted portion of the text. — Eds.]

from Louisiana. Ultimately the court established as Ida's next of kin some first cousins once removed (none of whom Ida had seen since her marriage to Wood sixty-five years before). Matter of Wood, 164 Misc. 425, 299 N.Y.S. 195 (1937). The whole fascinating story is recounted in Cox, The Recluse of Herald Square (1964).

Henrietta E. Garrett died intestate in Philadelphia in 1930, leaving an estate of over $17,000,000. Nearly 26,000 claims were filed by persons claiming to be her heirs. The testimony covered 390 volumes and over 115,000 pages. In addition, for 15 years the Attorney General of Pennsylvania vigorously contended that Henrietta died without heirs. Finally the Attorney General entered into a compromise which recognized that the three persons found by the Master to be first cousins of Henrietta were her heirs. In 1953 the Supreme Court of Pennsylvania finally ordered the Garrett estate closed. Estate of Garrett, 372 Pa. 438, 94 A.2d 357 (1953).

Escheat

The amount of property that escheats to each state each year is not insubstantial. For example, from 1966 to 1970 there escheated to the state of California:

Estates of deceased persons	$ 4,281,185
Abandoned property[53]	7,381,685
	$11,662,870[54]

The Semi-Annual Reports of the Public Administrator's Office in Los Angeles County indicate that the vast majority of escheated estates belonged to persons of very moderate means. This is not surprising. Relatives usually keep tabs on kinfolk of obvious wealth, and the heir-hunting firms do not find enough profit in finding heirs for small estates. A research assistant of one of the editors was told by employees in the Public Administrator's Office that a substantial amount of escheated property consisted of small homes in poorer areas of the city. How would you change the law to prevent escheat from falling so heavily on the poor, the ignorant, and persons psychologically afraid of making a will? Would it be a good idea to

[53] Statutes, such as the Uniform Disposition of Unclaimed Property Act, are found in most states, providing for escheats after a period of time of unclaimed bank deposits, insurance proceeds, corporate dividends, contents of safe deposit boxes and such. In State of Texas v. State of New Jersey, 379 U.S. 674 (1965), four states claimed an interest by escheat of intangible property interests held by the Sun Oil Company: the state of principal corporate activity (Texas), the state in which the corporate offices were located (Pennsylvania), the state of incorporation (New Jersey), and the state in which the last-known address of each creditor was located (Florida and Texas). Candidly recognizing "that this case could have been resolved [one of 4 ways], for the issue here is not controlled by statutory or constitutional principles . . . nor is it entirely one of logic," the Supreme Court ruled that the interests escheated to the state of last-known address of the creditor where the corporations' books showed a last-known address; otherwise to the state of incorporation. See generally, Note, Modern Rationales of Escheat, 112 U. Pa. L. Rev. 95 (1963).

[54] Annual Report of the State Controller, State of California A-63 (1967); id. at A-68 (1971).

permit death designees in deeds, checking accounts, and savings accounts — as is presently done with government bonds?

COOK, AMERICAN LAND LAW REFORM: LEGAL CO-OWNERSHIP, DOWER, AND CURTESY

1960 Duke L.J. 485, 488-490

Throughout the United States, there is a serious and growing shortage of fairly large tracts of contiguous land to which marketable title can be obtained readily and which are suitable for residential, commercial, industrial, or recreational uses. This shortage will become more acute each year as the population increases, its standard of living rises, and industry expands to meet the increasing demand for consumer goods by the people of the United States and of other countries. . . .

A substantial acreage of land between major cities or along waterfronts that not many years ago was considered of little value because vacant, unproductive, or not readily accessible, is now potentially valuable if marketable title to it can be obtained. One of the major factors that impairs the ready marketability of title to this land here too is common ownership (usually tenancy in common, or in coparceny), as well as dower and curtesy. And while co-ownership of land is certainly not the sole cause of slums and blighted vacant land, it is significant that a substantial number of such lots also are owned in common. Ira S. Robbins, Counsel, New York State Board of Housing, stated, with respect to problems in land assembly, in connection with slum clearance projects: "Surprising as it may seem, experience has shown that the failure to assemble large tracts of land by purchase alone is due as frequently to the need for clearing doubtful titles as it is to the demand of 'hold-outs' for exorbitant prices."

"The Resettlement Administration found it impossible to complete many transactions by direct purchase, for a variety of reasons, including:

"1. Cases where title is in the estate of a deceased person and the heirs either refuse, or are financially unable, to probate the estate.

"2. Cases where certain parties in interest cannot be located and the heirs of such persons are unknown. . . ."

In connection with an analysis of blighted vacant lots scattered throughout the City of Chicago, it is also significant that marketable title to many was not obtainable, owing to the virtual impossibility of locating the numerous owners and their heirs. The lots are often located in areas of new growth and are dormant "not because of the lack of demand for home sites, or because these subdivisions are undesirable for residential use, but because of diversity of ownership, etc." Thus, antiquated statutes of descent and the laws with respect to the administration of an intestate's real property have been and are a primary cause of the impractical and undesirable ownership of a single parcel of land by many persons.

5. Life Insurance, Social Security and Employee Benefits

SECTION A. Introduction

Adam Smith, like most persons similarly situated, has provided that his life insurance proceeds are to be paid outright to his wife if she survives him, otherwise to the Smith children. This plan for payment of the policy proceeds may be a sound one — or, at any rate, may be the method that Smith, having considered the alternatives, wants to employ. All too often, however, this beneficiary designation is made with little attention being given to the alternative planning arrangements that are available. Typically, the decision is made on the recommendation of a life insurance agent, and the lawyer who subsequently drafts the will gives little or no consideration to the client's life insurance coverage. Yet in terms of economic value, and of providing for his family's welfare in the event of an early death, life insurance is often the most valuable asset a man like Adam Smith owns.

Life insurance proceeds comprise a part of the assets in most estates, and are the principal asset in many estates. Integrating the disposition of insurance proceeds into the overall estate plan should be one of the major tasks of the attorney. In this chapter our primary focus is on the methods available for the settlement of life insurance proceeds. But before we consider this topic, in Section E, several related subjects merit our attention.

The attorney's role may call for more than the formulation of a plan for the client's present life insurance proceeds. It may be appropriate for the attorney also to give the client the benefit of his judgment on the effectiveness of the client's present insurance program. To this suggestion it might be objected that the role belongs to another member of the estate planning "team": the client's life insurance underwriter. The argument might run something as follows: The attorney's special competence is limited to his knowledge of the legal and tax implications of the client's estate problems, and to his ability to draft the documents needed to put the client's estate plan into operation. The attorney has no special competence in the area of life insurance or alternate investment arrangements, and this subject should be left to those who do, by training and experience, have such a special competence.

Without intending to disparage the role of the life underwriter in the planning process, it should be noted that there are two serious objections to relying solely on the underwriter as the source of recommendations on life insurance coverage. First, people do not "shop" for life insurance. About 99 percent of the persons who buy insurance buy a policy from the agent who first contacted them, based on the agent's recommendations as to the various policies issued by the one company.[1] Second, there is an inherent conflict of interest in the life insurance agent's relationship with his "client." He must sell a policy in order to earn a commission, and the higher the policy premium, the higher his commission. For this reason, an agent stands to gain more from the sale of a $10,000 policy with substantial investment features (such as an endowment or twenty-pay-life policy) than from the sale of an ordinary life policy. Similarly, the agent would much rather sell an ordinary life policy than a term policy that has no investment provisions. The particular agent may believe strongly in the value, to his client, of the savings feature of the policy he recommends, as against a less costly policy that provides the same insurance protection. But the fact remains that he stands to benefit more from the sale of such a policy. And the problem is that the client of moderate means has only so many dollars to spend for needed insurance coverage. The more he spends on investment-type policies, the less he has for purchasing true insurance coverage.

An attorney who is familiar with the various types of life insurance policies, their features and their cost, and who understands the methods commonly used to gauge insurance needs, can render a valuable service to his client by giving an informed and impartial appraisal of the client's present insurance program and of his insurance needs. These subjects are treated in Section D.

Among the factors that will affect an individual's insurance needs are the other sources of family support that will be available in the event of an early death. These include, in addition to owned assets, two programs that are taking on an increased importance in providing family protection: social security and employee benefit plans.

[1] Although all companies offer the same basic types of insurance policies, there are substantial variations in important details, most notably as to premium cost, policy interest rates, dividend rates, and cash surrender values. Best's Flitcraft Compend, a handbook that is published annually and is intended for use by insurance underwriters, gives data on policies issued by most major life insurance companies in the United States.

SECTION B. Social Security[2]

With life insurance, the amount and types of coverage, if any, a person wishes to buy, the designation of beneficiaries, and the selection of a plan for payment of the proceeds are, of course, all left to individual decision. This is not true of social security. The types and amounts of benefits under the social security program, and the manner of their payment to designated beneficiaries, are fixed by statute. The 100 million persons covered by social security[3] cannot opt out of the program; the only options they or their beneficiaries have relate to peripheral matters.[4] As a consequence, questions regarding social security benefits are not directly involved in the estate planning process. At the same time, the client (and hence his attorney) should be generally familiar with the benefits obtainable under social security. For the person who is planning for retirement, projected social security benefits are a factor to be considered in formulating an insurance/investments program. For an Adam Smith, projected "widow-with-dependent-children" survivor benefits will have a bearing on the decision as to the life insurance needed to cover the contingency of an early death.

The retirement and survivor benefits provided by social security are discussed below.[5] But first a word of caution, and then an observation. You should be warned that one of the immutable features of the social security program is that the schedule of benefits and the social security tax are subject to frequent change. For example, in 1965 all benefits under the program were increased a flat 7 percent; the "earnings base" upon which benefits and the social security tax are calculated was raised from $4800 to $6600; the age limit on dependent children entitled to benefits was raised from eighteen to twenty-two (if unmarried and a full-time student); the Medicare program was inaugurated; and the social security tax rate (the official literature calls this the "contribution rate") was increased. Two years later the Social Security Amendments of 1967 produced an additional 13 percent across-the-board increase in benefits, raised the earnings base to $7800 — and raised the "contribution rate." In 1970 benefits were again increased, this time by 15 percent. In 1971 the earnings base was increased to $9000. Thus it is safe to assume that the table of

[2] See Ball, Social Security: A Changing Program for a Changing World, 10 St. Louis U.L.J. 222 (1965).

[3] The only major groups of workers not covered by social security are railroad workers and federal civilian employees (covered by other federal retirement programs), clergymen who elect not to come under the program, and students working at schools where they regularly attend classes. Lawyers have been under the program since 1956, military personnel since 1957, and self-employed doctors since 1965.

For discussion of the various federal retirement programs see Comment, Federal Death Benefits, 5 Real Prop., Prob. & Trust J. 248 (1970).

[4] E.g., the option to take reduced retirement benefits at age sixty-two rather than age sixty-five; the optional insurance program under Medicare.

[5] In this summary, no discussion is given on two other important social security programs: benefits payable to workers who are permanently disabled, and the Medicare program.

benefits on page 175 will be out of date fairly soon. However, the basic definitions and concepts used to determine benefits (such as "earnings average" and "fully insured") have not been altered since 1951. The portion of this text note that explains the principles by which benefits are calculated should continue to apply for a number of years to come.

And now the observation. As you will soon discover, discussion of the social security program at anything more than a superficial level requires exposure to a number of narrow definitions and detailed computations. By the time you finish this note, you may feel that you've been told more about social security than you really wanted to know.[6] An effort has been made to outline the key features of this important program without getting bogged down in minutiae, but some of these minutiae must be presented if you are to have even a general understanding of the quantum of benefits obtainable under the program. If we do not succeed in giving you such a general understanding, at least we will have made a better effort than the official pamphlets promulgated by the Social Security Administration.

Retired Worker

The worker who is *fully insured* under the social security program at the time he or she reaches age sixty-five is entitled to monthly retirement benefits, the amount of which will be determined by his *earnings average* over the years in which he contributed to social security. To be fully insured, a person must have worked in employment covered by social security for a fixed number of years. For example, for a worker who reaches sixty-five, dies or becomes disabled in 1971, five years (twenty calendar quarters) are required. For a worker who reaches sixty-five, etc., in 1975, six years are required; in 1979, seven years are required.

A worker's earnings average is calculated by taking his *earnings base* against which the social security tax was levied in each year after 1950, subtracting the five lowest years, and then finding the arithmetic average of earnings for the remaining years. For a person attaining his twenty-first birthday after 1950, the first year counted is the calendar year in which he reached age twenty-two. The maximum earnings base has been increased a number of times: from $3600 in 1951-1954, to $4200 in 1955-1958, to $4800 in 1959-1965, to $6600 in 1966-1967, to $7800 in 1968-1971, and to $9000 beginning in 1972. This means that only persons who have entered the work force in the past few years will have been taxed at the higher earnings base and can expect to receive the benefits listed under the $7800 column in the table on page 175. For persons who have been employed since before 1960, the low earnings base applicable in their earlier years of employment will reduce their earnings average even though their five low years can be excluded.

Example: A, who is fully insured, retired upon attaining his sixty-fifth birthday

[6] You may be disposed to agree with Sam Weller: "Vether it's worth goin' through so much to learn so little, as the charity-boy said ven he got to the end of the alphabet, is a matter o' taste." — Dickens, Pickwick Papers, c. 27.

on December 30, 1971. In every year since 1950, A's salary exceeded the maximum earnings base for social security purposes. As a consequence, the social security tax paid by A and his employer was on the maximum allowable earnings in each year.

1951:	$3600	1961:	$4800
1952:	3600	1962:	4800
1953:	3600	1963:	4800
1954:	3600	1964:	4800
1955:	4200	1965:	4800
1956:	4200	1966:	6600
1957:	4200	1967:	6600
1958:	4200	1968:	7800
1959:	4800	1969:	7800
1960:	4800	1970:	7800
		1971:	7800

In calculating A's earnings average, the low five years (1951-1955) are dropped; the earnings average for the remaining years is $5667. Extrapolating from the table on page 175, A is entitled to a retirement benefit of approximately $214 per month. This retirement benefit, as with all other social security benefits, is not subject to income taxation.[7]

A worker may elect to receive retirement benefits at age sixty-two (or sixty-three or sixty-four). If such an election is made, the monthly benefit is permanently reduced: at sixty-two, to 80 percent of the benefit at age sixty-five; at sixty-three, 86.6 percent; at sixty-four, 93.3 percent. But this is not the only factor that reduces benefits for the worker who retires early. His earnings average is still computed to age sixty-five, with "zero earnings" credited for each year of early retirement. The effect is that only two (or three or four) early years of low earnings can be excluded instead of the usual five. In addition, he will not get the benefit of the three "high" years he would have had if he were to work to age sixty-five. If, in the example above, A had retired on his sixty-second birthday in 1968, he would not have received credit for three years at $7800, and he could exclude only two low years: 1951 and 1952. A's earnings average would be $4910. Since the retirement-at-sixty-five benefit for this average is approximately $193, A would be entitled to 80 percent of this amount, or $154 per month.

If a worker does not retire at sixty-five, his earnings continue to be subject to the social security tax. These earnings can be substituted for earnings earlier in his career, when the maximum earnings base was lower. For example, if A were to continue working until his seventieth birthday in 1976, and if his salary exceeded $9000 in each year, he could substitute an additional five years at $9000 for the lower earnings in 1956-1960. His earnings average would be $7090, and his monthly benefit would be $253.

Monthly benefits are also payable to the spouse of a retired worker. If she is sixty-five at the time her husband begins to draw monthly benefits or if (being

[7] I.T. 3447, 1941-1 Cum. Bull. 191.

younger) she waits until she reaches sixty-five before claiming benefits, she is entitled to a monthly benefit of one-half the "primary insurance benefit" (hereafter, p.i.) of her husband. Referring once again to the example above, if A's wife were sixty-five years old at the time A retired in 1971 and began drawing benefits, she would be entitled to a monthly benefit of one-half p.i., or $107 per month, making a total payment to the couple of $321 per month.

A retired woman worker who is fully insured as a result of her own earnings is entitled to retirement benefits in her own right. In this situation the married woman is entitled to the higher of (1) the one-half p.i. of her husband, or (2) her benefit as a retired worker, calculated in the usual manner.

Retirement Benefits for Widow of Insured Worker

If a fully insured worker dies before or after retirement, his widow is entitled to a monthly benefit of .82½ p.i. upon attaining age sixty-two or, if she elects, a reduced benefit beginning at age sixty. For example, if a fully insured worker dies survived by his fifty-two-year-old wife, and if the worker's earnings average was $6600, his widow will be entitled to a monthly benefit of $198.30 beginning at age sixty-two or, if she elects, a monthly benefit of $171.90 beginning at age sixty. (See table at page 175.)

Lump-Sum Death Benefit

Upon the death of a fully insured worker, a lump-sum death payment of $255 is made to his surviving spouse. If there is no surviving spouse, the death benefit goes toward defraying the worker's burial expenses. This sum is not subject to federal estate or state inheritance taxation.[8]

Survivor Benefits for Widow or Widower with Dependent Children

Prior to the Social Security Amendments of 1965, a widow under age sixty-two was entitled to monthly benefits if she had dependent children under age eighteen. Under the 1965 amendments, benefits to the widow still terminate when her youngest child reaches eighteen, but benefits to a child of a deceased worker can continue until the child reaches age twenty-two, provided he is unmarried and a full-time student. If a woman dies survived by her husband and children under age eighteen (or twenty-two), survivor benefits are payable to the children (but not the husband) if the mother was either "fully insured" or "currently insured" as described below.

Based on an earnings average of $5400, a widow with dependent children will receive monthly payments of $313.20 (¾ p.i. for the widow and ¾ p.i. for the child) if she has one dependent child under age eighteen, and $389.90 (an additional ¾ p.i. — but limited by a "maximum family payment" provision) if she has two or more dependent children under age eighteen. If the widow remarries or dies, the ¾ p.i.

[8] Rev. Rul. 67-277, 1967-2 Cum. Bull. 322.

benefit to her terminates, but all unmarried children under age twenty-two remain eligible for benefits. In examining the table on page 175, you will note that the survivor benefits listed under the right-hand columns are quite substantial. Once again, however, these benefits will be available only to the families of workers who do not have a number of early "low years" that reduce the earnings average.

As explained earlier, a worker is fully insured if he has credit for a certain number of years of covered employment. What happens if a person dies before he has been on the work force for the required number of years? The answer is that his family will still probably be eligible for survivor benefits, for one of two reasons. First, Congress has provided a more liberal (and more complicated) method for determining, in this situation, whether the worker was fully insured. Second, family benefits to a widow with dependent children are payable if the worker, although not fully insured, was "currently insured": He must have had at least six quarters of covered employment within the three years before his death.

How substantial are the survivor benefits provided by social security? The answer is that they are quite substantial — particularly for a person born after 1945, since the likelihood is that the wages used to compute his earnings average will be at the higher maximums permitted in recent years. Consider this example. B was born in January, 1945, and died in January, 1972, survived by his wife and two small children. In 1970 and 1971 B's annual salary exceeded the $7800 minimum for social security purposes. However, in the preceding three years B was a full-time graduate student, and earned wages only during the summer months. He earned $250 per month in June, July and August of each of those years.

Note first that B was "currently insured," since he had ten calendar quarters of covered work in the three years before his death. The amount of the monthly benefit payable to B's widow is determined by his earnings average.

1967:[9]	$750
1968:	750
1969:	750
1970:	7800
1971:	7800

In calculating B's earnings average, the low five years are dropped — provided that the resulting average is based on a minimum of two years. In this case the average is computed by using the two years in which B had the highest wages: 1970 and 1971. B's earnings average, then, is $7800. B's widow will be entitled to a monthly benefit of $482.70 until the oldest child attains age eighteen, and $413.80 until the youngest child attains age eighteen. In addition, the children will be entitled to benefits until age twenty-two, if they are unmarried and full-time students.

Had B lived for two more years, and if his annual salary for those years had exceeded $9000, his earnings average would be $9000, and the initial monthly

[9] For a person attaining his twenty-first birthday after 1950, in computing his earnings average, the first year counted is the calendar year in which he reached age twenty-two.

benefit to his widow would be $535. On the other hand, had B died in January, 1971, his earnings average would be $4275, and the initial monthly benefit to his widow would be approximately $310.

The survivor benefits payable under social security have several important implications in terms of estate planning for the young family man. The dollar amount of the benefits available under the program should be considered in assessing the individual's insurance needs, and also in selecting a plan for settlement of the insurance proceeds. If he should die survived by his wife and young children, the substantial benefits payable to his family (all tax-free), together with other sources of income (typically, benefits under his employer's retirement program and the income from insurance proceeds or other assets) should reduce the need to consume principal (e.g., the life insurance proceeds) until college expenses are faced. Moreover, since benefits may be payable to dependent children until age twenty-two, and the wife will be eligible for widow's benefits at age sixty, in many cases there will be only a few years in which no social security benefits are received.

Financing the Social Security Program

Increases in the social security tax come at least as often as do increases in benefits. Moreover, adjustments in the "contribution rate" are usually accompanied by an increase in the earnings base against which the tax is applied. Under the current law, the rates are programmed at 5.2 percent in 1972, 5.65 percent in 1973-1975, 5.85 percent in 1976-1979, 5.95 percent in 1980-1986, and 6.05 percent there-

Examples of Monthly Cash Payments

Average yearly earnings after 1950	*$923 or less*	*$1,800*	*$3,000*	*$4,200*	*$5,400*	*$6,600*	*$7,800**
Retired worker – 65 or older Disabled worker – under 65	70.40	111.90	145.60	177.70	208.80	240.30	275.80
Wife 65 or older	35.20	56.00	72.80	88.90	104.40	120.20	137.90
Retired worker at 62	56.40	89.60	116.50	142.20	167.10	192.30	220.70
Wife at 62, no child	26.40	42.00	54.60	66.70	78.30	90.20	103.50
Widow at 60	61.10	80.10	104.20	127.20	149.40	171.90	197.30
Widow or widower at 62	70.40	92.40	120.20	146.70	172.30	198.30	227.60
Disabled widow at 50	42.80	56.10	72.90	89.00	104.50	120.30	138.00
Wife under 65 and one child	35.20	56.00	77.10	131.20	181.10	194.90	206.90
Widowed mother and one child	105.60	167.90	218.40	266.60	313.20	360.60	413.80
Widowed mother and two children	105.60	167.90	222.70	308.90	389.90	435.20	482.70
One child of retired or disabled worker	35.20	56.00	72.80	88.90	104.40	120.20	137.90
One surviving child	70.40	84.00	109.20	133.30	156.60	180.30	206.90
Maximum family payment	105.60	167.90	222.70	308.90	389.90	435.20	482.70

*Revised table showing payments for $9,000 earnings average not available at time of publication.

after. The contribution donated by the employee is matched by an equal contribution by his employer. Thus for a worker earning more than $9000 in 1972, his social security tax for the year was $460; his employer also paid $460.

Social security benefits are the same for self-employed persons as for employees, but their tax rates differ. The tax for self-employed persons is 7.5 percent on net earnings (up to $9000) in 1972, 7.65 in 1973-1975, and increases (at the same intervals as for employees) to 7.9 percent in 1987 and thereafter.

PROBLEM

Assume that Adam Smith was born on July 12, 1936. Smith recently obtained a report from the Social Security Administration showing the earnings credited to his social security account in past years. This report showed low earnings for the years 1957 through 1962, reflecting Smith's earnings from summer jobs and while working part-time in college and graduate school.

1957:	$519
1958:	421
1959:	628
1960:	1025
1961:	910
1962:	2855

Smith began working full-time in the fall of 1962. Since that time his annual salary has exceeded the maximum earnings base allowable for social security purposes. If Smith were to die in January of next year, survived by his wife and three young children, what is the amount of the monthly survivor benefit to which Smith would be entitled?

SECTION C. Employee Benefit Plans

Employee benefit plans take a variety of shapes and forms. Several arrangements, most notably stock option plans, stock purchase agreements and deferred compensation agreements, are geared for high-level employees, not the toiling masses. These plans are used to provide capital gains incentives and deferred compensation (and thus deferred taxation) to corporate executives and key employees. Because of the specialized and complex features of these arrangements, their study is beyond the scope of this course.[10]

In this section our focus is on employee pension and profit-sharing plans,[11]

[10] See Havighurst, Deferred Compensation Plans for Key Employees: A Guide for Small Businessmen and Lawyers (1964); Rustigan, A Deferred Income Plan for the Corporate Executive, 54 A.B.A.J. 506 (1968).

[11] See Rothman, Establishing and Administering Pension and Profit Sharing Plans and

which are invariably open to all or most of a firm's employees. A *pension plan* is a plan established and maintained by an employer to provide for the payment of benefits over a period of years, usually for life, after retirement. Contributions to the plan by the employer (and, under some plans, the employee) are on a fixed schedule, typically geared to the employee's salary. Retirement benefits are determined by a formula based on such factors as years of service and average annual salary of the employee. Neither the employer's contributions nor benefits payable under the plan are dependent upon the firm's profits. Pension plans are *noncontributory* if only the employer contributes to the plan, and *contributory* if the employee is permitted or required also to make contributions. A *profit-sharing plan* provides for employees' participation in the employer's profits. The employer's contributions to the plan are pegged at a fixed percentage of the firm's profits in any year. Contributions are credited to each employee's account according to a predetermined formula; as with pension plans, the employee's share is typically determined by his years of service and salary level. Most profit-sharing plans are noncontributory.

The past three decades have seen a rapid growth, in both numbers and size, of employee pension and profit-sharing plans. In 1940, 5.5 million employees were enrolled in private, state and local government plans whose combined assets totalled \$4 billion.[12] In 1966, 38.6 million workers participated in such plans; assets totalled \$139.5 billion, or nearly fifteen percent of the slightly more than \$1 trillion in assets held by all institutional investors in the United States.[13] The majority of these plans are "trusteed"; that is, a corporate fiduciary manages the fund. In 1967 the five largest banks in New York City were managing pension and profit-sharing funds totalling \$29.3 billion. One bank alone (Morgan Guaranty Trust) holds \$10 billion in pension funds.[14] A substantial number of plans (in 1968, there were 168,000 plans covering 9.1 million persons) are administered by life insurance companies. In 1968 life insurance companies held \$34.9 billion in reserves under these plans.[15]

Viewed from one perspective, this concentration of wealth in the hands of fiduciaries raises significant questions as to the manner in which the resulting eco-

---

Trust Funds (1967); Symposium, Pension Plans: Current Problems, 1967 U. Ill. L.F. 691; 1968 id. 1.

Recent legislation has authorized retirement plans for the self-employed, which are designed to afford doctors, lawyers and other professionals the deferred compensation tax benefits of "qualified" employee retirement plans. See Taylor, Retirement Plans for Self-Employed — A Look at H.R. 10 as Amended, 34 Tenn. L. Rev. 632 (1967).

In this section, no discussion is given to two other significant employee benefits: disability insurance plans and health and accident insurance. While these are an important part of the family financial picture, they have no direct bearing on estate planning.

[12] Norman, Private Pensions: A Study of Vesting, Funding, and Integration, 21 U. Fla. L. Rev. 141, 144-145 (1968).

[13] H.R. Committee of Banking and Currency, Subcommittee on Domestic Finance, Commercial Banks and Their Trust Activities: Emerging Influence on the American Economy, 90th Cong., 2d Sess. 1 (1968).

[14] Id. at 35.

[15] Life Insurance Fact Book 39 (1969).

nomic power is exercised.[16] Viewed from the perspective with which we are immediately concerned, these data graphically demonstrate that employee benefit plans are a major source of retirement and family protection benefits.

An important reason for the growth of these deferred compensation arrangements is the favorable income tax and estate tax treatment accorded *qualified* plans. To be qualified, a plan must meet the detailed and technical requirements of §401 of the Internal Revenue Code of 1954. The major requirements are that the plan must be based upon a definite, permanent, written program that is communicated to the employees; it must be adequately funded; it must be maintained for the exclusive benefit of the employees and their beneficiaries; it must not discriminate in favor of officers, shareholders, supervisors or highly paid employees; and it must not be a subterfuge for the distribution of profits to shareholders.[17] If the plan meets these requirements, the following income tax and estate tax benefits will result:

(1) The employer's contributions to the plan are deductible from ordinary income for income tax purposes. Thus if the corporation's income is taxed in the 47 percent bracket, each dollar contributed to the plan "costs" the firm only fifty-three cents.

(2) The employer's contributions are not taxed as income to the employee in the year in which the contributions are made. The income taxation of these amounts is deferred until the benefits are distributed or made available to the employee or his survivors. When the benefits are not distributed until retirement, the result typically will be a lower tax or no tax at all: first, because the retired employee ordinarily will have less taxable income, meaning that the benefits will be taxed at lower rates; second, because the employee will have a second "over sixty-five" $750 personal exemption (and possibly also his spouse's $1500 in exemptions). Even if his other income is such that there turns out to be no reduction in the amount of the tax on these contributions, he will have benefitted from the tax deferral under the principle that "a tax dollar not paid today is a tax dollar not paid today."

Under a contributory plan, this tax deferral benefit does not apply to the employee's contributions unless the employer is a public school or some charitable organization.[18] Except for this one group of taxpayers, employees' contributions to a qualified contributory plan are paid out of after-tax dollars.

(3) The income earned from both the employer's and the employee's contributions (commonly referred to as the "build-up") is not subject to income taxation until benefits are distributed or made available to the employee.

[16] See page 41, supra; see also Lynn, Foreman & Wehr, The New Inheritance: Employee Benefit Plans as a Wealth Distribution Device, 11 Stan. L. Rev. 242 (1959); Lynn, Legal and Economic Implications of the Emergence of Quasi-Public Wealth, 65 Yale L.J. 786 (1956).

[17] See Comment, Qualification of Pension and Profit-Sharing Plans, 39 U. Cin. L. Rev. 726 (1970).

[18] Employees of charitable organizations exempt from taxation under Int. Rev. Code of 1954, §501 can enter into "salary reduction" agreements with their employers, and thereby obtain the same deferred income taxation benefits for their own contributions as for their employer's contributions. Treas. Reg. §1.403(b)-1(b)(3) (1971).

(4) Death benefits attributable to the employer's contributions are not subject to estate taxation if the benefits are payable to someone other than the employee's executor or his estate.

(5) Death benefits in an amount up to $5000 are exempt from income taxation, and amounts in excess of $5000 may qualify for capital gains treatment.

Under a *non-qualified* employee benefit plan (that is, one that fails to meet the requirements of §401), if the employer makes contributions to the plan these are taxed as income to the employee in the year in which the contributions are made. This is true even though the employee has no right to withdraw the funds or receive benefits until retirement: The employee is deemed to be in "constructive receipt" of the employer's contributions each year. Moreover, the employer is not entitled to an income tax deduction for its contributions to a non-qualified plan unless the employees' rights under the plan are "nonforfeitable" at the time the contributions are made. That is, an employee must have an indefeasible right to the retirement benefits provided by the contribution even if, for example, he is later fired. Finally, all death benefits paid under a non-qualified plan are subject to estate taxation in the employee's estate.

PROBLEM

Since an employee's contributions to a non-qualified plan may not be deductible for income tax purposes, why would any employer want to establish such a plan? Despite the seeming tax disadvantages, non-qualified plans are widely used. Wherein lies the explanation?

(First clue: What class of employers might be unconcerned about the loss of an income tax deduction for its contributions to a funded plan?)

(Second clue: Reread the requirements for a qualified plan; and see Hancock, Planning and Drafting Nonqualified Deferred Compensation Arrangements, 19 Case W. Res. L. Rev. 921 (1968).)

Income Taxation of Retirement Benefits

The relevance of employee benefits to the estate planning decision will turn on the age and circumstances of the client. If he is nearing retirement age his primary concern is, of course, with the retirement benefits under the plan and their tax treatment. The client must select one of the optional methods of payment authorized by the plan. Typically, these include a straight life annuity, a joint and survivor annuity, and an annuity-plus-years-certain plan under which fixed monthly payments are made for the annuitant's life or (e.g.) ten years, whichever period is longer.

If the benefits are paid under a qualified noncontributory plan, the full amount of the benefits will be taxed as income to the retired employee in the years in which they are received by him. If the payments are under a qualified contributory plan, the amount of the benefits over and above the employee's contributions will be taxed. This is the consequence of the tax deferral feature of a qualified plan, which permits postponement of the income tax on the employer's contributions, and on the "build-up" from both the employer's and the employee's contributions, until benefits are distributed at retirement. Under a contributory plan, the amount of each payment that represents a return of the employee's contributions (computed on a proportional basis with respect to each payment) is not taxed; these were already taxed to the employee at the time the contributions were made.

Some plans give the retired employee a further option of receiving a lump-sum payment of all the funds in his account. Since the entire sum (in excess of the employee's contributions) will be taxed as income in the year in which it is received, before this option is selected the client should determine whether any portion of the payment is eligible for capital gains treatment under §402(a)(2) or §403(a)(2) of the Internal Revenue Code of 1954, as amended by the Tax Reform Act of 1969.

In short, a number of important decisions and complex tax questions are faced — if the client is nearing retirement age. But for Adam Smith retirement is a long way off. His immediate concern is with the death benefits that will be available to his family if he should die before retirement. This means that we can postpone a more detailed study of the income tax treatment of retirement benefits and annuities to another day.[19]

Adam Smith's Pension Plan

Adam Smith's pension plan with the Tresco Machine Tool Company is fairly representative. It is a qualified, contributory plan under which Smith contributes 4 percent of his annual salary and Tresco contributes 8 percent. At Smith's present salary of $17,000, Smith contributes $680 per year via payroll deductions and the company contributes $1360. While this is a fairly hefty contribution on Smith's part and the amount is not deductible for income tax purposes, Smith sees this as a desirable forced savings program, and the aggregate contributions will ultimately provide substantial retirement benefits. Upon retirement at age sixty-five, Smith will be entitled to an annuity calculated under the following formula:

$$(\text{yrs. service}) \times (1\tfrac{1}{2}\%) \times (\text{average salary}) = \text{annuity}$$

Smith began working at Tresco six years ago, when he was thirty years old. His initial salary was $10,000. Smith's salary is likely to increase over the years, but those

[19] More pointedly, we can transfer that responsibility to another instructor in another course.

You should be grateful. If you don't believe us, try reading Int. Rev. Code of 1954 §72, taxing annuities and retirement benefits. Be sure to read all the way from §72(a) to §72(o), nine pages later. If you have any questions after reading the statute, read the thirty-two pages of crystal-clear regulations beginning at Treas. Reg. §1.72-1(a).

low early years will tend to keep his average salary down. Under this formula, if Smith works at Tresco until retirement at age sixty-five and his average salary over the years is \$18,000, he will retire with an annuity of

$$35 \times 1\tfrac{1}{2}\% \times \$18{,}000 = \$9450$$ [20]

The Tresco plan permits retirement at age fifty-five with thirty years' service, or retirement at age sixty with twenty years' service. If an early retirement option is selected, the annuity benefits are reduced by a factor that takes into account the longer life expectancy of the annuitant.

A Tresco employee's rights under the plan do not "vest" or become "nonforfeitable" (the terms are used interchangeably) until he has been employed for ten years. This means that if Smith were to terminate his employment at Tresco before ten years have elapsed, he would lose his right to all benefits under the plan represented by Tresco's contributions. (He would, however, be given a refund of his contributions, together with interest at 3 percent.) But once Smith has been on the job for ten years, if he should later sever his employment he will still be entitled to benefits at retirement, based upon Tresco's and his contributions to the plan prior to the severance date.

The Tresco pension plan does not provide any death benefits as such. Upon Smith's death before retirement, his designated beneficiary would receive a lump-sum payment of Smith's contributions to date, with interest compounded at 3 percent annually. In the six years Smith has contributed to the plan, this amount has grown to \$4200. To indicate the rate of growth of this fund, if Smith's annual salary stays at \$17,000, in six years (when Smith attains age forty-two) his accumulated contributions will total about \$8600.

In not providing greater death benefits, the Tresco pension plan is quite representative. One of the requirements for a qualified pension plan is that any death benefits payable under the plan must be "incidental" to its retirement features. While some pension plans provide death benefits that are measured in part by the employer's contributions, this is not a common feature. The "refund of contributions" feature of the Tresco plan is the typical death benefit found in contributory pension plans. In noncontributory plans, the death benefit may be a modest lump-sum payment (e.g., six months' salary, or \$5000, or \$1000), or a monthly payment to the surviving spouse or children (e.g., \$100 per month for each month the deceased worker was employed), or there may be no death benefit at all. Because of the "incidental" death benefit requirement Tresco, like most employers, has a separate fringe benefit program that provides death benefits. Each employee is covered by a group term life insurance policy whose premiums are paid by Tresco. The

[20] This annuity is guaranteed under the pension plan. The annuity will be higher if the pension fund enjoys a more favorable earnings experience than has been projected.

The amount indicated is for a straight annuity. A joint-and-survivor or years-certain annuity would pay smaller benefits.

amount of insurance provided by the policy is determined by the employee's salary level.

Profit-sharing plans, on the other hand, ordinarily do provide substantial death benefits. Under most profit-sharing plans, on an employee's death the amount in his account under the plan, together with accumulated earnings, is payable to his survivors, either in a lump sum or under an annuity arrangement.

Federal Estate Tax and Income Tax Treatment of Employee Death Benefits[21]

When death benefits are paid under a qualified pension or profit-sharing plan, the amount of the benefits attributable to the employer's contributions is not subject to estate taxation unless the proceeds are payable to the employee's executor or estate.[22] This exemption from the estate tax applies only to the employer's contributions and the build-up attributed to those contributions, and only if the plan is a qualified plan. Insofar as the payment represents the employee's contributions and the build-up thereon (computed on a straight pro rata basis), it will be taxed in his estate. All benefits paid under a non-qualified plan are subject to estate taxation regardless of the source of contributions.

Qualified pension and profit-sharing benefits over and above the employee's contributions are taxed as income to the employee when they are distributed to him at retirement. If the employee dies before retirement and death benefits are paid to his survivors, this incipient income tax liability does not disappear. The benefits are taxable as income to the survivors. Congress has eased this potential income tax burden by granting a $5000 exclusion for benefits paid by reason of the death of an employee.[23] If the death benefits are paid in a lump sum, a straight $5000 exclusion is permitted. If they are paid in installments (typically, under an annuity), the $5000 exclusion is spread out over the years in which the payments are to be made. Prior to 1970 a second income tax break was given to lump-sum payments. If death benefits were paid in a lump sum within one year of the employee's death, they were taxed as capital gains rather than at ordinary income rates. This rule was changed by the Tax Reform Act of 1969:[24] Lump-sum distributions allocable to contributions made before December 31, 1969, still qualify for capital gains treatment, but distributions allocable to contributions made after that date are taxed as ordinary income.

This income tax liability applies only to death benefits attributable to the employer's contributions and the build-up under a *qualified* plan. To the extent that the death benefits represent a return of the employee's contributions, or of the employer's contributions under a non-qualified plan, these will already have been

[21] For discussion of estate planning guidelines applicable to employee death benefits, see Rothman, Establishing and Administering Pension and Profit Sharing Plans and Trust Funds 73-104 (1967).

[22] Int. Rev. Code of 1954, §2039(c).

[23] Id. §101(b).

[24] Id. §§402(a)(5), 403(a)(2).

taxed as income to the employee during his lifetime;[25] they are not again taxed as income at his death.

Example: By reason of H's death, his wife (W) is entitled to death benefits under H's employer's qualified pension plan. The plan was contributory: H contributed 4 percent of his annual salary to the pension fund, and his employer contributed 6 percent. Over the years, H contributed \$15,300 to the plan. W has selected an option under which she will receive an annuity of \$250 per month for life. W is fifty-three years old at the time she begins receiving annuity payments. In determining the income tax consequences to W, the first step is to determine the "exclusion ratio": that portion of each annuity payment that is to be treated as a tax-free return of H's contributions. According to the tables prescribed for use for this purpose, the overall return that will be produced by a \$3000 annuity for a fifty-three-year-old woman who lives out her life expectancy is 27.1 times the annual payment. Treas. Reg. §1.72-9, Table I. Thus the expected return is 27.1 × \$3000, or \$81,300. Of this, \$15,300 (roughly 20 percent) is treated as the return of H's contributions.

W is also entitled to a \$5000 exclusion. For the purposes of this income tax computation, the \$5000 exclusion is treated in the same manner as the employee's contributions. Thus the "exclusion ratio" is:

$$\frac{\$15{,}300 + \$5000}{\$81{,}300} = .25$$

This exclusion ratio is applied to each annuity payment. As a consequence, one-fourth of each monthly payment, or \$750 per year, is excludable from W's gross income. The remaining \$2250 is taxed as income to her. As with the income taxation of annuities generally, this \$750 exclusion will apply to each annual payment whether W dies in five years or lives to age 100. If the former happens, W never will have received the full deduction for H's contributions or the full benefit of the \$5000 exclusion. If the latter happens, the taxpayer gets a break.

It will be recalled that because of the modest death benefits payable under the Tresco pension plan, the company has another fringe benefit program that provides each employee with group term insurance coverage. Although all of the life insurance premiums are paid by Tresco, the life insurance proceeds are *not* given the same tax treatment as death benefits under a qualified pension or profit-sharing plan. In fact, their tax treatment is just the opposite. The insurance proceeds are not taxed as income to the deceased employee or his beneficiary,[26] but they are subject to estate taxation in the estate of the employee.[27]

[25] Unless the employer is an educational institution or other charitable organization, and the employee has entered into a salary reduction agreement under a qualified plan. See footnote 18, supra.

[26] Int. Rev. Code of 1954, §101(a); Treas. Reg. §1.101-1 (1964).

[27] The estate tax treatment of life insurance proceeds is discussed in greater detail in Chapter 6.

PROBLEMS

1. Edward Elder, a resident of a common law state, died several months ago. He was survived by his fifty-year-old wife and three college-age children. By reason of Elder's death employee death benefits totalling $36,000 are payable to Mrs. Elder. These represent the aggregate employer's and employee's contributions to the Hemp Manufacturing Company's qualified pension plan, plus accumulated earnings on those contributions. Under the plan, Elder contributed 3 percent of his annual salary and his employer contributed 9 percent. In the twenty years in which he was employed at Hemp, Elder contributed a total of $8000 to the plan. What portion of the pension plan benefits is includible in Elder's gross estate for federal estate tax purposes?

2. Would the answer to Problem 1 be different if Elder's will named his wife executrix of his estate?

3. Under the Hemp pension plan, Mrs. Elder has the option of (1) receiving the entire $36,000 fund in a lump-sum payment, or (2) receiving a ten-years-certain annuity that will pay $175 per month for life or for ten years, whichever period is longer. Before Mrs. Elder selects one of these options, she wants to be apprised of the income tax treatment of each of these methods of payment. Advise her.

4. Assume that Adam Smith dies at age forty-two, and that by reason of his death Mrs. Smith is paid $8600 as a lump-sum death benefit under the Tresco pension plan. What are the income tax and estate tax consequences of this payment?

5. In what way, if any, will the benefits payable under the Tresco pension plan have a bearing on the formulation of an estate plan for Adam Smith?

SECTION D. Life Insurance: How Much and What Kinds?

1. *Life Insurance as a Funding Device*

A, B and C are the principal officers and only shareholders of a small corporation. As a group, they are concerned about the effect of the death of any one of them upon the management and operation of the business. None of them has children with the background or interest that would enable the children to take their father's place in the business. They have agreed that upon the death of either of them the survivors should succeed to management of the corporation. As individuals, each is concerned that if he is the first to die, his wife and children should be suitably provided for out of his interest in the corporation, which is his principal asset. An outright bequest of the stock to his wife or children would not suffice. The corporation has never paid dividends; instead, its earnings have always been distributed to A, B and C in the form of salaries. Taking A as an example, if his widow were to succeed to his 33-percent ownership interest, she would not be entitled to any salary, and her minority interest would not give her sufficient leverage to demand dividend distributions. If the stock produced no income, she would want to sell the shares — but to whom? Third persons would not likely want to buy a minority interest in the corporation, and Mrs. A would have little bargaining power if she wanted to sell her shares to the surviving owners. Furthermore, neither B nor C would have the cash with which to purchase her shares.

This frequently encountered business planning problem is typically resolved through the use of a buy-sell agreement under which the survivors (or the corporation) will purchase the shares of the deceased shareholder at a price fixed by some formula. Since the survivors (or the corporation) rarely would have the liquid assets needed to purchase the shares, life insurance is often the only available source of funding the buy-sell agreement.[28]

2. *Life Insurance as a Source of Liquid Funds*

D's net worth is close to a million dollars. However, little of this wealth is represented by liquid assets, such as securities listed on a stock exchange, government bonds, or money in the bank. Instead, D's wealth is primarily represented by his sole proprietorship business interest (or stock in a closely held corporation, or farm lands, or real estate being held for development purposes). On D's death his estate will be faced with a number of obligations, primarily personal loans, federal estate and state inheritance taxes, and the expenses of administering his estate. None of D's assets are readily salable, and a forced liquidation to meet these post-death obligations might prove disastrous to his family. D could solve this potential liquidity problem by buying enough life insurance to enable his executor to meet these obligations without the need for selling any of the other assets.

3. *Life Insurance as an Investment*[29]

E's salary and other income put him in the 55-percent income tax bracket. He is concerned about what he sees as an imbalance in his investment program: Most of his investments are in speculative ventures and "growth" common stocks. He wants diversification by investing in a secure, fixed dollar asset that will provide reasonable capital appreciation. He also wants to provide his family with a source of liquid funds on his death. E purchases a $25,000 Metropolitan Life Insurance Company endowment policy that will "endow" (that is, pay the face amount) at age sixty-five. E is forty-five years old at the time he takes out the policy; the annual premium is $1305 (less dividends). A portion of each premium goes toward purchasing pure insurance, so that the face amount of the policy will be paid to E's beneficiary if he should die before age sixty-five. The balance of each premium goes

[28] See Wojta, Life Insurance Funding of Stock Purchase Agreements, 48 Neb. L. Rev. 961 (1969).

[29] See Lucas, Life Insurance as a Personal Savings Vehicle, 48 Neb. L. Rev. 877 (1969).

toward building a cash surrender value — the investment portion of the policy. In five years, the cash surrender value will be $4300; in ten years, $10,400; in twenty years, $25,000.

All types of life insurance policies except term insurance have an investment feature. For an annual premium of $795 (less dividends), E could purchase a $25,000 "ordinary" life insurance policy from Metropolitan. In ten years, the cash surrender value under this policy would be $5500; in twenty years, $11,600.

Adam Smith does not fit into any of the above categories. Like most persons who buy life insurance, his concern is to provide for his family's welfare if they should be deprived of his earning power by an early death. While Smith has not given the subject much thought, he has a general notion that his social security and employee benefits, together with the modest investments he has accumulated, would not make adequate provision for his family. Smith has already demonstrated his awareness that he needs some insurance. On several occasions in the past, life insurance agents have persuaded him that he should purchase policies with an aggregate face value of $47,000. (See page 75.) When asked if he thought he had enough insurance, and the right kinds of policies, Smith replied, "I really can't say. I think it's enough. This is the figure we came up with when a Metropolitan Life agent ran an Electronic Family Security Check-Up[30] on me six years ago."

4. *Glossary of Life Insurance Policies and Policy Features*

There is a remarkable variety of life insurance policies available to the buying public. Moreover, there is an astonishing number of different features to be found in policies of the same general type. It is safe to say that except for term insurance, no two policies issued by different insurance companies are exactly alike. This makes price comparisons difficult, at best. Take the sophisticated buyer — the exception — who has compared the rates for $10,000 ordinary life insurance policies issued by company X and company Y. He points out to X's agent that he can obtain the same amount of insurance from company Y for a premium that is lower by $10 per year. The response: "Yes, but our policy endows at age ninety, while theirs endows at age 100. This means that the cash surrender value builds up at a faster rate." Or, "Yes, but our dividend experience has been much better than theirs in the past ten years" (pulling out chart). "Over the years you'll pay less." Or, "Yes, but we include a disability waiver of premium rider at no extra cost." Or, "Yes, but our policy pays double if you should die while participating in or watching a polo match."

[30] "This service is available at any local Metropolitan Life office. Using U.S. Dep't of Labor statistics, a computerized read-out compares the prospect's projected estimated needs for final expenses, emergencies, monthly family income and retirement income with provisions already made to meet these needs. The personalized program then shows how life insurance can meet any deficit." Creedon, Some Uses of Life Insurance in Estate Planning 6 (1968).

Most life insurance companies have similar computerized programs for measuring a prospect's insurance needs.

Following is a brief description of the basic types of policies and policy features. *Term insurance* provides pure insurance. That is, for a fixed premium the company contracts to pay a stated dollar amount to the named beneficiary if the insured should die within the year. The annual premium is computed on an actuarial basis; in general, it is based on the number of adult deaths per thousand for persons of a given age and sex — with an add-on, of course, for the salesman's commission and the company's operating expenses and profits. If the insured lives for the year, the insurance comes to an end. If he wants similar protection for the next year, he purchases a new policy at a slightly higher premium — provided he is still insurable.

Because of the uncertain protection given by this one-year-at-a-time approach, most companies sell term policies that are *guaranteed renewable*. That is, the insured has the right to purchase a term policy giving the same coverage in future years (usually to age sixty-five or seventy) without evidence of insurability.

One of the most popular term policies is *five-year-renewable term*, under which the face amount of the policy stays the same over the years, but with premium increases every five years. Under a *decreasing term* policy, the annual premium stays the same each year, but the face amount of the policy decreases. Less insurance for the same premium reflects the fact that the insured's life expectancy is shorter with each passing year (and his chances of dying within the year increased). Decreasing term is often sold as *mortgage cancellation insurance*, which assures that the family home will pass to the survivors free of encumbrances. As the loan balance decreases with each mortgage payment, the insurance coverage decreases correspondingly.

For a small additional premium, *a convertibility rider* can be included in the term policy. This gives the insured an option to convert his coverage to an ordinary life policy, at a higher premium, without evidence of insurability.

The most widely sold policy is *ordinary life* (also called "straight life" and "whole life"). This policy combines decreasing term insurance with an investment feature. When a person takes out a policy at a given age, the annual premium stays the same for the rest of his life (or for as long as he continues the policy in force). In this respect it differs from term insurance, which invariably calls for periodic increases in the premium for the same insurance coverage. A portion of each premium pays for pure insurance protection, to guarantee that the beneficiaries will be paid the face amount of the policy upon the insured's death. The balance goes toward building a cash surrender value in the policy. Referring back to E's $25,000 ordinary life insurance policy described on page 186, recall that aften ten years the policy would have a cash surrender value of $5500. If E were to surrender the policy after ten years, this amount would be paid to him — in effect, his investment return. While the policy is in force, the insured has the right to borrow an amount up to the cash surrender value, usually at 5 percent interest per annum.

It is commonly believed that under an ordinary life policy, the fixed annual premium purchases the same insurance coverage each year. This is not so. Referring once again to E and his $25,000 ordinary life policy, if E were to die after ten years his beneficiary would be paid the face amount of $25,000 — but $5500 of that amount would be a return of E's money in the policy. Thus E's premium in that tenth year would only have purchased $19,500 in pure insurance coverage. As the cash surrender value builds up, the amount of pure insurance provided by the policy goes down.

Other insurance-plus-savings policies have a more substantial investment feature, meaning that annual premiums are higher and the cash surrender value builds up at a faster rate. *Limited pay life* policies provide for the payment of all premiums in a given number of years (quite commonly, twenty years — thus a "twenty pay life" policy). The insured pays premiums for the designated number of years; thereafter the policy is "paid up" for its face amount. The higher premiums build up a fund that produces the income needed to pay the cost of the insurance after (e.g.) the twentieth year.

All investment-type policies are in reality endowment policies. For example, ordinary life policies typically endow at age 100, or age ninety. That is, if the insured were to live that long, the cash surrender value would equal the face amount of the policy. However, those policies actually designated as *endowment policies* endow within a person's expected lifespan — typically, at age sixty-five, or age sixty, or after twenty years.

Mutual life insurance companies are (nominally, at least) nonprofit organizations that are owned by the policyholders. These companies issue *participating* policies: The company's earnings over and above operating expenses are returned to the policyholders in the form of premium *dividends*. Policy dividends are actually rebates of the premiums charged, not income. The company charges more than actuarial experience would indicate is necessary, to cover the contingency of a "bad year." When this contingency does not materialize, at the end of the year the excess premiums are returned. It is for this reason that life insurance "dividends" are not taxable as ordinary income. Policy dividends tend to be low in the early years of the policy and increase with each passing year. To take the recent dividend experience of one company (New York Life), policy dividends were about 9 percent of the premium for two-year-old policies, 14 percent for five-year-old policies, 27 percent for ten-year-old policies, and over 50 percent of the premium for twenty-year-old policies.

Capital stock companies are, as the name implies, privately owned, with their securities usually listed on one of the national or regional stock exchanges. These companies issue *non-participating* policies: The premium charge for a particular policy is not reduced by premium-rebate dividends. The consequence is that the quoted premium for a non-participating policy will be substantially lower than the premium for a participating policy giving the same coverage. In the first years after the policy is issued, a non-participating policy will cost less. But as the years pass the dividends under a participating policy will bring its cost below that of a comparable non-participating policy. Many capital stock companies also issue participating policies, apparently to have a product that will compete with the dividend-paying mutual policies.

For an additional premium, the insured can obtain a *waiver of premium* rider.

Under this rider, if the insured should become permanently disabled, his insurance will be kept in force without the payment of premiums. Also for an additional premium, the insured can obtain a *double indemnity* rider: If he dies as the result of an accident, the policy pays double its face amount. Some companies offer a *double-triple indemnity* rider: If the insured dies as the result of an accident while on a public conveyance (e.g. aircraft, train, ship), the policy pays triple its face amount. These riders are apparently intended to supplant the need for playing the "slot machines" at airport terminals.

Under a *family income* rider the company agrees to pay the insured's family a specific monthly income for a specified period, such as the number of years from the date of the insured's death until the youngest child reaches age eighteen. At that

"Besides the woefully inadequate insurance money, I bequeath to my family all the beauties of earth and skies and seas, the marvels of creation; the birds, the brooks, the trees, the salt wind on the marshes, the primrose in the lane, the green and golden meadows, the heather on the moorlands, the snowdrop in the winter, the lilacs in the spring."

time the company will pay the face amount of the basic ordinary life policy. This plan actually involves a combination of decreasing term insurance and ordinary life insurance. With each passing month the guaranteed income feature of the policy decreases in value.

5. *How Much Life Insurance Is Enough?*

At the end of 1969, 92 percent of all American families with children under age eighteen had some life insurance coverage. The average coverage for families in this group was $20,900.[31] In 59 percent of these families, however, the head of the household was insured for less than $25,000; in 24 percent, for less than $10,000. With his $47,000 in life insurance coverage, Adam Smith is well above the national average. But does he have *enough* life insurance to suitably provide for his family? And how does one go about determining this?

The Consumer Union has outlined a do-it-yourself method of gauging insurance needs.[32] The method is essentially the same as that used by life insurance agents as a part of their sales presentation, in programming an individual's insurance requirements.[33] Under this approach, a dollar value is placed on the income needs of the individual's family if he should die within the next year, and on the insurance that would be required to produce the desired fund. The family's needs will generally fall into the following categories:

(1) Immediate cash, to meet possible costs of last illness, funeral expenses, expenses of estate administration, estate and inheritance taxes, etc.;
(2) Emergency fund, for medical and other unusual expenses that may arise in the future;
(3) Monthly income needed to raise the children;
(4) Amount needed to provide college education for the children;
(5) Monthly income needed by wife from time children leave home until wife reaches retirement (and social security) age;
(6) Retirement income for wife.

Specific dollar amounts are arrived at for each of these categories, and the present value of the fund needed to satisfy these requirements is determined. The next step is to subtract the value of the other sources of income that will be available for the family's support. At the top of the list are social security survivor benefits and employee death benefits. Also to be considered are savings accounts, investments in stocks and bonds, and other income-producing assets. Life insurance is needed to the extent that these other sources will not provide the funds deemed necessary.

This approach has its shortcomings. In calling for the determination of a monthly family income level, it assumes that, e.g., $500 per month ten years from now will provide the same level of support as $500 per month today. In measuring

[31] Life Insurance Fact Book 14 (1971).

[32] The Consumer Union Report on Life Insurance: A Guide to Planning and Buying the Protection You Need (1967).

[33] See footnote 30 supra.

the principal amount needed to produce this income, it requires that an estimate be made of the likely net return on money. Should this be 3 percent? 4 percent? 6 percent? If too low a figure is selected, this will tend to overstate the size of the required fund; if too high a figure is selected, the size of the fund will be understated. Furthermore, this approach does not take into account the many variables that a particular family may encounter. How is it possible even to guess what the family's circumstances will be ten years from now? Would the wife go to work if the husband dies? Does she have a specific vocation she might pursue? Would she remarry? Do any of the children have any special physical or health problems? Would the children go to college? What is the likelihood of financial assistance from the husband's parents, or from the wife's parents? Is there the prospect of a substantial inheritance on either side of the family? If so, should this be taken into account? Since every dollar spent on insurance means a dollar less for the savings account, or for the individual's equity investment program, or for current living expenses of the family, how generous (or how conservative) should an individual be in providing security for his family through life insurance protection?

The problem of determining a family's economic needs, if the chief provider were to be removed from the scene by a premature death, is a difficult one. Arbitrary judgments and guesstimates are inevitable. Some attempt to calculate these needs must be made, however. There is no other satisfactory way to gauge an individual's life insurance requirements. Better an informed guess than an uninformed one.

Appendix A (which begins on page 1093) illustrates how this approach might be used in measuring Adam Smith's life insurance requirements. The illustration is based on a plan that would provide Smith's wife with a monthly income of $750 per month during the child-raising years and $500 per month thereafter. The plan would also establish a college education fund for the children and an emergency fund that would enable Mrs. Smith to meet unusual expenses. Taking into account social security benefits and the income-producing assets presently owned by the Smiths, this illustration suggests that Smith, with his present life insurance coverage of $47,000, is underinsured by about $50,000. To provide his family with the desired level of support, Smith would have to increase his life insurance coverage to $97,000. At this point you should read Appendix A, and then consider the problems set out below.

PROBLEMS

1. "I appreciate your explaining this method of programming my insurance needs but, frankly, I think it's all a bit silly. Planning for contingencies that might arise in the next few years is one thing. But once the children are raised, how can I possibly know, or even guess, what my wife's needs would be? Maybe she'll have remarried, or gone back to work. And your plan talks about setting up a retirement fund for her in the year 2000! In short, this whole presentation is just too 'iffy' for me. Insurance coverage of $47,000 sounds about right; I can afford it; I think I'll leave it right there." How would you respond to this reasoning?

2. "You have convinced me that I don't need *any* more insurance. I am now thirty-six years old. Your calculations are premised on my dying within the next several years, while I still have young children. But statistics show that if I die before age forty-two or so, the probabilities are that it will be from accidental causes rather than illness or disease. As you know, three of my present life insurance policies have double indemnity provisions, meaning that if I die as the result of an accident the insurance proceeds would total $77,000. Two of those policies pay triple if I die from an accident while on a public conveyance; this would bring the proceeds up to $97,000. The odds are that if I do need insurance in the amounts we've been talking about, it will be there." How would you respond to this reasoning?

3. "I don't think I need any additional insurance; in fact, I may not need the insurance I now have. As I told you, Jane's parents, Dr. and Mrs. Preston, are fairly well off, and I'm sure that if anything ever happened to me, they would step in and help her financially. As you yourself told me, when I stated that Dr. Preston's net worth was around $200,000, anyone who knows a Boston doctor can be sure that that's an understatement. Dr. Preston's net worth provides all the insurance I need." How would you respond to this reasoning?

6. *What Type of Life Insurance Should Adam Smith Buy?*

If Smith does decide to purchase additional life insurance coverage, what type of policy should he buy? While there is a variety of policies to choose from, for most persons in Smith's circumstances the choice will be between ordinary life and some form of term insurance. Smith's primary concern is for protection, and endowment policies do not provide sufficient protection for the premium dollar.

FARR, AN ESTATE PLANNER'S HANDBOOK
39-41 (3d ed. 1966)

§6. *The value of life insurance for the average man.* As has been seen, the initial estate plan of the young man of business or professional life must depend chiefly upon life insurance. There is no reasonable possibility of provision for his family by any other method of accumulation of property. He need not in his early career be concerned by fear of wastage of his estate by taxes and expenses of administration; his aim is to provide means to carry his family group through the critical period which might ensue if anything were to happen to him. If he is well advised, he will arrange his financial affairs so that *first* he maintains at all times, in cash, government bonds, or in savings bank, a sufficient reserve to meet family expenses on a reduced scale for a period of six months to a year, this to safeguard against illness, loss or change of employment, and like emergency; *second,* he buys all the life insurance he possibly can assume, using for the latter purpose something on the order of 10 per cent of his income; and *third,* he makes whatever progress he can toward buying the kind of home he fairly can afford.

Proportions and amounts of life insurance may vary, depending upon the amount of his protection from other sources; but he will do well to discount all other possibilities of accumulation and eschew all other investment methods, however attractive, until he has made a sound beginning at least upon his protective life insurance program.

It is possible to argue that other methods of investment, regularly continued, will yield more, with more capital appreciation, than life insurance. But it is not possible to argue that any other investment may be depended upon to provide the unique service of life insurance — the marshaling of money in greatly enhanced sums at the contingency in early life where money is desperately needed. The wise young man places protection first in line, and investment second. The time for investment will come after protection in reasonable amount has been obtained.

Assume, for example, that a young man and his wife commence their life venture in employment by a bank, after graduation from college and perhaps a school of business, in their middle twenties. They will possess, if they are lucky enough to be on their own, a very small number of thousands of dollars and a modest collection of wedding presents and essential furnishings. In all likelihood they will earn not much in excess of $8000 a year in any of their first five years in business. The situation will be about the same if they are in a profession, except that the annual earnings are very likely to be less. They will be well advised to maintain a savings account as close to $3000 as they can manage. They naturally will wish, and ought to proceed, to buy some modest home on a rent payment basis. If they then place 10 per cent of their gross annual earnings in life insurance, they eventually will be able to acquire straight life insurance in increasing amounts (with larger early protection if they will buy some such policy forms as term insurance or policies of the family income type). Hopefully, they may have acquired by the age of thirty or thereabouts a minimum death protection of about $35,000 permanent coverage, made up probably of straight life policies and/or the permanent portion of the "family income" policies. In addition to these so-called face amounts of permanent insurance there may be a further and additional protection in the term insurance either separately or as a portion of the family income policies.

Given qualities of determination and intelligence and a reasonable amount of luck, our young family, by the time they have reached forty, will have moved ahead into earning brackets closer to $10,000 and upward. The $3000 in the savings bank has become a forgotten, or, at worst, a little-used reserve asset; the home has been largely, if not wholly, paid for. And the life insurance coverage is nearer $60,000 to $80,000 of permanent protection, with perhaps some additional coverage still remaining in the form of term insurance, either under the family income policies or independently.

What is more, the insurance policies with their accumulating values begin to look like an investment, as well as protection. Some of the policies are likely to be of the limited pay type, such as "life paid-up" at age sixty or sixty-five. Or, if the client is a professional man or an independent and self-employed producer, some of these policies may be of the retirement income type, under which intervening insurance protection is coupled with a specific amount of monthly annuity income to the insured, or perhaps to the insured and his wife after they have arrived at age sixty or sixty-five. Some partial or total disability coverage also may have been acquired.

If success is to be the lot of the family, the "break" is likely to appear sometime in the neighborhood of age forty or a few years later. Earnings mount rapidly and, while expenses seem to keep pace, there is not only enough for a better standard of living, and perhaps a larger house in a better neighborhood, but there is a substantially increased amount of life insurance. In all probability, all of the term insurance has either been converted or has expired. The total permanent coverage may now be $100,000 or more. The client, if he is a corporate employee or official, also may be protected by an additional substantial amount of intervening coverage under the provisions of the group, or pension trust or profit-sharing plan carried by his corporation. There also may be some securities and other types of investment which promise, if things continue to go well, to convert the enterprise into a well-to-do family.

PROBLEMS

1. Farr refers to the ordinary life insurance policy as "permanent insurance." In what way is an ordinary life policy more "permanent" than a guaranteed renewable term policy?

2. Observe that Farr recommends a "ten percent of gross income" approach as the means of determining how much a young family man should be spending on life insurance. Evaluate this proposal.

3. "The wise young man places protection first in line, and investment second. The time for investment will come after protection in reasonable amount has been obtained." Is Farr's recommended course of action consistent with this advice?

4. Farr suggests that "if success is to be the lot of the family," insurance coverage should continue to rise, and should be at the $100,000 level or higher by the time the individual reaches age 45 or thereabouts. At this point will the individual's insurance needs have increased or lessened?

A radically different approach is suggested by the Consumer Union booklet referred to earlier. The essence of its recommendations is *protection now* in the form of term insurance. Term is recommended because (1) it is the only type of insurance the young family man can afford to buy in sufficient quantities, and (2) the investment return on other types of life insurance does not compare favorably with investments of comparable safety, such as insured savings deposits or government bonds. The CU consultants recommend decreasing term or five-year-renewable term, with the overall insurance coverage reduced after the children have been raised and educated.

In a chapter entitled "Should Your Policy Be a Savings Account?" the CU consultants compare the rate of return from a representative ordinary life insurance policy and a "buy term and invest the difference" plan. Their study uses the premium cost of a $50,000 non-participating[34] ordinary life policy issued to a twenty-five-year-old male by the Connecticut General Life Insurance Company. The annual premium for this policy would be $632.50. The accumulation (that is, the cash surrender value) under this policy is then compared to a plan under which the twenty-five-year-old purchases a five-year-renewable policy from the same company (at a premium of $195.30 for the first five years), and invests the balance ($437.20 for the first five years) in a savings account that earns interest at a net rate of return of 3½ percent. Every five years the term insurance premium increases, and the amount deposited in the savings account decreases. Periodic reductions are made in the face amount of the term insurance policy to adjust for the fact that as the cash surrender value of the ordinary life policy increases, the amount of the pure insurance provided by that policy goes down. Their conclusion: The savings account is larger than the cash surrender value in the policy after ten years ($5370 vs. $4450), twenty years ($12,403 vs. $11,650), and thirty years ($20,609 vs. $19,950), but is lower after forty years ($27,747 vs. $28,500). What this indicates is that the build-up under this particular policy is slightly less than 3½ percent per annum.

On the other hand, the more complicated (and controversial) "Linton Method" of measuring the investment return on ordinary life insurance policies, widely quoted by representatives of the life insurance industry, has shown a net rate of return of close to 4.8 percent for participating policies issued by ten selected mutual life insurance companies.[35] While this yield figure is challenged by Consumer Union,[36] and the Linton Method has been criticized by other writers in the insurance field,[37] it does appear that for some policies issued by some companies, over the years the build-up may be a point or more higher than 3½ percent per annum.

GREGG, INFLATION, EQUITIES AND LIFE INSURANCE: A CONTEMPORARY VIEW

3, 18-19 (1965)

Inflation is the devastating foe of everyone — destructive of economic, social and moral fibers throughout the fabric of our society. Its insidious and cancerous

[34] Consumer Union concludes that the only comparison that can readily be made is with a non-participating policy: It is impossible to project future dividends under a participating policy, and the use of projections from past dividend experience for a particular company makes the comparison (1) inexact and (2) highly complicated. Representatives of the life insurance industry would no doubt contend, with some justification, that this biases the comparison. Over the years, the net premium cost of a participating policy ordinarily will be lower than the cost of a non-participating policy, and the cash surrender value under a participating policy typically will be larger.

[35] Linton, Life Insurance as an Investment, Life and Health Insurance Handbook 242 (1964).

[36] The Consumer Union Report on Life Insurance: A Guide to Planning and Buying the Protection You Need 110 (1967).

[37] Barth, The Rate of Return on the Savings Element in Cash-Value Life Insurance, 35 J. Risk and Ins. 569 (1968); Ferrari, Investment Life Insurance Versus Term Insurance and

growth has led many people into confused and disorderly financial thinking. Some of this financial thinking has questioned the value of permanent life insurance as good investment property in an inflationary era. Often a decision about life insurance is being made without study of all the factors a prudent investor should consider. By the same token, in some quarters equity investments are thought to be the panacea as a hedge against inflation. . . .

In a growth economy and in the economic climate of today, it is human nature for many of us to speculate, even gamble a little in the hope of hitting a bonanza. Mark Twain's advice on speculation might well be heeded here. He said: "There are two times in a man's life when he should not speculate: when he can't afford it, and when he can." Then, too, probably the best prescription ever given for doubling your money was "to fold it once and stick it in your pocket."

Realistically, however, speculation will happen as long as we are in a boom. There is no quarrel with this so long as people speculate only after they have protected their life value assets with appropriate insurance and attained a reasonably balanced investment program.

Those who urge individuals to put most of their savings into equity investments forget that the man who embarks on a systematic fixed-dollar plan such as life insurance, a savings account, bonds, and similar fields, makes his deposits in "average dollars," that is, dollars as they are at the time he makes each payment. In other words, he makes his payments with inflation dollars in inflationary periods and with deflation dollars in deflationary periods. . . .

With an adequate life and disability insurance program, even a conservative man can afford to run the inevitable risks of speculation. Life insurance can bring true security to men, women, and children in our society; it is a form of thrift of unique and workable force; it is an investment of untarnished strength and vitality. It is our good fortune to have within our reach this most remarkable financial device ever created by man.

CREEDON, SOME USES OF LIFE INSURANCE IN ESTATE PLANNING

7, 8 (*1968*)

Each of the kinds of insurance mentioned and their many permutations has its utility in particular circumstances. Frequently, however, the choice will be between a whole life and a term policy. Arguments wax and wane on whether to buy whole life or to buy term and invest the difference between the higher whole life premium and the lower term insurance premium. Those who favor term insurance maintain that it is better to buy all term insurance to meet one's insurance needs and to invest the difference in high yielding investments rather than in permanent values in life insurance policies which tend to reflect a more certain but relatively lower

---

Separate Investment: A Determination of Expected-Return Equivalents, 35 J. Risk and Ins. 181 (1968).

investment yield. It is clear, however, that the conclusion reached is necessarily based on the assumptions made. If one assumes that the "difference" is invested so as to produce an annual return of 10% after taxes, under present conditions buying term and investing the difference would be clearly preferable. If one's assumption as to the 10% return is erroneous and the "difference" is invested so as to produce a much lower return or perhaps even a loss — a negative return (which has been known to happen), the investment in permanent life insurance is considerably more attractive. To a certain extent, therefore, the decision between term and whole life is one of personal preference. A highly practical factor to be considered is that many people do not *in fact* invest the difference, whereas if they had taken the whole life insurance, they would have forced themselves to invest by paying the required premiums. This practical factor should frequently outweigh any assumed theoretical advantage of investing the difference.

If Adam Smith does decide to purchase additional insurance, his decision on what type of policy to buy may well turn on the factor of cost. At his present income and expenditure level, he does not have an unlimited number of dollars to spend for family protection, or investment, via life insurance. Following are some representative annual premium costs for policies issued to an insurable 36-year-old male.[38]

$25,000 *participating ordinary life policy:*

Aetna	$617.75
Canada Life	540.75
Connecticut Mutual	595.50
Prudential	623.50

$25,000 *non-participating ordinary life policy:*

Aetna	$433.75
Connecticut General	477.70
Southland Life	466.00
Travelers	445.75

$25,000 *five-year-renewable non-participating term policy:*

	36-40	*41-45*	*46-50*	*51-55*
Aetna	142.25	185.50	251.50	374.25
Southland Life	139.50	186.50	261.00	374.25
Travelers	137.75	176.75	257.25	387.75
Prudential *	182.50	237.25	337.25	500.00

* participating

[38] Source: Best's Flitcraft Compend (1970).

PROBLEMS

1. Adam Smith says to you, "I realize that any decision I make on life insurance has to be my own; no one can make it for me. However, I would appreciate your recommendations, or at least your guidance, in making that decision. On the questions of amounts of coverage and types of coverage, what factors do you think are the most important ones that I should take into account? If you were in my shoes, what would *you* do?" How would you respond?

2. A proposal: "Smith says he wants to increase his insurance coverage by $25,000. He shouldn't simply purchase an additional policy; instead he should retool his entire insurance program. Right now he has two term insurance policies totalling $27,000 in coverage. (See page 75.) These are all right. He also has two $10,000 ordinary life insurance policies. These are participating policies whose combined premiums total $435 per year — less current dividends, about $350 per year. The present cash surrender values under these policies total about $1900.

"Smith should dump these two policies and invest the $1900 in growth stocks. He should then take out a $50,000 five-year-renewable term policy from Southland Life. The premium rates for this policy are:

Age	
36-40:	$269.00
41-45:	363.00
46-51:	512.00
51-55:	738.50

Under this plan, over the next five years Smith can actually increase his insurance coverage by $30,000 for an annual cost of $80 or so less than he is now paying — and he can have that $1900 working for him in the market. At age forty-one the insurance premiums will go up (and the cost differential will be greater because the dividends under his present policies would have increased). But his salary will probably be higher, and he does have that $1900, so he'd still be money ahead. By the time Smith reaches age fifty-one, this plan doesn't look quite as good — but by that time the children will have been raised and educated, and Smith should start cutting back on his insurance coverage anyhow. Smith has already demonstrated that he knows how to invest prudently, and he doesn't need the low-yield forced savings under ordinary life policies. This plan will give him more insurance for less money over the next ten years."

Evaluate this proposal.

SECTION E. Life Insurance: How Should the Proceeds Be Settled?

Be advised that Adam Smith has decided to purchase a five-year-renewable term insurance policy, in a face amount of $25,000. As with his present policies,

Smith has — for now, at least — designated his wife, Jane, as primary beneficiary under the policy, and his children have been named as contingent beneficiaries.

This brings Smith's basic insurance coverage to $72,000: $20,000 in ordinary life policies, $35,000 in commercial term policies, and $17,000 in the group term coverage provided by his employer. As noted on page 75, three of these policies have double or double-triple indemnity riders, meaning that the proceeds payable by reason of his death might be as high as $122,000. Even without this additional policy, Smith's life insurance policies represent, in terms of economic value, his most important asset. He must now consider the manner in which these proceeds are to be paid at his death. How the life insurance proceeds are settled will have a decided bearing on the formulation of an estate plan for the rest of the Smith assets.

The distribution of the proceeds from life insurance policies can be handled in one of four ways. A lump-sum payment can be made to the named beneficiaries. A lump-sum payment can be made to the insured's estate, or to the executor or administrator of his estate. The policy proceeds can be left with the insurance company, to be paid out in installments under one of the policy settlement options. Finally, the proceeds can be placed in trust, the trustees to hold and administer the fund under the terms of a trust created either during the insured's lifetime or by his will.

1. *Lump-Sum Payment to Beneficiary*

The most frequently used method of settling life insurance proceeds is a lump-sum payment to the named primary beneficiary (usually the insured's wife) or secondary beneficiaries (usually the insured's children). The advantage of such an arrangement, when the insured is survived by his wife, is that it gives the wife immediate and unrestricted access to the insurance fund. This enables her to meet the expenses occasioned by the insured's death, and to manage the fund in the manner that she sees most fit. As compared to a settlement in trust, the lump-sum payment eliminates the expenses of trust administration and of trustee compensation. It also enables the wife to make her own decisions as to whether a particular expenditure is necessary or appropriate, without the requirement of a trustee's supervision or approval of her scale of living or pattern of expenditures. The principal advantage of a lump-sum payment over a policy settlement option is with respect to the investment return on the money. Since the interest rate under most insurance companies' settlement options is between 3 and 4.25 percent, the wife can get a better return on the money from almost any investment she might make, including such conservative investments as government bonds, corporate bonds, and insured savings deposits.

What are the disadvantages? "A lump sum payment accords protection to the surviving beneficiary at the time of the insured's death. Thereafter the continuance of the protection depends upon the personal actions of the survivor. She may be extravagant in her expenditures. She may be improvident in her investments. To too many people money in the pocket is an ever present temptation to spend or to take a chance. By arranging that the proceeds of life insurance be paid under [a policy settlement option or a trust], the insured makes certain that the protection he has provided is spread over the desired period of time." [39]

Most insureds name their children as secondary beneficiaries, with the children to receive a lump-sum payment if the insured is not survived by his spouse. If the children have all attained majority, this arrangement raises no problems. But if any of them are minors, this beneficiary designation is highly undesirable. As was indicated in Chapter 3, guardianship administration procedures in most states are too inflexible and cumbersome for the handling of even modest estates, let alone the substantial sums that might be payable from life insurance policies. Although the children's guardian might be permitted to select one of the policy settlement options as the least undesirable method of managing and investing the proceeds, the option payments themselves would have to be handled through the guardianship process. Even if Adam Smith decides to leave his wife as the primary beneficiary of a lump-sum payment, he would be well advised to establish some form of "contingent trust" for the policy proceeds, to be operative if his wife predeceases him.[40] If the fund will not be large enough to warrant naming a corporate fiduciary as trustee, a relative or family friend (usually the person named in the will as guardian) could be named as trustee. The guardian-trustee could then manage and administer the fund under the more liberal powers given to trustees. An example of such a trust, with commentary, is given in Appendix C.

2. *Lump-Sum Payment to Insured's Estate or Executor*

One method of integrating the disposition of life insurance proceeds with other owned assets is to designate the insured's executor or estate as beneficiary of his life insurance policies. This will cause the proceeds to pass by the insured's testamentary plan, and it assures that the funds will be available to the executor for the payment of funeral and administration expenses, death taxes, and other estate obligations. There are disadvantages to this approach, however. First, this will subject the proceeds to the delays — and the expenses — of probate. In most states the executor's fees (and typically the estate attorney's fees as well) are based on the size of the probate estate. Second, the proceeds will be subject to the claims of the insured's creditors. If, on the other hand, they are paid to a named beneficiary, they are free from creditors' claims. In some estates (but probably not many) this would be a significant factor. Finally, in a number of states payment to the executor or to the estate would result in the loss of the state's inheritance tax exemption for insurance proceeds.[41]

[39] Lourie, How to Use Insurance Settlement Options to Get the Marital Deduction, in 1 Lasser, Estate Tax Techniques 139, 140 (1967).

[40] See Hammond & Victor, Contingent Life Insurance Trusts, 104 Trusts & Estates 392 (1965); Corcoran, The Contingent Insurance Trust — A Hidden Bonanza For Minor Children, 55 Ill. B.J. 596 (1967).

[41] E.g., Tex. Tax-Gen. Ann. art. 14.01 (1969) (up to $40,000 in proceeds of insurance on decedent's life exempt from inheritance taxation when proceeds payable to someone other than

3. *Settlement Options*

The proceeds of a life insurance policy may be left with the company, to be paid out under one of the policy settlement options. These options are of two types: The interest option and the installment options. Under the interest option, the beneficiary receives only the interest on the proceeds until the time agreed upon for payment of the fund in a lump sum. While the interest rate on older policies was often higher, the guaranteed interest rate on policies issued by most major companies today is $2\frac{1}{4}$ to 3 percent. In addition, many companies pay something they call "excess interest." The company is obligated to pay the guaranteed interest rate, but payment of excess interest is by annual vote of the company's board of directors. The sources of excess interest payments are (as with premium-rebate dividends) increased profits stemming from a favorable mortality experience and the return from investment of the company's reserves. Many of the major companies have paid excess interest of 1 to $1\frac{1}{2}$ percent in every year for the past several decades.

Most insurance policies contain three or four different installment options. The most commonly offered installment options are the following:

Installments of Fixed Amounts

Under this option, a specified amount is paid periodically (e.g., $100 per month) until the policy proceeds, with interest, are exhausted. If the primary beneficiary dies before the fund has been consumed, the remaining payments are made to the secondary beneficiaries. This option can be used to provide a fixed (and relatively large, compared to other installment options) periodic payment to meet some specific, short-term need, as when the insured's children are being raised, or to cover the period when the wife is not entitled to social security benefits.

Installments for Fixed Period

(Sometimes called installments for years certain.) Under this option, a fixed amount is paid periodically for a predetermined number of years. The amount of each periodic payment is determined by (a) the amount of the insurance fund, plus interest, and (b) the number of years selected. As with the fixed amount option, if the primary beneficiary dies before the period has elapsed, payments are made to the secondary beneficiaries. This option can be used to provide maximum income at the time it is needed the most. It is often used to cover the time during which the insured's children are being raised and educated, or to fill the gap during which the insured's wife is not eligible for social security benefits.

---

decedent's estate, executor or administrator); Cal. Rev. & Tax Code §13724 (1970) ($50,000 exemption, when proceeds payable to other than estate, executor or administrator).

Straight Annuity

The effect of this provision is to purchase an annuity for the primary beneficiary's lifetime, with the policy proceeds constituting a single premium payment. The advantage of this option, as with all annuities, is that it insures periodic payments for the beneficiary's lifetime. The disadvantages are that the periodic payments are relatively low (unless the beneficiary is at a very advanced age), no provision can be made for secondary beneficiaries, and (as with all annuities) it involves a gamble that the beneficiary will outlive her life expectancy.

Installments for Fixed Period and for Life Thereafter

This option is a combination of the two preceding ones. It guarantees periodic payments for the designated time, and payments for life thereafter. This reduces to some extent the gamble connected with a straight annuity. If the period selected is ten years and the primary beneficiary dies in the fifth year, payments do not cease as they would under a straight annuity; the secondary beneficiaries will receive payments for an additional five years. At the same time, the primary beneficiary is assured of periodic payments during her lifetime. A disadvantage of this option is that the payments will be lower than for any other installment option, since the insurance proceeds are being used to pay for both annuity and guaranteed payment features.

Joint and Survivor Annuity

This option is intended for use by the insured who lives to retirement age, and who wants to settle the cash surrender value of the policy in a manner that will supplement his retirement income. The typical joint and survivor option provides for the payment of monthly installments in a set amount so long as both designated payees (usually the husband and wife) are living, with payments reduced to two-thirds of the original amount during the lifetime of the survivor.

Each installment payment to a beneficiary consists of a portion of the principal and an interest element. Most companies use a guaranteed interest factor that is $\frac{1}{4}$ to $\frac{1}{2}$ percent higher than the interest rate under the straight interest option. The guaranteed interest factor on policies currently being issued is $2\frac{1}{2}$ to 3 percent. Excess interest is payable under the installment options as well as under the interest option. In 1971 most major companies were paying total interest (i.e., guaranteed plus excess) of 4 to 4.4 percent under their installment options. This means that the actual installment payments will ordinarily be higher than those given by the various payment tables listed in the policy.

During his lifetime the insured may designate the option under which the proceeds are to be settled. If he selects the interest option, he must also make provision for lump-sum payment of the policy proceeds at some designated time, such as the attainment of a certain age or the death of the primary beneficiary. If he selects the interest option or an installment option not involving an annuity feature, he can specify whether it is to be binding on the beneficiary, or whether the beneficiary can modify the arrangement by selecting another option or by drawing down all or a portion of the policy proceeds. If the insured does not make a binding election during his lifetime, the beneficiary may select one of the options in lieu of a lump-sum payment of the insurance proceeds.

Set out below are the settlement option tables for policies currently being issued by the Mutual Life Insurance Company of New York.[42]

MUTUAL LIFE INSURANCE COMPANY OF NEW YORK, SETTLEMENT OPTION TABLES

Option 1. Interest only. For policies issued after 1/1/68, guaranteed interest is 2¾%. Participating (in excess interest declarations).

Option 2. Income for specified period. For policies issued after 1/1/64, guaranteed interest is 2¾%. Participating. Monthly income for each $1,000 of proceeds:

Years	*1*	*2*	*3*	*4*	*5*	*6*	*7*	*8*	*9*	*10*
Amt.	$84.37	42.76	28.89	21.96	17.80	15.03	13.06	11.58	10.42	9.50
Years	11	12	13	14	15	16	17	18	19	20
Amt.	8.75	8.13	7.60	7.15	6.76	6.41	6.11	5.85	5.61	5.39

Option 3. Life income with period certain. For policies issued after 1/1/68, guaranteed interest is 2¾%. Nonparticipating. The period certain elected may be (a) 10 years, (b) 20 years, or (c) the period required for the total income payments to equal the proceeds (refund period certain). Monthly income for each $1,000 of proceeds: [see next page].

Option 4. Income of specified amount. For policies issued after 1/1/64, guaranteed interest is 2¾%. Participating. The Company will pay an income of the amount elected, but not less each year than 6 percent of the amount originally settled under option and never less than $10 per installment.

(The Mutual of New York policies also offer several annuity options. The tables for these options have not been reproduced.)

Income Taxation of Settlement Option Payments

Section 101(d)(1)(b) of the Internal Revenue Code of 1954 grants the surviving spouse an exclusion for the first $1000 of interest paid under installment options in any year. This exclusion applies to excess interest as well as to the guaranteed interest paid under the options. However, it applies only to interest paid under one

[42] Best's Settlement Options Manual 339, 567 (30th ed. 1971).

Age	Male payee 10 years	Male payee 20 cert.	Male payee Ref. cert.	Female payee 10 years	Female payee 20 cert.	Female payee Ref. cert.
10	2.69	2.69	2.68	2.63	2.63	2.62
15	2.77	2.77	2.76	2.70	2.70	2.69
20	2.87	2.87	2.85	2.78	2.78	2.77
25	3.00	2.99	2.97	2.89	2.88	2.87
30	3.15	3.14	3.12	3.01	3.00	2.99
35	3.35	3.32	3.29	3.17	3.15	3.13
40	3.60	3.54	3.51	3.36	3.34	3.32
45	3.92	3.81	3.78	3.61	3.57	3.54
46	3.99	3.87	3.84	3.67	3.62	3.59
47	4.07	3.93	3.90	3.73	3.67	3.65
48	4.15	3.99	3.97	3.80	3.73	3.70
49	4.23	4.05	4.04	3.86	3.79	3.76
50	4.32	4.12	4.11	3.94	3.85	3.83
51	4.41	4.19	4.19	4.01	3.91	3.89
52	4.51	4.25	4.27	4.09	3.98	3.96
53	4.61	4.32	4.35	4.18	4.05	4.03
54	4.71	4.39	4.44	4.26	4.12	4.11
55	4.83	4.46	4.53	4.36	4.19	4.19
56	4.94	4.53	4.63	4.46	4.26	4.27
57	5.06	4.60	4.73	4.57	4.34	4.36
58	5.19	4.67	4.84	4.68	4.41	4.46
59	5.32	4.74	4.95	4.80	4.49	4.56
60	5.45	4.80	5.07	4.92	4.57	4.66
61	5.60	4.87	5.19	5.05	4.64	4.77
62	5.75	4.93	5.32	5.19	4.72	4.89
63	5.90	4.99	5.46	5.33	4.79	5.01
64	6.08	5.05	5.61	5.49	4.87	5.15
65	6.26	5.10	5.76	5.65	4.94	5.29
66	6.42	5.15	5.93	5.82	5.00	5.43
67	6.59	5.19	6.10	5.99	5.06	5.59
68	6.78	5.23	6.29	6.18	5.12	5.75
69	6.96	5.26	6.48	6.37	5.17	5.93
70	7.16	5.29	6.69	6.56	5.22	6.12
71	7.35	5.32	6.91	6.77	5.25	6.32
72	7.54	5.33	7.15	6.98	5.29	6.53
73	7.74	5.35	7.40	7.19	5.31	6.76
74	7.92	5.36	7.66	7.40	5.34	7.00
75	8.11	5.37	7.94	7.62	5.35	7.26
80	8.89	5.39	9.65	8.60	5.39	8.85
85	9.32	5.39	12.04	9.22	5.39	11.11

of the installment options, not to payments under the interest option, and it is available solely to the surviving spouse.

Example: An insured designates his wife as primary beneficiary under a $20,000 Mutual of New York policy. He later dies survived by his wife. She elects to settle the proceeds under a fixed period option, with installment payments for twenty years certain. According to the table for option 2, above, the monthly payments will be \$5.39 per \$1000, or \$107.80. This return is based on the guaranteed interest rate of $2\frac{3}{4}$ percent. In 1970, Mutual of New York paid excess interest of 1.6 percent under this option. At a 4.35 rate of return the monthly payment will be \$6.17 per \$1000, or \$123.40 per month. The annual payment will be \$1480.

In computing the portion of each payment that represents income and the portion that represents return of principal (and therefore not subject to income taxation), the Treasury Regulations take a straight pro rata approach. Since the \$20,000 of principal will be paid in twenty years, \$1000 of each yearly payment is treated as the return of principal. Thus the annual interest element is \$480 per year. Since this amount is less than the \$1000 exclusion granted by §101, it is not taxed.

4. *Settling Adam Smith's Life Insurance Proceeds Under a Settlement Option*

PROBLEMS

1. Adam Smith's primary concern is to provide for his wife's support needs during the child-raising years — roughly, the next twenty years. One plan Smith might employ would be to have \$10,000 in life insurance proceeds paid outright to Mrs. Smith as an emergency fund, and to settle the remaining \$62,000 in proceeds under a twenty-years-certain option. If Smith were to die in the next year, this plan would assure monthly payments to Mrs. Smith until she reached age fifty-four. At that point she would be nearing social security age and the children would have been raised and educated. If Mrs. Smith were to die before that time, the monthly payments would be made to the Smith children until the youngest child was in her mid-twenties. While Smith has policies with several companies, let us assume that their settlement option provisions are similar to those given by Mutual of New York policies. According to the table for option 2, the monthly payment under the twenty-years-certain option would be \$5.39 per \$1000, but current excess interest declarations would bring that amount up to \$6.17 per month.

If Smith were to select this option, what monthly income would his family receive after his death? What portion of the option payments would be subject to income taxation? Would this arrangement meet Smith's family income planning objectives? (See Appendix A.) Would you recommend that Smith select this settlement option plan?

2. One of the difficulties with the plan outlined in Problem 1 is that there will be no money left for Mrs. Smith after twenty years. (In the context of the Smith family situation, how serious a problem would this be?) Smith might settle all but \$10,000 of the proceeds under an option that assures Mrs. Smith a monthly income for life, but protects the children in the event of her early death by guaranteeing payments for at least twenty years.

If Smith were to select the "life income plus twenty-years-certain" option and Mrs. Smith is thirty-five years old at the time of his death, what monthly income would his family receive after his death? What portion of the option payments would be subject to income taxation? Would this arrangement satisfy Smith's family income planning objectives? Would you recommend that Smith consider using this option in his estate plan?

3. A slight variation on Problem 2. If Smith does select the "life income with period certain" option, would he be better advised to select the twenty-years-certain option or the refund-period-certain option?

4. Compare the foregoing plans with one under which Mrs. Smith would be paid the policy proceeds in a lump sum and would then invest them in 5 percent certificates of deposit with local banks. What monthly income (after taxes) would Mrs. Smith receive under this plan?

5. If Smith were interested in using one of the settlement option plans, he would have to decide how to put the plan into operation. He would have three choices.

(a) He could select the option plan and provide that it could not be modified or revoked by Mrs. Smith after his death. He would, of course, reserve the right to change the option designation during his lifetime.

(b) He could select the option plan but authorize Mrs. Smith to modify the plan (by selecting another settlement option, or by drawing down the entire proceeds in a lump sum) during her lifetime. This alternative is not available for any option with an annuity feature. If an annuity option is selected, it cannot be modified after the insured's death.

(c) Smith could provide for payment of the insurance proceeds in a lump sum, and let Mrs. Smith decide which option should be selected.

What are the advantages and disadvantages of each of these alternatives?

5. Settling Life Insurance Proceeds in a Trust

Since much of this course is concerned with trusts, and with the dispositive provisions of trusts, this is not the time or place for an extended treatment of the subject. For now it should suffice to outline the methods by which life insurance proceeds can be settled in a trust.

A person may create a *revocable* or *irrevocable* trust during his lifetime, and then designate the trustee as beneficiary of his life insurance policies. On his death the proceeds will be added to the corpus of the trust, to be administered in accordance with the trust's terms. If other assets have been settled in the trust during the person's lifetime, the trust is said to be *funded*. In many instances an individual will not own sufficient assets to warrant establishing a funded trust during his lifetime. This would certainly be true of Adam Smith. Additionally, many persons who own assets that might be placed in a trust are not inclined to relinquish their control and management to a trustee. Persons similarly situated who do want their life insurance proceeds to be administered in a trust can create an *unfunded revocable inter vivos trust*. Under this arrangement the trust instrument is drafted and signed by the settlor, and the trustee is named as beneficiary of the settlor's life insurance policies, but no other assets are transferred to the trustee during the settlor's lifetime. The trustee does not begin to administer the trust until the life insurance proceeds are received by the trustee after the settlor's death. As we shall see in Chapter 8, some courts have held that this arrangement runs afoul of three dogmas of trust law: There can be no trust without a trust *res* (assets that are the subject of the trust); an inter vivos trust must come into existence (and therefore must have a res) during the settlor's lifetime; and a trustee must have active duties to perform. (Do you see how you could set up an unfunded life insurance trust and avoid these dogmas?) Other courts have held that a valid trust is created, and in recent years most states have enacted statutes that expressly sanction the creation of unfunded revocable life insurance trusts.[43]

When a person establishes an inter vivos trust, funded or unfunded, revocable or irrevocable, he can integrate the disposition of his testamentary assets with the assets in the trust by using a *pour-over* provision.[44] This is done by devising the residue of his estate to the trustee of the inter vivos trust. On his death the residuary assets are added to the corpus of the trust, and the combined fund is managed and administered as one unit. This eliminates the inconvenience and added expense of having two trusts for the same beneficiaries.

A second method of settling life insurance proceeds in trust is available in some states. If a person does not want to create an inter vivos trust but does intend to establish a testamentary trust for his probate assets, he names the testamentary trustee as beneficiary of his life insurance proceeds. This eliminates the need to draft an inter vivos trust. It should also avoid the problems raised by payment of the proceeds to the insured's executor or estate,[45] since payment to the trustee is not the equivalent of payment to the executor. In some states there are problems with this approach, however. Several courts have held that this is not a valid transfer because the testamentary trust does not come into existence until some time after the insured-transferor's death.[46] In recent years a few states have enacted statutes authorizing this method of integrating life insurance proceeds and testamentary assets.[47]

If Adam Smith does decide to settle a portion of his life insurance proceeds in a trust, one of these methods — the revocable inter vivos trust or the testamentary trust — is likely to be available to him under his state's laws. We will take a closer look at the problems of trust creation in Chapter 8.[48]

[43] See page 420, infra.
[44] See page 419, infra.
[45] See page 200, infra.
[46] See page 394, infra.
[47] See page 397, infra.
[48] For discussion of the pros and cons of using trusts or settlement options as the mode of settling life insurance proceeds, see Huff, Life Insurance Trusts for Everyman, 39 Colo. L. Rev. 239 (1967); Krueger & Hinckley, Settlement Options and Trusts, 14 J. Am. Soc'y C.L.U. 350 (1960).

6. The Federal Estate and Gift Taxes and State Succession Taxes

> "It seems that our main objectives should be to avoid probate and to eliminate as many inheritance taxes as possible." — ADAM SMITH

Is the projected value of Adam Smith's estate of such size that he has to worry about the impact of the federal estate tax and state succession taxes? To what extent, if any, should tax considerations be taken into account in formulating a suitable dispositive plan for Smith's assets? In general, at what point on the economic scale do projected tax consequences begin to have relevance to the estate planning decision?

SECTION A. The Federal Estate Tax[1]

The federal estate tax is not a point of concern in planning most persons' estates. Under the Internal Revenue Code of 1954, the source of the current estate and gift tax statutes, the estate of every decedent is entitled to a $60,000 exemp-

[1] For more comprehensive treatment of the federal estate and gift tax laws see Lowndes & Kramer, Federal Estate and Gift Taxes (2d ed. 1962); Mertens, Law of Federal Gift and Estate Taxation (1959, with current pocket parts); Casner, Estate Planning (3d ed. 1961, with current supplements). An excellent summary treatment is given in Lowndes, An Introduction to the Federal Estate and Gift Taxes, 44 N.C.L. Rev. 1 (1965). Current compilations of the relevant statutes, regulations and cases are collected in the Commerce Clearing House and Prentice-Hall looseleaf services: CCH Fed. Est. & Gift Tax Rep.; P-H Fed. Est. & Gift Taxes.

tion.[2] The purpose of this exemption is to remove estates of modest size from the ambit of the estate tax. If a decedent's gross estate is less than $60,000, his personal representative does not have to file a preliminary notice or an estate tax return.[3] If the gross estate exceeds $60,000, it is still possible that no estate tax will have to be paid. While a preliminary notice and tax return would have to be filed, the return may show that allowable deductions, together with the $60,000 exemption, reduce the taxable estate to zero.

The basic purpose of the federal estate tax is to tax the transfer of property at death. This is accomplished by imposing a graduated tax rate on the decedent's *taxable estate.* In calculating the taxable estate, the first step is to include in the decedent's *gross estate* the value of all property owned by him at his death and passing by will or intestacy, plus the value of all other property that is made subject to the tax. The taxable estate is computed by subtracting from the gross estate the *$60,000 exemption* and various *deductions* to which the estate may be entitled. If the decedent is survived by a spouse, property passing to the spouse may qualify for a marital deduction. Charitable bequests will qualify for a charitable deduction. In addition, the estate is allowed deductions for funeral expenses, expenses of administration of the estate, claims against the estate, and losses incurred during administration of the estate.

After the estate tax has been calculated, it may be reduced by various *tax credits.* The credit for state death taxes permits a reduction in the federal estate tax for some, but by no means all, of the succession taxes paid to a state by reason of the decedent's death. Similarly, the credit for foreign death taxes permits a partial reduction in the estate tax when succession taxes have been paid to a foreign government. The credit for taxes on prior transfers gives some relief against double estate taxation when the property now being taxed has been taxed in the estate of another decedent within the preceding ten years. The credit for gift taxes affords relief against double taxation when a gift tax has been paid on property transferred by the decedent during his lifetime, but the value of the property transferred is for some reason includible in his gross estate.

Gross estate minus $60,000 exemption and allowable deductions equals the taxable estate. Taxable estate times the applicable tax rate equals the estate tax. Estate tax minus allowable credits equals the amount due the federal government. Thus stated in outline form, the structure of the federal estate tax is fairly simple and straightforward. But in actual operation the estate tax can be, and often is, quite complicated, "replete with nice refinements and delicate distinctions." [4] In the pages that follow, discussion is given to the basic provisions of the federal estate tax as they relate to will and trust drafting and estate planning.

[2] Int. Rev. Code of 1954, §2052. In 1969, less than 7 percent of all decedents' estates filed federal estate tax returns. See page 32, supra.

[3] Int. Rev. Code of 1954, §6018.

[4] Lowndes & Kramer, Federal Estate and Gift Taxes 5 (2d ed. 1962).

1. *The Gross Estate: Property Owned at Death*

Interests Owned at Death Transmissible by Will or Intestacy

Section 2033 of the Internal Revenue Code provides: "The value of the gross estate shall include the value of all property to the extent of the interest therein of the decedent at the time of his death." Section 2033 reaches all property owned at death that passes by will or intestacy. This includes real and tangible personal property, intangibles such as securities, patents, and copyrights, interests in an incorporated or unincorporated business, and undivided interests in property (such as the decedent's share of property held under a tenancy in common).

Property owned by the decedent may be taxed in his gross estate even though he did not have the power of disposition over it at his death. This is true, for example, of property set aside for the decedent's family under a state's homestead or exempt property laws. This is also true of property that passes to a surviving spouse because of dower or curtesy rights or because of a statute that gives her a "forced share" of the estate in lieu of dower. The full value of the property is includible in the decedent's gross estate, undiminished by the value of the spouse's dower or curtesy interest or statutory share.[5]

If the decedent owned a life estate in property transferred by another person,[6] nothing is includible in his gross estate under §2033. The life estate terminates at his death, and he owns nothing that can pass by will or intestacy.[7] This principle is of considerable importance in estate planning. It is possible to transfer property into a trust that gives a beneficiary the income from the property for life without causing anything to be taxed in the beneficiary's estate. It is even possible to give the beneficiary certain limited powers to invade the corpus of the trust for his own benefit, and also a special power to appoint the remainder interest at his death,[8] without estate tax cost. Upon the death of the income beneficiary the property passes to (or is held in further trust for) the remaindermen according to the terms of the original transfer. The only tax incurred is the gift tax or the estate tax imposed at the time

[5] Int. Rev. Code of 1954, §2034.

Section 2034 does not apply to community property. In community property states other than New Mexico each spouse is the owner of an undivided one-half interest in the common property, and has the power of testamentary disposition over only his one-half share. Only the value of the decedent spouse's community share is taxed as an owned interest under §2033. For the peculiar law of New Mexico, see Swihart, Federal Taxation of New Mexico Community Property, 3 Nat. Res. J. 104 (1963).

[6] If the decedent himself had made an inter vivos transfer with a retained life estate, the value of the transferred property would be taxed in his estate under §2036.

[7] If the decedent owned a life estate measured by the life of another person (a life estate pur autre vie), and the other person is still living at the decedent's death, the value of the remaining life estate, measured by the life expectancy of the other person, is includible in the decedent's gross estate. Millard v. Maloney, 121 F.2d 257 (3d Cir.), cert. denied, 314 U.S. 636 (1941).

[8] The tax treatment of limited invasion powers and special powers of appointment is discussed at page 231, infra.

the original transfer was made. The income beneficiary can be given many of the attributes of ownership without being taxed as the owner at his death.[9]

What is to prevent a transferor from creating a succession of life-income gifts in trust for his children, then his grandchildren, then his great-grandchildren, and so on, thereby removing the property from the ambit of estate or gift taxation for a number of generations? The answer is given by the Rule against Perpetuities, which prohibits the creation of interests in family settlements that may vest remotely. The practical effect of this rule of property law is to limit the permissible duration of family trusts. On this subject, more — much more — later.

Property Passing by Right of Survivorship[10]

Property that passes by right of survivorship is not taxed under §2033, since the decedent's interest terminates at death as a consequence of the survivorship arrangement. It is, however, taxed under §2040. This section requires the inclusion of all property passing by right of survivorship, to the extent that the decedent originally owned the property or furnished the consideration for its acquisition. It applies to property held under joint tenancy or tenancy by the entireties, joint bank accounts, and government bonds with survivorship provisions.

The decedent's personal representative has the burden of showing that all or a portion of the jointly held property should not be taxed to the estate. The statute requires inclusion of the entire value of the property, unless it is established that the survivor originally owned all or a portion of the property or furnished all or a portion of the consideration for its acquisition. When title to property is taken under a joint tenancy or tenancy by the entireties, it is important to keep records showing the source of the funds with which the property was acquired. Failure to do this may result in needless taxation if the survivor cannot satisfactorily establish the amount of the consideration furnished by him. With respect to joint bank accounts, the survivor must sustain the burden of showing the amount on deposit

[9] Under tax reform proposals presented to Congress by the Treasury Department in 1969, the favorable tax treatment now accorded the life estate-remainder arrangement would be substantially curtailed. Under the "generation-skipping transfer" portion of the proposed legislation, if a transferor created a trust for the benefit of his son for life with remainder to his grandchildren, a "substitute tax" would be imposed on the death of the life tenant. The basic objective of the proposed legislation would be to tax any transfer of an interest to the next generation, regardless of the form of the transfer. The Treasury proposals would also revise the estate tax marital deduction and gift tax laws, and would eliminate the tax-free "stepped-up basis" rule; these portions of the reform proposals will be discussed at later points in this chapter. See Kurtz & Surrey, Reform of Death and Gift Taxes: The 1969 Treasury Proposals, 70 Colum. L. Rev. 1365 (1970); Kinnebrew, Estate and Gift Tax Reform: A Compendium of Thought, 24 Sw. L.J. 608 (1970). Busy with income tax revisions that resulted in the Tax Reform Act of 1969, Congress took no action on estate and gift tax reform. The House Ways and Means Committee indicated, however, that it probably would reopen the subject in the near future. H.R. Rep. No. 413, 91st Cong., 1st Sess., pt. 1, at 2 (1969).

[10] See Dean, Federal Tax Consequences of Joint Ownership, 53 Geo. L.J. 863 (1965); Schwartz, Joint Tenancy and the Federal Tax Law, 101 Trusts & Estates 1038, 1151 (1962).

attributable to his contributions, or the full account is taxed in the decedent's estate.

Section 2040 does not apply to tenancies in common. Upon the death of a tenant in common the value of his undivided interest in the common property, as provided in the instrument of transfer or as fixed by local law, is includible in his gross estate regardless of who furnished the consideration for the property's acquisition.

PROBLEMS

1. Four years ago X contributed $10,000 and Y contributed $5000 for the purchase of Blackacre as joint tenants with right of survivorship. X died two months ago, survived by Y. At the time of X's death Blackacre was worth $12,000. What portion of Blackacre's value is includible in X's gross estate for federal estate tax purposes? See Treas. Reg. §20.2040-1(a)(2) (1958).

2. Consider the same facts and the same question as above, except that Blackacre was worth $30,000 at X's death.

3. F died eleven years ago. By his will he devised a 200-acre tract of land "to my two sons, A and B, as joint tenants with right of survivorship and not as tenants in common." This created a valid joint tenancy under the applicable state's laws. At the time of F's death the land was worth $15,000. A died two months ago, survived by B; at the time of his death the land was worth $30,000. What portion of the land's value (if any) is includible in A's gross estate for federal estate tax purposes? See Treas. Reg. §20.2040-1(a)(1) (1958). If B thereafter sells the land, what is his basis for federal income tax purposes? See page 235, infra.

Life Insurance

Section 2042 of the 1954 Code provides that the gross estate shall include the value of insurance proceeds on the life of the decedent (a) if he possessed at his death any of the *incidents of ownership* under the policies, or (b) if the policy proceeds were payable to his executor or estate. The incidents of ownership include such policy rights as the right to change the beneficiary, to surrender, cancel or assign the policy, to pledge the policy as security for a loan, or to borrow against the cash surrender value in the policy. In the ordinary situation where a person takes out a policy on his own life and names some member of his family as beneficiary, the proceeds will be taxed in the insured's estate since he will hold whatever incidents of ownership are given by the policy. This is true of even a term insurance policy that has no investment features and hence no cash surrender value, for the insured has the right to change the beneficiary designation, and also the right to assign or cancel the policy. The retention of only one incident of ownership causes the full value of the insurance proceeds to be taxed under §2042.[11] If the policy proceeds are payable to the insured's executor or estate, the proceeds are taxed in his estate whether or not he held incidents of ownership in the policy.

An insured can eliminate the estate tax on his life insurance proceeds by making an irrevocable transfer of the policy, and all incidents of ownership under the policy, to some other person. The wisdom of doing this, and also some of the problems that can be encountered in making the transfer, have been the subject of much debate.[12]

TREASURY REGULATIONS §20.2042-1(c) (1958): "(2) For purposes of this paragraph, the term 'incidents of ownership' is not limited in its meaning to ownership of the policy in the technical legal sense. Generally speaking, the term has reference to the right of the insured or his estate to the economic benefits of the policy. Thus, it includes the power to change the beneficiary, to surrender or cancel the policy, to assign the policy, to revoke an assignment, to pledge the policy for a loan, or to obtain from the insurer a loan against the surrender value of the policy, etc. Similarly, the term includes a power to change the beneficiary reserved to a corporation of which the decedent is sole stockholder.

"(4) A decedent is considered to have an 'incident of ownership' in an insurance policy on his life held in trust if, under the terms of the policy, the decedent (either alone or in conjunction with another person or persons) has the power (as trustee or otherwise) to change the beneficial ownership in the policy or its proceeds, or the time or manner of enjoyment thereof, even though the decedent has no beneficial interest in the trust. Moreover, assuming the decedent created the trust, such a power may result in inclusion in the decedent's gross estate under section 2036 or 2038 of other property transferred by the decedent to the trust if, for example, the decedent has the power to surrender the insurance policy and if the income otherwise used to pay premiums on the policy would become currently payable to a beneficiary of the trust in the event that the policy were surrendered."

---

[11] In community property states, life insurance policies that are classified as community property are accorded the same tax treatment as other community assets. To take the typical case in which the husband is the insured under a community policy that names the wife as primary beneficiary, if the husband predeceases his wife only one-half the value of the proceeds is includible in his gross estate. Although the husband, as manager of the community assets, can exercise the incidents of ownership over the entire policy, with respect to the wife's one-half interest in the policy he is deemed to hold these rights as her "agent." Commissioner v. Chase Manhattan Bank, page 527, infra; Note, 64 Mich. L. Rev. 1150 (1966). If the wife predeceases her insured husband, the value of her community one-half interest in the policy (valued at the time of her death) is includible in her gross estate. United States v. Stewart, 270 F.2d 894 (9th Cir.), cert. denied, 361 U.S. 960 (1959); Treas. Reg. §20.2042-1(c)(5) (1958). Since the insured husband would still be living, the amount includible in the wife's gross estate would be one-half the policy's interpolated terminal reserve value — roughly, the policy's cash surrender value.

[12] See Alembic, Transfers of Life Insurance, 106 Trusts & Estates 617 (1967); Miller & Martin, Hold That Transfer! 19 J. Am. Soc'y C.L.U. 160 (1965).

In 1954 Congress eliminated from the Internal Revenue Code a provision that insurance proceeds were includible in the decedent's estate if the decedent paid the premiums. The reason for this was that Congress wanted to treat life insurance like any other property, but some have doubted that life insurance should be treated like other property. See Lowndes & Kramer, Federal Estate and Gift Taxes §13.4 (2d ed. 1962); Groll, Some Federal Tax Aspects of Life Insurance, 15 De Paul L. Rev. 48 (1965).

ESTATE OF FRUEHAUF

United States Court of Appeals, Sixth Circuit, 1970
427 F.2d 80

Peck, Circuit Judge. Harry R. Fruehauf (hereinafter "the decedent") died on April 29, 1962, in Detroit, Michigan. An estate tax return filed with the district director of internal revenue for Detroit, Michigan, was subsequently determined by the Commissioner of Internal Revenue (hereinafter "the Commissioner") to disclose a deficiency in the tax upon the estate. The basis of the Commissioner's deficiency determination was the failure by the executors to include in decedent's gross estate the value of the proceeds of six insurance policies on decedent's life in which the Commissioner determined that decedent possessed "incidents of ownership" at the time of his death. This appeal is from the Tax Court's affirmance of the Commissioner's deficiency determination.

All six of the policies on decedent's life were applied for, paid for, and owned by decedent's wife, Vera Berns Fruehauf, who was also the primary beneficiary of each policy. She died testate approximately fourteen months prior to the date of decedent's death. Among other things, her will bequeathed her residuary estate to a trust, the net income of which was to be paid to her husband, the decedent, for life with a remainder over to her issue per stirpes. The will also assigned to the trust created from the residuary estate the life insurance policies owned by the wife at the date of her death and gave to the executors and trustees certain powers over those insurance policies. Finally, the will named decedent as a co-executor of his wife's estate and as a co-trustee of the trust created by her will. The pertinent provisions of the will are as follows:

> . . .
>
> Tenth: My Executors and my trustees may retain for such periods as they determine advisable any insurance policies owned by me at my death on the life of any other person, and pay the premiums on such policies whenever they become due out of income and/or principal as they shall see fit, and cause themselves to be designated as the beneficiaries thereof, or they may, at any time, sell and assign any of such policies to the person whose life is insured for the cash surrender value thereof, or they may surrender any of such policies for their cash surrender value, or they may, at any time, convert any of such policies into paid up policies in whatever amounts may be provided by the terms of such policies. With respect to any

policies retained by them, they may arrange for the automatic application of dividends in reduction of premium payments and they may borrow on any of such policies, make premium payments from the funds so derived, and repay such loans.

At the date of decedent's death the administration of his wife's estate had not been completed. There had been no distribution to the trust established under paragraph Eighth of his wife's will, and neither decedent nor the other trustees named in the will had been appointed by the probate court. All of the assets of the wife's estate which would have been distributed to the testamentary trust were distributed directly to the Fruehauf's son, Harry R. Fruehauf, Jr.

The Commissioner determined that the proceeds of the six insurance policies on decedent's life were includible in his gross estate under §2042(2) of the Internal Revenue Code of 1954 (hereinafter "the Code"), which provides in part as follows:

> Sec. 2042. Proceeds of Life Insurance.
>
> The value of the gross estate shall include the value of all property —
>
> . . .
>
> (2) Receivable by other Beneficiaries. — To the extent of the amount receivable by all other beneficiaries as insurance under policies on the life of the decedent with respect to which the decedent possessed at his death any of the incidents of ownership, exercisable either alone or in conjunction with any other person.

. . .

Comparison of [Treas. Reg. §20.2042-1(c)(2).] with the pertinent provisions of the wife's will, supra, readily discloses that decedent did possess a number of powers over the policies in the nature of "incidents of ownership" in his fiduciary capacity as executor of his wife's will and trustee-designate of the testamentary trust. The issue was thus narrowed, both in this Court and in the Court below, to the question of whether the powers over the policies which decedent here held constitute "incidents of ownership" in view of the fact that he held these powers in a fiduciary capacity only. The Tax Court answered this in the affirmative and held that therefore the proceeds of the policies were includible in his gross estate.

While the opinion of the Tax Court clearly related the holding to the facts of this case, certain language in that opinion is susceptible to interpretation as a broad per se rule that possession by a decedent of powers constituting incidents of ownership in insurance policies on his life, regardless of the capacity in which they are held, always requires inclusion of the proceeds of the policies in the decedent's gross estate. In reasoning to this conclusion the Tax Court placed heavy reliance on a number of cases which arose under §2038 (and its predecessor sections) of the Code. Section 2038 charges a decedent's gross estate with any property of which he made an inter vivos transfer if, at the date of his death, he possessed the power to "alter, amend, revoke, or terminate" the transfer. The statute also provides that the existence of the power is to be determined "without regard to when or from what source the decedent acquired the power." Thus, the Tax Court reasoned:

> There is no doubt at all but that sections 2038 and 2042 are parts of a tax pattern to make includable in the gross estate property over which the decedent held various powers affecting beneficial enjoyment. Since case law makes immaterial for purposes of section 2038 the capacity in which the powers are held, it is not logical to make capacity a significant factor as far as section 2042 is concerned.

and held that: "[T]he fact the powers over the policies were held by decedent in a fiduciary capacity is no bar to their constituting incidents of ownership under section 2042." 50 T.C. at 926.

We must disagree with the Tax Court's broad per se rule. We believe that there is a distinction between the issues arising under §2038 where the decedent, as transferor of certain property, possesses at his death the power, even though in a fiduciary capacity, to revoke or change the transfer, and the issues in a case arising under §2042 where the decedent is the transferee, in a fiduciary capacity, of powers constituting incidents of ownership in the insurance policies on his life. Where a decedent holds the requisite powers over policies on his life solely because he is a transferee, in a fiduciary capacity, of those powers, with no beneficial interest therein, such arrangement can hardly be construed as a substitute for testamentary disposition on decedent's part. Cf. Porter v. Commissioner of Internal Revenue, 288 U.S. 436, 444, 53 S. Ct. 451, 77 L. Ed. 880 (1933); Commissioner of Internal Revenue v. Chase National Bank, 82 F.2d 157, 158 (2d Cir. 1936).

Moreover, the Tax Court has previously held that where the decedent himself procured the policies on his life and transferred them to a trust, while retaining certain powers over the policies in a fiduciary capacity, the proceeds of the policies were not includible in the decedent's gross estate. In Estate of Newcomb Carlton, 34 T.C. 988 (1960), rev'd on other grounds, 298 F.2d 415 (2d Cir. 1962), the decedent originally procured 21 insurance policies on his life. He then transferred them to a trust, together with certain securities, with instructions to use the net income from the securities to pay the premiums on the life insurance policies. The decedent originally retained certain powers over the policies, but by a subsequent instrument he relinquished all rights over the trust except the right to the income from the trust in excess of that necessary to pay the premiums on the life insurance policies, and the right to appoint a co-trustee, including himself, for a co-trustee who had resigned. Decedent never exercised the power to appoint himself as co-trustee, but he retained that power until his death. Had he appointed himself as co-trustee he would have had, in conjunction with the other co-trustees, broad powers to borrow on the insurance policies or surrender them for their cash surrender value, powers which would constitute incidents of ownership in the policies. The Tax Court stated, however:

> Any control that decedent would have acquired over the insurance policies had he appointed himself co-trustee would have been control over the policies jointly with the corporate trustee as trustee only and such control would be solely for the benefit of the trust. Such control as trustee would not constitute incidents of ownership in

> the insurance policies in decedent except in his capacity as trustee for the benefit of the trust. 34 T.C. at 996.

In Estate of Bert L. Fuchs, 47 T.C. 199 (1966), the decedent was one of three business partners who funded a partnership purchase agreement with insurance policies on the lives of the respective partners. The purchase agreement provided that the beneficiaries would be the owners of the policies, that the beneficiaries would pay the premiums on the policies, and that the insureds would have no right, title or interest in the policies on their respective lives. Through inadvertence on the part of the insurance agent, the policies showed ownership to be in the insured rather than in the beneficiaries, thereby giving the insured the right under the policy to change the beneficiary and to surrender or assign the policies. Nevertheless the Tax Court held that the insured decedent did not possess any incidents of ownership in the policies on his life at the date of his death. While that determination was based on a finding that the insurance policies were subject to the provisions in the partnership purchase agreement, the Tax Court clearly recognized the nature of the fiduciary relationship:

> Assuming, arguendo, that the insured of each policy herein possessed the naked power to change beneficiaries or make an assignment, we cannot say, in view of the partners' agreement regarding the policies, that the insured herein should be treated in any way differently than a common trustee. Each insured herein was under no less of a legal duty to respect the terms of the partners' agreement than a common trustee legally obligated to respect the terms of a trust indenture. Decedent merely had the same type of power over the . . . policies as a trustee's power to affect trust proceeds. We do not believe that this type of naked power alone is sufficient to bring the insurance proceeds within decedent's gross estate. 47 T.C. at 204.

We believe that the Tax Court in this case ignored what it had clearly recognized in these prior cases, i.e., the fundamental nature of the fiduciary relationship. Accordingly, we decline to hold that mere possession by a decedent of any powers in the nature of incidents of ownership in a fiduciary capacity invariably requires inclusion of the proceeds of the policies on the decedent's life in his gross estate.

Our rejection of the per se rule of the Tax Court majority opinion does not dispose of the case, however. In an opinion in which three other judges joined, Judge Simpson of the Tax Court similarly rejected the per se rule of the majority opinion but concurred in the result because of the special facts of this case. Judge Simpson viewed the powers held by decedent in his fiduciary capacity as broad enough to permit their exercise for his individual benefit. Specifically, the concurring opinion concluded that decedent had the power as trustee under paragraph Eighth of his wife's will to surrender the insurance policies for their cash surrender values. The amounts so received could then have been added to the corpus of the trust, thereby increasing the income receivable from the trust by decedent as income beneficiary.

The estate's first response to this analysis of the facts is that decedent did not actually have any powers as trustee or any right to receive any increased income which would result from a surrender of the insurance policies because, at the date of his death, no distribution of assets had been made to the trust, and neither decedent nor any of the other co-trustees had been formally appointed as trustees of the testamentary trust by the state probate court. In support of this argument the estate contends that the normal period for the administration of decedents' estates in Michigan is eighteen months, and since decedent's death here occurred only fourteen months after his wife's death the testamentary trust could not reasonably have been created.

It appears, however, that eighteen months is the maximum period allowable by a Michigan probate court for the administration of an estate before the accrual of interest on pecuniary bequests begins. See In re Howlett's Estate, 275 Mich. 596, 602, 267 N.W. 743, 745 (1936). It does not appear that swifter administration of an estate is impossible. Decedent here had the power to become both trustee and life income beneficiary of the testamentary trust through the exercise of his powers as executor of the will. We believe that it is the existence of that power, not its exercise, which is determinative. Merely because decedent had not performed certain acts necessary to enable him to become trustee-beneficiary of the trust does not detract from his power to do so. Moreover, under the terms of paragraph Eighth of his wife's will decedent had the power in his capacity as *executor* as well as trustee to surrender the policies for their cash value. Accordingly, he could have surrendered the policies for their cash value while he was executor thereby enlarging the income producing ability of the corpus available for distribution in due course to the testamentary trust. We therefore do not consider it significant that decedent had not been formally appointed trustee by the probate court.

The estate's second line of argument is that the fiduciary duty of loyalty imposed upon decedent in his capacity as executor and trustee would have prevented him from exercising any of the powers granted to him in any manner which would benefit himself to the detriment of the remainderman; that any powers granted to decedent which would appear to give him authority to perform acts which would benefit himself to the detriment of the remainderman were void as a matter of law.

It is a well established rule of law that a fiduciary cannot use his position to benefit himself in his individual capacity. See e.g., Michigan Trust Co. v. Luton, 267 Mich. 547, 554, 255 N.W. 351, 353-354 (1934); Chambers v. Chambers, 207 Mich. 129, 136, 173 N.W. 367, 369-370 (1919); Sloan v. Silberstein, 2 Mich. App. 660, 673, 141 N.W.2d 332, 338 (1966); Bogert, Trusts and Trustees §129 (2d ed. 1965); II Scott on Trusts §170.23 (3rd ed. 1967). There is, however, an equally well established countervailing rule of law that a fiduciary may be authorized by the terms of the instrument creating his powers to do that which in the absence of such provision would be a violation of his fiduciary duty of loyalty. II Scott on Trusts §170.9 (3rd ed. 1967). Michigan courts have recognized this rule. See Waddell v. Waddell, 335 Mich. 498, 506-507, 56 N.W.2d 257, 260-261 (1953).

Under the provisions of paragraph Eighth of decedent's wife's will, decedent was authorized, both as executor and as trustee, to surrender the policies on his life for their cash value. If this had been done the policies would have been transformed from non-income producing assets designed to benefit primarily the ultimate beneficiary of the trust into income producing assets (since it must be assumed that such proceeds would not remain idle), which would benefit decedent when he assumed his capacity as trustee and income beneficiary of the trust. We must therefore hold that under the facts of this case decedent could exercise powers in the nature of incidents of ownership in the policies to his individual benefit, and that therefore the proceeds of the policies were includible in his gross estate.

The judgment of the Tax Court is affirmed.[13]

KEARNS v. UNITED STATES, 399 F.2d 226, 185 Ct. Cl. 227 (Ct. Cl. 1968): Oscar Kearns applied for and received a policy of life insurance on his own life. The policy named Kearns's family business, O. E. Kearns & Son, Inc., as beneficiary. Under the terms of the policy certain rights were granted the insured, including the right to change the beneficiary, to exercise a conversion privilege, and to elect a settlement option. The corporation had physical custody of the policy. All premiums were paid by the corporation. The policy was carried as an asset on the corporation's books. On several occasions the policy was assigned as collateral for loans by a bank, which assignments were consented to by the insured. In executing these assignments the corporation was designated as "owner-beneficiary." Oscar Kearns died. Held: The policy is includible in Kearns's estate under §2042 of the Internal Revenue Code. "[P]aragraph 25 of the policy indicates that . . . the insured's privilege . . . of assigning his right to change the beneficiary could not be validly exercised without written notification to the insurance company — that is the clear implication of the requirement that a change of beneficiary could not be made without a 'written notice to the company at the Home Office' — and no such notice of assignment or attempted assignment was ever given. . . .

"Several litigated cases present this same situation, with a decedent insuring his life, naming his business as beneficiary, and with the business thereafter paying the premiums and otherwise exercising dominion over the policy. Such cases hold almost uniformly that where the decedent retains rights under the policy he possesses incidents of ownership within the meaning of section 2042(2). . . . These cases further delineate the general rule that so-called 'policy facts' (i.e., reservation of rights in the contract of insurance) are not easily rebutted by reference to 'intent facts' or external circumstances. The advantage of such a well-defined rule for taxability of life insurance proceeds was succinctly stated by the court in United States v. Rhode Island Hospital Trust Co., 355 F.2d 7, 13 (1st Cir. 1966): 'While decisions against the estate of a passive but power-possessing decedent may often conflict with the honest intentions and understanding of premium-paying beneficiaries and insureds, the alternative of abandoning the insistence on the governing nature of the contract, in most cases, is less desirable. The drawing of a useful line would

[13] Noted 49 N.C.L. Rev. 539. — Eds.

be impossible; there would be a much wider range of varying decisions on similar facts; and there would be an invitation to unprincipled estate manipulation. As government counsel has pointed out, there could always be a formally executed side agreement under which the insured clearly surrenders to the beneficiary all his rights to the policy, such agreement to be brought to light only in the event of the decedent's dying before the beneficiary.' "

2. *The Gross Estate and Lifetime Transfers*

It should be obvious that if the estate tax reached only assets owned or transferred at death, this would encourage lifetime transfers designed to reduce the gross estate. It might even be possible to avoid the tax by making deathbed gifts, or transfers in which the transferor retained substantial economic benefits in the property. The federal tax laws respond to these possible means of estate tax avoidance in three ways. First, a gift tax is imposed on irrevocable lifetime transfers. Second, the gross estate is defined to include inter vivos transfers that are deemed to be "in contemplation of death." Section 2035 provides that an inter vivos transfer is presumed to have been made in contemplation of death if it was made within three years of the transferor's death. Third, the gross estate is also defined to include inter vivos transfers where the transferor retained certain controls or economic benefits. Section 2036 taxes transfers with a retained life estate and transfers in which the transferor retained the power to control the beneficial enjoyment of the property. Section 2037 reaches transfers "taking effect at death"—a phrase that has a highly technical meaning under the tax code. Section 2038 taxes revocable transfers, and also those transfers in which the transferor retained the power to control the beneficial enjoyment of the property.

Transfers in Contemplation of Death

The purpose of §2035 is to prevent avoidance of the estate tax through the use of inter vivos transfers intended as testamentary substitutes. Although these transfers are subject to the gift tax, because of the lower gift tax rates and other factors there would be a strong inducement to making gifts shortly before death if the assets thereby escaped estate taxation.

Transfers within three years of death are presumed to have been made in contemplation of death. The decedent's personal representative has the burden of showing that a transfer made within this period was motivated by considerations other than "contemplation of death," and that the assets should not be taxed in the decedent's estate. But if the transfer was made more than three years before death, the statute expressly provides that it is not subject to estate taxation regardless of the motives that may have prompted the transfer.

The tax law concept of "in contemplation of death" should not be confused with the common law gift causa mortis. The latter is a gift made in anticipation of impending death that is revocable by the donor and is automatically revoked if the donor survives the apprehended peril. Although the gift causa mortis is made "in contemplation of death" in the tax law sense, there is no need to resort to §2035 to subject the transfer to estate taxation. It is taxed under §2038 because of the donor's retention of the power to revoke.

When is a transfer "in contemplation of death"? The test that has been developed by the courts is a very general one. As stated by the Supreme Court in the leading case of United States v. Wells:[14]

> The dominant purpose [of the statute] is to reach substitutes for testamentary dispositions and thus to prevent the evasion of the estate tax. . . . As the transfer may otherwise have all the indicia of a valid gift inter vivos, the differentiating factor must be found in the transferor's motive. Death must be "contemplated," that is, the motive which induces the transfer must be of the sort which leads to testamentary disposition. . . .
>
> It is contemplation of death, not necessarily contemplation of imminent death, to which the statute refers. It is conceivable that the idea of death may possess the mind so as to furnish a controlling motive for the disposition of property, although death is not thought to be close at hand. Old age may give premonitions and promptings independent of mortal disease. Yet age in itself cannot be regarded as furnishing a decisive test, for sound health and purposes associated with life, rather than with death, may motivate the transfer. The words "in contemplation of death" mean that the thought of death is the impelling cause of the transfer. . . . If it is the thought of death, as a controlling motive prompting the disposition of property, that affords the test, it follows that the statute does not embrace gifts inter vivos which spring from a different motive. . . .
>
> It is apparent that there can be no precise delimitation of the transactions embraced within the conception of transfers in "contemplation of death," as there can be none in relation to fraud, undue influence, due process of law, or other familiar legal concepts which are applicable to many varying circumstances. There is no escape from the necessity of carefully scrutinizing the circumstances of each case to detect the dominant motive of the donor in the light of his bodily and mental condition, and thus to give effect to the manifest purpose of the statute.

It is hardly surprising that this test, based as it is upon the subjective state of mind of the donor at the time of the gift, has produced a considerable amount of litigation, with the courts "carefully scrutinizing the circumstances of each case to detect the dominant motive of the donor." In each case the attorney for the estate produces evidence by which he seeks to persuade the jury that the gift was induced by "lifetime" rather than "testamentary" motives. More often than not, the jury's decision is favorable to the taxpayer.[15] Various factors have emerged from the cases

[14] 283 U.S. 102, 116-119 (1931).

[15] The Commissioner has been singularly unsuccessful in persuading juries that particular transfers were made in contemplation of death. See 1 Casner, Estate Planning 191 (3d ed. 1961, Supp. 1967). In his 1967 Supplement, Casner cites and discusses thirty-two cases reported since 1961. In twenty-seven of the cases the courts reached decisions that the transfer was not made in contemplation of death. Eleven of the twenty-seven cases involved donors aged seventy-two or over, some of whom were in poor health at the time of the transfer.

as tending to show that the particular transfer was or was not in contemplation of death. Findings that the transfer was not in contemplation of death have been made when circumstances indicated that the decedent's dominant motive was to make his children financially independent, to establish his children in a business enterprise, to reduce his income taxes, or to carry out a long-continuing program of giving to his children. The physical condition of the transferor has been stressed in support of decisions that the transfer was or was not in contemplation of death. And while the advanced age of the donor would seem to point to a finding that the transfer was made in contemplation of death, in a substantial number of cases involving donors in their seventies, eighties, and even nineties, the courts have made findings favorable to the taxpayer.[16]

PROBLEM

In 1965 O takes out a policy of life insurance on his own life, naming his wife as beneficiary. O pays the annual premiums. In 1967 O transfers all his rights in the policy to his wife. O continues to pay the premiums. In 1972 O dies. If the premium payments made in the last three years before his death are deemed in contemplation of death, what amount is included in O's gross estate? First Nat'l Bank v. United States, 423 F.2d 1286 (5th Cir. 1970), noted 49 N.C.L. Rev. 548, 49 Texas L. Rev. 365; Gorman v. United States, 288 F. Supp. 225 (E.D. Mich. 1968), noted 82 Harv. L. Rev. 1765, 67 Mich. L. Rev. 812. In answering this question bear in mind that a gift of stock in contemplation of death is includible in the donor's gross estate at its value as of the date of his death; and that if O had transferred this policy in 1970, rather than in 1967, in contemplation of death the policy would be included in O's estate at its face value which became collectible at his death.

Transfers with a Retained Life Estate

Sections 2036, 2037, and 2038 of the Internal Revenue Code deal with lifetime transfers where the transferor retains some rights or controls or where beneficial enjoyment of the property is postponed until the transferor's death. These sections raise some of the most troublesome and complex problems encountered in estate taxation. They can cause the completely unexpected taxation of irrevocable transfers by which it was intended to remove assets from the transferor's estate. A consideration of all of the problems raised by these provisions is beyond the scope of this course. In the discussion that follows, the basic features of these sections are briefly outlined, and illustrations are given of some, but by no means all, of the complex problems that may be encountered.

Section 2036(a) provides: "The value of the gross estate shall include the value

[16] In Kniskern v. United States, 232 F. Supp. 7 (S.D. Fla. 1964), a gift made by a 99-year-old was held not to have been made in contemplation of death. In reviewing the evidence the court noted, inter alia, that movies taken on the donor's 100th birthday "revealed the decedent's extraordinary vitality, geniality and enjoyment of life."

of all property to the extent of any interest therein of which the decedent has at any time made a transfer (except in case of a bona fide sale for an adequate and full consideration in money or money's worth), by trust or otherwise, under which he has retained for his life or for any period not ascertainable without reference to his death or for any period which does not in fact end before his death —

"(1) The possession or enjoyment of, or the right to the income from, the property, or

"(2) The right, either alone or in conjunction with any person, to designate the persons who shall possess or enjoy the property or the income therefrom."

Note that §2036 imposes a tax on two types of transfers. Section 2036(a)(1) applies when the decedent retains a life estate in the transferred property. Although his reserved life estate terminates at his death, the transfer is subjected to estate taxation because the decedent retained the most important incident of property ownership: the right to possess and enjoy the property, or the right to its income, for life.

Section 2036(a)(2) reaches transfers in which the decedent retains the right to control beneficial enjoyment of the property, even though he cannot exercise that right for his own economic benefit. To take an obvious case, when the transferor designates himself as a co-trustee and the trustees have a discretionary power to accumulate trust income or distribute it to the beneficiary, or a power to distribute the income among several beneficiaries in such shares as the trustees shall determine, the transfer is taxed under this section. The transfer is also taxed even though the power is exercisable only with the consent of a person having an interest which could be adversely affected by the exercise of the power.

The retained powers that result in taxation under this section are not always obvious. They may be hidden in the administrative powers given to the trustees. In State Street Trust Co. v. United States,[17] O created three irrevocable trusts for the benefit of his children, naming himself and a corporate fiduciary as co-trustees. In all three trusts the trustees were given broad administrative powers, as follows: to exchange trust assets for other property without reference to the value of the properties involved in the exchange; to invest trust property in securities yielding either a high rate of income or no income at all, without limitation as to the percentage of trust corpus invested in either category; and to allocate trust receipts between income and corpus, with the power not limited to situations where the law governing apportionment of trust receipts was unsettled. The trust further provided that the trustees' decisions in good faith were binding on all parties, and that the trustees were liable only for willful acts or defaults and not for errors of judgment. O retained no direct or indirect right to the income from the trust, and he reserved no express power to control the beneficial enjoyment of the trust property. The court held, however, that the trust assets were includible in his gross estate because of the administrative powers that were exercisable by him as a co-trustee.[18]

[17] 263 F.2d 635 (1st Cir. 1959).

[18] See Gray & Covey, State Street — A Case Study of Sections 2036(a)(2) and 2038, 15 Tax L. Rev. 75 (1959).

OLD COLONY TRUST CO. v. UNITED STATES
United States Court of Appeals, First Circuit, 1970
423 F.2d 601

ALDRICH, Chief Judge. The sole question in this case is whether the estate of a settlor of an inter vivos trust, who was a trustee until the date of his death, is to be charged with the value of the principal he contributed by virtue of reserved powers in the trust. The executor paid the tax and sued for its recovery in the district court. All facts were stipulated. The court ruled for the government, 300 F. Supp. 1032, and the executor appeals.

The initial life beneficiary of the trust was the settlor's adult son. Eighty per cent of the income was normally to be payable to him, and the balance added to principal. Subsequent beneficiaries were the son's widow and his issue. The powers upon which the government relies to cause the corpus to be includible in the settlor-trustee's estate are contained in two articles. A third article, purporting to limit the personal liability of the trustees for acts of mismanagement, although relied on by the government, has no bearing on the questions in this case because it does not affect the meaning, extent or nature of the trustees' duties and powers. Briggs v. Crowley, 1967, 352 Mass. 194, 224 N.E.2d 417. We will not consider it further.

Article 4 permitted the trustees to increase the percentage of income payable to the son beyond the eighty per cent, "in their absolute discretion . . . when in their opinion such increase is needed in case of sickness, or desirable in view of changed circumstances." In addition, under Article 4 the trustees were given the discretion to cease paying income to the son, and add it all to principal, "during such period as the Trustees may decide that the stoppage of such payments is for his best interests."

Article 7 gave broad administrative or management powers to the trustees, with discretion to acquire investments not normally held by trustees, and the right to determine, what was to be charged or credited to income or principal, including stock dividends or deductions for amortization. It further provided that all divisions and decisions made by the trustees in good faith should be conclusive on all parties, and in summary, stated that the trustees were empowered, "generally to do all things in relation to the Trust Fund which the Donor could do if living and this Trust had not been executed."

The government claims that each of these two articles meant that the settlor-trustee had "the right . . . to designate the persons who shall possess or enjoy the [trust] property or the income therefrom" within the meaning of section 2036(a)(2) of the Internal Revenue Code of 1954, 26 U.S.C. §2036(a)(2), and that the settlor-trustee at the date of his death possessed a power "to alter, amend, revoke, or terminate" within the meaning of section 2038(a)(1) (26 U.S.C. §2038(a)-(1)).

If State Street Trust Co. v. United States, 1 Cir., 1959, 263 F.2d 635, was correctly decided in this aspect, the government must prevail because of the Article

7 powers. There this court, Chief Judge Magruder dissenting, held against the taxpayer because broad powers similar to those in Article 7 meant that the trustees "could very substantially shift the economic benefits of the trusts between the life tenants and the remaindermen," so that the settlor "as long as he lived, in substance and effect and in a very real sense . . . 'retained for his life . . . the right . . . to designate the persons who shall possess or enjoy the property or the income therefrom; . . . .' " 263 F.2d at 639-640, quoting 26 U.S.C. §2036(a)(2). We accept the taxpayer's invitation to reconsider this ruling.

It is common ground that a settlor will not find the corpus of the trust included in his estate merely because he named himself a trustee. Jennings v. Smith, 2 Cir., 1947, 161 F.2d 74. He must have reserved a power to himself [19] that is inconsistent with the full termination of ownership. The government's brief defines this as "sufficient dominion and control until his death." Trustee powers given for the administration or management of the trust must be equitably exercised, however, for the benefit of the trust as a whole. Blodget v. Delaney, 1 Cir., 1953, 201 F.2d 589; United States v. Powell, 10 Cir., 1962, 307 F.2d 821; Scott, Trusts §§183, 232 (3d ed. 1967); Rest. 2d, Trusts §§183, 232. The court in State Street conceded that the powers at issue were all such powers, but reached the conclusion that, cumulatively, they gave the settlor dominion sufficiently unfettered to be in the nature of ownership. With all respect to the majority of the then court, we find it difficult to see how a power can be subject to control by the probate court, and exercisable only in what the trustee fairly concludes is in the interests of the trust and its beneficiaries as a whole, and at the same time be an ownership power.

The government's position, to be sound, must be that the trustee's powers are beyond the court's control. Under Massachusetts law, however, no amount of administrative discretion prevents judicial supervision of the trustee. Thus in Appeal of Davis, 1903, 183 Mass. 499, 67 N.E. 604, a trustee was given "full power to make purchases, investments and exchanges . . . in such manner as to them shall seem expedient; it being my intention to give my trustees . . . the same dominion and control over said trust property as I now have." In spite of this language, and in spite of their good faith, the court charged the trustees for failing sufficiently to diversify their investment portfolio.

The Massachusetts court has never varied from this broad rule of accountability, and has twice criticized State Street for its seeming departure. Boston Safe Deposit & Trust Co. v. Stone, 1965, 348 Mass. 345, 351, n. 8, 203 N.E.2d 547; Old Colony Trust Co. v. Silliman, 1967, 352 Mass. 6, 8-9, 223 N.E.2d 504. See also, Estate of McGillicuddy, 54 T.C. No. 27, 2/17/70, CCH Tax Ct. Rep. Dec. 29, 1965. We make a further observation, which the court in State Street failed to note, that the provision in that trust (as in the case at bar) that the trustees could "do all things in relation to the Trust Fund which I, the Donor, could do if . . . the Trust had not been executed," is almost precisely the provision which did not protect the trustees from accountability in Appeal of Davis, supra.

[19] The number of other trustees who must join in the exercise of that power, unless the others have antagonistic interests of a substantial nature is, of course, immaterial. Treas. Reg. §20.2036-1(a)(ii), (b)(3)(i) (1958); §20.2038-1(a) (1958).

We do not believe that trustee powers are to be more broadly construed for tax purposes than the probate court would construe them for administrative purposes. More basically, we agree with Judge Magruder's observation that nothing is "gained by lumping them together." State Street Trust Co. v. United States, supra, 263 F.2d at 642. We hold that no aggregation of purely administrative powers can meet the government's amorphous test of "sufficient dominion and control" so as to be equated with ownership.

This does not resolve taxpayer's difficulties under Article 4. Quite different considerations apply to distribution powers. Under them the trustee can, expressly, prefer one beneficiary over another. Furthermore, his freedom of choice may vary greatly, depending upon the terms of the individual trust. If there is an ascertainable standard, the trustee can be compelled to follow it.[20] If there is not, even though he is a fiduciary, it is not unreasonable to say that his retention of an unmeasurable freedom of choice is equivalent to retaining some of the incidents of ownership. Hence, under the cases, if there is an ascertainable standard the settlor-trustee's estate is not taxed, . . . but if there is not, it is taxed. . . .[21]

The trust provision which is uniformly held to provide an ascertainable standard is one which, though variously expressed, authorizes such distributions as may be needed to continue the beneficiary's accustomed way of life. . . . On the other hand, if the trustee may go further, and has power to provide for the beneficiary's "happiness," Merchants Nat'l Bank v. Com'r of Internal Revenue, 1943, 320 U.S. 256, 64 S. Ct. 108, 88 L. Ed. 35, or "pleasure," Industrial Trust Co. v. Com'r of Internal Revenue, 1 Cir., 1945, 151 F.2d 592, cert. denied 327 U.S. 788, 66 S. Ct. 807, 90 L. Ed. 1014, or "use and benefit," Newton Trust Co. v. Com'r of Internal Revenue, 1 Cir., 1947, 160 F.2d 175, or "reasonable requirement[s]," State Street Bank & Trust Co. v. United States, 1 Cir., 1963, 313 F.2d 29, the standard is so loose that the trustee is in effect uncontrolled.

In the case at bar the trustees could increase the life tenant's income "in case of sickness, or [if] desirable in view of changed circumstances." Alternatively, they could reduce it "for his best interests." "Sickness" presents no problem. Conceivably, providing for "changed circumstances" is roughly equivalent to maintaining the son's present standard of living. . . . The unavoidable stumbling block is the trustees' right to accumulate income and add it to capital (which the son would never receive) when it is to the "best interests" of the son to do so. Additional payments to a beneficiary whenever in his "best interests" might seem to be too broad a standard in any event. In addition to the previous cases see Estate of Yawkey, 1949, 12 T.C. 1164, where the court said, at p. 1170,

> We can not regard the language involved ["best interest"] as limiting the usual scope of a trustee's discretion. It must always be anticipated that trustees will

[20] See, e.g., Old Colony Trust Co. v. Rodd, 1970 Mass. A.S. 25, 254 N.E.2d 886, trustee of trust to provide "comfortable support and maintenance," rebuked for "parsimonious" exercise of judgment.

[21] See Comment, The Doctrine of External Standards Under Sections 2036(a)(2) and 2038, 52 Minn. L. Rev. 1071 (1968). — Eds.

act for the best interests of a trust beneficiary, and an exhortation to act "in the interests and for the welfare" of the beneficiary does not establish an external standard.

Power, however, to decrease or cut off a beneficiary's income when in his "best interests," is even more troublesome. When the beneficiary is the son, and the trustee the father, a particular purpose comes to mind, parental control through holding the purse strings. The father decides what conduct is to the "best interests" of the son, and if the son does not agree, he loses his allowance. Such a power has the plain indicia of ownership control. The alternative, that the son, because of other means, might not need this income, and would prefer to have it accumulate for his widow and children after his death, is no better. If the trustee has power to confer "happiness" on the son by generosity to someone else, this seems clearly an unascertainable standard. Cf. Merchants Nat'l Bank v. Com'r of Internal Revenue, supra, 320 U.S. at 261-263, 64 S. Ct. 108.

The case of Hays' Estate v. Com'r of Internal Revenue, 5 Cir., 1950, 181 F.2d 169, is contrary to our decision. The opinion is unsupported by either reasoning or authority, and we will not follow it. With the present settlor-trustee free to determine the standard himself, a finding of ownership control was warranted. To put it another way, the cost of holding onto the strings may prove to be a rope burn. State Street Bank & Trust Co. v. United States, supra.

Affirmed.[22]

It might be thought that application of §2036(a)(2) to retained powers can be avoided by not naming the settlor as trustee or co-trustee. This alone is not enough, however. If the named trustee has these powers, and if the settlor has the power to remove the trustee and appoint himself as successor trustee, the settlor is deemed to possess the powers, and estate taxation results.[23] This may be true even though the trust instrument, in granting the settlor the power to remove the trustee and appoint a successor, is silent on whether the settlor can appoint himself as successor trustee, for the settlor may have this power under local law.[24]

The more difficult problems that can be encountered under §2036 are not limited to cases involving the "right . . . to designate the persons who shall possess or enjoy" language of §2036(a)(2). It is also possible that §2036(a)(1) can apply to an inter vivos transfer although the transferor did not expressly reserve a life interest. One such problem is raised by the so-called "support" trust. A transfer is taxed under §2036(a)(1) if the income from the transferred property is required to be used to discharge a legal obligation of the transferor.[25] This includes a legal obliga-

[22] Noted 49 N.C.L. Rev. 811. — Eds.

[23] Treas. Reg. §20.2036-1(b)(3) (1958); Van Beuren v. McLoughlin, 262 F.2d 315 (1st Cir. 1958), cert. denied, 359 U.S. 991 (1959).

[24] Clark v. United States, 267 F.2d 501 (1st Cir. 1959), on remand 180 F. Supp. 696 (N.D. Me. 1960).

[25] Treas. Reg. §20.2036-1(b)(2) (1958).

tion to support a dependent. If O creates a trust that directs the payment of trust income for the "maintenance and support" of his wife or children, and if under local law O is deemed to have a legal obligation to support his wife and children, the trust assets are taxed in O's estate. Although O had no direct right to the income, its use to discharge his support obligation is deemed to put the transfer within the intendment of §2036.

PROBLEMS

1. Settlor executes a trust instrument providing that the entire net income be paid to his wife for "her support and comfort." The trust is irrevocable. Upon settlor's death is the trust property included in the settlor's gross estate? Richards v. Commissioner, 375 F.2d 997 (10th Cir. 1967); First Nat'l Bank v. United States, 211 F. Supp. 403 (M.D. Ala. 1962). Would the trust property be includible if the trust terms did not require that the income be used for "her support and comfort," but only gave the trustee discretion to so use it? Commissioner v. Douglass' Estate, 143 F.2d 961 (3d Cir. 1944); Estate of Jack F. Chrysler, 44 T.C. 55 (1965), rev'd on other grounds sub nom. Estate of Chrysler v. Commissioner, 361 F.2d 508 (2d Cir. 1966). Would your answer to the last question be the same if the settlor were a trustee?

2. Settlor transfers property to himself and X Bank as co-trustees. Income is to be paid to the settlor's issue in such shares and amounts as the trustees in their discretion decide. The trust instrument contains a provision that upon the incapacity of the settlor-trustee, X Bank "shall act as sole trustee." Subsequently a conservator is appointed for the settlor by a court on the ground that he is "incapable of caring properly for his property." Will the value of the trust property be included in the settlor's gross estate? Round v. Commissioner, 332 F.2d 590 (1st Cir. 1964).

3. Joseph Grace executes a trust instrument providing for payment of income to his wife, Janet, for her life, with payment to her of any part of the principal which a majority of the trustees think advisable. Mrs. Grace is given a special testamentary power of appointment over the trust estate. Named as trustees are Joseph, his nephew, and a third party. Shortly thereafter Janet Grace, at Joseph's request, executes a virtually identical trust instrument naming Joseph as life beneficiary. Upon Joseph's death is the corpus of either of the trusts includible in Joseph's gross estate? United States v. Estate of Grace, 395 U.S. 316 (1969).

Revocable Transfers

Section 2038 overlaps §2036(a)(2) to a considerable extent, and so §2038 will be considered before §2037. Section 2038 includes in the decedent's gross estate lifetime gratuitous transfers "where the enjoyment thereof was subject at the date of his death to any change through the exercise of a power (in whatever capacity exercisable) by the decedent alone or by the decedent in conjunction with any other person (without regard to when or from what source the decedent acquired such power), to alter, amend, revoke, or terminate, or where any such power is relinquished in contemplation of decedent's death." The property is taxed in decedent's estate even though the power is exercisable only with the consent of a person having an interest which could be adversely affected by the power's exercise.

If the power to alter, amend, revoke, or terminate is given to some third person, the transfer is not taxed under §2038 even if the person given the power is a nonadverse party. It is for this reason that a trustee who is not the settlor can be given broad discretionary powers, including the power to distribute a portion or all of the trust corpus (thereby terminating the trust), without adverse tax consequences. This last statement is subject to the same qualification that was made in the discussion of §2036. If a trustee has such a power, and if the transferor has the right to remove the trustee and appoint himself as trustee, the transferor is treated as having the power and §2038 is applicable.[26]

Although §2038 is generally referred to as the provision that taxes revocable transfers, it reaches transfers over which the decedent held any one of the enumerated powers,[27] even though the power cannot be exercised in such a way as to benefit the transferor.[28] If O creates an irrevocable trust in which he, as co-trustee, has a discretionary power to accumulate or distribute trust income, or a discretionary power to distribute corpus to the income beneficiary, the transfer is taxed in O's estate under §2038; his discretionary power is a power to alter or amend.[29]

As with §2036, the retained powers that can result in taxation under §2038 are not always as obvious as the ones discussed above. For example, if the settlor of an irrevocable trust has a power to borrow from the trustee without furnishing adequate security,[30] or a power to substitute other assets in exchange for the assets originally placed in the trust,[31] he is deemed to have a power to remove assets from the trust — a power to revoke. Or if the settlor as co-trustee has such broad powers over the administration of the trust that he can alter the respective interests of the

[26] Treas. Reg. §20.2038-1(a)(3) (1958).

[27] In Rhode Island Hospital Trust Co. v. Commissioner, 219 F.2d 923 (1st Cir. 1955), the settlor created a trust under which he expressly retained the power to revoke, and also a power to "annul, change or modify" the terms of the transfer. Twelve years later he executed an instrument providing that "I hereby declare" the trust "to be irrevocable." On the settlor's death the trust was taxed in his estate. Although he had relinquished the power to revoke the trust, his amendment left him with the power to "alter or amend." Quaere: Would the attorney who drafted and supervised the amendment of the trust be liable for negligence?

[28] In Florida Nat'l Bank v. United States, 336 F.2d 598 (3d Cir. 1964), cert. denied, 380 U.S. 911 (1965), the settlor created an irrevocable trust in which he retained the power to alter or amend, but the trust expressly provided that this power could not be exercised in favor of the settlor or his estate. Held: the trust was taxed in the settlor's estate under the predecessor section to §2038.

[29] Note that O's reserved power would also cause taxation under §2036(a)(2). His discretionary power is a power to control the beneficial enjoyment of the property. For a discussion of the relationship between §2036 and §2038 see Lowndes & Kramer, Federal Estate and Gift Taxes 188-191 (2d ed. 1962).

[30] Cf. Estate of Garland v. Commissioner, 42 B.T.A. 324 (1940), 43 B.T.A. 731 (1941) (income tax).

[31] Commonwealth Trust Co. v. Driscoll, 50 F. Supp. 949 (W.D. Pa.), aff'd, 137 F.2d 653 (3d Cir. 1943), cert. denied, 321 U.S. 764 (1944).

income beneficiary and remaindermen, he may be deemed to have a power to alter or amend.[32] In drafting a trust by which it is intended to remove the assets from the transferor's estate, more is needed to avoid the operation of §2038 than a simple declaration that the trust shall be irrevocable. The attorney-draftsman must be on familiar terms with the many problems that lurk behind the seemingly innocuous language of "alter, amend, revoke, or terminate."

PROBLEMS

1. O transfers property to X in trust to pay the income to A for life, and on A's death to pay the trust assets to B. O retains the power to invade corpus for the benefit of B. What amount is includible in O's gross estate?

2. O transfers property to X in trust to pay the income to A for life, and on A's death to pay the trust assets to B. O retains the power to accumulate income and add it to corpus. What amount is includible in O's gross estate?

3. O transfers property to X in trust to pay the income to A until he reaches twenty-five, and at age twenty-five, or (if A dies under twenty-five) at the time A would have reached twenty-five had he lived, to pay the trust assets to A or his estate. O retains the power to accumulate income for A until he reaches twenty-one and the power to invade corpus for the benefit of A. What amount is includible in O's gross estate? Lober v. United States, 346 U.S. 335 (1953).

Transfers Taking Effect at Death

Section 2037 of the 1954 Code is titled "Transfers Taking Effect at Death." One might expect that a statutory provision so titled would encompass a broad range of lifetime transfers in which succession to an interest in property "took effect" at the transferor's death. In point of fact, however, the scope of §2037 is quite limited. And, somewhat surprisingly, neither the Code provision nor the supporting regulations so much as mention the phrase, "transfers taking effect at death." Instead, the detailed language of the statute and of the regulations is largely devoted to defining and illustrating the types of *reversionary interests* that can, in certain situations, invoke §2037. As this would indicate, the estate tax treatment of transfers "taking effect at death" has had a long and tortured history. The numerous cases and statutory changes that have led to the present language of §2037 all but defy comprehension. Certainly they defy summarization in this brief treatment of the estate tax laws. Our intention is to outline the narrow circumstances that can give rise to estate taxation under this provision.

Under §2037 the value of property transferred inter vivos is includible in the transferor's gross estate if (1) possession or enjoyment of the property can be obtained only by a transferee's surviving the transferor, *and* (2) the transferor retained a reversionary interest whose value, immediately before his death, was more than five percent of the value of the transferred property. For example, suppose O places

[32] Commissioner v. Hager's Estate, 173 F.2d 613 (3d Cir. 1949).

securities in an irrevocable trust, directing the trustee to pay the income to O's son A for life, and on A's death to pay the trust principal to O if he is then living, otherwise to B if B is then living. Observe that this transfer leaves two reversionary interests in O: one expressed in the trust (if O survives A), the other arising because of an incomplete disposition (if neither O nor B survives A). Note also that if O dies in the lifetime of A and B, the reversionary interest that was dependent upon his surviving A has no value. This does not affect the applicability of §2037, though, for the statute reaches transfers in which a reversionary interest is retained even though the reversion never takes in possession and enjoyment.

Whether O's reversionary interest exceeds five percent of the value of the transferred property will depend upon actuarial computations of the total value of the two reversions, made as of the moment immediately before O's death.[33] If the five-percent requirement is met, the entire value of the property (less the value of A's life estate), and not just the value of O's reversionary interests, is includible in O's gross estate. This is because the first requirement under §2037 is clearly met: since B takes only if he survives A, and O does not survive A, B will take under the trust only if he survives O.

What if, in the above example, the combined value of the two reversions does not exceed five percent? Even though the transfer imposes a requirement that B must survive the transferor in order to take, §2037 is not applicable since *both* of the requirements under the statute have not been met. In this situation, the expressly created reversion that was contingent upon O surviving A is not taxed under §2033: since O failed to survive A, the value of this interest at O's death is zero. However, the end reversion that will take if neither O nor B survives A is taxed as an owned interest under §2033. Do you see why this is so?

Although the tax consequences of bringing §2037 into play are serious, this provision is far less of a threat to the draftsman of an irrevocable inter vivos trust than its companion provisions, §§2036 and 2038. The draftsman can avoid the operation of §2037 by eliminating any possibility of a reversionary interest in the transferor — something that should be done in any trust. This is accomplished by making sure that there is some taker (other than the transferor or his estate) regardless of what contingencies occur, and by including an effective end limitation to heirs or to a charity, to take effect if all of the designated beneficiaries die before they become entitled to their interests. We'll be talking about reversions and end limitations at a point later in the course.

3. *The Gross Estate and Powers of Appointment*

Under §2041 the gross estate includes the value of assets over which the decedent held a general power of appointment.[34] Subject to some exceptions, a general

[33] The value of the express reversionary interest would be measured by the actuarial probability of a person O's age (the moment before his death) outliving a person A's age. The value of the reversionary interest arising by implication would be measured by the actuarial probability of a person A's age outliving both a person B's age and a person O's age. Treas. Reg. §20.2037-1(c)(3) (1958).

[34] Section 2041 applies to assets that were not owned by the decedent during his lifetime.

power of appointment is defined as a power exercisable in favor of the decedent, his estate, his creditors, or the creditors of his estate. The assets subject to the general power are taxed in the decedent's estate whether the power was exercisable during the decedent's lifetime or by his will, and (if the power was created after October 21, 1942),[35] whether or not the decedent actually exercised the power. Thus if H settles property in a trust providing for the payment of trust income to W for life, and on her death "to pay the trust corpus to such person or persons as W shall appoint by will," the value of the appointive assets is includible in W's gross estate. Although W is restricted to the income from the trust, and she cannot exercise the power of appointment in such a way as to benefit herself or her creditors during her lifetime, she has a testamentary power that can be exercised in favor of her estate or the creditors of her estate.

If the decedent holds a special power of appointment, the assets subject to the power are not taxed under §2041.[36] A special power of appointment is a power to appoint among a restricted class of persons that does not include the decedent, his estate, his creditors, or the creditors of his estate. If, for example, H settles property in a trust providing for the payment of trust income to W for life, and on her death "to pay the trust corpus to such one or more of her descendants as she shall appoint by deed or will," whether or not W exercises the power none of the trust assets are taxed in her estate. Since W's life estate terminates at her death, nothing is taxed under §2033. Since W's power of appointment is not a general power, §2041 is not applicable. As this example demonstrates, it is possible to give a beneficiary a life interest in property plus a limited power to control the devolution of the property at his death without subjecting the property to taxation in the beneficiary's estate.

Under several exceptions written into §2041, it is also possible to give the income beneficiary certain limited powers to appoint to himself during his lifetime without adverse estate tax consequences. The statute provides that if the decedent held a power to consume, invade or appropriate property for his own benefit, the power shall not be deemed a general power of appointment for estate tax purposes if the exercise of the power is "limited by an ascertainable standard relating to the health, education, support, or maintenance of the decedent." [37] Section 2041 further provides that if the decedent held a power to consume or invade that was limited to the greater of $5000 or 5 percent of the trust corpus each year, except for the year of death the decedent's failure to exercise the power in any year is not treated as a taxable lapse of the power.[38] If the beneficiary is given a "$5000 or 5

If the decedent made a transfer of assets over which he reserved the equivalent of a general or even a special power of appointment, the value of the assets is includible in his gross estate under §2036(a)(2) and §2038. Sections 2036 and 2038 apply to retained "grantor" powers; §2041 applies to powers given to the decedent by someone else.

[35] Property subject to a general power created on or before October 21, 1942, is taxed in the estate of the holder of the power only if the power is exercised. Int. Rev. Code of 1954, §2041(a)(1).

[36] Treas. Reg. §20.2041-1(c)(1) (1958). There is one important exception to this general rule. See the "Delaware Tax Trap," page 1044, infra.

[37] Int. Rev. Code of 1954, §2041(b)(1)(A). See page 875, infra.

[38] Int. Rev. Code of 1954, §2041(b)(2). In order to simplify the sentence in the text we

percent" limited invasion power, the only estate tax consequence is that in the year of death he is treated as having a taxable general power to that extent. Only 5 percent of the trust corpus or $5000 (whichever is greater) is includible in the beneficiary's gross estate.[39]

Special and limited powers given to a beneficiary, and also discretionary powers given to a trustee, can be employed to create a flexible estate plan that accommodates the foreseen needs of the transferor's family and yet allows for adjustments if circumstances should warrant. Contrast this with the traditional family settlement of property "to my wife for life, remainder to my issue then living per stirpes." At the time the transfer is made, the expected income from the property may appear to insure that the wife's support and other needs will be met. But if she (or the children) should encounter unusual medical or other expenses, or if the cost of living should rise over the years, the income from the property may prove to be inadequate. If, on the other hand, the trustee is given a discretionary power to distribute corpus to the wife whenever it is needed to supplement the trust's income, or if the wife is given a power measured by an ascertainable standard or a $5000 or 5 percent invasion power, the corpus of the trust can be used to satisfy the wife's support or other needs whenever trust income proves insufficient.

---

have written "the greater of $5000 or 5 percent of the trust corpus." The exact language of the Code is "the greater of the following amounts:

"(A) $5000, or

"(B) 5 percent of the aggregate value, at the time of such lapse, of the assets out of which, or the proceeds of which, the exercise of the lapsed powers could have been satisfied."

Reference to the exact language is helpful in drafting 5 percent powers, because it is in several respects ambiguous. See problem, page 877, infra.

[39] Treas. Reg. §20.2041-3(d)(3) (1958) illustrates the operation of this type of limited invasion power with the following example: "Assume that A transferred $200,000 worth of securities in trust providing for the payment of income to B for life with remainder to B's issue. Assume further that B was given a non-cumulative right to withdraw $10,000 a year from the principal of the trust fund (which neither increased nor decreased in value prior to B's death). In such case, the failure of B to exercise his right of withdrawal will not result in estate taxation with respect to the power to withdraw $10,000 which lapses each year before the year of B's death. At B's death there will be included in his gross estate the $10,000 which he was entitled to withdraw for the year in which his death occurs less any amount which he may have taken during that year. However, if in the above example B had possessed the right to withdraw $15,000 of the principal annually, the failure to exercise such power in any year will be considered a release of the power to the extent of the excess of the amount subject to withdrawal over 5% of the trust fund (in this example, $5,000, assuming that the trust fund is worth $200,000 at the time of the lapse). [Another provision explains that this "release" of the power would constitute a taxable gift to the remaindermen of $5000 in each year in which the power was allowed to lapse.] Since each lapse is treated as though B had exercised dominion over the trust property by making a transfer of principal reserving the income therefrom for his life, the value of the trust property (but only to the extent of the excess of the amount subject to withdrawal over 5 percent of the trust fund) is includible in B's gross estate [under §2036]."

In addition to the "ascertainable standard" and "$5,000 or 5%" invasion powers, several other exceptions to the general power of appointment rule are given in §2041. For example, a power created after October 21, 1942, is not deemed a general power (i) if it is exercisable only "in conjunction with the creator of the power," or (ii) if it is exercisable only "in conjunction with a person having a substantial interest in the property, subject to the power, which is adverse to exercise of the power in favor of the decedent." Int. Rev. Code of 1954, §2041(b)(1)(C). These types of powers are rarely used because of their limited utility. See 1 Casner, Estate Planning 714-715 (3d ed. 1961).

Upon the wife's death, a distribution of the remainder in equal per stirpital shares to the issue may, and ordinarily will, be appropriate. Yet it may turn out that life will have been kinder to some of the children than to the others, and various factors may point toward an unequal, rather than an equal, distribution. Through the use of a special testamentary power of appointment, a final determination of how the remainder should be distributed can be postponed until the wife's death.[40]

Under §2041, all of these powers can be given to the income beneficiary and trustee with little or no tax cost.

PROBLEMS

1. T bequeaths a fund in trust for A for life, and gives A the power to invade corpus to pay all A's family medical bills. When A dies, will the value of the trust property be included in A's gross estate? 1 Casner, Estate Planning 714, n. 46 (1962, Supp. 1968).

2. T bequeaths a fund to A in trust to pay A the income for her life, with the power in A as trustee to invade principal to the extent that "it is at any time necessary or advisable in order to provide for the reasonable needs and proper expenses or the benefit or comfort" of herself. At A's death is the trust property included in A's gross estate? Strite v. McGinnes, 330 F.2d 234 (3d Cir. 1964), cert. denied, 379 U.S. 836 (1964). Would the answer be different if A is a co-trustee with a bank? Miller v. United States, 387 F.2d 866 (3d Cir. 1968).

3. T bequeaths a fund in trust for A for life, remainder as A appoints by will to anyone except A's creditors, A's estate, and the creditors of A's estate; and in default of appointment the trust property is to be applied by A's executors "as if the same formed part of his personal estate at death." A dies intestate. H is his heir. Is the trust property included in A's gross estate? Estate of Robert E. Jones, 20 CCH T.C. Mem. 558 (1961).

4. *The Gross Estate: Valuation of Estate Assets*

For estate tax purposes assets are valued as of the date of death or, if the decedent's personal representative elects, as of the *alternate valuation date*. The alternate valuation date is the date six months after death, except for assets "distributed, sold, exchanged, or otherwise disposed of" during the six months' period, for which it is the date of distribution or sale.[41] The purpose of the alternate valuation date option is to give some protection against the hardship that could result if estate assets decline in value after the decedent's death. To take an extreme case, if the decedent's gross estate were valued at $1 million at the date of his death and declined to $500,000 six months later, and if the date-of-death value were used for

[40] In Chapter 13 we shall take a closer look at the use of special powers of appointment in estate planning, and at the problems encountered in drafting and exercising them.

[41] Int. Rev. Code of 1954, §2032.

estate purposes, the estate tax might well exceed the value of the assets on hand to pay the tax, due nine months after death. In such a case one would have to feel sorry even for a millionaire!

The personal representative must select either the date-of-death valuation date or the alternate valuation date for all assets. He cannot value some assets as of one date and other assets as of the other date.

In general, the personal representative will select the valuation date that produces the lowest gross estate valuation and hence the lowest estate tax. This will not always be the case, however, because selection of the valuation date also has income tax consequences. Under §1014 of the 1954 Code, property acquired from a decedent is given a new basis for federal income tax purposes. The new basis is the value of the assets as valued in the decedent's gross estate. Section 1014 applies to all property included in the gross estate, including lifetime transfers taxed under §§2035-2038.

Suppose O purchases 100 shares of common stock at $50 per share, and over the years their value increases to $150 per share. If O were to sell the stock, he would realize taxable capital gain of $100 per share. If he gives the stock to B, B would take the donor's basis of $50 per share, with an upward adjustment of the basis for any gift tax paid by reason of the transfer. If B then sells the stock, he will realize a substantial capital gain. If, on the other hand, O dies leaving a will that devises the stock to B, and if the date-of-death value of the stock is $150 per share, under §1014 the basis of the stock in B's hands is $150 per share. By O's holding the appreciated assets until death, the built-in income tax liability of the appreciated assets would be eliminated. The postulated example illustrates why this is often called the "stepped-up basis" rule.[42] But this is not a wholly accurate label. If assets have depreciated in value from the time of their acquisition, they will receive a lower basis at the owner's death — with the result that the potential tax savings of a deductible loss cannot be realized.

Since election of the alternate valuation date has income tax as well as estate tax consequences, the personal representative should take both taxes into account in making his election. Suppose 1000 shares of stock are valued at $150 per share at the decedent's death, and $160 per share six months later. If the date-of-death value is used, the amount includible in the gross estate will be $150,000. If the alternate valuation date value is used, the amount includible will be $160,000. Under the latter, the decedent's estate tax will be increased by an amount equal to $10,000 times the applicable estate tax rate. This of course points toward using the date-of-death value. On the other hand, this would mean that the devisee of the stock would receive the shares with a basis of $150, and a built-in capital gains liability of $10 per share. As far as this asset is concerned, the decision of which is the appropri-

[42] Under the Treasury Department's tax reform proposals (see note 9 supra), while appreciated assets would be given a new basis at death, the step-up in basis would not be tax free. The appreciation in value would be included in the decedent's final income tax return, and would be taxed at long-term capital gain rates. See Kurtz & Surrey, Reform of Death and Gift Taxes: The 1969 Treasury Proposals, 70 Colum. L. Rev. 1365, 1381-1389 (1970).

ate valuation date will turn, in part, on the effective estate tax rate as compared to the effective capital gains tax rate applicable to the asset in the hands of the devisee.[43] But of course selection of the appropriate valuation date affects not only this one asset but a wide variety of other assets, of which some may have increased in value, some may have declined in value, and some may have a value that is constant.

5. Sections 2053 and 2054 Deductions

Once the value of the gross estate has been determined, the next step in calculating the estate tax is to compute the value of the *taxable estate*. This figure is arrived at by deducting from the gross estate the estate's $60,000 exemption and any deductions to which the estate is entitled. Deductions are allowed under §2053 for "expenses, indebtedness, and taxes," under §2054 for "losses," and under §2055 for charitable transfers. Under §2056 a "marital deduction" is allowed for certain transfers to the decedent's spouse.

Section 2053 provides for the deduction of (1) funeral expenses, (2) expenses incurred in administering the estate, (3) claims against the estate, and (4) unpaid mortgages on, or any indebtedness in respect to, property included in the gross estate.[44] Administration expenses include such items as the commission paid to the executor or administrator as compensation for administering the estate, attorney's fees, court costs and appraiser's fees, and expenses incurred in preserving and distributing the assets in the estate. Claims deductible under §2053 are "personal obligations of the decedent existing at the time of his death, whether or not matured, and interest thereon which had accrued at the time of death."[45] Obligations incurred by the estate after the decedent's death are not deductible. If, for example, property taxes on real estate owned by the decedent accrue and become payable on October 1 and the decedent dies in September, the taxes are an obligation of the estate, not of the decedent, and they are not deductible under §2053. Taxes owed by

[43] The basis and capital gains treatment of the estate assets is not the only consideration that might point toward selection of a valuation date that produces a higher estate tax. If an estate includes depreciable assets that have increased in value, the higher estate tax caused by selection of the alternate valuation date may be more than offset by income tax savings resulting from increased depreciation deductions available to the beneficiary. See generally Blattmachr, Choosing Optional Valuation Date, 99 Trusts & Estates 714 (1960); Halbach, Post-Mortem Estate Planning, 1963 U. Ill. L.F. 212.

[44] In the eight community property states the extent to which expenses and claims are deductible from the decedent spouse's gross estate is determined by the state's community property laws. Only one-half of a claim that is classified as a community obligation is deductible under §2053. This extends to funeral expenses if, under the state's laws, these expenses are a charge against the entire community property. United States v. Collins, 399 F.2d 90 (5th Cir. 1968). Only one-half of the expenses resulting from administering community property is deductible under §2053 unless it can be shown that a particular expense is allocable to the deceased spouse's community share. For example, in Lang's Estate v. Commissioner, 97 F.2d 867 (9th Cir. 1938), the court held that one-half of the "general" administration expenses was deductible, but that attorney's fees and other expenses relating to settlement and adjustment of the estate's federal estate tax and state inheritance tax liability were deductible in full. The latter items "were incurred solely for and on behalf of that portion of the community estate which was subject to decedent's disposition and which made up the 'estate' subject to tax by the state and federal governments."

[45] Treas. Reg. §20.2053-4 (1958).

the decedent at his death are deductible as claims against his estate. Except for these, "any income taxes on income received after the death of the decedent, or property taxes not accrued before his death, or any estate, succession, legacy, or inheritance taxes, shall not be deductible under this section." [46]

Section 2054 allows a deduction for "losses incurred during the settlement of estates arising from fires, storms, shipwrecks, or other casualties, or from theft, when such losses are not compensated for by insurance or otherwise." In other words, the losses deductible under this section are limited to casualty losses. No deduction is allowed, for example, for a loss resulting from the sale of securities that have depreciated in value because of declining market conditions.[47]

Administration expenses and casualty losses are also deductible from estate income. Section 212 of the Internal Revenue Code of 1954 allows a deduction for expenses incurred "for the production or collection of income," or "for the management, conservation, or maintenance of property held for the production of income." The executor's commission and such items as attorney's fees, appraisers' fees, and court costs qualify for deduction under §212. In short, the same items can be taken as deductions in computing either the estate tax or the estate's income tax. Not surprisingly, the tax laws do not permit a single expense (or loss) item to be taken as a deduction against both taxes. Under §642(g) the personal representative is given an election. He can treat these items as deductions against the gross estate in computing the estate tax, as deductions against estate income, or he can split the deductions, taking some against the gross estate and the rest against estate income. How the deductions are taken will depend on which treatment produces the lowest overall tax bill.

PROBLEMS

1. On June 1 O borrowed $2000 from his local bank and signed a note promising to pay the principal amount, together with interest at 8 percent, on December 1. O died on September 1. On December 1, his executor paid the bank $2080 in satisfaction of the obligation. What portion of this amount, if any, is deductible under §2053? Would it make any difference if the executor selects the alternate valuation date as the date for valuing estate assets? See Treas. Reg. §20.2053-4 (1958). What portion of the $2080, if any, is subject to the §642(g) election?

2. Thomas dies leaving a will that devises his estate to his three children, Arnold, Betty and Carol, in equal shares. The will names Arnold as executor, and he has commenced serving in that capacity. It is anticipated that the statutory fee to which Arnold will be entitled as executor will be approximately $8000. Arnold wants your advice: should he "waive" his executor's fee? See Rev. Rul. 66-167, 1966-1 Cum. Bull. 20.

[46] Int. Rev. Code of 1954, §2053(c)(1)(B).

[47] In Lyman v. Comm'r, 83 F.2d 811 (1st Cir. 1936), the estate claimed a deduction of $254,000 for losses in the value of securities resulting from Great Britain's abandonment of the gold standard, on the ground that this was an "other casualty" within the meaning of the statute. The deduction was denied.

3. Would your answer to Problem 2 be any different if Arnold were Thomas's only child and the principal beneficiary of the estate?

4. Assume the same facts as in Problem 2, except that Thomas is still alive. Consider the advisability of including the following provision in Thomas's will: "I hereby devise to my son, Arnold, in lieu of any compensation to which he may be entitled as executor, the sum of $5000."

6. *The Charitable Deduction*

Section 2055 of the estate tax, like a similar provision under the income tax, allows a deduction for transfers for public, charitable or religious purposes. Unlike the income tax provision, §2055 has no percentage limitation on the amount that can qualify for a charitable deduction.

Just as under the income tax, the principal question concerning the estate tax charitable deduction is whether a particular bequest qualifies as a transfer for public, charitable, or religious purposes. The statute provides guidelines which, while taking care of the clear cases, leave the harder cases for resolution by revenue ruling or court decision. If a bequest is made to a corporation, to qualify as a "charity" the corporation must be "organized and operated exclusively for religious, charitable, scientific, literary, or educational purposes, including the encouragement of art and the prevention of cruelty to children or animals, no part of the net earnings of which inures to the benefit of any private stockholder or individual, and no substantial part of the activities of which is carrying on propaganda, or otherwise attempting, to influence legislation, and which does not participate in, or intervene in (including the publishing or distributing of statements), any political campaign on behalf of any candidate for public office." [48]

If a bequest is made to trustees, or to a fraternal society or lodge, the trust or association need not be organized and operated exclusively for charitable purposes, but the bequest itself must be used exclusively for these purposes.[49] Some examples: A bequest to a state medical society was denied a deduction, but a deduction was allowed for a bequest to a public hospital, and also for a bequest to provide free research facilities for young doctors. A bequest to a college fraternity was denied a deduction, but a bequest to a college to provide housing for the school's fraternity students was held deductible.

To qualify for a deduction, the bequest must be for public charity, not private charity. Some examples: A deduction was disallowed for a trust created to provide scholarships for decedent's children, grandchildren, nephews, and nieces, and for a trust providing for the maintenance of a park-like memorial for the family burial plot. A deduction was allowed for a trust providing for scholarships for student nurses, and for a trust to provide relief for the needy — even though, in the latter, preference was to be given to the decedent's friends and relatives.

Prior to the Tax Reform Act of 1969, a person could use a "charitable remainder trust" to make provision for his family while substantially reducing the amount

[48] Int. Rev. Code of 1954, §2055(a)(2).
[49] Id. §2055(a)(3).

of the estate tax on his death. For example, the residuary clause of T's will could establish a testamentary trust under which the income was to be paid to his sister for life, with the remainder passing to the American Cancer Society on her death. T's estate would receive a deduction for the value of the remainder given to charity. Its value was computed by determining the present, discounted value of the right to receive the fund X years from now, X being the income beneficiary's life expectancy.[50] The deduction would reduce T's estate tax, and hence increase the size of the fund from which his sister would receive the income.

If, however, the trustee or income beneficiary were given a discretionary power to invade corpus, difficulties were encountered in valuing the remainder. Because of the widespread use of invasion powers in trusts of this type, considerable litigation ensued in which allowance of a deduction turned on whether the court found that the invasion power was limited by an "ascertainable standard." [51] Concerned that the courts were granting deductions for interests which, through the liberal exercise of invasion powers, might never pass to charity, in 1969 Congress partially closed the door by providing that there shall be no income, gift, or estate tax deduction for a charitable remainder unless the trust takes the form of an "annuity trust," a "unitrust," or a "pooled income fund." [52] A charitable remainder annuity trust is one under which a fixed sum, which is no less than 5 percent of the initial value of the trust corpus, is paid at least annually to the beneficiary or beneficiaries. A unitrust is one under which a fixed percentage, which is not less than 5 percent of the trust corpus, valued annually, is paid to the beneficiaries. A pooled income fund is set up by a charitable organization to meet certain specific requirements of the Code. See Rev. Rul. 72-196. The objectives of these rules are to reduce the uncertainty involved in valuing the future interest given to charity, and to increase the likelihood that the interest for which a deduction is given will in fact pass to charity.

7. *The Marital Deduction*

Historical Background

Section 2056 of the 1954 Code allows a marital deduction for certain dispositions of property to a decedent's surviving spouse. The estate tax marital deduction was first enacted in 1948 as part of a broader plan to eliminate discrimination in the tax treatment of couples residing in common law states. Prior to that time the community property system operated to give income, gift, and estate tax advantages to couples residing in community property states. The husband living in a common

[50] See Treas. Reg. §2512-9, Table A-2 (1971).

[51] See, e.g., Estate of Schildkraut v. Comm'r, 368 F.2d 40 (2d Cir. 1966), cert. denied, 386 U.S. 959 (1967), noted 67 Colum. L. Rev. 371 (1967), 55 Calif. L. Rev. 937 (1967); see also Warm, "Ascertainable Standard"— Its Use and Misuse in Charitable Trust Remainders, 31 J. Taxation 32 (1969).

[52] Int. Rev. Code of 1954, §§664(d), 2055(e)(2), 2522(c)(2). For discussion of annuity trusts and unitrusts see Comment, The Charitable Mixed Trust After the Tax Reform Act of 1969, 45 Tul. L. Rev. 115 (1970); Sanders, How to Draft Charitable Remainder Trusts in View of New Proposed Regulations, 33 J. Taxation 258 (1970); Moore, Estate Planning Under the Tax Reform Act of 1969: The Uses of Charities, 56 Va. L. Rev. 565 (1970).

law state who had a salary of $15,000 paid income tax on the full $15,000 of gross income. His neighbor in a community property state, earning the same $15,000 salary, was treated as having received *community* income of $15,000. Under a state's community property laws each spouse is regarded as the owner of an undivided one-half of the community property (property acquired after marriage by other than gift, descent, or devise). This system of tax treatment creates two taxpayers with a gross income of $7500 each — and a lower tax bill because of the graduated income tax rates.

Discrimination also occurred under the estate tax. In a common law state, all property acquired from the husband's earnings was taxed in his estate; in a community property state only the husband's one-half community interest was includible in his gross estate. The surviving spouse's share of the community property was ultimately taxed in her estate, but this deferral of taxation left the wife with the use of the tax money during her lifetime. Moreover, the wife owning community property had property against which her own $60,000 estate tax exemption could be applied. Hence community property up to $120,000 in amount was exempt from estate taxes. By contrast, if a husband in a common law state acquired $120,000 in property from his earnings during marriage, $60,000 was exempt and $60,000 was taxed at his death.

In 1948 Congress equalized income tax consequences among the states by authorizing married couples to file a joint income tax return, in effect permitting couples residing in common law states to split their incomes and have them taxed in the same manner as community income. Congress attempted to end the discrimination under the estate and gift taxes by creating the marital deduction, which extends to residents of common law states the opportunity to split their gifts and their estates for tax purposes. Because of the estate tax marital deduction, there is now a strong inducement toward settling at least a portion of the husband's property in such a way that it will be includible in his wife's estate on her subsequent death, for this is a prerequisite to qualifying for the marital deduction.[53]

Section 2056 is one of the more complex provisions of a tax code not notable for its lucidity. The text, consisting of four pages of very small type, is replete with narrow definitions, numerous exceptions and detailed limitations on whether a particular transfer will or will not qualify for the deduction. The implementing Regulations begin with §20.2056(a)-1(a) and drone on to §20.2056(e)-3, twenty-six pages later. Presumably intended to clarify the operation of the statute, the regulations puzzle even the sophisticated attorney who deals with the marital deduction on a regular basis. Some of the major problems — the differences between a "formula" clause and a "non-formula" clause, the pros and cons of a "fractional share"

[53] Under the Treasury Department's tax reform proposals, note 9 supra, the present marital deduction rules would be eliminated and a 100-percent marital deduction would be allowed. The basic premise of the Treasury proposals is that estates should be taxed once a generation; a corollary to that proposition is that they should not be taxed more than once a generation. Thus all interspousal transfers of interests in whatever form, and whether by lifetime gift or at death, would qualify for the marital deduction. For further discussion see authorities cited note 9 supra.

gift versus a "pecuniary" gift, the questions raised by a "specific portion" gift — have been made the subject of a book,[54] chapters in treatises,[55] law review symposia,[56] and countless law review articles. What follows is an outline of the basic features of the estate tax marital deduction.

The Maximum Allowable Marital Deduction: Herein of the "Adjusted Gross Estate"

Section 2056 attempts to provide parity in the estate tax treatment of marital property by extending to spouses residing in common law states the estate-splitting feature that is a characteristic of the community property system. If a husband leaves roughly one-half of his property outright to his wife (or makes some other transfer that qualifies for the marital deduction), his estate is entitled to a marital deduction for this interest. The result is that only the remaining one-half of his property is taxed in his estate.

To provide the desired parity, §2056 imposes a ceiling on the maximum marital deduction to which the deceased spouse's estate is entitled. The maximum allowable marital deduction available to the estate is one-half the adjusted gross estate. The adjusted gross estate is an accounting concept whose sole function is to determine the maximum allowable marital deduction. When community property is not involved, the adjusted gross estate is computed by subtracting from the gross estate the deductions for expenses, indebtedness, taxes, and losses allowed under §§2053 and 2054.[57] If the husband [58] has transferred property to his wife that qualifies for the marital deduction, but the amount transferred exceeds the maximum allowable marital deduction, his estate is entitled to the maximum deduction. If he has transferred less than this amount, the marital deduction is limited to the value of the property that passes to the wife.

Using a $400,000 estate as an example, assume that the husband dies leaving a will that bequeaths "all my property" outright to his wife, and that §§2053 and 2054 deductions total $20,000.

[54] Covey, The Marital Deduction and the Use of Formula Provisions (1966).

[55] See 1 Casner, Estate Planning 783 (3d ed. 1961, with current supplements); Lowndes & Kramer, Federal Estate and Gift Taxes 368 (2d ed. 1962).

[56] See 16 W. Res. L. Rev. 237-305 (1965).

[57] The personal representative has an option of treating administration expenses and losses as deductions against either the estate tax or the income tax. See page 237, supra. If these deductions are taken against estate income, the §§2053 and 2054 deductions will be reduced and the adjusted gross estate will be increased — meaning that the maximum allowable marital deduction will also be increased. The personal representative's election thus affects the amount of the estate tax. Furthermore, if a marital deduction "formula gift" has been used, under which the surviving spouse is given a share or amount measured by "the maximum allowable marital deduction available to my estate," the representative's decision will affect the amount actually passing to the surviving spouse. See Halbach, Post-Mortem Estate Planning, 1963 U. Ill. L.F. 212, 246.

[58] The marital deduction is not limited to transfers by the deceased husband to his wife. Property passing from the wife to her surviving spouse can also qualify for the deduction. Simply for the purposes of illustration, we shall assume that the husband has predeceased his wife.

$400,000	gross estate
– 20,000	§§2053, 2054 deductions
$380,000	adjusted gross estate
$190,000	maximum allowable marital deduction

Because of the outright disposition of all of his property to his wife, the husband's estate is entitled to the maximum deduction.

$400,000	gross estate
– 190,000	marital deduction
– 20,000	§§2053, 2054 deductions
– 60,000	exemption
$130,000	taxable estate

If, on the other hand, the husband left property valued at only $100,000 outright to his wife, his estate would not be entitled to the maximum marital deduction. The deduction would be limited to $100,000. In short, the maximum allowable marital deduction, which is one-half of the deceased spouse's adjusted gross estate, places a ceiling on the marital deduction to which the estate may be entitled. The amount of the actual marital deduction (up to this ceiling) is measured by the value of the property that actually passes to the surviving spouse in a qualifying way.

PROBLEM

During his lifetime H transfers assets worth $200,000 in a trust under which the income is to be paid to H for life, then to W for life. Upon the death of the survivor of H and W, the trust corpus is to be distributed to H's issue then living per stirpes. The trust is irrevocable. H dies five years later; the value of the trust corpus at H's death is $200,000. H's will gives all his property outright to W. At his death the property owned by H is valued at $100,000. The deductions allowed by §§2053 and 2054 total $6000. Assuming that the date-of-death valuation date is chosen, what amount is includible in H's gross estate? What is the maximum marital deduction allowable in determining H's taxable estate?

Interests That Qualify for the Deduction: The Nondeductible Terminable Interest Rule

Section 2056 requires that in order to qualify for the marital deduction, an interest passing to the surviving spouse must be such that it is subject to taxation in her estate. An outright devise of property is the clearest example of an interest that qualifies. It is equally clear that a devise of property to the wife for life, with the remainder to pass to the couple's children at her death, does not qualify. In this latter situation, the life estate is disqualified by the *nondeductible terminable interest rule*:

> Where, on the lapse of time, on the occurrence of an event or contingency, or on the failure of an event or contingency to occur, an interest passing to the surviving spouse will terminate or fail, no deduction shall be allowed under this section with respect to such interest —
>
> (A) if an interest in such property passes or has passed (for less than an adequate and full consideration in money or money's worth) from the decedent to any person other than such surviving spouse (or the estate of such spouse); and
>
> (B) if by reason of such passing such person (or his heirs or assigns) may possess or enjoy any part of such property after such termination or failure of such interest so passing to the surviving spouse.[59]

Under this definition, the life estate in our example is a nondeductible terminable interest. On the occurrence of an event or contingency — the wife's death — her interest will fail. An interest in the property — the remainder interest — passes from the decedent to persons other than the surviving spouse or her estate. By reason of such passing the remaindermen may possess or enjoy the property on the termination of the wife's life estate.

PROBLEMS

1. H buys an annuity contract providing for payments to himself for life and then to W if she should survive him. On the death of H and W all payments will cease. H dies and the value of the annuity is included in his gross estate. Does the gift from H to W qualify for the estate tax marital deduction? Treas. Reg. §20.2056(b)-1(g), example (3) (1958).

2. H by will directs his executor to purchase an annuity paying $5000 a year to W. Does the annuity qualify for the estate tax marital deduction? Treas. Reg. §20.2056(b)-1(f) (1958).

There are three important exceptions to the nondeductible terminable interest rule. "The purpose of these exceptions is to prevent the marital deduction prejudicing the prudent disposition of an estate. Standing alone, the nondeductible terminable interest rule creates considerable pressure to give property outright to a surviving spouse in order to take advantage of the marital deduction, although wisdom might dictate a more conservative disposition. The exceptions to the terminable interest rule seek to ease this pressure by providing that certain restrictions upon the

[59] Int. Rev. Code of 1954, §2056(b)(1).

interest passing to a surviving spouse will not disqualify the interest given to her for the marital deduction."[60]

The first exception permits *limited survivorship* provisions. In drafting wills it is a common practice to include a clause requiring that a legatee must survive the testator by a stated period (say, thirty or sixty days) in order to take under the will. The purpose of this type of provision is to avoid double administration and possible double taxation of the same property in two estates in quick succession. A survivorship clause also causes the property to pass to alternate beneficiaries designated by the testator in his will, rather than to the heirs or devisees of a beneficiary who did not live long enough to enjoy the property himself. Under the definition of terminable interests given above, this type of condition appended to a devise to the wife makes it a terminable interest. Section 2056(b)(3) provides that such a devise is not a nondeductible terminable interest if (a) the condition of survival is for a period not exceeding six months and (b) the contingency (the wife's death within the period) does not in fact occur. In short, a requirement of survival for up to six months can be attached to the interest passing to the wife without disqualifying it for the marital deduction. If the wife does not survive for the stated period, of course no marital deduction will be available, since no interest will actually pass from the decedent to his surviving spouse.

PROBLEMS

1. Nearly every state has enacted the Uniform Simultaneous Death Act or its equivalent.[61] The Act provides that where the owner of property and the beneficiary (whether by will, intestate succession, right of survivorship, or life insurance beneficiary designation) die simultaneously or under circumstances that make it difficult or impossible to ascertain the order of deaths, in the absence of a will provision to the contrary "the property of each person shall be disposed of as if he had survived." H and W are residents of a common law state, and the projected value of H's gross estate is $400,000. H wants to draft a will that devises most of his estate outright to his wife. In light of the marital deduction, consider the advisability of (a) relying on the Simultaneous Death Act to provide an appropriate distribution in the event of a common disaster, or (b) drafting a clause that devises the property to the wife "if she survives me by sixty days." See Treas. Reg. §20.2056(e)-(2)(e) (1958); 2 Casner, Estate Planning 1240, clause 6 (3d ed. 1961).

2. H's will devises the residue of his estate to his wife "absolutely and in fee simple; provided, however, in the event my said wife should die before a decree of final distribution is entered in my estate, I then devise the said property to my sister, Agnes." H's will is probated immediately, and a final decree of distribution is entered five months after H's death. The residuary estate is distributed to his wife. Does the residuary devise qualify for the marital deduction? Bookwalter v. Lamar,

[69] Lowndes & Kramer, Federal Estate and Gift Taxes 394-395 (2d ed. 1962).

[61] See page 139, supra.

323 F.2d 664 (8th Cir. 1963), cert. denied, 376 U.S. 969 (1964); Pirrie v. United States, 318 F. Supp. 274 (D. Mont. 1970).

The *estate trust* exception to the terminable interest rule is included within the language of the statute defining a nondeductible terminable interest. Under subsection (A) of §2056(b)(1), the nondeductible terminable interest rule applies only when an interest passes to someone other than the surviving spouse *or her estate.* Consequently, a disposition of property "to my wife for life, and on her death to her estate" qualifies for the marital deduction. This exception applies to conveyances of a legal life estate and remainder as well as to settlements in trust. Since, however, legal life estates are rarely used in estate planning, this type of settlement is commonly referred to as the estate trust arrangement. The estate trust is seldom employed as the means of qualifying for the marital deduction because of its relative inflexibility.[62] Also, an estate trust causes the assets to be subject to administration expenses in the surviving spouse's estate. The estate planner's choice is usually between an outright gift to the surviving spouse or a power of appointment trust.

The third major exception to the nondeductible terminable interest rule is the *life estate with general power of appointment* in the surviving spouse. If the surviving spouse is given a life estate and also a power of appointment over the property, §2056(b)(5) declares that the interest passing to the spouse qualifies for the marital deduction — provided that five technical requirements imposed by the statute are met.

(a) The surviving spouse must be entitled to all of the income for life.[63]

(b) The income must be paid annually or at more frequent intervals.

(c) The power of appointment must be exercisable in favor of the spouse or her estate. In other words, the power must be a general power of appointment. It may be exercisable either during the spouse's lifetime or by her will.

(d) The power must be exercisable by the spouse alone and in all events.

(e) The spouse's interest must not be subject to a power in anyone else to divert the property to someone other than the spouse. In other words, the trustee cannot be given a discretionary power to distribute trust corpus to others (such as the couple's children).

[62] See Fox, Estate: A Word to Be Used Cautiously, If At All, 81 Harv. L. Rev. 992 (1968); Huston, Transfers to the "Estate" of a Named Person, 15 Syracuse L. Rev. 463 (1964).

[63] If the wife's income interest is conditioned upon her not remarrying, this disqualifies the trust.

If non-income-producing property is transferred to a power of appointment trust, the Regulations take the position that the entire trust does not qualify for the marital deduction unless the wife can compel the trustee to convert the property into something productive, or pay her a reasonable income from other property in trust. Treas. Reg. §20.2056(b)-5(f)(4), (5) (1958). This raises a potentially serious problem if, for example, the husband owns stock in a closely-held corporation that does not regularly pay dividends, or if he owns unimproved real estate that he is holding for future development.

You should *note well* the implications of these carefully delineated requirements. While the general test for qualification is that the interest passing to the surviving spouse must be such that it will be taxed in her estate, it by no means follows that *any* interest that will be includible in her gross estate automatically qualifies for the deduction. If the wife is not given an outright interest in the property or if her estate is not given a remainder, the interest passing to her qualifies for the marital deduction only if these five requirements are met.[64] It is quite possible — indeed, a host of cases indicate that it is altogether too easy — for a husband to give his wife an interest that will be taxed in her estate without getting the benefit of the marital deduction. For example, in Matteson v. United States[65] the husband's will created a trust giving his wife a life estate plus a power to withdraw corpus if she should ever find "that the income received by her from the Trust herein created for her benefit is not sufficient, and of its sufficiency she shall be the sole judge." The court held that under New York law "the only event which would allow the invasion of the corpus of the trust fund would be the sufficiency of the income as she decided it *in good faith*, and this seems far from a power to appoint the entire corpus free of the trust in her favor or to her estate without qualification as provided in the statute and regulations involved." Although the wife was given a power to appoint corpus to herself, it was not a power exercisable "in all events" as required under §2056. Note, however, that her power to appoint to herself was not limited by "an ascertainable standard relating to the health, education, support, or maintenance" of the wife, which meant that the wife did hold a general power of appointment for the purposes of including the property in her estate under §2041.

No single estate tax question has been so frequently litigated as the question whether the surviving spouse's power over the property has been limited in such a way as to disqualify the property for the marital deduction.[66] The precise language used in wills is carefully scrutinized by the Internal Revenue Service to see if the power held by the spouse is exercisable in all events. The Matteson case, referred to in the preceding paragraph, is an example. Piatt v. Gray[67] is another. In that case H devised the residue of his estate to W for life with power "whenever, in her opinion, it shall be necessary for her maintenance, comfort or well-being to expend all or any part of the principal . . . without being required to account therefor," and with power "to sell, lease, encumber or otherwise dispose of any and all items." On the wife's death the unconsumed portion of the estate went to others. The court held that under Kentucky law the wife could not dispose of the property by will or by gift, and that such a restricted power does not qualify the transfer for the marital deduction.

[64] It is not necessary to use a trust in order to qualify an interest for the marital deduction under §2056(b)(5). A legal life estate and a general power of appointment qualify for the marital deduction if the five technical requirements of the statute are satisfied. As a practical matter, though, legal life estates are rarely used in estate planning. See page 891, infra.

[65] 147 F. Supp. 535 (N.D.N.Y. 1956), appeal dismissed, 240 F.2d 517 (2d Cir. 1956).

[66] See Howard & Lederer, The Marital Deduction: Powers of Invasion and the "All Events" Requirement, 40 St. John's L. Rev. 179 (1966).

[67] 321 F.2d 79 (6th Cir. 1963).

PROBLEMS

1. H dies. His will establishes a trust and gives W a right to the income for her life and, in addition, "the power to consume my entire estate for any purposes which she shall deem advisable." In a state probate court proceeding this language is construed as giving W a life interest with "the unrestricted power exercisable at any time during her life — without accounting to any person whomsoever — to use all or any part of the trust property, and to dispose of or consume it in any manner, including the power to dispose of it by gift." Does the trust qualify for the marital deduction? Estate of Francis F. Field, 40 T.C. 802 (1963).

2. H dies. His wife is mentally incompetent and is confined in a mental hospital. H's will gives a sum in trust for W for her life, with a general inter vivos power of appointment in W over the principal. Does this gift qualify for the marital deduction? Stockdick v. Phinney, 65-2 U.S.T.C. ¶12351 (S.D. Tex. 1965); Townsend v. United States, 232 F. Supp. 219 (E.D. Tex. 1964).

Interests That Qualify for the Deduction: Modes of Transfer

Up to now we have discussed interests transferred to the surviving spouse by will. Needless to say, this is not the only form of transfer that can be used to qualify for the marital deduction. Outright interests passing to the spouse by intestacy, by right of survivorship, or by life insurance contract also qualify. If property passes to a spouse by reason of her dower rights or statutory share in lieu of dower, whether the interest qualifies will depend on the nature of the interest. If the wife receives only a life estate, the interest does not qualify because it is a terminable interest. If, on the other hand, she receives an outright interest, it will qualify.[68]

Lifetime transfers included in the husband's gross estate under §§2035-2038 can also qualify for the marital deduction. In fact, one of the commonly used means of satisfying the marital deduction gift is a revocable inter vivos trust funded with assets during the husband's lifetime.

[68] The widow's election to take a statutory share, discussed in Chapter 9, can be used to salvage the marital deduction and thereby produce tax savings. If the wife has a right under local law to take "against" the will, thereby receiving an outright statutory share in lieu of the interest given to her by the will, this share would qualify for the marital deduction, and the husband's estate tax liability would be reduced. See Estate of Kennedy v. United States, page 468, infra.

In Isaac Harter, Jr., 39 T.C. 511 (1962), the wife's will made no provision for her husband, as he was "otherwise well provided for." The will bequeathed all her property to her son. The husband exercised his statutory right of election under New York law and received property worth $78,000 outright. Because of the marital deduction, this reduced the wife's estate tax by $22,000. Shortly thereafter the husband gave the $78,000 to his three grandchildren (children of the will beneficiary — thus keeping the $78,000 out of the son's estate) at a gift tax cost of $5000. The government's contention that the wife's estate was not entitled to a marital deduction was summarily dismissed. (How's that for an effective job of lawyering?)

The Marital Deduction and Estate Planning in Common Law States

For couples residing in common law states, the tax benefits provided by the marital deduction are a strong inducement toward making a property settlement that will produce the maximum deduction. The overall estate tax liability is reduced since the combined taxes on two smaller estates is less than a single tax on one larger estate. Also, payment of a portion of the tax ultimately due is postponed until the death of the surviving spouse; in effect, the spouse has the use of this tax money during her lifetime.

The basic marital deduction estate plan used in common law states involves the creation of a "marital deduction trust" and a "family trust." The husband's will devises the family residence and all items of tangible personal property outright to his wife. After making other specific bequests (if any), the will [69] provides for a "formula" gift to the wife in a marital deduction trust — either a formula fractional share of his residuary estate or a formula pecuniary gift. The formula is designed to produce exactly the maximum marital deduction — no more, no less. A *formula fractional share gift* may read as follows:

> If my said wife survives me, I give to [trustee] the following described fractional share of my residuary estate: The numerator of the fraction shall be the maximum estate tax marital deduction (allowable in determining the federal estate tax payable by reason of my death) minus the value for federal estate tax purposes of all items in my gross estate which qualify for said deduction and which pass or have passed in a form which qualifies for the estate tax marital deduction from me to my said wife (the words "pass or have passed" shall have the same meaning as such words shall have under the provisions of the Internal Revenue Code in effect at the time of my death) under other provisions of this will, by right of survivorship with respect to jointly owned property, under settlement arrangements relating to life insurance proceeds, and otherwise than under this fractional share gift of my residuary estate (in computing the numerator, the values as finally determined for federal estate tax purposes shall control); and the denominator of the fraction shall be the value of my residuary estate (in computing the denominator, the value of my residuary estate shall be determined on the basis of the values as finally determined for federal estate tax purposes). If the numerator of the above-described fraction equals or exceeds the denominator, the entire residuary estate shall be placed in this marital deduction trust.[70]

Alternatively, the draftsman might use a *formula pecuniary gift* such as the following:

[69] If the husband uses a funded revocable inter vivos trust as the basic dispositive arrangement in his estate plan, his will would devise his residuary estate to the inter vivos trust by a "pour-over" provision. See page 419, infra. The inter vivos trust would contain the formula language creating the marital deduction and family trusts. See 2 Casner, Estate Planning 1237, 1278 (3d ed. 1961, with current supplements).

[70] 1 Casner, Estate Planning 797 (3d ed. 1961, Supp. 1969 at 883).

> If my said wife survives me, I give to [trustee] the following: An amount equal to the maximum estate tax marital deduction (allowable in determining the federal estate tax payable by reason of my death) minus the value for federal estate tax purposes of all items in my gross estate which qualify for said deduction and which pass or have passed in a form which qualifies for the estate tax marital deduction from me to my said wife (the words "pass or have passed" shall have the same meaning as such words shall have under the provisions of the Internal Revenue Code in effect at the time of my death) under other provisions of this will, by right of survivorship with respect to jointly owned property, under settlement arrangements relating to life insurance proceeds, and otherwise than under this pecuniary bequest. In making the computations necessary to determine the amount of this pecuniary estate tax marital deduction gift, values as finally determined for federal estate tax purposes shall control.[71]

Read the above clauses carefully, and you will observe that each is designed to assure that the husband's estate will receive the maximum allowable marital deduction. The clauses make automatic adjustments to take into account property passing to the wife by other means that qualify for the marital deduction. This includes the house and tangible personal property devised outright to the wife, life insurance proceeds, joint bank accounts, and so on. The remaining provisions of the marital deduction trust are drafted to give the wife a life income interest and a general power of appointment, with a gift in default of appointment to the family trust.

After making the marital deduction formula gift, the remainder of the residuary estate is settled in the "family trust." Under this trust the wife is given a life income interest and a *special* testamentary power to appoint the remainder among the couple's descendants, with a gift in default of appointment in further trust for the couple's descendants. The consequence is that the corpus of the marital deduction trust will be taxed in the wife's estate on her death, but the corpus of the family trust will not. In more substantial estates, where a mandatory income interest in the family trust would give the wife more income than she will need (and thus a larger income tax bill than is necessary or desirable), various alternatives are available. The trustee might be given the discretionary power to "spray" family trust income among the couple's descendants, or to accumulate trust income, thereby providing the income tax savings that this type of settlement makes possible.

PROBLEMS

1. Harold, a resident of Iowa, is seventy-one years old. His first wife, Velma, died several years ago. Two years ago he married Wanda, aged fifty-two. Ten years ago Harold established a revocable inter vivos trust (present value of corpus is $200,000) under which the trustees were directed to pay trust income to Harold for life, then to Harold's son Samuel for life, and on the death of Samuel to distribute the corpus of the trust to Samuel's children. At about the same time Harold drafted

[71] Id. at 794 (Supp. 1969 at 877).

a will devising his house and tangible personal property (present value $30,000) outright to his wife, Velma. The residuary clause of his will established a trust under which the trustees were directed to pay trust income to Velma for life, and on her death to distribute the trust corpus to Samuel. The present value of the assets that would be subject to this residuary clause is $210,000.

Shortly after his marriage to Wanda, Harold executed a codicil by which he deleted "Velma" from the will and substituted "Wanda" in her place. Harold has two life insurance policies. One (face value $20,000) names Samuel as principal beneficiary; the other (face value $10,000) names Wanda as principal beneficiary. Wanda owns no property other than various items of tangible personalty worth around $5000. Harold has asked you for an evaluation of his estate plan. Specifically, he wants to know whether it is a sound plan from a tax standpoint. Advise him.

2. Clause 3 of John's will devised to his wife Ellen "a portion of my estate equal in value to the maximum marital deduction allowable in the determination of the federal estate tax upon my death, less the value of any property which passed or is deemed to have passed to my wife under other provisions of this will or otherwise than under this will, but only to the extent that such property is included in my estate for the purpose of the federal estate tax and is allowable as a marital deduction." Clause 4 devised the residue of John's estate to his two children in equal shares.

John's executor selected the date-of-death valuation date. The amount of the allowable marital deduction in John's estate was $200,000. No other assets were given to Ellen under the will, but $40,000 in life insurance proceeds were paid to Ellen in a lump sum. As of John's death the assets on hand to satisfy the devises in clauses 3 and 4 were valued at $320,000; as of the date of final distribution twenty months later, these assets had appreciated in value to $400,000. Ellen contends that clause 3 is a "fractional share marital deduction gift," and that she is entitled to 50 percent of the assets now on hand, or assets worth $200,000. What result? See In re Nicolai's Estate, 232 Ore. 105, 373 P.2d 967 (1962); compare In re Estate of Kantner, 50 N.J. Super. 582, 143 A.2d 243 (1958).[72] Would Ellen be on firmer ground if her husband's will contained the first clause set out on page 248?

The Marital Deduction and Estate Planning in Community Property States

The estate of a deceased spouse is not allowed a marital deduction that is measured by any community property in his estate. The community property system has given the husband's estate the "split" that §2056 seeks to provide. Hence

[72] Formula gifts raise a host of very technical problems, and whether the formula fractional share gift or the formula pecuniary gift is preferable is a subject of much dispute. See Casner, Estate Planning 791-818 (3d ed. 1961, with current supplements); Covey, The Marital Deduction and the Use of Formula Provisions (1966); Polasky, Marital Deduction Formula Clauses in Estate Planning — Estate and Income Tax Considerations, 63 Mich. L. Rev. 809 (1965).

§2056(c)(2)(B) requires that in computing the adjusted gross estate, community property includible in the gross estate must also be deducted. At the same time it would be unfair to deny community property state residents any marital deduction, for the deceased spouse's estate might include separate property not subject to the community "split." Thus the estate is eligible for a marital deduction measured by the separate property in the estate.[73]

It is sometimes said that "community property does not qualify for the marital deduction." This is a misleading statement. It is true that the amount of the maximum allowable marital deduction is *measured by* the separate property in the estate. However, once the maximum allowable deduction has been determined, any of the husband's property — separate or community — that passes to his surviving spouse in a qualifying way can satisfy the marital deduction gift. Thus if a husband devises his separate property to third persons, or to his wife in a manner that does not qualify for the marital deduction, the estate may nonetheless be entitled to the maximum deduction if the husband devised sufficient community property outright to his wife (or left community property to her in some other manner that qualifies).

Since community property cannot be used to measure the maximum allowable marital deduction, the marital deduction does not play as significant a role in estate planning in community property states as it does in common law states. If the estate consists entirely of community property, the marital deduction is not involved at all. If, on the other hand, one of the spouses owns more than a modest amount of separate property, the tax-saving and tax-postponement features of the marital deduction should be considered in formulating a suitable estate plan. In this situation the will or trust draftsman in a community property state must be every bit as familiar with the nuances of §2056 as his common law state counterpart.

[73] Since the marital deduction is available to the extent of separate property in the deceased spouse's estate, what is to prevent the husband and wife from partitioning their community property into two equal shares of separate property (something that can be done in all the community property states except Louisiana), and thereby increasing the maximum allowable marital deduction? The answer: §2056(c)(2)(C)(i), which provides that community property "converted, by one transaction or a series of transactions, into separate property of the decedent and his spouse . . . shall" for the purpose of computing the adjusted gross estate "be considered as 'held as community property.' " In other words, "tainted" separate property (separate property that was created by partitioning community property) is also deductible in computing the adjusted gross estate.

In a community property state, the adjusted gross estate (and thus the maximum allowable marital deduction) is computed under the following formula:

Gross estate
— Community property included in gross estate
— "Tainted" separate property included in gross estate
— §§2053, 2054 deductions allocable to separate property

Adjusted gross estate

"Allocable" §§2053 and 2054 deductions are computed as follows:

$$\frac{\text{Separate property in gross estate}}{\text{Gross estate}} \times \text{§§2053, 2054 deductions} = \text{allocable deductions}$$

See Lowndes & Kramer, Federal Estate and Gift Taxes 372 (2d ed. 1962).

PROBLEM

H dies leaving a will that devises his community share of the family residence and tangible personal property outright to his wife, W. His will directs that "all the rest, residue and remainder of my property, including my separate property as well as my share of community property owned by my wife and me," shall be held in a trust from which the income is to be paid to the wife for her life, and on her death the corpus is to be distributed to the couple's children in equal shares. The family residence (date-of-death value $30,000) and tangible personal property ($10,000) are community property. The residuary estate consists of H's one-half share of community property (value of H's share is $170,000) and H's separate property ($50,000). By reason of H's death $20,000 in life insurance proceeds are paid outright to W; the life insurance policies were community property. Funeral expenses, claims and administration expenses deductible from H's gross estate under §2053 total $10,000. Compute H's taxable estate. See Johanson, Revocable Trusts, Widow's Election Wills, and Community Property: The Tax Problems, 47 Texas L. Rev. 1247, 1265 n. 82 (1969).

8. *Federal Estate Tax Rates*

The federal estate tax rates imposed by the Internal Revenue Code of 1954 are set out in §2001, as follows:

If the taxable estate is:	The tax shall be:
Not over $5000	3% of the taxable estate.
Over $5000 but not over $10,000	$150, plus 7% of excess over $5000.
Over $10,000 but not over $20,000	$500, plus 11% of excess over $10,000.
Over $20,000 but not over $30,000	$1600, plus 14% of excess over $20,000.
Over $30,000 but not over $40,000	$3000, plus 18% of excess over $30,000.
Over $40,000 but not over $50,000	$4800, plus 22% of excess over $40,000.
Over $50,000 but not over $60,000	$7000, plus 25% of excess over $50,000.
Over $60,000 but not over $100,000	$9500, plus 28% of excess over $60,000.
Over $100,000 but not over $250,000	$20,700, plus 30% of excess over $100,000.
Over $250,000 but not over $500,000	$65,700, plus 32% of excess over $250,000.

Over $500,000 but not over $750,000	$145,700, plus 35% of excess over $500,000.
Over $750,000 but not over $1,000,000	$233,200, plus 37% of excess over $750,000.
Over $1,000,000 but not over $1,250,000	$325,700, plus 39% of excess over $1,000,000.
Over $1,250,000 but not over $1,500,000	$423,200, plus 42% of excess over $1,250,000.
Over $1,500,000 but not over $2,000,000	$528,200, plus 45% of excess over $1,500,000.
Over $2,000,000 but not over $2,500,000	$753,200, plus 49% of excess over $2,000,000.
Over $2,500,000 but not over $3,000,000	$998,200, plus 53% of excess over $2,500,000.
Over $3,000,000 but not over $3,500,000	$1,263,200, plus 56% of excess over $3,000,000.
Over $3,500,000 but not over $4,000,000	$1,543,200, plus 59% of excess over $3,500,000.
Over $4,000,000 but not over $5,000,000	$1,838,200, plus 63% of excess over $4,000,000.
Over $5,000,000 but not over $6,000,000	$2,468,200, plus 67% of excess over $5,000,000.
Over $6,000,000 but not over $7,000,000	$3,138,200, plus 70% of excess over $6,000,000.
Over $7,000,000 but not over $8,000,000	$3,838,200, plus 73% of excess over $7,000,000.
Over $8,000,000 but not over $10,000,000	$4,568,200, plus 76% of excess over $8,000,000.
Over $10,000,000	$6,088,200, plus 77% of excess over $10,000,000.

9. *Estate Taxes in the Adam Smith Estate*

PROBLEMS

1. Assume that Adam Smith is a resident of a common law state, and that he dies leaving a will that devises all his property outright to his wife, Jane. He is survived by his wife and three minor children. At his death the assets listed on pages 74-76, together with the $25,000 life insurance policy taken out recently (page 198), are owned by the Smiths: These are set forth in the table on page 254. Values given are date-of-death values; the date of death is selected for asset valuation purposes. Funeral and administration expenses and claims other than the $19,000 mortgage debt, deductible under §2053, total $8000. Compute the federal estate tax due by reason of Adam Smith's death.

	Property acquired from H's earnings during marriage	H's property acquired by gift	W's property acquired by gift
Tangible personalty:	$ 8,000		
Real estate:			
Residence (title is in "Adam Smith and Jane Smith, husband and wife"); subject to mtge. of $19,000.	32,000		
Lot, Lake Murray (title is in Adam Smith alone)	5,000		
Bank accounts:			
Checking (joint or survivor)	1,000		
Savings (joint tenancy with wife)	4,000		
Securities:			
Varoom Mutual Fund (registered in Adam Smith's name alone)		$2,000	
General Corp. common (registered in Adam Smith's name alone)		560	
American Growth Fund (joint tenancy with wife)	2,185		
Union Nat'l Bank common (registered in Jane Smith's name alone)			$7,500
Life insurance: (wife is primary beneficiary; children are secondary beneficiaries)	72,000		
Tresco pension plan: (Smith's contributions)	4,200		
	$128,385	$2,560	$7,500

1a. Jane Smith dies five years after Adam, leaving a will that devises all her property to her children in equal shares. Assume that the assets owned by Jane, and the assets passing to her from Adam's estate, have neither increased nor decreased in value since Adam's death, and that the only reductions in the size of the Smith estate came from (a) the funeral and administrative expenses incurred at Adam's death, deducted under §2053, and (b) the federal estate tax paid at Adam's death. The mortgage indebtedness was not paid off during administration of Adam's estate; the balance now stands at $16,000. Funeral and administration expenses and other claims deductible under §2053 total $8000. Compute the federal estate tax due by reason of Jane Smith's death.

2. Given the same facts as in Problem 1, except that Adam Smith dies in the crash of a commercial airliner: The double-triple indemnity provisions in several of

the Smith life insurance policies increase the amount of the policy proceeds to $122,000. Compute the federal estate tax due by reason of Adam Smith's death.

2a. Given the same facts as in Problem 1a, but with the increased life insurance proceeds resulting from Adam Smith's accidental death: Compute the federal estate tax due by reason of Jane's death.[74]

3 and 3a. Consider the same facts as in Problems 1 and 1a, except that the Smiths are residents of a community property state. (In computing the tax at Adam's death, assume that expenses and claims allocable to Adam's community share of the assets in administration, deductible under §2053, total $8000.)

4 and 4a. Compute the federal estate tax, given the same facts as in Problems 2 and 2a, except that the Smiths are residents of a community property state.

SECTION B. The Federal Gift Tax

Section 2501 of the Internal Revenue Code of 1954 imposes a gift tax on "the transfer of property by gift during [each] calendar year by any individual." The statute's purpose is to tax lifetime transfers that remove assets from the transferor's estate and thereby escape estate taxation.[75] There are, however, strong tax inducements to making donative transfers by inter vivos gift rather than at death. By utilizing the donor's $30,000 lifetime exemption and the $3000 per-donee annual exclusions (which are doubled in the case of married couples who split their gifts), it is possible to give substantial amounts without incurring either a gift tax or an estate tax. If lifetime gifts exceed the exclusions and exemption so that a gift tax must be paid, the tax is smaller than under the estate tax for two reasons. First, the tax rates are lower under the gift tax than under the estate tax. Second, the transferred assets are removed from the transferor's top estate tax bracket and are taxed in the bottom brackets of the gift tax, where the graduated tax rates begin at $2\frac{1}{4}$ percent.[76]

[74] The credit for taxes on prior transfers, Int. Rev. Code of 1954, §2013, affords some relief against double taxation of assets that have been taxed in the estate of another decedent within the preceding ten years. If the prior decedent died within two years of the decedent whose estate tax is now being computed, a 100-percent credit is allowed. If he died within three to four years, the credit is 80 percent; if within five to six years, 60 percent; if within seven to eight years, 40 percent; if within nine to ten years, 20 percent. If T dies leaving a will that devises Blackacre to B, and B dies within two years, §2013 gives B's estate a 100-percent credit for that portion of T's estate tax attributable to his ownership of Blackacre. (Do you see why, in the context of the Adam Smith–Jane Smith problem, the relief afforded by §2013 often is illusory even if the deaths occur within two years?) The credit is limited, however, to the amount of B's estate tax that is attributable to his ownership of Blackacre. (You should be able to see the reason for this limitation if you consider that T may be a millionaire and B may have a very modest estate.)

The actual calculation of the tax credit in a particular case is quite complicated; §2013 has been called "the most complicated and confusing provision of the estate tax law." Rudick, The Estate Tax Credit for Prior Transfers, 13 Tax L. Rev. 3 (1957).

[75] It is possible, however, for a transfer to be taxed under both the gift tax and the estate tax. The most common example is the lifetime transfer held to be in contemplation of death under §2035. See page 220, supra. If assets transferred inter vivos are taxed in the decedent's gross estate, a credit is allowed for the gift tax paid. Int. Rev. Code of 1954, §2012.

[76] One of the major components of the Treasury Department tax reform proposals, note 9

After the gift has been made, income from the transferred property is taxed to the donee, typically a child or grandchild in a lower income tax bracket than the donor. Because the income tax savings are realized in each year after the transfer, in many instances the income-shifting feature of a lifetime gift, and not projected transfer tax savings, furnishes the tax motivation for the transfer.

1. *The Annual Exclusion*

Under §2503(b), a taxpayer is allowed an exclusion for the first $3000 given to any person during the calendar year. The purpose of the annual exclusion is to remove modest gifts, including wedding, Christmas, and birthday presents, from the ambit of the gift tax laws. If O makes gifts to a dozen persons during the year, but none of the gifts exceeds $3000 in value, no gift tax return need be filed and no tax is paid. If he gives $5000 each to A and B, he must file a gift tax return that reports these gifts, deducts the per-donee annual exclusions, and shows $4000 in gifts subject to the tax. (If O has not previously used up his $30,000 lifetime exemption he can, in his return, apply the exemption against these gifts and avoid payment of any tax.)

The annual exclusion is not available for gifts of future interests. Int. Rev. Code of 1954, §2503(b). If O gives property to A for life, and on A's death to his children in equal shares, O is entitled to an exclusion for his gift of the present income interest to A but not for the remainder interest given to A's children. "[T]he denial of the [exclusion] in the case of gifts of future interests is dictated by the apprehended difficulty, in many instances, of determining the number of eventual donees and the value of their respective gifts." [77]

Prior to 1954, the denial of an exclusion for gifts of future interests created problems for the donor who wished to give property to his minor child or grandchild. An outright gift qualified for the exclusion, but the child's disability necessitated a cumbersome and expensive guardianship administration for management of the donated property. If the donor established a trust under which the income was payable to the child until he attained age twenty-one, at which time the principal

---

supra, is that there be a unified transfer tax. "Under this proposal the existing estate and gift taxes with their separate schedules would be replaced by a single unified transfer tax with a single schedule of rates and exemptions. In determining the applicable tax rates on property transferred at death, all transfers made during lifetime would be taken into account. For example, if an individual made $100,000 in taxable gifts during lifetime and paid taxes on them and thereafter left an estate of $500,000 at death, assuming no deductions or exemptions the tax applicable to the $500,000 transferred at death would be computed at the rates beginning above $100,000. Stated differently, the lifetime and deathtime transfers would be aggregated so that the total tax at death would first be computed on $600,000, and then the amount of transfer taxes paid during lifetime would be credited against the tentative tax so computed, leaving the balance as the tax due on the estate." Kurtz & Surrey, Reform of Death and Gift Taxes: The 1969 Treasury Proposals, 70 Colum. L. Rev. 1365, 1375 (1970). The $3000 per-donee annual exclusions would be retained, but a single $60,000 exemption would replace the present $60,000 estate tax exemption and $30,000 gift tax exemption.

[77] H.R. Rep. No. 708, 72d Cong., 1st Sess. 29 (1939-1 Cum. Bull. Part 2, 478); S. Rep. No. 665, 72d Cong., 1st Sess. 41 (1939-1 Cum. Bull. Part 2, 526).

was to be distributed to him, the present income interest qualified for the exclusion but the future interest did not. To permit some flexibility in making gifts to minors that qualify for the exclusion, in 1954 Congress enacted §2503(c):

> *Transfer for the Benefit of Minor.* —
> No part of a gift to an individual who has not attained the age of 21 years on the date of such transfer shall be considered a gift of a future interest in property for purposes of subsection (b) if the property and the income therefrom —
> (1) may be expended by, or for the benefit of, the donee before his attaining the age of 21 years, and
> (2) will to the extent not so expended —
> (A) pass to the donee on his attaining the age of 21 years, and
> (B) in the event the donee dies before attaining the age of 21 years, be payable to the estate of the donee or as he may appoint under a general power of appointment as defined in section 2514(c).

Section 2503(c) is not limited to transfers in trust. Any transfer that satisfies the section's requirements qualifies for the annual exclusion. To provide a convenient form for gifts that qualify, every state has enacted its version of the Uniform Gifts to Minors Act.[78] Under the Act money, securities, life insurance policies, annuities, and (under some states' statutes) any other form of personal property can be transferred to a person (including the donor) or corporate fiduciary as custodian for the benefit of a minor. A transfer "to ________ as custodian for ________ under the [name of state] Uniform Gift to Minors Act," without more, gives the custodian broad fiduciary powers that permit a more flexible administration than is available under a guardianship. The custodian's distribution powers over income and principal, set out in the statute, meet the requirements of §2503(c).

OHIO REVISED CODE ANNOTATED §1339.34 (Page 1962): "(B) The custodian shall pay over to the minor for expenditure by him, or expend for the minor's benefit, so much or all the custodial property as the custodian deems advisable for the support, maintenance, education, and benefit of the minor in the manner, at the time or times, and to the extent that the custodian in his discretion deems suitable and proper, with or without court order, with or without regard to the duty of himself or of any other person to support the minor or his ability to do so, and with or without regard to any other income or property of the minor which may be applicable or available for any such purpose.

"(D) To the extent that the custodial property is not so expended, the custodian shall deliver or pay it over to the minor on his attaining the age of twenty-one years or, if the minor dies before attaining the age of twenty-one years, he shall thereupon deliver or pay it over to the estate of the minor."

[78] See page 455, infra. Generally on gifts to minors, see Ziegler, Gifts to Minors — Three Variations, 24 Tax Law. 297 (1971); Ehrlich, The Effective Use of Support Trusts: Trusts for Minors, Custodian Statutes, Gifts of Future Interests, N.Y.U. 19th Inst. Fed. Tax 729 (1961).

PROBLEMS

1. Over a five-year period, O transfers securities worth $15,000 to himself as custodian for his child, A. O dies four years after making the last transfer; A is sixteen years old at the time of O's death. Is any portion of the securities' value includible in O's gross estate? Rev. Rul. 59-357, 1959-2 Cum. Bull. 212; Dorothy Stuit, 54 T.C. 580 (1970).

2. In each year from 1965 through 1970, O transfers securities worth $5000 to his son X as trustee for the benefit of O's grandchild, G. G is ten years old at the time of the first transfer in 1965. Under the terms of the trust, "the trustee shall at least as often as quarterly pay over to G, or expend for G's benefit, all of the trust income until G attains the age of twenty-five, at which time the trustee shall distribute the trust corpus to G, free of trust. If G dies before attaining age twenty-five, the trustee shall distribute the trust corpus to such person or persons as G shall appoint by will, and in default of appointment the trustee shall distribute the corpus to G's estate."

(a) Is O entitled to an annual exclusion for the gifts to G in 1965 through 1970? Commissioner v. Herr, 303 F.2d 780 (3d Cir. 1962); Rev. Rul. 68-670, 1968-2 Cum. Bull. 413; see Treas. Reg. §2512-9, Table B (1971); Sugarman & Brucken, The Present Interest Trust for a Minor, 4 Real Prop., Prob. & Trust J. 651 (1969).

(b) In 1973 the trust produces income of $1600. How and to whom is the income taxed? Int. Rev. Code of 1954, §§141, 151, 6012(a); cf. Raymond H. Biggs, T.C. Mem. 240 (1968). But see Int. Rev. Code of 1954, §678(c).

2. *The Lifetime Exemption*

Every taxpayer is entitled to a $30,000 lifetime exemption under the gift tax. Unlike the annual exclusions, which recur each year, there is only one lifetime exemption — although the taxpayer may use portions of it from time to time. Suppose, for example, O (who is not married) gives $10,000 to A and $10,000 to B. He can take the $3000 exclusion against each gift, and then apply $14,000 of his lifetime exemption to the remaining portion of the gifts. If in the next year he again gives $10,000 each to A and B, he can apply $14,000 of his remaining exemption, and he will be left with a $2000 exemption that can be applied to gifts in future years.

3. *The Gift Tax Marital Deduction; Split Gifts*

As a part of the general plan to equalize the tax treatment of couples residing in common law states and community property states,[79] in 1948 Congress authorized

[79] See page 239, supra.

couples to split their gifts for tax purposes and provided for a marital deduction under the gift tax.

A gift of community property worth $10,000 is treated as a gift of $5000 from each spouse. Each can claim a $3000 exclusion and can apply his lifetime exemption to the balance of $2000. Section 2513 of the 1954 Code places the owner of separate property on an equal footing: "A gift made by one spouse to any person other than his spouse shall . . . be considered as made one-half by him and one-half by his spouse," if both spouses signify their consent to splitting the gift. The effect of §2513 is to double the available exclusions and exemptions applicable to a gift by a married couple, and also to lower the overall tax bill if a taxable gift is made. Because of the graduated tax rates, the tax on two taxable gifts of $25,000 is lower than the tax on a gift of $50,000.

PROBLEM

H gives property worth $100,000 to A, and his wife W signifies her consent to splitting the gift. Each files a gift tax return that reports a gift of $50,000, claims a $3000 annual exclusion and $30,000 exemption, and reflects a taxable gift of $17,000. The tax on a $17,000 taxable gift is $952.50; the total tax of $1905 is paid. H dies two years later; W dies two years after H; the gift by H is held to be in contemplation of death. What amount is includible in H's gross estate? Rev. Rul. 54-246, 1954-1 Cum. Bull. 179. Suppose, instead, that W dies two years after the gift, and H dies two years after W. What amount is includible in W's gross estate?

As with the estate tax marital deduction under §2056, §2523 allows a marital deduction for gifts to the transferor's spouse. While the two marital deduction provisions are generally similar, there are important differences in their operation. Most notably, the marital deduction under the estate tax is limited to one-half the decedent's adjusted gross estate, but the gift tax marital deduction is simply one-half the value of the gift. If H gives separate property[80] worth $10,000 outright to W, the marital deduction is one-half this amount, or $5000. H can then claim an annual exclusion of $3000, and he will pay a tax on a taxable gift of $2000 (unless he applies a portion of his lifetime exemption to the gift).

To qualify for the deduction, the gift must not be a nondeductible terminable interest. In general, the nondeductible terminable interest rule — and the exceptions to the rule — are the same under both taxes. For our purposes it suffices to note than an outright gift, an estate trust, and a life estate with general power of appointment are the most common means of qualifying for the gift tax marital deduction.

[80] Community property does not qualify for the gift tax marital deduction. Int. Rev. Code of 1954, §2523(f).

PROBLEM

A life insurance agent has recommended to H that he give his wife (who has no property of her own) securities worth \$66,000. The purpose of the transaction would be to insure that the benefit of the wife's \$60,000 estate tax exemption is not lost if she predeceases H. H wants your advice: What are the pros and cons of such a gift?

4. *Federal Gift Tax Rates*

After exclusions and the exemption have been exhausted and any deductions[81] have been taken, the balance comprises the donor's taxable gifts for the year. If he has not made any taxable gifts in earlier years, the gift tax is calculated by applying the tax rates set out in §2502. If you compare the table below with the one set out on page 252, you will note that the tax rates are 75 percent of those under the estate tax.

If the taxable gifts are:	The tax shall be:
Not over \$5000	2¼% of the taxable gifts.
Over \$5000 but not over \$10,000	\$112.50, plus 5¼% of the excess over \$5000.
Over \$10,000 but not over \$20,000	\$375, plus 8¼% of the excess over \$10,000.
Over \$20,000 but not over \$30,000	\$1200, plus 10½% of the excess over \$20,000.
Over \$30,000 but not over \$40,000	\$2250, plus 13½% of the excess over \$30,000.
* * * *	
Over \$100,000 but not over \$250,000	\$15,525, plus 22½% of the excess over \$100,000.

The gift tax is cumulative. That is, the rate of tax applicable to this year's gifts is determined by the total amount of taxable gifts the taxpayer has made during his lifetime. Suppose, for example, that in past years O has made taxable gifts of \$10,000 and has paid total gift taxes of \$375. This year he made taxable gifts of \$15,000. The tax is computed by first determining the tax on gifts totalling \$25,000, and then subtracting the gift tax paid in previous years.

Taxable gifts in earlier years	\$10,000
Taxable gifts this year	15,000
Total taxable gifts	\$25,000

[81] Only two deductions are allowed under the gift tax: the marital deduction and the charitable deduction. In general, the rules governing allowance of a gift tax charitable deduction under §2522 are the same as under the estate tax. This includes the deduction for a charitable remainder: Only a charitable remainder annuity trust or unitrust qualifies for deduction. See page 238, supra.

Tax on taxable gifts of $25,000	$1725
Tax paid on gifts in earlier years	– 375
Tax due this year	$1350

PROBLEM

Last November H gave 100 acres of land to each of his three adult sons. The land was worth $300 per acre. H's wife signified her consent to the gifts. H and his wife have never made any taxable gifts before last year, and they want to apply their lifetime exemptions to the gifts. What is the total amount of gift tax that must be paid? Could H have transferred the land to his sons without incurring any gift tax?

5. *What Transfers Are Subject to the Gift Tax?*

The gift tax reaches transfers with a donative element, even though there was consideration for the transfer. If O sells land worth $30,000 to his son for $15,000, the transaction is treated as part sale and part gift. As stated in the Regulations, "Transfers reached by the gift tax are not confined to those only which, being without a valuable consideration, accord with the common law concept of gifts but embrace as well sales, exchanges, and other dispositions of property for a consideration to the extent that the value of the property transferred exceeds the value in money or money's worth of the consideration given therefor." [82]

The statute taxes indirect as well as direct gifts. Some examples: O pays a debt of A; or forgives a debt owed to him by A. In both cases, unless the transaction arises in a business context in which consideration can be found, O has made a gift to A. If O renounces his intestate share in his ancestor's estate, and as a consequence the property that would have passed to O passes to A, O has made a gift of the property to A.[83] If O deeds land worth $20,000 to A on the condition that A give $10,000 to B, and A satisfies the condition, O is deemed to have made gifts of $10,000 each to A and B.[84]

Not all donative transfers are taxed, however. In order to incur a gift tax, the transfer must be "complete."

ESTATE OF SANFORD v. COMMISSIONER

United States Supreme Court, 1939
308 U.S. 39

MR. JUSTICE STONE delivered the opinion of the Court.

This and its companion case, Rasquin v. Humphreys, post, p. 54, present the

[82] Treas. Reg. §25.2512-8 (1958).

[83] See Problem 2, page 88, supra.

[84] A related problem was raised in United States v. Estate of Grace, 395 U.S. 316 (1969), Problem 3, page 228, supra.

single question of statutory construction whether in the case of an inter vivos transfer of property in trust, by a donor reserving to himself the power to designate new beneficiaries other than himself, the gift becomes complete and subject to the gift tax imposed by the federal revenue laws at the time of the relinquishment of the power. Corelative [*sic*] questions, important only if a negative answer is given to the first one, are whether the gift becomes complete and taxable when the trust is created or, in the case where the donor has reserved a power of revocation for his own benefit and has relinquished it before relinquishing the power to change beneficiaries, whether the gift first becomes complete and taxable at the time of relinquishing the power of revocation.

In 1913, before the enactment of the first gift tax statute of 1924, decedent created a trust of personal property for the benefit of named beneficiaries, reserving to himself the power to terminate the trust in whole or in part, or to modify it. In 1919 he surrendered the power to revoke the trust by an appropriate writing in which he reserved "the right to modify any or all of the trusts" but provided that this right "shall in no way be deemed or construed to include any right or privilege" in the donor "to withdraw principal or income from any trust." In August, 1924, after the effective date of the gift tax statute, decedent renounced his remaining power to modify the trust. After his death in 1928, the Commissioner following the decision in Hesslein v. Hoey, 91 F.2d 954, in 1937, ruled that the gift became complete and taxable only upon decedent's final renunciation of his power to modify the trusts and gave notice of a tax deficiency accordingly.

The order of the Board of Tax Appeals sustaining the tax was affirmed by the Court of Appeals for the Third Circuit, 103 F.2d 81, which followed the decision of the Court of Appeals for the Second Circuit in Hesslein v. Hoey, supra, in which we had denied certiorari, 302 U.S. 756. In the Hesslein case, as in the Humphreys case now before us, a gift in trust with the reservation of a power in the donor to alter the disposition of the property in any way not beneficial to himself, was held to be incomplete and not subject to the gift tax under the 1932 Act so long as the donor retained that power.

We granted certiorari in this case, 307 U.S. 618, and in the Humphreys case, id. 619, upon the representation of the Government that it has taken inconsistent positions with respect to the question involved in the two cases and that because of this fact and of the doubt of the correctness of the decision in the Hesslein case decision of the question by this Court is desirable in order to remove the resultant confusion in the administration of the revenue laws.

It has continued to take these inconsistent positions here, stating that it is unable to determine which construction of the statute will be most advantageous to the Government in point of revenue collected. It argues in this case that the gift did not become complete and taxable until surrender by the donor of his reserved power to designate new beneficiaries of the trusts. In the Humphreys case it argues that the gift upon trust with power reserved to the donor, not afterward relinquished, to change the beneficiaries was complete and taxable when the trust was created. It concedes by its brief that "a decision favorable to the government in either case will necessarily preclude a favorable decision in the other."

In ascertaining the correct construction of the statutes taxing gifts, it is necessary to read them in the light of the closely related provisions of the revenue laws taxing transfers at death, as they have been interpreted by our decisions. Section 319 et seq. of the Revenue Act of 1924, 43 Stat. 253, reënacted as §501 et seq. of the 1932 Act, 47 Stat. 169, imposed a graduated tax upon gifts. It supplemented that laid on transfers at death, which had long been a feature of the revenue laws. When the gift tax was enacted Congress was aware that the essence of a transfer is the passage of control over the economic benefits of property rather than any technical changes in its title. See Burnet v. Guggenheim, 288 U.S. 280, 287. Following the enactment of the gift tax statute this Court in Reinecke v. Northern Trust Co., 278 U.S. 339 (1929) held that the relinquishment at death of a power of revocation of a trust for the benefit of its donor was a taxable transfer, cf. Saltonstall v. Saltonstall, 276 U.S. 260; Chase National Bank v. United States, 278 U.S. 327; and similarly in Porter v. Commissioner, 288 U.S. 436 (1933), that the relinquishment by a donor at death of a reserved power to modify the trust except in his own favor is likewise a transfer of the property which could constitutionally be taxed under the provisions of §302(d) of the 1926 Revenue Act (reënacting in substance 302(d) of the 1924 Act) although enacted after the creation of the trust. Cf. Bullen v. Wisconsin, 240 U.S. 625; Curry v. McCanless, 307 U.S. 357; Graves v. Elliott, 307 U.S. 383. Since it was the relinquishment of the power which was taxed as a transfer and not the transfer in trust, the statute was not retroactively applied. Cf. Nichols v. Coolidge, 274 U.S. 531; Helvering v. Helmholz, 296 U.S. 93, 98.

The rationale of decision in both cases is that "taxation is not so much concerned with the refinements of title as it is with the actual command over the property taxed" (see Corliss v. Bowers, 281 U.S. 376, 378; Saltonstall v. Saltonstall, supra, 261; Burnet v. Guggenheim, supra, 287) and that a retention of control over the disposition of the trust property, whether for the benefit of the donor or others, renders the gift incomplete until the power is relinquished whether in life or at death. The rule was thus established, and has ever since been consistently followed by the Court, that a transfer of property upon trust, with power reserved to the donor either to revoke it and recapture the trust property or to modify its terms so as to designate new beneficiaries other than himself is incomplete, and becomes complete so as to subject the transfer to death taxes only on relinquishment of the power at death.

There is nothing in the language of the statute, and our attention has not been directed to anything in its legislative history to suggest that Congress had any purpose to tax gifts before the donor had fully parted with his interest in the property given, or that the test of the completeness of the taxed gift was to be any different from that to be applied in determining whether the donor has retained an interest such that it becomes subject to the estate tax upon its extinguishment at death. The gift tax was supplementary to the estate tax. The two are in pari materia and must be construed together. Burnet v. Guggenheim, supra, 286. An important, if not the main, purpose of the gift tax was to prevent or compensate for avoidance of death taxes by taxing the gifts of property inter vivos which, but for the gifts, would be subject in its original or converted form to the tax laid upon transfers at death.

Section 322 of the 1924 Act[85] provides that when a tax has been imposed by §319 upon a gift, the value of which is required by any provision of the statute taxing the estate to be included in the gross estate, the gift tax is to be credited on the estate tax. The two taxes are thus not always mutually exclusive as in the case of gifts made in contemplation of death which are complete and taxable when made, and are also required to be included in the gross estate for purposes of the death tax. But §322 is without application unless there is a gift inter vivos which is taxable independently of any requirement that it shall be included in the gross estate. Property transferred in trust subject to a power of control over its disposition reserved to the donor is likewise required by §302(d)[86] to be included in the gross estate. But it does not follow that the transfer in trust is also taxable as a gift. The point was decided in the Guggenheim case where it was held that a gift upon trust, with power in the donor to revoke it is not taxable as a gift because the transfer is incomplete, and that the transfer whether inter vivos or at death becomes complete and taxable only when the power of control is relinquished. We think, as was pointed out in the Guggenheim case, supra, 285, that the gift tax statute does not contemplate two taxes upon gifts not made in contemplation of death, one upon the gift when a trust is created or when the power of revocation, if any, is relinquished, and another on the transfer of the same property at death because the gift previously made was incomplete. . . .

There are other persuasive reasons why the taxpayer's contention cannot be sustained. By §§315(b), 324, and more specifically by §510 of the 1932 Act,[87] the donee of any gift is made personally liable for the tax to the extent of the value of the gift if the tax is not paid by the donor. It can hardly be supposed that Congress intended to impose personal liability upon the donee of a gift of property, so incomplete that he might be deprived of it by the donor the day after he had paid the tax. . . .

The argument of petitioner that the construction which the Government supports here, but assails in the Humphreys case, affords a ready means of evasion of the gift tax is not impressive. It is true, of course, that under it gift taxes will not be imposed on transactions which fall short of being completed gifts. But if for that reason they are not taxed as gifts they remain subject to death taxes assessed at higher rates, and the Government gets its due, which was precisely the end sought by the enactment of the gift tax. . . .

Affirmed.

PROBLEMS

1. O establishes an irrevocable trust that is funded with securities worth $200,000. Trust income is to be paid to O for life, "and on his death the trustee shall distribute the trust corpus to such of the Settlor's issue as he shall appoint by

[85] Now Int. Rev. Code of 1954, §2012. — Eds.
[86] Now Int. Rev. Code of 1954, §2036(a)(2). — Eds.
[87] Now Int. Rev. Code of 1954, §6324(b). — Eds.

will; and in default of such appointment the trustee shall distribute the corpus to the Settlor's issue then living, per stirpes." What are the gift tax consequences of this transfer? Treas. Reg. §25.2511-2(b) (1958).

2. Consider the same facts as in Problem 1, except that the trust further provides: "In the event that the income so payable to the Settlor does not in the sole judgment and discretion of the trustee provide for the comfortable well-being of the Settlor, the trustee may from time to time pay to the Settlor such part or all of the corpus of the trust estate as to the said trustee in its sole discretion shall seem advisable." O does not reserve a power of appointment over the trust corpus. Instead, the trust provides: "On the Settlor's death the trustee shall distribute the corpus to the Settlor's issue then living, per stirpes." What are the gift tax consequences of this transfer? Commissioner v. Vander Weele, 254 F.2d 895 (6th Cir. 1958); Rev. Rul. 62-13, 1962-1 Cum. Bull. 181. But see Herzog v. Commissioner, 116 F.2d 591 (2d Cir. 1941); Estate of Leon Holtz, 38 T.C. 37, 42 (1962) (dictum).

3. O places securities worth $200,000 in an irrevocable trust under which trust income is to be paid to his daughter D for life, "and on her death the trustee shall distribute the trust corpus to such of D's issue as she shall appoint by will; and in default of appointment the trustee shall distribute the corpus to D's issue then living, per stirpes." What are the gift tax consequences of this transfer?

6. *Gift Tax Treatment of Joint Tenancies and Tenancies by the Entireties*[88]

Special rules govern the gift taxation of joint tenancies and tenancies by the entireties, the two forms of concurrent ownership that have as their chief characteristic the right of survivorship. Operation of these rules is best illustrated by contrasting the tax treatment of the creation and termination of these survivorship interests with the tenancy in common.

> *Case 1.* A pays $40,000 for securities, taking title in the name of A and B as tenants in common. Under the state's laws, A and B each acquire an undivided one-half interest in the property. A has made a gift of one-half the property, worth $20,000, to B.

If A and B later sell the securities for $60,000 and split the sale proceeds, there are no gift tax consequences at the time of the sale. A paid the only gift tax that is due at the time he gave B an undivided one-half interest. (A and B would each realize capital gain of $10,000.) Similarly, if A predeceases B, and the value of the concurrently owned property is $60,000 at A's death, the value of A's one-half interest, or $30,000, is includible in his gross estate.

> *Case 2.* A pays $40,000 for securities, taking title in the name of A and B as joint tenants with right of survivorship. A is sixty-five years old and B is forty years

88 On this subject generally, see authorities cited note 10 supra.

old at the time the securities are purchased. A has made a gift of one-half the property, worth $20,000, to B. Treas. Reg. §§25.2515-2(b)(1), 25.2511-1(h)(5) (1958).

At first blush, it would appear that A has given B an interest worth more than half the value of the property. Because of A's advanced age, the probabilities are that B will outlive him and succeed to outright ownership of the securities. A joint tenancy is, however, severable by any joint tenant. If A conveys his interest in the joint tenancy to C, the right of survivorship is severed and B and C become tenants in common, each owning an undivided one-half interest in the property. Since a joint tenancy can be transformed into a tenancy in common by a lifetime transfer that severs the right of survivorship, creation of a joint tenancy is taxed in the same manner as creation of a tenancy in common — subject to two exceptions.

The first exception relates to joint bank accounts and United States government bonds.

Case 3. A deposits $10,000 in a joint bank account, taking title to the account in the form, "A and B, payable on death to the survivor." Under the state's laws this creates a joint tenancy account under which either party can withdraw funds at any time. On the death of one co-owner the survivor succeeds to the entire balance in the account. Since A can revoke the account by withdrawing all the funds on deposit, the transfer is incomplete for gift tax purposes. There will not be any gift until B withdraws funds from the account. Treas. Reg. §25.2511-1(h)(4) (1958).

Similarly, if A and B each deposit $5000 in the joint account, there will be no gift until either A or B withdraws more than the $5000 he deposited.

The same rule applies to United States government bonds registered in "A or B" form. Under this ownership designation, either A or B can present the bond for payment. If A cashes in the bond, there is no gift. If B cashes in the bond, or if A causes it to be reissued in B's name alone, the gift to B is complete.[89]

A second exception applies to real estate acquired by a husband and wife in joint tenancy or tenancy by the entireties form. "Frequently, real property is held in a tenancy by the entirety [or in joint tenancy] to insure the right of survivorship in the surviving spouse. Many couples who elect this method of buying a home have no intention of making a gift at the time of the creation of the tenancy . . . or any knowledge that they are considered as having done so." [90] To meet this problem, §2515 of the 1954 Code provides that the creation of a tenancy by the entireties or joint tenancy in land between husband and wife shall not be treated as a taxable gift unless the donor spouse elects to have it so treated.

Case 4. H buys land for $30,000, taking title in the form, "H and W, husband and wife." Under the state's laws this creates a tenancy by the entireties es-

[89] Rev. Rul. 55-278, 1955-1 Cum. Bull. 471.

[90] H.R. Rep. No. 1337, 83d Cong., 2d Sess. 4121; S. Rep. No. 1622, 83d Cong., 2d Sess. 4761.

tate under which, upon the death of one of the spouses, the survivor succeeds to outright ownership of the property. There is no taxable gift unless the husband elects to treat the transfer as a gift by including the value of the donated interest in his gift tax return for the year. Treas. Reg. §25.2515-1(b) (1958).

This exception, which is available only to spouses, applies to real estate, and not to personal property acquired in joint tenancy or tenancy by the entireties form.

The tenancy by the entireties form of ownership of real property between spouses is recognized in twenty jurisdictions,[91] and in most of these jurisdictions such an estate can be created with respect to personal property.[92] If the donor elects to treat the acquisition of tenancy by the entireties land as a gift, or if such an estate is created with respect to personal property, the gift tax treatment of the acquisition is complicated by the fact that the survivorship incident of the estate is indestructible. That is, in states that allow one of the spouses to transfer his interest in the entireties property, or that permit his interest to be reached by creditors, the grantee receives that spouse's interest subject to the other spouse's right of survivorship. If H transfers his interest in entireties property to B and H survives his wife W, on H's death B succeeds to outright ownership of the property. But if H predeceases W, on his death B's interest is extinguished and W succeeds to outright ownership of the property. Only a conveyance by both the husband and wife can eliminate the survivorship incident of the estate. Consequently, when H furnishes the consideration for the purchase of property in tenancy by the entireties form, the effect is to give his wife an interest in the property during their joint lives *plus* the chance of succeeding to absolute ownership upon H's death.

Case 5. H pays $40,000 for securities, taking title in the form, "H and W, husband and wife." Under the state's laws this creates a tenancy by the entireties estate. H is sixty-five years old and W is forty years old at the time the securities are purchased. H has made a taxable gift of a portion of the property to W. The amount of the gift is the difference between the value of the property and the value of H's retained interest in the property. The latter is determined by comparing the life expectancies of H and W. Treas. Reg. §25.2515-2(b)(2), (c), (d). The value of H's retained interest is .27 (of $40,000), or $10,800, and the amount of his gift to W is $29,200. Treas. Reg. §25.2512-9(e), Table ET6 (1971).

If the creation of a tenancy by the entireties or a joint tenancy between spouses is treated as a taxable gift, does the transfer qualify for the gift tax marital deduction? It would appear that it does not, since the donee spouse's interest is terminable: if she predeceases the donor spouse her interest is extinguished. However, §2523(d) exempts the creation of joint estates from the nondeductible terminable interest rule. Thus in *Case 5* H would be entitled to a gift tax marital deduction of $14,600 as well as a $3000 annual exclusion. If he has not used up his $30,000 lifetime exemption, he could apply $11,600 of the exemption to this gift and avoid the payment of any gift tax.

[91] See Phipps, Tenancy by Entireties, 25 Temp. L.Q. 24 (1951).
[92] See Note, 64 A.L.R.2d 8 (1959).

Suppose, in *Case* 5, that H dies survived by W some years after the securities are purchased, and that at H's death the value of the securities is $60,000. Since H furnished the entire consideration for the purchase of the property, under §2040 the full value of the assets, or $60,000, is includible in H's gross estate.[93] His estate is given a credit for any gift tax paid at the time the tenancy by the entireties was created.[94] Suppose, instead, that W predeceases H. Under §2040 no portion of the securities' value is includible in W's gross estate since the entire consideration for the property was furnished by H.

PROBLEMS

1. H purchases a new home for $40,000, paying $10,000 down and signing a secured note for the balance of $30,000. He takes title in the form, "H and W, as joint tenants with right of survivorship and not as tenants in common." He did this on the recommendation of his grantor's real estate agent, who told him, "most couples in our state do it this way, and a joint tenancy solves a lot of problems." What are the tax consequences of H's purchase, and what do you think of the broker's advice?

2. H purchases mutual funds for $20,000, and causes the securities to be registered in the form, "H and W, as joint tenants with right of survivorship and not as tenants in common." He did this on the recommendation of his stock broker, who told him, "most couples in our state do it this way, and a joint tenancy solves a lot of problems." What are the tax consequences of H's purchase, and what do you think of the broker's advice? See Dean, Federal Tax Consequences of Joint Ownership, 53 Geo. L.J. 863 (1965).

SECTION C. State Succession Taxes

All states except Nevada have succession taxes that take one of two forms: an inheritance tax or an estate tax.[95] Fifteen states impose a gift tax on lifetime transfers. The District of Columbia and three-fourths of the states have inheritance taxes under which the tax is levied on the amount passing to each legatee or heir, and the applicable tax rates and exemptions are determined by the relationship of the beneficiary to the decedent. Although the decedent's executor or administrator is personally liable for payment of the tax, the actual burden of the inheritance tax falls on and is payable from the amount passing to each beneficiary (unless the decedent's will provides otherwise).

The Illinois inheritance tax is representative. Under the Illinois statute[96] a tax is

[93] See page 211, supra.
[94] Int. Rev. Code of 1954, §2012.
[95] The succession tax laws of all states are compiled in CCH Inh., Est. & Gift Tax Rep., and a summary of the state tax laws is given in CCH State Tax Guide ¶89-000.
[96] Ill. Ann. Stat. c. 120, §375 (Smith-Hurd 1968, Supp. 1971).

imposed on property passing by will or inheritance or by right of survivorship. Also taxed are lifetime transfers made in contemplation of death, certain lifetime transfers in which the decedent retained controls or economic benefits, and property over which the decedent held *and exercised* a power of appointment (whether special or general). Life insurance proceeds are not taxed unless payable to the decedent's estate or personal representative.[97]

The applicable tax rates and exemptions turn on whether the transferee is a Class A, Class B, or Class C beneficiary. Class A beneficiaries include lineal ancestors, lineal descendants, daughters-in-law, sons-in-law, and the spouse of the decedent. (Adopted children are treated the same as natural children for purposes of determining a beneficiary's relationship to the decedent.) For each of the above Class A beneficiaries, there is a personal exemption of $20,000. Brothers and sisters of the decedent are also Class A beneficiaries, but their exemption is limited to $10,000. Class B beneficiaries include uncles, aunts, nephews, nieces, and their lineal descendants. The personal exemption for Class B beneficiaries is $500. Class C beneficiaries include all other persons or organizations (other than charitable organizations, for which a charitable exemption is granted). The Class C personal exemption is $100.

The Illinois inheritance tax rates are as follows:

Value of Share in Excess of Exemption		Class A		Class B		Class C	
		Tax on Col. 1	*Rate on Excess*	*Tax on Col. 1*	*Rate on Excess*	*Tax on Col. 1*	*Rate on Excess*
$ 0	$ 20,000	$ 0	2%	$ 0	6%	$ 0	10%
20,000	50,000	400	2%	1,200	8%	2,000	12%
50,000	70,000	1,000	4%	3,600	8%	5,600	16%
70,000	100,000	1,800	4%	5,200	12%	8,800	16%
100,000	150,000	3,000	4%	8,800	12%	13,600	20%
150,000	170,000	5,000	6%	14,800	12%	23,600	24%
170,000	250,000	6,200	6%	17,200	16%	28,400	24%
250,000	500,000	11,000	10%	30,000	16%	47,600	30%
500,000	......	36,000	14%	70,000	16%	122,600	30%

As with every other jurisdiction that has an inheritance tax, Illinois also has an estate tax designed to take advantage of the federal estate tax credit for state death taxes.[98] This tax is quite commonly (and appropriately) called the "take-up" or

[97] This is the treatment accorded life insurance proceeds in over half the states. In the other states life insurance proceeds in excess of a certain amount (ranging from $15,000 to Colorado's $75,000) are taxed.

[98] Int. Rev. Code of 1954, §2011.

The estate tax credit for state death taxes traces back to the 1920s, when efforts were made to repeal the federal estate tax on the ground that this source of revenue should be reserved to the states. In 1924 Congress granted a state tax credit of 25 percent of the federal tax, and in 1926 the credit was increased to 80 percent. Most states immediately revised their succession tax laws to take full advantage of the credit, since it permitted diversion of 80 percent of the federal tax revenues to the states without increasing the actual death tax burden on their residents. With the Great Depression came efforts to repeal the tax credit, but this proved to be

"sponge" tax. The amount of the estate tax is defined by statute as an amount equal to the difference between (1) the maximum tax credit allowed under the federal law and (2) the amount of tax due under the state's inheritance tax.[99] The maximum tax credits are set out in §2011(b) of the Internal Revenue Code of 1954, as follows:

If the taxable estate is:	The maximum tax credit shall be:
Not over $90,000	8/10ths of 1% of the amount by which the taxable estate exceeds $40,000.
Over $90,000 but not over $140,000	$400 plus 1.6% of the excess over $90,000.
Over $140,000 but not over $240,000	$1200 plus 2.4% of the excess over $140,000.
Over $240,000 but not over $440,000	$3600 plus 3.2% of the excess over $240,000.
Over $440,000 but not over $640,000	$10,000 plus 4% of the excess over $440,000.
* * * *	
Over $10,040,000	$1,082,800 plus 16% of the excess over $10,040,000.

Fourteen states have an estate tax as their basic succession tax. The estate tax is a charge against the estate and, in the absence of a will provision to the contrary, it is payable out of the residuary assets. In five of these states[100] the tax does no more than absorb the federal tax credit for state death taxes. Consequently, the table of maximum tax credits under §2011(b) also serves as the table of rates under the state

---

politically impossible since the states were reluctant to lose this revenue source. Congress resolved the impasse by allowing the credit to continue against the estate tax imposed by the Revenue Act of 1926, and by enacting an additional estate tax against which the credit was not applicable. This pattern has been carried down to the present day. Thus the Revenue Act of 1926 is still part of our estate tax laws, but its only function is to determine the amount of the credit for state death taxes. There is no tax credit unless the decedent's taxable estate exceeds $40,000. This stems from the fact that the Revenue Act of 1926 granted an estate tax exemption of $100,000.

[99] "In addition to the inheritance tax imposed by this Act, a tax is also imposed upon the transfer of the estate of every decedent dying subsequent to July 24, 1949, leaving an estate which is subject to the Federal estate tax imposed by the United States of America under the applicable provisions of the Internal Revenue Code and which has, in whole or in part, a taxable situs in this State. The tax hereby imposed upon the transfer of each such estate shall be equal to the maximum tax credit allowable for State death taxes against the Federal estate tax imposed with respect to the portion of the decedent's estate having a taxable situs in this State, less the inheritance taxes, if any, due this State under this Act, it being the purpose and intent of this Section to impose only such additional taxes hereunder as may be necessary to give this State the full benefit of the maximum tax credit allowable against the Federal estate tax imposed with respect to a decedent's estate which has a taxable situs in this State." Ill. Ann. Stat. c. 120, §403(a) (Smith-Hurd 1968, Supp. 1971).

[100] Alabama, Alaska, Arkansas, Florida, and Georgia.

estate tax. In these jurisdictions very few estates incur tax liability, since there is a $100,000 exemption under §2011(b) and thus under the states' tax laws.

The estate tax laws of the other nine jurisdictions[101] do not follow any one pattern, although each incorporates some features of the federal estate tax. For example, the New York estate tax laws are almost a paraphrase of the federal tax laws, while Vermont's statute follows the federal tax laws most closely and succinctly by imposing an estate tax equal to 30 percent of the federal estate tax. In these nine states, in addition to the basic estate tax there is a "sponge" estate tax designed to absorb the §2011(b) credit. The amount of this additional tax is the difference between (1) the maximum tax credit allowed under federal law and (2) the amount of tax due under the basic estate tax.

PROBLEM

Assume that Adam Smith is a resident of Illinois, and that he dies leaving a will that devises all his property outright to his wife, Jane. He is survived by his wife and three minor children. At his death the assets listed on page 254 are owned by the Smiths. Funeral and administration expenses and claims other than the $19,000 mortgage debt total $8000. Compute the Illinois inheritance tax due by reason of Adam Smith's death.

In re OGBURN'S ESTATE
Wyoming Supreme Court, 1965
406 P.2d 655

GRAY, Justice. The will of Alice R. Ogburn, deceased, disposed of real and personal property appraised in her probate estate in the sum of approximately $238,000. Out of that property a special devise was made to her foster son, Douglas Bell Ogburn, of certain real estate valued at $80,000 and a special bequest of certain stocks valued in the approximate sum of $62,000 was made to his children. A brother and five sisters of decedent were made the residuary devisees and legatees. In addition to the above-described property passing under the will, the foster son, as a result of the death of testatrix, acquired ownership of jointly held property valued at approximately $12,500 and proceeds of insurance policies in the sum of $20,000. The foster son was named as executor of the estate and qualified and acted as such during the times herein. In rendering his final account as executor, the foster son undertook to charge the residuary estate with the full amount paid for Federal estate tax and the full amount paid for Wyoming inheritance tax. Exceptions to the accounting treatment accorded such items were duly taken by the residuary legatees. After hearing, the trial court approved the final accounting in all respects and a decree of distribution was entered on that basis. From that decree the residuary

[101] Arizona, Mississippi, New York, North Dakota, Ohio, Oklahoma, South Carolina, Utah, and Vermont.

devisees and legatees appeal. For convenience we shall hereafter usually refer to the brother and sisters as appellants and to the foster son and his children as appellees.

The ultimate questions presented, as we view it, may be summarized as follows:

1. Did the will contain a sufficient directive against apportionment of the Federal estate tax in the manner prescribed by the Uniform Estate Tax Apportionment Act, Ch. 171, S.L. of Wyoming, 1959 (§§2-336 to 2-346, W.S. 1965 Cum. Supp.), with respect to (a) the testamentary gifts made to appellees and (b) to the nontestamentary gifts of the joint property to the foster son?

2. Did the will contain a sufficient directive against apportionment of that part of the Federal estate tax levied upon the proceeds of insurance policies in the manner prescribed by the Internal Revenue Code of 1954, 26 U.S.C.A. §2206 (1955)?

3. Did the will contain a sufficient directive to shift the burden of payment of State inheritance taxes from the devisees and legatees of property transferred by the will, as the statute provides, to the residuary estate?

In this connection we should state that the parties, for purposes of argument with respect to the questions relating to Federal estate taxes, made no effort to segregate into component parts the three classes of property that were included in decedent's taxable estate and, although recognizing that the enumerated specific questions exist, simply took the position that the language of the will either did, or did not, contain a directive against apportionment of the Federal tax as a whole. For reasons soon to be stated we believe that the views of the parties are not entirely correct and hence the necessity to state the questions with preciseness.

The clause of the will that brought about this controversy states: "First: I direct the payment of all my just debts, taxes, funeral expenses and expense of administration of my estate." Following this are articles "Third" and "Fourth" making the specific devises and bequests to the foster son and his children, and article "Fifth" granting the residuary estate to the brother and sisters of the testatrix. For our purposes that is the sum and substance of the will.

The Federal Taxes

As an initial approach to the matter of apportionment of Federal estate taxes we point out, as indicated above, that the public policy of this State, as declared by the legislature, is to apportion such taxes to the persons benefited. Section 2 of the Act, supra, succinctly lays down that proposition. It provides:

> Unless the will otherwise provides, the tax shall be apportioned among all persons interested in the estate. The apportionment shall be made in proportion that the value of the interest of each person interested in the estate bears to the total value of the interests of all persons interested in the estate. The values used in determining the tax shall be used for that purpose.

The statute accomplishes three general purposes. First, it preserves the inherent and recognized right of a testator or testatrix to designate the fund from which such taxes are to be paid. Secondly, it abrogates the common-law rule that, absent such a designation, the burden of payment was first to be imposed upon the residuary estate. Thirdly, and again absent a directive in the will to the contrary, it apportions the tax — without regard to special or general devises and bequests — commensurately to those benefited by the gifts of property upon which the Federal tax has been imposed.

We are one of three states which have adopted the Uniform Estate Tax Apportionment Act, as it relates to Federal estate taxes.[102] With one exception, so far as we can determine, In re Crozier's Estate, 105 N.H. 440, 201 A.2d 895, which is not particularly helpful here in view of the variance in the language used in the will, the Uniform Act has not been subjected to judicial scrutiny. Nevertheless, we are not without guidance in the matter. Over one-half of the states have enacted laws of similar import and the aim of the commissioners was to incorporate into the Uniform Act the most desirable features of the several state acts. There are innumerable cases[103] from those states construing directive tax clauses of a will in the light of statutory provisions, and while there is diversity in the result reached because of the variance in the language used, there is much unanimity in the observance of certain general principles for purposes of construction.

Practically all of the cases agree that a directive against apportionment should be expressed in clear and unambiguous language. Depending, of course, upon the complexity of the testamentary plan a few simple words may suffice to effectuate that purpose. It is essential, however, that the words, or combination of words, used in the will sufficiently indicate an intention against apportionment. In case of doubt the burden of the taxes must be left where the law places it. See A.L.R. Annotations, supra. It has been said that a sufficient tax clause should expressly state "(1) what gifts or beneficiaries are freed of the burden of taxes, (2) what taxes are affected, and (3) where the burden of taxes is shifted." 28 Am. Jur., Inheritance, Estate, and Gift Taxes, §488, p. 353. Surmounting the foregoing rules is the paramount rule that the intention of the testator or testatrix is to be ascertained, if possible, from the meaning of the words used in the context of the entire will. . . .

Beyond the foregoing aids to construction, the authorities are not too helpful. The results reached in all of the cases vary in accordance with the circumstances present. For example, our search and apparently the search of counsel for the parties have failed to disclose a case wherein an appellate court passed upon a tax clause essentially the same as the tax clause before us. To illustrate, appellees place great reliance upon the case of In re Bourquin's Estate, 87 Colo. 144, 286 P. 114, 115, which dealt with the State inheritance tax. The tax clause there said: ". . . 'After paying all court costs, taxes and administrators fees, I hereby give [et cetera] . . ." The court remarked that the phrase "all taxes" meant what it said. However, we would immediately point out that the phrase was in no way qualified by other

[102] The other states are New Hampshire and Michigan. 9A, Uniform Laws Annotated, §1(a), p. 183 (1964 Cum. Supp.).

[103] For example, see Annotations 37 A.L.R.2d 7, et sequitur, and 15 A.L.R.2d 1218, et sequitur.

language. That is not true in our case. Here the will goes on to say, "of my estate." The distinction is fully discussed in Norton v. Jones, Tex. Civ. App., 210 S.W.2d 820, 821, 822. We might also say that the cases cited to us by appellants, such as In re Grondin's Estate, 98 N.H. 313, 100 A.2d 160, 162, 163, are premised on language substantially different from the language contained in the tax clause before us.

It should be kept in mind also that the burden of establishing a basis for non-apportionment rests upon those contending against the statute. In re Pepper's Estate, 307 N.Y. 242, 120 N.E.2d 807, 811.

Turning now to article "First" of the will, stripped of irrelevant language in order to reach the tax clause, it is provided "I direct payment of all my . . . taxes . . . of my estate." We by no means commend this clause as a model directive against apportionment. It is a superficial, artless, and inept expression relating to this important and crucial element of a testamentary plan prepared by a non-resident attorney confessedly unfamiliar with the applicable laws of Wyoming.

As appellants point out, the tax clause fails by direct language clearly to specify the nature of the taxes embraced within the clause, the source from which the taxes affected were to be paid, and the persons interested in the estate who were to receive benefits freed of the burden of taxes. Such deficiencies, of course, prompted the present litigation. Furthermore, as we indicated above, there is some basis under the authorities for appellants' contention that such lack of clarity condemns the clause as an enforceable directive against apportionment or, at least, when related to the matter of the purpose intended, demonstrates that neither the testatrix nor the scrivener of the will had in mind the importance of fitting death taxes into the testamentary plan.

Nevertheless, we think appellants' concept is too narrow. To adopt it without reservation would be to ignore the critical question of just what testatrix did intend by use of the words "all my taxes of my estate." Surely, those words meant something more than appellants are willing to concede. To hold as appellants argue that the language embraced only ad valorem taxes would be improper for the reason that it would result in regarding such language as mere surplusage. The statutes treat ad valorem taxes as debts of a decedent, to be paid by the executor the same as any other debt, whether so directed or not. On the other hand, however, neither do we accept appellees' version that the word "all" because used in conjunction with the word "taxes" must be taken in a literal sense as embracing all taxes, including all death taxes. True, the word "all" is a general term, comprehensive in scope. If it stood alone with the word "taxes" it might possibly bear the stress which appellees place upon it. However, as previously noted, it does not stand alone. It is qualified by the words "my taxes" and the words "of my estate." To ignore the qualifying language would also be to ignore fundamental tenets of construction. In re Lendecke's Estate, 79 Wyo. 27, 329 P.2d 819; State Board of Equalization v. Courtesy Motors, Inc., Wyo., 362 P.2d 134, 136. As we view it, the proper answer lies somewhere between the divergent contentions of the parties.

Reminding that we are presently considering the relationship of the language used to the apportionment of the Federal estate taxes, an important consideration is the nature of the tax. Unlike our inheritance tax, the tax is not imposed upon the privilege of the devisees, legatees, and heirs to take and receive an interest in property from a decedent. Rather it is a tax imposed upon the interest of a decedent which ceased by reason of death thus causing the transfer of such interest to the recipients thereof. Young Men's Christian Ass'n of Columbus Ohio v. Davis, 264 U.S. 47, 44 S. Ct. 291, 292, 68 L. Ed. 558; In re Setrakian's Estate, 169 Cal. App. 2d 795, 338 P.2d 247, 250; Succession of Jones, La. App., 172 So. 2d 312, 316, writ of review refused 247 La. 718, 174 So. 2d 131. In other words, the tax might be described as a tax on the privilege of transferring an interest in the property upon death, In re Vanderbilt's Estate, 281 N.Y. 297, 22 N.E.2d 379, 387, affirmed Whitney v. State Tax Commission of State of New York, 309 U.S. 530, 60 S. Ct. 635, 84 L. Ed. 909, which generally is understood as an obligation imposed upon the transferor.

When the nature of the tax is taken into consideration, together with the fact that testatrix, over the years, was a successful and experienced businesswoman, we think it must be assumed that she had some familiarity with the impact of death taxes and that by the language "all my taxes of my estate" she did intend to embrace at least a portion of such taxes. Further, by inclusion of the tax clause in the usual ritualistic and introductory portion of the will directing payment of debts, expenses, et cetera, which when possible are ordinarily satisfied from the residuary estate, it seems clear that testatrix also intended that the death taxes embraced within the language were to be paid from the same source. Annotation 37 A.L.R.2d 124.

That leaves for consideration the portion of the taxes affected. As stated above, we think that question cannot be precisely answered without relating the tax clause to each segment of the testatrix's property transferred as a result of death and upon which the tax was levied, i.e., testamentary gifts, nontestamentary gifts, and proceeds of insurance policies.

In fact the necessity for so doing seems inherent in the distinction made under the laws of Wyoming between what we shall term the "taxable" estate defined in Ch. 171, §1(a), S.L. of Wyoming, 1959 (§2-337(a), W.S. 1965 Cum. Supp.), as being "the gross estate of a decedent as determined for the purpose of federal estate tax" and the "probate" estate, which as commonly understood consists of the property owned by a decedent at the time of death which is transferred in accordance with the provisions of the will or statute relating to intestacy through the processes of the probate court. While both estates have some interrelation, there is a substantial difference. The "probate" estate, as indicated, is concerned with the devolution of a decedent's interest in property at the time of death which does not occur otherwise than by the will or the intestacy statute. A property interest such as an unsevered interest in a joint tenancy forms no part of the "probate" estate. Witzel v. Witzel, Wyo., 386 P.2d 103, 109. On the other hand, Federal law for purposes of determining the "taxable" estate, while including all of the assets of the "probate" estate, is not concerned with the manner in which property interests of a decedent are otherwise transferred, and interests such as the joint tenancy mentioned are treated as integral parts of a decedent's estate for purposes of the Federal estate tax. That such a distinction has special significance in considering the question before us can readily be seen. A somewhat ambiguous tax clause may contain language sufficient to disclose an intent on the part of the testator or testatrix to shift the burden of the Federal estate tax levied upon decedent's property passing under the will and yet be insufficient to shift the tax levied upon the transfer of a decedent's interest in property which is not controlled by the will. Such a possibility is much too important to be overlooked. Furthermore, the authorities sustain the approach we are here taking, Union Trust Co. v. Watson, 76 R.I. 223, 68 A.2d 916, 919; In re Armstrong's Estate, 56 Cal. 2d 796, 17 Cal. Rptr. 138, 366 P.2d 490, 494; In re Cudahy's Will, 251 Wis. 116, 28 N.W.2d 340, 341, 342; Annotation 15 A.L.R.2d 1216; and we find nothing in the apportionment statute that would cause us to reject such an approach.

Relating the tax clause to the testamentary gifts, we are inclined to the view — based on the foregoing general discussion — that testatrix must be understood as having this portion of the taxes in mind when she referred to "my taxes of my estate" and that such language, although not entirely clear, sufficiently expressed the intention of testatrix to direct against statutory apportionment of the taxes imposed on such gifts. It is only by such an interpretation that force and effect can be given to such language, and as stated above we have concluded that this must be done. We are not disposed, however, to go further than that.

Just as testatrix must be assumed to have been familiar with the tax imposed upon the transfer of the property in her estate in accordance with the will, it must likewise be assumed she was familiar with the fact that a tax would be imposed upon the nontestamentary gift of the joint property to her foster son. As stated, such property formed no part of her probate estate, and that testatrix so understood can also be assumed. Yet no mention is made of an interest in property passing other than by the will, as a result of the death. Nor do we find language in the will from which a purpose to shift the burden of such tax to appellants can be inferred, a purpose which is required clearly to appear. The dominant words are "my estate." That such phrase fails to establish a basis for nonapportionment of the tax here being discussed seems well established by the authorities. In Union Trust Co. v. Watson, 76 R.I. 223, 68 A.2d 916, 919, the court had this to say:

> We think that the testator's expression "my estate" in his later will has a very definite and explicit meaning. Such expression, it has been said, "has a fixed and limited meaning; it is positive, clear-cut and free from doubt. It conveys an inference of existing title or ownership in the maker of the phrase and leads to the single conclusion that he had in mind the payment only of such taxes which might be levied upon his testamentary gifts or devises."

In In re Leonard's Estate, 9 A.D.2d 1, 189 N.Y.S.2d 422, 423, the court was confronted with even more direct language in that testator had provided for payment of estate taxes "as may be assessed against my estate." In holding such phrase insufficient as a directive against apportionment, the court said:

> The necessity of a direction against apportionment that will be both "clear and unambiguous" seems, in reason, even stronger in the case of taxable transfers *dehors* the instrument in which the supposed direction is sought. . . . (Italics in original.)

In view of the foregoing we think the only reasonable interpretation of the will which can be reached is that by the language testatrix could have intended nothing more than a shifting of taxes imposed upon the property passing under the will.

With respect to the proceeds of insurance policies we would remind that Congress has singled out this particular segment of a taxable estate for special treatment and has prescribed the manner in which the taxes imposed thereon are to be apportioned "unless the decedent directs otherwise in his will." 26 U.S.C.A. §2206 (1955).[104] Thus, the matter of insurance raises a Federal question rather than a question under our apportionment statute. A state statute "begins where the federal act leaves off." Hale v. Leeds, 28 N.J. 277, 146 A.2d 216, 221. However, that does not mean that the point cannot or should not here be decided. The question involves a surcharge to certain of the executor's accounts, a controversy fully within the jurisdiction of the probate court. Thus we perceive no sound reason why this court should not pass upon the question, in keeping with Federal law. As to this we find no decisions of the Federal courts authoritatively determining what is or what is not a sufficiently expressed directive.

Nevertheless, we are persuaded that those courts would subscribe to the general legal principles heretofore mentioned. As we view it, all that has been said above concerning nontestamentary gifts is equally applicable here. Probably more so because insurance policies are a special species of property. Johnson v. First Nat. Exchange Bank of Roanoke, 181 Va. 617, 26 S.E.2d 86, 88. Seldom are they spoken of as any part of an estate. In Priedeman v. Jamison, 356 Mo. 627, 202 S.W.2d 900, 903-904, the court emphasized such fact and pointed to the total lack of reference in the will to insurance beneficiaries or to the proceeds of such policies. It was principally on that basis that the court held the testator did not direct "otherwise in his will" and the Federal apportionment statute should apply. We hold that such is the case here.

State Inheritance Taxes

Of this, we think little need be said. The statutes imposing such taxes, §§39-337 and 39-355, W.S. 1957, clearly and specifically place the burden thereof upon the recipients of the testatrix's bounty. In re Young's Estate, 33 Wyo. 317, 239 P. 286,

[104] Int. Rev. Code of 1954, §2206, provides: "Unless the decedent directs otherwise in his will, if any part of the gross estate on which tax has been paid consists of proceeds of policies of insurance on the life of the decedent receivable by a beneficiary other than the executor, the executor shall be entitled to recover from such beneficiary such portion of the total tax paid as the proceeds of such policies bear to the sum of the taxable estate and the amount of the exemption allowed in computing the taxable estate. . . ."

The only other federal provision relating to apportionment is §2207, which applies the same apportionment rule with respect to assets passing by the exercise, nonexercise, or release of a general power of appointment. — Eds.

287. That such was to continue as the public policy of this State was clearly demonstrated when the legislature in adopting the Uniform Estate Tax Apportionment Act in 1959 deleted from the prescribed form any reference to inheritance taxes payable to the State. True, the inheritance tax statute does not take from a testator or testatrix the right to shift the statutory burden to a particular fund, but to accomplish such purpose the directive must clearly appear from the will. That the language here could not possibly constitute such a directive is self-evident. The testatrix refers only to "my taxes of my estate." These were not her taxes, nor were the taxes levied upon her estate. To hold such language to constitute a sufficient directive would be to reach a most inequitable result in clear contravention of the statute that is designed to prevent such a happening. The State taxes paid were attributable entirely to the gifts made to appellees. The amounts received by the appellants were entirely exempt. The executor was clearly wrong in attempting to charge appellants' accounts with such taxes. See Norton v. Jones, Tex. Civ. App., 210 S.W.2d 820; In re Cudahy's Will, 251 Wis. 116, 28 N.W.2d 340, 341, 342; In re Grondin's Estate, 98 N.H. 313, 100 A.2d 160, 162, 163.

Summation

Our conclusions with respect to the ultimate questions stated above are these:

1(a). The answer must be in the affirmative and the trial court's decree charging appellants with such portion of the Federal estate tax is affirmed.

1(b). The answer is "no" and the trial court is directed to surcharge the account of the foster son with the proper portion of the Federal estate tax and to relieve appellants from payment thereof.

2. The answer is "no" and the trial court is directed to apportion the tax in keeping with the provisions of 26 U.S.C.A. §2206 (1955).

3. The answer is "no" and the trial court is directed to surcharge the accounts of appellees with the full amount paid for State inheritance taxes and to relieve appellants from payment thereof.

As so modified the decree is affirmed.

PROBLEM

The first clause of T's will states, "I direct that my executor shall pay, out of my residuary estate, all of my just debts, funeral expenses, and the expenses of administration of my estate, as soon after my death as may be practicable." A, who is given a specific legacy under the will, and who is also the beneficiary under an insurance policy on T's life, contends that the federal estate tax is a "just debt" of the decedent, and that this clause is a sufficient directive against application of (a) the Uniform Estate Tax Apportionment Act, and (b) the apportionment rule under Int. Rev. Code of 1954, §2206. Is this contention sound? Thompson v. Thompson, 230 S.W.2d 376, 380 (Tex. Civ. App. 1950); In re Doerfler's Estate, 348 Ill. App. 347, 109 N.E.2d 230 (1952).

III. CONSTRUCTION OF THE ESTATE PLAN: THE LAW OF WILLS, TRUSTS AND FUTURE INTERESTS

7. Formalities of Transfer: Wills

SECTION A. Execution of Wills

1. *Attested Wills*

5 AMERICAN LAW OF PROPERTY §23.1 (Casner ed. 1952): "It is fundamental in our system that the owner of property may transfer it and, within limits, control its beneficial use after transfer. If A, having property, manifests an intent that it shall pass to B, it will do so. Although certain requirements as to capacity and formality have been imposed, these are basically steps in the process of determining whether A has manifested the intent to transfer; they protect, rather than restrict."

GULLIVER & TILSON, CLASSIFICATION OF GRATUITOUS TRANSFERS
51 Yale L. J. 1, 2-5, 9-10 (1941)

One fundamental proposition is that, under a legal system recognizing the individualistic institution of private property and granting to the owner the power to determine his successors in ownership, the general philosophy of the courts should favor giving effect to an intentional exercise of that power. This is commonplace enough, but it needs constant emphasis, for it may be obscured or neglected in inordinate preoccupation with detail or dialectic. A court absorbed in purely doctrinal arguments may lose sight of the important and desirable objective of sanctioning what the transferor wanted to do, even though it is convinced that he wanted to do it.

If this objective is primary, the requirements of execution, which concern only the form of the transfer — what the transferor or others must do to make it legally effective — seem justifiable only as implements for its accomplishment, and should be so interpreted by the courts in these cases. They surely should not be revered as ends in themselves, enthroning formality over frustrated intent. Why do these requirements exist and what functions may they usefully perform? . . .

In the first place, the court needs to be convinced that the statements of the transferor were deliberately intended to effectuate a transfer. People are often careless in conversation and in informal writings. . . . Casual language, whether oral or written, is not intended to be legally operative, however appropriate its purely verbal content may be for that purpose. Dispositive effect should not be given to statements which were not intended to have that effect. The formalities of transfer therefore generally require the performance of some ceremonial for the purpose of impressing the transferor with the significance of his statements and thus justifying the court in reaching the conclusion, if the ceremonial is performed, that they were deliberately intended to be operative. This purpose of the requirements of transfer may conveniently be termed their ritual function.

Secondly, the requirements of transfer may increase the reliability of the proof presented to the court. The extent to which the quantity and effect of available evidence should be restricted by qualitative standards is, of course, a controversial matter. Perhaps any and all evidence should be freely admitted in reliance on such safeguards as cross-examination, the oath, the proficiency of handwriting experts, and the discriminating judgment of courts and juries. On the other hand, the inaccuracies of oral testimony owing to lapse of memory, misinterpretation of the statements of others, and the more or less unconscious coloring of recollection in the light of the personal interest of the witness or of those with whom he is friendly, are very prevalent; and the possibilities of perjury and forgery cannot be disregarded. These difficulties are entitled to especially serious consideration in prescribing requirements for gratuitous transfers, because the issue of the validity of the transfer is almost always raised after the alleged transferor is dead, and therefore the main actor is usually unavailable to testify, or to clarify or contradict other evidence concerning his all-important intention. At any rate, whatever the ideal solution may be, it seems quite clear that the existing requirements of transfer emphasize the purpose of supplying satisfactory evidence to the court. This purpose may conveniently be termed their evidentiary function.

Thirdly, some of the requirements of the statutes of wills have the stated prophylactic purpose of safeguarding the testator, at the time of the execution of the will, against undue influence or other forms of imposition. . . . It may conveniently be termed the protective function.

. . . This [protective function] is difficult to justify under modern conditions. First, it must be reiterated that any requirement of transfer should have a clearly demonstrable affirmative value since it always presents the possibility of invalidating perfectly genuine and equitable transfers that fail to comply with it; there are numerous decisions interpreting these requirements, particularly with reference to the competency of attesting witnesses, wholly or partially invalidating wills that do not seem from the opinions to be in any way improper or suspicious. Secondly, there are appropriate independent remedies for the various forms of imposition, and these prophylactic provisions are therefore not, in the long run, of any essential utility except in instances where the imposition might not be detected. Thirdly, as indicated below, it is extremely doubtful that these provisions effectively accomplish any important purpose. Fourthly, they are atypical; no similar purpose is indicated in the requirements for inter vivos dispositions. Why should there be a differentiation between inter vivos and testamentary transfers in this respect? The purely legal elements of the two categories suggest no justification; in fact, the automatic revocability of a will presents a simpler and more uniformly prevalent means of nullifying the effect of imposition than exists for inter vivos transfers. In spite of the benevolent paternalism expressed in some of the decisions interpreting these requirements, the makers of wills are not a feeble or oppressed group of people needing unusual protection as a class; on the contrary, as the owners of property, earned or inherited, they are likely to be among the more capable and dominant members of our society. It is probable that the distinction originally arose because of a difference in the factual circumstances customarily surrounding the execution of the two types of transfer. The protective provisions first appeared in the Statute of Frauds, from which they have been copied, perhaps sometimes blindly, by American legislatures. While there is little direct evidence, it is a reasonable assumption that, in the period prior to the Statute of Frauds, wills were usually executed on the death bed. A testator in this unfortunate situation may well need special protection against imposition. His powers of normal judgment and of resistance to improper influences may be seriously affected by a decrepit physical condition, a weakened mentality, or a morbid or unbalanced state of mind. Furthermore, in view of the propinquity of death, he would not have as much time or opportunity as would the usual inter vivos transferor to escape from the consequences of undue influence or other forms of imposition. Under modern conditions, however, wills are probably executed by most testators in the prime of life and in the presence of attorneys. If this assumption is correct, the basis for any general distinction disappears. For these reasons, this article will proceed on the hypothesis that, while the provisions of the statutes of wills seeking to fulfill the protective function must be reckoned with doctrinally as part of our enacted law, this function is not sufficiently important in the present era to justify any more emphasis than these provisions require.

The formal requirements for execution of wills vary considerably in detail from state to state. Some of these variations result from the fact that England had two basic acts governing the execution of wills, the Statute of Frauds (1677) and the Wills Act (1837). Prior to enactment of the Statute of Frauds, personal property was transferable at death by either a written or oral will, perhaps given to the priest as part of the last confession.[1] Land was made devisable "by last will and testament, in writing," by the Statute of Wills in 1540, but the statute required no signature or other formalities. The Statute of Frauds, coming 137 years later, imposed stringent formalities upon the testamentary disposition of land. Less stringent formalities, which need not concern us here, applied to testamentary dispositions of personalty. Having different requirements for wills of realty and wills of personalty proved unsatisfactory, and in 1837 England passed a Wills Act requiring the same formalities for all wills.

The formalities required by the Wills Act of 1837 and by the Statute of Frauds were not the same. For example, the Wills Act required a signature "at the foot or end" of the will and attestation by two witnesses, both of whom had to be present when the will was signed or acknowledged. The Statute of Frauds did not require a signature in any special place but required three witnesses, and the witnesses could attest separately.

In the main, the American states have tended to copy the Wills Act of 1837 rather than the Statute of Frauds. It was not unusual, however, for a legislature to take something from each act, or to throw in an innovation such as that the testator must "publish" the will by declaring that it is his last will and testament.[2] The statutes governing execution of wills differ more in technical detail than in substance. Nonetheless, strict compliance with the specific requirements of a particular statute is a prerequisite for probate.

In re GROFFMAN
Court of Appeal
Probate, Divorce and Admiralty Division, 1968
[1969] 1 W.L.R. 733

SIR JOCELYN SIMON, P. In this case the executors of a will dated September 1, 1964, propound it in solemn form of law. The will is of the late Mr. Charles Groffman, who died on April 11, 1967. The first plaintiff, being the first executor named, is the son of the deceased testator. The second plaintiff, Mr. Block, is the second executor named and is the solicitor who prepared the will. The defendant, who claims that the will was not properly executed, is the widow of the deceased; and in

[1] Some American states permit nuncupative (oral) wills under very limited conditions. Typically, these wills can be used only to devise personal property of small value (say, up to $1000) by a person in extremis, who makes the declaration before three persons who must reduce the declaration to writing within a week. Atkinson, Wills 363-367 (2d ed. 1953). Soldiers, sailors, and airmen are in some states granted the privilege of making an oral will under limited circumstances. Id. at 368-374.

[2] See Comment, An Analysis of the History and Present Status of American Wills Statutes, 28 Ohio St. L.J. 293 (1967).

the circumstances, the estate being of the region of £8,000 or £9,000 in total, she takes the whole of it in the event of an intestacy. The estate consists partly of what was the matrimonial home (as to just over half the total estate). That house belonged to the deceased. There was also a building society account held by the deceased; the defendant claims that that was held jointly with her, or that at least she has some interest in it.

The defendant was the second wife of the deceased. They married about 1948, the deceased being a widower and the defendant a widow. The marriage was childless; but the deceased had two children, the first plaintiff and a daughter who is in America. The defendant has a daughter by her first marriage, a Miss Berenson.

Most of the relevant events took place in 1964; and I do not think any witness can really be expected to remember the details, even Mr. Block the solicitor who prepared the will. Indeed, I think that many of the witnesses now think that they can remember more than they actually can. But the rough outline of events was this.

Sometime in the summer of 1964, the deceased went to Mr. Block, the solicitor. He was senior partner in the firm of Maxwell and Lawson. The deceased was not a regular client of his, but had been recommended to him by another client. He gave instructions for a will and the instructions were put into a draft, which is exhibit 1 to the plaintiffs' affidavit of scripts. That appointed the executors and trustees; it devises the house to the trustees on trust to allow the defendant to have the use and enjoyment of this during her lifetime. It also bequeaths all chattels to her for use during her life. Then the residue — what was not disposed by the dispositions I have referred to — was disposed of in this way. It was to be divided between the first plaintiff, the daughter in America, and the step-daughter, Miss Berenson. There was in that draft a clause dealing with the advancement of the residuary estate in the interest of the defendant, which subsequently disappeared. That draft was handed by the second plaintiff to the deceased, who took it away to discuss it with his son, the first plaintiff. As a result of that discussion, in which the first plaintiff made no comment as to the dispositions, the draft was brought back to the second plaintiff; some nine corrections were made and the advancement clause to which I have referred was cancelled. The document as amended was then typed out, engrossed ready for execution.

The second plaintiff told the deceased very generally what was the right method of execution; but realising that the deceased was an intelligent man relied in the main on the attestation clause to be a guide to the deceased. That was in the usual form, and it seems to me to have been a perfectly reasonable course for the second plaintiff to have taken.

The deceased and his wife were close family friends of a Mr. and Mrs. David Block and a Mr. and Mrs. Julius Leigh. They spent at least the summer holidays of 1964 together, and it was their custom to meet alternately at their respective houses, generally on a Tuesday night. This was because Mr. Leigh was a taxi driver and the Tuesday was his free evening. On a number of occasions after the engrossed document was handed to the deceased, he mentioned the matter to Mr. David Block, saying that he would like Mr. Block and Mr. Leigh to be witnesses to his will. Mr. Block, in a very usual reaction, said: "There's no hurry about that; there's plenty of time to be thinking about that sort of thing" — or words to that effect.

The parties met on a Tuesday evening in September, 1964. That may have been September 1, which is the date that the will bears. They met at the house of Mr. and Mrs. David Block, and the will purports to have been executed that evening in circumstances to which I shall have to refer. It is sufficient to say that, as I have already indicated, the attestation clause is the normal one, and Mr. Block and Mr. Leigh signed as attesting witnesses. The document also bears what is admittedly the signature of the deceased, and the date, September 1, 1964.

I am perfectly satisfied that that document was intended by the deceased to be executed as his will and that its contents represent his testamentary intentions.

After he had obtained the signatures of his friends, he took the will and handed it to his son, the first plaintiff. He appears to have referred to it to Mr. Block on a number of occasions thereafter; but nothing turns on that, since the only question that arises in this suit is as to the execution of the document.

The deceased died, as I have said, on April 11, 1967. The funeral was on April 13, and thereafter the widow and the first plaintiff observed a period of ritual mourning, during which there was no discussion of any testamentary instrument or disposition. At the end of that period, within a matter of a few days, the first plaintiff handed the document to the second plaintiff. At some time towards the end of April, and again within a month or two, there were meetings between the plaintiffs and the defendant; . . . the defendant showed considerable dissatisfaction with the dispositions in the purported will. She used the words, "My Charlie wouldn't have done that to me." . . .

As I have said, the only question that arises for the determination of the court is whether this will was duly executed. That takes me back to the occasion in September, 1964, which may have been September 1 — the episode at the house of Mr. and Mrs. David Block.

Mr. Leigh, the second purported attesting witness, has suffered a disabling ailment; and his evidence has been placed before me only in the form of a statement, dated August 22, 1967, which was obviously taken for the purposes of litigation. It has, therefore, not been cross-examined to. Since I am satisfied that the document propounded represents the deceased's testamentary dispositions and intentions and since the document is in regular form, a very strong presumption arises in its favour. If I merely had the statement of Mr. Leigh and the other witnesses, except for Mr. David Block and his son, Stewart, I should pronounce for the validity of this will. But that is not all I have.

Mr. David Block and his son, Stewart, seem to me to be credible and reliable witnesses. I have it in mind that the evidence they have given contradicts the statement in the attestation clause. I have it in mind that they are friends of the defendant and desire her to succeed in this action. I have it in mind that there is some discrepancy between the evidence that they respectively gave, though no more than I should expect in perfectly honest witnesses trying to recollect what happened over four years ago. I accept the evidence of Mr. David Block, borne out as it is by Stewart, and indeed by what Mr. Leigh says in his proffered statement.

I think that what happened on the evening in question was this. I have already said that the deceased had previously indicated to Mr. David Block that he would like him and Mr. Leigh to witness his will. On the evening in question, which was in all probability a Tuesday and possibly September 1, 1964, the deceased and the defendant, Mr. and Mrs. David Block and Mr. and Mrs. Julius Leigh, were all together in the lounge of the Blocks' house. Mr. Block's son, Stewart, was also in the house, though not in the lounge at the commencement of the transaction to which I refer.

During the course of the evening, when the coffee table, the only available table, was laden with coffee cups and cakes, the deceased said words to this effect, which he addressed to Mr. David Block and Mr. Julius Leigh: "I should like you now to witness my will." I think he may well have gestured towards his coat. The will in question as engrossed was of the usual double foolscap folded in two and then in four, so as to be a convenient size for putting in an inside pocket of a coat. That is where it was on this occasion. However, it was not taken out by the deceased in the lounge. At the most, he gestured towards the pocket where it was. There seems to me to be an overwhelming inference that his signature was on the document at that time. There being no convenient space for the execution in the lounge, Mr. Block led the deceased into the adjacent dining room. That was just across a small hall. There the deceased took the document from his pocket, unfolded it, and asked Mr. Block to sign, giving his occupation and address. The signature, as I have already said, was on the document at the time and was visible to Mr. Block at the time; indeed, he noted this. Mr. Leigh, who seems to have been somewhat cumbrous in his movements, was left behind. He was not there when Mr. Block signed his name. Mr. Block then returned to the lounge, leaving the deceased in the dining room. He said to Mr. Leigh words to this effect: "It is your turn now, don't keep him waiting, it's cold in there." Mr. Leigh then went into the dining room and, according to his statement, and as is indeed borne out by the form of the document that we now have, signed his name beneath that of Mr. David Block. In the meantime Mr. Block had remained in the lounge.

In other words, we are left with this situation — that the signature of the deceased was on the document before he asked either Mr. Block or Mr. Leigh to act as his witnesses; that Mr. Block signed his name in the presence of the deceased but not in the presence of Mr. Leigh; and that Mr. Leigh signed his name in the presence of the deceased but not in the presence of Mr. Block. The deceased did not sign in the presence of either of them; and the question is whether he acknowledged his signature in the presence of both of them.

As must appear from the fact that I have been satisfied that the document does represent the testamentary intentions of the deceased, I would very gladly find in its favour; but I am bound to apply the statute, which has been enacted by Parliament for good reason. The provision with which I am concerned is section 9 of the Wills Act, 1837. That reads:

> . . . no will shall be valid unless it shall be in writing and executed in manner hereinafter mentioned; (that is to say,) it shall be signed at the foot or end thereof by the testator, or by some other person in his presence and by his direction; and such signature shall be made or acknowledged by the testator in the presence of two or more witnesses present at the same time, and such witnesses shall attest and shall subscribe the will in the presence of the testator, but no form of attestation shall be necessary.

The question, as I have indicated, is whether the testator acknowledged his signature in the presence of Mr. Block and Mr. Leigh, those two witnesses being present at the same time. The matter has been considered by a number of eminent judges, starting with Dr. Lushington, and followed by the members of the Court of Appeal in Blake v. Blake (1882) 7 P.D. 102 and Daintree v. Butcher and Fasulo (1888) 13 P.D. 102. It seems presumptious to say that I agree with their construction of the statute; but it appears to me to be clear. In any event I am bound by what was decided by the Court of Appeal, even if I were to disagree with it, which I do not. It seems to me that the authorities establish that the signature of the testator must be on the document at the time of acknowledgment (as I think it was), and that the witnesses saw or had an opportunity of seeing the signature at that time, in other words, at the time of acknowledgment.

In Blake v. Blake, 7 P.D. 102, Sir George Jessel M.R. gave a judgment in which he said, at p. 107: "The question, then, arises whether the testatrix acknowledged her signature before the witnesses." That was a case where the testatrix had signed and had asked two attesting witnesses to add their signature, but had covered her own signature with blotting paper, so they could not see it. Sir George Jessel in those circumstances posed the question, at p. 107-8:

"What is in law a sufficient acknowledgment under the statute?" — he answers —

> What I take to be the law is correctly laid down in Jarman on Wills, 4th ed. p. 108, in the following terms: "There is no sufficient acknowledgment unless the witnesses either saw or might have seen the signature, not even though the testator should expressly declare that the paper to be attested by them is his will";

He quotes Dr. Lushington in Hudson v. Parker (1844) 1 Rob. Eccl. 14, at p. 25

> What do the words import but this? "Here is my name written, I acknowledge that name so written to have been written by me; bear witness."

. . .

In deference, however, to the interest and vigour of Mr. Craig's argument, I must deal with various alternative ways in which he puts his case. He says, first, that Blake is to be distinguished in that there was a deliberate concealment by the testatrix of her signature, which, he says, is the very negation of acknowledgment. But there is nothing at all in the judgments of Blake v. Blake, 7 P.D. 102, to indicate that that was the ratio decidendi, which was indeed afterwards explained in Daintree v. Butcher and Fasulo, 13 P.D. 102.

Secondly, he says, there is sufficient acknowledgment if the attesting witnesses had an opportunity to see the will or the signature or both if they had wished to. Opportunity to see, says Mr. Craig, does not mean physical opportunity: it means that they could have seen if they expressed the desire to see. If that were so, it seems to me that Blake v. Blake, 7 P.D. 102, could not have been decided in the way it was. The attesting witnesses could have asked the testatrix to remove the blotting paper, just as in the present case Mr. Block or Mr. Leigh could have asked the testator to remove the paper from his pocket and show it to them, or at least show them his signature.

There is, however, one final argument. Having submitted originally that there was a sufficient acknowledgment to satisfy the statute in what happened in the lounge, when admittedly both attesting witnesses were present, Mr. Craig puts his argument alternatively in this way. He says that what happened was all part of one res gestae — there was no break in the continuity of the transaction. Both attesting witnesses had an opportunity of seeing the signature at the time they signed the will, which was within a matter of seconds of each other and within a matter of seconds of being asked to witness it. On that argument the acknowledgment started in the lounge but ended in the dining room. Now, it seems to me that there is one fatal flaw in that argument; namely, that if the acknowledgment was not completed until the dining room, then there was no completed acknowledgment in the presence of both attesting witnesses being present at the same time.

In the end, therefore, although I would gladly accede to the arguments for the plaintiffs if I could consistently with my judicial duty, in my view there was no acknowledgment or signature by the testator in the presence of two or more witnesses present at the same time; and I am bound to pronounce against this will.

Order accordingly.[3]

NOTES AND PROBLEMS

1. Specifically, why was Mr. Groffman's will denied probate? What formalities required by the Wills Act were not satisfied?

2. Were the ritual, evidentiary, and protective policies basing the Statute of Wills satisfied by the manner in which Groffman's will was executed and attested? If so, should Groffman's will have been denied probate? What policies were served by the court's decision denying probate of the will?

3. If Mr. Block, the solicitor who drew the will (to be distinguished from Mr. David Block, the witness), were sued by the beneficiaries named in the will, would he be liable under the reasoning of Heyer v. Flaig, page 21, supra? In Licata v. Spector, 26 Conn. Sup. 378, 225 A.2d 28 (1967), a Connecticut attorney was held liable to the intended will beneficiaries when he supervised the execution of a will

[3] Noted 114 Sol. J. 198. — Eds.

that had only two attesting witnesses. Connecticut is one of six states[4] that requires three witnesses to a will.

4. In England and in many American states the requirement that the witness sign in the "presence" of the testator is satisfied only if the testator can see the witness when he is in the act of signing. The testator does not actually have to see the witness, but he must be able to see him if he so desires. 1 Jarman, Wills 138 (8th ed. 1951). An exception is made for a blind man. In some American states the sight test has been rejected in favor of the "conscious presence" test. Under this test the witness is in the presence of the testator if the testator, through sight, hearing, or general consciousness of events, comprehends that the witness is in the act of signing. 2 Page, Wills §19.125 (Bowe-Parker rev. 1960).

5. Statutes in several states have adopted the Wills Act requirement that the testator sign the will "at the foot or end thereof." Suppose testator signs the will, then adds a provision naming an executor, and then the attesting witnesses sign. Is the will entitled to probate? See Matter of Winters, 302 N.Y. 666, 98 N.E.2d 477 (1951); N.Y. Estates, Powers & Trusts Law §3-2.1(a)(1) (1967); Walsh & Jones, Instruments Signed "At the End Thereof" and the Register of Wills, 71 Dick. L. Rev. 563 (1967); Note, 19 A.L.R.2d 926 (1951).

6. Is the order of signing important? Suppose the attesting witnesses sign the will, and then the testator signs immediately below their signatures? See Marshall v. Mason, 176 Mass. 216, 57 N.E. 340 (1900); compare Hopson v. Ewing, 353 S.W.2d 203 (Ky. App. 1962).

7. Another common requirement is that the testator publish his will, that is, declare to the witnesses that the document is his will. Suppose T asks two persons to "witness my signature," and further says, "I am going away on a trip. I have some instructions here that I want carried out if anything happens. With all the accidents that you have today, you never know what will happen." The two persons see T sign the document, then add their signatures. The document contains no attestation clause and there is no other indication that they are witnessing a will. Is the will entitled to probate? See In re Pulvermacher's Will, 305 N.Y. 378, 113 N.E.2d 525 (1953).

Section 47 of the Model Probate Code, promulgated in 1947, contains most of the formal requirements for the execution of wills found in the Statute of Frauds and the Wills Act of 1837. This section of the Code provoked the following reaction from Professor Philip Mechem.

MECHEM, WHY NOT A MODERN WILLS ACT?
33 Iowa L. Rev. 501-503 (1948)

The recently promulgated Model Probate Code has attracted wide attention and has evoked much favorable comment. The latter is amply deserved. In its en-

[4] The other states are Maine, Massachusetts, New Hampshire, South Carolina, and Vermont.

tirety the Code offers a sensible, liberal, carefully thought out, and expertly drafted code, covering every angle of probate procedure, conceived of as a whole, immensely superior to the grab bag of scattered provisions found in most states. . . . The writer, however, is a little disturbed by one portion of the Code, small but of great importance, namely, the provisions relating to the execution, revocation, and operation of wills. The draftsmen here seem to the writer to have displayed anything but imagination, resourcefulness, or audacity, restrained or otherwise. On the contrary, these provisions seem to him almost incredibly reactionary, unimaginative, and timid. The Statute of Frauds was passed in 1677. One is asked to think either that that famous enactment was so perfect as to need no improvement or that the framers of the Code have learned nothing from the experience of the intervening 270 years. . . .

The substance [of Section 47] is highly familiar. . . . With one striking exception (signed at the foot or end) all the familiar "safeguards" are present: publication, attestation in the presence of the testator, attestation by the witnesses in the presence of each other. Apparently, although the language is somewhat ambiguous, testator must sign or acknowledge in the presence of both witnesses at once. It is likewise not clear whether the "signature already made" must have been made by testator in person.

The philosophy of all this is likewise obvious and familiar. It assumes that the more "safeguards against fraud" the better. It is likewise big-law-office philosophy: every testator must be forced to execute his will just as it would be done if the matter were being handled by a high-powered law firm. This overlooks one very important fact, namely, that the only persons the execution of whose wills are likely to come into question are precisely those persons who do not have the job supervised by a high-powered law firm, but who instead have the matter looked after by some very bad lawyer or by the local J.P. or the local banker or the local real estate man or on the advice of those who happen to be gathered at some lonely deathbed. These persons have the same right to make wills as their more prosperous or sophisticated brothers and sisters who employ good lawyers; the governing philosophy should be to design a wills act that as far as is consistent with safety adapts itself to the knowledge (or ignorance), psychology, and habits of such people so as to create the minimum risk that their testamentary attempts will be frustrated by failure to have the witnesses attest in the presence of the testator, or the like.

Put slightly otherwise, the philosophy should be to impose only such requirements as seem so unmistakably essential to a safe will-making process as to justify running the known risk of defeating meritorious wills through failure of testators to know or comply with the requirements. In making this determination, careful attention should be given to the known habits of testators (particularly untutored ones) as illustrated by the thousands of cases decided since 1677.

This philosophy has been adopted by the Uniform Probate Code, which reduces the formalities for a witnessed will to a minimum. Section 2-502 of the Code provides:

> Except as provided for holographic wills, writings within Section 2-513, and wills within Section 2-506, every will shall be in writing signed by the testator or in the testator's name by some other person in the testator's presence and by his direction, and shall be signed by at least 2 persons each of whom witnessed either the signing or the testator's acknowledgement of the signature or of the will.

No self-respecting lawyer will rely on the minimum formalities required by his state's statute, however. A lawyer should assume that his client's will may be offered for probate in another state. The client may be domiciled elsewhere when he dies, or he may own real property in another state at the time of his death, or his will may exercise a power of appointment governed by the law of another state. Under the usual conflict of laws rules, the law of the decedent's domicile at death determines the validity of the will insofar as it disposes of personal property. The law of the state where real property is located determines the validity of a disposition of real property. If a man domiciled in Illinois executes his will, then moves to New Jersey and dies there, owning Arizona real estate, some tangible personal property, and some stocks and bonds, the law of Illinois does not govern the validity of the will at all. New Jersey law determines the validity of the disposition of the tangible and intangible personalty, and Arizona law governs the validity of the disposition of the real estate.[5] Many states have statutes recognizing as valid a will executed with the formalities required by the state where the will was executed or by the state where the testator was domiciled when he executed his will. Some of these statutes are ambiguous, however, and the lawyer should draft his wills so there is no need to resort to them. Hence the careful lawyer in our highly mobile society draws a will and has it executed in a manner that satisfies the formal requirements in all states.

Recommended Method of Executing Will

If the procedure set forth below[6] is followed, the instrument will be valid in all states, no matter in which state the testator is domiciled at the date of execution or at his death or where the property is located.[7] If all these steps are not followed to the letter, the will may be invalid in one or more states.

(1) If the will consists of more than one page, the pages should be fastened

[5] In states where the situs rule is not changed by statute, the doctrine of equitable conversion is sometimes of use in probating a will valid in the domiciliary state. Hancock, Equitable Conversion and the Land Taboo in Conflict of Laws, 17 Stan. L. Rev. 1095 (1965).

[6] This procedure is based upon the recommended format developed first by Professor Leach in his Cases on Wills 44 (2d ed. 1949), and subsequently refined by Professor Casner in his work, 1 Estate Planning 51 (3d ed. 1961).

[7] With one exception. If the will is executed in Louisiana by a Louisiana domiciliary, three witnesses are required, one of whom must be a notary public. La. Rev. Stat. §9.2442 (1965, Supp. 1971). The recommended procedure satisfies Louisiana law if the will is executed outside the state by a person then domiciled outside the state. Id. §9.2401. If you are interested in other ways of making a will in Louisiana, including a "mystic will," see La. Civ. Code §§1574-1596 (1952); Atkinson, Wills 375-378 (2d ed. 1953).

For the formal requirements of will execution in all states, see Rees, American Wills Statutes: I and II, 46 Va. L. Rev. 613, 856 (1960).

together securely. The will should specify the exact number of pages of which it consists.

(2) The testator should read the will and the lawyer should be certain that he understands its contents.

(3) The lawyer, the testator, and three persons who have no interest whatsoever in the property disposed of by the will should be brought together in a room, from which everyone else is excluded. The door to the room is closed. No one is to go in or out of this room until the ceremony is finished.

(4) The lawyer should ask the testator the following three questions:

(a) "Is this your will?"

(b) "Have you read it and do you understand it?"

(c) "Does it dispose of your property in accordance with your wishes?"

After each question the testator should answer "Yes" in a voice that can be heard by the three witnesses. It is neither necessary nor customary for the witnesses to know the terms of the will. If, however, the lawyer foresees a will contest, added precautions might be taken at this time. (See below.)

(5) The lawyer should ask the testator the following question: "Do you request Mr. ______, Mr. ______ and Mr. ______ (the three witnesses) to witness the signing of your will?" The testator should answer "Yes" in a voice audible to the three witnesses.

(6) The witnesses should be standing or sitting so that all three can see the testator sign. The testator should initial or sign on the margin of each page of the will. This is done for purposes of identification and to prevent subsequent substitution of pages. The testator should then sign his name at the end of the will.

(7) One of the witnesses should read aloud the attestation clause, which attests that the foregoing things were done. Here is an example: "The foregoing instrument, consisting of __ pages, including the page signed by the Testator, was subscribed on the date which it bears by the Testator, Adam Smith, and at the time of subscribing was declared by him to be his last Will. The subscription and declaration were made in our presence, we being present at the same time; and we, at his request and in his presence and in the presence of each other, have affixed our signatures hereto as witnesses." [8]

[8] No state's statute requires the use of an attestation clause. The requirement of due execution can be satisfied merely by having the witnesses sign below the testator's signature as "witnesses." Such a clause is very important, however. It makes out a prima facie case that the will was duly executed, and thus the will may be entitled to probate even though the witnesses predecease the testator or cannot recall the events of execution. Note, 40 A.L.R.2d 1223 (1955). Moreover, if one of the attesting witnesses testifies that the steps for due execution were not satisfied, the attestation clause gives the will proponent's attorney ammunition for a vigorous cross-examination, and the will can be admitted to probate on the presumption of due execution despite such testimony.

In In re Estate of Koss, 84 Ill. App. 2d 59, 228 N.E.2d 510 (1967), one of the attesting witnesses, a nurse, testified she did not know that the document was a will, that she was informed by the sole beneficiary that the document was a power of appointment so that the nurses could be paid, that she could not read any portion of the document she signed because her glasses were broken, and that the document she signed consisted of only one page instead of the three pages offered for probate. The court, in admitting the will to probate, said, "Where an attestation

(8) Each witness then signs his name and writes his address. The first witness to sign should write in his own handwriting under the spaces provided for the signature of the witnesses: "The foregoing attestation clause has been read by us and is accurate." He should place his initials under this line, as should the others when they sign. As each witness signs, the testator and the other two witnesses should watch the witness sign his name. (What is the reason for stating that the attestation clause has been read?)

(9) The ceremony is finished. The door to the room is opened.

Special Precautions When Will Contest a Possibility

Nearly all challenges to wills on grounds of undue influence or lack of testamentary capacity arise in one of two contexts. The first is the "divided family" situation in which there is a second wife (or husband) and children by a former marriage. If the testator leaves the bulk of his estate to his spouse, this may produce a challenge by the embittered children against the disposition in favor of the second wife. The second major source of will contests is the "unnatural" disposition in which the testator cuts off his heirs in favor of a charity, or gives some of his children a larger testate share than the other children. The excluded children's initial hurt and disappointment may grow into a conviction that "Dad must have been out of his mind" to make such a disposition, or that he was subject to the undue influence of the favored legatee. The well-documented tendency of juries to rewrite a will in accordance with their idea of what is a fair distribution, rather than testing the will's validity according to the court's instructions,[9] makes these cases fertile grounds for will contests. In drafting a will for a client who has children by a former marriage, or a will that makes an unnatural distribution, the attorney should assume that the will is going to be challenged, and he should plan the will execution ceremony accordingly.

JAWORSKI, THE WILL CONTEST
10 Baylor L. Rev. 87, 91-93 (1958)

The question thus arises: What can be done best to preserve for the benefit of the court and jury facts showing that the testator possessed the legal requisites of soundness of mind and was not under the subjugation of a preferred beneficiary? It is suggested that with careful planning many of the avenues otherwise open to the contestant may be blocked partially, if not wholly.

An elderly lady possessed of a considerable estate had three children: two

---

clause is in due form and the will bears the genuine signatures of the testatrix and of the witnesses this is prima facie evidence of the due execution of the will, which cannot usually be overcome by the testimony of a witness that there was not compliance with all of the statutory requisites. . . . The testimony of a subscribing witness which seeks to impeach a will is to be viewed with suspicion and received with caution." 84 Ill. App. 2d at 70, 228 N.E.2d at 515-516.

[9] See pages 584-589, infra.

daughters and a son. The daughters married and moved away, and the son remained at home with his mother. Although mentally strong, she was not in good health. Her son looked after her wants and cares and also looked after her property. At one time she had made a will leaving all three children equal shares, but as time went on and as she leaned more heavily upon her son, she concluded that the son was entitled to a greater share and to certain special considerations not accorded to the daughters under the terms of her will. In view of the opportunities for the exercise of undue influence on the part of the son, and the changing of the will from equal to unequal distributions, a factual situation existed suggestive of the possibility of a contest. These steps were taken to assist in preserving the will: All discussions with the testatrix were had in the absence of the favored beneficiary, the son. After the initial conference with the testatrix, she was requested to write me a letter in her own handwriting, setting forth in detail the disposition she wished to make of her estate and the reasons that motivated her desire to provide more favorably for her son than for her daughters. Upon receipt of this letter, a draft of the will was prepared and forwarded to her under a covering letter in which she was requested to give close and careful consideration to the inequality of the disposition as between her children and the reasons supporting such action. She was requested again to transmit her final decision in her own handwriting. This was done, and thereupon the will was placed in final form. Four persons were then selected in whose presence this will was to be reviewed, explained, discussed and executed. Two of these were to be used as attesting witnesses in keeping with the legal requirements of the laws of our state. The other two were not to sign as attesting witnesses and would be used only in the event of a contest. These four persons were carefully selected as to age and other qualifications as witnesses. Upon completion of the execution, each witness recorded the discussions that took place, and particularly the statements of the testatrix, for future reference in the event of a contest. When the testatrix died, the daughters were disappointed — one was embittered, and there was talk of a contest. She employed a reliable attorney, and in the course of his investigation, there was revealed to him a part of the somewhat elaborate steps that had been taken to discourage the filing of a contest. The daughter's attorney advised against a contest, and the will was probated. Perhaps it is fair to conclude that the detailed precautions that were exercised at the time the will was prepared and executed assisted in averting a contest.

PROBLEMS

1. If a will contest is anticipated, might it be desirable to make a videotape or a recording of the discussion between the testator and the witnesses? In Belfield v. Coop, 8 Ill. 2d 293, 134 N.E.2d 249, 58 A.L.R.2d 1008 (1956), where a will was challenged on grounds of mental incompetency, the court held that it was reversible error to exclude from evidence a sound recording taken at the scene of execution which revealed the testator's responses to questions asked.

2. If it is anticipated that the will may be attacked on the ground of lack of testamentary capacity, would it be advisable to use a psychiatrist as one of the attesting witnesses, or to obtain a psychiatric report on the mental condition of the testator at the time the will is executed? See Jaworski, The Will Contest, 10 Baylor L. Rev. 87, 93 (1958); page 589, infra.

Proving the Will in Probate

The procedure for proving due execution of a will varies from state to state. For example, the North Carolina statute[10] requires the testimony of at least two attesting witnesses. If only one witness is available, the statute requires that witness's testimony plus (a) proof of the handwriting of the witness who is dead or otherwise unable to testify, (b) proof of the handwriting of the testator, and (c) proof of "such other circumstances as will satisfy the clerk of the superior court as to the genuineness and due execution of the will." If none of the attesting witnesses is available to testify, the statute requires proof of the handwriting of at least two attesting witnesses and satisfaction of requirements (b) and (c). These stringent requirements show the importance of selecting witnesses who are likely to be available to testify or for whom testimony as to their handwriting can be obtained. By contrast, the Texas statute[11] requires the testimony of only one attesting witness, either in open court or by deposition. If none of the witnesses is living, due execution is proved by the testimony of two witnesses to the handwriting of any one of the signatories: the testator or either of the attesting witnesses.

The mechanics of proving a will can be a source of minor (and sometimes major) irritation. Even if all the witnesses are easily located and are available to testify, it becomes necessary to arrange for their court appearance at a set time of the day, and perhaps to endure a wait of several hours as other cases are called before their testimony can be offered. If none of the witnesses is in the jurisdiction, or in the county, their testimony must be taken by deposition or interrogatory at considerable cost and effort. (Can you see why, under the Texas statute, it is easier to prove a will if all the witnesses are dead than if they are alive and living in Argentina?) These problems are particularly aggravating if, as in the great majority of cases, the family situation is a harmonious one, no one objects to the will, and proof of due execution is a mere formality. These mechanical problems have prompted several states to adopt a "self-proving will" procedure under which, at the time the will is executed, the testator and the witnesses execute a sworn affidavit before a notary public. The affidavit recites, along the lines of a complete attestation clause, that all the requisites for due execution were complied with. After the testator's death the will is admitted to probate on the basis of the affidavit, without the need for testimony from the witnesses.[12]

[10] N.C. Gen. Stat. §31-18.1 (1966).

[11] Tex. Prob. Code §84(b) (1956).

[12] Uniform Probate Code §§2-504, 3-406 (1969); Conn. Gen. Stat. Ann. §45-166 (1960); Nev. Rev. Stat. §133.050 (1969); N.Y. Surr. Ct. Proc. Act §1406 (1967); Okla. Stat. Ann. tit. 84, §55 (1970); Tex. Prob. Code §59 (1956); W. Va. Code Ann. §4075 (1961).

PROBLEM

In a state that has a self-proving will statute, testator signs his will in a manner that satisfies the requirements for due execution (presence of witnesses, publication, etc.), and the testator and all three attesting witnesses execute the self-proving affidavit, which is on a separate page following the will. Through oversight, none of the attesting witnesses signs the will itself; when the will is offered for probate after testator's death, it is discovered that the witness signature lines beneath the will's attestation clause are blank. Probate of the will is challenged on the ground that the will, which was the only document executed with testamentary intent, was not signed by two witnesses as required by state law; and that the self-proving affidavit, admittedly signed by witnesses, was not executed with testamentary intent but was a procedural document relating to the proof of validly executed wills. What result? See Boren v. Boren, 402 S.W.2d 728 (Tex. 1966); compare Estate of Cutsinger, 445 P.2d 778 (Okla. 1968); In re Leitstein's Will, 46 Misc. 2d 656, 260 N.Y.S.2d 406 (Sur. 1965).

Some years ago, Professor Cavers recommended the ante-mortem probate of wills, under which due execution, testamentary capacity, and freedom from undue influence would be proved during the testator's lifetime. Cavers, Ante Mortem Probate: An Essay in Preventive Law, 1 U. Chi. L. Rev. 440 (1934). No American state has adopted this procedure, but a variation of it is followed in the Soviet Union. What are the advantages and disadvantages of ante-mortem probate?

GRIFFIN, THE ABOUT TURN: SOVIET LAW OF INHERITANCE, 10 Am. J. Comp. L. 431, 438 (1961): "There are detailed and specific provisions spelling out the formal requirements of a will. Soviet law recognizes only registered wills. A testator, if he would have a valid will, must sign it and present it to a notarial office for notarial certification. Wills of illiterates are signed by a third party non-beneficiary on the testator's behalf. When the will is presented, the notary examines it to ensure that it is in accordance with the testamentary provisions. If it complies, he enters it in the official record, this entry serving, if necessary, in place of the document itself. There are two means of revocation. The testator may simply file at the notarial office a revocation of the former will without making a new one. Alternatively, if he files a new will, this supersedes the old one, except to the extent that it does not dispose of property which was disposed of in the prior document. There is obviously a good deal of sense in these provisions which must eliminate the disputes which are so likely to arise where privately made wills are recognized, and which exclude the possibility of a disposition being given no effect because of invalidity. It can well be argued that the inhibition thereby created upon the freedom of testation is justifiable."

JUSTICE [SOCIETY], HOME-MADE WILLS 4-5 (1971): "5. It is our view that the relative lack of formality required for the making of an English will is in fact a serious disadvantage, because it conceals from the ordinary testator the difficulties inherent in disposing of his estate. The only property transaction of comparable importance which most people enter into is the purchase of a house. Because the procedure is more complex, usually involving applications to the Land Registry, negotiation of a mortgage, payment of stamp duty and so on, it is hardly ever handled without a solicitor. Yet far more thought is, or ought to be, involved in making a will than in buying a house, and in our view a procedure which supports the attitude that a will is something which can be botched up at home and witnessed by a couple of neighbours needs reform. In most countries with a legal system derived from civil law, wills have to be recorded or witnessed by a notary, though some systems allow holograph wills (with or without witnesses) in addition. We take the view that there is, on balance, much to be gained by substituting for the present system of attestation a rule that all wills which now require attestation should in future be witnessed by an English equivalent of a notary.

"6. The principal advantage of the notarial system, in our view, is that the need to have a will formally executed in the presence of a Commissioner for Oaths or probate official would indirectly lead more testators to take proper legal advice before executing their wills. In addition, the problems of formal invalidity would be completely eliminated, and while a notary could not be expected to make any serious investigation of the state of mind or circumstances of the testator we think his presence would still form a more effective barrier against the more blatant forms of undue influence than the present system provides. A notarial system would also make registration of wills much simpler if it were decided to introduce such a scheme, though we have not ourselves considered the merits of registration."

In re PAVLINKO'S ESTATE

Supreme Court of Pennsylvania, 1959

394 Pa. 564, 148 A.2d 528

BELL, Justice.

Vasil Pavlinko died February 8, 1957; his wife, Hellen, died October 15, 1951. A testamentary writing dated March 9, 1949, which purported to be the will of Hellen Pavlinko, was signed by Vasil Pavlinko, her husband. The residuary legatee named therein, a brother of Hellen, offered the writing for probate as the will of Vasil Pavlinko, but probate was refused. The Orphans' Court, after hearing and argument, affirmed the decision of the Register of Wills.

The facts are unusual and the result very unfortunate. Vasil Pavlinko and Hellen, his wife, retained a lawyer to draw their wills and wished to leave their property to each other. By mistake Hellen signed the will which was prepared for her husband, and Vasil signed the will which was prepared for his wife, each instrument being signed at the end thereof. The lawyer who drew the will and his secretary,

Dorothy Zinkham, both signed as witnesses. Miss Zinkham admitted that she was unable to speak the language of Vasil and Hellen, and that no conversation took place between them. The wills were kept by Vasil and Hellen. For some undisclosed reason, Hellen's will was never offered for probate at her death; in this case it was offered merely as an exhibit.

The instrument which was offered for probate was short. It stated:

"I, *Hellen* Pavlinko, of . . . , do hereby make, publish and declare this to be *my* Last Will and Testament, . . ."

In the first paragraph she directed her executor to pay her debts and funeral expenses. In the second paragraph she gave her entire residuary estate to "my husband, Vasil Pavlinko . . . absolutely." She then provided:

> Third: If my aforesaid husband, Vasil Pavlinko, should predecease me, then and in that event, I give and bequeath:
>
> (a) To my brother-in-law, Mike Pavlinko, of McKees Rocks, Pennsylvania, the sum of Two Hundred ($200) Dollars.
>
> (b) To my sister-in-law, Maria Gerber, (nee Pavlinko), of Pittsburgh, Pennsylvania, the sum of Two Hundred ($200) Dollars.
>
> (c) The rest, residue and remainder of *my* estate, of whatsoever kind and nature and wheresoever situate, I give, devise and bequeath, absolutely, to *my brother*, Elias Martin, now residing at 520 Aidyl Avenue, Pittsburgh, Pennsylvania.
>
> I do hereby nominate, constitute and appoint my husband, Vasil Pavlinko, as Executor of this my Last Will and Testament.

It was then mistakenly signed: "Vasil Pavlinko [Seal]".

While no attempt was made to probate, as Vasil's will, the writing which purported to be his will but was signed by Hellen, it could not have been probated as Vasil's will, because it was not signed by him at the end thereof.

The Wills Act of 1947 provides in clear, plain and unmistakable language in §2: "Every will, . . . shall be in writing and shall be signed *by the testator* at the end thereof," 20 P.S. §180.2, with certain exceptions not here relevant. The Court below correctly held that the paper which *recited* that it was the will of Hellen Pavlinko and intended and purported to give Hellen's estate to her husband, could not be probated as the will of Vasil and was a nullity.

In order to decide in favor of the residuary legatee, almost the entire will would have to be rewritten. The Court would have to substitute the words "Vasil Pavlinko" for "Hellen Pavlinko" and the words "my wife" wherever the words "my husband" appear in the will, and the relationship of the contingent residuary legatees would likewise have to be changed. To consider this paper — as written — as Vasil's will, it would give his entire residuary estate to "my husband, Vasil Pavlinko, absolutely" and "Third: If my husband, Vasil Pavlinko, should predecease me, then . . . I give and bequeath my residuary estate to my brother, Elias Martin." The language of this writing, which is signed at the end thereof by *Vasil* Pavlinko, is unambiguous, clear and unmistakable, and it is obvious that it is a meaningless nullity.

While no authority is needed to demonstrate what is so obvious, there is a case which is directly in point and holds that such a writing cannot be probated as the will of Vasil Pavlinko. This exact situation arose in Alter's Appeal, 67 Pa. 341. The facts are recited in the unanimous opinion of the Court, speaking through Mr. Justice Agnew (at page 344):

> This is a hard case, but it seems to be without a remedy. An aged couple, husband and wife, having no lineal descendants, and each owning property, determined to make their wills in favor of each other, so that the survivor should have all they possessed. Their wills were drawn precisely alike, mutatis mutandis, and laid down on a table for execution. Each signed a paper, which was duly witnessed by three subscribing witnesses, and the papers were enclosed in separate envelopes, endorsed and sealed up. After the death of George A. Alter, the envelopes were opened and it was found that each had by mistake signed the will of the other. To remedy this error the legislature, by an Act approved the 23rd day of February 1870, conferred authority upon the Register's Court of this county to take proof of the mistake, and proceed as a court of chancery, to reform the will of George A. Alter and decree accordingly. . . . Was the paper signed by George A. Alter his will? Was it capable of being reformed by the Register's Court? The paper drawn up for his will was not a will in law, for it was not "signed by him at the end thereof," as the Wills Act requires. *The paper he signed was not his will, for it was drawn up for the will of his wife and gave the property to himself. It was insensible and absurd.* It is clear, therefore, that he had executed no will, and there was nothing to be reformed. There was a mistake, it is true, but that mistake was the same as if he had signed a blank sheet of paper. He had written his name, but not to his will. He had never signed his will, and the signature where it was, was the same as if he had not written it at all. He therefore died intestate, and his property descended as at law.

The Court further decided that the Legislative Act was void because it had no power to divest estates which were already vested at law on the death of George A. Alter without a will.

. . .

Once a Court starts to ignore or alter or rewrite or make exceptions to clear, plain and unmistakable provisions of the Wills Act in order to accomplish equity and justice in that particular case, the Wills Act will become a meaningless, although well intentioned, scrap of paper, and the door will be opened wide to countless fraudulent claims which the Act successfully bars.

Decree affirmed. Each party shall pay their respective costs.

MUSMANNO, Justice (dissenting).[13]

[13] Justice Musmanno was one of our more flamboyant state court judges. This adjective applies to his language as well as his actions. In dissenting from a majority holding that Tropic of Cancer was not obscene, Musmanno wrote: " 'Cancer' is not a book. It is a cesspool, an open sewer, a pit of putrefaction, a slimy gathering of all that is rotten in the debris of human depravity. And in the center of all this waste and stench, besmearing himself with its foulest defilement, splashes, leaps, cavorts and wallows a bifurcated specimen that responds to the

Vasil Pavlinko and his wife, Hellen Pavlinko, being unlettered in English and unlearned in the ways of the law, wisely decided to have an attorney draw up their wills, since they were both approaching the age when reflecting persons must give thought to that voyage from which there is no return. They explained to the attorney, whose services they sought, that he should draw two wills which would state that when either of the partners had sailed away, the one remaining ashore would become the owner of the property of the departing voyager. Vasil Pavlinko knew but little English. However, his lawyer, fortunately, was well versed in his clients' native language, known as Little Russian or Carpathian. The attorney thus discussed the whole matter with his two visitors in their language. He then dictated appropriate wills to his stenographer in English and then, after they had been transcribed, he translated the documents, paragraph by paragraph, to Mr. and Mrs. Pavlinko, who approved of all that he had written. The wills were laid before them and each signed the document purporting to be his or her will. The attorney gave Mrs. Pavlinko the paper she had signed and handed to her husband the paper he had signed. In accordance with customs they had brought with them from the old country, Mrs. Pavlinko turned her paper over to her husband. It did not matter, however, who held the papers since they were complementary of each other. Mrs. Pavlinko left her property to Mr. Pavlinko and Mr. Pavlinko left his property to

---

name of Henry Miller. One wonders how the human species could have produced so lecherous, blasphemous, disgusting and amoral a human being as Henry Miller. One wonders why he is received in polite society. . . . From Pittsburgh to Philadelphia, from Dan to Beersheba, and from the ramparts of the Bible to Samuel Eliot Morison's Oxford History of the American People, I dissent." Commonwealth v. Robin, 421 Pa. 70, 100, 218 A.2d 546, 561 (1966).

In his first five years on the Pennsylvania Supreme Court, Musmanno filed more dissenting opinions than all the other members of that court had collectively filed in the preceding fifty years. One dissent got him into a lawsuit. Chief Justice Stern once ordered that Musmanno's dissent not be published in the official state reports because he had not circulated it among the court. Musmanno sought mandamus to compel the state reporter to publish his dissent. The supreme court denied the writ, Musmanno not sitting. Musmanno v. Eldredge, 382 Pa. 167, 114 A.2d 511 (1955). Justice Musmanno then moved his case to the court of last resort, the law reviews. His side of the controversy can be found in Musmanno, Dissenting Opinions, 60 Dick. L. Rev. 139 (1956). When asked whether he read Musmanno's dissents, Stern, C.J., replied that he was not "interested in current fiction." The New Republic, Feb. 3, 1968, p. 14.

Musmanno's ancestors came from Italy, and he was a leading force in establishing Columbus Day as a special day for Italian-Americans. When Yale accepted the Vinland map as evidence that Norsemen and not an Italian, Christopher Columbus, had discovered America, Musmanno immediately rose to the attack. He dropped all his duties and went to Yale to dispute the archeologists, embarked on a six-month speaking tour disputing the authenticity of the Vinland map, and wrote a book, Columbus Was Right!

Justice Musmanno's last opinion was a freewheeling dissent to a reversal of a rape conviction. The majority held that it was error for the judge to tell the jurors they would have to answer to God for their actions. Commonwealth v. Holton, 432 Pa. 11, 247 A.2d 228 (1968). Wrote Musmanno: "God is not dead, and judges who criticize the invocation of Divine Assistance had better begin preparing a brief to use when they stand themselves at the Eternal Bar of Justice on Judgment Day. . . . I am perfectly willing to take my chances with [the trial judge] . . . at the gates of Saint Peter and answer on our voir dire that we were always willing to invoke the name of the Lord in seeking counsel. . . . Miserere nobis Omnipotens Deus!" Id. at 41, 43, 247 A.2d 242-243. The next day, Columbus Day, 1968, Justice Musmanno dropped dead and presumably this voir dire took place. — Eds.

Mrs. Pavlinko. They also agreed on a common residuary legatee, Elias Martin, the brother of Mrs. Pavlinko.

. . .

We have also said time[s] without number that the intent of the testator must be gathered from the four corners of his will. Whether it be from the four corners of the will signed by Vasil Pavlinko or whether from the eight corners of the wills signed by Vasil and Hellen Pavlinko, all set out before the court below, the net result is always the same, namely that the residue of the property of the last surviving member of the Pavlinko couple was to go to Elias Martin. . . .

The Majority says that there is nothing we can do to effectuate the expressed intention of Vasil Pavlinko. But, I respectfully submit, the Majority does not make a serious effort to effectuate that expressed intent. The Majority contents itself with saying that "the facts are unusual and the result very unfortunate." But the results do not need to be unfortunate. . . . Elias Martin is being turned out of Court when there is no need for such a peremptory eviction. The Majority authorizes the eviction on the basis of a decision rendered by this Court in 1878 in the case of Alter's Appeal, 67 Pa. 341. There, wife and husband, also signed wrong papers and the Court in that post-Civil War period, held nothing could be done to correct the error. But even if we say that the Alter decision makes impossible the transferring of the signature of Vasil Pavlinko to the will written in his name, I still do not see how it prevents this Court from enforcing the provision in the will which *was* signed by Vasil Pavlinko. In the Alter case an attempt was made to reform the will "by striking off the signature 'Catherine Alter,' and causing the name 'George A. Alter' to be signed thereto" so that the paper so signed could be "admitted to probate as the will of George A. Alter." But in our case here, no such substitution is being sought. What Elias Martin seeks is admission to probate of a testamentary writing *actually signed by the testator Vasil Pavlinko.*

Moreover, in the Alter case, as distinguished from the Pavlinko will, George A. Alter left everything to himself. Even if we accept the Majority's conclusion, based on the Alter case, that all provisions in the Pavlinko will, which refer to himself, must be regarded as nullities, not correctible by parol evidence because they evince no latent ambiguities, it does not follow that the residuary clause must perish. The fact that some of the provisions in the Pavlinko will cannot be executed does not strike down the residuary clause, which is meaningful and stands on its own two feet. We know that one of the very purposes of a residuary clause is to provide a catch-all for undisposed-of or ineffectually disposed-of property.

. . .

I see no insuperable obstacle to probating the will signed by Vasil Pavlinko. Even though it was originally prepared as the will of his wife, Hellen, he did adopt its testamentary provisions as his own. Some of its provisions are not effective but their ineffectuality in no way bars the legality and validity of the residuary clause which is complete in itself. I would, therefore, probate the paper signed by Vasil Pavlinko. . . .[14]

[14] Noted 11 Mercer L. Rev. 229; 107 U. Pa. L. Rev. 1237. — Eds.

COMMENTS AND QUESTIONS

1. In Guardian, Trust, etc. Co. v. Inwood, [1946] N.Z.L.R. 614, a will was prepared for testatrix Jane Remington, which devised her property "to my sister Maude Lucy Remington" for life, remainder to B. A will was prepared for her sister Maude Lucy, which devised her property "to my sister Jane Remington" for life, remainder to B. Both wills named the same executor and were in all other essential aspects the same. The sisters signed the wrong wills. The court reasoned that there was testamentary intent with respect to the document signed. It granted probate of the will signed by Jane with the omission of the word "Jane" from the body of the will.[15] The New Zealand case is followed in Re Brander, [1952] 4 D.L.R. 688, 6 W.W.R. 702, noted in 31 Can. B. Rev. 185 (1953).

2. Can the problem in Pavlinko's Estate be separated into two inquiries? First, we ascertain whether Vasil intended the document he signed to have testamentary effect. If the answer is yes, then we inquire what substantive disposition he intended and fashion constructional techniques to carry out his intention. Consider this question in the light of the following three hypothetical cases.

(a) Suppose testator is preparing to sign the original copy of his will, in which his testamentary intentions are fully set forth. By mistake the lawyer supervising the ceremony substitutes a carbon copy for the original and the carbon copy is executed. Can the executed carbon copy be probated? Yes.

(b) Suppose the lawyer by mistake substitutes a will with entirely different dispositive arrangements, which is duly executed. Can this be probated as decedent's will? No.

(c) Suppose the lawyer is drawing a will for a client named Pavlov, who wants to leave everything to the Russian Orthodox Church. He also has a client named Pavlinko, who desires to leave his whole estate to the Russian Orthodox Church. Pavlinko comes in to execute his will. By mistake he executes the will drawn for Pavlov. The only difference between these two wills is in the first sentence: "I, Pavlov, hereby make my last will," reads the document signed by Pavlinko. The dispositive provisions of the paper signed by Pavlinko carry out his intentions exactly. Can this paper be probated as Pavlinko's will? Even if this particular paper was not the paper Pavlinko intended to sign, it was a paper which contained everything of substance that he wished included in the paper he intended to sign.

Is case (a), (b) or (c) analogous to what actually happened in Pavlinko's Estate? Can we tell whether the paper signed contained everything of substance Vasil wished to include before we know how the language will be construed? If the instrument cannot be admitted to probate until the language is construed, and the language cannot be construed until the instrument is admitted to probate, how can we get out of this circle? How did we get into it?

[15] A part of the description of property given or of the intended recipient, if shown by extrinsic evidence to be false, can be stricken. The maxim falsa demonstratio non nocet (meaning mere false description does not make the instrument inoperative) is applicable.

3. Is the majority's view in Pavlinko's Estate sound in terms of the ritual, evidentiary, and protective functions of the Statute of Wills? Henderson, Mistake and Fraud in Wills — Part I: A Comparative Analysis of Existing Law, 47 B.U.L. Rev. 303, 369 (1967). Professor Henderson believes that courts have been unduly restrictive in relieving from the effects of mistake, and has drafted a statute that would authorize judicial reformation of wills in many cases. Henderson, Mistake and Fraud in Wills — Part II: A Suggested Statutory Departure, 47 B.U.L. Rev. 461 (1967).

4. On testator's illiteracy or lack of knowledge of the language in which a will is written as affecting its validity, see Note, 37 A.L.R.3d 889 (1971).

Competency of Witnesses and Interested Witness Statutes

Under the English common law, any witness to a will who was beneficially interested in the will on the day of execution was barred from testifying as to the acts of execution. Such person was thus disqualified from acting as an attesting witness. Persons beneficially interested included, among others, a legatee or devisee and the spouse of a legatee or devisee. If three witnesses were required and one of the three witnesses was a legatee, the will could not be probated.

While all states have interested witness statutes, only a few adopt the harsh common law rule invalidating the entire will when an attesting witness is a legatee. Most of the statutes make a witness competent to testify, but either (a) invalidate any testamentary gift in his favor or (b) invalidate any such gift to the extent it exceeds the amount that would pass to the witness by intestacy. Although these purging statutes vary in detail, the Florida statute is illustrative.

FLORIDA STATUTES ANNOTATED §731.07(5) (1964): "All devises and bequests to subscribing witnesses are void unless there are at least two other disinterested subscribing witnesses to the will. If a subscribing witness would be entitled to any share of the estate of the testator in case the will were not established, he shall take such proportion of the devise or bequest made to him in the will as does not exceed the share of the estate which would be distributed to him if the will were not established."

Section 2-505 of the Uniform Probate Code provides that an interested witness is competent to testify to prove execution of the will, and that the witness does not forfeit the testamentary gift in his favor. This provision for nonforfeiture is novel. Is it sound? [16]

[16] See Mechem, Why Not a Modern Wills Act? 33 Iowa L. Rev. 501, 506 (1948); Gulliver & Tilson, Classification of Gratuitous Transfers, 51 Yale L.J. 1, 12 (1941).

PROBLEMS

1. T's typewritten will is witnessed by his friends, A, B, and C, who are not related to him. His will devises his entire estate "to my lifelong good friends, A and B." T, who never married, dies domiciled in Florida. His closest known relative is a third cousin thrice removed, Z. How is T's estate distributed?

(a) Suppose that after T's death A renounces his interest under the will. How is T's estate distributed? See Caesar v. Burgess, 103 F.2d 503 (10th Cir. 1939); Nixon v. Armstrong, 38 Tex. 297 (1873).

(b) Suppose, instead, that A predeceases T, leaving no issue surviving. How is T's estate distributed?

2. T's typewritten will is witnessed by X and S. X is a disinterested witness. S is T's son. T's will devises his entire estate to S for life, then to S's issue per stirpes who survive S. T, a widower, dies domiciled in Florida. He is survived by two children, S and D. How is T's estate distributed?

3. Can the person named in the will as executor be a disinterested subscribing witness? Pavletich v. Pavletich, 78 N.M. 93, 428 P.2d 632, 30 A.L.R.3d 1355 (1967); Appeal of Richburg, 148 Me. 323, 92 A.2d 724 (1952) (power in executor, who was witness, to dispose of clothing and other personal articles held to prevent probate of will; no purging statute in state).

4. If the will designates Jones, a lawyer, to serve as attorney for the estate, does Jones run any risks if he witnesses the will? If his partners witness the will? Re George's Estate, 11 Ill. App. 2d 359, 137 N.E.2d 555 (1956); American Bar Association Code of Professional Responsibility, Canon 5, EC 5-5, 5-6 (1969).

2. *Holographic Wills*

THE JOLLY TESTATOR WHO MAKES HIS OWN WILL[17]

Ye lawyers who live upon litigants' fees,
And who need a good many to live at your ease,
Grave or gay, wise or witty, whate'er your degree,
Plain stuff or Queen's Counsel, take counsel of me:
When a festive occasion your spirit unbends,
You should never forget the profession's best friends;
So we'll send round the wine, and a light bumper fill
To the jolly testator who makes his own will.

He premises his wish and his purpose to save
All dispute among friends when he's laid in the grave;
Then he straightway proceeds more disputes to create
Than a long summer's day would give time to relate.

[17] Reprinted in full in Prosser, The Judicial Humorist 246 (1952).

He writes and erases, he blunders and blots,
He produces such puzzles and Gordian knots,
That a lawyer, intending to frame the thing ill,
Couldn't match the testator who makes his own will.

Testators are good, but a feeling more tender
Springs up when I think of the feminine gender!
The testatrix for me, who, like Telemaque's mother,
Unweaves at one time what she wove at another;
She bequeaths, she repeats, she recalls a donation,
And ends by revoking her own revocation;
Still scribbling or scratching some new codicil,
Oh! success to the woman who makes her own will.

Tisn't easy to say, 'mid her varying vapors,
What scraps should be deemed testamentary papers.
Tisn't easy from these her intention to find,
When perhaps she herself never knew her own mind.
Every step that we take, there arises fresh trouble:
Is the legacy lapsed? Is it single or double?
No customer brings so much grist to the mill
As the wealthy old woman who makes her own will.

— Lord Neaves

In about half the American states, principally in the South and West, holographic wills are permitted.[18] Holographic wills are written in the testator's handwriting and require no witnesses. Most statutes require a holographic will to be dated,[19] signed, and written entirely in the testator's hand. Most statutes do not require that a holograph be signed "at the end." If a statute does not require signing at the end of a will, a signing at any place on the will is sufficient if the testator intended it as his signature. The signature may be at the beginning of the will, in the body of the will, or on the margin.

GULLIVER & TILSON, CLASSIFICATION OF GRATUITOUS TRANSFERS, 51 Yale L.J. 1, 13-14 (1941): "The exemption of holographic wills from the

[18] The states are Alaska, Arizona, Arkansas, California, Idaho, Kentucky, Louisiana, Mississippi, Montana, Nevada, North Carolina, North Dakota, Oklahoma, Pennsylvania, South Dakota, Tennessee, Texas, Utah, Virginia, West Virginia and Wyoming. Uniform Probate Code §2-503 permits a holographic will.

[19] What function is served by requiring that a holographic will be dated? Suppose a holograph is dated "May 1948." Should the document be admitted to probate as a will? See In re Estate of Carson, 174 Cal. App. 2d 291, 344 P.2d 612 (1959); Compare In re Irvine's Estate, 114 Mont. 577, 139 P.2d 489 (1943).

It has been held that "10/3/50" is not sufficient as a date, although "10/10/50" would be. Succession of Schellang, 144 So. 2d 896 (La. App. 1962). Do you see why? See Note, 22 A.L.R.3d 866 (1968).

usual statutory requirements seems almost exclusively justifiable in terms of the evidentiary function. The requirement that a holographic will be entirely written in the handwriting of the testator furnishes more complete evidence for inspection by handwriting experts than would exist if only the signature were available, and consequently tends to preclude the probate of a forged document. . . . [T]here seems no substantial guarantee of the performance of the protective function. . . . A holographic will is obtainable by compulsion as easily as a ransom note. While there is a certain ritual value in writing out the document, casual off-hand statements are frequently made in letters. The relative incompleteness of the performance of the functions of the regular statute of wills, and particularly the absence of any ritual value, may account for the fact that holographic wills are not recognized in the majority of the states, and for some decisions, in states recognizing them, requiring the most precise compliance with specified formalities."

NOTES AND PROBLEMS

1. Velma Lorenz was found unconscious in her home on May 18, 1964, and died on May 23, 1964. On May 18 a stamped envelope was found in her home; the envelope was addressed to her attorney, Mr. Grimes. The envelope, which was delivered to Mr. Grimes, contained the following letter in Mrs. Lorenz's handwriting:

> May 17, 1964
> Dear Mr. Grimes,
>
> I've been ill and unable to go to your office. I would like to make some changes in my will regarding the bonds and savings accounts. Fee enclosed.
>
> When you probate the will please have it done as I wish and take your fees and costs from the Lorenzs and not from my friends.
>
> Thank you.
>
> (signed) Velma B. Lorenz
>
> *page* 2
>
> May 17, 1964
> Changes to be made in my will:
> Government bonds to Lynette and Louann Huntsman.
> United Savings account to Mrs. Louise L. Huntsman.
> First Savings account to Mrs. Louise Lorenz.
> Robstown Savings Account to Miss Audrey Price.
> Corpus Christi Savings account to Mr. and Mrs. J. H. Philbrick.
> Pioneer account of Waco to Mr. W. Enloe Simmons of Hillsboro.
>
> (signed) Velma B. Lorenz

This letter was offered for probate as a codicil to Mrs. Lorenz's typewritten and attested will, executed in 1961. Its probate was contested by the legatees under the 1961 will. What result? Price v. Huntsman, 430 S.W.2d 831 (Tex. Civ. App. 1968).

2. The following letter was offered for probate by the deceased's sister, Nina.

Los Angeles
October 1, 1890

Nina:

I wrote you yesterday, hastily. Answer my letter at once. I want to know everything about mother, and all about you, — your children. I have reached the point of perfect independence, pecuniarily. My health is probably ruined, and I want to anticipate possibilities. You and your children get everything. Your boy I want given the best of educations. I would like him to go to Harvard. I would like to have him a lawyer. Don't bring him up a prejudiced southerner, but teach honor, — make it dearer than life, and he must, with the blood in his veins, be a man. Write me. As soon as I possibly can, I will be in Savannah.

(signed) Brother.

What result? In re Richardson's Estate, 94 Cal. 63, 29 Pac. 484 (1892).

Assuming the above letter was otherwise held to be a valid holographic will, would "Brother" satisfy the signature requirement? Would a testator's initials ("C.B.R.") satisfy the signature requirement? See Estate of Cook, [1960] 1 W.L.R. 353, 1 All Eng. 689, 75 A.L.R.2d 892; Note, 98 A.L.R.2d 841 (1964).

3. S. F. Thorn had a country place that he called Cragthorn. He had a rubber stamp made, inscribed "Cragthorn," that he used to embellish his stationery and other documents. Thorn wrote a holographic will that made various devises, among them: "To the California Academy of Sciences I leave my country place *Cragthorn* consisting of 241 64/100 acres located about $1\frac{1}{4}$ mile below Glenwood and about $9\frac{1}{4}$ miles from the City of Santa Cruz in Santa Cruz County, State of California in Sec. 6 Town. 10 S. Range 1 West." All of the holograph was in Thorn's handwriting except for the word "Cragthorn," which had been imprinted by Thorn's rubber stamp. After Thorn's death, probate of the holograph was challenged by Thorn's heirs on the ground that it was not entirely in the testator's handwriting as required by state law. What result: Should the word Cragthorn be excised and the remaining portion of the will be admitted to probate? Should the will be denied probate? In re Thorn's Estate, 183 Cal. 512, 192 P. 19 (1920); see Note, 89 A.L.R.2d 1198 (1963).

4. Chester Baker wrote a codicil to his witnessed will on printed stationery of the Hotel Covell, and crossed out part of the printed matter.

~~AAA~~
~~APPROVED~~

~~HOTEL COVELL~~
MODESTO, CALIFORNIA

Jan. 2, 1962

This is a codicil to my will. I bequeath all my interest in Insurance Securities Trust Fund to Laura Crosby.

(signed) Chester Baker

THE HOTEL THAT HAS EVERYTHING (ALMOST)

The printed matter is shown in small capitals; Chester crossed out "AAA APPROVED" and "HOTEL COVELL," which appear at the top of the page. He did not cross out "MODESTO, CALIFORNIA" or the slogan at the bottom. All else on the sheet was in Chester's handwriting. Is the codicil entitled to probate? In re Baker's Estate, 59 Cal. 2d 680, 31 Cal. Rptr. 33, 381 P.2d 913 (1963); see Note, 89 A.L.R.2d 1198 (1963). Would the result be different if the date were written above "MODESTO, CALIFORNIA"?

5. Purported holographic wills have taken myriad forms — and shapes. Wills have been written on a nurse's petticoat, inscribed on an eggshell, and scratched on a tractor fender. If you are interested in this sort of thing, there is a lot of humor and human interest to be found in Byrne, Curiosities of the Search Room (1880, 1969); Menchin, The Last Caprice (1963); Gest, Some Jolly Testators, 8 Temp. L.Q. 297 (1934). We offer a recent addition to the list, reported in the Austin (Texas) American-Statesman, October 15, 1968.

> Unusual Will Names Dancer
>
> PHILADELPHIA (AP) — A note to a belly dancer scribbled on a bedroom wall was offered Tuesday as a legal last will and testament.
>
> An 18-inch square section of the plaster wall was sawed out under the supervision of Register of Wills John E. Walsh and submitted to Probate Court.
>
> The note, signed by Hermann Schmidt, 49, who died Sept. 15, said in part:
>
> "Genevieve: You take care of all my belongings. This give's you authority. Love, Hermann, 8-14-1968."
>
> Attorney Leio T. Connor said he believes this entitles Genevieve — Genevieve Decker, 42, a belly dancer and Schmidt's fiancee — to Schmidt's $12,000 estate and plans to file it for this purpose.

Would you be as confident as attorney Connor that the piece of plaster is entitled to probate? That Genevieve takes all of Hermann's estate if it is admitted to probate? Compare In re Estate of Gasparovich, 487 P.2d 1148 (Mont. 1971).

3. *Conditional Wills*

In re PASCAL'S ESTATE

Surrogate's Court, New York (N.Y. County), 1956
2 Misc. 2d 337, 152 N.Y.S.2d 185, aff'd, 4 App. Div. 2d 941, 167 N.Y.S.2d 1002, Motion for leave to appeal denied, 4 App. Div. 2d 1021, 4 N.Y.2d 674

FRANKENTHALER, Surrogate.

There is offered for probate as decedent's last will and testament an instrument in his own hand in the following text:

To Zaya Kingman-Speelman

470 Park Avenue, N.Y.

This is my will if I
should die on this
my trip to India
You are my sol heiress.

Signed the 22 february 1954

Witnesses
[signatures]
Daisy Haang
Y. T. Kan
[oriental calligraphy]

[signature] Gabriel Pascal

Objections to the probate of this document were interposed by decedent's widow and his brother. Their objections asserting fraud, undue influence and lack of testamentary capacity were withdrawn prior to the trial so that the only remaining issues as to the validity of the paper's execution as a will are those asserting that the instrument was not duly published by decedent and that he did not request the witnesses to attest it.

Heretofore a motion was made by the widow for a summary judgment that the propounded paper was subject to a condition which never occurred and consequently the instrument never became effective as the decedent's will. It was urged in support of this motion that the propounded paper was intended to be operative only in the event of decedent's death on a particular trip to India and, inasmuch as he did not make a trip to India and died on July 6, 1954 in a New York City hospital, the instrument should not be admitted to probate. This court ruled that the motion for denial of probate would be held in abeyance for determination with other issues upon the trial (N.Y. Law Journal, November 8, 1954). The Court of Appeals affirmed the order of this court and held that the effect of the alleged condition upon the validity of the propounded paper should be determined on the trial of the probate or other hearing at which the parties would have an opportunity to develop extrinsic facts in aid of a construction of the testator's language, 309 N.Y. 108, 127 N.E.2d 835. In accordance with this holding the parties have been permitted to introduce evidence in support of their respective contentions as to the validity and effect of the propounded paper.

The question as to whether or not the propounded paper is a duly executed testamentary instrument is of first importance inasmuch as a negative answer would deprive the proponent of any further status in the estate and also would render construction of the paper unnecessary. The circumstances of the paper's execution have been established. Stated in brief the pertinent facts are that on the evening of February 22, 1954, at the apartment of the proponent, decedent stated to one Daisy Haang, a person whose signature appears as a witness on the propounded paper, that he was about to write his will and he further said "I want you girls to be my witnesses"; that Mrs. Y. T. Kan then came into the room; that Kan's knowledge of the English language was negligible; that the proponent said to Kan in the Chinese language that decedent was going to write a will; that decedent then wrote upon the paper, signed his name and handed the paper to Haang who wrote the word "witnesses" and signed her name; that Haang then handed the paper to Kan and stated to Kan in Chinese that the paper was decedent's will and that decedent wanted Kan to be one of the witnesses and that thereupon Kan signed her name below that of Haang. The testimony was that the witness Kan was unable to interpret any statement in English that decedent and others made at the time. It is contended that the manner in which the instrument was executed and attested was not in compliance with Decedent Estate Law, §21, for the reasons that, because language differences made it impossible for decedent to converse with Kan, there was no declaration by decedent to Kan that the instrument was his will and Kan did not sign as a witness at the request of decedent.

The fundamental purpose of the statutory requirement of publication is to prevent fraud and it has been said that the reasons for requiring publication are twofold; first, to assure that the testator is under no misapprehension as to the nature of the instrument he is executing and second, to impress upon the witnesses the importance of their act and their consequent duties to vouch for the validity of the instrument, Matter of Pulvermacher's Will, 305 N.Y. 378, 383, 113 N.E.2d 525, 526. Here the instrument is a holograph, the body of which opens with the words "This is my will." There can be no doubt of the testator's awareness of the nature and purpose of this instrument in his own hand. He orally identified the instrument to one of the witnesses, he requested her to witness it and he asked her to procure the subscription of the other witness. The nature of the instrument was conveyed to the second witness and she then subscribed her name below that of the first witness in the presence of the testator. It is perfectly clear that the testator was fully aware of what was occurring and that these acts of subscription were not only with his acquiescence but were completely in accord with his wishes. It also has been established that both witnesses were cognizant of the nature of the instrument and the function they were performing in attesting it. It can be said in the words employed in Peck v. Cary, 27 N.Y. 9, 26: ". . . the understanding of the witnesses that they came forward and signed because the testator desired them to do so, and the understanding of the testator that they came and signed at his instance was perfect, and the privity which was the purpose of the statute was secured."

There is no requirement that a testator's publication of his will be in a particular form and both a declaration of the character of the instrument and a request that the witnesses act may be communicated by signs and conduct as well as by words, Lane v. Lane, 95 N.Y. 494; Matter of Hunt's Will, 110 N.Y. 278, 18 N.E. 106; Matter of Mullenhoff's Will, 278 App. Div. 963, 105 N.Y.S.2d 675; . . .

Accordingly it is found that statements and events contemporaneous with the execution of the instrument established that the testator conveyed to both the witnesses the fact that the instrument was his will and his request that they sign the instrument as witnesses. It is held that the propounded paper was duly executed in accordance with Decedent Estate Law, §21. The competency of the decedent to make a will and his freedom from restraint also having been established, the paper is entitled to probate under Surrogate's Court Act, §144.[20]

Consonant with the opinion of the Court of Appeals, 309 N.Y. 113–114, 127 N.E.2d 837–838, the parties have been permitted to introduce in evidence extrinsic facts in aid of a construction of the will. The construction issue, referred to briefly hereinabove, arises because of the testator's employment of the words "if I should die on this my trip to India". The proponent contends that the quoted words are an expression of the testator's motive for the making of his will in that a then impending trip to India made the testator conscious of the uncertainty of life and the consequent need for a will. The proponent further urges that, if the will is susceptible of the construction that it was to be effective only in the event of the testator's death on his trip to India, the condition was fulfilled because the trip to India although postponed, was never abandoned. The contestants assert that the explicit condition of the will was that it be operative only in the event that the testator died on the scheduled trip to India which he was to undertake on the day following the will's execution.

The evidence established the facts hereinafter narrated. The testator and the proponent became acquainted in March 1953 and thereafter their relationship was a close one.[21] Prior to the date of the will the proponent had lent the testator $7,500, a substantial part of which she had procured by pledging jewelry, and at the date of the will the testator had not repaid the loan. The testator expressed great concern about this obligation and his inability to satisfy it. Some hours before the execution of his will the testator, with money borrowed from another source, had purchased a ticket for airplane passage from New York to Bombay, India, and had procured a reservation for a flight scheduled to leave New York at 5 P.M. on February 23, 1954. The testator for some time had entertained the idea of making motion pictures in India but his main purpose in making the flight on February 23rd was to interview a particular individual in connection with a contemplated motion picture. The will

[20] In Atohka's Estate, 282 P.2d 737 (Okla. 1955), decedent spoke little English, and there was no interpreter present. The will was denied probate on the ground that decedent did not request the attesting witnesses to witness his signature. There was also evidence that decedent was almost deaf, blind, and addicted to alcohol, and the circumstances surrounding the execution were not above suspicion. — Eds.

[21] Gabriel Pascal was a well-known theatrical producer. At the time of his death he held the exclusive right to produce a musical play based on George Bernard Shaw's "Pygmalion." Negotiations completed after his death resulted in production of the highly successful stage and movie musical, "My Fair Lady."

His widow, Valerie Pascal, subsequently wrote that Gabriel and Zaya Kingman-Speelman had entered into a passionate love affair after their March meeting. Pascal, The Disciple and his Devil 252 (1970). On June 16, 1954, Valerie was granted an interlocutory divorce decree, which was to become final one year later. One of the reasons for divorce was Gabriel's affair with Zaya. Id. at 315; N.Y. Times, June 17, 1954, p. 37, col. 1. Gabriel died within a month of the interlocutory decree. In her book, at pages 296-356, Valerie relates her version of the will contest and of the entangled relationships of the three parties.

On the same night that Gabriel executed his will, he made a handsome gift to Zaya, which Valerie also contested. See Speelman v. Pascal, page 385, infra. — Eds.

was executed in the proponent's apartment at about 10 o'clock on the night of February 22, 1954. On the morning of February 23rd the testator was advised by cablegram that the individual whom he expected to interview in India would not be available until the end of May and thereupon the testator cancelled his passage. The fare was returned to the testator by check of the airline in April but he returned the check to the airline and obtained a credit. On May 19th a ticket for passage from New York to London, England was issued to the testator which was turned in on May 20th when there was issued to him a round trip ticket from New York to Bombay via London. A reservation for a particular flight was not made. This ticket was not used and its cost was refunded to the estate after the testator's death. In March the testator had repaid to the proponent a substantial part of her loan to him and she then redeemed the jewelry. The testator was in failing health from early May 1954 and died on July 6th in a hospital in this city.

On February 23, 1954 the testator's wife verified a complaint in an action for divorce in the State of California. That complaint alleged that the parties had married in September 1947 and had separated on January 1, 1953. The complaint further alleged that a property settlement agreement then was in the contemplation of the parties. A property settlement agreement was signed by the testator and his wife on March 10, 1954.

Can it be said that the testator's will, considered in the light of the foregoing facts, was intended by him to be a disposition of his property regardless of the circumstances of his death? The Appellate Division has expressed the unanimous opinion that a reading of the testator's will, unaided by any extrinsic fact, leads to the conclusion that it was intended to be a conditional instrument effective to pass his property only in the contingency that he met his death on a trip to India. Basing a construction of the instrument on its language alone no other conclusion is to be reached and when due weight is given to the extrinsic facts that conclusion seems only to be fortified. The paper was hastily drawn on the eve of an impending trip to India. It was drawn at a time when the testator was troubled lest his inability to repay a sum borrowed from the proponent would result in a forfeiture of her pledged jewelry. It is not mere conjecture to say that the disposition in the will was prompted by the proponent's generosity to the testator and his consequent solicitude for her. To his mind the writing of the will was an expeditious means of protecting her in the event of his sudden death and there is nothing in the circumstances indicating that the testator was looking beyond the exigencies of the immediate situation. Knowledge of the extrinsic facts confirms the terse statement in the will that it was a disposition of the testator's property in the contingency that he met death on his planned trip to India. That particular trip was abandoned and, in view of the conclusion here reached as to the limited purpose of the will, it is inconsequential that the testator may not have abandoned the business venture which occasioned the trip or that he retained the hope of visiting India when his health permitted him to do so and the necessary business arrangements had been concluded. The condition of the will of February 22nd was that the testator meet his death on his contemplated trip to India on the following day. That condition did not occur and as a consequence the will does not provide a disposition of the testator's property.

The motion to dismiss the objections of the testator's widow was made by the proponent who under the foregoing construction of the will has no interest in the estate. The testator's brother has not attacked the status of the widow and inasmuch as he would be the only person to benefit were the widow to be deprived of an intestate share no purpose is to be served by a consideration of the issues raised by the proponent's motion. Accordingly the motion is dismissed.

The application of the widow for letters of administration has been opposed in the answer of the testator's brother solely upon the ground that a corporate fiduciary would serve the interests of the estate in a more efficient and competent manner. This answer does not allege a statutory basis for denial of letters of administration to the surviving spouse who has a prior right to administration under Surrogate's Court Act, §§118 and 133.

Submit decree on notice (1) admitting the propounded paper to probate, (2) construing the will as ineffectual to dispose of any part of the testator's property, (3) dismissing the proponent's motion seeking a dismissal of the widow's objections to probate, and (4) granting letters of administration with the will annexed to the widow.

On August 31, 1901, Caroline Holley executed the following instrument in Washington, D.C.:

> I am going on a Journey and may, not ever return. And if I do not, this is my last request. The Mortgage on the King House, wich is in the possession of Mr. H H Brown to go to the Methodist Church at Bloomingburgh All the rest of my properday both real and personal to My adopted Son L. B. Eaton of the life Saving Service, Treasury Department Washington D.C, All I have is my one hard earnings and I propose to leave it to whome I please.

Caroline went on her journey, returned to Washington, resumed her work as a clerk in the Treasury Department, and died there on December 17, 1901. The Supreme Court, per Holmes, J., ordered that the will be probated. "Obviously the first sentence, 'I am going on a journey and may not ever return,' expresses the fact which was on her mind as the occasion and inducement for writing it. . . . She was thinking of the possibility of death or she would not have made a will. But that possibility at that moment took the specific shape of not returning from her journey, and so she wrote 'if I do not return,' before giving her last commands." Eaton v. Brown, 193 U.S. 411, 414 (1904). Should the same reasoning have been applied to Gabriel Pascal's will?

Generally on conditional wills, see Note, 1 A.L.R.3d 1048 (1965).

SECTION B. Revocation of Wills

1. *Revocation by Writing or Physical Act*[22]

A will is an ambulatory document, which means that it is subject to modification or revocation by the testator during his lifetime. A testator can revoke his will in one of two ways: by a subsequent writing executed with testamentary formalities,[23] or by a physical act such as destroying or burning the will. On the assumption that oral revocations would open a wide door for fraud, an oral declaration that a will is revoked, without more, is inoperative in all states.[24]

Section 2-507 of the Uniform Probate Code is typical of statutes providing for revocation by a writing or by physical act:

"A will or any part thereof is revoked

"(1) by a subsequent will which revokes the prior will or part expressly or by inconsistency; or

"(2) by being burned, torn, cancelled, obliterated, or destroyed, with the intent and for the purpose of revoking it by the testator or by another person in his presence and by his direction."

PROBLEMS

1. Testatrix duly executes the following instrument:

Dr. O'Kennedy:

Dear Friend. — Please destroy the Will I made in favor of Thomas Hart.

Margaret McGill

Is the will revoked if Dr. O'Kennedy destroys the will? If he does not destroy it? Matter of McGill, 229 N.Y. 405, 128 N.E. 194 (1920).

2. In 1970 T executes a will giving all his property to A. In 1971 T executes a

22 See Hoffman, Revocation of Wills and Related Subjects, 31 Brooklyn L. Rev. 220 (1965); Rees, American Wills Statutes: II, 46 Va. L. Rev. 856, 871-80 (1960).

23 In states that recognize holographic wills, a holograph can revoke a typewritten, attested will. In re Salmonski's Estate, 38 Cal. 2d 199, 238 P.2d 966 (1951); In re Hengy's Estate, 53 Idaho 515, 26 P.2d 178 (1933).

24 Suppose testator executes a written, attested will that devises "all my property, real and personal," to A and B. Later, in his last illness, testator declares a nuncupative will that devises specifically described personal property to C. In effect, the nuncupative will is a codicil to testator's written will. A number of courts have held that the nuncupative will is invalid. To give it effect would result in a partial revocation of testator's written will that devised all his property, and oral revocations are invalid. In re Hadsell's Estate, 55 Ariz. 116, 99 P.2d 93 (1940); In re Carlton's Estate, 221 So. 2d 184 (Fla. 1969); In re Grattan's Estate, 157 Kan. 116, 138 P.2d 497 (1943); but see Ind. Ann. Stat. §6-504(c) (1953); Connor v. Purcell, 360 S.W.2d 438 (Tex. Civ. App. 1962).

will giving his diamond ring to B, his automobile to C, and all the rest of his property to A. The second will contains no words of revocation. In 1972 T revokes his 1971 will. H is T's heir. Can the first will be probated? Estate of Schnoor, 4 Cal. 2d 590, 51 P.2d 424 (1935).

With rare exceptions, the best way to revoke a will is by a subsequent will in which the testator states unequivocally that he revokes "any and all wills and codicils heretofore made." Revocation by physical act, as by burning, tearing, or cancelling, is not a recommended method of revoking a will because the physical act is inherently ambiguous. To be legally effective, the act must be accompanied by an intention to revoke. The act, without animus revocandi, does not revoke the will. Proof of intent must be found in the words or conduct of the testator — as recalled by others, as the principal is never present to testify. In many cases there is no direct evidence of intent, and various presumptions are brought into play. Further, there may be no direct evidence that it was the testator who cancelled or obliterated the will, giving rise to a nagging suspicion that someone else may have wielded the scissors or the marking pencil.

In re BAKHAUS' ESTATE

Supreme Court of Illinois, 1951
410 Ill. 578, 102 N.E.2d 818

FULTON, Justice. William F. Bakhaus, a resident of Crete, Illinois, died on July 9, 1947. A document purporting to be his last will and testament was found in a drawer in the harness shop which he operated in the basement of his home on July 14, 1947. The instrument consisted of two pages of typewriting, and is as follows:

> Page 1
>
> Know All Men By These Presents, That I, William F. Bakhaus, of Crete, Illinois, being of sound and disposing mind and memory do hereby make, publish and declare, this to be my Last Will and Testament, hereby revoking all Wills by me at anytime heretofore made.
>
> First; I order and direct, that my Executor hereinafter named pay my funeral expenses and just debts as soon after my decease as conveniently may be.
>
> Second; I give, devise and bequeath unto my beloved wife Bertha Bakhaus, all of my personal property and belongings, that I may die possessed of or may be entitled to.
>
> Third; My Home described as, Lot Number Two (2) in Seggebruchs Subdivision, in the Village of Crete, County of Will and State of Illinois, with the buildings thereon, I give, devise and bequeath unto my beloved wife Bertha Bakhaus, for her sole use during her lifetime and after her death, the same shall become the property of my Nephew, William Bakhaus, of Grant Park, Illinois.

Subject however to the payment of the following bequests which are to be paid after the death of my beloved wife, Bertha Bakhaus, as follows:

To my brother Fred Bakhaus, One Hundred Dollars
To my brother August Bakhaus, One Hundred Dollars
To my sister Emma Engelking, One Hundred Dollars
To my niece Velma Bakhaus, One Hundred Dollars

and I charge the aforesaid Real Estate with the payment of the above bequests.

Fourth: I hereby nominate and appoint, my nephew William Bakhaus of Grant Park, Illinois, sole Executor of this my Last Will and Testament and I do hereby exempt him from giving any Surety on any Bond that may be required of him as such Executor.

In Witness Whereof, I have hereunto set my hand and affixed my seal this *27th* day of October, A.D. 1941.

Page 2

The within instrument, consisting of two sheets of paper including this sheet, was at the date thereof, signed, sealed, published and declared, by the said Testator, William F. Bakhaus as and for his Last Will and Testament, in the presence of us and we at his request and in his presence and in the presence of each other, have affixed our names as witnesses thereto, the day and year first above written.

Witnesses	Address
Johanna Rohe	*Crete, Ill.*
Fred A. Rohe	*Crete, Ill.*

It was on legal size paper and the signature of the testator had been cut from the will. The cutting had apparently been done by a sharp instrument straight across the bottom of the page, and the cutting had removed not only the bottom of the first page together with the signature, but also the bottom of the second page of the will.

The executor named in the will offered the same for probate. The attesting witnesses appeared before the probate court and testified to the proper execution of the will by the testator, and that court admitted the will to probate. Two of the heirs appealed from the action of the probate court to the circuit court of Will County and after another hearing in that court the will was held to have been properly admitted to probate. These two heirs have brought this appeal contending that the will was improperly admitted to probate. A freehold being involved, the appeal has been taken directly to this court.

William F. Bakhaus, the testator, was a widower and was the owner of a house in Crete, where he lived, in the basement of which he conducted a harness shop. His wife had died in 1946 and after her death his nephew William Bakhaus and his nieces, Velma Bakhaus and Beatrice Bakhaus, children of his deceased brother, came and resided with him in this home. He was afflicted with palsy and during the last few months of his life he was quite shaky and had to be assisted while eating or cutting his food by his niece and at times it was necessary for her to assist him in the harness shop. The proponent of the will offered the testimony of the two attesting witnesses as to the due execution of the will on October 27, 1941, showing that the will was duly and properly executed in Crete, at the office of a real-estate broker who had prepared it at the request of the testator. After the execution of the will it appears that the testator took the will with him to his home and that it remained there until his death. No evidence was submitted by any of the parties as to the circumstances attending the mutilation of the will. The proponent, however, did introduce testimony of several witnesses who testified to statements and declarations made by the testator during his lifetime that he wanted his home to go to his nephew, the proponent, and that the deceased held the proponent in high regard. It was further shown by the evidence that the will was found in a drawer in the harness shop, while his other valuable papers were found in a safe which the testator kept in his bedroom closet. Evidence was admitted indicating that the harness shop was a gathering place for testator's many customers and numerous friends, that the entrance to the harness shop was unlocked and that persons other than the testator had access to the shop.

Two witnesses testified in behalf of the contestants. These witnesses were nieces of testator and daughters of one of the contestants. They testified that in December, 1946, about 7 months prior to testator's death, he stated to them that the home was not going to the nephew but that he desired to have all of his property divided equally between his heirs. Fred Rohe, the man who drew the will, testified that the last time the testator spoke to him about his affairs in detail was when the will was drawn in 1941, but that, about a week before testator died, testator had a conversation with him in which he told Rohe he wanted to see him sometime and that he would let him know when he should come, since he thought he might make some changes in his will.

The contestants argue that the will was revoked by the testator and therefore should not have been admitted to probate. They contend that where a will remains in the testator's possession until his death and is then found among his papers or effects with erasures, alterations or mutilations, the law presumes that the will was revoked by the testator with the proper intention. The proponent contends that the will was properly admitted to probate because the will was established as having been validly executed and, before the presumption of revocation by the testator exists, it must be established that the will was in the exclusive possession and control of the testator up until the time of death. He further argues that any presumption of destruction by the testator is a rebuttable one which can be overcome by declarations of the testator and other evidence. Likewise, he contends that this case presents purely a question of fact and that the decision of the trial court will not be disturbed unless manifestly against the weight of the evidence.

. . .

Cases wherein a will is torn or cut normally, fall in two categories, first, cases wherein certain provisions or portions of the will are removed by cutting or tearing, and second, cases where the signature is removed or obliterated. In the first type of case we have held that the tearing or cutting of a portion of the will was similar to cases wherein lines have been drawn through certain portions of the will. In these instances it has been held that the drawing of a line through certain portions of the will, or the cutting of a certain portion of it, was an attempt to revoke so much of the will as was crossed out or removed and that, in the absence of evidence of an intention on the part of the testator to revoke the entire will, such crossing out or cutting would be disregarded and the will admitted to probate as it originally existed, so far as legible. Fleming v. Fleming, 367 Ill. 97, 10 N.E.2d 641; Casey v. Hogan, 344 Ill. 208, 176 N.E. 257; Schmidt v. Bauermeister, 279 Ill. 504, 117 N.E. 49.

In the latter type of case the court has held that, where a signature of a testator had been cut from the codicil to the will, the codicil was revoked and, depending upon the intention of the testator as to the will itself, the whole will could be revoked by such action. Burton v. Wylde, 261 Ill. 397, 103 N.E. 976, 978.

In the case of Burton v. Wylde, we held that, if declarations by the testator are admissible to prove a lost will, they were admissible to explain the acts of revocation or to show the intent of the testator, and we stated, "If declarations of this nature are admissible to show the total destruction or cancellation of the will, there can be no escape from the conclusion that they are admissible to show partial mutilation, cancellation or tearing of the will."

In the case of Burton v. Wylde many statements had been made by a testatrix to various people, some indicating that she had destroyed her will and some indicating that she had a will. In that case, after discussing the various contentions of the parties and the conflicting evidence this court stated, "Intelligent, careful woman that she was shown to be, how should she expect the will to remain in force if she cut a portion out of it, even though that portion might be small? In view of all the evidence in the record, in the light of the condition in which the will was found among the papers of the testatrix at her death, we can reach no other conclusion, under the authorities, than that she herself cut out her signature with the intention of revoking the entire document."

It would appear to us from the record of this case that the cutting of the signature from the will must certainly be taken as an act of revocation. The signature is the most important part of the will and if one not familiar with the statute were to revoke a will, the cutting of the signature from the will would be an ordinary mode to adopt, since the cutting of signatures from documents is frequently used to indicate their cancellation.

Proponent has argued that the will was not in the possession or control of the testator until his death, and has attempted to avoid the presumption that when the will is found in the possession and control of testator in a mutilated condition the law presumes that the mutilation was done by the testator with the requisite intention. He asserts that, the will having been kept in a drawer in the harness shop, it was not in the exclusive possession of the testator as it would have been had it been in the testator's safe in his bedroom. We do not agree with this contention because we do not feel that the exclusive possession of the testator means that it must be kept under lock and key or in a safety-deposit box. This will appears to have been kept in a drawer where he kept other papers in connection with his business. The fact that the place where he kept the will was not as safe a place as he had available to him does not mean that the will was not in his exclusive possession and control. If the keeping of the will in the drawer rather than the safe means anything, it could easily mean that the testator, having revoked the will, thought that it was no longer a valuable paper and therefore did not keep it in his safe but rather in a drawer in his harness shop where he could look at it and decide whether or not he wanted to make a new will.

Under all of the circumstances shown by this record, we believe that the will should not have been admitted to probate, in view of the fact that it did not contain the signature thereon of the testator and it appearing that the will had, since its execution, remained in his possession and control.

The right of a person to dispose of his property by will did not always exist but was originally created by statute. In view of the fact that a will operates contrary to the statute of descent and permits a person to dispose of his property contrary to the way the law prescribes, we believe that the proponent of a will disposing of property contrary to the statute of descent has the burden of showing the will to be validly executed and effective, and that the presumption against the validity of a will which has been mutilated should not be lightly set aside. This court can see that in the case at bar it could well have been the intention of the testator to give his home to his nephew and namesake, and, while such an intention might be considered commendable, such an intention is contrary to the statute of descent and, therefore, any will which attempts to accomplish that purpose must be established by such evidence as to leave little doubt as to its validity.

For the reasons stated in this opinion, the judgment of the circuit court of Will County is reversed and the cause remanded, with directions to enter an order denying the probate of said will.

Reversed and remanded, with directions.

MATTER OF BONNER, 17 N.Y.2d 9, 266 N.Y.S.2d 971, 214 N.E.2d 154, 28 A.L.R.3d 990 (1966). A will found among decedent's papers had been cut in two and was contained in an envelope labeled "Last Will and Testament of Merritt Bonner," which also had been cut in two. The separate pieces were enclosed in a larger envelope which bore the words "My Will" in decedent's handwriting. Two witnesses were permitted to testify that about a year before he died the decedent had stated that he had cut his will by mistake while cutting up old insurance policies. One of these witnesses assured him that, since he had a copy of the document, its validity remained unimpaired and the witness testified that decedent appeared satisfied with this advice. On the other hand, another witness declared that the decedent had repeatedly spoken of his intention to change his will and mentioned that he had actually cut it. The court held that when the will was in testator's possession, the presumption that testator cut his will with the intent to revoke could not be overcome by declarations of the decedent unless they were made "in connection with some act under such circumstances as to become a part of the res gestae." The court denied probate to the will.

THOMPSON v. ROYALL

Supreme Court of Virginia, 1934
163 Va. 492, 175 S.E. 748

HUDGINS, Justice. The only question presented by this record is whether the will of Mrs. M. Lou Bowen Kroll had been revoked shortly before her death.

The uncontroverted facts are as follows: On the 4th day of September, 1932, Mrs. Kroll signed a will, typewritten on the five sheets of legal cap paper; the signature appeared on the last page duly attested by three subscribing witnesses. H. P. Brittain, the executor named in the will, was given possession of the instrument for safe-keeping. A codicil typed on the top third of one sheet of paper dated September 15, 1932, was signed by the testatrix in the presence of two subscribing witnesses. Possession of this instrument was given to Judge S. M. B. Coulling, the attorney who prepared both documents.

On September 19, 1932, at the request of Mrs. Kroll, Judge Coulling and Mr. Brittain took the will and the codicil to her home where she told her attorney, in the presence of Mr. Brittain and another, to destroy both. But, instead of destroying the papers, at the suggestion of Judge Coulling, she decided to retain them as memoranda, to be used as such in the event she decided to execute a new will. Upon the back of the manuscript cover, which was fastened to the five sheets by metal clasps, in the handwriting of Judge Coulling, signed by Mrs. Kroll, there is the following notation: "This will null and void and to be only held by H. P. Brittain instead of being destroyed as a memorandum for another will if I desire to make same. This 19 Sept. 1932.

"M. Lou Bowen Kroll."

The same notation was made upon the back of the sheet on which the codicil was written, except that the name S. M. B. Coulling was substituted for H. P. Brittain; this was likewise signed by Mrs. Kroll.

Mrs. Kroll died October 2, 1932, leaving numerous nephews and nieces, some of whom were not mentioned in her will, and an estate valued at approximately $200,000. On motion of some of the beneficiaries, the will and codicil were offered for probate. All the interested parties including the heirs at law were convened, and on the issue devisavit vel non the jury found that the instruments dated September 4 and 15, 1932, were the last will and testament of Mrs. M. Lou Bowen Kroll. From an order sustaining the verdict and probating the will this writ of error was allowed.

For more than 100 years, the means by which a duly executed will may be revoked have been prescribed by statute. These requirements are found in section 5233 of the 1919 Code, the pertinent parts of which read thus: "No will or codicil, or any part thereof, shall be revoked, unless . . . by a subsequent will or codicil, or by some writing declaring an intention to revoke the same, and executed in the manner in which a will is required to be executed, or by the testator, or some person in his presence and by his direction, cutting, tearing, burning, obliterating, canceling, or destroying the same, or the signature thereto, with the intent to revoke."

The notations, dated September 19, 1932, are not wholly in the handwriting of the testatrix, nor are her signatures thereto attached attested by subscribing witnesses; hence under the statute they are ineffectual as "some writing declaring an intention to revoke." The faces of the two instruments bear no physical evidence of any cutting, tearing, burning, obliterating, canceling, or destroying. The only contention made by appellants is that the notation written in the presence, and with the approval, of Mrs. Kroll, on the back of the manuscript cover in the one instance, and on the back of the sheet containing the codicil in the other, constitute "canceling" within the meaning of the statute.

Both parties concede that to effect revocation of a duly executed will, in any of the methods prescribed by statute, two things are necessary: (1) The doing of one of the acts specified, (2) accompanied by the intent to revoke — the animo revocandi. Proof of either, without proof of the other, is insufficient. Malone v. Hobbs, 1 Rob. (40 Va.) 346, 39 Am. Dec. 263; 2 Minor Ins. 925.

The proof established the intention to revoke. The entire controversy is confined to the acts used in carrying out that purpose. The testatrix adopted the suggestion of her attorney to revoke her will by written memoranda, admittedly ineffectual as revocations by subsequent writings, but appellants contend the memoranda, in the handwriting of another, and testatrix' signatures, are sufficient to effect revocation by cancellation. To support this contention, appellants cite a number of authorities which hold that the modern definition of cancellation includes "any act which would destroy, revoke, recall, do away with, overrule, render null and void, the instrument."

Most of the authorities cited that approve the above or a similar meaning of the word were dealing with cancellation of simple contracts, or other instruments that require little or no formality in execution. However, there is one line of cases which apply this extended meaning of "canceling" to the revocation of wills. The leading case so holding is Warner v. Warner's Estate, 37 Vt. 356. In this case proof of the intent and the act were a notation on the same page with, and below the signature of, the testator, reading: "This will is hereby cancelled and annulled. In full this 15th day of March in the year 1859," and written lengthwise on the back of the fourth page of the foolscap paper, upon which no part of the written will appeared, were these words, "Cancelled and is null and void. (Signed) I. Warner." It was held this was sufficient to revoke the will under a statute similar to the one here under consideration.

In Evans' Appeal, 58 Pa. 238, the Pennsylvania court approved the reasoning of the Vermont court in Warner v. Warner's Estate, supra, but the force of the opinion is weakened when the facts are considered. It seems that there were lines drawn through two of the three signatures of the testator appearing in the Evans will, and the paper on which material parts of the will were written was torn in four places. It therefore appeared on the face of the instrument, when offered for probate, that there was a sufficient defacement to bring it within the meaning of both obliteration and cancellation.

The construction of the statute in Warner v. Warner's Estate, supra, has been criticized by eminent text-writers on wills, and the courts in the majority of the states in construing similar statutes have refused to follow the reasoning in that case. Jarman on Wills (6th Ed.) 147, note 1; Schouler on Wills (5th Ed.) §391; Redfield on the Law of Wills (4th Ed.) 323-325; 28 R.C.L. 180; 40 Cyc. 1173; Dowling v. Gilliland, 286 Ill. 530, 122 N.E. 70, 3 A.L.R. 839; . . . .

The above, and other authorities that might be cited, hold that revocation of a will by cancellation within the meaning of the statute contemplates marks or lines across the written parts of the instrument or a physical defacement, or some mutilation of the writing itself, with the intent to revoke. If written words are used for the purpose, they must be so placed as to physically affect the written portion of the will, not merely on blank parts of the paper on which the will is written. If the writing intended to be the act of canceling does not mutilate, or erase, or deface, or otherwise physically come in contact with, any part of written words of the will, it cannot be given any greater weight than a similar writing on a separate sheet of paper, which identifies the will referred to, just as definitely as does the writing on the back. If a will may be revoked by writing on the back, separable from the will, it may be done by a writing not on the will. This the statute forbids. . . .

The attempted revocation is ineffectual, because testatrix intended to revoke her will by subsequent writings not executed as required by statute, and because it does not in any wise physically obliterate, mutilate, deface, or cancel any written parts of the will.

For the reasons stated, the judgment of the trial court is affirmed.

NOTES AND PROBLEMS

1. If Judge Coulling had been sued for negligence by Mrs. Kroll's heirs, would he have been held liable?

2. What policy is served by the court's decision in the Thompson case? Given the clear and uncontroverted evidence of Mrs. Kroll's intention that her will be revoked, how can the court's decision be justified?

3. Suppose Mrs. Kroll had written "VOID" across the face of an unexecuted typewritten carbon copy of her will. Would this be a valid revocation by physical act? In re D'Agostino's Will, 9 N.J. Super. 230, 75 A.2d 913 (1950); In re Wehr's Will, 247 Wis. 98, 18 N.W.2d 709 (1945). If she had written "9/19/32 — VOID — MLBK," would it have been a valid revocation? In re Kehr's Estate, 373 Pa. 473, 95 A.2d 647 (1953); Note, 22 A.L.R.3d 1346 (1968).

4. Suppose Mrs. Kroll had written "VOID" across the face of an executed duplicate carbon copy of her will. Could this be a valid revocation by act? Estate of Holmberg, 400 Ill. 366, 81 N.E.2d 188 (1948).

5. If a will is revoked by burning, are the codicils to that will which are not burned thereby revoked? 2 Page, Wills §21.17 (Bowe-Parker rev. 1960); Comment, Wills — Revocation by Act to the Document — Effect on Codicil, 60 Mich. L. Rev. 82 (1961).

6. In 1964 T executed a will devising his entire estate to A. In 1965 T informed his lawyer that he wanted to leave his property in equal shares to A and B. The lawyer thereupon, in the presence of T, removed the staples from the will and dictated to his secretary a new first page. The lawyer then directed the secretary to copy the remaining pages and instructed her to request another attorney in the same office to supervise the execution, as he had an appointment out of the office. The secretary typed the new page but, to save herself work, failed to carry out the other directions. She attached the new first page to the others, stapled them together, and had T initial all the pages. When the lawyer returned, she told him his instructions had been carried out. Is either the 1964 will or the 1965 will entitled to probate? In re Will of Robinson, 26 A.D.2d 306, 273 N.Y.S.2d 985 (1966). If the 1965 will cannot be probated, is the lawyer liable for negligence? See Wade, Tort Liability of Paralegals and Lawyers Who Utilize Their Services, 24 Vand. L. Rev. 1133 (1971); cf. In re Peterson, 178 N.W.2d 738 (N.D. 1970), holding attorney responsible in disciplinary proceeding for improper acts of secretary that he should have discovered in the exercise of appropriate supervision.

Partial revocations.

In many states a will cannot be revoked in part by an act of revocation; it can be revoked in part only by a subsequent instrument. If partial revocation by act is not recognized, the will must be admitted to probate in the form in which it was originally executed if the original language can be ascertained. New York does not recognize partial revocation by act,[25] but the rule has developed there that, if a partial revocation by act is attempted, the will is admissible to probate in its altered form if the contents of the missing or altered portion of the will cannot be ascertained, unless it is apparent that the unascertainable portions would materially affect the remaining parts and the probate of only the remaining provisions would do violence to the decedent's testamentary plans.[26] This rule constitutes in effect a limited recognition of partial revocation by act.

PROBLEMS

1.. T executes a will that devises the residue of his estate to six named relatives. After T's death some years later, his will is found in a stack of papers on his desk. Two of the six names in the residuary clause have been lined through with a black

[25] N.Y. Estates, Powers & Trusts Law §3-4.1 (1967).

[26] Matter of Dryer, 143 Misc. 310, 257 N.Y.S. 257 (Sur. Ct. 1932); N.Y. Temporary State Commission on the Law of Estates, 5th Report 415 (1966). The mere augmentation of the residuary by the partial revocation has been held not to preclude probate of the remaining parts of the will. Matter of Enright, 139 Misc. 192, 248 N.Y.S. 707 (Sur. Ct. 1931).

marking pen, and their names can be read only by holding the will up to a light. There is no direct evidence that T marked out the two names. The two relatives contend that the attempted partial revocation is ineffective — if, indeed, it was T who marked out the two names. Among their arguments is that recognition of the partial revocation would increase the other legatees' shares from one-sixth to one-fourth, thus "making a new gift," and that this can be done only by a subsequent writing executed with testamentary formalities. The other four relatives contend it should be presumed that T made the markings, and that his partial revocation should be given effect.

(a) What result in a state having a statute similar to §2-507 of the Uniform Probate Code? In re Byrne's Will, 223 Wis. 503, 271 N.W. 48 (1937); compare Leatherwood v. Stephens, 24 S.W.2d 819 (Tex. Comm. App. 1930). See Note, 34 A.L.R.2d 619 (1954).

(b) What result in a state where the revocation statute does not include the phrase, "or any part thereof"? In re Minsinger's Estate, 228 Ore. 218, 364 P.2d 615 (1961).

(c) Suppose the line drawn through the names was made with a No. 3 lead pencil rather than a marking pen. Would you expect the result to be different? See Note, 24 A.L.R.2d 514, 524 (1952).

2. T's typewritten will devises Blackacre to A for life, remainder to B in fee. After execution T lines out the words "for life, remainder to B in fee." What interest, if any, does A take? Atkinson, Wills 445 (2d ed. 1953).

2. *Safeguarding the Will; Proof of Lost Will Statutes*

What should be done with the client's will after it has been executed? The most common practice is to give the will to the client together with instructions that he keep it in a safe place, such as in his safety deposit box or among his valuable papers at his home. This may not be the most desirable practice, however. The many reported cases involving notations, interlineations, or other markings on wills, indicate that over the years a disturbing number of testators have attempted partial revocations or, perhaps, have used their wills as memo pads on which contemplated modifications have been noted. Also, an occasional testator has taken too seriously his lawyer's advice on safeguarding the will, with the result that the will cannot be located after his death.[27] These potential difficulties have prompted some attorneys

[27] Consider the case of Oscar P.'s will, a true story told in a letter to one of the editors from Mr. A. J. Robinson, an attorney in Amarillo, Texas. Mr. Robinson was counsel for one group of claimants under the will. "Two men walked into our office in late August and told us that they were Mr. P.'s nephews. They were completely covered with chigger bites from the top of their shoes to their belts. Their legs were swollen and red all over. They told us that their uncle had died in East Texas on a 40-acre farm. They said that he was found dead in his old house that did not have any doors or windows and that the floor was about to fall in, that he kept his eggs in a bucket hanging from a tree limb by wire to keep the snakes from stealing them, that he hung his milk from a tree limb, dangling in a creek, that there was no stove in the house and that he had a wheel barrow with the wheel running at about a 45 degree angle that he pushed to and from town to carry all his supplies. They had been informed that their uncle had left a will, and

to follow the practice of retaining the client's will in their files. The client is given an unexecuted carbon copy of his will, on which the location of the original will is noted. (Are there any problems connected with this approach?)

Many states have statutes permitting deposit of wills with the clerk of the probate court. This procedure has much to commend it. It protects the will against tampering by the testator (or perhaps by someone adversely affected by the will's terms), and it should insure that the will can be located after the client's death. Uniform Probate Code §2-901 provides for the deposit of a will in court for safekeeping.

What happens when it is known or believed that the decedent had a will, but the will cannot be located after diligent search? This situation raises a difficult problem for the courts. It may be that the testator did too good a job of safeguarding his will. Or the will may have been destroyed in a manner that did not effect a revocation, as by public calamity, fire or flood, by fraud or mistake, or by the testator when he was non compos mentis or under the undue influence of another. There is also the possibility that the will may have been destroyed or suppressed by someone adversely affected by its contents. A will destroyed without the intention to revoke it remains legally effective. If the decedent actually had a will and never revoked it, and if its contents and due execution can be established by some other means, to deny probate of the lost or destroyed will results in the decedent's property passing to persons other than those he intended.

On the other hand, the alleged lost will may be just that: an alleged will that is the product of the proponents' avarice and imagination. Or if there was a will, it may not have been validly executed, or there may be doubts as to its contents unless an exact copy is available. Finally, it may be that the reason the will cannot be found is that the testator destroyed it with the intention to revoke.

These considerations have prompted the courts and legislatures to impose restrictions on the probate of a lost or destroyed will. Subject to these restrictions, by statute in about half the states and by court-developed rules in the remaining states, a will that is not produced in court can be established.[28]

The proponents of an alleged lost will must satisfy stringent proof requirements. Typically, due execution of the will must be proved as in any other case,[29]

---

the entire family had descended on the place over the weekend to hunt for it. They had spent two days digging in every place that they could think of on the entire 40 acres, hunting for the will that they assumed was buried somewhere. When they were about to quit, someone decided to dig up the floor of the chicken house. Underneath the chicken house floor they found a gallon jar, and in the gallon jar was a half-gallon jar, and in the half-gallon was a quart, and in the quart was a pint, and in the pint was a half-pint, and in the half-pint was a key which appeared to fit some safety deposit box. Upon checking all the banks in the neighboring towns, they finally found a bank that had a safety deposit box that the key would fit. Upon opening the safety deposit box they found P.'s holographic will. The first sentence recited that this was Oscar P.'s last will. The second sentence read: 'You will find the key to my safety deposit box in a jar under the floor of the chicken house.' " Oscar P. left a substantial estate.

[28] See Evans, The Probate of Lost Wills, 24 Neb. L. Rev. 383 (1945); Comment, Probate of Lost Wills in New England, 42 B.U.L. Rev. 338 (1962); Comment, The Evidence Required to Probate a Missing Will, 29 Notre Dame Law. 444 (1954).

[29] "[P]apers of this character are not usually entrusted to those who are disconnected with

and the contents of the will must be substantially proved either by a copy of the will or by the testimony of one or more persons who have read it or heard it read. Statutes in several states also require that, in order to probate the will, it must have been in existence at the testator's death or fraudulently destroyed during his lifetime.

PROBLEM

T is known to have had a will that he kept in a desk in his home. T's home was destroyed by fire some months before his death. After T's death an unexecuted carbon copy of his will is offered for probate. X and Y, close friends of T, testify that they witnessed the original of T's will, and that all the required formalities of due execution were satisfied. The state's statute provides that a lost or destroyed will cannot be probated "unless the same be proved to have been in existence at the time of the death of the testator, or is shown to have been fraudulently destroyed in the lifetime of the testator." Wyo. Stat. Ann. §2-73 (1959).

Proponents of the will argue that since the will was never revoked by T during his lifetime, it was in "legal existence" at his death, and that this is all the statute requires; alternatively, they argue that destruction of T's will by fire amounted to a "constructive fraud." What result? See In re Havel's Estate, 156 Minn. 253, 194 N.W. 633 (1923); Matter of Fox, 9 N.Y.2d 400, 174 N.E.2d 499 (1961); compare In re Estate of Strickman, 247 Cal. App. 2d 469, 55 Cal. Rptr. 606 (1966).

3. *Dependent Relative Revocation*[30]

This is the rather ungainly name given to a doctrine abbreviated in law students' notes as DRR. It is a judge-made doctrine, recognized in many jurisdictions, that cancels a revocation. The doctrine is applied when a court determines that although testator revoked his will, the revocation would not have been made but for a mistaken belief that another disposition of his property had been effectively made. If the other disposition is for any reason ineffective, the revocation also fails, and the original will remains in force. Here are some examples.

(1) In 1965 T executes a will devising all his property to A. In 1968 T executes

---

their execution; and it is, therefore, generally a difficult matter, and often an impossible one, to know who are the subscribing witnesses to a lost will. And if they are known, it would seldom be the case that their handwriting could be proved. . . . If it is urged that the loss of the instrument renders proof of its due execution, in the manner directed by the statute, more difficult, . . . it may be answered, . . . a relaxation of the rule would afford greater facility to the perpetration of fraud, and make it more difficult to meet or repel it. . . . It surely cannot be maintained that facts which must be established in order to give effect to the testamentary instrument, if it were before the court, need not be proved if it is not produced. If so, the case derives presumptive strength from its intrinsic weakness." Tynan v. Paschal, 27 Tex. 286, 298-299 (1863).

[30] See Palmer, Dependent Relative Revocation and Its Relation to Relief for Mistake, 69 Mich. L. Rev. 989 (1971); Walsh & Jones, Dependent Relative Revocation, 67 Dick. L. Rev. 275 (1963); Warren, Dependent Relative Revocation, 33 Harv. L. Rev. 337 (1920).

a will devising all his property in trust for A until he attains the age of thirty, at which time the trust principal is to be distributed to him. T tears up the first will. The second will is invalid because it was not attested with the required formalities. Subject to compliance with the state's proof-of-lost-will procedure, the first will is entitled to probate. It is assumed that T would not have revoked the first will by physical act had he known the second will was invalid.

(2) In 1965 T executes a will devising all his property to A. In 1968 T executes a will devising all his property in trust for A until he attains age thirty, with a principal distribution to him at that time. This second will is validly executed. Its first sentence revokes "all wills heretofore made by me." T does not destroy the first will, but keeps the two wills together in his safe deposit box. In 1971 T again has a change of heart, and decides that he wants all his property to pass outright to A. He destroys the second will on the supposition that the earlier will is thereby reinstated. His supposition is erroneous: Since the earlier will has been expressly revoked by the second will, it cannot be revived without re-execution or republication by a later testamentary writing.[31] The second will is entitled to probate under the doctrine of dependent relative revocation.[32] Since the two wills are substantially similar, it seems clear that T would prefer a distribution under the second will to an intestate distribution.

LA CROIX v. SENECAL

Supreme Court of Errors of Connecticut, 1953

140 Conn. 311, 99 A.2d 115

Brown, Chief Justice. The plaintiff, a niece of the testatrix, who was left nothing under her aunt's will and codicil, brought this action for a declaratory judgment as heir and next of kin. She asked in effect for a decree that one-half of the residuary estate of the testatrix is intestate and that she, as heir, is entitled to that one-half

[31] When T destroys the second will, with its language of revocation of all prior wills, why isn't the first will revived? The English common law courts took the position that with respect to devises of land the prior will was revived. "A will is ambulatory till the death of the testator. If the testator lets it stand till he dies, it is his will; if he does not suffer it to do so, it has no effect, no operation; it is as no will at all, being cancelled before his death. But the former, which was never cancelled, still stands as his will." Goodright d. Glazier v. Glazier, 4 Burr. 2512, 98 Eng. Rep. 317 (K.B. 1770).

The American states differ considerably on when a revoked will is revived. A handful of jurisdictions apply the English "automatic revival" doctrine. The remaining states are about equally divided between two positions, on which there are several variations. (1) Revival of the first will depends on the intention of the testator, which can be shown by surrounding circumstances. This was the view of the English ecclesiastical courts. (2) A revoked will cannot be revived except by its re-execution or republication in a later testamentary writing. See Hoffman, Revocation of Wills and Related Subjects, 31 Brooklyn L. Rev. 220, 246 (1965); Comment, Revival of Revoked Wills, 19 Wyo. L. Rev. 223 (1965); Note, 162 A.L.R. 1072 (1946). Uniform Probate Code §2-509(a) provides that the first will is not revived "unless it is evident from the circumstances of the revocation of the second will or from testator's contemporary or subsequent declarations that he intended the first will to take effect as executed."

[32] Estate of Alburn, 18 Wis. 2d 340, 118 N.W.2d 919 (1963); In re Callahan's Estate, 251 Wis. 247, 29 N.W.2d 352 (1947).

interest. The plaintiff's claim of intestacy is predicated upon the fact that one of the three subscribing witnesses of the codicil was the husband of the defendant Aurea Senecal, to whom one-half of the residue was given by the express terms of both instruments. The court held that the residuary devise and bequest to the defendant under the codicil was void but that there was no resulting intestacy as to that portion of the residue, because the gift thereof under the will is valid. The plaintiff has appealed.

The testatrix, Celestine L. Dupre, died in Putnam on April 19, 1951, leaving as her heir at law and next of kin her niece, the plaintiff. The testatrix left a will dated March 26, 1951, and a codicil thereto dated April 10, 1951. These instruments were admitted to probate on May 22, 1951. Item five of the will reads as follows: "All the rest, residue and remainder of my property of whatsoever the same may consist and wheresoever the same may be situated, both real and personal, I give, devise and bequeath one-half to my nephew, Nelson Lamoth of Taftville, Connecticut, to be his absolutely; the other one-half to Aurea Senecal of 200 Providence Street, Putnam, Connecticut, to be hers absolutely."

The codicil reads as follows: "1. I hereby revoke Item Five of said will and substitute for said Item Five the following: Item Five: All the rest, residue and remainder of property of whatsoever the same may consist and wheresoever the same may be situated, both real and personal, I give, devise and bequeath one-half to my nephew Marcisse Lamoth of Taftville, Connecticut, also known as Nelson Lamoth, to be his absolutely; the other one-half to Aurea Senecal of 200 Providence Street, Putnam, Connecticut to be hers absolutely. 2. I hereby republish and confirm my said will in all respects except as altered by this Codicil."

Aurea Senecal is not related to the testatrix. One of the three subscribing witnesses to the codicil was Adolphe Senecal, who at the time he witnessed the codicil was, and still is, the husband of Aurea Senecal. Section 6952 of the General Statutes, so far as material, provides as follows: "Every devise or bequest given in any will or codicil to a subscribing witness, or to the husband or wife of such subscribing witness, shall be void unless such will or codicil shall be legally attested without the signature of such witness . . . ; but the competency of such witness shall not be affected by any such devise or bequest." As the court pointed out in its memorandum of decision, any bequest to Aurea Senecal in item five of the codicil was void because her husband was a subscribing witness. The question left to be answered, therefore, was whether the devise or bequest to the defendant Aurea under item five of the original will stands. It is to be noted that the only difference between item five of the will and item five of the codicil is the substitution for the words "my nephew, Nelson Lamoth of Taftville, Connecticut," in the former, of the words "my nephew Marcisse Lamoth of Taftville, Connecticut, also known as Nelson Lamoth," in the latter. It is also to be noted that by the second paragraph of the codicil the testatrix confirmed the will "in all respects except as altered by this Codicil."

The defendants' brief suggests that the issue on this appeal is whether the doctrine of dependent relative revocation may be invoked to sustain a gift by will, when such gift has been revoked in a codicil which substantially reaffirmed the gift but was void as to it, under §6952, by reason of the interest of a subscribing witness. The gist of the doctrine is that if a testator cancels or destroys a will with a present intention of making a new one immediately and as a substitute and the new will is not made or, if made, fails of effect for any reason, it will be presumed that the testator preferred the old will to intestacy, and the old one will be admitted to probate in the absence of evidence overcoming the presumption. . . . It is a rule of presumed intention rather than of substantive law; . . . and is applicable in cases of partial as well as total revocation. . . . That it can only apply when there is a clear intent of the testator that the revocation of the old is made conditional upon the validity of the new is well brought out in Sanderson v. Norcross, 242 Mass. 43, 45, 136 N.E. 170, and in Estate of Kaufman, 25 Cal. 2d 854, 858, 155 P.2d 831, where many cases are cited.

The doctrine has long been accepted in Connecticut, notwithstanding the plaintiff's claim that we should adopt the contrary view. In 1898, Justice Simeon E. Baldwin stated in a case involving a question of this nature: "It being [the testator's] manifest intention to revoke the provision in the will only for this purpose so far as the purpose fails of effect, the revocation must fall with it. . . . The rule of construction upon which we proceed is analogous to that governing a revocation which is grounded on a state of facts which proves not to exist. It falls when its foundation falls. Dunham v. Averill, 45 Conn. [61] 62." Security Co. v. Snow, 70 Conn. 288, 293, 39 A. 153, 155.

In a later case involving the principle, we stated: "The case, therefore, is within the reason of the rule that a writing purporting to revoke a will on account of the existence of a certain fact does not revoke it if there be no such fact. Dunham v. Averill, 45 Conn. 61, 80. It is true that the mistake is, at bottom, one of law. [The testatrix] supposed that her unsigned and unattested will would have full effect upon her decease. In law it had no effect. But as respects a question of this nature, it is immaterial whether the mistake under which the act of revocation was done were one of fact or law. The act was nothing unless done with the intent of revocation. If the intent to revoke was, as in this case, clearly dependent on a reliance upon a certain legal consequence attributed to certain circumstances, an error in attributing that effect to them is as effectual a bar to an actual revocation as if it were a pure error of fact. . . ."

So far as the factual situation is concerned, it would be difficult to conceive of a more deserving case for the application of the doctrine of dependent relative revocation than the one before us. There is no room for doubt that the sole purpose of the testatrix in executing the codicil was, by making the very minor change in referring to her nephew, to eliminate any uncertainty as to his identity. Obviously, it was furthest from her intention to make any change in the disposition of her residuary estate. When the will and codicil are considered together, as they must be, to determine the intent of the testatrix, it is clear that her intention to revoke the will was conditioned upon the execution of a codicil which would be effective to continue the same disposition of her residuary estate. Therefore, when it developed that the gift under the codicil to the defendant Aurea was void, the conditional intention of the testatrix to revoke the will was rendered inoperative, and the gift to Aurea under the will continued in effect. The situation is well summed up in this statement by the court in a case on all fours with the one at bar: "When a testator repeats the same dispositive plan in a new will, revocation of the old one by the new is deemed inseparably related to and dependent upon the legal effectiveness of the new." Estate of Kaufman, 25 Cal. 2d 854, 860, 155 P.2d 831, 834. In short, in the words of the court in Matter of Macomber's Will, 274 App. Div. 724, 728, 87 N.Y.S.2d 308, 312, "the facts here fit well within the classic pattern of the rule in its most reliable aspect, and it ought to be applied to the facts of this case."

It only remains to consider the plaintiff's further claim that, even though the doctrine of dependent relative revocation does prevail in Connecticut, it cannot be applied in the present case because of the reason for the invalidity of the gift under the codicil to the defendant Aurea. The claim is that, since the history of §6952 shows that from the beginning its purpose was to prevent the subversion of wills, the doctrine considered above cannot be utilized as a means of defeating the very purpose of this express statutory provision. There very likely could be a case where on the facts there would be force to this argument. However, this cannot be said to be so here. The history of the statute as traced in the plaintiff's brief shows that the subversion of wills which it was designed to prevent was that which results from the scheming activities of persons in a position to utilize the capacity of attesting witnesses to take advantage of testators by overpersuading them to make wills in favor of the scheming persons. There is no intimation of any such improper attempt or achievement in the case before us. As has already been pointed out, no change of beneficiaries or in the amount or nature of any of the gifts under the will was made by the codicil. The sole motivating cause of its execution was an attempt by the testatrix to confirm and make more certain the gift to her nephew which she had already expressly provided for in the will. Under these circumstances, the purpose of §6952 is neither challenged nor thwarted by applying the doctrine of dependent relative revocation in order to realize the obvious testamentary intent of this testatrix. As was well pointed out in a closely analogous case: "The doctrine of dependent relative revocation is basically an application of the rule that a testator's intention governs; it is not a doctrine defeating that intent. It should be applied in this case." Linkins v. Protestant Episcopal Cathedral Foundation, 87 U.S. App. D.C. 351, 187 F.2d 357, 360, 28 A.L.R.2d 521.

Since the defendants expressly stated that no claim is made under their cross appeal in the event that the plaintiff fails to prevail on her appeal, the former calls for no consideration.

There is no error.

In this opinion the other judges concurred.[33]

PROBLEMS

1. Helen Lubbe executed a will on August 15, 1958. The will contained thirty-two bequests and gave the residue to Brantley Burcham, the testatrix' attorney who

[33] Noted 1953 Wash. U.L.Q. 449. — Eds.

drew the will and the 1959 will. The will was attested by Burcham and two disinterested witnesses. On August 24, 1959 Helen Lubbe executed a new will, expressly revoking her prior wills. Twenty-four bequests were identical with those in the 1958 will, eight bequests were omitted, and one new bequest was added. Again Brantley Burcham was named residuary legatee. The 1959 will was witnessed by Burcham, one beneficiary who was left some furniture, and one disinterested witness. The jurisdiction requires two disinterested witnesses and has the Florida purging statute reproduced at page 302. Burcham is not an heir of the testatrix. Is he entitled to share in her estate? Estate of Lubbe, 142 So. 2d 130 (Fla. App. 1962), 95 A.L.R.2d 1246 (1962). See Note, Dependent Relative Revocation, 6 Sydney L. Rev. 394 (1971).

2. Clause 5 of T's typewritten will provides: "I bequeath the sum of $1000 to my nephew, Charles Blake." T crosses out the "$1000" and substitutes therefor "$1500." He then writes his initials and the date in the right-hand margin opposite this entry. After T's death some years later his will is admitted to probate. Blake contends that he is entitled to $1500 or, in the alternative, $1000.

(a) What result in a state that recognizes holographic wills?

(b) What result in a state that does not permit partial revocation by a physical act?

(c) What result in a state that permits partial revocations? Should the doctrine of dependent relative revocation be applied? Carpenter v. Wynn, 252 Ky. 543, 67 S.W.2d 688 (1934).

3. Suppose T crossed out "$1000" and substituted "$500."[34] In a state that permits partial revocations, should the doctrine of dependent relative revocation be applied? Ruel v. Hardy, 90 N.H. 240, 6 A.2d 753 (1939).

4. In his typewritten will, which contains a legacy of $5000 "to my nephew, John Boone," T crosses out the latter phrase and writes in "niece, Nancy Boone." Nancy cannot take because the gift to her is not attested. In a state permitting partial revocation by physical act, should the legacy to John be sustained under the doctrine of dependent relative revocation? In re Houghten's Estate, 310 Mich. 613, 17 N.W.2d 774 (1945); compare Thomas v. Thomas, 76 Minn. 237, 79 N.W. 104 (1899). See Note, 24 A.L.R.2d 514, 556 (1952).

In re ESTATE OF CUNEO

Supreme Court of California, 1963

60 Cal. 2d 196, 384 P.2d 1, 7 A.L.R.3d 1132

PEEK, J.

Multiple appeals are taken from a judgment admitting to probate a 1956 holographic will of Carolina Cuneo, deceased.

When Carolina died in 1958 she left surviving her six children: Julia Cuneo,

[34] If T does not cross out the whole of $1000 but merely cancels the last numeral, only the last numeral has been revoked and the legatee takes $100 where partial revocations are permitted.

Clara Mondani, Sarah Carboni, Louise Varni, Suzanne Dobbert and Andrew Cuneo. Her estate, appraised at $67,698.98, consisted primarily of farm properties, livestock, and cash deposits. Beginning in 1943 she made four successive wills, three of which have been offered for probate. With one exception the testamentary writings are holographic and written in Italian. They provide generally as follows:

(1) A 1943 will, not offered for probate, made specific gifts ($500) to each of her four children except Julia and Clara and to one grandchild, and left the residue to Julia and Clara.

(2) A 1951 will again made specific gifts ($25) to the same persons and provided for the residue to be divided between Julia and Clara in a manner specified. Clara was designated as executrix, and was to live with, care for and manage the affairs of Julia "when Guilia (Julia) comes home from the hospital." It appears that at all times herein mentioned Julia was an incompetent and a patient in a mental hospital.

(3) A 1954 will, prepared by an attorney, revoked "all wills by me heretofore made." A specific bequest of $500 was made to a former daughter-in-law, and the residue was set aside for Julia until her death or her marriage, at which time it was to be distributed equally to all of the deceased's children and the grandchild mentioned in prior wills. Angelo De Paoli, another attorney, was designated as executor.

(4) A 1956 testamentary document, decedent's last, provided as follows:

"October 15, 1956

"I, Carolina Cuneo, add this to my will. Upon my death my daughter, Clara, is to take my place and act in my stead as if it were I. I strongly recommend Guilia to her. She and Clara will be the owners of everything I possess. While they live no one will be able to disturb them.

"I sign myself Carolina Cuneo, nee Carolina Poggi.

"My will is in the possession of De Paoli. After my death Clara will be the manager because Guilia is not good at managing. She is to take my will from De Paoli and pay whatever is to be paid.

"I sign myself Carolina Cuneo."

A second translation of the foregoing document, submitted in evidence, varies the wording in minor respects only.

In 1957 De Paoli, who had possession of the 1954 will, surrendered it to Henry Mondani, Clara's husband, at decedent's request. The will was delivered to decedent who stated that "this is not what I want," and that she intended to burn it. The original will was not found. However a copy thereof was identified and introduced into evidence.

The 1956 instrument, when found with the 1951 will among decedent's valuable papers, contained penciled strike outs of the phrases "my will is in the possession of De Paoli," and "take my will from De Paoli."

Following decedent's death her daughter Sarah first petitioned for letters of administration, alleging that her mother died intestate. The litigation thereafter developed in the following order: Clara filed the 1951 holographic will and petitioned for probate thereof; Andrew filed a contest of the 1951 will; Clara filed the

1956 instrument, alleging it to be a codicil to the 1951 will and petitioned for probate of the two instruments together; Andrew filed a contest of the two instruments; De Paoli petitioned for probate of the 1954 will, alleging the 1956 instrument to be a codicil thereof, and opposing the other petitions; Andrew filed a contest of the 1954 will and alleged codicil.

After trial of the consolidated causes the court found that the 1951 will had been revoked by the general revocation clause of the 1954 will; that the 1954 will was destroyed by decedent with intention to revoke, and was so revoked; that it was the decedent who made modifications to the 1956 instrument, and as modified it was intended by decedent to remain in effect; that it was testamentary in character and was legally sufficient to stand by itself. The court concluded and ordered that the 1956 instrument alone be admitted to probate and that Clara be appointed administratrix with will annexed.

Turning first to Andrew's appeal it is his contention that since the 1956 instrument was intended only as a codicil, and since "[t]he revocation of a will revokes all its codicils" (Prob. Code, §79), it was therefore revoked by reason of the destruction of the 1954 will, and hence his mother died intestate.

De Paoli, who also appeals, contends that the 1956 instrument was originally intended as a codicil to the 1954 will; that the 1954 will was later destroyed and revoked only under the mistaken belief that the 1956 instrument could be given effect as a testatmentary instrument standing alone. He argues further that the 1956 instrument could not, by itself, be given the effect intended by the testatrix because the pretermitted heir statute (Prob. Code, §90) requires that the estate be distributed in part to those children not mentioned in the 1956 instrument. It is his conclusion that the doctrine of dependent relative revocation requires the revival of the 1954 will, and it should be probated as modified by the 1956 codicil.

Finally there is the appeal by Clara Mondani who also relies on the doctrine of dependent relative revocation. It is her contention that the 1951 will, revoked by the 1954 will, was revived by operation of the doctrine when the 1954 will was revoked and the decedent made modifications to the 1956 codicil.

It is apparent that all contentions raised herein relate, in one manner or another, to the propriety of the trial court's conclusion that the 1956 instrument became a self-contained will upon modifications thereto and the revocation of the 1954 will.

We cannot disregard the trial court's finding that the decedent intended the republished codicil to be her sole testamentary instrument. The modifications of the original instrument evidence a desire to divorce it from the 1954 will, and her revocation of the latter must be deemed in aid of her intention that the 1956 instrument stand alone. Although there is no direct evidence that the decedent destroyed her 1954 will, other substantial evidence supports such a conclusion. Similarly, there is no direct evidence as to who made the changes in the 1956 instrument, but where changes and alterations are made in a holographic will in the possession of the testatrix, the inference is that they were made by her. (Estate of Stickney, 101 Cal. App. 2d 572, 575, 225 P.2d 649.) Cancellations, modifications and interlineations made in a testator's hand in a holographic will do not render it invalid. Rather, they become a part thereof. (Estate of Finkler, 3 Cal. 2d 584, 600, 46 P.2d 149.)

Manifestly, the document is testamentary in character, and while it may have lost something in its translation and perhaps is inexpertly drawn, nevertheless it appears to be sufficiently clear on its face as to decedent's intentions to render them ascertainable and thus avoid intestacy. . . .

The contention herein urged by Andrew that the 1956 instrument must fall under section 79 of the Probate Code because, as a codicil, the will to which it related was revoked, is not tenable. As a codicil the statute would have required its revocation with that of the will heretofore determined to have been revoked on substantial evidence. But merely because it was intended as a codicil when first published does not compel its continuance as such. A document, originally a codicil, which is a complete testamentary instrument in all respects is not dependent upon the continued existence of its basic will to retain its testamentary character. (Estate of Benson, 62 Cal. App. 2d 866, 870, 145 P.2d 668.) Where the document satisfies the legal requirements of a testamentary instrument the discernible intent of the testator as to which instrument or instruments constitute the final testamentary expression must govern. (Estate of Danford, 196 Cal. 339, 342, 238 P. 76; Prob. Code, §101.) For reasons heretofore set out we are persuaded that the trial court properly concluded that the decedent intended her 1956 instrument to continue in effect as her final testamentary expression after revocation of the 1954 will. . . .

As previously noted De Paoli and Clara Mondani urge divergent views as to the effect of the application of the doctrine of dependent relative revocation when applied to the facts of the present case. "Under the doctrine . . . an earlier will, revoked only to give effect to a later one on the supposition that the later one will become effective, remains in effect to the extent that the latter proves ineffective. [Citations.] The doctrine is designed to carry out the probable intention of the testator when there is no reason to suppose that he intended to revoke his earlier will if the later will became inoperative. [Citations.]" (Estate of Kaufman, 25 Cal. 2d 854, 858, 859, 155 P.2d 831, 833.)

The doctrine thus requires that, in revoking a prior and executing a subsequent will, it be specifically intended that certain provisions in the former testament have a continuing effect, either through similar provisions in the new will or because it is intended to make only conditional changes which subsequently do not become effective for the reason that the conditions on which predicated fail to come into being. It is De Paoli's contention herein that the 1954 will was thus only conditionally revoked by the testatrix, the condition being that the 1956 instrument be legally sufficient to accomplish the testatrix's obvious purpose to provide for Clara and Julia to the full extent of the decedent's estate. This cannot be accomplished, it is claimed, because the pretermitted heir statute requires that each heir not mentioned in the 1956 instrument be distributed the share to which he would be entitled under the laws of succession.

In Estate of Kaufman, supra, 25 Cal. 2d 854, 155 P.2d 831, a testator wished to make minor changes not going to the dispositive provisions of the will, and executed a second will for this reason. His death occurred within 30 days thereafter, invalidating a substantial gift to a church under the applicable mortmain statute. The court concluded, 25 Cal. 2d at page 860, 155 P.2d at page 834: "The record makes clear the intention of the testator. He did not change his testamentary purpose but only minor details in its execution. . . . Since the second will was virtually identical with the first in the disposition of the testator's estate, it is clear that the first will was revoked only because the second duplicated its purpose and that the testator would have preferred the first will to intestacy as to a substantial part of his estate. Where a testator repeats the same dispositive plan in a new will, revocation of the old one by the new is deemed inseparably related to and dependent upon the legal effectiveness of the new." In that case the first will was ordered admitted to probate together with the second.

It is argued that in the instant case the testatrix's intention that the first will be admitted to probate in the event of the insufficiency of the second is not as clear. The 1956 instrument became effective as a self-contained will only at the time the testatrix republished it as a will, at which time or prior thereto the 1954 will must be deemed to have been revoked. The changes in dispositive provisions between the 1954 will and the republication of the 1956 instrument were to eliminate a $500 gift to a former daughter-in-law; provide at least life estates, if not gifts in fee, for Clara and Julia instead of an estate for Julia alone for her life or until she married; and eliminate provisions for remaindermen interests, whereas originally the six children and a grandchild were specifically named to share therein. A change in the person designated to administer the estate was also made and a clause disinheriting anyone who contested the will was eliminated.

The foregoing are, manifestly, substantial changes, and standing alone cannot be said to evidence an intention on the part of the testatrix that the 1954 will was to continue in effect in the event the 1956 instrument could not, as a self-contained will, be effective in accomplishing her purpose. It is significant, too, that upon the delivery of the 1954 will to her from De Paoli she stated that it was not what she wanted, and that she intended to burn it.

Consistent with the foregoing there are nevertheless, good and substantial grounds for the application of the doctrine of dependent relative revocation, if we recognize that it is not the 1954 will which is sought to be revived, but instead the 1954 will *as modified by the 1956 codicil*. Prior to her revocation of the 1954 will, and republication of the 1956 codicil as a will, the testatrix had effectively modified the 1954 will with the 1956 instrument, conceded by all parties to then be a codicil. Although such codicil did not formally modify specific provisions of the will, those provisions of the will were nevertheless effectively modified which were inconsistent with the codicil. (Estate of Salmonski, 38 Cal. 2d 199, 209, 238 P.2d 966.) This included the whole of the dispositive plan of the testatrix and the substitution of Clara to "manage" or administer the estate in the place of De Paoli.

In 1957 then, when the testatrix revoked the will, she substituted in its place a testamentary document which made identical provisions for disposition of the estate. It is not significant that the testatrix evidently misunderstood the effect of the 1956 codicil on her will and was thus under an impression that the dispositive provisions of the will continued to be effective. Only such a misunderstanding can account for her statement that the 1954 will was not what she wanted prior to her substitution in its place of the republished 1956 instrument, by which she sought to make the identical disposition as provided in the 1954 will as modified. Thus the will, as modified by the codicil, *was* what she wanted regardless of whether she so understood it to have that effect. Any conclusions as to her intentions when she revoked the 1954 will and republished the 1956 codicil as a will must be considered in the light of her knowledge at that time. (Estate of Kaufman, supra, 25 Cal. 2d 854, 861, 155 P.2d 831.)

The situation herein is not distinguishable in principle from that in the Kaufman case. The testatrix, in 1957, did not change her dispositive plan, but only minor details in its execution. As the 1956 instrument, republished as a will, was virtually identical with the 1954 will as modified, it is clear that the latter was revoked only because the testatrix thought that, by the republished instrument, she could accomplish what the 1954 will as modified did in fact accomplish. It must be deemed incontrovertible that the testatrix would have preferred the 1954 will, as modified, to intestacy as to a substantial portion of her estate. "When a testator repeats the same dispositive plan in a new will, revocation of the old one by the new is deemed inseparably related to and dependent upon the legal effectiveness of the new. [Citations.]" (Estate of Kaufman, supra, 25 Cal. 2d 854, 860, 155 P.2d 831, 834.)

It affirmatively appears that the 1956 instrument as republished by the testatrix, standing alone, will fail to accomplish her intended purposes. Those purposes are discernible over a period of years commencing in 1943. Since that time the testatrix has evidenced a continuous, consistent testamentary plan wherein she provided the bulk of her estate for Julia, her incompetent daughter, and Clara who was to care for Julia. This plan was reasserted when the testatrix published the 1956 codicil to the will, and again when she republished the codicil as a will in 1957. However, the 1956 instrument, standing alone, fails to mention four of the decedent's six issue. Section 90 of the Probate Code imposes intestacy upon a testatrix as to any child who is not provided for by the testator "in his will" unless it "appears from the will" that the omission was intentional. Extrinsic evidence is not admissible to establish the intent to omit. (Estate of Trickett, 197 Cal. 20, 239 P. 406.) On the other hand, if the 1954 will as modified is revived and admitted to probate together with the 1956 instrument as republished, the testatrix's intentions with respect to all her issue expressly appear within the testamentary documents, and such children do not achieve the status of pretermitted heirs. (Payne v. Payne, 18 Cal. 292.)

It is also urged herein that the 1951 will was revived by application of the doctrine of dependent relative revocation or otherwise, and that it should be admitted to probate together with the 1956 "codicil" thereto. The 1951 will was revoked by the 1954 will, and there is no substantial evidence which requires a conclusion that at such time the revocation was conditionally dependent upon the sufficiency of the 1954 will. The further facts that decedent kept the 1951 will with her other valuable papers and that after the strike outs in the 1956 instrument there still remained an implication that the document was a codicil, do not require that the trial court should have found, as a matter of law, an intent to republish the 1951 will through the alleged codicil thereto. In any event the admission of the 1951 will to probate would serve no purpose, in view of the conclusion herein that the later documents are to be admitted.

There remains unresolved at this time the question whether the dispositive provisions of the 1956 instrument conferred upon Julia and Clara life estates or full fee interests. The trial court made no findings thereon, and properly so. "When there is presented for probate one or more instruments claimed to constitute a will, the only question legitimately before the court is whether or not the propounded instrument or instruments constitute a will; and in determining that question the court ordinarily has nothing to do with the construction of the will, resolving inconsistencies in the disposition of property or interpreting the testamentary provisions." (Estate of Salmonski, supra, 38 Cal. 2d 199, 207, 238 P.2d 966, 971.)

The judgment is reversed with directions to admit the 1954 will to probate with the 1956 codicil as republished in 1957.

Gibson, Ch. J., and Traynor, Schauer, McComb, Peters, and Tobriner, JJ., concur.

NOTES AND PROBLEMS

1. In Estate of Cuneo the court did not mention California Probate Code §350, which provides: "No will shall be proven as a lost or destroyed will unless proved to have been in existence at the time of the death of the testator, or shown to have been destroyed by public calamity, or destroyed fraudulently in the lifetime of the testator, without his knowledge; nor unless its provisions are clearly and distinctly proved by at least two credible witnesses." On the facts of Estate of Cuneo there was no fraudulent destruction of the 1954 will, as that term is interpreted in California. In re Estate of Strickman, 247 Cal. App. 2d 469, 55 Cal. Rptr. 606 (1966). If the 1954 will could not be admitted to probate, could the 1951 will be admitted on the theory that it was republished by the codicil in 1957? If not, should the attorney for the losing parties in Estate of Cuneo be liable for negligence in not mentioning the above statute to the court?

For further litigation as to whether Clara and Julia took life estates or a fee simple, see Estate of Cuneo, 1 Cal. App. 3d 1008, 82 Cal. Rptr. 261 (1969).

2. When there has been a mistake in the inducement causing *execution* of a will, courts ordinarily have denied relief unless the will itself shows both the testator's mistaken belief and what the testator would have done had the mistake not occurred. Thus Carpenter v. Tinney, 420 S.W.2d 241 (Tex. Civ. App. 1967): T's will made token bequests to two of her children and devised the residue of her estate to her other two children. Testimony was offered which tended to show that T believed her husband had a will devising all his estate to the two children, that

her will was motivated by a desire to equalize distribution of their property among the four children, and that had T not been mistaken as to the terms of her husband's will (he died intestate), she would have devised her estate to all four children in equal shares. The trial court's refusal to submit the issue of mistaken inducement to the jury was sustained on appeal.

Why, then, have the courts been quite liberal in admitting parol evidence and giving relief where there has been a mistake in the inducement causing *revocation* of a will? Professor Henderson gives this answer: "The first important difference stems from the availability in most jurisdictions of revocation by physical act, a phenomenon without counterpart in the execution of testamentary intent. Under relevant provisions in the Statute of Wills, revocation may be accomplished by the testator's destruction or defacement of the instrument with intent to revoke. Clearly, it would be impossible to satisfy a requirement that evidence of mistake appear on the face of the instrument, since no instrument of revocation exists upon which such evidence might appear. Confronted with allegations in appropriate cases that such physical act revocations were the product of mistake in the inducement on the part of the testator, the courts have taken the position that because such acts are by their nature informal and ambiguous, extrinsic evidence should be admissible to show not only the required intent to revoke but also the source in mistake of such intent. As for the element of 'what the testator would have done,' because most of these fact patterns involve intestacy as the alternative to disposition by the will whose revocation is in question, the general presumption against intestacy operates to justify granting relief in doubtful cases. . . . In cases where the presumption against intestacy is unavailable, those courts willing to apply the dependent relative revocation doctrine . . . appear to be willing to make inquiry into the circumstances surrounding the revocation in order to determine whether the granting of relief conforms to what the testator would have intended in the absence of mistake in the inducement.

"It remains to consider judicial reaction to the question of granting relief from the effects of mistake where the revocation is accomplished formally by subsequent instrument. Here, at least, the requirement that both the mistaken belief and what the testator would have done must appear on the face of the instrument might more reasonably be imposed, for here there is an instrument of revocation upon whose face such indications might appear. . . . Most often, subsequent instrument revocation of prior dispositions is accompanied by alternative provisions disposing of the property in question. In many, if not all, such cases in which the testator may be said to have suffered a mistake in the inducement causing revocation, the erroneous belief will concern the validity of the substitutive dispositions attempted in the revoking instrument itself. In such cases the prior will is expressly revoked, accompanied by an alternative disposition which fails because of some substantive limitation upon the power of testation. Relief is at least theoretically supportable under these circumstances, for . . . the mistake in the inducement — i.e., the testator's belief concerning the validity of the alternative disposition — certainly appears impliedly on the face of the instrument in question; and the requirement with respect to what testator would have done is once again satisfied by the presumption that the testator would have preferred the prior will over intestacy." Henderson, Mistake and Fraud in Wills — Part I: A Comparative Analysis of Existing Law, 47 B.U.L. Rev. 303, 332-335 (1967).

3. T's will provides legacies for the grandchildren of his brother, John. T later executes a codicil as follows: "I revoke the legacies to the grandchildren of my brother, John, they being all dead." In fact, two of the grandchildren are still living, and both survive T. Do they get their legacies? Campbell v. French, 3 Ves. Jr. 321, 30 Eng. Rep. 1033 (Ch. 1797).

4. T's will provides legacies for the grandchildren of his brother, John. He later executes a codicil as follows: "I revoke the legacies to the grandchildren of my brother, John." After T's death John testifies that on the day the codicil was executed he told T that all his grandchildren were dead, and T replied, "in that case I may as well revoke the legacies to them." In fact, two of the grandchildren were still living, and both survive T. Do they get their legacies? In re Salmonski's Estate, 228 P.2d 860, aff'd, 38 Cal. 2d 199, 238 P.2d 966 (1951).

5. T's will provides: "I devise Blackacre to A and Whiteacre to B." At his death T owned Blackacre, worth $55,000. T at no time owned Whiteacre. Whiteacre, worth $25,000, has at all times been owned by A. What are the rights of A and B? Atkinson, Wills §138 (2d ed. 1953); 5 Page, Wills §§47.1, 47.2 (Bowe-Parker rev. 1960).

4. *Revocation by Operation of Law: Change in Family Circumstances*

LUFF v. LUFF
United States Court of Appeals, D.C. Circuit, 1966
359 F.2d 235

FAHY, Circuit Judge: The question is whether the last will and testament of Morris F. Luff, deceased, of whom appellant, Willard J. Luff, is a surviving brother and one of several heirs at law, was impliedly revoked. The will, dated April 7, 1953, provided that testator's entire estate should go to Ruth K. Luff, appellee, who then was his wife. Thereafter they separated. Some five years after the separation she sued for and obtained an absolute divorce upon the ground of five years consecutive separation without cohabitation. A property settlement agreement entered into between the parties during the pendency of the divorce proceeding was made a part of the decree of divorce.[35] There was no child, and neither remarried.

[35] This agreement set forth in some detail a division of particular items of personal property and provided that from the monies in the hands of the wife she would pay the husband the sum of $7,000 and give him the deed to a cooperative apartment. The agreement also provided that the wife "shall not claim any interest as Wife, widow, heir, next of kin or successor" in the property of the husband and that she would execute any papers necessary or convenient to enable him, his heirs, executors, administrators or assigns "to hold or dispose of his property, free and clear of all rights of hers which she might have had except for this covenant."

The will was found in testator's apartment after his death. At his request it had been sent to him by his former wife after their divorce. She offered the will for probate. Appellant filed a caveat, and the issue as to the validity of the will came on for trial before judge and jury. Appellant relied entirely upon the divorce and property settlement as impliedly revoking the will. Appellee introduced considerable testimony tending to show that decedent should not be held to have intended to revoke the will. At the close of all the evidence the motion of appellee for a directed verdict in her favor was granted, the will thus being given effect. We reverse, being of opinion that the divorce with property settlement revoked the will by implication of law. In so holding we follow the majority rule, which we think has the support of better reasoning.

We discuss first whether our Code provisions respecting revocation . . . allow revocation implied in law. At one time these provisions were thought not to do so [because there was no express authorization of revocation by implication]. See McGowan v. Elroy, 28 App. D.C. 188, and Morris v. Foster, 51 App. D.C. 238, 278 F. 321, cert. denied, 259 U.S. 582, 42 S. Ct. 586, 66 L. Ed. 1074. However, in Pascucci v. Alsop, 79 U.S. App. D.C. 354, 147 F.2d 880, decided in 1945 with an opinion by Chief Justice Groner, joined by Associate Justices Justin Miller and Edgerton, this court reconsidered and departed from Morris v. Foster. Following the common law the court held that where an unmarried testator, without child by a former marriage, executed a will which contained no provision for any child of a subsequent marriage, and remarried, followed by birth of a child, the will was impliedly revoked. The basis for the doctrine thus approved is that such change in the testator's condition or circumstances gives rise to a legal presumption of an intention inconsistent with a previously executed will.

Appellee contends, however, that the common law did not extend to an implied revocation by reason of divorce with a property settlement; and we find no case in the early common law, when divorce was rare, contrary to this contention. Moreover, courts have not infrequently stated that the principal grounds for implied revocation at common law were a subsequent marriage of a woman or subsequent marriage of a man with birth of a child. But this does not end our inquiry.

The doctrine of implied revocation due to change of condition or circumstances came to be recognized in a number of states by statute. Many state statutes, after specifying as does our Code the usual means of revoking a will, . . . go on to provide, "but nothing in this section will prevent the revocation implied by law from subsequent changes in the condition or circumstances of the testator." While this language did not appear in our Code when this case arose,[36] nevertheless, as we have seen, this court in Pascucci v. Alsop read the common law doctrine into our

[36] However, on January 1, 1966, Pub. L. No. 183, 89th Cong., 1st Sess. (Sept. 14, 1965) took effect and Title 18, D.C. Code, §109, (replacing the former §19-103 and other provisions), does now explicitly include the words authorizing revocation "by implication of law." S. Rep. No. 612, 89th Cong., 1st Sess. 10-11 (1965); H.R. Rep. No. 235, 89th Cong., 1st Sess. 8-9 (1965).

decisional law. It is urged, however, that since our Code did not contain explicit statutory authorization of revocation by implication the circumstances under which this occurred in this jurisdiction must be limited to those found in early common law decisions. We do not agree. Once the doctrine was accepted, as in Pascucci v. Alsop, we think it should not be limited to the particular circumstances which gave rise to it, if at this period of our history changes in marital relations in other respects, here divorce and property settlement, which were rarely known at the time of the early cases, bring the situation within the rationale of the doctrine. Accord, Rankin v. McDearmon, 38 Tenn. App. 160, 270 S.W.2d 660. . . .

The trend of statutory law in other jurisdictions is to include changes other than such as were present in Pascucci, including marriage alone and divorce alone. And the weight of decisional law is now to the effect that when a married man makes provision in his will for his wife, and is thereafter divorced, with a property settlement between them, such change in the condition and circumstances of the parties impliedly revokes the previously executed will in favor of the wife. The cases are numerous. While some are of an early period in our history, the weight of authority persists to the present time. Lansing v. Haynes, 95 Mich. 16, 54 N.W. 699; Wirth v. Wirth, 149 Mich. 687, 113 N.W. 306; In re Hall's Estate, 106 Minn. 502, 119 N.W. 219, 20 L.R.A., N.S., 1073; In re Battis, 143 Wis. 234, 126 N.W. 9; In re Martin's Estate, 109 Neb. 289, 190 N.W. 872; Younker v. Johnson, 160 Ohio St. 409, 116 N.E.2d 715; Caswell v. Kent, 158 Me. 493, 186 A.2d 581. In Caswell v. Kent, decided in 1962, it is stated:

> The majority rule clearly rests on the assumption based upon common knowledge and experience that it is so rare and so unusual for a testator under these circumstances [divorce and property settlement] to desire or intend that his divorced spouse should benefit further under his will, that it is not improper or unreasonable to require that such a testator make that extraordinary desire and intention manifest by a formal republication of his will or by the execution of a new will.

Caswell v. Kent, supra at 582-583. . . .

Respectable authority to the contrary is not lacking. Hertrais v. Moore, 325 Mass. 57, 88 N.E.2d 909; and see Baacke v. Baacke, 50 Neb. 18, 69 N.W. 303; Mosely v. Mosely, 217 Ark. 536, 231 S.W.2d 99, 18 A.L.R.2d 695; Codner v. Caldwell, 156 Ohio St. 197, 101 N.E.2d 901. The reasoning of the contrary rule is stated as follows by the Massachusetts court in Hertrais v. Moore, 88 N.E.2d at 912:

> It would be a serious matter to invalidate a will because of a supposed change in intention on the part of a testator not given formal expression by him. Our conclusion avoids the difficulties faced in those jurisdictions where the statutes permit the adoption of a contrary view, where the revocation is not presumptive but absolute, and evidence, not amounting to a republication, cannot be received of a testator's actual intent to continue his will in force, and where the prevailing standard seems to be what a reasonable testator would be deemed to have intended. [citations omitted] If the changes relied upon by the respondents were held

> to achieve a revocation implied in law, other changes can be imagined which with equal plausibility might be urged to have similar effect. Persons who have drawn wills or who are to draw wills are not now to be exposed to the risk that, in the present circumstances and perhaps others, the courts might decree revocation notwithstanding that such persons do not avail themselves of the easy means afforded by statute for accomplishing revocation by their own intentional acts.

The commentators recognize the division of authority,[37] but the majority support the position we now take. . . .

The doctrine of implied revocation is so ancient and widespread that the question simply comes down to the nature of the changed condition or circumstances which will bring it into operation. This court in Pascucci applied it to a subsequent marriage and birth of a child. We apply it to a subsequent divorce coupled with a property settlement, because that also creates such a change both in status and responsibility as to raise the presumption of change in intention which lies at the basis of the doctrine. A will in favor of a wife is a means by which a husband makes provision for her as wife. When there is a divorce and a formally agreed property settlement, as here, both the wifely status and the testamentary provision are replaced by such changed condition and circumstances that the law may well imply an intention no longer to give effect to the provision for the wife contained in the will.[38]

The intention to revoke is imputed and conclusive. It may not be overcome by evidence adduced subsequent to the death of the testator and then relied upon as indicative of an intention that the will should be effective. Inquiry into the state of mind of the testator is confined to that imputed to him by the divorce and property settlement. Lansing v. Haynes, supra; Wirth v. Wirth, supra; In re Battis, supra; In re Martin's Estate, supra; Caswell v. Kent, supra. Contra, Card v. Alexander, 48 Conn. 492; In re Jones' Estate, 211 Pa. 364, 60 A. 915, 69 L.R.A. 940; In re Arnold's Estate, 60 Nev. 376, 110 P.2d 204.

> At common law certain changes in the condition and circumstances of the testator worked a revocation by implication, and it was formerly held that this was prima facie only, and open to rebuttal by proof that the testator intended his will to remain, notwithstanding the change in his circumstances. The rule, however, by all modern authorities, is that the presumption of law arising from the changed conditions is conclusive, and no evidence is admissible to rebut it. . . .

[37] 2 Page, Wills §21.101 (Bowe-Parker Revision 1960); Atkinson, Wills §85, at 431 (2d ed. 1953); Annot., 18 A.L.R.2d 697, 705-710 (1951); Thompson, Wills §176 (3d ed. 1947); Mersch, "Implied Revocation of Wills Revised in the District of Columbia," 33 Geo. L.J. 182 (1945); Durfee, "Revocation of Wills by Subsequent Change in the Conditions or Circumstances of the Testator," 40 Mich. L. Rev. 406, 412-413 (1942); Note, 52 Harv. L. Rev. 332 (1938); Evans, "Testamentary Revocation by Divorce," 24 Ky. L.J. 1 (1935); Graunke and Beuscher, "The Doctrine of Implied Revocation of Wills by Reason of Change in Domestic Relations of the Testator," 5 Wis. L. Rev. 387 (1930).

[38] Divorce itself is not enough. See text and cases referred to in 2 Page, op. cit. supra note [37], at 521-522.

In re Hall's Estate, 106 Minn. 502, 119 N.W. 219, 220. This is the sounder rule, illustrated by the present case. There was evidence of strained relations between testator and appellant, one of his heirs. It was also urged that when at the divorced husband's request his former wife sent the will to him he kept it in a bureau drawer in his apartment where it was found after his death, and that this indicated an intention not to revoke it. Testator is not available to give his version of either of these matters. He has a sister and other brothers besides appellant; and he may have asked his former wife to send the will to him so that it would no longer be in her control. He may have retained it undestroyed as a memento of happier days, or because of indecision. It is safer to rely upon the divorce and carefully composed adjustment of property between the parties, by which the former husband was relieved of further legal obligation to his former wife with respect to his property. While he remained of course free to make additional provision for her if he desired to do so the law should require this to be done anew in a manner provided by statute for valid testamentary disposition.

Reversed and remanded for further proceedings not inconsistent with this opinion.

Leventhal, Circuit Judge, dissents.[39]

There is a clear trend toward statutory recognition of divorce as grounds for partial revocation by operation of law. Only three states had such legislation in 1942. By 1960 the number of states had grown to fourteen, and by 1971 to twenty-four. See Rees, American Wills Statutes: II, 46 Va. L. Rev. 856, 885 (1960); Comment, The Effect of Divorce on Wills, 40 S. Cal. L. Rev. 708 (1967). In another eight states the courts have found an implied revocation from this change in circumstances. In none of these states is the will revoked in its entirety. Only the dispositive and administrative provisions in favor of the ex-spouse are affected; the rest of the will stands. Some of the statutes specify how the will is now to be read: "Property prevented from passing to a former spouse because of revocation by divorce or annulment passes as if the former spouse failed to survive the decedent, and other provisions conferring some power or office on the former spouse are interpreted as if the spouse failed to survive the decedent." Uniform Probate Code §2-508 (1969). In the other states this question is left for the courts to resolve.

PROBLEMS

1. In 1964 T executes a will that devises his entire estate "to my wife, Madeline Cooper, if she survives me; if the said Madeline Cooper does not survive me, to my sister, Alice Jones." In 1967 T is divorced by Madeline. In 1972 T dies survived by Madeline, Alice Jones, and several other collateral relatives. The state's statute provides: "If the testator is divorced after making a will, all provisions in favor of the testator's spouse so divorced shall be null and void and of no effect." Tex. Prob.

[39] Noted 16 Am. U.L. Rev. 351; 12 N.Y.L.F. 158; 69 W. Va. L. Rev. 108. — Eds.

Code. §69 (1956). The collateral relatives contend that Madeline cannot take because of the statute, and that Alice cannot take because the condition to her taking (that Madeline predecease the testator) was not met. Therefore, T died intestate. What result? First Church of Christ, Scientist v. Watson, 286 Ala. 270, 239 So. 2d 194 (1970).

2. In 1965 T takes out a $25,000 life insurance policy that names his wife W as primary beneficiary "if she survives me." In 1968 W divorces T. In 1971 T dies; he is survived by W. The state has a statute providing for revocation of wills by subsequent divorce, but it has no statute governing the disposition of life insurance proceeds in this situation. Is W entitled to the $25,000? Rountree v. Frazee, 282 Ala. 142, 209 So. 2d 424 (1970); Gerhard v. Travelers Insurance Co., 107 N.J. Super, 414, 258 A.2d 724 (1969); compare Starbuck v. City Bank & Trust Co., 16 Mich. App. 152, 167 N.W.2d 601 (1968), rev'd, 384 Mich. 295, 181 N.W.2d 904 (1970), construing Mich. Stat. Ann. §552.101 (1967).

3. O, a bachelor, names his mother as beneficiary of his life insurance policy. Subsequently O marries and his wife bears a child. O then dies, leaving his insurance policy as his principal asset. Should the doctrine of implied revocation be applied to life insurance policies?

About half the states have statutes revoking a will if the testator subsequently marries. Under the California and Nevada statutes the will is revoked only "as to the spouse," and the rest of the will stands. See Heyer v. Flaig, page 21, supra. In the other states the will is revoked in its entirety. Rees, American Wills Statutes: II, 46 Va. L. Rev. 856, 882 (1960). In states not having such a statute, most courts hold that marriage, by itself, does not affect a previously executed will. However, a number of jurisdictions apply the common law rule that marriage followed by the birth of issue revokes a will. This was the decision in Pascucci v. Alsop, 147 F.2d 880 (D.C. Cir. 1945), discussed in the Luff opinion.

In states where marriage alone does not revoke a will, the newly acquired spouse may nonetheless obtain an interest in the testator's estate although not mentioned in the will. All but two common law states give the surviving spouse an election to take a "forced share" of the decedent's estate. See page 461, infra.

Finally, a number of states have pretermitted child statutes giving a child not mentioned in his parent's will his intestate share in the parent's estate. See page 557, infra. The effect of such a statute is to produce a partial revocation of the parent's will.

SECTION C. Components of a Will

In the first section of this chapter we considered the formalities with which a will must be executed. We saw that if a state's wills statute is not complied with in all its particulars, a testamentary instrument is not entitled to probate, no matter how clearly it reflects the testator's intention that it be his will. Yet despite these formal requirements of transfer, it is possible for documents and acts not executed with testamentary formalities to have the effect of determining the takers of a testator's assets. In this section we are concerned with two doctrines that can have this effect. These are (a) the doctrine of incorporation by reference and (b) the doctrine of facts of independent significance.[40] But before we consider these doctrines, we must examine two others that are sometimes confused with them.

1. *Integration of Wills*

Wills are often written on more than one sheet of paper. Under the doctrine of integration all sheets of paper present at the time of execution are integrated into one will where testator so intends. Typically there is no problem, for the pages of the will are physically connected by a staple or, failing this, there is a sufficient connection of language carrying over from page to page to show an internal coherence of the provisions. The litigated cases involving integration arise when, for example, the pages are not physically connected and there is no internal coherence, or there is evidence that a staple has been removed and page three is typed with elite type while the rest of the will is in pica.

In re ESTATE OF BEALE
Supreme Court of Wisconsin, 1962
15 Wis. 2d 546, 113 N.W.2d 380

The judgment admitted to probate the will of Howard Kennedy Beale dated June 22, 1959. The guardian ad litem of the youngest son, Thomas Beale, has appealed.

Howard Beale, about sixty years of age, and a resident of Shorewood Hills, Dane County, Wisconsin, died on December 27, 1959, leaving an estate inventoried at approximately one and one-quarter million dollars. His survivors include:

(1) Georgia Robison Beale, his widow, executrix of Beale's estate and a respondent in this case.

(2) Howard Kennedy Beale, Jr., age 16, his son, and a respondent in this case.

(3) Henry Barton Beale, age 15, his son, and a respondent in this case; and

(4) Thomas Wight Beale, age 10, his son, and appellant in this case.

During his lifetime Beale executed two documents, each of which is presented as his last will. On November 16, 1954, Beale and his wife executed similar wills drafted by an attorney. A short codicil was executed to this document on July 26, 1958. Under these (hereinafter called the "1954" will) all of Beale's children were treated equally.

[40] In a later chapter we will consider the power of appointment, a device whereby another person can be given the power to direct the distribution of testator's assets by a nontestamentary writing. See page 850, infra.

A petition for probate of the 1954 will was filed on April 29, 1960, on behalf of Thomas Wight Beale, the appellant. No objections to this will have been filed.

Beale also left a document of 14 typewritten pages not fastened together. These, too, are presented as his last will. The final page, bearing the signatures of the testator and the witnesses is dated June 22, 1959. A petition for probate of this, hereinafter called the "1959" will, was filed April 29, 1960, on behalf of Howard Kennedy Beale, Jr. and Henry Barton Beale, respondents herein. By this one the practical effect is to disinherit Thomas unless the widow makes provision for him from her share.

Objections to the 1959 will were filed June 10, 1960, on behalf of Thomas Wight Beale.

The 1959 will was executed in the following manner:

Beale, a history professor at the University of Wisconsin, planning to take a trip to Russia, dictated the document on either June 16 or June 17, 1959, to his part-time secretary, Mrs. Jessica Burleigh. This dictation took place in the Rathskeller of the Wisconsin Union late in the evening.

Mrs. Burleigh typed the will, 14 pages in all, with three complete carbon copies, and gave them, original and copies, to Beale on June 20, 1959, in his Bascom Hall office. Beale then left for New York with his two eldest sons on his way to Moscow.

On June 21, 1959, Beale attended a party in New York given in his honor at the apartment of a friend who was a history professor at Columbia University. During the festivities he asked three of his friends, all professors at various eastern colleges, one being his host, to witness his will. The four people went into an adjoining room where Beale placed some papers in a "pile" on the table, declaring this was his will. Two of the witnesses testified that they saw Beale sign the last page of the will, while the third remembered only that Beale's signature was on the document when the witness signed. All three testified that they signed the document at the usual attestation clause in the presence of the testator, in the presence of each other and at the testator's request. None of the witnesses were able to identify at the trial any of the pages except the page they had signed. Beale then picked up all the papers and replaced them in his briefcase.

Although the will is dated June 22nd it is undisputed that it was executed June 21st. By letter dated June 21, 1959, Beale sent Mrs. Burleigh pages 12 and 13 of the will, asking her to make certain changes and corrections. The only change affecting the meaning was the substitution of "my friend, Alexander H. McLeod" for "wife, Georgia Robison Beale" as co-executor. The others were corrections of grammar and punctuation. Mrs. Burleigh made the corrections on the original and sent the pages to Beale in Moscow. The envelope inclosing the letter to her and the two will pages has not been found and there is no positive proof of when or where it was mailed. At different times Mrs. Burleigh testified it was mailed to her from New York and at another she testified that she received the two pages in an envelope from Beale in London.

A sealed envelope, postmarked September 7, 1959, from London, was later found among Beale's possessions at his death. The envelope was self-addressed to Beale and contained pages 12 and 13 of a copy of the 1959 will. These pages, along with all other pages of the 1959 will, contained the initials "H.K.B." in the left hand margin.

After returning from Russia, Beale asked Mrs. Burleigh to re-type the entire two pages but she testified that she did not do this until after Beale's death and then did it at the later request of Beale's son, Henry. These pages also had the initials "H.K.B." on them.

After Beale's death all the will pages except page 1 were found in his office at the Wisconsin Library. The pages were in looseleaf form and located under other papers on his desk. Underneath these pages was a carbon copy of all the will pages, including a copy of the missing page 1. Then under these copy pages was the 1954 will and the 1958 codicil. The pages of the 1954 will and codicil were stapled together.

The missing first page of the 1959 will was located several months later in Beale's Bascom Hall office among some American History notes.

The trial judge admitted the 1959 will to probate as the will existed before any changes or corrections were typed. The appeal from the judgment was taken by Fred Risser, guardian ad litem for Thomas Wight Beale. . . .

BROWN, Justice. . . .

EXECUTION OF WILL

While appellant concedes, or at least does not dispute, that when Professor Beale signed the purported 1959 will he had testamentary capacity and was not subject to undue influence appellant vigorously denies that the 14 pages of the 1959 instrument were legally published and declared to be his will and legally signed and witnessed as such and, in the alternative, that these pages did not constitute his will at the moment of execution.

In this record there are a few indisputable facts. From them there are a number of conflicting inferences reasonably to be drawn.

It cannot be questioned that on June 16 or 17, 1959, Professor Beale dictated a 14 page document in the form of a last will, revoking all prior wills; that his secretary typed the original will, with three carbon copies, and delivered all of them to him in looseleaf form the afternoon of June 20th; that Beale was in New York City at the home of a friend, a professor of Columbia University, on the evening of June 21st and on that evening he exhibited "a pile" of sheets of paper and declared to his three friends that this was his will and desired them to witness his will; that they saw him sign the sheet which was on top of the pile and that immediately thereafter, at his request, they signed as witnesses in his presence and in the presence of each other; that the place where they put their signatures was immediately below the usual testamentary clause declaring this to be Professor Beale's will; that none of the witnesses paid any detailed attention to the number of pages in the pile nor could they identify later any of the pages except the one where they had written their names; that when all four participants had signed, Beale put all papers in his briefcase and the meeting ended.

It is uncontradicted that on the next day, or shortly thereafter, Beale and his two sons left by plane for Moscow; that a few days after June 21st Mrs. Burleigh, Beale's secretary, received a letter from him on Columbia University note paper, bearing date June 21, 1959, mailed in New York or in London on a day not given; that the letter asked Mrs. Burleigh to make several changes in pages 12 and 13 of the will which she had previously typed, to carry out marginal penciled notes in Beale's handwriting on those pages; that enclosed with the letter were the original pages 12 and 13; that Mrs. Burleigh made the alterations as directed and mailed them back to him in Moscow; that these pages were later found in a sealed envelope addressed to Beale in Beale's handwriting and mailed from London, England to him at his Madison address.

There is nothing legally invalid in the execution of a will because the separate pages of the will have not been fastened together. It is a requirement, though, that all the pages be present at the time of execution. . . .

In the case at bar the witnesses are unable to say whether or not the 14 pages were on the table before them when, on June 21st, they signed the last page. The determination then, comes down to the reasonable inferences to be drawn from the established facts. Appellant relies on the undisputed fact that two pages of the will were received in Madison within a few days following June 21st, enclosed in a letter dated June 21st. And appellant infers that those two pages had already been sent off to Madison when, late in the evening of June 21st, the testator and witnesses signed the last page.

On the other hand the trial court put weight on the fact that all 14 original pages are clearly identified and legible as they were dictated by Beale before the corrections or amendments. This intact original was handed to Beale by his secretary and was taken by him to New York. The very next day Beale presented "a pile" of papers to his witnesses and declared that such papers were his will. It is not impossible or improbable that Beale was speaking the truth and the pile of pages were the complete 14 page will, as the trial court found. The fact that Beale sent off two pages to Mrs. Burleigh with a letter dated June 21st may raise an inference that Beale did this before he went to the party and he had there only the remaining pages, which he falsely declared to be his will. Certainly that is not the only permissible inference. When Beale and his friends had signed the will and he had gathered up the pages and departed June 21st was not over; Beale could still have written the letter, less than 100 words, on that date after the party and enclosed with it pages 12 and 13. There is no evidence at all of when the letter and the pages were mailed and there is some evidence that they were mailed in London.

The question is one of inference and when the inferences can reasonably go either way the appellate court must adopt the view taken by the trial court. . . .

While the present facts permit the inference urged by appellant they do not compel that inference in opposition to the one drawn by the trial court, and the evidence and reasonable inferences sustain the trial court's conclusion that the entire original will, as dictated by Professor Beale to his secretary, was before the witnesses and the execution of that will complied with the requirements of law. . . .

EPILOGUE

At least one more mystery appears worth mentioning, although in our view it presents no fact to affect the outcome:

A few days before Christmas, 1959, Beale, who had returned to Madison, directed Mrs. Burleigh to re-type the altered pages 12 and 13 on the same typewriter she had used when she first typed the will. We may guess that Beale wanted pages which did not show they had been tampered with, as was apparent on the two original sheets now showing erasures and re-typed corrections. We may guess, further, that Beale intended to insert in the will without discovery the new pages without republication and re-execution of the will. This is no more than guesswork and is of no consequence. Before Mrs. Burleigh typed the two new sheets Beale's death intervened on December 27, 1959. Whatever his purpose, nefarious or not, he did not accomplish it. Mrs. Burleigh had not begun this final typing when she was told that Professor Beale had died. She then typed the two pages as Professor Beale directed and gave them to Beale's son, Henry. There were then no marginal initials on them. These pages are in evidence and, although Professor Beale never in his life had them or saw them, his initials are now on the margin of each of these pages and, as Mrs. Burleigh testified, are in his handwriting.

We began with a consideration of the unnatural. At the end we are confronted by the supernatural. We consider ourselves fortunate that this weird addition to the facts turns out to be immaterial.

We conclude that the trial court's findings and conclusions are not against the great weight and the clear preponderance of the evidence and the judgment admitting the will to probate as the will existed when it was executed and as Mrs. Burleigh first typed it must be affirmed.

Judgment affirmed.

2. *Republication by Codicil*

In its narrowest sense republication by codicil "means an implied restatement or rewriting of the language of a valid will as of the time of the republication." [41] This is accomplished by the execution of a valid codicil to a valid will. But courts have not so narrowly restricted the idea of republication. It has been used to revive an instrument that once had testamentary life, but for some reason became void.[42]

[41] Evans, Testamentary Republication, 40 Harv. L. Rev. 71, 103 (1926).

[42] In this way the doctrine differs from incorporation by reference, which technically applies only when instruments which never had testamentary life are incorporated into a will and given testamentary effect.

For example, suppose the testator revokes his first will by a second will and then executes a codicil to his first will. The first will is republished and thus the second will is revoked by implication ("squeezed out").[43] The doctrine of republication also covers the case where the testator declares to witnesses that his revoked first will once again embodies his intentions with respect to the disposition of his estate. If this declaration is made to the original witnesses, it may not be necessary for the witnesses to resubscribe;[44] if the declaration is made to new witnesses, resubscription is necessary.[45]

Republication by codicil has sometimes been used to validate a prior invalid will, though strictly speaking there cannot be a republication of a will which was never valid. One cannot restore life to that which never had life. Yet, used in this manner, the doctrine has enabled courts which do not permit incorporation of unattested documents by reference to give effect to instruments which are invalid for some reason other than faulty execution. In New York, for example, which does not in general permit incorporation by reference, a codicil can republish and thereby give testamentary effect to a will which was invalid because of mental incapacity or undue influence, but a codicil cannot republish an instrument never duly executed with the required formalities.

If a codicil republishes a will, the will is deemed to have been executed as of the date of the codicil. However, a codicil will not be deemed to have republished a will where updating the will would lead to a result contrary to the testator's intent. Today, application of the doctrine can arise in a number of contexts. Suppose, for example, a state has a pretermitted child statute that protects children born after execution of the will and not provided for therein. In 1965 T executes a will that devises his entire estate to his wife W and names his friend X as executor. The will makes no mention of children because the couple have no children at that time. In 1968 a son, S, is born to T and W. In 1971 T executes a codicil that substitutes Y National Bank for X as his executor. T dies in 1972. The pretermitted child statute does not apply. Under the doctrine of republication by codicil, S was born prior to execution of the will.

PROBLEM

In 1969 T executes a will which leaves his entire estate to X charity. In 1970 T executes a will which leaves his entire estate to Y charity. In 1971 T executes an instrument which reads: "This is a codicil to my 1969 will. I give $5000 to Norma Stein. Except for this gift I hereby confirm my 1969 will and it shall be given effect." T dies six days later. A state statute invalidates any bequest to charity made by a will executed within thirty days of death. Is X charity or Y charity entitled to

[43] Matter of Campbell, 170 N.Y. 84, 62 N.E. 1070 (1902); Matter of Fould, 13 App. Div. 2d 16, 212 N.Y.S.2d 519 (1961), aff'd, 10 N.Y.2d 1027, 225 N.Y.S.2d 46, 180 N.E.2d 434 (1962).

[44] Matter of Flynn, 174 Misc. 565, 21 N.Y.S.2d 496 (Sur. Ct. 1940).

[45] Matter of Stickney, 161 N.Y. 42, 55 N.E. 396 (1899).

share in T's estate? White v. Conference Claimants Endowment Commission, 81 Idaho 17, 336 P.2d 674 (1959); In re Estate of Ryder, 227 Cal. App. 2d 820, 39 Cal. Rptr. 178 (1964).

3. *Facts of Independent Significance*[46]

It is often necessary to resort to extrinsic evidence to identify the will beneficiaries or property passing under the will. Thus a devise of "all the land I own in Crabtree County to my nephews and nieces who shall be living at my death" requires the executor to "go outside the will" to determine the extent of testator's land holdings in Crabtree County and the identity of the nephews and nieces who survived him. In some cases the property or beneficiary designation may leave it in the testator's power to alter the gift or the beneficiaries by later unattested acts. So long as these acts have a lifetime motive and significance apart from their effect on the will, the gift will be upheld under the doctrine of facts of independent significance (also called the doctrine of nontestamentary acts).

Example: T's will devises "the automobile that I own at my death" to his nephew N, and gives $1000 "to each person who shall be in my employ at my death." At the time the will is executed T owns a Volkswagen. Shortly before his death T trades the Volkswagen in on a new Cadillac, with the result that T dies owning a $7000 automobile rather than one worth $1000. In the year before his death T fires two long-time employees and hires three new ones. The gifts are valid. While T's act in buying the Cadillac had the practical effect of increasing the value of his gift to N, it is unlikely that this is what motivated his purchase. It is more probable that he bought the car because he wanted to drive a Cadillac. Similarly, his acts in hiring and firing various employees were doubtless prompted by his business needs rather than a desire to make or unmake legatees under his will. Indeed, cases involving this form of devise typically assume the validity of the gift without discussion of the facts of independent significance doctrine. See, e.g., Shoup v. American Trust Co., 245 N.C. 682, 97 S.E.2d 111 (1957).

PROBLEMS

1. T's will devises "my mahogany hope chest and all its contents to my sister, Beatrice." After T's death her hope chest is opened and is found to contain three wool sweaters, two silver candelabra, several items of glassware, five uncirculated $1000 bills, and a certificate for 100 shares of General Electric common stock. Is Beatrice entitled to these items? See Note, 5 A.L.R. 3d 466 (1966).

2. T's will, executed in 1968, contains the following clause: "All my wearing apparel, jewelry and all other articles of personal adornment, linen, silver, books,

[46] See Evans, Nontestamentary Acts and Incorporation by Reference, 16 U. Chi. L. Rev. 635 (1949).

Uniform Probate Code §2-512 expressly adopts the facts of independent significance doctrine.

pictures and household effects, I give and bequeath to my sister, Florence, with the understanding that she shall distribute them to the persons named in a memorandum of instructions I shall leave addressed to her." After T's death an envelope is found containing her will and a typewritten memorandum addressed to Florence. The memorandum, dated June 5, 1970, makes various gifts of these tangible items to fifteen persons. It is signed by T but it is not witnessed. Are the gifts valid? Hastings v. Bridge, 86 N.H. 247, 166 A. 273 (1933); Ragland v. Wagener, 142 Tex. 651, 180 S.W.2d 435 (1944).[47]

4. *Incorporation by Reference*[48]

An unattested document may be incorporated into the will by reference so that it is considered a part of the will for purposes of construing the will and distributing testator's assets. In order to be incorporated by reference, the document must be in existence at the time the will is executed, it must (according to many courts) be referred to as being in existence, and it must be sufficiently described in the will to permit its clear identification. The incorporation by reference doctrine, which is recognized in all but a handful of states,[49] is particularly useful in validating a prior will that was defectively executed but is referred to in a duly executed codicil.

In re ESTATE OF DIMMITT
Supreme Court of Nebraska, 1942
141 Neb. 413, 3 N.W.2d 752, 144 A.L.R. 704

PAYNE, J. This is an appeal by contestants from an order of the district court admitting to probate, as the will of the decedent, two written instruments, one a

[47] Uniform Probate Code §2-513 provides: "Whether or not the provisions relating to holographic wills apply, a will may refer to a written statement or list to dispose of items of tangible personal property not otherwise specifically disposed of by the will, other than money, evidences of indebtedness, documents of title, and securities, and property used in trade or business. To be admissible under this section as evidence of the intended disposition, the writing must either be in the handwriting of the testator or be signed by him and must describe the items and the devisees with reasonable certainty. The writing may be referred to as one to be in existence at the time of the testator's death; it may be prepared before or after the execution of the will; it may be altered by the testator after its preparation; and it may be a writing which has no significance apart from its effect upon the dispositions made by the will."

Given the policy reasons underlying the formalities required for will execution, is this provision sound?

[48] Uniform Probate Code §2-510 provides: "Any writing in existence when a will is executed may be incorporated by reference if the language of the will manifests this intent and describes the writing sufficiently to permit its identification."

[49] Two exceptions are Connecticut and Louisiana. While New York and New Jersey are usually cited as not permitting incorporation of unattested instruments, cases from those jurisdictions sustained certain pour-overs from a will into an inter vivos trust prior to legislation authorizing pour-overs. See Clark v. Citizens Nat'l Bank, 38 N.J. Sup. 69, 118 A.2d 108 (1955); Comment, Incorporation by Reference and Independent Legal Significance in the New York Law of Wills, 29 Fordham L. Rev. 143 (1960); 2 Page, Wills §19.17 (Bowe-Parker rev. 1960). On pour-overs, see page 419, infra.

will and the other a warranty deed which the court found was incorporated into and made a part of the will by reference. . . .

There is practically no dispute about the following facts as shown by the evidence. V. L. Dimmitt, the testator, died March 4, 1939, at the age of 78 years, having resided about 50 years on his 320-acre farm northwest of Wisner in Cuming county. His wife predeceased him about two years. Their only child died in infancy, and testator left no issue. His heirs at law were two sisters, Lura Boney and Mary R. Cary, of Red Oak, Iowa; two nephews, Aldos D. Brouhard and Avan L. Brouhard, of Ames, Iowa, who were sons of Jennie Brouhard, a deceased sister; and two nieces and a nephew, Beulah M. Priest and Lillian L. McKeone, of Omaha, Nebraska and, and LeRoy Dimmitt, of Papillion, Nebraska, daughters and son of Elmer Dimmitt, a deceased brother.

Alta J. Pullman was a niece of the testator's wife, and was born in Mills county, Iowa, and lived with her parents until she was three years old. The testator and his wife had only one child, a daughter who died in infancy, and so they urged the parents of Alta J. Pullman to let her live with them, which they did, and at three years of age she was taken into their home in Iowa. When she was five years of age they removed to Nebraska, and as soon as they were settled they took her to their new home, and she lived with them continuously until she was married in 1907, at the age of 27 years. After her marriage she visited them in Nebraska two or three times a year, and they repeatedly visited her in her Iowa home. On November 30, 1936, before his wife's death, which occurred in 1937, testator and his wife executed a deed to the home quarter to Alta J. Pullman. This deed was sealed in an envelope and placed by testator in his safety deposit box in the First National Bank at Wisner, where it remained until his death. It is undisputed that the deed was never delivered, and never left testator's possession and control in his lifetime. Four or five months prior to the testator's death, Mrs. Pullman was notified that he was ill, and she went out to his home. She, together with Mr. and Mrs. Tucker, took him to a hospital at Wayne. As they commenced their journey, the testator said to her: "I am pretty sick and you know that. I may not come back and if I don't come back here is the key and you can have this place. Your aunt and I have always said that; and it is in the will."

Mrs. Pullman testified: "I have the key in my possession in my pocketbook. Q. He handed you the key at that time? A. Yes, sir. Q. That was the key to the dwelling house occupied by him located on the southeast quarter of section 8-24-4 in Cuming county? A. That is right.[50] . . ."

Lon Tucker, who is a farmer living northwest of Wisner, was a friend of the testator for more than 40 years. They had visited each other's homes hundreds of times, and he said that he had taken the deceased on a great many trips; in fact, for

[50] The delivery of a key may suffice for a gift causa mortis of personal property (Re Elliott, 312 Pa. 493, 167 Atl. 289 (1933)), but the doctrine of gifts causa mortis does not apply to real property. Wilson v. Jourdan, 79 Miss. 133, 29 So. 823 (1901). Why not? 1 Page, Wills §7.20 (Bowe-Parker rev. 1960). Suppose Dimmitt gave Alta the key to his safe deposit box which contained the deed? — Eds.

the last 15 or 20 years he took the deceased on practically every trip that he made.

Mr. Tucker testified that Mr. Dimmit always thought well of Mrs. Pullman "and I could not see any other way;" that the deceased told him many times of his intentions toward her, and Mr. Dimmitt told him that his feelings were just the same as any man's feelings would be toward his own child; that conversations in regard to these matters were over a period of 20 years; that some time prior to his death he took Mr. Dimmitt to the hospital at Wayne; that he had been quite sick and that none of his relatives were there except Mrs. Pullman and her daughter, and that he had quite a good deal of difficulty in persuading Mr. Dimmitt to go to the hospital at Wayne, some 14 miles away; that he was not addicted to taking advice, and was a rather stubborn sort of person; that he and his wife and Mrs. Pullman went to the hospital with him. "We got him ready and got out on the porch and he locked the door and he handed the key to Mrs. Pullman. 'Now,' he said, 'you know that this old home is yours. If anything happens to me and I don't get back here' he says, '[t]his old home is yours.' He says, 'Now, you know where the line of this place is, know all about it here.' And then we started and we got down to where the line was there — Q. Did he give her anything? A. He gave her the key. Q. At that time? A. Yes. He handed her the key. Q. This key to the house in which he lived, was it? A. Yes, sir. And when we got to the north line of the quarter he stopped on the road and showed her as near as he could where the line was, and he says, 'Now, there will probably have to be a fence through there between you and the boys' quarter.' "

The will, exhibit A, was dated December 31, 1937, and was properly executed. The first paragraph related to debts and funeral expenses. In the second paragraph, the northeast quarter of section 8-24-4 in Cuming county was given to the two nephews, Aldos D. Brouhard and Avan L. Brouhard. The third paragraph gave \$200 to the East Liberty Cemetery Association in Mills county, Iowa. The fourth paragraph gave all of testator's telephone stock to Lucille Genevieve Schultz. The fifth and sixth paragraphs read as follows:

"Fifth: All the rest and residue of my personal property I order and direct that my executor hereinafter named divide the same according to private instructions I have given him.

"Sixth: I have already deeded to my niece, Alta J. Pullman, the southeast quarter (SE$\frac{1}{4}$) of section eight (8), township twenty-four (24), north, range four (4), east of the 6th P.M. in Cuming county, Nebraska, and for that reason I do not devise any real estate to her in this Will."

The seventh paragraph appointed Clark B. Evans executor, and he is the appellee and proponent of the will.

The proponent contends that by the sixth paragraph the deed was incorporated into and made a part of the will. The contestants deny that the deed was ever delivered.

The deed, exhibit C, is a warranty deed, on a regular printed blank, filled in on a typewriter, and dated and acknowledged November 30, 1936, before Clark B. Evans, notary public, and is signed by the testator and his wife, and conveys the southeast quarter of section 8-24-4, Cuming county, to Alta J. Pullman, "for and in consideration of the sum of One Dollar ($1.00), Services performed over a period of years, and Love and Affection."

The deed was never recorded, but bears on the back, among other indorsements, these words: "Admitted to Probate and filed for record April 19-1939 as a part of the Last Will and Testament of V. L. Dimmitt. Homer A. McDonald Co. Judge."

Clark B. Evans testified that he lived in Wisner, Nebraska, and had been acquainted with the testator for about 50 years; that he drove out to see Mr. Dimmitt when called, and when he received the necessary instructions he drove back to town and prepared the warranty deed, and took it back to their farm, about seven or eight miles out, and they signed and executed the deed. Mr. Evans testified that he took the deed back to town, placed it in an envelope, and gave it to Mr. Dimmitt the next time he came to town, and he never saw it again until the will was read.

Neil D. Saville, cashier of the First National Bank of Wisner for 13 years, was well acquainted with the testator, who was a customer of the bank. He testified that Mr. Dimmitt did not have a safety deposit box, but had a box of his own, in which he kept his papers, and that he left his box in the bank simply for safe-keeping. He said the box was not locked, and on the order of the county judge he opened the box and forwarded the sealed envelope containing the deed to the county judge.

The contestants present, as the sole question, whether the deed was incorporated into and made a part of the will by the language of paragraph 6 thereof. It is insisted that the language contained no disposable words; it is not a devise, and the intent statute of Nebraska (Comp. St. 1929, sec. 76-109) is powerless to change that statement; that a mere recital in a will that testator has previously deeded realty, which recital proves to be erroneous because of the nondelivery of the deed in the testator's lifetime, does not disclose an intention to incorporate such undelivered deed, and does not operate as a devise of the realty. . . .

In this case we are faced with the question: Under what conditions may an extrinsic document be incorporated into the will, and admitted to probate with the will?

The first essential requisite in such cases is that the instrument must be in existence, which is admitted in this case. The next requisite is that it must be referred to in the will in a manner which will clearly identify the instrument. There can be no question in the case at bar as to the deed being the one referred to in the will.

The argument, therefore, seems to rest on the point: Can the words of the will be construed to be, or to imply, an intention on the part of the testator to incorporate this particular deed into and make it a part of his will? See 68 C.J. 640; Bottrell v. Spengler, 343 Ill. 476, 175 N.E. 781.

In Loring v. Sumner, 23 Pick. (Mass.) 98, a case was decided at the October term, 1839, in which the testator said in his will: "I have given to my son $1,000 by note, for his full part of my estate." This note was invalid as having no consideration, but it was held that on the whole the testator by his will had manifested an intention or determination that such amount should be paid out of his estate to his son, and therefore the court could see no good reason why the determination manifested in the will should not be carried into execution.

In Newton v. Seaman's Friend Society, 130 Mass. 91, 39 Am. Rep. 433, the testator directed that legacies should be paid according to the directions which had been written in a book by another and signed by him, and the book was finally admitted to probate, and the legacies were paid in accordance therewith, and it was held that a paper referred to in a will and containing directions for the disposition of the estate, but not executed nor witnessed as a will, *should be admitted to probate as a part of the will,* if it was in existence at the date of the will, and is clearly identified.

Of the many Nebraska cases on wills, we believe that one of them throws light on the question before us. It is In re Estate of Hopper, 90 Neb. 622, 134 N.W. 237, which came up from Douglas county. William Hopper, a widower, had nine children. He had his will prepared, and at the same time seven warranty deeds. In his will he made a specific bequest to a daughter and to one of his sons. The will recited that he had executed conveyances by warranty deed to seven of his children of land of approximately equal value, and directed that upon his death the executors should deliver the deeds to the seven grantees, and that the land so deeded to them should be held by them in fee simple thereafter.

Judge Sedgwick, in writing the opinion, held that oral evidence was admissible to prove the circumstances surrounding the execution of the instrument. It was further held that a writing in existence at the time of executing a will, and made at the same time and as a part of the same transaction, may by reference be made a part of the will. It was argued that the deeds were not made in compliance with the statute in relation to the execution of wills, and, never having been delivered to the grantees in the lifetime of the grantor, were ineffectual to pass title. But it was held that the deeds and the will taken together were intended and executed by the deceased as his will.

In this Hopper case, deeds were given effect, because by placing them away with the will the testator by this act, and by his reference in the will, intended to incorporate them into his will, and the deeds thereby had a testamentary effect. In the Hopper case the testator said: "I have made and executed conveyances by warranty deed." In the case at bar the testator said, "I have already deeded to my niece, Alta J. Pullman," and by the sixth paragraph of the will in the case at bar he gives her the last piece of his land, and in the seventh and last paragraph he appoints the executor. Aside from all extrinsic evidence, the language of that will discloses an intention on his part that Mrs. Pullman is to receive the home quarter-section as a part of his testamentary scheme.

Merritt Schultze was a witness for the contestants. He said his father and Mrs. Dimmitt were cousins. He visited the testator in the hospital at Wayne and testator told him he had *willed* the southeast quarter to Alta Pullman.

It is clear in this case that the testator and his wife had several years before decided to give to Alta Pullman the old home place, where she had been raised to womanhood, and in carrying that out a warranty deed was drawn up and executed by the grantors. . . .

This deed to his niece, Alta J. Pullman, was never delivered, but was kept off the record by the testator, for he intended to hold the title to that home place until he died. If he had intended that deed to be effective at the time he put it in his safety deposit box, he need not have mentioned it in his will at all. Therefore, at the time of its execution it was not intended to convey title, and standing by itself it cannot be given effect as a deed; however, at the time of the execution of the will the testator intended that the two instruments should be admitted to probate and convey title to his most valuable piece of property to the one to whom he had handed the key to the house when he locked the door when he left for the hospital, and said, in brief, I am pretty sick, I may not come back; if I don't, here is the key, and you can have this place; your aunt and I have always said that, and it is in the will.

Therefore, at his death his will conveyed a good title to his niece of the property described in the deed. It is an accepted rule that the will always speaks from the date of testator's death, and speaks conclusively as of that particular date.

Because of the reasons set forth in this discussion of the facts and the law, the decision of the district court is hereby Affirmed.

YEAGER, J., dissenting. In our consideration of this matter we must not lose sight of the fact that the question of whether or not this was sufficient as a devise is the sole and only question for determination in this case. We must not become confused by the discussion regarding delivery of the deed to the real estate, and the key to the house. The point of such discussion bears only on the question of whether or not there was passage of title under the deed, which is not an issue triable in this case.

Coming back then to the real issue presented, on the clear and specific language employed by the testator, can it be said that he intended a devise of the real estate to Alta J. Pullman? The will itself supplies the unequivocal answer. The testator said in language so plain and simple that it is not subject to construction, but only to acceptance, that he did not so intend. He said: "I do not devise any real estate to her in this will." The fact that he intended to convey to her real estate by deed, and that what he did in that connection was sufficient or insufficient to effect a conveyance, is beside the point and of no consequence here. Words could not have been selected to express the testamentary intention more clearly than those used. There was no ambiguity, latent or patent.

The case of In re Estate of Hopper, 90 Neb. 622, 134 N.W. 237, cited and commented upon in the majority opinion, is clearly not in point in the present situation. There, simultaneously with the making of the will, the testator executed seven warranty deeds. The deeds were admitted to probate. There by specific declaration in the will the testator made the deeds a part of the testamentary disposition. In the case at bar, by equally specific declaration, the testator removed the deed from his testamentary disposition.

The case of Noble v. Tipton, 219 Ill. 182, 76 N.E. 151, closely parallels this one. A father deeded his home farm to his son Thomas, and ten months later made a will in which he disposed of all his property by will except the home farm. In the will he said that he had deeded the farm to his son, Thomas Noble. He delivered the deed to the cashier of a bank where it was held subject to the order of the grantor. The court held that the deed operated neither as a conveyance nor a devise. Of like effect is Allenbach v. Ridenour, 51 Nev. 437, 279 Pac. 32.

The testator clearly had no intention of giving Alta J. Pullman anything by will and, in my opinion, this court has established a dangerous precedent in declaring the existence of a testamentary intent which is specifically negatived by the language of the will which is clear and plain.

Simmons, C.J., and Carter, J. concur in the dissent.[51]

PROBLEM

Charles Garrison inherited from his father the home place, divided as follows: 40 acres for life, remainder to Charles's daughter, Gladys, and 40 acres in fee simple. Charles's will provided: "I give and bequeath unto my daughter, Gladys Garrison, the sum of One Dollar ($1.00). This bequest is no indication of my love and affection for my daughter, Gladys Garrison, but inasmuch as she will receive at the time of my death 80 acres of land under the Last Will and Testament of my father, Robert Garrison, I have, therefore, reduced her gifts under this will." Gladys received only 40 acres of land under Robert Garrison's will. Does she now receive the other 40 acres devised to Charles Garrison in fee simple? In re Garrison's Estate, 374 S.W.2d 92 (Mo. 1964). See 2 Page, Wills §19.30 (Bowe-Parker rev. 1960); 4 id. §30.18 (1960).

JOHNSON v. JOHNSON

Supreme Court of Oklahoma, 1954
279 P.2d 928

Per Curiam. This is an appeal from a judgment of the District Court of Oklahoma County affirming the County Court of Oklahoma in denying probate to an instrument purporting to be the last will and testament of Dexter G. Johnson, who was sometimes known as D. G. Johnson.

The instrument in question was on a single sheet of paper and contained three typewritten paragraphs, started out with the words, "I, D. G. Johnson also known as Dexter G. Johnson, of Oklahoma City, Oklahoma County, State of Oklahoma do hereby make, publish and declare this to be my last Will and Testament . . ." and made numerous bequests and devises and concluded with recommending the employment of a certain attorney to probate the will. This typewritten portion was not dated nor did the testator sign his name at the conclusion thereof nor was it attested

[51] Noted 37 Ill. L. Rev. 425; 41 Mich. L. Rev. 751; 22 Texas L. Rev. 87. — Eds.

by two witnesses. At the end of the typewritten portion, at the bottom of the sheet of paper, appears the following, admitted to be in the handwriting of the deceased:

> To my brother James I give ten dollars only. This will shall be complete unless hereafter altered, changed or rewritten. Witness my hand this April 6, 1947. Easter Sunday, 2:30 P.M.
>
> D. G. Johnson
> Dexter G. Johnson.

On trial de novo in the District Court the proponents of this purported will, plaintiffs in error here, introduced evidence over objections (which objections were never ruled on by the court) showing that Dexter G., or D. G. Johnson for many years was a practicing attorney in Oklahoma City; that during his practice he prepared many wills, all in proper form, for various clients; that in October, 1946, deceased told Jack G. Wiggins, his insurance counselor, that he had a will but it was out of date and needed changing; that in March, 1947, deceased told this insurance counselor that he was working on his will, making changes, and expected to complete it right away and told Mr. Wiggins in general the disposition he intended to make of his property; that in the latter part of 1946 Lowell M. Wickham, deceased's rental agent, was shown the instrument here in question at which time it had only the typewritten portions on it; that at that time deceased told him that was his will and he wanted Wickham to witness it, but he and deceased started discussing other business and neglected to do it at that time; that when Wickham left the paper was lying on deceased's desk; that some months later Wickham asked deceased about witnessing the will and deceased replied he had changed his will by codicil and did not need Wickham to sign it as witness; an offer by statement of counsel was made to show the intention of the testator in leaving his property to the persons he named as beneficiaries which was rejected by the court and is not helpful in deciding the questions raised here.

The above is a summary of all the testimony that appears in the record. None of the testimony presented to the County Court appears in the record; defendant below, contestant of the will and defendant in error here, offered no testimony.

Is this instrument one complete, integrated writing, partly typed and partly handwritten; or is it an unexecuted nonholographic will to which is appended a valid holographic codicil? If it be the former it cannot be admitted to probate because it was not signed in the presence of two subscribing witnesses as required by law.

Defendant in error urges that the instrument shows on its face that it is but one instrument and that it cannot be divided into two parts, one, the typewritten part to be called a will and the other, the handwritten part, to be called a codicil. In support of his contention he says that the typewritten portion standing alone is not a will because, though admittedly testamentary in character, it is not dated, signed, nor witnessed; that it takes the handwritten portion to complete the instrument; that by definition to have a codicil there must first be a will.

There is no question in this case that the typewritten instrument which was not signed, dated, nor attested was prepared by D. G. Johnson and that it is testamentary in character, or that he intended same as his will or that it effectively makes complete disposition of his estate. A will may be so defective, as here, that it is not entitled to probate but if testamentary in character it is a will, nonetheless. . . . Nor is there any question that the handwritten words were wholly in the handwriting of the testator.

The question next arises, do these words meet the requirements of a codicil? By definition a codicil is a supplement to, an addition to or qualification of, an existing will, made by the testator to alter, enlarge, or restrict the provisions of the will, to explain or republish it, or to revoke it, and it must be testamentary in character. In re Whittier's Estate, 26 Wash. 2d 833, 176 P.2d 281. A codicil need not be called a codicil, In re Carr's Estate, 93 Cal. App. 2d 750, 209 P.2d 956; In re Atkinson's Estate, 110 Cal. App. 499, 294 P. 425. The intention to add a codicil is controlling. Allgeier v. Brown, 199 Ky. 672, 251 S.W. 851; Stewart v. Stewart, 177 Mass. 493, 59 N.E. 116; In re Whittier's Estate, supra. The handwritten words are admittedly testamentary in character. It is clear that they make an addition to the provisions of the will theretofore existing. This codicil is on the same sheet of paper and the terms thereof, the circumstances surrounding it, as shown by the evidence indicate that the testator intended it as an addition to and republication of his will.

If it be a codicil, then, is it a valid one? It is written, dated, and signed by the testator. It meets all the requirements of a valid holographic codicil. The fact that the codicil was written on the same piece of paper as the typewritten will will not invalidate the codicil. In re Atkinson's Estate, supra.

It is admitted that a codicil republishes a previous will as modified by the codicil as of the date of the codicil. Can a valid, holographic codicil republish and validate a will which was theretofore inoperative because not dated, signed, or attested according to law?[52]

The general principle of law is that a codicil validly executed operates as a republication of the will no matter what defects may have existed in the execution of the earlier document, that the instruments are incorporated as one, and that a proper execution of the codicil extends also to the will. Twenty-two states and England so hold. For citation of cases see Annotations 21 A.L.R.2d 823. That a properly executed codicil will give effect to a will which has never been signed has been specifically held in Kentucky, New Jersey, and England. See Beall v. Cunningham, 1843, 3 B. Mon. 390, 42 Ky. 390, in which it appeared that a paper wholly written

[52] Compare the reasoning of the White Knight in Carroll, Through the Looking Glass:

"Well, just then I was inventing a new way of getting over a gate — would you like to hear it?"

"Very much indeed," Alice said politely.

"I'll tell you how I came to think of it," said the Knight. "You see, I said to myself 'The only difficulty is with the feet: the head is high enough already.' Now first I put my head on the top of the gate — then the head's high enough — then I stand on my head — then the feet are high enough, you see — then I'm over, you see."

"Yes, I suppose you'd be over when that was done," Alice said thoughtfully: "but don't you think it would be rather hard?" — Eds.

by testator dated 1825 was denied probate, and thereafter there was offered for probate a typewritten will dated in 1827, which was unsigned and unattested, together with a codicil dated 1832 on the same sheet of paper which was signed and attested; the opinion holds that the properly executed codicil had the effect of giving operation to the whole as one will. See also Hurley v. Blankinship, 1950, 313 Ky. 49, 229 S.W.2d 963, 21 A.L.R.2d 817, in which a holographic will which was not signed was held validated by properly executed holographic codicils; Doe v. Evans, 1832, 1 Cromp. & M. 42, 129 Eng. Reprint 307, in which an unsigned typewritten will was held validated by a properly executed codicil on the same sheet of paper; see also McCurdy v. Neall, 1886, 42 N.J. Eq. 333, 7 A. 466 and Smith v. Runkle, 1916, 86 N.J. Eq. 257, 98 A. 1086, in both of which the signatures to the wills were defective because not placed on the will in the presence of witnesses but it was held that valid codicils thereafter executed gave operation to the entire will and codicils; Rogers v. Agricola, 176 Ark. 287, 3 S.W.2d 26, in which an invalid typewritten will (due to only one witness) was held validated by a subsequent holographic codicil; In re Plumel's Estate, 151 Cal. 77, 90 P. 192, an invalid holographic will because of printing thereon was held validated by a subsequent holographic codicil written on the back of the will. . . .

The only exception is New York which modifies the general rule by holding that a properly executed codicil validates a will originally invalid for want of testamentary capacity, undue influence, or revocation but does not validate a will defectively executed because of improper attestation. It will be noted, however, that Justice Cardozo in Re Fowles, 1918, 222 N.Y. 222, 118 N.E. 611, Ann. Cas. 1918D, 834, stated that the rule was malleable and uncertain and he anticipated that New York would abandon its limitations on the rule. . . .

We therefore hold that the valid holographic codicil incorporated the prior will by reference and republished and validated the prior will as of the date of the codicil, thus giving effect to the intention of the testator.

Reversed with directions to enter the will for probate.

Johnson, V.C.J. and Welch, Corn, Arnold and Blackbird, J.J., concur. Halley, C.J., Williams and Davison, J.J., dissent.

Corn, Justice (concurring specially.)[53] I concur in the per curiam opinion. In

[53] In 1964 Justices Corn and Welch were convicted of Federal income tax evasion and sentenced to prison terms of 18 months and 3 years respectively. New York Times, July 19, 1964, p. 44, col. 1; id., Nov. 14, 1964, p. 14, col. 6. Corn and Welch resigned their judicial positions. Subsequently Corn signed a statement in which Corn said Welch, Johnson, and he had accepted more than $150,000 in bribes for throwing cases. In 1965 Justice Johnson was convicted of corruption in office and removed from the Court. Id., May 14, 1965, p. 40, col. 1.

The newspaper accounts did not mention any evidence of bribery in the principal case of Johnson v. Johnson. Yet when a judge has been convicted of bribery in one case the public may suspect there was bribery in others. (Indeed, when Corn was asked if he could remember any year, in the twenty-four he served as Justice, when he did not take money for his votes, he replied: "Well, I don't know." Id., May 11, 1965, p. 18, col. 6.) The votes of Corn, Welch, and Johnson were decisive in Johnson v. Johnson. Although there is no report of bribery in this case, *and none is to be inferred from this note,* does the mere appearance of possible impropriety require that the case now be reheard upon petition of the losing party?

In Johnson v. Johnson, 424 P.2d 414 (Okla. 1967), the executor of the losing party in the original case (who had since died) petitioned to have the 1954 decision vacated in view of

so doing I have in mind the purpose of our law-makers in enacting statutes regulating the making of a Will. They require certain steps to be taken in the execution of a Will solely for the purpose of permitting a person to dispose of his property by Will, to take effect after his death the way he desired, and to prevent someone, through fraud or by other means, from permitting this to be done. It was the purpose of our lawmakers, in passing the Act, to make it impossible for fraud or undue influence to be practiced in the execution of the Will, and in the disposition of the property disposed of by the Will.

It was not the intent of our law-makers, in enacting these statutes, if substantially complied with, to ever allow a miscarriage of justice by a wrongful disposition of the testator's property contrary to his intent. 84 O.S. 1951 §151 provides: "Intention of testator governs. — A will is to be construed according to the intention of the testator. . . ."

In Munger v. Elliott, 187 Okl. 19, 100 P.2d 876, 877, in syllabus 1, we held:

> The cardinal rule for the construction of Wills is to ascertain the intent of the testator, and give effect thereto, if such intent does not attempt to effect that which the law forbids. All rules of construction are designed for this purpose, and all rules and presumptions are subordinate to the intent of the testator where that has been ascertained.

In the instant case, the intent expressed by the testator in the written instrument which he prepared, while of sound mind and disposing memory, is clear and beyond any question of doubt, free from fraud or undue influence of any kind. The only objection raised is that the statutes were not strictly complied with in the execution of the Will. I am of the opinion, when a person dies leaving a written

---

Justice Corn's participation in that decision. Five of the Supreme Court justices who were on the court in 1954 disqualified themselves, and five special justices were appointed in their stead. In a unanimous decision, two justices specially concurring, the court denied the petition since there was no allegation of wrongdoing in the particular case. Among the reasons given were the practical consequences of a contrary decision:

"It is apparent that if our holding were in the affirmative every decision from 1938 to January of 1959 in which Corn cast the deciding vote would have to be set aside. There are more than one thousand such cases. Rights of every kind have been settled by the decisions in such cases. Marriages have been contracted upon the basis of divorces granted, titles have been transferred and judgments paid. To now go back and reopen every such case for a possible new decision requiring new arguments and new hearings would cast intolerable and unjust burdens upon all the parties. Titles and status long thought put at rest would be thrown open to doubt. It would indeed create a 'shambles' as Respondent contends. And this would be so in every case in which Corn cast the deciding vote even though no corruption occurred in such case.

"To us this result seems unthinkable and contrary to the most elementary principles of justice. We think it more just that those cases in which no corruption can be found should be allowed to stand, at the same time giving full right to any person who believes that any such decision has been corruptly obtained, to petition this Court for a hearing, in which, if corruption can be shown, the decision may be set aside."

Cf. Electric Auto-Lite Co. v. P. & D. Mfg. Co., 109 F.2d 566 (2d Cir. 1940), where a rehearing was granted "because of the disqualification of one member of the original court [Judge Martin T. Manton, convicted of bribery in 1939], not known at the time."

For tales of other corrupt judges, including Sir Francis Bacon, see Borkin, The Corrupt Judge (1962). — Eds.

instrument which he intended to be his last Will, and it is free from fraud or undue influence and in harmony with the purpose of our law-makers for enacting statutes regulating the execution of Wills, and also in accord with the laws of England and twenty-two of our states, it would be a miscarriage of justice to not admit the Will to probate, and thereby allow the property to be disposed of contrary to the testator's intent.

To hold otherwise would, in effect, permit a contrary disposition of testator's property against the purpose for which the statutory provisions were aimed.

HALLEY, C.J., dissenting: . . . Counsel for the proponents of the purported will have come up with the ingenious idea that this instrument which is partly in typewriting and partly in handwriting is valid and should be admitted to probate for the fantastic reason that the handwriting is a codicil to the typewriting. It is my position that the typewritten part is not a will and the handwritten part is not a codicil. The handwritten part is only a continuation of the typewritten part and that combined, they constitute a will which was not attested and therefore cannot properly be admitted to probate.

. . . [T]here was nothing in the handwriting which referred to a previous will. It spoke of "this will" and not of a previous will. There is nothing about this handwriting to indicate that the testator intended it to be a codicil. He was completing his will with the handwriting.

I think he intended the typewritten portion to be a part of his will, not the completed will. A will is to be interpreted by what is found in its "four corners" and there is nothing to indicate that the testator intended it to be anything but one instrument. Parol or extrinsic evidence should not be admitted to show the contrary when the signed will is one instrument.

Under no circumstances should this be considered a codicil and I can never subscribe to the proposition that a holographic codicil will validate as a will an instrument that is typewritten, unfinished as to content, undated, unsigned and unattested. Not a case has been cited where a holographic codicil validates an instrument as a will which was not dated, signed or attested and no reference made in the purported codicil to the preceding will. . . .

Something is attempted to be made of the fact that the testator was a lawyer but that would prove nothing as many eminent lawyers have failed to properly prepare and execute their own wills. The will of Samuel J. Tilden is a notable example.

This will was one complete will unattested and therefore not admissible to probate and to give this will the construction that the majority has placed upon it is wholly unwarranted. Why make a mockery of the plain provision of our statutes? Property may only descend by will when the will is executed in conformity with the statutes.

I dissent.[54]

[54] Noted 8 Baylor L. Rev. 104; 7 Hastings L.J. 225; 44 Ky. L.J. 130; 30 N.Y.U.L. Rev. 1456; 9 Okla. L. Rev. 225; 34 Texas L. Rev. 148; 23 U. Chi. L. Rev. 316; 17 U. Pitt. L. Rev. 312; 8 Vand. L. Rev. 924. The careful dissection of the issues in the case in 23 U. Chi. L. Rev. 316 is especially good. — EDS.

NOTES AND PROBLEMS

1. In terms of the ritual and evidentiary functions of the statute of wills, is it better to view the problem in Johnson v. Johnson as one involving incorporation by reference or as one involving integration? Mechem, Integration of Holographic Wills, 12 N.C.L. Rev. 213 (1934).

2. Does incorporation of a typewritten document into a holographic will offend the requirement that a holographic will be entirely in the maker's handwriting? Hinson v. Hinson, 154 Tex. 561, 280 S.W.2d 731 (1955); Rogers v. Agricola, 176 Ark. 287, 3 S.W.2d 26 (1928). Does it matter whether testator uses one piece of paper or two?

3. If the holograph had not given James $10, could the holograph be probated? An instrument that does not dispose of property or appoint an executor cannot be probated as a will. If the holograph could not be probated, the typewritten part could not be incorporated by reference. Scott v. Gastright, 305 Ky. 340, 204 S.W.2d 367 (1947).

4. James Levin put his deceased wife's diamond ring in a jewelry box, and wrote on a piece of paper "Dec. 12, 1970. For Mary Korchek at my death. James Levin." He put the paper over the top of the box, and fastened them together by a string in the same manner as if he were wrapping the box for mailing. He then placed the box in a dresser drawer. At James's death is Mary entitled to the ring? Would it make any difference if inside the box were a stock certificate rather than a ring, or if James's signature were attested?

SECTION D. Contracts Relating to Wills

Questions respecting contracts to make wills can arise in a variety of fact situations, such as a claimed promise to make a will in exchange for an agreement not to contest a will, or to marry, or to serve as nurse and housekeeper. If a contract is found to exist, it is enforceable against the promisor's estate even though it was not executed with testamentary formalities. Contract law, not the law of wills, applies. Thus even an oral contract to make a will can be proved unless land is involved, in which case most courts require compliance with the Statute of Frauds provision governing contracts for the sale of land.

Application of contract law can also arise in the context of a claimed agreement not to revoke a will.[55] Typically, this question is raised where the parties have executed a joint will or mutual wills. A joint will is the will of two or more persons executed as one instrument and intended to serve as the will of each, as in the

[55] Where the first party to die has revoked his will and dies in breach of contract, the majority of courts deny the surviving party relief on the theory that the survivor has not been damaged. Thus a contract to make a will can be unilaterally terminated until one party dies. In a minority of jurisdictions a contract to make a will is treated like an ordinary bilateral contract.

". . . And to my faithful valet, Sidney, who I promised to remember in my will—Hi there, Sidney!"

Question: Does Sidney have an enforceable claim against his master's estate? See Kennedy v. Bank of America, 237 Cal. App. 2d 637, 47 Cal. Rptr. 154 (1965).

Rubenstein case, page 371. Mutual wills are the separate wills of two or more persons that contain similar or reciprocal provisions, as in the Oursler case, below.

Given these definitions of joint wills and mutual wills, it would appear to be impossible to have a "joint and mutual" will. Yet this term is commonly used by courts to describe a joint will that devises "our" property, and under which each testator gives an interest to his co-testator and to the same third persons.

There are no legal consequences peculiar to joint or mutual wills unless they are executed pursuant to a contract between the testators to devise their property in a given manner. The initial problem is proof of the contract. Most courts have adopted a rule that contracts not to revoke will not be enforced unless they are proved by clear and convincing evidence, and that the mere execution of a joint will or of mutual wills does not give rise to a presumption of contract. The difficulty, however, is that the existence of a common dispositive scheme and, in the case of a joint will, the expression of the scheme in a jointly executed instrument, strongly suggests an understanding or underlying agreement and thus invites a claim of contract, the terms of which can be inferred from the will or wills. The danger of litigation can be reduced by inserting in every mutual will a provision declaring that the will was or was not executed pursuant to a contract. This advice also applies to joint wills — but the lawyer who is astute enough to be aware of this problem will doubtless also know that joint wills are notorious litigation-breeders that shouldn't be used at all. The problems following the Rubenstein case explore some of the constructional problems raised by joint wills.

UNIFORM PROBATE CODE §2-701: "A contract to make a will or devise, or not to revoke a will or devise, or to die intestate, if executed after the effective date of this Act, can be established only by (1) provisions of a will stating material provisions of the contract; (2) an express reference in a will to a contract and extrinsic evidence proving the terms of the contract; or (3) a writing signed by the decedent evidencing the contract. The execution of a joint will or mutual wills does not create a presumption of a contract not to revoke the will or wills."

OURSLER v. ARMSTRONG

Court of Appeals of New York, 1961

10 N.Y.2d 385, 223 N.Y.S.2d 385, 179 N.E.2d 489

VAN VOORHIS, Judge. Charles Fulton Oursler had two children by his first wife and two children by his second wife.[56] In 1951 Oursler and his second wife, Grace

[56] Charles Fulton Oursler was the author of many books, including The Greatest Book Ever Written and The Greatest Story Ever Told. The latter, an account of the life of Jesus, was made into a motion picture. His first book, published in 1924, was entitled, prophetically, Behold This Dreamer! On his tombstone are carved the words, "Behold these Dreamers."

Fulton's second wife, Grace, also was an author, but she wrote books of an entirely different kind under the pseudonym of Dora May. They include Boy Crazy, Ex-Mistress, Promiscuous, Night Nurse, Modern Lady, Marry To-morrow, and Twilight Cheats. Oursler also wrote, under another name, Confessions of an Ex-Cabaret Girl. — EDS.

Perkins Oursler, executed wills at the same time before the same attesting witnesses. His will provided that his residuary estate would go to Grace; but if he survived her it would go to the four children of both his marriages, or their children; the will of Grace provided that her residuary should go to Oursler but, if she survived him, the property coming to her from Oursler would go to the same four children of both marriages, or to their children.

Oursler died in 1952. Grace survived him. On January 21, 1955, in the year of her death, she made a new will which was admitted to probate in which she left everything to her two children and nothing to the children of Oursler's first marriage. In this action in the Supreme Court the children of the first marriage and their children seek to impress a trust on the property received by Grace under Oursler's will.

The trial court impressed such a trust on the basis of a promise found to have been made by Grace Oursler that she would deal with the property received by her under her husband's will so that the children of both marriages would share alike in the property. The Appellate Division affirmed, stating that "On the whole record we are thus of opinion that Grace took the property by Fulton's will in a relationship of confidence from which Fulton believed she would dispose of the property 'as he would do it himself'; and that it was the implicit understanding between them that such a distribution was an obligation, based on confidence, which Grace undertook. The imposition of a constructive trust upon the estate of Grace is thus well grounded in equitable principle." One Justice dissented on the ground that the proof did not support a promise by Grace on which a constructive trust could be founded. We are in accord with the latter view.

Grace may have had a moral obligation to give the property which she inherited from Fulton to all four of the children, but a moral obligation alone is not enough to set the court in motion in a case of this kind (Amherst College v. Ritch, 151 N.Y. 282, 45 N.E. 876, 37 L.R.A. 305). The only basis on which a court can intervene is that a promise was made by Mrs. Grace Oursler not to alter or revoke her 1951 will and that by reason of her promise to that effect her husband gave and bequeathed to her what he did. The power to dispose of one's property by will is not lightly to be denied even if Judges think that the testatrix should have disposed of her estate differently. No express promise or representation was proved in writing or orally to have been made by Grace Oursler that she would not change her testamentary intent as expressed in the will which she executed contemporaneously with the will of her husband. Nor does the evidence from which such a promise is sought to be implied establish anything more than a 1951 intention on Mrs. Oursler's part to dispose of her property as she provided by her 1951 will.

The law does not view the renunciation of the right to alter or revoke a will as a casual matter (Matter of Bekker, 283 App. Div. 609, 129 N.Y.S.2d 126) and, regardless of whether the Statute of Frauds (Personal Property Law, §31, subd. 7) controls this case, as quite possibly it does not . . . , the spirit of it as well as the decisional law requires clear evidence of the existence of a promise of this nature. . . . In Edson v. Parsons, 155 N.Y. 555, 571, 50 N.E. 265, 269, after mentioning the similarity in lives, thoughts, emotions, and testamentary plan of two elderly maiden sisters whose wills were executed on the same day before the same witnesses, the court said in regard to a subsequent change in the will of the survivor: "Was the surviving sister not to be free, in all the contingencies of life, with all the possible mutations in her relations to others, or in the worthiness of the destined objects of their bounty, to make such other testamentary dispositions as might seem wise, or in better accord with her sentiments? These are most serious questions for consideration upon the plaintiff's appeal to a court of equity for relief."

The Appellate Division appears to have realized the weakness of the evidence in this record of any binding agreement or promise by Grace Oursler to renounce her future power of testamentary disposition. The opinion at the Appellate Division states that "It is clear that there is no remedy for plaintiffs to be laid in contract; they are unable to show either an enforcible contract by Grace to make a will for their benefit; or an enforcible contract by Grace to assume a trust in their interest."

The opinion then states: "The theory of constructive trust does not depend necessarily upon proof of the actual undertaking of a trust obligation by the party charged. He may have intended to become a trustee, and the proof of his undertaking either is barred by statutory or other rules of evidence, or direct proof of intent may be absent altogether. On the other hand he may have had no intention at all of becoming a trustee." This is followed by the statement that a constructive trust may embrace situations "where all reasonable probabilities point to an intended trust which cannot be proved," as well as "situations in which equity spells out a trust not at all intended by the trustee."

Thus a constructive trust for the testamentary disposition of assets received from another is equated with a quasi contract implied in law, contrary to actual fact, as thus described in Miller v. Schloss, 218 N.Y. 400, 407, 113 N.E. 337, 339: "A *quasi* or constructive contract rests upon the equitable principle that a person shall not be allowed to enrich himself unjustly at the expense of another. In truth it is not a contract or promise at all. It is an obligation which the law creates, in the absence of any agreement, when and because the acts of the parties or others have placed in the possession of one person money, or its equivalent, under such circumstances that in equity and good conscience he ought not to retain it, and which ex aequo et bono belongs to another. Duty, and not a promise or agreement or intention of the person sought to be charged, defines it. It is fictitiously deemed contractual, in order to fit the cause of action to the contractual remedy."

This is evidently the reasoning behind the statement by the Appellate Division in the case at bar that "It is the weight of judicial power that imposes the constructive trust; it is a trust fashioned by the moral mandate of equity."

This is all very well in instances where a defendant is charged as a trustee ex maleficio without intending to become a trustee in fact and in instances where he has misappropriated property belonging to another. It has no application to the present case where no property has been misappropriated and it is admitted that a moral obligation alone is not enough to set a court in motion to compel the devolution of property in a certain way (Amherst College v. Ritch, supra; Oursler v. Armstrong, 8 A.D.2d 194, 197, 186 N.Y.S.2d 829, 831, citing Wood v. Rabe, 96 N.Y. 414, 421).

Although at one point it was stated that on the whole record "it was the implicit understanding between them that such a distribution was an obligation, based on confidence, which Grace undertook" (8 A.D.2d 194, 200, 186 N.Y.S.2d 829, 836), the decision of this appeal depends upon the existence of an actual promise by Grace, express or implied, that she would not afterward change her will. Any conclusion based on analogy with the law of quasi contract is inadmissible. Courts do not have that much power over the devolution of other people's property. That is made clear by the cases which are cited in support of the existence of a confidential relationship in order to escape the impact of the Statute of Frauds, such as Sinclair v. Purdy, 235 N.Y. 245, 139 N.E. 255, and Foreman v. Foreman, 251 N.Y. 237, 167 N.E. 428, where, in writing the opinion, Judge Cardozo repeated the language used by him at Special Term in Golland v. Golland, 84 Misc. 299, 306, 147 N.Y.S. 263, 268, that "It is not the promise only, nor the breach only, but the promise and the breach combined with the extortion of property from the owner upon faith of the engagement, which puts the court in motion." The existence of a promise, express or implied, is a vital necessity; the mere fact of a confidential relationship is not enough. In the present instance Grace Oursler appropriated no property belonging to others, within the rule of quasi contract. She had the legal right to dispose of her property by will as she chose, unless she obtained her deceased husband's estate on the strength of a promise that she would bequeath it equally among his four children, in which event only could a constructive trust come into being covering what she inherited from him.

Where a testator has received property from others, now deceased, equity will intervene under certain circumstances to declare the surviving testator a trustee in order to carry out a promise on the strength of which the property has been received (Ahrens v. Jones, 169 N.Y. 555, 62 N.E. 666; Amherst College v. Ritch, supra); the existence of a joint will where the same document is signed by both husband and wife has been held to constitute a sufficient basis for the existence of such a promise (Rastetter v. Hoenninger, 214 N.Y. 66, 108 N.E. 210; Tutunjian v. Vetzigian, 299 N.Y. 315, 87 N.E.2d 275). An antenuptial contract has been held sufficient to the purpose (Phalen v. United States Trust Co., 186 N.Y. 178, 78 N.E. 943, 7 L.R.A., N.S., 734). Nevertheless, "To attribute to a will the quality of irrevocability demands the most indisputable evidence of the agreement which is relied upon to change its ambulatory nature, and that presumptions will not, and should not, take the place of proof." (Edson v. Parsons, supra, 155 N.Y. p. 568, 50 N.E. p. 268; Lally v. Cronen, 247 N.Y. 58, 63, 159 N.E. 723, 726; Wallace v. Wallace, 216 N.Y. 28, 109 N.E. 872; Matter of Bekker, supra). The same is true of the existence of a promise, express or implied from circumstances, in the case of a constructive trust of the nature sought to be established in this case. Such a promise is not established by the mere confidentiality of the relationship between the persons involved.

None of the testimony adduced to sustain the judgment establishes a promise by Grace Oursler to renounce her power of testamentary disposition. The witnesses

Farrar and Denker merely testified to conversations of a general nature, which have no tendency to establish a promise by Grace. The testimony of the attorney, Mr. Morris L. Ernst, indicates that there was a friendly relationship between Fulton and his two children by his first wife. Mr. Ernst did not testify to any promise made by Grace nor did he even testify that the memorandum which Grace sent to him outlining the contents of portions of her 1951 will was ever seen or mentioned by Fulton Oursler. If the intention had been that Mrs. Grace Oursler was renouncing her power to alter or revoke her 1951 will, as regards the property which she stood to inherit from her husband, it is remarkable that it was not put in writing or even mentioned orally in joint consultation by so experienced and competent a lawyer as Mr. Ernst. Instead of there being a promise to sustain a constructive trust of this kind, binding Grace Oursler during the rest of her life to the same testamentary disposition, it is plain that Fulton Oursler gave his property to her by will absolutely believing that in her own good judgment she would do whatever was the right thing. Many another husband has done the same.

The circumstance that Fulton Oursler once discussed the formation of a corporation to do a television production of "The Greatest Story Ever Told" whereas such corporation was never formed has no operative effect, nor the pre-incorporation agreement embodying an arrangement at one time desired by him. Nothing in the memorandum which Grace Oursler submitted to their attorney, Mr. Ernst, amounts to a promise that she would refrain from later exercising her prerogative of revoking or altering her 1951 will to which it relates. This memorandum has no more probative force than the will itself, the substance of portions of which it incorporates. The mere inclusion of statements that her 1951 will is "as he would wish it," or that "should he not survive me then I would wish my estate handled as he would wish matters to be handled, except that anything of my own would go directly to my own children and grandchildren, knowing that my husband's loved ones have been, are and will be well remembered," do not alter the situation. She was stating her present wish with regard to the contents of her 1951 will. The mere circumstance that she executed this will contemporaneously with the will of her husband, and that both contained similar provisions with respect to the gift over to Fulton Oursler's children in 1951, does not constitute an agreement as was recognized by the Appellate Division's citing Edson v. Parsons (supra) (8 A.D.2d 196, 186 N.Y.S.2d 831).

The judgment appealed from should be reversed and the complaint dismissed, with costs in all courts.

Froessel, Burke and Foster, JJ., concur with Van Voorhis, J.

Desmond, C.J., and Dye and Fuld, JJ., dissent and vote to affirm upon the opinion of Justice Bergan in the Appellate Division.[57]

---

[57] Noted 28 Brooklyn L. Rev. 336; 12 Buffalo L. Rev. 155; 13 Syracuse L. Rev. 621; 36 Tul. L. Rev. 885. In 1963 Justice Bergan, who wrote the opinion for the Appellate Division, succeeded Judge Foster on the Court of Appeals. Had the case come up thereafter, presumably it would have gone the other way. — Eds.

Will Oursler, Fulton Oursler's son by his first wife, Rose, recounts his version of the will contest in his book, Family Story 279-291 (1963):

> It was a battle I did not seek, did not want — brother and sister against brother and sister, love against love, hate against hate.
>
> I did not seek it, but I had no escape. The challenge was there. And if I did not wish battle for myself, I still could not leave Helen and her children to go the road alone.
>
> To accept it passively would be to believe that my father did not love my sister Helen and me, that he loved only the children of his second marriage, April and Tony. It would be to believe that my father wanted two of his children to live in luxury on the money he had earned, and the other two to know nothing but the earnings they struggled for. I've told the family story now; I can believe this no more now than I could before I began this retelling, this search of time past.
>
> It is an experience to be disinherited. Of a sudden there is a brand upon you, the letter etched into your flesh.
>
> You should feel quilty. But guilty of what? Of being born? For if you had not been born, Grace would have faced no problem, no lonely set of children to remind her of another wife.
>
> You turn to lawyers and courts to seek a remedy, if remedy there be. Could I go to them and ask them to give us money their mother left to them?
>
> In the hands of the law, lawyers, legalism, of procedures, delays, and tactics, you are no longer yourself or even your own master. Abruptly, you are a part of this too, and your lawyer informs you that introducing testimony about some of the facts might be painful. But this is the way of the law and courts, this is the meaning of conflict between human beings, the bitterness of conflict.
>
> We made our claim for a share in our father's estate.
>
> It went on for five years, the battle that hung above our lives like a smoky cloud. Helen and I were asking only for the share that would have come to us, and for our children the share that would have come to them, under the terms of Grace's original will. . . .
>
> While the battle of brother and sister against brother and sister went on in the courts, so also it went on in our lives, with no word between these two sets of children beyond the legalisms of complaints and answers and pretrial interrogations. . . .
>
> All this time the case went on, the battle of briefs and counterbriefs. There was an effort at settlement, and April and Tony and Helen and I had several meetings, through which would occasionally glow the feeling that we were truly brothers and sisters.
>
> For a few weeks it almost seemed as though a settlement were possible; it almost seemed as though the flickering flame of brotherhood was coming alive. But it, too, died in the suffocating questions that arose — lawyers' bills and which side was to pay them, questions of who was right and wrong at this time or that. The lawyers tried to work it out and failed, we all tried to work it out and failed. The staggering legal fees remained to be met, and unanswered questions that dogged us remained.
>
> Grimly, like a Greek tragedy, the plot went on and we returned to court. For this breakdown in negotiations that could have made us all more content I don't

blame April and Tony. I blame the four of us — and Grace and Fulton, the past, all our lives.

There were too many problems, too much involvement with lawyers and fees and bills to be paid. And below the surface perhaps the chasm had become too great to bridge.

We were brothers and sisters, but we could not agree. Once more the case went back into the courts, but now it was a higher court — the New York Court of Appeals. And there April and Tony won, four to three, and it was over.

There are no villains in this family story. What can I be but sorry for what Grace has done to Helen and to me, to April and to Tony, to Fulton's grandchildren, most of all for what she did to herself? Can I find it in my heart to hold rancor, where there is only pity and sorrow for the woman of many gifts and accomplishments who suffered bitter insecurity and guilt? She was bewildered and confused, torn by conflict. And her last gesture, incomprehensible to Helen and me, left our family irreparably estranged.

RUBENSTEIN v. MUELLER

Court of Appeals of New York, 1967

19 N.Y.2d 228, 278 N.Y.S.2d 845, 225 N.E.2d 540

Burke, Judge. On October 23, 1961, Bertha and Conrad Mueller, after nearly a half century of marriage, executed a joint will providing that the estate of the first to die should go to the survivor, and on the survivor's death their property should go to certain named beneficiaries. Nine months later in July of 1962, Bertha died and Conrad, pursuant to the joint will, received her entire net estate. The following month Mueller's cousin, Martha Louise Mueller, the defendant herein, came to live with him, keeping house for him and after he became ill, nursing him until his death in June, 1964. Conrad and Martha were married on March 12, 1963, and a week later on March 20 Conrad executed a new will naming his second wife sole beneficiary. This latter will has been admitted to probate.

On this appeal we are asked to determine the respective rights of the widow and the beneficiaries under the joint will to Muellers' property, consisting of a house and lot acquired by Bertha and Conrad as tenants by the entirety in 1919, and a joint bank account in Conrad and Martha's names, but funded with money received by Conrad as the surviving owner of joint bank accounts in the names of Bertha and himself. There is unanimity of opinion in this court that Conrad's final will was ineffective to alter the testamentary arrangement provided for in the joint will, but we are divided over the question of whether this decedent's earlier covenant with his first wife respecting the disposition to be made of their collective property on the death of the survivor should take precedence over the claim of the widow to a right of election to take against the earlier joint will.[58]

[58] The widow does not actually assert a right of election, as provided in section 18 of the Decedent Estate Law, Consol. Laws, c. 13, since under the later will, properly admitted to probate as the last will and testament of her husband, she takes all, though subject to the claims of

On the first issue raised herein, the revocability of the joint will, the language in the instrument clearly indicates the Muellers' intention that its provisions should be binding upon the survivor. It "imports the joint disposition of the collective property of both, not the independent disposition by each of his own." (Rastetter v. Hoenninger, 214 N.Y. 66, 72, 108 N.E. 210, 211; see, also, Rich v. Mottek, 11 N.Y.2d 90, 94, 226 N.Y.S.2d 428, 430, 181 N.E.2d 445, 446; Tutunjian v. Vetzigian, 299 N.Y. 315, 320, 87 N.E.2d 275, 277.) The recently decided case of Matter of Zeh 24 A.D.2d 983, 265 N.Y.S.2d 257, affd. 18 N.Y.2d 900, 276 N.Y.S.2d 635, 223 N.E.2d 43, wherein we held that the joint will in question was not binding upon the survivor, is distinguishable from the present case. In Zeh the survivor was given all the property, "meaning thereby that *the survivor of us shall be the absolute owner*, to him or to her to have and to hold, his or her heirs and assigns *absolutely and forever*, of all that both of us possess." (Emphasis added.) Under the rule that before the right to alter or revoke a will may be curtailed prior to the testator's death his intention to so bind himself must be manifested clearly and unambiguously (see Oursler v. Armstrong, 10 N.Y.2d 385, 389, 223 N.Y.S.2d 477, 478, 179 N.E.2d 489, 490), the use of language such as "absolutely" barred our finding that the survivor was bound to the testamentary plan found in that joint will. In the instant case, on the other hand, the Muellers' intention is clear and unambiguous. The phrasing used in paragraph "Third", providing that "[u]pon the death of the second one of us to die, or in the event of our simultaneous deaths or deaths resulting from a common disaster, then the estate of the second decedent, or of both of us as the case may be, is hereby bequeathed, devised and disposed of as follows", is in the present tense, and thus implies a present joint intention to make a gift of the collective property to the named beneficiaries, effective upon the survivor's death, but binding as of the signing of the joint will. The entire context of the will is plural, the pronoun "we" is used instead of "I", "our" instead of "my" and "us" instead of "me". (See Rich v. Mottek, supra, 11 N.Y.2d p. 94, 226 N.Y.S.2d p. 430, 181 N.E.2d p. 446; Tutunjian v. Vetzigian, supra, 299 N.Y. p. 320, 87 N.E.2d p. 277.) Moreover, this will contains an express revocation of a prior joint will and it *omits* the provision in that prior will describing the survivor's right to alter the disposition made of the signatories' property. The omission of this provision in the later joint will is persuasive evidence that the second joint will was intended to be irrevocable. (Compare the analysis employed by this court in Tutunjian, supra, 299 N.Y. p. 320, 87 N.E.2d p. 277, where we took note of the fact that the joint will there in question "preserved and repeated the same dispositions without substantial change" that were contained in an earlier will.)

---

the beneficiaries named in the joint will. Her argument is, rather, that the public policy finding expression in section 18, seeking to guarantee the widow a distributive share in her husband's estate, constitutes a limitation upon the right of a party to a joint will to bind himself to a testamentary arrangement which would not provide a surviving spouse with such a share in his estate. Consequently, equity should decline to specifically enforce an otherwise binding obligation of the survivor under a joint will where such specific enforcement will frustrate this legislatively declared public policy.

On the other issue raised here, the effect of section 18 of the Decedent Estate Law on the right of the beneficiaries under the joint will to obtain specific enforcement of the covenant by Mueller contained in that will, we are of the opinion that the named beneficiaries under the joint will are entitled to prevail and a constructive trust in their favor was properly impressed upon the property received by the widow under the later will.

As to property received by Mueller under the joint will there can be no question but that upon his acceptance of such benefits under that instrument a trust was impressed in favor of the beneficiaries to the extent expressed in Tutunjian. As to such property Mueller really took but an interest during his life with a power to use or otherwise dispose of principal, and the named beneficiaries took the interest which remained. Under such circumstances he had no property interest in these assets against which his widow's right of election could operate.

The bulk of the property involved did not come to Mueller under the joint will. His interest in the real property, for example, commenced as a tenant by the entirety, ripening into sole ownership through his surviving his first wife. Similarly, his formal title to most of the personalty, consisting of savings accounts, derived from his surviving Bertha, with whom he had these joint accounts. In addition, it is not clear from the stipulated facts whether any of this jointly held property represented the independent estate of Bertha Mueller or whether, as is typical, it represented the jointly held fruits of Conrad's labors outside the home aided by Bertha's efforts within the home for their lifetime together. In any event we do not attempt a segregation of assets of husband and wife after a marriage of this duration. For all practical purposes, equity may content itself with considering the assets as their collective property, as if their estates had merged.

As to this collective property we feel that, on the death of one party to the joint will, the survivor was bound by the mutual agreement that the named beneficiaries should receive the property remaining when the survivor died. (See Hermann v. Ludwig, 186 App. Div. 287, 297, 174 N.Y.S. 469, 474, affd. 229 N.Y. 544, 129 N.E. 908.) As we pointed out above, the agreement embodied in the joint will provides that "Upon the death of the second . . . the estate of the second . . . is hereby bequeathed, devised and disposed of as follows." The survivor's right to full ownership of the collective property is transformed and modified by this joint agreement, effective upon the other's death as stated above, into but an interest during the life of the survivor with power to use the principal. "While neither a husband nor a wife can dispose of property owned by them as tenants by the entirety so as to affect the right of survivorship, they may do so by acting in concert, as by a joint will, or by a contract." (Azzara v. Azzara, 1 A.D.2d 1012, 1013, 151 N.Y.S.2d 458, 460; see, also, Swerdfeger v. Swerdfeger, 4 A.D.2d 535, 167 N.Y.S.2d 775.) After Bertha's death, then, the property received by Conrad was his but subject to an interest enforcible specifically as to so much of it as he did not consume during his lifetime.

Contrary to the result which we here reach, the defendant urges that the widow's right of election constitutes a limitation on the freedom of an individual to so incumber his estate. In support of this contention she directs our attention to a number of lower court cases involving marital separation agreements under which husbands covenanted to make a will leaving all or a portion of their property to the estranged wife or to their children and later remarried, leaving widows. In these cases the learned Surrogates correctly held that the former wife's right to specific enforcement of the agreement must give way to the widow's statutory right to a share in her husband's estate. (Matter of Lewis' Will, 4 Misc. 2d 937, 123 N.Y.S.2d 859; Matter of Erstein's Estate, 205 Misc. 924, 129 N.Y.S.2d 316; Matter of Hoyt's Estate, 174 Misc. 512, 21 N.Y.S.2d 107.) These cases are, however, distinguishable from the instant case and they present different equitable considerations. Separation agreements are usually attended by a present division of any jointly held property, and any provision for a future legacy is usually but an incident to the over-all settlement to be made with respect to the husband's individual property and his obligation of support. In the case of the joint will, however, this instrument typically represents the sole attempt by the signatories to effect a distribution of their collective property in a fashion agreeable to both. Most importantly, in those separation agreements there was no irrevocable obligation concerning the collective property. The husband did not, as Mueller did here, become sole owner of jointly owned property by virtue of surviving the former wife. As the divorced husband's property after the agreement remains his own individual property, to which he holds beneficial as well as legal title, his widow's right of election may be asserted against such assets.

Accordingly, the order of the Appellate Division affirming the judgment of Special Term should be affirmed, without costs.

BERGAN, Judge (dissenting). . . . The basic legal effect of the execution of the superseding will is to be seen in Tutunjian v. Vetzigian, 299 N.Y. 315, 87 N.E.2d 275. There it was held that when there is a breach by one of the parties of an agreement expressed in a joint will not to revoke it, the court will recognize the legal power of the testator to do this, but equity will compel his executor and beneficiaries "to perform the contract" of their decedent (299 N.Y. 315, 319, 87 N.E.2d 275, 276, per Fuld, J.).

This means in legal theory that the property is deemed in the estate and subject to testamentary disposition, but the court will control the disposition posthumously. It follows that the surviving spouse's right of election to an intestate share is assertable against the estate and against any will which would cut her off. . . .

When it comes to a matter of the equities involved in this equitable action, the surviving spouse who seeks to make the election which the statute gives her is possessed of superior equitable rights. She married decedent on March 12, 1963. In August, within six months of this marriage, decedent became ill of cancer from which he died 10 months later, on June 28, 1964.

It is expressly stipulated that the surviving spouse "took care of him and nursed him until he died." As far as the record shows, the plaintiff, a niece of the first wife, did nothing for the testator, and it seems not unreasonable that the surviving widow's share, at least, of the property which decedent had accumulated and which is not shown to have been derived individually from the first wife, go to the surviving spouse on her election. No one would suggest that, had dower been continued in New York, this joint will could have defeated the surviving wife's dower and the right of election, as a statutory substitute for dower, is much the same thing.

The order should be modified to allow the appropriate scope to be given to the right of election of the surviving spouse.

Van Voorhis, Scileppi, Keating and Breitel, JJ., concur with Burke, J.

Bergan, J., dissents in an opinion in which Fuld, C.J., concurs.

Order affirmed.

NOTES AND PROBLEMS

1. When a person enters into a valid contract to *convey* land and then marries before execution of the conveyance, the authorities are unanimous in holding that the surviving spouse cannot, upon the death of the contracting spouse, claim dower or curtesy or a statutory forced share in the property. Where the contract is to *make a will*, however, many courts hold that knowledge of the contract by the surviving spouse is a material factor, and that the survivor's claim will be denied where knowledge is shown, and will be allowed in the absence of knowledge. Thus in Barkley v. Barkley, 314 F.2d 188, 8 A.L.R.3d 562 (5th Cir., 1963), the court held that under Florida law a will, executed pursuant to a contract between the decedent and his first wife, did not cut off the surviving second wife's dower rights, since she had no notice of the will or the contract when she married the decedent.

2. Suppose a state statute provides that if the testator marries after executing a will, the will is revoked as to the surviving spouse unless the spouse is mentioned or provided for in the will, and that the surviving spouse will take her intestate share. Can the surviving spouse claim her intestate share under such a statute where, before marriage, the testator contracts to devise all his property to his stepchildren and his will fulfills the contract? In Simpson v. Dodge, 220 Ga. 705, 141 S.E.2d 532 (1965), it was held that the surviving spouse took her intestate share. In re Estate of Stewart, 69 Cal. 2d 296, 70 Cal. Rptr. 545, 444 P.2d 337 (1968) is contra.

3. The exact language of the Mueller will was as follows:

> SECOND: The first deceased hereby bequeaths and devises all real and personal property of whatever kind and wherever situated to the survivor of us outright.
>
> THIRD: Upon the death of the second one of us to die, or in the event of our simultaneous deaths or deaths resulting from a common disaster, then the estate of said second decedent, or both of us as the case may be, is hereby bequeathed, devised and disposed of as follows: . . . .
>
> FOURTH: All the rest, residue and remainder of the estate or estates . . . we hereby give, devise and bequeath equally between Ruth Hanzlicsek and Wilma Rubenstein aforesaid.

263 N.Y.S.2d 349, 351 (1965). In its opinion the Court of Appeals made no mention of the second clause, with its language of gift to the survivor "outright." (Is the implication from this word different from the language of "absolute owner" in the Zeh case, cited and distinguished by the court?) Instead, the court laid heavy emphasis on the words "we" and "us" in the third and fourth clauses, making a gift over on the death of the survivor, in finding that the will was contractual.

In Matter of Zeh, 18 N.Y.2d 900, 276 N.Y.S.2d 635, 223 N.E.2d 43 (1966), decided by the same court four months before, the will read as follows:

> SECOND: We give, devise and bequeath all of the Estate, of whatsoever kind and nature and wheresoever situated, of which we, or either of us, may die seized and/or possessed . . . each unto the other, meaning thereby that the survivor of us shall be the absolute owner, to him or to her . . . absolutely and forever of all that both of us possess.
>
> THIRD: Upon the death of the survivor of us, or in the event that our deaths should occur simultaneously, or approximately so, or in the same common accident or disaster, . . . we, or the survivor of us, give, devise and bequeath unto our children Fanny Rebecca Howell and William Arthur Zeh all of the Estate of which we, or said survivor, shall die seized and/or possessed. . . .

In its opinion the court made no mention of the third clause, with its gift over on the death of the survivor. Instead, the court laid heavy emphasis on the words "absolute owner" and "absolutely and forever" in the second clause in finding that the will was not contractual. Three judges dissented.

4. After Bertha Mueller's death, what were Conrad's rights in the property during his lifetime? Since he had been given the property "outright," did he have the rights of a fee simple owner, with the gift on his death being only of what he had not consumed, spent, or given away during his lifetime? Or did Conrad have only a life estate? Suppose that Conrad gave all the property to his second wife Martha after he learned that he was terminably ill, or suppose that he set up an inter vivos revocable trust for himself for life, remainder to Martha. Could the contract beneficiaries set aside these transfers (a) in their entirety, or (b) as to Bertha's share of the property transferred, during Conrad's life or after his death? Estate of Chayka, 47 Wis. 2d 102, 176 N.W.2d 561 (1970).

Does the contract apply only to Conrad's property as of Bertha's death? (If so, will there be any problem in identifying the property subject to the contract?) Or does the contract also apply to property acquired by Conrad thereafter? Note that the will (and thus the contract?) speaks of "the estate of the second decedent."

These and other constructional problems are discussed in Sparks, Contracts to Make Wills (1956); Comment, The Contractual Will: Invitation to Litigation and Excess Taxation, 48 Texas L. Rev. 909 (1970).

5. The estate and gift tax problems arising from contracts to make a will are slippery and far from settled.

a. *At Bertha's death:*

(1) Does the transfer from Bertha to Conrad qualify for the marital deduction

under the federal estate tax? Or is it disallowed because Conrad received a terminable interest? Treas. Reg. §20.2056(e)-2(a) (1970) provides: ". . . The deduction may not be taken with respect to a property interest which passed to such spouse . . . subject to a binding agreement by the spouse to dispose of the interest in favor of a third person." Estate of Awtry v. Comm'r, 221 F.2d 749 (8th Cir. 1955); Sparks, Application of the Marital Deduction to Joint and Mutual Wills, 37 Miss. L.J. 226 (1966).

In Estate of Saul Krampf, 56 T.C. No. 25 (1971), H and W entered into a joint, mutual, and contractual will providing that on the death of either the property of the deceased would become the "sole and separate property of the surviving party for his or her use and benefit forever" and upon the death of the survivor, the property of both H and W would pass to their children. H died. The Tax Court held that the property received by the wife did not qualify for the marital deduction because the wife was contractually bound to devise any unconsumed portions of it to her children.

Revenue Ruling 71-51, 1971 Int. Rev. Bull. No. 5 at 15, deals with the tax treatment of jointly owned property and life insurance proceeds that are restricted by a contract to will. A husband and wife owned certain property as joint tenants. The husband owned several insurance policies on his life in which his wife was designated beneficiary. In 1955 the husband and wife executed a joint, mutual, and contractual will that provided that all their property was to be held by the survivor during his or her life with the right to the income therefrom, remainder to their children upon the death of the survivor. The husband died in 1964; the wife died in 1968. The ruling stated:

"Under the general rule relating to joint tenancies, a joint tenant who survives does not take the interest of the other tenant from him as his successor, but takes it by right under the instrument by which the tenancy was created. Thus, joint tenancy property passes outside of a will even though the interest that vests in the surviving tenant is limited by the terms of the instrument. Similarly, the proceeds of life insurance pass to the named beneficiary by reason of the designation in the insurance contract and not under the will or pursuant to any contractual provision in the will. Any restriction limiting the surviving tenant's (beneficiary's) interest to a life estate is not placed on the property by the decedent, but arises out of the contract voluntarily entered into by the survivor. . . .

"Accordingly, it is held . . . that complete ownership passed from the decedent to the surviving wife. . . . Such complete ownership is a nonterminable interest that qualifies for the marital deduction under section 2056(a) of the Code notwithstanding that such property is subject to the restriction of the joint and mutual will as to its ultimate distribution.

"The surviving wife's survivorship interest in the jointly held property and the insurance proceeds ripened into absolute ownership upon the death of her husband. However, under the contractual aspects of the joint and mutual will that were irrevocable at the death of the husband, the wife's fee interest in the property was reduced to a life estate, the remainder interest passing to the children. Thus, the wife is deemed to have made a transfer . . . of the entire value of the property, under which she retained for her life the right to the income from the property.

"Accordingly, it is held . . . that the entire value of the . . . property . . . is includible in the deceased wife's gross estate under section 2036 of the Code."

Do you see how the Internal Revenue Service has given a time sequence as to when the contract becomes binding if the property is jointly held property which differs from the time sequence given if the property passes to the wife under the husband's will? In the former case the contract becomes binding on the wife one moment of time after the husband dies. In the latter case the contract becomes binding on the wife simultaneously with the husband's death. Should tax consequences turn upon what time sequence is given to purely conceptual events?

(2) If under Bertha's will Conrad were given only a life estate, without power to consume principal, would Conrad make a taxable gift to the contract beneficiaries of a remainder interest in his own property? Revenue Ruling 71-51 apparently assumes the answer is yes. Conrad has given up a remainder interest in *his* property in exchange for a life estate in *Bertha's* property. In determining the amount of the gift, is Conrad entitled to deduct the value of such life estate from the value of the remainder interest that he has given in his own property? Johanson, Revocable Trusts, Widow's Election Wills, and Community Property: The Tax Problems, 47 Texas L. Rev. 1247, 1267-1269 (1969). If Conrad is given the power to consume principal, no gift results. Id. 1269-1274; S. E. Brown, 52 T.C. 50 (1969).

b. *At Conrad's death:*

Is the value of the property received from Bertha included in Conrad's federal gross estate? The property which passed to Conrad as a tenant by the entirety or as a joint tenant would be included. Revenue Ruling 71-51. What about Bertha's separate property which passed to Conrad under her will? If Conrad received in such property the equivalent of a life estate coupled with a general power of appointment not limited by an ascertainable standard relating to his health, education, support, or maintenance, the value of such property is includible. Internal Rev. Code of 1954, §2041(b)(1)(A); Phinney v. Kay, 275 F.2d 776 (5th Cir. 1960).

6. Given the frequency with which joint wills are litigated on the question of whether they are contractual, and given the constructional and tax problems raised if they are found contractual, is the lawyer who drafts a joint will liable for negligence if the will is later litigated?

8. Formalities of Transfer: Trusts and Gifts

SECTION A. The Requisites of a Trust

1. *Introduction*

In the words of the Restatement (Second) of Trusts, a trust is "a fiduciary relationship with respect to property, subjecting the person by whom the property is held to equitable duties to deal with the property for the benefit of another person." [1] It is basically a device whereby one or more persons manage the property for the benefit of others. The usual kind of trust is an express trust created by a written instrument.

Just as there is separation of management from benefits in a trust, there is a correlative separation of rights in the property held subject to trust. The trustee ordinarily has legal title to the property, and the beneficiaries have equitable title. Generally speaking, equitable title can be broken into as many conceptual parts as legal title can be. You can create equitable life estates, equitable remainders, equitable executory interests, etc. Hence:

> *Case 1.* O, the settlor, transfers $100,000 to X in trust to pay the income to A for life, and on A's death to distribute the trust property to A's issue then living per stirpes. X has legal ownership equivalent to a fee simple. A has an equitable life estate, A's issue have an equitable contingent remainder in fee simple, and O has an equitable reversion (often called a resulting trust).

[1] Restatement (Second) of Trusts §2 (1959). Maitland characterized the law of trusts as a "vast appendix" to the law of property. Maitland, Equity 20 (1909).

These equitable interests are the result of the accidental circumstance that in England there were separate courts of law and equity. What started out as the mere enforcement of personal duties of the trustee by the Chancellor grew into ownership forms closely analogous to legal interests in property. Today most future interests are equitable rather than legal interests; they are created in trust property. Legal future interests in chattels are rare, and always inadvisable. Legal future interests in land are sometimes encountered. They too are almost always inadvisable. A trust with equitable future interests is much more flexible and useful than legal future interests.

A trustee is held to a very high standard of conduct in handling the property. He is under a duty to administer the trust solely in the interest of the beneficiary. He must preserve the property, make it productive, and, where required by the terms of the trust, pay the income to the beneficiary. His more important duties include duties to keep the trust property separate from his own, to keep accurate accounts, to invest prudently, and not to delegate his powers. Banks are frequently named as trustee. Almost every large bank has a trust department set up to manage trusts and carry out the duties expected and required of a trustee. If the trustee improperly manages the trust property he may be denied his commissions, subjected to personal liability, or removed as trustee by a court.

In order to have a trust, it is necessary for the trustee to have some duties to perform. If he has no duties at all, there is no reason to have a trust. The trust is then said to be "passive," rather than active, and the trust fails. When a trust fails because the trustee has no active duties, the beneficiaries acquire legal title to the trust property.

A trust ordinarily involves at least three parties: the settlor, the trustee, and the beneficiary. But three different persons are not necessary for a trust. One person can wear two, or even all three, hats. The settlor may be trustee. He may simply declare himself trustee of certain property for the benefit of designated beneficiaries. A declaration of trust requires no delivery. Thus:

> *Case* 2. O executes a deed of trust declaring himself trustee of Blackacre, to pay the income to A for life, and upon the death of A to convey Blackacre to B. This is a valid trust. Neither consideration nor delivery of the deed of trust is necessary. All that is required is that O manifest an intention to hold the property in trust.

Moreover, the settlor also may be a beneficiary and at the same time trustee. Thus:

> *Case* 3. O executes a deed of trust declaring himself trustee of Blackacre, to pay the income to himself for life, and upon his death Blackacre is to go to A. This is a valid trust. If O were the sole beneficiary and the trustee, the trust would not be valid because no one can hold O accountable under the trust. O must owe equitable duties to someone other than himself.

Just as the settlor may be trustee, the beneficiary of a trust may be a trustee. Thus:

Case 4. By will, T devises property to X in trust to pay the income to X for life, and upon the death of X the property is devised to A. This trust arrangement is preferable to a legal life estate in X, remainder in A. X as trustee must keep the trust property separate from his own property. A trustee has broader powers of sale and reinvestment than a legal life tenant has.

A trust may be created by an instrument executed by the settlor during his life. This *trust deed* will create an *inter vivos* (or *living*) trust. Or a trust may be created by will, in which case it is a *testamentary* trust. An *inter vivos* trust is a non-court trust, i.e., it comes into being without the intervention of any court, and in most states it is not subject to court orders unless the beneficiary or the trustee comes into court to settle some trust matter. A testamentary trust, on the other hand, is a court trust. It is brought into being by the probate court which supervises the administration of the estate, and this court continues to supervise the administration of the trust after the estate is closed. One of the primary differences between a court and a non-court trust relates to the accounting. Judicial approval of a trustee's accounts is often a time-consuming and expensive procedure. It may require the appointment of guardians ad litem to represent unborn and unascertained beneficiaries. To avoid this, a provision may be inserted in a trust instrument that certain beneficiaries have the power to approve the trustee's accounts without a court proceeding. This provision is effective in non-court trusts, but whether it is effective in court trusts is open to question. The probate court, having brought the trust into being, may refuse to be deprived of its authority to oversee the trustee's work.

The usual definition of a trust includes three elements: a trustee, a trust res, and a beneficiary. All three are sometimes stated to be necessary, but this must be taken with an appropriate amount of salt. If there is an intention to create a trust by will, but no trustee is named, or if the trustee dies, a trustee will be appointed by a court. This result is stated in this rule: *a trust will not fail for want of a trustee.* If the attempted trust is inter vivos, however, and no trustee is named, the trust may fail for want of a transferee or for want of delivery.

With respect to the necessity of beneficiaries, the beneficiaries may be unborn or unascertained. A trust by O, an unmarried man, for the benefit of his children would be a valid trust, and the court would protect the unborn children from improper acts of the trustee. On the other hand, if at the time the trust becomes effective, the beneficiaries are not definite and they can never be ascertained, then the attempted trust may fail for want of ascertainable beneficiaries. Thus in a transfer to X as trustee "to pay the income to my best friends," no trust is created. The class of takers is too indefinite to permit identification of the beneficiaries.[2] We shall discuss the problem of unascertainable beneficiaries in Chapter 13, when we take up powers of appointment. The problem is best understood in the context of whether an instrument creates a trust or a power.

[2] A charitable trust may be created for the benefit of indefinite beneficiaries, described as broadly as this: "any corporations, trusts, or community chests, funds, or foundations, which are organized and operated exclusively for religious, charitable, scientific, literary, or educational purposes, with respect to which no part of the net earnings inures to the benefit of any private shareholder or individual." See Chapter 14.

2. *The Requirement of a Res*

A trust res is said to be necessary to a trust. If the trust has no res — if the trustee has no property to manage — the trust is "dry" (as a well is dry, not as a wine is dry). A dry trust fails. When the meaning of res is examined, however, we find that it may refer to something other than a piece of land or a hefty bit of boodle, such as $100,000. The res can be one dollar or one cent or it can be *any* "interest" in property that can be transferred.[3] Contingent remainders, leasehold interests, choses in action, royalties, et cetera, can be put in trust. The critical question is whether the particular claim will be called an "interest" by a court. When one ventures beyond what are historically conceded to be "interests," the circumstances that lead a court to classify a claim as an "interest" rather than an "expectancy" require a careful analysis of many variables.[4]

BRAINARD v. COMMISSIONER OF INTERNAL REVENUE

United States Court of Appeals, Seventh Circuit, 1937
91 F.2d 880

SPARKS, Circuit Judge. This petition for review involves income taxes for the year 1928. The question presented is whether under the circumstances set forth in the findings of the Board of Tax Appeals, the taxpayer created a valid trust, the income of which was taxable to the beneficiaries under section 162 of the Revenue Act of 1928.

The facts as found by the Board of Tax Appeals are substantially as follows: In December, 1927, the taxpayer, having decided that conditions were favorable, contemplated trading in the stock market during 1928. He consulted a lawyer and was advised that it was possible for him to trade in trust for his children and other members of his family. Taxpayer thereupon discussed the matter with his wife and mother, and stated to them that he declared a trust of his stock trading during 1928 for the benefit of his family upon certain terms and conditions. Taxpayer agreed to assume personally any losses resulting from the venture, and to distribute the

[3] In Kutner, Due Process of Euthanasia: The Living Will, A Proposal, 44 Ind. L.J. 539 (1969), it is suggested that the settlor's body be the res of a trust providing that if the settlor becomes vegetative, medical treatment of the body shall cease.

[4] See 4 Powell, Real Property ¶512 (1970); 1 Scott, Trusts §§74-88 (3d ed. 1967). Cf. Elliott v. Elliott, 231 Cal. App. 2d 205, 41 Cal. Rptr. 686 (1964): "Defendant tells us no res is involved here, simply an indebtedness which became unenforceable by reason of the statute of limitations. It should hardly be necessary to point out that the note which evidenced the indebtedness satisfied any technical requirement that there be 'a thing' or a res, in the sense that a res is a necessary integrant of the concept 'constructive trust.'" What if the note burned up? Would you still have a "thing"?

A transfer of an expectancy is enforceable in equity as a contract to transfer if an adequate consideration was given. 3 Powell, Real Property ¶383 (1970).

profits, if any, in equal shares to his wife, mother, and two minor children after deducting a reasonable compensation for his services. During 1928 taxpayer carried on the trading operations contemplated and at the end of the year determined his compensation at slightly less than $10,000, which he reported in his income tax return for that year. The profits remaining were then divided in approximately equal shares among the members of his family, and the amounts were reported in their respective tax returns for 1928. The amounts allocated to the beneficiaries were credited to them on taxpayer's books, but they did not receive the cash, except taxpayer's mother, to a small extent.

In addition to these findings the record discloses that taxpayer's two children were one and three years of age. Upon these facts the Board held that the income in controversy was taxable to the petitioner as a part of his gross income for 1928, and decided that there was a deficiency. It is here sought to review that decision.

In the determination of the questions here raised it is necessary to consider the nature of the trust, if any, that is said to have been created by the circumstances hereinbefore recited. It is clear that the taxpayer, at the time of his declaration, had no property interest in "profits in stock trading in 1928, if any," because there were none in existence at that time. Indeed it is not disclosed that the declarer at that time owned any stock. It is obvious, therefore, that the taxpayer based his declaration of trust upon an interest which at that time had not come into existence and in which no one had a present interest. In the Restatement of the Law of Trusts, vol. 1, §75, it is said that an interest which has not come into existence or which has ceased to exist can not be held in trust. It is there further said: "A person can, it is true, make a contract binding himself to create a trust of an interest if he should thereafter acquire it; but such an agreement is not binding as a contract unless the requirements of the law of Contracts are complied with . . .

"Thus, if a person gratuitously declares himself trustee of such shares as he may thereafter acquire in a corporation not yet organized, no trust is created. The result is the same where instead of declaring himself trustee, he purports to transfer to another as trustee such shares as he may thereafter acquire in a corporation not yet organized. In such a case there is at most a gratuitous undertaking to create a trust in the future, and such an undertaking is not binding as a contract for lack of consideration . . .

". . . If a person purports to declare himself trustee of an interest not in existence, or if he purports to transfer such an interest to another in trust, he is liable as upon a contract to create a trust if, but only if, the requirements of the law of Contracts are complied with." See, also, Restatement, §30b; Bogert, Trusts and Trustees, vol. 1, §112. In 42 Harvard Law Review 561, it is said: "With logical consistency, the courts have uniformly held that an expectancy cannot be the subject matter of a trust and that an attempted creation, being merely a promise to transfer property in the future, is invalid unless supported by consideration." Citing Lehigh Valley R.R. Co. v. Woodring, 116 Pa. 513, 9 A. 58. Hence, it is obvious under the facts here presented that taxpayer's declaration amounted to nothing more than a promise to create a trust in the future, and its binding force must be determined by the requirements of the law of contracts.

It is elementary that an executory contract, in order to be enforceable, must be based upon a valuable consideration. Here there was none. The declaration was gratuitous. If we assume that it was based on love and affection that would add nothing to its enforceability, for love and affection, though a sufficient consideration for an executed conveyance, is not a sufficient consideration for a promise. . . .

What has been said, however, does not mean that the taxpayer had no right to carry out his declaration after the subject matter had come into existence, even though there were no consideration. This he did and the trust thereby became effective, after which it was enforceable by the beneficiaries.

The questions with which we are concerned are at what times did the respective earnings which constitute the trust fund come into existence, and at what times did the trust attach to them. It is obvious that the respective profits came into existence when and if such stocks were sold at a profit in 1928. Did they come into existence impressed with the trust, or was there any period of time intervening between the time they came into existence and the time the trust attached? If there were such intervening time, then during that time the taxpayer must be considered as the sole owner of the profits and they were properly taxed to him as a part of his income.

It is said in the Restatement of the Law of Trusts, §75c: "If a person purports to declare himself trustee of an interest not in existence or if he purports to transfer such an interest to another in trust, no trust arises even when the interest comes into existence in the absence of a manifestation of intention at that time." This we think is especially applicable where, as here, there was no consideration for the declaration. It is further stated, however, in the Restatement, §26k: "If a person manifests an intention to become trustee at a subsequent time, his conduct at that subsequent time considered in connection with his original manifestation may be a sufficient manifestation of intention at that subsequent time to create a trust. . . . The act of acquiring the property coupled with the earlier declaration of trust *may be* a sufficient manifestation of an intention to create a trust at the time of the acquisition of the property." (Our italics, here and hereafter.) In subsection 1 it is said ". . . Mere silence, however, ordinarily will not be such a manifestation. Whether silence is or is not such a manifestation is a question of interpretation." In such interpretation, subsection m is quite pertinent and controlling: "A promise to create a trust in the future is *enforceable*, if . . . the requirements for an enforceable contract are complied with. Whether a promise to transfer property in trust or to become trustee creates in the promisee a right to recover damages for breach of the promise, and whether such a promise is specifically enforceable, are determined by the law governing contracts. Thus, if the owner of property transfers the property in trust and agrees to pay a sum of money to the trustee to be held upon the same trust, he is not liable for failing to pay the money if the promise was made gratuitously . . . but if the promise was made for consideration . . . the promisor is liable thereon. So also, a promise to create a trust of property if thereafter acquired by the promisor imposes no liability upon the promisor if the promise was gratuitous. . . ."

. . .

From what has been said we are convinced that appellant's profits in question were not impressed with a trust when they first came into existence. The Board was obviously of the impression that the trust first attached when appellant credited them to the beneficiaries on his books of account. This act, it seems to us, constituted his first subsequent expression of intention to become a trustee of the fund referred to in his original and gratuitous declaration. Prior to that time we think it is clear that the declaration could not have been enforced against him, and that his mere silence with respect thereto should not be considered as an expression of his intention to establish the trust at a time earlier than the credits. . . .

The order of the Board is affirmed.[5]

SPEELMAN v. PASCAL

Court of Appeals of New York, 1961

10 N.Y.2d 313, 222 N.Y.S.2d 324, 178 N.E.2d 723

Chief Judge Desmond. Gabriel Pascal, defendant's intestate who died in 1954, had been for many years a theatrical producer. In 1952 an English corporation named Gabriel Pascal Enterprises, Ltd., of whose 100 shares Gabriel Pascal owned 98, made an agreement with the English Public Trustee who represented the estate of George Bernard Shaw. This agreement granted to Gabriel Pascal Enterprises, Ltd., the exclusive world rights to prepare and produce a musical play to be based on Shaw's play "Pygmalion" and a motion picture version of the musical play. The agreement recited, as was the fact, that the licensee owned a film scenario written by Pascal and based on "Pygmalion." In fact Pascal had, some time previously, produced a nonmusical movie version of "Pygmalion" under rights obtained by Pascal from George Bernard Shaw during the latter's lifetime. The 1952 agreement required the licensee corporation to pay the Shaw estate an initial advance and thereafter to pay the Shaw estate 3% of the gross receipts of the musical play and musical movie with a provision that the license was to terminate if within certain fixed periods the licensee did not arrange with Lerner and Loewe or other similarly well-known composers to write the musical play and arrange to produce it. Before Pascal's death in July, 1954, he had made a number of unsuccessful efforts to get the musical written and produced and it was not until after his death that arrangements were made, through a New York bank as temporary administrator of his estate, for the writing and production of the highly successful "My Fair Lady." Meanwhile, on February 22, 1954, at a time when the license from the Shaw estate still had two years to run, Gabriel Pascal, who died four and a half months later, wrote, signed and delivered to plaintiff a document as follows:

> Dear Miss Kingman
>
> This is to confirm to you our understanding that I give you from my shares of profits of the Pygmalion Musical stage version five per cent (5%) in England,

[5] Noted 36 Mich. L. Rev. 1041. — Eds.

and two per cent (2%) of my shares of profits in the United States. From the film version, five per cent (5%) from my profit shares all over the world.

As soon as the contracts are signed, I will send a copy of this letter to my lawyer, Edwin Davies, in London, and he will confirm to you this arrangement in a legal form.

This participation in my shares of profits is a present to you, in recognition for your loyal work for me as my Executive Secretary.[6]

Very sincerely yours,
Gabriel Pascal.

The question in this lawsuit is: Did the delivery of this paper constitute a valid, complete, present gift to plaintiff by way of assignment of a share in future royalties when and if collected from the exhibition of the musical stage version and film version of "Pygmalion"? A consideration was, of course, unnecessary (Personal Property Law, §33, subd. 4). . . .

The only real question is as to whether the 1954 letter above quoted operated to transfer to plaintiff an enforcible right to the described percentages of the royalties to accrue to Pascal on the production of a stage or film version of a musical play based on "Pygmalion". We see no reason why this letter does not have that effect. It is true that at the time of the delivery of the letter there was no musical stage or film play in existence but Pascal, who owned and was conducting negotiations to realize on the stage and film rights, could grant to another a share of the moneys to accrue from the use of those rights by others. There are many instances of courts enforcing assignments of rights to sums which were expected thereafter to become due to the assignor. A typical case is Field v. Mayor of New York (6 N.Y. 179). One Bell, who had done much printing and similar work for the City of New York but had no present contract to do any more such work, gave an assignment in the amount of $1,500 of any moneys that might thereafter become due to Bell for such work. Bell did obtain such contracts or orders from the city and money became due to him therefor. This court held that while there was not at the time of the assignment any presently enforcible or even existing chose in action but merely a possibility that there would be such a chose of action, nevertheless there was a possibility of such which the parties expected to ripen into reality and which did afterwards ripen into reality and that, therefore, the assignment created an equitable title which the courts would enforce. A case similar to the present one in general outline is Central Trust Co. v. West India Improvement Co. (169 N.Y. 314) where the

[6] Pascal's loyal "Executive Secretary" is painted scarlet by Pascal's widow, Valerie, in her book, The Disciple and his Devil (1970). Marianne Speelman, also known as Zaya Kingman, was half Chinese and half Irish and the exotically beautiful widow of a Dutch banker who had made a fortune in China. She invited Gabriel Pascal to dinner in March of 1953, and that same night began a torrid love affair (id. at 252). As a result of her herb teas and food prepared with "life elixir," Pascal experienced "prodigious sexual powers" and felt as if he were flying. Marianne wrote that anybody who had ever made love to her could never again be satisfied with any other woman (id. at 255). Valerie states that soon after delivering the document in this case (id. at 297), Pascal attempted to break off his volcanic affair and, under the influence of an Indian mystic, renounced his fleshly desires forever (id. at 299). Pascal died some four months later. — Eds.

assignor had a right or concession from the Colony of Jamaica to build a railroad on that island and the courts upheld a mortgage given by the concession owner on any property that would be acquired by the concession owner in consideration of building the railroad if and when the railroad should be built. The Court of Appeals pointed out in Central Trust Co., at page 323, that the property as to which the mortgage was given had not yet come into existence at the time of the giving of the mortgage but that there was an expectation that such property, consisting of securities, would come into existence and accrue to the concession holder when and if the latter performed the underlying contract. This court held that the assignment would be recognized and enforced in equity. The cases cited by appellant (Young v. Young, 80 N.Y. 422; Vincent v. Rix, 248 N.Y. 76; Farmers' Loan & Trust Co. v. Winthrop, 207 App. Div. 356, mod. 238 N.Y. 477) are not to the contrary. In each of those instances the attempted gifts failed because there had not been such a completed and irrevocable delivery of the subject matter of the gift as to put the gift beyond cancellation by the donor. In every such case the question must be as to whether there was a completed delivery of a kind appropriate to the subject property. Ordinarily, if the property consists of existing stock certificates or corporate bonds, as in the Young and Vincent cases (supra), there must be a completed physical transfer of the stock certificates or bonds. In Farmers' Loan & Trust Co. v. Winthrop (supra) the dispute was as to the effect of a power of attorney but the maker of the power had used language which could not be construed as effectuating a present gift of the property which the donor expected to receive in the future from another estate.[7] The Farmers' Loan & Trust Co. case does not hold that property to be the subject of a valid gift must be in present physical existence and in the possession of the donor but it does hold that the language used in the particular document was not sufficient to show an irrevocable present intention to turn over to the donee securities which would come to the donor on the settlement of another estate. At page 485 of 238 New York this court held that all that need be established is "an intention that the title of the donor shall be presently divested and presently transferred" but that in the particular document under scrutiny in the Farmers' Loan & Trust Co. case there was lacking any language to show an irrevocable intent of a gift to become operative at once. In our present case there was nothing left for Pascal to do in order to make an irrevocable transfer to plaintiff of part of Pascal's right to receive royalties from the productions. . . .

The judgment should be affirmed, with costs.

Judges Dye, Fuld, Froessel, Van Voorhis, Burke and Foster concur.

Judgment affirmed.[8]

[7] In Farmers' Loan & Trust Co. v. Winthrop the settlor executed an inter vivos trust with Farmers' Loan as trustee of $5000 "and all other property hereafter delivered." On the same day she gave a power of attorney to Farmers' Loan authorizing it to collect the assets she was entitled to receive from the estate of Jabez Bostwick, "and to transfer such securities and property to yourself as trustee." Before the executor of the Bostwick estate delivered the property to Farmers' Loan, the settlor died. The court held that the attempted transfer failed. — Eds.

[8] Noted 11 Catholic U.L. Rev. 115; 13 Syracuse L. Rev. 481. — Eds.

QUESTION

What doctrinal, factual, or other distinction justifies the different results reached in the Brainard case and the Speelman case? In terms of the ritual and evidentiary policies, are the cases consistent?

The Trustee's Own Promise as a Trust Res

The requirement of an identifiable trust res distinguishes a trust from a debt. A trust involves a duty to deal with some specific property. A debt involves an obligation to pay a sum of money to another. For example, a life insurance company holding the proceeds of a matured policy under either an annuity option or an interest option is a debtor, not a trustee. Pierowich v. Metropolitan Life Ins. Co., 282 Mich. 118, 275 N.W. 789 (1937). The proceeds are not segregated and invested separately from the company's funds. The annuitant under the policy could, of course, transfer the annuity into a trust, and the annuity would then serve as a trust res. But an obligation to pay an annuity is not a res in the hands of the company. Similarly, money deposited in a bank ordinarily creates a debt, for the money is not segregated from the bank's general funds. However, the chose in action against the bank can serve as a res if the depositor transfers it in trust to another. The characterization of a relationship as a trust rather than a debt governs the consequences in several problems. See 1 Scott, Trusts §12 (3d ed. 1967).

KLEIN v. BRYER

Court of Appeals of Maryland, 1962
227 Md. 473, 177 A.2d 412, 3 A.L.R.3d 1411

Prescott, J. The plaintiff below has appealed from an order entered by the Circuit Court for Montgomery County, sitting as a Court of Equity, in a special case by consent.

The petition requested the trial judge to determine two questions:

(1) Is all, or any portion of the $5,850 now held by defendant Montgomery Title Company for the estate of Leo A. Bryer, held in trust for plaintiff by virtue of a written agreement dated October 1, 1956, between plaintiff and Leo A Bryer?; (2) If the answer to the preceding question is in the affirmative, is such trust property the sole property of plaintiff, and not subject to claims of third parties against the trustee, Leo A. Bryer, or his legal representative?

The agreement between Bryer and the plaintiff, mentioned in question 1 above, contained the following paragraph:

> 5. . . . In no case shall the Broker be personally liable to the Salesman for any commission, nor shall said Salesman be personally liable to said Broker for any commissions, but when the commission shall have been collected from the party

or parties for whom the service was performed, said Broker, in the event such commissions are paid to him, shall hold the same in trust for said Salesman and himself to be divided according to the terms of this agreement.

The parties then stipulated:

> (1) Of the $5,850.00 held for Leo A. Bryer by Montgomery Title Company, $4,950 represents sales commissions on homes sold in 1959 by Grace Wills Klein while acting as a salesman for Leo A. Bryer, pursuant to an employment agreement filed as Exhibit I herein.
>
> (2) According to the terms of said agreement, Grace Wills Klein's commissions on the aforementioned sales amount to 50% of $4,950, or $2,475, and were never received by her.

This was followed by an agreement of the parties that, if questions 1 and 2, above, were answered in the affirmative, the court should enforce the trust and order the Title Company to pay the plaintiff the amount due her, and direct that any funds remaining in the hands of the Title Company be paid to the representative of the estate of Leo A. Bryer; but in the event that the answers were in the negative, the whole sum held by the Title Company should be paid to the estate of Leo A. Bryer.

The trial judge determined that both questions should be answered in the negative, and ordered the Title Company to pay the full amount of $5,850 to the said estate.

This is the entire record as the case is presented to us. The appellant contends it discloses that $2,475 of the $5,850 held by the Title Company for the estate of Leo A. Bryer is impressed by an express trust for her benefit; the appellees, in their brief, content themselves by claiming the record fails to show any question or decision made by the trial judge, and, therefore, it raises no question for our decision.

With this proposition of the appellees, we are unable to agree. Maryland Rule 886a specifically provides that when an action has been "tried by the lower court without a jury," this Court will review the case upon both the law and the evidence.

Thus, the simple question for our determination is whether any portion of the fund held by the Title Company to the credit of the Leo A. Bryer estate is impressed with a trust for the benefit of the appellant. The decision turns upon a careful analysis of the provisions of the contract quoted above, which will be made below, after a very brief reference to the law.

The facts do not call for a lengthy or elaborate discussion of the law relating to trusts. It will suffice, at this point, to say that they may be created for any purpose, not illegal; and, in a broad sense, they are either express, or the result of the operation of law. Restatement, Trusts 2d, §2, says a trust (excluding charitable, resulting and constructive trusts) is a fiduciary relationship with respect to property, subjecting the person by whom the title is held to equitable duties to deal with the property for the benefit of another person, which arises as a result of a manifestation of an intention to create it.

We turn now to a consideration of the contract. Of course, every trust must have a trust res, and it is obvious that when the contract was executed, there was no trust property in existence and ascertainable; hence our problem is to determine the relationship between the appellant and Bryer (or his agent) when the commissions were collected. The situation here is not the same as that in Century Indemnity Co. v. State of Maryland, D.C., 144 F Supp 671, wherein Judge Thomsen dealt with a deposit made upon a sale, which was held by a broker. A relationship of debtor and creditor between the broker and his saleswoman did not arise when the settlements for the properties were made. The contract expressly provides that "in no case shall the Broker be personally liable to the Salesman"; and it is difficult to conceive of a more explicit or clearer manifestation of the intention of the parties that Bryer should not have the free and unrestricted use of the money received as commissions resulting from sales made by the appellant, which would have been necessary for the relationship of debtor and creditor to have arisen. Dunlop Sand & Gravel Corp. v Hospelhorn, 172 Md 279, 288, 191 A 701; 1 Scott, Trusts (2d Ed), §14.1; Restatement, op cit, §14. It is apparent that if the parties intended such a relationship to arise, the whole of paragraph 5 set forth above is meaningless; for the debtor-creditor relationship would have been created by the provision in the contract to pay the appellant a portion of the commissions, even if paragraph 5 had not been inserted in the contract.

A careful reading of the provisions of paragraph 5 discloses that Bryer did not promise to create in the future a trust in property owned by him. Such a situation is discussed and considered in 1 Scott, Trusts (2d Ed) §26.5, and in Restatement, op cit, §§26, 30. Nor did he promise to create in the future a trust in a res to be then brought forth by him. On the contrary, he promised to act as trustee of property to be produced in the future by the efforts of the appellant; and his promise to act as such trustee was supported by a valuable consideration, for he was to receive one-half of the commissions. In this situation — with the promise of Bryer to act as trustee contained in a valid and enforceable contract, supported by a valid and valuable consideration, furnished by the appellant-promisee — a trust arose, and we so hold, in one-half of the commissions in favor of the appellant, when the commissions were collected by the Title Company; and the appellant was the settlor of said trust. 1 Scott, Trusts, §17.3; Restatement, op cit, §26 comment n. The mere fact that the trust property was not in existence (as a fund) at the time of the execution of the contract did not prevent a trust from later arising. Restatement, op cit, comments, a, b and c. Nor did the collection of the commissions by the Title Company, instead of by Bryer personally, prevent the same. When the commissions were actually paid to the company as Bryer's agent, it was, in legal contemplation, a fulfillment of the provision in the contract that reads, "in the event such commissions are paid to him [Bryer]," which provision was followed by a statement that in such an event, the commissions would be held in trust. And, likewise, the further fact that Bryer died did not stop the trust from arising. Restatement, op cit, §32(2) and comment j.

Hence, the trial judge's answer to question (1) should have been in the affirmative. And, as we have held that a valid trust was created instead of a debtor-creditor relationship between Bryer (or his estate) and the appellant, the answer to question (2) also should have been in the affirmative, for the rights of the appellant in the trust property are superior to the rights of Bryer's general creditors. Restatement, op cit, §74 comment a.

Order reversed, and case remanded for the entry of a decree not inconsistent with this opinion; the appellee, Bryer, to pay the costs.

RESTATEMENT (SECOND) OF TRUSTS §26, Comment j (1959): "If a person declares his intention or promises to be trustee of property from and after a future date without further manifestation of intention on his part, but does not manifest an intention to be trustee in the meantime, a trust arises at the subsequent time if, but only if, at that subsequent time he manifests an intention then to create a trust. It is immaterial whether the property is owned at the time of the declaration or promise or is thereafter acquired."

RESTATEMENT (SECOND) OF TRUSTS §26, Comment n (1959): "A promise to create a trust in the future is to be distinguished from the creation of a present trust of a promise to be performed in the future. A promisee of an enforceable promise to be performed in the future can hold his rights as promisee in trust for a third person. See §17(e). If a person makes an enforceable promise to pay money or to make a conveyance of property to another person as trustee a present trust is created, the rights of the promisee being held by him as trustee, provided that the person creating the trust manifested an intention to create an immediate trust of the promisee's rights, and not merely to create a trust of the money when paid or of the property when conveyed."

1 SCOTT, TRUSTS
(3d ed. 1967)

§87. Obligor cannot be trustee of obligation. As has been stated, a chose in action can be held in trust by the obligee. It is clear, however, that the obligor has no such interest in his own obligation as can be held in trust. A debtor may, indeed, make himself trustee for his creditor of specific property held by him; but he cannot be trustee of the debt itself. It might be suggested that a person may be indebted individually to himself as trustee, and that as trustee he holds a claim against himself individually in trust for another. This, however, seems to be a mere playing with words; a person cannot have a legal claim against himself, whether for his own benefit or for the benefit of another.

Where a creditor directs his debtor to pay to a third person the amount which he owes to the creditor, the debtor does not thereby become trustee for the third person, since he holds no property for the third person. The creditor may become trustee of the obligation, but the debtor is at the wrong end of the obligation; the debtor has only a liability not an asset. Thus in Bair v. Snyder County State Bank[9] the owner of a certificate of deposit in a bank directed the bank to pay the amount of the deposit to such person as he might name in a check. On his death a check was found in his safe-deposit box covering the amount of the deposit and payable to the plaintiff. It was held that the plaintiff was not entitled to the deposit. The court said that the bank could not be a trustee, because there was no segregation by it of any part of its assets, and "a trust without a *res* is impossible." The bank could not be trustee of its own obligation.[10] So also in Samuels v. E. F. Drew & Co., Inc.[11] the court said: "The defendant could not be a trustee of its obligation to the appellant, nor could its obligation to the creditor be held as security, for security presupposes the existence of property." It is immaterial that the parties use the language of trust. Thus in Molera v. Cooper[12] the holder of a note made an agreement with the maker that in consideration of the extinguishment of the note the maker would hold the amount in trust for certain third persons. The court held that no trust was created since there was no property which would be the subject of the trust. The debtor could not be trustee of the debt.[13] . . .

Although the notion that an obligor may be trustee of the obligation has been repudiated in many cases, there are occasional cases in which the courts have asserted the opposite, usually in order to evade some rule of law which is applicable to other situations but which is not applicable to trusts. Thus in England, as we have seen, in order to avoid the English rule that the beneficiary of a contract cannot enforce it, the courts have sometimes treated a contract for the benefit of a third party as a trust; and although they do not make it clear who is supposed to be trustee and what he is supposed to hold in trust, the language of the decisions sometimes seems to indicate that the promisor is regarded as trustee of his promise. So also in order to avoid the rule that a gratuitous promise is not binding as a contract, the courts have sometimes tortured such a promise into a trust, apparently treating the promisor as trustee of his promise. They are particularly likely to do this where the parties happen to use the language of trust in connection with the promise. In all these cases the courts have used the language of trusts as a verbal device for evading a rule of law which they are not prepared to set aside.

HICKOK v. BUNTING, 67 App. Div. 560, 73 N.Y.S. 967 (1902). Defendant signed and delivered to Geraldine H. Hickok an instrument reading: "Having

[9] 314 Pa. 85, 171 Atl. 274 (1934).

[10] . . . It might have been held that although no trust was created there was a contract for the benefit of a third party. It would seem, however, that the disposition was in substance testamentary.

[11] 296 Fed. 882, 887 (C.C.A.2d, 1924).

[12] 173 Cal. 259, 160 Pac. 231 (1916).

[13] Although undoubtedly no trust was created, it would seem that there was a contract for the benefit of a third party, made in consideration of the extinguishment of the debt. The court said, however, that there could not be a novation, substituting such a contract for the debt, unless the beneficiaries agreed. This is contrary to the great weight of authority, which holds that the beneficiary of such a contract need not have notice of the contract.

been cause of a money loss to my friend Geraldine H. Hickok, I have given her three thousand dollars. I hold this amount in trust for her, and one year after date or thereafter on demand I promise to pay to the order of Geraldine H. Hickok, her heirs or assigns, three thousand dollars, with interest." Held: no trust was created and in the absence of consideration the instrument was not enforceable as a promissory note. Said the court: "The language following contains what would be a good declaration of trust, assuming that there was a res to which it could attach. It is not claimed by the plaintiff, nor does the evidence establish, that the deceased had, at the time of the execution of the instrument, assuming that she executed it, $3000, or any other sum of money, or other property representing it, which was set apart, or in any manner placed so that it could become the subject of a trust. In order to constitute a trust there must be a res to which it can attach, and where that does not exist there is nothing which can be made the subject of a trust."

Matter of IHMSEN, 253 App. Div. 472, 3 N.Y.S.2d 125 (1938). Jay George Ihmsen entered into a written custodian agreement with a bank, whereby the bank agreed to hold securities for safekeeping and to collect and pay the income to Ihmsen. The agreement further provided that any property in the hands of the bank at the time of Ihmsen's death should be regarded as a trust fund and held by the bank for Ihmsen's widow for life and then distributed to others. Held: the bank was an agent, and the agency terminated on Ihmsen's death. No trust was created inter vivos because it was to arise only on Ihmsen's death. The agreement was not executed in accordance with the Statute of Wills; therefore it was without testamentary effect.

PROBLEM

Three days before his death C. P. Craft penned a lengthy personal letter to Mrs. Iva Rippstein. A portion of the letter read:

> Used most of yesterday and day before to "round up" my financial affairs, and to be sure I knew just where I stood before I made the statement that I would send you $200.00 cash the first week of each month for the next 5 years, ~~provided I live that long,~~ also to send you $200.00 cash for Sept. 1960 and thereafter send that amount in cash the first week of the following months of 1960, October, November and December.

Opposite which in the margin there was written:

> I have stricken out the words "provided I live that long" and hereby and herewith bind my estate to make the $200.00 monthly payments provided for on this Page One of this letter of 9-17-60.

Craft enclosed the first payment with the letter.

After Craft's death Mrs. Rippstein attempted unsuccessfully to probate the writing as a codicil to the will of Craft. She then filed suit against the executors claiming that Craft had established a voluntary trust under which Craft bound his property to the extent of the promised payments. What result? Unthank v. Rippstein, 386 S.W.2d 134 (Tex. 1964).

3. *The Necessity of a Trustee: Testamentary Trustee as Insurance Beneficiary*

FROST v. FROST
Supreme Judicial Court of Massachusetts, 1909
202 Mass. 100, 88 N.E. 446

Bill in Equity, filed in the Supreme Judicial Court by the widow of Albert G. Frost, late of Boston, who died on October 24, 1907, and whose will was admitted to probate, the defendants being named therein as trustees and executors and having qualified by giving bonds as required by law, praying to have the defendants declared to be trustees for the plaintiff's sole benefit under assignments of five life insurance policies alleged to have been made by her husband on May 17 and August 4, 1898, and that the defendants be ordered to pay to her the amounts of life insurance received by them as executors and trustees under the policies in question.

The case was refered to William H. H. Emmons, Esquire, as master. He filed a report in favor of the plaintiff. The defendants filed ten exceptions to the report, of which only the second and sixth are now material. Those exceptions were as follows:

2. To the master's ruling that "Upon the foregoing facts I rule as matter of law that the prayer of the bill should be granted and that the plaintiff is entitled to recover of the defendants as trustees $17,327.69 and also such interest thereon as may accrue after it was received by them."

6. To the master's report because he did not rule, as requested, that the assignments of said policies were inoperative and void.

The assignments, which were brief, are described in the opinion.

The case came on to be heard before Loring, J., who reserved it upon the pleadings, the master's report and the exceptions thereto for determination by the full court, such decree to be entered as justice and equity might require.

Hammond, J. One of the questions is whether the assignments were valid. The plaintiff does not contend that there was a gift, but insists . . . that the assignments were operative as a perfected trust. . . .

Was the trust perfected during the lifetime of the assignor? There were five policies, of which two were each payable to his executors, administrators and assigns, and three were each payable to his legal representatives. Each assignment was of all his right, title and interest "in and to said policy, subject to all its terms and conditions," and each was made to "the trustees to be named in my will," for the sole use and benefit of the plaintiff. The master has found that the plaintiff was informed of these assignments and that she assented thereto; and we think the facts reported by him warrant such findings. But she testified that she never saw any of these policies, nor any of the assignments, until after her husband's death; and the master has further found that "these insurance policies and assignments were matters of common knowledge among the brothers and sisters of the testator; also that they discussed them at times with the plaintiff; also that they were mistaken in supposing that these assignments gave to the plaintiff only the income of the proceeds of these policies for her life, and that the plaintiff had knowledge that her husband had made provision of some kind for her, by means of these policies and assignments, and that she was willing to accept, and did accept, such provision, whatever it might be, just as her husband made it, but did not see these policies and assignments and was not informed about the details of the provision made for her therein until after his death."

Who were the assignees? They were to be named in his will. What will? Was it to be the first testamentary document he should thereafter make, whether or not revoked before his death, or was it to be the one which should finally be admitted to probate as his will? The assignor actually made three wills after the assignments were executed and "the trustees named in the different wills were not exactly the same." There can only be one sensible interpretation of the phrase "my will." It must be held to mean the document finally admitted to probate as the will of the assignor. It is certain, therefore, that the trustees could not be finally ascertained until after his death. The assignment could not be delivered to the assignees until after his death. There is nothing to indicate that he intended to make any delivery to any third person to hold for the trustees until they were finally ascertained, nor is it shown upon the facts in the case that he intended to hold the policies himself as trustee. While it is true, as contended by the plaintiff, that the trustees when finally ascertained would derive their appointment under the assignment and not under the will, still it remains equally true that they could not be appointed, nor even ascertained, until after the death of the assignor. It is to be noted that the papers were all retained by the assignor.

Here then is a case where no assignments are delivered to the assignees, nor can they be delivered until after the assignor's death, where also there is no delivery to any one for them and where it does not appear that the assignor intends to hold for them. The language of the assignments seems to point to a testamentary intention, and the whole scheme is manifestly not to take effect as an operative assignment during the lifetime of the testator. The assignments were of a testamentary nature, and, not being witnessed as required by the statutes concerning wills, were inoperative after his death.

Nor is the defect cured by the assent of the cestui que trust to the assignments. While such an assent might have a bearing upon the validity of the trust if there was any question as to notice or acceptance, still it has no effect upon the validity of the assignments upon which the trust depends. The question is not simply whether, assuming the validity of the assignments, the trust was good, but is much deeper, and is whether the assignments upon which alone the trust depends ever became operative in law. The case is plainly distinguishable from Kendrick v. Ray, 173 Mass. 305, upon which the plaintiff relies. There the trustee was the beneficiary named in the policy; and the question was as to the terms of the oral trust upon which he received the insurance, and not as to the validity of the appointment of the trustee. See also Gould v. Emerson, 99 Mass. 154.

Upon the facts in the case these assignments never took effect within the lifetime of the assignor, for want of assignees, and never took effect after his death for want of proper attestation. There was therefore nothing upon which to base the contemplated trust, and it never was perfected. . . .

It follows that the second and sixth exceptions of the defendant to the master's report must be sustained. It becomes unnecessary to consider the other exceptions. The order must be: Bill dismissed.

NOTES

1. On the problems involved in Frost v. Frost, see Haskell, Testamentary Trustee as Insurance Beneficiary: An Estate Planning Gimmick, 41 N.Y.U.L. Rev. 566 (1966); Note, The Testamentary Life Insurance Trust, 51 Minn. L. Rev. 1118 (1967).

2. Frost v. Frost did not discuss the question of whether the beneficiary designation violated the Rule against Perpetuities. Does it? See page 979, infra. To avoid this problem how would you draw the beneficiary designation of a testamentary trustee?

3. Designating as beneficiary of a life insurance policy "The trustee to be named in my will" may have estate and inheritance tax disadvantages. In many states proceeds from life insurance policies payable to a named beneficiary are exempt, up to a specified maximum, from inheritance tax. It may be held that payment to a testamentary trustee does not qualify for the exemption if the testamentary trustee is obligated to pay the debts and expenses of the estate. In Estate of Anderson, 236 Cal. App. 2d 214, 45 Cal. Rptr. 852 (1965), the policies were made payable to "Bank of America Trust Department, as stipulated in my Will, dated 1961." The court held that the proceeds of the policies were the subject of an inter vivos trust because the reference was to a will already executed, and thus the proceeds qualified for the inheritance tax exemption.

Section 2039(c) of the Internal Revenue Code of 1954 provides that the employer-financed portion of the benefits payable under a qualified employee pension plan are not includible in the gross estate of the employee if such benefits are "receivable by any beneficiary (other than the executor)" of the decedent's estate. If local law is clear that such benefits payable to a testamentary trustee are not reachable by creditors of the estate, they will not be includible in the employee's gross estate. Brorby, Designation of Inter Vivos or Testamentary Trustee as Beneficiary of Employee Benefits, 24 Tax Lawyer 141 (1970).

4. In recent years a number of states have enacted statutes authorizing the payment of life insurance proceeds to a testamentary trustee. The statutes have been drafted to preserve the proceeds' inheritance tax exemption and immunity from creditors' claims. The Wisconsin statute set forth below is representative.

WISCONSIN STATUTES ANNOTATED
§231.49 (1957, Supp. 1971)

§231.49 Trustees appointed

(1) A policy of life insurance may designate as beneficiary a trustee or trustees named or to be named by will, if the designation is made in accordance with the provisions of the policy and the requirements of the insurance company. The trustee or trustees may be appointed immediately after the proving of the will, and upon appointment and qualification the proceeds of such insurance shall be paid to the trustee or trustees to be held and disposed of under the terms of the will as they exist at the death of the testator and in accordance with ch. 323; but if no qualified trustee makes claim to the proceeds from the insurance company within one year after the death of the insured, or if satisfactory evidence is furnished the insurance company within such one year period showing that no trustee can qualify to receive the proceeds, payment shall be made by the insurance company to the executors, administrators or assigns of the insured, unless otherwise provided by agreement with the insurance company during the lifetime of the insured. The proceeds of the insurance as collected by the trustee or trustees shall not be subject to debts of the insured and inheritance tax to any greater extent than if such proceeds were payable to any other named beneficiary other than the estate of the insured. For purposes of trust administration such proceeds shall be subject to the court jurisdiction over the trust . . . but shall not otherwise be considered as payable to the estate of the insured. Such proceeds shall be listed for tax purposes only . . . in the general inventory of the estate. Such insurance proceeds so held in trust may be commingled with any other assets which may properly come into such trust as provided in the will. Enactment of this section shall not invalidate previous life insurance policy beneficiary designations naming trustees of trusts established by will.

(2) Benefits under an employe benefit plan conforming to the requirements of s. 272.18(31) or under an annuity contract purchased for an employe by an employer which is a religious, scientific, educational, benevolent or other corporation or association not organized or conducted for pecuniary profit may be made payable to a trustee or trustees named or to be named in a will and such benefits shall be treated in the same manner as insurance proceeds are treated under sub. (1) except that if no qualifying trustee asserts a claim to any such benefits within one year after the employe's death or if satisfactory proof is furnished the disbursing authority under the plan or the contract within such period showing that no trustee can qualify to receive the benefits, the benefits shall be paid in accordance with any alternative disposition provided for under the plan or the contract.

(3) Interests other than those described in sub. (1) and (2) may be made

payable to or transferred to a trustee or trustees named or to be named in a will in the same manner and to the same extent they could be made payable to or transferred to any other person.

4. The Use of Trusts in Estate Planning

The trust is one of the most flexible and useful devices developed by English law. It can be used for almost any purpose. The trustee's powers of management and of distribution of income and principal can be tailored to fit a wide variety of situations. The trust is often used in business transactions as a substitute for the corporation, in corporate finance, in financing and developing real estate. It may also be used to devote huge sums to charity, thus avoiding the necessity of applying for a legislative charter. One of the most important uses of the trust is in the distribution of family wealth.[14] It is this last use that concerns us here.

The powers of a trustee over the distribution of income and principal are subject to as many variations as draftsmen can imagine. Nonetheless the powers given trustees over income and principal fall into patterns, and trusts may be classified according to these recurring patterns. These classifications are very important in determining tax consequences and creditors' rights. The most important kinds of trusts can perhaps be best distinguished by illustrative cases.

> *Case* 5. O transfers property to X in trust, to distribute all the income currently to A (or in equal shares to B and C). This is known as a *simple mandatory* trust. The trustee has no discretion to choose either the persons who will receive the income or the amount to be distributed.
>
> *Case* 6. O transfers property to X in trust, to distribute all the income currently to one or more members of a group consisting of A, A's wife, and A's issue in such amounts as the trustee determines. This is a kind of discretionary trust known as a *mandatory spray* trust. The trustee must distribute all the income currently, but he has discretion to determine who gets it and in what amount. A mandatory spray trust is a useful device to lessen the impact of income taxation upon family wealth. Instead of distributing the income to the head of the family, who is in a high tax bracket, the trustee may distribute it among all members, thus obtaining a lower tax rate.
>
> *Case* 7. O transfers property to X in trust, to accumulate the income or pay the income to A, in X's discretion, and upon the death of A, to pay to B the accumulated income, if any, and the principal. This is known as a *discretionary accumulation* trust.
>
> *Case* 8. O transfers property to X in trust, to accumulate the income or distribute the income to one or more members of a group consisting of A, A's wife,

[14] For a summary of the different types of trusts used in estate planning see Rogers, Express Personal Trusts and Trust Clauses in Estate Planning: A Functional Analysis, 14 Kan. L. Rev. 461 (1966).

and A's issue in such amounts as the trustee determines. This is known as a *discretionary spray* and *accumulation* trust.

With respect to the principal of the trust, the terms may specify that the trustee has power to spray principal to the income beneficiary. Such a power may be limited by a standard ("such amounts as are necessary to support my wife in the style of living to which she has become accustomed"), or the trustee may be given wide discretion.

Corporate Trustees: Investment Practices and Fees

Among the factors that should be considered in deciding whether to settle property in a trust are the investment practices of corporate fiduciaries and the expenses of trust administration.

There is no single criterion by which the performance of trust accounts can be measured. The performance sought for a particular trust will turn on the objectives of the settlor and on the needs of the trust beneficiaries. For example, the person of moderate wealth who establishes a funded revocable inter vivos trust for his own benefit may be using the trust department of a bank as, in effect, the manager of his private mutual fund. He may be relying on the bank's investment expertise to produce a high income yield, in which case the trust's investments will lean toward corporate bonds and real estate mortgages. Alternatively, he may be more interested in growth, in which case the investments will lean toward common stocks. If he is in a high income tax bracket, he may want the bulk of the trust fund invested in tax-free municipal bonds, or he may want a mix between growth common stocks and municipals.

If the settlor creates a testamentary trust or an unfunded revocable life insurance trust, his objective is to provide for the income and other needs of his wife and children, and perhaps grandchildren. If his concern is to assure his wife of as much income as possible, this would point toward investment in mortgages, high-yield bonds, and utility stocks. At the same time, he may be concerned about the long-term protection accorded by the trust fund in an inflationary economy; this would point toward investment in high-yield, medium-yield, or low-yield common stocks.

Another factor that makes "performance" difficult to evaluate is the changing nature of the economy. As recently as the 1940s and early 1950s many common stocks listed on the national exchanges gave a higher yield, in the form of dividends, than corporate bonds or debentures, on the theory that equity investments involved greater risks. In the growth-oriented 1960s and 1970s all this changed. Common stocks with yields that matched the return from corporate bonds were not to be found. The yields on many blue chip stocks were about the same as the interest rates on commercial bank deposits, and some highly regarded stocks paid no dividends at all.

There is, in short, no Barron's Report on the investment activities of bank trust departments. While it is possible to obtain information on an individual trust department's past investment experience, there is no industry-wide reporting of these data. At the same time, it is possible to make some generalizations.

If the trust estate is very large, or if it includes assets of an unusual nature (such as commercial real estate or stock in a closely held corporation), it may be managed and invested as a separate unit. For smaller trusts, the corpus may be placed in one of the trust department's common trust funds. Most states have enacted the Uniform Common Trust Fund Act, under which the assets of many trusts can be pooled and invested as a unit, with each separate trust sharing in the income and growth (or decline) of the fund on a pro rata basis. In effect, the fiduciary creates its own mutual funds. This gives each separate trust the advantages of a broadly based investment program, and reduces the risks involved if the corpus of each trust were invested in the securities of only a few corporations. Smaller banks have just one common fund. For these the investment formula typically calls for a 50-50 split between investments in high-yields (corporate bonds and mortgages) and common stocks. An increasing number of banks have at least two common trust funds. In one fund the emphasis is on high yield. Eighty to 90 percent of the assets are invested in bonds and mortgages. The other fund concentrates on growth and capital gains. The bulk of this fund is invested in common stocks that produce a lower dividend income but have growth (and hence capital gain) potential. Many of the larger banks have a third common fund that invests exclusively in tax-free municipal bonds.

The paragraph that follows is taken from a letter written to one of the editors in 1971. The correspondent was a trust officer at a large Texas bank.

> $10,000 placed in our Equity Fund of Common Trust Fund A on December 1, 1960, would have grown to $16,162 on November 30, 1970. (This assumes that all earnings were distributed and not reinvested.) In addition, the fund would have distributed income of $4,171 on this original $10,000 investment. In 1970 the income yield for this fund was 3.93 percent. Over the same ten-year period the unit value of shares in our Income Fund of Common Trust Fund A declined from $6.63 to $5.67, but the income yield for this fund increased from 4.27 percent in 1961 to 6.67 percent in 1970.

How much do corporate fiduciaries charge as compensation for their services? Following are the rates being charged by a large bank in Philadelphia:

Individual Invested Trusts

On the first $200,000 of principal, $5.00 per $1000

On the next $500,000, $4.00 per $1000

On the next $500,000,
$3.00 per $1000
On the next $800,000,
$2.00 per $1000
On excess over $2,000,000,
a special study is required.
Minimum fee $300.

Trusts fully invested in Common Trust Funds
On the first $200,000 of principal,
$4.00 per $1000
On the next $500,000,
$3.00 per $1000
On the next $500,000,
$2.25 per $1000
On the next $800,000,
$1.50 per $1000
On excess over $2,000,000,
a special study is required.
Minimum fee $100.

5. *Resulting and Constructive Trusts*

Up to this point in this chapter, we have been talking about private express trusts. Two other fiduciary relationships, closely related to the express trust, require comment here. The first is a *resulting trust.* It is a trust which arises by operation of law in one of two situations: (a) where the express trust fails or makes an incomplete disposition;[15] (b) where one person, A, pays the purchase price for property, and title to the property is taken in the name of B, a person who is not a natural object of the bounty of A. In these two situations the circumstances are such that the law assumes that the settlor did not intend for the person taking legal title to have the beneficial interest. Situation (b) is known as a "purchase money" resulting trust. The purchase money resulting trust is deemed to arise whenever title is taken in the name of another, who is not a natural object of the bounty of the person who paid the consideration. Thus:

> *Case* 9. O owns Blackacre. A pays O $10,000 for Blackacre; O transfers title to B. If B is not a natural object of A's bounty, B is presumed to hold on a resulting trust for A. If B is A's son, it is presumed that A intended to make a gift to B. The presumption can, of course, be rebutted by evidence.[16]

Many of the rules applicable to express trusts are applicable to resulting trusts, but the Statute of Frauds is not. Even though the subject matter is real property, it

[15] Where the instrument makes an incomplete disposition, the resulting trust is the equivalent of an equitable reversion.
[16] See 4 Powell, Real Property ¶592 (1970); 5 Scott, Trusts §442 (3d ed. 1967).

is usually held that resulting trusts, as well as constructive trusts, are trusts arising by operation of law, and hence without the Statute of Frauds.

A second fiduciary relationship, sometimes confused with a resulting trust, is the *constructive trust*. This trust also arises by operation of law and not by the express terms of an instrument. It is basically a relationship which courts impose upon a person to prevent his unjust enrichment. When the circumstances justify the imposition of a constructive trust, the constructive trustee is held to a duty to convey the property to another on the ground that his retention of it is wrongful. A constructive trust, being remedial in character, can be imposed in a great number of situations outside of, as well as within, the family wealth transactions area.[17]

SECTION B. Trust Formalities

1. *Oral Inter Vivos Trusts*

If the subject matter of an inter vivos trust is land, a written instrument is commonly required to make the trust effective. Section 7 of the English Statute of Frauds[18] required "all declarations or creations of trusts . . . of any lands" to be in writing.[19] Where O conveys land to X upon an oral trust to pay the income to A for life, and upon A's death to convey the land to B, the Statute of Frauds prevents enforcement of the express trust. Is X permitted to keep the land? The cases go three ways: (a) X retains the land, because the Statute of Frauds forbids proof of the oral trust; (b) to prevent unjust enrichment of X, X holds on a constructive trust for the settlor; (c) to prevent unjust enrichment of X, X holds on a constructive trust for the beneficiaries. The older cases tended to favor solution (a). The scholars have divided between solutions (b) and (c). Professor Scott favors solution (b): "The policy of the Statute of Frauds, which does indeed forbid going forward with the transaction, does not forbid going back and putting the parties in statu quo." [20] A constructive trust for the beneficiaries will be imposed where the transfer was wrongfully obtained by fraud or duress, or where the transferee, X, was in a confidential relation to the transferor, or where the transfer was made in anticipation of the transferor's death.

More common than an oral trust for a third party is an oral trust for the benefit of the transferor. Indeed, judging by the cases, [21] an amazing number of persons

[17] See pages 622-626, infra. Generally on constructive trusts, see 4 Powell, Real Property ¶¶593-594 (1970); 5 Scott, Trusts §§461-552 (3d ed. 1967).

[18] Stat. 29 Car. 2, c. 3 (1676). In most American jurisdictions similar statutes have been enacted. 1 Scott, Trusts §40.1 (3d ed. 1967). In a few states which have no such statute, oral trusts of land are permitted. 4 Powell, Real Property ¶509 (1970).

[19] An inter vivos oral trust of personalty, not being within the Statute of Frauds, is enforceable in a large majority of states. In a few states, however, an express trust of personal property is required to be in writing.

[20] 1 Scott, Trusts §45 (3d ed. 1967).

[21] See id. §44.

from time to time put title to land in another, relying upon the transferee's oral promise to reconvey. Some of the transferors are attempting to avoid their creditors or to achieve some property tax benefit. Others transfer title to a member of the family for one reason or another. Of course, any lawyer knows these transferors are asking for trouble and, human nature being what it is, they usually get it. Most of the older cases took a strict view of the Statute of Frauds and permitted the transferee to keep the land.

1 SCOTT, TRUSTS
(3d ed. 1967)

§44. Effect of failure of oral trust for the settlor.

. . .

In England it has been held that where a conveyance of land is made upon an oral trust in favor of the transferor or upon an oral contract to reconvey to the transferor, and the transferee, relying upon the Statute of Frauds, refuses to perform the trust or contract, a constructive trust will be raised in favor of the transferor. If the transferee were allowed to retain the land he would be unjustly enriched; a constructive trust is imposed in order to prevent this unjust enrichment. The Statute of Frauds prevents the courts from enforcing the intention of the parties as such; it does not prevent them from putting the parties in statu quo. The statute forbids going forward; it does not forbid going back. It is true that the results of going forward and of going back may be, although they will not necessarily be, the same, but that should not affect the result.

. . .

By the weight of authority in the United States, however, the transferee of land upon an oral trust or contract is allowed to retain the land. But there are a number of American cases which seem to follow the English view. The argument in favor of the prevailing American view is that, though it might not violate the letter of the Statute of Frauds to show the oral trust or contract for the purpose of raising a constructive trust, yet it would violate the policy underlying it; that the purpose of the statute is to prevent proof of an oral trust or contract, not merely for the purpose of enforcing it, but also for the purpose of restoring the status quo.

It is clear, however, that the policy of the Statute of Frauds does not prevent showing an oral trust or contract for all purposes. As will appear in the sections which follow, where a transfer of land upon an oral trust or contract to reconvey it is procured by fraud, duress or undue influence, the courts have had no difficulty in imposing a constructive trust, even though in order to prove that the transferee was guilty of a wrong in obtaining the land it is necessary to prove the oral trust or contract. So also the courts have enforced a constructive trust where land is conveyed to a person who is in a confidential relation to the transferor for whom he has orally agreed to hold it. So also a constructive trust is enforced where the transfer is made as security for an indebtedness of the transferor to the transferee. Moreover, it is held by the weight of authority that an oral agreement by a purchaser upon an involuntary sale to reconvey the property to the owner, although not enforceable as such, affords a sufficient basis for imposing a constructive trust. If it is possible to show an oral trust under these circumstances, it would seem that the policy of the Statute of Frauds should not forbid showing the oral trust for the purpose of establishing an unjust enrichment. Indeed there are many cases in which it has been held that even in the absence of fraud or undue influence or a confidential relation, it is permissible to show an oral trust or contract for the purpose of preventing unjust enrichment. Thus it has been held that if money is paid in consideration of an oral agreement to transfer land, there is a quasi-contractual obligation to restore the money; and if services are rendered or chattels given in return for an oral promise to convey land, there is a quasi-contractual obligation to pay for the services or chattels. Similarly, if one piece of land is conveyed in consideration of an oral promise to convey another piece of land, the former piece of land may be recovered in equity.

In all these cases an obligation is imposed in order to prevent unjust enrichment; it is held that the Statute of Frauds is not violated by allowing proof of the oral agreement for the purpose of showing that the defendant would be unjustly enriched if he were allowed to refuse to perform his promise and retain the consideration which he has received. It would seem, therefore, that where land is transferred upon an oral trust for the transferor, the policy of the statute should not forbid evidence of the oral trust for the purpose, not of enforcing the trust, but of preventing unjust enrichment by restoring the status quo.

In the original Restatement of Trusts §44, a caveat was inserted stating that the Institute takes no position on the question whether the transferee will be compelled to hold the land upon a constructive trust for the transferor where he orally agreed to hold it in trust for the transferor. In the Restatement of Trusts Second the caveat is omitted and in the comment the argument is presented that a constructive trust should be imposed, since there is a growing body of authority to that effect.

. . .

§44.2. *Where the transferee is in a confidential relation to the transferor.* There are numerous cases to the effect that, where at the time of the transfer the transferee was in a confidential relation to the transferor, and the transferor relied upon his oral promise to reconvey the land, he is chargeable as constructive trustee of the land for the transferor. In these cases it is held that the constructive trust will be imposed even though at the time when he acquired the property the transferee intended to perform his promise and was not therefore guilty of fraud in acquiring it; and even though the transferee did not take improper advantage of the confidential relation in procuring the transfer and was not therefore guilty of using undue influence. The abuse of the confidential relation in these cases consists merely in his failure to perform his promise. A constructive trust is imposed even though there is no fiduciary relation such as that between attorney and client, principal and agent, trustee and beneficiary; it is sufficient that there is a family relationship or other personal relationship of such a character that the transferor is justified in believing that the transferee will act in his interest.

. . .

Although the result reached in cases like this is sound, it is difficult to see why a constructive trust should not be imposed on the ground of the existence of a confidential relation in every case where land is transferred upon an oral trust for the transferor, since the transfer would never be made except for the confidence which the transferor places in the transferee. There are, however, numerous cases in which there was a close family relationship between the transferor and the transferee, and yet it was held that no constructive trust arose. In many of these cases there seems to be as clear a confidential relation as in the cases in which the courts have imposed a constructive trust, but the existence of the relation was either ignored or the particular relationship was said to be insufficient as a ground for imposing a constructive trust. The truth of the matter seems to be that whenever a court wishes to compel the transferee to reconvey the property, it can always do so by laying stress upon the confidential relation existing between the transferor and transferee, and by stating that the Statute of Frauds is a shield and not a sword, that it was intended to prevent fraud and not to promote fraud, and that the transferee was guilty of "constructive fraud" in refusing to reconvey the land. On the other hand, if the court wishes to deny relief to the transferor, it can always do so by laying stress upon the policy of the Statute of Frauds and saying that if injustice results this is to be attributed to the legislature and not to the court, and it can emphasize the possibility of fraudulent claims which might be made if relief were to be given in the absence of a writing.

2. *Secret and Semisecret Testamentary Trusts*

OLLIFFE v. WELLS

Supreme Judicial Court of Massachusetts, 1881
130 Mass. 221

[Ellen Donovan died leaving a will devising her residuary estate to the Rev. Eleazer M. P. Wells "to distribute the same in such manner as in his discretion shall appear best calculated to carry out wishes which I have expressed to him or may express to him." Wells was named executor. Ellen's heirs brought suit, claiming the residue should be distributed to them. In his answer Wells stated that the testatrix, before and after the execution of the will, had orally expressed to him her wish that her estate be used for charitable purposes, and especially for the poor, aged, infirm, and needy under the care of Saint Stephen's Mission of Boston. Wells further stated that he desired and intended to distribute the residue for these purposes. The parties agreed that the facts alleged in the answer should be taken as true.]

Gray, C.J. Upon the face of this will the residuary bequest to the defendant gives him no beneficial interest. It expressly requires him to distribute all the property bequeathed to him, giving him no discretion upon the question whether he shall or shall not distribute it, or shall or shall not carry out the intentions of the testatrix, but allowing him a discretionary authority as to the manner only in which the property shall be distributed pursuant to her intentions. The will declares a trust too indefinite to be carried out, and the next of kin of the testatrix must take by way of resulting trust, unless the facts agreed show such a trust for the benefit of others as the court can execute. Nichols v. Allen, 130 Mass. 211. No other written instrument was signed by the testatrix, and made part of the will by reference, as in Newton v. Seaman's Friend Society, 130 Mass. 91. . . .

In any view of the authorities it is quite clear, and is hardly denied by the defendant's counsel, that intentions not formed by the testatrix and communicated to the defendant before the making of the will could not have any effect against her next of kin. Thayer v. Wellington, 9 Allen 283. Johnson v. Ball, 5 De Gex & Sm. 85. Moss v. Cooper, 1 Johns. & Hem. 352. But assuming, as the defendant contends, that all the directions of the testatrix set forth in the answer are to be taken as having been orally communicated to the defendant and assented to by him before the execution of the will, we are of opinion that the result must be the same.

It has been held in England and in other States, although the question has never arisen in this Commonwealth, that, if a person procures an absolute devise or bequest to himself by orally promising the testator that he will convey the property to or hold it for the benefit of third persons, and afterwards refuses to perform his promise, a trust arises out of the confidence reposed in him by the testator and of his own fraud, which a court of equity, upon clear and satisfactory proof of the facts, will enforce against him at the suit of such third persons. . . .

Upon like grounds, it has been held in England that, if a testator devises or bequeaths property to his executors upon trusts not defined in the will, but which, as he states in the will, he has communicated to them before its execution, such trusts, if for lawful purposes, may be proved by the admission of the executors, or by oral evidence, and enforced against them. . . . And in two or three comparatively recent cases it has been held that such trusts may be enforced against the heirs or next of kin of the testator, as well as against the devisee. . . . But these cases appear to us to have overlooked or disregarded a fundamental distinction.

Where a trust not declared in the will is established by a court of chancery against the devisee, it is by reason of the obligation resting upon the conscience of the devisee, and not as a valid testamentary disposition by the deceased. Cullen v. Attorney General, L.R. 1 H.L. 190. Where the bequest is outright upon its face, the setting up of a trust, while it diminishes the right of the devisee, does not impair any right of the heirs or next of kin, in any aspect of the case; for if the trust were not set up, the whole property would go to the devisee by force of the devise; if the trust set up is a lawful one, it enures to the benefit of the cestuis que trust; and if the trust set up is unlawful, the heirs or next of kin take by way of resulting trust. . . .

Where the bequest is declared upon its face to be upon such trusts as the testator has otherwise signified to the devisee, it is equally clear that the devisee takes no beneficial interest; and, as between him and the beneficiaries intended, there is as much ground for establishing the trust as if the bequest to him were absolute on its face. But as between the devisee and the heirs or next of kin, the case stands differently. They are not excluded by the will itself. The will upon its face showing that the devisee takes the legal title only and not the beneficial interest, and the trust not being sufficiently defined by the will to take effect, the equitable interest goes, by way of resulting trust, to the heirs or next of kin, as property of the deceased, not disposed of by his will. Sears v. Hardy, 120 Mass. 524, 541, 542. They cannot be deprived of that equitable interest, which accrues to them directly from the deceased, by any conduct of the devisee; nor by any intention of the deceased, unless signified in those forms which the law makes essential to every testamentary disposition. A trust not sufficiently declared on the face of the will cannot therefore be set up by extrinsic evidence to defeat the rights of the heirs at law or next of kin. . . .

Decree for the plaintiffs.

NOTES

1. In Estate of Liginger, 14 Wis. 2d 577, 111 N.W.2d 407, 3 A.L.R.3d 1372 (1961), the testatrix devised her residuary estate to her executor, an attorney who drafted her will. The will provided: "My executor shall pay the sums in his hands in his sole discretion to the person or persons which I have previously indicated to him." The executor testified, "I know full well what is to be done with these funds," but he did not state who the intended beneficiaries were. It was held that parol declarations of the testatrix to the scrivener were not admissible, and the trust failed for lack of a beneficiary.

2. In In re Colin Cooper, [1939] Ch. 811, testator bequeathed £5000 to his executors "upon the trusts which I have already communicated to them with respect thereto." He had instructed them to hold the money for the benefit of a certain woman. In a subsequent will testator increased the sum to £10,000 "they knowing my wishes regarding this sum." He did not tell the executors of the increase. It was held that the trust was enforceable only as to the £5000, and as to the balance there was a resulting trust.

3. The Restatement (Second) of Trusts §55, Comment h (1959), adopts the English view, which imposes a constructive trust in both the secret and semisecret trust situations. Many states also follow that view.

RESTATEMENT (SECOND) OF TRUSTS
§55, Comment h (1959)

h. *Where intention to create a trust appears in the will.* If a testator devises or bequeaths property to a person, and the will states that the property is to be held upon such trust as the devisee or legatee had agreed with the testator to hold it, and the devisee or legatee had agreed to hold the property upon a particular trust, he can be compelled to hold it upon a constructive trust for the purposes for which he agreed to hold it. In such a case it is clear that the devisee or legatee will not be permitted to keep the property since it appears in the will that he was not to take it beneficially, and he would be unjustly enriched if he were permitted to keep it. Although it would be possible to impose a resulting trust for the benefit of the estate of the testator, the reasons for compelling him to hold it upon a constructive trust for the intended purposes are as strong as where the devise or bequest is absolute in its terms.

As in the case where the devise or bequest is absolute on its face, it is immaterial whether the agreement of the devisee or legatee was made prior to or at the time of or after the execution of the will, and whether the agreement by the devisee or legatee was made in specific words, whether written or oral, or was shown by his conduct.

If the devisee or legatee did not agree with the testator to hold the property upon trust, he cannot be compelled to hold it upon a constructive trust, nor will he be permitted to keep the property since it appears in the will that he was not to take it beneficially, but a resulting trust will be imposed for the benefit of the estate of the testator. Even if the devisee or legatee is willing to perform the intended trust he cannot do so.[22]

If by the terms of the will it appears that although the testator desired that the property should be devoted to certain purposes he did not intend to impose any legal obligation upon the devisee or legatee, the devisee or legatee can hold the property free of trust, unless he agreed to hold it upon trust.

George Pfahl executed a will devising all his property to his sister Gertrude Ida Pfahl absolutely. Thereafter he and Gertrude signed a "Mutual Understanding," which reads as follows:

> Due to the fact that my beloved sister, Mrs. Margaret Lortcher, has not been mentioned nor provided for in my Last Will and Testament, my beloved sister, Gertrude Ida Pfahl, and I, George Pfahl, have entered into a mutual understanding this 17th day of July, 1966, that when and if my estate, real, personal or otherwise, is disposed of in the event of my decease, said estate will be divided (after settlement of all debts and liabilities) as follows:
>
> Two-thirds of the estate is to go to my beloved sister, Gertrude Ida Pfahl, who has looked after me all these past years.
>
> One-third of the estate is to go to my beloved sister, Mrs. Margaret Lortcher.
>
> *George Pfahl*
>
> Agreed to:
> *Gertrude Ida Pfahl*

George died in 1966. On petition for a declaratory judgment it was held that the "Mutual Understanding" was of no effect and that Gertrude took the entire estate. Quoting from 55 Ohio Jurisprudence 2d, the court said, "The rule is that if the

22 Why is a constructive trust not imposed when the devisee makes no promise? — Eds.

obligation prescribed by an instrument in the form of a written contract is revocable and the vesting of an interest thereunder is postponed until the death of the obliger, the instrument is testamentary in character and ineffective unless executed in the manner prescribed by statute for the execution of wills." Pfahl v. Pfahl, 10 Ohio Misc. 234, 225 N.E.2d 305 (1967).

SECTION C. Will Substitutes

The Statute of Wills provides that "every will" must be executed with certain formalities. The words "every will" are not, however, self-defining. Courts must determine what documents, other than a formal will, come within the Statute of Wills. Many documents signed by a person can have testamentary effect in the sense that at such person's death an economic benefit passes to another person. Will substitutes are growing both in extent of use and in variety. Avoidance of probate, with its expenses and delays, is a common objective of estate planners.

1. *Revocable Trusts*

Under the typical revocable inter vivos trust, the settlor transfers assets to another person as trustee pursuant to a writing in which he retains the power to revoke, alter or amend the trust and the right to trust income during his lifetime. On the settlor's death the assets are distributed to or held in further trust for other beneficiaries. While several early cases held these trusts invalid unless executed with testamentary formalities, all American jurisdictions now recognize the validity of a trust in which the settlor reserves the power to revoke and an income interest, and even a power to control devolution of the remainder interest by retention of a testamentary power of appointment.

Can the settlor retain more than the aforementioned powers without running the risk that the trust may be held invalid? In recent years this question has arisen in one of two contexts. A "control" trust is one in which the trustee's power to administer the trust assets is subject to the settlor's approval. Even though legal title is transferred to the trustee, if he is given no managerial, investment or other administrative powers that can be exercised without the settlor's approval, is he a trustee or an agent? If the arrangement is characterized as an agency, it will not be effective to pass title to assets at death, for an agency terminates at death.

The second question concerns the validity of revocable declarations of trust, under which the settlor declares himself trustee for the benefit of himself during his lifetime, with the remainder to pass to others at his death. During his lifetime the "transferor" wears all three hats: settlor, trustee, beneficiary. Since there is little discernible change in the owner's relation to his property during his lifetime, should the courts give effect to this arrangement to the extent that it causes assets to pass to others at the owner's death? Several objections might be raised against such an arrangement. (1) No lifetime purpose is served by the so-called trust since the owner does not change his ability to deal freely with the assets during his lifetime. The sole purpose of the arrangement is to cause assets to pass to another at death. The policy of the Statute of Wills is to require a transfer with solely a testamentary purpose to be executed with testamentary formalities. (2) If the settlor is the sole beneficiary of a trust, there is no trust. (See *Case* 3, page 380.) If the declaration of trust purports to create a remainder in third persons, the remaindermen's interest is so tenuous that as a practical matter they could never hold the settlor-trustee accountable to perform trust duties. It is not simply that the remainder interest may be defeated by exercise of the power to revoke, for this is true of a conventional revocable trust that names another person as trustee. Rather, it is that because of the owner's retention of possession of the assets and of broad powers as both settlor and trustee, any action he might take as trustee, even if inconsistent with the trust terms or beyond the trustee's stated powers, could be construed as a partial revocation. Thus the settlor-trustee can do no wrong, and can never be held accountable to anyone. (3) The owner retains possession and enjoyment of the property, full power to manage it as before, and the power to determine who shall succeed to the property at his death. A trust presupposes a separation of equitable title and legal title with the attendant duty to manage the assets. Here the separation exists in form only and not in substance.

FARKAS v. WILLIAMS

Supreme Court of Illinois, 1955

5 Ill. 2d 417, 125 N.E.2d 600

HERSHEY, Justice. . . . The plaintiffs asked the court to declare their legal rights, as coadministrators, in four stock certificates issued by Investors Mutual Inc. in the name of "Albert B. Farkas, as trustee for Richard J. Williams" and which were issued pursuant to written declarations of trust. The decree of the circuit court found that said declarations were testamentary in character, and not having been executed with the formalities of a will, were invalid, and directed that the stock be awarded to the plaintiffs as an asset of the estate of said Albert B. Farkas. Upon appeal to the Appellate Court, the decree was affirmed. See 3 Ill. App. 2d 248, 121 N.E.2d 344. We allowed defendants' petition for leave to appeal.

Albert B. Farkas died intestate at the age of sixty-seven years, a resident of Chicago, leaving as his only heirs-at-law brothers, sisters, a nephew and a niece. Although retired at the time of his death, he had for many years practiced veterinary medicine and operated a veterinarian establishment in Chicago. During a considerable portion of that time, he employed the defendant Williams, who was not related to him.

On four occasions (December 8, 1948; February 7, 1949; February 14, 1950; and March 1, 1950) Farkas purchased stock of Investors Mutual, Inc. At the time of each purchase he executed a written application to Investors Mutual, Inc., instructing them to issue the stock in his name "as trustee for Richard J. Williams." Investors Mutual, Inc., by its agent, accepted each of these applications in writing by signature on the face of the application. Coincident with the execution of these applications, Farkas signed separate declarations of trust, all of which were identical except as to dates. The terms of said trust instruments are as follows:

> Declaration of Trust — Revocable. I, the undersigned, having purchased or declared my intention to purchase certain shares of capital stock of Investors Mutual, Inc. (the Company), and having directed that the certificate for said stock be issued in my name as trustee for Richard J. Williams as beneficiary, whose address is 1704 W. North Ave. Chicago, Ill., under this Declaration of Trust Do Hereby Declare that the terms and conditions upon which I shall hold said stock in trust and any additional stock resulting from reinvestments of cash dividends upon such original or additional shares are as follows:
>
> (1) During my lifetime all cash dividends are to be paid to me individually for my own personal account and use; provided, however, that any such additional stock purchased under an authorized reinvestment of cash dividends shall become a part of and subject to this trust.
>
> (2) Upon my death the title to any stock subject hereto and the right to any subsequent payments or distributions shall be vested absolutely in the beneficiary.
>
> (3) During my lifetime I reserve the right, as trustee, to vote, sell, redeem, exchange or otherwise deal in or with the stock subject hereto, but upon any sale or redemption of said stock or any part thereof, the trust hereby declared shall terminate as to the stock sold or redeemed, and I shall be entitled to retain the proceeds of sale or redemption for my own personal account and use.
>
> (4) I reserve the right at any time to change the beneficiary or revoke this trust, but it is understood that no change of beneficiary and no revocation of this trust except by death of the beneficiary, shall be effective as to the Company for any purpose unless and until written notice thereof in such form as the Company shall prescribe is delivered to the Company at Minneapolis, Minnesota. The decease of the beneficiary before my death shall operate as a revocation of this trust.
>
> (5) In the event this trust shall be revoked or otherwise terminated, said stock and all rights and privileges thereunder shall belong to and be exercised by me in my individual capacity.

. . .

The applications and declarations of trust were delivered to Investors Mutual, Inc., and held by the company until Farkas's death. The stock certificates were issued in the name of Farkas as "trustee for Richard J. Williams" and were discovered in a safety-deposit box of Farkas after his death, along with other securities, some of which were in the name of Williams alone. . . .

It is conceded that the instruments were not executed in such a way as to satisfy the requirements of the statute on wills; hence, our inquiry is limited to whether said trust instruments created valid inter vivos trusts effective to give the purported beneficiary, Williams, title to the stock in question after the death of the settlor-trustee, Farkas. To make this determination we must consider: (1) whether upon execution of the so-called trust instruments defendant Williams acquired an interest in the subject matter of the trusts, the stock of defendant Investors Mutual, Inc., (2) whether Farkas, as settlor-trustee, retained such control over the subject matter of the trusts as to render said trust instruments attempted testamentary dispositions.

First, upon execution of these trust instruments did defendant Williams presently acquire an interest in the subject matter of the intended trusts?

If no interest passed to Williams before the death of Farkas, the intended trusts are testamentary and hence invalid for failure to comply with the statute on wills. Oswald v. Caldwell, 225 Ill. 224, 80 N.E. 131; Troup v. Hunter, 300 Ill. 110, 133 N.E. 56; Restatement of the Law of Trusts, section 56. But considering the terms of these instruments we believe Farkas did intend to presently give Williams an interest in the property referred to. For it may be said, at the very least, that upon his executing one of these instruments, he showed an intention to presently part with some of the incidents of ownership in the stock. Immediately after the execution of each of these instruments, he could not deal with the stock therein referred to the same as if he owned the property absolutely, but only in accordance with the terms of the instrument. He purported to set himself up as trustee of the stock for the benefit of Williams, and the stock was registered in his name as trustee for Williams. Thus assuming to act as trustee, he is held to have intended to take on those obligations which are expressly set out in the instrument, as well as those fiduciary obligations implied by law. In addition, he manifested an intention to bind himself to having this property pass upon his death to Williams, unless he changed the beneficiary or revoked the trust, and then such change of beneficiary or revocation was not to be effective as to Investors Mutual, Inc., unless and until written notice thereof in such form as the company prescribed was delivered to them at Minneapolis, Minnesota. An absolute owner can dispose of his property, either in his lifetime or by will, in any way he sees fit without notifying or securing approval from anyone and without being held to the duties of a fiduciary in so doing.

It seems to follow that what incidents of ownership Farkas intended to relinquish, in a sense he intended Williams to acquire. . . . It is difficult to name this interest of Williams, nor is there any reason for so doing so long as it passed to him immediately upon the creation of the trust.[23] As stated in 4 Powell, The Law of Real Property, at page 87: "Interests of beneficiaries of private express trusts run the gamut from valuable substantialities to evanescent hopes. Such a beneficiary may

[23] The idea of an interest smaller than any interest you can name, but nonetheless an interest, brings to mind the mathematical concept of the infinitesimal, developed by Isaac Newton and Gottfried Wilhelm von Leibniz. Although scorned by Bishop Berkeley as "ghosts of departed quantities," infinitesimals proved very useful in differential calculus.

Would it be a good idea for the Illinois legislature to settle the matter by passing a statute providing that, if a settlor retained the powers Farkas retained, the beneficiary would be deemed to receive an infinitesimal interest? Should the legislature give the interest a name, such as a farkas, since the court finds naming so difficult? — Eds.

have any one of an almost infinite variety of the possible aggregates of rights, privileges, powers and immunities."

An additional problem is presented here, however, for it is to be noted that the trust instruments provide: "The decease of the beneficiary before my death shall operate as a revocation of this trust." The plaintiffs argue that the presence of this provision removes the only possible distinction which might have been drawn between these instruments and a will. Being thus conditioned on his surviving, it is argued that the "interest" of Williams until the death of Farkas was a mere expectancy. Conversely, they assert, the interest of Farkas in the securities until his death was precisely the same as that of a testator who bequeaths securities by his will, since he had all the rights accruing to an absolute owner.

Admittedly, had this provision been absent the interest of Williams would have been greater, since he would then have had an inheritable interest in the lifetime of Farkas. But to say his interest would have been greater is not to say that he here did not have a beneficial interest, properly so-called, during the lifetime of Farkas. The provision purports to set up but another "contingency" which would serve to terminate the trust. The disposition is not testamentary and the intended trust is valid, even though the interest of the beneficiary is contingent upon the existence of a certain state of facts at the time of the settlor's death. (Restatement of the Law of Trusts, section 56, comment f.) In an example contained in the previous reference, the authors of the Restatement have referred to the interest of a beneficiary under a trust who must survive the settlor (and where the settlor receives the income for life) as a contingent equitable interest in remainder. . . .

Second, did Farkas retain such control over the subject matter of the trust as to render said trust instruments attempted testamentary dispositions?

In each of these trust instruments, Farkas reserved to himself as settlor the following powers: (1) the right to receive during his lifetime all cash dividends; (2) the right at any time to change the beneficiary or revoke the trust; and (3) upon sale or redemption of any portion of the trust property, the right to retain the proceeds therefrom for his own use.

Additionally, Farkas reserved the right to act as sole trustee, and in such capacity, he was accorded the right to vote, sell, redeem, exchange or otherwise deal in the stock which formed the subject matter of the trust.

We shall consider first those enumerated powers which Farkas reserved to himself as settlor.

It is well established that the retention by the settlor of the power to revoke, even when coupled with the reservation of a life interest in the trust property, does not render the trust inoperative for want of execution as a will. . . .

A more difficult problem is posed, however, by the fact that Farkas is also trustee, and as such, is empowered to vote, sell, redeem, exchange and otherwise deal in and with the subject matter of the trusts.

. . .

In the instant case the plaintiffs contend that Farkas, as settlor-trustee, retained complete control and dominion over the securities for his own benefit during his lifetime. It is argued that he had the power to deal with the property as he liked so long as he lived and owed no enforceable duties of any kind to Williams as beneficiary. . . .

That the retention of the power by Farkas as trustee to sell or redeem the stock and keep the proceeds for his own use should not render these trust instruments testamentary in character becomes more evident upon analyzing the real import and significance of the powers to revoke and to amend the trust, the reservation of which the courts uniformly hold does not invalidate an inter vivos trust.

It is obvious that a settlor with the power to revoke and to amend the trust at any time is, for all practical purpose, in a position to exert considerable control over the trustee regarding the administration of the trust. For anything believed to be inimicable to his best interest can be thwarted or prevented by simply revoking the trust or amending it in such a way as to conform to his wishes. Indeed, it seems that many of those powers which from time to time have been viewed as "additional powers" are already, in a sense, virtually contained within the overriding power of revocation or the power to amend the trust. Consider, for example, the following: (1) the power to consume the principal; (2) the power to sell or mortgage the trust property and appropriate the proceeds; (3) the power to appoint or remove trustees; (4) the power to supervise and direct investments; and (5) the power to otherwise direct and supervise the trustee in the administration of the trust. Actually, any of the above powers could readily be assumed by a settlor with the reserved power of revocation through the simple expedient of revoking the trust, and then, as absolute owner of the subject matter, doing with the property as he chooses. Even though no actual termination of the trust is effectuated, however, it could hardly be questioned but that the mere existence of this power in the settlor is sufficient to enable his influence to be felt in a practical way in the administration of the trust. . . .

In the case at bar, the power of Farkas to vote, sell, redeem, exchange or otherwise deal in the stock was reserved to him as trustee, and it was only upon sale or redemption that he was entitled to keep the proceeds for his own use. Thus, the control reserved is not as great as in those cases where said power is reserved to the owner as settlor. For as trustee he must so conduct himself in accordance with standards applicable to trustees generally. It is not a valid objection to this to say that Williams would never question Farkas' conduct, inasmuch as Farkas could then revoke the trust and destroy what interest Williams has. Such a possibility exists in any case where the settlor has the power of revocation. Still, Williams has rights the same as any beneficiary, although it may not be feasible for him to exercise them. Moreover, it is entirely possible that he might in certain situations have a right to hold Farkas' estate liable for breaches of trust committed by Farkas during his lifetime. In this regard, consider what would happen if, without having revoked the trust, Farkas as trustee had given the stock away without receiving any consideration therefor, had pledged the stock improperly for his own personal debt and allowed it to be lost by foreclosure or had exchanged the stock for another security or other worthless property in such manner as to constitute gross impropriety and gross negligence. In such instances, it would seem in accordance with the terms of these instruments that Williams would have had an enforceable claim against Farkas' estate for whatever damage had been suffered. Contrast this with the rights of a legatee or devisee under a will. The testator could waste the property or do anything with it he wished during his lifetime without incurring any liability to those designated by the will to inherit the property. . . .

Another factor often considered in determining whether an inter vivos trust is an attempted testamentary disposition is the formality of the transaction. Restatement of the Law of Trusts, section 57, comment g; Stouse v. First National Bank, Ky., 245 S.W.2d 914, 32 A.L.R.2d 1261; United Building and Loan Association v. Garrett, D.C. 64 F. Supp. 460; In re Sheasley's Trust, 366 Pa. 316, 77 A.2d 448. Historically, the purpose behind the enactment of the statute on wills was the prevention of fraud. The requirement as to witnesses was deemed necessary because a will is ordinarily an expression of the secret wish of the testator, signed out of the presence of all concerned. The possibility of forgery and fraud are ever present in such situations. Here, Farkas executed four separate applications for stock of Investors Mutual, Inc., in which he directed that the stock be issued in his name as trustee for Williams, and he executed four separate declarations of trust in which he declared he was holding said stock in trust for Williams. The stock certificates in question were issued in his name as trustee for Williams. He thus manifested his intention in a solemn and formal manner.

For the reasons stated, we conclude that these trust declarations executed by Farkas constituted valid inter vivos trusts and were not attempted testamentary dispositions. It must be conceded that they have, in the words of Mr. Justice Holmes in Bromley v. Mitchell, 155 Mass. 509, 30 N.E. 83, a "testamentary look." Moreover, it must be admitted that the line should be drawn somewhere, but after a study of this case we do not believe that point has here been reached. . . .

Reversed and remanded, with directions.[24]

NOTES

1. In terms of the ritual, evidentiary, and protective functions of the Statute of Wills, how do you evaluate the trust set up by Albert B. Farkas? How do the policies underlying the Statute of Wills apply to (a) creation of the trust; (b) amendment of the trust; (c) revocation of the trust? 1 Scott, Trusts §57.2 (3d ed. 1967). For discussion of the issues raised by the Farkas case see Johanson, Revocable Trusts and Community Property: The Substantive Problems, 47 Texas L. Rev. 537, 548-558 (1969).

2. Where the settlor is not the trustee but retains the right to control the trustee in the administration of the trust, some courts have viewed the arrangement as an agency rather than a trust. Inasmuch as the powers of an agent cease at death, if the trustee is viewed as an "agent," the trust likewise will cease at death. In that

[24] Noted 5 De Paul L. Rev. 153; 23 U. Chi. L. Rev. 289, 303. — Eds.

case the trust property will be paid to testator's estate and not to beneficiaries under the trust deed. Denver Nat'l Bank v. Von Brecht, 137 Colo. 88, 322 P.2d 667 (1958); 1 Bogert & Bogert, Trusts and Trustees §104 (2d ed. 1965, with supplements); 1 Scott, Trusts §57.2 (3d ed. 1967). This view, which was reflected in the first Restatement of Trusts, was abandoned in the second Restatement. Restatement (Second) of Trusts §57 (1959). See also Merchants Nat'l Bank v. Weinold, 12 Ill. App. 2d 209, 138 N.E.2d 840 (1956), upholding revocable trust which provided that "the trustee shall not exercise any of the powers granted without first obtaining the written consent of the settlor."

3. O transfers property to X in trust to pay the income to O for life, and on the death of O to pay the corpus as O by will appoints, and in default of appointment to pay the corpus to O's issue then living per stirpes. O retains the right to revoke or amend the trust. What are the advantages and disadvantages of this arrangement?

a. *During the settlor's life, these may be advantages:*

(1) The settlor is relieved from the burden of financial management.

(2) The settlor can evaluate the trustee's performance and name a new trustee if he is not satisfied — an opportunity not available in the case of his executor.

(3) In case of the settlor's incompetency, the trustee can use the income for his support and no guardian nor conservator need be appointed.

(4) The settlor retains complete control during his competency and can accommodate changing conditions in his family.

b. *During the settlor's life, these may be disadvantages:*

(1) Attorneys who make a relatively nominal charge to prepare a will may make substantially higher charges to prepare an inter vivos trust.

(2) Trustees' fees may be payable.[25]

(3) Stock transfer taxes may be payable when the transfer is made to the trustee.

c. *During the probate period, these may be advantages:*

(1) Income and even principal may be disbursed relatively promptly after the settlor's death.[26]

(2) The trustee can change investments if desirable, and invest in common stocks, whereas in many states executors can invest only in savings accounts, federal or state bonds, or similar investments deemed very safe.

(3) Unlike a will, the trust instrument is not a public record and the amount of the settlor's assets and his beneficiaries need not be disclosed to anyone except the tax authorities.

(4) The trust assets do not become part of the probate estate and are excluded in computing the executor's fee, the attorney's fee, and the fees of any guardian ad litem or appraiser (where required).

(5) If the settlor owned any real property located outside his domiciliary

[25] Such compensation is generally deductible for income tax purposes, except to the extent that it relates to tax-exempt income. Int. Rev. Code of 1954, §212.

[26] Deferring disbursement of income and principal may be desirable for income tax reasons or to preserve the alternate valuation date under the estate tax. Int. Rev. Code of 1954, §2032.

state, and put such property into the trust, ancillary administration and its attendant expenses are avoided.

(6) In many states the surviving spouse cannot reach the trust assets to satisfy her claim to a statutory forced share of the decedent's property.[27]

(7) Children omitted from the settlor's will cannot reach the trust assets under a pretermission statute.[28]

(8) Statutes giving decedent's heirs a right to upset gifts to charity do not apply to charitable gifts under an inter vivos trust.[29]

d. *During the probate period, these may be disadvantages:*

(1) An executor or testamentary trustee has ready access to probate court to seek instructions or settle accounts, because of the court's retained jurisdiction. An inter vivos trust is a non-court trust and the trustee cannot so easily get into court.[30]

(2) The opportunity for post-mortem tax planning is more limited in the case of a revocable trust. Such matters as the alternate valuation date for federal estate tax purposes and the splitting of income between the decedent and his surviving spouse during his last year of life may be adversely affected by the use of an inter vivos trust.[31]

e. *After the probate period, these may be advantages* resulting from the fact that the settlor of an inter vivos trust is permitted to choose the state law to govern the trust whereas a testator may not be able to so choose:

(1) The settlor can select a corporate fiduciary in another state, perhaps where the beneficiaries live.

(2) The settlor can select a trustee in a state which has the most permissive period of perpetuities.[32]

(3) The settlor can select a trustee in a state which permits spendthrift trusts if his domiciliary state does not.

(4) The settlor can select a trustee in a state which denies the surviving spouse a right to set aside an inter vivos trust to satisfy her forced share, and which applies its own law regardless of where the settlor and spouse are domiciled.[33]

The rights of creditors to reach a revocable inter vivos trust are not the same in all states. Where the settlor has reserved the right to the income and a general power of appointment over the property, in addition to the power to revoke, the weight of authority holds that creditors of the settlor can reach the trust assets.[34]

[27] See pages 477-494, infra.
[28] See pages 555-566, infra.
[29] See pages 633-635, infra.
[30] Wile, Judicial Assistance in the Administration of California Trusts, 14 Stan. L. Rev. 231 (1962).
[31] See pages 234-235, supra.
[32] Wisconsin has abolished the common law Rule against Perpetuities and permits a trust to endure indefinitely if the trustee has the power of sale. See pages 1079-1080, infra.
[33] Massachusetts is such a state. Nat'l Shawmut Bank v. Cumming, 325 Mass. 457, 91 N.E.2d 337 (1950), discussed at page 492, infra.
[34] 4 Scott, Trusts §330.12 (3d ed. 1967).

Generally speaking, a revocable inter vivos trust does not avoid death taxes. Section 2038 of the Internal Revenue Code of 1954 requires the inclusion of the value of the trust assets in the settlor's estate if the settlor retains the power to revoke the trust. However, in certain situations there may be special tax advantages and disadvantages.[35]

For the details of the benefits and detriments of the revocable inter vivos trust, see 1 Casner, Estate Planning 120-147 (3d ed. 1961, Supp. 1971); Casner, Estate Planning — Avoidance of Probate, 60 Colum. L. Rev. 108 (1960); Bostick, The Revocable Trust: A Means of Avoiding Probate in the Small Estate? 21 U. Fla. L. Rev. 44 (1968).

4. The revocable declaration of trust is the key feature of Norman F. Dacey's book, How to Avoid Probate! (1965). Upon publication the book became a best seller. Dacey, who is not a lawyer, was sharply critical of the probate system and of the lawyers who tolerate and maintain its existence. He refers to the expenses of probate as "a private tax imposed by one group of citizens on another, a form of tribute privately levied by the legal profession" (id. at 14), and adds, "Remember, the racket persists only because it hasn't occurred to the public to call a halt to this looting of estates" (id. at 15). Having made a case that probate should be avoided, Dacey goes on to suggest that it can be avoided through use of "a legal wonder drug," the revocable inter vivos trust. The remainder of the book consists of some 300 pages of will and trust forms printed in duplicate, with instructions for their use.

Prior to being catapulted to fame and fortune, Dacey, a resident of Bridgeport, Connecticut, had as his principal business selling shares in mutual funds, including the Wellington Fund. He devised a form of inter vivos trust which became known as a "Dacey trust." He helped his mutual fund customers establish trusts by filling in the blanks in his will and trust forms, and he supervised their execution. In some cases he prepared documents that deviated from his forms. In 1964 the Grievance Committee of the Bar of Fairfield County filed suit for an injunction to restrain Dacey from preparing wills and trusts, or otherwise participating in the practice of law. A lower court issued an injunction. The Connecticut Supreme Court of Errors found that Dacey's activities involved the practice of law and accordingly sustained the injunction. Grievance Committee v. Dacey, 154 Conn. 129, 222 A.2d 339, 22 A.L.R.3d 1092 (1966). In its opinion the court described how Dacey profited from the use of his forms:

"Although it did not clearly appear that Dacey ever charged for the preparation of a trust or will, as such, he did provide in the will form that upon the death of the testator the entire estate, except for tangible personal property, should go into the corpus of the trust and that substantially the entire corpus should be invested in shares of the Wellington Fund which should be purchased from Dacey. Under his contract with the Wellington Fund, Dacey received a 6 percent commission on all sales of shares of the Wellington Fund. Thus, as a direct consequence of his prepa-

[35] A revocable inter vivos trust of community property presents unusual tax problems. These are treated at pages 526-546, infra.

ration of the Dacey trust arrangement, Dacey virtually assured himself of what amounted to a 6 percent sales commission on almost the entire assets of each estate. Compensation may have been frequently deferred, but it was substantial when received. The court found that the money involved in the trust arrangements prepared by Dacey amounted to several million dollars. On most, if not all, of this sum, he would receive a 6 percent commission."

In 1967 the New York County Lawyers' Association filed suit to have Dacey, his publisher, and two booksellers judged in criminal contempt for the unauthorized practice of law and to have the sale and distribution of How to Avoid Probate! enjoined. Special Term adjudged Dacey in contempt and enjoined the sale and distribution of his book. The Appellate Division affirmed. However, the Court of Appeals dismissed the suit on the grounds that the book was sold to the public at large, and that no relationship of personal trust and confidence arose between Dacey and the purchasers of the book. New York County Lawyers' Ass'n v. Dacey, 21 N.Y.2d 694, 287 N.Y.S.2d 422, 234 N.E.2d 459 (1967).

While pursuing his state court appeals, Dacey brought suit in federal court against the New York County Lawyers' Association, alleging that the criminal contempt proceedings deprived him of his First Amendment right to free speech, and requesting that the Association be enjoined from further prosecution of the state court proceeding. After the New York Court of Appeals ruled in his favor, Dacey amended his complaint in federal court to demand $1,500,000 in compensatory damages and $4,500,000 in punitive damages. The Court of Appeals for the Second Circuit dismissed Dacey's suit on the ground that the Lawyers' Association had probable cause to initiate unauthorized practice proceedings against Dacey. Dacey v. N.Y. County Lawyers' Ass'n, 423 F.2d 188 (2d Cir. 1969), cert. denied, 398 U.S. 929 (1970).

Dacey's book was reviewed in an article in the March, 1967, issue of the Florida Bar Journal by Boyd Anderson, Jr. The article defended the Florida probate system and contained statements which Dacey viewed as libelous. Dacey sued both the Florida Bar and Anderson for libel, and lost both cases. Dacey v. Florida Bar, Inc., 414 F.2d 195 (5th Cir. 1969), cert. denied, 397 U.S. 909 (1970); Dacey v. Florida Bar, Inc., 427 F.2d 1292 (5th Cir. 1970).

How to Avoid Probate! received wide attention in the law reviews. Most of the reviewers found that Dacey's forms contained errors and ambiguities and concluded that they would breed litigation. See 46 B.U.L. Rev. 417; 16 Buffalo L. Rev. 517; 54 Calif. L. Rev. 2189; 42 Calif. St. B.J. 63; 16 De Paul L. Rev. 276; 41 Fla. B.J. 26; 35 Geo. Wash. L. Rev. 853; 55 Ill. B.J. 220; 36 J. Kan. B. Assn. 181; 55 Ky. L.J. 733; 42 Notre Dame Law. 445; 29 Tex. B.J. 897; 28 U. Pitt. L. Rev. 128; 42 Wash. L. Rev. 311.

The Pour-Over

Along with the increasing use of the revocable trust as an estate planning device has come the development of the "pour-over" will. In concept it is simple. O sets up a revocable inter vivos trust with X as trustee. O transfers to X, as trustee, his stocks and bonds. O then executes a will devising the residue of his estate to X, as trustee, to hold under the terms of the inter vivos trust. The pour-over is a useful device where O wants to establish an inter vivos trust of some of his assets, and wants to merge after his death his testamentary estate, insurance proceeds, and other assets into a single trust receptacle subject to unitary administration. (*Note:* Not all assets are suitable for an inter vivos trust. Closely held businesses, the settlor's residence, and unimproved real estate, if put into the trust at all, should be made subject to special provisions governing their management and administration. Also, of course, clothes, automobiles, and most items of tangible personal property are not suitable for trust management at all.)

Prior to the 1960s there was considerable uncertainty about the validity of pour-over provisions, particularly where the trust had been amended after the will had been executed. Some courts held that a revocable trust could not be incorporated by reference, and the pour-over failed. Other courts permitted a pour-over into the trust to be disposed of in accordance with the terms of the trust deed as it stood at the time of execution of the will and not as subsequently amended. Still other courts, in the later cases, permitted the pour-over into the trust as amended on the theory that the inter vivos trust had independent significance.[36] Bowing to the demands of estate planners, legislatures in every state except Louisiana and Missouri[37] have enacted statutes permitting a will to pour over estate assets into an inter vivos trust as amended on the date of death. The Uniform Testamentary Additions to Trusts Act is typical of these statutes, though in some states the pour-over act is not as broad as the Uniform Act.

UNIFORM TESTAMENTARY ADDITIONS TO TRUSTS ACT

Section 1 (Testamentary Additions to Trusts)

A devise or bequest, the validity of which is determinable by the law of this state, may be made by a will to the trustee or trustees of a trust established or to be established by the testator or by the testator and some other person or persons or by some other person or persons (including a funded or unfunded life insurance trust, although the trustor has reserved any or all rights of ownership of the insurance contracts) if the trust is identified in the testator's will and its terms are set forth in a written instrument (other than a will) executed

[36] See Bogert & Bogert, Trusts and Trustees §§105-107 (2d ed. 1965, with supplements); 1 Scott, Trusts §54.3 (3d ed. 1967); Flickinger, The "Pour-Over" Trust and the Wills Statutes: Uneasy Bedfellows, 52 Ky. L.J. 731 (1964); Polasky, "Pour-Over Wills": Use with Inter Vivos Trust, 17 Sw. L.J. 410 (1963).

[37] In Louisiana a pour-over into a trust as amended on the date of the execution of the will is permitted. La. Rev. Stat. §9:1754 (1965). If the trust is amended after the execution of the will, the amendment cannot be given effect as to probate assets unless executed in accordance with the Statute of Wills. The law in Missouri appears to be similar to that in Louisiana. Prudential Insurance Co. of America v. Gatewood, 317 S.W.2d 382 (1958).

before or concurrently with the execution of the testator's will or in the valid last will of a person who has predeceased the testator (regardless of the existence, size, or character of the corpus of the trust). The devise or bequest shall not be invalid because the trust is amendable or revocable, or both, or because the trust was amended after the execution of the will or after the death of the testator. Unless the testator's will provides otherwise, the property so devised or bequeathed (a) shall not be deemed to be held under a testamentary trust of the testator but shall become a part of the trust to which it is given and (b) shall be administered and disposed of in accordance with the provisions of the instrument or will setting forth the terms of the trust, including any amendments thereto made before the death of the testator (regardless of whether made before or after the execution of the testator's will) and, if the testator's will so provides, including any amendments to the trust made after the death of the testator.[38] A revocation or termination of the trust before the death of the testator shall cause the devise or bequest to lapse.

Section 2 (Effect on Prior Wills)

This Act shall have no effect upon any devise or bequest made by a will executed prior to the effective date of this Act.

NOTES

1. For comment on the Uniform Act, see McClanahan, The Pour-Over Device Comes of Age, 39 S. Cal. L. Rev. 163 (1966); Hawley, The "Statutory Blessing" and Pour-Over Problems, 102 Trusts & Estates 896 (1963).

2. Section 2 of the Uniform Act, included by a 28 to 25 vote of the commissioners, was not adopted in some states. Is it a good idea? Osgood, Pour Over Will — Appraisal of Uniform Testamentary Additions to Trusts Act, 104 Trusts & Estates 768 (1965).

3. Assume the Uniform Testamentary Additions to Trusts Act is the law in this jurisdiction. O executes a trust deed which names X as trustee and provides that X shall pay the income to O's daughter, D, for life, remainder in fee to D's issue per stirpes. The trust deed provides that the trust can be revoked or amended at any time by a written or oral communication to X from O. O transfers to X one dollar as the trust property. O subsequently makes a will pouring over all his property into this trust. Then O invites X to come by his house for a drink one afternoon. O takes X on a tour of the house and tells X exactly what item he wants to go to whom. He also tells X he wants $1000 to go each to M and N. A few days later O writes X a letter telling X that he wants M to have $2000 rather than $1000; he adds that with respect to the family silver, he is preparing a memorandum which will

[38] Cf. N.Y. Estates, Powers & Trusts Law §3-3.7 (1967), which requires that the trust and any amendments be executed with the formalities required for recording a deed in order to pour over into a trust as amended. — Eds.

state who is to get which teapot, creamer, platter, etc. upon his death. Upon O's death, such a memorandum is found. What disposition is made of O's estate?

4. When a will attempts to pour over assets into an inter vivos trust, it is possible to hold (a) that the combined assets form one trust, which is an inter vivos trust; or (b) that the combined assets form one trust, which is a testamentary trust,[39] or (c) that the assets cannot be combined but must be administered as two different trusts, one inter vivos and one testamentary.

A single trust simplifies administration and also may result in lower trustee's fees. An inter vivos (or non-court) trust has a number of advantages over a testamentary (or court) trust. Two are particularly pertinent here. First, a provision that certain beneficiaries can approve the trustee's accounts is usually effective if the trust is an inter vivos trust.[40] This provision may avoid an expensive and time-consuming judicial accounting, with the necessity of appointing guardians ad litem to represent all unborn and unascertained beneficiaries. If the trust is testamentary, it is a court trust, brought into being by the probate court which retains jurisdiction. It may not be possible by a provision in the will to oust the court from jurisdiction to approve the trustee's accounts.[41] The second basic advantage of treating the poured-over assets as part of the inter vivos trust is the greater flexibility possible in the choice of law and of the trustee. For example, an out-of-state corporate trustee cannot act as testamentary trustee in many states. These restrictions can be avoided if the assets poured over are treated as poured into one inter vivos trust. Where the beneficiaries reside in another state, the testator may wish to avoid the retained jurisdiction of the probate court, especially if the trustee is domiciled elsewhere. A foreign trustee will usually be desirable where there are foreign beneficiaries and the trustee is given discretionary powers which can be soundly exercised only on the basis of personal contact with the beneficiaries. The Uniform Testamentary Additions to Trusts Act adopts the view that one trust is created by a pour-over and this is a non-court trust. A few courts have also come to this conclusion. See 4 Powell, Real Property ¶510 (1970); 1 Scott, Trusts §54.3 (3d ed. 1967).

ESTATE PLANNING PROBLEM

Adam Smith is married to Jane Smith. They have three minor children. Adam has five life insurance policies, with a face value of $72,000. Three of the policies have double or triple indemnity provisions.[42] The policies name Jane as primary

[39] In Estate of Meskimen, 39 Ill. 2d 415, 235 N.E.2d 619 (1968), the husband of the decedent argued that the trust was incorporated by reference, that the combined assets formed a testamentary trust, and that he was entitled to a forced statutory share from the combined trust. The court held that the inter vivos trust had independent significance and that the surviving spouse could neither reach the receptacle trust nor take it into account in determining his forced share.

[40] Westfall, Nonjudicial Settlement of Trustees' Accounts, 71 Harv. L. Rev. 40 (1957).

[41] Why not? What public policy forbids giving effect to a provision in a will or trust instrument that certain beneficiaries shall have power to approve the trustee's accounts?

[42] For details, see pages 72-77, supra.

beneficiary. If Jane predeceases him, Adam wants the proceeds to go to his brother Henry to be held in trust for the benefit of Adam's three minor children, with the children receiving the principal when the youngest child reaches twenty-one. Which of the following plans do you recommend to carry out Adam's wishes?

Plan A. The proceeds of the policies are made payable to Jane if she survives Adam. If Jane does not survive Adam, the proceeds are made payable to a testamentary trustee. Thus the secondary beneficiary will be designated on the policies as "the trustee named as beneficiary in the Will of Adam Smith." Adam then executes a will devising his residuary estate to his brother Henry in trust if Jane predeceases Adam.[43]

Plan B. The proceeds of the policies are made payable to Jane if she survives Adam. If Jane does not survive Adam, the proceeds are made payable to Henry as trustee to be held in trust pursuant to the terms of a trust instrument executed by Adam. The secondary beneficiary will be designated on the policy as "the trustee under the Adam Smith Insurance Trust, executed on (date)." Adam then executes a will pouring over into this trust his residuary estate, if Jane predeceases him.[44]

Plan C. The policies are assigned and delivered to Henry as trustee to be held in trust pursuant to the terms of a trust instrument executed by Adam. The trustee is named as beneficiary under the policies and holds legal title to the policies. This inter vivos trust is revocable by Adam. Under the terms of the trust, the proceeds are payable to Jane if she survives Adam, and if she does not they are held on trust for the children. Adam then executes a will pouring over into this trust his residuary estate, if Jane predeceases him.[45]

2. *Bank Arrangements*

In Matter of Totten, 179 N.Y. 112, 71 N.E. 748 (1904), O made deposits in a savings account in the name of "O as trustee for A." O had the right to withdraw the funds at any time during his life and use them as he saw fit. The court upheld this arrangement, declaring it not testamentary. At O's death any funds in the account belong to A. Savings account trusts, often known as Totten trusts, have now been accepted in a majority of jurisdictions and by the Restatement of Trusts.[46]

[43] Review pages 394-398, supra.

[44] Review pages 206-207, supra.

[45] If the policies are assigned to a trustee, unless the trust instrument is carefully drafted it may not be possible for the trustee to elect any installment option; he may have to draw down the proceeds in a lump sum. An installment option or an interest option may not be a proper investment for a trustee. If he elects the life annuity, for example, how is this to be apportioned between the life tenant and the remaindermen? If he elects the interest option, has he improperly delegated to the insurance company his control over the principal? If the client wishes the trustee to have the power to elect among the options, the trust instrument should specifically authorize him to do so and further provide how the payments are to be apportioned between the life tenant and remaindermen. To protect itself, an insurance company usually will not allow a trustee to elect any installment or interest option until it looks at the trust instrument to make certain that the trustee is specifically authorized to make such an election.

[46] Restatement (Second) of Trusts §58 (1959). See 1 Scott, Trusts §§58.2 to 58.5 (3d ed. 1967); Christopher, Totten Trust: The Poor Man's Will, 42 N.C.L. Rev. 214 (1963).

Notice to the beneficiary is not essential to the creation of any kind of trust, and a Totten trust beneficiary frequently does not know of the existence of the trust until the depositor dies. Creditors of the settlor of a Totten trust can reach the trust property before and after his death; a Totten trust can be revoked by the will of the settlor and another beneficiary named to take the proceeds.[47]

ESTATE OF SCHNEIDER

Supreme Court of Illinois, 1955

6 Ill. 2d 180, 127 N.E.2d 445

Mr. Justice Schaefer delivered the opinion of the court:

This case turns upon the admissibility of parol evidence to show the actual ownership of funds deposited in a joint bank account "with right of survivorship." Prior to May 10, 1952, Edward Schneider had two accounts aggregating $5850.81 in the North West Federal Savings and Loan Association of Chicago. On that date he took William M. Ralston with him to the association, withdrew the money from his accounts and deposited it in two joint accounts in his name and Ralston's. The following document was signed by Schneider and Ralston:

> Joint Savings Account. One signature only required for withdrawal. Account No. 17434.
>
> Schneider, Edward (Mr.) or
> Ralston, William M. (Mr.)
> Type all names: ....
> (Last name) (First name) (Middle name)
>
> As joint tenants with right of survivorship and not as tenants in common, the undersigned hereby apply for a membership and for a.................... savings account in the North-West Federal Savings and Loan Association and for issuance of evidence of membership in the joint names of the undersigned as joint tenants with right of survivorship and not as tenants in common. The signatures of the undersigned are shown below, and the Association is hereby authorized to act without further inquiry in accordance with writings bearing any such signature; it being understood and agreed that any one of the undersigned who shall first act shall have power to act in all matters related to the membership and any savings account in said Association held by the undersigned, whether the other person or persons named hereon be living or not. Payment or delivery of a receipt or acquittance signed by any one of the undersigned shall be a valid and sufficient release and discharge of said Association. The undersigned hereby authorizes the said Association to accept drafts, checks, money orders and other credit instruments for credit

[47] In re Vertroock's Will, 34 Misc. 2d 1073, 230 N.Y.S.2d 485 (1962), held that a Totten trust was revoked by the testatrix's will, but that a survivorship provision in a joint bank account could not be revoked by will.

of this account, whether payable to either one or all of the undersigned, and if not endorsed to supply such endorsement as may be required.

(1) /s/ Edward Schneider	(2) /s/ Wm. M. Ralston
550 N. Mason Ave.	2456 N. Normandy
Chicago 30	Chicago 35

Dated May 10, 1952 Introduced by RO3-8628

* The names on any membership certificate, issued pursuant to this application, must be followed by the words "as joint tenants with right of survivorship and not as tenants in common." Space for Identification Information on reverse side.

After Schneider's death his executor filed a petition in the probate court of Cook County alleging that the funds in the accounts belonged to the estate and not to Ralston. The probate court dismissed the petition. Upon appeal to the superior court of Cook County there was a trial de novo. Ralston was called as an adverse witness and testified over objection that all of the money in the accounts was deposited by Schneider and none by Ralston, that Schneider at no time told Ralston that he wanted Ralston to have any of the money in the accounts, and that when they went to the bank on May 10, 1952, Schneider said to him, "I want your name on these bank accounts so that in case I am sick you can go and get the money for me." The superior court found that the funds were the property of the estate. The Appellate Court affirmed, (2 Ill. App. 2d 560) and we granted leave to appeal, primarily because of a conflict in the decisions of the Appellate Courts with respect to this problem. See Cuilini v. Northern Trust Co. 335 Ill. App. 86; Johnson v. Mueller, 346 Ill. App. 199.

Appellant's position is that the instrument executed by him and Schneider was a contract between them, the terms of which establish appellant's right to the funds deposited, and that parol evidence is inadmissible to vary the terms of that agreement.

We note initially we are here concerned only with the rights of the depositors between themselves. That an instrument such as that executed by Schneider and the appellant protects a bank against a claim by either of the depositors if payments are made to them in accordance with the terms of the agreement, is settled by statute. Ill. Rev. Stat. 1953, chap. 76, par. 2.

The familiar joint bank account has had an uneasy career in the courts because the relationships which it contemplates do not fit readily into common-law categories. The four unities of the common-law joint tenancy, the notion of an undivided moiety in each joint tenant, and the difficulty of applying the common-law concept of joint tenancy to a fluctuating res have caused difficulties. Common-law doctrines governing gifts of personal property have contributed their share to the complex of legal problems stemming from joint bank accounts, for the common law required a complete relinquishment of ownership by the donor in order to achieve an effective gift, while the joint bank account contemplates power of withdrawal by both parties. The varying methods adopted by the courts in meeting these problems appear in the cases collected and discussed in the following annotations: 48 A.L.R. 189; 66 A.L.R. 881; 103 A.L.R. 1123; 135 A.L.R. 993; 149 A.L.R. 879.

The particular problem involved in this case has not been before this court. Basic to its solution is an analysis of the transaction between the parties and the bank. This case is typical of many others in which the sole owner of funds in a bank account desires to establish a joint account with another person, and the question of the right of the survivor arises upon the death of the original owner of the funds. In such cases generally, as in this case, it is not seriously suggested that there was any consideration for the transfer of an interest in the funds from the original owner to the survivor. To say, as appellant here says, that the agreement is a third party beneficiary contract, begs the question by assuming that the contract is for the benefit of the beneficiary. If any interest in the funds was transferred, the transfer must have been by gift or bequest. If the transfer was by bequest, it was testamentary in character and ineffective under the Statute of Wills. (L.R.A. 1917C 550.) If the transfer was by gift, the problem of consideration is of course eliminated.

This court has held that the relationship established by a joint bank account is not that of joint tenancy, but rather is one which is governed by the provisions of the agreement between the bank and the depositors. (Erwin v. Felter, 283 Ill. 36; Illinois Trust and Savings Bank. v. VanVlack, 310 Ill. 185; Reder v. Reder, 312 Ill. 209.) The difficulties involved in reaching this result are disclosed in the dissenting opinions of Mr. Justice Thompson in the VanVlack and Reder cases. These decisions, as the dissenting opinions make clear, were intended to meet the objections that the statute then in effect did not permit joint tenancies in personal property, and that a joint tenancy could not exist when the property was unspecified and when one joint tenant could terminate the right of survivorship by withdrawing the entire amount. Under these decisions the subject of the gift is not the funds on deposit in the account, but rather an interest in the account, or a power to deal with the funds on deposit. This is also the view which has been taken by courts of other jurisdictions which have also rested the right to create a joint bank account upon contract. Goldston v. Randolph, 293 Mass. 253, 199 N.E. 896, 899; Beach v. Holland, 142 Pac. 2d 990.

Appellant's argument that these decisions also hold that evidence bearing upon donative intent is inadmissible is not correct. The court, in characterizing the relationship as one arising out of contract, was concerned only with the minimum legal sufficiency of the agreement to create that relationship and not with necessity or manner of showing the donative intent which is required to sustain a valid inter vivos gift. . . .

To establish a gift, the proof must be clear and convincing, (People v. Polhemus, 367 Ill. 185; Rothwell v. Taylor, 303 Ill. 226,) and the burden is upon the alleged donee to establish the existence of a donative intent. (Bolton v. Bolton, 306 Ill. 473.) The decisions of this court relied on by appellant go no further than to indicate that the deposit agreement tends to show a donative intent on the part of the original owner of the funds, and that the intention so manifested, in the absence of contrary evidence, is sufficient to establish ownership in the survivor by virtue of the contract upon the death of the original owner. The form of the agreement, however, is not conclusive as to the intention of the depositors between themselves.

It is also suggested by the appellant that his testimony was insufficient to establish that the joint accounts were created for Schneider's convenience in the event of anticipated illness. But we agree with the trial court and the Appellate Court that his testimony was sufficient to show that the actual ownership of the money in the accounts remained in Schneider. . . .

In our opinion the judgment of the Appellate Court was correct and it should be affirmed.

Judgment affirmed.

MR. JUSTICE HERSHEY, dissenting: I dissent from the majority opinion for the following reasons: (1) Until the instant case, the reviewing courts of Illinois have consistently refused to approve the admission of parol evidence to show an intent contrary to that expressed in a clear, unambiguous agreement creating a joint bank account with right of survivorship, unless the evidence tended to establish mental incapacity, mistake of fact, fraud, undue influence or duress. (2) There is a reasonable basis for both the theory heretofore adopted by the courts of Illinois (the contract theory) and the substantive rule of contract law applied (the so-called parol evidence rule). (3) In the absence of legislation so requiring, the overruling and qualifying of precedent which is clearly determinative of the issue will create uncertainty and confusion in this field of law, and because of implications that may logically be derived from the majority opinion, cause uncertainty and confusion in other analogous situations. (4) Even under the theory adopted by the majority opinion, the evidence adduced is insufficient to overcome the clearly expressed intent of the deceased as to the disposition of the property.

In this case, there is nothing to establish that at the time Schneider signed these instruments he did not intentionally and knowingly sign them with the object of being bound by the clear, unambiguous provisions thereof. Moreover, it is recognized that the instruments were contracts, which are not said to be void or voidable because of illegality, fraud, mistake or any other reason. Nor is there any showing that the parties did not assent to these writings as the complete and accurate integration of their agreements. Such being this particular case, I do not believe parol evidence should be admitted to show an intent on the part of Schneider contrary to that expressed in the agreements.

In the application of the parol evidence rule to joint tenancy accounts, where the funds belonging to the depositor are placed in a bank account in his name and the name of another as joint tenants with the right of survivorship, courts of various jurisdictions have adopted different theories.

In a few States, notably New York and California, there are statutes which express the public policy of the State to prohibit parol evidence in the absence of fraud or undue influence. (N.Y. Banking Law, McKinney, 1950, §§134, subd. 3, 394, subd. 1; California Banking Code, Deering, 1949, §852.) In States where there is no specific statute in force, courts generally have adopted one of three theories:

(1) a gift theory (48 A.L.R. 191-202; 66 A.L.R. 882-90; 103 A.L.R. 1124-32; 135 A.L.R. 994-1006); (2) a trust theory (48 A.L.R. 202-3; 66 A.L.R. 890-1; 103 A.L.R. 1132-3; 135 A.L.R. 1006-7); or (3) a contract theory (103 A.L.R. 1140-1; 135 A.L.R. 1021-3).

In jurisdictions where the gift theory is relied upon, parol evidence may often be introduced to show an intent different from that expressed in the instrument. Where the trust theory is adopted, limited to cases where the depositor alone signs the instrument, parol evidence may be introduced to show he intended to create a trust with respect to the deposit. Under the contract theory, however, the rights of the parties are governed by rules applicable to written contracts generally. This means that if the terms of the agreement are clear and unambiguous, parol evidence is inadmissible to vary those terms or to show an intent contrary to that expressed in the agreement, in the absence of grounds such as mental incapacity, mistake of fact, fraud, undue influence or duress.

With the exception of the instant Appellate Court decision, the reviewing courts of Illinois have consistently applied the contract theory to determine the rights of parties who have signed an agreement creating a joint account with the right of survivorship. . . .

There is a reasonable basis for the theory invoked in the Illinois cases (the contract theory) and the rule of contract law applied. For these instruments *are* contracts and have repeatedly been recognized as such. The refusal to admit evidence (whether parol or otherwise) for the purpose of showing an intention contrary to that expressed in a written contract, a rule of substantive contract law, is calculated to prevent the perpetration of fraud and the litigation of groundless claims. . . .

Finally, even if it be decided that parol evidence may properly be considered, these signed agreements warrant the executor being required to negative by clear and convincing evidence the donative intent expressed therein. Perhaps there is too quick a tendency to categorize this transaction as but another of the cases wherein the depositor does utilize the arrangement solely and exclusively for convenience and in fact does not intend the survivor to have the proceeds remaining. This case cannot so easily be fitted to the somewhat usual form. Viewing the matter retrospectively it does appear Ralston would be paid very well for the services he undertook to perform. But had Schneider lived longer and the money, through repeated withdrawals made by Ralston for Schneider's benefit, dwindled to a mere nominal amount, the appearances of unjust enrichment and violations of so-called equitable rights would have all but vanished. Moreover, the facts disclose that Schneider was Ralston's uncle by marriage, and Schneider always referred to him as his nephew. And at the time these agreements were signed, Ralston was the closest relative Schneider had in Chicago. True, there is Ralston's statement that he contributed none of the money, and that Schneider asked him to go with him to the bank so that if he became ill Ralston could make withdrawals for him. But there is nothing to negate the fact that Schneider, while remaining cognizant of the convenience of the arrangement, may still have intended Ralston to have the money remaining in the account upon his death just as the instruments provide. Certainly, in view of the signed agreements, the burden should be upon the executor to negate this possibility. Since the executor has not done this, I believe that even under the theory adopted by the majority opinion, (the gift theory,) the evidence adduced is insufficient to overcome the clearly expressed intent of the deceased as to the disposition of this property.

Mr. Justice Klingbiel concurs in the foregoing dissenting opinion.[48]

NOTES

1. Where a person wants a relative to be able to draw on his bank account to pay his bills, why might a bank advise a joint account with the relative rather than giving the relative a power to draw on the account? Are all the problems solved by Uniform Commercial Code §4-405?

"§4-405. *Death or Incompetence of Customer*

"(1) A payor or collecting bank's authority to accept, pay or collect an item or to account for proceeds of its collection if otherwise effective is not rendered ineffective by incompetence of a customer of either bank existing at the time the item is issued or its collection is undertaken if the bank does not know of an adjudication of incompetence. Neither death nor incompetence of a customer revokes such authority to accept, pay, collect or account until the bank knows of the fact of death or of an adjudication of incompetence and has reasonable opportunity to act on it.

"(2) Even with knowledge a bank may for 10 days after the date of death pay or certify checks drawn on or prior to that date unless ordered to stop payment by a person claiming an interest in the account."

See also Beaucar v. Bristol Federal Savings & Loan Assn., 268 A.2d 679 (Conn. Cir. Ct. 1969); Uniform Probate Code §5-501.

2. Since Estate of Schneider there have been numerous cases involving joint bank accounts in Illinois. In about one-half of them the courts have ruled in favor of the surviving joint tenant, in the other one-half in favor of the estate of the deceased joint tenant. Hunt, What About That Joint Bank Account? 52 Ill. B.J. 30, 41 (1963). What advice would you give a sick client who wants a relative to be able to pay the client's bills? Kepner, Five More Years of the Joint Bank Account Muddle, 26 U. Chi. L. Rev. 376 (1959).

3. Where a joint bank account is established by O (the depositor) and A (the donee), can A's creditors reach the joint account? Kepner, The Joint and Survivorship Bank Account — A Concept Without a Name, 41 Calif. L. Rev. 596, 617 (1953).

4. O deposits funds in a bank in his own name, payable on his death to A. This is a payable-on-death, or P.O.D. account. Most courts have struck down P.O.D. accounts as testamentary because O had no intention to give A a present interest

[48] Noted 23 U. Chi. L. Rev. 289; 1955 U. Ill. L.F. 782. — Eds.

and O did not surrender any dominion and control over the funds. Young v. McCoy, 152 Neb. 138, 40 N.W.2d 540 (1950); Blais v. Colebrook Guaranty Savings Bank, 220 A.2d 763 (N.H. 1966) (Kenison, C.J., dissenting). What policy reasons can you suggest for refusing to give effect to P.O.D. designations on bank accounts? See Wellman, The Joint and Survivor Account in Michigan — Progress Through Confusion, 63 Mich. L. Rev. 629 (1965); McGovern, The Payable on Death Account and Other Will Substitutes, 67 Nw. U.L. Rev. 7 (1972). By statute P.O.D. designations on savings accounts are permitted in a few states. Ill. Rev. Stat. c. 32, §770(c) (1970); Iowa Code §534.11(8) (1970); N.J. Stat. Ann. §17:9A-217 (1963); Ohio Rev. Code §2131.10 (1971). P.O.D. accounts are authorized by Uniform Probate Code §6-104(b).

Uniform Probate Code §6-104(a) states that the surviving payee of a joint account is entitled to the balance "unless there is clear and convincing evidence of a different intention at the time the account is created." Similarly, the surviving beneficiary of a trust account is entitled to the balance at the death of the trustee "unless there is clear and convincing evidence of a contrary intent." Id. §6-104(c). If the account is a P.O.D. account, however, there is no provision for admitting extrinsic evidence to vary the terms of the account or deposit agreement. Id. §6-104(b). Why this difference?

5. M opens a savings account in the form, "M and N, payable on death to the survivor," and deposits $10,000 in the account. Representing the bank in the transaction is a young lady whose official title is "Assistant Cashier for New Accounts." The state's supreme court has held that although it is permissible to create a joint and survivor bank account if a certain verbal formula is employed ("as joint tenants with right of survivorship and not as tenants in common"), a "payable on death to the survivor" designation is ineffective to vest title to the fund in the survivor upon the depositor's death. One year later M dies intestate, and the $10,000 plus interest on deposit is paid to M's heir, H, rather than to N. N sues the bank, citing Heyer v. Flaig, page 21, supra, as authority. What result? See Robinson v. Colebrook Guaranty Savings Bank, 109 N.H. 382, 254 A.2d 837 (1969).

6. A person often leases a safe deposit box jointly with another person. To protect itself, the bank may include a provision in the rental agreement that property deposited in the box becomes joint property of the lessees. Professor Atkinson says this provision may be perilous, "for a momentary deposit in the 'magic box' might make the object joint property." Atkinson, Wills 167 (2d ed. 1953). Some of the cases have held the surviving lessee is entitled to the contents of the safe deposit box; some have held to the contrary.

3. *Joint Tenancies*

A joint tenancy, particularly between husband and wife, is a common method of avoiding probate. There are, however, two tax disadvantages of joint tenancies. First, §2040 of the Internal Revenue Code of 1954 provides that all property owned by a decedent as a joint tenant must be included in the decedent's estate except to the extent that it can be proved that the survivor contributed to the joint tenancy. The burden of proving the survivor's contribution is on the decedent's personal representative, and it is often difficult to meet. Second, unnecessary taxation may occur at the death of the surviving joint tenant. The surviving spouse has a fee simple in jointly held property, and the property is taxed at the survivor's death. The use of the joint tenancy precludes giving the survivor a life estate and avoiding taxation on the survivor's death.[49] Despite these disadvantages, Professor Hines has found that joint tenancies between husband and wife are increasing — a trend he views with favor.[50]

Two additional features of joint tenancies commonly unknown to laymen: (1) The decedent cannot dispose by will of his interest in a joint tenancy; the survivor takes all. (2) Creditors of a deceased joint tenant cannot reach the property; to subject the property to their claims, creditors must sever the joint tenancy during the debtor's life.

4. *Contracts*

WILHOIT v. PEOPLES LIFE INSURANCE COMPANY

United States Court of Appeals, Seventh Circuit, 1955

218 F.2d 887

MAJOR, Circuit Judge. The plaintiff, Robert Wilhoit, instituted this action against the defendants, Peoples Life Insurance Company (sometimes referred to as the company) and Thomas J. Owens, for the recovery of money held by the company. Roley Oscar Wilhoit was the insured and Sarah Louise Wilhoit, his wife, the beneficiary in a life insurance policy in the amount of $5,000, issued by Century Life Insurance Company and later reinsured in Peoples Life Insurance Company of Frankfort, Indiana. Mr. Wilhoit died prior to October 22, 1930 (the exact date not disclosed by the record), without having changed the beneficiary designated in the policy, and the proceeds thereof became due and payable to Mrs. Wilhoit. The amount due was paid to her and the policy surrendered, as is evidenced by the following receipt appearing on the back of the policy:

> $4,749.00 Indianapolis, Ind., Oct. 22-1930.
>
> Received from Century Life Insurance Company Forty Seven hundred forty nine Dollars in full for all claims under the within policy, terminated by death of Roley O. Wilhoit.
>
> Sarah Louise Wilhoit.

[49] See 1 Casner, Estate Planning 409-415 (3d ed. 1961); Riecker, Joint Tenancy: The Estate Lawyer's Continuing Burden, 64 Mich. L. Rev. 801 (1966).

[50] Hines, Real Property Joint Tenancies: Law, Fact and Fancy, 51 Iowa L. Rev. 582 (1966); Hines, Personal Property Joint Tenancies: More Law, Fact and Fancy, 54 Minn. L. Rev. 509 (1970).

The main body of the policy contained a provision entitled "The Investment, as follows:

> Upon the maturity of this policy, the amount payable hereunder, or any portion thereof, not less than One Thousand Dollars, may be left on deposit with the Company, and the Company will pay interest annually in advance upon the amount so left on deposit at such rate as the Company may declare on such funds so held by it, but never at a rate less than three per cent, so long as the amount shall remain on deposit with the Company. The said deposit may be withdrawn at the end of any interest year; or upon the death of the payee the amount of said deposit will be paid to the executors, administrators or assigns of said payee.

On November 14, 1930, Mrs. Wilhoit (twenty-three days after she had acknowledged receipt of the amount due her under the policy) from her home in Indiana signed and addressed a letter to the company in the same State, which in material parts reads as follows:

> I hereby acknowledge receipt of settlement in full under Policy No. C172 terminated by the death of Roley O. Wilhoit, the Insured, and I direct that the proceeds of $4,749.00 be held in trust by the Peoples Life Insurance Company under the following conditions:
>
> (1) Said amount or any part thereof (not less than $100.00) to be subject to withdrawal on demand of the undersigned.
>
> (2) While on deposit, said amount or part thereof shall earn interest at the rate of 3½%, compounded annually, plus any excess interest authorized by the Board of Directors of the Company. Interest may be withdrawn at the end of each six months period or whenever the principal of the fund is withdrawn or may be allowed to accumulate compounded annually. Interest on this trust fund shall begin as of October 9th, 1930.
>
> (3) In the event of my death, while any part of this trust fund is still in existence, the full amount, plus any accrued interest, shall be immediately payable to Robert G. Owens (Relationship) Brother.

The proposal contained in this letter was, on November 17, 1930, accepted by the company in the following form:

> The above agreement creating a trust fund is hereby accepted and we acknowledge receipt of the deposit of $4,749.00 under the above specified conditions.

Robert G. Owens, a brother of Mrs. Wilhoit and the person mentioned in her November 14 letter to the company, died January 23, 1932, and Mrs. Wilhoit died April 12, 1951, each leaving a last will and testament. The will of the former by a general clause devised all his property to Thomas J. Owens, a defendant, and was admitted to probate in Marion County, Indiana. The will of Mrs. Wilhoit was admitted to probate in Edgar County, Illinois, and contained the following provision:

> I now have the sum of Four Thousand Seven Hundred Forty Nine Dollars ($4,749.00), or approximately that amount, which is the proceeds of an insurance policy on the life of my deceased husband, Oscar Wilhoit, on deposit with the insurance company, the Peoples Life Insurance Company of Frankfort, Indiana. This I give and bequeath to Robert Wilhoit, now of Seattle, Washington, who is another son of my said stepson, the same to be his property absolutely. . . .

The fund in controversy, deposited with the company by Mrs. Wilhoit on November 17, 1930, remained with the company continuously until the date of her death, April 12, 1951. The company refused to recognize the claim to the fund made by the executor of her estate. Thereupon, the executor assigned his interest to Robert Wilhoit, the legatee named in the will of Mrs. Wilhoit and the plaintiff in the instant action. On petition, the Probate Court of Marion County, Indiana, on June 2, 1953, entered an order reopening the estate of Robert G. Owens, appointed Lee C. Emmelman administrator de bonis non with the will annexed and authorized him to petition for leave to intervene in the instant action. Such intervention was allowed on July 3, 1953. The intervenor joined Thomas J. Owens as a counterclaimant. The former claimed the fund as administrator de bonis non of the estate of Robert G. Owens, while the latter claimed the fund as the legatee under the will of Robert G. Owens. There is no controversy between the intervenor and Thomas J. Owens. They are both represented by the same counsel, and it is conceded that if the defendants prevail the fund should be payable to the intervenor.

The company, after the institution of the action, paid the fund into court by interpleader and is no longer an active party to the litigation. The parties on both sides filed motions for a summary judgment. There was no dispute as to the facts and no question but that the situation was such that the issue in controversy could properly be disposed of in that manner. The District Court, on March 11, 1954, without opinion sustained the motion of the plaintiff for summary judgment and at the same time denied the motion of the defendant, Thomas J. Owens, and the intervenor, Emmelman. Thereupon, judgment was entered in favor of the plaintiff in the sum of $4,749.00, together with interest and costs. From this judgment the defendant, Thomas J. Owens, and the intervenor, Emmelman, appeal.

Defendants (this includes the intervenor-appellant) advance two theories in support of their argument for reversal, both of which are firmly grounded upon the premise that the agreement of November 17, 1930, between Mrs. Wilhoit and the company, was an insurance contract or a contract supplemental thereto. Thus premised, they argue (1) that the rights of the parties must be determined by the law of insurance and not by the statute of wills, and (2) that Mrs. Wilhoit as a primary beneficiary named Robert G. Owens as the successor beneficiary irrevocably, without right to revoke or change and without a "pre-decease of beneficiary" provision, and that as a result the rights of such successor beneficiary upon his death prior to the death of the primary beneficiary did not lapse but passed on to the heirs and assigns of such successor beneficiary.

On the other hand, plaintiff argues, in support of the judgment, that the disposition of the fund is not controlled by the law of insurance because the agreement between Mrs. Wilhoit and the company was not an insurance contract or a supplement thereto but was nothing more than a contract of deposit, and that the provision in the agreement by which Robert G. Owens was to take the funds in the event of her death was an invalid testamentary disposition. Further, it is argued that in any event any interest acquired by Robert G. Owens was extinguished upon his death, which occurred prior to that of Mrs. Wilhoit.

Defendants cite many cases from numerous jurisdictions which have held under a variety of circumstances that the proceeds of a life insurance policy are to be disposed of in accordance with its provisions, and that a beneficiary, if authorized by the policy, may designate a successor beneficiary to take on the death of the primary beneficiary.

. . . Obviously, defendants' contention is without merit and the cases cited in support thereof are without application unless we accept the premise upon which the contention is made, that is, that the agreement between Mrs. Wilhoit and the company was an insurance contract or an agreement supplemental thereto. While there may be room for differences of opinion, we have reached the conclusion that the premise is not sound, that the arrangement between the parties was the result of a separate and independent agreement, unrelated to the terms of the policy. There are two cases which support this conclusion. Mutual Ben. Life Ins. Co. v. Ellis, 2 Cir., 125 F.2d 127, 130, 138 A.L.R. 1478, certiorari denied Eisenlord v. Ellis, 316 U.S. 665, 62 S. Ct. 945, 86 L. Ed. 1741, and Gram v. Mutual Life Ins. Co. of New York, 300 N.Y. 375, 91 N.E.2d 307.

The "investment" provision was an offer by the company by which Mrs. Wilhoit, on maturity of the policy, could have left the proceeds with the company on the terms and conditions therein stated. It is plain, however, that she did not take advantage of this offer. Instead, she accepted the proceeds, surrendered the policy and receipted the company in full "for all claims under the within policy," and presumably the proceeds were paid to her at that time. At any rate, it was not until twenty-three days later that she, by letter, made her own proposal to the company, which differed materially from that contained in the policy. The company proposed to pay interest annually in advance on the amount left on deposit, at a rate of interest not less than 3%. Her proposal provided for interest at the rate of $3\frac{1}{2}$%, compounded annually, with a right to withdraw interest at the end of any six-month period. The company proposal provided that Mrs. Wilhoit could withdraw the deposit only at the end of any interest year, it made no provision for the withdrawal of any amount less than the total on deposit, while the offer of Mrs. Wilhoit provided for the right to withdraw, on demand, any amount or part thereof (not less than $100). Undoubtedly the company was obligated, upon request by Mrs. Wilhoit, to comply with the terms of the investment provision and, upon refusal, could have been forced by her to do so. On the other hand, it was under no obligation to accept the proposal made by her and, upon its refusal, she would have been without remedy.

Having concluded that the agreement between Mrs. Wilhoit and the company was neither an insurance contract nor an agreement supplemental thereto, we might dispose of the case without further discussion; however, we think other cases upon which defendants rely should be considered. In Mutual Ben. Life Ins. Co. v. Ellis, 2 Cir., 125 F.2d 127, 138 A.L.R. 1478, the court held, under circumstances similar to those here, that the agreement in dispute was not an insurance contract or an agreement supplemental thereto because the beneficiary had not accepted any of the options provided for in the policy but instead made a proposal of her own which was accepted by the company. There, the insured, Mrs. Addie, made an agreement with the insurance company by which the proceeds remained with it, with the right to receive interest and to withdraw the funds on three months' notice. She directed the company to pay the fund to her three sisters-in-law upon her death. When Mrs. Addie died, conflicting claims to the fund were made by her administrator and the sisters-in-law. Notwithstanding that the court had held that the agreement between Mrs. Addie and the insurance company was separate and independent, it sustained the right of the sisters-in-law to the fund on the theory that they were third party donee beneficiaries under the contract. That case is distinguishable from the instant case in several respects. The court there appears to have emphasized the fact that Mrs. Addie could only withdraw the fund on three months' notice, while here it could be withdrawn upon demand. There, the court was applying what it found to be the rule of the State of Colorado, with which we are not here concerned. The so-called donee beneficiaries in that case were living at the death of Mrs. Addie, while here the death of Robert G. Owens occurred some nineteen years before that of Mrs. Wilhoit. In any event, we are not impressed with the reasoning by which the result was reached in that case.

. . .

Irrespective of whether the agreement in the instant case be characterized as an assignment, a contract for the benefit of a third party or an attempted gift causa mortis, no reason is discernible why any different rule of law should be applied. Mrs. Wilhoit deposited her money with the company, which obligated itself to pay interest and return the principal to her on demand. Only "in the event of her death" was the deposit, if it still remained, payable to Robert G. Owens. If Mrs. Wilhoit had deposited her money with a bank rather than with the insurance company under the same form of agreement, we think that it would have constituted an ineffectual disposition because of failure to comply with the Indiana statute of wills.

In conclusion, we think it not immaterial to take into consideration what appears to have been the intention of the parties. . . . As already shown, Robert G. Owens, through whom defendants claim, died in 1932, and in his will made no mention of the funds in controversy. After the death of Mrs. Wilhoit almost twenty years later, the estate of Robert G. Owens was reopened for the express purpose of making claim to the fund. On the other hand, Mrs. Wilhoit in her will specifically devised the fund in controversy to plaintiff, Robert Wilhoit. It thus appears plain that Mrs. Wilhoit did not intend that the fund go to the successors of Robert G. Owens but that after his death she thought she had a right to dispose of the fund as she saw fit, as is evidenced by the specific bequest contained in her will. We recognize that the intention of the parties or the belief which they entertained relative to the fund is not controlling, but under the circumstances presented, we think it is entitled to some consideration.

The judgment of the District Court is affirmed.[51]

QUESTION

The rule is that one cannot change the beneficiary of a life insurance policy by will. However, a gift of the rights of the donor under the policy may be effectuated by handing over the written policy. In Stepson v. Brand, 213 Miss. 826, 58 So. 2d 18, 33 A.L.R.2d 267 (1952), the insured took out a life insurance policy and named his wife Emma beneficiary. The policy certificate provided that the insured could designate a new beneficiary by written notice to the insurance company. The insured then made a gift of the policy to Emma by delivering it to her. Subsequently the insured notified the company that he was designating Rosie Lee the beneficiary of the policy. The insured then died. The court held that the provisions in the policy requiring written notification to the insurance company do not bar a gift without notification, since they are intended only for the protection of the company. The insurance company could properly pay Rosie Lee, but, as between Emma and Rosie Lee, Emma was entitled to the proceeds. If a gift of the policy can be made without notifying the company, why is not a testamentary change of beneficiary given effect so that although the insurance company can lawfully pay the beneficiary named in the policy, the beneficiary named in the will can recover the proceeds from the beneficiary named in the policy?

ESTATE OF HILLOWITZ

Court of Appeals of New York, 1968

22 N.Y.2d 107, 238 N.E.2d 723

FULD, Chief Judge. This appeal stems from a discovery proceeding brought in the Surrogate's Court by the executors of the estate of Abraham Hillowitz against his widow, the appellant herein. The husband had been a partner in an "investment club" and, after his death, the club, pursuant to a provision of the partnership agreement, paid the widow the sum of $2,800, representing his interest in the partnership. "In the event of the death of any partner," the agreement recited, "his share will be transferred to his wife, with no termination of the partnership." The executors contend in their petition that the above provision was an invalid attempt to make a testamentary disposition of property and that the proceeds should pass under the decedent's will as an asset of his estate. The widow maintains that it was a valid and enforcible contract. Although the Surrogate agreed with her, the Appellate Division held that the agreement was invalid as "an attempted testamentary disposition" (24 A.D.2d 891, 264 N.Y.S.2d 868).

[51] Noted 50 Nw. U.L. Rev. 796. — EDS.

A partnership agreement which provides that, upon the death of one partner, his interest shall pass to the surviving partner or partners, resting as it does in contract, is unquestionably valid and may not be defeated by labeling it a testamentary disposition. . . . We are unable to perceive a difference in principle between an agreement of this character and one, such as that before us, providing for a deceased partner's widow, rather than a surviving partner, to succeed to the decedent's interest in the partnership. . . .

These partnership undertakings are, in effect, nothing more or less than third-party beneficiary contracts, performable at death. Like many similar instruments, contractual in nature, which provide for the disposition of property after death, they need not conform to the requirements of the statute of wills. . . . Examples of such instruments include (1) a contract to make a will . . . ; (2) an inter vivos trust in which the settlor reserves a life estate . . . ; and (3) an insurance policy. . . .

In short, members of a partnership may provide, without fear of running afoul of our statute of wills, that, upon the death of a partner, his widow shall be entitled to his interest in the firm. This type of third-party beneficiary contract is not invalid as an attempted testamentary disposition.

The executors may derive little satisfaction from McCarthy v. Pieret (281 N.Y. 407, 24 N.E.2d 102),[52] upon which they heavily rely. In the first place, it is our considered judgment that the decision should be limited to its facts. And, in the second place, the case is clearly distinguishable from the one now before us in that the court expressly noted that the "facts . . . indicate a mere intention on the part of the mortgagee to make a testamentary disposition of the property and not an intention to convey an immediate interest" and, in addition, that the named beneficiaries "knew nothing of the provisions of the extension agreement" (p. 413, 24 N.E.2d p. 104).

The order of the Appellate Division should be reversed, with costs in this court and in the Appellate Division, and the order of the Surrogate's Court reinstated.

Burke, Scileppi, Bergan, Breitel and Jasen, JJ., concur with Fuld, J.

Keating, J., concurs in result in the following memorandum: I concur in reversal but find it difficult to distinguish McCarthy v. Pieret, 281 N.Y. 407, 24 N.E.2d 102, and am not prepared to overrule that authority. I prefer to rest reversal on the ground that respondent widow is entitled to interest in the partnership by right of survivorship as set forth in the second opinion of the Surrogate (51 Misc. 2d 666, 273 N.Y.S.2d 607).

Order reversed, etc.

In his concurring opinion Judge Keating refers to the opinion of the Surrogate in Matter of Hillowitz. Surrogate Silver stated:

"The record is clear and convincing that the funds, or the greater part of them,

[52] In McCarthy v. Pieret a mortgage provided that if any installments remained unpaid at the mortgagee's death they should be paid to A. The provision was held to be testamentary and void. — Eds.

used for the purchase of the partnership interest had their source in the joint account of the decedent and the respondent. The record is also clear and convincing that all securities purchased during the marriage — with the single exception of a bank account created by respondent from funds received from her first husband in trust for their son — were taken in joint ownership of the decedent and respondent. In entering into the partnership agreement, from the layman's point of view, the decedent provided for the very result that would have happened if the interest in the partnership were taken in his name jointly with his wife with the right of survivorship. It taxes one's logic to infer from the known circumstances that he was charged with the knowledge that upon his death the transfer of the interest to his wife upon her survival would be held to be ineffective as an invalid testamentary disposition. Decedent can be charged only with the expectation of the average man when he entered into the partnership agreement.

"On the basis of the agreement inferable from the facts and circumstances herein, respondent would be entitled to a judgment . . . reforming the partnership contract to evidence her husband's intention to purchase the interest in the joint names of decedent and respondent with the right of survival." 51 Misc. 2d 666, 669, 273 N.Y.S.2d 607, 611 (1966).

UNIFORM PROBATE CODE

Section 6–201. [Provisions for Payment or Transfer at Death.]

(a) Any of the following provisions in an insurance policy, contract of employment, bond, mortgage, promissory note, deposit agreement, pension plan, trust agreement, conveyance or any other written instrument effective as a contract, gift, conveyance, or trust is deemed to be nontestamentary, and this Code does not invalidate the instrument or any provision:

(1) that money or other benefits theretofore due to, controlled or owned by a decedent shall be paid after his death to a person designated by the decedent in either the instrument or a separate writing, including a will, executed at the same time as the instrument or subsequently;

(2) that any money due or to become due under the instrument shall cease to be payable in event of the death of the promisee or the promissor before payment or demand; or

(3) that any property which is the subject of the instrument shall pass to a person designated by the decedent in either the instrument or a separate writing, including a will, executed at the same time as the instrument or subsequently.

(b) Nothing in this section limits the rights of creditors under other laws of this state.

COMMENT

This section authorizes a variety of contractual arrangements which have in the past been treated as testamentary. For example most courts treat as testamentary a provision in a promissory note that if the payee dies before payment is made the note shall be paid to another named person, or a provision in a land contract that if the seller dies before payment is completed the balance shall be cancelled and the property shall belong to the vendee. These provisions often occur in family arrangements. The result of holding the provisions testamentary is usually to invalidate them because not executed in accordance with the statute of wills. On the other hand the same courts have for years upheld beneficiary designations in life insurance contracts. Similar kinds of problems are arising in regard to beneficiary designations in pension funds and under annuity contracts. The analogy of the power of appointment provides some historical base for solving some of these problems aside from a validating statute. However, there appear to be no policy reasons for continuing to treat these varied arrangements as testamentary. The revocable living trust and the multiple-party bank accounts, as well as the experience with United States government bonds payable on death to named beneficiaries, have demonstrated that the evils envisioned if the statute of wills is not rigidly enforced simply do not materialize. The fact [is?] that these provisions often are part of a business transaction and in any event are evidenced by a writing to eliminate the danger of "fraud."

Because the types of provisions described in the statute are characterized as nontestamentary, the instrument does not have to be executed in compliance with Section 2-502; nor does it have to be probated, nor does the personal representative have any power or duty with respect to the assets involved.

The sole purpose of this section is to eliminate the testamentary characterization from the arrangements falling within the terms of the section. It does not invalidate other arrangements by negative implication. Thus it is not intended by the section to embrace oral trusts to hold property at death for named persons; such arrangements are already generally enforceable under trust law.

5. *Deeds*

Deeds on condition and revocable deeds have proved very troublesome to the courts. Typically these deeds have been used by persons of modest wealth who want to avoid probate and lawyers. Where the grantor delivers the deed to the grantee and annexes to it an oral condition, the great weight of authority holds that the delivery is absolute. The oral condition violates the Statute of Frauds and is void. Even if the condition is in writing, however, the deed may be held in violation of the Statute of Wills.

Case 10. O executes a deed conveying Blackacre to A and his heirs. A provision of the deed reads: "This conveyance is made upon the following conditions: (1) this deed is not effective if A predeceases O; (2) this deed is not to take effect until O's death; and (3) this deed is revocable by O at any time." The deed is delivered to A. Is the deed valid? [53]

[53] The deed in Butler v. Sherwood, 196 App. Div. 603, 188 N.Y.S. 242 (1921), aff'd, 233

Courts traditionally have analyzed the problem in *Case 10* as whether O intended presently to create an interest in A. With respect to condition (1) there should be no problem. The condition is analogous to a springing executory interest, valid in law since 1536. An early use of the springing interest occurred in English marriage settlements. In order to give the intended groom, G, assurances that the bride, B, would come to the marriage endowed with property, the father of the bride would convey land, prior to the wedding ceremony: "to B and her heirs if she marries G." Condition (1) in *Case 10* is analogous, but because the event upon which the grantee takes possession, if ever, is the grantor's death, some courts have held that the deed is testamentary and void. Others have held that an interest passed to the grantee during the grantor's lifetime.[54]

Condition (2) also should be valid. Many courts have so held, construing "take effect on death" to mean that the grantor reserves a life estate and creates a remainder in the grantee. A few courts, on the other hand, have construed the condition to mean that the deed was intended not to take effect at all until death; thus construed, the deed is void.[55]

Condition (3) — the reservation of a power to revoke — has in most cases been held to prevent an effective delivery, and, of course, without delivery the deed is void.[56] Yet it is not easy to give policy reasons why a revocable trust should be valid and a revocable deed void. It may well be that a decision to strike down the deed in *Case 10* rests solely on anachronistic "thing-thinking" and primitive formalism.

Where the grantor does not deliver the deed to the grantee but delivers the deed to an escrow agent, the transfer may be effective if the grantor does not retain the right to recall the deed. Thus:

> *Case 11.* O executes a deed of Blackacre to A and his heirs. O delivers the deed to B, an escrow agent, and tells B to hand the deed to A on O's death. If O retains no right to recall the deed, this is a valid escrow; B is the agent of the donee. If O retains the right to recall the deed, B is the agent of the donor; the agency ceases at death; the deed passes nothing to A. If O tells B to deliver the deed to A only if A survives O, the cases are divided, and the reasoning usually ambiguous.[57]

In these cases little effort is expended on an analysis of whether the deeds satisfy the ritual, evidentiary, and protective policies of the Statute of Wills. Much is made of whether the grantor had a present donative intent and intended to create presently an interest in the grantee. And in the escrow cases much is said about

---

N.Y. 655, 135 N.E. 957 (1922), contained all three conditions as in *Case 10*. The court held the deed void.

[54] 1 Page, Wills §6.6 (Bowe-Parker rev. 1960).

[55] Id. §6.5.

[56] 6 Powell, Real Property ¶896 (1970).

[57] Id., ¶898.

whose agent the escrowee is. If revocable trusts are valid, should revocable deeds delivered to the grantee or to an escrow agent also be valid?

See in general Ballantine, When Are Deeds Testamentary? 18 Mich. L. Rev. 470 (1920); Gulliver & Tilson, Classification of Gratuitous Transfers, 51 Yale L.J. 1 (1941); Ritchie, What Is a Will? 49 Va. L. Rev. 759 (1963).

SECTION D. Gifts

BAUGH v. HOWZE
Supreme Court of Arkansas, 1947
211 Ark. 222, 199 S.W.2d 940

HOLT, J. Dr. Enoch Howze died testate January 6, 1944. By the terms of his will, the validity of which is in no way questioned, he left all of his property to his widow, appellee here. Dr. Howze and appellee were married in March, 1943. In addition to appellee, two sisters, one of whom is the wife of appellant, Stanley T. Baugh, a Methodist minister, and two brothers survived Dr. Howze. A very close relationship had, for many years, existed between the Baughs and Dr. Howze, and Dr. Howze's confidence in, and friendship for them, were of the highest order, and on one occasion after Dr. Howze and Mr. and Mrs. Baugh had returned from a vacation trip, which they had made together, Dr. Howze made Mrs. Baugh a present of $5,000.

In July, 1939, Dr. Howze placed in the hands of his brother-in-law, Mr. Baugh, then pastor of a Pine Bluff church, $5,000 with directions that he deposit it to Baugh's credit in a bank in that city and take care of it. In August of this same year, Dr. Howze gave Mr. Baugh another $5,000 with directions to deposit it in a Pine Bluff bank in the name of Thomas Baugh, one of Mr. Baugh's children, and take care of it for him, Dr. Howze. Mr. Baugh complied with both requests. At the time this $10,000 was entrusted to Mr. Baugh and deposited in the Pine Bluff bank, nothing was said by Dr. Howze as to its disposition other than the admonition to take care of it.

In the latter part of December, 1940, after Mr. Baugh had moved to a church in Prescott, Mr. Baugh testified that while he and Mrs. Baugh were visiting Dr. Howze, and were in his office: "A. Of course I kept wondering what Doctor Enoch wanted to do with that (meaning the $10,000). So after we moved from Pine Bluff to Prescott, in his office the last of December — I think it must have been right after Christmas — he took us back in his office again and closed the door to the outer waiting room and he said, 'I want that ten thousand dollars you hold on deposit in Pine Bluff for my brothers and sisters. I want you to take it out of the bank and put it in a lock box and hold it and deliver it to them at my death.' . . . And when he said, 'I give it to you for my brothers and sisters,' he said, 'nobody knows a thing about that, but we three,' and Mrs. Baugh, he and I were standing there. 'Nobody knows about it but we three,' and after that he cautioned about that, 'Nobody knows a thing about this, and nobody is to ever know it but we three.' "

Following these instructions from Dr. Howze, Mr. Baugh removed the $10,000 in currency from the Pine Bluff bank, and on December 22, 1941, placed it in a lock box in the Worthen bank, Little Rock. The box was procured in the names of Mr. and Mrs. Baugh.

Following the marriage of appellee and Dr. Howze in March, 1943, Dr. Howze spent several thousand dollars in remodeling and improving his residence, and in April, 1943, Dr. Howze, according to the testimony of both Mr. and Mrs. Baugh, asked Mr. Baugh to loan him $1,000 of the $10,000 in the lock box and promised to repay it in the fall. Mr. Baugh promptly delivered this $1,000 to Dr. Howze. No note or other evidence of this transaction appears. December 12, 1943, Dr. Howze told Mrs. Baugh to have Mr. Baugh get $5,000 additional from the lock box and place it to Dr. Howze's account in a Malvern bank. Mr. Baugh, without question, immediately complied with this request, no loan being mentioned in connection with this transaction.

After the delivery of the $6,000 to Dr. Howze, there remained in the lock box $4,000, which remained in the box until Dr. Howze died, January 6, 1944, and shortly thereafter Mr. Baugh distributed this $4,000 by giving to each of Dr. Howze's sisters and two brothers $1,000.

The present action was brought by Dr. Howze's widow, appellee, against Mr. Stanley Baugh and the other appellants to recover the $4,000 and any other property that appellants might have that belonged to Dr. Howze.

From a decree in favor of appellee, Dr. Howze's widow, for $4,000 comes this appeal.

The sole question presented, say appellants, "is whether or not Dr. Enoch Howze made a gift to his brothers and sisters of $10,000 in December, 1940, when he instructed Brother Stanley T. Baugh to hold that money for them." In other words, was it a valid gift inter vivos?

Appellants earnestly contend that a valid gift was made. It is our view, however, that no gift was effected and that the decree of the trial court must be upheld.

The material facts, which are practically undisputed, are in effect as above detailed.

To constitute a valid gift inter vivos certain essential elements must be present, these include actual delivery of the subject-matter of the gift to the donee or to some one as agent or trustee for the donee, with a clear intent to make an immediate present and final gift beyond recall, and at the same time unconditionally releasing all future dominion and control by the donor over the property so delivered.

As we view the record before us, Mr. Baugh was acting as the trusted agent of Dr. Howze in caring for and handling the $10,000 in question, which had been entrusted to his care, was not the agent of the donees, and Dr. Howze never relinquished dominion and control over this money. In fact, all the alleged donees, with the exception of Mrs. Baugh, were kept in ignorance of this alleged gift until after the death of Dr. Howze. That he did not relinquish control and dominion, a necessary requisite to a completed gift, is, we think, clearly evidenced by Dr. Howze's actions in demanding, and receiving, as above noted, 60 per cent. of this $10,000 after Mr. Baugh had placed it in a lock box in the Worthen bank, and without any objections on the part of his agent, Mr. Baugh. . . .

In 24 Am. Jur., §30, pp. 747, 748, the text writer on the question of agency said: "While delivery may be made by an agent of the donor, delivery to the agent is not enough. The gift is not complete until there is an actual delivery to the donee or to someone for him, and until the gift is completed by delivery, the donor may reassert title to the property. Moreover, since the authority of an agent is revoked by the death of his principal, the death of the donor before the actual delivery of the property to the donee terminates the authority of the agent to make such delivery, and works a revocation of the gift"; and in 28 C.J., §31, p. 640, we find this language: "While a delivery may be made to a third party in order that the latter may deliver the subject of the gift to the donee as agent of the donor, the gift is not complete until there is an actual delivery to the donee, and until the gift is completed by delivery the donor can revoke the agent's authority and resume possession of the gift. As the authority of an agent is revoked by the death of his principal, the death of the donor before the actual delivery of the property to the donee terminates the authority of the agent to make such delivery, and the gift, therefore, fails for want of delivery. So, also, the delivery of property to an agent to be delivered to an intended donee after the donor's death is not sufficient to sustain a gift inter vivos, and such a disposition is void as being in contravention of the statute of wills." See, also, 38 C.J.S., Gifts, §25.

On the question of agency, this court again said in Newton v. Snyder, 44 Ark. 42, 51 Am. Rep. 587: "Delivery to a third person for a donee is as effective as delivery to the donee, but delivery to an agent in the character of an agent for the giver, to perform the act or make the delivery only after the giver's death, would amount to nothing. (2 Redf. Wills, chapter 12, §§42, 45.)"

As indicated above, the question here simply stated is, do the facts show a gift of the $10,000 to Dr. Howze's brothers and sisters? Conceding that Dr. Howze wanted this money to go to his sisters and brothers after his death, still unless he took proper or legal steps to carry out such intention, this court cannot act for him and give legal effect to the donor's wishes when the donor himself has failed to comply with the essential requirements necessary to effectuate the gift.

Finding no error, the decree is affirmed.[58]

Robins and Millwee, JJ., dissent.

NOTES

1. 1 Scott, Trusts §8 (3d ed. 1967): "Whether a relationship of trust or of agency is created depends upon the intention of the parties. The mere fact that a person describes himself as agent does not necessarily mean that an agency rather

[58] Noted 1 Ark. L. Rev. 316. — Eds.

than a trust is created. Thus where A deposited money in a bank in the name of 'A, agent for B,' it has been held that a trust and not a mere agency was created. . . .

"An agent does not ordinarily have title to the property of the principal, although he may be entrusted with possession and although he may have power to pass title; but a trustee has title to the trust property. . . ."

2. In Baugh v. Howze the court states that an agency terminates upon the principal's death, and the agent cannot thereafter deliver the property. Why does not the agent become, simultaneously with the donor's death, the agent of the donee? In a few other situations courts have used a theory of simultaneity to escape an undesirable result caused by giving a time sequence to conceptual events. See page 745, note 81, infra.

3. If Dr. Howze had told Baugh that he was going to leave him $4000 in his will and he wanted Baugh to divide this among Dr. Howze's sisters and brothers, and Baugh had promised to do so, Baugh's promise would be enforceable as an oral trust if Dr. Howze left him $4000 by will. Why is a secret oral testamentary trust enforceable and oral directions to an agent to perform an act after death not enforceable?

4. Aurilla Ballou gave $300 to Henry L. Sheldon and took back a writing as follows:

> For value received I promise to pay Aurilla Ballou three hundred dollars with annual interest, on demand, if she called for it before she deceased, if not to be paid to Daniel M. Blanchard by her order.
>
> January 12, 1867
>
> Henry L. Sheldon
> Miranda Hines

Aurilla's intention was that Daniel would have whatever she should not use of the $300. During her lifetime she did not call for any of the $300. Held: Sheldon took the $300 as agent for Daniel, subject to being defeated by Aurilla calling for it back. Blanchard v. Sheldon, 43 Vt. 512 (1871).

Garvey, Revocable Gifts of Personal Property: A Possible Will Substitute, 16 Catholic U.L. Rev. 119, 256 (1966), argues that revocable gifts should be recognized, and collects many cases which uphold gifts even though the donor can revoke. At least on a verbal level, however, the overwhelming weight of authority does not recognize revocable gifts. The donor, it is said, must suffer the wrench of delivery, whereby he recognizes that the property is no longer his.

FOSTER v. REISS

Supreme Court of New Jersey, 1955

18 N.J. 41, 112 A.2d 553, 48 A.L.R.2d 1391

Vanderbilt, C.J. On April 30, 1951 the decedent, Ethel Reiss, entered a hospital in New Brunswick where she was to undergo major surgery. Just prior to going to the operating room on May 4, 1951, she wrote the following note in her native Hungarian language to her husband, the defendant herein:

> My Dearest Papa:
>
> In the kitchen, in the bottom of the cabinet, where the blue frying pan is, under the wine bottle, there is one hundred dollars. Along side the bed in my bedroom, in the rear drawer of the small table in the corner of the drawer, where my stockings are, you will find about seventy-five dollars. In my purse there is six dollars, where the coats are. Where the coats are, in a round tin box, on the floor, where the shoes are, there is two hundred dollars. This is Dianna's. Please put it in the bank for her. This is for her schooling.
>
> The Building Loan book is yours, and the Bank book, and also the money that is here. In the red book is my son's and sister's and my brothers address. In the letter box is also my bank book.
>
> Give Margaret my sewing machine and anything else she may want; she deserves it as she was good to me.
>
> God be with you. God shall watch your steps. Please look out for yourself that you do not go on a bad road. I cannot stay with you. My will is in the office of the former Lawyer Anekstein, and his successor has it. There you will find out everything.
>
> Your Kissing, loving wife,
> Ethel Reiss 1951-5-4.

She placed the note in the drawer of a table beside her bed, at the same time asking Mrs. Agnes Tekowitz, an old friend who was also confined in the hospital, to tell her husband or daughter about it — "In case my daughter come in or my husband come in, tell them they got a note over there and take the note." That afternoon, while the wife was in the operating room unconscious under the effects of ether, the defendant came to the hospital and was told about the note by the friend. He took the note from the drawer, went home, found the cash, the savings account passbook, and the building and loan book mentioned in the note, and has retained possession of them since that time.

The wife was admittedly in a coma for three days after the operation and the testimony is in dispute as to whether or not she recovered consciousness at all before her death on the ninth day. Her daughter, her son-in-law, Mrs. Waldner, an old friend and one of her executrices who visited her every day, and Mrs. Tekowitz, who was in the ward with her, said that they could not understand her and she could not understand them. The defendant, on the other hand, testified that while she was "awful poor from ether" after the operation, "the fourth, fifth and sixth days I thought she was going to get healthy again and come home. She talked just as good as I with you." The trial judge who saw the witnesses and heard the testimony found that

> After the operation and until the date of her death on May 13, 1951 she was in a coma most of the time; was unable to recognize members of her family;

and unable to carry on intelligent conversation . . . Mrs. Reiss was never able to talk or converse after coming out of the operation until her death.

The decedent's will gave $1 to the defendant and the residue of her estate to her children and grandchildren. The decedent's personal representatives and her trustees under a separation agreement with the defendant, brought this action to recover the cash, the passbook, and the building and loan book from the defendant, who in turn claimed ownership of them based on an alleged gift causa mortis from his wife. The trial court granted judgment for the plaintiffs, concluding that there had been no such gift. The Appellate Division of the Superior Court reversed, 31 N.J. Super. 496, 107 A.2d 24, and we granted the plaintiff's petition for certification to the Appellate Division, 16 N.J. 221, 108 A.2d 211.

The doctrine of donatio causa mortis was borrowed by the Roman law from the Greeks, 2 Bl. Com. 514, and ultimately became a part of English and then American common law. . . .

. . . Blackstone has said that there is a gift causa mortis "when a person in his last sickness, apprehending his dissolution near, delivers or causes to be delivered to another the possession of any personal goods, to keep in case of his decease." 2 Bl. Com. 514. . . .

The modern description is similar:

> A donatio causa mortis is a gift of personal property made by a party in expectation of death, then imminent, and upon the essential condition that the property shall belong fully to the donee in case the donor dies as anticipated, leaving the donee surviving him, and the gift is not in the meantime revoked, but not otherwise. . . . To constitute a valid gift causa mortis, it must be made in view of the donor's impending death; the donor must die of the disorder or peril; and there must be a delivery of the thing given. The donor must be competent to make the gift; there must be an intent upon his part to do so; and an acceptance by the donee. . . . The delivery must be such as is actual, unequivocal and complete during the lifetime of the donor, wholly divesting him of the possession, dominion, and control thereof. Weiss v. Fenwick, 111 N.J. Eq. 385, 387-388, 162 A. 609, 610 (E. & A. 1932). . . .

Gifts causa mortis are not favored in the law. As stated in Buecker v. Carr, 60 N.J. Eq. 300, 305, 47 A. 34, 35 (Ch. 1900), "gifts mortis causa are not favored in the law, for the reason that this mode of disposition permits property without limit of value to be transferred by mere delivery, and the proof thereof to be made when death has closed the lips of the claimed donor." In Parker v. Copland, 70 N.J. Eq. 685, 691, 64 A. 129, 131 (E. & A. 1906), the highest court of this State had this to say:

> Of all legal rules, however, those that have grown up around the doctrine of donatio causa mortis should be the least subject to relaxation. Formed, as these rules were at a period when personal property consisted for the most part of

tangible chattels or private choses in action, they have survived to do duty at a time when fortunes of unprecedented dimensions are evidenced solely by documents that fall within their operation and effect.

. . .

The first question confronting us is whether there has been "actual, unequivocal, and complete delivery during the lifetime of the donor, wholly divesting him [her] of the possession, dominion, and control" of the property. . . .

In Cook v. Lum, . . . 55 N.J.L. 373, 26 A. 803, 804, our former Supreme Court stated that where choses in action were concerned delivery of the "donor's voucher of right or title" would be sufficient:

> The general legal principle regulating the subject of gifts of choses in action has long been established. It is to the effect that with respect to things both tangible and intangible mere words of donation will not suffice. With regard to the former class, — that is things corporeal, — there must be, in addition to the expression of a donative purpose, an actual tradition of the corpus of the gift whenever, considering the nature of the property and the circumstances of the actors, such a formality is reasonably practicable. In some instances, when the situation is incompatible with the performance of such ceremony, resort may be had to what has been called a "symbolical delivery" of the subject. Touching things in action, as there can be no actual delivery of them, the legal requirement is that the donor's voucher of right or title must be surrendered to the donee. Such surrender is deemed equivalent to an actual handing over of things corporeal. To this extent the law of the subject is neither doubtful nor obscure. The difficulty supervenes as soon as the attempt is made to apply these rules to the ever variant conditions of the cases that are being presented for judicial examination. Even when the thing given has been a personal chattel, whether certain acts show a purpose to give consummated by a delivery of it has often been, and doubtless will be, a vexed question. The uncertainty in construing the circumstances is even greater when we have rights of action to deal with. There are a multitude of decisions which demonstrate the embarrassment inherent in this class of cases, but as these decisions, while all acknowledging the rules just indicated, are in truth nothing more than interpretations respectively of the facts of the particular case, and as such facts are unlike the juncture now present, it would serve no useful purpose to review or quote them in detail. There is no observed precedent, so far as circumstances are concerned, for the matter now before us. Many of these decisions may be found in the Encyclopedia of English and American Law, tit. "Gift," and any person who will examine this long train of cases will at once perceive that the principal difficulty has been to decide whether the evidence in hand in the given case showed a delivery of the subject of the gift in a legal point of view. But this was a maze not without its clue, for the cardinal principal as to what constituted a delivery that would legalize a gift was on all sides admitted, and was generally applied. The test was this: that the transfer was such that, in conjunction with the donative intention, it completely stripped the donor of his dominion of the thing given, whether that thing was a tangible chattel or a chose in action. (55 N.J.L. at pages 374-376, 26 A. at page 804).

Thus, under New Jersey law actual delivery of the property is still required except where "there can be no actual delivery" or where "the situation is incompatible with the performance of such ceremony." In the case of a savings account, where obviously there can be no actual delivery, delivery of the passbook or other indicia of title is required. . . .

Here there was no delivery of any kind whatsoever. We have already noted the requirement so amply established in our cases, . . . of "actual, unequivocal and complete delivery during the lifetime of the donor, wholly divesting her of the possession, dominion, and control" of the property. This requirement is satisfied only by delivery by the *donor*, which calls for an affirmative act on her part, not by the mere taking of possession of the property by the donee.

Delivery itself, which we have been considering, is to be distinguished from donative intent, another element in gifts causa mortis. . . .

We must not forget that since a gift causa mortis is made in contemplation of death and is subject to revocation by the donor up to the time of his death it differs from a legacy only in the requirement of delivery. Delivery is in effect the only safeguard imposed by law upon a transaction which would ordinarily fall within the statute of wills. To eliminate delivery from the requirements for a gift causa mortis would be to permit any writing to effectuate a testamentary transfer, even though it does not comply with the requirements of the statute of wills.

Here we are concerned with three separate items of property — cash, a savings account represented by a bank passbook, and shares in a building and loan association represented by a book. There was no actual delivery of the cash and no delivery of the indicia of title to the savings account or the building and loan association shares. Rather, the donor set forth in an informal writing her desire to give these items to the defendant. Although the writing establishes her donative intent at the time it was written, it does not fulfill the requirement of delivery of the property, which is a separate and distinct requirement for a gift causa mortis. The cash, passbook, and stock book remained at the decedent's home and she made no effort to obtain them so as to effectuate a delivery to the defendant.

We disagree with the conclusion of the Appellate Division that the donee already had possession of the property, and therefore delivery was unnecessary. Assuming, but not deciding, the validity of this doctrine, we note that the house was the property of the deceased and, although defendant resided there with her, he had no knowledge of the presence of this property in the house, let alone its precise location therein; therefore it cannot be said that he had possession of the property. . . .

But it is argued that the decedent's note to her husband in the circumstances of the case was an authorization to him to take possession of the chattels mentioned therein which when coupled with his taking of possession thereof during her lifetime was in law the equivalent of the delivery required in the Roman and common law alike and by all the decisions in this State for a valid gift causa mortis. Without accepting this contention, it is to be noted that it has no application to the present case, because here at the time the defendant obtained her note the decedent was in the operating room under ether and, according to the finding of the trial court, supra,

> after the operation and until the date of her death on May 13, 1951 she was in a coma most of the time; was unable to recognize members of her family; and unable to carry on intelligent conversation . . . Mrs. Reiss was never able to talk or converse after coming out of the operation until her death.

In these circumstances the note clearly failed as an authorization to the defendant to take possession of the chattels mentioned therein, since at the time he took the note from the drawer the decedent was under ether and according to the findings of the trial court unable to transact business until the time of her death. See section 122 of the Restatement of the Law of Agency:

> The authority of the agent to make the principal a party to a transaction is terminated or suspended upon the happening of an event which deprives the principal of capacity to become a party to the transaction or deprives the agent of capacity to make the principal a party to it.

and comment (b) thereunder:

> The power of the agent terminates although he has no notice of the principal's loss of capacity or of the event causing it. It also terminates although the contingency has been provided for and it has been agreed that the authority would not thereupon terminate.

. . .

The judgment of the Appellate Division of the Superior Court is reversed and the judgment of the Chancery Division of the Superior Court will be reinstated.

For reversal: Chief Justice Vanderbilt and Justices Heher, Oliphant and Burling — 4.

For affirmance: Justices Wachenfeld, Jacobs and Brennan — 3.

Jacobs, J. (with whom Wachenfeld and William J. Brennan, Jr., JJ., agree) dissenting.

The decedent Ethel Reiss was fully competent when she freely wrote the longhand note which was intended to make a gift causa mortis to her husband Adam Reiss. On the day the note was written her husband duly received it, located the money and books in accordance with its directions, and took personal possession of them. Nine days later Mrs. Reiss died; in the meantime her husband retained his possession and there was never any suggestion of revocation of the gift. Although the honesty of the husband's claim is conceded and justice fairly cries out for the fulfillment of his wife's wishes, the majority opinion (while acknowledging that gifts causa mortis are valid in our State as elsewhere) holds that the absence of direct physical delivery of the donated articles requires that the gift be stricken down. I find neither reason nor persuasive authority anywhere which compels this untoward result. See Gulliver and Tilson, Classification of Gratuitous Transfers, 51 Yale L.J. 1, 2 (1941):

> One fundamental proposition is that, under a legal system recognizing the individualistic institution of private property and granting to the owner the power to determine his successors in ownership, the general philosophy of the courts should favor giving effect to an intentional exercise of that power. This is commonplace enough but it needs constant emphasis, for it may be obscured or neglected in inordinate preoccupation with detail or dialectic. A court absorbed in purely doctrinal arguments may lose sight of the important and desirable objective of sanctioning what the transferor wanted to do, even though it is convinced that he wanted to do it.

Harlan F. Stone in his discussion of Delivery in Gifts of Personal Property, 20 Col. L. Rev. 196 (1920), points out that the rule requiring delivery is traceable to early notions of seisin as an element in the ownership of chattels as well as land; and he expresses the view that as the technical significance of seisin fades into the background, courts should evidence a tendency to accept other evidence in lieu of delivery as corroborative of the donative intent. See Philip Mechem, The Requirement of Delivery in Gifts of Chattels, 21 Ill. L. Rev. 341, 345 (1926). Nevertheless, the artificial requirement of delivery is still widely entrenched and is defended for modern times by Mechem (supra, at 348) as a protective device to insure deliberate and unequivocal conduct by the donor and the elimination of questionable or fraudulent claims against him. But even that defense has no applicability where, as here, the donor's wishes were freely and clearly expressed in a written instrument and the donee's ensuing possession was admittedly bona fide; under these particular circumstances every consideration of public policy would seem to point towards upholding the gift.

The delivery requirement has, for the most part, been applied in like fashion to gifts causa mortis and gifts inter vivos. See Brown, Personal Property (1936), 76, 137; Atkinson, Wills, (1937), 157. Cf. 4 Page, Wills (1941), 757. And although some courts have suggested that stricter attitude is called for in gifts causa mortis than in gifts inter vivos, other courts have adopted the opposite point of view. See e.g., In re Wasserberg (1915) 1 Ch. 195; Begovich v. Kruljac, 38 Wyo. 365, 267 P. 426, 60 A.L.R. 1046 (Sup. Ct. 1928); Devol v. Dye, 123 Ind. 321, 24 N.E. 246, 7 L.R.A. 439 (Sup. Ct. 1890). In the Begovich case, supra [38 Wyo. 365, 267 P. 429], the court said:

> . . . gifts causa mortis are ordinarily resorted to by intending donors because the facilities for executing the more formal testamentary disposition are not available, or the death of the donor is so imminent in point of time as to preclude preparation of the formal documents. They are in their very nature emergency measures. Hence, though delivery cannot be dispensed with, since words may be easily misrepresented (Drew v. Hagerty, supra [81 Me. 231, 17 A. 63, 3 L.R.A. 230]), still we should naturally expect the courts to hold the requirements as to

such delivery to be less strict than in connection with gifts inter vivos, and that, in fact, is the holding of at least many of the courts. . . .

No helpful purpose would be served by further discussion of the history or wisdom of the delivery rule or its sympathetic or hostile application to gifts causa mortis; it would seem that under any reasoned point of view the particular facts in the instant matter should be deemed to constitute the required delivery. It must be remembered that the gift to Adam Reiss did not rest upon delivery of the note alone; it rested on the acknowledged fact that in accordance with the terms of the note the donee took physical possession of the donated articles and retained them until after the death of the donor. In his article on Gifts of Chattels without Delivery, 6 L. Quar. Rev. 446 (1890), Sir Frederick Pollock said:

> On principle it would seem that where A by word of mouth purports to give B a certain chattel, this will have the effect of a license to B to take that chattel peaceably wherever he may find it. For it would not be reasonable for A to treat B as a trespasser for acting upon A's expressed intention. The license is no doubt revocable until executed, and may be revoked either by the communication to B, by word or act, of A's will to that effect, or by A's death (which was the case of Irons v. Smallpiece) or perhaps by A's becoming insane. If without any revocation the license is executed by B taking possession of the chattel, then, it is submitted, the property is irrevocably transferred to B. There would be great and obvious inconvenience in holding otherwise.

Similarly, Stone, supra, at 198, noted that "If the donor make oral gift of a chattel in the donor's possession to the donee, and the donee avails himself of the donor's license to possess himself of the chattel, the gift then becomes complete" without further delivery. Page in his treatise on Wills, supra, at 759, states flatly that "If the donor authorizes the donee to take physical possession of the property in question and the donee takes such possession before the donor dies, the donee's act in taking possession is sufficient delivery." Commonsensible decisions in England and in this country have applied these views to sustain gifts causa mortis where, as in the instant matter, the donee properly acquired possession before the donor's death. See Cain v. Moon (1896) 2 Q.B. 283; Champney v. Blanchard, 39 N.Y. 111 (1868); Davis v. Kuck, 93 Minn. 262, 101 N.W. 165 (Sup. Ct. 1904); In re Gordon's Will, 238 Iowa 580, 27 N.W.2d 900 (Sup. Ct. 1947). Cf. Brown, supra, at 102; Mechem, supra, at 364.

The Davis case related to a causa mortis gift of a team of horses from a father to a son who lived with him; the court sustained a charge that where the donee and donor lived together, as in the case of husband and wife or parent and child, it was not necessary that the donated article be removed from the common residence and it was "sufficient if it appear that the donor has relinquished and the donee acquired a control of the property." See 101 N.W., at page 166. In the Champney case the court, in sustaining a gift causa mortis, held that where the donee already had possession no further formal delivery was necessary. See 39 N.Y., at page 116:

> Delivery of the subject-matter is, no doubt, essential to a gift, either inter vivos or mortis causa; but the object of delivery is to give possession, and, in this case, possession was already complete in the donee. No further delivery was necessary, nor was it possible, without first returning the property to the donor, that it might be redelivered to thé donee, an idle and unmeaning ceremony.

To the same effect was the upholding of the gift causa mortis in the Cain case, where Justice Wills remarked (2 Q.B., at 289):

> Suppose a man lent a book to a friend, who expressed himself pleased with the book, whereupon the lender, finding that he had a second copy, told his friend that he need not return the copy he had lent him; it would be very strange if in such a case there were no complete gift, the book being in the possession of the intended donee.

When Ethel Reiss signed the note and arranged to have her husband receive it, she did everything that could reasonably have been expected of her to effectuate the gift causa mortis; and while her husband might conceivably have attempted to return the donated articles to her at the hospital for immediate redelivery to him, it would have been unnatural for him to do so. It is difficult to believe that our law would require such wholly ritualistic ceremony and I find nothing in our decisions to suggest it. The majority opinion advances the suggestion that the husband's authority to take possession of the donated articles was terminated by the wife's incapacity in the operating room and thereafter. The very reason she wrote the longhand note when she did was because she knew she would be incapacitated and wished her husband to take immediate possession, as he did. Men who enter hospitals for major surgery often execute powers of attorney to enable others to continue their business affairs during their incapacity. Any judicial doctrine which would legally terminate such power as of the inception of the incapacity would be startling indeed — it would disrupt commercial affairs and entirely without reason or purpose.

The New Jersey decisions dealing with gifts causa mortis, including the leading cases of Cook v. Lum, 55 N.J.L. 373, 26 A. 803 (Sup. Ct. 1893), and Keepers v. Fidelity Title & Deposit Co., 56 N.J.L. 302, 28 A. 585, 23 L.R.A. 184 (E. & A. 1893), relied upon by the majority, do not bear on the actual issue presented in the instant matter. In the Cook case the court held that delivery of a slip of paper referring to a sum of money which the donor had on deposit did not constitute delivery of the deposit (see Brown, supra, at 183); the donee there did not take possession of the deposit before the donor's death. In the Keepers case the court held that delivery of the key to a box did not constitute delivery of its contents (see Brown, supra, at 95); the donee there likewise did not take possession of the contents before the donor's death.

In the Cook case [55 N.J.L. 373, 26 A. 804] Chief Justice Beasley set forth the supposedly controlling principles which have been followed in our later cases and which do not in anywise impair the validity of the gift in the instant matter. Thus he noted that "there must be, in addition to the expression of a donative purpose, an actual tradition of the corpus of the gift whenever, considering the nature of the property and the circumstances of the actors, such a formality is reasonably practicable"; and further in his opinion he stated that "the test was this: that the transfer was such that, in conjunction with the donative intention, it completely stripped the donor of his dominion of the thing given." When the husband took possession of the donated articles in accordance with his wife's wishes and the decent dictates of the circumstances, he acquired complete dominion to the exclusion of the donor; in all justice this should satisfy the delivery requirement even in the eyes of those who adhere most technically to its ancient terms and tenor.

I would affirm the judgment of the Appellate Division.[59]

NOTES

1. In essence delivery is the transfer of possession from one party to another with the intention of making a gift. On the functions of delivery see Fuller, Consideration and Form, 41 Colum. L. Rev. 799 (1941); Gulliver & Tilson, Classification of Gratuitous Transfers, 51 Yale L.J. 1 (1941); Mechem, The Requirement of Delivery in Gifts of Chattels and of Choses in Action Evidenced by Commercial Instruments, 21 Ill. L. Rev. 341, 457, 568 (1926) ((a) makes vivid and concrete to the donor the significance of the act he is doing, (b) makes unequivocal to actual witnesses, if any, the nature of the act done, and (c) gives to the donee, subsequently to the act, at least prima facie evidence in favor of the alleged gift); Rohan, The Continuing Question of Delivery in the Law of Gifts, 38 Ind. L.J. 1 (1962); Rohan, Some Problems of Constructive Delivery, Agency and Proof in Gift Litigation, 38 Ind. L.J. 470 (1963).

2. Suppose that Ethel Reiss had mailed the note to her husband by dropping it in a hospital mail chute before she went into the operating room. Would there have been a sufficient delivery? Pikeville Nat'l Bank & Trust Co. v. Shirley, 281 Ky. 150, 135 S.W.2d 426, 126 A.L.R. 919 (1939); Waller v. Capper, 143 Kan. 164, 53 P.2d 836 (1936).

3. In addition to manual delivery, delivery of a chattel can be effectuated by an instrument of gift or by constructive delivery. In the fifteenth century it was established that the gift of a chattel may be made by the delivery of a sealed instrument, without delivery of the chattel. 3 Holdsworth, History of English Law 354 (1923). With the abolition of the necessity for seals, an unsealed instrument of gift became efficacious in transferring a chattel.

Constructive delivery contemplates the transfer of some object which gives to the donee physical access or control over the subject of the intended gift. The classic example is a key which opens a safe deposit box or a heavy chest. Constructive delivery does not suffice, however, when the article is easily delivered manually. Constructive delivery is permitted only when it would be difficult or impracticable

[59] Noted 54 Mich. L. Rev. 572; 10 Rutgers L. Rev. 457; 17 U. Pitt. L. Rev. 105. — Eds.

to deliver the article manually because of its bulk or inaccessibility. Brown, Personal Property §§41, 42 (2d ed. 1955). Thus if O, in New York, wishes to give A a diamond ring and an antique secretary which are in his house in East Hampton, and hands over the key to the house to A with the words, "The ring and secretary are yours," O has delivered the secretary to A but not the ring. "The consequence is that while the small thing requires a special journey, the big thing can be 'transferred' at home." Stoljar, The Delivery of Chattels, 21 Mod. L. Rev. 27, 42 (1958).

4. *Choses in action.* "In considering gifts of choses in action it is necessary to differentiate between two classes of such choses: 1, those evidenced by written instruments, which either by law or business custom are accepted as representative of the obligation itself, so that assignments of the obligation are usually made through the medium of a manual delivery of the instrument, which instrument is also surrendered to the obligor when the obligation is satisfied; and 2, those not evidenced by such instruments. Among the obligations of the first class are those embodied in bonds, promissory notes, bills of exchange, stock certificates, insurance policies, savings account books and the like. . . . Gifts of choses in action of the first class follow closely the analogy of gifts of tangible property; a delivery of the instrument evidencing the obligation is treated as a delivery of the obligation itself. . . .

"When the chose in action is not embodied in a bond, bill of exchange, promissory note, or other instrument which . . . is in a particular sense the tangible representative of the obligation, the difficulty of discovering in a gift thereof something analogous to the delivery of tangible chattels is immeasurably increased. The modern tendency . . . is to sustain gifts of such choses in action where evidenced by the written assignment of the donor. . . .

"Whether gifts of choses in action not evidenced by written instruments of the character, discussed in the previous section, may be effected by delivery of the written contract embodying their terms, or by the memorandum or account book kept by the donor-creditor, is a difficult question. . . . The surrender of such documents is not required as a condition of the satisfaction of the obligations they evidence. For this reason the scholars who restated the law of contracts refuse to accept such a delivery as constituting a sufficient gift." Brown, Personal Property §§59, 61 (2d ed. 1955).

5. A check is treated as an order to pay, not as an assignment, and until payment the gift can be revoked by stopping payment and is revoked by the donor's death. Why does delivery of a check fail to effect an irrevocable gift? Havighurst, Gifts of Bank Deposits, 14 N.C.L. Rev. 129 (1936).

6. A purchases U.S. government bonds in the name of "A or B." Under government regulations, payment of such bonds will be made to either co-owner, and if either dies before requesting payment, the survivor is recognized as the sole and absolute owner. A endorses the bonds and hands them to C, stating that he wishes C to have them. A dies. Who owns the bonds, B or C? In Neglia Estate, 403 Pa. 464, 170 A.2d 357 (1961), noted 110 U. Pa. L. Rev. 440 (1962), the court held for C on the ground that the regulations apply only to payment by the United States, and not to the eventual disposition of the proceeds under state law. Most courts

have held to the contrary, either on the theory (a) that the federal regulations are part of the contract between the government and the purchaser and are therefore binding on the purchaser or (b) that federal law prevails over state law.

Gifts to Minors

The gift of income-producing property to a child produces a number of difficulties. These may include arranging for a person other than the minor to manage, sell, and reinvest the proceeds from such property. Since a minor can disaffirm the sale, buyers deal with a minor at their peril. Exceptions to the disability of minors to deal with property have been made in some instances, particularly in the case of United States Savings Bonds and deposits in banking institutions. Each state has also enacted a custodianship statute, which permits the donor of a gift to a minor to place certain kinds of property in the name of a selected custodian.

ESTATE DISTRIBUTIONS TO MINORS

5 Real Prop., Prob. & Trust J. 486, 491-492 (1970)

Each state has now enacted its version of the Uniform Gifts to Minors Act whereby provision is made for a simple, inexpensive, but not exclusive method of making a gift of property by an adult person to an infant to be held in the name of a qualified custodian followed by the words, in substance, "as custodian for . . . . (name of infant) under the . . . . (name of state) Uniform Gifts to Minors Act." The gift once made as prescribed by the statute is irrevocable and indefeasibly vests legal title to the property in the minor, subject to the custodian's broad powers contained in the statute. He has the duty to collect the property and to pay over to the minor for expenditure by the minor, or to expend for the minor's benefit, so much or all of the custodial property as he deems advisable for the minor's support, maintenance, education and benefit. The custodian has complete discretion as to the time and amount of such payment. Unused property must be paid to the minor when he reaches 21 years of age, or to his estate if he sooner dies.

Reference must be made to the particular state statute to determine what property may be the subject of a gift, the manner in which it must be made and who may act as custodian. Some statutes permit the donor, an adult member of the minor's family, a guardian of the minor or a trust company to act as custodian when the gift is money, a security in registered form, a life insurance policy or annuity contract, but excludes the donor from so acting when the gift is a bearer security. Other statutes are much broader and permit all types of personal property as well as an interest in real estate to be the subject of the gift; and the adult person who may be custodian is not restricted to a member of the minor's family. The gift is limited to one minor and only one person may be custodian.

Again, the custodian's compensation, if any, depends upon the particular statute. In New York a custodian, other than a trust company or a guardian of the property, receives no compensation for his services. Other statutes are broader, and the custodians who may be compensated are not so limited. A custodian not compensated for his services is not liable for losses to the custodial property unless they result from his bad faith, intentional wrongdoing or gross negligence or from his failure to maintain the standard of prudence in investing the custodial property.

A custodian is not required to give a bond for the performance of his duty, except with respect to a successor custodian designated by the court and then only if the court in its discretion so directs. Third persons are exempt by the statute from liability when dealing with any person purporting to act as a donor or in the capacity of a custodian. Provision is made for a compulsory accounting when deemed necessary.

The statute provides for the resignation, death or removal of a custodian and the designation of a successor custodian. A custodian may designate his successor by executing an instrument of designation before a subscribing witness other than the successor. If the custodian does not so designate his successor before he dies, the minor if he has attained the age of 14 years may designate a successor custodian by executing an instrument of designation, otherwise the guardian of the minor becomes the successor custodian, and if he has no guardian, a donor, his legal representative, the legal representative of the custodian or an adult member of the minor's family may petition the court for the designation of a successor custodian.

In almost all jurisdictions the custodian provisions apply only to inter vivos transfers to a minor, and therefore the statute is of no special significance in the distribution of a minor's interest in a decedent's estate. Nevertheless, it is important to bear in mind that such a lifetime transaction in effect is a substitute for a dispositive will provision by the donor. Four jurisdictions,[60] however, have extended the statute to include testamentary dispositions. In Maryland, for example, the gift may be made by will by stating that the devise or bequest is made under the Maryland Uniform Gifts to Minors Act.[61] If the testator does not designate the custodian in his will his personal representative has the power, without court order, to name a custodian and make distribution to the custodian. Such an extension of the statute is significant and of great advantage in making distribution of a legacy to a minor.

PROBLEM

T dies domiciled in a state in which the Uniform Gifts to Minors Act does not extend to testamentary dispositions. T's will provides: "I give my 100 shares of IBM stock to my nephew, N, to be held for him by his father, F, as custodian under the Uniform Gifts to Minors Act." N, aged 3, and F survive T. In T's estate is a certificate for 100 shares of IBM stock. Does F hold the stock as custodian or as guardian?

[60] Conn. Gen. Stat. §45-102; Md. Ann. Code art. 93A, §302; Neb. Rev. Stat. §38-101; N.J. Rev. Stat. §46:38-22.

[61] Md. Ann. Code art. 93A, §302, subd. 7.

9. Restrictions on the Power of Disposition: Protection of the Family

In this chapter we examine the various statutes and doctrines that impose restrictions on the power of disposition in order to protect the family. We shall consider this subject from two vantage points. First, from the standpoint of the individual: Adam Smith's attorney must be familiar with these rules to avoid drafting a will or trust that is subject to possible challenge. Second, in terms of social policy: To what extent and under what circumstances should a person have power to disinherit his spouse, his children, and his extended family? How effective are the rules and doctrines that have been fashioned to protect the family?

The chapter begins with an assessment of statutes enacted in common law states specifically to protect an individual's spouse from disinheritance. We then take a look at statutes in community property states designed to protect the spouse. We shall find that the law in the fifty states differs widely — from North and South Dakota, which offer little protection to the surviving spouse, to Massachusetts, which gives the surviving spouse substantial statutory rights but permits the statutes to be evaded by use of a revocable inter vivos trust (an avoidance device open to residents of all common law states provided a Massachusetts trustee is used), to California, which gives the greatest protection to the decedent's spouse of any state. After examining the problems related to protection of the spouse, we take a look at pretermission statutes protecting children from unintentional disinheritance. Finally, to close the chapter, we examine homestead laws, small estate statutes, and family maintenance legislation, all designed to protect needy and dependent members of the decedent's family.

"Now read me the part again where I disinherit everybody."

SECTION A. Protection of the Surviving Spouse — Common Law States

All the American states attempt to give the surviving spouse some protection against disinheritance. In the eight community property states this protection is given by the system of marital property ownership itself. Each spouse is owner of an undivided one-half interest in the community property. The death of one of the spouses dissolves the community, and the surviving spouse becomes a tenant in common with the estate of the deceased spouse, whose power of disposition extends only to his one-half community share.

In the common law states, all property acquired from the husband's earnings during marriage is his property.[1] As a consequence, in the typical case of the nonworking wife all or most of the marital assets belong to the husband, and the starting point is that he has full power of disposition over them. Only when the wife owns substantial property before marriage, or acquires property after marriage by gift or devise or from her own earnings, does she have any built-in protection against being left without means of support upon her husband's death.

To protect the wife against disinheritance, all but two[2] of the common law states give her a share of her husband's estate, either in the form of *dower* or a *statutory forced share*. Of course, these are not the only sources of economic protection of the surviving spouse. We saw in Chapter 5 that the federal social security program gives substantial benefits to widows with dependent children, and more modest benefits to widows age sixty and over. Retirement plans for federal, state, and municipal government employees not only secure funds for the retired worker but also provide pensions for his widow and dependent children after his death.[3] Ordinarily, the employee cannot divert the pension payments to anyone other than his spouse and other dependent relatives. This is often a feature of private pension plans as well. State homestead laws and the family allowance in probate are also sources of protection.[4] The various restrictions on gifts to charity that exist in several states[5] are intended to protect the testator's family against charitable bequests prompted by an undue concern for the hereafter.

While the state and federal tax laws can hardly be said to give affirmative protection to the testator's spouse and children, they certainly encourage him to make gifts and devises to members of the family unit. In states that have an inheritance tax, larger exemptions and lower tax rates apply to bequests to the decedent's immediate family.[6] For the wealthy, the exclusions, exemptions and lower tax rates under the federal gift tax serve as an inducement to making lifetime transfers, as do the income tax savings that may be available through use of additional tax entities within the family.[7] The estate tax marital deduction provides an incentive to making transfers to the surviving spouse that qualify for the deduction.[8]

Our immediate focus, though, is on dower, the forced share, and other restric-

[1] For background information on the capacity of married persons to acquire, control and deal with property, see 1 Powell, Real Property ¶¶116-123 (1970).

[2] North and South Dakota have abolished the wife's common law dower interest without providing a statutory substitute. North Dakota Cent. Code §§14-07-09, 56-01-02 (1960); S.D. Code §§25-2-9, 29-1-3 (1967). See In re Vetter's Estate, 75 S.D. 417, 66 N.W.2d 519 (1954). In these states the wife's only protection comes from liberal family allowance provisions and homestead rights.

[3] In Dunham, Sixty Different Succession Laws in Illinois, 46 Ill. B.J. 741 (1958), the author points out that Illinois has forty separate statutes providing pension plans for such groups as state and municipal government employees, teachers, firemen, and policemen, and that there are over twenty federal programs that may apply to Illinois residents, including servicemen, veterans, railroad workers, and lighthouse keepers.

[4] See pages 568-573, infra.

[5] See page 633, infra.

[6] See page 269, supra.

[7] See pages 255-261, supra.

[8] See page 239, supra.

tions on the power of testation, for these are the arrangements with which lawyers, judges and courts deal most frequently.

1. *Dower*

At common law, a wife had dower in all lands of which her husband was seised during marriage and which were inheritable by her issue. Dower was a life estate in an undivided one-third of each parcel of land. A husband had a comparable interest in his wife's lands, called curtesy. It differed from dower in two substantial ways. Curtesy was not acquired unless issue was born alive of the marriage "and heard to cry within the four walls"; curtesy gave the surviving husband a life estate in the whole parcel. Except for these two differences, curtesy and dower functioned alike in protecting the surviving spouse. In modern statutes curtesy and dower have usually been assimilated, and the single term "dower" is used hereinafter.

Where dower exists, the dower interest arises when the real property is acquired. It is "inchoate" until the other spouse dies, which means that the dower interest gives no right to possession until that time. If the wife predeceases her husband, her inchoate dower interest is extinguished. If she survives her husband, she becomes entitled to possession of a one-third life estate in his lands.

Dower cannot be barred by an inter vivos transfer unless the spouse consents to the transfer. If the husband owns Blackacre and sells it to A, and his wife survives him, she can claim dower in Blackacre unless she has previously released it to A. Consequently, in a state that still recognizes dower, the buyer of real property should always require that the grantor's spouse sign the deed, thereby relinquishing her inchoate dower interest.

In a society where land was the principal form of wealth and the rents and profits from land were the principal source of income, dower worked reasonably well in protecting the surviving spouse against disinheritance. Dower has priority over creditors and no inter vivos transfer can defeat it. On the other hand, dower has two disadvantages, which grew larger when a landed society changed into a mercantile society. A surviving spouse has dower in land only, not in personal property. Today the principal form of wealth is personalty, not land, and a system that assures the surviving spouse a share of her husband's real property may give her no protection at all. The other disadvantage of dower appeared with the development of the corporation. Instead of taking title to land directly, the husband could have a corporation, in which he owned most of the stock, take title. Thus he could prevent dower from attaching by interposing a corporation between himself and the land.

In a society where land is freely bought and sold and is not a reification of Family History, Status, and Ambitions, as it was in England, dower is a clog on marketability. Purchasers of land must assure themselves that there are no outstanding dower interests in their chain of title. This often requires search outside the record for facts such as marriage or divorce dates or whether the grantor (who declared himself to be an unmarried man) was really married.

Dower has been abolished in England and in about a dozen American states, among them Colorado, Connecticut and New York. In the other common law states dower still exists in some form or other.[9] In many states, especially in the Midwest, the surviving spouse's dower interest has been increased from a life estate in one-third of the land to an absolute interest in one-third of the land or to a life estate in all the land.

2. *Forced Share*

Concern for the wife's possible disinheritance and the limited protection given by dower has prompted the legislatures of all but seven[10] common law states to enact statutes giving the surviving spouse an unbarrable share of the deceased spouse's assets, real and personal. These statutes give the surviving spouse an election. She can take under her spouse's will, or she can renounce the will and take a "forced share" of his estate. The forced share may be a fraction (usually one-third or one-half) of the decedent's estate, or a fixed figure plus a fraction (e.g., $5000 plus one-half of what remains), or a sliding scale inverse fraction (i.e., the fraction grows smaller as the decedent's estate becomes larger). In most states the right of election is given to the surviving spouse, whether husband or wife; in a few states only the wife is given a forced share election.[11] While the statutes vary greatly in detail, the Colorado statute is fairly typical:

COLORADO REVISED STATUTES ANNOTATED §153-5-4 (1964): "*Surviving spouse may elect.* (1) Notwithstanding the provisions of a testator's will, his surviving spouse shall have the option to take and receive one-half of the testator's estate, as provided in section 153-14-10; provided, that such surviving spouse exercises such option by filing in the court in which the testator's will is admitted to probate, within six months thereafter, his election in writing to take and receive one-half of said estate. The failure to exercise such option within said period of six months shall be conclusive evidence of the consent of the surviving spouse to the provisions of such will."

§153-14-10: "*Surviving spouse renounces will — payment of benefits.* (1) In any case in which an election is made pursuant to section 153-5-4, the court shall order the distribution to the surviving spouse of the property specifically devised and bequeathed to him by the testator, and of such additional property the value of which on the date of the order, when added to the value on said date of the property specifically devised and bequeathed to such spouse, will equal the value on said

[9] For a summary of statutory provisions on dower and curtesy see Phipps, Marital Property Interests, 27 Rocky Mt. L. Rev. 180 (1955).

[10] The holdouts are North and South Dakota, which have neither dower nor a forced share system, and Delaware, Georgia, New Jersey, Rhode Island, and South Carolina, all of which give the surviving spouse some form of dower interest in the deceased spouse's realty. See 6 Powell, Real Property ¶971.9 (1970).

For contrasting views on the need for statutory protection of the widow see Haskell, The Power of Disinheritance: Proposal for Reform, 52 Geo. L. Rev. 499 (1964), and Plager, The Spouse's Nonbarrable Share: A Solution in Search of a Problem, 33 U. Chi. L. Rev. 681 (1966).

[11] The statutes are collected and discussed in Comment, Election by the Surviving Spouse, 2 Real Prop., Prob. & Trust J. 310 (1967).

date of one-half the testator's estate. The additional property distributed shall be selected by the court from other property of the estate following the order of abatement provided in section 153-14-17, and so far as feasible, in kind, proportionately. If the property specifically devised and bequeathed to said spouse exceeds one-half of the value on said date of the testator's estate, the court shall order the distribution to the spouse of a part of said property equal to one-half of said value. Except with respect to property specifically devised and bequeathed, none of the provisions of the will in favor of the spouse shall be effective."

There are several disadvantages to the forced share approach of protecting the surviving spouse. First, the statutes give her a fraction or other portion of the deceased spouse's *net* estate. Creditors' claims thus have priority over the widow's forced share.[12] Second, the forced share is fixed and arbitrary, and some take the position that the surviving spouse's share should be limited to the amount needed for support. Professor Macdonald is an articulate spokesman for this position. He writes:

"[T]he overall picture is one of fixed, unalterable, arbitrary positions. Relief is standardized; no attention is paid to individual equities or unusual circumstances.

"There are, of course, some isolated instances of flexibility. A Vermont statute provides that the surviving spouse may take, out of the intestate property or upon waiving the will, such part of the personalty 'as the probate court assigns . . . according to his or her circumstances and the estate and degree of the decedent, which shall not be less than a third, after the payment of the debts, funeral charges, and expenses of administration.' In Mississippi there is a proviso that the wife may not elect against the will if her separate estate is equal to the share of the realty and personalty that she would take under the will. A comparable position exists in Alabama. . . . In the main, however, the pattern is one of unyielding rigidity.

"The statutory share almost inevitably entails a lump sum payment. No thought is given to the possibility — indeed, the probability — that the widow will be inexperienced in money matters and that the lump sum will soon be dissipated." [13]

The third disadvantage of the forced share is that when the spouse elects against the will and pulls her assets out of the testator's estate, problems are often encountered in applying the remaining provisions of the will to the remaining assets. These problems are rarely resolved by the statutes.

Finally, the legislatures of the various states have not shown much foresight or imagination in protecting the surviving spouse against the husband who is deter-

[12] However, the widow's homestead rights and family allowance, discussed in Section E, pass to the widow free of claims of her husband's creditors.

Several states that have enacted a forced share statute and have not abolished dower give the surviving spouse a three-way election. She can take under her husband's will, she can renounce the will and claim her statutory share, or she can renounce the will and statutory share and claim her dower interest. As a practical matter, the dower election is attractive only when the deceased spouse owned a substantial amount of real estate and his estate is insolvent, for only the dower interest takes priority over creditors' claims.

[13] Macdonald, Fraud on the Widow's Share 21-23 (1960).

mined to disinherit her. The typical statute gives the spouse a fractional share of her husband's "estate," as in the Colorado statute, or a share of "property owned at death." This leaves open the possibility of defeating the statute's objective through inter vivos transfers — perhaps even revocable transfers in which the husband retains a life estate — that remove the assets from the husband's "estate."

PROBLEMS

1. H's estate totals $1 million. H's wife W is an incompetent and is confined to a mental hospital. H's will leaves $300,000 in trust for W for life, with the power in the trustee to use principal to support W. The surviving spouse's forced share is one-half of her spouse's estate. Can a guardian appointed for W elect to take $500,000 outright? Suppose H's will had left W nothing? 5 Page, Wills §47.18 (Bowe-Parker rev. 1960).

2. The will of H's aunt creates a trust giving H a life income interest and a general power of appointment exercisable by deed or will, with a gift in default of appointment to H's brother B. By his will H exercises the power by appointing the trust principal to H's three children in equal shares. H is survived by his wife W, who elects to take her forced share under a statute that gives her a one-third share of property "owned by the deceased spouse at his death." Is W entitled to a one-third share of the appointive assets? See In re Kate's Estate, 282 Pa. 417, 128 A. 97 (1925); Fiske v. Fiske, 173 Mass. 413, 53 N.E. 916 (1899); Macdonald, Fraud on the Widow's Share 252 (1960).

3. *The Widow's Election to Take Her Statutory Share: Effect on the Husband's Will*

PROBLEMS

1. H's will gives Blackacre (worth $50,000) to his son S, securities worth $50,000 (a general legacy) to his daughter D, and the residue of his estate to his wife W. The net value of the residuary estate is $50,000. W elects to take her forced share under a statute that gives her one-half of her husband's estate: property worth $75,000. This leaves Blackacre and securities worth $25,000 as the assets remaining in H's estate. To whom should these assets be distributed?

Should the statutes provide (or, in the absence of a controlling statutory provision, should the courts hold) that the wife's share is to be treated as an ordinary debt of the estate? " 'Abatement' is the reduction of legacies on account of the insufficiency of the estate to pay testator's debts and other legacies. Intestate property should be first applied for these purposes. In absence of testamentary indication as to order of abatement, legacies ordinarily abate in the following order: (1) residuary legacies, (2) general legacies, (3) specific and demonstrative legacies, which give way together ratably." Atkinson, Wills 754 (2d ed. 1953); compare id. at 123-126.

2. If the surviving spouse elects to take against the will and, independent of her election, there is a partial intestacy, should she be entitled to claim (in addition to her statutory share) a portion of the intestate propery as an heir?

The third clause of H's will devises property worth $100,000 in trust, from which trust income is to be paid to his wife W for her life, with the remainder on her death to H's brother B. The fourth clause of H's will devises the residue of his estate (valued at $200,000) one-half to his son S and one-half to his daughter D. D predeceased her father by six months. She was not survived by any descendants, and the devise to her lapses. W elects to take her statutory share of one-third of her husband's estate, or $100,000.

Under the state's intestacy laws, when a person dies intestate survived by his spouse and one child, his real and personal property descend one-half to the spouse and one-half to the child. In distributing H's property, the only thing that is clear to the court is that W is entitled to property worth $100,000 under the state's forced heir statute. How should the remaining $200,000 be distributed? What arguments should be made by B, S and W, and who should prevail? See Sellick v. Sellick, infra; see also Phelps, The Widow's Right of Election in the Estate of Her Husband, 37 Mich. L. Rev. 236, 401-408 (1939).

3. If the surviving spouse elects to take under the will and there is a partial intestacy, should she be entitled to claim (in addition to the bequest in the will) a portion of the intestate property as an heir?

Consider the same facts as in Problem 2, except that W elects to take under her husband's will. How should H's residuary estate be distributed? See Ness v. Lunde, 394 Ill. 286, 68 N.E.2d 458 (1946); compare Trafton v. Trafton, 96 N.H. 188, 72 A.2d 457 (1950). See also Phelps, supra, at 255-272.

SELLICK v. SELLICK

Supreme Court of Michigan, 1919

207 Mich. 194, 173 N.W. 609

Fellows, J. This case involves the construction of the will of William J. Sellick, late of Paw Paw, Van Buren County, and the effect as between certain of the legatees of the election of the widow to take under the statute. Mr. Sellick left real estate inventoried at $8,500, and personal property inventoried at upwards of $176,000. He left a widow, Caroline Sellick, and one son, William R. Sellick, the plaintiff, now grown to manhood, who was the child of a former wife. He also left collateral kindred, including the defendants Arthur F. Sellick, a nephew, and Gertrude Sellick, a niece. To his collateral kindred other than defendants he gave varying sums aggregating $15,000. By the second clause of his will he gave to each of the defendants $5,000. The first clause of his will is as follows:

> I give, devise and bequeath to my wife, Caroline Sellick, twenty-five thousand dollars ($25,000), to be used and enjoyed by her during her life and at her death

to be equally divided between my nephew, Arthur F. Sellick, and my niece, Gertrude Sellick.

The residue of his estate he gave to his son, the plaintiff. The widow elected to take under the statute. The trial judge construed the first clause of the will, when taken in connection with the second clause, which gave each defendant $5,000, and the residuary clause, as giving the widow absolutely $25,000, and accordingly held that the defendants took nothing under such clause. This rendered unnecessary the determination of the other questions involved. From a decree in accordance with these views the defendants appeal, and it is here urged by their counsel that the first clause of the will gave the widow a life estate, with remainder over to them; that by the election of the widow to take under the statute her life estate is at an end, and that, applying the doctrine of acceleration of remainders, they are now entitled to said sum of $25,000. On the other hand, it is insisted by counsel for the appellee that the bequest to the widow gave her an absolute estate, . . . and that the decree should be affirmed. It is further insisted by appellee's counsel that if we decline to follow this contention and accept the view that a life estate only was given to the widow, still we should not apply the doctrine of acceleration of remainders, but that such life estate, given to the widow by the will, should be sequestered to reimburse the plaintiff in part for the depletion of his bequest occasioned by the payment out of it of the sums necessary to make up the widow's statutory share. In short, that he is known in the law as a disappointed legatee, and that the doctrine of acceleration of remainders should not be adopted at the expense of disappointed legatees. . . .

Under the repeated decisions of this court the clause of Mr. Sellick's will above quoted gave the widow the use of $25,000 for her life, a life estate, and it gave her no more. . . .

This brings us at once to the interesting and novel questions in the case. It must be conceded at the outset that the decisions of the court of last resort of the state of Pennsylvania sustain the contention of defendants' counsel unequivocally.[14] Coover's Appeal, 74 Pa. 143; Ferguson's Estate, 138 Pa. 208, 20 Atl. 945; Vance's Estate, 141 Pa. 201, 21 Atl. 643, 12 L.R.A. 227, 23 Am. St. Rep. 267. Is the rule laid down by the Pennsylvania court supported by the weight of authority and by equitable principles? Should the doctrine of acceleration of remainders be applied where by its application the remainderman gets more than the will gave to him and legatees either specific or residuary get less? To these questions we shall now direct our attention. . . .

We are persuaded that under the great weight of authority the contention of plaintiff's counsel in this regard must prevail. While the doctrine of acceleration of the time of taking effect of the remainder upon the termination of the life estate by

[14] The Pennsylvania rule is that unless a will expressly states there shall be no acceleration, when a spouse elects her statutory forced share the balance of the estate is disposed of as if the spouse had predeceased the testator. See Bach v. McGinnes, 218 F. Supp. 914 (E.D. Pa. 1963). The same rule is provided by statute in Ohio. Ohio Rev. Code Ann. §2107.39 (Page 1954). — Eds.

act other than the death of the life tenant (i.e., by the election of the widow to take under the statute) must be recognized and applied in proper cases, such doctrine should not be applied where by the election a portion only of the legacies are diminished in order to make up the amount required by the statute to satisfy the widow's statutory rights. And that this should be true whether the legacy diminished be a specific or a residuary one. Under such circumstances the disappointed legatee may in a court of equity compel the sequestration of the legacy to the refractory legatee for the purpose of diminishing the amount of his disappointment.

Manifestly this is in consonance with equitable principles. In the instant case the residuary fund given to the plaintiff has been diminished by many thousand dollars in order to discharge the claim of the widow resulting from her election. To adopt defendants' claim would give to them the $25,000 many years before the time fixed by the testator for its payment. They would not only receive the amount given them by the will, but they would also receive the widow's life estate renounced by her to the disadvantage of the plaintiff. Equitable principles do not require that this should be done.

We are asked to fix the present worth of the widow's life use of the $25,000 with a view of finally closing the estate and disposing of all matters at once. The parties interested are all of age, and may make such adjustment as they may desire, but we do not feel empowered to fix the present worth of the widow's use and direct its present payment. We see no occasion, however, to longer hold the estate open. A trustee may be appointed to handle this fund of $25,000. He shall annually pay the income thereon to the plaintiff during the life of the widow, and upon her death pay the corpus to defendants in equal shares.

It follows that the decree must be reversed, and one here entered in conformity with this opinion. The defendants will recover costs of this court. Neither party will recover costs of the circuit court.

PROBLEMS

1. Suppose the first clause of Sellick's will gave W a life estate and then provided:

(a) "and at the death of W, to the children of my nephew, Arthur."
(b) "and at the death of W, to my issue who shall survive W per stirpes."
(c) "and at the death of W, to such of the children of my nephew, Arthur, as shall reach the age of twenty-one."

W renounces. Who will be the claimants and what will be their arguments? See Matter of Byrnes, 149 Misc. 449, 267 N.Y.S. 627 (Sur. 1933). Would it make a difference if the gift were of the residue of Sellick's estate rather than of a $25,000 general pecuniary legacy? 5 American Law of Property §§21.41 to 21.43 (Casner ed.

1952). See generally Simes, Acceleration of Future Interests, 41 Yale L.J. 659 (1932); 2 Powell, Real Property ¶310 (1967).

2. What do the Sellick case and the problems preceding and following it suggest to the draftsman of a will in a common law state? How might the respective wills have been drafted to avoid the need for litigation to resolve the consequences of the widow's election against the will?

3. To avoid the possible disruption of his testamentary plan, can a husband secure his wife's agreement that she accepts the terms of his will and waives her statutory right of election? Statutes in several states authorize a lifetime waiver of the election. Ind. Ann. Stat. §6-306 (1953, Supp. 1970); Kan. Stat. Ann. §§59-602, 59-603 (1964, Supp. 1970); N.Y. Estates, Powers & Trusts Law §5-1.1(f) (1967, Supp. 1970). In the absence of a statute, should such a lifetime agreement be held enforceable? See Horney v. Rhea, 152 Fla. 817, 12 So. 2d 302 (1943); In re Beat's Estate, 25 Wis. 2d 315, 130 N.W.2d 739 (1964).

4. You are an attorney in a common law state, and you have just drafted H's will. It devises the residue of H's estate in trust, with the income to H's wife for life, remainder to the couple's children. H wants his wife to sign an agreement electing to take under the will. He wants you to explain the will and the election agreement to his wife, and he wants you to secure her signature. If you do advise the wife, who is your client? Would it be better to advise the wife that she should retain independent counsel? What are the advantages and disadvantages of this approach? Cf. Cantor v. Palmer, 166 So. 2d 466 (Fla. Ct. App. 1964); Hartz v. Hartz, 248 Md. 47, 234 A.2d 865 (1967).

4. *Estate Tax Consequences of the Widow's Election to Take Her Statutory Share*

The surviving spouse's election to take against her husband's will alters the amount passing to her, and may affect the amount of the marital deduction in the husband's estate. Before she decides to elect under or against the will, the tax consequences of her decision should be examined.

If the testamentary gifts in her favor do not qualify for the marital deduction, can the forced share be used to increase the marital deduction and thus reduce the estate tax bill?

PROBLEM

After making specific devises of property worth $50,000, H's will places the residue of his estate (worth $450,000) in a trust from which the income is to be paid to his wife W for life, with remainder to the couple's children. Since the devise to W is a terminable interest, it does not qualify for the marital deduction. The entire $500,000 will be taxed in H's gross estate:

$500,000	H's gross estate
−20,000	§§2053, 2054 deductions
−60,000	Exemption
$420,000	Taxable estate
$120,100	Federal estate tax

W renounces the will and elects to take her statutory share, which is one-third of H's real and personal property. Does the amount passing to W via the forced share qualify for the marital deduction?

ESTATE OF KENNEDY v. UNITED STATES

United States District Court, D. South Carolina, 1969
302 *F. Supp.* 343

DONALD RUSSELL, District Judge. This action to recover federal estate taxes, allegedly erroneously and illegally assessed and collected of the plaintiff, involves the right of the estate to a marital deduction for property awarded the widow of the testator by way of dower.

The facts have been stipulated between the parties and such stipulation is hereby adopted as the Findings of Fact herein.

From such stipulation, it appears that, on account of property awards, partially in cash and partially in land, to the widow by way of dower, the plaintiff, as executor of the estate of the deceased, claimed a marital deduction in the amount of $31,291.70, upon its estate tax return. The Commissioner disallowed $28,291.70 of such deduction and imposed an estate tax thereon, which was paid by the plaintiff. Thereafter plaintiff filed a claim for refund, which was timely only with respect to those payments made by plaintiff on August 23, 1963, in the respective amounts of $9,783.15 and $4,214.02. It is to recover such payments that this suit is brought.

It is conceded by both parties that the right of the plaintiff to claim a marital deduction for property awarded the testator's widow by way of dower turns on a construction of Section 2056, 26 U.S.C.A.

In computing the estate tax, Section 2056, authorizes a marital deduction from the gross estate, not to exceed 50 per cent of the adjusted gross estate, to the extent of the value of nonterminable property interests passing from a decedent to his surviving spouse at the time of death. It includes a definition of the term "property interests." Among the property interests "considered as passing from the decedent to any person" the statute specifically defines "the dower or curtesy interest (or statutory interest in lieu thereof) of such person as surviving spouse of the decedent."

The purpose of Section 2056 was to equalize federal estate tax results in community property and common law jurisdictions. In Dougherty v. United States (C.C.A. Ky. 1961) 292 F.2d 331, 337, the Court expressed this purpose thus:

> The purpose of the provision (i.e., Section 2056) was to extend to married taxpayers in common law states the advantages of residents of community property jurisdictions by permitting a surviving spouse to acquire, free from estate tax exaction, one-half of what is referred to as the adjusted gross estate of the deceased spouse. Generally speaking, the "terminable interest" concept was devised for the purpose of assuring that if the property bequeathed to the spouse was to be excluded from the gross estate of the decedent, it would be adequately integrated in the spouse's estate so that on her death, it would not escape the death tax a second time. "The basic principle . . . is that the spouse first to die shall be permitted to pass on to the surviving spouse free of estate tax up to one-half of his or her estate, provided only that the terms of the transfer are such that this property will be taxable in the estate of the surviving spouse."

Consonant with this Congressional purpose, the Courts have sought to give the statute a liberal construction, looking more to substance than to form. Accordingly, if the estate passing to the surviving spouse is such that it satisfies the purpose of the statute (i.e., becomes taxable in the estate of the surviving spouse, or as one Court has phrased, "gains only a respite and not absolution" from estate taxes), the disposition of the Courts, as evidenced in repeated decisions, is to sustain the right to a marital deduction therefor.

In this case, the widow petitioned under Sections 19-161, Chapter 3, Code of South Carolina (1962) for the admeasurement of her dower. In her petition she asked that it be assigned her in the form of a one-sixth interest in fee absolute in all lands possessed by the decedent at his death or, in case such lands were sold, in one-sixth of the proceeds of sale. Such petition was agreed to and assignment of land and cash was made to the widow. There thus passed to, and became vested in, her, from the estate of her husband, an absolute nonterminable one-sixth interest in all lands of the decedent owned by him at his death and not sold by his executor and in the proceeds of all sales of land made by the executor. It is this interest in land and in cash thus passing to the widow, which the plaintiff contends qualifies for a marital deduction under Section 2056.

The defendant argues that the property received by the widow fails to qualify, because her dower interest was, at the time of her husband's death, a terminable interest, being contingent upon her survival until dower had been definitely allotted to her. It urges that the terminability of the widow's dower interest is fixed as of the date of decedent's death and, if terminable at that time, it cannot qualify as a marital deduction. Following this reasoning, it argues that the right of the widow to the land and cash allotted to her subsequently by way of dower was contingent at the time of the decedent's death upon her survival until actual allotment of dower was made to her and that, at best, until such allotment was made, her interest by way of dower was a mere one-third life-estate, terminable, of course, on her death.

It is the general rule at common law and in most jurisdictions that (1) dower does not vest until it has been properly allotted and (2) it normally is defined as a one-third life interest. It is plain, then, that, if the statute is to be given the strict interpretation urged by the defendant, the allowance of dower as a marital deduction in any instance is precluded. Such a strict interpretation seems clearly contrary to the Congressional purpose in enacting Section 2056. It, if adopted, would make meaningless and would nullify that portion of the statute which defines "dower" as a property interest which may qualify under Section 2056. The Courts, taking a more realistic view and deferring to the obvious purpose of the statute, have with an almost complete uniformity held that dower interests, allotted, whether in cash or in land, in absolute fee qualify as a marital deduction. It is generally stated that, while, at the husband's death, the vested right of the widow to dower is "merely a right to sue for and compel the setting aside to her of her dower interest," such right, when recognized by an allotment, becomes a "vested estate" which relates back to the date of her husband's death. United States v. Crosby, supra, at p. 520 (257 F.2d); Bradham v. United States, supra, at p. 16 (287 F. Supp.). Indeed, in First National Exchange Bank of Roanoke v. United States (C.C.A. Va. 1964) 335 F.2d 91, 93, note 7, "The Government concedes (d) that the widow's election to take against her husband's will and to take her dower relates back to the date of the husband's death." Likewise, while, at time of the husband's death, the right by way of dower in the widow in practically all jurisdictions is normally spoken of as a life estate, the Courts look to the estate finally acquired by the widow in the allotment of her dower and determine then its quality under Section 2056; and, if it is represented in an absolute fee, whether in cash or in land, it qualifies. The widow in this case at no time had a life estate in the lands owned by her husband; the only estate ever allotted to her (and until allotment she had no estate) was an absolute fee and as such it qualified under Section 2056.

Actually, in South Carolina, by whose law the widow's right to dower in this case is controlled, it is traditionally assumed that the widow may, by way of dower, claim either a one-third life estate in her deceased husband's lands or a one-sixth interest in fee simple. Thus in Geiger v. Geiger (1900) 57 S.C. 521, 529, 35 S.E. 1031, the Court said that, "The rule is to allow *one-sixth absolutely* in lieu of one-third for life" (Italics by Court). This principle originated in the cases where it was not convenient to set-off in kind and a cash assessment or commutation was made. Wright v. Jennings (1829) 1 Bailey (17 S.C. Law) 277, 280; Stewart v. Pearson (1872) 4 S.C. 4, 8. But, in Asbill v. Asbill (1886) 24 S.C. 355, 359, the principle was held equally applicable, whether the allotment was a cash settlement under Section 19-166 or represented an assignment of an interest in land. Accordingly, the widow herein had a right, upon renouncing her rights under the will, to demand dower either in the form of a life estate or an estate in fee simple. Exercising her election, she chose an absolute estate; upon that election, her title in fee simple related back to the decedent's death and met the requirements of Section 2056 for a marital deduction.

It is argued by the defendant that the decisions sustaining the deductibility of dower interests under Section 2056 either antedated or failed to give proper effect to Jackson v. United States (1964) 376 U.S. 503, 84 S. Ct. 869, 11 L. Ed. 2d 871, which, under defendant's construction, proscribes dower as a marital deduction. That argument was considered and dismissed by our Circuit Court in First National Exchange Bank of Roanoke v. United States (C.C.A. Va. 1964) 335 F.2d 91, 93-94.

The Court in that case clearly distinguished between a widow's allowance under California law, which was the issue in the Jackson Case, and the widow's dower which is specifically provided for in the statute. Wachovia Bank & Trust Company v. United States (D.C.N.C. 1964) 234 F. Supp. 897, decided shortly after and on the basis of the First National Exchange Bank Case, recognized the difference between dower, when assigned as an absolute estate, and the widow's allowance, and, after giving proper effect to the Jackson Case, held that the widow's allowance in that case failed to qualify but that the dower, assigned as an absolute interest, did qualify as a marital deduction under Section 2056. (pp. 899-900) See, also, Bradham v. United States, supra, p. 17 (287 F. Supp.).

For the reasons given, I am of opinion that the allotment of dower made the widow herein qualifies as a marital deduction in the calculation of estate taxes due by the plaintiff, and that plaintiff is entitled to recover all payments made on account of its disallowance, so far as timely claim was filed therefor. Let the parties submit an order for judgment herein in conformity with this conclusion.

PROBLEM

Refer back to the problem preceding the Kennedy case. Under that decision, the wife's forced share qualifies for the marital deduction provided it is not a terminable interest. What is the amount of her share, and consequently the amount of the marital deduction? One-third of $480,000 (H's gross estate less debts, funeral and administrative expenses)? Or one-third of $480,000 minus the federal estate tax and state succession tax payable by the estate? The answer to this question has significance on two counts. First, it affects the amount actually passing to the wife as a result of her election. Does she receive $160,000, or considerably less than $160,000? Second, it affects the tax payable by the estate, since the amount passing to W determines the marital deduction.

First possibility:	$500,000	H's gross estate
	– 20,000	§§2053, 2054 deductions
	–160,000	Marital deduction
	– 60,000	Exemption
	$260,000	Taxable estate
	$ 68,900	Federal estate tax

Second possibility, in which the wife's forced share bears a pro rata burden of the federal estate tax: (This raises the "circle" problem in which there are two mutually dependent variables. The federal estate tax affects the size of the wife's share and consequently the amount of the marital deduction; the wife's share, which determines the marital deduction, affects the computation of the tax. The Regulations give guidance. Reg. §20.2056(b)-4(c)(4).)

$500,000	H's gross estate
– 20,000	§§2053, 2054 deductions
–134,290	Marital deduction
– 60,000	Exemption
$285,710	Taxable estate
$ 77,130	Federal estate tax

. . .

$500,000	H's gross estate
–20,000	Deductions
–77,130	Estate tax
$402,870	H's net estate
$134,290	W's $\frac{1}{3}$ share

CAMPBELL v. LLOYD

Supreme Court of Ohio, 1954

162 Ohio St. 203, 122 N.E.2d 695

Charles E. Roseman, Jr., herein referred to as decedent, died on March 26, 1952, leaving a will which was admitted to probate. Decedent was survived by a widow and by an infant daughter who is his only lineal descendant.

Under the terms of item II of decedent's will, his widow was given "one-half of" his "net estate . . . to be hers absolutely and in fee simple." The will gave the remainder of the estate, after certain specific bequests, to a trustee for the benefit of decedent's child with the proviso that, if the child should not live to receive all the benefits provided for her, what was left should be distributed to certain charitable organizations.

Pursuant to Section 10504-55, General Code, decedent's widow duly elected to take under the statute of descent and distribution.

Decedent's gross estate had a value of approximately $2,275,326.36. Its amount is such as to involve a substantial federal estate tax.

Plaintiff, as the duly qualified executor of decedent's estate, instituted an action in the Probate Court of Cuyahoga County for a declaratory judgment to determine whether the amount of the federal estate tax should or should not be deducted from the estate before computing the widow's one-half share of the estate.

The Probate Court rendered a judgment holding that it should be deducted.

On appeal to the Court of Appeals, 117 N.E.2d 45, that judgment was reversed and the Court of Appeals held that the amount of the federal estate tax should not be deducted from the estate before computing the widow's one-half share of the estate.

The cause is now before this court on appeal from the judgment of the Court of Appeals, pursuant to allowance of a motion to certify the record.

TAFT, Judge. As it did in Miller v. Hammond, 156 Ohio St. 475, 104 N.E.2d 9, the question to be determined in the instant case arose because of the enactment of Section 812(e), Title 26 U.S. Code, effective in 1948, by which Congress created the so-called "marital deduction" under which bequests and certain transfers to a surviving spouse qualify as deductions from the gross estate of a decedent in the computation of the federal estate tax.

Decedent's widow contends that the decision of this court in Miller v. Hammond, supra, requires affirmance of the judgment of the Court of Appeals. On the other hand, the guardian ad litem of decedent's daughter, who will be herein referred to as the guardian, contends that, because of certain provisions of Section 10504-55, General Code, pursuant to which the widow made her election, the decision of this court in Miller v. Hammond, supra, does not apply.

Section 10504-55, General Code, reads so far as pertinent:

> After the probate of the will and filing of the inventory, appraisement and schedule of debts, the probate court on the motion of the executor or administrator, or on its own motion, forthwith shall issue a citation to the surviving spouse, if any, to elect whether to take under the will or under the statute of descent and distribution. In the event of election to take under the statute of descent and distribution, *such spouse shall take not to exceed one-half of the net estate*. . . . (Emphasis added.)

The guardian contends that "the net estate" is what remains of the estate after all debts and obligations of decedent and of the estate, including the federal estate tax, have been paid; and that the widow's election can entitle her to no more than one-half of that.

We are in agreement with the Court of Appeals that the words "net estate," as used in Section 10504-55, General Code, describe the same property as do those words of Section 10503-4, General Code, which describe the property to be distributed and to descend and pass pursuant to the provisions of the latter statute. We are further of the opinion that the decision of this court in Miller v. Hammond, supra, fully supports the judgment which the Court of Appeals rendered in the instant case.

Such a decision, however, results in the widow receiving as her "one-half of the net estate," somewhere between $286,000 and $296,000 (or between 37 per cent and 42 per cent) more than all the others entitled to share in the estate. In view of this result, we are inevitably though reluctantly led to a reconsideration of our decision in Miller v. Hammond, supra. . . .

It is arguable that, in the absence of statutory provisions which would be inconsistent with such a result, this court should require an equitable apportionment of the estate tax which would relieve this widow's share of her husband's estate from part or all of the burden of the federal estate tax on his estate. The question remains whether the statutes, which provide for the rights which she claims in his estate, would be consistent with such a result.

The rights of the widow are admittedly dependent upon the provision of Section 10504-55, General Code, that she may "elect whether to take under the will or under the statute of descent and distribution" and on the provisions of the statute of descent and distribution. The applicable portion of the latter statute is Section 10503-4, General Code, which provides so far as pertinent:

> When a person dies intestate having title or right to any personal property, or to any real estate or inheritance in this state, such *personal property* shall be *distributed, and* such *real estate* or inheritance shall *descend and pass* in parcenary, except as otherwise provided by law, in the following course:
>
> . . .
>
> 2. If there be a spouse and one child, or its lineal descendants, surviving, *one-half to* the *surviving spouse* and one-half to such child or its lineal descendants, per stirpes.
>
> 3. If there be a spouse and more than one child, or their lineal descendants, surviving, one-third to the surviving spouse and the remainder to the children equally, or to the lineal descendants of any deceased child, per stirpes.
>
> . . . (Emphasis added.)

As to personal property, the statutes of this state require an executor or an administrator to pay the debts or make provision for their payment before distribution of such personal property can be made. See Sections 10509-121, 10509-181 and 10509-182, General Code. As stated in the syllabus in Tax Commission ex rel. Price v. Lamprecht, 107 Ohio St. 535, 140 N.E. 333, 31 A.L.R. 985, "in determining the value of the succession of any . . . beneficiary the *amount of* the *federal estate tax should* first *be deducted, like other debts* and expenses of administration." . . .

Under the words of Section 10503-4, General Code, applicable in the instant case, the widow will be entitled to none of the personal property of her husband until it is to "*be distributed.*" At that time, its amount will necessarily be diminished by the payment "like other debts" or provision for such payment of the federal tax on his estate. Thus, the statute gives her only one-half of that diminished amount. If therefore the personal property of the estate is sufficient to pay all charges against the estate, it would obviously be inconsistent with that statute to give her more than one-half of that diminished amount of personal property.

As in Miller v. Hammond, supra, it does not appear from the record in the instant case that the personal property available was insufficient to pay all charges against the estate. However, it may be observed that even though, under the words of Section 10503-4, General Code, "any real estate" of decedent did "descend and pass in parcenary" one-half to his widow, such real estate would be fully available to the executor to pay charges against the estate, if the personal property were insufficient. . . .

The widow further contends that "the concept of equitable apportionment . . . established" in Miller v. Hammond, supra, was "restated and applied" in McDougall v. Central National Bank of Cleveland, 157 Ohio St. 45, 104 N.E.2d 441. That case dealt with apportionment of the estate tax between assets which were a part of the decedent's estate under the law of this state (referred to therein as "probate assets") and assets which were not but which were taxed by the federal government as though they were (referred to therein as "nonprobate assets").

There was no statute which was inconsistent with an equitable apportionment of the federal estate tax burden between the probate and the nonprobate assets. See paragraph one of the syllabus and the opinion at pages 51, 52 and 55, of 157 Ohio St., at pages 444, 446 of 104 N.E.2d. Although the opinion does state that Miller v. Hammond, supra, would require the result there reached, at pages 50 and 51 of 157 Ohio St., at page 444 of 104 N.E.2d, the reasons thereafter given in the opinion and the principles of law stated in the syllabus are sufficient to sustain that decision without reference to Miller v. Hammond, supra.

Because we are of the opinion that they are inconsistent with the provisions of the statutes hereinbefore referred to, paragraphs two, three and four of the syllabus and the decision in Miller v. Hammond, supra, must be overruled. Because we are of the opinion that those statutory provisions require such a result, the judgment of the Court of Appeals is reversed and that of the Probate Court is affirmed.

Judgment reversed.

Weygandt, C.J., and Hart, Zimmerman and Lamneck, JJ., concur.

Middleton and Stewart, JJ., dissent.

Stewart, Judge (dissenting). In the case of Riggs v. Del Drago, 317 U.S. 95, 98, 63 S. Ct. 109, 87 L. Ed. 106, the Supreme Court of the United States held that Congress had not undertaken to determine the thrust of the federal estate tax, and that that thrust should be borne as the state law provides.

By Section 812(e), Title 26 U.S. Code, Congress undertook to place property of married persons residing in common-law states upon an equal basis with property of married persons residing in community-property states, so far as the federal estate tax is concerned. Where a married resident dies in a community-property state, the surviving spouse is considered to own one-half of the entire community estate in the name of the deceased spouse, which one-half is not subject to the estate tax. In a common-law state, where a surviving spouse is entitled under the statute of descent and distribution to a portion of the deceased spouse's estate, up to one-half of the estate is not, under the doctrine of equitable apportionment, subject to the federal estate tax, and, therefore, should not bear the thrust of that tax which is levied against the decedent's estate.

The other states of the Union are divided with reference to whether the surviving spouse's estate should bear any of the thrust of the tax.

On January 30, 1952, this court, in the case of Miller v. Hammond, 156 Ohio St. 475, 104 N.E.2d 9, adopted as the law of Ohio the theory of equitable apportionment and relieved a surviving spouse's share in the deceased spouse's estate from the thrust of the federal estate tax. That has been the rule in this state since that time and doubtless a large number of estates have been administered under that rule. Now, with nothing having happened in the meantime to change the atmosphere or the situation with reference to the settlement of estates, we overrule Miller v. Hammond, supra, and adopt a contrary rule, taking away from surviving spouses the advantage of the rule of equitable apportionment and giving the resulting advantage to other beneficiaries of the estate. If this were a new question in Ohio, there would be much to be said in favor of either of the rules. The rule which we adopt today might well have been originally adopted.

I am in thorough accord with the idea that it is highly proper for this court to overrule one of its former decisions, where conditions have changed, making the former decision inapplicable to the present times, or where the former decision is manifestly or clearly wrong, but it seems to me that, under the doctrine of stare decisis, where this court has laid down a rule of property, where nothing has intervened to change the conditions under which it was laid down and where the principle enunciated is overruled within a little over two years, there results an uncertainty of reliance upon our decisions. Surely the surviving spouse whose rights were settled since January 30, 1952, must rejoice that such rights are not being settled now, whereas, from now on, the other beneficiaries of a deceased spouse whose rights have been determined within the last two years must wonder why they fare so much worse than those in a similar situation to their own will fare in the future.

Middleton, J., concurs in the foregoing dissenting opinion.

NOTES AND PROBLEMS

1. The Court of Appeals decision gave the widow her share free of any burden of the federal estate tax. Why was that decision appealed? The controversy was between the decedent's wife and his infant daughter (represented by a guardian ad litem). While it is true that the reversing Ohio Supreme Court decision decreased the widow's share by some $290,000, it does not follow that it increased the child's share by a like amount. As shown by the problem preceding the Campbell case, reduction of the widow's share leads to a reduction in the marital deduction unless other offsetting assets (such as life insurance proceeds or funds in a joint bank account) have passed to the surviving spouse in a manner that qualifies for the deduction.

Suppose the decedent's child had been an adult, and that the result of burdening the widow's share with the estate tax would be to increase the tax by $120,000, and to increase the child's share by $170,000. Would you have advised the child to appeal the intermediate court decision?

2. What do you think of the dissenting judge's conception of stare decisis? Are the reasons he gave for following Miller v. Hammond persuasive? He refers to that decision as establishing "a rule of property," but he makes no mention of any reliance factor as a possible reason for following the earlier decision. Is this a relevant factor in deciding whether to follow or overrule an earlier decision in a "property" case? If so, was this factor present in the Campbell case?

3. Suppose the decedent's will provided: "I direct that all of my debts, expenses of administration and funeral expenses, and all taxes payable by reason of my death in respect of all of my property, whether passing under this will or otherwise, be paid out of my residuary estate." His wife, having elected against his will, contends that she is entitled to her forced share free of the estate tax burden, since her husband's will directed that all taxes be paid out of the assets passing under the will's residuary clause. What result? See Herson v. Mills, 221 F. Supp. 714 (D.D.C. 1963); Weeks v. Vandeveer, 13 Ohio St. 2d 15, 233 N.E.2d 502 (1968); compare In

re Barnhart Estate, 102 N.H. 519, 162 A.2d 168 (1960). See Note, 37 A.L.R.2d 7, ¶12 (1954).

4. As the dissenting opinion points out, "The other states of the Union are divided with reference to whether the surviving spouse's share should bear any of the thrust of the tax." Only a few of the forced share statutes deal with the apportionment problem. Thus the courts are forced to reach a decision by construing language in a statute that did not address itself to the problem, or by seeking guidance in the language of a will that was drafted on the premise that the widow would take under, not against, it.

With the principal case compare Estate of Jones, 376 S.W.2d 210 (Mo. 1964) and Lincoln Bank & Trust Co. v. Huber, 240 S.W.2d 89 (Ky. 1951). See generally Kahn, The Federal Estate Tax Burden Borne by a Dissenting Widow, 64 Mich. L. Rev. 1499 (1966).

5. What is the message of these tax cases for the draftsman of a husband's will in a common law state?

5. *Lifetime Transfers to Defeat the Widow's Share*

A major difficulty with the forced share statutes in most states is that property transferred inter vivos may not be subject to the forced share. Few statutes expressly deal with inter vivos transfers, which have greatly increased since the days when the forced share statutes were passed and deemed to protect the spouse. The pattern of donative transfers has changed. Inter vivos transfers in general have become more frequent. Among the reasons for this: (1) There is greater awareness of the favorable tax treatment accorded lifetime transfers in the form of exclusions, exemptions and lower tax rates. (2) Because the amount of wealth has greatly increased, and because more persons are more conscious of the tax and other advantages of trusts, the number of trusts has risen sharply in recent years. Today's lawyers, and their clients, are more sophisticated about the various devices that can serve as alternatives or supplements to a will. (3) Probate, with its attendant costs, delays and restrictions, can be avoided by various dispositions that permit retention of controls over and economic benefits from the property transferred. At the top of the list are the joint tenancy, the joint bank account, and the funded revocable trust.

In addition, there apparently have been changes in society which result in an increasing number of husbands desiring to avoid the widow's forced share.[15] (1) The higher divorce rate in contemporary society may indicate an increase in family disharmony.[16] (2) A very high percentage of divorced or widowed persons re-

[15] For the view that very few spouses are disinherited and elect to take against the decedent's will, see Plager, The Spouse's Nonbarrable Share: A Solution in Search of a Problem, 33 U. Chi. L. Rev. 681 (1966).

[16] In the United States one out of every eleven marriages ended in divorce in 1900. By the 1940s one out of every three marriages ended in divorce. See Macdonald, Fraud on the Widow's Share 10-15 (1960).

"The increase in divorces and annulments continued in 1969 for the seventh consecutive year. The national total was 639,000, larger by 55,000, or 9.4 percent, than the comparable figure for 1968 (584,000). The 1969 total was more than 50 percent larger than the 1962 total (413,000).

marry.[17] This often results in a conflict between the second wife and children of the first wife. The husband cannot leave his property to his spouse with any assurance that she will leave it to her stepchildren.[18] (3) Remarriages are frequently for convenience or companionship. This is partly attributable to the fact that the basic family unit which lives together no longer commonly includes grandmother and grandfather. The aged, no longer welcome among the young, may find companionship through remarriage. Fifty years ago it was a rare case when a man's widow was not the woman he had been married to for many years and who had borne his children. Today it is not unusual to find that a man's widow is his second wife, or that he was her second husband.

What effect do these changes in the American family, and in the pattern of donative transfers, have upon judicial decisions? What effect *should* they have upon decisions and upon statutes dealing with the forced share and its avoidance?

NEWMAN v. DORE

Court of Appeals of New York, 1937

275 N.Y. 371, 9 N.E.2d 966

LEHMAN, Judge. Ferdinand Straus died on July 1, 1934, leaving a last will and testament dated May 5, 1934, which contained a provision for a trust for his wife for her life of one-third of the decedent's property both real and personal. In such case the statute did not give the wife a right of election to take her share of the estate as in intestacy.[19] She receives the income for life from a trust fund of the amount of the intestate share, but does not take the share. That share is one-third of the decedent's estate. It includes no property which does not form part of the estate at

---

The recent increases cannot be explained by the growth of the population, since the divorce rates increased considerably during the same period.

"The national divorce rate was 3.2 per 1,000 population in 1969 as compared with 2.9 in 1968 and 2.2 in 1962. The growth of the rate from 1962 to 1969 was 45 percent, only slightly less than that for the number of divorces. The rate per 1,000 married women was 13.4 in 1969, 12.4 in 1968, and 9.4 in 1962, an increase of 43 percent from 1962 to 1969.

"From 1968 to 1969 divorce totals increased in the District of Columbia and in all States except Indiana and Texas. In eight States the annual growth was very pronounced, between 20 and 50 percent. In some of these States this increase was due to the liberalization of divorce laws." Public Health Service, U.S. HEW Dept., Monthly Vital Statistics Report, July 22, 1971.

[17] "In the period 1960 to 1966, about 3 out of 10 divorced men remarried in the first year after divorce. Approximately one-fourth of those not remarried by the end of the first year remarried by the end of the second year. Thus, by the end of the second year of divorce, about one-half of the men were remarried. . . .

"Between 1960 and 1966, one in four divorced women remarried in the first year after divorce. By the end of the third year of divorce, one-half of the divorced women were remarried." Bureau of the Census, U.S. Commerce Dept., Current Population Reports — Special Studies, July 29, 1970.

[18] Cf. Oursler v. Armstrong, page 365, supra.

[19] At the time of this case N.Y. Decedent Estate Law §18 gave the surviving spouse a right to elect his or her intestate share, unless "the testator has devised or bequeathed in trust an amount equal to or greater than the intestate share, with income thereof payable to the surviving spouse for life." Under id. §83, Mrs. Straus's intestate share was one-third of her husband's estate. — EDS.

the decedent's death. The testator on June 28, 1934, three days before his death, executed trust agreements by which, in form at least, he transferred to trustees all his real and personal property. If the agreements effectively divested the settlor of title to his property, then the decedent left no estate and the widow takes nothing. The widow has challenged the validity of the transfer to the trustees. The beneficiary named in the trust agreement has brought this action to compel the trustees to carry out its terms. The trial court has found that the "trust agreements were made, executed and delivered by said Ferdinand Straus for the purpose of evading and circumventing the laws of the State of New York, and particularly sections 18 and 83 of the Decedent Estate Law." Undoubtedly the settlor's purpose was to provide that at his death his property should pass to beneficiaries named in the trust agreement to the exclusion of his wife. Under the provisions of the Decedent Estate Law the decedent could not effect the desired purpose by testamentary disposition of his property. The problem in this case is whether he has accomplished that result by creating a trust during his lifetime.

The validity of the attempted transfer depends upon whether "the laws of the State of New York and particularly sections 18 and 83 of the Decedent Estate Law" prohibit or permit such transfer. . . . The statute gives to a spouse a property right. The question is, how far the statute protects that right even while it remains only expectant and contingent. . . . Here, we should point out that the courts below have not based their decision primarily upon the finding that the trust agreements were executed for the purpose of evading and circumventing the law of the state of New York. The courts have also found, and the evidence conclusively establishes, that the trust agreements were made for the purpose of depriving the decedent's widow of any rights in and to his property upon his death. Under the trust agreements executed a few days before the death of the settlor, he reserved the enjoyment of the entire income as long as he should live, and a right to revoke the trust at his will, and in general the powers granted to the trustees were in terms made "subject to the settlor's control during his life," and could be exercised "in such manner only as the settlor shall from time to time direct in writing." Thus, by the trust agreement which transferred to the trustees the settlor's entire property, the settlor reserved substantially the same rights to enjoy and control the disposition of the property as he previously had possessed, and the inference is inescapable that the trust agreements were executed by the settlor, as the court has found, "with the intention and for the purpose of diminishing his estate and thereby to reduce in amount the share" of his wife in his estate upon his death and as a "contrivance to deprive . . . his widow of any rights in and to his property upon his death." They had no other purpose and substantially they had no other effect. Does the statute intend that such a transfer shall be available as a means of defeating the contingent expectant estate of a spouse?

In a few states where a wife has a similar contingent expectant interest or estate in the property of her husband, it has been held that her rights may not be defeated by any transfer made during life with intent to deprive the wife of property, which under the law would otherwise pass to her. Thayer v. Thayer, 14 Vt. 107, 39 Am. Dec. 211; Evans v. Evans, 78 N.H. 352, 100 A. 671; Dyer v. Smith, 62 Mo. App.

606; Payne v. Tatem, 236 Ky. 306, 33 S.W.(2d) 2. In those states it is the intent to defeat the wife's contingent rights which creates the invalidity and it seems that an absolute transfer of all his property by a married man during his life, if made with other purpose and intent than to cut off an unloved wife, is valid even though its effect is to deprive the wife of any share in the property of her husband at his death. Dunnett v. Shields & Conant, 97 Vt. 419, 123 A. 626; Patch v. Squires, 105 Vt. 405, 165 A. 919. The rule has been stated that "while the wife cannot complain of reasonable gifts or advancements by a husband to his children by a former marriage, yet, if the gifts constitute the principal part of the husband's estate and be made without the wife's knowledge, a presumption of fraud arises, and it rests upon the beneficiaries to explain away that presumption." Payne v. Tatem, supra, 236 Ky. 306, at page 308, 33 S.W.(2d) 2, 3.[20]

Motive or intent is an unsatisfactory test of the validity of a transfer of property. In most jurisdictions it has been rejected, sometimes for the reason that it would cast doubt upon the validity of all transfers made by a married man, outside of the regular course of business; sometimes because it is difficult to find a satisfactory logical foundation for it. Intent may, at times, be relevant in determining whether an act is fraudulent, but there can be no fraud where no right of any person is invaded. "The great weight of authority is that the intent to defeat a claim which otherwise a wife might have is not enough to defeat the deed." Leonard v. Leonard, 181 Mass. 458, 462, 63 N.E. 1068, 1069, 92 Am. St. Rep. 426, and cases there cited. Since the law gives the wife only an expectant interest in the property of her husband which becomes part of his estate, and since the law does not restrict transfers of property by the husband during his life, it would seem that the only sound test of the validity of a challenged transfer is whether it is real or illusory. That is the test applied in Leonard v. Leonard, supra. The test has been formulated in different ways, but in most jurisdictions the test applied is essentially the test of whether the husband has in good faith divested himself of ownership of his property or has made an illusory transfer. "The 'good faith' required of the donor or settlor in making a valid disposition of his property during life does not refer to the purpose to affect his wife but to the intent to divest himself of the ownership of the property. It is, therefore, apparent that the fraudulent intent which will defeat a gift inter vivos cannot be predicated of the husband's intent to deprive the wife of her distributive . . . share as widow." Benkart v. Commonwealth Trust Co., of Pittsburgh, 269 Pa. 257, 259, 112 A. 62, 63. . . . In other jurisdictions transfers in trust have been upheld regardless of their purpose where a husband retained a right to enjoy the income during his life. . . . In some of these cases the settlor retained, also, a power of revocation. In no jurisdiction has a transfer in trust been upheld where the conveyance is intended only to cover up the fact that the husband is retaining full control of the property though in form he has parted with it. Though

[20] In jurisdictions applying the "motive" or "intent" test, the following criteria are often used in place of, or in addition to, "subjective intent": (a) proportion of decedent's property included in the inter vivos transfer; (b) proximity of the transfer to the date of death; (c) provision by the decedent for the surviving spouse by will or by inter vivos transfer; (d) closeness of relationship between decedent and donee; and (e) relative equities of the spouse and donee. See Macdonald, Fraud on the Widow's Share 98-119, 145-174, 379-400 (1960). — Eds.

a person may use means lawfully available to him to keep outside of the scope of a statute, a false appearance of legality, however attained, will not avail him. Reality, not appearance, should determine legal rights. Cf. Jenkins v. Moyse, 254 N.Y. 319, 172 N.E. 521, 74 A.L.R. 205.

In this case the decedent, as we have said, retained not only the income for life and power to revoke the trust, but also the right to control the trustees. We need not now determine whether such a trust is, for any purpose, a valid present trust. It has been said that, "where the settlor transfers property in trust and reserves not only . . . a power to revoke and modify the trust but also such power to control the trustee as to the details of the administration of the trust that the trustee is the agent of the settlor, the disposition so far as it is intended to take effect after his death is testamentary. . . ." American Law Institute, Restatement of the Law of Trusts, §57, subd. 2. We do not now consider whether the rule so stated is in accord with the law of this state or whether in this case the reserved power of control is so great that the trustee is in fact "the agent of the settlor." We assume, without deciding, that except for the provisions of section 18 of the Decedent Estate Law the trust would be valid. . . . Perhaps "from the technical point of view such a conveyance does not quite take back all that it gives, but practically it does." That is enough to render it an unlawful invasion of the expectant interest of the wife. . . .

Judged by the substance, not by the form, the testator's conveyance is illusory, intended only as a mask for the effective retention by the settlor of the property which in form he had conveyed. We do not attempt now to formulate any general test of how far a settlor must divest himself of his interest in the trust property to render the conveyance more than illusory. Question of whether reservation of the income or of a power of revocation, or both, might even without reservation of the power of control be sufficient to show that the transfer was not intended in good faith to divest the settlor of his property must await decision until such question arises. In this case it is clear that the settlor never intended to divest himself of his property. He was unwilling to do so even when death was near.

The judgment should be affirmed, with costs.

Crane, C.J., and Hubbs, Loughran and Rippey, JJ., concur.

Finch, J., concurs in result.

O'Brien, J., takes no part.[21]

NOTES AND PROBLEMS

1. The decision in Newman v. Dore truly merits the label, "leading case." The "illusory transfer" test laid down by the court quickly spread to other states. The entry for the case in Shepard's Citator runs for three columns and includes citations to decisions in sixteen other states, as well as a host of later New York cases that

[21] Noted 7 Brooklyn L. Rev. 241; 37 Colum. L. Rev. 1219; 23 Cornell L.Q. 457; 7 Fordham L. Rev. 115; 26 Geo. L.J. 784; 36 Mich. L. Rev. 496; 12 St. John's L. Rev. 355; 5 U. Chi. L. Rev. 504. — Eds.

have applied, explained, followed, distinguished away or questioned the holding of Newman v. Dore. See the parade of cases from many jurisdictions in Ackers v. First National Bank, 192 Kan. 319, 387 P.2d 840 (1963), which held a revocable trust illusory and permitted the surviving spouse to take her forced share out of its assets.

2. In the last paragraph of its opinion the New York court chose not to formulate a general test of "illusoriness." Instead, it left the scope of the doctrine to be resolved on a case-by-case basis. Decisions from other jurisdictions have seen as one of the advantages of the doctrine that it "expressly avoids the formulation of a fixed test for defining an illusory trust, but instead, states a general and flexible test which is more adaptable to varied situations." Land v. Marshall, 426 S.W.2d 841, 848 (Tex. 1968).

What are the advantages and disadvantages of this approach? Is it desirable from the standpoint of a widow who is thinking about challenging a particular lifetime transfer? From the standpoint of a husband, or his attorney, who wants to make a disposition that will secure the husband's planning objectives? Johanson, Revocable Trusts and Community Property: The Substantive Problems, 47 Texas L. Rev. 537, 561-562 (1969).

3. What kind or degree of control retained by a transferor will cause the transfer to be illusory? Consider the following transfers (the donor is designated as H, the donee as A):

(1) inter vivos trust for benefit of A except
  (a) income retained by H.
  (b) power to consume principal retained by H.
  (c) power to appoint by will retained by H.
  (d) power to revoke retained by H.
  (e) control over administration of the trust retained by H.
(2) deed of real estate to A
  (a) with life estate retained by H.
  (b) in escrow with B with directions to B to deliver deed to A upon death of H.
  (c) with power to revoke retained by H.
(3) gift causa mortis to A.
(4) joint tenancy in real property (H and A).
(5) joint bank account (payable to H or A or survivor).
(6) joint safe deposit box (H and A each have access).
(7) Totten trust (savings account in name of H, in trust for A).
(8) U.S. government savings bonds (in name of H, payable on death to A).
(9) transfer of partnership interest to surviving partner under the partnership agreement (H and A are partners).
(10) designation of A as beneficiary of life insurance policies on H's life.
(11) designation of A as beneficiary of pension plan or employee death benefits.

The cases, which leave little room for dogmatic statement, are collected in Macdonald, Fraud on the Widow's Share 181-245, 401-405 (1960); Notes, 49 A.L.R.2d

521 (1956); 157 A.L.R. 1184 (1944); 112 A.L.R. 649 (1937); 64 A.L.R. 466 (1929).

4. If a lawyer advises a husband to use one of the above devices, and expressly or impliedly represents that it will not be subject to the wife's forced share, will the lawyer be liable to the donee if the transfer is held illusory? Cf. Heyer v. Flaig, page 21, supra.

KERWIN v. DONAGHY

Supreme Judicial Court of Massachusetts

317 Mass. 559, 59 N.E.2d 299 (1945)

LUMMUS, Justice. [William J. Kerwin had four children by his first wife: William, Jr., Harold, Gladys, and Ernest. He married his second wife, Lillian, in 1926 when he was fifty-seven and she was thirty-nine. At that time Kerwin was worth half a million dollars. William, Jr., predeceased his father, leaving a widow but no issue. William J. Kerwin died in 1941. His will, executed in 1928, gave his residuary estate in five equal parts to Lillian, William, Jr., Harold, Gladys, and Ernest. Lillian (the widow) waived the will and claimed the share that she would have taken had William J. Kerwin died intestate. Lillian and Ernest then brought this petition in equity against Gladys and the executors (the executors having refused to bring suit) to recover for the estate a large number of stocks, bonds, and deposits in banks, standing in the name of Gladys, but allegedly owned by William J. Kerwin. The Probate Court ordered Gladys to deliver the stocks, bonds, and bank deposits to the executors of the estate. Gladys appealed.]

The judge found in substance that from a time as early as 1923 William J. Kerwin was addicted to the folly of carrying most of his property in the names of some of his children, with the understanding that it should remain his and should be turned back to him at his request. His purpose was to defraud the Federal government by pretending to divide his income so as to avoid large surtaxes. The parts of his property held by his children other than Gladys were conveyed either to Gladys or back to him. In 1929 and thereafter the bulk of his property was held by and in the name of Gladys, and was kept in a safe deposit box of which she was the proprietor, although he had access to the box and kept the key to it in his desk. Many of the stock certificates, standing in her name, bore and still bear her indorsement in blank. In 1934, apparently with his consent, she cancelled his right of access, but that, the judge found, "was entirely consistent with a desire on Mr. Kerwin's part to make it appear, in case it should be questioned, that Gladys and not he was the owner of the contents of the box. He would have no difficulty in having Gladys go to the box with him and he kept the key to the box in his desk. It was customary when Mr. Kerwin wanted money to telephone Gladys to put it in his bank account which she promptly did whenever he called, excepting towards the last" of his life, during his last illness. During 1940 she paid him at his request about $15,000. It is hard to see how the surtaxes could be lessened by holding the bulk of his property in the name of Gladys after he ceased in 1927 to earn money, unless upon the tax returns the income was divided between him and Gladys. Whether it was or not does not appear.

Nothing in the relations of William J. Kerwin with his children made it likely that he would wish at any time to give all his property to Gladys and cut the others off. The judge found that "Mr. Kerwin and his wife got along well excepting for occasional times when there were some disagreements, but not very serious, and towards the last of his life they were very close to each other and he was solicitous for her welfare." Nevertheless the judge found that "he told Harold that he had put stock in Gladys' name because Mrs. Kerwin made so many demands for money he was going to see when he passed on that his children were going to have the money." It was, the judge found, "as a result of a temporary disagreement between William J. Kerwin and his wife" that he executed two trust agreements in August, 1936.

At that time William J. Kerwin consulted John D. Kenney, Esquire, a lawyer in New Bedford. Kerwin came alone at the first visit to the lawyer, but on later occasions Gladys accompanied him. He told the lawyer that he wished to make sure that at his death Gladys would own the property that she was holding for him. The lawyer advised him that a will would be ineffective, for his wife could waive the will. The lawyer advised a trust, and two formal trust agreements were drawn, and were executed by William J. Kerwin and by Gladys. One agreement dealt with the stocks and bonds, the other with the bank deposits. The agreements were substantially identical in their terms.

In these agreements Gladys declared herself trustee of a large number of specified stocks, bonds and bank deposits "to pay the net income therefrom to said William J. Kerwin, for and during the term of his natural life . . . and upon the decease of said William J. Kerwin to hold said fund, together with any undistributed income therefrom, to her own use and behoof absolutely forever." He reserved the right during his life "to alter, amend or revoke this agreement in whole or in part, by giving written notice thereof to said Gladys M. Donaghy." He covenanted, agreed and declared that he had no interest in the trust property except that set forth in the agreements. It was provided that "this trust agreement shall be binding upon the heirs, executors and administrators of the parties hereto." It was provided that the trustee "shall not be obligated to disclose the existence of this trust to any person, nor shall she be required to have said securities registered or recorded in her name as trustee, nor shall she be forbidden to mingle said securities or the income therefrom with her own funds." . . .

The property covered by the two trust agreements comprised substantially all the property that William J. Kerwin had. . . . Late in 1940 he was disturbed about the condition of his affairs, and was trying to reach Gladys for the purpose of arranging his affairs so that what he considered his property would form part of his estate if he should die, to the end that his wife and all his children would be protected. Gladys apparently avoided any considerable talk with him. He was in bad health, and entirely dependent on Gladys for money. On October 9, 1940, he got Gladys and Harold together, and asked them whether they would do the "right thing" by his wife. When they said they would, he fell on his knees and said "Thank God for that." He apparently rested content with that vague assurance, and did not then remember or appreciate the fact that under the trust agreements he had reserved a power of revocation of the trusts. Not unlikely he was then too ill to take decisive action, and still trusted Gladys, although he was beginning to doubt her. When he died there was little if anything remaining in his hands. . . .

Lillian A. Kerwin and Ernest W. Kerwin claim under William J. Kerwin. They stand in his shoes. If title passed to Gladys as against William J. Kerwin, it passed to her as against his legatees. When the trust agreements were executed, the property to which they related was already in the possession of Gladys, and most if not all of it stood in her name. Those agreements contemplated the holding by her of the legal title. Under those circumstances no formal delivery of the property itself was necessary to vest the legal title in her. . . .

The trust agreements furnish incontrovertible internal evidence that they were intended to express the whole transaction between Gladys and her father. He covenanted, agreed and declared under seal that he had no right, power or interest in the trust property except such as was set forth in the trust agreements. The beneficial interest was completely disposed of by giving him an equitable life estate and Gladys the "remainder to her own use and behoof absolutely forever." His apparent purpose to render a will practically unnecessary, and his reserved power to alter, amend or revoke the trust, did not make the trust testamentary in its nature. National Shawmut Bank v. Joy, 315 Mass. 457, 469, 475, 477, 478. The reserved power could be exercised only according to its terms and since there was never even an attempt to exercise it there was no impairment of the rights in remainder given to Gladys. Kelley v. Snow, 185 Mass. 288, 298. Coates v. Lunt, 210 Mass. 314; Clune v. Norton, 306 Mass. 324; National Shawmut Bank v. Joy, 315 Mass. 457, 462, 474, 475. There was no mistake in drafting the trust agreements. Plainly they conformed to the purpose of William J. Kerwin at the time, that of disinheriting his wife. He could hardly have been so obtuse as to fail to see that they disinherited his sons also in plain words.

As matter of law the trust instruments must be taken as intended to accomplish the very purpose of the so-called "parol evidence rule," that of fixing beyond all question the rights of the parties to those agreements in accordance with their terms, and to preclude resort to extrinsic evidence apart from exceptional and strictly limited instances of need that are not applicable to this case. As to trusts, a learned author has said, "Under the parol evidence rule, if the manifestation of intention of the settlor is integrated in a writing, that is, if a written instrument is adopted by him as the complete expression of his intention, extrinsic evidence, in the absence of fraud, duress, mistake or other ground for reformation or rescission, is not admissible to contradict or vary it." Scott, Trusts (1939) §§38, 164.1. That statement finds support in our decisions. Coolidge v. Loring, 235 Mass. 220; Gorey v. Guarente, 303 Mass. 569, 573, 574. Though often stated in terms of the admissibility of evidence, the so-called "parol evidence rule" is really a rule of substantive law. Extrinsic evidence, even though admitted, cannot control the words of a document that purports to express the whole transaction. . . .

It is true that a written contract or other instrument may be invalidated by extrinsic proof that it was executed as a joke or even in some instances as a pretence, with no intention on the part of either party that it should create any legal right or obligation. Williston, Contracts (Rev. ed. 1936) §21; Beaman-Marvell Co. v. Gunn, 306 Mass. 419, 422, 423; Zell v. American Seating Co., 2 Cir., 138 F.2d 641, 644. . . . [I]n our opinion an inference of fact could not properly be drawn that the trust agreements were intended merely as shams. The evident purpose at the time was to disinherit the wife. The husband was careful to reserve the right to revoke the trusts, and revest the trust property in himself. The correct conclusion, we think, is that the trust agreements express the actual intention of the parties at the time.

Even if, notwithstanding the terms of the trust agreements, the remainder passing to Gladys under those agreements might be subjected to a trust in favor of her brothers and Lillian A. Kerwin by proof of an oral promise by Gladys to share the remainder with them, . . . the difficulty in this case would be that there is little evidence of such an oral promise. The trust agreements themselves, and all that was said when they were drawn and executed, negative any promise that would benefit Lillian A. Kerwin, for the plain purpose was to disinherit her. Neither was there anything said or done at that time to show a promise to hold for the other children. If there had been such a promise, it would not support the present petition which is brought for the benefit of the estate generally. The only conduct of Gladys that might be thought to recognize the claim of Lillian A. Kerwin was her promise, jointly with Harold who had no property in his hands, made on October 9, 1940, when their father was in his last illness and mentally disturbed, to "do the right thing" by Lillian. Such a promise by Harold could hardly have reference to a money settlement out of property of his father in his hands, for there was no such property. The promise by Gladys was in identical words. We cannot find that such a vague promise amounted to an understanding to hold for the distributees of the father's estate the remainder given to Gladys by the trust agreements. . . .

The judge found that the trust agreements "constituted an illusive device to deprive the wife of any substantial interest in her husband's estate as his widow." It has been shown already that that "device" was not "illusory," but was one that fixed the rights of the parties to those agreements. The judge found further that William J. Kerwin, if the trust agreements were intended to be effective, "intended to cheat his wife." He could not "cheat" her in any legal sense by means of those agreements unless she had rights that were paramount to his right to do what he pleased in his lifetime with his own personal property. . . .

The limitation found in some of our cases upon the right of a husband to disinherit his wife by a conveyance or gift of personal property inter vivos, that the conveyance or gift must not be "colorable," . . . means merely that the conveyance or gift must be one legally binding on the settlor or donor, accomplished in his lifetime, and not testamentary in its effect. In other words, it must be an actual conveyance or gift. Potter Title & Trust Co. v. Braum, 294 Pa. 482, 64 A.L.R. 463. In Newman v. Dore, 275 N.Y. 371, 112 A.L.R. 643, complete control of the trustee, reserved to the settlor, was held to make testamentary and invalid a settlement designed to disinherit his wife. See also Krause v. Krause, 285 N.Y. 27; Brown v.

Crafts, 98 Me. 40, 45. The soundness of that ground was recently left open by us in National Shawmut Bank v. Joy, 315 Mass. 457, 476. In the present case no such control was reserved.

Cases are not in point that hold invalid a conveyance by a husband to defeat a possible decree for the support of his wife. Shepherd v. Shepherd, 196 Mass. 179. Doane v. Doane, 238 Mass. 106, 112. Caines v. Sawyer, 248 Mass. 368, 374. Neither are cases holding invalid a gift made by a husband for the purpose of reducing the share of his estate to which his wife is entitled under an antenuptial contract. Eaton v. Eaton, 233 Mass. 351, 369, et seq. Nor are cases in which a woman married a man of supposed means in ignorance of the fact that on the eve of marriage he had conveyed away all his property for the purpose of defeating her expectations. Gedart v. Ejdrygiewicz, 305 Mass. 224. LeStrange v. LeStrange, 242 App. Div. (N.Y.) 74. Collins v. Collins, 98 Md. 473.

. . . [The] findings and orders contained in the final decree upon [the petition of Lillian A. Kerwin,] . . . are to be stricken out.

So ordered.

NOTES AND PROBLEMS

1. With the reasoning of the court in Kerwin v. Donaghy compare the reasoning of the Red Queen:

> "Try another subtraction sum. Take a bone from a dog; what remains?"
>
> Alice considered. "The bone wouldn't remain of course, if I took it — and the dog wouldn't remain; it would come to bite me — and I'm sure I shouldn't remain!"
>
> "Then you think nothing would remain?" said the Red Queen.
>
> "I think that's the answer."
>
> "Wrong, as usual," said the Red Queen. "The dog's temper would remain."
>
> "But I don't see how —"
>
> "Why, look here!" the Red Queen cried. "The dog would lose its temper, wouldn't it?"
>
> "Perhaps it would," Alice replied cautiously.
>
> "Then if the dog went away, its temper would remain!" the Queen exclaimed triumphantly.
>
> — Carroll, Through the Looking Glass

2. In Kerwin v. Donaghy the court holds that if the husband had made a "transfer" of property during his lifetime, his widow cannot reach it. By what criteria do we determine whether a "transfer" has been made? By the same criteria used to determine whether an inter vivos transfer is "testamentary"? Is the problem the same, and are the policies the same, when the question is (a) whether the spouse can avoid the forced share and (b) whether the transfer must comply with the formal requirements of the Statute of Wills? What policies are relevant here? See Macdonald, Fraud on the Widow's Share 20-46 (1960); Simes, Public Policy and the Dead Hand 28-31 (1955).

Statutory Solutions

Only a few states have statutes dealing with the problem of the lifetime transfer. The Model Probate Code §33 (1946) would enable the surviving spouse to reach any transfer "in fraud of the marital rights of his surviving spouse," and would raise a presumption that any transfer made within two years of death is in fraud of her rights. The fraud test, but not the two-year presumption, has been adopted in Missouri and Wisconsin. Mo. Ann. Stat. §474.150(1) (1956); Wis. Stat. Ann. §861.17 (1971). The commentary on the Wisconsin statute states that "[t]he problem is essentially left to the courts to apply a flexible concept to meet unusual cases where one spouse depletes the probate estate deliberately to avoid the election." 40H Wis. Stat. Ann. 458 (1971). The "fraud" test weighs a wide variety of factors. See, e.g., Merz v. Tower Grove Bank & Trust Company, 344 Mo. 1150, 130 S.W.2d 611 (1939); Note, 21 Mo. L. Rev. 151 (1956).

The Vermont statute allows the widow to reach conveyances of real estate by her husband "made during coverture and not to take effect until after his decease, and made with the intent to defeat his widow in her claim to her share of his real estate." Vt. Stat. Ann. tit. 14, §473 (1958). Cases have extended the "intent" test to transfers of personalty. See, e.g., Patch v. Squires, 105 Vt. 405, 165 Atl. 919 (1933). A Tennessee statute combines the "fraud" and "intent" tests by giving the surviving spouse the right to reach conveyances "made fraudulently . . . with an intent to defeat the widow of her dower, or distributive share." Tenn. Code Ann. §31-612 (1955).

The New York statute, applicable to transfers made after August 31, 1966, allows the surviving spouse to reach gifts causa mortis, savings accounts payable on death to another person, assets held in joint tenancy, and any other disposition of property "to the extent that the decedent at the date of his death retained . . . by the express provisions of the disposing instrument, a power to revoke such disposition or power to consume, invade or dispose of the principal thereof." N.Y. Estates, Powers & Trusts Law §5-1.1(b)(1) (1967). Section (b)(2) of the New York statute excludes payments under pension funds and trusts, insurance proceeds, and United States government bonds. See Note, 33 Brooklyn L. Rev. 530 (1967). The Third Report of N.Y. State Commission on Modernization of the Law of Estates, Leg. Doc. 19 (1964), is a comprehensive study basing the New York legislation.

The Pennsylvania statute, which also has been enacted in Minnesota, provides: "A conveyance of assets by a person who retains a power of appointment by will, or a power of revocation or consumption over the principal thereof, shall at the election of the surviving spouse, be treated as a testamentary disposition so far as his surviving spouse is concerned to the extent to which the power has been reserved." Pa. Stat. Ann. tit. 20, §301.11 (1950, Supp. 1971); Minn. Stat. Ann. §525.213 (1969, Supp. 1971), noted, 54 Minn. L. Rev. 1029 (1970). Both statutes exclude life insurance proceeds.

UNIFORM PROBATE CODE

§2-201. [Right to Elective Share.] (a) If a married person domiciled in this state dies, the surviving spouse has a right of election to take an elective share of one-third of the augmented estate under the limitations and conditions hereinafter stated.

(b) If a married person not domiciled in this state dies, the right, if any, of the surviving spouse to take an elective share in property in this state is governed by the law of the decedent's domicile at death.

§2-202. [Augmented Estate.] The augmented estate means the estate reduced by funeral and administration expenses, homestead allowance, family allowances and exemptions, and enforceable claims, to which is added the sum of the following amounts:

(1) The value of property transferred by the decedent at any time during marriage, to or for the benefit of any person other than the surviving spouse, to the extent that the decedent did not receive adequate and full consideration in money or money's worth for the transfer, if the transfer is of any of the following types:

(i) any transfer under which the decedent retained at the time of his death the possession or enjoyment of, or right to income from, the property;

(ii) any transfer to the extent that the decedent retained at the time of his death a power, either alone or in conjunction with any other person, to revoke or to consume, invade or dispose of the principal for his own benefit;

(iii) any transfer whereby property is held at the time of decedent's death by decedent and another with right of survivorship;

(iv) any transfer made within two years of death of the decedent to the extent that the aggregate transfers to any one donee in either of the years exceed $3,000.

(2) Any transfer is excluded if made with the written consent or joinder of the surviving spouse. Property is valued as of the decedent's death except that property given irrevocably to a donee during lifetime of the decedent is valued as of the date the donee came into possession or enjoyment if that occurs first. Nothing herein shall cause to be included in the augmented estate any life insurance, accident insurance, joint annuity, or pension payable to a person other than the surviving spouse.

(3) The value of property owned by the surviving spouse at the decedent's death, plus the value of property transferred by the spouse at any time during marriage to any person other than the decedent which would have been includible in the spouse's augmented estate if the surviving spouse had predeceased the decedent, to the extent the owned or transferred property is derived from the decedent by any means other than testate or intestate succession without a full consideration in money or money's worth. For purposes of this subsection:

(i) Property derived from the decedent includes, but is not limited to, any beneficial interest of the surviving spouse in a trust created by the decedent during his lifetime, any property appointed to the spouse by the decedent's exercise of a general or special power of appointment also exercisable in favor of others than the spouse, any proceeds of insurance (including accidental death benefits) on the life of the decedent attributable to premiums paid by him, any lump sum immediately payable and the commuted value of the proceeds of annuity contracts under which the decedent was the primary annuitant attributable to premiums paid by him, the commuted value of amounts payable after the decedent's death under any public or private pension, disability compensation, death benefit or retirement plan, exclusive of the Federal Social Security system, by reason of service performed or disabilities incurred by the decedent, and the value of the share of the surviving spouse resulting from rights in community property in this or any other state formerly owned with the decedent. Premiums paid by the decedent's employer, his partner, a partnership of which he was a member, or his creditors, are deemed to have been paid by the decedent.

(ii) Property owned by the spouse at the decedent's death is valued as of the date of death. Property transferred by the spouse is valued at the time the transfer became irrevocable, or at the decedent's death, whichever occurred first. Income earned by included property prior to the decedent's death is not treated as property derived from the decedent.

(iii) Property owned by the surviving spouse as of the decedent's death, or previously transferred by the surviving spouse, is presumed to have been derived from the decedent except to the extent that the surviving spouse establishes that it was derived from another source.

COMMENT

Although the system described herein may seem complex, it should not complicate administration of a married person's estate in any but very unusual cases. The surviving spouse rather than the executor or the probate court has the burden of asserting an election, as well as the burden of proving the matters which must be shown in order to make a successful claim to more than he or she has received. Some of the apparent complexity arises from Section 2-202, which has the effect of compelling an electing spouse to allow credit for all funds attributable to the decedent when the spouse, by electing, is claiming that more is due. This feature should serve to reduce the number of instances in which an elective share will be asserted. Finally, Section 2-204 expands the effectiveness of attempted waivers and releases of rights to claim an elective share. Thus, means by which estate planners can assure clients that their estates will not become embroiled in election litigation are provided.

Uniformity of law on the problems covered by this Part is much to be desired. It is especially important that states limit the applicability of rules protecting spouses so that only estates of domiciliary decedents are involved.

. . .

The purpose of the concept of augmenting the probate estate in computing the elective share is twofold: (1) to prevent the owner of wealth from making arrangements which transmit his property to others by means other than probate deliberately to defeat the right of the surviving spouse to a share, and (2) to prevent the surviving spouse from electing a share of the probate estate when the spouse has received a fair share of the total wealth of the decedent either during the lifetime of the decedent or at death by life insurance, joint tenancy assets and other nonprobate arrangements. Thus essentially two separate groups of property are added to the net probate estate to arrive at the augmented net estate which is the basis for computing the one-third share of the surviving spouse. In the first category are transfers by the decedent during his lifetime which are essentially will substitutes, arrangements which give him continued benefits or controls over the property. However, only transfers during the marriage are included in this category. This makes it possible for a person to provide for children by a prior marriage, as by a revocable living trust, without concern that such provisions will be upset by later marriage. The limitation to transfers during marriage reflects some of the policy underlying community property. What kinds of transfers should be included here is a matter of reasonable difference of opinion. The finespun tests of the Federal Estate Tax Law might be utilized, of course. However, the objectives of a tax law are different from those involved here in the Probate Code, and the present section is therefore more limited. It is intended to reach the kinds of transfers readily usable to defeat an elective share in only the probate estate.

In the second category of assets, property of the surviving spouse derived from the decedent and property derived from the decedent which the spouse has, in turn, given away in a transaction that is will-like in effect or purpose, the scope is much broader. Thus a person can during his lifetime make outright gifts to relatives and they are not included in this first category unless they are made within two years of death (the exception being designed to prevent a person from depleting his estate in contemplation of death). But the time when the surviving spouse derives her wealth from the decedent is immaterial; thus if a husband has purchased a home in the wife's name and made systematic gifts to the wife over many years, the home and accumulated wealth she owns at his death as a result of such gifts ought to, and under this section do, reduce her share of the augmented estate. Likewise, for policy reasons life insurance is not included in the first category of transfers to other persons, because it is not ordinarily purchased as a way of depleting the probate estate and avoiding the elective share of the spouse; but life insurance proceeds payable to the surviving spouse are included in the second category, because it seems unfair to allow a surviving spouse to disturb the decedent's estate plan if the spouse has received ample provision from life insurance. In this category no distinction is drawn as to whether the transfers are made before or after marriage.

Depending on the circumstances it is obvious that this section will operate in the long run to decrease substantially the number of elections. This is because the statute will encourage and provide a legal base for counseling of testators against schemes to disinherit the spouse, and because the spouse can no longer elect in cases where substantial provision is made by joint tenancy, life insurance, lifetime gifts, living trusts set up by the decedent, and the other numerous nonprobate arrangements by which wealth is today transferred. On the other hand the section should provide realistic protection against disinheritance of the spouse in the rare case where decedent tries to achieve that purpose by depleting his probate estate.

The augmented net estate approach embodied in this section is relatively complex and assumes that litigation may be required in cases in which the right to an elective share is asserted. The proposed scheme should not complicate administration in well-planned or routine cases, however, because the spouse's rights are freely releasable under Section 2-204 and because of the time limits in Section 2-205. Some legislatures may wish to consider a simpler approach along the lines of the Pennsylvania Estates Act. . . .

PROBLEMS

1. Which of the transfers listed on page 482 could be reached by the surviving spouse under the Missouri statute? Under the Vermont statute? Under the New York statute? Under the Pennsylvania statute? Under the Uniform Probate Code?

2. Your client, in his late fifties, wants to disinherit his wife, whom he constantly refers to, in the course of your interview, as "that woman." He wants to give his wife a life income interest in a small fund, and he wants the bulk of his estate to go "to my faithful and efficient secretary," a lady in her early thirties. He is willing to make a lifetime transfer to his secretary provided he can retain some controls and economic benefits in the assets transferred.

a. Should you take this case when the client's objective is to defeat his wife's statutory rights? Are any ethical problems raised?

b. Assuming your answer to the first question is yes, can you accomplish the client's objectives if the client resides in Missouri? In Vermont? In New York? In Pennsylvania? In a state that has enacted the Uniform Probate Code?

3. H and W, both sixty-five years of age, move to New York from Massachusetts. They were married some forty years before. W has little property of her own. H made a great deal of money in Massachusetts during their marriage. After a fuss between H and W, H flies from New York to Boston and sets up an inter vivos trust, retaining the right to the income, the power to appoint by will, and the power to revoke. He names a Boston bank as trustee and transfers to the trustee title to practically all his assets. H dies domiciled in New York. Can W reach the assets in the Boston trust by virtue of N.Y. Estates, Powers & Trusts Law §5-1.1? How should she go about it?

In answering these questions, consider National Shawmut Bank v. Cumming, 325 Mass. 457, 91 N.E.2d 337 (1950). In that case a Vermont husband, after nineteen years of marriage, set up an inter vivos trust in Boston, retaining the income, the power to withdraw principal, and the power to revoke. He transferred to the trustee the greater part of his property. After his death, his widow attempted to set aside the trust. Bringing suit in Massachusetts, she contended that Vermont law was applicable, and that the transfer was made with the intent to deprive her of her statutory share. The Massachusetts court held that the law of the situs of the trust controlled, and that the Vermont wife could claim no more interest in the trust property than a Massachusetts wife. Said the court:

> The general tendency of authorities elsewhere is away from the adoption of the law of the settlor's domicil where the property, the domicil and place of business of the trustee, and the place of administration intended by the settlor are in another state [citing a great many authorities applying the law of the situs where the problem involves ease of administration of the trust]. . . . The situation is unchanged by the fact that the one seeking to set aside the transaction is the widow of the settlor.[22]

Do you see how the court here, as in Kerwin v. Donaghy, fell into the fallacy of the transplanted category?

CLARK, THE RECAPTURE OF TESTAMENTARY SUBSTITUTES TO PRESERVE THE SPOUSE'S ELECTIVE SHARE: AN APPRAISAL OF RECENT STATUTORY REFORMS

2 Conn. L. Rev. 513, 543-545 (1970)

It is obvious that the author believes that a case is not made out for the adoption of this statute in any of the several forms discussed herein. The danger is too great that the remedy will operate to the detriment of the family's overall welfare and that it will be productive of massive administrative problems. . . .

Up to now the criticism has focused on alleged deficiencies in the statutes and the lack of any showing that these kinds of solution are needed. The starting point of all these developments is the proposition that a man should not disinherit his wife. This postulate does not seem as compelling in today's world as it might once have.[23] Our system has developed a number of guarantees to insure that a widow will not be left destitute. About 100 million persons are insured under social security, and almost every person in the United States is in line to receive some benefits from it. The death benefits are not yet adequate, but they have increased significantly in recent years and show every sign of continuing to do so. It is important to note in this context that the payments are directed to the widow and family and that the wage-earner cannot by will, gift or assignment divert them to other people. Private and governmental pension plans, which have also enjoyed a tremendous growth in recent years, frequently contain similar guarantees on behalf of the widow and family.

The stereotyped portrait of the wronged and impoverished widow will elicit a

[22] 325 Mass. at 463-464, 91 N.E.2d at 341. Compare Hilaire Belloc's Captain Blood:

> Whatever happens, we have got
> The Maxim Gun, and they have not.
> — Belloc, The Modern Traveller 41

[23] For an earlier suggestion along these lines, see Garland, The "Non-Barrable" Share: Some Comments Regarding a Reappraisal, 32 St. John's L. Rev. 218 (1958).

variety of reactions in today's society. To the Women's Liberationists and their legions of sympathizers she may appear to be a symbol of past exploitation who needs to be liberated rather than bought off by a forced inheritance;[24] to the husband of a tragic second marriage she is a parasite out after the last pound of flesh who is deserving of nothing,[25] and to countless others she is seen as a character out of a nineteenth century novel who no longer exists, if she ever did. The law's concern for her, which found its origins in the conditions existing centuries ago, has not reflected this change in contemporary realities and attitudes. The injunction against disinheritance, as it is expressed in the statutory right of election, is probably a useful device, along with such tax incentives as the marital deduction, to remind a husband to include his wife in his estate plan. The law, however, exceeds its proper goals when it seeks to not just prod the husband but to reshape the distribution of the family's wealth by intervening massively on the side of the widow even though there has been no showing that she needs, deserves or will be greatly benefited by its action.

SECTION B. Protection of the Surviving Spouse — Community Property States

1. *An Overview of the Community Property System*

The eight community property states are Arizona, California, Idaho, Louisiana, Nevada, New Mexico, Texas, and Washington.[26] Statutes in all these states define separate property as property owned by either spouse before marriage and property acquired after marriage by gift, descent or devise. All other property acquired after

[24] For another perspective on woman's property and support rights, see Kanowitz, Women and the Law c. 3 (Law and the Married Woman) (1969).

[25] The policy perspective must take into account that many of the problems involved in this kind of litigation arise out of a second marriage where litigants are the step-mother and her step-children. Macdonald [Fraud on the Widow's Share], 383-386. Needless to say, the equities do not always favor the widow as the law basically assumes.

[26] Between 1939 and 1947, Hawaii, Michigan, Nebraska, Oklahoma, Oregon and Pennsylvania enacted statutes converting their systems of marital property ownership from the common law system to the community property system. The switch was prompted by the favorable income tax treatment then being given to residents of community property states. In a community property state the husband's earnings are community property, in which each spouse has an undivided one-half interest; one-half is taxed to the husband and one-half to the wife. Several other common law states were about to follow suit when Congress, in the Revenue Act of 1948, authorized income splitting by couples in common law states via the joint income tax return. See page 239. Five of the six states immediately repealed their community property statutes and went back to the common law regime with which they were familiar — but the consequence was that for several years they were community property states, and couples in those states had several years' worth of community property. This created no little confusion, and an occasional community property case still crops up. See, e.g., Catron v. First Nat'l Bank & Trust Co., 434 P.2d 263 (Okla. 1967); see generally Comment, Epilogue to Community Property Scramble — Problems of Repeal, 50 Colum. L. Rev. 332 (1950). The Supreme Court of Pennsylvania declared the Pennsylvania statute unconstitutional, with the result that Pennsylvania "never was" a community property state.

marriage is community property. In Idaho, Louisiana and Texas, the income from separate property is community property; in the other states the income from separate property retains its separate character. With relatively minor exceptions, the husband is manager of all the community assets. Except for transactions involving community real estate (which generally require the wife's joinder), the husband has full power to buy, sell, encumber, invest, manage and otherwise deal with community assets without his wife's approval or participation. But while he has the power to manage the assets, he does not own them. Rather, each spouse owns an undivided one-half interest in every community asset.

The basic idea underlying the community property system is that while the husband's earnings may be the immediate source of the couple's income and acquisitions, the labor, efforts, and industry of both spouses contribute to the acquisition of property during the marriage.[27] Community property began among the common folk of continental Europe at a time when both husband and wife typically contributed to the economic welfare of the family. "[I]n origin it was based on the customs of those low on the social and economic scale. On the Continent these customs slowly made their way among the nobles. In England the opposite was true. As Pollock and Maitland put it: 'In England, the law for the great becomes the law for all.' "[28] Community property gained acceptance in most of western Europe except England. And lately an English Law Commission has suggested the adoption of community property in that bastion of male supremacy.[29]

In six of the American states a French or Spanish-Mexican community property system already existed when the states joined the Union; adoption of the community property system in Idaho and Washington is traceable to the influence of California law on the framers of those states' constitutions. But although the states' laws have a common history and are similar in broad outline, diverse judicial interpretations of essentially the same statutes have produced substantial differences on fundamental points.[30] Generalization is both difficult and dangerous. A further complicating factor is that in the less populated states of Arizona, Idaho, Nevada and New Mexico, a sizable number of fundamental questions concerning the nature of community property rights have yet to be litigated and thus resolved.

Without going into the pros and cons of the community property system on other counts,[31] it is quite clear that it gives the surviving wife more substantial pro-

[27] Stated more lyrically, although not addressed to this precise issue:

> "[T]here is not and cannot be any question of *un*equality between us [husband and wife]. Whatever I have achieved is at least one half due to her liberation of me for my work and her inspiration and loving kindness and patience and labor and sympathy. All that I have is as much hers as mine." — Lewisohn, The Vehement Flame 140

[28] Kirkwood, Historical Background and Objectives of the Law of Community Property in the Pacific Coast States, 11 Wash. L. Rev. 1 (1936).

[29] Law Commission, Public Working Paper No. 42, Family Property Law (1971).

[30] See Lay, Survey of Community Property, 51 Iowa L. Rev. 625 (1966).

[31] Lawyers in common law states who delve into community property laws are quick to declare their exasperation at what they see as the needless complexity of the unfamiliar community property system. Few have done so as pungently as Professor Richard R. B. Powell: "[T]he lawyers and courts of Washington have not yet explored and revealed the creaking joints of this institution as thoroughly as have the lawyers and courts of California. This is not due to any dearth of litiga-

tection than does the common law system. This is because the wife does not have simply a claim on her husband's property at his death; during the existence of the marriage relation and upon its dissolution by divorce or death she is the *owner* of an undivided one-half of the community assets. Each spouse has unrestricted power of disposition over his or her separate property, and the surviving spouse has no claim against separate assets.[32] In the typical case of a couple where neither has been previously married, however, most or all of the assets on hand at one spouse's death

---

tion in Washington. Professor Mechem asserts that in the decade from 1922 to 1932 the Supreme Court of Washington decided more than one hundred cases involving the law of community property. Rather it is due to a plethora of litigation in California. It is true that Washington has struggled with the lines of demarcation between separate and community property; has sought to construe conveyances and gifts between spouse and spouse; has worried over imputing the negligence of the husband so as to bar an action for wrongful death brought by heirs of the wife; has fixed the fractions in ownership upon the basis of proportions contributed by separate and community funds; and has figuratively tossed the dice to fix the instant of acquisition when acquisition was not confined to an instant but occupied a period. But the end is not yet. This field of law touches the intimate lives of a very large percentage of the population. It is replete with difficult and as yet unsolved problems inviting litigation. The continuance of such a system in California and Washington may be profitable to the pockets of their lawyers but is certain to cause headaches to their judges and economic waste to their non-lawyer citizens.

". . . [T]he writer finds the community property system lacking as a system of marital property. Its complexity is such as not to be offset by those values claimed for it by its most ardent protagonists. It injects useless uncertainty and unjustifiable barriers into transactions between the spouses as a unit and third persons. It submerges the individual husband or wife in a purely imaginary third entity — the family, in a fashion promoting the ultimate welfare of no one except those parasites who live on litigation-breeding rules of law and have no care for the social implications of the statutes and decisions of their jurisdiction. The writer realizes that many may be shocked at his disregard of the alleged protection of helpless wives implicit in this system. . . . The vaunted protection of married women is an intellectual hang-over from the time when woman was a salable chattel and ill consorts with the modernity and wisdom otherwise so characteristic of the West Coast." Powell, Community Property — A Critique of Its Regulations of Interfamily Relations, 11 Wash. L. Rev. 12, 37-38 (1936).

Professor Powell taught law for thirty-seven years at Columbia University in New York, where the state appellate courts, between 1935 and 1957, grappled with seventy-one cases concerning the widow's forced share on the evasion issue alone. See Macdonald, Fraud on the Widow's Share 430-436 (1960).

In The Community Property Law of Idaho 39 (1962), Brockelbank rushes to the defense of the community property system by slamming the common law marital property system. Brockelbank attacks the common law system as unfair to the wife because the function of bearing and raising children is assigned to her, while the economic function of making money and saving is assigned to the husband. "Twenty of the most productive years taken from the career of a woman plays the same kind of havoc with it economically that the same time would play if taken from the career of a man. . . . [I]t is stated that the married woman now has the ownership, possession, and management of property she acquires during the marriage the same as her husband. But this principle is naive, for it takes no account of the fact that the average married woman who is bearing and rearing children and keeping house during a good part of her married life has little opportunity 'to acquire property,' while the opportunity and capacity of her husband remains not only complete in itself but is greatly enhanced by the intangible values of the very home, the making of which has incapacitated the wife."

[32] Except, under certain circumstances, in Louisiana. La. Civ. Code Ann. art. 2382 provides, in characteristically quaint language, "if either the husband or the wife die rich, leaving the spouse in necessitous circumstances," the survivor is entitled to one-fourth of her spouse's assets.

In several of the other states the surviving spouse's homestead and family allowance claims are sometimes satisfied out of the deceased spouse's separate property.

will be community property. Furthermore, all of the assets owned at death are presumptively community property, and the burden of establishing otherwise is on the party asserting their separate character. As cases in this section show, the "community presumption" is not easily overcome.

At the death of the first spouse to die, the surviving spouse takes his or her one-half share of the community assets outright — not by succession from the other spouse, but because death dissolves the community and effects a partition of the assets into the respective one-half shares. Each spouse has the power of testamentary disposition over only his or her community share.[33] This share can be devised to whomever the decedent spouse pleases,[34] but in all cases the surviving spouse ends up with at least one-half of the marital assets. Added protection is given in California, Idaho, Nevada, and New Mexico by provision that if one spouse dies intestate, his or her community share descends to the surviving spouse.[35]

It is only when most or all of the assets are the separate property of one spouse that the surviving spouse faces the possibility of disinheritance. There are several situations in which this possibility might be encountered. If the couple were married only a short time before the husband's death, there would be little time in which to accumulate a community estate. This case does not present a serious problem, however. It probably doesn't arise very often; and in view of the short span of the marriage, the widow's case is not a very compelling one. Moreover, the decisions suggest that the short-term spouse doesn't fare too badly; given the presumption that all property on hand at the dissolution of the marriage belongs to the community, a complaisant court may come up with a surprising amount of community property.[36]

The possibility also arises if the marriage takes place after the husband has retired, or if the husband lived on inherited income and never worked. In a state in which the income from separate property after marriage is treated as community property, this rule together with the community presumption would operate to protect the widow. In the other states, however, the husband might die owning no community assets.

The most serious problem arises when a couple move from a common law state to a community property jurisdiction, bringing with them what might be called "conflict of laws separate property." Because of two conflict of laws rules that don't

[33] In New Mexico this is true if the husband predeceases his wife, but not if the wife predeceases her husband. In this latter situation the wife has no power of disposition over the community assets; the husband succeeds to all the community property without administration. N. Mex. Stat. Ann. §§29-1-8, 29-1-9 (1954, Supp. 1971).

[34] In Idaho, only the decedent's community share in excess of $25,000 "may be disposed of as the testator sees fit." The first $25,000 can be devised only to the testator's spouse, his descendants, or the parents of either spouse, and the last group cannot be given more than one-half of this amount. Idaho Code Ann. §14-113 (1948).

[35] See Gibson, Inheritance of Community Property in Texas — A Need for Reform, 47 Texas L. Rev. 359 (1969), in which the author recommends that Texas adopt the same intestacy scheme. In Texas and Arizona the intestate's share of community assets passes to descendants, or, if there are no descendants, to the surviving spouse.

[36] See, e.g., Duncan v. United States, 247 F.2d 845 (5th Cir. 1957); Stanley v. Stanley, 294 S.W.2d 132 (Tex. Civ. App. 1956).

mesh, the surviving spouse loses the forced share protection she had in the former state, and doesn't pick up the protection given by the community property system in the new state. This problem is treated at page 546, infra.

2. *Classification of Assets as Community or Separate Property*

For the estate planner, a number of consequences turn on whether assets are classified as community or separate property. Community property states have different schemes of intestate distribution for separate and community property. And, as we have already indicated, each spouse's power of testamentary disposition extends only to his one-half share of community assets, but is unlimited with respect to his separate assets. Thus it is important to know which items of property will pass under which spouse's will. If one spouse's will purports to devise the other's share of community property as well as his own, the surviving spouse obviously does not have to go along with the arrangement. In this situation the surviving spouse is put to an election. She can take under her husband's will, allowing her community share to be governed by the terms of the will. Alternatively, she can elect against the will and claim her community share outright — but in so doing she must relinquish any of the will provisions in her favor.

With respect to lifetime transfers, in California and Washington one spouse cannot make a gift of community assets without the other's consent. If the husband attempts to do so, the wife can void the transfer entirely during his life or set it aside to the extent of one-half after his death. The other states give the wife some protection (but by no means absolute protection) against lifetime gifts of community assets by the husband.

Classification of assets as community or separate property has a decided bearing on their tax treatment. Under the federal estate tax, the entire value of a spouse's separate property, but only his one-half share of community property, is taxed in his gross estate. Consequently, when one spouse owns a substantial amount of separate property, to obtain the estate-splitting benefits of the marital deduction he must leave sufficient assets (community or separate) to his spouse in a manner that qualifies for the deduction.[37] Also, classification of the assets determines the total tax bite. Suppose, for example, the wife predeceases her husband. To the extent that assets are classified as community property, one-half their value will be taxed in her estate. To the extent they are classified as the husband's separate property, they will not be taxed at all. This situation, in which the tax bill cannot be determined until the character of the assets is established, is a commonly encountered one since some commingling of community and separate assets is likely to have occurred over the years of marriage.

The assets of the deceased spouse acquire a new basis at death whether they are classified as separate or community property.[38] If separate property, they are given a new basis because of their inclusion in the decedent's gross estate. If com-

[37] At this point you should reread pages 250-252, on availability of the marital deduction in a community property state.

[38] For discussion of the "new basis" rule, see page 235.

munity property, §1014(b)(6) of the 1954 Code provides that the entire property (including the surviving spouse's community share) acquires a new basis although only the deceased's one-half interest is taxed in his estate.

Classification of the assets also has an impact on their state inheritance tax treatment. Most of the states give some preferred treatment to community property. For example, in California and Idaho community property that passes to the surviving spouse is not taxed at all.[39] Texas gives no such break to interspousal transfers; however, a $40,000 exemption for life insurance proceeds is construed to apply to the deceased's community share of the proceeds. If life insurance policies are classified as the husband's separate property, $40,000 in proceeds are exempt; if classified as community property, $80,000 in proceeds are exempt.[40]

In short, it does make a difference to the estate planner whether assets are classified as community or separate property. In addition to the above, each of the states has indigenous rules of significance to the estate planner. A few examples: Texas takes the singular position that it is unconstitutional to use community funds to create a joint tenancy with right of survivorship between the spouses.[41] If community funds are deposited in a joint and survivor bank account, the survivorship provision is presumably ineffective to pass the deceased's share of the fund to the surviving spouse; theoretically, it passes under his will or by intestacy.[42] If, on the other hand, the deposit is classified as separate property the survivorship provision is effective. In California, when community assets are placed in a joint tenancy form of ownership, unless the transaction has been handled carefully it is difficult to tell whether the assets are still community property, or whether they have been partitioned into the separate property of the spouses and a true joint tenancy created. This is because the spouses can agree — even orally — that the assets are to remain community property despite the joint tenancy designation.[43]

[39] Cal. Rev. & Tax Code §§13551, 13694 (1970, Supp. 1971); Idaho Code Ann. §14.408-(2a) (1948, Supp. 1969).

[40] Tex. Tax-Gen. art. 14 (1969).

[41] Hilley v. Hilley, 161 Tex. 569, 342 S.W.2d 565 (1961).

If, however, community funds are deposited in the name of the husband and some third party as joint tenants, the survivorship provision is effective. On the death of the husband the entire fund belongs to the named co-owner unless the wife can establish that the transfer was "in fraud of her community rights." Krueger v. Williams, 163 Tex. 545, 359 S.W.2d 48 (1962).

[42] The words "presumably" and "theoretically" are used advisedly. A statute provides that banks may pay over funds to the surviving co-owner of an account, without liability if it turns out that payment was made to the wrong person. As a practical matter, the survivorship designation is effective unless someone challenges it.

"There is no evidence that this decision [Hilley v. Hilley] has discouraged the use of joint bank accounts with community funds — or even impaired their effectiveness to vest title to the community funds in the survivor. Since the surviving spouse has the authority to withdraw the funds unless someone challenges him, as a practical matter the Hilley doctrine frustrates the parties' intention in only two situations: (1) in the divided family situation, where children by a former marriage — claiming either as heirs or as residuary legatees under the deceased spouse's will — are determined to enforce their rights as to one-half of the fund; and (2) where the deceased spouse's will names a corporate fiduciary as executor or testamentary trustee, and the fiduciary is aware of its obligation to claim one-half of the fund for the estate or trust." Johanson, Revocable Trusts and Community Property: The Substantive Problems, 47 Texas L. Rev. 537, 557 n. 74 (1969).

[43] This California rule has prompted an occasional surviving spouse to "remember" that she

How does one determine whether assets are separate property or belong to the community? The straightforward definitions of separate and community property given on page 494 resolve the easy classification problems, but give little guidance in resolving the frequently encountered situation in which the spouses have commingled community and separate assets and have failed to keep adequate records. All it takes is a little separate property, a little community property, a little commingling, no records, and the passage of time — and it becomes difficult, if not impossible, to determine whether assets are community or separate property, or perhaps a little bit of each.

PROBLEMS

1. Prior to his marriage to B, A owns securities worth $100,000. After the marriage A continues to earn $20,000 a year from his job. A is a fairly active investor. He keeps abreast of the stock market, occasionally buying, occasionally selling, regularly investing dividends. (The dividends from securities owned as separate property are community property in Idaho, Louisiana, and Texas; separate property in the other states.) In one year, anticipating a drop in the market, A sells about half his securities and deposits the proceeds in the family checking and savings accounts, the accounts in which he regularly deposits his salary check. Six months later A goes back into the market. A dies after six years of married life. At his death the securities portfolio is worth $180,000. Part of the increase in value has come from added investments of both dividends and salary; part of the increase is attributable to a rise in the securities' market value. At A's death he holds shares in only five of the fifteen companies whose securities made up his portfolio prior to his marriage, and even here the number of shares has changed. A's records are of little help. All he had was a notebook (and an account ledger at Merrill, Lynch) listing his holdings

---

and her husband had agreed that the property was to remain community property. Tax considerations tend to promote this recollection. If the assets are community and pass to the survivor by other than survivorship (as under the husband's will), they are not subject to inheritance taxation; if a true joint tenancy was created, the husband's *separate* property passing by right of survivorship is taxed. If the assets are community, they receive a new basis on the death of one of the spouses. If a joint tenancy was created, only the deceased's *separate* property (his one-half interest in the joint tenancy) is given a new basis. To illustrate: Assume H and W purchase land with $20,000 of community funds, taking title in joint tenancy form. On H's death some years later the land is worth $50,000, and several years after that, W sells the land for $60,000. If the land was held as community property despite the joint tenancy designation, W will pay a tax on $10,000 capital gains. If a true joint tenancy was created, W will have incurred capital gains of $25,000 (since the basis was $10,000 for half the property and $25,000 for the other half).

In Perkins v. West, 122 Cal. App. 2d 585, 265 P.2d 538 (1954), at H's death record title to land was in H and W in joint tenancy form. H's will devised a portion of his community estate to B, and a portion to W. W, upon advice of her attorney, submitted a sworn affidavit to the state inheritance tax department stating that H and W had orally agreed that the land was community property. As a result, no inheritance tax was paid on the devise of the land. Thereafter B sued W and relied on the inheritance tax affidavit in claiming a portion of the land as devisee under H's will. W then testified that there was no such oral agreement, and that a joint tenancy with right of survivorship really had been created. The court agreed. Thus the land was treated as community property for tax purposes, but as separate property in joint tenancy form for devolution purposes. (Anything wrong with that?)

and changes in his holdings from time to time. There is no clear showing of where he put the funds when he sold, or of the source of the funds when he bought. A's income tax returns show the amounts of his salary, dividends and capital gains over the years.

What portion of the securities should be classified as A's separate property, what portion should be classified as community property — and how does one go about determining this? See Duncan v. United States, 247 F.2d 845 (5th Cir. 1957); See v. See, 51 Cal. Rptr. 888, 415 P.2d 776 (1966), 19 Stan. L. Rev. 661 (1967), 14 U.C.L.A.L. Rev. 935 (1967); Johanson, Community Property: Common Law Assets, 252 Tax Management 36 (1971).

2. Prior to his marriage to D, C owns an unincorporated business (a liquor store) that nets about $25,000 per year. After the marriage the business continues to prosper. Three years after marriage C opens a second store, buying the land, refurbishing the building, etc., partly out of the accumulated earnings from the first store, and partly out of the savings he had accumulated before marriage. Family income goes up to about $40,000 per year. Over the years C, who works full-time at one or the other of the liquor stores, takes no salary; he simply takes home the "net," as most sole proprietors do. In the early years of the marriage D works at the store, sometimes keeping the books, sometimes working behind the counter. She of course gets no salary or wages; she's simply working at "the family store." C dies after eight years of married life. The value of the two stores (taking into account the value of the two properties and their improvements, C's very valuable liquor license, the business inventory, and the intangible but real value of a prosperous going business) is around $300,000. Are the two stores C's separate property, community property, or a mixture of the two? If the latter, what's the mix?

3. In 1953 E takes out an ordinary life insurance policy with a face value of $10,000. In 1957 he takes out a $25,000 ordinary life policy; in 1959 he takes out a $25,000 five-year renewable term policy. Since 1955 E has been covered by a group term policy (face amount $15,000) whose premiums are paid by E's employer. In 1961 E marries F; thereafter he pays the annual policy premiums out of his salary (except, of course, for the group term policy). E dies in 1970, survived by F. The proceeds from the $10,000 policy and the $25,000 term policy are payable to E's mother. The proceeds from the other two policies are payable to F — but not in a lump sum, for E selected a ten-years-certain option that is irrevocable by F. F is infuriated; she wants to collect all of the proceeds from all of the policies, and she wants the proceeds in a lump sum. What are F's rights?

SOMPS v. SOMPS

California Court of Appeal
First District, California, 1967
250 Cal. App. 2d 328, 58 Cal. Rptr. 304

Harold C. Brown, Associate Justice. The plaintiff Judy Somps appeals from certain portions of an interlocutory judgment of divorce which awards the stock in

MacKay & Somps, a corporation, and other assets, to defendant George Somps as his separate property.

Judy Somps (hereinafter referred to as wife) and George Somps (hereinafter referred to as husband) were married on April 28, 1954, and lived together until April of 1963, the date of commencement of this divorce proceeding. Wife had three children by a prior marriage who were subsequently adopted by husband. The parties had three children by this marriage. Prior to marriage wife had no financial assets. Husband had a 50% partnership interest with one Donald MacKay in an engineering business which had been in existence for a period of one year. Husband also had some cash and stocks.

On November 13, 1964, an interlocutory judgment of divorce was entered granting both parties a divorce on the grounds of extreme cruelty. The decree awarded the business and certain other assets to husband as his separate property. It declared a $15,000 indebtedness to First Valley Bank to be a community indebtedness. An accumulation of cash from husband's earnings from the business was allocated as 60% separate property of husband and 40% community property.

Other joint tenancy and community assets possessed by husband and wife at the time of divorce consisted of two residences, household furniture, real property, cash in bank, and automobile, all of which were evaluated at approximately $463,000. This property was awarded one-half to husband and one-half to wife. Wife's total award amounted to approximately $250,000.

Wife claims that the trial court erred in holding (1) that the business (MacKay & Somps) was the separate property of husband; (2) that the Binkley property was purchased with separate funds of husband and therefore the profit realized from the sale was his separate property; (3) that certain income and salaries of husband be allocated 60% to husband as his separate property and 40% to the community; . . . .

(1) Did the trial court err in holding that the business of MacKay & Somps was husband's separate property?

Husband and a Donald MacKay as equal partners commenced a civil engineering business in 1953. Each of the parties contributed $5,000, tools, and his personal automobile to the original capital. The firm specialized in single-family residences. When husband and wife married in 1954, husband's equity in the business was approximately $16,000. At the time of divorce the net worth of husband's one-half was $222,433. In 1959 the assets of the partnership were transferred to two corporations formed by husband and MacKay in exchange for stock. MacKay and husband each received 50% of the stock in the new corporations. It was conceded that the two corporations were a continuation and reorganization of the original partnership formed in 1953.

Wife contends that the large increment to the business accruing after marriage should be declared community property because husband's education, abilities and labors contributed substantially to its growth and success. Husband had a degree in engineering from Utah State University and a master's degree in business administration from Stanford. She testified that the business was in existence only one year prior to marriage, that they did not go on a honeymoon and rarely took a vacation and that husband worked overtime in the early part of their marriage. Husband admitted that he occasionally worked nights and on week ends.

The general rule is that "The time, efforts, and skill of the husband are assets of the community and when they are used for the enrichment of the separate property of the husband, the community must be compensated." (Strohm v. Strohm, 182 Cal. App. 2d 53, 62, 5 Cal. Rptr. 884, 889.)

Wife introduced evidence to show that husband treated the business as community property. This evidence disclosed that husband and his partner MacKay used business assets to purchase several investment properties, particularly those parcels known as (1) the Cook ranch, (2) the Wisner property, consisting of two parcels of land (which had not been sold at time of divorce, one parcel was adjudged to be community property and the other joint tenancy property of husband and wife), and, (3) the Goldhammer property. Title to all these properties, with the exception of one portion of the Wisner property which was in husband's and Donald MacKay's name only, was taken in the names of Mr. and Mrs. MacKay as to an undivided one-half interest and to husband and wife as joint tenants as to an undivided one-half interest. The properties were carried on the books of the business as assets and the balances due on the purchase prices were listed as liabilities. All installments due on the balance were paid by the business. The Cook ranch was sold at a substantial profit. The Goldhammer property was sold at a profit to a joint venture owned by the corporation MacKay & Somps. The proceeds of the sale of these properties was apparently deposited to the account of the business. Wife and husband jointly paid capital gains taxes on these transactions. Wife claims that this commingling of community assets with the property of the business made segregation impossible, and was evidence that husband himself considered the business to be community property.

The reason MacKay and husband had title to the Cook, Wisner and Goldhammer properties, deeded to themselves jointly with their wives and thereafter listed the properties as assets of the business, is not clear. It is clear, however, that the purchase price of the properties and all installments were paid by the business and the risk of loss was borne by the business. No community funds were used to purchase these properties. The trial court was not persuaded that community funds were so commingled with business assets so as to evidence an intent by husband to make the business community property.

Husband produced expert testimony to the effect that the growth of the business was due to the tremendous demand for single-family residences, to the phenomenal population growth in Santa Clara County, to his partner MacKay's ability and to the efforts of the loyal staff of employees. An expert witness (another civil engineer from that locality) testified that MacKay and husband could not have picked a better time to commence the business. Two employees stated the business would have operated just as well without husband so great was the market for single-family homes. Husband and MacKay testified that one-half of the first year of business was spent for promotional activities. Husband testified that 60% of the money earned by the firm between 1954 and 1964 could be traced to husband's and MacKay's efforts in soliciting clients during the year prior to the Somps' marriage.

The court's opinion that the business was the separate property of husband was fortified by testimony that husband and wife had orally agreed that it should remain his separate property and the court so found. This finding was based on the testimony of husband. It was denied by wife. Husband and wife may alter the character of their property by oral agreement. A transmutation from community to separate property occurs when the spouses agree to change the character of the property. Originally only a written agreement would suffice but more recently oral transmutations have been upheld. . . .

. . . It is unnecessary to consider the propriety of this finding, however, as there was substantial evidence for the trial court's holding that the increase in the partnership assets or in the value of the stock after the business was incorporated was attributed to a reasonable return upon the separate property of husband invested by him before marriage, and the faithful, loyal and effective services of his partner MacKay and the employees, together with the unprecedented population growth in Santa Clara County, causing an abnormal demand for residential subdivisions and other favorable business factors not related to husband's abilities or labors.

Although the court found that the business was the separate property of husband, there is no doubt that husband's efforts, educational training and ability contributed to some extent to its success. The community was entitled to compensation for this contribution.

Wife contends that the community should be compensated by adopting the method of apportionment between separate and community property as set forth in Pereira v. Pereira, 156 Cal. 1, 103 P. 488, 23 L.R.A., N.S., 880. There the court held that the husband's separate property amounted to his original investment plus a fair return thereon measured by the usual interest on a long investment well secured, which was fixed at 7%. The increment due to the personal efforts of husband belonged to the community estate. This rule was followed in In re Estate of Neilson, 57 Cal. 2d 733, 740, 22 Cal. Rptr. 1, 5, 371 P.2d 745, 749 and other cases cited therein. The courts, however, recognize that "Departures from the Pereira formula have been made when husband introduced evidence that 'a larger return on his capital had in fact been realized.' (Gilmore v. Gilmore, 45 Cal. 2d 142, 150, 287 P.2d 769 [great increase in automobile business as a whole accompanied by increase in value of husband's dealer franchises; husband did not take active part in conducting routine operations of the business]; Harrold v. Harrold, 43 Cal. 2d 77, 80, 271 P.2d 489 [same]; Huber v. Huber, 27 Cal. 2d 784, 792, 167 P.2d 708 [custom broker business required considerable capital since money was advanced for customers]; Tassi v. Tassi, 160 Cal. App. 2d 680, 691, 325 P.2d 872 [high profits realized in meat business generally]; Logan v. Forster, 114 Cal. App. 2d 587, 601, 250 P.2d 730 [increase in population and economic development of community; wife played inactive role in conducting her business].)" In re Estate of Neilson, supra, 57 Cal. 2d p. 740, 22 Cal. Rptr. p. 5, 371 P.2d p. 749.

The court in Owens v. Owens, 219 Cal. App. 2d 856, 858, 33 Cal. Rptr. 599, 600 said: " 'It has frequently been held that a proper method of making such allocation [between separate and community property] is to deduct from the total earnings of the business the value of the husband's services to it. The remainder, if any, represents the earnings attributable to the separate property invested in the business.' [Citation.] . . . [Citations] . . . The court found that the salaries paid by the corporation to defendant for his services during the marriage, were sufficient to fully compensate both defendant and the community. . . ."

"It is primarily a question of fact 'for the court to determine what portion of the profits thereafter arises from the use of this (separate) capital and what part arises from the activity and personal ability of the husband.' "

There was substantial evidence to justify the court's finding that the husband and the community were fairly and adequately compensated for husband's services to the business. Husband withdrew extensive sums as salary from the business. During the marriage husband and wife maintained a high, if not luxuriant, standard of living. The parties owned community and joint tenancy assets in excess of $450,000 at the time of divorce, and the source of all money expended for living expenses and used to acquire these assets was the earnings husband received from the business. (The trial court awarded this property equally to husband and wife.)

Since the evidence adequately supports the findings that the business was the separate property of husband and the community had been compensated for his contribution, it cannot be disturbed on appeal.

(2) Did the trial court err in holding the Binkley property was purchased with husband's separate assets and that the profits realized from the sale were his separate estate?

Husband, with MacKay and a Mr. Rodrigues, purchased and sold a parcel of property known as the Binkley property. When acquired, title to husband's interest was conveyed in husband's name alone. Husband in purchasing the property used $5,000 received from the sale of stock which was his separate property and $8,000 which he borrowed from a bank on his note. Wife was not a co-signer on the note. The banker who made the loan to husband testified that he did so on the basis of husband's credit and the credit of the business of MacKay & Somps. Husband testified that the loan was personal and was granted on the basis that the Binkley venture was sound. Wife contends that the bank in extending this credit relied on the financial statement given by husband to the bank which listed husband's and wife's community and joint tenancy properties as assets in addition to husband's separate property.

"There is a rebuttable presumption that property acquired on credit during marriage is community property. Civ. Code, §164; Hogevoll v. Hogevoll, 59 Cal. App. 2d 188, 193-194, 138 P.2d 693. But 'funds procured by the hypothecation of separate property of a spouse are separate property of that spouse.' In re Estate of Abdale, 28 Cal. 2d 587, 592, 170 P.2d 918, 922. The proceeds of a loan made on the credit of separate property are governed by the same rule. In re Estate of Ellis, 203 Cal. 414, 416-417, 264 P. 743. In accordance with this general principle, the character of the property acquired by a sale upon credit is determined according to the intent of the seller to rely upon the separate property of the purchaser or upon a community asset.

"The burden rests on the party asserting that property acquired after marriage is separate to establish that fact. (Wilson v. Wilson, supra, 76 Cal. App. 2d 119, at page 126, 172 P.2d 568 at page 572.) There are expressions in the decisions to the effect that the separate character of property acquired after marriage is to be established by 'clear and convincing evidence,' 'clear and decisive proof,' 'clear and satisfactory proof.' [Citations.] These expressions state a rule of evidence directed to the trial court; and if that court finds that the evidence meets the rule, a reviewing court must accept that determination as conclusive if there is substantial evidence to support it." (Thomasset v. Thomasset, 122 Cal. App. 2d 116, 123, 264 P.2d 626, 630, overruled on other grounds; also see See v. See, supra.)

Here the presumption that property purchased after marriage is community property was rebutted. The trial court was justified in accepting the testimony of the banker and in finding that the property was purchased with husband's separate estate.

Wife argues that all transactions between persons in confidential relationship, and particularly between husband and wife, by which one obtains an advantage from the other are presumed to be entered into without consideration and [under] undue influence. (Barney v. Fye, 156 Cal. App. 2d 103, 319 P.2d 29.) She further contends that husband breached a fiduciary relationship between husband and wife in that he should have purchased the property with community funds which were available. The fact that husband purchased the Binkley property with his separate funds, as the trial court found, is not evidence of taking any undue advantage nor is it a breach of a fiduciary relationship which would invoke a presumption of fraud or undue influence. There is no reason why husband should be compelled to keep his separate funds idle. Husband apparently had made many investments benefitting the community during the marriage which resulted in the substantial estate owned by the parties at the time of divorce.

Wife further introduced evidence that husband used $6,450 of salary checks to improve the Binkley property and that by reason thereof she should have an interest in the entire Binkley profits. A husband may improve his separate property and if he uses community funds the wife is entitled to compensation to the extent that her share of the community funds increased its value. (In re Estate of Chandler, 112 Cal. App. 601, 297 P. 636; deFuniak, Improving Separate Property (1957-58) 9 Hastings L.J. 37.) Here husband used the community funds for taxes and incidental expenses. Where funds have been used for taxes and the like, the wife is limited in recovery to the actual amount used. (In re Estate of Turner, 35 Cal. App. 2d 576, 96 P.2d 363.) Husband testified that the use of community funds was a loan which he repaid to the community. The trial court could and did accept husband's testimony.

There was sufficient evidence to support the trial court's findings that the purchase of the property was consummated with husband's separate funds, which he received from the sale of stock he owned prior to marriage, with money borrowed from the bank loan on the strength of the Binkley transaction itself, the reliability and financial stability of the firm of MacKay & Somps, husband's separate property and that there was no fraud or duress practiced on wife.

(3) Did the trial court err in determining that certain income and salary from the business were 60% husband's separate property and 40% community property?

At the time of trial husband had (1) salary due from MacKay & Somps in the sum of $13,112, (2) $7,128 he received as salary which was on deposit in the First Valley Bank, and (3) in his possession salary accumulations (uncashed checks and cash) in the sum of $34,285. This latter amount was reduced by his payment of $29,325 in community income taxes, leaving husband with the balance of $4,960 at the time of trial. The trial court allocated 60% of these sums to husband as his separate property and 40% to the community. There is no specific finding by the court as to the means of arriving at this allocation. A witness testified that a reasonable salary for his services would be between $30,000 and $50,000 per year. There is also evidence that husband gave wife $3,000 per month for household expenses. ($36,000 is 40% of the $90,000 salary.) The record is silent as to whether the court considered salaries for the years preceding 1960.

MacKay & Somps permitted withdrawals from the business for three years preceding the divorce at $90,000 per year each. They made no allocation as to whether this was salary or dividends. They determined the amount which would reasonably compensate them for their services. During the approximate ten years of marriage salary withdrawals were treated as the property of the community. In the absence of contrary evidence salary withdrawals to the time of divorce should have been treated in the same manner and declared to be community property. Further, it was inconsistent for the trial court to hold that the community was adequately compensated for husband's contribution to the success of the business by reason of the community receiving his salary withdrawals and other emoluments and then to declare that the balance of salary on hand at the time of divorce should be 60% husband's separate property and 40% community property.

The judgment of the trial court allocating 60% to husband and 40% to the community of the salary in possession of husband at the time of the divorce totalling $25,200 is reversed with directions that this sum should be declared community property to be equally divided between husband and wife.

McCURDY v. McCURDY
Texas Court of Civil Appeals, 1963
372 S.W.2d 381

Wilson, Justice. The problem we are required to solve is whether proceeds of life insurance policies issued to the insured husband before marriage naming his estate as beneficiary (a) belong to the separate estate of the husband after his death, only in proportion to the amount of premiums paid by him before marriage;

or (b) belong entirely to his separate estate, with right of reimbursement to the community based on the amount of premiums paid from community funds during marriage. Appellant urges the first solution; appellee the second, adopted by the trial court, and by us.

The facts are stipulated. Insured and his wife were married August 3, 1960, and their marriage continued until his death, March 16, 1962. Both policies of life insurance were issued to the insured husband before marriage, naming his estate beneficiary. One policy was issued May 22, 1956; the other, February 13, 1959. The 1959 policy was "converted" February 12, 1962, as authorized by the original policy. The nature of the conversion is not shown. Of the total premiums on the two policies, $1094.66 was paid by the husband before marriage; $657.60 was paid during coverture from community funds. The executor named in the husband's will listed the proceeds as a part of the husband's separate estate. The widow's action against the executor sought determination of the status of the proceeds. The trial court concluded the proceeds constituted a part of the husband's separate estate and decreed that the community estate of husband and wife should be reimbursed on the basis of the payments made out of community funds for premiums. The policies are not in evidence. No issue of fraud is suggested by the parties. There is no other evidence. The pleadings allege insured's will made specific bequests of $3000 each to his widow and their two children, of $5000 to his parents, with the rest of his estate to be held in trust for the use of his parents, his brother and his widow, who is appellant here.

The problem is directly presented for the first time in this State under these facts. In all other cases we have examined which reached the question, and where the beneficiary was insured's estate, the policies were issued during marriage. Our decision is restricted to the stated facts.

In Brown v. Lee, Tex., 371 S.W.2d 694, 7 S. Ct. J., 10, The Supreme Court said that by amendment of the definition of "property" in Art. 23(1), Vernon's Ann. Tex. Stats., to include "life insurance policies, and the effects thereof," the Legislature has "aligned Texas with other community property states in adhering to the theory that the right to receive insurance proceeds payable at a future but uncertain date is 'property.' Such property is said to be in the nature of a chose in action which matures at the death of the insured." In that case, however, the policy was also issued during coverture.

In approaching solution to this problem we must look somewhat beyond the immediate consequences of decision in this case. A dominant factor in our conclusion is an effort, within the broad principles of dissonant precedent, to fit life insurance proceeds under the present facts to the pattern of Texas community property law as applied to other types of property. This the Legislature has apparently sought to do by amending Art. 23, Sec. 1.

That pattern, as to realty, title to which is acquired before marriage, and a portion of the consideration for which is thereafter paid from community, fixes the character of title at the time of its inception or acquisition. It "depends upon the existence or nonexistence of the marriage at the time of the incipiency of the right in virtue of which the title is finally extended." Creamer v. Briscoe, 101 Tex. 490, 109 S.W. 911, 912, 17 L.R.A., N.S., 154, 130 Am. St. Rep. 869. In such a case as this, realty is held to be the husband's separate property. Colden v. Alexander, 141 Tex. 134, 171 S.W.2d 328, 334.

The Supreme Court of Louisiana had settled the present problem in 1886 in In re Moseman's Estate, 38 La. Ann. 219, by holding that where a life insurance policy was acquired before marriage, payable to the insured husband's estate, under community property law the right to proceeds remained the insured's separate estate, as vested before marriage, notwithstanding part of the premiums were paid thereafter from the community. Twelve years later Chief Justice Gaines utilized that very holding to establish the analogy to realty similarly acquired, Welder v. Lambert, 91 Tex. 510, 44 S.W. 281, 284; and to sustain the holding that a fixed contract right acquired before marriage was property the "character [of which] takes its impress from the date of the contract." The Texas pattern is not generally different as to personalty. Schmidt v. Huppman, 73 Tex. 112, 11 S.W. 175. See Hilley v. Hilley, 161 Tex. 569, 342 S.W.2d 565, 568.

The grappling by Texas courts with the community property aspects of life insurance has been admirably analyzed by William O. Huie, 5th Ann. Taxation Conf., II Texas Institutes, 104, 109 (1957), 17 Tex. L. Rev. 121, 146; 18 Tex. L. Rev. 121, 147 (1940); by Judge Wisdom, Commissioner of Int. Rev. v. Chase Manhattan Bank, 5 Cir., 259 F.2d 231, cert. den., 359 U.S. 913, 79 S. Ct. 589, 3 L. Ed. 2d 575; and by George E. Ray, 26 Tex. Bar Journal 835. It is not necessary to repeat the analysis.

Why do we not adopt the California solution formula of proportionate premium payments suggested by the respected author of the first cited treatises? California has done what we think should here be done; it has made its solution as to life insurance proceeds consonant with its other community property law. In Modern Woodmen of America v. Gray, 113 Cal. App. 729, 1931, 299 P.754, where it first considered the problem, the California court stated it would apply the apportionment method so as to follow the California rule as to realty: that the inception of title doctrine does not apply (citing Vieux v. Vieux, 80 Cal. App. 222, 251 P.640, where the latter principle was reflected). In Forbes v. Forbes, 118 Cal. App. 324, 257 P.2d 721, 722, the same court confirms its reason: "Contrary to the rule adopted in most community property states, under which the community has only the right of reimbursement for payments made with community funds," it is stated, "California gives to the community a pro tanto community property interest in such property in the ratio" which the separate and community payments bear to each other in the case of other types of property; and "[t]he same rule has repeatedly been applied in the case of life insurance policies procured by the husband before marriage." Apparently Washington also has followed its general tracing rule, see Jacobs v. Hoitt, 119 Wash. 283, 205 P.414; In re Coffey's Estate, 195 Wash. 379, 81 P.2d 283, 286.

We think our decision harmonizes with what is said to be elsewhere the general rule: "If either spouse before marriage procures a policy of life insurance on his own or another's life, in his favor or in favor of his estate, the policy and its proceeds are his separate property. His rights to the proceeds date from the policy." McKay, Community Property (2d ed.) Sec. 479, p. 316. It is consistent with the holdings of the Supreme Court of New Mexico, In re Miller's Estate, 44 N.M. 214, 100 P.2d 908, 910 syl. 2; and of Louisiana, In re Moseman's Estate, 38 La. Ann. 219.

Two reasons for applying the tracing principle to give proportionate ownership of proceeds are suggested, II Texas Institutes, supra, 111: (a) simplicity; (b) just results. These are good reasons, and we have carefully considered others. It does not appear that the inception of title rule is less simple: each method requires computation of the amount of premiums paid out of community funds. Many incidental problems resulting from attempted application of the proportionate ownership rule are avoided. If simplicity be a virtue, we think the inception of title rule is simpler. It facilitates application of general principles of community property law. The inception of title rule is not less equitable in results. While in this case the proceeds which would be proportionately attributable to the community under the tracing theory happened to exceed the community premium payments, in another case the gross premiums so paid out might well exceed the total proceeds. To permit the nature of the property to be determined by the monetary result is not necessarily equitable; and apparent inequity may result under either method, depending on the facts in each case.

In II Texas Institutes, above, the query is presented: "How are orthodox principles to be applied when there is a change of marital status?" We believe the inception of title test applied to other forms of property, though arbitrary, is more conducive to uniformity and a degree of certainty under the present facts; and that (although there is much to be said for the proportionate method) this is the best method by which orthodox principles may be here applied.

In our opinion the proceeds of the policies constitute the separate estate of the deceased insured, and the community estate is entitled to reimbursement on the basis of premiums paid with community funds. Affirmed.[44]

NOTE

In Parson v. United States, 308 F. Supp. 1159 (E.D. Tex. 1970), the court concluded that "the McCurdy case is not binding and determinative regarding this area of the law and particularly when applied to the facts of this case." While a resident of Texarkana, Arkansas, Dr. Parson took out fourteen life insurance policies in which he was named as the insured. Two were taken out before marriage, and twelve were acquired after marriage. In 1945 Parson and his family moved to Texarkana, Texas, where he resided until his death in 1961. Relying on the McCurdy inception of title rule, the Internal Revenue Service argued that the entire proceeds were includible in Parson's gross estate as his separate property since the policies were acquired in a common law state and the first premiums

[44] Noted 15 Baylor L. Rev. 425; 42 Texas L. Rev. 747. — Eds.

were therefore paid from separate funds. The court held that only a proportionate part of the proceeds were includible in the gross estate. Concluding that the Texas law on the question was unsettled notwithstanding the McCurdy case, and noting that the case had been criticized in the law reviews as arbitrary and inequitable, the court applied the tracing or proration formula that had been used in another federal tax case that antedated McCurdy. "The McCurdy case involved life insurance policies taken out before marriage on which premiums paid after marriage were paid from community funds; thus, in McCurdy there was a much stronger inclination to hold the policies to be the decedent's separate property, because taken out before marriage, than in the present case where all but two of the life insurance policies were taken out after marriage. . . . If applied in this case, the inception of title rule would surely bring about inequitable results. Schedule A of the Stipulation of Facts cites the percentage of premiums paid for with separate and community funds. On eight of the fourteen policies over 70% of the premiums were paid for with community funds. Only the two policies acquired before marriage were paid for with less than 50% community funds."

In Estate of Bryan Wildenthal, T.C. Mem. 1970-119, yet another forum had occasion to express its view concerning the proper method of classifying life insurance policies in Texas. The insured acquired four life insurance policies before his marriage, paying $660 in premiums before marriage and $8500 (93 percent of the total premiums paid) after marriage. The Tax Court held that the entire proceeds were separate property and includible in the insured's gross estate, subject to a right of reimbursement to the community for premiums paid out of community funds. Refusing to follow the Parson case, the court concluded: "In our opinion [the McCurdy case] states the correct rule in Texas. It is the most recent statement of the law in this area by the Texas courts, and it is consistent with the 'inception of title' doctrine and the general body of community property law in Texas."

Question: What is the Texas law concerning classification of life insurance policies as separate or community property (a) for the purpose of making distribution of the proceeds, (b) for tax purposes? Should the rules be different for these two classes of cases? [45]

3. *The Widow's Election in a Community Property State*

In a common law state, the "widow's election" refers to a surviving spouse's option to take either under her husband's will or against the will by claiming a statutory forced share of his estate. Whether she takes under or against the will, her election affects the disposition of her husband's property. In the community property states, there are no forced share statutes.[46] In these states the term "widow's

[45] See Commissioner v. Estate of Bosch, 387 U.S. 456 (1967).

[46] Exception: California has a forced share for the surviving spouse in property acquired by the decedent spouse from earnings during marriage before the couple moved to California. See page 543, infra.

election" refers to the situation in which the deceased spouse's will purports to devise the entire interest in community assets, and not just his undivided one-half share. Since the husband does not have the power of disposition over his wife's community interest, she can defeat this usurpation of testamentary power by claiming her community interest. But if she does so, she must renounce all interests given to her by the will as a condition to taking "against" it. Unlike the widow's election in a common law state, the community property widow's election affects the disposition of the electing spouse's own property.

The community property widow's election involves the application of a well-established common law doctrine:

> An election is required when the testator purports to devise A's property to B by the will and also gives other property to A. Here A must decide whether he will accept the property given him by the will in which case he relinquishes his own property devised to B, or whether he, A, will claim his own property, thereby losing the testamentary gift in his favor. It is not material whether the testator was in error as to his ownership, or whether he knew he had no title thereto. It is enough, if a reasonable interpretation of the will discloses a situation which should equitably put the beneficiary to an election; an express testamentary requirement of an election is not necessary.[47]

To make this statement applicable to the community property situation, all that needs to be done is to delete "A's property" and substitute "his wife's community interest" in its stead.

The widow's election can work either way; that is, the wife's will can also put her husband to an election by attempting to devise the entire interest in community assets. Because women usually outlive men, the "widower's election" is not commonly encountered, however. In our discussion we shall assume the typical case in which the husband has died leaving a will that puts his wife to an election.

There are two important differences between the common law widow's election and the community property widow's election. (1) In a common law state, if the widow elects to claim her statutory share she receives a share of *her husband's property;* in a community property state, if the widow elects against the will she is making claim to *her own property.* (2) In a common law state, if the widow elects to take under the will, the husband's will operates to transfer all *his property.* In a community property state, if the widow elects to take under the will, the will operates to transfer both the husband's and *the wife's property.* Although at first blush it appears that the husband has made a testamentary transfer of all the property, in reality there are two transfers and two transferors. The husband's will makes a testamentary transfer of his property; the wife makes a lifetime transfer of her community share. By electing to take under the will, in effect the wife agrees to make a transfer of her community interest pursuant to the will's terms, in exchange for receiving an interest in her husband's property under the will. Since the wife, by

47 Atkinson, Wills 768 (2d ed. 1953); see Problem 5, page 338, supra.

electing, is a transferor, this has a profound impact on the tax treatment of her election.

Accidental Elections

As suggested by the above quotation from Atkinson on Wills, the election may arise by mistake. The husband, in devising an asset by his will, may think it is his separate property and not a community asset. The courts do not, however, stretch to find that a husband's will was intended to put his wife to an election.

COMMISSIONER v. CHASE MANHATTAN BANK

United States Court of Appeals, Fifth Circuit, 1958
259 F.2d 231, cert. denied, 359 U.S. 913, 1959

Wisdom, Circuit Judge. . . . Because of a long history of stoutly supporting a wife's vested ownership of half the community, Texas courts are loath to divest a widow of her share of the community on loose inferences. A study of the cases shows five major obstacles standing in the way of an election.

(1) *A presumption exists that a testator intends to dispose of his property only.* In Whaley v. Quillin, Tex. Civ. App. 1941, 153 S.W.2d 969, 971, involving a will in which the testator left his residuary estate in trust for his wife, the court held that the will disposed of the testator's share only; that "the law presumes that no man will attempt to dispose of another's property through the instrumentality of a will . . . the law will deprive no man of his property by conjecture." . . .

(2) *Only where the testator's intention to dispose of property that is not his own is shown by clear and unequivocal language is a husband's will construed to devise his wife's property.* Pope v. Pope, Tex. Civ. App. 1943, 175 S.W.2d 289. "In order that the necessity of an election shall take place, the testator must affect to dispose of property which is not his own, and also make a valid gift of his own property." McFarland v. Campbell, 5 Cir., 1954, 213 F.2d 855, 857. . . .

(3) *The language of the will must be susceptible of no other construction.* ". . . [The law] deprives no man of his property merely by conjecture. . . . For a will to be given the effect of an attempted disposition of property not owned by the testator, it is required that the language of the will conclusively evidence such a purpose. In such cases it is not sufficient that the will may be construed as revealing such an intention. It is necessary that it be open to no other construction." Avery v. Johnson, 1917, 108 Tex. 294, 192 S.W. 542, 544. If a will is ambiguous as to whether a testator attempted to dispose of both halves of the community, only the testator's half passes under his will. "[I]f this will should be construed to be ambiguous on the question as to whether the testator intended to bequeath the entire community estate, or merely the interest he owned therein, then the law furnishes a solution by requiring that it be given the construction that only the property owned by the

testator was intended to pass thereunder." Schelb v. Sparenburg, 1939, 133 Tex. 17, 124 S.W.2d 322, 326. . . .

(4) *Use of the first person singular pronoun shows an intention to dispose of the testator's property only.* In Haley v. Gatewood, 74 Tex. 281, 12 S.W. 25, 26, the testator used the language, "I will and bequeath all the estate I now own and possess." The Texas Supreme Court held: "We do not think this language indicates an intention on the part of the testator to dispose of any part which he did not own or possess." In Sailer v. Furche, Tex. Com. App. 1930, 22 S.W.2d 1065, 1066, the same result was reached where the testator made a testamentary disposition to his wife of "all property, real, personal, and mixed, of which I may die seized and possessed, wherever situated." A devise of "my" property is construed as referring only to the testator's interest in the community property. Sauvage v. Wauhop, Tex. Civ. App. 1912, 143 S.W. 259.

(5) *Finally, the will must give some benefit to replace the property surrendered by the election.* . . .

PROBLEMS

1. "I give and bequeath to my son, William, eleven lots owned by me in Block Thirteen, Somerset Addition, City of Waco; and also fifteen acres of land owned by me adjoining said City of Waco; and I give and bequeath to my wife, Rebecca, the twenty-five acres of land deeded to me by the State of Texas." All the described lands are community property. Does the will put the testator's widow to an election? See Chace v. Gregg, 88 Tex. 52, 32 S.W. 520 (1895); In re Wolfe's Estate, 48 Cal. 2d 570, 311 P.2d 476 (1957).

2. "I devise the land bounded and described by [metes and bounds description] as follows: The north half of said tract to my wife, Mary. The south half of said tract to my son, John." The described land is community property. Does the will put the testator's widow to an election? See Harkey v. Lackey, 259 S.W.2d 641 (Tex. Civ. App. 1953).

3. "I give, devise and bequeath all of the rest, residue and remainder of the property, both real and personal, which I shall own or to which I may be entitled at the time of my death, as follows: . . ." Does the will put the testator's widow to an election? See Commissioner v. Chase Manhattan Bank, supra; LaTourette v. LaTourette, 15 Ariz. 200, 137 Pac. 426 (1914).

4. "I give, devise and bequeath unto my wife, Effie May, one-half of all the property, real, personal and mixed, which I own or may be entitled to at the time of my death; and the remaining one-half of my property I give to the Church of Christ at Lott, Texas." Does the will put the testator's widow to an election? Church of Christ v. Wildfong, 265 S.W.2d 622 (Tex. Civ. App. 1954); compare In re Emerson's Estate, 82 Cal. App. 2d 510, 186 P.2d 734 (1947).

The "accidental election" cases, in which it is not clear whether the will puts the wife to an election, are not encountered very often. If the husband wants to put his wife to an election, the well-drafted will will make it abundantly clear that an election is required. The following clarifies matters: "It is my intention to dispose of not only my share of the community property of myself and my wife but of our entire community property, including my wife's share thereof, and my wife shall elect whether she shall take under this Will or shall take the share of our community property given her by law. Regardless of the election made by my wife, she shall be entitled to a probate homestead, exempt property, and family allowance out of my estate. If my wife elects to take the share of our community property given her by law, the provisions of this Will in her favor, except the bequest of tangible personal property and the devise of our residence, shall be of no effect and the remaining provisions of this Will shall be fully effective as if my wife had predeceased me."

The Widow's Election Will as an Estate Planning Arrangement

The above provision makes it clear that the wife is put to an election. But why would a husband want to use this arrangement? Why shouldn't he be satisfied with making a disposition of all his separate property and his one-half community interest? Isn't it overreaching on his part to impose his will on his wife's property?

The answer comes from comparing the posture of a husband in a community property state with that of his common law state counterpart. In a common law state, the husband has full power of disposition over his property, usually most or all of the marital assets. While he must be mindful of his wife's statutory share rights, and while the marital deduction tends to encourage a disposition that secures the maximum deduction, basically he is free to devise all the assets in the manner he sees best for the benefit of his family.

The husband in a community property state may be every bit as desirous of settling all the marital assets in a single dispositive plan. He may be satisfied, for example, that he is providing his spouse with greater financial security by leaving her an income interest in the entire community estate rather than outright ownership of her one-half share. He may see it as desirable to have the entire community state managed by a corporate fiduciary and thereby protect his wife against improvident investments, bad advice from importuning relatives — or perhaps gentle persuasions from a possible second husband. By restricting his wife to an income interest in the total community estate (plus, perhaps, limited invasion powers) the husband can be assured that the trust fund will give substantial protection to the wife during her lifetime, and will ultimately pass to the couple's children without undue or unfortunate dissipation. Finally, the nature of the assets (a business interest owned by the community, for example) may be such that their integrated management is seen as highly desirable, if not indispensable.

Viewed in this light, the husband's desire to settle all the community assets can hardly be said to amount to heinous overreaching on his part, or an unwarranted usurpation of his wife's testamentary power. While his decision may be motivated by paternalistic considerations, his paternalism is at least understandable. In short, the husband may be quite satisfied to make a testamentary disposition of only his one-half share of community assets — as, in fact, the great majority of husbands are. Alternatively, he may want to make an integrated disposition of all the community assets. If he chooses the latter, the widow's election will is one of the two planning arrangements he can employ. (The other is the funded inter vivos trust, in which the community assets are transferred to the trustee during the couple's lifetime.) While this arrangement is subject to the wife's "veto," in the form of an election to take against the will, it can serve as the basis for a sound estate plan.

Making Sure the Widow Elects

One of the risks in using a widow's election will is that the wife may elect against the will, and thereby disrupt the husband's dispositive plan. In addition, her election to pull her assets out of the will, thereby renouncing all will provisions in her favor, may raise many of the same mechanical problems as were litigated in the Sellick case.[48] Is there any way these problems can be avoided?

Provisions might be made in the will for what is to happen if the wife elects against the will. Another way is to secure the wife's signature on an "inter vivos agreement to elect." Here is an example:

> I, Jane Smith, wife of Adam Smith, hereby certify that I have read the foregoing Will of my husband and fully understand that he disposes not only of his separate property but also of our community property now owned or hereafter to be acquired, if any, including my half of that property. Being fully satisfied with its provisions, I hereby elect to accept and acquiesce in the provisions of the Will, waiving all claims to my share of any community property and all other claims that I may have upon any of the property disposed of by the Will, but not including my right to a family allowance out of my husband's estate during probate (*optional: or to a probate homestead and to property exempt from execution*). This instrument is not a transfer or release of my right, title or estate in any property now owned or hereafter acquired by me, is revocable by written instrument executed by me and delivered to my husband during his lifetime, and shall be effective and valid for any purpose only after the decease of my husband and provided I survive him, and upon the condition that the foregoing Will shall be duly admitted to probate by a court of competent jurisdiction and that it shall not be successfully contested or probate revoked.
>
> Dated at ____________, California, the _____ day of _______________, 19___.
>
> ____________________

[48] See page 464, supra. For a comprehensive discussion of the effects of a widow's election in a community property state, see Ray, The Widow's Election — A Study in Three Parts, 15 Sw. L.J. 85, 123 (1961).

PROBLEM

You are the attorney who drafted Adam Smith's widow's election will, and Adam and Jane Smith are coming into your office tomorrow: Adam to execute the will, and Jane to execute the inter vivos agreement to elect, reproduced above. Jane attended an earlier conference at which you outlined the dispositive plan that you were setting up at Adam's request: except for the family residence and tangible personal property, which are to pass to Jane outright, all the community property is to be placed in a trust from which Jane is to receive the income for life. On her death the trust corpus is to be distributed to the Smiths' descendants, per stirpes. At that earlier conference, Jane indicated that she had a general understanding of the testamentary plan and said, "I think it sounds all right to me."

One of your associates has suggested that it would be strongly desirable for Mrs. Smith to secure independent legal advice — from another law firm in town — in connection with her execution of the waiver. Do you think this is necessary? Desirable? See Gaines v. California Trust Co., 48 Cal. App. 2d 709, 121 P.2d 28 (1942); compare Opp v. Fry, 70 Cal. App. 2d 478, 161 P.2d 235 (1945).

4. *Lifetime Transfers of Community Property*

The widow's election doctrine protects the wife against testamentary transfers of her community interest. But what about lifetime gifts? Suppose the husband gives community assets to his mother, or to his children by a former marriage, or to his mistress. Can his wife have the transfer set aside in its entirety? As to her one-half community share? Does it make any difference whether the wife's challenge is made (a) during the husband's lifetime, (b) after her husband's death?

PROBLEMS

1. H, in his middle fifties, begins to show an unusual amount of interest in his "cousin" Samantha, a divorcee in her early forties. It is as though a long-lost member of the family has been found. H, who has grandchildren of his own, shows as much attention to his cousin's two children as he does to his own descendants. Several years after this new "family relationship" blossoms, H dies. His wife W discovers (1) that six months before his death H changed the beneficiary designation on a $25,000 community life insurance policy from W to "my dear friend, Samantha"; (2) that over the past three years H gave Samantha securities (community property) worth $20,000; and (3) that while there certainly was a relationship between H and Samantha, it was a quite different one from what W had supposed — Samantha wasn't a cousin!

W brings an action against Samantha, seeking to recover the entire $25,000 in life insurance proceeds and the securities (which have increased in value to

$25,000). The total value of the couple's community estate, as of H's death, was $250,000; H's will left all of his estate (as it existed at his death) to W. Is W entitled to all or any portion of the life insurance proceeds or securities?

2. On L's death, his wife M discovers that the beneficiary of a $25,000 community life insurance policy is L's mother. (Another $25,000 community policy is payable to M.) In addition to the two life insurance policies, the community estate of L and M consisted of a house and tangible personal property ($30,000), cash and securities ($40,000). L's will leaves "all my property" to his wife M. L and M have no children. L's mother is a widow who, while hardly a poverty case, lives in an apartment and has no source of income other than social security benefits and a $100/month annuity under her late husband's life insurance policies.

Assessing the situation, M concludes that L did her wrong — at least her mother-in-law (whom M never really liked) is on social security. She brings an action against L's mother, seeking recovery of the $25,000 in life insurance proceeds. What result?

3. P transfers community assets worth $200,000 to a local bank, naming it as trustee of a revocable inter vivos trust. Under the trust's terms, trust income is to be paid to P (in his capacity as "community manager") during his lifetime. P reserves the power, acting alone, to revoke, alter or amend the trust. On P's death the trust is to become irrevocable, and the trustee is to pay the income to P's wife Q for life. On Q's death the corpus is to be distributed to the couple's descendants, per stirpes. During Q's lifetime the trustee has the power to distribute so much of the trust corpus as in its discretion is deemed necessary for Q's support and maintenance.

These $200,000 in assets comprise almost the entire community estate. Q did not participate in creating the trust; in fact, she didn't even learn about it until P's death, some five years after the trust was created. P's will devises "all my property" to his wife Q — but the only probate assets consist of a house and tangible personalty (total value of this community property: $30,000), and $3,000 cash.

Q is sixty-eight years old at the time of P's death, and she is terribly upset (a) that her husband never told her about having set up the trust, and (b) that at age sixty-eight, a life estate in the assets doesn't appear to be much of a bargain. She comes to you, her attorney, and wants to know whether she can set the trust aside in whole or in part. Advise her.

4. Assume the same facts as in Problem 3, except that Q predeceases P. Q leaves a will that devises "all my property" to her two children by a former marriage. Your client is the Acme National Bank, named in Q's will as executor of her estate. Q's two sons are demanding that the executor challenge the trust and claim one-half the assets in the trust on behalf of Q's estate. The sons have threatened to "hold you fully responsible" if the executor doesn't challenge the trust. Advise the executor as to its rights and responsibilities. See Johanson, Revocable Trusts and Community Property: The Substantive Problems, 47 Texas L. Rev. 537, 570 (1969).

FIELDS v. MICHAEL

California Court of Appeal, Second District, 1949
91 Cal. App. 2d 443, 205 P.2d 402

Shinn, Presiding Justice. This is an appeal from a judgment in favor of defendant after an order sustaining a demurrer to plaintiff's complaint without leave to amend.

The complaint set forth the following allegations: Defendant is the duly appointed and acting executrix of the estate of W. C. Fields, who died on December 25, 1946. Plaintiff married decedent in California on April 8, 1900, and was his wife at all times thereafter until his death. At the time of the marriage decedent had no assets or estate of any kind whatsoever, and all of the estate which he acquired subsequent to marriage was from compensation for personal services rendered during marriage together with the increment thereon. Several years subsequent to their marriage, decedent deserted plaintiff. He never discussed his financial affairs with her and wilfully withheld from her all information concerning the extent of his assets and any gifts or transfers made by him out of the community property. Solely from his personal earnings for services rendered during marriage, decedent secretly and without plaintiff's knowledge or consent made extensive transfers of money by way of gifts. Ten separate gifts in stated amounts, made to named individuals are set out, all of which "were illusory and were transferred and set over by said decedent wilfully and fraudulently, secretly and clandestinely, from the community property of plaintiff and said decedent with intent to defraud plaintiff of her interest in her and his estate." The total amount of these gifts was $482,450. Upon information and belief, six additional gifts in unknown amounts to fictitiously named defendants are alleged. The complaint states that "plaintiff has not at any time consented to the making of said gifts or to any one or more of them and said gifts and each of them were made without her knowledge and approval and are all disaffirmed by plaintiff"; and alleges that plaintiff did not learn of any of the gifts until after the death of her husband. . . .

This action was thereafter brought against the estate for the reason that "many of said donees are deceased and that those remaining alive reside at divers places, some of them away from the State of California, and that they have used up and dissipated the sums of money by way of gift transferred and set over to them as aforesaid, and would not be able to pay a judgment, if one were rendered against them for return to plaintiff of said gifts or of some part thereof. Plaintiff is without any means of collecting in full from said donees those portions of said gifts which she is entitled to." It is also alleged that defendant executrix has possession and control of the financial records and papers of decedent; that she has refused to permit plaintiff to inspect them; and that these records disclose to a large extent detailed information concerning the alleged gifts of money as to which plaintiff is without information. The prayer for relief was twofold: (1) "By reason of plaintiff's disaffirmance of the gifts hereinbefore described, that defendant pay the plaintiff the sum of $241,225.00." (2) An accounting be had to determine the amount of any additional gifts made by decedent from community funds, and upon such accounting judgment be rendered for plaintiff to the extent of her interest therein.

Defendant's demurrer set forth some seven grounds upon which it was claimed the complaint was insufficient. The written opinion of the trial judge . . . discloses that the sole ground upon which the demurrer was sustained was that the complaint did not state a cause of action maintainable against defendant as executrix of the estate of W. C. Fields. The paramount issue presented is whether plaintiff may proceed directly against the estate of her husband to secure relief from his dissipation of the community funds through secret and unauthorized inter vivos gifts, or must seek recourse solely against the donees.

Section 574 of the Probate Code provides that "any person, or the personal representative of any person, may maintain an action against the executor or administrator of any testator or intestate who in his lifetime has wasted, destroyed, taken, or carried away, or converted to his own use, the property of any such person. . . ."

The facts alleged in the complaint are in our opinion sufficient to bring the action within these provisions. Even before the husband was forbidden by statute to make a gift of community property without his wife's consent, his power of disposition had never been deemed to include the privilege of acting in fraud of the rights of the wife in the community property. Smith v. Smith, 12 Cal. 216, 225, 73 Am. Dec. 533; Lord v. Hough, 43 Cal. 581, 585. Where actual fraud is alleged, as it is here, it would seem clear that a husband who has made unauthorized gifts of a large share of the community property may be held accountable to the offended wife as in the case of any other person who has wrongfully disposed of the property of another.

The position of the husband, in whom the management and control of the entire community estate is vested by statute, Civ. Code, secs. 161a, 172, 172a, has been frequently analogized to that of a partner, agent, or fiduciary. . . . Section 2219 of the Civil Code provides: "Everyone who voluntarily assumes a relation of personal confidence with another is deemed a trustee . . . as to the person who reposes such confidence. . . ." It is clear that, being a party to the confidential relationship of marriage, the husband must, for some purposes at least, be deemed a trustee for his wife in respect to their common property. Cf. Vanasek v. Pokorny, 73 Cal. App. 312, 320, 238 P. 798; Arnold v. Leonard, 114 Tex. 535, 273 S.W. 799, 804. Fundamental principles governing trust relationships are set forth in sections 2228 and 2229 of the Civil Code: "In all matters connected with his trust, a trustee is bound to act in the highest good faith toward his beneficiary, and may not obtain any advantage therein over the latter by the slightest misrepresentation, concealment, threat, or adverse pressure of any kind. A trustee may not use or deal with the trust property for his own profit, or for any other purpose unconnected with the trust, in any manner." Section 2234 declares: "Every violation of the provisions of the preceding sections of this article [i.e. sections 2228 through 2233] is a fraud against the beneficiary of a trust." Disregarding the allegations of intent to defraud, it is abundantly clear from those remaining that Fields must be held to have consummated a fraud against plaintiff. Nine years prior to their marriage, section 172 of the Civil Code was amended to provide that the husband could not make a gift of community property without the written consent of his wife. Stats. 1891, p. 425. Fields' disregard of this affirmative duty imposed upon him as manager of the community estate was a violation of his fiduciary obligations as defined in sections 2228 and 2229 of the Civil Code, supra. Even if good faith were to be shown, he would nevertheless be subject to personal liability for disposing of trust property in an unauthorized manner. Civ. Code, sec. 2238.

It is well settled, of course, that a gift made in violation of section 172 is, as against the donee, voidable by the wife in its entirety during the husband's lifetime, Matthews v. Hamburger, 36 Cal. App. 2d 182, 97 P.2d 465; Lynn v. Herman, 72 Cal. App. 2d 614, 165 P.2d 54, and to the extent of one-half after his death. Trimble v. Trimble, 219 Cal. 340, 26 P.2d 477; Ballinger v. Ballinger, 9 Cal. 2d 330, 70 P.2d 629. The beneficiary of a trust, however, is not required to pursue the trust property, but may elect to hold the trustee (or after his death, his estate) personally liable, McElroy v. McElroy, 32 Cal. 2d 828, 831, 198 P.2d 683; Lathrop v. Bampton, 31 Cal. 17, 23, 89 Am. Dec. 141; and the latter may not escape such liability by showing that the trust property has been dissipated. 54 Am. Jur., sec. 253, p. 196. Manifestly, a wife whose community property rights have been violated, as plaintiff alleges hers have been, is entitled to pursue whatever course is best calculated to give her effective relief. Where the amount of the gifts and identity of the donees are known, and the property can be readily reached, the former remedy may be decidedly more advantageous to the plaintiff than an action against the husband's estate, since the assets of the latter may be insufficient to satisfy a judgment. On the other hand, where recourse against the donees would be ineffective to give relief, as in the present instance, a denial of the alternative remedy would not only be in disregard of rudimentary principles applicable to persons acting in a fiduciary capacity, insofar as the husband stood in that relation, but would also amount to a concession that the law is powerless to accord to the wife's community interest the full protection which section 172 was evidently designed to ensure. We think the law is not so toothless. Whether the action is viewed as one based upon actual fraud, or as one based upon a violation of a statutory limitation upon the husband's power of control and management, is immaterial, for the dissipation of community assets by means of unauthorized gifts is in either view a conversion of the "property" of the wife such as would subject the husband's estate to suit under section 574 of the Probate Code. The statutory language is sufficiently comprehensive to include any wrongful conduct resulting in a loss of "property" to another.

. . .

The sole question we decide is that the complaint states a cause of action for compensatory relief. If plaintiff should prevail it will be for the trial court to decide the form the judgment should take and for the court in probate to give proper effect to it in exercising its jurisdiction with relation to claims to the community property.

The judgment is reversed with directions to overrule the demurrer and permit defendant to answer.[49]

PROBLEMS

1. Acting without his wife's knowledge or participation (quite possibly because it didn't occur to him to ask her), a California husband changes the beneficiary designation under a $25,000 community life insurance policy from a lump-sum payment to his wife to a life-plus-years-certain option. Under this option, fixed monthly payments are to be made to the wife for her lifetime or for ten years, whichever period is longer. If the wife dies before ten years have elapsed, the remaining payments are to be made to the couple's children in equal shares. In making the designation, the husband expressly reserves the right to change the beneficiary designation during his lifetime, but upon his death the option is to be irrevocable by his wife.

After the husband's death, the wife demands that the policy proceeds be paid in a lump sum rather than under the installment option. The life insurance company takes the position that the proceeds must be paid under the option. It contends that the case is governed by contract rules, and a husband has the power, as community manager, to enter into binding contracts on behalf of the community. What result? See Tyre v. Aetna Life Ins. Co., 54 Cal. 2d 399, 6 Cal. Rptr. 13, 353 P.2d 725 (1960).

Would it make any difference if the wife's life expectancy (either under mortality tables or because of some affliction) is less than ten years?

2. In 1948 W is adjudged an incompetent and H, her husband, is appointed her guardian. H serves in that capacity until 1957, when he resigns and the couple's son S is appointed guardian. Between 1948 and 1957 H makes gifts totalling $30,000 to the couple's grandchild, G. Between 1958 and 1961 H gives an additional $20,000 to G. All gifts are of community assets.

In 1961 H and W both die. W's will, executed long before she became incompetent, names her son S as executor. He sues G to recover one-half the gifts made by H, or $25,000. G makes the following arguments:

a. The gifts were voidable by the wife, not void, and only W could bring an action to set them aside. Since she died without having avoided the gifts (or without her guardian having taken steps to challenge them during her lifetime), her right to set the gifts aside is extinguished.

b. As for the gifts made between 1948 and 1957, H had the power, as W's guardian, to make these "reasonable" gifts to the grandchild, a natural object of both H's and W's bounty. W, acting through her guardian, consented to these gifts.

What result? See Harris v. Harris, 57 Cal. 2d 346, 19 Cal. Rptr. 793, 369 P.2d 481 (1962).

[49] Noted 23 S. Cal. L. Rev. 84. — Eds.

3. Suppose W had not been incompetent, and H had made these same lifetime gifts from community property. W dies, and her executor attempts to set the gifts aside. The grandchild argues that the gifts were voidable by W during her lifetime; and since she took no steps to avoid the gifts, it should be conclusively presumed that she acquiesced in them. Hence her right to set the gifts aside is extinguished. What result? Would it make a difference if W actually knew (or perhaps *probably* knew — she is now dead, and we don't really know) that H had made the gifts?

JOHANSON, REVOCABLE TRUSTS AND COMMUNITY PROPERTY: THE SUBSTANTIVE PROBLEMS

47 Texas L. Rev. 537, 563-564, 566-568 (1969)

Only in California and Washington is the wife given the same protection against lifetime donations of community property [that she has against testamentary transfers]. By statute in California and case decision in Washington, if a husband makes a gratuitous transfer of community property without obtaining his wife's joinder or consent, she can elect to set the transfer aside either during the husband's lifetime or after his death. This position has much to commend it, in terms both of clarity and of policy. Unlike the situation faced in the other community property states, the husband's power to make a gift of community property is not subject to a vague and ill-defined test that invites future challenge. Rather, the husband knows that unless the gift is a "mere trifle" that can be "sustained under the rule of de minimis," [50] he must obtain his wife's consent to the transfer. Furthermore, the wife *is* the owner of a one-half interest in the community assets. A gratuitous transfer does not involve the "management" of the community property, but rather results in a depletion of the community estate. The wife is protected against attempted testamentary dispositions of her community interest; it is both logical and desirable that she be given the same protection against inter vivos donative transfers that reduce her community share.

In the remaining community property states [other than Texas] the husband's sole management power over community assets other than homestead property[51] is held to include the power to make gifts, subject only to the requirement that the transfer not be "in fraud of the wife's rights." However, there are so few decisions discussing or applying this doctrine that its scope is unclear. Since none of the reported cases involve revocable transfers, in these states it is not clear whether the doctrine of "fraud on the wife" gives the wife a basis for challenging settlements of community property by revocable trust. . . .

[50] Marston v. Rue, 92 Wash. 129, 130, 159 P. 111, 112 (1916).

[51] The wife's joinder is required on deeds affecting homestead property. See, e.g., Idaho Code Ann. §55-1006 (1957); Nev. Rev. Stat. §115.040 (1967). In Arizona and New Mexico the wife's joinder is required on all deeds or mortgages affecting community real estate. Ariz. Rev. Stat. Ann. §33-452 (1956); N.M. Stat. Ann. §57-4-3 (1962).

Under the Matrimonial Property Act of 1967 the Texas husband has "sole management, control and disposition" over community property derived from his personal earnings and the revenues from his separate property. In the typical family situation most, if not all, of the community property is of this type, and will continue to be subject to the husband's sole management power. This includes the power to make gratuitous transfers of the property, subject to the two safeguards formulated by the Texas courts to protect the wife's community interest: The transfer must not be "in fraud of the wife's rights," and the transfer must not be "illusory." [52]

> Texas recognizes the right of the husband to make moderate gifts for just causes, but excessive or capricious gifts made with intent to defraud the wife are void or at least voidable upon her insistence.[53]

This statement of the "fraud on the wife" doctrine needs amplification in one respect. While a showing that the husband intended to defeat the wife's rights will enable the wife to challenge the transfer, proof of an actual intent to defraud need not be established: The circumstances surrounding the transfer and the amount of the gift may support a finding of "constructive" fraud.[54] But while the foregoing gives a satisfactory statement of the general principle, it leaves much to be desired as a workable test. What kinds of gifts are for just causes, and which ones are capricious? When is a gift moderate in amount, and when does it become excessive? What kinds of circumstances will lead to a finding of constructive fraud? Assessing

[52] In Land v. Marshall, 426 S.W.2d 841 (Tex. 1968), the Texas Supreme Court invoked the "illusory trust" doctrine of Newman v. Dore, page 478, supra, in allowing a widow to reach community assets in a revocable trust that became irrevocable on her husband's death. Although the facts of the case may have supported a challenge on "fraud on the wife" grounds, that issue had not been preserved on appeal and was not before the court. The case and problems engendered by it are discussed in the excerpted article at 571-578; Jones, The Illusory Trust and Community Property: A New Twist to an Old Tale, 22 Sw. L.J. 447 (1968).

In Texas there may be another basis on which the wife can challenge a lifetime transfer by her husband. Assets classified as "mixed community property" are "subject to the joint management, control and disposition of the spouses." Texas Family Code §5.22(b) (1971). Apparently, a transfer of such property without the wife's participation would be void as to her community share. See the excerpted article at 564. — Eds.

[53] Kemp v. Metropolitan Life Ins. Co., 205 F.2d 857, 863 (5th Cir. 1953). See also Stamler v. Coe, 15 Tex. 211, 215 (1855).

[54] Davis v. Prudential Ins. Co., 331 F.2d 346 (5th Cir. 1964); Land v. Marshall, 426 S.W.2d 841 (Tex. 1968); Kreuger v. Williams, 163 Tex. 545, 359 S.W.2d 48 (1962).

Where the wife attacks the gift during her husband's lifetime, a finding that the transfer was in actual or constructive fraud of the wife's rights will enable her to set the transfer aside in its entirety. Mahoney v. Snyder, 93 S.W.2d 1219 (Tex. Civ. App. — Amarillo 1936, no writ). Where the challenge does not come until after dissolution of the community by divorce or by the death of the husband, there is a conflict in the Texas decisions as to the remedy available to the wife. There is authority to support three different positions: (1) the transfer may be set aside in its entirety and the property restored to the community; (2) the transfer may be set aside as to the wife's one-half interest, and given effect as to the husband's community interest; and (3) the transfer may be set aside only if and to the extent that the wife cannot be compensated out of the husband's share of community property still on hand. See Huie, Texas Marital Property Rights 18 (1966).

the scope of the doctrine, and the likelihood of its application to a transfer by revocable trust, is not an easy task. None of the reported cases involve revocable transfers, and many of them deal with fact situations not ordinarily faced by the estate planner: transfers made while a divorce was pending or when the couple were separated, and instances in which title to assets was taken in a third party's name with an intent to defeat the wife's rights.

As a group the cases do not give clear guidelines. At best, they point up the factors that bear on the decision whether a transfer is likely to be held in constructive fraud of the wife's rights. Among the factors that have been emphasized are the relationship of the transferee to the transferor or his wife; whether there are special circumstances that tend to justify the transfer; the value of the assets transferred in relation to the total value of the community estate; and whether the wife has adequately been provided for out of the remaining community property and the separate property of the husband.

NOTES AND QUESTIONS

1. Certain transfers do not fall neatly into either category of outright gift or testamentary transfer. The most important of these are life insurance policies, revocable trusts, and joint bank accounts. While these are established during the transferor's lifetime, they have testamentary characteristics in that (a) the transferor retains an interest in the property until his death, (b) he can modify or revoke the arrangement, and (c) someone succeeds to ownership of the property upon his death. In California and Washington[55] the wife is given the same protection against these transfers that she has against testamentary transfers of community assets: She has an election to set them aside, wholly or partially.

In the other six states, which apply different rules to lifetime transfers and testamentary transfers, should the wife's power to challenge the transfers listed above be governed by the lifetime rules or by the testamentary rules?

2. The eight community property states have developed these various tests designed to give the wife some degree of protection against lifetime transfers of community property by the husband. From the standpoint of the estate planner, how serious are the problems raised by these doctrines? Suppose you are an attorney (a) in California or Washington, (b) in Texas, (c) in one of the other states, for a husband who wants to transfer a substantial amount of community assets in a revocable inter vivos trust. The trustee, a local bank, is to pay the trust income to the husband ("as community manager") for life, then to the wife for life, with remainder to the couple's children. How would you proceed (a) if the husband thinks his wife would go along with the arrangement if it were satisfactorily explained to her; (b) if the husband is concerned about his wife's temperament, mental stability, and capacity to manage money?

[55] And Idaho? See Anderson v. Mutual Benefit Assn., 77 Idaho 373, 292 P.2d 760 (1956).

5. *Tax Problems Raised by Transfers of the Entire Interest in Community Property*

In a common law state, the full value of a husband's property is taxed in his estate even though his wife claims a dower interest or elects to take a statutory share in lieu of property given to her by his will.[56] Her election to take under or against the will affects the amount of the husband's property passing to her, and thus may affect the amount of the marital deduction in his estate,[57] but it does not cause a transfer of any of the wife's property. While her election affects the amount of property that passes to other beneficiaries, it still passes to them from the husband's estate and not from the wife. In sum, the common law widow's election has no tax consequences to the wife.

In a community property state, the wife's decision to take *against* her husband's election will has no unusual tax consequences. The husband's one-half community interest is taxed in his gross estate as in the ordinary case, and the wife, by asserting a claim to her community share, does not make a transfer. But if the wife elects to take *under* the will, a transfer of her property takes place. By not asserting a claim to her community interest, she in effect transfers that interest pursuant to the terms of her husband's will. Her election also involves an element of exchange. She makes a transfer of her interest in exchange for receiving an interest in her husband's property under the will.

There are thus two distinctive tax characteristics of the community property widow's election. By electing to take under her husband's will, the wife makes a transfer — meaning that she may incur gift tax liability if by the transfer an interest in her property passes to third persons. Also, since her "election-transfer" involves an exchange, it may be treated as a transfer for a partial consideration under §§2512(b) and 2043(a) of the Internal Revenue Code of 1954 — meaning that she may be entitled to a "consideration offset."

What if the transfer of community assets is by inter vivos gift rather than by will? Suppose the husband places community assets in a revocable inter vivos trust under which the trust income is to be paid to the husband (on behalf of the community) during his lifetime, then to his wife for her lifetime. On the death of the survivor the trustees are to distribute the corpus to the couple's children in equal shares. The wife does not join in or assent to the transfer.

In California and Washington it is clear that the transaction will be treated, for tax purposes, the same as a widow's election will. In those states the wife has the same protection against lifetime donations of community property that she has against testamentary transfers: She has an election.[58] In the other community prop-

[56] Int. Rev. Code of 1954, §2034.
[57] See Estate of Kennedy v. United States, page 468, supra.
[58] See page 523, supra.

erty states, where the husband's power to make lifetime gifts is limited only by the "fraud on the wife" doctrine (and, in Texas, also by the "illusory trust" test), the wife cannot challenge a transfer if it does not fall within the protection of these doctrines. It is not as easy to visualize the wife as a transferor in this situation, since she did not join in the creation of the trust and is powerless to challenge it. Yet she is treated as a transferor for tax purposes. The case that established this proposition is Commissioner v. Chase Manhattan Bank.

COMMISSIONER v. CHASE MANHATTAN BANK

United States Court of Appeals, Fifth Circuit, 1958
259 F.2d 231, cert. denied, 359 U.S. 913, 1959

omit to 539

WISDOM, Circuit Judge. This case turns on the community property law of Texas. Stated broadly, the question before us is the gift tax effects of trusts and insurance in a community property state where the wife has a present, vested ownership of half the marital community in her own right.

The proceedings are brought to this Court by a petition and a cross-petition for review of a Tax Court decision concerning the transferee liability of the taxpayer, Chase Manhattan Bank, successor to Chase National Bank of New York, for gift taxes for the year 1948. 25 T.C. 617 (1955). The alleged transferor is Mrs. Marie Elizabeth Moran, widow of Daniel J. Moran. Marie is alleged to have made gifts of her share of her community property by "acquiescing" in the benefits of three trusts — an insurance trust, a living trust, and a testamentary trust — established by her husband.

I. The Three Trusts.

Daniel James Moran and Marie Elizabeth Moran were married before 1922 and remained husband and wife until Daniel died April 3, 1948. Their legal domicile was Texas during their entire married life. Daniel had no separate property.

November 2, 1928, in New York, Daniel created a living trust, naming as trustee, The Equitable Trust Company, a predecessor to Chase. The trust estate consisted of securities belonging to the community. Income was payable to Daniel for life, then to Marie for life, with the remainder to the settlor's descendants. Daniel reserved the right to modify or revoke the trust. He reserved no powers of control over the administration of the trust.

November 2, 1928 Daniel also created an insurance trust with the same trustee. The trust estate consisted of insurance policies on Daniel's life. Daniel paid the insurance premiums with community funds. He reserved the right to modify or revoke the trust; and under the policies he had the right to change the beneficiaries. Upon Daniel's death the insurance proceeds were payable to the trustee. Income was payable to Marie for life, with the remainder to the settlor's descendants. . . .

Daniel's will provided for a testamentary trust of his residuary estate, Marie to receive the income for life, the remainder to be divided among Daniel's descendants. Chase, the trustee, was given broad discretionary power to distribute principal to any beneficiary.

II. Conflicting Contentions.

A. The Commissioner held that on Daniel's death the living trust and insurance trust became irrevocable and the testamentary trust came into being. (1) As to the testamentary trust, the Commissioner took the position that Marie was put to an election under Daniel's will and that she elected to take under the will, relinquishing her half of the community for a life estate in that half. (2) As to the living trust, the Commissioner held that it became a completed gift by husband and wife when Daniel died without having exercised his right of revocation. (3) Section 86.2(a) of Treasury Regulations 108 specifically covers insurance payable revocably to a third person and purchased with community funds. The Commissioner held that on the husband's death there was a gift by the wife of one-half the amount of the proceeds of the insurance.

The Commissioner valued the gift to each trust as the difference between what he concluded that Marie gave up (her community one-half share of the trust estate) and what she retained (a life estate in her one-half). The resulting deficiency for the three trusts amounted to $133,378.88. This was assessed against Chase as trustee and transferee under Section 1025 of the Internal Revenue Code of 1939.

B. Chase, represented by the same New York lawyers who drew the trusts and the will, filed a petition in the Tax Court contending that Marie had made no taxable gifts; but, if she had, that the Commissioner's measure of each gift should be reduced by the value of the life estate she received in her husband's one-half of each trust. . . .

IV. The Community Property System.

For many years taxpayers in common law states, with a legitimate interest in tax uniformity, and taxpayers in community property states, with a legitimate interest in tax recognition of the realities of the community property system, were at cross purposes. Finally, Congress enacted the equalization provisions of the Revenue Act of 1948 — to put taxpayers in all states on the same tax basis and at the same time recognize the logical tax effects of community property principles. It is important therefore that we weigh the issues carefully, in the interest of giving full weight to the community property law of Texas — while we give full weight to the tax laws of the United States. This takes a little doing.

A few basic principles characterize the community property system. Their application here is determinative of the issues in this case.

The community property system comes from the custom of the women of the Visigoths and other Germanic tribes sharing the fighting and the spoils of war with their men; it owes its strength to the civilized view that marriage is a full partnership. Husband and wife are equal partners. Each has a present, vested half interest in all community property. All property accumulated during marriage is community property, unless it is received by gift, devise, or inheritance. In Texas even income derived from separate property belongs to the community, including interest and dividends from separately owned securities. The husband is the manager of the community. But this management is not equivalent to ownership. He acts as a managing agent or trustee or managing partner of a limited partnership. The husband may sell or donate community property but not in fraud of his wife's rights. The earnings of the husband during marriage are community, and property purchased with such earnings is also community. The wife's rights, aside from managerial control, are the same as the husband's. Thus, on death or divorce the community is divided equally. Neither spouse has testamentary disposition over the other's half of the community. The wife has complete testamentary disposition over her half and may leave it even to her paramour. Upon the death of either spouse, a community property state levies an inheritance tax on the decedent's half of the community. Since 1948 (and prior to 1942), only the decedent's half is includible in his gross estate for federal tax purposes.

V. The Testamentary Trust.

[In an omitted portion of the opinion the court held that Daniel's will did not put Marie to an election because it did not purport to devise the entire interest in community assets. See page 513, supra.]

VI. The Insurance Trust.

The Commissioner's position is that on Daniel's death Marie made a taxable gift of one-half of the value of the proceeds of the insurance policies less the value of a life estate in that half. Chase, the trustee, contends (on appeal) that, although Daniel could revoke the trust and change beneficiaries, Marie could not, and as to her the trust was complete and irrevocable in 1928 when it was created, and therefore there is no tax. . . .

In a community property state where insurance on the husband's life is purchased with community funds, payable revocably to a third person beneficiary, the husband's right to change the beneficiary and all other control over the property are held as agent of the community. The bundle of rights in the policy is owned by the community. Something happens to this bundle when the insured dies, thereby terminating his control over the property and bringing the community to an end. What happens is, that the community's property interests in the policy-rights are transformed into the beneficiary's right to the proceeds. It is a shift in control and a shift of beneficial interest. This is the transfer that is taxed.

Up to the time of his death, Daniel, as managing agent of the community, had the right to change beneficiaries. When he died without exercising this right, the transfer to the trustee was a completed gift from the community: one-half therefore should have fallen in the taxable estate of the deceased husband. The other half is a taxable gift from the surviving spouse.

Under the terms of the trust agreement Marie was the income beneficiary for life. Accordingly, the measure of her gift was half the amount of the proceeds less a life estate in that half. . . .

VIII. The Living Trust.[59]

. . .

It must be borne in mind that *Daniel did not create the trust. The community created it.* Any rights that were reserved in the settlor were rights held by the community. . . . Daniel's control (in his case restricted to the right of revocation and modification) could be exercised only as *agent for the community.*

. . .

We hold that the Moran living trust was not ambulatory; it was a present, valid trust created in 1928. Marie is the income beneficiary under the express terms of that trust and not because she receives the income in exchange for relinquishing her half of the community as part of an assumed election to accept the benefits of the trust. We do not have before us, therefore, the question at issue in Commissioner of Internal Revenue v. Siegel, 9 Cir., 1958, 250 F.2d 339, that is, whether the wife's election to take under the will should be considered as a gift by the wife or a purchase of an annuity supported by consideration.

Our holding does not mean that gift tax consequences attached at the time the trustee took title in 1928. In a transfer of property valid under state law, state law focuses on title. The federal gift and estate tax law focuses on transfer of the beneficial enjoyment of the property. One who creates a trust during his lifetime, even though he reserves a life estate, parts with legal title to the trustee and grants to the beneficiaries (including remainderman) an immediate equitable title. Transfer of the possession and enjoyment of the property may be deferred until some future time. It is this very situation that causes the application of the gift and estate tax laws. Treasury Regulation 108, Section 86.3 provide therefore: "A gift [for tax purposes] is incomplete in every instance where a donor reserves the power to revest the beneficial title to the property in himself." The taxable incident is the shifting of the beneficial enjoyment in the trust property, no matter when title is vested. See Brady v. Ham, 1 Cir., 1930, 45 F.2d 454.

Since Daniel retained the power of revocation (for the community), there was no taxable gift until the shift in beneficial enjoyment at his death. Estate of Sanford v. Commissioner, 1939, 308 U.S. 39, 60 S. Ct. 51, 84 L. Ed. 20; Burnet v. Guggenheim, 1933, 288 U.S. 280, 52 S. Ct. 369, 77 L. Ed. 748. When Daniel died the trust became irrevocable. His community one-half should have been included in his gross estate under Section 811(c) and 811(d) of the 1939 Code, and Marie made a taxable gift of the other half under Treasury Regulations, Section 86.2 and 86.3 less her retained life estate in such one-half.

Had Daniel been acting for himself instead of for the community, and had the

[59] In an omitted portion of the opinion the court held that the transfer by revocable trust was not in fraud of the wife's rights under Texas law. The Chase Manhattan Bank case antedated Land v. Marshall, note 52 supra, applying the illusory transfer doctrine to a revocable trust funded by the husband with community property. — Eds.

right of revocation been retained by him individually the taxpayer would have been on stronger ground to urge that, as to Marie, the gift was complete in 1928.[60] But it was as agent for the community, that Daniel held the right of revocation. For tax purposes the gift was incomplete until the right of revocation ceased on Daniel's death.

IX. Conclusion.

Summarizing, we hold as follows: . . .

2. As to the insurance trust, we hold in favor of the Commissioner. On the death of the insured, for tax purposes half of the proceeds of the insurance belonged in Daniel Moran's gross estate and the other half was a taxable transfer from Mrs. Moran, less her retained life interest in that half.

3. As to the living trust, we hold partly in favor of the Commissioner and partly in favor of the taxpayer. We hold that on Daniel Moran's death the trust became irrevocable. His half of the community belonged in his gross estate and his wife's half was a taxable gift to the trust less her retained life interest in that half.

Accordingly, the judgment is Reversed and the case Remanded for any appropriate proceedings not inconsistent with this opinion.

Gift Tax Problems

In the Chase Manhattan Bank case the court held that Mrs. Moran made a gift of the remainder interest in her community share of the trusts' assets. The beneficiaries of the gift were the couple's children, named as remaindermen under the trusts. The amount of the gift was determined by computing the present value of the right to receive the trust corpus X years from now, X being Mrs. Moran's life expectancy.

To illustrate: H creates a revocable inter vivos trust that is funded with community assets. At his death some years later the value of the trust corpus is $450,000. The value of H's community interest (after being reduced by death taxes and other charges) is $200,000; the value of W's community interest is $250,000. The trust, which became irrevocable on H's death, provides that trust income is to be paid to W for life, and on W's death the trust corpus is to be paid to the couple's children, A and B. W, who is sixty-five years old at the time of her husband's death, elects not to challenge the trust. By taking under the trust W is deemed to have made a transfer of her $250,000 community interest, retaining a life estate therein. The value of the remainder interest she has transferred to A and B is the value of the right to receive $250,000 on her death. Under the Treasury tables used for valuing future interests, which employ an interest factor of 6 percent, the right to receive a fund on the death of a 65-year-old woman is .44 times the present value of the fund.

[60] The taxpayer argued that if the wife ever made a gift, it was in 1928, at the time the trust was created — a very convenient argument, since the present gift tax was not enacted until 1932. — Eds.

Treas. Reg. §2512-9, Table A (2) (1971). Thus the value of the remainder interest in W's community share is .44 times $250,000, or $110,000. Stated another way, $110,000 deposited at 6 percent compound annual interest will grow to $250,000 in X years, X being a 65-year-old woman's life expectancy. The older the life tenant, the larger the present value of the remainder interest that follows her life estate, and the larger the amount of the gift.[61]

If the transfer is by widow's election will rather than by revocable trust, and the wife elects to take under the will (thereby transferring her community interest pursuant to the will's terms), the wife's gift is computed in the same manner.

Can the gift tax occasioned by the wife's election-transfer be avoided? Certainly — by making the wife's transfer incomplete for gift tax purposes. This could be done by giving her a power of appointment over her community share of the trust assets, or a power to revoke as to her share of assets in the trust.

PROBLEM

Suppose the revocable trust (or the testamentary trust created by H's election will) gives W the power to revoke the entire trust, including the portion funded by H's share of assets. What are the estate tax consequences on W's subsequent death? (A clue: Is W's power over the corpus funded with H's assets a power to revoke or a power of appointment?) See Johanson, Revocable Trusts and Community Property: The Substantive Problems, 47 Texas L. Rev. 537, 590 (1969).

Up to this point we have explained how the wife's election to take under a widow's election will, or her "transfer" under a revocable trust funded with community property, may generate a taxable gift of the remainder interest in her share of the assets. But that's only half the story. In the Chase Manhattan Bank case the taxpayer's attorney contended "that Marie had made no taxable gifts; but, if she had, that the Commissioner's measure of each gift should be reduced by the value of the life estate she received in her husband's one-half of each trust." [62] The latter contention, that Marie was entitled to a "consideration offset," was rejected by the court. Perhaps it would be more appropriate to say that the question was not fully considered by the court, as the primary thrust of Judge Wisdom's landmark opinion was to recognize the wife as a transferor for gift tax purposes. Commissioner v. Siegel and a group of more recent cases[63] have established the wife's right to an offset for the value of the interest received from her husband's estate. On the con-

[61] Since the gift is of a future interest, the $3000-per-donee annual exclusions are not available to W. Int. Rev. Code of 1954, §2503(b). She could, however, apply her $30,000 lifetime exemption to the gift if she has not previously used the exemption. See pages 256-258, supra.

[62] See page 528, supra.

[63] Widow's election will: Estate of Emma Brassani, 45 T.C. 373 (1966); Zillah Mae Turman, 35 T.C. 1123 (1961). Revocable trust: cf. United States v. Gordon, 406 F.2d 332 (5th Cir. 1969).

sideration offset question, then, the Chase Manhattan Bank decision is no longer the law.

COMMISSIONER v. SIEGEL

United States Court of Appeals, Ninth Circuit, 1957
250 F.2d 339

Yankwich, District Judge. The question involved in this petition by the Commissioner of Internal Revenue to review a decision of the Tax Court rendered October 3, 1956, turns on the correctness of the determination by the Tax Court of a deficiency, arising under the federal gift tax law for the taxable year 1950, of the respondent Mildred Irene Siegel, to be referred to hereinafter as the taxpayer.

On February 8, 1954, the Commissioner of Internal Revenue mailed to the taxpayer a notice of a deficiency in the total amount of $51,144.24. The assessment was based on a determination which read in part:

> The transfer by the above-named donor to her son of a remainder interest in her one-half interest in community property which she transferred to a testamentary trust established under the last will and testament of Irving Siegel, Deceased, is determined to constitute a transfer by said donor without consideration in money or money's worth, and a gift within the meaning of Section 1000 of the Internal Revenue Code.

On April 29, 1954, the taxpayer filed a petition with the Tax Court for a redetermination of the deficiency. The Tax Court entered its decision on October 3, 1956, determining, in effect, that the taxpayer's transfer having been made in consideration of her waiver of her community rights and her acceptance of the benefits under the will, only the excess of the value of her transfer over what she received was a taxable gift. The Tax Court determined the amount to be $4,314.87, which has been paid.

I. Facts Admitted or Uncontroverted.

In the main, the facts are not in dispute, either because they were stipulated or found by the Court on evidence which stands uncontradicted. So, unless the facts warrant different legal conclusions, the decision of the Tax Court must stand.

In outline, the facts are:

The taxpayer and Irving Siegel, to be referred to as Siegel, were husband and wife and residents of the State of California. Siegel died in California on January 4, 1949. The Siegels had an adopted son, Richard Bruce Siegel, who was born on May 14, 1943, and who resides with the taxpayer. Siegel left an estate consisting entirely of community property acquired by him, as the Tax Court found, and his wife since 1927. The Tax Court also found that on the date of Siegel's death, the gross value of the community property was $1,422,897.14, and the gross value of the taxpayer's half share in it was $711,448.57. At the time of the hearing, the Tax Court determined that on January 5, 1950, the date of the taxpayer's election to take under the Will, to be referred to later on, the net value of Siegel's share to be $295,076.54 and that of the taxpayer's $584,035.44. . . .

Siegel left a Will, dated March 28, 1948, which was admitted to probate in the Superior Court of Los Angeles County, California, on February 3, 1949. The will contained a provision bequeathing to the taxpayer, in addition to some minor gifts, the sum of $35,000 ("to offset," as the will stated, a like sum bequeathed to his "sisters and nephew") and created a trust to pay to her during her lifetime, and to the son, thereafter, the income of the estate. The instrument provided that the payments shall be such as the trustees

> deem proper to maintain at least the same standard of living to which she has been accustomed in recent years, but in no event less than the sum of $1000.00 per month.

The taxpayer was named one of three trustees and the will specifically provided that should she determine to take her community property share, "she should take nothing as a beneficiary under the trust". . . . The reference to the standard of living in the will is important in view of the fact that the Tax Court found that in 1948, the year preceding his death, the living expenses of the taxpayer and her husband before income taxes were $46,500.

On January 5, 1950, the taxpayer executed and filed with the Superior Court an instrument electing to take under Siegel's last will and testament in lieu of all community property rights which she had in the estate. . . .

[T]he Tax Court made the following additional findings:

> Included in the above total expenditures were sums expended by petitioner for the support of her and Irving's son which averaged well under $3,000 per year.
>
> Under the economic conditions existing during the years subsequent to decedent's death and prior to this hearing it would cost petitioner $45,000 per year, including income taxes to maintain the standard of living to which she was accustomed in recent years prior to decedent's death.

On the basis of these findings, it concluded that the surrender by the taxpayer of her community property rights was a gift to the estate to the extent that the value of the interest thus surrendered exceeded the value of the interest she acquired under the terms of the will.

In determining the values the Tax Court ruled that the amount of the gift should be measured by the taxpayer's community interest reduced by the present value of her life interest in the entire community property and a specific bequest of $35,000 granted to her by the terms of the will.

In sum, the Tax Court treated the transfer as being one in which what the taxpayer surrendered *was the consideration* for what she received.

In this petition for review, the Commissioner contests this basic principle and the reasons upon which it is grounded.

II. The Problem of Consideration.

It is the contention of the Commissioner that in this manner the Tax Court misapplied to the facts Section 1002 of the Revenue Code of 1939, which reads:

> Where property is transferred for less than an adequate and full consideration in money or money's worth, then the amount by which the value of the property exceeded the value of the consideration shall, for the purpose of the tax imposed by this chapter, be deemed a gift, and shall be included in computing the amount of gifts made during the calendar year.[64]

We are of the view that the Commissioner's contention that the transaction was donative and that, as his brief puts it, "the taxpayer received no consideration whatsoever, adequate or not, for making the election" is without merit. The issue must be determined in the light of the community property law of California and the law of wills.

The election made by the taxpayer reads:

> Election of Widow to Take Under Will
>
> I, the undersigned, Mildred I. Siegel, widow of Irving Siegel, deceased, do hereby elect to take under the Last Will and Testament of said deceased *in lieu of any and all community property rights which I have* in said estate. (Emphasis added.)
>
> Dated this 5th day of January, 1950.

Elections to take under a will by one of the spouses instead of property that he or she may be entitled to under state law have long been recognized as transactions in which the property surrendered is considered the consideration for the offer made in the will and accepted at the time of the execution of the will in a contemporaneous instrument or thereafter. In all instances, the effect of the election is determined by the status of the property under the law of the state. "The gift by will in lieu of the other right is said to be equivalent to an offer, and to offer something to the devisee in return for his property or interest." [65]

Most writers on the law of contracts and Courts which have dealt with the matter are in accord that the property surrendered is a consideration for that which is accepted, and what may begin as a unilateral offer turns into a binding contract upon such acceptance.

In the present case, the Tax Court found that the property left by Siegel was community property acquired by Siegel and the taxpayer in California since 1927. *This date is of utmost importance.* For, since 1927, the interests of husband and wife in community property in California are declared to be "present, existing and equal interests." . . .

The husband and wife may alter their legal relations as to property and only

[64] 26 U.S.C., 1952 Ed., §1002. [Int. Rev. Code of 1954, §2512. — Eds.]
[65] Page on Wills [3d (Lifetime) ed. 1941] §1346.

one-half of the community property is subject to the testamentary disposition of the decedent. When the husband makes a testamentary disposition of more than half of the community property and the wife chooses to take under the will, the half interest in the estate which she surrenders is a contract supported by adequate consideration. As stated by the Supreme Court of California in a noted case:

> The "waiver" was in fact a contract, by the terms of which plaintiff accepted certain devises and bequests under the will in lieu of any right she might have in any community property. Such an agreement is clearly supported by consideration and is binding upon the plaintiff, irrespective of any element of estoppel arising from the testator's change of position in reliance upon the representation contained in the instrument.[66]

And the rule is the same whether the waiver be attached to the will or is contained in a separate instrument. The wife is not put upon her election until the estate is ready for distribution.

In view of the vested character of the interest of the wife in community property under California law even before death, if the property was, *as was the case here,* acquired since July 29, 1927, decisions arising in states in which the wife has a mere dower right are not controlling. . . .

California law gives to each spouse a "present, existing and equal" interest in community property acquired since July 29, 1927. During the lifetime of the husband, the entire community property is subject to his management and control. Upon his death the property is released of his limited managerial and control powers and one-half of it, as the statute says, "belongs to the surviving spouse." The other half is subject to the testamentary disposition of the decedent. . . .

This Court, in interpreting California law, as changed by the Act of July 29, 1927, has held that the wife's interest being vested, her half never became a part of his estate:

> The Tax Court appears to have assumed that, upon decedent's death, petitioner's half of the community property ceased to be hers and became a part of decedent's estate. The assumption is incorrect. Petitioner's half, like decedent's half, was subject to administration, but, unlike his half, her half never became a part of his estate.[67]

III. The Events Which Led to Surrender.

Factually, the record shows that the decision to accept the legacy under the will in lieu of the community property which she surrendered to the trust chiefly for the benefit of her son was arrived at by the taxpayer after full consultation between her and the trustees. In the hearing before the Tax Court, she testified in substance:

[66] Flanagan v. Capital National Bank of Sacramento, 1931, 213 Cal. 664, 666, 3 P.2d 307, 308.

[67] Bishop v. Commissioner, 9 Cir., 1945, 152 F.2d 389, 391.

Her husband was only forty-seven years of age at the time of his death, dying of a coronary thrombosis which was sudden and unexpected. He had been a builder and contractor for over twenty-five years. They had been married for twenty-seven years, residing in California during the entire period of marriage except four years. The property accumulated was community property. She did not own any separate property of any consequence before marriage and neither of them had acquired any property by gift or inheritance at the time of her husband's death. The home they occupied cost $62,500, on which they made repairs amounting to $30,000, the furnishings of the house having been appraised in 1950 on the replacement basis as $60,000. They also owned a home at Palm Springs, completely furnished. For the calendar year 1947, the net income for federal tax purposes was $479,422.99 and for the year 1948, $230,399. Their living expenses, including the taxes for the year 1948 — as shown by excerpts from the books — were $46,551.49.

At the time of Siegel's death, the adopted son was five and one-half years of age.

Of the two persons named as co-trustees, one Ben Weingart was a close friend and associated in business with Siegel. The other, N. B. Allison, was also a close friend whom the taxpayer and Siegel had known since arriving in California in 1926. They were suggested as trustees with her because Siegel considered them the most capable men to administer his estate and to be trustees of the trust. Although she was named as one of the co-trustees, Siegel did not discuss with her the terms of his Will prior to his death. About two weeks after his death, Weingart and the attorney for the estate explained the Will to her. She understood that if she took her half of the community property, she received nothing under the Will.

The matter was also discussed with the other co-trustees and finally, on the advice of Weingart, she decided to take under the will, for by so doing, she would have the benefit of the advice of the co-trustees as to investment and the entire estate would be under one management instead of two.

She summed up her testimony by saying that she took under the will because she could not maintain her standard of living on the income from her half and did not wish to lose control of the other half.

These facts were, in the main, confirmed by Weingart, who was consulted by Siegel about the terms of the will. He also corroborated the taxpayer's statement that he advised her to take under the will.

A good portion of the estate consists of the ownership of apartment properties.

In the light of this recital of facts, it is quite evident to us that the Tax Court's determination that there was a transfer, the consideration for which was the value of the community property interest that she surrendered taxable only to the amount of the excess of the value of her transfer over what she received, is not clearly erroneous. Indeed, we believe that no contrary conclusion is warranted. And, as the foregoing discussion discloses, we are also of the view that the Tax Court applied the law correctly to the facts.

The petition for review is denied and the order of the Tax Court affirmed.[68]

[68] Initially, the Commissioner issued a nonacquiescence to the Siegel decision, indicating he

---

The Tax Court had held that "a gift was made to the remainderman to the extent of petitioner's community one-half of the principal less the life estate reserved by her therein, reduced by the value of the life estate received by her in the husband's part of the community property conveyed to the testamentary trust, plus the $35,000 bequest in cash which she received under the will." It refused to allow an offset for discretionary distributions of principal that might be made "to maintain at least the same standard of living to which she has been accustomed," on the ground that the amount of trust income would likely make distributions of principal unnecessary.

To illustrate computation of the consideration offset under the gift tax, let us return to the example on page 531. There the value of the remainder interest in W's $250,000 community share was determined to be $110,000. However, in exchange for making the transfer W received an income interest in her husband's community share of $200,000. Computation of the present value of that life income interest is given by the same Treasury table. Since the value of a remainder interest following a 65-year-old woman's life estate is .44 times the fund's present value, the present discounted value of a 65-year-old woman's life estate is (1.00 minus .44 =) .56 times the fund's value. Thus the value of W's income interest in H's community share is .56 (times $200,000), or $112,000. Stated another way, a fund of $112,000 invested at 6 percent compound annual interest will return annuity payments of (.06 times $200,000 =) $12,000 for X years, X being a 65-year-old woman's life expectancy.

$110,000	Value of remainder interest transferred by W
−112,000	Value of income interest received from H
$ 0	Taxable gift.

Since the value of the interest received by W exceeds the value of the interest she transferred in exchange, there is no taxable gift.[69] The older the widow at the time of her husband's death, the greater the likelihood of a taxable gift. Another factor increasing the likelihood of a taxable transfer is that in the typical case the wife's interest will exceed the value of the husband's interest since death taxes and other

---

would refuse to follow the case in making gift tax assessments. 1957-1 Cum. Bull. 6. He later reversed his position, and issued an acquiescence. 1964-2 Cum. Bull. 7. — Eds.

[69] "That this should be the result can be seen by viewing the wife's economic position immediately before and immediately after her election. Before her election, she had outright ownership of assets worth 250,000 dollars. After the election she has a life income interest in the entire 450,000-dollar fund. According to the Treasury tables used to value life income interests for tax purposes, the present value of this income interest for a person her age is [.56 times $450,000, or $252,000]. . . . [I]n terms of present value the wife's economic position has not changed. What has changed is the nature of her ownership interest. [The gift tax applies to transfers that deplete the transferor's estate.] Since the wife's election-transfer has not depleted her estate, there is no taxable gift." Johanson, Revocable Trusts, Widow's Election Wills, and Community Property: The Tax Problems, 47 Texas L. Rev. 1247, 1268-1269 (1969).

expenses will have reduced the husband's share. In the Siegel case, for example, the husband's community share was reduced by taxes and other charges to $295,000; the wife's share in the trust was $584,000.

Estate Tax Problems

When a husband creates a revocable trust funded with community property, on his death only his one-half community interest is taxed in his estate.[70] If the transfer is by an election will and his widow elects to take under the will, the tax consequences in his estate are the same. Although his will purports to dispose of the entire community interest, only the value of his one-half interest is includible in his gross estate.[71] As we have already seen, in this situation the wife is treated as the transferor of her community interest.

In determining the estate tax consequences on the wife's subsequent death, the starting point is that the wife's community share in the trust is includible in her gross estate. She made an inter vivos transfer of her interest, and in that transfer she retained a life estate. Just as in the gift tax situation, though, she is deemed to have made that transfer *in exchange for* receiving an interest in her husband's estate. Section 2043(a) of the estate tax code, which contains a companion provision to the "transfers for insufficient consideration" provisions of the gift tax code,[72] has been held to apply to the wife's election-transfer, whether that transfer was by election will or revocable trust.[73] Consequently, the wife's estate is given a "consideration offset" for the value of the income interest she received from her husband's estate. The amount of the offset is based on the value of that interest as of the husband's death — in our example, $112,000 — without regard to the amount of income the wife actually received from the husband's share during her lifetime.[74]

[70] See Commissioner v. Chase Manhattan Bank, page 527, supra.

[71] Pacific Nat'l Bank, 40 B.T.A. 128 (1939), acquiesced in, 1939-2 Cum. Bull. 28; Coffman-Dobson Bank & Trust Co., 20 B.T.A. 890 (1930), acquiesced in, X-1 Cum. Bull. 13 (1931).

[72] "If any one of the transfers, trusts, interests, rights, or powers enumerated and described in sections 2035 to 2038, inclusive, and section 2041 is made, created, exercised, or relinquished for a consideration in money or money's worth, but is not a bona fide sale for an adequate and full consideration in money or money's worth, there shall be included in the gross estate only the excess of the fair market value at the time of death of the property included on account of such transaction, over the value of the consideration received therefor by the decedent." Int. Rev. Code of 1954, §2043(a).

[73] Election will: Estate of Vardell v. Comm'r, 307 F.2d 688 (5th Cir. 1962); Whiteley v. United States, 214 F. Supp. 489 (W.D. Wash. 1963); Estate of Daisy F. Christ, 54 T.C. 493 (1970); Estate of Lillian B. Gregory, 39 T.C. 1012 (1963). Revocable trust: United States v. Gordon, 406 F.2d 332 (5th Cir. 1969).

[74] In applying the estate tax consideration offset to the example in the text, assume that the trust corpus, valued at $450,000 at H's death, neither increased nor decreased in value from that date to the wife's death some years later.

$250,000	Includible in W's gross estate under §2036
–112,000	Consideration offset under §2043(a)
$138,000	Taxed in W's estate

Lane, The Widow's Election as a Private Annuity: Boon or Bane for Estate Planners? 44 S. Cal. L. Rev. 74 (1970), questions this method of computing the estate tax consideration offset.

This result, of taxing substantially less than the wife's community share on her death, has provoked a heated controversy. Critics have argued that application of §2043(a) to the wife's election-transfer produces an unwarranted tax bonanza, since the consequence is that a substantial portion of the marital estate — the amount of the offset — passes to the next generation without having been taxed in either spouse's estate.[75] Its defenders argue that the widow's receipt of a life estate in her husband's property does augment her estate, and thus allowance of an offset for this interest is justified. To the extent that income from the husband's share is accumulated by the wife, it will in fact be taxed in her estate. To the extent that it is consumed by her, it makes unnecessary the depletion of her other assets for the purpose of meeting her income needs, and thus tends to preclude her reducing the amount of her estate that will be taxed at her death.[76]

To date, all the cases agree with the proponents of this tax treatment of the election-transfer. There are, however, a number of unresolved questions concerning the terms a transfer must include to qualify for the offset. It is generally agreed that if the wife is given a power to revoke her share of the trust, or if she has a general power of appointment over that share, she has not made a transfer that qualifies for the offset.[77] By retaining one of these powers she has not agreed to give anybody anything. Her decision to exercise or not exercise the power will come in the future, and the decision will not be for a consideration. But what if the wife is given a lesser power?

PROBLEMS

1. M transfers community assets in trust, reserving (on behalf of the community) the right to trust income for life and the power to revoke, alter, or amend the trust. On M's death the trust is to become irrevocable; trust income is to be paid to M's wife N for life, and on N's death the corpus is to be distributed to the couple's three children. On M's death some years later, the value of his share of trust assets is $200,000; the value of N's share is $250,000. N is fifty-eight years old at M's death. (The factor used to value a remainder interest following a life estate in a 58-year-old woman is .34. Treas. Reg. §25.2512-9, Table A-2 (1971).)

a. Has N made a taxable gift to the remaindermen? If so, in what amount?

[75] See dissenting opinion of Wisdom, J., in Estate of Vardell v. Comm'r, 307 F.2d 688, 694 (5th Cir. 1962); Lowndes, Consideration and the Federal Estate and Gift Taxes: Transfers for Partial Consideration, Relinquishment of Marital Rights, Family Annuities, the Widow's Election, and Reciprocal Trusts, 35 Geo. Wash. L. Rev. 50 (1966); Westfall, Estate Planning and the Widow's Election, 71 Harv. L. Rev. 1269 (1958).

[76] Morrison, The Widow's Election: The Issue of Consideration, 44 Texas L. Rev. 223 (1965); Schwartz & Liker, The Widow's Election, in U. Miami 1st Institute on Estate Planning 10-1 (1967).

[77] However, in Estate of Vardell v. Comm'r, note 73 supra, the first case to allow an estate tax consideration offset, the wife held a general inter vivos power of appointment over the trust assets. In a dissenting opinion Judge Wisdom argued that this retained power of consumption and disposition disqualified the transfer as one for a consideration.

b. N dies some years later; the value of the trust corpus on her death has remained unchanged at $450,000. What amount is includible in N's gross estate? Is her estate entitled to a consideration offset? If so, in what amount?

2. Consider the same facts, except that the trust authorizes the trustee to distribute to N "all or so much of the trust corpus, at any one time or from time to time, as the trustee, in its sole discretion, deems appropriate for N's comfortable support and benefit."

a. Answer the same questions as in Problem 1a.[78]

b. Answer the same questions as in Problem 1b.[79]

3. The facts are the same as in Problem 1, except that W is given a power to appoint her share of the trust assets "among such one or more of our descendants as she shall appoint, outright or in further trust, by her last will and testament; and in default of appointment, to our descendants per stirpes."

a. Answer the same questions as in Problem 1a.

b. Answer the same questions as in Problem 1b.

Income Tax Problems

If the wife's election-transfer is treated as one for a consideration under the gift and estate taxes, should it also be treated as a transfer for a consideration for income tax purposes? If so, some interesting possibilities and problems arise. The wife might be regarded as having purchased a life estate — a "wasting asset" — for which she could amortize the cost of her "purchase" with deductions against future receipts of income.[80] But if the wife purchases an income interest in her husband's assets, who sells her that interest, and what are the consequences to the seller? [81] You should be relieved to know that we only raise these sophisticated and complex income tax questions; we do not propose to discuss them.

[78] See Johanson, Revocable Trusts, Widow's Election Wills, and Community Property: The Tax Problems, 47 Texas L. Rev. 1247, 1277 (1969).

[79] Id. at 1307.

[80] Anticipating this argument, Judge Wisdom, in his dissent in the Vardell case, note 75 supra, sarcastically referred to the possibility of tax-free income (to the extent of the amortization deduction) as a "taxpayer's Utopia." 307 F.2d at 699, 700. That Utopia now exists — in the Ninth Circuit. Gist v. United States, 296 F. Supp. 526 (S.D. Cal. 1969), aff'd, 423 F.2d 1118 (9th Cir. 1970). Accord, Estate of Christ, 54 T.C. 493 (1970). The Commissioner did not appeal the Christ decision because the appeal would be to the Ninth Circuit, where the Gist decision had been handed down some months before.

Arguing that this result is sound, see Miller & Martin, Voluntary Measured Election: Nationwide Planning for the Million Dollar Estate, 1 Cal. W.L. Rev. 63 (1965). Criticizing the result, see Lane, The Widow's Election as a Private Annuity: Boon or Bane for Estate Planners? 44 S. Cal. L. Rev. 74 (1970); Schwartz & Liker, The Widow's Election, in U. Miami 1st Institute on Estate Planning 10-1 (1967).

[81] One commentator has suggested that the trust funded with the husband's interest is the seller, and that the adverse income tax consequences to that trust will offset, and possibly outweigh, any advantages obtained from the amortization deduction. The problem is believed to involve the "immediate recognition of income" doctrine under Commissioner v. P. G. Lake, 356 U.S. 260 (1958), in which case the trust would be taxed, at ordinary income rates, for the amount received in exchange for its sale of the income interest. Lane, note 80 supra.

Putting the Tax Problems in Perspective

The foregoing tax problems (and tax-saving possibilities) all stem from treatment of what is essentially a donative transaction as a sale or exchange for a consideration. Now that you have been exposed to this maze of sophisticated tax concepts and problem areas, an understandable reaction would be to conclude that widow's election wills and revocable trusts funded with community property are arrangements that you should stay away from. But let's put these problems in perspective. First, recall from page 515 that there will be instances in which planning considerations point toward settlement of the entire interest in community assets, and not just the spouse's one-half share. If, in a particular case, this is a sound planning objective, these tax problems should not discourage the use of such a plan. Second, to date all the tax decisions have been in the taxpayer's favor. Transfers that qualify as "transfers for a consideration" can, for the cost of a small gift tax or none, generate substantial estate tax and income tax savings. It may be that this favorable tax treatment will continue for some time.

Most important of all, most election wills and revocable trusts do not qualify as "transfers for a consideration," and do not even raise these distinctive tax questions. To make a transfer for a consideration, or an "exchange" for income tax purposes, the widow must transfer something of value — and something capable of being valued — to the remaindermen; and she must receive, in exchange, a measurable interest in her husband's property. But most trusts include invasion powers over the trust corpus and powers of appointment over the remainder interest, permitting adjustments for contingencies that may arise in the future. The consequence of including these powers, so sound from a planning standpoint, may be to preclude characterization of the widow's election-transfer as one for a consideration. In any case, if the wife is given the power to revoke as to her share of assets in the trust, all these tax problems are avoided.

PROBLEMS

1. P, a resident of Arizona, is the insured under a $25,000 community life insurance policy that names P's mother as primary beneficiary and his wife as secondary beneficiary. P dies survived by his mother and his wife. Assume that, under the facts of the case, designation of P's mother as primary beneficiary is not "in fraud of his wife's rights," and that the $25,000 is paid to P's mother. What are the tax consequences?

2. Is the election will doctrine limited to transfers of the entire interest in community property, or can the widow's election also involve transfers of the spouses's separate property? Suppose a husband's will purports to devise his separate property, the entire interest in community assets, and his wife's separate property,

with the terms of the transfer similar to those given in the example on page 531. Are the same problems raised?

3. To what extent can these same problems be encountered in a common law state? Can a widow's election will be drafted in, say, Kentucky? See Kentucky Trust Co. v. Kessel, 464 S.W.2d 275 (Ky. 1971); Miller & Martin, Voluntary Measured Election: Nation-wide Planning for the Million Dollar Estate, 1 Cal. W.L. Rev. 63 (1965).

SECTION C. Protection of the Spouse — Migrating Couples

1. *Separate Property Brought into a Community Property State*

> All marital property is . . . either separate or community. If acquired before marriage by any method, or after marriage by gift, devise or descent, it is separate; otherwise it is community. There are only two exceptions. Property purchased with separate funds is separate, . . . and community property partitioned in the manner provided in [the statutes] becomes separate property.[82]

This statement, a fairly representative judicial paraphrase of the statutory definitions, purports to list all the circumstances in which assets can be characterized as the separate property of one of the spouses. And yet the list is incomplete. It fails to include a source of separate property that is the product of our mobile society, as couples move from one state to another with increasing frequency. This is what might be called "conflict of laws separate property."

In a common law state, property acquired as a product of the husband's efforts during marriage belongs to the husband. If the couple thereafter move to a community property state, "his property" becomes "his separate property." Decisions in all the community property states recognize and apply the standard conflict of laws rule: For marital property rights purposes, the character of assets is determined according to the laws of the state of marital domicile at the time the property is acquired, and that character is not altered when the couple move to another state.[83] This conflicts rule, when combined with a second conflict of laws rule, produces a serious gap in the protection of widows against disinheritance. The second rule is this: The devolution of property at death is governed by the laws of the state in which the person was domiciled at the time of his death.[84] Thus for purposes of testamentary disposition, intestate succession, and federal or state taxation, a com-

[82] Hilley v. Hilley, 161 Tex. 569, 573, 342 S.W.2d 565, 567 (1961).

[83] See Lay, Marital Property Rights of the Non-Native in a Community Property State, 18 Hastings L.J. 295 (1967); Marsh, Marital Property in the Conflict of Laws 225-233 (1952).

[84] Except for real estate located in another jurisdiction, which, according to conventional conflict of laws analysis, is governed by the laws of the situs state. For a critical analysis of the situs rules see Weintraub, An Inquiry Into the Utility of "Situs" as a Concept in Conflicts Analysis, 52 Cornell L.Q. 1 (1966).

munity property state treats this conflict of laws separate property the same as any other separate property.

To illustrate the problem, suppose H and W marry in Iowa and live there for a number of years, accumulating a sizable estate from H's salary or wages. If H died while the couple were still living in Iowa, W would be protected against disinheritance by that state's statutory forced share and dower laws. Suppose, though, the couple move to Texas. Since the Texas courts recognize the character of the marital assets as determined by the Iowa rules, all the assets brought from Iowa are H's separate property in Texas.

A few years later H dies leaving a will that devises the bulk of his estate to a newfound Texas "friend." The Iowa forced share law no longer applies, for H was not domiciled in Iowa at the time of his death. Instead, the Texas rules apply — and H has the unrestricted power of testation over his separate property. Thus W has lost the forced share protection she had in Iowa, and (at least with respect to the assets brought from Iowa) she has not gained the built-in protection of the community property system. The possibility of total disinheritance would be present if the couple moved to the community property state after retirement, for there would be no salary or wages to build up to the community estate. In three of the states the wife would get some protection from the rule that income from separate property is community. But in the other five states, it is quite possible that the couple would own no community property at all.

When some community property is accumulated in the new state, the wife may receive nondoctrinal protection against disinheritance from the presumption that all assets on hand on dissolution of the marriage belong to the community, with the burden of proving otherwise on the party seeking to establish their separate character. This presumption is not easily overcome, and operates to strongly favor the community.

Only one state has moved to fill this gap in the widow's protection. This is California, with its quasi-community property statute.[85] Quasi-community property is property owned by the husband or wife which was acquired while the couple were domiciled in another state, and which would have been characterized as community property had it been acquired while the couple were domiciled in California. (Real property situated outside the state of California is not treated as quasi-community property.) The acquiring spouse may dispose of only one-half his quasi-community property by will. The other one-half passes to the surviving spouse; she cannot be deprived of this amount by will. In the absence of a will, all the quasi-community property passes to the surviving spouse.

In other words, for devolution purposes quasi-community property is treated the same as community property — with this difference: If the nonacquiring spouse predeceases, she has no power of testation over the other spouse's quasi-community property. The statute does not give the nonacquiring spouse an interest in the prop-

[85] Cal. Prob. Code §201.5 (1956, Supp. 1971). For a comprehensive analysis of the statute see Abel, Barry, Halsted & Marsh, Rights of a Surviving Spouse in Property Acquired by a Decedent While Domiciled Outside California, 47 Calif. L. Rev. 211 (1959).

erty. Instead, it limits the acquiring spouse's power of testamentary disposition over the assets. The statute is analogous to a common law state's forced share statute.

It is not difficult to understand why California should be the first state to fill this gap in the widow's protection. "The major portion of the burgeoning population of California consists of persons who have migrated to this state from other parts of the country. Statistics show that 'Most Californians come to this state from somewhere else.' And most of these migrants have been married adults." [86] It is a little surprising, though, that California should be the only state to address itself to the problem. While it is perhaps less true of the other community property states, certainly Arizona and New Mexico have attracted large numbers of couples from colder climes — particularly retired couples, where the potential of total disinheritance is the greatest. To date, though, no movements are afoot to follow the California pattern.[87]

In order to prevent a spouse from attempting to defeat the survivor's forced share in quasi-community property by making inter vivos transfers with economic benefits retained, California has enacted legislation similar to that enacted in some common law states.[88] Probate Code §201.8 provides that whenever a married person dies domiciled in California and has made a gratuitous transfer of quasi-community property, "the surviving spouse may require the transferee to restore to the decedent's estate one-half of such property, its value, or its proceeds, if the decedent had a substantial quantum of ownership or control of the property at death." What is a "substantial quantum of ownership"? The California Law Revision Commission Report, which recommended this statute, states: "[I]t seems entirely just to subject to Section 201.5 any property transferred inter vivos by gratuitous transfers which are commonly considered will substitutes — e.g., joint tenancy in real or personal property, joint bank accounts, Totten trust bank accounts, revocable trusts, transfers in trust with right to the income reserved for life in the settlor, and legal transfers with life estate reserved in the conveyor." [89]

PROBLEM

While living in Massachusetts and married to W, H purchases an insurance policy on his life with a face amount of $50,000. He pays the premiums out of his earnings. He names his daughter, D, as beneficiary of the policy. H and W move to California. H then changes the beneficiary of the policy to S, his son. H dies domiciled in California. Can W reach the proceeds of the policy? Would it make any

[86] Abel, id. at 211.

[87] Advocating that the California pattern be followed are Comment, Rights of a Surviving Spouse in Texas in Marital Property Acquired While Domiciled Elsewhere, 45 Texas L. Rev. 321 (1966); Comment, Rights of Surviving Spouse in New Mexico, in Property Acquired by Decedent Spouse While Domiciled Elsewhere, 5 Nat. Res. J. 373 (1965).

[88] See page 488, supra.

[89] California Law Rev. Comm'n, Study Relating to Rights of Surviving Spouse in Property Acquired by Decedent While Domiciled Elsewhere E-31 (1956).

difference if W had been named beneficiary of the policy while the couple lived in Massachusetts, and after moving to California H changed the beneficiary to S? [90]

2. *Community Property Brought into a Common Law State*

In the preceding subsection we examined the problems that can arise when a couple move from a common law state to a community property jurisdiction. What happens when the move is in the other direction? Suppose a couple live in California for a number of years and then move to Ohio. In addition to their household furnishings and other items of tangible personalty, transported by moving van, the couple bring to Ohio their U.S. Government bonds, securities, life insurance policies, and other intangibles, and they transfer their checking and savings accounts to an Ohio bank. About three months after their move the couple finally sell their home in Santa Monica, and deposit the sale proceeds in their Ohio savings account. Let us assume that all these items were community property under California law.

What is the effect of this change of domicile on the marital property rights of the spouses? The answer — at least in theory — is given by the standard conflict of laws rules. For marital property rights purposes, the character of assets is determined according to the laws of the state of marital domicile at the time the property is acquired, and that character is not altered when the couple move to another state. Accordingly, what was community property in California remains — or should remain — community property in Ohio.

Moving from the theoretical to the actual, it doesn't take much perception to realize that there are going to be problems with this approach. Ohio doesn't have a community property system, and Ohio's judges and lawyers are not likely to have any real understanding of the distinctive features of the community property form of ownership. It is probable that, when called upon to do so, they will view community property through a common law lawyer's eyes, and they will analogize it to the common law concepts with which they are familiar.

Common law judges and lawyers have taken varying attitudes toward community property. In some instances they have seen the community form of ownership as akin to a tenancy in common, or a tenancy by the entireties, or a joint tenancy. Sometimes they have viewed the husband's managerial powers, over assets that somehow belong to his wife, as analogous to the husband's jure uxoris (estate by the marital right) at early common law. Alternatively, they have seen the husband's managerial powers as indicative of ownership, and the wife's community rights as a "mere expectancy." They have taken these varying positions, however, only when the problem of possible community property rights has been recognized at all.[91] In

[90] Id. at E-10 states that the Commission does not favor applying §201.8 to transfers made by a spouse prior to moving to California since the spouse "could not reasonably have anticipated that the transfer would later be subjected to California law."

[91] Lay, Community Property in Common Law States: A Comparative Analysis of Its Treatment in Foreign Jurisdictions, 41 Temp. L.Q. 1 (1967), observes that "while the interests of each marital partner has been accorded some form of protection, no common law state has treated the property as still being community." Id. at 4.

making an extensive study of this problem, Professor Norvie Lay found a half-dozen cases decided in the 1840s and 1850s, five cases and an attorney general's opinion handed down since 1951, and almost nothing in the 100 years between those clusters of dates.[92] In only a handful of states is there any authority, old or recent, on how community assets are treated after they are brought into a common law state.

This situation creates problems for the estate planner in a common law state, when one of these "migratory clients" comes into the office. The first and most important step in planning an estate is to ascertain the assets owned by the clients and their value, and to determine which spouse has the power of disposition over which assets. The attorney may have his own views on the proper classification of these assets, but will his state's courts, and the state and federal tax commissioners, arrive at the same conclusions? And how can he tell, when his state's courts have never passed on the problem, and other state courts have offered divergent views?

PROBLEMS

1. H and W, in their late forties, moved from San Francisco to Cleveland two years ago. H has come to your law office to have his will revised. His present will, drafted in California, takes the form of something called a "widow's election will," whatever that is, and purports to devise "my wife's interest in community assets as well as my own." (What would an Ohio probate court *do* with such a will, if H died in Ohio without ever having revised it?) Your interview discloses that H and W brought with them from California, all community property at the time of the move:

Proceeds from sale of California home, now in Certificates of Deposit with an Ohio bank	$ 25,000
Securities	200,000
Tangible personal property	15,000

The couple also own a $50,000 home in Shaker Heights, purchased with a $15,000 cash downpayment three weeks after having arrived from California. Title to the home was taken in the form, "H and W, husband and wife." In addition to these assets, the couple have acquired others (mostly securities) worth $30,000 in the two years they have been in Ohio. These new assets have been acquired partly from H's salary and partly from the income from the California-source securities and certificates of deposit. (Note: In all the community property states, the income from community property is itself community property.)

[92] Ibid. See also Lay, Community Property and the Kentucky Attorney, 31 Ky. B.J. 53 (1967); Lay, Migrants from Community Property States: Filling the Legislative Gap, 53 Cornell L.Q. 832 (1968); Lay, A Survey of Community Property, 51 Iowa L. Rev. 625 (1966); Lay, Community Property and the Migrant Executive, 108 Trusts & Estates 1043 (1969). These articles appear in revised form in Lay, Tax and Estate Planning for Community Property and the Migrant Client (1971).

Let us assume the unlikely: That the couple have kept their "California assets" and "Ohio assets" separate, and that the only complicating factor is that there have been a number of changes in the securities portfolio over the past two years. Some of the "California securities" were sold, and the proceeds were immediately reinvested in the market.

The general question is: Who owns what?

a. The will that you draft for the husband will devise "all my property." Which assets, or portions thereof, will pass by this devise?

b. For a client with an estate this large, an Ohio attorney ordinarily would recommend that the will be drafted in a manner that assures qualification for the maximum estate tax marital deduction. Is the marital deduction a factor here? If so, how much of a factor, and how would you recommend that the advantages of the marital deduction be secured?

c. If H predeceases W, which of the foregoing assets will be taxed in H's gross estate for federal estate tax purposes? What portion of the assets will be used in computing the adjusted gross estate, and thus the maximum allowable marital deduction? What portion of the assets will be taxed under Ohio's inheritance tax?

d. On the husband's death, which assets (or portions thereof) will acquire a new basis under Int. Rev. Code of 1954, §1014? Would it matter, for this federal income tax purpose, that in other cases the Ohio courts have treated community property brought into the state as "something akin to a tenancy in common"?

e. Assume that under some theory the Ohio court treats the California assets as belonging one-half to the husband and one-half to the wife. W exercises her right under Ohio law to claim a statutory share in lieu of the provisions in her husband's will. Does her forced share extend to the husband's one-half interest in these assets — meaning that the wife ends up with three-fourths?

2. How about the house the couple purchased in Shaker Heights? The down-payment presumably came from California funds, but the mortgage payments presumably came from H's salary in Ohio. How does this affect the marital property classification of this asset?

Does (should) the manner in which title was taken affect the classification of this asset? (In resolving this question, would you want to hear from title examiners, title insurance companies, and other groups concerned about the stability of land titles in Ohio?)

3. How about the $200,000 securities portfolio? Is the classification of these assets affected by the fact that the husband "dealt with" them after coming to Ohio? See Restatement (Second), Conflicts §259 (Tent. Ed. 1969); 40 Op. Att'y Gen. 526 (Md. 1955).

4. Refer back to Subquestions (c) and (d) of Question 1. Would you expect (want) the answers to these questions to be different if the wife predeceased the husband?

5. Assume that you are properly concerned about the uncertainties involved in classifying the couple's property, but that you are also concerned that your estate plan for the couple be premised on a solid fact situation, so that its dispositive and

tax consequences are predictable. You decide that the best thing to do is to put the assets into a form of ownership with which you — and the Ohio courts — are familiar. You advise the couple to partition their California assets, making them tenants in common with respect to these assets.

a. If the couple had moved to Ohio from Louisiana, will the partition be effective? (All community property states except Louisiana permit partitioning of community property into the separate property of the spouses, although the procedure for partitioning varies from state to state. But Louisiana law prohibits partitioning of community property so long as the couple are married, in the absence of some form of antenuptial agreement. See Lay, Transmutation of Community Property, 18 S.C.L. Rev. 755 (1966).)

b. Will the partition result in a taxable gift by the husband?

COMMONWEALTH v. TERJEN

Supreme Court of Appeals of Virginia, 1956

197 Va. 596, 90 S.E.2d 801

HUDGINS, Chief Justice. Henry A. Terjen and his wife, Jean F. Terjen, while domiciled in and residents of the State of California, accumulated personal property of substantial value held by them under the law of California as community property. In 1950 they moved from California to Virginia bringing this property with them. In September of the same year $19,000 of this community property was used in the payment for a home in the City of Norfolk, title to which was taken in the name of Jean F. Terjen, the wife.

In March, 1953, Henry A. Terjen filed a tax return with the Department of Taxation of the Commonwealth of Virginia showing a gift from him to his wife in the amount of $9,500, one-half the purchase price of the home, and paid the correct amount of the gift tax thereon. Later the Department of Taxation assessed the petitioner an additional gift tax on the ground that the value of the gift was $19,000 and not $9,500. Thereafter Henry A. Terjen filed a petition under the provisions of Section 58-234 of the Code of Virginia praying that he be exonerated from paying the additional assessment. The trial court upheld this contention and entered judgment accordingly. The Department of Taxation, being of the opinion that the judgment was erroneous, filed a petition for rehearing, which was denied. This appeal granted the Commonwealth brings these judgments under review.

The only question presented is whether the husband as donor is chargeable with a gift tax (less personal exemptions) on $9,500, one-half the purchase price of the home, or $19,000, the full purchase price.

The husband conceded in his petition filed in the lower court that the Virginia statutes, 1950 Code, §§58-218, 58-219, 58-223, imposing a tax upon him as donor of a gift to his wife in excess of the value of $5,000 are valid and applicable to the agreed facts. His contention in the lower court (he made no appearance in this Court) was that the $19,000 (accumulated from his own earnings) was held as community property in California where his wife had a present vested interest in one-half, and that this one-half interest was not divested by the transfer of the property and domicile from California to Virginia.

The general rule is that "A change of domicil from a state where the community property law prevails to a common-law state does not affect the community character of property previously acquired. The law of the state to which the parties remove will regulate their future conduct and acquisitions, but the removal will not alter the rights of either to property then in possession, the title to which had vested under the community property law." 11 Am. Jur., Community Property, Sec. 16, p. 185; Annotation 92 A.L.R. 1352; Am. Law Inst., Restatement, Conflict of Laws, Sec. 292.

Whether the wife had a present vested interest in community property in California depends upon the California statutes as construed by the courts of that state. [Section 161a of the Civil Code of California, as amended in 1927,] provides:

> The respective interests of the husband and wife in community property during continuance of the marriage relation are present, existing and equal interests under the management and control of the husband as is provided in sections 172 and 172a of the Civil Code. This section shall be construed as defining the respective interests and rights of husband and wife in the community property.

The California courts in construing this section have held (1) that the statute defining the interest of spouses in community property did not change existing rules vesting in the husband the exclusive management and control of community property with absolute power of disposition other than a disposal without consideration, and (2) that all community property except the earnings of the wife were liable for the obligations of the husband, including liability for torts committed by him. Grolemund v. Cafferata, 17 Cal. 2d 679, 111 P.2d 641; Dandini v. Dandini, 82 Cal. App. 2d 263, 186 P.2d 41.

In Bose v. Mills, 101 Cal. App. 2d 782, 226 P.2d 5, at page 8, it is said: "There is no question, of course, that under the provisions of the Civil Code in respect to community property the husband has the exclusive management and control of community personal property, with like absolute power of disposition other than testamentary, as he has of his separate estate. Civil Code, §172."

A wife may have a transfer of community property by the husband set aside if it is without consideration or fraudulently made, but even if she is successful in such an action the property returns to the control of the husband. She cannot gain possession or control, enjoy or use the property during coverture. While the husband cannot convey the property without consideration, he may squander it, or invest it unwisely without violating the rights of the wife therein. McClain v. Tufts, 83 Cal. App. 2d 140, 187 P.2d 818; Stratton v. Superior Court, 87 Cal. App. 2d 809, 197 P.2d 821; In re Marinos' Estate, 39 Cal. App. 2d 1, 102 P.2d 443.

The question whether a wife domiciled and residing in California took or held a present vested right or interest in the community property was discussed at some length and many of the California decisions were reviewed by the Supreme Court of Montana in In re Hunter's Estate, 125 Mont. 315, 236 P.2d 94. The facts were that William J. Hunter and his wife, Thelma D. Hunter, while residents of the State of California acquired valuable assets held as community property. The husband invested $156,000 of this property in two tracts of land, one thousand head of livestock and other personal property located in the State of Montana. His wife was not a party to the contracts of purchase or to the title papers. Hunter died devising and bequeathing all the property in Montana to his wife. She, as executrix of her husband's estate, claimed that the Montana property was purchased with funds acquired by her and her husband while residents of the State of California and was community property. The trial court upheld her contention and imposed an inheritance tax on only one-half the value of the property. On review by the Supreme Court of Montana the contention of the surviving spouse was rejected and the judgment of the trial court reversed.

The executrix conceded that the law of the situs of the land (Montana) governs the incidence of an inheritance tax on the death of the owner, but she contended that by virtue of the law of California the money used by the husband to pay for the Montana property was community property, and that vested rights in property are not lost simply because the property is transported into another state and exchanged there for other property. Therefore, she said that since her property had been used for the purchase of the Montana land, a trust therein resulted. It was said in the opinion, 236 P.2d 96 and 99:

> In determining what the state law of California is upon the question before us, we are endeavoring to define the nature of the interest a husband and wife have in California community property prior to the dissolution of the marriage and then apply the Montana tax statutes to a transfer of that interest if applicable. In so doing we have no definitive decision of the highest court of California to guide us. Further we are compelled to analyze a system of ownership adopted largely from Spanish sources and foreign to our common law. For a discussion of the origin and extent of the community property system, see de Funiak, "Principles of Community Property," Vol. 1, and the article by Evans, The Ownership of Community Property, 35 Harv. L. Rev. 47. In applying our taxing law to the interest growing out of a different system of law in a different jurisdiction we must also reserve the integrity of our own system and protect our residents whose rights in both tax matters and ownership of property are fixed by Montana law. . . . At the same time we give protection to the property of California citizens just as they protect the rights and property of our citizens. In re Thornton's Estate, 1 Cal. 2d 1, 33 P.2d 1, 92 A.L.R. 1343; Tomaier v. Tomaier, supra [23 Cal. 2d 754, 146 P.2d 905].
>
> . . .
>
> Ownership of property has been defined as a "bundle of privileges," Henneford v. Silas Mason Co., 300 U.S. 577, 582, 57 S. Ct. 524, 527, 81 L. Ed. 814, or a "conglomerate of jurisdiction and substantive legal rights." United States v. Gossler, D.C., 60 F. Supp. 971, 973.
>
> By the various amendments to California's community property law, the wife's "bundle of privileges" has been enlarged. However, an examination of the decisions

indicates that it is not yet that of ownership so that the wife has a vested title sufficient to overcome the presumption that title is where the record puts it and to bear the burden of proof necessary to impress a resulting trust. At most section 161a seems to be only another amendment giving a wife rights not possessed by an heir. But these "rights were given her in order that she might protect herself against the fraudulent and inconsiderate acts of her husband, and thereby preserve the community property intact until the dissolution of the marriage."

The rights of the spouses during the continuance of the marriage relation in the $19,000 before the change of domicile from California to Virginia were that the husband was entitled to the exclusive possession, use, control, and disposal of it, except that he could not give or will it to a third party. It was subject to the payment of his debts, including his liability for torts. It was not subject to any obligations of the wife. Her only rights seem to have been the right to have any transfer made by the husband without consideration set aside, and possession and control restored to him.

When the husband disposed of the $19,000 in question by payment for Virginia realty, title to which was taken in the name of the wife, he thereby transferred to her all the exclusive rights theretofore owned by him in the $19,000 converted from personal property to real estate. This real estate is held by the wife as her separate estate with the exclusive right to possession, use, enjoyment and disposal (subject to the husband's continued right of courtesy) of it under the laws of Virginia. The value of the wife's separate estate so acquired is not $9,500, but the whole purchase price used in payment of the real estate. It is upon the transfer of these rights in and to the $19,000 converted into realty that the Virginia statute, §58-218, imposes the gift tax.

The judgment of the trial court is reversed and final judgment entered for the Commonwealth in the sum of $140, plus penalty, interest and costs.

Reversed and final judgment.[93]

See also In re Kessler's Estate, 177 Ohio St. 136, 203 N.E.2d 221 (1964), subjecting the entire value of assets acquired in California as community property to inheritance taxation upon the husband's death. Noting the husband's broad managerial powers, the court held that although the wife's interest in the assets was "vested," "it is equally certain that the interest accorded her by the community-property law generally, and more specifically by the California statute, is certainly not in the nature of outright ownership until the dissolution of the marriage, as upon the death of the husband. The nature of the wife's interest in community property is summarized in Willcox v. Penn. Mutual Life Ins. Co. (1947), 357 Pa. 581, 55 A.2d 521, 174 A.L.R. 220, wherein the Supreme Court of Pennsylvania found legislation attempting to establish the principle of community property in that state to be unconstitutional. The court observes: '. . . it is obvious that an

[93] Noted 34 N.C.L. Rev. 564; 42 Va. L. Rev. 724. See also De Funiak, Commonwealth v. Terjen: Common Law Mutilates Community Property, 43 Va. L. Rev. 49 (1957).

alleged interest in property over which another person has the right of control, management and disposal, which the creditors of such other person can take in satisfaction of his debts, and as to which there is no practical means of protection, is not a genuine right of property no matter what name or alleged title of ownership may have been given to it.' "

But in People v. Bejarano, 145 Colo. 304, 358 P.2d 866 (1961), the court held that only one-half of a deceased husband's interest in an employee pension fund, acquired while the couple resided in Texas and later in California, was subject to inheritance taxation in Colorado.

To what extent will resolution of this classification problem be affected by the nature of the issue before the court?

POLASKY, MULLIN & PIGMAN, ESTATE PLANNING FOR THE MIGRATING CLIENT: PROBLEMS WHEN COUPLE MOVES FROM COMMUNITY PROPERTY STATE TO COMMON LAW STATE, 101 Trusts & Estates 876, 878 (1962): "The particular cause, the relationship of the parties, the particular [forum], will be determinative of the manner in which 'property' will be treated. In a divorce action in a state where the community property interests of the wife exceed her common law rights, and if the court believes that the wife has received a bad deal from her husband, the court will find the community property doctrine a handy way to allocate one-half or more of the property to the wife. Conversely, if a taxing authority would be faced with less revenue by the recognition of community property, the court in the taxing jurisdiction would be disinclined to recognize the community property."

Now that you have been furnished all this helpful information, you should be ready to handle H's situation in Problem 1, page 547. (At least you are as ready as you'll ever be.) How should you proceed? Consider the following approaches:

1. In view of the uncertainty of the law and the complexity of the problem, treat it as though no problem exists. That is, plan H's estate as though he were a long-time Ohio resident and all the assets are his. After all, it has been pointed out that these problems often go undetected. Why volunteer for an Excedrin headache? H is a young man, and it is likely that he will live for a long time. The passage of time will obscure the trail leading from California, and everyone will have forgotten about the somewhat confusing history of "a few" of H's assets. Or perhaps more accurately, in twenty or so years it will not occur to anyone to look into the history or source of the assets.

Two very practical considerations support this approach. First, you bill on an hourly rate, and the client couldn't really afford to have you spend the time needed to straighten out this mess. Moreover, the client is one of those mobile executive types. Isn't it likely that in another five years or so his company will move him again — to who knows where?

All things considered, let sleeping dogs lie.

2. Partition the community property into a tenancy in common between the

spouses. The Terjen case poses no problem: There the husband made the mistake of making an unequal partition, and he "red-flagged" the problem by filing a gift tax return. But you propose that H and W make an equal partition. Since under your interpretation of California law an equal partition produces no taxable gift, there is no need to file a state or federal gift tax return, and neither the Ohio nor the federal tax people will even learn about the transaction. You certainly have no legal, ethical or moral obligation to tell the tax people that "my clients have made this partition, but no tax is due, so we're not filing any gift tax return." Right?

While a partition into a tenancy in common loses any chance for a stepped-up basis under Int. Rev. Code of 1954, §1014(b), this possible tax benefit is worth sacrificing in the interest of clarifying H's and W's asset situation.

3. Do nothing with the assets, draft "conventional" Ohio wills for H and W, and see what happens. If W predeceases H, take the position that most if not all the assets are H's property under Ohio law. The reason? There will be no assets to tax in her estate. If H predeceases W, work vigorously to establish that most of the California-source assets are community property if it is in the wife's interest to get a new basis for all the assets, and if the result is a lower federal and state succession tax. This "do nothing" approach provides maximum flexibility, and will permit a little "post-mortem estate planning."

4. "The [clients'] interests may best be served by placing their property within the physical jurisdiction of the state that will most likely apply the rules that you wish to have applied to their affairs. Thus, if you wish to preserve the community property, place stocks, bonds and bank accounts in California, where they would be subject to ancillary proceedings. Such a step would counter the danger of taking the property to [a common law state], where a probate court might not apply community property principles. On the other hand, if the [clients'] interests would be best served by doing away with the community property concept, it would be better to remove the property entirely from California and have it in a forum where the court would disregard the community property history." Polasky, Mullin & Pigman, Estate Planning for the Migrating Client: Problems When Couple Moves from Community Property State to Common Law State, 101 Trusts & Estates 876, 879 (1962).

5. For discussion of these approaches, see Polasky, Mullin & Pigman, supra; Lay, Tax Aspects of Estate Planning for the Migrant Client from a Community Property State, 35 Tenn. L. Rev. 262 (1968).

UNIFORM DISPOSITION OF COMMUNITY PROPERTY RIGHTS AT DEATH ACT (1971)[94]

SECTION 1. [*Application.*] This Act applies to the disposition at death of the following property acquired by a married person:

(1) all personal property, wherever situated:

[94] For discussion of the Uniform Act and its background, see Comment, Property Problems of the Peripatetic Client, 5 Real Prop., Prob. & Trust J. 526 (1970).

(i) which was acquired as or became, and remained, community property under the laws of another jurisdiction; or,

(ii) all or the proportionate part of that property acquired with the rents, issues, or income of, or the proceeds from, or in exchange for, that community property; or

(iii) traceable to that community property;

(2) all or the proportionate part of any real property situated in this state which was acquired with the rents, issues or income of, the proceeds from, or in exchange for, property acquired as or which became, and remained, community property under the laws of another jurisdiction, or property traceable to that community property.

SECTION 2. [*Rebuttable Presumptions.*] In determining whether this Act applies to specific property the following rebuttable presumptions apply:

(1) property acquired during marriage by a spouse of that marriage while domiciled in a jurisdiction under whose laws property could then be acquired as community property is presumed to have been acquired as or to have become, and remained, property to which this act applies; and

(2) real property situated in this State and personal property wherever situated acquired by a married person while domiciled in a jurisdiction under whose laws property could not then be acquired as community property, title to which was taken in a form which created rights of survivorship, is presumed not to be property to which this Act applies.

SECTION 3. [*Disposition upon Death.*] Upon death of a married person, one-half of the property to which this Act applies is the property of the surviving spouse and is not subject to testamentary disposition by the decedent or distribution under the laws of succession of this State. One-half of that property is the property of the decedent and is subject to testamentary disposition or distribution under the laws of succession of this State. With respect to property to which this Act applies, the one-half of the property which is the property of the decedent is not subject to the surviving spouse's right to elect against the will [and no estate of dower or curtesy exists in the property of the decedent].[95]

SECTION D. Protection of Children and Descendants

In all states except Louisiana,[96] which has a legitime (forced share for issue) derived from civil law, a child or other descendant has no statutory protection

[95] Other sections of the Act (a) protect purchasers for value and lenders who deal with the spouse having apparent title to the property, (b) make creditors' claims superior to the surviving spouse's claim, and (c) authorize the spouses to sever or alter their interests in the property.

[96] In Louisiana a testator can dispose of only one-third of his estate if he is survived by three or more children, one-half if he is survived by two children, and two-thirds if he is survived by one child. Children cannot be deprived of their statutory portions except for one of ten "just causes" set forth in the Civil Code. Among them: refusing to ransom a parent held in captivity, and refusing to bail a parent out of jail. La. Civ. Code Ann. arts. 1493, 1621 (West 1952). See Yiannopoulis, Testamentary Dispositions in Favor of Surviving Spouse and the Legitime of Descendants, 28 La. L. Rev. 509 (1968).

against disinheritance by his parent. There is no requirement that a testator leave any property to his child, not even the proverbial one dollar.[97] But while a parent has the power to disinherit his children, he should think twice, or better three times, before exercising the power. Although no statute or judicial decision flatly prohibits conscious disinheritance, the law does not favor cutting children out of the distributive plan. A number of doctrines have been flexibly used to protect children, with the consequence that disinheritance is almost always a risky affair. A will disinheriting a child virtually invites a will contest. As we shall see in the next chapter, "lack of testamentary capacity," "undue influence" and "fraud" are subtle and elastic concepts that can be used by judges and juries to rewrite the testator's distributive plan in order to "do justice." In contests by disinherited children, judges and juries are frequently influenced by their sympathies for the children. This is well known to practicing lawyers, who will often advise the devisees to agree to an out-of-court settlement with a disinherited child. Also protecting children is the rule that disinheritance is not possible by a simple declaration that "my son John shall receive none of my property." To disinherit, it is necessary that the entire estate be devised to other persons. If there is a partial intestacy for some reason, the child will take his intestate share notwithstanding such a provision in the will.[98]

Having been given these caveats, you should understand what is meant by "disinheriting" a child. As part of a family law study conducted in Nebraska, persons were asked whether they thought it was proper for a parent to disinherit his children. Of the respondents, 93.4 percent would not permit disinheritance of children under the age of twenty-one; 63.4 percent would not permit disinheritance of children over the age of twenty-one. The question asked, however, was whether a parent *whose spouse was deceased* should be allowed to disinherit his children.[99] In point of fact, many parents who die testate do disinherit their children — by leaving their entire estate to their surviving spouse. "Most laymen do not consider that there is any disinheritance until the death of the surviving spouse, so it is only upon the passing of property from one generation to the next that the question of excluding one or more descendants becomes relevant in most people's thinking. So long as the property remains in the family unit for the support of the surviving spouse, there is nothing suggesting the denial of the children's birthright." [100]

[97] At common law a child omitted from his parent's will had no remedy. It may have been thought that it was necessary to leave the heir a shilling to disinherit him effectively, but Blackstone says that this was an error. 2 Blackstone, Commentaries *502. Blackstone says "cutting the heir off with a shilling" is traceable to a Roman law notion that the testator had lost his memory or mind unless he gave some legacy to each child.

[98] Suppose T's will devises one-half of his estate to A and the other half to B, and expressly provides that "my son John shall receive none of my property." A predeceases T, and the gift to A lapses. The result will be that B takes one-half the estate by will — and John takes the other one-half by inheritance. John takes "by force of law," and the will's expression of disinheritance is ineffective. See Comment, Right of Disinherited Heir to Share Upon Intestacy, 41 Calif. L. Rev. 758 (1953); Note, 100 A.L.R.2d 325 (1965).

Another protective rule, provided by statute in a dozen states, is that marriage followed by birth of issue revokes a will made before marriage. Rees, American Wills Statutes: II, 46 Va. L. Rev. 856, 884-885 (1960).

[99] Cohen, Robson & Bates, Parental Authority: The Community and the Law 44 (1958).

[100] Gibson, Inheritance of Community Property in Texas — A Need for Reform, 47 Texas L. Rev. 359, 366 (1969).

Pretermitted Child Statutes

All but three states[101] have pretermitted child statutes that operate to protect a child against being left out of his parent's will. These statutes are designed to prevent inadvertent, not intentional, disinheritance. Generally, a child is "pretermitted" if he is omitted from the will.

The pretermitted child statutes follow one of two patterns. In about half the states the statutes give protection only to "after-borns"; that is, to children born (or adopted) after execution of the will. The North Carolina statute is representative:

NORTH CAROLINA GENERAL STATUTES §31-5.5(a) (1966): "*After-born or after-adopted child; effect on will.* — (a) A will shall not be revoked by the birth of a child to or adoption of a child by the testator after the execution of the will, but any such after-born or after-adopted child shall be entitled to such share in testator's estate as it would be entitled to if the testator had died intestate unless:

"(1) The testator made some provision in the will for the child, whether adequate or not, or

"(2) It is apparent from the will itself that the testator intentionally did not make specific provision therein for the child." [102]

These statutes raise no problem for the will draftsman, and they have produced little litigation. A parent's will usually makes some provision for his present children, if only as takers "if my wife does not survive me." To avoid the application of this type of statute, and the resulting partial disruption of a plan to leave everything to the surviving spouse, for example, all that need be done is to add a clause along the following lines: "The term 'children' as used in this will includes any child or children hereafter born to or adopted by me, as well as the children, David, Susan Jane, and Barbara Carolyn, that I now have."

In the remaining states the statutes operate in favor of children alive when the will was executed as well as after-borns. Nearly all of these latter statutes emphasize intention, and permit the child who was alive when the will was executed to take his intestate share "unless it appears that the omission was intentional and not occasioned by accident or mistake." [103] Intent usually can be shown by extrinsic evidence, but some statutes, such as the California statute discussed in Estate of Torregano, restrict the evidence of intent to omit to the face of the will itself. In states

[101] The three states are Hawaii, Kansas and Wyoming. The District of Columbia also does not have such a statute.

[102] The New York pretermission statute is especially well drafted. N.Y. Estates, Powers & Trusts Law §5-3.2 provides that if the testator has a child living when he executes his will and makes no provision for such child, an after-born pretermitted child does not share in the estate. If, on the other hand, the testator does make some provision for a child living when he executes his will, an after-born pretermitted child takes a share equal to that of the living child. If the testator has no child living when he executes his will, each after-born pretermitted child takes his intestate share.

[103] Mass. Ann. Laws c. 191, §20 (1958, Supp. 1971).

with this type of statute, the clause suggested above takes care of possible after-born or after-adopted children, but it does not preclude a claim by a child alive at the time the will was executed.

Typically, statutes of both types give the child his intestate share, and the will is operative with respect to the testator's remaining assets. The statutes vary considerably in detail, and many of them leave open subsidiary problems in statutory interpretation. Among them: Does the statute apply to grandchildren? To adopted children? Will the naming or express disinheritance of a child cut off such child's issue if he predeceases the testator? These and other questions are discussed in the standard reference works.[104]

PROBLEMS

1. H dies leaving a will that devises "all of my property to my beloved wife, Gertrude, knowing that she will make ample provision for our children." H is survived by Gertrude and by two children (Andy and Bob), both of whom were alive at the time the will was executed. Do Andy and Bob have a claim under the North Carolina pretermitted child statute? Under the California statute (page 560 of the Torregano opinion)?

2. Consider the same facts, except that another child (Carl) was born to H and Gertrude after H's will was executed, and Carl also survived H. Does Carl have a claim?

3. Consider the same facts as in Problem 2, except that the will devised "all of my property to my beloved wife, Gertrude, knowing that she will make ample provision for our children, Andy and Bob."[105] Does Carl have a claim?

4. M, twenty years old and unmarried, becomes pregnant by F. The principals agree to put the child out for adoption. Several months later a child (C) is born. C is adopted; M and F go their separate ways.

Years pass. C somehow learns who his natural parents are — or were, for he also learns that they have died a short time ago, leaving wills that make no mention of C. Armed with proof that he is the natural child of both M and F, he makes a claim as a pretermitted child against both their estates. All this takes place in a state that protects omitted children alive at the time the will is executed, "unless it appears that the omission was intentional and not occasioned by accident or mistake."

a. What result, as against M's estate? See Note, 142 A.L.R. 1447 (1943); In re Nelthropp's Estate, 129 F. Supp. 609 (D. Virgin Is. 1955); but cf. Estate of Jensen, page 157, supra.

[104] In addition to the Rees article cited in footnote 98, see Atkinson, Wills 138-145 (2d ed. 1953); Touster, Testamentary Freedom and Social Control — After-born Children, 6 Buffalo L. Rev. 251, 7 id. 47 (1957); von Briesen, The Problem of Pretermitted Heirs, 1948 Wis. L. Rev. 474.

[105] The entire will of Calvin Coolidge, who was noted for economy of words, read: "Not unmindful of my son, John, I give all my estate, both real and personal, to my wife, Grace Coolidge, in fee simple." No child was born to Coolidge after the will was executed.

b. What result, as against F's estate? See In re Glick's Estate, 346 P.2d 987 (Mont. 1959).

5. Suppose it is held that the reasoning of the North Dakota court in the Jensen case applies to pretermitted child statutes, and you are in a state whose statute protects children alive at the time of will execution. How do you handle the initial office interview with your client? Is there any easy or tactful way to ask a client, "Do you have any illegitimate children?" Should you recommend that the following clause be added to his will, "just in case"? "I intentionally make no provision for any person who claims to be an illegitimate child of mine."

In Estate of Peterson, 74 Wash. 2d 92, 442 P.2d 980 (1968), the testator stated: "I declare that I have no children, no children of deceased children, and no adopted children." The court held that this did not disinherit a child of testator, whose paternity he denied. "[T]he mistaken denial that he has children seems to us a clear example of a situation in which the statute was intended to operate to protect a forgotten child from being disinherited. There is no indication in the will that the testator remembered the petitioner and intended to disinherit him."

6. J is a judgment creditor of S, the only child of T, and S has no assets to pay the judgment. T dies, leaving a one-sentence will written years ago before S's birth: "I give all of my property to my wife, W." S's intestate share of T's estate is one-half. S refuses to claim as a pretermitted child. Can the judgment creditor reach the property devised to W? Does it matter how title passes at the death of T? Farmer's Co-op Assn., Inc. v. Webb, 249 Ark. 277, 459 S.W.2d 815 (1970); Barker v. Hayes, 347 Mo. 265, 147 S.W.2d 429 (1941). Suppose that during T's life S had assigned for a fair consideration all his right, title, and interest in T's estate to B. Can B claim S's share as a pretermitted child? 2 Page, Wills §21.110 (Bowe-Parker rev. 1960); 5 id. §47.16.

ESTATE OF TORREGANO

Supreme Court of California, 1960

54 Cal. 2d 234, 352 P.2d 505

PETERS, J. — Plaintiff appeals from a decree dismissing her petition for determination of heirship. The trial court held that, as a matter of law, plaintiff is not a pretermitted heir of Ernest J. Torregano, deceased.

Torregano, a San Francisco attorney, died on January 18, 1954. His will was dated June 25, 1947. It was duly admitted to probate on February 5, 1954. By the terms of that will decedent left the bulk of his estate to his brother, Alfred Torregano, the defendant herein. Plaintiff was not specifically named in the will, nor was she mentioned in any manner unless the trial court was correct in holding that she is a person who is included in the general class mentioned in clause Thirteenth of the will. Clauses Second, Thirteenth and Fourteenth (the only portions of the will involved in this appeal) read as follows:

"Second: I declare that I am a widower and that I have no children, issue of my marriage; that my deceased wife's name was Pearl C. Torregano; that my entire estate is separate property. . . .

"Thirteenth: I give, devise and bequeath to any person or persons who may contest this my Last Will and Testament, or assert any claim to share my estate by virtue of relationship or otherwise the sum of One Dollar ($1.00) each in settlement of their said claim or claims.

"Fourteenth: I give, devise and bequeath all the rest and residue of my estate of whatsoever kind or nature and wheresoever situate which I may die seized and possessed of, to my dearly beloved brother, Alfred Torregano, . . ." There follow provisions for contingent residuary beneficiaries in the event of Alfred's prior death.

On January 8, 1957, the estate then being in the process of probate, plaintiff filed a "Petition for Decree Determining That Gladys Torregano Stevens is a Pretermitted Heir," therein alleging that she is the lawful child of decedent and Viola Perrett, that she was not provided for by settlement or advancement, that she was not mentioned in decedent's will, that such omission was unintentional, and that she is entitled to the entire estate under the provisions of Probate Code, sections 90. . . . [California Probate Code §90 provides: "When a testator omits to provide in his will for any of his children, or for the issue of any deceased child, whether born before or after the making of the will or before or after the death of the testator, and such child or issue are unprovided for by any settlement, and have not had an equal proportion of the testator's property bestowed on them by way of advancement, unless it appeared from the will that such omission was intentional, such child or such issue succeeds to the same share in the estate of the testator as if he had died intestate."]

On May 15th the matter came on for trial. . . . Both parties produced witnesses and documentary evidence which, because of the nature of the ultimate action of the trial court, need not be set forth in detail. It is sufficient for the purposes of this opinion to state that plaintiff produced evidence from which the jury, if it believed the evidence, could have found that the following facts were true:

Testator, Ernest J. Torregano, was born November 21, 1882, a member of a fairly large Negro family. During 1902 or 1903 he married Viola Perrett, a member of his minstrel troupe, and brought her to live at his mother's house in New Orleans, Louisiana. On February 7, 1904, plaintiff, Gladys Torregano Stevens, was born the issue of such marriage, in the home of her grandmother (decedent's mother). When plaintiff was less than a year old testator (having established his family in a separate residence) took a position as a porter on a railroad train running between New Orleans and San Francisco, California. For the next year or more he continued in such work, residing with his wife and child during the periods of stopover in New Orleans. He then found permanent work in San Francisco, but did not immediately terminate his infrequent visits to his family. Some time after the earthquake and fire of 1906 he took up the study of law, and "commenced to pass for white." During this period, he sent for his brother Alfred, presumably the only other member of his family so capable of "passing," and the two of them ultimately succeeded. Testator ultimately became a successful member of the bar in San Francisco. Prior to 1915 testator had ceased his infrequent visits to New Orleans, but maintained contact with various members of his family by correspondence. During this period, he maintained two addresses in San Francisco, one for a "white" establishment and the other as an address to receive his mail from his colored family. During the year 1915 (or thereabouts), testator's mother and his half-brother, Edgar, visited him in San Francisco. On that occasion testator's mother told him that his wife and daughter, the plaintiff, were dead. On her return to New Orleans, testator's mother told the wife and child that testator was dead. On that date plaintiff was a child of tender years, incapable of producing issue, which testator then knew. The testator never had any other issue. After the date of the visit from his mother there was no further contact (by mail or otherwise) between testator and his wife (Viola) or plaintiff, although there was subsequent contact between testator and at least one of his sisters. On March 15, 1917, testator married Pearl C. Bryant, of Oakland, California, the marriage certificate indicating that he and his parents were white. In 1922 Viola remarried (presumably relying upon the misinformation given to her by testator's mother). Pearl died prior to June 25, 1947.

The will was introduced into evidence. From all of the foregoing facts, including the subsequent remarriage, the fact that testator was a successful practicing attorney who was versed in the law, and the fact that the will made no specific mention of plaintiff, and, in fact, inferred lack of any issue, there is no doubt that a jury could have found — if such evidence is admissible and relevant under the law — that testator, when executing his will, believed plaintiff to have been dead for many years, and that she had died at a time when she could not possibly have had issue.

Much of the evidence upon which the foregoing statement is based was received over the objection of defendant. He took the attitude that extrinsic evidence was inadmissible. The trial court admitted all of the evidence subject to such objection, which it took under submission along with the motions made at the commencement of the trial.

After all the evidence had been received, but prior to giving the case to the jury, the trial judge entered a minute order and a memorandum opinion, both granting defendant's "motion to dismiss." [106] The court then entered its decree, by the terms of which it held, in effect, that, as a matter of law, plaintiff is not a pretermitted heir of testator, and is entitled as a claimant to receive but the sum of $1.00 as mentioned in paragraph Thirteenth of testator's will. It also held that defendant is entitled to the residue of the estate, after payment of all specific bequests. From this decree, and from the denial of her motions for new trial and for order vacating the decree, plaintiff has appealed.

. . . The single question thus posed in this case is whether, under all of the

[106] The San Francisco Chronicle, May 25, 1960, p. 2, col. 1, reported that after granting the defendant's motion to dismiss, the trial judge said, "All our sympathies are with this girl," and urged Alfred Torregano to make a settlement on Gladys. The Chronicle also stated that the jurors staged a "corridor revolt" and said they stood 100 percent behind Gladys. Torregano's estate was worth around $350,000. At the time of the case Gladys was working as a domestic in Los Angeles. — Eds.

circumstances presented, there were factual issues which required the case to go to the jury. We are of the opinion that this question must be answered in the affirmative. We are of the further opinion that such determination requires conclusions which are, to some extent, matters of first impression.

Our first such conclusion is that extrinsic evidence is admissible to prove a testator's *lack* of intent to omit from his will any provision for a presumptive heir.

In contending that evidence *dehors* the will was not admissible herein, respondent relies upon that portion of Probate Code, section 90, which states that a child who is not provided for succeeds to a portion of the estate "unless it appears from the will that such omission is intentional." The quoted phrase specifically bars the introduction of evidence, other than that found on the face of the will, in proving that testator intentionally omitted provision for his child. The significant fact is that the code section makes no reference to the method of proving *lack* of intent to exclude a child. . . .

Upon a review of all of the California cases dealing with this subject, it will be discovered that no appellate decision in this state has ever held, in a case where the point was involved, that extrinsic evidence is inadmissible for the purpose of proving *lack* of intent to omit provision for a presumptive heir. . . .

Although no California case has directly barred the use of extrinsic evidence to prove lack of intent to omit provision for testator's child, it is also true that we have found no California authority expressly authorizing its use for such purpose . . . Therefore, the point is one of first impression.

From a standpoint of reason and common sense, it is obvious, by very definition, that a pretermission can exist only through oversight. It occurs only when there has been an omission to provide, absent an intent to omit. As pointed out in Matter of Estate of Garraud, 35 Cal. 336, the mistake or accident which caused the testator to omit provision for his child cannot possibly appear from the will itself. Extrinsic evidence for this purpose must be contemplated by the statute. Otherwise pretermission could never be proven.

There are other grounds for holding that evidence of this type is admissible. Extrinsic evidence is always admissible for the purpose of proving the circumstances under which a will was executed (Estate of Smith, 145 Cal. 118, 123, 78 P. 369; Estate of Spreckels, 162 Cal. 559, 123 P. 371; Estate of Pierce, 32 Cal. 2d 265, 196 P.2d 1; Prob. Code, §105). In the instant case petitioner produced evidence of relationship and family circumstances from which the jury could have found that for some 32 years testator and his daughter each believed the other dead. Should the trier of fact accept that evidence as true, it could further find that the erroneous belief continued to and including the date of making the will. Such evidence is then part of the "circumstances" under which the will was executed, and thus admissible. Extrinsic evidence is also admissible to explain any ambiguity arising on the face of a will, or to resolve a latent ambiguity which does not so appear. . . . In the instant case the testator declared: ". . . that I am a widower and that I have no children, issue of my marriage"; (clause Second). He also declared that his deceased wife's name was Pearl, and made no mention of a previous wife, or of any issue by such.

Granting appellant's right to offer evidence that she is testator's daughter, by a wife named Viola, a latent ambiguity immediately appears, which ambiguity must be resolved by recourse to extrinsic evidence.

. . . [T]he Legislature has intended . . . to bar only that method of proof which is easily susceptible to perjury, or which requires conjecture and speculation, . . . except in certain cases of necessity. This is why section 90 expressly denies the proponent the right to offer extrinsic evidence to prove *intentional omission.* Such proof would be tantamount to allowing parol declaration of intent to conflict with a written statement thereof. But such reason does not exist where the offeror of the evidence desires to show *lack of intent.* Of necessity, such must be proved by circumstances other than the testator's declaration of intent.

Appellant's entire case must rest on the contention that appellant was omitted from the will because the testator thought her dead. If true, that explains rationally his failure to provide for her, absent an intent to disinherit her. Since such a lack of intention could not appear from the face of the will, she is entitled to prove such by resort to extrinsic evidence.

We now turn to the language of clause Thirteenth. By the terms of that clause testator left $1.00 "to any person or persons who may contest . . . or assert any claim . . . by virtue of relationship or otherwise . . ." The trial court held (and respondent contends) that this language includes appellant, as a matter of law. Such general language, referring as it does to a large class of persons, cannot be deemed, as a matter of law, necessarily to include a close relative [whom] the testator mistakenly thought dead. . . .

Appellant is obviously not included in that class for whom clause Thirteenth provides $1.00 should they *contest* the will. This is so, for the obvious reason that appellant is not a contestant. She is a petitioner for distribution, claiming to be a pretermitted heir, and such a person has never been held to be a contestant. . . .

In order to bring appellant within the remaining provisions of clause Thirteenth respondent reads into that clause an intent to include the specific person within the general class of persons claiming "by virtue of relationship." It is true that the cases cited by respondent have held that, under the circumstances therein, the words "relation" or "relationship" were deemed to include testator's child. But, as we have shown, words of kinship may not be interpreted solely on the basis of previous definition under another set of facts. Here it is shown that the jury could have found that testator believed appellant to be dead. Hence it cannot be said with utter finality that he intended the phrase "by virtue of relationship" to apply to her.

The will must be interpreted as a whole, giving effect to all of its clauses. While Torregano did not say in so many words that he never had issue, the language of clause Second is meaningless unless it was intended to convey the impression that Torregano was childless. To give it any effect whatsoever, we must presume that testator thought he was without lineal issue. Hence the word "relationship" may not be said, as a matter of law, to have been used with intent to exclude his child. . . .

Directly applicable to the case under consideration is the rule that before a testator may be said to have intentionally omitted his child, it must appear on the face of the will that he had such child in mind at the time of executing the will, and having the child in mind he omitted to provide. . . . If a jury may find from the facts herein that Torregano thought appellant dead, he could not be said to have her in mind for the purpose of excluding her from his estate. One does not disinherit a deceased person.

Respondent argues that such an interpretation gives little or no effect to clause Thirteenth. We cannot agree. Clause Thirteenth is a typical clause intended to prevent contest. Under the construction of the will in this opinion the clause is given full effect as a no contest clause. Such a clause differs radically from a clause of disinheritance. The true disinheritance clause often fails to name a specific presumptive heir, and yet may be interpreted to exclude the same because of the use of words expressly indicating an intent to disinherit. Typical examples of general disinheritance clauses are: "I purposely leave nothing to anyone not mentioned in this will . . ."; "I intentionally leave nothing to any other person, with full knowledge . . ." Perhaps that most widely used (and most often interpreted to exclude presumptive heirs, even though unnamed) is some form of the clause found in Van Strien v. Jones, 46 Cal. 2d 705, 299 P.2d 1, wherein the testator expresses his intent to exclude or leave a nominal sum to any person, not named in the will, "who if I died intestate would be entitled to share in my estate." Such language was also in the will under scrutiny in Estate of Fernstrom, 157 Cal. App. 2d 380, 321 P.2d 25, relied upon by respondent. Often a testator combines in one clause provisions intended to bar contest with general language of disinheritance; but we have found no case in which the unnamed presumptive heir was held to be excluded from the will unless that will contained either some express language of intention to omit provision for all but those named, or a complete testamentary plan from which it clearly appeared that testator would adhere to such plan even in the event that it should later appear that he had a presumptive heir who was unknown to him. The Torregano will contains no direct or indirect language of disinheritance, and no inference that testator would adhere to his testamentary scheme in the event that he had a daughter whose existence was unknown to him. While he did leave $1.00 to anyone who might claim by reason of relationship, this clause must be viewed in light of the language of Estate of Carroll, 138 Cal. App. 2d 363, 291 P.2d 976 (hearing by Supreme Court denied), wherein it was said, at page 366: "We have been unable to find, nor have we been cited to, any case holding that the mere bequest of a nominal sum constitutes an intent to disinherit under other circumstances than those contemplated in the will."

We have read and analyzed each case cited by respondent for the proposition that appellant is excluded from the Torregano estate as a matter of law, and we find that although the language of some appears to give comfort to respondent's contention, none actually resulted in judgment against the claiming pretermitted heir unless the will included: (a) a specific clause of disinheritance, (b) a general clause expressing an intention to disinherit all those not named, (c) a clause affecting all persons who might have taken in the event that testator died intestate, (d) a clause expressing some doubt regarding the identity of testator's heirs and providing for disinheritance or nominal sums to such persons who may prove to be his heirs, (e) reasons for leaving the entire estate to the named beneficiaries, which reasons exclude the intent to leave anything to other presumptive heirs, or (f) a complete testamentary plan from which the court was bound to find that testator would have left nothing to any other person even though there were presumptive heirs of whose existence he was unaware. We find none of these elements in the Torregano will.

For the reasons assigned, it cannot be said as a matter of law that the language found in clause Thirteenth clearly indicates an intention to omit provisions for testator's daughter. It should require more than such general language to exclude from the operation of section 90 a daughter of whose existence testator was unaware.

Under the circumstances here presented the question of whether or not appellant is a pretermitted heir is one of fact, and the trial court erred in taking it from the jury. Whether appellant is the person she claims to be, whether or not Torregano believed her dead, and whether he intended, under the facts, that the phrase "by relationship or otherwise" should include appellant, are issues which must be determined by the trier of fact. Under the facts of this case such questions are not matters of law.

The judgment is reversed and the cause remanded for a new trial.

Gibson, C.J., Traynor, J., and White, J., concur. Spence, J., Schauer, J., and McComb, J., dissent.[107]

PROBLEMS

1. Based on your reading of the Torregano case, would you agree that Gladys was omitted from the will by mistake? That her father really thought she was dead?

2. If Ernest Torregano wanted to disinherit Gladys without advertising the fact, he didn't do too well. Note the implications of footnote 106. How would you have drafted Torregano's will to accomplish this objective? Would the following clause be effective?

> "Except as otherwise provided in this will, I have intentionally and with full knowledge omitted to provide for my heirs who may be living at the time of my death."

Van Strien v. Jones, 46 Cal. 2d 705, 299 P.2d 1 (1956), criticized 45 Calif. L. Rev. 220, 8 Hastings L.J. 342; Taylor v. Cammack, 209 Ark. 983, 193 S.W.2d 323 (1946).

3. Would you advise a client who wants to disinherit a child that he should give the reason in the will? In Brown v. DuFrey, 1 N.Y.2d 190, 134 N.E.2d 469 (1956), testatrix' will contained the following paragraph: "Fifth: I am mindful of

[107] Noted 13 Stan. L. Rev. 663. — Eds.

the fact that I have made no provision for John H. Brown, my husband. I do so intentionally because of the fact that during my lifetime he abandoned me, made no provision for my support, treated me with complete indifference and did not display any affection or regard for me."[108] Testatrix died in 1951. She had married John H. Brown in 1901, who had secured a divorce from her in 1917 on grounds of adultery. Brown remarried in 1924 and was living with his second wife at the time of testatrix' death. Brown sued testatrix' estate for testamentary libel and recovered as damages a sum approximately equal to one-half the estate.

See Reynolds, Defamation from the Grave: Testamentary Libel, 7 Cal. W.L. Rev. 91 (1971); Fuson, Testamentary Libel, The Case of the Vindictive Testator, 57 Ill. B.J. 840, 938 (1969); Note, 21 A.L.R.3d 754 (1968).

4. What policies base the pretermission statutes? Do the statutes carry out these policies effectively? See Touster, note 104 supra; von Briesen, note 104 supra.

La Réserve Héréditaire et L'Affaire Lacaze

The Civil Code of France provides that a testator may not dispose of all his property either by inter vivos gifts or by will if he is survived by direct descendants or ascendants.[109] He may only dispose of that portion of his assets designated as the disposable portion (la quotité disponible). If he has one legitimate child living at his death, the disposable portion is one-half; if two, one-third; if three or more, one-fourth. The remaining portion, usually called a legitime but in France called the réserve héréditaire, goes to the descendants per stirpes. There are no reserved rights in collaterals, while adopted children have the same rights as natural children of succession to the estate of the adopting parents.

A testator cannot avoid this statutory scheme by making inter vivos gifts, although he may alienate his assets in excess of the disposable portion during life by contracts with adequate consideration. The validity of a contract for this purpose (such as the sale of assets for a nominal sum) turns on whether or not it can be classified as a "liberality" or "donation." In such cases the courts will not be bound by the form of the transaction, but will examine the adequacy of the consideration received, and, if it finds that such alienations have taken place, it will calculate the estate as follows in a process called the "réduction des libéralités": 1. The value of assets in the hands of the deceased at the time of his death is determined. 2. Inter vivos donations are ascertained. 3. The value of all these assets is added up. 4. The debts of the estate are deducted. The remaining amount is then divided into the disposable portion and the réserve or réserves as indicated above. Devises and legacies in excess of the disposable portion are reduced first, then inter vivos gifts are reached, the most recent first. The testator may, however, decide to make up the

[108] Heinrich Heine, the German expatriate poet who died in France in 1856, also used his will to fire a parting shot at his spouse. His will closed with these words: "I leave all my estate to my wife on the express condition that she remarry. I want at least one person to sincerely grieve my death." Reported in 74 Case & Comment 21 (March-April 1969).

[109] Code Civil art. 913, 914 (67e ed. Petits Codes Dalloz 1967-1968). On the réserve héréditaire see Amos & Walton, Introduction to French Law 341 (1935); 5 Planiol & Ripert, Traité Pratique de Droit Civil Française §674 (1957).

disposable portion and the réserve with whatever assets he wishes, since the law restricts him only as to the proportionate value of his dispositions. He can, for example, devise real property and leave only personal property to his heirs.

In the ordinary case a man wants to leave something to his children, and there is no problem with the réserve héréditaire, but there is always the exception. Avoiding the réserve héréditaire, or any forced heir scheme, can lead to murder. A notable scandal arose in France in the 1950s over attempts to cut off a ne'er-do-well son. It was known as L'affaire Lacaze. The events were these.[110]

In 1934 Paul Guillaume died, leaving an estate of $40 million and a fabled collection of modern art to his wife Domenica (born Juliette Lacaze). Ten months after Paul's death Domenica adopted a baby boy, called Polo, whose birth certificate named neither a mother nor a father.

In 1941 Domenica married Jean Walter, an international tycoon who owned a vast empire of lead and zinc mines in Morocco, known as the Zellidja mines. Walter died in 1957, leaving the Zellidja mines to Domenica. Domenica was then immediately faced with a dilemma: how to prevent Zellidja mines (which accounted for 10 percent of France's foreign revenue) from being inherited by Polo, the adopted son who had grown up to be an inconsequential young man, already in trouble for passing bad checks. Under French law he could not be deprived of his forced share of his mother's property unless the adoption could be revoked. An adoption can be revoked only for "very grave reasons." [111] One leading commentator, Planiol, states that most of the successful petitions complain of egregious behavior of the child that disgraces the parents.[112]

According to the reports in the popular press, Domenica's brother, Jean Lacaze, masterminded a scheme to deprive Polo of his réserve héréditaire. Lacaze's friend and intermediary, Dr. Lacour, hired an ex-parachutist, Rayon, to kill Polo. But Rayon, seeing Polo in a paratrooper's uniform, felt sorry for his victim and, instead of killing him, warned him of the plot. Polo then disappeared, and Rayon told Dr. Lacour that he had strangled Polo and thrown his body into the Seine. He received $20,000 for supposedly knocking off Polo.

Some months later Polo turned up living in Paris with "une call girl" (as the French newspapers referred to her). According to the prostitute's story, Lacaze offered her $30,000 if she would complain to the police that Polo was living off her earnings. A conviction for pimping would provide grounds for annulling the adoption. Having the traditional heart of gold, the chippy told Polo of the plot. They went to the police, who arrested Lacaze when he handed over a $4000 advance to the prostitute in a Paris bar. Lacaze's story was that the prostitute had tried to blackmail him by threatening to report his nephew Polo for procuring. He turned the tables on her: he agreed to pay her, but only if she would indeed go ahead and report Polo.

Once Lacaze was arrested, the script turned into a French farce. Everybody

[110] Accounts of the affair, differing widely in details, can be found in Newsweek, vol. 53, Feb. 16, 1959, p. 46; The New Yorker, vol. 35, Feb. 21, 1959, p. 105; Time, vol. 73, Feb. 2, 1959, p. 20.

[111] Rouast, Révocation de l'adoption, [1923] Recueil Périodique et Critique [D.P.] IV. 262, col. 1.

[112] 2 Planiol & Ripert, Traité Pratique de Droit Civil Français §1049 (1957).

started talking at once; no one was sure what crime, if any, Lacaze had committed; Lacaze sued the investigating judge, who committed him to jail, for false imprisonment; it was announced that Dr. Lacour had committed no crime under French law because there was no corpse; Dr. Lacour threatened to sue Rayon for defamation of character; the prostitute changed her story and agreed with Lacaze's version. While everyone was talking, Domenica sold to the Louvre for a small sum (but reserving lifetime use) her collection of 8 Cézannes, 9 Renoirs, 5 Rousseaus, 3 Matisses and other masterpieces. The Louvre agreed to carve her two husbands' names on the facade of the Musée de l'Orangerie. But no way had yet been found to deprive Polo of control of the Zellidja mines after Domenica's death, unless, of course, Domenica sold them. In that case Polo's réserve héréditaire would be payable out of the assets that replaced the Zellidja mines.

SECTION E. Protection of Dependents

Dower, forced share, community property, and pretermission statutes are methods of protecting members of the decedent's family upon an arithmetic theory of justice. In most instances the statutes operate quite mechanically with arbitrary results, and they make no attempt to allocate family wealth according to the needs of the individual family members. For example, the forced share of a surviving spouse is given to the widow of a poor man as well as to the widow of a millionaire. It applies equally to a wife of forty years and to a wife of forty days; to a wife with a half-dozen minor children and to a wife with no children.

It is arguable that after a man's death his property should continue to be used to support those who were dependent upon him during his lifetime, and in England and several Commonwealth nations this objective is achieved with family maintenance legislation. No American state has taken this approach, however. Apart from the protection methods we already have considerered in this chapter, the only sources of economic protection obtainable from the decedent's property are those listed below.

1. *Homestead Rights*[113]

1 AMERICAN LAW OF PROPERTY §§5.75, 5.76 (Casner ed. 1952): "*General Characteristics*. Most jurisdictions in the United States have legislative provisions, commonly referred to as homestead laws, which are designed to preserve the family home from certain classes of creditors and to prevent the alienation thereof by the owner without the consent of his spouse. Although exemptions from execution,

[113] See 1 American Law of Property §§5.75 to 5.120 (Casner ed. 1952); Comment, The Probate Homestead in California, 53 Calif. L. Rev. 655 (1965); Comment, Nature of the Probate Homestead, 10 Okla. L. Rev. 106 (1957); Haskins, Homestead Rights of a Surviving Spouse, 37 Iowa L. Rev. 36 (1951); Haskins, Homestead Exemptions, 63 Harv. L. Rev. 1289 (1950).

On the tax treatment of homestead awards see Berg, Tax Aspects of Homestead and Family Allowance Awards, 37 Wash. L. Rev. 435 (1962).

embracing real and personal property, were known in England at common law and also in this country at an early date, homestead legislation appears to be an uniquely American contribution to the law of real property and traces its origins to a statute of the Republic of Texas, enacted in 1839. The generally announced purpose of the homestead laws is the security of the family, which in turn enures to the benefit of the community to the extent that such security prevents pauperism and provides the persons benefited thereby with some measure of stability and independence. In addition, the homestead laws have been regarded as devices to encourage home ownership and to attract settlers to areas in which the home is accorded maximum protection.

"The policy of the homestead laws is reflected in the three principal consequences which follow when particular property constitutes a homestead: (1) the property is exempt from execution for certain kinds of debts; (2) the owner's freedom of disposition is limited, since the consent of the spouse is required for a conveyance or encumbrance of the property; and (3) the use and disposition of the homestead, after the owner's death, is regulated for the benefit of his family.

"*Nature of the Homestead: Scope and Treatment.* . . .

"Although it is of little value to regard a homestead right as 'attaching' to particular property except in view of the three consequences enumerated in the preceding section, it is helpful for purposes of analysis to consider that property becomes a homestead upon the concurrence of certain conditions prescribed by the applicable statute. Those conditions may include requirements that the owner have a family, that the property be occupied and used as a residence, that the owner have a specified interest in the property, that the property not exceed a stated value or extent, or that some formal, unequivocal act of dedication be placed on record to identify the property as a homestead which is under the protection of the statute.

"The homestead provisions in all states are amenable to analysis in accordance with the foregoing requirements. It should be emphasized, however, that the homestead provisions do not by any means include all of the characteristics enumerated, which are as varied as the considerations which have prompted the different legislatures in their enactment. Consequently, generalizations with respect to these statutes as a whole, or concerning any aspect of their application, is [*sic*] often impossible and usually unwise. Definitions of homestead laws, based on conceptions of their proper scope, have been formulated so as to place certain state statutes outside the scope of homestead provisions; but it is misleading to exclude from consideration any statutory provisions which have as their apparent purpose the preservation of the home. Consequently, it may be said that there are, in addition to other exemptions from execution, homestead laws throughout the United States with the exception only of Delaware, the District of Columbia, Maryland, Pennsylvania, and Rhode Island."

Consideration of homestead laws as affording protection against creditors' claims, and as requiring a spouse's joinder on conveyances of real property, are the concerns of other courses in the law school curriculum. Our concern is with the third consequence of classifying property as a homestead: what is commonly referred to as the *probate homestead.* Typically, homestead statutes provide that upon the death of one of the spouses the surviving spouse (and, under many statutes, minor children and unmarried daughters) shall be entitled to occupancy of the homestead for the duration of her life (or, for minor children, until they attain legal age); and that the property shall be exempt from creditors' claims just as it was during the deceased spouse's lifetime. Under this approach the spouse has what amounts to a life estate determinable: She is entitled to occupy the homestead for so long as she occupies it, but she "abandons" it if she moves away, and she cannot convey or lease her interest.

In many states the widow may petition for and have set aside a cash award in lieu of homestead. Under statutes giving this option, the amount of the award is typically limited to the value of property that would otherwise have qualified as a homestead (e.g., $1000, or $5000, or $15,000).

While in theory the homestead laws appear to give assurance that the widow will at least have a roof over her head, and that the family home cannot be reached by creditors, in most states these statutes give no real protection to the widow. Under most statutes the value of property that can be set aside as a homestead is limited to a fixed dollar amount — usually $5000 or less.[114] A few statutes set the amount at $1000. Such statutes are hopelessly out of date: How many houses are there today valued at $1000 — and who would want to live in them? In other states, however, the statutory amount is, if not substantial, at least worth talking about.[115] In still others the limit is on lot size or acreage, and any dollar limit applies to the value of the land without improvements.[116] The Texas provisions are the most liberal of any state. There the homestead may consist of rural property of up to 200 acres, without regard to improvements, *or* an urban homestead consisting of a lot or lots not exceeding $10,000 in value, without regard to improvements. The urban homestead may include residential property and business property.[117] It is quite possible (and it has happened) that property worth several hundred thousand dollars can qualify as a homestead: If there's oil under those 200 acres, so much the better!

In short, whether a state's homestead laws give any substantial economic protection to a widow or minor children will turn on the acreage restrictions or (more typically) the dollar restrictions on the size of a homestead under that state's statute. Of course, if the husband has devised his entire estate to his wife, she needn't be concerned about homestead rights unless the estate is insolvent. But where the husband has devised a substantial portion of the estate to others, a homestead, or a cash award in lieu of homestead, may permit a partial reordering of the husband's dispositive plan in favor of his widow.

[114] E.g., Ind. Ann. Stat. §2-3501 (1968) ($1000); N.Y. Civ. Prac. §5206(a) (1963, Supp. 1970) (1969 amendment increased amount of homestead exemption from $1000 to $2000); Va. Code Ann. §34-4 (1970) ($2000).

[115] E.g., Cal. Civ. Code §1260 (1954, Supp. 1971) ($20,000); Ariz. Rev. Stat. Ann. §33-1101 (1956) ($8000).

[116] E.g., Iowa Code Ann. §561-2 (1950) (40 acres).

[117] Tex. Const. art. 16, §51.

Related to the homestead laws are the statutes in a number of states authorizing the probate court to "set aside" for the widow or minor children various items of tangible personal property, such as furniture, wearing apparel, farm implements, cars, and so on.[118] Generally, the items that can be given to the widow or children are those items of personal property that are exempt by statute from execution and forced sale by creditors. If the widow asserts a claim to these items, they pass outright to her, even though the husband's will may have devised them to some other party. It is a commentary on the inadequacy of the homestead laws, in states fixing a dollar limit on the amount of the homestead, that a widow's "exempt personal property" award will often exceed the value of her homestead rights.

2. *Family Allowance During Probate*

Every state has a statute authorizing the probate court to fix a family allowance on behalf of the surviving spouse (and, in most states, minor children) designed to provide temporary support while the decedent's assets are being administered.[119] In a few states the allowance is limited to a fixed — and modest — amount.[120] In most states the widow is entitled to an amount sufficient for her "support," or "maintenance," sometimes for a fixed period,[121] but more typically for the entire period during which the estate is in administration.[122]

[118] E.g., Kan. Stat. Ann. §59-403(1) (1964); Tex. Prob. Code §287 (1956). These statutes are often outmoded. New York's statute, originally enacted in 1829, was reenacted, with minor changes, in the general updating of the law of estates in 1966. N.Y. Estates, Powers & Trusts Law §5-3.1 (1967):

"(a) If a person dies, leaving a surviving spouse or minor children, the following items of property are not assets of the estate but vest in, and shall be set off to such surviving spouse, unless he is disqualified, under 5-1.2, from taking an elective or distributive share of the decedent's estate. In case there is no surviving spouse or such spouse, if surviving, is disqualified, such items of property vest in, and shall be set off to the decedent's minor children:

"(1) All housekeeping utensils, musical instruments, sewing machine, household furniture and appliances used in and about the house, fuel, provisions and clothing of the decedent, not exceeding in aggregate value one thousand dollars.

"(2) The family bible, family pictures and school books, used by such family, and books, not exceeding in value one hundred and fifty dollars, which were part of the family library.

"(3) Domestic animals with their necessary food for sixty days, farm machinery, one motor vehicle and one tractor, not exceeding in aggregate value five thousand dollars.

"(4) Money or other personal property not exceeding in value one thousand dollars, except that where assets are insufficient to pay the reasonable funeral expenses of the decedent, the personal representative must apply such money or other personal property to defray any deficiency in such expenses.

"(b) No allowance shall be made in money or other property if the items of property described in subparagraphs (1), (2) or (3) are not in existence when the decedent dies.

"(c) The items of property, set off as provided in paragraph (a), shall, at least to the extent thereof, be deemed reasonably required for the support of the surviving spouse or minor children of the decedent during the settlement of the estate."

[119] The statutes are collected in Comment, Widows' Allowances and Marital Deductions — The Date-of-Death Rule, 63 Mich. L. Rev. 924 (1965).

[120] E.g., Kan. Stat. Ann. §59-403(2) (1964) ($750).

[121] E.g., Ga. Code Ann. §113-1002 (1959, Supp. 1970) (one year); Minn. Stat. Ann. §525.15(4) (1969) (eighteen months).

[122] E.g., Cal. Prob. Code §680 (1956) (no time limit unless estate insolvent); Conn. Gen. Stat. Ann. §45-250 (1960, Supp. 1971).

In states where there is no dollar limit on the amount of the award, the family allowance can do more than provide for the widow's interim support needs. It can be used to increase the amount of property passing outright to the wife. Typically, the allowance is over and above the amount passing to the widow by her husband's will; it is not treated as a prepayment of any legacies in her favor. Furthermore, the reported decisions indicate that courts tend to be generous in fixing these awards.[123]

But while the family allowance statutes permit a partial reordering of the husband's dispositive plan in favor of his widow and minor children, they are designed to meet short-term, not lifetime, support needs. It appears that in only one state, Maine, has such a statute been construed to authorize the grant of a permanent support allowance,[124] although a handful of states permit support allowances to continue for minor children after the estate has been closed.[125]

PROBLEM

H, a resident of your state, dies leaving a will that devises $5000 to W, his wife of ten years, and the residue of his estate to S, his adult son by a former marriage. H owned the following property:

House and lot (value of lot: $4000)	$25,000
Print shop (value of lot on which print shop stands is $4500)	50,000
150-acre farm	30,000
Tangible personalty (car, furniture, personal effects, etc.)	10,000
Securities	35,000

In the year preceding his death, H's gross income amounted to $15,000. Under your state's laws, what homestead or exempt personal rights does W have in any of this

[123] Note, 90 A.L.R.2d 687 (1963); see Moore v. Moore, 430 S.W.2d 247 (Tex. Civ. App. 1968) (court upheld allowance of $42,366 as amount sufficient for maintenance of widow for one year). In the estate of William Randolph Hearst, his widow was given a family allowance of $10,000 per month for eighteen months. N.Y. Times, Feb. 26, 1952, p. 29.

The family allowance also offers limited opportunities for tax planning in administering the husband's estate. The Supreme Court's decision in Jackson v. United States, 376 U.S. 503 (1964), precludes qualification of a family allowance for the estate tax marital deduction in most states. See Comment, supra note 119. However, fixed dollar awards specified by a statute will qualify for the marital deduction. In such states the family allowance can be used to increase the amount qualifying for the deduction if the husband's will did not leave sufficient assets in a qualifying way. For discussion of the qualification of homestead and exempt personal property awards for the marital deduction, see Berg, supra note 113. Of greater importance, how the family allowance award is drafted (i.e., whether it is to be paid out of principal or out of estate income) may determine the income tax burden on estate income. That is, it may determine whether income is taxable to the estate as a separate tax entity, or whether satisfaction of the family allowance "carries out distributable net income," causing it to be taxed as income to the widow. Ferguson, Freeland & Stephens, Federal Income Taxation of Estates and Beneficiaries 575 (1970).

[124] Me. Rev. Stat. Ann. tit. 18, §801 (1965); see Gilman v. Gilman, 53 Me. 184 (1865) (widow's allowance increased on appeal to $85,000 — in 1865 dollars!).

[125] E.g., Neb. Rev. Stat. §30-103(3) (1965) (support for child until age fourteen); Wash. Rev. Code Ann. §11.52.030 (1967) (support for children until they attain legal age).

property? Are these rights subject to any election on her part? That is, must she choose between her forced share rights and homestead rights; or must she choose between the will provisions and her homestead rights? To what family allowance is W entitled? What further information would you need before advising W how to proceed?

3. *Small Estate Administration Statutes*

We have discussed this topic earlier, when we were assessing the need for a formal, court-supervised administration of a decedent's estate.[126] These "small estate" statutes, found in a growing number of states, do not simply provide a short-cut administration procedure. In many instances they permit distribution of the entire probate estate to the surviving spouse or minor children irrespective of the provisions of the deceased's will or of the state's intestacy statutes. Typically, they provide that estates which do not exceed a certain figure (varying from $500 in the District of Columbia to $5000 in California and Nevada) shall, upon petition, be set apart for the surviving spouse or minor children. For example, the California statute provides that an estate of less than $5000 may be set aside to the surviving spouse (or, if there is no surviving spouse, to the minor children) if the surviving spouse (or children) owns property worth less than $20,000.[127] The statutes protect the spouse and children against most creditors. They also supersede the provisions of a will, and thus they may eliminate the testamentary power of a relatively poor man who dies survived by a spouse or minor children. They also supersede the intestacy statutes, with the result that the widow may take all to the exclusion of the children.

While the small dollar amounts suggest that these statutes are applicable only to families on the lowest rungs of the economic ladder, this is not always the case. In the first place, the statutory limit ordinarily applies only to the value of the probate estate, meaning that such items as employee death benefits, life insurance proceeds, and bank accounts or other assets that pass by right of survivorship are excluded. Second, many of the statutes provide that the dollar limit is exclusive of property that can be set aside as a homestead or as exempt personal property, and exclusive of the amount set aside as a family allowance. Given a state whose homestead and family allowance provisions are on the generous side, it is quite possible for an estate of substantial dollar value to qualify as a "small" estate.

4. *Family Maintenance Legislation*

The most important application of the policy that a man's property should be used to support his dependents after his death is found in the family maintenance legislation originating in New Zealand and now adopted in Australia, England and Canada.

[126] See page 89, supra.
[127] Cal. Prob. Code §§640, 645 (1956, Supp. 1971).

LAUFER, FLEXIBLE RESTRAINTS ON TESTAMENTARY FREEDOM — A REPORT ON DECEDENT'S FAMILY MAINTENANCE LEGISLATION, 69 Harv. L. Rev. 277, 282-283 (1955): "[F]lexible restraints on testamentary freedom in their modern form seem an independent creation of New Zealand's legislative genius. Its statute, first enacted in 1900, remains the most comprehensive and uncompromising version of this approach.

"In substance, it assures to a decedent's surviving family, above all his spouse and children, adequate maintenance whenever his will does not provide it. Maintenance may only be granted out of the net estate, i.e., after all claims have been discharged. A dependent who claims that the will failed to make proper provision for him may apply to the court within twelve months of probate. Eligible dependents are not only the testator's spouse, child, or grandchild, but also his parents and his adopted and illegitimate children. Upon application the court will determine whether the testator has adequately provided for the dependent. If it finds that he has not, it may in its discretion order that suitable provisions be made out of the estate, or it may refuse an order if it finds that the dependent's character or conduct 'disentitles' him. It may order that provision shall be made in the form of periodic payments or in a lump sum. It may attach any conditions it deems fit to its order. It may provide that the incidence of the order shall fall ratably on the entire estate or it may exonerate certain portions, either completely or partially. Save where the dependent has been granted a lump sum, the court may later set aside, vary, or suspend its order where it finds that the dependent's situation has improved. The court's power extends over the entire estate even if the will disposes of only a part of the estate."

NEW YORK TEMPORARY COMMISSION ON THE LAW OF ESTATES, FOURTH REPORT, SHARES DISTRIBUTABLE — MINORS, INCOMPETENTS AND OTHER DEPENDENT CHILDREN
(*Appendix 17, 1965*)

In summary, the [1963 report on the power of a New York testator to disinherit his children] submits that — "In contrast with the solicitude for the welfare of children of a neglectful testator revealed in the legitime of those jurisdictions following the civil law and in the maintenance programs of England and the Commonwealth nations, the continued complete freedom of the New York testator to disinherit his dependent children appears to reflect an indifference to moral and social irresponsibility and is certainly out of harmony with the vast social legislation which has characterized the last half century in this state and country."

The report criticizes the remedies proposed by the "forced share" or "legitime" concept of the Civil Law as having no relationship to need and seriously interfering with estate planning. Instead, it recommends the "flexible restraints" of maintenance legislation first enacted in New Zealand and finally in England in 1938 and largely re-enacted and extended to intestacy in 1952.

The benefit of the recommended statute can only be obtained on behalf of a legitimate or adopted minor child, an illegitimate minor child where the decedent is the mother, or where paternity has been proved or acknowledged by a father, or any other child who because of physical or mental disability cannot maintain himself. The draft [accompanying this supplemental report, proposing adoption of a family maintenance scheme], consistent with the English Act, provides for maintenance for a child upon order of the surrogate by periodic payments of income until the child is twenty-one or the disability ceases.

Any child within the definition of the statute would be entitled to such maintenance except where: —

1. The surviving spouse is the parent of such child and is given "substantially all of the estate or substantially all of the income therefrom."
2. The surrogate in his discretion denies the application.

The burden of the maintenance award is to be borne by all of the interested parties proportionately unless it would result in an increase in estate taxes and an application for such an award must be made within a fixed time after the will is admitted or letters of administration are issued.

The outstanding feature of the recommendation, as well as the similar legislation enacted in England, is the broad discretion of the court to vary the will of a testator or the laws of intestacy to comply with the testator's moral if not legal obligations. The implicit sanction against an unjust will vis-a-vis dependent children is that a man will not make an unjust will if he and his lawyer know that the court will not permit it to be carried out. At the same time the court is authorized to take into consideration the present or future income of the child, the decedent's reasons for his testamentary disposition, the conduct of the child and any other relevant matter.

The primary difficulties with the proposed legislation appear to be: —

1. *The administration of the estate would have to be kept open.* It would appear that this difficulty could be solved by payment to a guardian. In addition, in all wills where there is any possibility of property passing to an infant, a careful lawyer either creates a trust by the will or permits it to be held by the executor under a power in trust. Under the former method the estate terminates but the grantee of the power (usually the executor) is accountable to the beneficiaries until they become twenty-one. The recommended plan is only the equivalent of a statutory trust.

2. *Every surrogate would have a different idea of need.* The answer to this objection is that this type of legislation has worked very well in England for over twenty-five years and in New Zealand for over sixty years without any real problems and with restraint by the courts.

Several other proposals were advanced: —

1. *Something similar to the right of election with an arbitrary but definite share for children.* This would appear to raise the same problems and complications now faced in section eighteen [now N.Y. Estates, Powers & Trusts Law §5-1.1, giving the surviving spouse a forced share], would treat all children regardless of need the same, and interfere with freedom of testamentary disposition even more than the

recommendation. Unless the statute could be satisfied by a trust, in which case all of the requirements of a real trust would have to be set forth in detail as in section eighteen, a guardian would have to be appointed in every case. In addition, either the court, a guardian or the special guardian would have to make the election in every case on behalf of the child.

2. *It could be limited to an adjudicated incompetent.* This would not remedy the plight of the dependent who has never been adjudicated because he has no estate to be conserved.

3. *Section twenty-six could be extended to require that a testator must specifically disinherit a child in his will.* This would not appear to be a meaningful sanction against conduct which in itself would appear to be morally reprehensible.

4. *The need test should be retained but the award distributed under the formula of Matter of Kaiser, 198 Misc. 582.* The difficulty is that the amount of the award would first have to be fixed by some means, and a withdrawal from the estate of the amount of the award would more seriously interfere with testamentary freedom than the recommendation. Under the maintenance system, payments are made out of income (unless the estate is so small that this would be impractical) until the cessation of the disability which is either when the child attains majority or his death if there is a physical or mental disability. If the estate is large, the principal is preserved for the legatee. While the legatee might have to wait for it, it can be assigned during the disability for its value. While this is inconvenient to the legatee, the law should be more concerned with the decedent's dependent child than a stranger.

It should be noted that the act will not apply where the surviving parent is given the income or substantially all the income of the estate. In the vast majority of estates, this is the case. It would not even apply in the usual "second spouse with children of the first spouse situation" since most litigation in such circumstances arises out of the favoring of the children of the first marriage over the subsequent spouse. It will only apply where the decedent has neglected the obligations to his children which the law had imposed during his lifetime. As a practical matter, it would only be giving statutory authority and guidelines to the common practice of the surrogate using his prestige and power to encourage settlements of will contests where there is a patently unjust will but only questionable evidence of undue influence or lack of testamentary capacity. In the absence of any such evidence most surrogates feel helpless to act even in the face of the obvious and unquestionable equities of the case.

Other proposals to limit the power of disinheritance of children of the decedent or parents have been made. Professor Simes (Simes, Public Policy and the Dead Hand) proposes a right to take against the parent's will in the event the child is unable to support himself and only for the amount necessary for support. This proposal, however, requires the same determination as to need and support as the proposal of the recommendation in the report. However, it requires an election to be made by or on behalf of the child.

Professor Macdonald (Macdonald, Fraud on the Widow's Share) proposes a family maintenance act similar to this recommendation but including nontestamentary transfers. This recommendation has the flexibility of and is based upon the English maintenance statutes and is practically identical to the recommendation of this report with the exception that it would include non-testamentary assets. Similar proposals have been made by the late Professor Cahn of New York University Law School (Cahn, Restraints on Disinheritance, 85 Pa. L. Rev.).

Professor Paul G. Haskell of Georgetown Law School (The Power of Disinheritance — Proposal for Reform, 52 Georgetown Law Journal 499 [1964]) proposes a limited and variable forced share for children with provision for needy parents. He would require protection against disinheritance by inter vivos disposition by requiring matching trusts for the post mortem support of the family. He would include all property required to be included in the federal gross estate for tax purposes. The forced share for children would not be based upon need, would apply to the child until twenty-one unless he is in school in which case it would terminate at the age of twenty-six. His forced share for children would be one-third of the first $200,000 of the estate after debts and expenses with a supplemental forced share equal to the basic forced share. In the event that the child is between the ages of twenty-one and twenty-six, both shares would be placed in trust until he became twenty-six and upon attaining the age of twenty-six, the forced share would be payable outright to the child, and the supplemental forced share would be payable to the legatees.

It is obvious that Professor Haskell's proposal is not based upon need. It would seriously interfere with freedom of alienation and estate planning. It does not seem to take into consideration inter vivos or testamentary benefits which have been given to the child. It does have the advantage of a definite standard for determining the amount of the share for the child but since it includes all property which would be included in the gross estate of the decedent (including gifts in contemplation of death), it would seem to be unduly restrictive of the power of both inter vivos and testamentary alienation.

Another proposal which has been made is to increase the amount of property which is to be set off to the surviving spouse and children under Section 200. Under the present statute all of such property is to be set off to the surviving spouse. Where the surviving spouse is the parent of the child, there is no problem. Where the surviving spouse is not the parent, however, the children have no right to have exempt property set off to them. Many states have much more generous homestead and widow's allowances than New York. The problem with this method, however, is that such property is exempt from creditors, would affect all the children the same regardless of their respective needs, and if substantially increased would more seriously interfere with freedom of testamentary disposition than the recommendation.

To paraphrase the words of the Foley Commission, the law compels a man to support his dependent children during his lifetime and enables him to leave them penniless at his death. That Commission specifically left this problem to a future commission, and Surrogate Slater specifically pointed to family maintenance legislation as a workable method.

> The Commission has left to be considered by others whether a parent has a moral duty, which should be made a legal duty, to provide for the support and

maintenance of children during the period of their dependence. Should the law compel a parent at death to provide for his helpless dependents? The right of a testator to pauperize his helpless dependents now exists under our law. When will the State step in and take away that privilege? When will such public policy be changed? The State is vitally interested in the care of minor children from both a pecuniary and a social viewpoint.

The report of the Commission refers to those states having statutory exemptions for minor children. It is the hope of the speaker that this subject may be studied by a Commission and the law of the State humanized so that at least minor children may be permitted to share in a parent's estate. Lord Astor's bill will be a workable guide to such an end.

The Commission is unanimous in agreeing that this anomaly should no longer continue and has requested further study of the means to end it. Upon reflection and reconsideration, it is the considered opinion of the Commission that this recommendation is the most workable method.

The family maintenance legislation recommended by the Temporary State Commission on the Law of Estates was not enacted by the New York legislature.

On the English family maintenance legislation, see Albery, The Inheritance (Family Provision) Act 1938 (1950), reprinted as Chapter 5 of Jarman on Wills, 8th ed. (1951); Theobald on Wills 114 (13th ed. 1971); Crane, Family Provision on Death in English Law, 35 N.Y.U.L. Rev. 984 (1960). Albery includes in the Appendix a form of trust deed entitled "Settlement upon Mistress and Illegitimate Child for Purpose of Evading the Provisions of the Act."

10. Restrictions on the Power of Disposition: the Transferor, the Survivors, and Social Policy

In this chapter we examine various restrictions on the power of disposition, other than restrictions relating to formalities of transfer, direct protection of the family, and the Rule against Perpetuities. First we deal with capacity to make a will and then with transfers prohibited because of the conduct or nature of the beneficiary. Next, after a brief look at disposition of the decedent's body, we turn to several areas where the decedent attempts to project his control of property long after his death with resulting conflict between his wishes and those of the beneficiaries. The transferor may attempt to interfere with the conduct of the beneficiaries, or restrain their free alienation of the property, or prevent them from terminating a trust. The common question running through the various fact situations in this chapter is: When should the transferor's wishes not be honored because another competing interest is of more importance to society?

SECTION A. Capacity to Make a Will

1. *Legal Capacity*

At early English law a person convicted of certain types of felonies lost his right to devise his lands and bequeath his chattels. For some felonies, including suicide, property was forfeited to the crown. Forfeiture by attainder does not now exist in the United States, although in a few states by statute imprisoned convicts cannot execute a valid will, and in Hawaii, Michigan, and Rhode Island certain prisoners are divested of their property.[1] Generally in the United States the only persons legally incapable of making a will are persons under age or of unsound mind. However, American Indians still remain under certain disabilities.

In 1970 Indian reservation lands totaled approximately 50 million acres. Not all of this land is remote and isolated. Phoenix, Seattle, Albuquerque, and Tulsa have substantial tracts of Indian land located near them, and much of Palm Springs, California, is built on land owned by the Agua Caliente Indians. Almost 80 percent of Indian lands is held in trust by the federal government for the benefit of individual tribes. The tribes may assign trust land to individual members, generally for life, with the approval of the Secretary of the Interior. The balance of Indian lands is held in individual allotments authorized by the General Allotment Act (Dawes Act) of 1887, 24 Stat. 388. The Dawes Act authorized the President to partition Indian land into tracts of 40, 80, or 120 acres and allot them to individual Indians. The title to these lands is held by the United States in trust for the allottee. Although further allotment of land was forbidden by Congress in 1934, approximately 11 million acres of reservation lands are beneficially owned by individual allottees. Allotments are generally devisable by will subject to the approval of the Secretary of the Interior. Although allotments are theoretically subject to sale with Secretarial consent, such consent is very rarely given. For a full discussion of Indian property see U.S. Dept. of the Interior, Federal Indian Law c. 9 (1958).

TOOAHNIPPAH v. HICKEL

United States Supreme Court, 1970

397 U.S. 598

[George Chahsenah, a Comanche Indian, died owning three Comanche allotments in Oklahoma. Chahsenah devised his estate to a niece, Viola Atewooftakewa Tate, and her three children. Chahsenah had resided with this niece during a considerable portion of the later years of his life. His will made no mention of his surviving daughter, Dorita High Horse, but stated that he was leaving nothing to his heirs at law "for the reason that they have shown no interest in me." The beneficiaries under the will sought to have it approved by the Secretary of the Interior, as required by 25 U.S.C. §373.[2] Dorita High Horse contested. The Examiner

[1] Project, The Collateral Consequences of a Criminal Conviction, 23 Vand. L. Rev. 929, 1035-1037, 1079-1086 (1970).

[2] Section 2 of the Act of June 25, 1910, 36 Stat. 856, amended by Act of February 14, 1913, 37 Stat. 678, 25 U.S.C. §373, provides in pertinent part:

"Any persons of the age of twenty-one years having any right, title, or interest in any allotment held under trust or other patent containing restrictions on alienation or individual Indian moneys or other property held in trust by the United States shall have the right prior to the expiration of the trust or restrictive period, and before the issuance of a fee simple patent or the removal of restrictions, to dispose of such property by will, in accordance with regulations to be prescribed by the Secretary of the Interior: *Provided, however,* That no will so executed shall be

of Inheritance in the Department of the Interior found that the testator was competent and not acting under undue influence and that the will was properly executed; he approved the will and ordered distributions in accordance with its provisions. An appeal was taken to the Regional Solicitor of the Department of the Interior, who had final authority to act on behalf of the Secretary. The Regional Solicitor viewed his authority as requiring him to examine all the circumstances to determine whether "approval will most nearly achieve just and equitable treatment of the beneficiaries thereunder and the decedent's heirs-at-law." Under this standard he found that Chahsenah was an alcoholic and had ceased cohabiting with Dorita's mother shortly before her birth, thus failing to provide Dorita with a "normal home life during her childhood." The Regional Solicitor concluded that although Dorita was a married adult "it is inappropriate that the Secretary perpetuate this utter disregard for the daughter's welfare." Accordingly he disapproved the will and ordered the entire estate distributed to Dorita High Horse as sole heir at law.

The beneficiaries under the will then brought an action against the Secretary of the Interior in the United States District Court, contending that the action of the Regional Solicitor exceeded the authority conferred upon the Secretary by 25 U.S.C. §373. Dorita High Horse was allowed to intervene as a party defendant. Both the Secretary and Dorita High Horse moved for summary judgment, contending that the action of the Regional Solicitor was final and unreviewable and, in addition, did not involve an abuse of discretion. The District Court held that the Secretary's action could be reviewed, and that he had exercised his power too broadly. The case was remanded to the Secretary with directions to approve the will. On appeal the Court of Appeals for the Tenth Circuit reversed, holding that the Secretary's action under 25 U.S.C. §373 was unreviewable. The beneficiaries appealed to the United States Supreme Court, which held that the Secretary's action was subject to judicial review. The Court then dealt with the scope of the Secretary's power to grant or withhold approval of the instrument.]

Mr. Chief Justice BURGER. . . . The Regional Solicitor's view of the scope of the Secretary's power is reflected in his statement:

> When a purported will is submitted for approval and it has been determined that it meets the technical requirements for a valid will, further consideration must be given before approving or disapproving it to determine whether approval will most nearly achieve *just and equitable treatment of the beneficiaries thereunder and the decedent's heirs-at-law*. App. 84-85. (Emphasis added.)

The basis of the Regional Solicitor's action emerges most clearly from his reliance on the legal relationship of the testator to his daughter and his failure to support her. From this he concluded that failure to provide for the daughter in the

---

valid or have any force or effect unless and until it shall have been approved by the Secretary of the Interior: *Provided further,* That the Secretary of the Interior may approve or disapprove the will either before or after the death of the testator. . . . *Provided also,* That this section and section 372 of this title shall not apply to the Five Civilized Tribes or the Osage Indians."

will did not meet the just and equitable "standard" that he considered the Secretary was authorized to apply in passing on an Indian will. The Regional Solicitor related the failure to support the daughter in her childhood to the absence of provision for her in the will and declared that the decedent "had an obligation to his daughter which was not discharged either during his lifetime or under the terms of his purported will. *For this reason* it is inappropriate that the Secretary perpetuate this utter disregard for the daughter's welfare. . . ." (Emphasis added.) While thus stressing the natural ties with Dorita High Horse, the Regional Solicitor neither challenged nor gave weight to the predicate of the Examiner's determination which was that the decedent had a close and sustained familial relationship with his niece and had resided in her home, while, in contrast, he had virtually no contact with his natural daughter.

To sustain the administrative action performed on behalf of the Secretary would, on this record, be tantamount to holding that a public officer can substitute his preference for that of an Indian testator. We need not here undertake to spell out the scope of the Secretary's power, but we cannot assume that Congress, in giving testamentary power to Indians respecting their allotted property with the one hand, was taking that power away with the other by vesting in the Secretary the same degree of authority to disapprove such a disposition.

In reaching our conclusions it is not necessary to accept the contention of the petitioners that the Secretary's authority is narrowly limited to passing on the formal sufficiency of a document claimed to be a will. The power to make testamentary dispositions arises by statute; here we deal with a special kind of property right under allotments from the Government. The right is not absolute; the allottee is the beneficial owner while the Government is trustee. 25 U.S.C. §348. The Indian's right to make inter vivos dispositions is limited and requires approval of the Secretary. The legislative history reflects the concern of the Government to protect Indians from improvident acts or exploitation by others, and comprehensive regulations govern the process of such inter vivos dispositions. No comparable regulations govern the right to make testamentary dispositions, and from this one might argue that the power of an Indian relating to testamentary disposition of allotted property is uninhibited. The legislative history on this score is perhaps no more or less reliable an indicator of what Congress intended than is usual when the scope of administrative discretion is in question.

Whatever may be the scope of the Secretary's power to grant or withhold approval of a will under 25 U.S.C. §373, we perceive nothing in the statute or its history or purpose that vests in a governmental official the power to revoke or rewrite a will that reflects a rational testamentary scheme with a provision for a relative who befriended the testator and omission of one who did not, simply because of a subjective feeling that the disposition of the estate was not "just and equitable." The Regional Solicitor's action was based on nothing more that we can discern than his concept of equity and in our view this was not the kind or degree of discretion Congress vested in him. . . .

The Secretary's task is not always an easy one and perhaps is rendered more difficult by the absence of regulations giving guidelines. It is not difficult to conceive of dispositions so lacking in rational basis that the Secretary's approval could reasonably be withheld under §373 even though the same scheme of disposition by a non-Indian of unrestricted property might pass muster in a conventional probate proceeding; on this record, however, we see no basis for the decision of the Regional Solicitor and must hold it arbitrary and capricious. There being no suggestion that the record need or could be supplemented by added factual material, the case is remanded to the Court of Appeals with directions to reinstate the judgment of the District Court.

NOTE

Chief Justice Burger states that "it is not difficult to conceive of dispositions so lacking in rational basis" that Secretarial approval might lawfully be withheld. This, however, assumes that testamentary dispositions by Indians must be "rational." Why should the Secretary be empowered to pass on more than "the formal sufficiency" of an allottee's will? In other words, why should the Secretary function as more than a state probate court, deciding, for example, whether the will was properly witnessed and determining whether fraud or duress was involved? Since state court jurisdiction often does not extend to Indian real property, it may be reasonable for the Secretary to act as a surrogate government in these respects.

In thinking about these questions, consider whether there is a distinct nature to Indian property rights. Suppose, for example, that an Indian allottee wished to will his allotment to a non-Indian. This might be invalidated by the Secretary as compromising the value of the reservation as a cultural homeland for tribal members. Or if the Indian allottee were to will his land to ten relatives in equal shares, this might so divide the ownership of the allotment as to render it unsuitable for use. Federal policy, on the other hand, may favor unitization of Indian allotments as a means of providing income to the Indians. The Secretary might, consequently, adopt a policy of disapproving wills that pass the property to more than two devisees.

Divided ownership of allotted land is a severe problem on many reservations. Land allotted to a single owner in the 1890s, for example, may now have over 100 owners, each holding a fractional share of the acreage. The splintered ownership becomes worse as time progresses, and the land becomes of greatly diminished value. Various schemes for land consolidation have been suggested and attempted, such as landowners' committees with powers-of-attorney from all allottees of a particular parcel, or the holding of title to substantial parts of a reservation by one corporate entity, which issues stock in proportion to an allottee's interest in the land and pays out lease income as dividends. In 1940, Congress empowered the Secretary to arbitrate disputes among heirs of an allottee, and to lease the entire parcel if the allottees could not agree among themselves how it should be used within a three-month period. See Comment, Too Little Land, Too Many Heirs — The Indian Heirship Land Problem, 46 Wash. L. Rev. 709 (1971); Comment, The Problems of

Indian Poverty: The Shrinking Land Base and Ineffective Education, 36 Albany L. Rev. 143 (1971).

Procedural regulations governing the testamentary disposition of allotted Indian lands may be found in 43 C.F.R. §§4.260 to 4.262, which were published in Part II of the April 15, 1971 Federal Register, 36 F.R. 7198, as amended on Nov. 5, 1971, 36 F.R. 21284. As of 1972 substantive regulations regarding testamentary disposition of allotted land by an Indian had not been adopted.

2. *Mental Capacity*

NOTE, TESTAMENTARY CAPACITY IN A NUTSHELL: A PSYCHIATRIC RE-EVALUATION

18 Stan. L. Rev. 1119, 1123-1143 (*1966*)

Though the exact nature of the original policy which was thought to necessitate testamentary capacity limitations is unclear, it was probably a product of the medieval conception of the will. Denoting testamentary instruments as "wills" obviously implies that the disposition is to be such as is intended by the testator, that is, that which conforms to the testator's "will" in the philosophical-assertive sense of the term. Thus, if the testator, as a result of insufficient capacity, is unaware of the significance of his act or of the effect it will have on the post-mortem disposition of his property, he cannot, in any real sense, be said to be exercising his "will." This legalistic approach has been attacked by writers as a vestige of an earlier era of the law "when mind was considered a separate and distinct entity . . ."[3] yet some experts still refuse to relinquish this relic of Cartesian dualism. They insist that the public policy underlying the voiding of a will on testamentary capacity grounds is that "the law seeks to enforce what it considers to be the decedent's true testamentary desires."[4] This conceptualization, however, merely abstracts the notion of mind, as though it were something separate and distinct from the organism that we call the "testator." One might be tempted, therefore, to turn to a somewhat related rationale — that the purpose of testamentary capacity limitations is to protect the testator. Two considerations, however, lead to a rejection of this approach. First, such a rationale would have no valid basis since the person we are claiming to protect is dead at the time we determine that he needs protection. Moreover, this rationale for testamentary capacity limitations overlooks the countervailing need to protect the testator during his lifetime from the fear of malignment after death by his unrewarded and ungrateful heirs. If a satisfactory justification for testamentary capacity is to be found, then, one should look elsewhere than to the protection of the testator or of his "true testamentary desires."

[3] Green, Public Policies Underlying the Law of Mental Incompetency, 38 Mich. L. Rev. 1189, 1205 (1940).

[4] E.g., Epstein, Testamentary Capacity, Reasonableness and Family Maintenance: A Proposal for Meaningful Reform, 35 Temp. L.Q. 231, 233 (1962).

A more rational basis for testamentary capacity limitations is the desire of the law to protect society from the acts of the mental incompetent. In the case of wills the protection of society is furthered by preventing disinheritance of the testator's heirs who, if they could be disinherited, might become wards of the state. The primary purpose of testamentary capacity, however, is the protection of the family. The concern here is with the family as an end in itself; that is, as a moral — as well as sociological — entity which is entitled to make certain demands upon its members. Within this moral construct the family is to be given due consideration before property is devised upon death to someone outside the unit. . . .

II. Testamentary Capacity and the Courts

A. *The Formal Elements of Testamentary Capacity*

The limitation of testamentary capacity to those of "sound mind" is far too vague to be of any real utility. Forced to give content to this provision, the courts have concluded that in order to possess the mental capacity necessary to make a will the testator must have, at the time of execution of the will, the ability to understand and remember in a general way: (1) The nature and extent of his property, (2) the persons who are the natural objects of his bounty, and (3) the disposition he is making of his property. Further, the testator must be capable of: (4) Appreciating these elements in relation to each other, and (5) forming an orderly desire as to the disposition of his property. Given the policies underlying testamentary capacity limitations, the requirements of understanding and memory necessary to effectuate these policies are fairly obvious. In theory, then, if the testator meets these five requirements, the policies underlying freedom of testation can be said not to be outweighed by policies favoring protection of the family and society, except to the extent otherwise provided for by family maintenance provisions. If, on the other hand, the testator fails to meet any one of the five requirements, the protection of society and the family outweighs freedom of testation. While, arguably, these five requirements draw a line between those who have a testamentary capacity and those who have not at too low a level, this is necessary in order to allow the great majority of people to stand above the line. Only if the substantial majority are above the line can testation continue to fulfill its philosophical and social purposes. . . .

B. *The Use and Misuse of Relevant Criteria: A Psychiatric Critique*

[The author analyzes the types of evidence that are relevant in determining mental capacity. These include evidence of abnormal behavior, of senility, and of disease, and opinion evidence of laymen and physicians as to testamentary capacity.]

Another form of symptomatic conduct, closely related to abnormal behavior, is evidence of what the law terms "insane delusions." Most often, the concept arises in those instances that psychiatry has come to characterize as "paranoid delusions."

As in the case of abnormal behavior, the question to be asked is whether the insane delusion prevented the testator from fulfilling one of the five necessary elements of testamentary capacity. Thus, the insane delusion test may be regarded as simply a special application of the understanding test — the testator is prevented from understanding because of his insane delusion. The insane delusion test may also be treated as supplementary to the understanding test, that is, as a case where disinheritance is the result of improper motivation. Whichever way the insane delusion rule is conceptualized a problem arises as to precisely what constitutes an insane delusion. Professor Green expressed the view held by most authorities that an insane delusion is "a belief in the reality of facts which do not exist and in which no rational person would believe." [5] The problem, however, is that by this definition differentiation between an insane delusion and a simple mistake of fact is extremely difficult. This difficulty has led at least one authority to conclude that the determination of whether a belief is simply false or is an insane delusion is purely subjective. The consideration such criticism fails to take into account, however, is that the definition of delusion as simply a false belief is "fallaciously inadequate." Much of the thinking that is characterized as normal is to some extent controlled by feelings and emotion rather than logic or reason. The difference, therefore, is one of degree. What is characterized as insane delusion differs from "healthy" thinking primarily in its irrational fixity, "even in the face of what would be considered incontrovertible evidence to the contrary." Thus, courts generally say that where there is "some basis" for the testator's beliefs, such beliefs are not the product of an insane delusion.

. . .

4. *The abnormality of the disposition.*

If an individual possesses testamentary capacity, freedom of testation allows him, within very broad limits, to make his will as unjust and capricious as his desires may dictate. While courts and commentators pay lip service to this rule, they also contend that the idiosyncrasy of the disposition is a proper element to be considered in determinations of testamentary capacity. The reasons for this treatment seem to be twofold: (1) It accords with the basic policy of testamentary capacity to protect the family of the testator, and (2) a disposition which is idiosyncratic should be treated as having the same probative value as any other abnormal behavior.

While these contentions are true so far as they go, certain fundamental objections may be raised to the use of the will as an element of probative value. First, a judgment on the issue of testamentary capacity which is based on the testamentary instrument itself involves certain elements of circularity. As one authority points out, "Where competence vel non to make a will is inferred from the will itself, the

[5] Green, Fraud, Undue Influence and Mental Incompetency — A Study in Related Concepts, 43 Colum. L. Rev. 176, 192 (1943). For others holding the same view see Murphy, Personality, A Bisocial Approach to Origins and Structure 402 (1947); 1 Page, Wills §§12.29 to 12.35 (Bowe-Parker rev. 1960); Comment, 11 Ark. L. Rev. 84, 88-89 (1957); Comment, Psychology and Law: An Examination of the Concept of Insane Delusions, 1960 Wis. L. Rev. 54, 60-61.

threefold subjective test is circumvented." [6] Notions of reasonableness which commend themselves to the trier of fact may not accord with notions of justness held by the testator. If the law is to allow freedom of testation, the practice of allowing the trier of fact to substitute his own moral values for those of the testator can only be regarded as an arbitrary limit upon the testator's right of disposition. Second, the use of the will as evidence of capacity may overlook the fact that the testator had sufficient secret reasons for desiring to dispose of his estate as he did. Further, while it is true that the treatment of the will as evidence accords with the basic policy of protection of the testator's family, as will be pointed out in the following section, this is the least desirable means of affording such protection. Last, and most important, the primary objection to the use of the will as evidence of capacity or incapacity is not so much that it is a factor — one to be applied along with other factors — but that it often becomes the primary factor in the determination of testamentary capacity — a factor which is sufficient to override substantial evidence to the contrary.

As others have pointed out, there is no suggestion that courts always use the standard of reasonableness in determining testamentary capacity. In many cases where the evidence of testamentary incapacity is weak, the orthodox test will serve to uphold the disposition in spite of its moral repugnancy. Similarly, where the evidence of testamentary incapacity is overwhelming, even the fairest disposition will probably fall before the pressure of a will contest. The problem, however, is that cases which reach the trial stage usually fall somewhere between these extremes; there will be evidence both pro and con. It is here that courts unfortunately utilize the standard of reasonableness to reach their conclusions.

C. *The Undesirability of Manipulation*

The reader may, at this juncture, be tempted to question why the use of the reasonableness rationale to determine testamentary capacity is not proper judicial action. Should courts be compelled to reach results which are shocking in the sense that they allow testators to pauperize their families? Whatever the merits of the policy arguments as to what testators should or should not be allowed to do to their families, the process of civil litigation is not the appropriate setting in which to resolve these fundamental issues. There are several reasons for this conclusion. First, this type of will contest is considered one of the most fertile grounds for champerty. Second, the tax upon the assets of the estate is considerable, especially when one considers the limited guidance to be obtained from judicial decisions. Third, the lack of predictability makes it easier for unscrupulous relatives to exact settlements from the beneficiaries designated under the will. Lastly, one may argue that the postmortem stigmatization of the testator's reputation is undesirable. While the designation of "unsound mind" will have no effect upon the testator at the time it is made, the undesirability stems more from the testator's anticipatory fear of the designation while he is alive. The opponents of this argument contend that fear of

[6] Smith & Hager, The Senile Testator: Medicolegal Aspects of Competency, 13 Clev.-Mar. L. Rev. 397, 402 (1964).

will contests is exaggerated and that their incidence is of no great consequence. Nonetheless, as one commentator points out, "The number of contested wills in proportion to the number offered for probate may not be large, but that is a misleading index of the evil's extent. The threat of the caveat is potent. . . ." [7]

Given the undesirability of the use of the reasonableness rationale to determine testamentary capacity, one is compelled to examine some of the means that might be utilized to alleviate this problem.

III. Suggestions for Reform

One solution that has been proposed to the problem of testamentary capacity is the institution of extensive family maintenance legislation, or "forced heirship." The proponents of this solution contend that such legislation would alleviate the need to use the "testamentary capacity" rubric to equalize distribution. However, assuming that such a proposal involves less than one hundred per cent of the decedent's assets, the problems of testamentary capacity would still remain.

A second solution that has been proposed is to hold a complete antemortem probate proceeding. The issue of testamentary capacity could be raised at this proceeding along with the other issues pertaining to the validity of the will. Though the suggestion has a certain attractiveness, it would not be feasible for several reasons. First, in most cases where the testator disinherits the natural objects of his bounty, he probably does not want them informed of the fact. Yet this proposal would require the will to be made public so the heirs could contest it. That second, and far more substantial, problem is the burden such a solution would cast on probate administration. As the present system works, the only will that is probated is the will executed closest to the death of the testator. However, it is impossible to know prospectively which will is going to be the last. Thus, each will executed during the life of the testator would have to be probated even though it might, at some later date, be superseded by a new will. There would thus be a meteoric increase in the number of wills probated each year.

The suggestion most often made to alleviate the undesirable consequences of will contests is the use of antemortem psychiatric examination of testators. Should the examining psychiatrist die before the will is probated, his notes could be used as the basis for a hypothetical question asked of a living expert called as an opinion witness. This could be accomplished if the examining psychiatrist enters the report of his examination in a book of records kept in the regular course of his professional business.

The use of antemortem psychiatric examination is supported by its proponents on two grounds: First, it will contribute to the peace of mind of the testator, who will worry less about his capacity being attacked after he is dead, and, second, it will discourage lawyers from taking will contests on a contingent fee basis, thus assuring

[7] Cavers, Ante Mortem Probate: An Essay in Preventive Law, 1 U. Chi. L. Rev. 440, 442-443 (1934).

"a decided decrease in the number of cases of contesting of wills. . . ."[8] The cost of such an examination would be relatively small, especially as compared with the amount usually at stake under the testamentary disposition.

Though the proposal of antemortem psychiatric examination is seemingly sound, three criticisms have been raised against its use. First, the drafting attorney may fear that the elderly person is not competent and might think it better to take his chances in court. The difficulty with his argument, however, is that it would probably be a breach of professional ethics for the attorney to draw a will for an individual whom he believed to be of unsound mind. The other two arguments made against the use of antemortem psychiatric examination are: (1) That the lawyer may fear that the very use of the examination will suggest to opposing counsel that the testator's own attorney doubted his mental competence, and (2) that the lawyer will simply "shop around" until he finds a psychiatrist who will declare his client of sound mind. . . .

In light of the thesis of this Note that the primary determinant of testamentary capacity is presently the reasonableness of the disposition, the major criticism which may be levied against antemortem psychiatric examination is that it fails to solve the real problem. The proposal is sound only if one first concludes that courts reach their decision on the basis of psychiatrically relevant data. Yet the cases are replete with evidence that this is not so. The proposal for antemortem psychiatric examination does, however, provide the basis for a sound solution to the problem of testamentary capacity. A solution that would alleviate the major criticism of this proposal — that it does not prevent courts from using the reasonableness rationale — might take the form of a legislative enactment along the following lines. . . .

[The author proposes establishing a statewide psychiatric council of ten psychiatrists who would conduct an examination of the testator before his death. Their determination of whether the testator is of sound mind would be conclusive and could be appealed only by the testator.]

NOTES

1. If a testator has no close relatives, should mental capacity be required?

2. When mental capacity is in issue, a study of California cases indicated that the jury found for the contestant in over 75 percent of the cases, and over one-half of the verdicts for contestants were reversed upon appeal on grounds of insufficient evidence. Note, Will Contests on Trial, 6 Stan. L. Rev. 91, 92 (1953). The note suggested that the jury serves a useful function in protecting against rules governing testamentary disposition that "no longer accord with the community's notions of justice." Id. at 102. On the other hand, in order to eliminate the jury's own notions of fairness, it has been suggested that the dispositive provisions of the will

[8] Stephens, Probate Psychiatry — Examination of Testamentary Capacity by a Psychiatrist as a Subscribing Witness, 25 Ill. L. Rev. 276, 282-283 (1930).

should not be revealed to the jury when the issue is mental capacity. The dispositive provisions could be revealed when the issue is undue influence. Comment, A Case Against Admitting Into Evidence the Dispositive Elements of a Will in a Contest Based on Testamentary Incapacity, 2 Conn. L. Rev. 616 (1970).

3. *Lynn v. Ada Lodge No. 146 of I.O.O.F., 398 P.2d 491 (Okla. 1965).* T, a bachelor, died in 1960 survived by a sister, a brother, and a half-sister. He devised his estate to his mother for life, then to the Odd Fellows. T's mother predeceased him. His heirs contested on the grounds of general mental incapacity and of an insane delusion. In August, 1947, T's mother had him committed to the state mental hospital. Shortly thereafter his mother and sister secured his release. After release from the hospital T stated that the Odd Fellows had secured his release, and although that was untrue, for the rest of his life T believed his sister and their mother were trying to commit him and the Odd Fellows were keeping him out of the asylum. In November, 1947, T executed the disputed will. The court ordered the will to probate, pointing out that there was no evidence to justify the conclusion that the will would have been different if decedent's delusion had not existed.

4. In Estate of Teel, 14 Ariz. App. 371, 483 P.2d 603 (1971), the testator, fifty-four years old, was mentally retarded, having the mentality of a ten- to twelve-year-old. Shortly after making the will, testator was declared incompetent and a guardian appointed. It was held that the testator had the mental capacity to make a will.

5. *Estate planning by the guardian of an incompetent.* Can the guardian of a rich insane person make gifts of principal to charity or to other members of the family in order to achieve tax savings? In In re duPont, 41 Del. Ch. 300, 194 A.2d 309 (1963), the court authorized a guardian to make gifts of an incompetent's assets by way of an inter vivos trust for his children and grandchildren. The trust's terms and beneficiaries were identical to those contained in the incompetent's will, executed before he became incapacitated. The guardian offered proof that the ward intended to make such gifts prior to his incapacity, and that the transfer would result in a tax saving of at least $16 million. In In re Trusteeship of Kenan, 262 N.C. 627, 138 S.E.2d 547 (1964), the court authorized the guardian to make gifts if the evidence showed that the incompetent, if then of sound mind, would have made the gift. In its first opinion (261 N.C. 1, 134 S.E.2d 85, 99 A.L.R.2d 934), the court required a determination of what the incompetent would have done from evidence of his prior conduct or practice. Although there was no evidence of a pattern of gifts or of methodical estate planning while sane, in its second opinion the court strained to find the desired conclusion in testimony that the incompetent had taken, and would take if sane, the advice of the witnesses who recommended the program. In In re Guardianship of Christiansen, 248 Cal. App. 2d 398, 56 Cal. Rptr. 505 (1967), the court rejected the subjective standard used in duPont and Kenan and decided it could authorize gifts upon a determination of what a reasonable and prudent person would do. The Christiansen case was followed in In re Morris, 281 A.2d 156 (N.H. 1971), and Strange v. Powers, 260 N.E.2d 704 (Mass. 1970) (upholding the constitutionality of Mass. Gen. Laws c. 201, §38, which authorizes the Probate Court to permit gifts by the conservator to minimize income,

estate, and gift taxes). In In re Guardianship of Estate of Neal, 406 S.W.2d 496, 24 A.L.R.3d 851 (Tex. Civ. App. 1966), the court held that it had no authority to make a gift of an incompetent's property to minimize estate taxes. See Comment, The Application of the Substitution of Judgment Doctrine in Planning an Incompetent's Estate, 16 Vill. L. Rev. 132 (1970). In England a court may authorize a person to make a will for a mentally incompetent person. Administration of Justice Act 1969, c. 58, pt. III.

SECTION B. Transfers Prohibited Because of the Conduct of the Beneficiary

1. *Undue Influence*

LIPPER v. WESLOW
Texas Court of Civil Appeals, 1963
369 S.W.2d 698

McDonald, Chief Justice. This is a contest of the will of Mrs. Sophie Block, on the ground of undue influence. Plaintiffs, Julian Weslow, Jr., Julia Weslow Fortson and Alice Weslow Sale, are the 3 grandchildren of Mrs. Block by a deceased son; defendants are Mrs. Block's 2 surviving children, G. Frank Lipper and Irene Lipper Dover (half brother and half sister of plaintiffs' deceased father). (The will left the estate of testatrix to her 2 children, defendants herein; and left nothing to her grandchildren by the deceased son, plaintiffs herein.) Trial was to a jury, which found that Mrs. Block's will, signed by her on January 30, 1956, was procured by undue influence on the part of the proponent, Frank Lipper. The trial court entered judgment on the verdict, setting aside the will.

Defendants appeal, contending there is no evidence, or insufficient evidence, to support the finding that the will was procured by undue influence.

Testatrix was married 3 times. Of her first marriage she had one son, Julian Weslow (who died in 1949), who was father of plaintiffs herein. After the death of her first husband testatrix married a Mr. Lipper. Defendants are the 2 children of their marriage. After Mr. Lipper's death, testatrix married Max Block. There were no children born of this marriage. Max Block died several months after the death of testatrix.

On 30 January, 1956, Sophie Block executed the will in controversy. Such will was prepared by defendant, Frank Lipper, an attorney, one of the beneficiaries of the will, and Independent Executor of the will. The will was witnessed by 2 former business associates of Mr. Block. Pertinent provisions of the will are summarized as follows:

> "That I, Mrs. Sophie Block, . . . do make, publish and declare this my last will and testament, hereby revoking all other wills by me heretofore made."

1, 2, 3 and 4.

(Provide for payment of debts; for burial in Beth Israel Cemetery; and for minor bequests to a servant, and to an old folks' home.)

5.

(Devises the bulk of testatrix's estate to her 2 children, Mrs. Irene Lipper Dover and Frank Lipper (defendants herein), share and share alike.)

6.

States that $7000. previously advanced to Mrs. Irene Lipper Dover, and $9300. previously advanced to Frank Lipper be taken into consideration in the final settlement of the estate; and cancels such amounts "that I gave or advanced to my deceased son, Julian."

7.

Appoints G. Frank Lipper Independent Executor of the estate without bond.

8.

Provides that if any legatee contests testatrix's will or the will of her husband, Max Block, that they forfeit all benefits under the will.

9.

":My son, Julian A. Weslow, died on August 6, 1949, and I want to explain why I have not provided anything under this will for my daughter-in-law, Bernice Weslow, widow of my deceased son, Julian, and her children, Julian A. Weslow, Jr., Alice Weslow Sale, and Julia Weslow Fortson, and I want to go into sufficient detail in explaining my relationship in past years with my said son's widow and his children, before mentioned, and it is my desire to record such relationship so that there will be no question as to my feelings in the matter or any thought or suggestion that my children, Irene Lipper Dover and G. Frank Lipper, or my husband, Max, may have influenced me in any manner in the execution of this will. During the time that my said son, Julian, was living, the attitude of his wife, Bernice, was at times, pleasant and friendly, but the majority of the years when my said son, Julian, was living, her attitude towards me and my husband, Max, was unfriendly and frequently months would pass when she was not in my home and I did not hear from her. When my said son, Julian, was living he was treated the same as I treated my other children; and, my husband, Max, and I gave to each of our children a home and various sums of money from time to time to help in taking care of medical expenses, other unusual expenses, as well as outright gifts. Since my said son Julian's death, his widow, Bernice, and all of her children have shown a most unfriendly and distant attitude towards me, my husband, Max, and my 2 children G. Frank Lipper and Irene Lipper Dover, which attitude I cannot reconcile as I have shown them many kindnesses since they have been members of my family, and their continued unfriendly attitude towards me, my husband, Max, and my said children has hurt me deeply in my declining years, for my life would have been much happier if they had shown a disposition to want to be a part of the family and enter into a normal family relationship that usually exists with a daughter-in-law and grandchildren and great grandchildren. I have not seen my grandson, Julian A. Weslow, Jr. in several years, neither have I heard from him. My granddaughter, Alice Weslow Sale, I have not seen in several years and I have not heard from her, but I heard a report some months ago that she was now living in California and has since married William G. Sale. My granddaughter, Julia Weslow Fortson, wife of Ben Fortson, I have not seen in several years and I was told that she had a child born to her sometime in December 1952, and I have not seen the child or heard from my said granddaughter, Julia, up to this writing, and was informed by a friend that Julia has had another child recently and is now living in Louisiana, having moved from Houston; and needless to say, my said daughter-in-law, Bernice, widow of my deceased son, Julian, I have not seen in several years as she has taken little or no interest in me or my husband, Max, since the death of my son, Julian, with the exception that Christmas a year ago, if I remember correctly, she sent some flowers, which I acknowledged, and I believe she had sent some greeting cards on some occasions prior to that time. My said daughter-in-law, Bernice Weslow, has expressed to me, on several occasions, an intense hatred for my son, G. Frank Lipper, and my daughter, Irene Lipper Dover, which I cannot understand, as my said children have always shown her and her children every consideration when possible, and have expressed a desire to be friendly with her, and them. My said children, G. Frank Lipper, and Irene Lipper Dover, have at all times been attentive to me and my husband, Max, especially during the past few years when we have not been well. I will be 82 years old in June of this year and my husband, Max, will be 80 years of age in October of this year, and we have both been in failing health for the past few years and rarely leave our home, and appreciate any attention that is given us, and my husband, Max, and I cannot understand the unfriendly and distant attitude of Bernice Weslow, widow of my said son, Julian, and his children, before mentioned."

10.

(Concerns personal belongings already disposed of.)

"In Testimony Whereof, I have hereunto signed my name. . . .

"(S) Sophie Block"

(Here follows attestation clause and signature of the 2 witnesses.)

The record reflects that the will in question was executed 22 days before testatrix died at the age of 81 years. By its terms, it disinherits the children of testatrix's son, who died in 1949. Defendant, Frank Lipper, gets a larger share than would have been the case if the plaintiffs were not disinherited. Defendant Lipper is a lawyer, and is admittedly the scrivener of the will. There is evidence that defendant Lipper bore malice against his dead half brother. He lived next door to testatrix, and had a key to her house. The will was not read to testatrix prior to the time she signed same, and she had no discussion with anyone at the time she executed it. There is evidence that the recitations in the will that Bernice Weslow and her children were unfriendly, and never came about testatrix, were untrue. There is also evidence that the Weslows sent testatrix greeting cards and flowers from 1946 through 1954, more times than stated in the will.

Plaintiffs offered no direct evidence pertaining to the making and execution of the will on January 30, 1956, and admittedly rely wholly upon circumstantial evidence of undue influence to support the verdict.

All of the evidence is that testatrix was of sound mind at the time of the execution of the will; that she was a person of strong will; that she was in good physical health for her age; and that she was in fact physically active to the day of her death.

Mrs. Weslow's husband died in 1949; and after 1952 the Weslows came about testatrix less often than before.

The witness Lyda Friberg, who worked at the home of testatrix from 1949 to 1952, testified that in 1952 she had a conversation with Bernice Weslow in which Mrs. Weslow told her if her children didn't get their inheritance she would "sue them through every court in the Union"; that she told testatrix about this conversation, and that testatrix told her "she would have those wills fixed up so there would be no court business", and that she wasn't going to "leave them (the Weslows) a dime." The foregoing was prior to the execution of the will on January 30, 1956.

Subsequent to the execution of the will, testatrix had a conversation with her sister, Mrs. Levy. Mrs. Levy testified:

> Q. Who did she say she was leaving her property to?
> A. She was leaving it to her son and her daughter.
> Q. What else did she say about the rest of her kin, if anything?
> A. Well she said that Julian's children had been very ugly to her; that they never showed her any attention whatever; they married and she didn't know they were married; they had children and they didn't let her know. After Julian passed away, she never saw any of the family at all. They never came to see her.
> Q. Did she make any statement?
> A. Yes she did. When she passed away, she didn't want to leave them anything; that they did nothing for her when she was living.

Shortly before she passed away, testatrix told Mrs. Augusta Roos that she was going to leave her property to her 2 children, and further:

> Q. Did she give any reason for it?
> A. Yes. She said that Bernice had never been very nice to her and the children never were over.

Again, subsequent to the making of her will, testatrix talked with Effie Landry, her maid. Mrs. Landry testified:

> Q. Did Mrs. Block on any occasion ever tell you anything about what was contained in her will?
> A. Yes.
> Q. What did she tell you about that?
> A. She said she wasn't leaving the Weslow children anything.

The only question presented is whether there is any evidence of undue influence. The test of undue influence is whether such control was exercised over the mind of the testatrix as to overcome her free agency and free will and to substitute the will of another so as to cause the testatrix to do what she would not otherwise have done but for such control. Scott v. Townsend, 106 Tex. 322, 166 S.W. 1138; Curry v. Curry, 153 Tex. 421, 270 S.W.2d 208; Boyer v. Pool, 154 Tex. 586, 280 S.W.2d 564.

The evidence here establishes that testatrix was 81 years of age at the time of the execution of her will; that her son, defendant Lipper, who is a lawyer, wrote the will for her upon her instruction; that defendant Lipper bore malice against his deceased half brother (father of plaintiffs); that defendant Lipper lived next door to his mother and had a key to her home; that the will as written gave defendant Lipper a larger share of testatrix's estate than he would otherwise have received; that while testatrix had no discussion with anyone at the time she executed the will, she told the witness Friberg, prior to executing the will, that she was not going to leave anything to the Weslows; and subsequent to the execution of the will she told the witnesses Mrs. Levy, Mrs. Roos, and Mrs. Landry that she had not left the Weslows anything, and the reason why. The will likewise states the reasons for testatrix's action. The testatrix, although 81 years of age, was of sound mind and strong will; and in excellent physical health. There is evidence that the recitation in testatrix's will about the number of times the Weslows sent cards and flowers were incorrect, to the extent that cards and flowers were in fact sent oftener than such will recites.

The contestants established a confidential relationship, the opportunity, and perhaps a motive for undue influence by defendant Lipper. Proof of this type simply sets the stage. Contestants must go forward and prove in some fashion that the will as written resulted from the defendant Lipper substituting his mind and will for that of the testatrix. Here the will and the circumstances might raise suspicion, but it does not supply proof of the vital facts of undue influence — the substitution of a plan of testamentary disposition by another as the will of the testatrix. Boyer v. Pool, supra.

All of the evidence reflected that testatrix, although 81 years of age, was of sound mind; of strong will; and in excellent physical condition. Moreover, subsequent to the execution of the will she told 3 disinterested witnesses what she had done with her property in her will, and the reason therefor. A person of sound mind has the legal right to dispose of his property as he wishes, with the burden on those attacking the disposition to prove that it was the product of undue influence. Long v. Long, 133 Tex. 96, 125 S.W.2d 1034, 1035; Curry v. Curry, 153 Tex. 421, 270 S.W.2d 208.

Testatrix's will did make an unnatural disposition of her property in the sense that it preferred her 2 children over the grandchildren by a deceased son. However, the record contains an explanation from testatrix herself as to why she chose to do such. She had a right to do as she did, whether we think she was justified or not.

Plaintiffs contend that the record supports an inference that testatrix failed to receive the cards and flowers sent to her, or in the alternative that she failed to know she received same, due to conduct of defendant Lipper. Here again, defendant Lipper had the opportunity to prevent testatrix from receiving cards or flowers from the Weslows, but we think there is no evidence of probative force to support the conclusion that he in fact did such. Moreover, the will itself reflected that *some* cards and flowers were in fact received by the testatrix, the dispute in this particular area, going to the number of times that such were sent, rather than to the fact that any were sent. See also: Rothermel v. Duncan et al., Tex. Sup., 369 S.W.2d 917.

We conclude there is no evidence of probative force to support the verdict of the jury. The cause is reversed and rendered for defendants.

NOTES AND PROBLEMS

1. Under Texas' procedural rules the Court of Civil Appeals, an intermediate appellate court, can reverse and remand for a new trial when there is some evidence to support the jury verdict, but the verdict is against the great weight of the evidence. It can reverse and render decision for the appellants only when there is no evidence to support the verdict. In Lipper v. Weslow the court reversed and rendered decision for the appellants. Would you agree that there was *no* evidence to support the jury finding of undue influence?

2. Mrs. Block's will included a statement setting forth the reasons why she was not making provision for Julian's children. When the possibility of a will contest is anticipated, is this a desirable practice to follow?

3. The will was drafted by Mrs. Block's son, an attorney and a principal beneficiary under the will. Why wasn't this, by itself, "some evidence" of undue influence? The general rule is that if there is a suspicious circumstance in making a testamentary gift to the testator's attorney, there is a presumption that the gift was procured by undue influence. The mere existence of the attorney-client relationship does not by itself ordinarily raise a presumption of undue influence. Attorneys sometimes win, sometimes lose their bequests. The cases are collected in Note, 19 A.L.R.3d 575 (1968). See also Note, Attorney Beware — The Presumption of Undue Influence and the Attorney-Beneficiary, 47 Notre Dame Law. 330 (1971).

Should an attorney who draws a will containing a bequest to himself be subjected to disciplinary action? See State v. Collentine, 39 Wis. 2d 325, 159 N.W.2d 50 (1968), noted 1969 Wis. L. Rev. 627; Note, 98 A.L.R.2d 1234 (1964). ABA Code of Professional Responsibility Canon 5, EC 5-5: "A lawyer should not suggest to his client that a gift be made to himself or for his benefit. If a lawyer accepts a gift from his client, he is peculiarly susceptible to the charge that he unduly influenced or overreached the client. If a client voluntarily offers to make a gift to his lawyer, the lawyer may accept the gift, but before doing so, he should urge that his client secure disinterested advice from an independent, competent person who is cognizant of all the circumstances. Other than in exceptional circumstances, a

"My goodness! Your dear old uncle seems to have left everything to me."

lawyer should insist that an instrument in which his client desires to name him beneficially be prepared by another lawyer selected by the client."

4. *No-contest clauses.* No-contest clauses are designed to discourage the institution of will contests. These clauses provide that beneficiaries who contest the will shall take nothing, or a token amount, in lieu of the provisions made for them in the will. The states generally split between two positions: (1) no-contest clauses are enforceable, and (2) no-contest clauses are enforceable unless there is probable cause for contest. Where the probable clause exception is applied, it may be limited to contests based on forgery, lack of due execution, or revocation by a subsequent instrument. In a few jurisdictions no-contest clauses are enforceable only if the will makes an express gift over to another person of the property given the contesting beneficiary.

In enforcing these clauses the courts are carrying out a policy of discouraging unmeritorious litigation. The probable cause exception is supported on the ground that it permits just litigation to protect the testator's family and detect frauds. For a comprehensive discussion of the problem see the majority and dissenting opinions in Barry v. American Security & Trust Co., 135 F.2d 470 (D.C. Cir. 1943); see also Jack, No-Contest or In Terrorem Clauses in Wills — Construction and Enforcement, 19 Sw. L.J. 722 (1965); Leavitt, Scope and Effectiveness of No-Contest Clauses in Last Wills and Testaments, 15 Hastings L.J. 45 (1963).

In the Lipper case, how effective was the draftsman's use of the no-contest clause?

In re KAUFMANN'S WILL

New York Supreme Court, Appellate Division, First Dept., 1964
20 App. Div. 2d 464, 247 N.Y.S.2d 664

McNally, J. This will contest is limited to the issue of undue influence. The contestants are the distributees of, and the proponent is unrelated to, the decedent. Two juries have found undue influence. On the prior appeal, by a divided court, the decree denying probate was reversed and a new trial directed because of error (14 AD2d 411). Appellant argues the proof in its totality fails to establish a jury question on the issue of undue influence. . . .

The instrument offered for probate is dated June 19, 1958. The decedent, Robert D. Kaufmann, was then 44, unmarried, a millionaire with a substantial income. Robert's sole distributees were two brothers, Joel and Aron. Joel is married and his sons are Richard and Lee, infants over 14 years of age. Aron is unmarried and an invalid.

Robert had inherited all his wealth from his parents. He had no liking or aptitude for business. His inherited wealth consisted principally of minority interests in various family enterprises in which he did not actually participate.

In and prior to 1947 Robert was intimately and warmly associated and identified with his relatives; he lived with his brother Joel in Washington and was particularly attached to and fond of his nephews, Richard and Lee. In 1947 Robert took up painting, an interest which he pursued and developed with increasing involvement with the passage of time and with a great measure of artistic success. During the latter part of 1947 or early 1948, Robert came to New York City and set up his own establishment. He was then about 34.[9]

[9] Many of Kaufmann's paintings are reproduced in a book published by Weiss, The Work of Robert Kaufmann (1961). In an introduction to the book the novelist Isidor Schneider wrote: "In addition to this inheritance of wealth and status, Robert Kaufmann had exceptional natural endowments. He had good looks, intelligence, and personal charm. . . . Nevertheless, there were signs to read, of tensions and discontent. Edmund Kaufmann, a kindly but forceful and regal man, appears to have been overwhelming to his son — a not uncommon case in father-and-son relationships in 'good families,' especially where the son has drives toward art. Discerning unusual gifts in the young man, the father sought to direct them into what seemed to him the natural course for

Until about 1951 Robert maintained his apartment at 965 Fifth Avenue. In 1951 he purchased a five-story town house at 42 East 74th Street. In addition, in 1955 Robert acquired a Summer house in Quogue, Long Island, and in 1958 a Winter home in Key West, Florida.

It would appear that Robert and the proponent, Walter A. Weiss, met in 1948. Weiss was the senior of Robert by five years. Weiss did not testify at either of the two trials. In his pretrial examination Weiss stated he was an attorney who did not practice. His pedigree, resources and means of income in 1948 do not appear.

On June 15, 1948 an agreement prepared by Weiss was entered into between Robert and Weiss whereby Weiss was retained as "financial advisor and business consultant" at an annual "retainer" of $10,000 for the period of one year with the right in Weiss to terminate the arrangement on "one weeks' notice, if he [Weiss] finds conditions make it impossible in his opinion to function effectively". The

---

a son of his, a good position in business, a good position in society, a good position in every life situation.

"This, and its possibilities for repressed conflict, are suggested in the younger Kaufmann's war experiences. On his own, he rose from private to master sergeant and enjoyed wide popularity at Fort Bragg, where he was stationed in 1942. In his father's opinion, however, an officer's rank was the suitable status for his son, and Robert enrolled in an Army Officer Candidate School. The day before he was to be commissioned he suffered a heart attack diagnosed as a coronary occlusion. . . .

"A more serious and significant manifestation of his tension was his drinking. He drank heavily, though never to the point of losing control over the habit. He could stop when he wanted to, or when he knew that it was necessary. He stopped drinking altogether in the last five or six years of his life. . . . (p. 6).

"It was in New York, though he began his stay there in a business approved by his father, that Kaufmann was first freed of direct family supervision and pressure. . . .

"There is probable significance in the first painting he did in his New York studio. The subject was a cock proudly crowing to the dawn. This was not a sight he could have seen from his office window nor a sound he could have heard in the traffic jangle down below. Could it not have risen from his unconscious, among other symbols of regeneration, a greeting to what he may have felt to be the dawn of a new existence for him?

"With so much that had hitherto been repressed emerging into consciousness, Kaufmann felt it desirable to uncover and face the unconscious conflicts he had now become aware of. In 1950, he undertook psychoanalysis with the late Dr. Leonard Blumgart. For about a year he had five sessions a week, without missing one. After another year spent without analysis he resumed sessions, three a week with Dr. Janet Rioch, for about a year. In the next two years he had sporadic consultations with her. After 1955, he relied on his own insights to meet strains or extend his self-knowledge. . . . (p. 9).

"More marked than any other feeling about money was his wish to be free of any concern over it. . . . It was with a feeling of liberation that he had given up business to devote himself to painting." (p. 12).

Robert also wrote poetry. The following poem, appearing on page 32, was written in 1956, a presage of his own will contest:

But it still takes over a year
to get a will probated

Lawyer! Unveil the personal monuments
Solid record of solemn thought.
Family and loving kin, stunned but watchful
Inwardly eyeing the car just bought.

— Eds.

agreement recites the purpose of Weiss to advise Robert as to his then investments and towards the end of "developing new opportunities for financial profit," it also recites: "It is contemplated an office will be maintained and probably a corporation will be formed, as dictated by maximum business gain."

Robert paid Weiss annually thereafter the sum of $10,000; in addition, he made tax-free gifts to Weiss of about $3,000 during the years 1956, 1957 and 1958. Weiss also received from Robert $4,500 for his services in the sale of a hotel owned by Robert.

Soon after June, 1948 the books and records of Robert were transferred from Washington to New York. Theretofore Robert's records had been kept by employees of Robert's family in Washington at no expense to Robert. Washington was the main business headquarters of the family.

During the latter part of 1948 offices were established at 630 Fifth Avenue and announcements printed of the opening on January 6, 1949 of offices as "financial consultants" by "Walter A. Weiss and Robert D. Kaufmann." Robert paid all office expenses; Weiss contributed his time. The venture earned no fees for financial consultations during the 10 years of its existence. The sole investment made was in a garage construction enterprise adverted to as "Multi-Deck" in which Weiss' brother was the principal. On Weiss' advice Robert invested $120,000 therein and the end result was a total loss.

In 1949 Weiss moved into Robert's apartment at 965 Fifth Avenue. Weiss lived with Robert until the latter's death on April 18, 1959.

The five-story town house at 42 East 74th Street, purchased in 1951, was extensively renovated. The top floor was made an office, a full-time secretary employed; the remainder of the building was elaborately furnished and appointed as living quarters. A full-time cook was employed. Weiss took full charge of the establishment, its furnishing, the employment of help and the maintenance of the household. All mail and incoming telephone calls were routed to and through Weiss.[10]

Robert and Weiss travelled to Paris in 1950 for a few months; to Europe, West Indies, the Virgin Islands, Haiti, Greece and other countries during 1952 and 1953 and around the world in 1956. Robert paid all expenses. Weiss claims to have paid his share of living and travel expenses but we have no evidence other than his declaration on that score.

On April 19, 1950 Robert made a will providing for bequests to his father's and brother's wives, his father's secretary who had for many years been in charge of Robert's records, his housekeeper and art teacher, the Institute for Psycho-Therapy,

[10] A rather similar ménage de vieux garçons was the celebrated villa, The Pines, occupied by Algernon Charles Swinburne, English poet, novelist, and sage, and Theodore Watts-Dunton, a country solicitor. In 1879, at the age of 42, Swinburne moved in with Watts-Dunton, who had rescued him from delirium tremens and from a house of pleasure in St. John's Wood where a couple of blonde amazons flagellated the customers. Watts-Dunton laid down the rules, managed all of Swinburne's business affairs, ran the household, and doled out the pin money. Swinburne stayed at home and wrote. The two men lived together until 1909, when Swinburne died, leaving everything to Watts-Dunton. Swinburne's family were hurt and indignant, but they did not sue. Panter-Downs, At The Pines (1971). — Eds.

Inc., and the Lillian Swope Foundation. To Weiss he devised the stock in Multi-Deck. In addition, Robert cancelled Weiss' indebtedness to him. The will recited provision had been made for an aunt of Robert by way of insurance. The residue was divided into four parts: two for the benefit of his brothers and two for the benefit of his two nephews. Three executors were nominated — Robert's father, his brother Joel and his cousin Donald.

The 1950 will reflects a natural testamentary disposition in the light of the nature and extent of Robert's estate, his family and his known relations to and with others.

Weiss had made efforts to insinuate himself into the good graces of Robert's family without success. The investment counseling project was his brainchild. In his view it contemplated the exploitation of his knowledge by Robert's family. Weiss' pretrial deposition is that "he [Robert] understood that on the facts his main contribution would be his contacts and the possibility for new business that might arise through his family and his companies, or through other connections that he might have. And we sent announcements of the opening of this business to all of his friends and business connections".

No business was forthcoming. Robert's family was unimpressed. Weiss was frustrated. He had succeeded in inducing Robert to place the utmost confidence in him but had been totally rejected by Robert's family. On April 4, 1951 Weiss' confidential memorandum to Robert states:

> It would be a good thing for me if I were able to achieve polite, formal business relations with your brother [Joel]. What he thinks of me personally cannot concern my business life. I have always felt that he has no faith in me and his surface facade was a "double-dealing", painful, and embarrassing to us both. It would surprise me if we were able to work well together, in the light of the record. At your request I am willing to try, and a full discussion of these present communications is a likely starting point. I repeat — Joel's personal appraisal of me is not in issue since I feel he does not know me. Your own continued confidence is naturally very gratifying, particularly in the face of so much family unpleasantness. That, too, however, I must reject from my door, as an inevitable part of your own family set-up. . . .
>
> Does Joel inherit your Dad's position as sole and unquestioned business authority for you? Does he want that responsibility? Unquestionably he craves it and you don't want to give it to him. Do you have to? Is there any insult implied in your refusing to assume Aron's status business-wise? If not, do you have the right to choose an adviser? Has Joel made any active honest effort to work with him? Why would he not welcome such a release from discretionary responsibility? . . . It is only lately when Joel was willing to show his hostility openly that you stated to me, if you did not have me advising you independently of your family, you would seek someone else. I believe Joel finds it most acceptable to his pride to consider that I have instigated an independent will in you for my own purposes; that you serve my selfish desire to mix into his all-important, fascinating business machinations — all out of some kind of misguided weakness of will! How distorted and ridiculous can a situation get? . . .
>
> There is certainly a lot of resentment and a fundamental lack of understand-

ing. I think you are finally growing up and realize you are not playing marbles. Each of you seems to think he is being treated like a child, and that the other is acting like a spoiled child. A free exchange of real feelings would clear the air and might lead to harmony and mutual respect — even admiration; very different qualities from the love always talked about in families and unfortunately so seldom present. We tried this speaking out earnestly and openly last Christmas in Washington and were woefully defeated. Your Dad and I finally came to cases, and that in a few days, only when we were willing to talk openly and assume good faith. I'm ready to meet on that basis if you want me to, but I've turned in my whipping-boy outfit and have no more stomach for that thankless role. Stop arguing so much about me and my abilities. Work out the hard facts of your own relationships and objectives, then you can easily enough agree on the mechanics. Joel has only one brother in Aron's circumstances, not two; you must make him understand that and be glad of it.

. . .

Joel presented an insurmountable obstacle to Weiss' full and complete control of Robert's financial affairs. Weiss accused Joel of "double-dealing" and of resenting the fact that he, Weiss, had "instigated an independent will" in Robert.

If, in fact, Weiss had aroused in Robert a drive for independence, had persuaded him to inform himself and assume the right to make his own decisions in matters of business and otherwise, there could be no objection even though Robert saw fit to be advised by Weiss. However, if Robert was unwilling or unable to assume responsibility in financial and other matters, and Weiss was aware of it and using Robert against Joel and his family to further his own selfish ends and purposes, then the question arises whether thereby Robert's testamentary disposition was influenced and whether it was permissible or undue influence.

It cannot be doubted that prior to 1948 Robert was dependent on Joel in financial matters; that Robert was not involved in decision making; he had shown no interest in such involvement; that he was warmly attached to his family and had no serious differences with them. Weiss' pretrial statement does not suggest otherwise.

Shortly after taking up with Weiss, Robert's financial records were transferred from Washington to New York; Robert employed Weiss as financial adviser, and they launched the venture of financial consultants. . . .

Weiss' pretrial statement is: "I remember his [Robert] asking me if I would undertake to represent him and to handle his affairs and to help him be independent so that he could take his affairs unto himself." In addition, Weiss said that Robert was obsessed with the idea of independence and Weiss offered to help him towards that end. If Weiss successfully persuaded Robert that he was achieving independence when, in fact, Weiss was extending and exploiting Robert's dependence and estranging Robert from his family, then he violated his undertaking and the issue is presented whether the instrument offered for probate is a product of the breach of faith.

In 1949 Robert opened a checking account with Bankers Trust Company.

Weiss was given power to draw against this account. Soon thereafter a similar arrangement was made as to an account with Chemical Bank New York Trust Co. Thereafter, until Robert's death, Weiss had the power to draw against all Robert's bank accounts. In 1951 Weiss acquired a general power of attorney from Robert. Weiss had unrestricted access to Robert's safe-deposit box.

The record establishes that since 1950 those selected by Weiss rendered medical and legal services to Robert. In 1951 Robert changed his attorneys. On June 13, 1951 he executed a new will. This enlarged Weiss' share of Robert's estate. In addition to personal effects and paintings, the will devises to Weiss the 74th Street residence and one half of the residue, and he is made the trustee of several trusts and one of three executors, the others being Robert's brother, Joel, and Robert's psychiatrist, Dr. Janet M. Rioch. Weiss' expectancy under the provisions of this will was over $500,000.

Contemporaneously with the will of June 13, 1951 Robert signed a letter of the same date purporting to explain his will. The letter affirms the will contains unusual provisions in that "a sizeable portion" of Robert's estate is devised to a man "not a member of my family". The letter to Robert's brothers proceeds to state the reasons for the provisions. It recites that Robert first met Weiss in 1946; that Robert's outlook was then "approaching the nadir"; he was a "frustrated time-wasting little boy"; he was "terribly unhappy, highly emotional and filled to the brim with a grandly variegated group of fears, guilt and assorted complexes". It states that Robert fortunately met Walter who encouraged him to submit to psychoanalysis. In addition, the letter goes on to state:

> Walter gave me the courage to start something which slowly but eventually permitted me to supply for myself everything my life had heretofore lacked: an outlet for my long-latent but strong creative ability in painting . . . a balanced, healthy sex life which before had been spotty, furtive and destructive; an ability to reorientate myself to actual life and to face it calmly and realistically. All of this adds up to Peace of Mind — and what a delight, what a relief after so many wasted, dark, groping, fumbling immature years to be reborn and become adult!
>
> I am eternally grateful to my dearest friend — best pal, Walter A. Weiss. What could be more wonderful than a fruitful, contented life and who more deserving of gratitude now, in the form of an inheritance, than the person who helped most in securing that life? I cannot believe my family could be anything else but glad and happy for my own comfortable self-determination and contentment and equally grateful to the friend who made it possible.
>
> Love to you all,
> Bob.

The letter is accompanied by an envelope addressed to Robert's brothers and the Kaufmann family. The envelope is unsealed. The letter and envelope thereafter accompanied the three succeeding wills prepared by attorneys other than the one who drew the will of 1951. Prior to 1954, the 1951 letter was in the possession of the attorney who had drawn the 1951 and the 1953 wills. In or about May, 1954, the letter of June 13, 1951 and the letter of October 23, 1952, hereafter described, came into the possession of Weiss who caused them to be delivered with the 1953 will to the attorneys who thereafter prepared the last two wills.

The letter of 1951 fixes the year 1946 as the year of meeting between Robert and Weiss. The record evidence is that this event occurred in 1948. The anticipation of their meeting by more than one year is significant in that it was during 1947 and before Robert met Weiss that Robert took up and commenced his career in art. It is in the artistic area that Robert was productive and accomplished. Weiss was not an artist. Robert's art teacher was provided for in the wills prior to but was excluded from the will offered for probate.

The 1951 letter is not based on reality. Robert had become aware of his desire to paint, had received instruction and had started painting prior to his meeting with Weiss. The will of 1950 provides for a bequest of $2,500 to Leo Steppat "my art teacher". Weiss had nothing to do with Robert's creative ability in painting. In attributing to Weiss the "start [of] something which slowly but eventually permitted me to supply for myself everything my life had heretofore lacked: an outlet for my long-latent but strong creative ability in painting", the letter is not in accord with the record. Weiss in his pretrial statement acknowledged he did not know why Robert attributed to him his painting career.

The letter refers to the "courage" acquired from Weiss "to supply for myself . . . a balanced, healthy sex life which before had been spotty, furtive and destructive". The implication is that Weiss in some fashion was identified with Robert's sex life. Weiss' pretrial statement emphatically denied it.

To the extent that the letter implies or suggests a marked improvement of a previously disoriented and fearful personality, it is again at odds with reality as will appear.

Assuming, however, the content of the letter, it completely fails to explain the extent of the testamentary gift to Weiss tantamount to over a half million dollars.

On March 11, 1952 Weiss prepared a memorandum to Robert which stated: "9. INSURANCE Life and other insurance should be transferred to New York to Frenkel Bros." In force at the time were insurance policies in the face amount of $100,000 on the life of Robert issued between 1937 and 1940. As a result of correspondence between Weiss and Frenkel & Co., Inc., insurance brokers, between June and September, 1952, Weiss was substituted as primary beneficiary as to policies in the face amount of $75,000, and as to the $25,000 policy initially payable to Birdie Ross, Weiss was designated the secondary beneficiary.

Weiss' pretrial deposition falsely denies he was in any way involved in the transfer of the life insurance policies from Washington to New York; denies knowledge of any details concerning the change of beneficiaries, except as to the policy naming Aunt Birdie; and denies recollection of the communications whereby the changes were effected. On the death of Robert, because of double indemnity provisions in some of the policies, Weiss collected $117,290.17. No explanation appears for the change in beneficiaries in 1952.

On October 23, 1952, Robert executed a most unusual document. Thereby

Weiss was granted exclusive power over Robert's corporeal remains, and the authority to make all funeral arrangements; in addition, in the event he was incapacitated by reason of mental or physical disability, Weiss was granted the power to consent in Robert's behalf to the performance of any operation he deemed necessary after consultation with Robert's physicians. The instrument provides Weiss is to act as "though he [Weiss] were my nearest relative . . . and that his instructions and consents shall be controlling, regardless of who may object to them". Robert was then 38 and so far as appears, physically well, and the profound concern with death, illness and hospitalization and the complete, almost sacrificial surrender of his corporeal remains to Weiss is most unusual.

The will of April 8, 1953 designates Weiss sole executor. Shortly thereafter, on May 28, 1953, Weiss' confidential memorandum to Robert states: "6. WILLS — Your will should be gone over, since there is at least one point needs changing."

On December 11, 1953 Robert wrote to Joel regarding the Fairfax situation. The Kaufmann brothers, including Robert, owned blocks of stock in a chain of 80 to 90 jewelry stores, established by their father, operating as Kay Jewelry Stores. The Fairfax Company was the purchasing agency of the jewelry stores. The Kaufmanns also owned stock of Fairfax Company. A merger was proposed. Weiss was opposed to and strongly advised Robert against it. At the core of the opposition was the ratio at which the shares in the new Fairfax corporation were to be exchanged for the shares of the old Fairfax corporation. The required percentage of shares had consented to the merger and included the members of the Kaufmann family other than Robert. Robert so advised by Weiss objected to the merger. As minority stockholder he was entitled to a statutory appraisal.

The letter of December 11, 1953 acknowledges that amicable negotiations between Joel and Weiss do not seem possible; that Robert does not wish to get involved in the unpleasant business controversy with his brother and he has therefore retained counsel so that it will obviate his role as a "go-between". Robert then observes: "Perhaps now, with no such matters between us, we can devote our time to being real friends, because the source of irritation, namely business friction, will no longer be present."

The Fairfax litigation ranged over a period of about four years. The original valuation of Robert's shares was about $225,000 and the ultimate award was $285,000. . . . [T]he record abundantly shows Weiss resented Joel and had conveyed to Robert uncomplimentary opinions as to Joel's integrity.

The emotional base reflected in the letter of June 13, 1951 is gratitude utterly unreal, highly exaggerated and pitched to a state of fervor and ecstasy. The jury could have found, in addition, that Weiss conveyed to Robert false accusations as to Joel's integrity and mismanagement of the family enterprises. If the accusations were intended to and did cause Robert to disinherit members of his family in whole or in part, Weiss exercised undue influence. (Matter of Anna, 248 N.Y. 421, 427; Matter of Budlong, 126 N.Y. 423, 432.)

On May 5, 1954 Weiss forwarded to attorney Lloyd Garrison the will of April 8, 1953 together with the letters of June 13, 1951 and October 23, 1952, and a covering letter stating that Robert "wants to make a new will as soon as possible". Mr. Garrison, by letter dated May 10, 1954, acknowledged the documents and stated he had discussed the matter with his partner, Mr. Rochlin. A draft of the proposed will was transmitted to Robert with Rochlin's letter dated May 21, 1954. The draft provided for the appointment of Weiss and Garrison as executors and trustees. The draft followed a conference between Robert and Rochlin on May 6, 1954. On May 25, 1954 Robert signed a letter to Rochlin returning the draft and requesting changes including a provision for the appointment of Weiss as sole executor instead of the provision in the draft appointing Weiss and Garrison jointly.

The May 6 conference was solely between Robert and Rochlin. Among the matters discussed was Robert's investment in the Multi-Deck Corporation. At the time Robert was still persuaded the corporation had good possibilities although it was in difficulties. Robert said he wanted the stock in the company to go to Weiss with provision in his will that it was to bear its share of the estate tax. Robert directed that one half of the residuary go to his two nephews, Richard and Lee. They also discussed the executors to be named and Rochlin was told to designate Weiss and Garrison executors and trustees. The 1953 will contained an in terrorem clause providing that the devise to one contesting the will shall lapse. Rochlin informed Robert his firm's policy was to recommend to a client not to put such a clause in his will.

Significantly, Robert at the time spoke of the letter of June 13, 1951. Rochlin read the letter. Robert inquired whether it was advisable to leave the letter with his will. Rochlin said he would talk with Garrison about it. Rochlin's office memorandum of June 10, 1954 states that on the previous day, when the 1954 will was executed, Robert again read the letter and on Rochlin's recommendation it was placed with the will together with the burial instructions of October 23, 1952. It does not appear what, if any, discussion was had between Robert and Rochlin; Robert did not discuss the letter with Garrison.

In July, 1955 Robert took title to a Summer home in Quogue, Long Island. Title closed July 22, 1955. Two days prior thereto a letter signed "E. Goldstein, secretary" was mailed to Garrison requesting in behalf of Robert that a codicil be prepared devising the property to Weiss. On July 29, 1955 Garrison responded advising a new will. It counsels as follows: "This will necessitate retyping the whole will, but it will simplify matters in the end because if you have a codicil, the executors will have to give notice to your residuary legatees, when the will and codicil are offered for probate, and give them a chance to come in and object to the codicil on the grounds of undue influence."

On October 21, 1955 a new will was executed substantially like the 1954 will with the additional provision for the devise of the Quogue property to Weiss.

Following the Fairfax litigation Weiss raised questions regarding the Kaufmann family venture in Reading, Pa. The Kaufmann Furniture Company was engaged in the furniture business and occupied property owned by Swope Realty Company. . . .

On March 3, 1958 a letter was addressed to Joel signed "Bob." It reads, in part:

> I appreciate the way you set out the position on Kaufmann Furniture and certainly regret for you all the work and effort you have put into this sick business. You know from long back, and I told Surrey long ago, that I want to be so far from any business kind of situations or any need to read reports or make decisions that I am perfectly content to see my money in tax exempt bonds. This I think, is about the last business situation where you and I alone (plus Aron, of course) are involved together so that we have to agree on a course, and I want to put it to you that in all fairness, you are overdue in giving me a break. You have had everything pretty much your way in all the business things which God knows, you are well entitled to and seem to want in your life; and I feel now it is high time you listen to my vote in this furniture situation — which is to get out.
>
> If you don't want to sell the business for what it will bring, then pay me out.

On February 25, 1958 Weiss also dictated a letter to his secretary which sets forth in detail his financial analysis of the furniture company and is highly critical of and implies improprieties on the part of Joel.

Joel's letter of March 12, 1958 in response to the letter of March 3, 1958 is informative, moderate and receptive to the suggestion of final liquidation of Robert's family interests. Negotiations towards that end proceeded to and past June 19, 1958 on which date Robert executed the instrument sought to be propounded as his will.

On April 18, 1958 Robert wrote to Joel a warm card of congratulations on his being designated "Man of the Year". On May 20, 1958 a letter allegedly dictated by Robert and signed "Bob" by Weiss' secretary was addressed to Garrison reciting:

> the personal situation with my family has changed considerably since the Fairfax suit. I now wish you to make a new, very simple will for me, leaving all property, real estate, tangible assets, etc., plus a beneficial life interest in the Kay Jewelry Store stocks stamped "To be offered to the Kay Stores before selling" to Walter A. Weiss. . . .
>
> Also, if not previously disposed of, I wish to give my nephews Richard D. and Lee S. Kaufmann, my one-third share of the Kaufmann Furniture Company. . . . Furthermore, I think there should be a non-contesting clause written in, and also a paragraph saying that in the event of my marriage, my widow and heirs should receive three-quarters of the above estate and one-quarter would go to Walter A. Weiss. In either case, I name him as sole executor.

A postscript inquired: "Can't all this be done on one page?"

. . .

The letter of May 20, 1958 is inconsistent with the facts. The Fairfax suit had terminated, allegedly to the satisfaction and profit of Robert. During the period the suit was in spirited litigation, on June 9, 1954 and October 21, 1955, Robert executed wills providing for his brother Aron, his nephews, various friends, his art teacher and The Arts Fund Inc., who were to be completely excluded by the proposed will. The Fairfax litigation involved only Joel. Moreover, nothing in the record suggests a marriage of Robert at that or any other time. In addition, Robert had been told by Rochlin in 1954 that his firm advised against a "non-contesting clause".

On May 22, 1958 Garrison caused to be delivered to Robert a five-page memorandum directing his attention to the fact that his then will provided for Aron, his father's former secretary, his former art teacher and other provisions. Other questions were raised. The final paragraph reads: "My suggestion is that you consider these questions with Walter [Weiss] and that then we should get together for a brief discussion, because I know from experience that in the course of discussion other questions will arise, and that we cannot work this all out by correspondence."

On June 5, 1958 there was a telephone conversation between Garrison and Robert. Garrison's memorandum of that date states Robert desired to modify the proposal of May 20, 1958 by leaving the Kay stores stock outright to Weiss, omitting the provisions for a wife and children and providing that the furniture stock go to Weiss if the nephews predecease Robert.

No draft of the will was submitted to Robert; he did not meet with Garrison as suggested by the latter and they had no discussion or talk regarding the radical departure from the testamentary plan of the 1955 will. The execution of the will on June 19, 1958 offered for probate took 15 to 20 minutes and involved only the formalities.

. . .

Weiss and Robert lived together from 1949 to the date of Robert's death. The evidence enabled the jury to find that Robert became increasingly dependent on Weiss socially and businesswise. Moreover, it supports the view that this dependence was encouraged and that Weiss took affirmative steps to insulate Robert from his family and persons he sought to cultivate.

Robert gave Weiss his unbounded confidence and trust. Weiss exploited Robert, induced him to transfer to him the stewardship formerly exercised by Joel, increased Robert's need for dependency, prevented and curtailed associations which threatened his absolute control of Robert and alienated him from his family.

. . .

Weiss was responsible for the displacement of the attorneys who prepared the 1950 will; he introduced Robert to Garrison who prepared the instrument offered for probate. Weiss recommended the doctors who treated Robert; he employed all help who came in contact with Robert. Mail and telephone communications were routed through Weiss. Family mail at times was destroyed and did not reach Robert. Correspondence purporting to be from Robert was dictated by Weiss.

Weiss saw to it none other than himself took advantage of Robert. Weiss warned Mapson, Robert's companion on the trip, not to take advantage of Robert during their stay in Paris in 1953. Finally, Weiss arrived in Paris unannounced and in the presence of Robert, who stood by mutely, told Mapson to remove himself. Robert attempted to maintain secretly his contact with Mapson in New York but was found out by Weiss who physically intervened. Again Robert submitted silently.

Anne McDonnell, the housekeeper and cook, testified Weiss was master of the household and brooked no interference from Robert. She also testified there were occasions when Weiss insisted that Robert sign papers without opportunity to read them and that Robert complied.

Watkins, a banker friend of Robert's father, testified he talked at length with Robert about the Fairfax matter. On one occasion Weiss was present and did all the talking while Robert was mute. On another occasion Watkins was alone with Robert and his only response was: "That's the way Walter [Weiss] wants it."

Robert perceptibly lost weight during the latter years, in part due to a low cholesterol diet. He became disinterested in his attire and appearance. After 1950 he received extensive psychiatric treatment, the nature of which does not appear.

In 1955 Robert complained of inability to sleep. His inability to sleep continued until his death. He took large quantities of pills for the condition which included doriden, miltown, seconal and nembutal — medication to reduce tension and induce sleep. He was unable to sleep without medication. On April 18, 1959, asleep at his home in Key West, Robert died in a fire which destroyed the house.

. . .

Robert and Weiss lived lavishly, travelled and entertained extensively. Despite the scale of living, which would appear to have been at the expense of Robert, and the ill-advised financial ventures, he left an estate of over one million dollars.

. . .

The documents of record, ostensibly emanating from Robert, which tend to explain his testamentary disposition, are in all important aspects at odds with the facts. The Fairfax suit is the sole reason assigned in the letter of May 20, 1958 for the testamentary scheme reflected in the instrument offered for probate and in the light of the facts it fails to explain it.

. . .

The record becomes clear if it is viewed in the light of a skillfully executed plan by Weiss to gain the confidence of Robert, displace Joel as manager of his financial affairs, assume control of Robert's bank accounts, safe-deposit box, household and property as if it were his. The only impediment against completely relieving Robert of his worldly goods was the circumstance that his investments in the main were closely tied in with those of Joel and his brother Aron. To overtly seize Robert's property would risk a challenge by his family. So long as Robert was under his control and influence, Weiss was assured of a life of ease and luxury. He, therefore, need only direct Robert toward making him his principal beneficiary in the event of his death. This he could do without the knowledge of the family. The result was to be substantiated by written declarations of Robert assigning reasons for the unnatural disposition.

. . .

Following the death of Robert, Weiss disclaimed knowledge of the letter of June 13, 1951; disclaimed knowledge of the details of the change of beneficiaries as to the insurance policies and averred initial knowledge after Robert's death of the instrument offered for probate. In all of these respects the jury could have found Weiss lied deliberately.

Contestants' medical expert testified the record evidence delineated a personality with pathological dependency; one unable to deal with reality, insecure, unstable and who tends to submit unreasonably to the will of another. There was no expert medical testimony to the contrary.

One may make testamentary disposition of his worldly goods as he pleases. The motives and vagaries or morality of the testator are not determinative provided the will is the free and voluntary disposition of the testator and is not the product of deceit. There are two principal categories of undue influence in the law of wills, the forms of which are circumscribed only by the ingenuity and resourcefulness of man. One class is the gross, obvious and palpable type of undue influence which does not destroy the intent or will of the testator but prevents it from being exercised by force and threats of harm to the testator or those close to him. The other class is the insidious, subtle and impalpable kind which subverts the intent or will of the testator, internalizes within the mind of the testator the desire to do that which is not his intent but the intent and end of another. (Marx v. McGlynn, 88 N.Y. 357; Rollwagen v. Rollwagen, 63 N.Y. 504, 519.)

If it appeared to the satisfaction of the jury that Weiss willfully alienated Robert from his family by falsely accusing Joel of fraud and mismanagement in the conduct of the family business enterprises for the purpose of causing Robert to disinherit members of his family, then the jury properly could have found undue influence. (Matter of Anna, 248 N.Y. 421, supra; Tyler v. Gardiner, 35 N.Y. 559, 595.)

The fact that the relation between Robert and Weiss may have afforded Robert some satisfaction did not enable Weiss deceitfully, improperly and insidiously to turn Robert against his family. (Matter of Budlong, 126 N.Y. 423, 432, supra; Rollwagen v. Rollwagen, supra, p. 520.)

We are concerned with the testamentary mind, intent and purpose of Robert on June 19, 1958, when the instrument offered for probate was executed. To what extent Weiss affected Robert's mind and whether, if at all, he influenced his testamentary intent can only be determined upon a close examination of the interaction between the two over the course of the period between 1948 and the time of death, April 18, 1959. When the influence, if any, is ascertained, we can then address ourselves to the question whether it was within legally permissible bounds or exceeded them and was therefore undue influence.

. . .

Appellant does not seriously urge that the change of the life insurance beneficiaries, the various gifts and the prior wills may not have been influenced by Weiss. He strenuously urges that the evidence fails to show he influenced the will of June 19, 1958.

The first of the four wills in which provision is made for Weiss is dated June 13, 1951. The letter signed by Robert the same day is cogent evidence of his complete domination by Weiss. Its exposure, implications and distortions can be understood only as an attempt to justify what is obviously unnatural and utterly inconsistent with reality and what the record establishes was the warm and close relation between Robert and his family. Apart from the content of the letter, two significant factors are present: a change from the attorneys who prepared the 1950 will and the substantial provisions for Weiss. The letter came into existence long before the Fairfax affair and evidences the presence of forces operating on Robert's mind in favor of Weiss to the detriment of Robert's family. The same forces continued to operate with ever-increasing potency to the date of Robert's death and at all times in favor of Weiss and against Robert's family and ultimately against his friends and persons who had served him faithfully.

Weiss sought to disassociate himself from the letter of June 13, 1951. Weiss on April 23, 1959 wrote to Aunt Birdie enclosing a copy with the comment: "I never saw this letter and I am amazed he was moved to write it as far back as '51." This was a false statement made by one with guilty knowledge of its origin and purpose, one of many similar statements with which this record is replete.

Weiss' deliberately false pretrial testimony is that he first learned he was a testamentary beneficiary of Robert after his death. The record shows indisputably Weiss' involvement with each of the wills since 1950; copies were in the vault to which he had the right of access he frequently exercised. In May, 1954 Weiss caused the prior will and the letters of June, 1951 and October, 1952 to be delivered to Garrison. Here, again, Weiss disassociates himself from circumstances cogently pointing to his involvement in and responsibility for the testamentary disposition made by Robert.

The record enabled the jury to find that the instrument of June 19, 1958 was the end result of an unnatural, insidious influence operating on a weak-willed, trusting, inexperienced Robert whose natural warm family attachment had been attenuated by false accusations against Joel, subtle flattery suggesting an independence he had not realized and which, in fact, Weiss had stultified, and planting in Robert's mind the conviction that Joel and other members of the family were resentful of and obstructing his drive for independence.

The fact that the instrument offered for probate was prepared by reputable, competent attorneys is a relevant circumstance but does not preclude a finding that the undue influence here involved was active, potent and unaffected by the interposition of independent counsel. (Matter of Anna, 248 N.Y. 421, 425, supra.) Far more extensive interposition by independent counsel has been held not to be conclusive on the existence of undue influence. (Smith v. Keller, 205 N.Y. 39, 43.)

If Weiss was in Europe at the times he became beneficiary of the life insurance policies and at the times when the four wills were executed in which he is named, and Robert was living in New York near or with his family, much of the argument made by counsel for appellant would be compelling. The assumed situation is what was present in Marx v. McGlynn (88 N.Y. 357, supra). There, Bradley was in

Europe, 3,000 miles away from the testatrix in New York when she executed the will. The testatrix lived with her sister and was among friends with whom she was brought up. However, there had been a long close relation between Bradley and the testatrix. Bradley had been spiritual advisor of the testatrix; had been her traveling companion and had shown great influence over her. The court there observed that Bradley did not influence the testatrix as to her property, or alienate her from her relatives; that at all times she had and kept control and that Bradley was given no control over her property; moreover, that Bradley was not her agent with respect to her property.

All of the elements adverted to in Marx and not present there are here conclusively established. In addition, there is here proximity to the point of oneness, and the presence of Weiss within the same household at the times the wills were made and the beneficiaries displaced in respect of the life insurance.

In Marx the court held there was a presumption of undue influence on the part of Bradley which, however, the Surrogate held had been overcome and the Court of Appeals affirmed, saying (p. 371): "But there are certain cases in which the law indulges in the presumption that undue influence has been used, and those cases are . . . a will . . . of . . . a ward in favor of his guardian, or any person in favor of his priest or religious adviser, or where other close confidential relationships exist."

Here, the circumstances spell out a confidential relation between proponent and the decedent which gave rise to an obligation on the part of the proponent-devisee to offer an explanation. The language of this court in Matter of Satterlee (281 App. Div. 251, 254) is apropos: "Surely, in the light of the unusual setting and the highly fiduciary relationship which proponent had assumed toward decedent, it was incumbent on him to come forward and explain his becoming the principal beneficiary under her will."

. . .

The issue of undue influence was submitted to the jury without the benefit to the contestants of any presumption. The charge placed the unrelieved burden of establishing undue influence upon the contestants. The issue was given to the jury in the aspect most favorable to the appellant; appellant made no exception to the charge. The record overwhelmingly sustains the verdict on undue influence on the basis of the charge made.

The decree denying probate of the instrument dated June 19, 1958 should be affirmed, with costs to respondents payable out of the estate.

Witmer, J. (dissenting). This case comes to us upon appeal by the proponent from the decree of New York County Surrogate's Court denying probate of the propounded will, entered upon the jury's verdict declaring that the instrument was procured by undue influence practiced upon the testator. A prior jury had reached the same conclusion, and this court (Matter of Kaufmann, 14 AD2d 411) reversed and ordered a new trial, saying in part (p. 413): "the verdict of the jury is against the weight of the credible evidence, and, in fact, some of us in the majority are of the opinion that upon the authority of Matter of Walther (6 NY2d 49) there was not sufficient evidence of undue influence to justify the submission of the question to the jury, and that the most that was shown was the existence of lawful influences arising from the claims of a close relationship which were not inconsistent with an assumption that the will expressed the voluntary intent of the testator." We agree with that expression of opinion. Upon the second trial each side added to the proof of the factual contentions in its favor made upon the first trial. It is not disputed that the testator was competent to make a will nor that the will was executed in accordance with the required legal formalities. There is no claim nor evidence of coercion.

The case for the contestants is grounded completely upon circumstantial evidence, and consists of evidence of a relationship between the testator and the proponent Weiss begun in the late 1940's and continuing until testator's death in April, 1959. No specific act is relied upon as constituting the alleged undue influence inducing the propounded will; but the claim is that from about 1950 testator was under the complete domination of Weiss.

. . .

"Undue influence is a fact which must be proved by the contestant and not merely assumed to exist. (Matter of Smith, 95 N.Y. 516; Matter of Ruef, 180 App. Div. 203, aff'd, 223 N.Y. 582; Matter of Rundles, 216 App. Div. 658.) Like any other fact, it may be proved by circumstantial evidence but the circumstances must lead to it not only by fair inference but as a necessary conclusion. To avoid the will of a competent testator on the ground of undue influence, the contestant must show facts entirely inconsistent with the hypothesis of the execution of the will by any means other than undue influence. [Cases cited.]" (Matter of Henderson, 253 App. Div. 140, 145.)

. . .

The verdict in this case rests upon surmise, suspicion, conjecture and moral indignation and resentment, not upon the legally required proof of undue influence; and it cannot stand.

The record shows that the testator was intelligent and generally healthy. The evidence that he lost weight was explained by his doctor who said that he had placed him upon a no-fat diet. True, the testator was not wholly like other people. He had little zest for business, which fact set him apart from his family. He had artistic ability, and particularly loved to paint. So did Weiss. They had common interests. Testator felt and said that he had uncommon ability as a painter and that some day he would be known for his artistic work. In this, he was not wholly wrong, for it appears that eighty museums have accepted his work for permanent display.

The record is replete with evidence of the friendly relation, indeed love and affection, that existed between testator and Weiss for a decade. There is no substantial evidence that their relationship was not one of mutual esteem and self-respect. The isolated incidents of testator bowing to Weiss' wishes on certain occasions over this period fall far short of conclusively pointing to a subserviency, when viewed in the light of all the evidence. True, testator relied upon Weiss in business and administrative matters, but that is not to say that testator was not essentially in command. There is evidence that at times testator made his own business decisions. The fact that Weiss advised testator in his business dealings with his brothers is not inconsistent with his position as testator's financial advisor. Moreover, the record shows that under the proposed Fairfax deal testator's brother Joel was to be paid more per share than the testator, which the testator did not like, and that by reason of testator's lawsuit against his brother, testator collected about $70,000 more than he had been offered. Certainly, that affords no ground for suspicion of Weiss. The testator did not overlook his nephews; and the evidence shows that in 1955 at a time when he changed his will the testator had spent considerable money refurbishing Aunt Birdie's apartment; and chided his brothers with reference to their lack of concern for her. Substantial evidence also shows that for years prior to his death testator acted normally in his outward relations toward Weiss and other people in Weiss' presence. And within a few weeks of his death, in Key West, Florida, when Weiss wanted to return to New York City testator declined to do so at the time, and Weiss came on to New York alone. Such conduct on the part of the testator by no means permits of "a necessary conclusion" that the testator was dominated by Weiss. Although testator placed confidence in Weiss, the relationship was not that of attorney and client, and Weiss had no part, directly at least, in the preparation and execution of these wills. The prior decision of this court disposes of that aspect of this case (14 AD2d 411, 413). . . .

The letter written by testator on June 13, 1951, proponent's Exhibit 19, and placed with his will of that date, and later reviewed with his attorney and placed with later wills, shows the regard which testator had for Weiss. This letter appears to lay bare the fact and prove the suspicion which members of testator's family had of the intimate relationship which existed between the two men. That and the falsehoods told by Weiss may have been among the reasons why Weiss failed to take the witness stand upon the trial. In our opinion, however, there was no legal compulsion upon Weiss to testify beyond the testimony which he gave on the examination before trial and which was read at length upon the trial of this case.

The issue in this case is not what were the morals of these men, nor whether testator led a normal life, nor whether Weiss has been proved a liar. The issue is, does the propounded instrument represent the intrinsic wishes and will of the testator, or was it the product of the command of Weiss which the testator did not really want to follow, but was unable to resist? The veracity of Weiss, it is true, may not be ignored in considering this issue.

Every act of the testator from the date of Exhibit 19, June 13, 1951, to the time of his death was consistent with what he expressed in that letter. Contestants' argument that Weiss induced testator to write said letter, Exhibit 19, to build a case for leaving his estate to Weiss, does not ring true. It is not reasonable that the letter would have contained the candid statement about sex, if it were written for such ulterior motive. It is true that contestants claim that at every stage testator was dominated by Weiss; but the period of time alone negates that claim. It is not claimed that the testator was hypnotized by Weiss during all this period, and certainly no evidence thereof has been presented. The record shows that for years testator had business differences with his brother Joel; and it shows also that he rarely saw his relatives in the years in question. In the meantime his attachment for Weiss apparently grew; and testator openly proclaimed his friendship for Weiss. In Exhibit 19 testator expressed for the eventual information of his relatives why he wished to leave his assets to Weiss. As far as the motive is concerned the relationship may be likened to that of one who has a mistress. Morals aside, upon the facts in this case "Proof of the circumstance that the will was an unnatural one is lacking." (Matter of Henderson, 253 App. Div. 140, 145, supra.) Of course, the court does not condone the relationship, but the moral law may not be substituted for the law of wills; and it should not be overlooked that difficult cases tend to make bad law. Undoubtedly the testator was influenced, but the evidence in this case is entirely consistent with the complete lack of undue influence. Yet, because of the suspicious circumstances involved, the majority of this court as well as the court below would deny him his legal right to dispose of his property as he has chosen to do.

Contestants' psychiatrist, Dr. Herman, testified that he did not know for what reason the testator was psychoanalyzed; that the testator was an introvert; and that another psychiatrist could reach a different conclusion than did Dr. Herman concerning testator's independence. However misguided testator was, in view of his admitted competence and the equivocation by Dr. Herman "The evidence is in no way inconsistent with the assumption that the will expresses the voluntary intent of the [testator] and does not satisfy the test that intervention and undue influence can only be established by evidence that is not inconsistent with a contrary hypothesis". (Matter of Walther, 6 N.Y2d 49, 56, supra.)

There was, thus, no question of fact for the jury; and proponents' motion for a directed verdict should have been granted. . . .

Breitel, J.P., and Rabin, J., concur with McNally, J.; Witmer, J., dissents and votes to reverse, in opinion, in which Stevens, J., concurs.

In re KAUFMANN'S WILL

Court of Appeals of New York, 1965

15 N.Y.2d 825, 257 N.Y.S.2d 941, 205 N.E.2d 864

Appeal from an order of the Appellate Division of the Supreme Court in the First Judicial Department, entered March 19, 1964, which, by a divided court, affirmed, insofar as appealed from, a decree of the New York County Surrogate's Court (S. Samuel Di Falco, S.) denying probate of the purported will of Robert D. Kaufmann, deceased, following a finding by a jury that said purported will was procured by undue influence.

Order affirmed, with costs to respondents payable out of the estate, in a memorandum: Where, as here, the record indicates that testator was pliable and easily taken advantage of, as proponent admitted, that there was a long and detailed history of dominance and subservience between them, that testator relied exclusively upon proponent's knowledge and judgment in the disposition of almost all of the material circumstances affecting the conduct of his life, and proponent is willed virtually the entire estate, we consider that a question of fact was presented concerning whether the instrument offered for probate was the free, untrammeled and intelligent expression of the wishes and intentions of testator or the product of the dominance of the beneficiary (Matter of Smith, 95 N.Y. 516; Marx v. McGlynn, 88 N.Y. 357; Matter of Putnam, 257 N.Y. 140; Matter of Satterlee, 281 App. Div. 251, 254).

Concur: Chief Judge Desmond and Judges Dye, Fuld, Van Voorhis, Burke, Scileppi and Bergan.

NOTES

1. The 1955 will gave bequests to various persons and one-half the residue of Robert's estate to Walter and one-half to Robert's two nephews, Richard and Lee. Is the clause in the 1958 will revoking all prior wills effective if the 1958 will is denied probate because of undue influence? If it is not effective, can the 1955 will be admitted to probate in whole or in part? Atkinson, Wills 289 (2d ed. 1953).

Suppose that, after Walter had left Robert in Key West and had returned to New York, Robert had gone to a lawyer in Key West and had him draw a codicil to his will giving $10,000 to his friend Sally Avery. Can a will invalid for undue influence be made valid by a later codicil? Note, 21 A.L.R.2d 821 (1952).

2. If a homosexual relationship had existed between Robert and Walter, would you have advised Walter to take the witness stand and admit it? If Robert had come to you in 1958 and said he wanted to leave everything to Walter, and feared his family would object, what would you advise him to do?

It has been held that influence which results from an immoral relation is not undue if it springs from affection rather than domination. Faulkes v. Brummett's Admr., 305 Ky. 434, 204 S.W.2d 493 (1947) (beneficiary was testator's mistress for twelve years); In re Swartz's Will, 79 Okla. 191, 192 P. 203, 16 A.L.R. 450 (1920) (beneficiaries and testatrix were inmates of a house of prostitution).

Do you think the jury and courts would have found undue influence on the facts in the Kaufmann case if (a) Robert had been a woman, or (b) Walter had been a woman, or (c) Walter had been a woman and the parties were married?

"It is impossible to be both a self-accepting homosexual and live a conventional life in American society. . . . This form of discrimination may be of declining importance as marriage itself becomes less important, yet there remain important legal and taxation difficulties that result from the inability of homosexuals to establish legalized relationships. These difficulties can be of major consequence. In A Single Man the hero experiences the death of his lover of many years, and realizes that he has less status for the man's family than would a casual girlfriend. And if their relationship had been open, what then? If his lover died intestate, what court would treat him as it would a widowed de facto wife? A report in the London Times referred to a lesbian dying in a hospital who 'was only allowed visits from her immediate family, and her partner of twenty years was excluded. When a lesbian loses her partner she can expect little or no comfort from conventional sources of support like neighbors, a priest or doctor who would try to ease the hurt of a heterosexual faced with bereavement or divorce.' " Altman, Homosexual Oppression and Liberation 38 (1971).

3. "*Displacement* is a kind of projection in which feelings toward one person are refocused on another person, or even on an animal or inanimate object. For example, a patient has feelings for his doctor that were originally (and are really) the feelings he has for his father. Displacement is also defensive, as all projections are; by displacing his feelings a person may avoid confronting in a realistic way his relationship toward significant people. [Both Freudian and Jungian psychological traditions see *transference* as a species of *projection*. Projection is the identification of attitudes, feelings, and pressures in another person which are in fact, or also, in oneself.] . . . Even Carl Rogers, who is no Freudian, sees transference as involving 'attitudes transferred to the therapist which were originally directed, with more justification, toward a parent or other person.'

". . . Freud's view of transference was tied to his view of the Oedipus complex. Feelings transferred by the patient originated in competition between the patient and his father for the love of the patient's mother — a necessarily contrasexual relationship. It is possible to exaggerate the importance of the sexual element in transference — especially in a limited discussion, for nonmedical purposes. . . . However, the evidence for some contrasexual tendency in transference is at least strong enough to justify seeking a parallel between clinical experience with the phenomenon and the apparent incidence of contrasexual transference in undue influence wills cases. . . .

"In re Kaufmann's Will made two trips to the appellate division of the New York Supreme Court and was finally resolved, by a divided court, against legacies made by Robert Kaufmann to his friend Walter Weiss. . . .

"Kaufmann appears to be a clear case of manipulation. Evidentiary sophistication in dealing with it — most notably the sophistication of a presumption or shift in the burden of proof — is not necessary to the decision. The majority alluded to the New York rule on presumption of undue influence, but its holding does not rest on a presumption nor on an esoteric view of burden of proof; the case was decided solely on the record. Psychological sophistication is not necessary either, given the majority's view of the evidence. A transference clearly existed, and it was clearly contrasexual, even though both parties were male. It was a strong transference, an emotional lever Weiss could have exploited in all of the ways the family pointed out. It probably gripped Weiss, too, but the majority could not discuss that because it was too intent on finding a villain. Moral judgments about Weiss and his power over Robert Kaufmann were doubtless made by the jury. They were made expressly by appellate judges on both sides of the issue; they were made by the majority in such a way as to resolve the evidence into both a finding and a righteous condemnation. Transference theory illuminates this sort of case; it would temper judicial rhetoric to have the theory out in the open — if only because the judges would see that we all manipulate and are manipulated — but it would probably not change the decision.

". . . Cases like Kaufmann may even be disposed of as involving fraud in the inducement. Fraud theory requires a showing of false representation, but the manipulation of a transference is false representation. Love is as much a fact as residence, age, or digestion. It is just as capable of being falsely represented. If the law can take cognizance of false representations about the loyalty or honesty of third persons it can take cognizance of the falsity in a person who pretends love in order to gain property. But even if the law of fraud won't do that, the law of undue influence has shown itself capable of dealing with cases like Kaufmann." Shaffer, Death, Property, and Lawyers 229-257 (1970).

4. "The description of the masochistic character as weak, dependent, easily influenced, helpless, continues to amaze us. All these features serve the purpose of concealing the utmost determination and stubbornness. What the masochist has to say to the existent ruling forces sounds like slavish submissiveness. It is, however, a scornful 'No' to the world of appearances that became dominant. He submits — in order never to yield. He remains in opposition, especially where he is servilely devoted. When Dr. Horney keeps emphasizing the dependence of masochistic characters, their tendency to cling to the loved person, she overlooks the fact that one can draw somebody down by clinging to him. . . .

"It is obvious that the forbidden sexual satisfaction is the aim of such defiance in perverse masochism. The driving power, however, that leads to masochism is not solely of a sexual nature. It receives mighty support from the efforts of the ego to maintain itself against superior forces, to save its internal independence when it has to give up the external one. . . . And it does not make any difference psychically whether the person of the opponent is still alive or has been dead for a long time. As in compulsory neurosis, the strong unconscious affects of defiance and rebellion remain attached even to persons who have left this world a long time ago. The late attainment of the instinctual aim must give such profound satisfaction — just as it does in the sexual sphere — that the masochist gladly submits to all sufferings and pain." Reik, Masochism in Modern Man 159, 164 (1941).

5. In MacDonald v. Joslyn, 275 Cal. App. 2d 282, 79 Cal. Rptr. 707, 35 A.L.R.3d 641 (1969), the testator's eldest son contested testator's will on grounds of fraud and undue influence. Pending determination of this contest, a special administrator was appointed to administer the estate. The son lost the contest. The executor then sued the son for malicious prosecution of his lawsuit. The court held that the son had no probable cause for his suit and acted maliciously. It awarded the executor $123,000 in compensatory damages for fees the executor did not earn because of the delay in his appointment and $50,000 punitive damages.

6. For a study illustrating the difficulty in predicting undue influence cases, see Note, Undue Influence — Judicial Implementation of Social Policy, 1968 Wis. L. Rev. 569.

A PEARL OF GREAT PRICE [11]

In October 1966 a 95-year-old South Pasadena millionaire, Albert Otis Birch, with an estate estimated at $200 million, married his 59-year-old nurse, Pearl Choate. This was the climax of a wild fifteen-month chase across California, Mexico, and Texas — Birch and his first wife periodically disappearing with Pearl, only to be found by investigators hired by Birch's prospective legatees.

Pearl Choate was many times married. She had six husbands, one of whom she married twice. She also had a lengthy criminal record including an acquittal for murder in 1938 (she shot a ranch hand in the back, but was successful in her claim of self-defense). She spent twelve years in a Texas prison for murdering a carpenter who had obtained a civil judgment against her. Pearl had come to work for Birch and his 93-year-old wife, Estelle, in the summer of 1965. They procured her through a nurses' registry after Estelle developed cancer.

In April of 1966 Pearl moved the Birches from their thirty-two-room South Pasadena mansion to her small home in Compton so she could better attend them. Two months later the Birches and Pearl disappeared. They were discovered in Mexico, where Otis Birch told investigators he had come of his own volition for his health. Not satisfied with this state of affairs, several distant relatives of the Birches (they had no close relatives) petitioned in Los Angeles to have a guardian of the persons and conservator of the property appointed for the couple. A cousin of Estelle, Martha Tulleys, was appointed guardian, and a bank was appointed conservator. Meanwhile the Birches and Pearl had disappeared again and were traced to Harlingen, Texas, where Birch fractured his hip in a fall. A local physician ordered Birch not to be moved for thirty days.

Dr. C. Adrian Heaton, president of California Baptist Theological Seminary, which had received large sums of money from Birch during his life and presumably would come in for a handsome gift at his death, flew to Harlingen only to find that Birch had been taken from the hospital and driven by Pearl 500 miles across Texas to Midland. There the trail was lost, and the whereabouts of the trio was not discovered until after Estelle died in Breckenridge, Texas, on October 7, 1966. Estelle's body was returned to Los Angeles and buried in Inglewood Park Cemetery.

After Estelle died, Harlan Moehn of Iowa, a relative of Estelle Birch, located Pearl and Otis Birch in Breckenridge, Texas, where one of Pearl's brothers ran a tavern. Moehn and Dr. Heaton discovered that Pearl had filed an adoption application to be named Birch's daughter. Moehn arranged to see Birch on October 25; the discussion became heated and Pearl attacked Moehn with a butcher knife, screaming, "I'll cut your heart out." He filed a complaint against Pearl, and she was arrested and booked on suspicion of assault with intent to commit murder. After posting bond in the case, Pearl put Otis Birch in a car and drove across the border

[11] This phrase, from the King James Version (Matt. 13-46), is changed to "one pearl of great *value*" in the Revised Standard Version. The facts are taken from various issues of the Los Angeles Times during 1966-1970.

to Altus, Oklahoma, where they were married in a flashy red sedan by a justice of the peace. Birch, recovering from hip surgery, was lying on a mattress in the back seat of the car when the ceremony was performed. "This was not a marriage of passion . . . he suggested it to protect my interests," Pearl told newsmen. She described the churchmen and relatives seeking to wrest Birch from her as "a bunch of vultures."

Harlan Moehn then sought a writ of habeas corpus in a Breckenridge court to release Birch from the control of his new wife. Pearl brought Birch to court, where he was the star witness. Almost totally deaf, he heard little of the proceedings. He had a new hearing aid, but Pearl had not yet obtained batteries for it. When handed questions in writing, Birch answered in a booming voice that he was not being restrained against his wishes and that he did not want to return to California where, he said, the "authorities" wanted to test him for insanity. The judge ruled that Birch was not being held against his will by his bride. Pearl put her arm around Otis Birch, and they both smiled broadly for photographers.

In the meantime the attorney general of California, overseer of charitable trusts, entered the case. His investigators turned up a very interesting bit of information: Pearl had married a Compton car-wash worker in a proxy marriage in Tijuana, Mexico, on Sept. 2, 1965. Thus informed, the attorney general of California asked the county attorney in Oklahoma to prosecute Pearl for bigamy. But the information proved not wholly accurate. It was discovered that Mexican authorities had failed to record the marriage certificate, and under Mexican law this final step is required for a valid proxy marriage. Hence the bigamy suit was called off.

In November, 1966, Birch and his bride disappeared from Breckenridge. Her relatives refused to say where they had gone. They were spotted briefly in Wichita Falls. The Harlingen law firm Birch had hired during his one-month stay there — with an unpaid bill of $7500 for legal services — discovered them in December occupying a house trailer in Odessa, Texas. From there they moved the trailer to Dallas, where Birch died on March 16, 1967. The next day Pearl had Birch's body entombed at the Laurel Land Mausoleum in Dallas.

By a handwritten will dated May 14, 1966, Birch devised all his property to Pearl. A prior will of September 7, 1965, had left his estate to sixteen charitable organizations, mainly Baptist institutions. The charitable organizations claimed Birch was mentally incompetent and unduly influenced by Pearl when he made the 1966 will, but, after an extended lawsuit, in 1970 the 1966 will was ordered probated by the district court in Dallas. Soon thereafter the Los Angeles Times reported that the Birch estate was vastly overestimated; it might not be worth more than $50,000. No one seemed to be able to find Otis' reputed assets.

After entombing her husband's body in Dallas, the widow Birch returned to her home in Compton, California, where she promptly had another run-in with the law. She quarreled with the tenant in her duplex, alleging the rent was overdue. When a neighbor called the police, she fired a .22-caliber rifle, barely missing a policeman and a bystander. On January 23, 1968, a jury found Pearl Choate Birch guilty of assault with a deadly weapon. She served twenty months in prison and was released in March 1970.

The Birch case raises a whole complex of interesting issues. Let us approach them from the viewpoint of the lawyer giving advice. Suppose you are an attorney practicing in Breckenridge, Texas. Soon after Estelle died Pearl Choate comes into your office and says Birch wants to leave her all his property and she wants to take care of him for the rest of his life. "He wants to protect me, and I want to look after him," she tells you. What do you advise Pearl Choate and Otis Birch to do? To draft a will for an incompetent person is a breach of professional ethics.[12] Although it is by no means clear that Birch is incompetent and that you must ethically refuse to draft a will for him, under the circumstances of the case a will might be attacked successfully on grounds of mental incompetency or undue influence. Hence consider the following alternatives.

(a) You advise an adoption proceeding, and draw a petition for adoption which Pearl and Otis Birch sign. The petition is approved by the court, which decrees that Pearl is the daughter of Otis. Birch's nearest relatives are not notified of the adoption proceeding. After Birch's death can his next of kin or his executor set aside the adoption? In re Adoption of Sewall, 242 Cal. App. 2d 208, 51 Cal. Rptr. 367 (1966); In re Adoption of Russell, 166 Pa. Super. 590, 73 A.2d 794 (1950).

(b) You advise Pearl and Otis to marry. They do. Under the laws of Texas and California, which have community property systems, Pearl would not be entitled to a forced share in Otis' estate. However, the surviving spouse does take a share if Otis dies intestate. Assume Otis dies intestate. Could the marriage be annulled by his next of kin? [13] Before or after Otis' death? McClure v. Donovan, 33 Cal. 2d 717, 205 P.2d 17 (1949); Greathouse v. Vosburgh, 19 Ill. 2d 555, 169 N.E.2d 97 (1960); Rattray v. Huntting, 11 App. Div. 2d 785, 205 N.Y.S.2d 232 (1960). Would you advise Pearl and Otis to move to Florida, which gives the surviving spouse a forced share in the decedent's estate? By what criteria would the domicile of Otis be determined at his death? Estate of Phillips, 269 Cal. App. 2d 656, 75 Cal. Rptr. 301 (1969); Kanowitz, Women and the Law 52 (1969).

(c) You recommend an inter vivos trust. You draw a trust instrument, which Otis signs, transferring all his property to Pearl as trustee to pay all the income to Otis for life, and on the death of Otis to pay the principal to Pearl. Can either Otis' next of kin or the executor of his will set aside the trust on grounds of undue influence? (Sure, the settlor can rescind for undue influence, but can third parties?) 4 Scott, Trusts §333.3 (3d ed. 1967); Hall v. Crouch, 341 S.W.2d 591 (Ky. 1960); Note, Undue Influence in Inter Vivos Transactions, 41 Colum. L. Rev. 707 (1941).

(d) You recommend a contract to devise. The agreement, signed by Pearl and

[12] In Gilmer v. Brown, 186 Va. 630, 44 S.E.2d 16 (1947), the attorney-draftsman was reprimanded for failing to make sufficient inquiry as to competence.

[13] In McKinney v. Clarke, 32 Tenn. 321 (1852), a widow had a life estate determinable upon remarriage; her children had the remainder. She ran up a lot of debts. Then she married the town drunk, who apparently had few sober moments. An outraged creditor unsuccessfully sought to annul the marriage.

Otis, provides that Pearl promises to take care of Otis for the rest of his life and, in exchange therefor, Otis promises to devise all his property to Pearl. Pearl fulfills her promise and Otis either (1) dies intestate or (2) devises all his property to Pearl, which devise is set aside on grounds of undue influence. What are Pearl's rights on the contract? Mutz v. Wallace, 214 Cal. App. 2d 100, 29 Cal. Rptr. 170 (1963); Henderson v. Fisher, 236 Cal. App. 2d 468, 46 Cal. Rptr. 173 (1965).

(e) You recommend a contract for services rendered. The agreement, signed by Pearl and Otis, provides that Otis will pay Pearl $50,000 a month for taking care of him. Six months later, after paying Pearl $300,000 pursuant to the contract, Otis dies. What are the rights of the next of kin or Otis' executor against Pearl? Green, The Operative Effect of Mental Incompetency on Agreements and Wills, 21 Texas L. Rev. 554 (1943); Green, Proof of Mental Incompetency and the Unexpressed Major Premise, 53 Yale L.J. 271 (1944); Note, Wills and Contracts — Degree of Mental Capacity Requisite for Each, 34 N.C.L. Rev. 155 (1955).

(f) Would any of the above alternatives be unethical for an attorney to advise? Would the attorney who advised any of these actions be subject to liability? Consider the following excerpt from Lysick v. Walcom, 258 Cal. App. 2d 136, 147, 65 Cal. Rptr. 406, 414 (1968):

> Where an attorney represents two clients with divergent or conflicting interests in the same subject matter, the Lucas rule [Lucas v. Hamm, supra page 15] demands that the attorney must disclose all facts and circumstances which, in the judgment of a lawyer of ordinary skill and capacity, are necessary to enable his client to make free and intelligent decisions regarding the subject matter of the representation. Accordingly, when an attorney attempts dual relationship without making the full disclosure required of him, he is civilly liable to the client who suffers loss caused by lack of disclosure.

Compare Hiemstra v. Huston, 12 Cal. App. 3d 1043, 91 Cal. Rptr. 269 (1970), which held that it was not actionable negligence for an attorney to *draft* a will without instructions from the testator and, allegedly, in ignorance of testator's true wishes.

2. *Fraud*

LATHAM v. FATHER DIVINE

Court of Appeals of New York, 1949

299 N.Y. 22, 85 N.E.2d 168, 11 A.L.R.2d 802

DESMOND, Judge. The amended complaint herein has, in response to a motion under rule 106 of the Rules of Civil Practice, been dismissed for insufficiency. Its principal allegations are these: plaintiffs are first cousins, but not distributees, of Mary Sheldon Lyon, who died in October, 1946, leaving a will, executed in 1943, which gave almost her whole estate to defendant Father Divine,[14] leader of a religious cult, and to two corporate defendants in some way connected with that cult, and to an individual defendant (Patience Budd) said to be one of Father Divine's active followers; that said will has been, after a contest instituted by distributees, probated under a compromise agreement with the distributees, by the terms of which agreement, to which plaintiffs were not parties, the defendants just above referred to will receive a large sum from the estate; that after the making of said will, decedent on several occasions expressed "a desire and a determination to revoke the said will, and to execute a new will by which the plaintiffs would receive a substantial portion of the estate", "that shortly prior to the death of the deceased she had certain attorneys draft a new will in which the plaintiffs were named as legatees for a very substantial amount, totalling approximately $350,000"; that "by reason of the said false representations, the said undue influence and the said physical force" certain of the defendants "prevented the deceased from executing the said new Will"; that, shortly before decedent's death, decedent again expressed her determination to execute the proposed new will which favored plaintiffs, and that defendants "thereupon conspired to kill, and did kill, the deceased by means of a surgical operation performed by a doctor engaged by the defendants without the consent or knowledge of any of the relatives of the deceased."

Nothing is better settled than that, on such a motion as this, all the averments of the attacked pleading are taken as true. For present purposes, then, we have a case where one possessed of a large property and having already made a will leaving it to certain persons, expressed an intent to make a new testament to contain legacies to other persons, attempted to carry out that intention by having a new will drawn which contained a large legacy to those others, but was, by means of misrepresentations, undue influence, force, and indeed, murder, prevented, by the beneficiaries named in the existing will, from signing the new one. Plaintiffs say that those facts, if proven, would entitle them to a judicial declaration, which their prayer for judgment demands, that defendants, taking under the already probated will, hold what they have so taken as constructive trustees for plaintiffs, whom decedent wished to, tried to, and was kept from, benefiting.

We find in New York no decision directly answering the question as to whether or not the allegations above summarized state a case for relief in equity. But reliable texts, and cases elsewhere, see 98 A.L.R. 474 et seq., answer it in the affirmative. Leading writers, 3 Scott on Trusts, pp. 2371-2376; 3 Bogert on Trusts and Trustees, part 1, §§473-474, 498, 499; 1 Perry on Trusts and Trustees [7th ed.], pp. 265, 371, in one form or another, state the law of the subject to be about as it is expressed in comment *i* under section 184 of the Restatement of the Law of Restitution: "*Preventing revocation of will and making new will.* Where a devisee or legatee under a will already executed prevents the testator by fraud, duress or undue

[14] For the story of this colorful and unorthodox religious leader, who proclaimed his own divinity and established Heavens across the country for his followers, see Harris, Father Divine: Holy Husband (1953); Hoshor, God in a Rolls Royce (1936); Parker, The Incredible Messiah (1937). Father Divine's given name was George Baker. — Eds.

influence from revoking the will and executing a new will in favor of another or from making a codicil, so that the testator dies leaving the original will in force, the devisee or legatee holds the property thus acquired upon a constructive trust for the intended devisee or legatee."

A frequently-cited case is Ransdel v. Moore, 153 Ind. 393, at pages 407-408, 53 N.E. 767, at page 771, 53 L.R.A. 753, where, with listing of many authorities, the rule is given thus: "when an heir or devisee in a will prevents the testator from providing for one for whom he would have provided but for the interference of the heir or devisee, such heir or devisee will be deemed a trustee, by operation of law, of the property, real or personal, received by him from the testator's estate, to the amount or extent that the defrauded party would have received had not the intention of the deceased been interfered with. This rule applies also when an heir prevents the making of a will or deed in favor of another, and thereby inherits the property that would otherwise have been given such other person." To the same effect, see 4 Page on Wills [3d ed.], p. 961.

While there is no New York case decreeing a constructive trust on the exact facts alleged here, there are several decisions in this court which, we think, suggest such a result and none which forbids it. Matter of O'Hara's Will, 95 N.Y. 403, 47 Am. Rep. 53; Trustees of Amherst College v. Ritch, 151 N.Y. 282, 45 N.E. 876, 37 L.R.A. 305; Edson v. Bartow, 154 N.Y. 199, 48 N.E. 541, and Ahrens v. Jones, 169 N.Y. 555, 62 N.E. 666, 88 Am. St. Rep. 620, which need not be closely analyzed here as to their facts, all announce, in one form or another, the rule that, where a legatee has taken property under a will, after agreeing outside the will, to devote that property to a purpose intended and declared by the testator, equity will enforce a constructive trust to effectuate that purpose, lest there be a fraud on the testator. In Williams v. Fitch, 18 N.Y. 546, a similar result was achieved in a suit for money had and received. In each of those four cases first above cited in this paragraph, the particular fraud consisted of the legatee's failure or refusal to carry out the testator's designs, after tacitly or expressly promising so to do. But we do not think that a breach of such an engagement is the only kind of fraud which will impel equity to action. A constructive trust will be erected whenever necessary to satisfy the demands of justice. Since a constructive trust is merely "the formula through which the conscience of equity finds expression" Beatty v. Guggenheim Exploration Co., 225 N.Y. 380, 386, 122 N.E. 378, 380; . . . its applicability is limited only by the inventiveness of men who find new ways to enrich themselves unjustly by grasping what should not belong to them. Nothing short of true and complete justice satisfies equity, and, always assuming these allegations to be true, there seems no way of achieving total justice except by the procedure used here. . . .

Nor do we agree that anything in the Decedent Estate Law, Consol. Laws, c. 13, §1 et seq., or the Statute of Frauds stands in the way of recovery herein. This is not a proceeding to probate or establish the will which plaintiffs say testatrix was prevented from signing, nor is it an attempt to accomplish a revocation of the earlier will as were Matter of Evans' Will, 113 App. Div. 373, 98 N.Y.S. 1042 and Matter of McGill's Will, 229 N.Y. 405, 411, 128 N.E. 194, 195, 196. The will Mary

Sheldon Lyon did sign has been probated and plaintiffs are not contesting, but proceeding on, that probate, trying to reach property which has effectively passed thereunder. See Ahrens v. Jones, 169 N.Y. 555, 561, 62 N.E. 666, 667, 668, 88 Am. St. Rep. 620, supra. Nor is this a suit to enforce an agreement to make a will or create a trust or any other promise by decedent, Personal Property Law, Consol. Laws, c. 41, §31; . . . This complaint does not say that decedent or defendants promised plaintiffs anything or that defendants made any promise to decedent. The story is, simply, that defendants, by force and fraud, kept the testatrix from making a will in favor of plaintiffs. We cannot say, as matter of law, that no constructive trust can arise therefrom. . . .

We do not agree with appellants that Riggs v. Palmer, 115 N.Y. 506, 22 N.E. 188, 5 L.R.A. 340, 12 Am. St. Rep. 819, completely controls our decision here. That was the famous case where a grandson, overeager to get the remainder interest set up for him in his grandfather's will, murdered his grandsire. After the will had been probated, two daughters of the testator who, under the will, would take if the grandson should predecease testator, sued and got judgment decreeing a constructive trust in their favor. It may be, as respondents assert, that the application of Riggs v. Palmer, supra, here would benefit not plaintiffs, but this testator's distributees. We need not pass on that now. But Riggs v. Palmer, supra, is generally helpful to appellants, since it forbade the grandson profiting by his own wrong in connection with a will; and, despite an already probated will and the Decedent Estate Law, Riggs v. Palmer, supra, used the device or formula of constructive trust to right the attempted wrong, and prevent unjust enrichment. . . .

This suit cannot be defeated by any argument that to give plaintiffs judgment would be to annul those provisions of the Statute of Wills requiring due execution by the testator. Such a contention, if valid, would have required the dismissal in a number of the suits herein cited. The answer is in Ahrens v. Jones, 169 N.Y. 555, 561, 62 N.E. 666, 668, 88 Am. St. Rep. 620, supra: " 'The trust does not act directly upon the will by modifying the gift, for the law requires wills to be wholly in writing; but it acts upon the gift itself as it reaches the possession of the legatee, or as soon as he is entitled to receive it. The theory is that the will has full effect by passing an absolute legacy to the legatee, and that then equity, in order to defeat fraud, raises a trust in favor of those intended to be benefited by the testator, and compels the legatee, as a trustee ex maleficio, to turn over the gift to them.' "

The judgment of the Appellate Division, insofar as it dismissed the complaint herein, should be reversed, and the order of Special Term affirmed, with costs in this court and in the Appellate Division.

Loughran, C.J., and Conway and Fuld, JJ., concur with Desmond, J.

Lewis and Dye, JJ., dissent and vote for affirmance upon the grounds stated by Vaughan, J., writing for the Appellate Division.[15]

---

[15] Noted 35 Cornell L.Q. 654; 63 Harv. L. Rev. 108; 48 Mich. L. Rev. 1048; 34 Minn. L. Rev. 80; and 1 Syracuse L. Rev. 146. — Eds.

POPE v. GARRETT, 147 Tex. 18, 211 S.W.2d 559 (1948): Carrie Simons, who was very ill, asked her neighbor to have a will prepared for her leaving all her property to her friend Claytonia Garrett. When the will was brought to Carrie for signing, some, but not all, of her expectant heirs "by physical force or by creating a disturbance, prevented her from carrying out her intention to execute the will." Shortly after this incident Carrie suffered a severe hemorrhage and lapsed into a coma; she died four days later without having recovered from the coma. The court imposed a constructive trust in favor of Claytonia not only on the heirs who had participated in the disturbance but also on the innocent heirs. The court reasoned that the innocent heirs would be unjustly enriched if they were permitted to keep the property, since but for the wrongful acts they would have inherited nothing.

3. *Killers of the Decedent*

UNITED TRUST CO. v. PYKE
Supreme Court of Kansas, 1967
199 Kan. 1, 427 P.2d 67

FATZER, Justice. This appeal involves claims of inheritance, joint tenancy survivorship, and proceeds under life insurance contracts in the estates of two decedents, Isaac Pyke and Della Pyke, husband and wife, and to collect damages for the wrongful death of Della by the alleged willful and intentional shooting of her by Isaac, who then committed suicide.

Actions were filed by the administrators of both estates in the probate and district courts of Dickinson County to obtain an award and distribution of the property claimed to belong to the respective decedents' estates. Claims filed in the probate court were transferred to and consolidated with those filed in the district court. (K.S.A. 59-2402a and 59-2402b.) A trial was had by the district court which made findings of fact, and rendered judgment in favor of Delbert V. Pyke, administrator of Isaac's estate. The plaintiff, The United Trust Company, administrator of Della's estate, has appealed.

Isaac and Della Pyke had been married for many years and resided in Abilene; they were childless, and both died intestate. Isaac was 85 years of age and was of sound mind and body. Della was 79 years of age and was of sound mind, but was physically impaired in that she had chronic leukemia (cancer of the blood), and adeno carcinoma (cancer of the throat glands) for which she had been hospitalized prior to her death. She also had a left facial paralysis preventing her closing her eyelid and a blindfold was placed over her eyes when she slept. Her personal physician and two doctors testified they could not say with reasonable medical certainty what effect, if any, her physical impairments had on her normal life expectancy.

Isaac was last seen alive about 7:30 P.M., September 5, 1962, when he walked to the home of a neighbor, Clara Rhodes, and asked her to come by the next morning and drive Della and him to a doctor in Salina. Isaac told Clara "she needn't knock," but to "come right in." When Clara arrived the following morning, September 6, 1962, at about 7:50 A.M. she called to Isaac. Receiving no answer, she went into the Pyke home and found Isaac's body lying on the kitchen floor. She immediately telephoned the police, and waited outside until they arrived. The police found both Isaac and Della dead at about 8:00 A.M. on September 6, 1962.

On October 4, 1962, Della's estate was admitted to probate, and the plaintiff-appellant, The United Trust Company, was appointed administrator. On June 28, 1963, the plaintiff filed identical petitions in the probate and district courts, alleging that Della survived Isaac and that all the property (their residence, certain jointly and separately owned stocks, bonds and checking accounts, and various life insurance proceeds) should be awarded and distributed to the heirs at law of Della. It was also alleged that in the event the time of death could not be established, all of the property should be awarded and distributed in accordance with the simultaneous death statute. (K.S.A. 58-701 et seq.) A second cause of action alleged that Della's death was the result of the willful acts of Isaac and that his estate was liable to Della's estate in the amount of $25,000.

On October 5, 1962, Isaac's estate was admitted to probate and the defendant-appellee, Delbert V. Pyke, was appointed administrator. The petition for administration alleged that Isaac was unmarried at the time of his death; that his wife, Della, had predeceased him, and that his only surviving heirs at law were his brothers and the nieces and nephews stated therein. On July 3, 1963, Delbert V. Pyke, as administrator of Isaac's estate filed identical petitions in the probate and district courts, repeating the allegation that Isaac had survived the death of Della, and praying that the property in issue be surrendered and awarded to the administrator of Isaac's estate. . . .

[T]he district court found that Isaac shot Della sometime between 8:30 P.M. on September 5, 1962, and 7:50 A.M. on September 6, 1962, and that Della predeceased Isaac. It also concluded the simultaneous death statute (K.S.A. 58-701 et seq.) was not applicable, and rejected the theory of constructive trust, finding no foundation for it in the case law or the statutes of Kansas. In a post-trial motion, the plaintiff requested the district court to expressly find that Isaac intentionally inflicted the fatal injuries upon Della, without legal justification, but the court specifically refused to make such finding. . . .

The facts that form the circumstantial and indirect evidence of the manner in which Della was killed by Isaac are essentially undisputed. The parties are agreed that a summary of those facts and the inferences to be logically drawn therefrom, may be stated as follows: Between the hours of 8:30 P.M. on September 5, and 7:50 A.M. on September 6, 1962, Isaac and Della were alone in their home in Abilene. Some time during this span of time (the exact time being completely immaterial), Isaac took an H & R .22 caliber revolver to the bedroom of his wife. Della was asleep at the time with a blindfold over her eyes. Isaac then proceeded to fire three bullets into Della's forehead and two bullets into the left temporal region, one above the ear and one above and behind the ear. Isaac then proceeded out of the bedroom, through the living room, through the dining room, and into the kitchen, a distance estimated at 35 to 40 feet. Isaac then emptied the spent cartridges from the revolver into the wastebasket in the kitchen, removed fresh cartridges from a box of shells on the kitchen table and reloaded the empty chambers in the revolver. At some time thereafter, Isaac shot himself once near the center of his forehead with the revolver.

The medical testimony with respect to the relative time of death of Della and Isaac is set forth at length in the record. Dr. Weber's report to counsel, which was introduced in evidence, states:

> "It is my opinion that Mrs. Pyke died almost immediately following the shooting. My opinion is based upon the extensive injury to the brain found at the autopsy. The brain injury is more extensive than that found in Mr. Pyke's brain. It is my opinion that Mrs. Pyke died before Mr. Pyke and any other interpretation would be improbable."

Dr. Carter testified that Della died almost instantaneously after five bullets had been shot into her head and that he could be reasonably medically certain she died prior to Isaac. It is evident there was ample evidence to support the finding that Della predeceased Isaac.

Likewise, the Kansas simultaneous death statute (K.S.A. 58-701 et seq.) is not applicable where there is "sufficient evidence that the persons concerned have died otherwise than simultaneously." Based upon the record, we are of the opinion the district court's conclusion of law that the foregoing statute was not applicable to the facts of this case was correct, and there is nothing to warrant a reversal of that conclusion.

The plaintiff strenuously contends the district court erred in refusing to find that Isaac intentionally and willfully inflicted the fatal injuries upon Della. . . .

It is conceded there was no charge, accusation, trial or conviction of Isaac for any felonious killing arising out of the occurrence which is the subject of this litigation. We do not speculate as to reasons why the district court refused to make the requested finding, except to say it was aware Isaac had not been convicted of feloniously killing Della, and had such a finding been made, it would have been contrary to some of our more traditionally poignant principles of justice. Deeply rooted in our system of jurisprudence is the principle that one cannot be tried in absentia, and this court has yet to sanction the practice of trying a man in his grave for the commission of a crime. (Bill of Rights, §10.) Furthermore, such a finding would have been immaterial, and contrary to the public policy of this state as declared in K.S.A. 59-513 which reads: "No person who shall be convicted of feloniously killing, or procuring the killing of, another person shall inherit or take by will or otherwise from such other person any portion of his estate."

. . .

As enacted in 1939, K.S.A. 59-513 modifies the statutes of descent and distribution and bars the wrongdoer from taking by inheritance or otherwise from a person feloniously killed by him, but makes conviction of the offense a condition precedent to the operation of the bar of the statute. The statute was applied in Rosenberger v.

Northwestern Mutual Life Ins. Co., D.C., 182 F. Supp. 633, where it was said the only inquiry for a court in a civil action by a widow who had been convicted of fourth degree manslaughter of involuntarily killing her husband, was whether the conviction was for a degree of homicide wherein intent to kill was a necessary ingredient. It was held that conviction of fourth degree manslaughter was not a felonious killing making the bar of the statute operative. We do not pass upon the correctness of the federal court's application of K.S.A. 59-513. Since Isaac was not charged, tried or convicted of any offense, it is unnecessary to determine what criminal homicides are included in the term "feloniously killing" as used in the statute, and we leave the question open.

The right to succeed to property as a surviving joint tenant is another field and subject matter pre-empted by the legislature. The same legislature which enacted K.S.A. 59-513, also enacted The Property Act of 1939. The first section of that Act, K.S.A. 58-501, amended and clarified G.S. 1935, 22-132 so as to apply to both real and personal property in harmony with opinions of the court construing the section. In 1951 the legislature enacted what is now K.S.A. 59-2286. By these statutes the legislature has provided for the creation and termination of estates in joint tenancy and the requirements necessary for succeeding to such property by right of survivorship. The statutes were applied in In re Estate of Foster, 182 Kan. 315, 320 P.2d 855, and it was said that in none of them has the legislature seen fit to limit or restrict the right of a surviving joint tenant to succeed to the property because of criminal conduct on his part, and it was held:

> The distinctive characteristic of joint tenancy is survivorship, and a surviving joint tenant of real property does not take as a new acquisition under the laws of descent and distribution, but under the conveyance by which the joint tenancy was created, his estate merely being freed from participation of the other.
>
> A husband and wife owned real estate as "joint tenants with right of survivorship and not as tenants in common." He killed her and was convicted of second degree murder. A dispute arose concerning whether the husband, as surviving joint tenant, succeeded to the entire interest in the property so owned, or whether he was barred by the provisions of G.S. 1949, 59-513, which reads:
>
> "No person who shall be convicted of feloniously killing, or procuring the killing of, another person shall inherit or take by will or otherwise from such other person any portion of his estate."
>
> *Held:* For reasons fully set forth in the opinion, the statute is inapplicable, and the husband, as surviving joint tenant, succeeded to the entire interest in the property in question. (Syl. ¶¶1, 2.)

In view of the foregoing, and the plaintiff's concession the provisions of K.S.A. 59-513 are not applicable since Isaac was not convicted of feloniously killing Della, we conclude the property owned by Della passed to Isaac in three different ways. First, the title to the residence in Abilene and nine shares of corporate stock having a combined appraised value of approximately $8,900, was in Della. Under the applicable law of descent and distribution, this property was inherited by Isaac as the surviving spouse of Della, pursuant to K.S.A. 59-504. (McAllister v. Fair, supra; Hogg v. Whitham, supra.) Second, at the time of their death, Della and Isaac owned property as joint tenants with right of survivorship and not as tenants in common, of the approximate value of $44,321, consisting of Series "E" United States Savings Bonds and checking accounts. Upon Della's death, Isaac became the surviving joint tenant and sole owner of this property. His ownership of the whole interest did not result from inheritance, but rather from the contracts of acquisition. (In re Estate of Foster, supra.) Third, the total approximate value of the proceeds of life insurance contracts amounted to $9,400. Isaac became entitled to those proceeds under the terms of the contracts and by virtue of his being the survivor or being designated as beneficiary therein. (Noller v. Aetna Life Ins. Co., supra.) The district court properly concluded the property heretofore described and the proceeds of the life insurance policies were owned by the appellee-administrator of Isaac's estate.

The plaintiff forcefully argues that, assuming Isaac's administrator may be the owner of the property in question, the court, in the exercise of its equity power, should impress a constructive trust on the property for the benefit of the victim's heirs, excluding the felonious killer. It is asserted the constructive trust remedy permits the murderer to take the legal title and then declares him trustee of the beneficial title for the heirs of the victim, excluding the killer; that the only possible time the equitable remedy of constructive trust would conflict with K.S.A. 59-513 is when the murderer has been convicted of his crime which then disqualifies him from taking any portion of the victim's estate, and, as applied to the instant case, the application of the equitable remedy would merely supplement the remedy under K.S.A. 59-513, since the statutory remedy does not provide appropriate relief for the intentional killing.

The theory of a constructive trust is merely a method by which this court is asked to by-pass existing rules established by the legislature relating to the descent of property, to succession of estates in joint tenancy, and to life insurance proceeds. Exceptions to those statutes are not to be made or arbitrarily declared by this court. In all our prior decisions, the court has expressed reluctance in enforcing the legislative enactments, but it has followed the laws as enacted by the legislature. The reasoning used by the court has varied, but it may be said that in each case considered, the contention the court should impress a constructive trust was urged in one form or another, and rejected upon the ground the power to declare the rules for the descent, succession or distribution of all property was vested in the legislature, and, where no exception was made on account of criminal conduct, or where the condition creating the bar was not established, this court was not justified in reading into the statutes a clause disinheriting a spouse because of a felonious killing. And so here. In passing, we note that when the legislature has considered conditions barring a convicted felon from taking by inheritance or otherwise from a person feloniously killed by him, it has raised, not lowered, the degree of homicide, and has made no other provision for the descent of property where an intestate married couple has no children and one spouse kills the other, and then commits suicide. In view of the foregoing, we reject the plaintiff's contention the court should impress the property in question with a constructive trust in favor of Della's heirs. . . .

We have fully reviewed the record and finding no reversible error, the judgment of the district court is affirmed.

NOTES

1. In Matter of Bobula, 45 Misc. 2d 745, 257 N.Y.S.2d 645 (1965), John Bobula killed his wife Marian and then committed suicide. The surrogate found that the pair died simultaneously. Under the simultaneous death act, the proceeds of a life insurance policy on John's life, payable to Marian, went to John's estate, and the joint property was divided equally between the estates of John and Marian. The surrogate refused to impose a constructive trust for Marian's estate on the insurance proceeds and joint property because in committing the crime John was not motivated by a desire to profit himself or his estate. The finding of simultaneous death was not appealed, but the holdings with respect to the life insurance and joint property were. The Appellate Division held that a constructive trust for Marian's estate should be imposed on the joint property on the ground that neither the wrongdoer nor his estate should be permitted to profit from his wrong. With respect to the life insurance, the Appellate Division reversed and remanded for findings as to whether John reserved the right to change the beneficiary. Matter of Bobula, 25 App. Div. 2d 241, 269 N.Y.S.2d 599 (1966). Upon further appeal, the Court of Appeals (4 to 3) in a memorandum opinion reversed the Appellate Division and remanded the case to the Surrogate's Court to determine whether the killing occurred under circumstances which would exculpate the killer from criminal liability (e.g., if he were insane). If it be determined that there could be no successful prosecution of John had he lived, then the property should be distributed as originally provided for by the surrogate. Estate of Bobula, 19 N.Y.2d 818, 227 N.E.2d 49, 280 N.Y.S.2d 152 (1967). Burke, J., said in dissent: "The question, as we see it, is not whether John Bobula was *criminally* liable for his wife's death, but rather whether he perpetrated a *wrong* upon her in taking her life whereby he changed and terminated her interest in their jointly owned property. . . . The majority's disposition of this case presents further difficulties: it imposes upon a Surrogate the duty of determining whether John Bobula was *criminally* liable for his wife's death. . . . [T]he Surrogate's Court is not a proper tribunal for such a proceeding."

2. If one joint tenant murders another, and the court agrees to impose a constructive trust on the surviving joint tenant, what should be the terms of the trust? 5 Scott, Trusts §493.2 (3d ed. 1967).

3. Suppose A's will leaves $50,000 to B. B murders A. There is a lapse statute in

the state which provides that if a legatee predeceases the testator the legatee's issue take the bequest. Under the Uniform Probate Code, infra, would B's issue take the $50,000? Cf. McGhee v. Banks, 115 Ga. App. 152, 154 S.E.2d 37 (1967).

4. The rights of a killer in the estate of a victim are usually covered by a state statute. These statutes vary in many details; there is by no means unanimous agreement as to what provisions are desirable. McGovern, Homicide and Succession to Property, 68 Mich. L. Rev. 65 (1969). For a summary of the law, see Turrentine, Wills and Administration, 61-69 (2d ed. 1962).

UNIFORM PROBATE CODE §2-803

(a) A surviving spouse, heir or devisee who feloniously and intentionally kills the decedent is not entitled to any benefits under the will or under this Article, and the estate of decedent passes as if the killer had predeceased the decedent. Property appointed by the will of the decedent to or for the benefit of the killer passes as if the killer had predeceased the decedent.

(b) Any joint tenant who feloniously and intentionally kills another joint tenant thereby effects a severance of the interest of the decedent so that the share of the decedent passes as his property and the killer has no rights by survivorship. This provision applies to joint tenancies [and tenancies by the entirety] in real and personal property, joint accounts in banks, savings and loan associations, credit unions and other institutions, and any other form of co-ownership with survivorship incidents.

(c) A named beneficiary of a bond, life insurance policy, or other contractual arrangement who feloniously and intentionally kills the principal obligee or the person upon whose life the policy is issued is not entitled to any benefit under the bond, policy or other contractual arrangement, and it becomes payable as though the killer had predeceased the decedent.

(d) Any other acquisition of property or interest by the killer shall be treated in accordance with the principles of this section.

(e) A final judgment of conviction of felonious and intentional killing is conclusive for purposes of this section. In the absence of a conviction of felonious and intentional killing the Court may determine by a preponderance of evidence whether the killing was felonious and intentional for purposes of this section.

(f) This section does not affect the rights of any person who, before rights under the section have been adjudicated, purchases from the killer for value and without notice property which the killer would have acquired except for this section, but the killer is liable for the amount of the proceeds or the value of the property. Any insurance company, bank, or other obligor making payment according to the terms of its policy or obligation is not liable by reason of this section unless prior to payment is has received at its home office or principal address written notice of a claim under this section.

Draftsman's Comment

A growing group of states have enacted statutes dealing with the problems covered by this section, and uniformity appears desirable. The section is confined to intentional and felonious homicide and excludes the accidental manslaughter killing.

At first it may appear that the matter dealt with is criminal in nature and not a proper matter for probate courts. However, the concept that a wrongdoer may not profit by his own wrong is a civil concept, and the probate court is the proper forum to determine the effect of killing on succession to property of the decedent. There are numerous situations where the same conduct gives rise to both criminal and civil consequences. A killing may result in criminal prosecution for murder and civil litigation by the murdered person's family under wrongful death statutes. While conviction in the criminal prosecution under this section [is] treated as conclusive on the matter of succession to the murdered person's property, acquittal does not have the same consequences. This is because different considerations as well as a different burden of proof enter into the finding of guilty in the criminal prosecution. Hence it is possible that the defendant on a murder charge may be found not guilty and acquitted, but if the same person claims as an heir or devisee of the decedent, he may in the probate court be found to have feloniously and intentionally killed the decedent and thus be barred under this section from sharing in the estate. An analogy exists in the tax field, where a taxpayer may be acquitted of tax fraud in a criminal prosecution but found to have committed the fraud in a civil proceeding. In many of the cases arising under this section there may be no criminal prosecution because the murderer has committed suicide.

SECTION C. Transfers Prohibited Because of the Nature of the Beneficiary

1. *Gifts to Charity*

In feudal times in England certain feudal incidents (comparable to modern inheritance taxes) were due to the king upon the death of the tenants of land. When land passed into the hands of the church or the monasteries, which never died, the feudal incidents were lost to the Crown. To preserve his revenues and to prevent the church from owning more land, upon which the civil power structure was based, Edward I passed the Statute of Mortmain in 1279. This statute declared that all land thereafter conveyed to the church or monasteries would be forfeited to the king. With great ingenuity the clerics subsequently evaded this statute by developing the conveyance to uses, the earliest forerunner of the modern trust.

The Statute of Mortmain has never been held to be applicable in the American states. Nonetheless, the apprehension of vast wealth held in perpetuity by a church has caused legislatures in some states to pass statutes restricting transfers to charity by gift, by conveyance, or by will. These statutes fall into three types.

(a) Limitation of amount of real or personal property which may be owned. In a few states churches, and sometimes non-religious charities, are limited in the amount of land or personal property they may own.[16] The limitation may be stated in terms of land acreage, or yearly income, or valuation of all property owned.[17] A limitation upon owning farm land has sometimes been extended to non-charitable corporations. (What social objectives are accomplished by prohibiting corporations from owning farm land?) These statutes may be enforced by declaring the transfer void or by providing for escheat to the state.[18]

(b) Limitation of amount of testator's estate which may be devised to charity. Six states have statutes which limit the percentage of testator's estate that he may devise to charity.[19]

(c) Deathbed wills. In eight American jurisdictions there are statutes which prohibit testamentary gifts to charity unless the will is executed more than a designated time (thirty days to one year) before testator's death.[20] Four of these jurisdictions also have statutes of type (b) above, limiting the amount devisable to charity.

Out of the ten jurisdictions having type (b) or type (c) statutes, eight provide that the statutory limitation is effective only if the testator is survived by certain designated relatives, such as spouse or issue. In these eight states the statute is not against charities as such, but rather it is designed to protect testator's family and heirs.

Statutes of type (b) and (c) can be easily circumvented. None of these statutes prohibits inter vivos gifts to charity, even the gift of a man's entire property on his deathbed. Consequently, an inter vivos transfer that removes the property from the testator's probate estate, including an inter vivos revocable trust, will avoid any statutory restriction upon testamentary gifts to charity. The problem here is similar

[16] See 4 Scott, Trusts §362.4 (3d ed. 1967).

[17] E.g., in North Dakota no religious or charitable corporation may hold land valued in excess of $50,000, except such land as is actually used for educational, hospital, charitable, or religious purposes. N.D. Cent. Code §10-28-19 (1960). In North Dakota there also are restrictions on farming by any corporation. See McElroy, North Dakota's Anti-Corporate Farming Act, 36 N.D.L. Rev. 96 (1960).

[18] State v. Spink Hutterian Brethren, 77 S.D. 215, 90 N.W.2d 365 (1958), noted 4 S.D.L. Rev. 157, upheld the constitutionality of a statute prohibiting "the expansion of any activity or power" of any communal corporation. The Hutterian Societies, believing in and living religious communism, are the only communal corporations of any consequence in South Dakota. Their continued purchase of land has caused the spectre of mortmain to rise in that state.

[19] See Atkinson, Wills 135-138 (2d ed. 1953); 6 Powell, Real Property ¶969 (1970). The limitation in New York is one-half; in Georgia, Idaho, Mississippi, and Montana one-third; in Iowa one-fourth.

[20] See authorities cited supra note 19. The eight jurisdictions are Florida, Georgia, Idaho, Mississippi, Montana, Ohio, Pennsylvania, and the District of Columbia. The statutes are collected in Comment, Restrictions on Charitable Testamentary Gifts, 5 Real Prop., Prob. & Trust J. 290 (1970), where it is recommended that all restrictions on the amount or time of charitable devises be eliminated.

to the problem of avoiding a spouse's forced share by inter vivos gifts, discussed in Chapter 9.

Moreover, in many of these states the statutory restriction can be avoided by careful draftsmanship. For example, N.Y. Estates, Powers & Trusts Law §5-3.3 (1967) provides that a devise to charity can be contested only by surviving issue or parents, and they can void the gift only if they would take the property if the gift to charity is invalidated. Hence the statute can be nullified by coupling the gift to charity with a provision that if the gift to charity is ineffective, the property shall go to someone other than issue or parents of the testator. The following provision in a will effectively nullifies the statutory restriction in New York: "If any gift to any charity under this will shall be ineffective, such bequest shall go instead to my friend X."

---

4 SCOTT, TRUSTS §397.2 (3d ed. 1967): "If a devise or bequest is made in trust for a particular charitable purpose and the testator names as trustee an unincorporated charitable association which has no capacity to take title to the property, the trust does not fail, but the court will appoint a trustee to administer the trust. By the great weight of authority the result is the same where a devise or bequest is made to the association directly without mention of the purposes for which the property is given to it. A bequest to such an association is a bequest to be applied to the purposes for which the association is created and is in substance if not in form a bequest in trust for the purposes of the association. It is immaterial that the bequest is in the form of a direct gift to the association and that the association has no capacity to take title to the property given to it."

2. *Gifts to Non-Charitable Associations*

At common law an unincorporated association was not recognized as a legal entity and lacked the capacity to take legal title to property. By statute or decision most states now permit charitable and certain other unincorporated associations to take title. In Estate of Carlson, 9 Cal. App. 3d 479, 88 Cal. Rptr. 229, 41 A.L.R.3d 833 (1970), testator devised his entire estate to the Socialist Labor Party of California, an unincorporated association. California Probate Code §27 permitted testamentary gifts to any corporation and to "unincorporated religious, benevolent or fraternal societies or associations or lodges." The court held that the Socialist Labor Party was not a religious, benevolent, or fraternal association and could not take the estate. In 1970 the Probate Code was amended by striking out the words "religious, benevolent or fraternal." Cal. Acts c. 965, §1 [1970]. Would a devise of property to the Yale Whiffenpoofs[21] or Hog Farm commune[22] be valid under California

[21] "The Whiffenpoofs are a noncharitable, unincorporated association. Each year is a whole new operation with 15 new members. They do not assume the debts of their predecessors but apparently sometimes buy at a discount any albums left over from the previous year and try to sell them at a profit before issuing their own album. Any money earned during the year is divided

Probate Code §27, as it existed before or after the 1970 amendment? See Ford, Dispositions of Property to Unincorporated Non-Profit Associations, 55 Mich. L. Rev. 67, 235 (1956).

In Bacon v. Pianta, (1966) 114 Commonwealth Law Reports 634, noted 40 Australian L.J. 283 (1966), the High Court of Australia held that a bequest "to The Communist Party of Australia for its sole use and benefit" was invalid. The Communist Party of Australia is an unincorporated, non-profit-making, non-charitable association. The court concluded that the bequest was not to the existing members of the Party individually but was a bequest to the members, both present and future, in trust for the purposes of the Party. Thus construed the trust failed because (a) the interests of future members may not vest within the time allowed by the Rule against Perpetuities, and (b) the purposes of the association were not charitable and there were no beneficiaries to enforce the trust. See Hogg, Testamentary Dispositions to Unincorporated Associations, 8 Melbourne U.L. Rev. 1 (1971).

Restatement (Second) of Trusts §119 states, "An unincorporated association has capacity to be the beneficiary of a trust," but a few American cases have refused to sustain trusts for unincorporated non-charitable associations on the ground of absence of beneficiaries to enforce the trust. Professor Scott's view is that such trusts ought to be valid, provided that they cannot continue beyond the period of the Rule against Perpetuities. 2 Scott, Trusts §119 (3d ed. 1967).

---

up among the members or applied to other uses in accordance with the decision of the group. It is my understanding that a new checking account is opened each year.

"I asked their informal historian (George Vaill, Assistant Secretary of the University) what would happen if a testator left the Whiffenpoofs a $50,000 bequest. He said that a call would go out to all living members back to 1908 for a meeting to decide how to regularize their association to put such a bequest to proper use." — Letter to the editors from Professor Elias Clark of Yale.

[22] *Los Angeles Daily Journal, July 6, 1970, p. 1:*

God Does Not Own Farm California Judge Rules

Santa Rosa (UPI) — The Superior Court of Sonoma County ruled Friday that God does not own the Morning Star Ranch.

Lou Gottlieb does, said Judge Kenneth Eymann. And he'd better get it cleaned up fast, the judge ruled, because it's a mess.

Eymann gave Gottlieb, onetime folksinger with the Limeliters, 30 days to remove the hippie-type structures built on the 30-acre ranch since Gottlieb "deeded it to God" last year and opened it to the world's "religious people."

Gottlieb had been ordered before to clear the structure off but said in a memorandum to the court that he could not comply because he was no longer the owner.

The judge ruled the deed, which Gottlieb notarized and which had been reluctantly recorded May 7, 1969, by County Recorder Herbert Snyder, was not valid.

"It is the law of the state that in order for an instrument purporting to be a deed to be operative as such, the grantee designated therein must be a person either natural or artificial, in existence at the time of the conveyance and capable of taking title," the judge said.

Eymann said the ranch is "unfit for human habitation." He gave Gottlieb until July 30 to clean it up.

Gottlieb had been in trouble with county authorities for two years because of the living quarters improvised by his hippie friends.

When he signed the ranch over to the Deity last year, he said he would continue to pay the property taxes, however.

"It's preposterous to pay taxes for God," he said. "But for God's sake I'll pay them."

3. *Gifts to Aliens*

In feudal times landowners wielded great power, and hence an alien could not inherit land as an heir. Any conveyance or devise of land to an alien was forfeited to the Crown, at the king's pleasure. These common law disabilities of aliens have generally been followed in the United States, except as they have been removed by statute.[23] In about one-half the states there are statutes removing the disabilities of aliens under various circumstances and frequently drawing distinctions between resident and nonresident aliens. As to personal property, aliens were under no disability at common law and are under none in the United States today, except insofar as they are affected by a reciprocity or impounding statute.[24]

Reciprocity and impounding statutes were enacted prior to and during World War II and were applied to communist countries with such zeal that Professor Heyman dubbed them "Iron Curtain" statutes.[25] Reciprocity statutes provide for escheat of property devised or bequeathed to, or inherited by, nonresident aliens unless the alien's country grants reciprocal rights of inheritance to United States citizens or unless the foreign heirs will receive the property without confiscation. Impounding statutes permit a court to impound property left to a nonresident alien if it is shown that such person would not have the benefit or use of the property. In Zschernig v. Miller, 389 U.S. 429 (1968), the Supreme Court held that the Oregon reciprocity statute, as applied, was unconstitutional as an intrusion by the state into the field of foreign affairs, which was solely the concern of the federal government.[26]

Mr. Justice Douglas, speaking for the court, said:

> This provision came into Oregon's law in 1951. Prior to that time the rights of aliens under the Oregon statute were defined in general terms of reciprocity, similar to the California Act which we had before us in Clark v. Allen, 331 U.S., at 506, n. 1.
>
> We held in Clark v. Allen that a general reciprocity clause did not on its face intrude on the federal domain.
>
> . . . At the time Clark v. Allen was decided, the case seemed to involve no more than a routine reading of foreign laws. It now appears that in this reciprocity

[23] See 1 Powell, Real Property, ¶¶101-106 (1970). In Shames v. Nebraska, 323 F. Supp. 1321 (D. Neb. 1971), the plaintiffs, residents of Syria and sole heirs of an intestate owning Nebraska land, sued to enjoin enforcement of Nebraska statutes barring nonresident aliens from inheriting Nebraska land and providing for escheat when there were no resident citizens or aliens capable of inheriting. A three-judge federal court upheld the statutes and refused to issue an injunction. The court held the statutes did not constitute an intrusion by the state into the federal government's field of foreign affairs and were not unconstitutional under the due process and equal protection clauses. See Comment, Nonresident Alien Inheritance of Nebraska Land: 1854-1971, 4 Creighton L. Rev. 304 (1971).

[24] Approximately one-third of the states now have such statutes. Fallwell, State Probate Laws and Alien Heirs — The Zschernig Legacy, 21 Baylor L. Rev. 450, 453 (1969).

[25] Heyman, The Non-Resident Alien's Right to Succession Under the "Iron Curtain" Rule, 52 Nw. U.L. Rev. 221 (1957).

[26] The Oregon statute was repealed by [1969] Ore. Acts c. 591, §305.

area under inheritance statutes, the probate courts of various States have launched inquiries into the type of governments that obtain in particular foreign nations — whether aliens under their law have enforceable rights, whether the so-called "rights" are merely dispensations turning upon the whim or caprice of government officials, whether the representation of consuls, ambassadors, and other representatives of foreign nations is credible or made in good faith, whether there is in the actual administration in the particular foreign system of law any element of confiscation.

. . . It seems inescapable that the type of probate law that Oregon enforces affects international relations in a persistent and subtle way. The practice of state courts in withholding remittances to legatees residing in Communist countries or in preventing them from assigning them is notorious. The several States, of course, have traditionally regulated the descent and distribution of estates. But those regulations must give way if they impair the effective exercise of the Nation's foreign policy.

In Estate of Kish, 52 N.J. 454, 246 A.2d 1 (1968), the court held that the New Jersey impounding statute had been unconstitutionally applied in the past, but held the statute valid "to the extent that shares of foreign beneficiaries may be ordered withheld and deposited in court when transmission or delivery is prohibited by our federal government or where it is clear that receipt or use is forbidden or made impossible by the law of the beneficiary's country, in whatever form such law may take under that nation's governmental or jurisprudential system, to be ascertained by what Mr. Justice Douglas referred to as 'a routine reading of foreign laws.' "

In Bjarsch v. Di Falco, 314 F. Supp. 127 (S.D.N.Y. 1970), a three-judge federal district court held that New York's impounding statute (N.Y. Sur. Ct. Proc. Act §2218) was not unconstitutional on its face and that the only reported post-Zschernig construction of the statute (Matter of Leikind, 22 N.Y.2d 346, 239 N.E.2d 550 (1968)) did not show unconstitutional application.

These reciprocity and impounding statutes have now been construed by most state courts to permit residents of communist countries to inherit. See Note, Rights of Alien Beneficiaries in the Post-Zschernig Era, 16 N.Y.L.F. 889 (1970).

In re ESTATE OF DANILCHENKO, 37 App. Div. 2d 587, 323 N.Y.S.2d 150 (1971). Testatrix died leaving a net residuary estate of $450,000. Her will devised the residue in equal shares to a brother, seventy-six, and a sister, seventy-two, living in the Soviet Union, and named Irving Trust Company executor. The will further provided: "If, at my death, it shall appear, to my Executor in its sole and uncontrolled judgment, that . . . [my brother or sister] would not, because of residence in a foreign country or state, have the benefit or use or control of the money or other property if distributed to him or her, I direct that he or she shall be deemed to have predeceased me, and I further direct that any share or portion of my estate which shall not be effectively disposed of . . . [under the residuary clause] shall be paid over in equal shares to . . . [named charitable organizations]." The executor employed Professor Harold Berman of the Harvard Law School to visit the brother and sister in the Soviet Union, to estimate what would be the practical consequences of sending this large estate to the Soviet heirs, both of whom were living in relatively humble circumstances, and to determine whether such a large gift would be so embarrassing to the heirs that they would relinquish a substantial portion of the bequest to Soviet public agencies and charities. Professor Berman reported that $40,000 sent to the sister would enable her to live comfortably for the next ten years and would not so conspicuously change her style of living as to embarrass her. The brother's statement of what he would do with the money "is comparable to Tevye, the milkman, singing 'If I Were a Rich Man,' a fantasy of building many houses for himself and for many others, and similar illusionary acquisitions." 323 N.Y.S.2d 158 (dissenting opinion). The executor decided that the Soviet beneficiaries could have the benefit or use of the legacies. The surrogate upheld the executor's decision, finding that it was made in good faith and that §2218 of the Surrogate's Court Procedure Act did not bar payment of the bequests. Upon appeal, the surrogate's decision was affirmed 3 to 2. The minority thought it was clear that a portion of the legacies could be used by the brother and sister, but that sending the total amount to them was an improvident exercise of discretion.

SECTION D. Disposition of Decedent's Body

Until the twentieth century an Englishman had no power to direct disposition of his body at death. The reason given for this rule was that there was no property in a dead body. As Lord Justice Kay said in the leading case of Williams v. Williams:[27]

> Several legal points have been raised, on which I have not felt a moment's doubt, and which I will dispose of in the first instance. It is quite clearly the law of this country that there can be no property in the dead body of a human being. . . .
>
> It follows that a man cannot by will dispose of his dead body. If there be no property in a dead body it is impossible that by will or any other instrument the body can be disposed of.

The proposition never doubted by His Lordship rests upon some dubious dicta of Lord Coke and some questionable reading of early cases by Sir William Blackstone.[28] More important, it begs the question to say that there is no right to dispose because there is no property in a cadaver. This is simply to say there is no right to dispose because the court refuses to recognize such a right.

Why did the English courts refuse to give effect to a decedent's wishes respecting disposition of his body? The answer is not hard to find. During the reign of William the Conqueror the law courts abdicated jurisdiction over burials to the ecclesiastical courts. Disposition of bodies was regarded as a matter of "sentiment and superstition," a dominion left to ecclesiastical courts. In America some courts

[27] 20 Ch. Div. 659 (1881).

[28] See Jackson, The Law of Cadavers 125-129 (2d ed. 1950).

followed the English rule; most courts, however, exercised a benevolent discretion and attempted to carry out the decedent's wishes if they were reasonable and equitable.[29]

With the advent of cadaver organ transplantation the first principle of law, medicine, and ethics — saving human life — became a relevant consideration in the disposition of the dead. To increase the quantity of cadaver organs for transplantation almost all states have enacted the Uniform Anatomical Gift Act, verbatim or in some modified version. This act permits a person to give his body to any hospital, physician, medical school, or body bank for research or transplantation. It also permits a gift of a body, or parts thereof, to any specified individual for therapy or transplantation needed by him. The gift can be made by a duly executed will or by a card carried on the person if the card is "signed by the donor in the presence of two witnesses who must sign the document in his presence." [30] Section 6 of the Uniform Anatomical Gift Act provides for methods of revoking the gift:

> *Section 6.* [*Amendment or Revocation of the Gift.*]
>
> (a) If the will, card, or other document or executed copy thereof, has been delivered to a specified donee, the donor may amend or revoke the gift by:
>
> (1) the execution and delivery to the donee of a signed statement, or
>
> (2) an oral statement made in the presence of 2 persons and communicated to the donee or
>
> (3) a statement during a terminal illness or injury addressed to an attending physician and communicated to the donee, or
>
> (4) a signed card or document found on his person or in his effects.
>
> (b) Any document of gift which has not been delivered to the donee may be revoked by the donor in the manner set out in subsection (a), or by destruction, cancellation, or mutilation of the document and all executed copies thereof.
>
> (c) Any gift made by a will may also be amended or revoked in the manner provided for amendment or revocation of wills, or as provided in subsection (a).

PROBLEMS

If organs are to be transplanted after death, the transplant surgeons must be able to establish quickly and conclusively that the gift ceremony has been properly performed and that the document has not been revoked. What ritual and eviden-

[29] In Holland v. Metalious, 105 N.H. 290, 198 A.2d 654, 7 A.L.R.3d 742 (1964), the will of Grace Metalious, the author of Peyton Place, forbade funeral services and gave her body to Dartmouth School of Medicine. Dartmouth declined the gift, and the court refused to enjoin funeral services by the family.

Jean Tanburn, who successfully defied the marriage restrictions imposed by her great-grandfather's trust (In re Rosenthal's Will, 307 N.Y. 715, 121 N.E.2d 539 (1954), infra page 651), was not successful in her bid to dispose of her father's remains contrary to his wishes. The court thought it relevant that Jean was "haughty" and had rebuked her father, telling him that he was acting "like a cheap adolescent instead of a decent father" when he brought his mistress to resorts frequented by herself and her mother. Feller v. Universal Funeral Chapel, 124 N.Y.S.2d 546 (1953).

[30] Uniform Anatomical Gift Act §4(a).

tiary problems may arise under the Uniform Act? Consider the following problems:

(1) T duly executes a card donating his body to the County Hospital. Subsequently he writes a will which states that he revokes all prior wills. At T's death the card is found in his wallet. Is the gift revoked?

(2) T duly executes a donation card. The card is carried in his wallet for several years and at death it is found that the card has been separated at the fold into two pieces. Is the gift revoked?

(3) T signs a donation card when he enters the hospital. The witnesses are two employees of the hospital. Is the gift good? [31]

(4) In his physician's office in the presence of his wife W, T signs a card donating his body to the County Hospital. Nurse A witnesses T's signature; then she takes the card to a back room where, outside of T's presence, Bookkeeper B witnesses T's signature. Nurse A then returns the card to T and tells him that everything has been taken care of. T dies. Before T's organs are removed W objects to removal and tells the transplant surgeons what happened in the physician's office. A quick check with a lawyer produces an opinion that the document is invalid. The surgeons do not remove the organs. Is the nurse liable to the County Hospital and, if so, on what theory and in what amount? Dukeminier, Supplying Organs for Transplantation, 68 Mich. L. Rev. 811, 827, n. 53 (1970). Is the physician liable? Toth v. Community Hospital, 22 N.Y.2d 255, 292 N.Y.S.2d 440, 239 N.E.2d 368 (1968), held that a physician may be liable to patients for failure to supervise adequately the implementation of his directions by nurses.

One important question concerning the Uniform Act is whether it will ease the shortage of organs by enrolling enough donors. People have psychological barriers to making wills, and carrying around a donation card might raise fearful anxieties of one's own death.[32] The best donors are young persons who die accidentally or from a heart attack or brain tumor; they are also the ones who think the least about death and the need for wills or donation cards.

If the Uniform Anatomical Gift Act fails to supply a sufficient quantity of organs for transplantation, what are the alternatives? A Note, Compulsory Removal of Cadaver Organs, 69 Colum. L. Rev. 693, 703-705 (1969), suggests that statutes should authorize the compulsory removal of cadaver organs. The ethical basis for this proposal is that neither a dead person nor his next of kin should have the power to deny a lifesaving resource, such as a kidney, to another. Would "nationalization

[31] Officers of a charitable corporation to which a gift has been made have been held to be incompetent subscribing witnesses, while employees of a private corporation to which a gift has been made have been held competent. 2 Page, Wills §19.100 (Bowe-Parker rev. 1960). Now you figure that one out.

[32] "Our own death is indeed unimaginable, and whenever we make the attempt to imagine it we can perceive that we really survive as spectators. Hence . . . at bottom no one believes in his own death, or to put the same thing in another way, in the unconscious every one of us is convinced of his own immortality." Freud, Our Attitude Towards Death, in 4 Collected Papers 304 (1925).

of the dead" require compensation for property taken? Would it be unconstitutional as an interference with First Amendment rights?

Another solution to the problem of an inadequate quantity of cadaver organs for transplantation would be to rewrite the law in favor of the living. A statute could authorize the removal of cadaver organs for transplantation unless, before removal, an objection had been entered, either by the decedent during his life or by his next of kin after the decedent's death. This "implied consent" or "opting out" approach would overcome any First Amendment objections to removal of cadaver organs. By making the basic presumption one which favors life, and by putting the burden of objecting upon persons who would deny life to another, the policy of saving human life is given first priority and the wishes of persons to preserve a corpse inviolate are also accommodated. In several European countries cadaver organs may be removed without permission of the family if the person dies in a hospital authorized to perform transplantation operations.[33]

Routine salvaging of usable cadaver organs unless there is objection has been widely debated in England. It was first proposed in that country by Lord Kilbrandon.[34] A bill to authorize removal of cadaver kidneys if no objection is lodged was introduced in Parliament in 1968, and a bill to authorize removal of any transplantable organ if no objection is lodged was introduced in 1969 by the leading Catholic layman Norman St. John Stevas, M.P. These private bills failed because the government took the position that the public was not yet ready for routine salvaging.

In 1968 in the New England Journal of Medicine one of the editors, together with Dr. David Sanders of Cedars-Sinai Medical Center, proposed routine salvaging of cadaver organs unless a prior objection is registered. This proposal brought the following delicious riposte.

ANTHROPOPHAGY: SWIFT REPRISAL

279 New England Journal of Medicine 890 (1968)

To the Editor: As the author, some time ago, of a certain modest proposal,[35] I find that the recent essay,[36] "Salvaging of Cadaver Organs," has presented, to my edification and delight, the prospect of an abundant annual harvest from (definably) dead bodies of gratifying numbers of "usable" kidneys, hearts and other viscera, no longer consigned to futile decay.

My enthusiasm is such that I have been moved to wonder whether the same arguments and approach might not, with a little imagination, be extended to the

[33] Dukeminier, Supplying Organs for Transplantation, 68 Mich. L. Rev. 811, 838 (1970).

[34] CIBA Foundation Symposium: Ethics in Medical Progress 213 (1966). See also Daube, Transplantation: Acceptability of Procedures and the Required Legal Sanctions, id. at 188; Kennedy, Alive or Dead? in Current Legal Problems 102, 120 (Keeton & Schwarzenburger ed. 1969).

[35] Swift, J. Modest Proposal for Preventing the Children of the Poor People from Being a Burden to their Parents or the Country. 1729.

[36] Dukeminier, J., Jr., & Sanders, D. Organ transplantation: proposal for routine salvaging of cadaver organs. New Eng. J. Med. 279: 413-419, 1968.

solution of a social and medical problem even more portentous than those of end-stage uremia, congestive heart failure and so forth. I refer to the vast suffering and annual thousands of premature deaths occasioned by protein malnutrition.

Although I would not pretend that, either for sophistication or for enduring benefit, a kidney stew could successfully compete with the transplanted organ, nevertheless, when the problems of supply and demand are placed in perspective, I am sure that the following arguments will commend themselves to you.

> Recently, the use for transplantation of kidneys, heart, lung and pancreas from a single cadaver was so impressive for its economy. "Waste not want not." In my proposal, not only could all these be salvaged, but also liver, intestines, spleen, bone marrow, muscles even brain — indeed, almost the whole of the otherwise useless cadaver.
>
> The problem of skilled personnel and equipment would be so much the less, able butchers and cooks being so much more numerous than surgeons, and cleavers and pots than equipped operating rooms. The advantage in undeveloped countries needs no emphasis.
>
> With this form of introduction into living persons of the remnants of the dead the problem of immunologic rejection could be readily solved. By enzymatic attack upon the whole proteins, antigenicity could be removed. It should be possible, without elaborate equipment, to employ the in situ enzymatic apparatus of the digestive tracts of the recipients for this purpose. With the elimination of the need for immunologic matching, the number of potential donors would be vastly increased.
>
> The exact definition of the moment of death would become less critical. Although I do not doubt that freshness would still be important, the urgency would be removed.

I am not insensible that the unthinking mob may cry, "Why this, Sir, is cannibalism!" Surely, we who believe in progress should not be dissuaded by appeals to outmoded legalisms and superstitions. We will keep in mind your authors' repeated assurances that the preservation of life is a primary good.

Recognizing that neither the route of introduction, nor the form of particular cadaver moieties is an ethically or scientifically important distinction, any objection could easily be met with such safeguards as those proposed by your authors — namely, a suitably limited right of objection by involved parties, acceptance of such salvage as routine, thereby sparing the bereaved needless participation in the process of decision. My friend Lemuel Gulliver, noted surgeon and world traveler,[37] assures me that the selection of donors and recipients could properly be left in the hands of the medical profession.

Religious authority, already being, we are told, not averse to one form of use of the dead, should not long withhold its approval from another.

Your Obedient Servant,
Jonathan Swift

Elysian Fields, Paradise 00000

[37] Gulliver, L. Travels into Several Remote Nations of the World. 1726.

Come to think of it, what *is* the difference between a starving man eating human flesh to stay alive and a doctor inserting a cadaver heart or kidney in an otherwise dying patient? Is it that eating is pleasurable and a surgical operation painful, or is there some more satisfactory distinction?

Should sales of cadaver organs be prohibited? Suppose a young man, with dependents, dying of a brain tumor, agrees to exchange all his cadaver organs for free medical and hospital services to him during his life. Or suppose the surviving spouse gives the decedent's kidneys in exchange for a certificate entitling her and her children to a kidney if one of them ever needs it (similar to blood insurance plans). Should these exchanges be prohibited? Dukeminier, Supplying Organs for Transplantation, 68 Mich. L. Rev. 811, 847-866 (1970). What would be the income, estate, and gift tax consequences of these exchanges? Sanders & Dukeminier, Medical Advance and Legal Lag: Hemodialysis and Kidney Transplantation, 15 U.C.L.A.L. Rev. 357, 391 (1968).

Who should determine who should receive the available cadaver organs, applying what standards? Should selection between two persons of equal medical suitability be made by random selection, a social worth judgment, or the market place? The ethical and legal issues involved in allocation of scarce lifesaving resources are unusually refractory. See Abram & Wadlington, Selection of Patients for Artificial and Transplanted Organs, 69 Ann. Intern. Med. 615 (1968); Dukeminier & Sanders, Legal Problems in Allocation of Scarce Medical Resources, 127 Arch. Intern. Med. 1133 (1971); Note, Scarce Medical Resources, 69 Colum. L. Rev. 620 (1969); Note, Patient Selection of Artificial and Transplanted Organs, 82 Harv. L. Rev. 1322 (1969).

SECTION E. Interference with Conduct of Beneficiaries

UNITED STATES NATIONAL BANK v. SNODGRASS

Supreme Court of Oregon, 1954
202 *Ore.* 530, 275 *P.2d* 860, 50 A.L.R.*2d* 725

[In 1929, when his daughter Merle was ten years old, C. A. Rinehart executed a will creating a testamentary trust for the benefit of Merle and others. Rinehart died in 1932. The terms of the trust provided for payments of the income to Merle until she reached thirty-two years of age, when the trustee was directed to distribute the trust estate to Merle "provided she shall have proved conclusively to my trustee and to its entire satisfaction that she has not embraced, nor become a member of, the Catholic faith nor ever married to a man of such faith. In the event my daughter . . . becomes ineligible to receive the trust fund then I direct the principal of such trust fund to be divided" among testator's mother, sisters, nephews, and nieces living in South Carolina. It was stipulated that Merle reached the age of thirty-two in 1951, and that at age twenty-four she had married a man, named Snodgrass, who was a member of the Catholic faith but she had not herself become a member of the Catholic faith. Upon the trustee's suit for instructions the lower court upheld the provision in the will and decreed forfeiture of Merle Rinehart Snodgrass' interest in the trust. Merle appeals.]

WARNER, J. . . . The appellant asserts that the court erred in holding as valid that provision of the will which disinherited her because of her marriage to a member of the Catholic faith before she was 32 years old. She leans heavily upon the proposition that such a provision violates public policy.

Mrs. Snodgrass did not join the Catholic church and therefore the clause restraining membership in that faith is not before us. Her loss, if any, accrues by reason of the restriction on her marriage to a Catholic within the time limitation. If the provision is valid, then the defendants-respondents take the entire corpus of the trust set up in the contested paragraph 7, and testator's daughter takes nothing.

The problem here is one of the validity of testamentary restraints upon marriage. While there is an abundance of law on the subject from other jurisdictions, the question and its solution are one of first impression in this court.

The briefs of both parties and some of their citations unavoidably employ various words and phrases which bring into focus the presence of religious prejudice which apparently dictated the contents of the paragraph occasioning this appeal. There we find, among other significant phrases, references to "religious tolerance," "religious freedom" and the "bigotry reflected by the will." No one will venture to gainsay that the father and his daughter in adulthood had entertained antipodal beliefs in the area of religious thought and faith. Indeed, it was the militant hostility of the father to the religion of Mrs. Snodgrass' husband that kindled the flames of the controversy from which this appeal arises.[38] . . .

While one may personally and loudly condemn a species of "intolerance" as socially outrageous, a court on the other hand must guard against being judicially intolerant of such an "intolerance," unless the court can say the act of intolerance is in a form not sanctioned by the law. We are mindful that there are many places where a bigot may safely express himself and manifest his intolerance of the viewpoint of others without fear of legal restraint or punishment. With certain limitations, one of those areas with a wide latitude of sufferance is found in the construction of the pattern of one's last will and testament. It is a field wherein neither this court nor any other court will question the correctness of a testator's religious views or prejudices. In re Lesser's Estate, 158 Misc. 895, 287 N.Y.S. 209, 216. . . .

We therefore have no intention or disposition to disturb the provisions of Mr. Rinehart's will unless it can be demonstrated that they do violence to some legal rule or precept. Two general and cardinal propositions give direction and limitation to our consideration. One is the traditionally great freedom that the law confers on the individual with respect to the disposition of his property, both before and after

[38] No evidence or explanation of Rinehart's hostility to Catholicism, except the words in the will, appears in the record or briefs on appeal. Nor is the religion of Rinehart and his wife disclosed in the record and briefs. — EDS.

death. The other is that greater freedom, the freedom of opinion and right to expression in political and religious matters, together with the incidental and corollary right to implement the attainment of the ultimate and favored objectives of the religious teaching and social or political philosophy to which an individual subscribes. We do not intend to imply hereby that the right to devise or bequeath property is in any way dependent upon or related to the constitutional guarantees of freedom of speech. . . .

No one has had the temerity to suggest that Mr. Rinehart in his lifetime could not have accomplished the equivalent of what he sought to accomplish by his will. It was within his power, with or without assigning any reason therefor, to have completely disinherited his daughter and left her in a state of impecunious circumstances. He could have gone even further and given all his fortune to some institution or persons with directions to propagandize his views adverse to any certain religion or creed for which he harbored antipathies. . . .

To sustain the contention that the contested provision of the will is against the public policy of the United States, appellant depends upon the First and Fourteenth Amendments to the United States Constitution; 42 U.S.C.A. §§1981-1983, relating to civil rights (formerly, and as cited by appellant, 8 U.S.C.A. Ch. 3, §§41-43); and Shelley v. Kraemer, 334 U.S. 1, 68 S. Ct. 836, 92 L. Ed. 1161, 3 A.L.R.2d 441.

The First Amendment prohibits Congress from making any law respecting the establishment of a religion. Everson v. Board of Education, 330 U.S. 1, 15, 67 S. Ct. 504, 91 L. Ed. 711, 168 A.L.R. 1392. That amendment is a limitation upon the power of Congress. It has no effect upon the transactions of individual citizens and has been so interpreted. McIntire v. Wm. Penn Broadcasting Co. of Philadelphia, 3 Cir., 151 F.2d 597, 601, certiorari denied 327 U.S. 779, 66 S. Ct. 530, 90 L. Ed. 1007; In re Kempf's Will, 252 App. Div. 28, 297 N.Y.S. 307, 312, affirmed 278 N.Y. 613, 16 N.E.2d 123. Neither does the Fourteenth Amendment relate to individual conduct. The strictures there found circumscribe state action in the particulars mentioned and in no way bear on a transaction of the character now before us. In re Civil Rights Cases, 1883, 109 U.S. 3, 3 S. Ct. 18, 27 L. Ed. 835. . . .

Shelley v. Kraemer, supra, is authority only for the proposition that the enforcement by state courts of a covenant in a deed restricting the use and occupancy of real property to persons of the Caucasian race falls within the purview of the Fourteenth Amendment as a violation of the equal protection clause, but, said the court, "That Amendment [Fourteenth] erects no shield against merely private conduct, however discriminatory or wrongful." 334 U.S. 1, 68 S. Ct. 842, 3 A.L.R.2d 460. . . .

It is not clear to us from appellant's argument whether she reads the offending provision of the will as an invasion of her constitutional right to religious freedom or views it as an unconstitutional act of discrimination; but whether one or the other, we are content that it does no violence to public policy arising from either category. If the contested portion is to fall, it must be by force of some precept of public policy resting upon different grounds from those here urged by appellant. . . .

The general rule seems to be well settled that conditions and limitations in partial restraint of marriage will be upheld if they do not unreasonably restrict the freedom of the beneficiary's choice. In 35 Am. Jur. 357-358, Marriage, §256, we find:

> . . . where the restraint is not general, but is merely partial or temporary, or otherwise limited in effect, then the condition may or may not be void, according to whether it is considered reasonable or otherwise, and does not operate merely in terrorem.
>
> . . .
>
> Among the restrictions which have been held reasonable are: Conditions to marry or not to marry . . . a person of a particular . . . religion. . . .

Of the same tenor is 1 Restatement, Trusts, 194, §62(g), reading, so far as pertinent:

> . . . such a provision is not invalid if it does not impose an undue restraint on marriage. Thus, a provision divesting the interest of the beneficiary if he or she should marry . . . a person of a particular religious faith or one of a different faith from that of the beneficiary, is not ordinarily invalid.

We turn to an examination of the controverted provision and note that the condition is not one of complete restraint, in which character it might well be abhorrent to the law. It is merely partial and temporary and, as we shall show later, is not in terrorem. Mr. Rinehart's daughter is not thereby restrained from ever marrying a Catholic. This inhibition as a condition to taking under the will at the age of 32 lasts only 11 years, that is, from the legal marriageable age without parental consent (in this state, 21 years). After the age of 32 she is free to marry a Catholic or become a Catholic if she so pleases and have her estate, too. Moreover, the condition imposed does not restrict the beneficiary from enjoying marital status either before or after attaining the age of 32. Here, unfortunately, appellant would eat her cake and have it, too.

In 25 A.L.R. 1523 will be found an ably-edited annotation respecting wills with gifts conditioned that the beneficiary renounce, embrace or adhere to a specified religious faith. At page 1524 the editor makes this statement: "The weight of authority, however, is to the effect that a testator has the right to make the enjoyment of his bounty dependent on the condition that the recipient renounce, embrace, or adhere to a particular religious faith." The following illustrative cases are cited: [Citations to thirteen cases omitted.] . . . To this list we add three more recent cases: Delaware Trust Co. v. Fitzmaurice, 1943, 27 Del. Ch. 101, 31 A.2d 383; In re Kempf's Will, 1937, 297 N.Y.S. 307; In re Lesser's Estate, supra, 1936, 287 N.Y.S.

209. Only three cases to the contrary are found in the annotation and are the only ones employed by the appellant in support of a contrary rule. . . .

In the case of In re Lesser's Estate, supra, the provision of the will construed created a trust for the following purposes, 287 N.Y.S. 211-212:

> To pay said sums to the children, that may survive me, of my son, Max Lesser, on their respective twenty-first birthdays, provided these children are given a normal Jewish, liberal education including an ability to read Hebrew, up to and including at least their fourteenth year: and, further, provided that the Jewish dietary laws are observed by their parents up to and including the confirmation of these my present grandchildren. . . . If these conditions are not complied with to the complete satisfaction of my executor or his successor or successors, then the funds herein bequeathed are to go to the "Federation for the Support of Jewish Philanthropic Societies of New York City". . . .

The objections there raised were disposed of by the court in these words, 287 N.Y.S. 216:

> Conditions involving the personal habits and traits of character of a potential recipient of a testator's bounty have frequently been sustained. [Citing cases.] The conditions here postulated respecting maintenance of the Jewish faith are analogous. The testator has in effect stipulated that to participate in his bounty, his grandchildren must live in the Orthodox Jewish manner which he may have deemed essential for their eternal salvation. It is not for this or any other court or person to question the correctness of his views or prejudices. His evident object was to see to it that the recipients of his bounty adhered at least to the outward manifestations of the religious faith in which he believed. Since they are all infants of tender years, it was obvious that the only method by which their desired faith could be assured would be through the co-operation of their parents. All of the conditions in this regard were conducive to this end and were, indeed, the only conceivable means of attaining it. There is nothing any more contrary to our policy in the requirement of a testator that his beneficiary should espouse and be trained in a certain religious faith, than in a stipulation that he shall marry one of a certain belief, which has been sustained. Matter of Seaman's Will, 218 N.Y. 77, 81, 112 N.E. 576, L.R.A. 1917A, 40, Ann. Cas. 1918B, 1138.

. . .

So far as we are able to ascertain, only two states — Pennsylvania and Virginia — have invalidated testamentary provisions committing the beneficiary to adhere to the doctrines of a particular religion. This departure from the majority rule is reflected by Drace v. Klinedinst, 1922, 275 Pa. 266, 118 A. 907, 25 A.L.R. 1520; and Maddox v. Maddox's Adm'r, 1854, 11 Grat., Va., 804.

The appellant can garner no comfort from the Pennsylvania case wherein the testamentary provision is declared invalid on the basis of an entirely different theory from the one here present. It rests upon a state of facts wholly unlike those apparent in the instant matter. In the Maddox case the condition was that the testator's daughter should marry a member of the Society of Friends. There were only five or six marriageable males of that faith within the circle of her acquaintances, and under the circumstances peculiar to that case the court held that the condition was an unreasonable restraint on marriage.

The last contention of Mrs. Snodgrass requiring consideration is that the offending provision is in terrorem and therefore invalid.

The phrase "in terrorem" is not new to the law of wills, although infrequently applied. It has been defined as "In terror, or warning; by way of threat. The term is applied to gifts or legacies given on conditions subsequent, because it is said that the possibility of losing the gift tends to inspire fear or dread." 42 C.J.S. p. 491. It is a rule designed to test the validity of gifts with certain conditions subsequent.

Generally, conditions in restraint of marriage are said to be in terrorem and therefore invalid when the subject of the gift is personal property and *there is no gift over;* but such a condition is not void as being in terrorem when there is a gift over. It is the absence of a gift over which supplies the quality of a coercive threat necessary to bring the condition under the in terrorem rule. 35 Am. Jur. 367, Marriage, §266. . . .

Affirmed.

Brand, J., dissents.

NOTES AND PROBLEMS

1. Our society permits a person during his life to exercise wide discretion in controlling resources so as to influence the behavior of another person. Does it follow from this that the same control after death should be allowed? Does the fact that C. A. Rinehart is permitted by law to disinherit Merle for any reason he chooses, including a capricious reason such as disapproval of her hair style, by itself support a holding that Rinehart can disinherit her for conduct long *after* his death?

At bottom the validity of the condition imposed by C. A. Rinehart is a question of public policy. It does not rest upon any supposed power of a testator to give away property upon such terms as he may choose to impose. For, of course, the testator has no such power. Only slight reflection is needed to note some of the many actions a person can take during his life, designed to influence behavior of others, which he is not permitted to require other persons to take after his death. Examples: inducing a married person to divorce his spouse, Note, 28 A.L.R.3d 1325 (1968); 1 Scott, Trusts §62.4 (3d ed. 1967); neglecting parental duties, such as forbidding a parent to let his child live with him, 1 id., §62.5; disrupting the family unit, Girard Trust Co. v. Schmitz, 129 N.J. Eq. 444, 20 A.2d 21 (1941) (holding invalid a condition that T's brothers and sisters must shun contacts with a brother and sister T disapproved of); requiring beneficiary to attend certain school, Matter of Carples, 140 Misc. 459, 250 N.Y.S. 680 (1931), Burke v. Burke, [1951] I.R. 216; inducing beneficiary not to enter military service, In re Edgar, [1939] 1 All E.R. 635; inducing beneficiary to procure a peerage, Egerton v. Earl Brownlow, 4 H.L.C.

1 (1853); directing trustee to block up house for twenty years, Brown v. Burdett, 21 Ch. Div. 667 (1882); directing trustee not to erect downtown buildings more than three stories in height, Colonial Trust Co. v. Brown, 105 Conn. 261, 135 A. 555 (1926); conditioning gift upon adding the surname of testator to beneficiary's surname (condition struck down as unreasonable in Cast v. Nat'l Bank of Commerce, 183 N.W.2d 485 (Neb. 1971)). Hence the validity of a condition against marriage to a person of a particular religion does not turn upon what power the donor has, which begs the question. It turns on whether or not such a condition offends public policy.

Our basic social hypothesis is that the totality of values in society (wealth, power, education, well-being, etc.) will be increased by giving wide discretion to private individuals in making decisions respecting the use of wealth. Honoring private volition rests upon an assumption that private individuals will use continuing intelligence in solving problems as they arise and that they will be accountable to the opinions of their relatives and friends for their decisions. What social objectives are accomplished by honoring control of a beneficiary's behavior by the dead hand, a hand which does not have a live mind controlling it and making a continuously informed, intelligent judgment as circumstances change, and which can no longer be affected by the opinions of mankind?

2. Does the restriction imposed by C. A. Rinehart tend to disrupt the relation of parent and infant child by interfering with the parent's right to determine the child's religion? After Rinehart's death who would determine Merle's religion? In Re Blake, [1955] I.R. 89, decedent set up a trust to provide support for his grandchildren, provided that they should be brought up in the Roman Catholic faith, and to pay them the principal on reaching twenty-one if they should have been brought up in that faith. The highest court in Ireland held the condition void as against public policy because it attempted to interfere with the rights of parents to control the religious education of their children. However, the court further held that the condition was a condition precedent and the whole gift failed. But cf. Matter of Kempf, 278 N.Y. 613, 16 N.E.2d 123 (1938) which upheld a condition that the beneficiary be brought up in the Roman Catholic faith.

3. Conditions which tend to induce divorce have been held in many cases to be against public policy. Might the forfeiture provision imposed by C. A. Rinehart tend to induce a divorce? Suppose Merle married a man who was a high Episcopalian (sometimes known as an Anglo-Catholic); after this marriage, and before Merle reached age thirty-two, her husband joined the Roman Catholic Church. Would Merle now be penalized for his conduct? In Holmes v. Conn. Trust & Safe Dep. Co., 92 Conn. 507, 103 A. 640 (1918), testator devised property in trust for his two daughters, provided their husbands abstain from the use of tobacco and liquor. The court held the conditions invalid on the grounds that the beneficiaries would be penalized by conduct out of their control, that the husbands, by threatening noncompliance with the conditions, could figuratively hold a sword over their wives' heads, and that the result might be marital discord and, ultimately, divorce. In Trustees v. Ebbeck, 104 C.L.R. 394 (Aus. 1960), testator provided that

bequests to two of his sons married to Roman Catholics would be forfeited if the wives failed to profess the Protestant faith. The provision was held void as against public policy because it tended to disrupt the family. Would the forfeiture provision in C. A. Rinehart's will give to any non-Catholic husband of Merle an improper control over her or tend to disrupt the marriage?

4. Assume $2000 is given to each of testator's grandchildren who marries a person "of the Greek Orthodox religion." Estate of Keffalas, 426 Pa. 432, 233 A.2d 248 (1967). Testator's granddaughter desires to marry Kelly, who declares that he is of the Greek Orthodox religion. Can a civil court go beyond his personal declaration and determine whether Kelly is of the Greek Orthodox religion? In Presbyterian Church v. Mary Elizabeth Blue Hull Mem. Presbyterian Church, 393 U.S. 440 (1969), the Supreme Court held that in accordance with the First Amendment civil courts could not determine ecclesiastical or doctrinal questions in resolving property disputes between church factions. Cf. Comment, A Reconsideration of the Religious Element in Adoption, 56 Cornell L. Rev. 780, 809-812 (1971).

5. *In re Rosenthal's Will, 307 N.Y. 715, 121 N.E.2d 539 (1954)*. Abraham Rosenthal died in 1938. His will created a trust of $675,000 for the benefit of his daughter Rhea and his grandson Stephen Tanburn. Stephen was given a testamentary power to appoint the corpus of the trust. Rosenthal's will further provided: "In case any child or descendant of mine shall marry a person who was not born in the Jewish faith and who shall not be of Jewish blood, upon such marriage all legacies and devises whether of income or of principal to such child or descendant of mine, so marrying, shall be cancelled, annulled and revoked." In 1952 Stephen Tanburn died. His will appointed income from the Rosenthal trust to his daughter Jean. In 1953 Jean decided to marry a young Princeton graduate by the name of Donelson Morrison Kelley, Jr., who was not of the Jewish faith. She brought suit for a declaratory judgment. Held, 4 to 3: Jean could have both her man and her great-grandfather's money. She was an "appointee," and Rosenthal's will cut off only "legatees" and "devisees."

6. Should a condition providing for forfeiture upon marriage to a person of a stated religion be void for indefiniteness? In Clayton v. Ramsden, [1943] A.C. 320, 1 All E.R. 16, the testator provided for forfeiture of a devise to his daughter if she married "a person who is not of Jewish parentage and of the Jewish faith." The court held the forfeiture condition void for indefiniteness. Lord Romer suggested that parentage meant "Hebraic blood" [39] and that testator had not indicated how much Hebraic blood was required for a permissible husband. He claimed that faith was not totally subjective but nonetheless held that condition void on the ground that testator had not indicated which branch of the Jewish faith was meant.[40] Sub-

[39] Miscegenation statutes, ruled unconstitutional in Loving v. Virginia, 388 U.S. 1 (1967), usually defined "Negro" as a person with some specified fractional amount of "Negro blood," without ever defining "Negro blood." Wadlington, The Loving Case: Virginia's Anti-Miscegenation Statute in Historical Perspective, 52 Va. L. Rev. 1189 (1966). What does Lord Romer mean by "Hebraic blood"? If a Jew receives a blood transfusion using blood from Gentile donors, does he remain a Jew?

[40] Determining who is Jewish has provoked continuing controversy in Israel. Note, Who Is

sequently the English courts have drawn a distinction between religious conditions *precedent* and religious conditions *subsequent*. A much higher degree of certainty is required in the latter case than in the former. For example, a provision that any beneficiary who "shall marry out of the Jewish faith shall [not] take any interest" was held to state a condition precedent or qualification and was held valid,[41] but the same provision stated as a condition subsequent would be void under Clayton v. Ramsden. Even if the provision is a condition precedent, however, it is not easy to predict judicial results. In Re Allen, [1953] 1 All E.R. 308, testator devised real property to the eldest of the sons of B "who shall be a member of the Church of England and an adherent to the doctrine of that church." [42] The condition was held to be precedent and void for uncertainty. Hence the gift failed. The uncertainty doctrine of the English courts was considered and rejected in Gordon v. Gordon, 332 Mass. 197, 124 N.E.2d 228, cert. denied, 349 U.S. 947 (1955), upholding "born in the Hebrew faith."

In Lynch v. Uhlenhopp, 248 Iowa 68, 78 N.W.2d 491 (1956), a divorce decree awarded custody of a five-year-old boy to his mother, a Protestant, and provided that the child "shall be reared in the Roman Catholic Religion." The father was a Roman Catholic. When the father attempted to enforce this provision, it was held void for uncertainty (5 to 4).

SECTION F. Restraints on Alienation

1. *Restraints on Legal Interests*

ANDREWS v. HALL
Supreme Court of Nebraska, 1953
156 Neb. 817, 58 N.W.2d 201

Carter, J. This is a suit for the partition of real estate devised to the plaintiff by her father, N. J. Hall. The appellant, Hilda B. Robinson, is the widow of Frank B. Hall, a son of the testator, N. J. Hall. The only question for determination is whether or not Frank B. Hall, who was devised a one-ninth interest in the real estate here involved, forfeited such interest when he attempted to sell, mortgage, and dispose of his interest in such real estate contrary to the provisions of the will of his father, N. J. Hall. The trial court held that Frank B. Hall had forfeited the

---

a Jew? A Determination of Ethnic Status for Purposes of the Israeli Population Registry Act, 10 Colum. J. Transnational Law 133 (1971).

[41] Re Selby's Will Trusts, [1965] 3 All E.R. 386; Re Abrahams' Will Trusts, [1967] 2 All E.R. 1175.

[42] See Bicknell, Member of the Church of England, 117 New L.J. 933 (1967).

interest in the real estate devised to him under the will of his father, N. J. Hall, and consequently that the appellant, the former wife of Frank B. Hall, acquired no interest therein under a deed from her husband. From a decree so holding, Hilda B. Robinson appeals.

The record shows that N. J. Hall died testate on January 28, 1930. By his will the real estate here involved could not be sold during the life of his wife, Minta A. Hall, the owner of the life estate. The will then provided: "After the death of my wife Minta A. Hall I wish all of my property both personal and real estate devided (divided) share and share alike with my children, with the following understanding that should any of my children during the life of my wife Minta A. Hall attempt to break this will or change the terms stated therein or attempt to sell, mortgage or dispose of their interest in my estate before the death of my wife Minta A. Hall, it is my will that such heir shall forfeit all of his or her share except ten dollars, and that the balance of their share shall be divided share and share alike with the other children."

The answer discloses that Frank B. Hall, during his lifetime and prior to the death of Minta A. Hall, widow of the testator, conveyed his interest in the real estate to his wife, Hilda B. Hall, now Hilda B. Robinson, the appellant. It is the contention of appellant that the provision of the will herein quoted devised an undivided one-ninth interest in and to the real estate involved, in fee simple absolute, which interest vested in said Frank B. Hall upon the death of his father, subject to the life estate of his mother. It is then urged that the restriction imposed by the will against selling, mortgaging, or disposing of such interest in the real estate before the death of testator's widow, Minta A. Hall, is invalid and ineffectual for that purpose, and null, void, and repugnant to the fee simple estate devised. . . .

The intent of the testator is clear in the present case. He gave a life estate to his widow and the remainder in fee simple to his children, share and share alike. It is clear, also, that testator intended to restrict the alienation of the vested remainders he had devised to his children. The question is whether or not his plainly expressed intent against alienation can properly be given effect under controlling rules of law. . . .

The children of the testator were devised a fee simple title to the remainder. It was alienable and devisable by the remaindermen, unless the restriction in question prevents. The will of the testator was effective at the death of the testator and it devised the entire interest of the testator to his wife and children. It is the general rule that a grant or devise of real estate to a designated person in fee simple, with provisions therein that are inconsistent or repugnant thereto such as a restriction against the power to sell, mortgage, or otherwise encumber, conveys an absolute fee and such restrictions are void. Watson v. Dalton, on rehearing, 146 Neb. 86, 20 N.W.2d 610; State Bank of Jansen v. Thiessen, 137 Neb. 426, 289 N.W. 791. One of the primary incidents of ownership of property in fee simple is the right to convey or encumber it. It is the general rule that a testator may not create a fee simple estate to vest at his death and at the same time restrict alienation thereof. Restatement, Property, §406, subd. e, p. 2397.

Appellee cites the case of Peters v. Northwestern Mutual Life Ins. Co., 119 Neb. 161, 227 N.W. 917, 67 A.L.R. 1311. There can be no question that it supports the position taken by appellee. The rule therein cited does not conform to the general rule applicable to restrictions upon alienation of fee simple estates. We do not agree that there has been a judicial relaxation of rules governing the creation and vesting of fee simple estates. The validity or extent of one's title to real estate ought not to rest upon considerations of reasonableness in the imposing of restrictions. Such a relaxation by judicial interpretation can only bring confusion where certainty ought to exist. We think the case of Peters v. Northwestern Mutual Life Ins. Co., supra, is unsound in its reasoning on this question and that it should be overruled. The general rule that restrictions against alienation of real estate vested in fee simple are against public policy and void is a rule of substantive law which remains unaffected by the intent statute. It is a rule to be applied in all cases falling within it.

We do not say that a testator may not create a vested fee simple estate subject to a condition subsequent, or a determinable or defeasible fee. What we do say is that a restriction against alienation of a vested fee simple estate is not any one of these, nor, since it is void, can it be used as the sole basis for the creation of any of these estates. A restraint on alienation in the form of a condition subsequent, forfeiting or terminating the fee simple estate, or providing for a limitation over upon breach of the condition, is void. 41 Am. Jur., Perpetuities and Restraints on Alienation, §70, p. 111; 31 C.J.S., Estates, §8, p. 20. The right of alienation is inherent in the vested fee simple estate and it arises by virtue of the fact that such an estate is created. The nature of estates in fee simple determinable, estates in fee simple subject to a condition subsequent, and estates in fee simple defeasible upon a condition subsequent, are fully discussed in Ohm v. Clear Creek Drainage Dist., 153 Neb. 428, 45 N.W.2d 117. A perusal of that case will demonstrate that a restriction against alienation of a vested estate in fee simple is no part of, nor incidental to, any one of these estates. Consequently, cases dealing with the creation of recognized common-law estates have no application to a restriction against alienation of a vested fee simple estate. The rules announced in Sandberg v. Heirs of Champlin, 152 Neb. 161, 40 N.W.2d 411, Watson v. Dalton, supra, State Bank of Jansen v. Thiessen, supra, and Myers v. Myers, 109 Neb. 230, 190 N.W. 491, control in the present case and require a holding that Frank B. Hall was the owner in fee simple of a one-ninth interest in the real estate in question and that the purported restriction against alienation contained in the will is against public policy and void. This being so, the conveyance made by him to Hilda B. Robinson was valid and operated to convey his interest in the real estate to her.

The judgment of the district court is reversed and the cause remanded with directions to enter a decree in conformity with the holdings of this opinion.

Reversed and remanded with directions.[43]

[43] Noted 52 Mich. L. Rev. 616. — Eds.

NOTES

1. Compare the following devises:

(a) To Minta in fee, but if she attempts to alienate her interest, to Frank. Frank's interest is void.

(b) To Minta in fee, but if Frank marries, to Frank. Frank's interest is valid.

(c) To Minta in fee, but if Minta fails to use the property personally, to Frank. Frank's interest has been held valid. Mountain Brow Lodge No. 82 I.O.O.F. v. Toscano, 257 Cal. App. 2d 22, 64 Cal. Rptr. 816 (1967) (2 to 1 decision).

Why is social policy offended by direct restraints on alienation but not offended by indirect restraints such as those in (b) and (c)? Should a direct restraint on alienation be valid if it cannot endure longer than the period permitted by the Rule against Perpetuities?

At 6 American Law of Property §26.3 (Casner ed. 1952) Professor Schnebly says: "Restraints which make it impossible for the owner of property to transfer his interest have grave social and economic consequences. Such restraints take the property out of commerce. . . . A more important objection to restraints is their tendency to concentrate wealth. . . . Another evil growing out of a restraint is its effect to discourage improvements when it is imposed upon an interest in land. . . . The concluding argument against the validity of a restraint is based upon its possible effect in respect to creditors of the owner of the property subject to the restraint. . . . A system of restraints which permits a debtor to continue in the enjoyment of the benefits of property of substantial value, and at the same time to refuse payment of his just debts, does not commend itself to the ideas of moral justice entertained by a considerable portion of society." [44]

2. Restraints on alienation can be divided into forfeiture restraints and disabling restraints. A forfeiture restraint provides that if the transferee attempts to transfer his interest he forfeits it to another person. A forfeiture restraint is less objectionable than a disabling restraint because the person who has the benefit of the forfeiture can, if in existence, release his interest and the land can thus be made marketable. A disabling restraint withholds from the transferee the power of voluntary or involuntary alienation of his interest or both. If the disabling restraint is valid, the transferee's interest simply cannot be conveyed. (A promissory restraint is a promise by the transferee that he will not convey his interest; it is usually treated the same as a disabling restraint.) An absolute forfeiture or disabling restraint upon a legal fee simple is almost always held void. 6 id. §§26.13 to 26.41. By the weight of authority a disabling restraint on a *legal* life estate is void, but a forfeiture restraint on a legal life estate is valid. Professor Schnebly says: "A forfeiture restraint upon a legal life estate is not so objectionable. While a forfeiture in some instances may disappoint the expectation of creditors unaware of the restraint, usually the risk of

[44] For a defense of the minority doctrine permitting reasonable restraints on the fee, see Bernhard, The Minority Doctrine Concerning Direct Restraints on Alienation, 57 Mich. L. Rev. 1173 (1959); Dukeminier, Perpetuities Law in Action 114-145 (1962).

loss of the property will suffice to induce the life tenant to pay his debt if possible. A forfeiture restraint does not give rise to the unpleasant spectacle of a debtor enjoying all the benefits of property and at the same time denying payment of his just debts." 6 id. §26.50.

3. "A forfeiture restraint might well be permitted where in fact there would be inalienability regardless of the restraint. Where a fee simple is subject to a valid executory limitation over, as upon the death of the first taker without issue surviving him, the defeasible fee is in practice inalienable, unless joinder of the person entitled by the gift over can be procured. If the gift over is contingent until the death of the first taker, as in the illustration given, there is for practical purposes entire inalienability during his life. If, therefore, a forfeiture restraint upon alienation be imposed for the life of the first taker, it produces no additional inalienability." 6 id. §26.27.

Which of the following restraints add practical inalienability?

(a) To Minta for life, then to testator's children, with a forfeiture restraint on alienation of any remainder interest in favor of testator's other children.

(b) To Minta for life, then to testator's issue then living per stirpes, with a forfeiture restraint on alienation of any remainder interest in favor of testator's other issue per stirpes living at Minta's death.

2. *Spendthrift, Support, and Discretionary Trusts*

In almost all American states a disabling restraint on an *equitable* life estate is valid. Usually the restraint is against both voluntary and involuntary alienation. A trust in which the equitable life estate is subject to a disabling restraint is known as a spendthrift trust. Spendthrift trusts are not recognized in England.

The two decisions that were largely responsible for the spendthrift trust doctrine are Nichols v. Eaton, 91 U.S. 716 (1875), and Broadway National Bank v. Adams, 133 Mass. 170 (1882). In the first case Justice Miller inserted an elaborate dictum upholding spendthrift trusts. He reasoned: "Why a parent, or one who loves another, and wishes to use his own property in securing the object of his affection, as far as property can do it, from the ills of life, the vicissitudes of fortune, and even his own improvidence, or incapacity for self-protection, should not be permitted to do so, is not readily perceived." [45] In the second case the Massachusetts court upheld a restraint on alienation of an equitable life estate.

John Chipman Gray was so outraged at the introduction of spendthrift trusts that he was moved to write his Restraints on Alienation in refutation of Nichols v. Eaton. He said, "If there is one sentiment, therefore, which it would seem to be the part of all in authority, and particularly of all judges, to fortify, it is the duty of

[45] "The Missouri court has even cited the Scriptures to justify the dubious morality of this doctrine. In Matthews v. Van Cleve, [282 Mo. 19, 221 S.W. 34 (1920)], there appears the following quotation from 1 Timothy 5, 8: 'But if any provide not for his own, and especially for those of his own house, he hath denied the faith and is worse than an infidel.' It is not likely that the Apostle Paul had the spendthrift trust doctrine in anticipation at the time when he wrote this epistle." 6 American Law of Property §26.100 n. 7 (Casner ed. 1952).

keeping one's promises and paying one's debts." [46] He also suggested that the judges who aided in the introduction of spendthrift trusts were influenced, unconsciously perhaps, "by that spirit, in short, of paternalism, which is the fundamental essence alike of spendthrift trusts and of socialism." [47] Yet in spite of Gray's strictures, spendthrift trusts have come to be recognized in all but a very few states. The question of public policy is still debated, however. See 2 Scott, Trusts §152 (3d ed. 1967); 6 American Law of Property §26.100 (Casner ed. 1952); Griswold, Spendthrift Trusts (2d ed. 1947); Bushman, The (In)Validity of Spendthrift Trusts, 47 Ore. L. Rev. 304 (1968); Note, A Rationale for the Spendthrift Trust, 64 Colum. L. Rev. 1323 (1964).

It is sometimes assumed that if spendthrift trusts were not recognized the creditors of trust beneficiaries could reach their interests. However, if the trust is broadly discretionary so that *any* right of *any* income beneficiary is subject to the condition precedent of the trustee having first exercised his discretion, the income of the trust is immune to creditors. They cannot compel the trustee to exercise his discretion to make payments to a particular beneficiary.

PROBLEM

"The most notable cause of Boston's commercial . . . decline is the 'spendthrift trust' decision of Massachusetts courts . . . that a man could tie his children's inheritance up, either by deed or will, so that they could not spend or risk the principal. . . . Immense wealth had been accumulated in Boston in the first sixty years of the republic; instead of trusting their sons and sending them out at their own risks . . . they distrusted their ability . . . and had them all trusteed. No new enterprise could be undertaken by them, for under the court decision they had no capital to risk. Perforce they became coupon-cutters — parasites, not promoters." Stimson, My United States 76-77 (1931). Do you agree? See Friedman, The Dynastic Trust, 73 Yale L.J. 547 (1964).

SHELLEY v. SHELLEY

Supreme Court of Oregon, 1960

223 Ore. 328, 354 P.2d 282

O'Connell, Justice. This is an appeal from a decree of the circuit court for Multnomah county establishing the rights of the parties to the income and corpus of a trust of which the defendant, the United States National Bank of Portland (Oregon) is trustee.

The assignments of error are directed at the trial court's interpretation of the trust. The trust involved in this suit was created by Hugh T. Shelley. The pertinent parts of the trust are as follows:

[46] Gray, Restraints on the Alienation of Property iii (2d ed. 1895).

[47] Id. at ix.

Ninth: All of the rest, residue, and remainder of my said estate, . . . I give, devise, and bequeath to the United States National Bank of Portland (Oregon), in trust, . . . upon the following trusts:

. . .

(2) I direct that, all income derived from my trust estate be paid to my wife, Gertrude R. Shelley, as long as she lives, said income to be paid to her at intervals of not less than three (3) months apart; . . . .

(4) If my said wife, Gertrude R. Shelley, shall predecease me, and my said son is then alive, or upon my wife's death after my death and my son being alive, it is my desire, and I direct, that, the United States National Bank of Portland (Oregon), as trustee, shall continue this estate in trust and pay all income derived therefrom to my son, Grant R. Shelley, as long as he lives, said income to be paid to him at intervals not less than three (3) months apart; Provided, Further, That when my son, Grant R. Shelley, arrives at the age of thirty (30) years, my trustee may then, or at any time thereafter, and from time to time, distribute to said son absolutely and as his own all or any part of the principal of said trust fund that it may then or from time to time thereafter deem him capable of successfully investing without the restraints of this trust; Provided, However, That such disbursements of principal of said trust so made to my son after he attains the age of thirty (30) years shall be first approved in writing by either one of my brothers-in-law, that is: Dr. Frank L. Ralston, now of Walla Walla, Washington, or Russell C. Ralston, now of Palo Alto, California, if either of them is then living, but if neither of them is then living, then my trustee is authorized to make said disbursements of principal to my son in the exercise of its sole and absolute judgment and discretion; Provided, Further, That, said trust shall continue as to all or any part of the undistributed portion of the principal thereof to and until the death of my said son.

(5) I further direct and authorize my trustee, from time to time (but only upon the written approval of my said wife if she be then living, otherwise in the exercise of my trustee's sole discretion) to make disbursements for the use and benefit of my son, Grant R. Shelley, or his children, in case of any emergency arising whereby unusual and extraordinary expenses are necessary for the proper support and care of my said son, or said children.

. . .

(8) Each beneficiary hereunder is hereby restrained from alienating, anticipating, encumbering, or in any manner assigning his or her interest or estate, either in principal or income, and is without power so to do, nor shall such interest or estate be subject to his or her liabilities or obligations nor to judgment or other legal process, bankruptcy proceedings or claims of creditors or others.

The principal question on appeal is whether the income and corpus of the Shelley trust can be reached by Grant Shelley's former wives and his children.

Grant Shelley was first married to defendant, Patricia C. Shelley. Two children were born of this marriage. Patricia divorced Grant in 1951. The decree required Grant to pay support money for the children; the decree did not call for the payment of alimony. Thereafter, Grant married the plaintiff, Betty Shelley. Two children were born of this marriage. The plaintiff obtained a divorce from Grant in August, 1958. The decree in this latter suit required the payment of both alimony and a designated monthly amount for the support of the children of that marriage.

Some time after his marriage to the plaintiff, Grant disappeared and his whereabouts was not known at the time of this suit. The defendant bank, as trustee, invested the trust assets in securities which are now held by it, together with undisbursed income from the trust estate. The plaintiff obtained an injunction restraining the defendant trustee from disbursing any of the trust assets. Patricia Shelley brought a garnishment proceeding against the trustee, by which she sought to subject the trust to the claim for support money provided for in the 1951 decree of divorce. . . .

The defendant bank finally brought a bill of interpleader tendering to the court for disbursement all of the funds held in trust, praying for an order establishing the respective rights of the interpleaded parties to the trust assets.

The trial court entered a decree subjecting the accrued income of the trust to the existing claims of the plaintiff and Patricia Shelley; subjecting future income of the trust to the periodic obligations subsequently accruing by the terms of the decrees in the divorce proceedings brought by plaintiff and Patricia Shelley; and further providing that in the event that the trust income was insufficient to satisfy such claims, the corpus of the trust was subject to invasion.

We shall first consider that part of the decree which subjects the income of the trust to the claims of plaintiff and of defendant, Patricia Shelley. The trust places no conditions upon the right of Grant Shelley to receive the trust income during his lifetime. Therefore, plaintiff and Patricia Shelley may reach such income unless the spendthrift provision of the trust precludes them from doing so.

The validity of spendthrift trusts has been established by our former cases. . . . The question on this appeal is whether the spendthrift provision will be given effect to bar the claims of the beneficiary's children for support and the plaintiff's claim for alimony.

In Cogswell v. Cogswell et al., 1946, 178 Or. 417, 167 P.2d 324, 335, we held that the spendthrift provision of a trust is not effective against the claims of the beneficiary's former wife for alimony and for support of the beneficiary's child. In that case the court adopted the rule stated in 1 Restatement, Trusts, §157, which reads in part as follows:

"§157. Particular Classes of Claimants.

"Although a trust is a spendthrift trust or trust for support, the interest of the beneficiary can be reached in satisfaction of an enforceable claim against the beneficiary,

"(a) by the wife or child of the beneficiary for support, or by the wife for alimony";

The defendant bank concedes that the Cogswell case is controlling in the case at bar, but asks us to overrule it on the ground that it is inconsistent with our own cases recognizing the testator's privilege to dispose of his property as he pleases and, further, that it is inconsistent with various Oregon statutes expressing the same policy of free alienation. If we should accept the premise urged by the defendant bank, that a testator has an inviolable right to dispose of his property as he pleases subject only to legislative restriction, the conclusion is inevitable that the testator may create in a beneficiary an interest free from all claims, including those for support and alimony.

But the premise is not sound. The privilege of disposing of property is not absolute; it is hedged with various restrictions where there are policy considerations warranting the limitation. . . . Not all of these restrictions are imposed by statute. The rule against perpetuities, the rule against restraints on alienation, the refusal to recognize trusts for capricious purposes or for illegal purposes, or for any purpose contrary to public policy, are all instances of judge-made rules limiting the privilege of alienation. Many others could be recited. . . . It is within the court's power to impose upon the privilege of disposing of property such restrictions as are consistent with its view of sound public policy, unless, of course, the legislature has expressed a contrary view. Our own statutes do not purport to deal with the specific question before us, that is as to whether there should be limitations on the owner's privilege to create a spendthrift trust. . . .

In holding that a spendthrift trust is subject to claims for alimony and support the court, in Cogswell v. Cogswell et al., supra, did not disclose the reasoning by which it reached its conclusion. This failure to examine the question of public policy in the area of spendthrift trusts is not unusual, for as Griswold, Spendthrift Trusts (2d Ed.), p. 634 points out in discussing the validity of spendthrift trusts, "examination [of public policy] has rarely, if ever, been attempted by the courts," and he admits that "it is obviously a matter difficult to approach and one about which dogmatic conclusions cannot be reached." But once having recognized the validity of spendthrift trusts, which we have and which conclusion defendant bank endorses, the more specific question of the validity of the restraint of such a trust as against the claims of children for support and of the beneficiary's former wife for alimony presents a narrower question of policy which, we believe, is easier to answer. The question is whether a person should be entitled to enjoy the benefits of a trust and at the same time refuse to pay the obligations arising out of his marriage.

We have no hesitation in declaring that public policy requires that the interest of the beneficiary of a trust should be subject to the claims for support of his children. . . . Certainly the defendant will accept the societal postulate that parents have the obligation to support their children. If we give effect to the spendthrift provision to bar the claims for support, we have the spectacle of a man enjoying the benefits of a trust immune from claims which are justly due, while the community pays for the support of his children. Wetmore v. Wetmore, 1896, 149 N.Y. 520, 44 N.E. 169, 33 L.R.A. 708. We do not believe that it is sound policy to use the welfare funds of this state in support of the beneficiary's children, while he stands behind the shield of immunity created by a spendthrift trust provision. To endorse such a policy and to permit the spectacle which we have described above would be to invite disrespect for the administration of justice. . . .

The justification for permitting a claim for alimony is, perhaps, not as clear. The adjustment of the economic interests of the parties to a divorce may depend upon a variety of factors, including the respective fault of the parties, the ability of the wife to support herself, the duration of the marriage, and other considerations. Whether alimony is to be granted and its amount are questions which are determined in light of these various interests. It is probably fair to say that the duties created by the marriage relation, at least as they are evaluated upon the termination of the marriage, are conceived of as more qualified than those arising out of the paternal relationship. On the theory that divorce terminates the husband's duty to support his former wife and that she stands in no better position than other creditors, some courts have held that the spendthrift provision insulates the beneficiary's interest in the trust from her claim. Lippincott v. Lippincott, 1944, 349 Pa. 501, 37 A.2d 741. Recognizing the difference in marital and parental duties suggested above, it has been held that a spendthrift trust is subject to the claims for the support of children but free from the claims of the former wife. Eaton v. Eaton, 1926, 82 N.H. 216, 132 A. 10, commented upon in 35 Yale L.J. 1025 (1926). . . . A majority of the cases, however, hold that a spendthrift provision will not bar a claim for alimony. . . .

As we have already mentioned, the case of Cogswell v. Cogswell, supra, is in accord with this latter view. We are of the opinion that the conclusion there reached should be reaffirmed. The duty of the husband to support his former wife should override the restriction called for by the spendthrift provision. The same reason advanced above for requiring the support of the beneficiary's children will, in many cases, be applicable to the claim of a divorced wife; if the beneficiary's interest cannot be reached, the state may be called upon to support her. . . .

We hold that the beneficiaries' interest in the income of the Shelley Trust is subject to the claims of the plaintiff for alimony and to the claims for the support of Grant Shelley's children as provided for under both decrees for divorce. These claims are not without limit. We adopt the view that such claimants may reach only that much of the income which the trial court deems reasonable under the circumstances, having in mind the respective needs of the husband and wife, the needs of the children, the amount of the trust income, the availability of the corpus for the various needs, and any other factors which are relevant in adjusting equitably the interests of the claimants and the beneficiary. Griswold, Spendthrift Trusts (2d Ed.) §339; 2 Scott on Trusts, §157.1; Note, 28 Va. L. Rev. 527 (1942). . . .

The question of the claimants' rights to reach the corpus of the trust involves other consideration. For the reasons heretofore stated, the beneficiary's interest in the corpus is not made immune from these claims. But, by the terms of the trust, the disbursement of the corpus is within the discretion of the trustee (or, in some instances subject to the approval of others), and, therefore, Grant Shelley's right to receive any part of the corpus does not arise until the trustee has exercised his discretion and has decided to invade the corpus. Until that time, the plaintiff and Patricia Shelley cannot reach the corpus of the trust because the beneficiary has no realizable interest in it. Mattison v. Mattison, 1909, 53 Or. 254, 100 P. 4, 133 Am. St. Rep. 829. It has been held that a discretionary trust for the "sole benefit" of the testator's son was enforceable by the son's destitute wife and children on the ground that the support of the son's family fell within the terms of the trust. Gardner v.

O'Loughlin, 1912, 76 N.H. 481, 84 A. 935, 936. But, assuming without deciding that such an interpretation is reasonable, it has not been extended to a case where there has been a divorce and the wife has ceased to be a member of the family and, therefore, has ceased to be a beneficiary of the trust. Eaton v. Eaton, supra. There is nothing in the trust before us which would indicate the testator's intent to make the plaintiff, either directly or indirectly, the beneficiary of the trust. Patricia Shelley could not be regarded as a beneficiary because the decree under which she claims called only for the payment of support money for the children and not alimony. In some jurisdictions a creditor of the beneficiary of a discretionary trust may attach the potential interest of the beneficiary. . . .[48] There is no such procedure in Oregon available to the creditor. And at least with respect to the corpus, ORS 29.175(2) makes the interest constituting the subject matter of the trust free from attachment. It follows that the decree of the lower court in making the corpus of the Shelley Trust subject to the plaintiff's claim for alimony was erroneous.

The claims for the support of Grant Shelley's children, provided for in the two divorce decrees, involve a different problem. The trust directed and authorized the trustee, in the exercise of its sole discretion upon the death of settlor's wife, to make disbursements for the use and benefit not only of Grant Shelley, but also for his children. The disbursements were to be made "in case of any emergency arising whereby unusual and extraordinary expenses are necessary for the proper support and care of my said son, or said children." Here the children are named as beneficiaries of the trust and need not claim derivatively through their father. However, they are entitled to a share of the corpus only if, in the trustee's discretion, it is determined that an emergency exists. The defendant bank contends that the expenses of supporting Grant Shelley's children claimed in this case were for the usual and ordinary costs of support and do not, therefore, constitute "unusual and extraordinary expenses" within the meaning of the trust provision. It is contended that there was no "emergency" calling for "unusual and extraordinary expenses" because there was no proof of an unexpected occurrence or of an unexpected situation requiring immediate action. We disagree with defendant's interpretation. We construe the clause to include the circumstances involved here, i.e., where the children are deserted by their father and are in need of support. We think that the testator intended to provide that in the event that the income from the trust was not sufficient to cover disbursements for the support and care of either the son or his children an "emergency" had arisen and the corpus could then be invaded. The decree of the lower court would permit the corpus to be employed if the "assets in the hands of the Executor [trustee] and the income cash from said trust shall be insufficient to pay the obligations of Defendant Grant R. Shelley" to plaintiff and Patricia Shelley. The decree is too broad; first because, as we have already indicated, it improperly includes the plaintiff's claim for alimony; second, because it permits

[48] The Restatement (Second) of Trusts §155 provides that a creditor cannot compel the trustee of a discretionary trust to pay him, but that, after the trustee has been served in a proceeding to reach the trust fund, the trustee must pay the creditor before he pays the debtor-beneficiary. — Eds.

encroachment upon the corpus without reference to whether the trustee has exercised his discretion or whether there has been an emergency as contemplated by the testator.

It is to be noted that the children of Grant Shelley are not beneficiaries of the income of the trust; they may reach it only as persons having claims against the beneficiary, Grant Shelley. If, for example, Grant Shelley should decide to support his children out of assets other than income of the trust, the children would have no claim whatsoever against his interest in the trust. The decree, therefore, should have permitted an invasion of the corpus only if it was necessary to first reach the income under the circumstances just mentioned and such income was insufficient. And further, the decree should have made such corpus available only in the event of the trustee's exercise of discretion authorizing the disbursement for the support of the children under the emergency circumstances provided for in the trust. After the entry of such a decree, if the trustee should refuse to exercise his discretion, or if it is claimed that he exercised it unreasonably, relief may be sought in a court of equity by the children.

The decree of the lower court is affirmed and the cause remanded with directions to modify the decree in accordance with the views expressed in this opinion.

ESTATE OF VOUGHT, 25 N.Y.2d 163, 250 N.E.2d 343, 303 N.Y.S.2d 61 (1969). Chance Vought created a testamentary trust to pay income to his widow for her life, and on her death to pay the principal in equal shares to his two sons. The settlor provided that both the life estate and the remainders were inalienable. One of his sons, Chance Jr., needed money badly and sought funds from companies that buy up remainder interests and expectancies from devisees and heirs. He executed four assignments of shares in his remainder, receiving approximately $180,000 therefor. At the death of his mother Chance Jr.'s interest in the principal of the trust was worth about $900,000. Chance Jr. predeceased his mother by eighteen months. He left a widow and children surviving. If the assignments were valid, his widow and children would receive nothing. The court held that the restraint on the equitable remainder was valid and the assignments were void.[49] In commenting on this case Professor Niles says: "If Chance Jr. had had a clearly alienable vested remainder, he could have borrowed at more reasonable rates or he could have sold his interest at something nearer to its actuarial value. . . . Now that some $900,000 has been held payable to Chance Jr.'s estate, it may soon be necessary to decide whether the companies that advanced the money and took the assignments will be able to enforce Chance Jr.'s contractual obligation which he presumably made to pay over the entire sum when he received it. In deciding whether the assignees are entitled to all that Chance Jr. promised them or only the amount paid to him plus interest and legal expenses, the Court might shape a modern law of unconscionability." Niles, Matter of Vought's Will: A Tighter Grip by the Dead Hand, 45

[49] For the law generally on restraints on alienation of principal, see 2 Scott, Trusts §153 (3d ed. 1967).

N.Y.U.L. Rev. 421, 439-440 (1970). Professor Powell is sharply critical of Estate of Vought. He believes the doctrine of spendthrift trusts should be confined exclusively to restraints on income. Powell, The Rule Against Perpetuities and Spendthrift Trusts in New York: Comments and Suggestions, 71 Colum. L. Rev. 688, 701 (1971).

NEWSWEEK, SPECULATION
January 25, 1971, p. 66

Betting on Death:

"At first I thought it was a rather cold-blooded business," said a London solicitor. "But if you think about it rationally, it's a rather practical way of raising and investing money."

He was referring to the practice known in British financial circles as the selling of reversions, a somewhat prim term for what is basically a speculation on the death of a total stranger. In one form or another, such investments have probably existed since property was invented, and they persist little-noticed in several countries. . . .

In Britain . . . what is sold is an actual inheritance — and such transactions occur every month at the London Auction Mart, in the heart of the City, in an atmosphere of fusty gentility and soft-voiced discretion comparable to the auctioning of an art collection at Sotheby's. The bidding sometimes runs to hundreds of thousands of pounds.

Bare Facts:

It works this way. A young man has been named in his grandfather's will as the heir to £60,000 ($144,000). But he will actually get the money only after the death of his grandmother, who has the income from the estate for as long as she lives. Unfortunately, the grandmother shows every sign of living indefinitely, and the young man is in need of money. If he sells his expected inheritance, known as a reversion, for whatever it will fetch at auction, the successful bidder will get the entire £60,000 when the grandmother dies.

The bare facts of this example are taken from the actual catalogue of a recent auction. And only bare facts are given — no names or personal details. The listing simply read: "Reversion receivable on the decease of a lady aged 80, provided the reversioner, a gentleman aged 30, is then living." That, plus an appraisal of the estate, was all the purchaser knew. The "gentleman aged 30" could have been a gay blade beset by gambling debts or an industrious husband who needed money for his children's education. No matter. The purchaser was simply betting that the "lady aged 80" would die before the 30-year-old "reversioner," a reasonable probability. And in the actual event, the highest bidder obtained the reversion for £32,000, only a little more than half of its assessed value.

"It was a particularly good investment," says Guy Enriquez, the auctioneer who handled the sale. Enriquez, a dignified, bespectacled man of 48 and a partner in the 127-year-old auctioneering firm of H. E. Foster and Cranfield, conducts the sales with an antique ivory gavel and the quiet, repeated question: "Can I tempt you, sir? You, sir?" And he is quick to resent what he considers "gross exaggerations" of the firm's activities. Some months ago, he recalls with annoyance, a Yugoslav magazine wrote that "old ladies were being sold in the streets of London." "Ridiculous," says Enriquez. "This is merely an investment, just like any other. It's nothing personal."

NOTES AND PROBLEMS

1. There are statutory provisions in many states permitting a creditor to reach some portion of the beneficiary's income interest in a spendthrift trust. The New York Revisers of 1830 inserted in their statutes a provision permitting creditors to reach the part of the beneficiary's income in excess of the amount necessary for the support and education of the beneficiary. Similar statutes exist in California, Connecticut, Michigan, Minnesota, Montana, North Dakota, Oklahoma, South Dakota, and Wisconsin, but in many of those states the statutes apply to trusts of land only. In determining what is necessary for the support of the beneficiary, courts developed a "station-in-life" rule. A high-living beneficiary was given a larger exemption than a frugal beneficiary. The "station-in-life" rule rendered these statutes relatively useless to creditors. Spendthrift trusts are usually created only by persons of considerable wealth who have raised their children in substantial luxury. The accustomed manner of living of the child-beneficiary is likely to require the full income from the trust.

In a few states a creditor is permitted to reach a certain percentage (usually 10 percent) of the income of the beneficiary. In other states a ceiling is placed upon the amount of exempt income. See 2 Scott, Trusts §152.1 (3d ed. 1967). American Security & Trust Co. v. Utley, 382 F.2d 451 (D.C. Cir. 1967), held that the income of a spendthrift trust could be reached for debts incurred for the necessities of life.

2. In 1931 Anna Knauth created a spendthrift trust for her son Oliver. Subsequently Oliver married Mary, and they had two daughters. In 1947 Mary instituted suit for a divorce. While the suit was pending Oliver made an irrevocable assignment to Mary of all income from the trust in excess of $100 a month. Mary was granted a divorce in 1948 and awarded alimony of $1 a month. A copy of the assignment was delivered to the trustees, and they henceforth paid the income in accordance with its terms. Prior New York cases had held that where a wife obtains a judgment of divorce directing the payment of alimony, the wife may require the trustees of a spendthrift trust to pay such alimony. Upon the trustees' suit for settlement of their accounts some ten years later, Oliver contended the assignment was void on the theory that it was voluntary and not directed by a court decree. In Matter of Knauth, 12 N.Y.2d 259, 189 N.E.2d 482 (1963), the court held that the voluntary assignment, in recognition of the husband's legal duty, was valid.

Suppose Mary remarries in 1964. A husband has no legal duty to support his divorced wife after she remarries, although he may have a duty imposed by a contractual agreement between the parties. Would you advise the trustees that they should continue to make payments to Mary? Matter of Goelet, 28 App. Div. 2d 149, 283 N.Y.S.2d 545 (1967), 31 App. Div. 2d 921, 298 N.Y.S.2d 604 (1969).

3. T, a resident of Rhode Island, which does not permit spendthrift trusts, bequeaths $500,000 to a Boston trust company, in trust, to pay the income to his daughter Mary for her life, then to convey the principal to the daughter's children. The trust contains a spendthrift clause. Mary, who lives in Rhode Island, runs up some debts. Can her creditors reach the income from the Boston trust? Scott, Spendthrift Trusts and the Conflict of Laws, 77 Harv. L. Rev. 845 (1964).

4. O transferred property to X in trust to pay the income annually during his lifetime "to O personally, to be for O's support," and on O's death, to pay the principal to A. One year later O gratuitously wrote, signed, and delivered to his cousin, B, the following memorandum: "I hereby assign to my cousin B all my right to receive future income for my lifetime from the trust," identifying the above trust in the memorandum. X, who had no notice of the assignment, paid the next annual installment of income, $5000, to O, who, having meanwhile become angry with B, refused to pay this sum over to B. Instead O used it to buy stock for himself. The stock is now worth $10,000. Does B have any claim against O? 2 Scott, Trusts §154 (3d ed. 1967). If the trust had contained a spendthrift clause, could C, a creditor of O, reach any portion of the trust fund? Id. §156.

5. Spendthrift trusts are not always wise. Consider the following case. In 1904 Levi Z. Leiter by will set up a spendthrift trust for the benefit of his children and grandchildren. One of his children, Lady Suffolk, in the 1960s paid income taxes on income in excess of $200,000, and, to reduce taxes, she executed assignments of her right to the income to members of her family. Held: The income tax situation is not an emergency which will justify a court of equity in deviating from the terms of the will; the assignments are void. Howard v. Chapman, 101 Ill. App. 2d 135, 241 N.E.2d 492 (1968).

UNITED STATES v. TAYLOR

United States District Court, N.D. California, 1966

254 F. Supp. 752

[Lee Jones died in 1964, leaving a will that devised assets worth $146,784 in a spendthrift trust that provided: "VI(a) The Trustees shall pay to or apply for the benefit of my son, Lee Jones, Jr., so much of the net income of said trust, up to the whole thereof, as the Trustees may from time to time deem necessary or advisable for his proper care, maintenance and support. The balance of said net income, if any, shall be accumulated by the Trustees, and from time to time added to the principal of the trust estate. VI(b) If at any time, in the absolute discretion of the Trustees, my son, Lee Jones, Jr., should for any reason be in need of funds for his proper care, maintenance and support, the Trustees may in their absolute discretion, pay to or apply for his benefit, in addition to the payments hereinabove provided for him, such amounts from the principal of his share of the trust estate, not to exceed Fifteen Thousand Dollars ($15,000.00) per annum, as the Trustees may from time to time deem necessary or advisable for his use and benefit." The will also provided that if any income or principal became payable to any creditor of the son, the son forfeited all his rights under the trust; "Provided, further, that notwithstanding any forfeiture by a beneficiary as aforesaid, my trustees in their uncontrolled discretion, but without any obligation to do so, may from time to time apply or direct the application of said income forfeited as aforesaid, or so much thereof as seems to them best to the use of the beneficiary so forfeiting the same." The United States had in 1964 an unpaid tax judgment against T's son for $143,624. Under federal law this judgment was a lien upon "all property and rights to property" of the son. In May, 1964, the trustees began making regular weekly payments to the son, but when the government filed suit against the trustees in February, 1965, the payments were discontinued.]

George B. Harris, Chief Judge. . . . Under paragraph VI(a), the taxpayer has a lifetime, enforceable, equitable right to support from the income of the trust. The discretionary feature is limited to the trustees' determining the amounts they deem "necessary" for the taxpayer's proper care, maintenance and support. The provision that the "trustees shall pay" is *mandatory* and conveys the intent of the testator that his son is to receive support payments from the net income of the trust if he needs support.

If the trustees refuse to act or act unreasonably, a court of competent jurisdiction may be invoked to obtain an order compelling the trustees to act in the exercise of discretion. §2269 California Civil Code; Estate of Lackmann, 156 Cal. App. 2d 674, 320 P.2d 186 (1958).

The courts have devised means of determining a beneficiary's reasonable needs, i.e., the station in life test, wherein the beneficiary receives enough to recover reasonable needs of a typical man of his station in life. See, e.g., Canfield v. Security-First Nat'l Bank, 13 Cal. 2d 1, 87 P.2d 830 (1939).

Paragraph VI(b), although phrased as a grant of absolute discretion, is geared to the taxpayer's need for support. The trustees have the power under this provision to invade the principal when the trust income is inadequate to meet the taxpayer's needs. This provision is enforceable whenever the trust income fails to meet the taxpayer's reasonable needs. In this regard, the courts will compel an honest exercise of discretion by the trustees. California Civil Code §2269; Estate of Lackmann, supra; Halbach, Problems of Discretion in Discretionary Trusts, 61 Colum. L. Rev. 1425, 1430-33 (1961).

The trust being one fundamentally for support, the taxpayer has a basic beneficial right to receive payments from income to the extent needed for his support. It follows that the government liens have attached to and subsist against that right.

The taxpayer's property right in the trust at bar differs from any other property right only in that it has no permanently fixed dollar value. It is variable according to the taxpayer's needs. At any given point in time it can be assigned a reasonably accurate dollar value by assessing the taxpayer's current needs and living demands. It may be assumed that his current needs are at least comparable in amount to the weekly payments which were terminated by the trustees in February, 1965. . . .

Does the forfeiture clause terminate the taxpayer's property right and therefore defeat the tax lien? . . . [This] proviso creates no real forfeiture and gift over to other beneficiaries for the reason that the *third* paragraph of the same article *gives back* to the "forfeiting beneficiary" by the device of the trustees' "uncontrolled discretion," essentially the same right to receive payments that he would have before the so-called "forfeiture." . . .

It should be abundantly clear that this is not a case of an *absolute* forfeiture, with a gift over upon the happening of a condition. It is quite transparent from the phrasing and verbiage employed that the draftsmanship resorted to was designed to insulate the interest of the spendthrift son from the admittedly valid government lien. Subtle or not, the provisions of the trust in question represent an exercise in circumlocution in attempting to draft around the well-settled law in the Ninth Circuit on spendthrift trusts. . . .

In Mercantile Trust Co. v. Hofferbert, D.C., 58 F. Supp. 701, at 705, Judge Chesnut concisely stated the issue and a sound resolution:

> The reasons which have actuated some courts, as in Maryland, to uphold spendthrift trusts against the claims of creditors do not necessarily apply to tax claims of the government either federal or State. . . . The public policy is quite different. In the one case the donor of the property has the right to protect the beneficiary against his own voluntary improvident or financial misfortune; but in the other the public interest is directly affected with respect to collection of taxes for the support of the government. . . . It is said . . . that in making the gift the donor had the absolute right to impose limitations on the application of the income. (Citations omitted.) But I am unable to concur in the soundness of the distinction sought to be made. Public policy is the determining factor. . . . If, as is conceded, the public policy of the State expressed in a statute must yield to federal taxes, so also must trust instruments created by a donor. In many States spendthrift trusts are not validated either by judicial decision or by statute; but federal income taxes are intended to be uniform in their application throughout the Nation. See Lyeth v. Hoey, 305 U.S. 188, 59 S. Ct. 155, 83 L. Ed. 119. . . . Cf. Commissioner of Internal Revenue v. Procter, 4 Cir., 142 F.2d 824, 154 A.L.R. 1215.

. . . [I]n the case at bar, the defendants' contentions surrounding the so-called "forfeiture" provisions, represent no more nor less than a trifling with the judicial process, and they cannot be sustained under any theory.

For the reasons hereinabove set forth:

(a) Neither the spendthrift trust nor the so-called "forfeiture" provisions of the trust, are valid as against the government liens which encumber the taxpayer's beneficial rights and interests under the trust;

(b) Summary judgment should be granted in the government's favor and against the trustees and other parties upon the terms particularly set forth in the prayer of plaintiff's complaint. . . .[50]

Naomi M. Swallow was the beneficiary of a trust which provided: "[T]he trustee shall distribute, in its sole and absolute discretion, so much of the income and the principal of her share as it, in its sole and absolute discretion, determines to be necessary for her care, comfort, maintenance and general well-being for and during her lifetime." Naomi was a mentally incompetent patient of the Dayton State Hospital. Under Ohio law the Department of Mental Hygiene and Correction is entitled to recover the cost of maintenance from the patient.[51] The court held that the trust was neither a purely discretionary trust nor a support trust, but that the words "care, comfort, maintenance and general well-being" were to be deemed to give the beneficiary an enforceable claim to minimal support. The parties agreed that the institutional care furnished Naomi was minimal, and hence the trust fund was liable. Bureau of Support v. Kreitzer, 16 Ohio St. 2d 147, 243 N.E.2d 83 (1968).

Suppose the trustee's power is wholly discretionary with no purpose nor standard mentioned, e.g., to X Bank in trust to accumulate the income or distribute the income to one or more members of a group consisting of the settlor's issue and spouses of issue in such amounts as the trustee determines.[52] Can the state or the federal tax authorities reach the trust for debts of the settlor's grandson? If the settlor's grandson owns no assets of his own can he qualify for Medicaid to pay for the $15,000 annual cost of hemodialysis? [53] Scott says: "By the terms of the trust the requirement of reasonableness in the exercise of a discretionary power by the trustee may be dispensed with. In such a case the exercise by the trustee of his discretion will not be interfered with by the court, even though he acts beyond the bounds of

[50] Noted 35 Geo. Wash. L. Rev. 615. — Eds.

[51] The courts are split over whether the state can, without a statute, require reimbursement from the trustee of a discretionary trust for institutional care furnished the beneficiary. Powell, Freedom of Alienation — For Whom? The Clash of Theories, 2 Real Prop., Prob. & Trust J. 127, 137 (1967).

[52] The power in the bank is the equivalent of a special power of appointment, and, to be valid, it will have to be limited so that it cannot be exercised more than twenty-one years after some life in being at the creation of the power. See page 1042, infra.

[53] "The federal statutes which authorize grants to the states for medical assistance programs, generally leave to the states the definition of medically indigent persons. E.g., 42 U.S.C. §§302(a)(10), 602(a)(7), 1382(a)(14) (1964); id. §1396 (Supp. I, 1966). The California Welfare and Institutions Code contains vague 'property' qualifications for public assistance. One section denies public assistance to an applicant unless 'the *property he owns*' is of a specified exempt kind or is valued below a specified amount. Cal. Welf. & Inst'ns Code §11151 (West 1966) (emphasis added). The California Medi-Cal program, id. §§14000-157, 14500-653, provides basic health care and extended health services to recipients of public assistance and to medically indigent persons whose average monthly income is not sufficient to provide for 'the cost of health care or coverage less any amount by which the value of his other resources, *owned by him alone or in combination with his spouse* exceeds' a specified value. Id. §14005 (emphasis added). It is far from clear that 'owned property' includes property in a discretionary trust of which the applicant is a possible income beneficiary. . . ." Dukeminier, Perpetuities Revision in California: Perpetual Trusts Permitted, 55 Calif. L. Rev. 678, 691 n. 33 (1967).

a reasonable judgment, if he acts in good faith and does not act capriciously." 3 Scott, Trusts §187.2 (3d ed. 1967). In McNiff v. State Dept. of Public Welfare, 287 Minn. 40, 176 N.W.2d 888 (1970), the beneficiary of a discretionary support trust, containing provisions similar to those in the trust for Naomi Swallow, was held ineligible for public medical assistance.

On the questions of how absolute is "absolute discretion" and how discretionary is a support trust, see pages 894-909, infra.

SECTION G. Termination of Trusts

In England a trust can be terminated if all the beneficiaries consent.[54] It can be terminated even though there is an express clause prohibiting termination. In the United States, if the settlor and all the beneficiaries consent, the beneficiaries can compel termination of the trust even though it is a discretionary trust or it contains a spendthrift clause. Of course, "all the beneficiaries" means every person with a present or future interest, vested or contingent, in the property. Where some of the possible beneficiaries are presently unborn or are legally incapacitated, a court may appoint a guardian to represent them, and may on their behalf approve a termination of the trust.[55] (See page 820, infra.)

If, however, the settlor does not give his consent or is dead, the great weight of authority holds that a trust cannot be terminated prior to the time fixed for termination, even though all the beneficiaries consent, if termination would be contrary to the purpose of the settlor. The leading case establishing this rule is Claflin v. Claflin, 149 Mass. 19, 20 N.E. 454 (1889), and the rule is often referred to as the Claflin doctrine. Although the rule is easy to state, there is considerable disagreement about the circumstances under which termination would be contrary to the purpose of the settlor.[56] Generally, a trust cannot be terminated if it is a spendthrift trust, if the beneficiary is not to receive the principal until he reaches a specified age, if it is a discretionary trust, or if it is a trust for support of the beneficiary. Such provisions are usually deemed to state a material purpose of the settlor. The cases are collected at Bogert & Bogert, Trusts and Trustees §§1007-1008 (2d ed. 1960); 4 Scott, Trusts §§337-337.8 (3d ed. 1967).

ADAMS v. LINK

Supreme Court of Errors of Connecticut, 1958
145 Conn. 634, 145 A.2d 753

KING, Associate Justice. The defendants Link and the United States Trust Company of New York are the executors and trustees under the will and codicil of

[54] Saunders v. Vautier, 4 Beav. 115, 49 Eng. Rep. 282 (Rolls 1841).

[55] Note, Trust Termination and Unborn Beneficiaries, 29 Ohio St. L.J. 741 (1968).

[56] The unpredictability of decisions in one state is documented in Wright, Termination of Trusts in Pennsylvania — Some Current Trends, 115 U. Pa. L. Rev. 917 (1967).

Mildred A. Kingsmill, late of Darien. Mrs. Kingsmill left, as her sole heirs at law, two brothers, Orson Adams, Jr., and Alvin P. Adams, and a sister, Ethel A. Martin. This action grows out of, although it is distinct from, an appeal by Orson Adams, Jr., and Alvin P. Adams, two of the three heirs at law, from the admission of the will and codicil to probate.

In the view which we take of the case, only the right to terminate the trust created in paragraph sixth of the will need be considered. This paragraph disposed of the residue by a trust. It provided for the payment of the net income for life, in monthly or quarterly instalments at their written election, to Joan K. Pringle and Mayes M. Foeppel, neither of whom was an heir at law. At the death of the survivor, the trust was to terminate and distribution of the corpus was to be made to the New York Association for the Blind. In fact, Joan K. Pringle predeceased the testatrix, leaving Mayes M. Foeppel as the sole income beneficiary and entitled, under the terms of the trust, to the entire net income for life.

During the pendency of the appeal from probate, a so-called compromise agreement was entered into between Mayes M. Foeppel, party of the first part, the New York Association for the Blind, party of the second part, and the three heirs at law of the testatrix, parties of the third part. The agreement in effect provided that (1) the appeal from the admission of the will and codicil to probate would be withdrawn; (2) 15 per cent of the residuary estate, i.e., the trust corpus, would be paid outright to the three heirs at law in equal shares; (3) 37 per cent would be paid outright to the New York Association for the blind; and (4) 48 per cent would be paid outright to Mayes M. Foeppel less a deduction of $15,000 which would be used to establish a new trust, the precise terms of which are not material. Basically, it was for the education of a son of Alvin P. Adams, and upon completion of his education the trust would terminate and any unused corpus and interest would be returned to Mayes M. Foeppel.[57] The compromise agreement was by its express terms made subject to the approval of the Superior Court. The defendant executors and trustees refused to participate in the agreement or to carry it out. The present action, the plaintiffs in which include all parties to the agreement except the New York Association for the Blind, which was made a party defendant, seeks in effect (a) the approval of the agreement by the Superior Court, and (b) a decree compelling the defendant executors and trustees to carry it out. Since the provision for the New York Association for the Blind was a charitable gift, the attorney general was made a defendant to represent the public interest, under the provisions of §212 of the General Statutes. The court refused to approve the agreement, and from this action the plaintiffs took this appeal.

[57] Who is the settlor of this trust for the son of Alvin P. Adams? If Mayes is the settlor, certain unexpected tax consequences may follow. For example, Section 673(a) of the Internal Revenue Code of 1954 provides that the settlor will be taxable on the income if the reversion to her may reasonably be expected to take effect in possession within ten years. Numerous other tax problems can arise out of will compromises, e.g., has any claimant made a gift to another by way of the agreement? See Comment, Post Mortem Estate Planning, 4 Real Prop., Prob. & Trust J. 209 (1969).

Could a will compromise be used to avoid claims of the beneficiary's creditors or spouse as well as to lessen taxes? — Eds.

While the parties have extensively argued and briefed a number of questions, one basic proposition is dispositive of, and fatal to, the position taken by the plaintiffs. No corrections of the finding which could benefit them in this view of the case can be made.

The fundamental effect of the compromise agreement, if approved by the court, would be to abolish the trust. Our rule as to the right of the beneficiaries of a testamentary trust to have it terminated has been set forth in a number of cases, including Ackerman v. Union & New Haven Trust Co., 90 Conn. 63, 71, 96 A. 149; De Ladson v. Crawford, 93 Conn. 402, 411, 106 A. 326, and Hills v. Travelers Bank & Trust Co., 125 Conn. 640, 648, 7 A.2d 652, 173 A.L.R. 1419. The rule has also in effect been applied to the right of the beneficiaries to terminate an inter-vivos trust. Gaess v. Gaess, 132 Conn. 96, 101, 42 A.2d 796, 160 A.L.R. 432. Here a testatrix, in her will, established a trust in admittedly clear and unambiguous language; she has now died; and the trust beneficiaries and the heirs at law have joined in a plan to set aside the trust and substitute a distribution of the testatrix' estate more to their liking. Such a testamentary trust may be terminated only by a decree of a court of equity, regardless of any stipulation by all parties in interest. Peiter v. Degenring, 136 Conn. 331, 336, 71 A.2d 87. Our rule as set forth in Hills v. Travelers Bank & Trust Co., supra, is: Conditions precedent which should concur in order to warrant termination of a testamentary trust by judicial decree are (1) that all the parties in interest unite in seeking the termination, (2) that every reasonable ultimate purpose of the trust's creation and existence has been accomplished, and (3) that no fair and lawful restriction imposed by the testator will be nullified or disturbed by such a result. "The function of the court [of equity] with reference to trusts is not to remake the trust instrument, reduce or increase the size of the gifts made therein or accord the beneficiary more advantage than the donor directed that he should enjoy, but rather to ascertain what the donor directed that the donee should receive and to secure to him the enjoyment of that interest only." Hills v. Travelers Bank & Trust Co., supra; Peiter v. Degenring, supra. The underlying rationale of our rule is the protection, if reasonably possible, of any reasonable, properly expressed, testamentary desire of a decedent. 3 Scott, Trusts (2d Ed.) §337.

It appears that all the interested beneficiaries have joined in the agreement under consideration. For the purposes of this case only, we will assume, without in any way deciding, that the plaintiffs are correct in their claim that the defendant executors and trustees have no standing to attack the compromise. This assumption is permissible because the compromise was in terms made contingent upon court approval, and this approval could not be compelled by any agreement of the trust beneficiaries among themselves. Peiter v. Degenring, supra. Thus we may assume, without deciding, that the first condition precedent under our rule is satisfied. But see Loring, A Trustee's Handbook (5th Ed.) §122 p. 316, §123 p. 318. The second and third conditions precedent have not, however, been satisfied. The obvious objectives of the testatrix were to provide (a) an assured income for life for Mayes M. Foeppel, and (b) at her death an intact corpus for the New York Association for the Blind. In carrying out these objectives, the testatrix took two important steps.

In the first place, the management of the trust corpus was committed to trustees selected by her and in whose financial judgment she is presumed to have had confidence. Secondly, expenditure of any principal by the life beneficiary was precluded. Taken together, these two steps would tend to achieve, and in all reasonable probability would achieve, the testatrix' two basic objectives. To abolish the trust and turn over a fraction of the corpus outright to the life beneficiary would be to enable her in a moment to lose the protection of the practically assured life income provided by the testatrix. The two basic objectives of the trust's creation and existence were reasonable and commendable and cannot be fully accomplished prior to the death of the life beneficiary. Peiter v. Degenring, supra, 136 Conn. 337, 71 A.2d 90; 3 Scott, op. cit., §337.1, p. 2454. Obviously, had the testatrix intended to entrust the life beneficiary with the handling of any part of the corpus, she would have so provided by a simple, outright gift.

The plaintiffs attempt to avoid the impact of our rule by two main claims. The first is that since the protection accorded the life beneficiary could be lost by her voluntary alienation of the income or by its involuntary alienation through attachment or seizure under an order in equity, the testatrix could not have intended to protect the beneficiary. This amounts in effect to a claim that only a spendthrift trust is protected from termination by agreement of all interested beneficiaries. The case against termination under our rule is of course even stronger where a spendthrift trust is involved, as in Mason v. Rhode Island Hospital Trust Co., 78 Conn. 81, 84, 61 A. 57. 3 Scott, op. cit., §337.2. But the operation of our rule is not restricted to such trusts. The mere fact that the testatrix failed to provide the maximum possible protection for the life beneficiary by creating a spendthrift trust under the terms of what is now §3195d of the 1955 Cumulative Supplement[58] does not warrant a conclusion that she intended no protection at all, so that we can consider that the trust no longer has any purpose. Id., p. 2454.

There is no merit in the plaintiffs' claim that in Peiter v. Degenring, supra, there was a change in, or a relaxation of, our rule. The facts in that case were peculiar. The testator's brother was seventy-eight years old and under a conservator. The testator created a trust for the payment to the brother or his conservator of "so much of the income and principal of my estate as may be necessary for his support and comfort, using the income first." In other words, the beneficiary was given neither principal nor income except as necessary for his support and comfort. The parties stipulated that the brother owned personal estate the annual income of which was greatly in excess of his needs for comfort and support, that he had not been entitled to receive and had not received any money from the trust, and that there was no possibility that he would be entitled to receive any money from it at any time. The proposal of all interested parties was that the trust be terminated

[58] Sec. 3195d provides a procedure for the attachment of such an unrestricted life estate as was here created, but further provides: "When any such trust shall have been expressly provided to be for the support of the beneficiary or his family, a court of equity having jurisdiction may make such order regarding the surplus, if any, not required for the support of the beneficiary or his family, as justice and equity may require."

upon the payment to the brother of $10,000, which of course would be under the management of the conservator. We held that a decree terminating the trust could not be granted on any stipulation of the parties but only, if at all, upon the basis of facts found by testimony offered before the court, and that the trust should not be terminated "unless those facts clearly establish that no purpose it was designed to serve would be defeated or jeopardized." Id., 136 Conn. 340, 71 A.2d 91. There is nothing in the decision inconsistent with our rule as set forth in the other cases cited by us. The Peiter cases does hold that evidence may be offered of facts, not apparent from the provisions of the trust instrument itself, which, if proved, would warrant a conclusion that the trust does not serve a legal and useful purpose and should be terminated. Ibid. We also held in the Peiter case that if satisfactory proof was made of the peculiar facts therein, it might warrant a conclusion by the court that in all reasonable probability the trust would remain inactive during the beneficiary's life and, if so, a termination might be ordered, as in the case of any useless trust. The Peiter case in nowise helps the plaintiffs here. . . .

The plaintiffs also claim that whatever the rule may be in cases involving no will contest, a more liberal rule applies where, as here, the termination of the trust is a part of the settlement of such a contest. Some support for this position may be found in cases cited in 3 Scott, Trusts (2d Ed.) §337.6. The rationale of our rule as to the power to set aside or terminate a trust is not, however, such that its applicability would be affected by the mere fact that the motivation of a trust termination agreement is the compromise of a will contest. It is true that such contests are not infrequently compromised by agreements involving the transfer of legacies or devises, in whole or in part, by beneficiaries under the will. Where such gifts are alienable this is permissible, since no violence is done to the provisions of the will. But that is not this case. Here the provisions of the will itself are being drastically changed so as to abolish a trust contrary to our rule. This cannot be done. It follows that the court below was not in error in denying approval of the agreement. Indeed, it was the only decision which could properly have been made. This conclusion makes unnecessary the consideration of the other grounds of appeal.

There is no error.

In this opinion the other judges concurred.[59]

NOTES

1. By his will David Rosen left the residue of his estate in trust to pay the income to his sister Rebecca for life, with power in the trustees to spend principal for her support if the income should prove insufficient. What remained on Rebecca's death was to go to her children. By a codicil David purported to change his will by giving Rebecca a life estate, eliminating the power to pay her principal, giving Rebecca's children a secondary life estate, and giving the ultimate remainder to a synagogue. The will and codicil were probated, and Rebecca then filed a peti-

[59] Noted 39 B.U.L. Rev. 274. — EDS.

tion to revoke the decree allowing the codicil. Rebecca, Rebecca's children (medical evidence was allowed to show Rebecca could have no more children), and the synagogue then entered into a compromise agreement. The agreement provided the residue was to be distributed free of trust, approximately one-fourth to the synagogue and three-fourths to Rebecca. In upholding the compromise the court said: "Such an agreement of compromise as to interests which might be received from an estate is apart from the provisions of the will. Rights under the agreement are wholly contractual and in no sense testamentary. . . . Indeed, the result may be quite contrary to the testator's intent. This means that before the allowance of a will a trust may be changed or even eliminated by a compromise otherwise valid and approved by the court." Budin v. Levy, 343 Mass. 644, 180 N.E.2d 74 (1962).

2. On termination of trusts by family settlement of testator's estate, see Note, 29 A.L.R.3d 8 (1970).

3. T bequeaths the residue of his estate in a spendthrift trust to pay the income to A for life, then to pay the principal to A's estate. A is the sole heir of T. A renounces all her interest in the trust. Does A take T's residue free and clear of the trust? In re Nicely's Estate, 235 Cal. App. 2d 174, 44 Cal. Rptr. 804 (1965); Halbach, Post Mortem Estate Planning, 1963 U. Ill. L.F. 212, 222.

4. Saddad transferred his stock in Playgirl Corporation to Beetle to use the income therefrom for the support and education of Saddad's daughter, Merry, so long as she remained married to her husband, Herbert. At the death of Herbert or if Merry sooner divorced him, Merry was to receive the principal free of the trust. A spendthrift limitation was attached to Merry's life and remainder interests.

Several years after creating this trust, Saddad died intestate, survived by Merry as his only heir.

Merry finds the income of the trust insufficient to finance ballet lessons in France which she considers vital to her professional career. She wishes to reach all or part of the principal of the trust for this purpose but has no intention at this time of divorcing Herbert.

Merry comes to you for advice as to how she might reach all or part of the principal during Herbert's lifetime and without divorcing him. Advise her. 1 Scott, Trusts §65.3 (3d ed. 1967); 2 id. §168; 4 id. §§337.2 to 337.4. (California Bar Examination Question, Fall, 1967.)

11. Future Interests

SECTION A. Introduction

In Chapter 8 we studied the trust, an arrangement whereby property ownership is divided into legal and equitable interests. Property is conveyed to a trustee, who holds legal title to the assets and manages and controls them for the benefit of the trust beneficiary, who has equitable title. In this chapter and the ones that follow we study another, quite different, means whereby ownership can be divided: into time segments. Our legal system permits the creation of *present interests* — giving the owner a right to present possession or enjoyment of the property, and *future interests* — giving the owner an interest that may entitle him to possession or enjoyment of the property at some future point in time.

Even though these two ways of dividing ownership involve totally different concepts, they are functionally related in that today future interests ordinarily arise in the context of trust settlements.[1] We have already commented on the increased use of the trust as a means of settling family wealth, and on the favorable estate tax treatment accorded life estates and power of appointment trusts, as contributing factors in this growth in the use of trusts.[2] But observe that whenever a life estate is given, a future interest is also created: someone is going to get the property on termination of the life estate. A trust settlement invariably involves the creation of one or more future interests. This necessitates that the trust draftsman be familiar

[1] We will take a look at *legal* life estates and future interests — and the substantial problems attendant to their use in estate planning — at page 891.

[2] See discussion at pages 209-210 and 231-233, supra.

with the types of future interests that can be employed, and with the constructional and other problems attendant to their use. Adam Smith's estate is a case in point.

Assume that Smith has decided to establish an unfunded revocable life insurance trust, which is to be funded at Smith's death by receipt of the proceeds of his life insurance policies. The residuary assets in his probate estate are to be added to the trust via a pour-over provision in his will. As with most persons considering this type of plan, Smith wants the trust income to be paid to his wife during her lifetime, and on her death he wants the trust corpus to be distributed to his children in equal shares. One way to provide for this would be simply to draft the trust like this:

> The Trustee shall pay the trust income to my wife, Jane Smith, during her lifetime, and on my wife's death the Trustee shall distribute the trust corpus then on hand to my children in equal shares.

Alas, more than a few wills and trusts have been drafted just that way. The result? A dispositive plan that *lacks flexibility,* and one that *fails to provide for contingencies* that may occur to change both the make-up of the Smith family and the respective needs of the family members. Consider:

"The Trustee shall pay the trust income to my wife, Jane Smith, during her lifetime, . . ." As presently planned, on Smith's death the trust will be funded with about sixty to seventy thousand dollars in life insurance proceeds. If the trust produces a net return (after taxes and the expenses of trust administration and trustee compensation) of five percent, it will provide income of about three thousand to thirty-five hundred dollars a year. Will this amount, together with social security benefits and the income from other assets, be sufficient to maintain the Smith family? Moreover, emergency needs and educational expenses are bound to arise; whence the funds to pay these bills? Obviously, the trust corpus must be reachable to meet necessary expenditures that are not satisfied from trust income. Hence the need to provide invasion powers over principal, exercisable either by the trustee or by Mrs. Smith. We shall study the use of invasion powers, which are a form of power of appointment, in Chapter 13.

". . . and on my wife's death the Trustee shall distribute the trust corpus to my children in equal shares." It takes no great vision to foresee that this plan for the disposition of principal fails to provide for a number of contingencies that may arise in the future. It is possible that Mrs. Smith may die while the Smith children (or some of them) are still minors. If this were to occur, Smith would undoubtedly want the trust to continue at least until the children attain legal age. Moreover, if he is like most parents, he would probably want trust corpus to be distributed to the children at age twenty-five, or perhaps at age thirty, rather than at the relatively tender age of twenty-one.

Then there is the matter of terminating the trust. All of the Smith children are not going to reach the age of twenty-five at the same time (unless they are twins, or triplets). Will Smith want a distribution of each child's share as that child attains age twenty-five? Or will he, instead, want the trust to continue until the youngest child attains age twenty-five? What are some of the factors that you, as Smith's attorney, would suggest that he consider in deciding how to handle this? Should Smith establish a separate trust for each child, or a single trust for all the children? What are the tax and other factors that bear on this question? (In Smith's case the relatively small size of his estate would point toward a single trust. In more substantial estates, this question would have to be explored.)

Then, too, suppose that all the Smith children do not live to attain the age of twenty-five. If one of them dies under that age, what is to be done with the share that otherwise would have passed to him? Would it make a difference if that child left a young widow? A young widow and an infant child?

Finally: to the Smith children "in equal shares"? This proposed disposition of course reflects the common parental sentiment that all children should be treated fairly and equally. But an equal distribution may not turn out to be a fair one. Looking far into the future — which is when this distribution will take place — it is possible that life will have been kinder to some of the Smith children than to the others. Would Adam Smith want an equal distribution if it turns out that one of his children has prospered in his career (or has "married well"), while another has suffered a financial setback, or a bad marriage, or a disabling illness or injury? These questions point up the undesirability of establishing now, in Smith's trust or will, a fixed plan for the distribution of trust corpus to the children. It is not enough to say that as circumstances change, Smith can exercise his reserved power to revoke, alter, or amend the trust, for the changed circumstances may occur after, not before, his death. It is for these reasons that Smith should consider giving his wife a testamentary power of appointment over trust corpus.

If the foregoing are valid questions[3] that Adam Smith should consider in working out a dispositive plan for his trust, we have raised a fairly substantial number of questions for such an uncomplicated family and asset situation. This points up the inherent difficulty in drafting wills and trusts that contain future interests. Drafting a legal document that is to cover an immediate transaction, such as a contract for the sale of goods, is relatively easy: The transaction is to take place at a fixed point in time, and the circumstances surrounding the transaction are known or can be predicted fairly accurately. But drafting for the future, as is inherent in drafting a will or a trust, requires that the instrument cover not only what is likely to occur "if all goes well," but also what may possibly occur at some uncertain time in the future.

And so we now take a look at the law of future interests — not because we professors find any unusual enchantment in the antiquarian base of the subject, or because we get some kind of perverse satisfaction in pushing students through the quirks and quiddities and sometimes infuriating distinctions that make up this area of the law. Rather, we study future interests because we must, for they are the stuff of which the dispositive provisions of trusts are made. On the positive side, we shall seek to gain an understanding of those facets of future interests law that are relevant and useful to the draftsman. On the negative side we must be able to identify,

[3] Are they? Or, given the Smith family situation, is the likelihood of these contingencies occurring so negligible as to make the stated concerns more imaginary than real?

so that we can avoid, (a) those intent-defeating technical rules of future interests law that are still with us, and (b) some commonly encountered problems of construction.

SECTION B. Present Interests

1. *Introduction*

The English developed, and gave to America, a unique system for dealing with claims of persons to resources — what Maitland called the wonderful calculus of estates. "We thus come upon a characteristic," wrote Maitland, "which, at all events for six centuries and perhaps for many centuries more, will be the most salient trait of our English land law. Proprietary rights in land are, we may say, projected upon the plane of time. The category of quantity, of duration, is applied to them. The life-tenant's rights are a finite quantity; the fee-tenant's rights are an infinite, or potentially infinite quantity; we see a difference in respect of duration, and this is the one fundamental difference. In short, to use a term that we have as yet carefully eschewed, we are coming to a law of 'estates in land.' " [4]

In our exploration of the estates system we must go back to the beginning — or almost to the beginning, somewhere around the eleventh or twelfth century — for the central characteristic of modern future interest law is its heavy reliance on its historical underpinnings: on vocabulary and concepts developed over several centuries in feudal and medieval England. When this nation was founded, our courts adopted the English common law system of estates in land and future interests, and in doing so adopted the bad along with the good. At that time lawyers and judges "read law," and the law they read was Blackstone, or perhaps the "Americanized" tome, Kent's Commentaries. In an era when the law was seen as a closed system of fixed rules, it was not the temper of the times for judges to conclude, or for lawyers even to argue, that some of the more peculiar rules and concepts of estates law related to a feudal system that had never existed in this country; or that the reasons for various intention-frustrating rules had long since disappeared and so the rules themselves should be abandoned.

Interests in property can be divided into present and future interests. The essential idea basing the distinction is that the owner of a present interest is presently entitled to possession, while the owner of a future interest will or may be entitled to possession at some time in the future. In this chapter we sketch the types of present interests and future interests recognized by our legal system. It is by no means definitive, nor is it intended to be. In fact a good part of this course is devoted to rendering these terms more intelligible by considering problems in which the terms are used. The terms stand for "interests," which are abstract concepts representing congeries of rights. They, like all words, are symbols, but they do not bring to mind when we see them concrete experiences or relations. Instead they bring to

[4] 2 Pollock & Maitland, History of English Law 10 (2d ed. 1911).

mind circles in the air, "things" you can think of but can neither feel nor see. This results from our continued adherence to the medieval mode of thinking which mistook the abstraction for concrete reality. The medieval mind reified (made things of) its abstractions, in much the same way as the primitive mind thought of a golden calf or of the sun when it thought of God.[5] Many paradoxes arise from this "fallacy of misplaced concreteness," to borrow a phrase from Alfred North Whitehead. Some of them appear recurrently throughout these materials.

2. *Fee Simple Absolute*

The fee simple absolute connotes absolute ownership of land, so far as it is known to our law. Expressed in the durational sense that is the essential characteristic of the "estates" concept, the fee simple absolute is an estate of infinite duration.

One way to understand what this means is to use a process of "thing-thinking" known as the reification of abstractions. This is the way our learned ancestors in this field thought. Here is a simplified illustration of how it is done. Consider first a plane of time running through space to infinity, like this:

We shall divide this plane sequentially according to who has the right to possession of Blackacre. Now think of a fee simple absolute in Blackacre. Reify it. (What did you think of when you were told to think of a fee simple absolute? Can you think of a fee simple without thinking of it as a thing, such as a circle in space or a "bundle of rights"? [6]) Having made a thing of a fee simple, you must now ascribe to it "qualities" or "characteristics" of things. One of the characteristics of this reified fee simple absolute is that it is of infinite duration. The owner of this fee, O, is entitled to possession of Blackacre unto infinity. We can show this on the plane of time, in this manner:

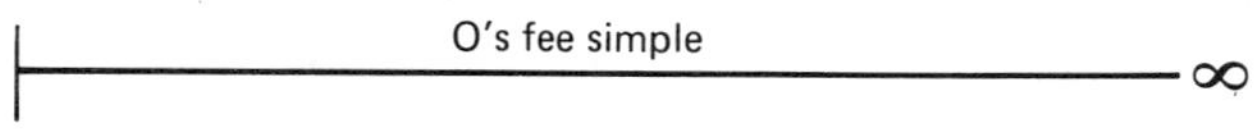

[5] Digby, History of the Law of Real Property 266 (1875): "The tendency of philosophical thought prevailing at the period in question was to invest all abstract ideas with a real and substantial existence, to treat of them not merely as collective names for a variety of particular facts and circumstances agreeing in the points designated by the general name, but as having a real existence, apart from the particular or individual instances, and possessing definite attributes or properties necessarily inherent in their essence."

[6] Cf. [The White King] ". . . And I haven't sent the two Messengers, either. They're both gone to the town. Just look along the road, and tell me if you see either of them."

"I see nobody on the road," said Alice.

"I only wish *I* had such eyes," the King remarked in a fretful tone. "To be able to see Nobody! And at that distance too! Why, it's as much as *I* can do to see real people, by this light!" — Carroll, Through the Looking Glass

Now we have an apparent conceptual difficulty: while O's estate will last forever, O most certainly will not. Yet there is no problem. What is meant, here, is that O's fee simple is an estate of general inheritability. If O never conveys the land during his lifetime and dies intestate, his fee simple will pass by intestacy to his heirs. If they never convey the land and die intestate, it will pass by intestacy to their heirs — and so on down the generations. The fee simple is the only estate capable of descending by intestacy from generation to generation until the end of time.

O's fee simple is also freely transmissible by him during his lifetime: He can deed his estate to A, in which case A will own an estate of infinite duration. O can also devise Blackacre by will, in which case his devisee will take the fee simple. (The estate in fee simple is not unique in these respects, however. Other "lesser" estates are also freely transferable during lifetime or by will. But only the fee simple is generally inheritable until the end of time in the manner that we have described.)

O can also convey a "lesser" estate, and thereby carve the fee into sequential interests that follow each other on the plane of time. Suppose O conveys to A the right to possession of Blackacre during A's lifetime. We take this right, call it a life estate, add some consequential rights, and reify it. In this case we may cut up the plane of time and designate on it who has the right of possession, thus:

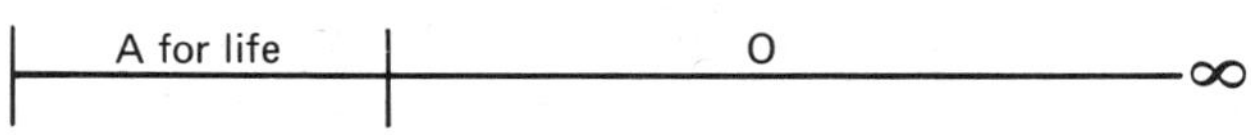

A has a life estate. O has a reversion in fee simple. When A dies and his life estate terminates, O will again have a present possessory estate in fee simple absolute.

Note on "to A and His Heirs": Words of Purchase and Words of Limitation

Suppose O transfers Blackacre "to A and his heirs." What does A get by this conveyance, and what do his heirs get? The answer is that A takes an estate in fee simple absolute, and the heirs take nothing. The explanation is that the words "and his heirs" are not *words of purchase;* they are *words of limitation.*

Words of purchase designate the taker or takers of an estate by grant or by will. The words of purchase in this conveyance are "to A." This does not mean that A bought Blackacre from O, paying a consideration for the transfer. As used in this sense, the term purchase means that A acquired the real property by grant or devise, rather than by inheritance.[7]

Words of limitation are the terms of the conveyance that define or delimit the durational extent of the estate that has been granted. Thus in a conveyance "to B

[7] "The word [*purchase*], in form and meaning born of the *chase* for wild animals, implied a personal effort to get something. The earliest law uses in French of the twelfth or thirteenth centuries adopted this common understanding. In the thirteenth century law French forms of *purchase* were used in the more specialized senses of obtaining (a writ), and acquiring property other than by inheritance. Since then the law has been refining and expounding this last sense." Mellinkoff, The Language of the Law 108 (1963).

for life," the words "to B" are words of purchase; the words "for life" are words of limitation that define the estate granted to B as one that is to last for the duration of B's lifetime.

Now let's go back to the conveyance "to A and his heirs." The words "and his heirs" are words of limitation denoting that A has been granted a fee simple absolute estate. *The phrase "and his heirs" is the legal equivalent of "in fee simple."* To understand how this came about, we have to go back to the early days of the feudal period, when virtually all the land in England was held in a tenurial relationship between the king and his various chief lords, between these lords and their tenants, between these tenants (mesne lords) and their tenants, and so on. A chief lord (tenant in capite) who had been granted lands by the king in return for an undertaking to render certain services (such as furnishing knights for a specified period) and an oath of homage, or loyalty, would in turn grant lands to various persons as tenants — again in return for an undertaking to furnish services and an oath of homage.[8]

Because of the highly personal nature of the lord-tenant relationship, in the beginning the tenant's interest in the land was not transferable inter vivos without his lord's consent. Of greater significance to our story, the tenant's interest was not inheritable; in effect he had a life estate. On the tenant's death his estate reverted to the lord, who was under no obligation to recognize the tenant's heir as successor to the estate. Customarily, though, for an appropriate fee (known as a relief — you might say the historical antecedent of our modern inheritance tax) the lord would regrant the land to the heir, securing from him an oath of homage. In time, tenants began to bargain for an advance agreement by the lord that on the tenant's death the lord would recognize the tenant's heir as successor to the estate; that is, that the estate granted to the tenant would be inheritable. When this was done, the phraseology used to denote that the tenant was being given an inheritable estate was "to A and his heirs." Still later, inheritance of a fee simple became a matter of right, but the payment of relief to the lord continued.

So long as the estate of the fee simple tenant was not freely transferable and was not devisable by will, the practical effect of a conveyance "to A and his heirs" was to give A an interest that would pass to his heir, to the heir's heir, and so on down the centuries. Once land became freely transferable and devisable, it became settled that the heirs took nothing by the conveyance. A can transfer his fee simple to B; if he does so, his heirs will receive nothing at his death. Or, A can devise his fee simple by will and thereby defeat the heirs' expectancy. It is true that if A doesn't make an inter vivos transfer and dies without a will, his fee simple will pass by intestacy to his heirs. If this occurs, the estate passes by intestacy *from* A; it does not pass by the language of "and his heirs" in the initial grant. The heirs take because A died intestate owning a fee simple, not because they were given an interest in the grant of that estate to A.

[8] "[T]his was felt to be a solemn and sacred bond. . . . The obligations of mutual aid and support which grew out of it may perhaps owe their sacred character to the fact that they were so absolutely necessary to the preservation of society." Plucknett, A Concise History of the Common Law 507 (5th ed. 1956).

For many centuries in England, in order to grant an estate in fee simple it was absolutely essential to use the verbal formula, "and his heirs." [9] A conveyance "to A and his successors and assigns forever," and even a conveyance "to A in fee simple," gave A a life estate only. Happily, this formalism is no longer a part of our law — except in South Carolina.[10] A number of states have statutes similar to the following:

> Every deed conveying lands shall, unless an exception be made therein, be construed to include all the estate, right, title, interest, use, possession, property, claim and demand whatsoever, both in law and equity, of the grantor, including the fee simple if he had such an estate, of, in and to the premises conveyed, with the appurtenances, and the word "heirs" shall not be necessary to effect the conveyance of the fee simple; . . .[11]

In states not having a statute, this result has been reached by judicial decision. While the phrase "and his heirs" is no longer required, lawyers, being creatures of habit, continue to insert it.

PROBLEMS

1. O conveys Blackacre "to A for life, and on his death to B." What interests are created by this conveyance? Does O have a reversion? Which words in the conveyance are words of purchase, and which are words of limitation?

2. O conveys Blackacre "to the heirs of A," and A is dead at the time of the conveyance. Which are words of purchase and which are words of limitation?

3. *Defeasible Fees*

Defeasible fee is the generic term that denotes an estate of *potentially* infinite duration; that is, an estate that may last forever, but can also come to an end at some point in time short of infinity because of the happening or failure to happen of some event.

> *Case 1.* O conveys Blackacre to the Board of Education, its successors and assigns, for so long as the premises are used for school purposes.

[9] In a will "and his heirs" was never necessary. It was assumed that the testator intended to dispose of as large an estate as he had.

[10] Grainger v. Hamilton, 228 S.C. 318, 90 S.E.2d 209 (1955).

In Cole v. Steinlauf, 144 Conn. 629, 136 A.2d 744 (1957), the Connecticut Supreme Court of Errors cited the common law rule in holding a title unmarketable when a 1945 deed in the chain of title ran to the grantee "and assigns forever." Since the "and his heirs" formula had not been used, it was doubtful whether that deed conveyed a fee simple title. Four years later the Court held that the "heirs" formula was not required under Connecticut law, but that the Steinlauf case had nonetheless been correctly decided because the issue in that case involved marketability of title and the case law was then unclear. Dennan v. Searle, 149 Conn. 126, 176 A.2d 561 (1961).

[11] N.J. Stat. Ann. §46:3-13 (1940).

In *Case 1* the Board of Education has a *fee simple determinable.* It is a fee simple, for the estate will last forever if the premises are used for school purposes until the end of time. But if at some point in the future the premises cease to be used for school purposes, the Board of Education's estate will come to an end, or "determine," and title will revert back to the grantor in fee simple absolute. The grantor has a *possibility of reverter.* (Why is the grantor's future interest a possibility of reverter, and not a reversion? A good question — and if you can't wait for an answer, skip to page 728.)

To project this on the plane of time,

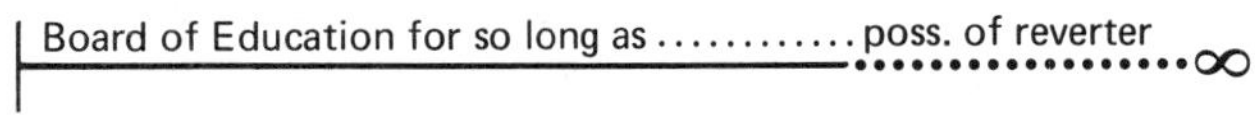

Another type of defeasible fee is the *fee simple on a condition subsequent.*

> *Case 2.* O conveys Blackacre to the Board of Education, its successors and assigns; provided, however, that if the premises shall ever cease to be used for school purposes, the grantor shall have the right to re-enter and retake the same.

Observe that we have here expressed the same condition as in the preceeding example, only this time we have used a different verbal formula. We have expressed the divesting event as a condition subsequent. Once again, the Board of Education's estate may last forever, and so it is a fee simple. But it may be cut short; if the Board, or its successors or assigns, ever cease to use the premises for school purposes, *and if* the grantor asserts his *right of entry for condition broken,* he can yank back the fee simple.

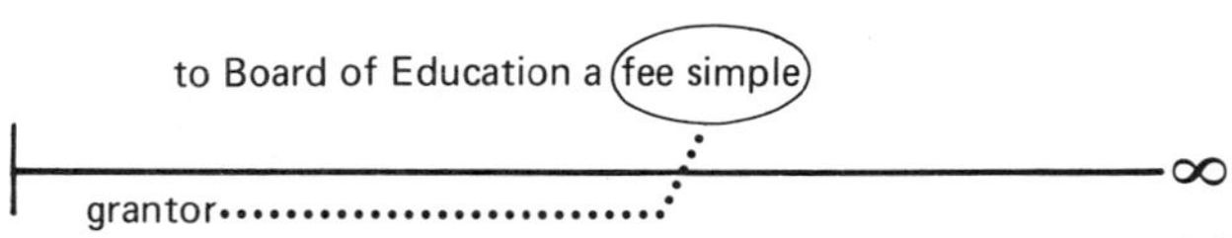

In the last section of this chapter we will give an extended discussion to the fee simple determinable (with its correlative future interest, the possibility of reverter) and to the fee simple on a condition subsequent (with its correlative future interest, the right of entry for condition broken).

4. *Fee Tail*

The fee tail has never been a viable form of land ownership in America. Still, it is necessary to make some reference to it: not simply to round out the list of present interests, but because two of its vestiges are still with us.

In England, from 1066 to the nineteenth century, land was more than merely the principal form of wealth; it also represented power and status. The nobility very much desired to keep their ancestral properties in the family and free from creditors and from forfeiture (a practical consideration in turbulent times). The estate in fee tail, recognized soon after the Statute de Donis Conditionalibus in 1285, was the chief instrument by which this was done. A conveyance "to A and the heirs of his body" gave A a fee tail.[12] The fee tail had two distinctive features. First, it was an estate that lasted only so long as there were descendants of the original tenant in fee tail, A. Second, it could be inherited only by A's descendants. In practical effect, A had what amounted to a life estate, for on his death the estate passed to A's lineal heir — under the doctrine of primogeniture then prevailing in England, to A's eldest son. During his lifetime, A could make no conveyance or take any other action that would defeat the fee tail. On A's death his eldest son succeeded to the fee tail; on the death of the eldest son it passed to such son's eldest son, and so on. If a tenant in tail died not survived by a son, the fee tail passed to his daughters. Observe that this arrangement was highly effective in keeping the ancestral property in the family line — so long as there were any descendants. If a tenant in tail died not survived by any descendants of the original tenant in tail, the estate came to an end.

PROBLEM

In 1325 O conveys Blackacre "to A and the heirs of his body." The estate in fee tail stays in A's family line for several generations; then in 1425 a tenant in tail dies not survived by any descendants of A. Who owns Blackacre after this tenant's death?

This early form of a "perpetuity" stood little chance of being curtailed by Parliament, which was controlled by the nobility. But the king's judges perceived many mischiefs attending settlements when there was no power of alienation, and in Taltarum's Case, Y.B. 12 Edw. 4, Mich. Term p. 25 (1472), they countenanced a method by which a tenant in tail could "bar the entail." By engaging in a fictitious lawsuit known as the common recovery, the fee tail tenant in possession could convert the fee tail into a fee simple absolute, cutting off all interests of other persons.[13] To counteract Taltarum's Case, lawyers for landowners drew conveyances prohibiting the tenant in tail from suffering a common recovery, but the judges forthrightly invented a rule that the power to suffer a recovery was an inseparable incident of every fee tail, and the attempt to hamper this power in any way was void.[14]

[12] The estate was a *fee* because it was an estate of *potentially* infinite duration; A's bloodline might never run out. It was a fee *tail* because it was especially tailored (from the French *tailler*, meaning "to carve") out of the fee simple.

[13] For a description of how the common recovery worked, and of other devices subsequently invented to bar the entail, see Megarry & Wade, The Law of Real Property 87-102 (3d ed. 1966).

[14] Taltarum's Case did not mean the end of the usefulness of the fee tail, however. Only a fee tail tenant *in possession* could suffer a common recovery. Lawyers for landowners used this

Modern Legacies from the Fee Tail

Although the estate in fee tail has never been a significant form of property ownership in America, two of its vestiges are still with us. The first is the *indefinite failure of issue* construction given to the words "die without issue." Recall that when O conveyed "to A and the heirs of his body," O was left with a reversion in fee simple. For a number of reasons O would usually not want the property to return to him or his estate when the fee tail expired but would want the property to go to the second or other son's descendants. Thus it was usual to provide "to A and the heirs of his body, but if A die without issue to B and his heirs." Read out of context by the modern student, the phrase "die without issue" appears to refer to facts existing at the death of A. But read in the context of O's granting A a fee tail, "die without issue" meant "when A's descendants become extinct." This was the standard construction given by the English courts to the phrase "die without issue," even in cases where it did not follow a fee tail.

PROBLEM

In England in 1500 O conveys "to A and the heirs of his body, but if A die without issue to B and his heirs." What is the state of the title? Is B's interest subject to a condition precedent and thus contingent?

In America more than half the states by statute have abolished the constructional preference for indefinite failure of issue and have substituted a constructional preference for *definite failure of issue*. Definite failure of issue means failure of issue at a definite time, for example at the death of the named ancestor. Applying this construction to the above problem, the gift over to B will take effect if, but only if, A is not survived by any issue at his death. If A is survived by issue, B is completely cut out.

In states without statutes, most courts have adopted a constructional preference for definite failure of issue. Professor Powell finds only five states in which substantial importance is still given to a constructional preference for indefinite failure of issue: Arkansas, Delaware, Florida, Indiana, and Maine.[15]

The second legacy from the fee tail is: What estate or estates are created by a grant "to A and the heirs of his body"? This quaint language continues to crop up

---

requirement as the keystone in creating what became known as a "strict settlement." In brief, land was limited to A for life, then to A's eldest son in tail, then to A's second son in tail, and so forth. When A's eldest son, B, became of age, A surrendered possession to B who suffered a common recovery and made a new limitation to A for life, then to B for life, then to B's eldest son in tail, and so forth. Thus inalienability was pushed forward generation by generation.

[15] 3 Powell, Real Property ¶340, n. 20 (1970).

in an occasional deed or will, usually homemade. There are several statutory solutions to the problem, and where no statute exists courts have come to one or another of these solutions. The majority of states divide between solutions (d) and (e).[16]

(a) The language creates a fee tail. Delaware, Maine, Massachusetts, and Rhode Island still have the fee tail. The fee tail tenant can convey a fee simple absolute by deed, and the creditor of the owner of such estate can reach the entire property to satisfy his claim.

(b) The language creates a fee tail in A, which becomes a fee simple in A's issue. A has no power to execute a disentailing conveyance.

(c) The language creates a life estate in A, remainder in fee simple in A's issue. States adopting this solution are split over whether A's children take vested interests when born or must survive A in order to take.

(d) The language creates a fee simple absolute in A.

(e) The language creates a fee simple in A, preserving any attempted limitation over on A's death without issue as an executory interest effective if A dies without issue surviving him. Thus if O grants Blackacre "to A and the heirs of his body, but if A dies without issue to B," A acquires a fee simple defeasible in favor of B if A dies without surviving issue. If A dies with issue, B's executory interest is cut off.

PROBLEM

T devises Blackacre "to my son John and his bodily heirs, and if he dies without bodily heirs to my daughter Mary and her heirs." John is aged twenty-four, married, with one child aged two. John wants to sell Blackacre to Henry, who is willing to pay a good price for a fee simple absolute. Advise Henry.

5. *Life Estate*

You will no doubt be relieved (and perhaps a little surprised) to learn that there are no unusual problems, conceptually or otherwise, attendant to the creation of a life estate. A conveyance "to A for life" gives A an estate that lasts for the duration of A's life. A can transfer his life estate to B, in which case B has a *life estate pur autre vie* — that is, an estate that is measured by A's life-span, not B's.

PROBLEMS

1. T devises his estate "to my wife, W, for so long as she remains unmarried, and if she remarries it is my will that my property shall, in that event, be distributed

[16] See 2 id. ¶¶196, 198.

to my son A." W does not remarry. She dies leaving a will that devises all her property to B. Does B take any of the property that came from T's estate? Saunders v. Saunders, 490 P.2d 1260 (Ore. 1971); Dickson v. Alexandria Hospital, Inc., 177 F.2d 876 (4th Cir. 1949).

2. In 1970 O conveys Blackacre "to A for life." In 1971 A conveys "all my right, title and interest in Blackacre to B and his heirs."

a. If in 1972 B dies, survived by A and O, what is the state of the title?

b. If, instead, in 1972 A dies, survived by B and O, what is the state of the title?

Seisin

The fee simple, fee tail, and life estate are *freehold* estates. (Perhaps it would be more accurate to say that they *were* freehold estates, for this term has no modern significance and is not a part of the vocabulary of today's lawyer.) The significance of this, at common law, was that the holder of a present freehold estate had *seisin*, and that before 1536 a freehold estate could be created or transferred only by a highly formalized ceremonial known as a *feoffment with livery of seisin*. This involved both the grantor and grantee going on the land and the grantor, before witnesses, delivering seisin to the grantee either by some symbolic act such as handing over a twig or a clod of dirt, or by uttering some words such as "Enter into this land and God give you joy." In a society where few could read and write, this ceremony performed important ritual and evidentiary functions.

Seisin was a very important concept in feudal times. Maitland has written: "In the history of our law there is no idea more cardinal than that of seisin. Even in the law of the present day it plays a part which must be studied by every lawyer; but in the past it was so important that we may almost say that the whole system of our land law was about seisin and its consequences." [17] The meaning of seisin changed through the centuries. But for our purposes it is sufficient to say that a person was seised if he held an estate of freehold and either had physical possession of the land or a leaseholder held the land from him. Except where the land was leased and the landlord held the seisin, "possession by a freeholder" embodied the fundamental idea of seisin. But more important than attempting to define seisin is to understand the way the concept of seisin functioned in the feudal system of government. In feudal times order was maintained by lords with great tracts of land. In exchange for the protection of the lord and the possession of some acreage, the lord was entitled to certain services. The persons responsible for these services, and against whom any default of services had to be enforced, were the persons seised of the land. Moreover, feudal death taxes were levied upon the death of a person seised of land. If seisin could be in abeyance, the feudal system could not work. Hence someone must always be seised, and feudal land law decreed that there must never be a moment of time when seisin could not be located in someone owning a freehold estate. This requirement of continuity of seisin had a decided impact on the evolution of the law of future interests.

[17] 2 Pollock & Maitland, History of English Law 17 (2d ed. 1911).

6. *Term of Years*

The term of years is a nonfreehold estate, and the termor could not hold seisin at common law. The term of years began as a moneylender's device. O would borrow a sum of money from A, and to pay A back O would grant A a term of years during which A would receive the profits from the land. The length of the term was calculated to produce a substantial profit above the amount loaned. Perhaps because of the way the term of years was initially used, the termor was not considered to be seised of the land. As it turned out, this proved to be extremely useful to conveyancers who wanted to avoid various rules and restrictions applicable to freehold estates. Among other things, conveyancers discovered that a 999-year term could be created, out of which could be carved estates more or less similar to estates that can be carved out of a fee. (The phrase "more or less" permits us to avoid a lot of history and a morass of technical details irrelevant today. Outside of Maryland, carving up a long term of years was never a prevalent practice in the United States.)

You should now be in a position to appreciate another group's reaction to these materials on estates and future interests. A few years ago one of the editors had occasion to schedule an evening make-up class at about this point in our coverage of the estates system. When he arrived at the classroom that evening, he found tacked to the door the notice reproduced on page 690.

SECTION C. Future Interests

1. *A List of Possible Kinds of Future Interests*

The future interests that are recognized in our legal system are:

A. Interests in the transferor known as:
   1. Reversion
   2. Possibility of reverter
   3. Right of entry (also known as power of termination)

B. Interests in a transferee known as:
   1. Vested remainder (which can be further divided into):
      a. Indefeasibly vested remainder
      b. Vested remainder subject to open (also known as vested remainder subject to partial divestment)
      c. Vested remainder subject to total divestment
   2. Contingent remainder
   3. Executory interest

TONITE! Room 1425!

"A MAN FOR ALL SEISINS"

Starring:

FREDDIE FREEHOLD — IVAN ISSUE

RUTH REMAINDERMAN — F.E. SIMPLE

and introducing:

DEE TERMINABLE!

Cast of Thousands! Cost of Millions!

SEE —
Men and women feoffing together!

SEE —
Beautiful girls in the act of livery!

SEE —
What grantors did with their fee tails!

SEE —
Inside the infamous seignories!

SEE —
The passion of subinfeudation!

REIFY THAT!

These interests are called "future interests" because the person who holds one of them is not entitled to present possession or enjoyment of the property, but he may or will become entitled to possession in the future. There are other interests (such as inchoate dower and a lien) where the holder may become entitled to possession in the future, but these interests are not called "future interests." The phrase "future interests" is useful simply as a shorthand way of referring to six specific interests which, for historical reasons, have been thought of as segments of ownership on a plane of time that are not now, but may or will in the future become, possessory. All future interests in property must be placed in one of the above categories.

In one sense future interests are present interests. A person who has a future interest has present rights and liabilities. Take this case: "To A for life, then to B and his heirs." B can sell or give away his remainder; his creditors can reach it; he can enjoin A from committing waste or doing other acts which impair the value of his right to future possession; and if B dies before A his remainder is subject to the federal estate tax. A person who has a future interest has a complex of present rights, privileges, duties, liabilities, and immunities, and in that sense he owns a present interest. But he does not have perhaps the most important right in the bundle — the right to present possession — and it is because of the absence of this right that we call his interest "future."

2. *Future Interests in the Transferor*

a. Reversion

"Reversionary interest" is the generic term sometimes used to denote the three future interests that a transferor may have: reversion, possibility of reverter, and right of entry for condition broken. The most important of these is the reversion. "A reversion is," in the words of Professor Lewis Simes, "the interest remaining in the grantor, or in the successor in interest of a testator, who transfers a vested estate of a lesser quantum than that of the vested estate which he has." [18] This interest is never created; it is a retained interest that always arises by operation of law because the transferor has conveyed away a lesser estate than he had.[19]

Suppose that O, the owner of Blackacre in fee simple absolute, conveys "to A for life, then to B for life, then to C for life." O has a reversion, thus:

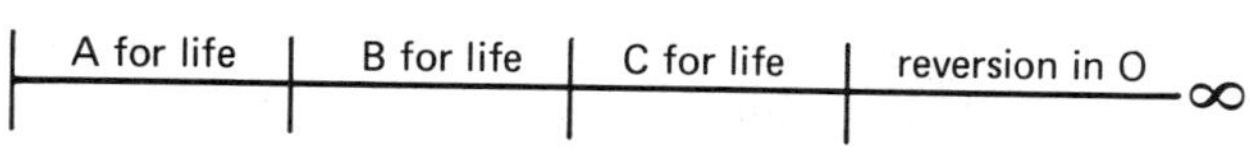

[18] 1 American Law of Property §4.16 (Casner ed. 1952).

[19] When O, holding a fee simple absolute, conveys "to A for life," this is fairly easy to see. But suppose O conveys "to A for life, and on A's death title to the property shall revert to O." Although it here appears that O has expressly created a reversion in fee simple absolute, the language beginning with "and on A's death" is stricken as surplusage; it adds nothing to the conveyance that is not inherent in the fact that O conveyed away only a life estate.

The reversion is the part of the fee, divided into sequential parts on the plane of time, that has not been transferred away. The right to possession is first in A, then in B, then in C; it will return to the transferor at the expiration of the life estates in A, B, and C.

But suppose that at the time of the transfer A, B, and C are all in their thirties, and O is seventy years old. Does O have a reversion when the odds are decidedly against his ever being entitled to present possession and enjoyment of Blackacre on the termination of the three life estates? The answer is yes. As a result of this conveyance, O has retained an interest that will entitle him to present possession of Blackacre on the termination of the preceding life estates. O can convey that interest to some other person during his lifetime, in which case the transferee will hold the reversion in fee simple absolute. If he doesn't make this conveyance and dies during the lifetime of A, B, or C, his interest will pass by will or intestacy, and his successors will hold a reversion in fee simple absolute.

Suppose that the above conveyance is not made in O's lifetime; instead O dies leaving a will that devises Blackacre "to A for life, then to B for life, then to C for life." Since the testamentary transfer takes effect at O's death, O, being dead, does not have a reversion. If O's will contains no residuary clause, O's heirs have the reversion. If O's will contains a residuary clause, the residuary legatee takes upon the death of A, B, and C, but the name of the residuary legatee's interest is much disputed.[20]

A reversion cannot be created in a transferee. If by deed or will a future interest is created in a transferee, that future interest must be given one of the labels that we give to future interests in transferees: it is either a remainder or an executory interest. However, after the transferor has *retained* a reversion, he may transfer it away to a third party. Thus if O wants to transfer Blackacre to A for life and after A's death to D in fee, he may do it in either of two ways:

(1) By one instrument reading, "to A for life, then to D and his heirs." This creates a life estate in A and a *remainder* in D.

(2) By two pieces of paper, the first reading "to A for life," and the second assigning the *reversion* to D.

O can choose the label attached to D's interest, and thereby perhaps affect the legal consequences.

Case 3. O conveys "to A for life, then to B and his heirs if B survives A." A has a life estate, B has a contingent remainder in fee simple absolute — and O has a reversion in fee simple absolute. O has not made a complete disposition of the total fee simple estate, for he has not provided for the contingency that B may predecease A. Since B's taking a present, possessory fee simple is contingent on his surviving A, if B predeceases A, O will take by reversion on A's death. We can diagram this on the plane of time thus:

[20] See Problem 4, page 706. Do you see why the interest of the residuary legatee cannot properly be called a reversion?

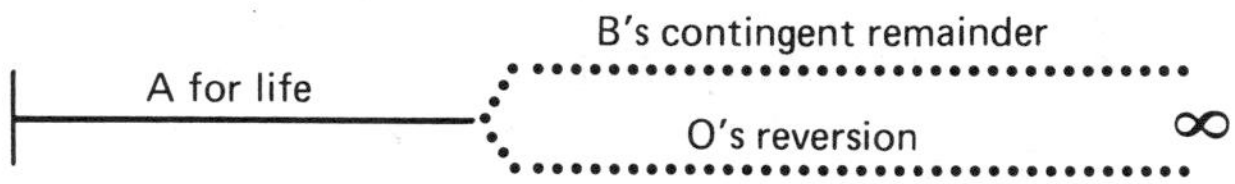

In *Case* 3, since O's taking a present, possessory interest in Blackacre is contingent on B's predeceasing A, does this mean that O's interest is a "contingent reversion"? NO! We do not apply the vested/contingent dichotomy to reversions. In the one instance where it clearly makes a difference whether future interests are vested or contingent — the Rule against Perpetuities, which voids future interests that "vest" too remotely — *all reversions are vested.* While at first blush this might appear strange, it is really quite consistent with the theory that reversions are never created; they arise from an incomplete disposition when the transferor conveys away a lesser estate than he had.[21]

Since the various future interests have different characteristics and often produce different legal consequences, it is important to call an interest by its proper name. Failure to do so may produce confusion or worse. In *Case* 3 it is *not* correct to call O's interest a "contingent reversion," for there is no such thing. It is *not* correct to call O's interest a "possibility of a reversion," for no such future interest is recognized in the law. It is *not* correct to call O's interest a "possibility of reverter," for that type of future interest in the transferor is the correlative of a fee simple determinable estate, and arises only when such an estate has been conveyed.[22] In *Case* 3 O has a reversion, nothing else.

To determine when a transferor has a reversion, you may if you wish go through all the possible ways of carving up the fee into interests which can be put on the plane of time. However, you can save yourself that trouble if you will memorize this simple rule: *An owner of a fee simple will not have a reversion in fee if he transfers a possessory fee or a vested remainder in fee; in all other cases where he transfers a present possessory interest, he will have a reversion in fee.* Hence, whenever the owner of a fee simple transfers a life estate or a term of years, not followed by a vested remainder in fee, he has a reversion. He may transfer a life estate followed by one or more contingent remainders in fee, but he still retains a reversion, since he has not transferred away a vested remainder in fee.

You will see why this rule operates if you consider a "reversion" a shorthand way of saying that when a vested estate of the same size is not transferred, "there is either a certainty or a possibility that the right to possession will return to the

[21] See Waggoner, Reformulating the Structure of Estates: A Proposal for Legislative Action, 85 Harv. L. Rev. 729, 747 (1972).

[22] Helvering v. Hallock, 309 U.S. 106, 118 n. 6 (1939) (Frankfurter, J.): "The confusion apt to be engendered by judicial forays into this field is well illustrated by the use of the term 'possibility of reverter' by the majority in Helvering v. St. Louis Union Trust Co. 'A possibility of reverter' is traditionally defined as the interest remaining in a grantor who has conveyed a determinable fee. The definition has not been thought to have any relation to the reversionary interest of a grantor who has transferred either a vested or contingent remainder in fee. See Gray, Rule Against Perpetuities (2nd ed.), §§13-51." (Question: What kind of reversionary interest after a vested remainder in fee does Justice Frankfurter have in mind?)

grantor."[23] According to feudal theory, a fee simple was longer in duration than a fee tail, a fee tail longer than a life estate, and a life estate longer than a term of years.[24] Thus when the owner of an estate in Blackacre carves out a smaller estate and does not add a vested remainder the same size as the owner's estate, there is a possibility that Blackacre will be his again.

PROBLEMS

1. O conveys property to X in trust "to pay the income to my wife for her life, and on her death to pay the income to me for life, and on the death of the survivor of my wife and me the trustee shall distribute the principal of the trust to A." Does O have a reversion?

2. O conveys "to A for life." Two years later A conveys "to B for B's life." What is the state of the title?

a. If B then dies, survived by A and O, what is the state of the title?

b. If, instead, A dies, survived by B and O, what is the state of the title?

3. In which of the following cases is there a reversion?

a. O conveys "to A for life, then to B for a term of ninety-nine years."

b. O conveys "to A for life, then to B and his heirs; but if at B's death he is not survived by any children, then to C and his heirs."

c. O conveys "to A for life, then to B and his heirs if he lives to attain the age of twenty-five years." At the time of the conveyance, B is fifteen years old.

4. "A gift of a consumable for life is commonly held to transfer an absolute interest, unless there is coupled with the gift a power to sell and convert the consumable into a nonconsumable, to which the future interests limited after the life estate are to attach. . . .

[23] Suppose O conveys "to A for life, then to B if B survives A, and if B does not survive A to C." Does O have a reversion here, when it is certain that either B or C will take depending on whether B survives A? Under the italicized rule in the text, O has a reversion — and this was the classification given at common law. You must always assume the life estate can terminate prior to the death of the life tenant, a realistic assumption in feudal times when A could forfeit his life estate in a number of circumstances. After the abolition of forfeiture the assumption continued to be made. For the explanation, see the problem on page 711.

[24] Because of this principle, if A, the owner of a life estate, conveyed a ninety-nine-year term to B, A had a reversion. Yet in the converse situation the courts did not carry this principle to its logical extreme. After much backing and filling, it was finally held (without explanation) in Eyres v. Faulkland, 1 Salk. 231, 91 Eng. Rep. 204 (K.B. 1697), that if A owned a term of years and granted B a life estate, the property reverted to A at B's death within the period of the term even though a life estate was a "larger" estate.

Medical science may some day confirm that a life estate is longer than a ninety-nine-year term; indeed, if the cryonics movement is successful, a life estate in the future may be of infinite duration, matching the fee simple. See Ettinger, The Prospect of Immortality (1964); Henderson & Ettinger, Cryonic Suspension and the Law, 15 U.C.L.A.L. Rev. 414 (1968). The property problems resulting from freezing and reviving the "dead" will require ingenious solutions. For a starter: What property arrangements would you recommend for your client, a firm believer in cryonic suspension, who wants to be assured that his frozen body is maintained indefinitely? Could a trust be worked out? Could the Rule against Perpetuities be avoided?

"Not too satisfactory reasons are given by the courts for the prevailing view. Apparently, it was thought that, if the use of the thing necessitated a consumption of the corpus, then ownership of the corpus could have no existence apart from the right to the use." Simes, Future Interests 15 (2d ed. 1966).

T bequeaths his farm to A for life together with 7 horses, 27 sheep, 1 cow, 40 fat hogs, 5 bushels of corn, and all the farming implements. Do T's heirs have a reversion? Davison's Adm'r v. Davison's Adm'x, 149 Ky. 571, 149 S.W. 982 (1912). Compare Seabrook v. Grimes, 107 Md. 410, 68 A. 883 (1908), holding a printing press to be a consumable because it wears out in a short time.

Suppose T, a professor of torts, bequeaths to A for life 200 copies of a casebook edited by T. Do T's heirs have a reversion?

b. Possibility of Reverter; Right of Entry

A possibility of reverter is the future interest that remains in the grantor when he conveys a fee simple determinable estate. (*Case 1*, supra.) A right of entry for condition broken is the future interest that arises in the grantor when he conveys a fee simple subject to a condition subsequent *and* expressly reserves a right of entry. (*Case 2*, supra.) We will examine these interests in Section E of this chapter. We mention them now to round out our list of future interests as well as to distinguish them from reversions. Do you see why the following statement is implicit in this paragraph? There can be no reversion where the owner of a fee simple has transferred a vested fee simple of any type (fee simple absolute, fee simple determinable, fee simple subject to condition subsequent) either in possession or in remainder.[25]

3. *Future Interests in Transferees*

There are three types of future interests in transferees: vested remainders, contingent remainders, and executory interests; and vested remainders are further broken down into indefeasibly vested, vested subject to open, and vested subject to total divestment. So: any time you have a remainder, it has to be either vested or contingent; any time you have a future interest in a transferee that is not a remainder, then it has to be an executory interest. As we shall see shortly, it is often quite difficult to classify a future interest created in a transferee. With respect to indefeasibly vested remainders and vested remainders subject to open, there is little difficulty in appending the appropriate label. But when it comes to future interests whose taking is subject to the happening or nonhappening of some event, in many cases it is no easy task to determine whether a particular interest is a contingent remainder, a vested remainder subject to divestment, or an executory interest. In this area the labeling of future interests turns on distinctions that sometimes all but defy comprehension and are difficult to justify today. But before we approach those problems, let us first define what is meant by the term "remainder."

[25] For further explanation see page 728, infra.

a. Remainders

"A remainder," says the Restatement of Property, "is any future interest limited in favor of a transferee in such manner that it can become a present interest upon the expiration of all prior interests simultaneously created, and cannot divest any interest except an interest left in the transferor." [26] Here are some examples.

Case 4. O conveys "to A for life, then to B and his heirs."

B's future interest is a remainder. It is a future interest limited in favor of a transferee. It can become a present interest (here it *will* become a present interest) on the expiration of A's life estate. When B's future interest takes in present possession and enjoyment, it will not divest A's estate; it will follow immediately upon the natural termination of the life estate. Thus it is portrayed on the plane of time:

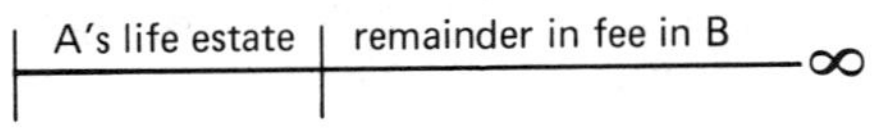

Contrast the above case with B's future interest in the following two cases.

Case 5. O conveys "to A and his heirs, but if B marries C, to B and his heirs."

In this case we have a future interest limited in favor of a transferee, B, but the future interest can become possessory only by divesting the fee simple in A. Since B's future interest cannot become a possessory estate on the natural termination of the preceding estate, it cannot be a remainder. What is it, then? Any interest that divests a *transferee* is a shifting executory interest. Here is a shifting executory interest in relation to the plane of time:

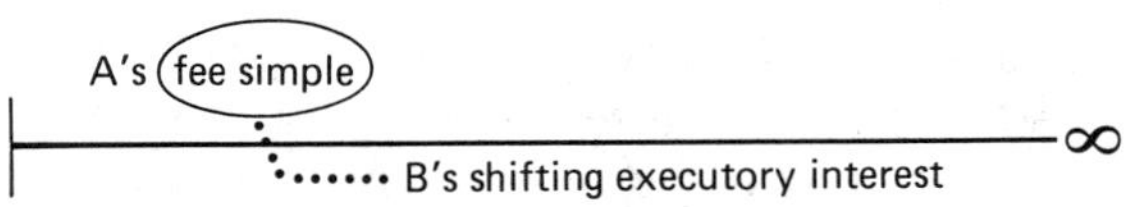

Case 6. O conveys "to A for life, and one year after A's death to B and his heirs."

Here B's future interest is not a remainder, because it cannot become a present interest on the expiration of A's prior interest; there is a one-year gap between the two estates, during which time O is entitled to possession. An interest that must divest the *transferor* of his possessory fee simple at some future date, if it takes effect, is a springing executory interest. B's future interest is an executory interest.

[26] 2 Restatement of Property §156(1) (1936).

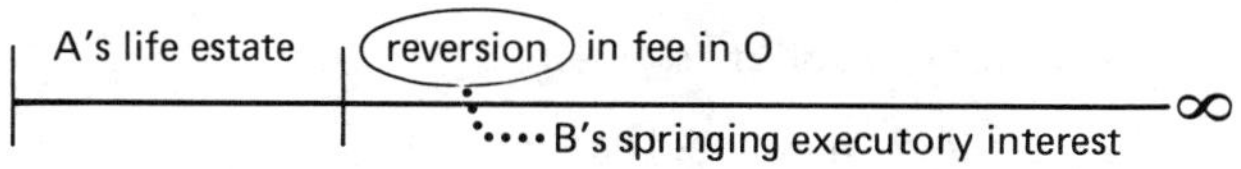

What is the significance, in the Restatement definition, of the phrase "that it *can* become a present interest upon the expiration of all prior interests"? This is shown by the following example.

> *Case* 7. O conveys "to A for life, then to B and his heirs if B lives to attain the age of twenty-five years." B is fifteen years old at the time of the conveyance.

Here B's taking is subject to a condition precedent that he attain the age of twenty-five years. But B's interest is a remainder, for it *can* take immediately on the expiration of the preceding estate. If B attains age twenty-five during A's lifetime, thereby satisfying the condition precedent, there will be no gap between the termination of A's life estate and B's taking a present, possessory estate. Thus B's interest is a remainder — a contingent remainder.

Note that if B attains the age of twenty-five during A's lifetime, his contingent remainder becomes a vested remainder. B (or his successors, if he should thereafter die in A's lifetime) will be sure to take upon the termination of A's life estate. O's reversion in fee simple absolute (which would have taken had B died before attaining the age of twenty-five) will be divested. But this divesting of a reversion is not inconsistent with the Restatement's definition of a remainder: see the last clause in the definition.

(1) *Indefeasibly vested remainder*

In general, a remainder is "vested" when it is given to an ascertained person and there is no condition precedent to its becoming a present possessory interest other than the natural termination of the preceding estate or estates. But there are different types of vested remainders.

An indefeasibly vested remainder is defined by the Restatement as one where "the remainderman is certain to acquire a present interest at some time in the future, and is also certain to be entitled to retain permanently thereafter the present interest so acquired. This remainderman, as an individual, may die before his interest can become present but a present interest is certain to come to this remainderman, or to those who are his grantees, distributees or devisees." [27] The classic example of an indefeasibly vested remainder is *Case* 4 above. In that case B's remainder is certain to take on A's death; there is no condition precedent to B's taking other than the natural termination of A's life estate. Nothing can happen to defeat or diminish B's remainder in fee simple absolute.

[27] Id. §157(a), Comment f.

(2) *Vested remainder subject to open*

This is a vested remainder in a class that has not closed.

Case 8. O conveys "to A for life, then to A's children and their heirs." A has a child, C, alive at the time of the conveyance.

In this case C has a vested remainder subject to open up and let in other children born to A. As with the indefeasibly vested remainder, C (or his successor) is certain to acquire a present interest at some time in the future, but C's share of the remainder will be diminished if A has any more children. The amount of C's share will depend on how many children, if any, are subsequently born to A. If at some time in the future A has another child — let's call him D — the class of remaindermen "opens," and C and D will have vested remainders subject to open. The class will remain "open" until A is no longer capable of having more children — which means until A's death.

PROBLEM

O conveys "to A for life, and on A's death to his children in equal shares." At the time of the conveyance A has two children, B and C. Two years later D is born to A. A year after that B dies, then A dies. What is the state of the title?

(3) *Vested remainder subject to divestment; contingent remainder*

Remainders that are not certain to become possessory interests, or to remain possessory interests after having become such, are either vested remainders subject to divestment or contingent remainders. A contingent remainder is a remainder either (1) given to an unascertained person or persons or (2) subject to a condition precedent. For a remainder to be vested it must be given to ascertained persons and not be subject to a condition precedent.

Case 9. O conveys "to A for life, then to A's children and their heirs." A has no children at the time of the conveyance. The remainder is contingent because the takers are unascertained.[28]

[28] Contingent remainder in whom? A remainder is a concept standing for legal relations between persons. Can unborn persons have legal relations? 2 Restatement of Property §153, Comment a (1936), says we cannot accurately say that an unborn person has a future interest. Yet it is quite clear that the law treats the limitation as if a future interest has been created. Some say the correct terminology is, "*There is* a contingent remainder in the unborn children of A," rather than, "The unborn children of A have a contingent remainder," and if that helps you get the idea, fine.

Some 500 years ago the common law courts got around a similar conceptual impasse by simply declaring that the remainder was in nubibus (in the clouds) or in gremio legis (in the bosom of the law). Megarry & Wade, The Law of Real Property 189-190 (3d ed. 1966). In this course the sky is the limit for a truly imaginative mind!

PROBLEMS

1. O conveys "to A for life, and on A's death to the heirs of B." At the time of the conveyance A and B are both alive, and B has two children, C and D. If B were to die intestate immediately after the conveyance, C and D would be B's heirs. One year after the conveyance D dies, leaving a minor son, E, and a will devising all his property to his wife, W. One year later B dies, devising all his property to his wife, M. A dies, survived by C, E, W, and M. Who owns the property? What would be the result if B had died before D?

2. O conveys "to A for life, then to the first child of A who reaches twenty-one." A has a daughter, C, aged eighteen, and a son, D, aged twelve. What interests are created?

If the taker of the remainder is ascertained, but the remainder will be defeated if a specified event occurs, whether the remainder is vested subject to divestment or is contingent depends upon whether the conditional event is expressed as a condition subsequent or a condition precedent.[29] In some cases this distinction is apparent — and understandable.

> *Case 10.* O conveys "to A for life, then to B and his heirs; but if at B's death he is not survived by any children, then to C and his heirs."

B's interest is a remainder in fee simple, for it is capable of taking upon the natural termination of A's life estate. It is a vested remainder, for there is no condition precedent to B's taking other than the natural termination of that preceding estate. B's interest is, however, subject to a condition subsequent: If at his death he is not survived by any children, his fee simple will be divested in favor of C. C has a shifting executory interest.

> *Case 11.* O conveys "to A for life, then to B and his heirs if B is then living."

In *Case 11* B has a contingent remainder in fee simple. In order to take on A's death he must meet the condition precedent of having survived A.

[29] Gray put it this way: "Whether a remainder is vested or contingent depends upon the language employed. If the conditional element is incorporated into the description of, or into the gift to, the remainder-man, then the remainder is contingent; but if, after words giving a vested interest, a clause is added divesting it, the remainder is vested. Thus on a devise to A. for life, remainder to his children, but if any child dies in the lifetime of A. his share to go to those who survive, the share of each child is vested, subject to be divested by its death. But on a devise to A. for life, remainder to such of his children as survive him, the remainder is contingent." Gray, The Rule Against Perpetuities §108 (4th ed. 1942).

PROBLEMS

1. O conveys "to A for life, then to B for life, then to C and his heirs." Two years later B dies, survived by A and C. Did B ever own anything? If the answer is yes, what did he own, and was it worth anything?

2. O conveys "to A for life, then to B for life if B is then living, then to C and his heirs." What interests are created? Webb v. Hearing, Cro. Jac. 415, 79 Eng. Rep. 355 (K.B. 1617); Simes & Smith, The Law of Future Interests §142 (2d ed. 1956).

3. O conveys "to A for life, and after A's death to B and his heirs." What interests are created? Id. §585.

In still other cases, the distinctions drawn between conditions precedent and conditions subsequent become quite tricky.

> *Case 12.* O conveys "to A for life, then to B and his heirs, but if B does not survive A, then to C and his heirs."

B has a vested remainder in fee simple subject to divestment; C has a shifting executory interest in fee simple. Contrast this case with:

> *Case 13.* O conveys "to A for life, then if B survives A, to B and his heirs, but if B does not survive A, then to C and his heirs."

Here B has a contingent remainder in fee simple; C has an alternative contingent remainder in fee simple.

The difference between *Case 12* and *Case 13* is solely in the verbal formula employed. In *Case 12* the condition of B's survival is expressed only as a condition subsequent in introducing the gift over to C. In *Case 13* the condition of B's survival is expressed as a condition precedent to B's taking an interest; this makes B's interest a contingent remainder, and C's interest an alternative contingent remainder.

But what of the fact, in *Case 13*, that there is both a condition precedent ("if B survives A") and a condition subsequent ("but if B does not survive A")? Why not stress the condition subsequent, and thus call B's interest a vested remainder subject to divestment? The simple — although not totally satisfactory — answer is that the interests are classified in sequence. A has a life estate. Next, B has a remainder that is subject to a condition precedent — it is a contingent remainder. Having thus classified B's interest, we then turn to the next interest, in C. Since we have decided that B has a contingent remainder, C's interest is an alternative contingent remainder.

We shall return to the distinction between conditions precedent and subsequent in Section D of this chapter, where we shall find some gossamer-thin lines drawn.

b. Executory Interests

We have already given a practical definition of "executory interest." These words stand for any future interest in a transferee that does not have the characteristics of a remainder. More precisely, an executory interest is a future interest that must, in order to become possessory,

(a) divest or cut short some interest in another transferee (this is a shifting executory interest), or

(b) divest the transferor following a certain period of time during which no transferee is entitled to possession (this is a springing executory interest).[30]

To understand how the classification of "executory interests" developed, it is necessary to turn a few pages of history. Executory interests grew out of feudal notions of conveyancing, the efforts of lawyers to bypass certain feudal rules, and an attempt by Henry VIII to replenish his treasury.

Two rules: No shifting interests; no freeholds to commence in futuro

Prior to 1536 the common law courts laid down two rules based upon their ideas of estates and of conveyancing. The first of these was that *no future interest could be created in favor of a third person if the interest could operate to cut short a freehold estate.* This was a rule against shifting interests.

> *Case 14.* Prior to the Statute of Uses (1536), O enfeoffs "to A and his heirs, but if B returns from Rome, then to B and his heirs."

Under this conveyance, A took a fee simple absolute and B took nothing. The reason for the rule probably was that if A took a fee simple (the whole estate), the judges thought that there was nothing left to give to B.

The second rule was that *no freehold estate could be created to commence in futuro.* A freehold estate could not be created unless seisin was simultaneously transferred. This was a rule against interests springing out of the grantor at some future date.

> *Case 15.* Prior to the Statute of Uses, O enfeoffs "to A and her heirs when A marries B."

[30] "A springing use is a forward pass; a shifting use is a lateral after a forward." Gulliver, Clark, Lusky & Murphy, Gratuitous Transfers 749 (1967). Although we differentiate here between a shifting executory interest and a springing executory interest because we think it helps the student better understand what an executory interest is, there is no difference in legal consequences between the two.

The distinction between "uses" (executory interests created by deed) and "executory devises" (interests created by will) is rarely made today and is of no consequence.

Under this conveyance, A took nothing; O was left with the fee simple. The reason for this rule lay in the feudal notions of conveyancing. A freehold estate could not be created unless a feoffment with livery of seisin took place on the land. The grantor had to hand over seisin (symbolized by a clod of dirt, a twig, or some other object) to the grantee. In *Case 15*, by the terms of the conveyance, A was not to be seised of a freehold estate until some time in the future. Therefore, seisin could not pass to A now.

This rule did not prevent the creation of a remainder to commence in the future, provided there was a freehold estate in a transferee to support it. Thus in a grant "to A for life, then to B and his heirs," livery of seisin to A was sufficient to create A's freehold life estate, and also to sustain B's remainder. A held seisin for his life and on A's death seisin immediately passed to B according to the terms of the original grant. But compare the following case:

> *Case 16.* Prior to the Statute of Uses, O enfeoffs "to A for life, and one year after A's death to B and his heirs."

In *Case 16* A took a life estate, B took nothing, and O was left with a reversion in fee simple. The attempted creation of a future estate in B violated the rule against creating freehold estates *in futuro*. By this conveyance seisin passed to A, and on A's death reverted to O. It could not spring out of the grantor one year later; only another feoffment with livery of seisin could move seisin to B. The one-year gap distinguished this case from the preceding one, and that gap was fatal to the future interest.

The rise of the use

The foregoing two rules concerning the continuity of seisin were rules of the law courts before 1536. The chancellor, sitting in equity, paid no attention to them. When he thought persons should be required to perform their *moral* duties, the chancellor would step in and protect a transferee, regardless of what his *legal* rights might be. He commanded persons to obey, and if they refused he threw them into jail. Hence there developed in equity a protected interest known as the "use" (from a corruption of the Latin word *opus*, meaning benefit).

> *Case 14a.* Before the Statute of Uses, O enfeoffs "to X and his heirs *to the use of* A and his heirs, but if B returns from Rome, then to the use of B and his heirs." (Compare *Case 14.*)

So far as the law courts were concerned, this conveyance was perfectly satisfactory. There had been a feoffment with livery of seisin that was effective to create a fee simple absolute in X. X was seised of the land and was obligated to perform the tenurial services attached to the land. The remaining language of the conveyance meant nothing to the law courts.

But it was not so in Chancery. To carry out the intention of O, the chancellor deemed that X had a moral duty to hold seisin for the benefit of A or, if the shifting event happened, for the benefit of B. By accepting this conveyance on these terms, X had undertaken a duty that was enforceable in equity. The state of title: Legal title in X in fee simple absolute, holding to the use of A, who had equitable title in fee simple subject to a shifting use in B in fee simple.

Another common method of creating a use was the bargain and sale deed. Suppose O and his grantee did not go out to the land (perhaps many miles removed from London) and perform livery of seisin; instead, in the London office of his solicitor, O sold Blackacre to A for £50 and gave a bargain and sale deed "to A and his heirs." So far as the law courts were concerned, nothing had happened. Since there had been no feoffment with livery of seisin, legal title and seisin were still in O. But here again, to enforce the bargain the chancellor stepped in and required O to hold legal title to Blackacre for the benefit of A, who had equitable title in fee simple absolute.

Legal historians have traced the "use" back to the time of the Crusades, when a man might dispose of his property to the use of his wife or dependents while he went on a Crusade. As time passed, it became increasingly evident to an increasing number of landowners that all sorts of benefits could be accomplished by "raising a use." We have already seen how shifting uses could be created by raising a use, notwithstanding the law courts' rule against conditions in strangers (*Case 14a*). Springing uses could also be created. For this, let's go back to *Case 15*. O's daughter (A) is soon to marry a virile young knight (B), and O wishes to endow A with a suitable tract of land. What with the vagaries of life in medieval England, he does not want to make a present conveyance of a fee simple to A; yet a conveyance "when A marries B" — in the form of *Case 15* — violates the law courts' rule against springing interests. Enter the use. O simply enfeoffs X and his heirs "to the use of O and his heirs and then to the use of A and her heirs when A marries B." X holds seisin and legal title to the use of O, who has equitable title in fee simple subject to a springing use in A.

The above examples illustrate how the use was employed to get around the common law technical rules governing conveyancing and the creation of future interests. But this device had a staggering number of other uses as well.[31] Prior to 1540 land could not be devised by will — but O might enfeoff "to X and his heirs to the use of O during O's lifetime and then to the use of such persons as O shall appoint by will." By this conveyance X held legal title to the use of O during O's lifetime; after O's death X held to the use of O's devisees. Or, O might enfeoff "to X and his heirs to the use of A and his heirs," and thereby immunize A's equitable title in fee simple from his wife's dower claim (dower applied to lands of which a husband was *seised* during marriage), from A's creditors, from forfeiture by A for high treason, from relief and other feudal incidents due at A's death. Particularly because of its success in evading feudal death duties, the use became universally popular.[32] Much

[31] See Fratcher, Uses of Uses, 34 Mo. L. Rev. 39 (1969).

[32] Feudal death duties were levied when seisin changed hands upon the death of a *sole* feoffee

of the legal business pertaining to land shifted from the law courts to the equity courts, and from the common law lawyers to lawyers who practiced before Chancery (a separate, and smaller, bar). The common law courts and lawyers did not at all like what was happening, but they were stuck with their rules and with an inflexible attitude toward those rules. As they saw it, the only remedy lay in legislation — and they controlled Parliament.

The Statute of Uses

As the result of a political bargain struck between Henry VIII and the lawyers who practiced before the law courts, the Statute of Uses was passed in 1535, becoming operative in 1536. To restore the king's feudal revenues and to return the conveyancing practice to the law courts, this statute operated to "execute" (that is, convert) equitable interests into legal interests, thus permitting springing and shifting interests in law. What were "springing uses" and "shifting uses" in equity before 1536 became "springing executory interests" and "shifting executory interests," thus:

> *Case 14b.* After 1536 O enfeoffs "to X and his heirs to the use of A and his heirs, but if B returns from Rome, then to the use of B and his heirs."

Here the conveyance "raised a use" — which was immediately "executed" by the Statute, dropping X out of the picture and leaving as the state of *legal* title: Fee simple in A subject to a shifting executory interest in B in fee simple.

> *Case 15a.* After 1536 O bargains and sells "to A and his heirs when A marries B."

Here the bargain and sale deed "raised a use" — which was immediately "executed" by the Statute, leaving as the state of *legal* title: Fee simple in O subject to a springing executory interest in A in fee simple.

For a time after the Statute of Uses, in order to create these new types of *legal* future interests it was necessary to "employ the machinery of the Statute." That is, a use had to be raised on which the Statute could operate. Thus back to *Case 14*.

> *Case 14.* After 1536 O enfeoffs "to A and his heirs, but if B returns from Rome, to B and his heirs."

The state of title? Fee simple in A, period. Here O attempted to create a shifting interest in B, but the "no conditions in a stranger" rule continued to apply. O did

---

to uses. But this catastrophe could be avoided by ensuring that there would never be less than two feoffees. Thus O would enfeoff H, I, J, K, and L as joint tenants to the use of A and his heirs. Upon the death of H no seisin passed to I, J, K, and L, who were, under the theory of joint tenancy, already seised of the whole. When the number of joint tenants grew dangerously low, others could be enfeoffed jointly with them. The trick was never to let seisin pass on a person's death.

not make a feoffment to uses, and O did not employ a bargain and sale deed; hence no use was raised which could be executed. *This formalism is no longer a part of our law.* Today, in any jurisdiction, springing and shifting executory interests can be created by deed, trust, or will; no special form of conveyance and no magic formula of words has to be employed.

That's the story of how executory interests came to be recognized. What were springing and shifting uses in equity before 1536 became thereafter executory interests that were recognized in the law courts. Hence, as incredible as it may seem, what are called executory interests today are interests that would have been void at law prior to the Statute of Uses because they violated the two seisin rules stated above. Four hundred years after the concept of seisin ceased to have any importance, we are still classifying future interests as if it did.

PROBLEMS

1. In 1970 O conveys "to A for life, and one year after A's death to B and his heirs." The state of the title is: Life estate in A, reversion in fee simple in O, springing executory interest in B. How can O have a reversion in fee simple, when the fee simple is certain to end one year after the death of A? The essence of a fee simple is that it may last forever. Why is not the state of the title a life estate in A, reversion for a one-year term in O, vested remainder in fee simple in B? If the deed were "to A for life, then to K for one year, then to B and his heirs," A would have a life estate, K would have a remainder for a one-year term, and B would have a vested remainder in fee simple. Why the difference when the one-year period of possession is given to a transferee rather than retained by the transferor? Simes, Future Interests 12 (2d ed. 1966). (Hint: The Statute of Uses did not change old valid estates; it merely permitted new interests, formerly prohibited.)

2. In 1970 O conveys "to A for life, then to B and his heirs, but if B does not survive A, then to C and his heirs." If B dies before A, C will take upon the natural termination of A's life estate. Why isn't C's interest a remainder?

3. What interests are created by the following conveyances?

   a. O conveys "to A for life, then to A's children and their heirs, but if at A's death he is not survived by any children, then to B and his heirs." At the time of this conveyance, A has no children.

   b. Consider the same facts as in Problem a. Two years after that conveyance, a child (C-1) is born to A. (See 3 Restatement of Property §278, Comment e, Illustration 5 (1940).)

   c. O conveys "to A for life, then to such of A's children as survive him, but if none of A's children survive him, then to B and his heirs." At the time of this conveyance, A has two children: C-1 and C-2.

   d. O conveys "to A for life, then to B and his heirs, but if A is survived at his death by any children, then to such surviving children and their heirs." At the time of this conveyance, A has two children: C-1 and C-2.

   e. O conveys "to A for life, then to the heirs of B, but if at A's death B is still living, then to D and his heirs." At the time of this conveyance, B is alive and has two children: C-1 and C-2.

4. T devises Blackacre to A for life, then to A's children who survive him. The residuary clause of T's will devises to B "all of the rest and residue of my property of whatever kind and wherever located that I own at my death, including any of the foregoing gifts in this will which for any reason fail to take effect." What is the state of the title? Egerton v. Massey, 3 C.B.(N.S.) 338, 140 Eng. Rep. 771 (1857), and Gray, The Rule Against Perpetuities §113.1 (4th ed. 1942), say A's children have a contingent remainder and B has a reversion. Do you see how this classification assumes that T can die twice? 2 Tiffany, Real Property §333 (3d ed. 1939), says A's children have a contingent remainder in fee, and B has a vested remainder in fee, but this classification runs into the rule of Loddington v. Kime, 1 Salk. 224, 91 Eng. Rep. 1031 (K.B. 1697), that there can be no vested remainder in fee after a contingent remainder in fee. Kales, Estates, Future Interests and Illegal Conditions and Restraints in Illinois §95 (2d ed. 1920), says we should read the clauses in reverse order, giving B a vested remainder, and A's children an executory interest. 3 Restatement of Property §278, Comment d (1940), says A's children and C have alternative contingent remainders. Which of the above answers is correct?

The label "executory interest" may also be applied in two situations that do not fit the definition of executory interests previously given. These are exceptions to that definition. One situation is where there is a fee simple determinable followed by a future interest in a transferee.

Case 17. O conveys "to Trinity Church for so long as the premises are used for church purposes, then to Mercy Hospital."

The interest given to Mercy Hospital should logically be classified as a remainder if the ordinary definition of a remainder is accepted. It stands ready to take on the natural termination of the preceding estate; it does not divest that preceding estate. Yet it is perfectly clear that under modern orthodoxy the future interest is called an executory interest. We do not know the reason for this anomaly and probably never shall. The reason usually given is that there can be no remainder following a fee simple. This statement is logically valid when a fee simple absolute is involved, for such a fee simple by definition is of infinite duration. But it is not a convincing explanation in the case of a determinable fee, for that estate may end some time short of infinity.[33] Remainders could follow other historic fee estates, such as the fee tail. The logical enigma is further confounded by the rule that a future interest

[33] Simes & Smith, The Law of Future Interests §35, p. 41 (2d ed. 1956) offer the following rationalization: "The totality of legal relations in any given piece of land consisted in one and only one fee-simple estate. . . . As a corollary to this proposition, it was only natural to conclude that there could be no remainder or reversion after a fee simple. If the totality of legal relations had been granted, obviously there was nothing left to give." What, if anything, is wrong with this explanation?

must be construed as a remainder rather than an executory interest, if possible.[34] Yet in spite of the difficulties in rationalization the result is fortunate. The holder of an executory interest following a determinable fee has substantially the same rights as the holder of an executory interest following a fee simple subject to a condition subsequent, so it is just as well that the labels are the same.

The other exception to our definition is where there is a contingent future interest (in fee or for life) following a term of years.

> *Case 18.* O conveys "to A for a term of ten years, then to B and his heirs if B is then living."

At early common law the state of title in *Case 18* was: Fee simple in O subject to a term of years in A, period. B took no interest. There could be no contingent future interest in a freehold estate following a possessory term of years, because the creation of a freehold estate required a present transfer of seisin. A, the termor, could not take seisin because he did not have a freehold estate. B could not take seisin because his interest was not sure ever to take effect in possession. Since a present transfer of seisin was required for an effective transfer of a freehold, the attempted contingent remainder in B was void.[35]

After the Statute of Uses, the contingent future interest in B could be created — but it was called an executory interest. Hence after 1536 the state of title in *Case 18* was: Fee simple in O subject to a term of years in A, subject also to a springing executory interest in B in fee simple. With the decline in the significance of seisin, the interest began to be called a contingent remainder. According to most modern commentators, this is its proper label.

c. Shifting Use Executory Vested Limitation

In teaching courses on estates and future interests, over the years each of the editors has been the recipient of bits and snatches of student doggerel, some of it very good, some of it very, very bad. We reproduce some of these verses from time to time, leaving it for you to decide whether we have shared with you the good ones or the bad ones. At this point we offer a dithyramb that provides a needed break before we proceed to the next section, as well as some practical advice concerning classroom recitation on the materials we have just covered.

[34] This is known as the Rule of Purefoy v. Rogers, 2 Wms. Saund. 380, 85 Eng. Rep. 1181 (K.B. 1670).

[35] A vested remainder after a term of years could be created, although it was not called that. Suppose in 1500 O conveyed "to A for ten years, then to B and his heirs." Seisin passed from O to B, not A. Thus B held a fee simple subject to a term of years in A. In modern times we say A has a term of years and B has a vested remainder.

(*to be sung to the tune of*
SUPERCALIFRAGILISTICEXPIALIDOCIOUS)

4. *Future Interests in Personal Property; Equitable Future Interests*

The estate practitioner is ordinarily concerned with equitable life estates and future interests in personal property held in trust. Although the law of future interests grew out of dispositions of land, the courts permitted the same kinds of future interests to be created in personal property. Equitable future interests as well as legal future interests can be created in any kind of property.

A *note about "fee simple" ownership of personal property:* Technically there is a fee simple only in land, not in personal property. The analogue to fee simple ownership of land is "absolute ownership" of personalty. You will observe, though, that an occasional court, commentator—and law professor—will refer to fee simple ownership of personalty. While technically imprecise, so far as we can tell there is no harm in the use of this colloquialism.

SECTION D. Consequences of Classification

If you do not find the law of future interests a wonderful calculus at all, but rather (as William James viewed algebra) a peculiarly low sort of cunning, you may wonder whether the preceding trip was worth the effort. What different consequences follow from giving an interest one label rather than another? In the next section of this chapter you will find that it matters greatly in some cases whether the interest is retained by the transferor or is created in a transferee. This is because the Rule against Perpetuities applies to contingent remainders and executory interests, but does not apply to reversions, possibilities of reverter, rights of entry, or vested remainders. Indeed, today the most important consequence of classification is in the application of the Rule against Perpetuities. In this section we deal with some other differences in consequences.

1. *Destructibility of Contingent Remainders*

One great historical difference was that contingent remainders were destructible by a gap in seisin, whereas vested remainders and executory interests were not so destructible. This recondite subject, which in 1772 warranted the great classic treatment given it by Charles Fearne,[36] is no longer part of our law except in a few states. Nonetheless, the doctrine of destructibility of contingent remainders had a great impact on the classification of interests because of the linguistic distinctions the courts developed to avoid application of the doctrine. The principal way of avoiding the doctrine was to construe a remainder as vested subject to divestment rather than contingent, by construing a condition as subsequent rather than precedent. Linguistic distinctions that were used to construe interests as vested, once made, were applied to other problems (perpetuities, acceleration of remainders, undisposed-of income, etc.) where the same language was used in a limitation, but otherwise the context and policies were different.[37]

[36] Fearne, An Essay on the Learning of Contingent Remainders and Executory Devises (1772). This work went through ten editions, the last published in 1845.

[37] ". . . [T]he distinction between vested and contingent remainders continues to be used by the courts because the two interests are given different legal characteristics. In some jurisdictions the question arises in determining whether or not the remainder is destructible — it being asserted that contingent remainders are destructible, while vested remainders are not. In some, it may arise on a question of alienability, since local precedent declares contingent remainders to be inalienable. Again, it may be a question of classification for the purposes of taxation or the application of the rule against perpetuities, when the court finds that the two interests are to be treated differently, or, the right to partition may be involved, and the court may, in the past, have denied a contingent remainderman the right to maintain such an action. In any of the foregoing cases, this question may be asked: Is there a tendency for the court to first decide whether it wants the

The doctrine of destructibility of contingent remainders is this: *If a remainder does not vest before or at the termination of the preceding freehold estate, the remainder is destroyed.* A remainder had to follow hard on the heels of the prior possessory estate. If there was a moment of time between the termination of the possessory estate and the time when the remainderman could rightfully demand possession, the remainder was destroyed. Since a vested remainder was by definition ready to take whenever and however the preceding estate ended, a vested remainder was not subject to destruction by a gap in seisin. Not so the contingent remainder. If perchance the contingent remainderman was not ready to take when the life estate ended, because he was unborn or unascertained or some prescribed event had not happened, he could never take.

> *Case 19.* O conveys "to A for life, then to B and his heirs if B lives to attain the age of twenty-five years." B is fifteen years old at the time of the conveyance. If B attains the age of twenty-five during A's lifetime, by virtue of having satisfied the condition precedent his remainder will become indefeasibly vested, and B will take on the natural termination of A's life estate. If, however, A's life estate comes to an end before B's twenty-fifth birthday, there will be a gap, and at common law that gap was fatal. (A "gap in seisin" means a period of time when no transferee is seised of the property.) The necessity of continuity of seisin required that B's remainder be destroyed if B could not take seisin on the termination of the life estate. If seisin reverted to O, and B's remainder was given effect when B reached twenty-five, it would have to take effect as a springing interest — forbidden at the time the doctrine was developed.

Case 19 illustrates how a remainder could be destroyed if it was still contingent at the natural termination of the preceding estate. A contingent remainder could also be destroyed by merger. Suppose O conveys "to A for life, then to B and his heirs"; thereafter, B conveys his remainder in fee simple to A. A now has a life estate and a remainder in fee simple absolute. Because A has the entire ownership of the property, it makes no sense to say that A has both a life estate and the remainder in fee. Enter the doctrine of merger. The life estate merges into the fee and ceases to exist as a separate estate; A has a present possessory fee simple estate.

---

particular remainder to have the necessary characteristic and then reach that legal result by classifying the interest accordingly? Phrased in another way, the question may be whether a remainder may be vested for the purpose of one legal result and contingent for another?

"It is entirely conceivable that the questions might both be answered in the affirmative, and one may certainly find decisions where it appears that the court has simply achieved a result it thought desirable by warping the classification of interests. The tendency of the courts, however, seems to be to maintain rather uniform concepts of vested and contingent remainders. . . . To the lawyer the significance of this tendency lies in the fact that it is possible to predict, with considerable certainty, the classification which will be given to a remainder merely by an examination of the *form* of the limitation. It is for that reason that the emphasis in this chapter relates to the differences in form which will result in the creation of the vested or contingent remainder. One must constantly bear in mind, however, that classification will not necessarily decide the issue, because the court may feel free to attribute a new legal characteristic to the particular interest." Simes & Smith, The Law of Future Interests §134 (2d ed. 1956).

But suppose *Case 19.* O conveys "to A for life, then to B and his heirs if B lives to attain the age of twenty-five years." Thereafter, but before B attains age twenty-five, O conveys his reversion in fee simple to A. The common law courts held that A's life estate merged with A's reversion in fee simple, thereby giving A a fee simple absolute — destroying B's contingent remainder in the process. The "logic" behind this result? A's life estate terminated by reason of the merger doctrine; B's remainder was still contingent when the life estate terminated. B could not take seisin; therefore seisin passed to A and B's remainder was destroyed.[38] (Which comes first in this explanation: the reason or the result?)

PROBLEM

O, owner of Blackacre in fee simple, conveys Blackacre to A for life, then to B and his heirs if B survive A, and if B does not survive A, to C and his heirs.

(a) Does O have a reversion if the doctrine of destructibility of contingent remainders is in effect? Gulliver, Cases on Future Interests 233 (1959). Do you see why this problem is like a circle of weary soldiers who rest themselves in a bog by each sitting on the lap of the man behind?

(b) Does O have a reversion if the doctrine of destructibility of contingent remainders has been abolished? If O has a reversion, does it have any economic value?

The destructibility rule did not apply to executory interests, which were by definition indestructible by a gap in seisin.[39] If executory interests are recognized at all, they must be indestructible. This can best be understood by looking at a couple of examples.

> *Case 20.* After the Statute of Uses, O bargains and sells "to A for life, and one year after his death to B and his heirs." After the Statute of Uses, this springing executory interest in B could be created. To say that B has an executory interest is to say that it will follow a certain gap in seisin: the one-year period following A's death. If a gap destroyed the interest, it would be impossible to create a springing executory interest.

[38] At common law B's remainder could also be destroyed by A's forfeiture. In *Case 19* suppose that A, while holding the life estate, purports to convey a fee simple title. Under the rules of the common law, this was a "tortious feoffment," a wrong to the overlord, and A forfeited his life estate. This would cause A's life estate to come to an end while B's remainder was still contingent, and the remainder was destroyed. Forfeiture is wholly obsolete in the United States.

[39] Pells v. Brown, Cro. Jac. 590, 79 Eng. Rep. 504 (K.B. 1620), is sometimes cited as so holding. In fact, Pells v. Brown decided that an executory interest following a fee simple was indestructible by a common recovery suffered by the fee simple tenant. A common recovery was a means used by a fee tail tenant to cut off all future interests, and in Pells it was argued unsuccessfully that this device should be extended to a fee simple owner. By blocking this means of untying land, the decision made a rule against perpetuities inevitable (so sayeth John Chipman Gray). Gray, The Rule Against Perpetuities §159 (4th ed. 1942).

Case 21. After the Statute of Uses, O bargains and sells "to A and his heirs, but if B returns from Rome, then to B and his heirs." B has a shifting executory interest, which shifts seisin out of A if B returns from Rome. By definition no gap is possible between the preceding estate and the shifting executory interest.

As the above two cases illustrate, enactment of the Statute of Uses in 1536 made possible the creation of indestructible interests. This, together with the decline in the significance of seisin, might have led the courts to do away with the destructibility doctrine, but in fact the scope of the destructibility doctrine was thereafter expanded. Prior to 1536 the doctrine applied only to contingent remainders that failed to vest at the natural termination of the preceding life estate. In Chudleigh's Case, 1 Co. Rep. 120a, 76 Eng. Rep. 261 (K.B. 1594), and Archer's Case, 1 Co. Rep. 66b, 75 Eng. Rep. 146 (K.B. 1599), the courts approved destruction of contingent remainders by merger of the life estate into the reversion. And in Purefoy v. Rogers, 2 Wms. Saund. 380, 85 Eng. Rep. 1181 (K.B. 1670), the court held that if it was possible for a future interest to take effect as a contingent remainder rather than as an executory interest, it should be classified as a contingent remainder. The reason for the continued adherence to the doctrine — even though it was easily evaded by careful draftsmanship creating indestructible executory interests — was the judicial desire to keep land alienable. Not until the Rule against Perpetuities developed in the eighteenth century was there much sentiment for treating contingent remainders and executory interests alike. The drafting devices used to avoid the doctrine are illustrated in the following problems.

PROBLEMS

1. O conveys Blackacre "to A for 100 years if he so long live, then in fee to B's issue who survive B, per stirpes." Thereafter, O conveys his interest to A. What is the state of title?

2. O conveys Blackacre "to A for life, and one day after A's death to B and his heirs if B lives to attain the age of twenty-five." B is fifteen years old at the time of the conveyance. Three years later A dies. What is the state of title?

3. O conveys Blackacre "to A for life, then if A's life estate shall terminate prior to A's death, to M, N, P, Q and R and their heirs in trust for the life of A to preserve contingent remainders, then to A's issue per stirpes who survive A." A conveys his life estate to O. What is the state of the title?

4. T devises Blackacre "to A for life, then to such of A's children as attain the age of twenty-one *before or after* A's death." A has three children and dies before any of them attain the age of twenty-one. What is the state of title? Dean v. Dean, 3 Ch. 150 (1891). If the gift to A's children is valid with the "before or after" language, can you make an argument that it should be valid without it? If this argument is accepted, do you see how it could be extended to eliminate completely

the destructibility doctrine? Kales, Contingent Future Interests After a Particular Estate of Freehold, 21 L.Q. Rev. 118 (1905).

Since the destructibility doctrine was concerned with gaps in seisin, it did not apply to conveyances that did not involve seisin. Specifically, the doctrine applied only to *legal* contingent remainders in *land*. Since the chancellor paid no attention to seisin, the doctrine did not apply to equitable interests, and there is no seisin in personal property.

PROBLEM

In a jurisdiction that applies the destructibility doctrine, O conveys securities worth $100,000 in trust "to pay the income to A for life, and then to distribute the trust corpus to such of A's children as reach the age of twenty-one." Two years later A dies, leaving two minor children. What is the state of the title to the trust fund?

Modern Status of the Destructibility Doctrine

After the development of the Rule against Perpetuities to curb executory interests that did not vest within lives in being plus twenty-one years, it appeared a good idea to have one time period governing the creation and existence of all contingent interests and to abolish the destructibility doctrine, which operated capriciously and was easily avoided by draftsmanship. In England destructibility of contingent remainders by merger was abolished in 1845, and destructibility by failure to vest upon natural termination of the prior estates was done away with in 1877. In about three-fourths of the states the destructibility rule has been abolished by statute or judicial decision.[40] What of the other jurisdictions? It is not easy to say. Professor Powell says, "Florida, Oregon, Pennsylvania, and Tennessee are reasonably certain to have the doctrine. Arkansas, North Carolina, and South Carolina have dicta, but no decisions, that the doctrine exists in those states." [41] Yet this appraisal is open to question. There are Tennessee cases which indicate that that state does not recognize destructibility.[42] And in Arkansas there are many cases where the doctrine should have been applied, but no mention of it was made.[43] In all these states except Florida, which clearly recognizes the doctrine,[44] the last cases noticing destructibility

[40] 1 American Law of Property §4.63 (Casner ed. 1952); Simes & Smith, The Law of Future Interests §209 (2d ed. 1956).

[41] 2 Powell, Real Property ¶314 (1970).

[42] Dukeminier, Contingent Remainders and Executory Interests: A Requiem for the Distinction, 43 Minn. L. Rev. 13, 34 (1958).

[43] Id. at 35; Fetters, Destructibility of Contingent Remainders, 21 Ark. L. Rev. 145 (1967).

[44] Popp. v. Bond, 158 Fla. 185, 28 So. 2d 259 (1946); In re Rentz' Estate, 152 So. 2d 480 (Fla. 1963); Smith, Destructibility of Contingent Remainders in Florida, 3 U. Fla. L. Rev. 319 (1950).

are more than sixty years old. Professors Simes and Smith have written: "This decisive trend away from the destructibility rule, evidenced by the legislative and judicial abolition thereof, should be influential in other jurisdictions where the matter has not yet been settled by either statute or decision. It would seem that those courts would be justified in holding that the destructibility rule no longer exists, just as the Restatement of Property has taken that position. Based purely upon a conception of continuity of seisin which has no practical significance today and has had none for centuries, the rule cannot be justified today." [45]

PROBLEM

In a jurisdiction in which the destructibility rule has been abolished by statute, O conveys land "to A for life, then to such of A's children as attain the age of twenty-one." Two years later A dies leaving two children: C (aged eight) and D (aged four). What is the state of title? When C reaches age twenty-one will he take any interest in Blackacre?

2. *Undisposed-of Income*

EDWARDS v. HAMMOND
Court of Common Pleas, 1684
3 Lev. 132, 83 Eng. Rep. 614

Ejectment upon not guilty, and special verdict, the case was. A copyholder of land,[46] burrough English,[47] surrendered to the use of himself for life, and after to the use of his eldest son and his heirs, if he lived to the age of 21 years: provided, and upon condition, that if he die before 21, that then it shall remain to the surrenderer and his heirs. The surrenderer died, the youngest son entered; and the eldest son being 17 brought an ejectment; and the sole question was, whether the devise to the eldest son be upon condition precedent, or if the condition be subsequent; scil. that the estate in fee shall vest immediately upon the death of the father, to be divested if he die before 21. For the defendant it was argued, that the condition was precedent, and that the estate should descend to the youngest son in the mean time, or at least shall be in contingency and in abeyance 'till the first son shall attain to one and twenty; and so the eldest son has no title now, being no more than 17. On the other side it was argued, and so agreed by the Court; that though by the first words this

[45] Simes & Smith, The Law of Future Interests §209, at 246 (2d ed. 1956).

[46] The land involved was copyhold, not freehold. The lord held seisin. Hence contingent remainders in copyhold land were not destructible by a gap in seisin. — Eds.

[47] In some parts of England, notably Sussex and Surrey, primogeniture did not prevail; land passed to the youngest son instead of the eldest according to the custom of "borough English." What reasons can you give for this reversal of the order of descent? Some have imagined it associated with the jus primae noctis. See 2 Blackstone, Commentaries *82; Cairns, The Explanatory Process in the Field of Inheritance, 20 Iowa L. Rev. 266, 277 (1935). — Eds.

may seem to be a condition precedent, yet, taking all the words together, this was not a condition precedent, but a present devise to the eldest son, subject to and defeasible by this condition subsequent, scil. his not attaining the age of 21. . . . Accordingly this case was adjudged in Mich. term next following.

NOTES

1. For ease of discussion, the conveyance in Edwards v. Hammond can be paraphrased as follows: "to A for life, then to A's eldest son B and his heirs if he attains the age of twenty-one; but if B dies under twenty-one, to A and his heirs." A died when B was seventeen. C, A's youngest son, was the heir of A. (a) Exactly what was the practical problem facing the court? What policies support the court's decision to put B into possession rather than C? (b) Assuming that it makes more sense to put B into possession, why could the court not put a contingent remainderman in possession? (c) If the court were to create a new rule to cover this situation, do you think the following New York statute suggestive of an appropriate solution? New York Estates, Powers & Trusts Law §9-2.3 (1967): "When income is not disposed of and no valid direction is given for its accumulation it passes to the persons presumptively entitled to the next eventual estate."

2. The rule of Edwards v. Hammond ("If an age contingency is Janus faced, look at it rear-end-to") is adopted by 2 Restatement of Property §253, Comment e (1940). It is discussed in 5 American Law of Property §21.32 (Casner ed. 1952), which says: "Furthermore, the rule of Edwards v. Hammond has been applied in situations where the divesting contingency is less comprehensive than the condition precedent. For example, the gift may be 'to *B* at twenty-one, but if *B* dies under twenty-one without issue, to *C*.' " Here, if it is determined that since both a condition precedent (attainment of twenty-one) and a divesting contingency (death without issue under twenty-one) are present, only the latter is operative, the effect is to enhance substantially the value of *B*'s gift. If he dies under twenty-one with issue, under this interpretation, his interest is not divested and the property will pass to his estate."

3. Another case where the courts do not classify the interests in sequence is when remainders in default of appointment are created. For example, O conveys Blackacre "to A for life, then to such persons as A by will appoints, and in default of appointment to the children of A and their heirs." A has one child, B. This conveyance is read as if it were "to A for life, then to A's children and their heirs, but if A otherwise appoints by will, to such appointees." Thus B has a vested remainder subject to open and also subject to complete defeasance by A's exercise of his power of appointment. Doe dem Willis v. Martin, 4 T.R. 39, 100 Eng. Rep. 882 (K.B. 1790). Professor Gulliver suggests that this reversal of grammatical sequence was influenced by the judges' desire to avoid the doctrine of destructibility of contingent remainders. Gulliver, Cases on Future Interests 259 (1959).

4. The English courts limited the rule of Edwards v. Hammond in two ways.

First, they restricted it to *age contingencies*, although, as Jarman says, "the rule of construction appears to be as reasonably applicable where the contingency is that of the devisee being alive when the remainder naturally falls into possession, as where it is the attainment by him of the age which presumably in the testator's mind qualifies him for the possession and legal control." Jarman, Wills 1367 (8th ed. 1951). Second, they limited its application by the distinction made in the following case, Festing v. Allen, where it was held that the age condition could not be ignored as surplusage when it was an essential part of the description of the beneficiaries. Why do you suppose the courts were so hostile to the rule of Edwards v. Hammond, especially in view of the stated preference for a vested construction?

FESTING v. ALLEN

Court of Exchequer, 1843

12 Mees. & Wels. 279, 152 Eng. Rep. 1204

[Roger Belk died devising land by a testamentary clause that went on for more than 550 words without a stop. Simplified, the devise was "to my wife for life, and after her death to my grand-daughter Martha Hannah Johnson for life, and after her death to the children of Martha Hannah who shall attain the age of 21, and for want of any such issue to [Ann Johnson and others]." Testator's widow died. Then Martha died survived by three minor children.]

ROLFE, B. . . . [T]he main question is, whether those children took on her death any interest in the devised estates.[48]

We think that they did not. It was contended on their behalf that they took vested estates in fee immediately on the death of their mother, subject only to be devested in the event of their dying under twenty-one, and the case, it was said, must be treated as coming within the principle of . . . [Edwards v. Hammond]. To this, however, we cannot accede. In all those cases there was an absolute gift to some ascertained person or persons, and the Courts held, that words accompanying the gift, though apparently importing a contingency or contingencies, did in reality only indicate certain circumstances on the happening or not happening of which the estate previously devised should be devested, and pass from the first devisee into some other channel. The clear distinction in the present case is, that here there is no gift to any one who does not answer the whole of the requisite description. The gift is not to the children of Mrs. Festing, but to the children who shall attain twenty-one, and no one who has not attained his age of twenty-one years is an object of the testator's bounty, any more than a person who is not a child of Mrs. Festing. . . . We think that Mrs. Festing was tenant for life, with contingent remainders in fee to such of her children as should attain twenty-one; and as no child had attained twenty-one when the particular estate determined by her death, the remainder was necessarily defeated. It is equally clear that all the other limitations were defeated by the same event, namely, the death of Mrs. Festing leaving several infant chil-

[48] If Martha Hannah's children had a *contingent* remainder, it was destroyed at Martha Hannah's death by failure to vest prior to the termination of the life estate. — EDS.

dren, but no child who had then attained the age of twenty-one years. For the limitations to take effect at her decease were all of them contingent remainders in fee, one or other of which was to take effect according to the events pointed out. . . . If . . . there had at her decease been a failure of her child or children who should attain twenty-one, then the alternative limitations would have taken effect; but this did not happen, for though she left no child of the age of twenty-one years, and therefore capable of taking under the devise in favour of her children, yet neither is it possible to say that there was at her decease a failure of her issue who should attain the age of twenty-one years, for she left three children, all or any of whom might and still may attain the prescribed age; so that the contingency on which alone the alternative limitations were to take effect had not happened when the particular estate determined, and those alternative limitations, all of which were clearly contingent remainders, were therefore defeated. On these short grounds, we think it clear, that neither the infant children of Mrs. Festing, nor the parties who were to take the estate in case of her leaving no child who should attain twenty-one, take any interest whatever, but that on her death the whole estate and interest vested in the heir-at-law [of Roger Belk].

NOTES

1. Apply the principles of Edwards v. Hammond and Festing v. Allen to the following cases. At the time of the conveyance A and B are alive and A has a son, C, aged 5, and a second son, D, aged 3.

(a) To A for life, then to B if B reaches 21.
(b) To A for life, then to B if B reaches 21, but if B does not reach 21 to C.
(c) To A for life, then to the first son of A if he reaches 21, and if he does not reach 21 to B.
(d) To A for life, then to the first son of A who reaches 21, and if no son of A reaches 21 to B. (See Re Astor, [1922] 1 Ch. 364.)
(e) To A for life, then to the children of A if they reach 21, but if none reach 21 to B. (See Randall v. Roake, 5 Dow. 202, 3 Eng. Rep. 1302 (H.L. 1817); Hawkins, Wills 286 (3d ed. 1925).)
(f) To A for life, then to the children of A who reach 21, but if none reach 21 to B.
(g) To A for life, then to such children of A as reach 21, but if none reach 21 to B.

2. Festing v. Allen did not go down well with the losing counsel in the case, who later became Vice Chancellor Malins. "It is said that the court's failure to see his argument that these children had an interest vested subject to condition subsequent so soured the disposition of this able lawyer and so distorted his mental processes that in this case we have the explanation for later events when Malins was on the bench, at which time a statement that the lower court decision had been by

Malins seemed to give an appellant a prima facie right to a reversal." Powell, Cases on Future Interests 159 n. 13 (1928). In Astley v. Micklethwait, 15 Ch. Div. 59 (1880), Malins remarked: "Why am I to go out of my way to destroy the will instead of preserving it? Anything that would enable the court to get out of the monstrous doctrine of Festing v. Allen . . . ought to be adopted."

3. Professor Schuyler developed a thesis, held by many other scholars as well,[49] that the preference for a vested construction arose primarily as a means of saving contingent remainders from destruction by a gap in seisin. Schuyler, Drafting, Tax, and Other Consequences of the Rule of Early Vesting, 46 Ill. L. Rev. 407 (1951). If this thesis is correct, how do you explain Festing v. Allen?

4. The difficulties encountered in classifying remainders as vested subject to divestment or as contingent are legendary. The Restatement of Property, §157, Comment p (1936), says the difference is this: If "it is possible to point to a person and to say that such person would take, if all interests including a prior right to a present interest should now end," the remainder is vested subject to divestment; if it is not possible to do so, the remainder is contingent. But unhappily the Restatement does not tell us *who* does the pointing (judge, lawyer, law professor, law student?). It does not separate the prescriptive function of a judge from the predictive function of a lawyer. Nor does it tell us *what conditions move* the person to point and say the magic words when the actual language being considered is not in the terse, pristine form of a Restatement (or casebook) example, but is the possibly verbose and probably ambivalent phraseology of some inspired draftsman's deed, trust or will. The phrase "it is possible" covers countless cases where, as a result of judicial genius, ignorance, ingenuity, or sheer humbug, we find almost anything conceivable. As Bentham observed, "Error is never so difficult to be destroyed as when it has its root in language."

For an interesting proposal to simplify the law of estates by, inter alia, treating all vested remainders subject to complete defeasance as contingent, see Waggoner, Reformulating the Structure of Estates: A Proposal for Legislative Action, 85 Harv. L. Rev. 729 (1972).

3. *Acceleration of Future Interests*

ESTATE OF REYNOLDS
Supreme Court of Wisconsin, 1968
39 Wis. 2d 155, 158 N.W.2d 328

The only question on this appeal is whether, under the circumstances, the renunciation of the income of a trust by a life tenant accelerates the distribution so that the remaindermen are presently entitled to their share of the trust corpus.

The settlor of the trust was Gladys Lampert Reynolds. Her will left a residue of approximately $106,000 in trust. Her dispositive scheme was to give her brother,

[49] Perhaps the first to advance this view was Kales, Estates, Future Interests and Illegal Conditions and Restraints in Illinois §328 (2d ed. 1920).

Harold Lampert, Sr., the income from the trust during his lifetime, and upon his death the corpus was to be distributed to Harold's children. This expected plan was disrupted when Harold Lampert, Sr., renounced his interest in his rights that arose under the will and in the trust created by that will. After the filing of that renunciation, Harold Lampert, Jr., who was to receive three-fifths of the corpus upon the termination of the life estate, and Barbara Lampert Fenster, who was to receive two-fifths, petitioned for the immediate distribution of the corpus to them.

The relevant terms of the will are:

> Article III
>
> . . .
>
> 2. The trustee shall pay the net income of the trust to or for the benefit of my said brother, Harold Lampert, Sr., so long as he shall live . . .
>
> 3. The trust shall terminate upon the death of my brother, Harold Lampert, Sr., and the trustee shall distribute the remaining assets of the trust, including any undistributed income, as hereinafter provided:
>
> (a) If my nephew, Harold Lampert, Jr., is living upon the termination of the trust, the trustee shall distribute three-fifths of the remaining assets of the trust to my said nephew.
>
> (b) If my nephew, Harold Lampert, Jr., is not living upon the termination of the trust, the trustee shall distribute three-fifths of the remaining assets of the trust to his then living children in equal shares by right of representation.
>
> . . .
>
> (d) If my niece, Barbara Lampert Fenster, is living upon the termination of the trust, the trustee shall distribute two-fifths of the remaining assets of the trust to my said niece.
>
> (e) If my niece, Barbara Lampert Fenster, is not living upon the termination of the trust, the trustee shall distribute two-fifths of the remaining assets of the trust to her then living children in equal shares by right of representation.
>
> . . .
>
> Article IV
>
> 1. If my brother, Harold Lampert, Sr., does not survive me, but my nephew, Harold Lampert, Jr., does survive me, I give, devise and bequeath three-fifths of the residue of my estate to my said nephew.
>
> . . .
>
> 4. If my brother, Harold Lampert, Sr., does not survive me, but my niece, Barbara Lampert Fenster, does survive me, I give, devise and bequeath two-fifths of the residue of my estate to my said niece.

Prior to any determination in the probate court, a guardian ad litem was appointed to represent the interests of the six infant children of Harold Lampert, Jr., who would, together with the possible, though non-existent, children of Barbara Lampert Fenster, be precluded from the opportunity to take if a present distribution were ordered. The guardian ad litem has appealed from the order of the probate court directing an immediate distribution.

HEFFERNAN, Justice. The general rule is set forth in Restatement, 2 Property, p. 961, sec. 231, wherein it is stated:

> When an attempted prior interest fails because the person to whom it is limited renounces it, succeeding interests are accelerated except when (a) the terms and circumstances of the limitation manifest a contrary intent . . .

In Will of Uihlein (1953), 264 Wis. 362, 378, 59 N.W.2d 641, 649, 38 A.L.R.2d 961, we quoted with approval from 4 Page, Wills (lifetime ed.), p. 89, sec. 1390:

> Where the enjoyment of possession by the remainderman is postponed until after the determination of the particular estate and for no other purpose, and such tenant elects to take against the will, the remainderman enters into enjoyment at once. This principle is called acceleration of the remainders. Renunciation by the particular tenant is said to be equivalent to his death with reference to the remainder's taking effect in possession.[50]

. . .

The appellant herein stresses that the right to have the terms of a will carried out is a sacred obligation of the court and that to permit the acceleration of the remainders would defy the testator's intent. Wisconsin cases, and the texts generally, give preeminence to the intent of the testator, and it is universally held, even in those jurisdictions permitting the acceleration of the remainder distribution, that such can be permitted only when it is consonant with the testator's intent. . . .

While there is substantial authority to the contrary in other jurisdictions,[51] we are satisfied that the Wisconsin law permits the acceleration of the remainder under the circumstances of the instant cases.

Our statutes (sec. 231.23) provide that, "When the purposes for which an express trust shall have been created shall have ceased the estate of the trustee shall also cease."

It would appear that, since the purpose of the trust — to assist in the support of Harold Lampert, Sr. — ceased to exist upon his renunciation, the only purpose for which the trust was created has ceased to exist, and, under the statutes, the trust should be terminated unless it is determined that such termination is contrary to the testatrix's intent.

The Restatement, 2 Property, p. 554, sec. 157, comment p, would also permit the acceleration of the remainder where the remaindermen are ascertainable at the time the prior interest is renounced. Hence, since both Harold, Jr., and Barbara are living and constitute the entire class of remaindermen designated in the will, under the Restatement rule the trust should be terminated and the remainders accelerated.

[50] This quotation from Page presently appears in 5 Page, Wills (Bowie-Parker [*sic*] Rev. 1962), p. 684, 686, sec. 47.45.

[51] In re Graham's Will (1932), 145 Misc. 628, 260 N.Y.S. 585; Walsh v. Hulse (1952), 23 N.J. Super. 573, 93 A.2d 230; In re Bauer's Estate (1959), 19 Misc. 2d 707, 192 N.Y.S.2d 252; Sueske v. Schofield (1941), 376 Ill. 431, 34 N.E.2d 399; Ajax Electrothermic Corp. v. First Nat. Bank (1951), 7 N.J. 82, 80 A.2d 559.

Perhaps the most satisfactory rationalization of the acceleration of remainders appears in Simes and Smith, The Law of Future Interests (2d ed.), p. 273-275, sec. 796.

> When the prior interest is renounced, this unanticipated event frustrates the dispositive scheme of the testator. It would seem that if he has clearly indicated a condition precedent which must occur before the next interest takes effect in enjoyment, the court would merely be adding to the disruption of the dispositive scheme by ignoring the express condition precedent. Hence, it would seem that as a starting point in the analysis, one should assume that a contingent remainder will never be accelerated. Yet, where the renunciation is unanticipated, this rule may work out unjustly if we were to apply the ordinary rules of construction in deciding whether the remainder is contingent. Nearly all of the cases in which remainders which appear to be contingent have been accelerated fall into the same class. They are remainders in which the apparent condition precedent is survivorship of the life tenant. Thus, suppose property is devised to the widow for life, and on her death to the children of the testator then surviving. Even though we concede that the gift to the children can be regarded as an executory interest, the accepted doctrine of property law would lead us to say that the children cannot take until the widow actually dies and they are left surviving. Yet the context of the will may indicate that the testator postponed the gift to the children solely to make adequate provision for his widow, and that, the moment she is otherwise provided for, it would be reasonable to assume that the testator wished his children to take. It is true he used the word "surviving," but that may be because he did not wish heirs or issue to take, although he had no intention of requiring his children actually to survive his wife if they could take before that time without injury to her. Hence in this situation many courts have said, and some have held, that the children who survive the widow's renunciation take a present interest on that event. What they really are doing is construing the will in the light of the widow's renunciation so that the limitation in remainder reads: To my children living at the termination of the life estate.
>
> It is believed, therefore, that although the courts may state that contingent remainders are accelerated they are likely to do so only in circumstances when it is reasonable to conclude that the particular condition precedent was not important to the testator in the light of the unanticipated renunciation. Such a conclusion is most likely to be reasonable when the expressed condition precedent is survival of the life tenant.

Applying this test, we conclude that the distribution of the remainder by the use of a trust was postponed solely to take care of Harold Lampert, Sr., during his lifetime, if he so desired.

This conclusion is borne out by the fact that the will provided for outright distribution of all of the residue of the estate to Harold, Jr., and Barbara in the event Harold, Sr., predeceased the testatrix.

It is thus apparent that the testatrix postponed the gift to Harold, Jr., and Barbara, her niece, only to assure that provision was made for her brother, Harold, Sr. Under the circumstances, it is reasonable to assume that the testatrix wished the remaindermen to take once the object of the trust had been fully accomplished.

Since the trust is now without purpose, it is reasonable, to paraphrase the words of Simes, to construe the will to read: "To Harold Lampert, Jr., and Barbara Lampert Fenster at the termination of the life estate."

We conclude that under the circumstances the mere holding of the residue in trust until Harold, Sr., should at last die was unimportant to the testatrix, and her testamentary intent is better carried out by affirming the trial judge's order accelerating the remainder.

Judgment affirmed.

2 RESTATEMENT OF PROPERTY (1936)

§233. When an attempted prior interest fails because it is renounced by the person to whom it is limited, a succeeding interest is not accelerated so long as a condition precedent to such succeeding interest continues unfulfilled.

Comment:

c. *Construction problem as to existence of condition precedent.* The rule stated in this Section applies only when the language of a limitation is construed to create a succeeding interest subject to a condition precedent which remains unfulfilled at the time when the creating conveyance becomes operative. Language which under other circumstances is appropriate for the creation of a condition precedent is sometimes employed in such manner that the conveyor does not manifest an intent to create a condition precedent for such succeeding interest, but rather, to refer thereby to the course of events which is to be significant *if* the attempted prior interest takes effect. Thus a description of the persons to take after the attempted prior interest as the "then surviving descendants" of a named person or as "such children of (a named person) as are then living" is not necessarily sufficient to create the condition precedent which is required for the operation of the rule stated in this Section. In resolving this preliminary problem of construction, the criterion is whether the terms and circumstances of the limitation manifest an intent to benefit persons living at the termination of the preceding interest or at the death of the person to whom such preceding interest was limited. . . .

4. *Alienability and Creditors' Rights*

HALBACH, VESTED AND CONTINGENT REMAINDERS: A PREMATURE REQUIEM FOR DISTINCTIONS BETWEEN CONDITIONS PRECEDENT AND SUBSEQUENT, in PERSPECTIVES OF LAW *152, 157-161 (Pound ed. 1964)*

The distinction between vested and contingent remainders continues to be significant in a number of jurisdictions in matters of inter vivos alienability of future interests. For purposes of transmission by will or intestacy no distinction is drawn between conditions precedent and conditions subsequent because it is clear in all states that remainders and executory interests of all types are freely alienable on death. . . . The importance of the distinction remains in the area of inter vivos transferability. Contingent remainders and executory interests are still not freely alienable in a number of states.[52] The reasons for this are principally traceable to the early common law notion that contingent remainders were not estates but merely expectancies or "possibilities." Even in jurisdictions which have retained the view that contingent remainders are inalienable inter vivos, all vested remainders are freely transferable. This is true even of remainders which are vested subject to complete defeasance. Consequently, in these states it is necessary to decide whether a particular condition is precedent or subsequent in order to determine the contingent or vested classification upon which inter vivos alienability turns. . . . Contingent remainders and executory interests have now become fully transferable inter vivos by statute or by judicial decision in most of the states. Even in those states where these interests are still deemed inalienable, the significance of the distinction between technically vested and contingent future interests is considerably lessened by the recognized exception for transfers by release and also by giving effect to certain purported transfers either as contracts to convey or through application of the doctrine of estoppel by deed. . . .

A more common rule requiring distinctions to be drawn between conditions precedent and subsequent is the rule under which the rights of a remainderman's creditors are made to depend upon the vested or contingent classification of his interest. The traditional view has been that all vested remainders, including those which are subject to complete defeasance, can be reached by whatever creditor process is appropriate in the jurisdiction but that contingent remainders and executory interests are not subject to creditors' claims. The immunity of contingent future interests readily follows from their inalienability in jurisdictions where this is the case; but immunity exists in a substantial number of other states in which contingent future interests are voluntarily alienable. The principal reason for not allowing involuntary alienation of these interests, even though voluntarily alienable, stems from an opposition to the forced sale of an interest which is not readily marketable. Thus the contingent remainder would be sold at a great sacrifice to the debtor while producing a disproportionately small return for the creditor. Another reason occasionally given for withholding alienable contingent future interests from creditors is the frustration of the grantor's intent which would result from sale of the interest. Yet these policies are implemented by a rule which distinguishes between interests subject to conditions precedent and those which are defeasibly vested. This technical distinction of the property law has no logical relationship to

[52] In a few states all contingent remainders are inalienable. E.g., Deener v. Watkins, 191 Ark. 776, 87 S.W.2d 994 (1935); Johnson v. Herrin, 383 Ill. 598, 50 N.E.2d 720 (1943). In a larger number of states a distinction is drawn between remainders "contingent as to person" and those "contingent as to event"; the latter being held alienable and the former not. E.g. Maine Rev. Stat. Ann. c. 168, §3 (1954); In re Clayton's Estate, 195 Md. 622, 74 A.2d 1 (1950).

the policy considerations involved. The element of sacrifice and the frustration of intent are the same whether a condition is precedent or subsequent in form. The distinction again represents a temptation for courts to manipulate results by strained classification of the interests in litigation. Examination of cases suggests that this temptation has not always been resisted, and most frequently it appears that conditions have been construed to be precedent rather than subsequent in order to avoid sacrifice sale of the interest. . . . If the policy against forced sale precludes changing the traditional rule with respect to contingent remainders, then the rule regarding defeasibly vested remainders should be changed to grant the same immunity to such interests, but this has rarely been done.[53] Thus the question may logically be resolved either by allowing or denying creditors the right to reach all uncertain future interests, or by some intermediate or more flexible position, but in order to eliminate the distinction between contingent and defeasibly vested interests it is necessary for these functional equivalents to be placed on an equal footing. This is, of course, the result of making contingent future interests available to creditors, since that has traditionally been the rule for defeasibly vested remainders. Even where individual creditors cannot reach contingent remainders and executory interests, however, the Federal Bankruptcy Act tends somewhat to reduce the significance of vested or contingent construction because it provides that all interests which are voluntarily alienable shall be available to the creditors in bankruptcy.[54] Nevertheless we are far from being rid of the distinction in this area; in the creditor cases outside bankruptcy the distinction is still controlling in about half of the states, while in bankruptcy the importance of the distinction is limited to those relatively few states in which contingent interests are not transferable voluntarily.

5. *Distinctions Between Contingent Remainders and Executory Interests*

DUKEMINIER, CONTINGENT REMAINDERS AND EXECUTORY INTERESTS: A REQUIEM FOR THE DISTINCTION
43 Minn. L. Rev. 13, 51-55 (1958)

Executory interests can be divided into two groups: (1) those that are in an ascertained person on an event certain to happen, and (2) those that are given to unascertained persons or on an uncertain event. Executory interests of the first type are rare. Examples are "to A thirty years from date," "to A after my death." The first is analogous to a vested remainder after a term of years, the second to a vested remainder after a life estate. These executory interests are treated like vested re-

[53] One of the rare examples is Anglo California National Bank v. Kidd, 58 Cal. App. 2d 651, 655, 137 P.2d 460, 462 (1943).

[54] Bankruptcy Act §70a(5), 30 Stat. 565 (1898), 11 U.S.C. §110(a)(5) (1952); Maclachlan, Bankruptcy §178 (1956). Where contingent interests are inalienable, courts still strain to avoid the availability of an interest in bankruptcy by finding that a particular condition is precedent. E.g., Spengler v. Kuhn, 212 Ill. 186, 72 N.E. 214 (1904).

mainders under the Rule Against Perpetuities,[55] and, although the cases are scarce, it is believed that they would also be treated as "vested" for other purposes as well. If they do not differ in consequences from vested remainders, they may as well be called vested future interests or vested remainders. . . .

Executory interests of the second type are analogous to contingent remainders. It is with these executory interests that we have been primarily concerned. The foregoing analysis indicates there is no difference between them and contingent remainders except where the issue is destructibility and, possibly, where the Rule in Shelley's Case is involved. No court has refused to apply Shelley's Case to an executory interest because it was an executory interest, and for the reasons given above, the distinction between the two interests under the Rule in Shelley's Case is either nonexistent or, if theoretically existent, of no substantial importance. We are left with destructibility as the only distinguishing feature. That relic of feudalism exists in Florida and, viewed in the friendliest fashion, possibly, although certainly not probably, in less than a dozen other states. In three-quarters of the states destructibility has been wholly done away with. Thus, in at least three-quarters of the states, there is no discernible difference between executory interests and contingent remainders. Only in Florida are we sure of any difference between them. . . .

It is enchantment with labels that is the hidden cause of most of the law's failure in the field of future interests. So long as we concern ourselves with labels and purely verbal distinctions, we can have no doctrinal structure that is more than a play with words, no doctrines that can justify themselves in terms of policy, no doctrines that can recognize the important factors, that can give predictability. All in all, the way to a useful, critical analysis of future interests seems to lead, not through gaps in seisin, but around them.

Is it possible to create an executory interest in New York?

NEW YORK ESTATES, POWERS & TRUSTS LAW (1967)

§6-4.2. A future estate is an estate limited to commence in possession at a future time, either without the intervention of a precedent estate, or on the determination, by lapse of time or otherwise, of a precedent estate created at the same time.

§6-4.3. A remainder is a future estate, as defined in 6-4.2, created in favor of a person other than the creator.

§6-4.7. A future estate indefeasibly vested is an estate created in favor of one or more ascertained persons in being which is certain when created to become an es-

[55] Professor Dukeminier admits that he was here too sanguine about rational results being achieved in perpetuities cases. See Burton v. Hicks and the notes following at pages 1032-1035. — EDS.

tate in possession whenever and however the preceding estates end and which can in no way be defeated or abridged.

§6-4.10. A future estate subject to a condition precedent is an estate created in favor of one or more unborn or unascertained persons or in favor of one or more presently ascertainable persons upon the occurrence of an uncertain event.

6. A Narrow Escape: The Tax Cases

For a period in the 1930s, the United States Supreme Court got itself gorgeously entangled in "the niceties of the art of conveyancing" (the court's phrase) in construing an estate tax statute taxing transfers "taking effect at death." In Klein v. United States,[56] O conveyed land to his wife A for life; the deed further provided that if A predeceased O the property was to revert to O, but *if* A *survived* O the property was to be hers in fee. A survived O. The court held that the value of the land was includible in O's gross estate: He had made a transfer "intended to take effect in possession or enjoyment at or after his death." Why so? Because, reasoned the court, A was given a life estate and a contingent remainder. A's taking was subject to a condition precedent; she had to survive O.

Then came the two St. Louis Union Trust cases, four years later. In Becker v. St. Louis Union Trust Company,[57] O settled property in a trust under which the income was to be paid to A for her lifetime. If A predeceased O the trust corpus was to revert to O; but *if O predeceased* A the corpus was to go to A absolutely. Compare this dispositive language with that in the Klein case. Exactly the same, right? Wrong! The court found a basis for distinction in the italicized portions of the two dispositions. In Klein, A was given a life estate and a contingent remainder, "and whether that should ever become vested in the grantee depended upon the *condition precedent* that the grantor die during the life of the grantee." But in Becker the court concluded that O made an absolute transfer to A, with A's interest subject to being divested by the operation of a *condition subsequent*. "Unlike the Klein Case, where the death was the generating source of the title, here . . . the trust instrument and not the death was the generating source. The death did not transmit the possibility, but destroyed [the possibility that A's title might be divested]. . . ." Hence this disposition was not taxable as a transfer taking effect at death.

Had this distinction between conditions precedent and conditions subsequent been preserved in the tax laws, it could well have prompted the publishers to bring out an eleventh edition of Fearne on Contingent Remainders. But this approach to transfer tax problems was short-lived. The St. Louis Union Trust cases were overruled by Helvering v. Hallock, decided in 1940:

[56] 283 U.S. 231 (1931).

[57] 296 U.S. 48 (1935); see also Helvering v. St. Louis Union Trust Co., 296 U.S. 39 (1935), handed down the same day.

> [T]he statute taxes not merely those interests which are deemed to pass at death according to refined technicalities of the law of property. It also taxes *inter vivos* transfers that are too much akin to testamentary dispositions not to be subjected to the same excise. . . . [This Court has] refused to subordinate the plain purposes of a modern fiscal measure to the wholly unrelated origins of the recondite learning of ancient property law. . . .
>
> The law of contingent and vested remainders is full of casuistries. . . . The importation of these distinctions and controversies from the law of property into the administration of the estate tax precludes a fair and workable tax system. Essentially the same interests, judged from the point of view of wealth, will be taxable or not, depending upon elusive and subtle casuistries which may have their historic justification but possess no relevance for tax purposes. These unwitty diversities of the law of property derive from medieval concepts as to the necessity of a continuous seisin. Distinctions which originated under a feudal economy when land dominated social relations are peculiarly irrelevant in the application of tax measures now so largely directed toward intangible wealth.[58]

Helvering v. Hallock was followed by the Spiegel case,[59] in which an inter vivos trust worth $1 million was taxed in the settlor's gross estate as a "transfer taking effect at death" because of the inadvertent retention of a reversion whose value (based on the actuarial probability of the settlor surviving all trust beneficiaries) was less than $70. This decision prompted Congress to enact what is now §2037 of the Internal Revenue Code, a provision of little concern to the estate practitioner.[60] Thus was the distinction between "contingent" and "vested" future interests written out of the federal estate tax laws.

In a few states, though, the inheritance tax treatment of a transfer may turn on whether a future interest is vested or contingent; and more than a few practitioners have on occasion found themselves citing the Restatement, Simes & Smith, and similar works in arguing that a particular interest is "contingent" and therefore should not be taxed in the estate of the holder.

SECTION E. Forfeiture Interests in a Transferor

1. *Creation of Possibilities of Reverter and Rights of Entry*

In this section we deal with two kinds of future interests previously given short shrift: possibilities of reverter and rights of entry. A *possibility of reverter* is the

[58] 309 U.S. 106, 112, 117-118 (1940).

[59] Spiegel's Estate v. United States, 335 U.S. 701 (1949). The contemptuous disdain of ancient property law displayed in Hallock did not extend, the taxpayer found to his dismay in Spiegel, to the law of reversions.

[60] Section 2037 is discussed at page 230, supra.

future interest that the owner of a fee simple absolute retains when he transfers to another person a *fee simple determinable.*

> *Case* 22. O conveys "to the Board of Education, its successors and assigns, for so long as the premises are used for school purposes." By this conveyance the Board of Education has a fee simple determinable; O has a possibility of reverter.

A determinable fee is created by a grant of a fee until an event happens. Apt words are "so long as," "while," "during," "until." Note the durational aspect of these words. When the event happens (e.g., the premises cease to be used for school purposes), the estate comes to an end, or determines, and the transferor has the right to possession. According to orthodox doctrine, it is not necessary to put in any specific words reserving a possibility of reverter. This future interest automatically arises in the grantor because, in conveying a determinable fee, he has transferred away "less" than he has.

The idea that the transferor retains an interest when he gives away less than he has is the theoretical explanation of both the reversion and the possibility of reverter. Both terms are simply legal ways of expressing the factual possibility that the transferor will be entitled to possession again. One word, "reversion," would do for both interests, but two labels we have. The reason is lost in history. Whatever the origin of the distinction, certainty of possession has nothing whatever to do today with the classification of an interest as a "reversion" or as a "possibility of reverter." Although there is no certainty that a possibility of reverter will become possessory in the future, this uncertainty does not make the interest a possibility of reverter. *An interest is called a possibility of reverter solely because it follows a determinable fee.* Indeed, many reversions are likewise uncertain to become possessory, such as one retained by an instrument creating a contingent remainder. But that uncertainty does not change the reversion, which is a conceptual interest retained when no vested fee has been transferred, into a possibility of reverter.

A *right of entry for condition broken* is an interest in the grantor that follows a *fee simple subject to a condition subsequent.* Strictly speaking, it is a power to terminate the granted estate upon the happening of a stated event. Under the terminology devised some fifty years ago by Professor Wesley N. Hohfeld, a distinction was made between a right and a power, and the right of entry was classified as a "power." When the Restatement of Property adopted the Hohfeldian terminology, the American Law Institute thought it necessary to change the name "right of entry" to "power of termination" in order to avoid confusion. While doubtless the Restatement name is more exact, the old one continues to be used.[61]

A right of entry is created by transferring away a fee simple and then adding a condition subsequent: "provided that," "on condition that," or "but if" a specified event happens, the transferor may re-enter the premises.

[61] Because right of entry was deemed inappropriate for personal property, by statute in New York the right is called a right of reacquisition. N.Y. Estates, Powers & Trusts Law §6-4.6 (1967).

Case 23. O conveys "to the Board of Education, its successors and assigns; provided, however, that if the premises shall ever cease to be used for school purposes, the grantor shall have the right to re-enter and re-take the same." O has a string (a "power of termination," a "right of entry") attached to the fee. If the premises ever cease to be used for school purposes, O can exercise his power and retake the fee.

As the above cases suggest, these interests are employed as a means of restricting land use.[62] They are not ordinarily found in family wealth dispositions, but (a) in conveyances of land to a charity (church, school, hospital), with the use of the land restricted to a specified charitable purpose, and (b) in conveyances of residential or commercial property subject to use restrictions, with the right of entry or possibility of reverter inserted to deter breach of the restrictions. Around the turn of the century there was a third source of these conveyances. As railroad operations expanded across the country, a landowner would convey a tract "to the Santa Fe Railroad for so long as the premises shall be used for railroad right of way purposes." The landowner's objective was to cause the railroad to locate a main line, or perhaps a trunk line, in such a way as to benefit his retained lands.

The problems raised by these interests are land use problems, and their study is more appropriately the subject of a Real Estate Transactions or Land Use Planning course. Why, then, the coverage here? First, to round out our study of future interests law and the types of future interests recognized by our legal system. Second, to introduce you to the Rule against Perpetuities. Third, to illustrate the importance of classifying future interests properly when grave consequences turn on the classification. And finally, to demonstrate that these future interests should not be used in family wealth dispositions — and to do a little evangelizing. An occasional practitioner who calls himself a lawyer will recommend that his client make a donative transfer "to the Georgetown YMCA, provided and upon condition that the property shall be the grantee's for so long as the premises shall be used for YMCA purposes; but if the land shall ever cease to be so used, then the premises shall revert to the grantor herein." In so doing, the attorney will have done a singular disservice . . .

To His Client:

(a) It is difficult to determine, without resort to litigation, what interests are created by this type of conveyance. Few such conveyances employ the pristine language of the Restatement or the hornbooks, and the typical deed will, like our example, contain elements both of condition or forfeiture (suggesting a right of entry) and of "so long as" or "revert" (suggesting a possibility of reverter). Moreover, courts have shown a pronounced hostility toward recognition of either of these interests. Given any plausible justification, a court may find that the interest retained by a grantor is a right of entry rather than a possibility of reverter; or (even

[62] There are a few — and only a few — cases involving possibilities of reverter and rights of entry in personal property. Simes & Smith, The Law of Future Interests §§361, 362 (2d ed. 1956).

better, it seems) that the grantor has not retained a future interest at all but is merely the beneficiary of a covenant, and that the grantee has a fee simple absolute. Hence litigation may be necessary to determine just what interest, if any, the client has retained.

(b) If, at some point in the future, a breach allegedly occurs, the grantor's re-entry may not be as simple as the conveyance would indicate. In many jurisdictions a grantee who has violated the condition has a broad range of defenses against enforcement of the forfeiture provision.

(c) If, as in the example, the transfer is to a charity, the federal income tax and gift tax consequences may be disastrous. On the client's death an amount may be includible in his gross estate for federal estate tax purposes, and may be subject to a state succession tax, because of his ownership of the forfeiture interest. Moreover, the interest will pass at death by will or intestacy (say, to his son), and will be taxed in his son's estate, and his son's son's estate, and his son's son's son's estate, and so on down the generations, since possibilities of reverter and rights of entry are not subject to the Rule against Perpetuities.

To the Grantee:

What does it mean to "use the premises for YMCA purposes?" Must the grantee conduct some official YMCA program or activity on the land? Would it be permissible to use the ground floor for YMCA purposes and rent out the second floor? To rent out the entire premises and use the rental proceeds for YMCA purposes? If the land is vacant, to hold for *future* YMCA purposes? To let the YWCA or the YMHA use the premises?

In the spring of 1970, the YMCA chapter near the University of Texas campus allowed the publishers of an underground radical newspaper to use a room in their building when the group was kicked out of leased premises and couldn't find other space. If the YMCA held title under a "so long as" deed, would this result in a forfeiture of its estate?

Observe that the YMCA must know the answer to these questions before it commences the activity. The penalty for its making an incorrect judgment as to permissible user is rather severe.

To Society:

Since possibilities of reverter and rights of entry are not subject to the Rule against Perpetuities, the restrictions on land use that trigger their taking can last forever. A restriction that arguably serves a useful purpose at the time the land is conveyed is not likely to make much sense a century or even a generation later. Even if surrounding circumstances make a violation of the restriction unlikely or impossible, the restriction remains as a cloud on title. Thus Van Vliet & Place, Inc. v. Gaines:[63] An 1834 deed conveying land on Eighth Avenue in Manhattan provided that "if the grantee, his heirs or assigns, should permit upon the premises a cemetery, slaughter house, manufactory of gunpowder, glue, varnish, vitriol, turpen-

[63] 249 N.Y. 106, 162 N.E. 600 (1928).

tine, a tannery, blacksmith shop, forge, or furnace, or any other occupation usually deemed unwholesome, noxious, or offensive, then said premises and every part thereof shall revert to said party of the first part and their heirs." A century later, a New York court declared that Mrs. Gaines's vendee under a real estate contract calling for "marketable title" was not obligated to perform because of this restriction in the deed records. A title insurance company had refused to issue a title policy or to loan money secured by a mortgage on the land. The court held, however, that Mrs. Gaines was obliged to compensate her real estate broker, who had found "a willing buyer."

PROBLEM

Since the court in Van Vliet & Place, Inc. v. Gaines found that Mrs. Gaines did not have a marketable title, does this mean that she cannot sell the land? What can she do with it? If you were Mrs. Gaines's attorney, what would you advise her with regard to (a) what she can do to clear her title, or (b) what she can do with the land if she cannot clear her title? Assume the jurisdiction is not New York, which now has legislation dealing with stale restrictions on land use. See page 747, infra.

Is it sound public policy that a person who owned a piece of land in 1834 should be permitted to restrict the user of that land for all time to come? What justification can be given for requiring compliance with the mandate of a grantor who has been dead for a hundred years?

Determinable Oil and Gas Leases; Rights of Entry in Leases

A jurisdictional note. The "so long as" phraseology is widely used in oil and gas leases. The typical lease is for a primary term (e.g., five years), "and as long thereafter as oil, or gas of whatsoever nature or kind, or either of them is produced from said land." [64] The determinable lease created by this language is beneficial to the developer because it permits him to keep the lease so long as it is productive, but enables him to terminate when the lease becomes unprofitable. It is beneficial to the landowner in that the primary term encourages prompt exploration and development, and thereby the chance of royalties if a producing well is brought in.

"Rights of entry" appurtenant to a landlord's reversion are commonly found in conventional leases. The tenant's various covenants (to pay rent, to keep the premises insured, to suffer no waste or injury to the premises, etc.) are invariably reinforced by a condition that if default is made in the performance of a covenant, "Lessor or its representatives may re-enter the premises by force, summary proceedings or otherwise, and remove all persons therefrom, and Lessee hereby waives the service of any notice in writing of intention to re-enter."

These interests serve a useful purpose in important commercial transactions.

[64] 3 Williams & Meyers, Oil and Gas Law §602 (1969).

They have different characteristics and raise altogether different problems from the ones we are now discussing, and are the subject of other courses in the law school curriculum. Our focus in this section, and our condemnatory remarks, are directed at the two forfeiture interests that can arise when a grantor conveys a defeasible fee.

STEVENS v. GALVESTON, H. & S.A. RY. CO.

Commission of Appeals of Texas, 1919
212 S.W. 639

[Deed construction suit involving three deeds. The first deed, executed on January 25, 1881, conveyed a certain tract "unto said (grantees) forever. On condition, nevertheless, that said real estate shall be used exclusively for railroad depot grounds and railroad business purposes . . . and that if said premises shall cease wholly to be used for the purposes herein contained they shall revert to the grantors or their successors."

The second deed, executed on April 9, 1881, conveyed several tracts, "The said tracts or parcels to be used for depot grounds and railway purposes. . . . And in case the said parcels of land are not used by said railway company for passenger and freight depots and railway purposes, then in that case all the right, title and interest therein conveyed shall revert to and again be vested in the (grantors)."

The third deed, executed on June 8, 1881, conveyed "the right of way for said company's railway through Main Street extending to the eastern boundary line of the lands" of the grantors, "to have and to hold, all and singular, the premises, with all the rights, privileges, and appurtenances thereunto appertaining unto the said (grantee) and its successors and assigns so long as the said land shall be used as a railroad right of way and if not so used shall revert to the grantor herein."]

McClendon, J. The only consideration expressed in the deeds was $1, but the trial court found that the real consideration for the conveyances was the expected enhancement in value of other property owned by the grantors at the time of the conveyances, by reason of the uses to be made of the property. . . .

The contentions of the respective parties may be briefly summarized as follows:

Plaintiffs and interveners contend: (1) That the deeds, being to a railway company and for railway purposes, must be construed as intending to pass only an easement, and not the fee to the property; (2) that if the deeds be construed as passing the fee, it was upon limitation, and not upon conditions subsequent; and upon failure to use the property for the purposes designated, the title of the grantee terminated and revested in the grantors, their heirs and assigns.

The defendant contends, on the other hand, that the deeds, properly construed, vested in the railway company a fee-simple title upon conditions subsequent, and that upon conveyance by the grantors of all the lands to be benefited by the conveyances their interest in the conditions of defeasance was forever lost.

We will consider these questions in the order named.

[In an omitted portion of the opinion the court ruled that interests in fee, and not merely easements, were conveyed by the three deeds.]

In Maddox v. Adair, 66 S.W. 811, the purpose to be accomplished, as shown by the real consideration for the deed, namely, the enhancement of other property by the erection of a school building on the property conveyed, was held to be controlling in determining the construction to be placed upon the language in the deed. In that case, Post v. Weil, 115 N.Y. 361, 22 N.E. 145, 5 L.R.A. 422, 12 Am. St. Rep. 809, is cited with approval and commented on as follows:

> It was ruled that the language of the deed, although importing a condition subsequent, should be considered as a covenant, in view of the fact that it was the evident intention of the grantor to protect his remaining property from depreciation in value by reason of the erection adjacent thereto of undesirable structures. Having parted with all his interest in both estates, he was no longer concerned in the condition, and it was held that no burden rested upon the title of the first purchaser. In this case, when Maddox disposed of his lots adjoining the lot in controversy, the purpose of the condition was satisfied, and he had no further interest in the continued maintenance of the school.

In Olcott v. Gabert, 86 Tex. 121, 23 S.W. 985, the deed was by a railway company upon consideration of $5, conveying certain town lots. The grantee was C. M. Dubois, bishop of Galveston, and his successors in office, "for the use of the Roman Catholic Church." The habendum clause read: "To have and to hold, all and singular, the premises above mentioned unto the said C. M. Dubois, bishop of Galveston, for the use aforesaid, and to his successors and assigns forever."

In holding that this deed passed a fee-simple title in trust, the court [said]:

> When the declared purpose for which the property shall be used is a matter that will inure to the special benefit of the grantor, the courts are more inclined to treat the conveyance as conditional than when, as in this case, the use is for the benefit of a special class of persons or of the public at large. In this case it does not appear that the maintenance of the church upon the lots was a matter specially advantageous to the railway company, who made the grant. Upon these propositions the authorities are numerous and in substantial accord.

It will thus be seen that in determining the character of the estate granted, the court took into consideration not merely the uses for which the property was designated in the conveyance, but the relation of the grantor to these uses. . . .

Passing to the question whether the conveyance of the fee is upon limitation or condition subsequent, we have reached the conclusion that the latter construction must prevail. . . .

The distinction between a conveyance upon limitation and upon condition subsequent is thus stated by Kent:

> Words of limitation mark the period which is to determine the estate; but words of condition render the estate liable to be defeated in the intermediate time,

> if the event expressed in the condition arises before the determination of the estate, or completion of the period described by the limitation. The one specifies the utmost time of continuance, and the other marks some event which, if it takes place in the course of that time, will defeat the estate. The material distinction between a condition and a limitation consists in this: That a condition does not defeat the estate, although it be broken, until entry by the grantor or his heirs. But it is in the nature of a limitation to determine the estate when the period of limitation arises without entry or claim. Wiederanders v. State, 64 Tex. 140.

Under the common law and the great weight of authority in our American courts, it is held that the reversionary interest of the grantor in a deed conveying a fee-simple estate upon condition subsequent is not assignable, can only be enforced by the original grantor and those connected with him in blood, and determines upon an assignment of the right or subsequent deed to the property. It is earnestly urged by counsel for plaintiffs that this rule is not in force in Texas. The decision of this question, however, is rendered unnecessary by the conclusion we have reached as expressed below.

While the legal attributes of the two estates under consideration are well defined and clearly distinguished, difficulty often arises when construing particular instruments in determining whether they fall within one or the other class. In this question of construction the chief difficulty lies. Certain general principles have from time to time been laid down, but it is not always easy to apply these principles to the particular case.

Aside from the general rules of construction above announced in passing upon the first question considered, it has been held that certain technical words denote a limitation, and certain other technical words denote a condition subsequent. But, as said by Mr. Washburn in his able work on Real Property (5th Ed. p. 26):

> It is apprehended that the mere use of any of these terms, ordinarily expressive of a condition or a limitation, would be an unsafe test of the true nature of the estate. The word "proviso" or "provided," itself, may sometimes be taken as a condition, sometimes as a limitation, and sometimes as a covenant.

Effect to this rule was given in Maddox v. Adair, above, in commenting upon the New York Case.

There is another rule generally applied in construing deeds where the language used may ordinarily import a limitation or condition subsequent, namely, that these provisions are strictly construed against the grantor, on the ground that the law does not favor forfeitures. . . . We think a correct application to be that where there is a doubt from the language of the entire instrument whether its fair construction imports a limitation which would absolutely determine the estate, or a condition subsequent determining the estate only upon some act of the grantor tantamount to a re-entry, the deed must be construed to import the latter as being in a sense less onerous upon the grantee. This conclusion, we think, is in harmony also with the rule that the greatest estate of which the language of the deed is susceptible of conveying will be held to have been intended by the parties, because, although both estates are generally regarded as fees, the former determines absolutely upon the happening of the condition, and is, therefore, more circumscribed than the latter, which requires some act on the part of the grantor for its determination, in addition to the breach of the condition.

To our mind, there is little doubt as to the effect of the deeds of January 25th and April 9th. There is nothing in the language of these deeds which would reasonably imply a limitation. The language used is, we believe, that ordinarily employed in deeds construed to be upon condition subsequent. It is contended by plaintiffs and interveners that the words in the deed of January 25th reading, "If said promises [*sic*] shall cease wholly to be used for the purposes herein contained, they shall revert to the grantors or *their successors*" (underscoring ours), import a limitation, in that the fair construction of said language is that the estate should determine ipso facto when the properties should cease to be used. We do not think this is a fair construction of this language. On the contrary, we find practically the same language used in deeds construed to import only a condition subsequent. Maddox v. Adair, above; Jeffery v. Graham, 61 Tex. 481. . . .

More difficulty arises in construing the deed of June 8th. The granting clause in that deed without question purports to convey an absolute fee-simple title. The first part of the habendum clause, namely, "so long as said land shall be used as a railroad right of way," is in the technical language of a limitation; but this is immediately followed by this language, "and if not so used shall revert to the grantors herein." The latter quotation, as we have seen, is the language usually employed to express the grantor's right of re-entry upon a condition subsequent broken.[65]

Having in mind all the foregoing considerations, we think the proper construction of each of the three deeds, when viewed in the light of the surrounding circumstances, and the purposes sought to be attained, is that they convey upon condition subsequent, and not upon limitation. To give them this construction, to our mind, reasonably harmonizes all the terms of all the deeds, and gives to the grantors that which they bargained for, as found by the trial court.

Having reached the above conclusions, the disposition to be made of the case, in our opinion, is controlled by the decision in Maddox v. Adair. In that case Mad-

[65] ["Revert" is the language usually employed to express the grantor's right of entry??? In conveying a determinable fee it is generally held that it is unnecessary to insert specific words expressly reserving a possibility of reverter. Here the grantor *did* put in express words of "revert," and the court used this as the basis for finding that the retained interest was a right of entry.

Compare In re Copps Chapel Methodist Episcopal Church, 120 Ohio St. 309, 166 N.E. 218 (1929), in which land was conveyed to the church "so long as said lot is held and used for church purposes." Held, the church had a fee simple absolute because the grantor *did* not insert express words of "revert" or re-entry. See also Washington City Bd., of Education v. Edgerton, 244 N.C. 576, 94 S.E.2d 661 (1956), where a deed "so long as the said property shall be used for school purposes," without a reverter clause, was held to convey a fee simple absolute. The quoted words were said merely to express the motive and purpose of the transfer.

In some jurisdictions, then, if the "so long as" language is followed by "revert," the latter phrase leads to a "right of entry" construction. In other jurisdictions, it is not possible to create a possibility of reverter *without* using express "reverter" language. — EDS.]

dox conveyed to certain school trustees a tract of land by deed in the usual form, except that it contained the following clause:

> But should the said land fail to be used for the purposes for which it is sold, viz., the establishment and maintenance of a first-class seminary of learning thereon, then it shall revert to me, the said J. W. Maddox.

The recited consideration in the deed was $100 cash; but the evidence showed that the real consideration was the expected enhancement in value to adjacent property owned by Maddox, as a result of the establishment of the school provided for. After the school was established, Maddox sold all of his adjacent property. The school was later abandoned, and Maddox sued to recover the property conveyed. The court in that case [said]:

> In ascertaining the intention it is proper to look at the circumstances surrounding the transaction. Railway v. Beller [90] Tenn. [548] 18 S.W. 391. Maddox desired the school to be used in order that the value of his property might be increased. This was the consideration for the conveyance, and he had no interest in having the school maintained for any other purpose. . . . When he sold his adjacent lots he ceased to be concerned in the continuance of the school, and the purpose of the condition was accomplished. This construction is also in harmony with the language of the condition.

The Supreme Court refused a writ of error in that case, and we think the decision therein is controlling here. The grantors in the several deeds do not appear to have had any interest whatsoever in the conditions expressed in the several deeds, other than the enhancement in value of their other property through compliance with such conditions. The trial court found that they had conveyed all their other property which was expected to be benefited, from which it conclusively appears that their interest in a further compliance with the conditions had determined.

Having reached the foregoing conclusions, the other questions raised by plaintiffs and interveners become immaterial.

We conclude that the railway company has an indefeasible fee-simple title to the property involved in this suit and that the judgment of the Court of Civil Appeals should be reversed, and the judgment of the trial court affirmed.

Phillips, C.J. The judgment recommended by the Commission of Appeals is adopted and will be entered as the judgment of the Supreme Court.

PROBLEMS

In the conveyances that follow, what interests are created? [66]

a. O conveys "to Trinity Church, its successors and assigns, the premises to be used for church purposes."

[66] See 1 American Law of Property §4.7 (Casner ed. 1952).

b. O conveys "to Trinity Church, its successors and assigns, subject to its using the premises for church purposes and for no other purposes."

c. O conveys "to Trinity Church, its successors and assigns, upon the express condition that the premises shall be used for church purposes."

d. O conveys "to Trinity Church, its successors and assigns, but if the land shall ever cease to be used for church purposes, it is to revert to the grantor or his heirs." See Oldfield v. Stoeco Homes, Inc., 26 N.J. 246, 139 A.2d 291 (1958); compare Mountain City Missionary Baptist Church v. Wagner, 193 Tenn. 625, 249 S.W.2d 875 (1952); Second Church v. Le Prevost, 67 Ohio App. 101, 35 N.E.2d 1015 (1941).

e. O conveys "to the Georgetown YMCA, provided and upon the condition that the property shall be the grantee's for so long as the premises shall be used for YMCA purposes; and if the land shall ever cease to be so used, then the premises shall revert to the grantor herein."

2. *Differences in Consequences of Classification*

The treatises set forth several possible situations where different legal consequences would result from classifying an interest as a possibility of reverter rather than as a right of entry.[67] One primary difference relates to alienability. These interests were inalienable inter vivos at common law because they were thought of as "possibilities of becoming an interest" rather than as interests. Nonetheless, these interests were descendable. In most American states today possibilities of reverter are alienable, but rights of entry are not.[68] Just why this distinction is made is hard to say, for the cases do not give any satisfactory reasons. In many states the right of entry has been given even harsher treatment: The mere attempt to transfer a right of entry destroys it.[69] These interests are descendable and in a large majority of states are devisable as well.[70]

The other primary difference between a possibility of reverter and a right of entry is that the former becomes possessory "automatically," while the exercise of the right of entry is optional, and requires an affirmative act by the grantor or his successors. What different consequences flow from automatic and optional termination? [71] Does automatic termination serve any useful purpose?

[67] See 1 id. §§4.68 to 4.75; 2 Powell, Real Property ¶¶281, 282, 284 (1970).

[68] Simes, Future Interests 73 (2d ed. 1966).

[69] The leading case is Rice v. Boston & Worcester Railroad Co., 94 Mass. (12 Allen) 141 (1866). But see Pickens v. Daugherty, 217 Tenn. 349, 397 S.W.2d 815 (1965): "It is difficult for us to understand the logic of this rule. How can it be said the right of re-entry upon condition broken is inalienable but an attempt to convey it destroys the right altogether? How can it be said that [that] which does not pass does not remain?" The Tennessee court went on to hold that the interest (variously described in the opinion as a possibility of reverter, a possibility of reversion, and a right of re-entry) was not transferable by a deed that purported to transfer the interest, and instead passed to the grantor's heirs. The court apparently had no difficulty understanding the logic of *that* rule!

[70] Simes, Future Interests 76 (2d ed. 1966).

[71] See 2 Powell, Real Property ¶190[2] (1970); Williams, Restrictions on the Use of Land:

Kentucky has the distinction of being the only jurisdiction to abolish by statute any difference between these interests. Kentucky Revised Statutes §381.218 (1962) provides: "The estate known at common law as the fee simple determinable and the interest known as the possibility of reverter are abolished. Words which at common law would create a fee simple determinable shall be construed to create a fee simple subject to a right of entry for condition broken. In any case where a person would have a possibility of reverter at common law, he shall have a right of entry." Why was the possibility of reverter converted into the right of entry, rather than vice versa? [72]

3. *Equitable Defenses to Enforcement*

Courts often give operative effect to the language of user by construing it as a covenant of which the grantor is beneficiary. But when the grantor, or his successor, attempts to enforce the covenant, he may be unsuccessful. If he sues for damages, he must prove monetary loss resulting from the breach. If he seeks to enjoin a violation of the covenant, he will be met by the traditional notion that an injunction will not be granted unless the defendant's conduct threatens substantial harm to the plaintiff. Moreover, his suit will be subject to the numerous defenses available to a grantee in an action to enforce a restrictive covenant: estoppel, waiver, laches, change of conditions in the neighborhood, material compliance, etc.

Even if the grantor persuades the court that the deed reserved a right of entry, or perhaps a possibility of reverter, he may be required to hurdle these same equitable defenses. Several jurisdictions — principally in the western states — permit equitable defenses, traditionally associated with restrictive covenants, to be raised in a suit to enforce a right of entry or a possibility of reverter. These defenses include showing that changed circumstances make the purpose of the condition no longer possible of fulfillment,[73] that there has been substantial compliance with the condition,[74] that the condition was intended to operate for only a reasonable period of time, which has elapsed,[75] that no damage is shown by noncompliance,[76] or that in

---

Conditions Subsequent and Determinable Fees, 27 Texas L. Rev. 158 (1948). Compare Dunham, Possibility of Reverter and Power of Termination — Fraternal or Identical Twins? 20 U. Chi. L. Rev. 215 (1953).

[72] An opponent of the legislation claimed that the act was, in effect, civil rights legislation. Do you see why? See Charlotte Park & Recreation Comm'n v. Barringer, 242 N.C. 311, 88 S.E.2d 114 (1955). And apparently he was right. See Evans v. Abney, 396 U.S. 435 (1970).

[73] Cole v. Colorado Springs Co., 381 P.2d 13 (Colo. 1963); Townsend v. Allen, 114 Cal. App. 2d 291, 250 P.2d 292 (1952); but see Murray v. Trustees of Lane Seminary, 1 Ohio Op. 2d 236, 140 N.E.2d 577 (C.P. 1956).

[74] Lassiter v. Town of Oxford, 234 F.2d 217 (4th Cir. 1956); Savanna School District v. McLeod, 137 Cal. App. 2d 491, 290 P.2d 593 (1955); Jordan v. Hendricks, 91 Ind. App. 678, 173 N.E. 288 (1930); J. M. Carey & Brother v. City of Casper, 66 Wyo. 437, 213 P.2d 263 (1950).

[75] Board of Commissioners v. Russell, 174 F.2d 778 (10th Cir.), cert. denied, 338 U.S. 820 (1949); Scheller v. Tacoma Ry. & Power Co., 108 Wash. 348, 184 P. 344 (1919).

[76] Atkins v. Anderson, 139 Cal. App. 2d 918, 294 P.2d 727 (1956).

not enforcing the covenant at an earlier date the plaintiff was guilty of laches or has waived the breach.[77] Where these defenses are permitted against the holder of a possibility of reverter, the possibility of reverter no longer becomes possessory "automatically."

PROBLEM

In 1862 O conveys land to a school board "on condition that the premises shall be used for school purposes; and if said Board, or their successors in office, shall at any time hereafter, refuse or neglect to use said premises for school purposes, then the said land shall revert to the grantor herein." The land is used for school purposes until 1959, when access to the land from the north and east is lost due to construction of an interstate highway that borders the tract. Plaintiffs, successors two generations removed from O, seek to enforce the right of entry which they contend was reserved in the 1862 deed. The School Board concedes that the deed reserved a right of entry, but contends (a) that the condition should not be enforced because the Board complied with the condition for a long period of time, and that should be enough; (b) that changed conditions over which the grantee had no control render such use of the land impractical and ineffectual; and (c) that nonuse of the premises for school purposes was not due to the Board's "refusal" or "neglect," but rather was due to the action of the state and federal governments in building the highway. What result? McArdle v. School District of Omaha, 179 Neb. 122, 136 N.W.2d 422 (1965). See Browder, The Condemnation of Future Interests, 48 Va. L. Rev. 461 (1962); Note, Compensation for Possibilities of Reverter and Powers of Termination Under Condemnation Law, 20 Hastings L.J. 787 (1969).

4. *Application of the Rule against Perpetuities*

Most of the problems created by rights of entry and possibilities of reverter stem from the fact that these interests are exempt from the Rule against Perpetuities and run on forever.[78] They are every bit as objectionable as interests subject to the Rule, in that they tie up property for long periods of time, potentially forever. With the passage of time and the change of conditions they leave the owner of the fee in a straitjacket. Title held subject to one of these interests is not marketable, and frequently the property is not improvable because a mortgage cannot be obtained upon it. The land may remain undeveloped or limited to uneconomic uses,

[77] Robinson v. Cannon, 346 Mo. 1126, 145 S.W.2d 146 (1940); Tough v. Netsch, 83 N.H. 374, 142 A. 702 (1928); Goodman v. Southern Pacific Ry. Co., 143 Cal. App. 2d 424, 299 P.2d 321 (1956). See generally Bianchi, Effect of Change of Conditions on Rights of Entry and Possibilities of Reverter Created to Control the Use of Land, 53 Mich. L. Rev. 246 (1954).

[78] In England possibilities of reverter and rights of entry are now subject to the Rule. Perpetuities and Accumulations Act, 1964, §12.

and the restrictions cannot be released because of the difficulty in ascertaining who now holds the right of entry or possibility of reverter created by a long-dead grantor.

Although possibilities of reverter and rights of entry are exempt, executory interests following determinable fees and fees subject to condition subsequent are subject to the Rule. This difference leads to the magnification in importance of slight differences in the language used by the draftsman. The resulting picture is wondrously bizarre and completely unbelievable by anyone except the student who has traveled this far through the wonderful calculus of estates and has learned to believe all kinds of amazing things.

The Rule against Perpetuities is: "No interest is good unless it must vest, if at all, not later than twenty-one years after some life in being at the creation of the interest." The problems and cases that follow introduce you to this important rule. Its vast intricacies will be explored in Chapter 15.

The Rule invalidates any executory interest (or contingent remainder) if there is any possibility that the interest might vest more than twenty-one years after some life in being at the date the instrument becomes effective. These principles are pertinent in applying the Rule: (1) We do not wait and see. If there is any possibility of remote vesting, judged from the date the instrument becomes effective, the interest is void ab initio. (2) An executory interest following a possessory fee simple cannot vest before it becomes possessory. (3) Any interest that violates the Rule is struck out — as with a blue pencil — and the remainder of the limitation stands as written. The next two cases are basic to understanding the materials that follow.

Case 24. O conveys Blackacre to the Board of Education for so long as the premises are used for school purposes, then to A. The purported executory interest in A violates the Rule against Perpetuities and is stricken. This leaves a determinable fee in the Board and a possibility of reverter in O. First Universalist Society v. Boland, 155 Mass. 171, 29 N.E. 524 (1892): Institution for Savings v. Roxbury Home for Aged Women, 244 Mass. 583, 139 N.E. 301 (1923).[79]

Case 25. O conveys Blackacre to the Board of Education, but if it ceases to use the land for school purposes to A. The purported executory interest in A violates the Rule and is stricken. This leaves a fee simple absolute in the Board. Proprietors of the Church in Brattle Square v. Grant, 69 Mass. (3 Gray) 142 (1855).

Can you justify the different results in the above cases on policy grounds? If you are advising O, how can he accomplish his wishes by using two pieces of paper rather than one? Is O's lawyer liable for negligence if he doesn't use two pieces of paper?

In the problems that follow, pay close attention to the precise language used.

[79] The rule in the First Universalist Society case is sharply criticized in Agnor, A Tale of Two Cases, 17 Vand. L. Rev. 1427 (1964), where it is suggested that courts without precedent directly in point should treat *Case 24* like *Case 25*. Professor Agnor concludes that "the rule from the First Universalist case has been accepted by most secondary authorities and by a half dozen states, largely without any real consideration of the principles involved." For a recent case applying this rule without any examination of underlying policy, see City of Klamath Falls v. Bell, 490 P.2d 515 (Ore. App. 1971).

Remember that the label of an interest always depends upon the person in whom it is initially created. A possibility of reverter or a right of entry can, by orthodox doctrine, be created only in the grantor, if the creating instrument is a deed, or in the testator's heirs, if the instrument is a will. A comparable interest in a transferee is an executory interest.

PROBLEMS

1. A conveys a one-acre tract, part of his eighty-acre farm, "to the Board of Education for so long as the premises are used for school purposes, and when they shall cease to be used for school purposes the tract is to revert to the owner of the farm from which it is taken." A subsequently conveys thirty-nine acres adjacent to the school tract to B and the remaining forty acres to C. A dies, devising his entire estate to his widow. H is the heir of A. Fifty years later the Board of Education ceases to use the one-acre tract for school purposes. Who owns the one-acre tract? Jones v. Burns, 221 Miss. 833, 74 So. 2d 866 (1954). Suppose the last clause had read ". . . is to revert to the heirs of A"? Standard Knitting Mills, Inc. v. Allen, 221 Tenn. 90, 424 S.W.2d 796 (1967).

2. For $5000 A conveys Blackacre "to the Board of Education for so long as it is used for school purposes, and when the land ceases to be used for school purposes A, his heirs, or assigns may repay the purchase price and demand a reconveyance of the property." The Board ceases to use the property for school purposes. A claims he now owns Blackacre and refuses to pay the Board $5000. Is A's claim sound? Merrihew v. Jensen, 272 Cal. App. 2d 619, 77 Cal. Rptr. 606 (1969); Gange v. Hayes, 193 Ore. 51, 237 P.2d 196 (1951); Simes & Smith, The Law of Future Interests §1245 (2d ed. 1956). Why is public policy violated if A has to pay $5000 to reclaim Blackacre and not violated if he can re-enter free?

3. Monawa Tribe No. 352 of the Improved Order of Red Men conveyed to St. Paul Building Association a certain tract of land and the building thereon. The deed provided that the Tribe retained the upper story "so long as they comply strictly with" certain restrictions on the use of the upper story. In the event the restrictions were not complied with "the rights of Monawa Tribe to said upper story shall cease and the use and occupancy of said upper story shall revert to and become the absolute right and property of the owners of the fee of said real estate." The Tribe did not comply with the restrictions. Is St. Paul Building Association entitled to eject the Tribe? Monawa Tribe No. 352 v. Wiley, 127 Ind. App. 660, 142 N.E.2d 488 (1957); compare Walker v. Marcellus & Otisco Lake Ry. Co., 226 N.Y. 347, 123 N.E. 736 (1919). (Remember: a fee simple in air space can be created. And keep the grantor and grantee straight.)

Exception: Gift over from one charity to another charity. If there is a gift to Charity A followed by a gift over to Charity B if a specified event happens, the executory interest in Charity B is exempt from the Rule against Perpetuities. Thus:

Case 26. O deeds Blackacre to the Board of Education for so long as used for school purposes, then to the County Hospital. The executory interest in the County Hospital is valid.

This exemption applies only if both the possessory estate and the future interest are in charitable organizations. It does not apply if either the possessory estate or the future interest is in a private individual. Do you think this exemption is sound? Should it matter whether the remote contingency is related to a charitable purpose or not? Suppose that in *Case* 26 the gift were to the Board of Education so long as the Board maintains O's family home. A perpetual endowment to maintain O's family home would be void. Should O be able to do indirectly what he cannot do directly? Morris & Leach, The Rule against Perpetuities 189-194 (2d ed. 1962); 4 Scott, Trusts §401.5 (3d ed. 1967).

BROWN v. INDEPENDENT BAPTIST CHURCH OF WOBURN

Supreme Judicial Court of Massachusetts, 1950

325 Mass. 645, 91 N.E.2d 922

QUA, C.J. The object of this suit in equity, originally brought in this court, is to determine the ownership of a parcel of land in Woburn and the persons entitled to share in the proceeds of its sale by a receiver.

Sarah Converse died seised of the land on July 19, 1849, leaving a will in which she specifically devised it "to the Independent Baptist Church of Woburn, to be holden and enjoyed by them so long as they shall maintain and promulgate their present religious belief and faith and shall continue a Church; and if the said Church shall be dissolved, or its religious sentiments shall be changed or abandoned, then my will is that this real estate shall go to my legatees hereinafter named, to be divided in equal portions between them. And my will further is, that if my beloved husband, Jesse Converse, shall survive me, that then this devise to the aforesaid Independent Church of Woburn, shall not take effect till from and after his decease; and that so long as he shall live he may enjoy and use the said real estate, and take the rents and profits thereof to his own use." Then followed ten money legacies in varying amounts to different named persons, after which there was a residuary clause in these words, "The rest and residue of my estate I give and bequeath to my legatees above named, saving and except therefrom the Independent Baptist Church; this devise to take effect from and after the decease of my husband; I do hereby direct and will that he shall have the use and this rest and residue during his life."

The husband of the testatrix died in 1864. The church named by the testatrix ceased to "continue a church" on October 19, 1939.

The parties apparently are in agreement, and the single justice ruled, that the estate of the church in the land was a determinable fee. We concur. First Universalist Society of North Adams v. Boland, 155 Mass. 171, 174. Institution for Savings v.

Roxbury Home for Aged Women, 244 Mass. 583, 585-586. Dyer v. Siano, 298 Mass. 537, 540. The estate was a fee, since it might last forever, but it was not an absolute fee, since it might (and did) "automatically expire upon the occurrence of a stated event." Restatement: Property, §44. It is also conceded, and was ruled, that the specific executory devise over to the persons "hereinafter named" as legatees was void for remoteness. This conclusion seems to be required by Proprietors of the Church in Brattle Square v. Grant, 3 Gray, 142, 152, 155-156, First Universalist Society of North Adams v. Boland, 155 Mass. 171, 173, and Institution for Savings v. Roxbury Home for Aged Women, 244 Mass. 583, 587. See Restatement: Property, §44, illustration 20. The reason is stated to be that the determinable fee might not come to an end until long after any life or lives in being and twenty-one years, and in theory at least might never come to an end, and for an indefinite period no clear title to the entire estate could be given.

Since the limitation over failed, it next becomes our duty to consider what became of the possibility of reverter which under our decisions remained after the failure of the limitation. First Universalist Society of North Adams v. Boland, 155 Mass. 171, 175. Institution for Savings v. Roxbury Home for Aged Women, 244 Mass. 583, 587. . . . A possibility of reverter seems, by the better authority, to be assignable inter vivos (Restatement: Property, §159; Simes, Future Interests, §715; see Tiffany, Real Property [3d ed.] §314, note 31) and must be at least as readily devisable as the other similar reversionary interest known as a right of entry for condition broken, which is devisable, though not assignable. . . . It follows that the possibility of reverter passed under the residuary clause of the will to the same persons designated in the invalid executory devise. It is of no consequence that the persons designated in the two provisions were the same. The same result must be reached as if they were different.

The single justice ruled that the residuary clause was void for remoteness, apparently for the same reason that rendered the executory devise void. With this we cannot agree, since we consider it settled that the rule against perpetuities does not apply to reversionary interests of this general type, including possibilities of reverter. Proprietors of the Church in Brattle Square v. Grant, 3 Gray, 142, 148. . . . For a full understanding of the situation here presented it is necessary to keep in mind the fundamental difference in character between the attempted executory devise to the legatees later named in the will and the residuary gift to the same persons. The executory devise was in form and substance an attempt to limit or create a new future interest which might not arise or vest in anyone until long after the permissible period. It was obviously not intended to pass such a residuum of the testatrix's existing estate as a possibility of reverter, and indeed if the executory devise had been valid according to its terms the whole estate would have passed from the testatrix and no possibility of reverter could have been left to her or her devisees. The residuary devise, on the other hand, was in terms and purpose exactly adapted to carry any interest which might otherwise remain in the testatrix, whether or not she had it in mind or knew it would exist. Thayer v. Wellington, 9 Allen, 283, 295. Wellman v. Carter, 286 Mass. 237, 249-250.

We cannot accept the contention made in behalf of Mrs. Converse's heirs that the words of the residuary clause "saving and except therefrom the Independent Baptist Church" were meant to exclude from the operation of that clause any possible rights in the *land* previously given to the church. We construe these words as intended merely to render the will consistent by excluding the church which also had been "above named" from the list of "*legatees*" who were to take the residue.

The interlocutory decree entered December 16, 1947, is reversed, and a new decree is to be entered providing that the land in question or the proceeds of any sale thereof by the receiver shall go to the persons named as legatees in the will, other than the Independent Baptist Church of Woburn, or their successors in interest. Further proceedings are to be in accord with the new decree. Costs and expenses are to be at the discretion of the single justice.

So ordered.[80]

LEACH & TUDOR, THE RULE AGAINST PERPETUITIES
191-192 (1957)

The practical problem of judicial administration. A receiver sold Sarah Converse's land for $34,000 under a court order. By 1939 all of Sarah's ten residuary legatees and twenty-five heirs (as of 1849) had been dead for decades. The process of rounding up the parties to the litigation was a formidable one. Did this heir leave a will? Whom did that legatee marry? Where did she go, and is she still alive? There had been three or four devolutions of the fractional shares in Sarah's possibility of reverter, with split-ups into subfractions and sub-subfractions. To handle this situation counsel agreed that a professional genealogist and searcher for missing heirs should be employed and that his charges should be paid out of the fund; this arrangement was approved by Spalding, J. The prevailing counsel, Guy Newhall, has described in a letter to me his problem of finding out who his clients were: "As to two of the legatees, mother and daughter, my list of modern descendants looks like a genealogy of the descendants of Methuselah, scattered all the way from California to Buenos Aires. Their shares will be very small, hardly worth bothering about. The other lines vary from a few to a lot." As a consequence of the litigation the court awarded a total of $9,091.25 for counsel fees and disbursements, $1,500 for a genealogist, $4,017.50 for a receiver, and divided the balance into more than one hundred shares ranging from $774.20 to $6.25.

Whether the testatrix's objectives were attained. No one can believe that this distribution of small fractional sums to remote descendants of residuary devisees was expected by Sarah Converse or would be desired by her if she could control the matter. Above all she wanted to benefit her church. In 1849 the land devised was on the village street in Woburn — just the place for a church. The church building was erected on the lot. But as time passed Woburn grew. The village street became Main Street in a busy, noisy commercial center. Other churches sold their land, greatly increased in value for commercial use, and with the proceeds of sale erected

[80] Noted 64 Harv. L. Rev. 864. — Eds.

church buildings in areas more appropriate to religious services. But not Sarah Converse's church, for it had no marketable title to sell. It tried to struggle along at the same old location by renting the first floor to a tailor and a grocery and living off the rents; the second floor provided adequate space for the shrinking congregation. A church cannot live unless it attracts new members; and new members are not attracted to a makeshift place of worship over a block of stores in a commercial district. As early as 1898 the end of the Church's useful life was in sight. During the last years services were held every fifth Sunday, for the rents could not support more frequent services. Finally in 1939, at the death of an elderly lady who seemed the last of those to whom the church had a real meaning, the organization simply passed out of existence. It is at least possible that the dissolution of this church, where others survived, is directly attributable to the unmarketable title of the Church caused jointly by Sarah's determinable fee and the exemption of her possibility of reverter from the Rule against Perpetuities.

PROBLEMS

The decision in the Woburn Church case is said to be based upon an assumption that a person can die twice. Simes & Smith, The Law of Future Interests §1241 (2d ed. 1956). Do you see why? The following three illustrations are variations on the problem whether an interest can simultaneously be created in the transferor and transferred to a transferee, or whether there must be a moment of time between creation and transfer.[81]

1. Suppose the specific devise in Sarah Converse's will had read:

> Article Two: I give Blackacre to the Independent Baptist Church of Woburn, but if it ceases to use the land for church purposes the land shall revert to my estate. And I give the possibility of reverter to Robert Simms and his heirs. [The draftsman expressly calls the interest a possibility of reverter and uses two sentences rather than one.]

Sarah's residuary estate is devised to ten named persons. Upon Sarah's death what is the state of the title to Blackacre? Held, on similar facts, that Robert Simms

[81] Controversies arising from giving a time sequence to purely conceptual events have an ancient history. The great "scintilla juris" controversy raged in England for three hundred years before Parliament settled the matter in 1860. The issue was whether a feoffee to uses had seisin for any amount of time before seisin was taken by the Statute of Uses and transferred to the cestui que use. See 7 Holdsworth, History of English Law 137-141 (1925).

Another momentous dispute arose with the invention of simultaneous seisin to protect the purchase money mortgagee from dower, liens, and other prior claims against the mortgagor. "The idea is that title shot into the grantee and out of him again into the purchase money mortgagee so fleetingly — quasi uno flattu, in one breath, as it were — that no other interest had time to fasten itself to it." Osborne, Mortgages 390 (2d ed. 1970).

Giving a time sequence to conceptual events also bases the rule that an express forfeiture restraint against involuntary alienation will be given effect. As soon as a creditor executes his judgment on the debtor's interest the interest ceases "eo instanti," and the creditor has nothing. See Dukeminier, Perpetuities Law in Action 136 (1962).

has a possibility of reverter. Knowles v. South County Hospital, 87 R.I. 303, 140 A.2d 499 (1958).

2. Suppose Sarah Converse had executed a will, without a residuary clause, devising Blackacre to the Baptist Church so long as used for church purposes. Subsequently she executed a *codicil* which provided that if the Baptist Church ceased to use Blackacre for church purposes, she gave Blackacre to ten named persons. The codicil contained no residuary clause. After Sarah's death, what is the state of the title to Blackacre? Held, on similar facts, that testatrix' heirs have a possibility of reverter. In re Pruner's Estate, 400 Pa. 629, 162 A.2d 626 (1960), noted 109 U. Pa. L. Rev. 433 (1961).

3. O conveys Blackacre to A reserving all oil, gas, and minerals "for a period of twenty-five years and as long thereafter as oil or gas or minerals" should be produced. A subsequent clause in the deed provides, "Subject to the reservations and conditions aforesaid, O hereby grants to A all of said real property, together with the reversion and reversions thereof." Later O conveys to B "all oil and gas" under Blackacre. The twenty-five-year period elapses, and no oil or gas is ever produced. A sues B to quiet title in the oil and gas. B brings a cross action asking the court to quiet title in him. Held: For A. By the second clause of the deed O conveyed his reversionary interest in the oil, gas, and mineral rights to A. Brown v. Terra Bella Irrigation District, 51 Cal. 2d 33, 330 P.2d 775 (1958), noted 58 Mich. L. Rev. 285 (1959).

The parties who lose these cases must surely regard the law with a bruised sort of amazement. Can you explain this law to a layman intelligibly, and support it with policies he can understand? What policies are involved here? From the viewpoint of policy is it preferable to rule in favor of (a) simultaneous creation and transfer, (b) requiring two pieces of paper, or (c) requiring two clauses in a will or deed? [82] Is there an alternative to any of these that will free us from the hieroglyphics of classification? Waggoner, Reformulating the Structure of Estates: A Proposal for Legislative Action, 85 Harv. L. Rev. 729, 750, 759 (1972).

A Few Legislatures Strike Back

Everyone seems to agree that possibilities of reverter and rights of entry should be extinguished at some point in time. The need for remedial action has been discussed extensively, but there is considerable disagreement as to what form the remedy should take.[83] Three general solutions have been advanced: (1) Subject pos-

[82] See, generally, Chaffin, Reverters, Rights of Entry, and Executory Interests: Semantic Confusion and the Tying Up of Land, 31 Fordham L. Rev. 303 (1962); Lynn & Ramser, Applying the Rule Against Perpetuities to Functional Equivalents: Copps Chapel and the Woburn Church Revisited, 43 Iowa L. Rev. 36 (1957); Boyer & Spiegel, Land Use Control: Pre-emptions, Perpetuities and Similar Restraints, 20 U. Miami L. Rev. 148 (1965).

[83] See Simes & Taylor, Improvement of Conveyancing by Legislation 201-217 (1960); Webster, The Quest for Clear Land Titles — Whither Possibilities of Reverter and Rights of Entry? 42 N.C.L. Rev. 807 (1964); Gwin, Proposed Restrictions on Possibilities of Reverter and Rights of Entry, 34 Miss. L.J. 176 (1963); Comment, Legislative Limitation of Reverter and Forfeiture Provisions in Conveyances and Devises of Land — A Proposed Statute for Kansas, 15 U. Kan. L. Rev. 346 (1967). Each of these authors presents a draft of a model act.

sibilities of reverter and rights of entry to the Rule against Perpetuities, as is done in England. No American jurisdiction has taken this approach. (2) Subject these interests to any equitable defense that might be interposed against a covenant, such as changed circumstances, substantial compliance and waiver. As we have seen, the courts in a number of jurisdictions have adopted this approach unaided by statute.[84] A New York statute prohibits enforcement of a restriction that triggers a forfeiture interest if "it appears that the restriction is of no actual and substantial benefit to the persons seeking its enforcement . . . either because the purpose of the restriction has already been accomplished or, by reason of changed conditions or other cause, its purpose is not capable of accomplishment, or for any other reason." [85] Another provision of the statute subjects actions to enforce a reverter or right of entry "to any defense that might be interposed in an action to enjoin a violation of the restriction if it were created by covenant." [86] (3) Terminate possibilities of reverter and rights of entry after a fixed number of years. The following Massachusetts statute is an example of this approach.

MASSACHUSETTS GENERAL LAWS ANNOTATED c. 184A, §3 (1956, Supp. 1971):[87] "A fee simple determinable in land or a fee simple in land subject to a right of entry for condition broken shall become a fee simple absolute if the specified contingency does not occur within thirty years from the date when such fee simple determinable or such fee simple subject to a right of entry becomes possessory. If such contingency occurs within said thirty years the succeeding interest, which may be an interest in a person other than the person creating the interest or his heirs, shall become possessory or the right of entry exercisable notwithstanding the rule against perpetuities. [But if a fee simple determinable in land or a fee simple in land subject to a right of entry for condition broken is so limited that the specified contingency must occur, if at all, within the period of the rule against perpetuities, said interests shall take effect as limited. This section shall not apply where both such fee simple determinable and such succeeding interest, or both such fee simple and such right of entry are for public, charitable or religious purposes; nor shall it apply to a deed, gift or grant of the commonwealth or any political subdivision thereof.] "

The Massachusetts statute was originally enacted in 1954 as reproduced above. In 1961 the Massachusetts statute was amended by striking out the third and fourth

[84] See pages 738-739, supra. A Florida statute converts forfeiture and reverter provisions into covenants after twenty-one years. Fla. Stat. Ann. §689.18(7) (1969).

[85] N.Y. Real Prop. Actions & Proc. Law §1951 (1963). Similar statutes applying to "conditions annexed to a grant" have been enacted in Arizona, Michigan, Minnesota and Wisconsin, but it is not clear that these statutes apply to possibilities of reverter as well as to rights of entry.

[86] N.Y. Real Prop. Actions & Proc. Law §1953 (1963). A separate statute governs enforcement of possibilities of reverter and rights of entry tied to grants of land for charitable purposes, and affords several lines of defense to the charity that wants to free the land from the restrictions. Id. §1955.

[87] The act is explained in Leach, Perpetuities Legislation, Massachusetts Style, 67 Harv. L. Rev. 1349, 1362-1365 (1954).

sentences, bracketed above. (What are the arguments against having an alternative perpetuity period and against exempting gifts over from one charity to another charity?) The original statute was copied verbatim in Connecticut and Maine. Similar time limitations have been imposed in Illinois (40 years), Kentucky (30 years), Minnesota (30 years), Nebraska (30 years), and Rhode Island (20 years). The Kentucky statute[88] does not apply to "any lease present or future or any easement, right of way, mortgage or trust, or any communication, transmission, or transportation lines, or any public highway, right to take minerals, or charge for support during the life of a person or persons, or any restrictive covenant without right of entry or reverter." Are these exceptions a good idea? [89]

PROBLEMS

1. Which of the three approaches mentioned above in dealing with possibilities of reverter and rights of entry is best from the standpoint of (a) marketability of land, (b) predictability of result, (c) eliminating manipulation of labels, (d) the title searcher's problems, and (e) eliminating only undesirable or useless restrictions?

2. Apply the Massachusetts statute to the following conveyances:
   (a) to Trinity Church so long as used for church purposes;
   (b) to Trinity Church so long as used for church purposes, then to X and his heirs;
   (c) to Trinity Church, but if the land ceases to be used for church purposes the grantor and his heirs shall have a right of entry;
   (d) to Trinity Church, but if the land ceases to be used for church purposes, then to X and his heirs;
   (e) to B and his heirs, but if B at any time dies without issue surviving him, then to X and his heirs;
   (f) to B for life, then in fee to B's issue per stirpes who survive B, but if B at any time dies without issue surviving him, then to X and his heirs.

By functional criteria the future interests in 2(c) and 2(d) above should be subject to the same rule limiting duration. By functional criteria the future interests in X in 2(e) and 2(f) above should be subject to the same rule limiting duration. However, the future interests in 2(d) and 2(e) are both executory interests. If two rules with different time periods are involved, the problem arises how to divide up executory interests into (1) those that are functional equivalents of possibilities of reverter and rights of entry (and subject to a fixed-period rule) and (2) those that are functional equivalents of remainders (and subject to the Rule against Perpetuities). How would you solve this problem? Dukeminier, Perpetuities: The New Empire, 77 Yale L.J. 159, 167 (1967).

Would the following restriction avoid the Massachusetts statute? O conveys to Trinity Church, but if the land ceases to be used for church purposes within

[88] Ky. Rev. Stat. §381.222 (1962).
[89] See 2 Williams & Meyers, Oil and Gas Law §335 (1970).

twenty-one years after the death of the survivor of A, B, C, D, E, F, G, H, I, J, K, and L (twelve healthy babies), then to X. If the Massachusetts statute does not apply to this, then a forfeiture restriction on land use can be imposed for approximately one hundred years if the right verbal formula is used. Suppose X conveys his executory interest back to O. Does the statute apply?

In an effort to cut off pre-existing claims and make land marketable, several states have statutes terminating possibilities of reverter and rights of entry created prior to the enactment of the statute. Some of these statutes permit the pre-existing interest to continue if it is re-recorded within a short period of time. Do these retroactive statutes deprive the owner of a possibility of reverter or right of entry of property without due process of law? The courts are split. Holding the statutes constitutional: Trustees of Schools v. Batdorf, 6 Ill. 2d 486, 130 N.E.2d 111 (1955) (no re-recording period provided); Chicago & North Western Ry. Co. v. City of Osage, 176 N.W.2d 788 (Iowa 1970) (one-year re-recording period); Atkinson v. Kish, 420 S.W.2d 104 (Ky. 1967) (five-year re-recording period); Town of Brookline v. Carey, 355 Mass. 424, 245 N.E.2d 446 (1969) (seven-and-one-half-year re-recording period); Wichelman v. Messner, 250 Minn. 88, 83 N.W.2d 800 (1957) (nine-month re-recording period). Holding the statutes unconstitutional: Biltmore Village v. Royal, 71 So. 2d 727 (Fla. 1954) (no re-recording period provided); Board of Education v. Miles, 15 N.Y.2d 364, 207 N.E.2d 181 (1965) (one-year re-recording period). See Comment, Retroactive Termination of Burdens on Land Use, 65 Colum. L. Rev. 1272 (1965).

5. Tax Problems Raised by Possibilities of Reverter and Rights of Entry

Thus far we have pointed up the problems raised by these interests from the standpoint of grantees and their successors, who wish to use the land free of restrictions, and from the standpoint of land use policy, since these interests have the potential of tying up land forever. We close by taking a look at possibilities of reverter and rights of entry from the standpoint of the grantor. Specifically, we examine some thorny problems produced by the fact that these interests just don't fit our system of taxing transfers of property.

As we have pointed out, many of these defeasible fees arise in transfers of land to a charity for some charitable purpose. Ordinarily, a lifetime transfer of property to a charity produces a charitable deduction against the transferor's income tax, and there is no gift tax because the transfer qualifies for a charitable deduction. A charitable transfer at death produces a charitable deduction against the decedent's estate tax. But here we have a transfer of less than the total interest in the property, and it is difficult to give a valuation to the interest being transferred. (There are no actuarial tables showing how long churches use land conveyed to them "for so long as the land shall be used for church purposes.") What does this do to the transferor's charitable deduction against the income tax, the gift tax, and the estate tax?

Suppose O transfers land worth $20,000 "to the Georgetown YMCA, its successors and assigns, for so long as the premises shall be used for YMCA purposes." If this transfer were made before January 1, 1970, there was considerable doubt whether O was entitled to a full $20,000 deduction against his income tax for that year, and whether the entire $20,000 was exempt from gift taxation as a charitable contribution.[90] If the transfer were by O's will, one line of authority supported the allowance of a $20,000 charitable deduction in computing the estate tax against O's estate; another line of decisions supported the total disallowance of any deduction.[91]

This uncertainty under the old law was eliminated — with devastating consequences to the taxpayer — by the Tax Reform Act of 1969. In an earlier chapter we discussed the 1969 Act's treatment of the "charitable remainder" trust.[92] Prior to 1970 O might establish a trust under which the income was paid to A for life, with the remainder passing to a charity on A's death. O (or O's estate, if the transfer were by will) would claim a charitable deduction for the present, discounted value of the charitable remainder — but the trust would contain invasion powers or powers permitting investment in high-risk, high-return assets which would increase the life tenant's interest at the expense of the charitable remaindermen. These powers, if exercised to the hilt, would reduce the amount ultimately passing to the charity. To curb these abuses the 1969 Act provided that there shall be no deduction for a charitable remainder gift, against either the income tax, the gift tax, or the estate tax, unless the transfer meets the very specific requirements of an "annuity trust," "unitrust," or "pooled income fund."

In formulating a statute imposing these requirements, Congress employed language that applies to transfers of a fee simple determinable or a fee on a condition subsequent. For example, the income tax statute provides:

> In the case of a contribution (not made by a transfer in trust) of an interest in property which consists of less than the taxpayer's entire interest in such property, a deduction shall be allowed under this section only to the extent that [the transfer takes a form comparable to a charitable remainder annuity trust or unitrust].[93]

[90] In Fargason v. Commissioner, 21 B.T.A. 1032 (1930), the court stated that the donor of land subject to a condition subsequent was entitled to a substantial charitable deduction against his income tax, but not to a deduction for the full market value of the property. However, the pre-1970 regulations under the income tax provided that there was to be a deduction only "if the interest would be defeated by the performance of some act or the happening of some event the occurrence of which appeared to be highly improbable on the date of the gift." Treas. Reg. §1.170-1(e). The pre-1970 gift tax regulations (Treas. Reg. §25.2522(a)-2(b)) contained the same language as in the income tax regulations — meaning that a valuable interest passing to a charity might not qualify for any deduction if the occurrence of the divesting condition were not "highly improbable."

[91] In E.T. 13, 1939-2 Cum. Bull. 326, it was ruled that since the grantee was an established charitable institution, the condition attached to the gift was so remote as not likely to occur. However, in three cases it was held that the divesting condition was not so remote as to be negligible; the consequence was that the estate tax charitable deduction was denied in full. Delaware Trust Co. v. Handy, 53 F.2d 1042 (D. Del. 1931); St. Louis Union Trust Co. v. Burnet, 59 F.2d 922 (8th Cir. 1932); Churchill v. United States, 68 F. Supp. 267 (E.D. Wis. 1946).

[92] See page 238.

[93] Int. Rev. Code of 1954, §170(f)(3).

The provisions authorizing charitable deductions under the gift tax and the estate tax contain similar language.[94]

What does all of this mean? If O makes his "so long as" transfer to the Georgetown YMCA after January 1, 1970, he gets no charitable deduction against his income tax. Furthermore, he must pay a gift tax on the full value of the property transferred. If the transfer is by will, O's estate gets no charitable deduction against the estate tax. Thus O's transfer of a valuable interest to the YMCA receives none of the tax benefits normally accorded charitable donations. Quaere: Is the attorney who counselled O in making the transfer, and who drafted the deed, liable to O for negligence?

And that's not the end of the story.

PROBLEMS

1. O dies several years after having transferred the property to the YMCA. At the time of his death, the value of the property has increased from \$20,000 to \$25,000. The YMCA is using the land (located two blocks away from one of its gyms) as a parking lot for its guests and employees. Is any amount includible in O's gross estate by reason of his ownership of the possibility of reverter? If so, what amount? Cf. Rev. Rul. 61-88, 1961-1 Cum. Bull. 417; Adriance v. Higgins, 113 F.2d 1013 (2d Cir. 1940).

2. A continuation of Problem 1. O's will devises "all the rest, residue and remainder of my property" to his son, O Jr. Five years later O Jr. dies leaving a will that devises "all the rest, residue and remainder of my property" to *his* son, O III. These will provisions are construed to pass the possibility of reverter to the named devisees. Is any amount includible in O Jr.'s gross estate by reason of his ownership of the possibility of reverter? If so, what amount?

3. It dawns on O III that something strange is going on here. He decides to give the possibility of reverter to someone.

(a) O III deeds the possibility of reverter to the Georgetown YMCA. In computing O III's income tax for that year, is he entitled to a charitable deduction? If so, in what amount? Commissioner v. Sternberger's Estate, 348 U.S. 187 (1955); cf. Rev. Rul. 67-363, 1967-2 Cum. Bull. 118.

(b) Alternatively, O III offers to deed the possibility of reverter to Paul, a neighbor whom O III dislikes intensely. O III persuades Paul that he is doing Paul a favor. If you were advising Paul, would you recommend that he accept the gift?

(c) Do we have, in the possibility of reverter and right of entry, successors to the Siamese white elephant? Is this a way to take care of a "friend": By giving him one of these interests that is not really worth anything as a practical matter, but that will be taxed in his estate, and in the estate of his family line for all time to come?

[94] Int. Rev. Code of 1954, §§2522(c)(2), 2055(e)(2).

12. Securing the Transferor's Intent: Lessons in Amphibology

SECTION A. Introduction

"I do not know of any more unsatisfactory duty for a Judge than that of being called upon to put a construction on an instrument with respect to which, it may be presumed, the framer of the instrument had himself no very definite notion. It is a duty, however, of necessity, imposed on the Judges of this Court, who, as Lord Mansfield has observed, must sometimes feel that they are the only authorized interpreters of nonsense." — Lord Chancellor Cranworth in Cookson v. Bingham, 3 DeG. M. & G. 668, 674, 43 Eng. Rep. 263 (Ch. 1853).

2 POWELL, REAL PROPERTY ¶317 (1970): "In every jurisdiction, the circumstances of an instrument's formulation are relevant factors for the resolution of a found ambiguity in its meaning. Thus it is permissible to show that the conveyor used words in a fashion peculiar to himself; or, put in other words, that he had a special vocabulary. It is permissible to show the utilization of a drafting agent and to show the presence or absence of skill in the use of language and of legal phraseology on the part of either the conveyor or his drafting agent. It is proper to show that a will expressed in terms of request or desire or other precatory language has the force of a command by evidence of the relationship of the testator to the party addressed plus evidence of a prevailing manner of expression. Normally, however, precatory language does not suffice to create a future interest. Courts constantly turn to the facts known or believed by a testator for light as to the meaning of his dispositive language. The law of the place where the testator lived at the time of the

drafting of his will can be shown as a part of the testator's background and hence as helpful in determining the meaning of his language found in the instrument."

HALBACH, STARE DECISIS AND RULES OF CONSTRUCTION IN WILLS AND TRUSTS

52 Calif. L. Rev. 921, 922-925 (1964)

The principal contentions of this Article may be summarized briefly. The first is that many recurring types of construction cases should be resolved by resort to rule, rather than by a particularistic, case-by-case approach which falsely claims to discover actual intention. This position is based only in part on the belief that decision by rule minimizes costly and fruitless litigation. It is primarily based on the conviction that in many situations the most likely route to appropriate results in individual cases is through the consistent application of sound rules of construction. This is because a particular, recurring problem of construction so often involves policy factors and strong probabilities of intention which coincide sufficiently to make one construction, in terms of the results it tends to produce, distinctly preferable to other permissible constructions.

Second, especially because of the peculiar constructional backdoor of "discovered" contrary intention, adherence to unsound constructional precedent cannot be justified in the name of stare decisis. In fact, to stand on unsound rules of construction is to forfeit the expected advantages of a practice of adhering to precedent. When a presumption conflicts with common sense, adherence to the rule becomes largely nominal; litigation is invited, and results contrary to the rule are frequent and based on unpersuasive details of particular cases. This produces a pattern of actual decision that is irregular and unpredictable. In fact, it is the hallmark of an unsound rule that it yields to faint indications of contrary intention. Actual decision by rule and fulfilment of the objectives of stare decisis thus depend on the existence of reasonably sound rules which courts can accept.

Finally, despite the usual assumption that reliance is an obstacle to overruling in areas regarded as involving property law, it follows from the preceding conclusion that reliance upon precedents which are demonstrably unsound — and thus ripe for overruling — is peculiarly *unlikely* in the case of rules of construction applicable to wills and trusts. This is not to dismiss reliance altogether as a factor in construction cases. It is simply to urge that a court, instead of assuming the reliance factor, at least consider whether realistic possibilities of reliance actually exist with respect to the type of constructional problem before it.

In large measure these contentions conflict with several widespread notions about the role of precedent in construction. . . . One is that precedents have little value in determining the meaning of individual wills or trust instruments since each is unique — often expressed in terms of not construing one man's nonsense by another's. This attitude is sometimes valid, as in misdescription cases, where the problem is essentially confined to "interpretation" and for which there is no serious temptation to rely on rules of construction. It is not valid, however, in those recurring situation-types within which the cases are similar in language and context and where the transferor apparently formed no actual intention, as in the typical future interest case. Nor is the value of precedent undetermined by the underlying argument that there are endless variations of intention and objectives, for the refusal of courts to "rewrite" wills limits the issue to selecting one of several recognized constructions. A second notion is that, when a particular type of constructional question must be settled, *a* rule is needed, and that one rule is about as good as another. While a few situations are sufficiently "neutral" to permit such an approach, it must not be assumed that this is true of others. The cases falling within a given situation-type frequently involve common considerations of policy and intention, a weighing of which will reveal that one construction is distinctly better than others. A third notion, that stare decisis is particularly sacred in property law, has been mentioned previously. Again, the notion has some validity, especially where a reasonable degree of certainty exists and where worthy reliance interests are likely. But the reliance factor is neither peculiar to property law nor necessarily weighty in all of the so-called property areas, and when carried over into construction it should not receive more emphasis than it deserves.

McDOUGAL, FUTURE INTERESTS RESTATED: TRADITION VERSUS CLARIFICATION AND REFORM

[A *review of* V*olume III of the Restatement of Property*]
55 Harv. L. Rev. 1077, 1077-1084 (*1942*)

Here in this third of five projected volumes of restatement of property "law as it is" — that is, of rules which purportedly predict what an intelligent court will do if properly harangued — the American Law Institute brings to a close its clear expression and authoritative crystallization of our traditional confusion about Future Interests.

. . . It still defines and classifies its problem largely in terms not of facts and social objectives but of legal concepts of high-level abstraction. It still offers but little explicit consideration of alternative social objectives and but little justification in terms of policy norms for the objectives which it implicitly prefers. It still seeks to investigate relations of cause and effect — the responses of judges to certain practical problems — by a completely inadequate analysis and observation of environmental and predispositional factors. . . . Formulated in symbols laden with the ambiguities of centuries, its rules are not so much a restatement of the "law as it is" as of the confusion that was, is, and inevitably will be until investigators of future interests problems clarify their purposes, improve their methods of analysis and observation, and widen the range of their efforts to be influential.

To expedite documentation of so sweeping an indictment, let us look first at the [American Law] Institute's avowed objective of determining predictive rules and consider some of the methods which would have to be employed for the achievement of such a formidable objective. . . .

What are some of these variables which, from the perspective of most practicing lawyers and even of most law teachers, are presumptively relevant? Let us undertake — as the Institute did not — to specify a list of classes of variables which an investigator must carefully distinguish, index, and observe if he is justifiably to entertain even faint hope of being able to discover predictive rules. However low our estimate of the possibilities of prediction, such inquiry need not be waste effort: some similar analysis is indispensable even to attainment of clarity of communication about unpredictable alternatives, and hence also to meaningful appraisal of what the Institute has actually done. Here in rough, tentative form is a list which may help to dispel confusion:

A. *The Practical Problem: Competing Claims Presented to the Court.* — In language redolent with legalistic justifications such problems would be described as problems in "destructibility," "perpetuities," "alienability," "partition," "taxation," "survivorship," "acceleration," "eminent domain," "statute of limitations." In more popular idiom, such problems pose the question of: Who wants what from whom and why? The "who" and the "whom" can include people claiming identification under the donor's language or their creditors, vendees or spouses, people purporting to represent the public interest (e.g., the tax collector), and even people who cannot identify themselves other than as intermeddling strangers; the "what" most often involves a demand for the "property" in whole or in part; and the "why," the justifications for the demand, may include a pronouncement of either legal norms or policy norms or both. At the very inception of our search for predictability we are confronted with the unfortunate fact that appellate opinions and even trial court records are often very meager in the information they yield about all of these quarreling people (their relations, blood and otherwise, to the donor and to each other) and how they identify themselves and what they want.

B. *The Language of the Dispositive Instrument.* — This is sometimes called "the limitation." For clarity of analysis it is indispensable that this variable, emphasized by a major heading here because of its apparent preeminent importance in most future interests problems, be kept quite distinct from the variable following (the donor's reference). As certain shapes on paper, certain manifest syllabic patterns — such as "heirs," "issue," "surviving children," "descendants" — the donor's language may unfortunately point equivocally to various and competing groups of claimants. Different verbal patterns may, conversely, make the same factual reference to person, time, event, and subject matter. Sometimes, furthermore, the language of the donor may be so devoid of factual reference that it gives no direction at all.

C. *The Donor's Reference in the Instrument to Facts of Person, Time, Event, and Subject Matter.* — Here it is important to keep distinct three very different observational standpoints. By the donor's reference is meant his reference as a scientific observer, or a majority of scientific observers, would determine it. Such determination may or may not coincide with the self-serving identifications of the claimants under heading A. And it may or may not coincide with the final determination by the court, which is part of the response sought. When, as in most problems of "survivorship," the words of the donor are so devoid of reference that they give little or no direction and a court must of necessity create its own reference as part of its response, our chief concern must be to observe whether the court smuggles in such response as a part of the "facts" ("intent of the donor"), and if so, what policy norms it is actually following in its distribution of the property.

D. *Legal Norms.* — These are the conventional justifications of judicial decisions, the answers which judges have become conditioned to give to losing counsel. They are the propositions which appear in most appellate opinions or textbooks discussing the specific practical problem in question and are usually in terms of a peculiar and distinctive vocabulary of lawyers: "vested," "contingent," "possibility of reverter," "class," "condition precedent," "remainder," "executory interest," "title." Often it is difficult to ascribe meaning to such propositions; they point to no identifiable goals and give no directions for action; they are tautological in the sense that they can be given "meaning" only by circular reference to the very behavior which they are supposed to justify and predict. Some contemporaries assume that such propositions have no effect on the decision, but affect only the style of justification; others by obsessive concern with such propositions seem to assume that they are all important. Our problem (that is, the Institute's) is of course to determine, if possible, just what effect they do have. . . . The one point which an investigator should never forget — and which the Institute appears never to have recognized — is that these norms are not themselves the statement of scientific laws but rather a part only of the data from which such laws might be formulated.

E. *Policy Norms.* — These are all of the other significant ideological propositions (social, economic, religious, ethical) of our culture which could conceivably bear on a judge's response to a practical problem in future interests. Such propositions purport to state how values (income, power, deference, safety, knowledge) ought to be distributed among people, and point to goals of varying degrees of abstraction. Some of these may be immediately presented to the court by counsel in argument or may even get mention in appellate opinions (carrying out intent of donor, limiting duration of future interests, promoting free alienability, preventing tax evasion, keeping in blood line); if they get enough mention in such opinions they may eventually qualify for classification as "legal norms." Other such norms are more free-floating in our culture and beat upon the judge from the rostrum, the printed page, and the radio, or are urged by family, friends, and colleagues. It is an axiom of contemporary jurisprudence that such norms are of the greatest significance for the prediction of behavior. Yet our techniques for classifying such norms and for determining which have been brought to a judge's attention over what period of time and by whom are still in the most rudimentary stages.

F. *Other Nonideological Factors: Environmental and Predispositional.* — This class is added for the sake of systematic completeness even though our techniques of observation and analysis have not yet been sufficiently refined to take many such variables into account. Our list here could include, for more or less random examples: personality type, social and class affiliations, group memberships of all kinds, skills of judges, parties, counsel, jurors, and witnesses; trial or hearing conditions, such as duration of proceedings, length of individual sessions, frequency of recesses; bribery and intimidation; shifts in the relative importance of symbols, goods, violence, and institutional practices as methods of social control generally; changes in technology, population, and resource utilization; and so on. Commonsense and unsystematic knowledge of such variables is of course a part of the working equipment of any successful practitioner.

Such in vague outline are some of the initial discriminations which a scientific observer in serious search of predictability would have to make. As appalling as it may seem to frame categories and subcategories for all of these key variables in terms of such precision that their influence and interrelations can be tested, it is nevertheless a task which cannot be ignored by anyone who pretends to seek scientific laws about judicial behavior. It is, furthermore, not so much the Institute's aspiration as it is its method — a "one factor, one result" analysis in terms of only a part of the relevant data — which is subject to question. Prediction which is useful for policy implementation (for securing, for example, certain desired responses from judges) cannot safely be left to clairvoyance by legal doctrine.

SECTION B. The Requirement of Survival

1. *Death of a Transferee Before Death of Testator: Lapse*

ESTATE OF RUSSELL
Supreme Court of California, 1968
69 Cal. 2d 200, 444 P.2d 353, 70 Cal. Rptr. 561

Sullivan, Associate Justice. Georgia Nan Russell Hembree appeals from a judgment (Prob. Code, §1240)[1] entered in proceedings for the determination of heirship (§§1080-1082) decreeing inter alia that under the terms of the will of Thelma L. Russell, deceased, all of the residue of her estate should be distributed to Chester H. Quinn.

Thelma L. Russell died testate on September 8, 1965, leaving a validly executed holographic will written on a small card. The front of the card reads:

Turn
the card March 18-1957
I leave everything
I own Real &
Personal to Chester
H. Quinn & Roxy Russell
Thelma L. Russell

[1] Hereafter unless otherwise indicated all section references are to the Probate Code.

The reverse side reads:

> My ($10.) Ten dollar gold
> Piece & diamonds I leave
> to Georgia Nan Russell.
> Alverata, Geogia [*sic*].

Chester H. Quinn was a close friend and companion of testatrix, who for over 25 years prior to her death had resided in one of the living units on her property and had stood in a relation of personal trust and confidence toward her. Roxy Russell was testatrix' pet dog which was alive on the date of the execution of testatrix' will but predeceased her.[2] Plaintiff is testatrix' niece and her only heir-at-law.

In her petition for determination of heirship plaintiff alleges, inter alia, that "Roxy Russell is an Airedale dog";[3] that section 27 enumerates those entitled to take by will; that "Dogs are not included among those listed in . . . Section 27. Not even Airedale dogs"; that the gift of one-half of the residue of testatrix' estate to Roxy Russell is invalid and void; and that plaintiff was entitled to such one-half as testatrix' sole heir-at-law.

At the hearing on the petition, plaintiff introduced without objection extrinsic evidence establishing that Roxy Russell was testatrix' Airedale dog which died on June 9, 1958. To this end plaintiff, in addition to an independent witness, called defendant pursuant to former Code of Civil Procedure section 2055 (now Evid. Code, §776). Upon redirect examination, counsel for Quinn then sought to introduce evidence of the latter's relationship with testatrix "in the event that your Honor feels that there is any necessity for further ascertainment of the intent above and beyond the document." Plaintiff's objections on the ground that it was inadmissible under the statute of wills and the parol evidence rule "because there is no ambiguity" and that it was inadmissible under section 105, were overruled. Over plaintiff's objection, counsel for Quinn also introduced certain documentary evidence consisting of testatrix' address book and a certain quitclaim deed "for the purpose of demonstrating the intention on the part of the deceased that she not die intestate." Of all this extrinsic evidence only the following infinitesimal portion of Quinn's testimony relates to care of the dog: "Q [Counsel for Quinn] Prior to the first Roxy's death did you ever discuss with Miss Russell taking care of Roxy if anything should ever happen to her? A Yes." Plaintiff carefully preserved an objec-

[2] Actually the record indicates the existence of two Roxy Russells. The original Roxy was an Airedale dog which testatrix owned at the time she made her will, but which, according to Quinn, died after having had a fox tail removed from its nose, and which, according to the testimony of one Arthur Turner, owner of a pet cemetery, was buried on June 9, 1958. Roxy was replaced with another dog (breed not indicated in the record before us) which, although it answered to the name Roxy, was, according to the record, in fact registered with the American Kennel Club as "Russel's [*sic*] Royal Kick Roxy."

[3] In his "Petition for Probate of Holographic Will and for Letters of Administration with the Will Annexed," Quinn included under the names, ages and residences of the devisees and legatees of testatrix (§326, subd. (3)) the following: "Roxy Russell, A 9 year old Airedale dog, [residing at] 4422 Palm Avenue, La Mesa, Calif."

tion running to all of the above line of testimony and at the conclusion of the hearing moved to strike such evidence. Her motion was denied.

The trial court found, so far as is here material, that it was the intention of testatrix "that CHESTER H. QUINN was to receive her entire estate, excepting the gold coin and diamonds bequeathed to" plaintiff and that Quinn "was to care for the dog, ROXY RUSSELL, in the event of Testatrix's death. The language contained in the Will, concerning the dog, ROXY RUSSELL, was precatory in nature only, and merely indicative of the wish, desire and concern of Testatrix that CHESTER H. QUINN was to care for the dog, ROXY RUSSELL, subsequent to Testatrix's death." [4] The court concluded that testatrix intended to and did make an absolute and outright gift to Mr. Quinn of all the residue of her estate, adding: "There occurred no lapse as to any portion of the residuary gift to CHESTER H. QUINN by reason of the language contained in the Will concerning the dog, ROXY RUSSELL, such language not having the effect of being an attempted outright gift or gift in trust to the dog. The effect of such language is merely to indicate the intention of Testatrix that CHESTER H. QUINN was to take the entire residuary estate and to use whatever portion thereof as might be necessary to care for and maintain the dog, ROXY RUSSELL." Judgment was entered accordingly. This appeal followed.

Plaintiff's position before us may be summarized thusly: That the gift of one-half of the residue of the estate to testatrix' dog was clear and unambiguous; that such gift was void and the property subject thereof passed to plaintiff under the laws of intestate succession; and that the court erred in admitting the extrinsic evidence offered by Quinn but that in any event the uncontradicted evidence in the record did not cure the invalidity of the gift.

We proceed to set forth the rules here applicable which govern the interpretation of wills.

First, as we have said many times: "The paramount rule in the construction of wills, to which all other rules must yield, is that a will is to be construed according to the intention of the testator as expressed therein, and this intention must be given effect as far as possible." (Estate of Wilson (1920) 184 Cal. 63, 66-67, 193 P. 581, 582.) The rule is imbedded in the Probate Code. (§101.) Its objective is to ascertain what the testator meant by the language he used.

[4] The memorandum decision elaborates on this point, stating in part: "The obvious concern of the human who loves her pet is to see that it is properly cared for by someone who may be trusted to honor that concern and through resources the person may make available in the will to carry out this entreaty, desire, wish, recommendation or prayer. This, in other words, is a most logical example of a precatory provision. It is the only logical conclusion one can come to which would not do violence to the apparent intent of Mrs. Russell."

The trial court found further: "Testatrix intended that Georgia Nan Russell Hembree was not to have any other real or personal property belonging to Testatrix, other than the gold coin and diamonds." This finding also was elaborated on in the memorandum decision: "In making the will it is apparent she had Georgia on her mind. While there is other evidence in the case about Thelma Russell's frame of mind concerning her real property and her niece, which was admitted by the Court, over counsel's vigorous objection, because it concerned testatrix' frame of mind, a condition relevant to the material issue of intent, nevertheless this additional evidence was not necessary to this Court in reaching its conclusion." The additional evidence referred to

When the language of a will is ambiguous or uncertain resort may be had to extrinsic evidence in order to ascertain the intention of the testator. We have said that extrinsic evidence is admissible "to explain any ambiguity arising on the face of a will, or to resolve a latent ambiguity which does not so appear." (Estate of Torregano (1960) 54 Cal. 2d 234, 246, 5 Cal. Rptr. 137, 144, 352 P.2d 505, 512, 88 A.L.R.2d 597 citing §105.) A latent ambiguity is one which is not apparent on the face of the will but is disclosed by some fact collateral to it. (See 4 Page on Wills (Bowe-Parker Rev.) §32.7, p. 255; Comment: Extrinsic Evidence and the Construction of Wills in California (1962) 50 Cal. L. Rev. 283, 284-291).

As to latent ambiguities, this court in the Donnellan case said: "Broadly speaking, there are two classes of wills presenting latent ambiguities, for the removal of which ambiguities resort to extrinsic evidence is permissible. The one class is where there are two or more persons or things exactly measuring up to the description and conditions of the will, . . . The other class is where no person or thing exactly answers the declarations and descriptions of the will, but where two or more persons or things in part though imperfectly do so answer." (Estate of Donnellan (1912) 164 Cal. 14, 20, 127 P. 166, 168.) Extrinsic evidence always may be introduced initially in order to show that under the circumstances of a particular case the seemingly clear language of a will describing either the subject of or the object of the gift actually embodies a latent ambiguity for it is only by the introduction of extrinsic evidence that the existence of such an ambiguity can be shown. Once shown, such ambiguity may be resolved by extrinsic evidence. . . .

A patent ambiguity is an uncertainty which appears on the face of the will. . . . "When an uncertainty arises upon the face of a will as to the meaning of any of its provisions, the testator's intent is to be ascertained from the words of the will, but the circumstances of the execution thereof may be taken into consideration, excluding the oral declarations of the testator as to his intentions." (Estate of Salmonski, supra, 38 Cal. 2d 199, 214, 238 P.2d 966, 975.) This is but a corollary derived from an older formalism. Long before Salmonski it was said in Estate of Wilson, supra, 171 Cal. 449, 456, 153 P. 927, 930: "The rule is well established that where the meaning of the will, on its face, taking the words in the ordinary sense, is entirely clear, and where no latent ambiguity is made to appear by extrinsic evidence, there can be no evidence of extrinsic circumstances to show that the testatrix intended or desired to do something not expressed in the will." However, this ancient touchstone has not necessarily uncovered judicial material of unquestioned purity.

In order to determine initially whether the terms of *any written instrument* are clear, definite and free from ambiguity the court must examine the instrument in the light of the circumstances surrounding its execution so as to ascertain what the parties meant by the words used. Only then can it be determined whether the seemingly clear language of the instrument is in fact ambiguous. "Words are used in an endless variety of contexts. Their meaning is not subsequently attached to them by the reader but is formulated by the writer and can only be found by inter-

---

included an address book of testatrix upon which she had written: "Chester, Don't let Augusta and Georgia have one penny of my place if it takes it all to fight it in Court. Thelma."

pretation in the light of all the circumstances that reveal the sense in which the writer used the words. The exclusion of parol evidence regarding such circumstances merely because the words do not appear ambiguous to the reader can easily lead to the attribution to a written instrument of a meaning that was never intended." (Universal Sales Corp. v. Cal., etc., Mfg. Co. (1942) 20 Cal. 2d 751, 776, 128 P.2d 665, 679 (Traynor, J., concurring).) "The court must determine the true meaning of the instrument in the light of the evidence available. It can neither exclude evidence relevant to that determination nor invoke such evidence to write a new or different instrument." (Laux v. Freed (1960) 53 Cal. 2d 512, 527, 2 Cal. Rptr. 265, 273, 348 P.2d 873, 881 (Traynor, J., concurring); see also Corbin, The Interpretation of Words and the Parol Evidence Rule (1965) 50 Cornell L.Q. 161, 164: "[W]hen a judge refuses to consider relevant extrinsic evidence on the ground that the meaning of written words is to him plain and clear, his decision is formed by and wholly based upon the completely extrinsic evidence of his own personal education and experience"; Corbin, op. cit. supra, pp. 189-190. . . .

The foregoing reflects the modern development of rules governing interpretation, for in the words of Wigmore "The history of the law of Interpretation is the history of a progress from a stiff and superstitious formalism to a flexible rationalism." (9 Wigmore, op. cit. supra, §2461, p. 187.) While "still surviving to us, in many Courts, from the old formalism . . . [is] the rule that you *cannot disturb a plain meaning*" (9 Wigmore, op. cit. supra, p. 191, original emphasis) nevertheless decisions and authorities like those cited above bespeak the current tendency to abandon the "stiff formalism of earlier interpretation" and to show the meaning of words even though no ambiguity appears on the face of the document. . . .

Accordingly, we think it is self-evident that in the interpretation of a will, a court cannot determine whether the terms of the will are clear and definite in the first place until it considers the circumstances under which the will was made so that the judge may be placed in the position of the testator whose language he is interpreting. (Cf. Code Civ. Proc. §1860.) Failure to enter upon such an inquiry is failure to recognize that the "ordinary standard or 'plain meaning,' is simply the meaning of the people who did *not* write the document." (9 Wigmore, op. cit. supra, §2462, p. 191.)

Thus we have declared in a slightly different context that extrinsic evidence as to the circumstances under which a written instrument was made is " 'admissible to interpret the instrument, but not to give it a meaning to which it is not reasonably susceptible' (Coast Bank v. Minderhout, 61 Cal. 2d 311, 315, 38 Cal. Rptr. 505, 507, 392 P.2d 265, 267; . . .), and it is the instrument itself that must be given effect. . . ." "If the evidence offered would not persuade a reasonable man that the instrument meant anything other than the ordinary meaning of its words, it is useless." (Estate of Rule (1944) 25 Cal. 2d 1, 22, 152 P.2d 1003, 1014 (Traynor, J., dissenting), disapproved on other grounds, Parsons v. Bristol Development Co., supra, 62 Cal. 2d 861, 866, fn. 2, 44 Cal. Rptr. 767, 402 P.2d 839.)[5] On the other

[5] We recognize that in contract cases . . . the standard of interpretation is normally the "mutual standard of parties to a bilateral act" whereas in will cases, such as the instant one, it is the individual standard of the testator." (See 9 Wigmore, op. cit. supra §2458, p. 181.)

hand an ambiguity is said to exist when, in the light of the circumstances surrounding the execution of an instrument, "the written language is fairly susceptible of two or more constructions." (Hulse v. Juillard Fancy Foods Co. (1964) 61 Cal. 2d 571, 573, 39 Cal. Rptr. 529, 394 P.2d 65; . . .)

. . . [W]hat is here involved is a general principle of interpretation of written instruments, applicable to wills as well as to deeds and contracts. Even when the answer to the problem of interpretation is different for different kinds of written instruments, "it appears in all cases as a variation from some general doctrine." (9 Wigmore, op. cit. supra, §2401, p. 7.) Under the application of this general principle in the field of wills, extrinsic evidence of the circumstances under which a will is made (except evidence expressly excluded by statute)[6] may be considered by the court in ascertaining what the testator meant by the words used in the will. If in the light of such extrinsic evidence, the provisions of the will are reasonably susceptible of two or more meanings claimed to have been intended by the testator, "an uncertainty arises upon the face of a will" (§105) and extrinsic evidence relevant to prove any of such meanings is admissible (see §106),[7] subject to the restrictions imposed by statute (§105). If, on the other hand, in the light of such extrinsic evidence, the provisions of the will are not reasonably susceptible of two or more meanings, there is no uncertainty arising upon the face of the will . . . and any proffered evidence attempting to show an intention *different* from that expressed by the words therein, giving them the only meaning to which they are reasonably susceptible, is inadmissible. In the latter case the provisions of the will are to be interpreted according to such meaning. In short, we hold that while section 105 delineates the manner of ascertaining the testator's intention "when an uncertainty arises upon the face of a will," it cannot always be determined whether the will is ambiguous or not until the surrounding circumstances are first considered. . . .

Examining testatrix' will in the light of the foregoing rules, we arrive at the following conclusions: Extrinsic evidence offered by plaintiff was admitted without objection and indeed would have been properly admitted over objection to raise and resolve the latent ambiguity as to Roxy Russell and ultimately to establish that Roxy Russell was a dog. Extrinsic evidence of the surrounding circumstances[8] was properly considered in order to ascertain what testatrix meant by the words of the will, including the words: "I leave everything I own Real & Personal to Chester H. Quinn & Roxy Russell" or as those words can now be read "to Chester H. Quinn and my dog Roxy Russell."

[6] As for example, under section 105 . . . which specifically excludes "the oral declarations of the testator as to his intentions." This opinion does not disturb the statutory proscription against the use of such evidence.

[7] Section 106 provides: "The words of a will are to be taken in their ordinary and grammatical sense, unless a clear intention to use them in another sense can be collected, and that other can be ascertained. Technical words are not necessary to give effect to any species of disposition by a will; but technical words in a will are to be taken in their technical sense, unless the context clearly indicates a contrary intention, or unless it satisfactorily appears that the will was drawn solely by the testator, and that he was unacquainted with such technical sense."

[8] Excluding however the oral declarations of testatrix as to her intentions. . . . It is to be noted that no such declarations are herein involved.

However, viewing the will in the light of the surrounding circumstances as are disclosed by the record, we conclude that the will cannot reasonably be construed as urged by Quinn and determined by the trial court as providing that testatrix intended to make an absolute and outright gift of the entire residue of her estate to Quinn who was "to use whatever portion thereof as might be necessary to care for and maintain the dog." No words of the will give the entire residuum to Quinn, much less indicate that the provisions for the dog is [*sic*] merely precatory in nature. Such an interpretation is not consistent with a disposition which by its language leaves the residuum in equal shares to Quinn and the dog. A disposition in equal shares to two beneficiaries cannot be equated with a disposition of the whole to one of them who may use "whatever portion thereof as might be necessary" on behalf of the other. (See §104; cf. Estate of Kearns (1950) 36 Cal. 2d 531, 534-536, 225 P.2d 218.) Neither can the bare language of a gift of one-half of the residue to the dog be so expanded as to mean a gift to Quinn in trust for the care of the dog, there being no words indicating an enforceable duty upon Quinn to do so or indicating to whom the trust property is to go upon termination of the trust. "While no particular form of expression is necessary for the creation of a trust, nevertheless some expression of intent to that end is requisite." (Estate of Doane, supra, 190 Cal. 412, 415, 213 P. 53, 54. . . .)

Accordingly, since in the light of the extrinsic evidence introduced below, the terms of the will are not reasonably susceptible of the meaning claimed by Quinn to have been intended by testatrix, the extrinsic evidence offered to show such an intention should have been excluded by the trial court. Upon an independent examination of the will we conclude that the trial court's interpretation of the terms thereof was erroneous. Interpreting the provisions relating to testatrix' residuary estate in accordance with the only meaning to which they are reasonably susceptible, we conclude that testatrix intended to make a disposition of all of the residue of the estate to Quinn and the dog in equal shares; therefore, as tenants in common. . . . As a dog cannot be the beneficiary under a will (§27; see 1 Page on Wills, op. cit. supra, §17.21, p. 851) the attempted gift to Roxy Russell is void. . . .[9]

There remains only the necessity of determining the effect of the void gift to the dog upon the disposition of the residuary estate. That portion of any residuary estate that is the subject of a lapsed gift to one of the residuary beneficiaries remains undisposed of by the will and passes to the heirs-at-law. . . . The rule is equally applicable with respect to a void gift to one of the residuary beneficiaries. . . . Therefore, notwithstanding testatrix' expressed intention to limit the extent of her gift by will to plaintiff . . . , one-half of the residuary estate passes to plaintiff as testatrix' only heir-at-law (§225). We conclude that the residue of testatrix' estate should be distributed in equal shares to Chester H. Quinn and Georgia Nan Russell Hembree, testatrix' niece.

[9] As a consequence, the fact that Roxy Russell predeceased the testatrix is of no legal import. As appears, we have disposed of the issue raised by plaintiff's frontal attack on the eligibility of the dog to take a testamentary gift and therefore need not concern ourselves with the novel question as to whether the death of the dog during the lifetime of the testatrix resulted in a lapsed gift. (§92.)

The judgment is reversed. . . .

Traynor, C.J., and Peters, Tobriner, Mosk, and Burke, JJ., concur.

McComb, J., dissents.

NOTE

What is the reason for the rule that if one of several residuary legatees predeceased the testator and an anti-lapse statute does not save the legacy, the portion of the predeceased residuary legatee goes by intestacy and not to the surviving residuary legatees? Comment, 55 Mich. L. Rev. 1202 (1957); Note, 31 Yale L.J. 782 (1922). In an increasing number of states this rule is rejected by statute (e.g., N.J. Stat. Ann. §3a:3-14 (1953); Pa. Stat. Ann. tit. 20, §253 (1950)) or by judicial decision (e.g., In re Estate of Jackson, 471 P.2d 278 (Ariz. 1970); In re Slack Trust, 220 A.2d 472 (Vt. 1966)). The rule may yield to a contrary intent gathered from the will, but exactly what indicates a contrary intent is the subject of much litigation. Compare Estate of Dammann, 12 N.Y.2d 500, 191 N.E.2d 452 (1963), with Matter of Urchs, 15 N.Y.2d 893, 206 N.E.2d 358 (1965) and Estate of Denison, 49 Misc. 2d 714, 268 N.Y.S.2d 165 (Sur. Ct. 1966). After great confusion, illustrated by these three cases, the New York legislature abolished the rule of no-residue-of-a-residue. N.Y. Estates, Powers & Trusts Law §3-3.4 (1967).

In re MOSS

Court of Appeal

[1899] 2 Ch. 314

Walter Moss by his will dated in 1876, after appointing his wife Elizabeth Moss and his niece Elizabeth Jane Fowler his executrixes, and making sundry devises and bequests, gave all his share or interest in the Daily Telegraph newspaper unto the said E. Moss and E. J. Fowler "upon trust to pay the income thereof to my said wife for her life, and after her decease, upon trust for the said E. J. Fowler and the child or children of my sister Emily Walter who shall attain the age of twenty-one years equally to be divided between them as tenants in common." And he gave the residue of his estate and effects to his wife. . . .

The testator died in 1893, and his will was proved by his widow, Elizabeth Moss, alone. At the date of his will there were living his niece Elizabeth Jane Fowler, who was then slightly under twenty-one, his sister Emily Walter, and five children of Emily Walter.

Elizabeth Jane Fowler died in 1891, in the testator's lifetime, a spinster. Emily Walter and her five children survived the testator.

The testator's widow, Elizabeth Moss, the tenant for life of his Daily Telegraph share and his residuary legatee, died in 1897, having by her will given her residuary estate . . . in trust for William George Kingsbury absolutely. . . .

At her death all the five children of Emily Walter were living and had attained twenty-one.

The question was whether, in consequence of the death of Elizabeth Jane Fowler in the lifetime of her uncle, the testator, the share bequeathed to her in his Daily Telegraph share had lapsed and fallen into his residuary estate, or whether the entirety passed to Emily Walter's five children: in other words, whether the gift by the testator of his Daily Telegraph share was a gift to a class, so that these five children, as the survivors of the class, took the whole.

To have this question decided, an originating summons was taken out by W. G. Kingsbury . . . to have it declared that the bequest of the testator's share in the Daily Telegraph newspaper upon trust, after the death of his wife, for Elizabeth Jane Fowler and the child or children of Emily Walter who should attain twenty-one equally, was not a gift to a class, but that the share bequeathed to Elizabeth Jane Fowler had lapsed by her death in the testator's lifetime and thus fell into the residue of the estate.

The summons was heard on December 14, 1898, by North J., who, after saying the cases upon the point were so irreconcilable that he should act independently of them, held that, as he could find nothing in the will to shew that Elizabeth Jane Fowler was included in the class, the share given to her lapsed by reason of her death in the testator's lifetime, and so passed to the plaintiffs.

The defendants, the five children of Emily Walter, appealed.

Lindley M.R. It is very difficult to construe this will by the light of the authorities. I entirely agree with North J. that the authorities do not help one much, because they are in inextricable confusion. I do not think there is any case which can be cited by either side which cannot be matched by a case on the other side more or less difficult to distinguish from it. The practical question which we have to decide on this will is, Who are the persons now entitled to the share of the testator in the Daily Telegraph newspaper? There are several rival views. One view is, and that is the one adopted by the learned judge below, that the share which Elizabeth Jane Fowler would have taken if she were alive — that is, one-sixth, as I understand it — has lapsed and has fallen into the residuary estate, so that, according to that view, one-sixth of that share has gone to persons who were certainly never intended to take it. That is obvious. That may be the legal result of the gift, but it is obvious it was never dreamt of by the testator. What he intended was that his share should go amongst the persons he has named and to no one else.

Now the difficulty lies in this. We hear about classes, and gifts to classes, and definitions of classes. You may define a class in a thousand ways: anybody may make any number of things or persons a class by setting out an attribute more or less common to them all and making that the definition of the class. We have been referred, and not improperly at all, to Mr. Jarman's definition of a class for the purpose for which lawyers want it — that is, in construing a will — and I think Mr. Swinfen Eady is right in saying that, looking at that definition, this case does come within it. But after all, whether you call this a class or whether you call it a number of persons who are treated by the testator as if they were the class, appears to me to be merely a matter of language. One is very reluctant to frame definitions unless one can make a law to accord with the definitions, which judges cannot do. Now what is to be done with the share of this lady who has died? The testator says it is to be equally divided between her and the children of Emily Walter, to be equally divided between them all. If some of them are dead, are the shares of those who are dead to go to those who survive, or are they to go to someone else? That is the practical question; and whether you call the persons a class or "in effect" a class — as Mr. Theobald does in a passage of his work on wills, where he says (4th ed. p. 645), "it is clear that a gift to A., and the children of B., may in effect be a gift to a class, if the testator treats the legatees as a class" — or whether you call them a number of persons who are to be treated as a class, is quite immaterial. The guiding question here is, What is to be done with this Daily Telegraph share which is to be divided amongst these legatees? It seems to me that it is to go to such of them as shall be living. That is the obvious intention. The alternative view takes the share away where it was never intended to go, and upon that ground it appears to me that we ought to differ from the learned judge. I confess, and I say so frankly, that if this case had come before me in the first instance I should have decided it as North J. did, but my brother Romer has convinced me that is not right.

SIR F. H. JEUNE. I agree. I do not propose to add anything that may tend to make the decisions which are already contradictory and complicated still more so.

ROMER L.J. In the absence of any context negativing this view, I think that, when a testator gives property X. to A. and a class of persons — say the children of B. — in equal shares, he intends that the whole of X. shall pass by his gift if any one of the children of B. survive him, even although A. does not. Clearly, if A. survived and none of the children of B. survived so as to share, then A. would take the whole, for A. would either have to take the whole or nothing, unless indeed it could be said that you are to look at the number of children of B. living at the date of the will and say there is an intestacy as to the share of each child dying between the date of the will and the testator's death; but that to my mind is clearly an untenable proposition. If then the testator intended that A. should take the whole if none of the children of B. survived him to share, I think also he intended the children of B. to take the whole if A. did not survive so as to share. There is no satisfactory distinction, to my mind, between those two cases. I think that, in such a gift as I have mentioned, what the testator really means is that the property is to be shared equally by a body constituted of such of the following as should be existing at the date of the testator's death, that is to say, A. and the children of B. And generally, when the testator — there being nothing to negative the view in the rest of the will — gives property to be shared at a particular period equally between a class properly so called and an individual or individuals, I think that what the testator primâ facie must be taken to mean is that you are to see which part of that aggregated body is to share in that property at the time it comes for distribution, and that such a gift is really a gift to a class: and though I am perfectly well aware of the danger there is in attempting to lay down general propositions — and few judges would more shrink from doing so than I, knowing as I do how a general proposition laid down often hampers judges in dealing with succeeding cases — yet I do think in the present case I may venture to make the following statement, especially as the cases are so complicated and there is no express decision of the Court of Appeal or of the House of Lords upon the point. In my opinion it is correct to say that a gift by will to a class properly so called and a named individual such as A. equally, so that the testator contemplates A. taking the same share that each member of the class will take, is primâ facie a gift to a class.

For those reasons, applying those principles to the case before us, I have no hesitation in saying that, in my opinion, the gift here was a gift to a class, and that Elizabeth Jane Fowler was only intended to share as one of a class; and that inasmuch as she did not survive so as to share, the rest of the class takes the whole of the property.

3 POWELL, REAL PROPERTY (1970)

¶352. *Prerequisite groupmindedness of the conveyor — General criterion*

The definition of a class given by Jarman is frequently quoted by American courts. Writing originally in 1843 this author said

> A number of persons are popularly said to form a class when they can be designated by some general name, as "children," "grandchildren," "nephews"; but in legal language the question whether a gift is one to a class depends not upon these considerations but upon the mode of gift itself, namely, that it is a gift of an aggregate sum to a body of persons uncertain in number at the time of the gift, to be ascertained at a future time, and who are all to take in equal or in some other definite proportions, the share of each being dependent for its amount upon the ultimate number of persons.[10]

In one particular this definition is too restrictive. A limitation of a specific sum to each of the "children of John Jones" fails to satisfy the "aggregate sum" factor of this definition, but has customarily been regarded by the profession as creating a class gift.

It is believed that the general prerequisite for the existence of a class gift can be simply stated. When a conveyor is found to have intended that there be the possibility of fluctuation in the number of takers, the limitation constitutes a class gift rather than a gift to individuals.[11] Hence the efficacy of a conveyance to limit property to a class, rather than to individuals distributively, can be equally well tested by an inquiry described in any one of three ways. One can ask whether the conveyor was "groupminded." One can ask whether there was a possibility of fluctuation in

[10] Jarman, Wills 336 (6th ed. 1910).

[11] Rest., Prop. §279, Comment a. For an excellent discussion of what constitutes a class gift, see Annot., 61 A.L.R.2d 212 (1958).

the number of takers under the limitation. One can ask whether the conveyor intended the consequences peculiar to a class gift. All three descriptions are merely different modes of presenting an identical search for the same ultimate fact.[12]

The consequences of finding a class gift are important. Suppose that A, by will, limits Blackacre "to the children of my friend B, namely, C and D." C dies before A. No lapse statute is applicable. The size of the interest acquired by D, on the death of A, depends upon whether the quoted language is construed to limit Blackacre to the class "children of B" or to limit an undivided half interest in Blackacre to each of the definite persons C and D. If the class gift construction is adopted, D acquires the entire subject matter of the gift. If, however, the individual gift construction is adopted, the modern preference for tenancies in common over joint tenancies causes D to acquire ownership of the undivided one-half interest in Blackacre and the other undivided one-half interest in Blackacre passes either to the residuary devisee, or to the heir, of A. A similar choice has to be made when the limitation in question concerns a future interest, as for example, when A limits Blackacre "to B for life and then to the surviving children of B, that is, C and D." Here again, if C dies after A but before B, the size of the interest acquired on B's death by D depends upon the acceptance or rejection of the class gift construction. The effect of failure to survive to the time of distribution depends upon whether the person so dying was one of a class or an individual distributee. Then let us suppose the same limitation as is given above followed by a codicil, duly executed by A, revoking the interest theretofore limited by the will in favor of C. If the original limitation is found to have created a class gift, D now gets the whole of Blackacre. Otherwise he gets one-half. The third important consequence of finding a class gift concerns the expansibility of the group of takers under the limitation. Thus if A, by will, limits property "to my wife B for life, thereafter to my grandchildren," and at the time of A's death he has three grandchildren, C, D, and E, but before B dies, two more grandchildren, F and G, are born, then F and G share in the property under a class gift construction but are excluded from sharing under an individual gift construction. This expansibility of the group of takers, which results from a class gift construction, has its dangers. If the expansibility of the group of takers is not certain to end within the permissible period of the applicable rule against perpetuities, the entire limitation to the class is usually invalid. Hence the validity or

12 "What 'ultimate fact' is this? Inquiries one and three are stated in terms of donor's intent; yet the problem before the court exists only because the donor has failed to indicate his intent — because his factual reference is inadequate to identify his beneficiaries. 'The doctrine that the testator ever "intends a class" when he does not say so in so many words,' wrote an acute commentator in a relatively recent issue of this Review, [Cooley, What Constitutes a Gift to a Class (1936) 49 Harv. L. Rev. 903, 912.] 'is in any case a beneficent fiction. The vast majority of testators in all likelihood have never even heard of a class.' Inquiry two is equally fruitless. Surely, if the task of a judge is to determine whether a group of 'possible takers' fluctuates, it helps him no whit to tell him that if it is a 'class' it fluctuates but that if it is not a 'class' it does not fluctuate. Given such a meaning, the word 'class' is obviously a tautological label to describe the judge's own behavior. Any group of persons, as Professor Cooley again points out, can, in a factual sense fluctuate; the question for a judge is should a particular group be held to fluctuate for a specified legal purpose and why." McDougal, Future Interests Restated: Tradition Versus Clarification and Reform, 55 Harv. L. Rev. 1077, 1102-1103 (1942). — Eds.

invalidity of this part of a limitation can depend upon the finding or refusal to find a class gift.

DAWSON v. YUCUS, 97 Ill. App. 2d 101, 239 N.E.2d 305 (1968). Testatrix' will provided: "Through the Will of my late husband I received an undivided one-fifth interest in farm lands located in Sangamon County, Illinois, and believing as I do that those farm lands should go back to my late husband's side of the house, I therefore give, devise and bequeath my one-fifth interest as follows: One-half of my interest therein to Stewart Wilson, a nephew, and one-half of my interest to Gene Burtle, a nephew." Stewart and Gene were her husband's nephews. Gene predeceased testatrix, who died without issue. The court held that this was not a gift to a class and that the devise to Gene lapsed and passed under the residuary clause of the will. "In this case the testatrix named the individuals, Stewart Wilson and Gene Burtle, and gave them each a one-half portion of her interest in the farm, thus making certain the number of beneficiaries and the share each is to receive. The shares in no way depend upon the number who shall survive the death of the testatrix. There is nothing in the language of the will that indicates the testatrix intended to create a class or survivorship gift. The only other provision of the will, also contained in clause two, that has any bearing on the question is the statement, '. . . believing as I do that those farm lands should go back to my late husband's side of the house . . . .' While it is true that this language recites testatrix' desire that the one-fifth interest in the farm go back to her husband's side of the house, it does not indicate a survivorship gift was intended. Her intention to return the farm to her husband's side of the house was fulfilled when she named Stewart Wilson and Gene Burtle as the donees of the interest. . . .

"Further emphasis for the result we have reached is supplied by other factors found in the will and extrinsic evidence. First, the testatrix created a survivorship gift of the residue of her estate in the ninth clause of her will, thus indicating she knew how to manifest an intent to create a class or survivorship gift; hence, the language of clause two, phrased differently, was intended to create a gift to individuals distributively. Restatement of Property, Future Interests, Sec. 280, Comment g., No. 1. Paragraph No. 2 of the same Restatement citation provides, 'The specification . . . of an exact proportion in the subject matter of the conveyance, which is to be received by each of the named and described persons, is strongly indicative of an intent to make a gift to individuals distributively whenever the [total of] . . . proportions so specified equals the entire subject matter given by the limitation in question.' Secondly, the common characteristic of the alleged class described by plaintiffs is that of relation to Dr. Stewart, or, in the words of clause two, the class is of 'my late husband's side of the house.' However, this characteristic is also shared by three other heirs of Dr. Stewart of the same degree of relationship to him as Stewart Wilson and Gene Burtle. It thus appears that Gene Burtle and Stewart Wilson do not constitute the alleged class but are individuals named from the class."

EPPES v. LOCKLIN, 222 Ga. 86, 149 S.E.2d 148 (1966). Testatrix devised certain real property "to George S. and Mrs. Mamie D. Crane," who were husband and wife. Mamie Crane died before the testatrix. Held: the devise was to George S. and Mamie D. Crane as a class, and George S. took the entire fee.

5 AMERICAN LAW OF PROPERTY
(*Casner ed. 1952*)

§22.49. *Lapse Statutes and Their Effect.* The lapse statutes that exist in England and in all but a few states in this country vary considerably in their wording, but the Massachusetts statute is typical of a number of them:

"If a devise or legacy is made to a child or other relation of the testator, who dies before the testator, but leaves issue surviving the testator, such issue shall, unless a different disposition is made or required by the will, take the same estate which the person whose issue they are would have taken if he had survived the testator." [13]

In some states the lapse statutes are narrower than the Massachusetts statute in that they apply only if the devisee or legatee is a descendant of the testator or other described relative. In other states the statutes are broader: in some they apply no matter who is the legatee or devisee, and in a very few they allow the heirs of the deceased devisee or legatee to be substituted in his place without regard to whether he left issue.

When the beneficiaries in a will are described only by a group designation, unless the described class members are related to the testator as required by the lapse statute and the class member who dies before the testator leaves surviving him the required substitutional group, the lapse statute obviously is of no effect, and the entire subject matter of the gift goes to the surviving members of the class in the absence of a contrary manifestation of intent. But even though the lapse statute is otherwise applicable, there still remains the question whether these lapse statutes have any applicability to class gifts at all.

It is believed that the correct answer to this question is not to be found in the literal wording of the statutes except in the few instances discussed later. In the main the statutes have been drawn without full appreciation of the ambiguity of the language employed in relation to a class gift. Under these circumstances, a court should feel completely free to apply a lapse statute to class gifts or not, as seems to be necessary to accomplish the legislative objective.

The contention may be made that lapse statutes were enacted only to provide substitutional takers where there would have been a technical lapse of the gift but for the statute. Under this view they are not applicable to class gifts, unless all the class members die before the testator, because no lapse results from the death of a

[13] Mass. Gen. Laws (1933), c. 191, §22. Arnold v. Helmer, 100 N.E. (2d) 886 (Mass. 1951), held that an adopted child of a legatee was not an "issue" of the legatee under the lapse statute.

class member before the testator since the surviving class members take the whole gift. In one case this position was taken because the local lapse statute specifically provides that the devise or legacy "shall not lapse" but shall go to the descendants of the deceased devisee or legatee. The court said:
". . . the natural force of the language employed in the act is that the provision is intended to be operative in case of a gift or devise to the persons mentioned, when formerly, on the occurrence of the death of a legatee or devisee, it lapsed." [14] Other courts have refused to apply the lapse statutes to class gifts, however, where the words of the local statute did not thus support this conclusion.

It may also be contended that these lapse statutes do not apply to class gifts because no devisee or legatee is described by the class designation except the members of the class who survive the testator. This thought has been expressed by the New Hampshire court as follows:

> . . . If a devise be to two or more and to the survivor of them, or to be held by them as joint tenants, or to such of a class of persons as may be living at the testator's death, and one die in the testator's lifetime leaving issue, a holding that such issue takes under the statute as the parent would have taken had he survived would defeat the expressed intention of the testator. . . . If a devise generally to a class of persons, and a devise to such individuals of the class as may survive the testator, are in legal effect equivalent, the statute can no more be applied in one case than in the other without thwarting the testator's intention.[15]

This approach to the applicability of lapse statutes to class gifts may be characterized as the "intention approach" and the other as the "lapse approach." Under either approach the same result is reached except in the situation where all class members predecease the testator. Logically, under the "intention approach" the lapse statute is not applicable to a class gift, even though all the class members predecease the testator, because no devisees or legatees are described whose interests can pass under the statute; whereas under the "lapse approach" there is then a technical lapse and the statute should become applicable. The cases, however, do not seem to have recognized this difference consistently.

Neither the "intention approach" nor the "lapse approach" to the applicability of lapse statutes to class gifts is believed to be sound. In the first place, the presumption that the testator intends the class members who survive him to take the whole gift represents a choice of results made at a time when the result set forth in the lapse statutes was not available. Therefore, to hold the lapse statute inapplicable on the basis of this presumption involves the erroneous assumption that the intention of the testator is the same although the basic facts are materially changed. In the second place, to determine the scope of applicability of lapse statutes by the answer to the highly technical question whether the gift would have lapsed before the passage of the statute shows a complete lack of appreciation of the unfair result

[14] Trenton Trust & Safe Deposit Co. v. Sibbets, 62 N.J. Eq. 131, 138, 49 Atl. 530, 533 (Ch. 1901).

[15] Campbell v. Clark, 64 N.H. 328, 331, 10 Atl. 702, 703-704 (1887).

which usually occurs when a devisee or legatee dies before the testator and which these lapse statutes are designed to cure. That unfair result is the inequality of the distribution of the testator's property among the objects of his affection, an inequality manifested not only when a single named beneficiary dies and his share goes to the testator's heirs or the residuary takers but also, many times, when a class member dies and his share goes to the surviving class members. The lapse statutes, if liberally applied, correct this unfair result by giving the share of a deceased beneficiary to his descendants, who naturally represent him and are within the scope of the benefit which the testator intended to confer.

This approach, which gives full effect to the purpose of the lapse statutes, may be called the "equality of distribution approach." Upon this analysis the applicability of lapse statutes to class gifts becomes clear. The probabilities are that the testator does not desire to leave out the issue of a deceased class member and thus cause the indicated distortion of distribution among the branches of the family. The courts, therefore, which have analyzed the situation thoroughly have applied the lapse statutes to class gifts. In a few states the lapse statute provides specifically that it is applicable to class gifts. No state, however, has enacted a lapse statute which provides specifically that it is not applicable to class gifts.

PROBLEMS

1. T's holographic will provides: "Should anything happen to me Mr. Gus Weiss is to open my safe deposit box and dispose of contents as he sees fit to." Weiss predeceases T, leaving one son, S, as his sole heir. S survives T. Does it make any difference whether the attempted gift to Weiss is classified as a fee simple or as a power of appointment? Weiss v. Broadway Nat'l Bank, 204 Tenn. 563, 322 S.W.2d 427 (1959).

2. Bessie Hesla bequeathed the residue of her estate to her brother, William, and her three sisters, Emma, Carrie, and Luella, "to share and share alike . . . in fee and as joint tennants and not tennants in common." William and Emma predeceased Bessie, each leaving issue who survived Bessie. Do Carrie and Luella split the residue if there is an anti-lapse statute? If there is not? Larson v. Anderson, 167 N.W.2d 640 (Iowa, 1969).

DELAWARE CODE ANNOTATED Title 12, §2313 (1953): "No devise or legacy in favor of a child or other lineal descendant of any testator, dying after March 15, 1909 [and] . . . no devise or legacy in favor of a brother, sister or children of a brother or sister of any testator dying after March 15, 1909, such testator not leaving a lineal descendant, shall lapse or become void by reason of the decease of the devisee or legatee in the lifetime of the testator if the devisee or legatee shall leave issue surviving the testator; but such devise or legacy shall be good and available in favor of such surviving issue with like effect as if such devisee or legatee had survived the testator, saving always to every testator the right to direct otherwise."

Omit to 781

JACKSON v. SCHULTZ

Court of Chancery of Delaware, New Castle, 1959
38 Del. Ch. 332, 151 A.2d 284

Marvel, Vice Chancellor. Plaintiffs, who are children of the late Bessie H. Bullock, have contracted to sell to defendant a house formerly owned by their stepfather the late Leonard S. Bullock, claiming to hold title to such property at 1012 Kirk Avenue in Wilmington under the terms of Mr. Bullock's will. Mr. Bullock, who had no children of his own, married plaintiffs' mother in 1918, caring for and supporting her three children during their minority, and continuing to support Beatrice after his wife's death some five years ago, a fact which is reflected in his income tax returns. He died on September 8, 1958.

Defendant has refused to perform the contract, claiming that plaintiffs' mother having predeceased the testator, plaintiffs took nothing under their stepfather's will of January 13, 1937, the controversial clause of which provides as follows:

"Second: I give, bequeath and devise unto my beloved wife, Bessie H. Bullock, all my property real, personal and mixed wheresoever situate and of whatever nature and kind, to her and her heirs and assigns forever."

Defendant contends that when a devise is made to a named person, "his heirs and assigns forever," the heirs as such normally take nothing by way of substitution if the devisee predeceases the testator, such expression being deemed one of limitation defining the quantity of the estate devised, Burton v. Masten, 18 Del. Ch. 242, 158 A. 136, 137. In the absence of "something further" in the language used in a will the same rule has been applied in cases where the word "and" appears before the clause "heirs and assigns," dictum in Burton v. Masten, supra, and 57 Am. Jur. Wills §1430. However, when "or" is used following a primary devise, the subsequent reference to "heirs" or the like has been deemed to designate those who will take by way of substitution in the event the primary devisee predeceased the testator, and a lapse is thereby avoided. See Annotations in 78 A.L.R. 992 and 128 A.L.R. 94; Delaware County Trust Co. v. Hanby, 19 Del. Ch. 228, 165 A. 568, and Fisher v. Barcus, 14 Del. Ch. 324, 127 A. 53.

It has also been held that the words "or" and "and" may be substituted for each other in arriving at a proper construction of a will, "and" having been read as "or" for the purpose of carrying out an obvious testamentary purpose in the cases of Kerrigan v. Tabb, N.J. Ch., 39 A. 701, and Huntress v. Place, 137 Mass. 409. In the case of Burton v. Masten, supra [18 Del. Ch. 242, 158 A. 137], the Chancellor, while distinguishing the facts of these cited cases, could not have applied their holding in any event because the word "and" was not used following the primary devise, the pertinent language in the will before him in that case being ". . . to them (him) their (his) heirs and assigns forever. . . ."

According to the uncontroverted facts before me on plaintiffs' motion for summary judgment, the testator's father, a widower, died on January 7, 1936. He was survived by a brother, Harry, a step-son, Frederick, and his own son, Leonard. On January 18, 1936 these three survivors entered into an agreement which was designed to insure, inter alia, that in the event of Leonard's death during the settlement of his father's estate his share of such estate would go to his wife, Bessie, and not to his Uncle Harry, the latter agreeing to such arrangement. Thus, while the legal theory of the agreement is dubious, it demonstrates Leonard S. Bullock's clear intent that his share of his father's estate should go to his wife and not to his only living blood relative. In his 1937 will, executed following settlement of his father's estate, he expressly directed that his entire estate should go to his wife, "to her and her heirs and assigns forever," and named her executrix.

In addition to this evidence of intent that his sole surviving blood relative should not share in his estate (Harry Bullock being the only one who would take in the absence of a will, there being no living brothers or sisters of either John, Harry or Leonard or descendants of any of them) there is the further fact that in 1939 Harry died. His wife having predeceased him and there being no known next of kin of the testator at the time of his death, his will should be read not only so as to carry out his intent but construed, if possible, so as to avoid not merely intestacy but a total escheat.

While the granting of a decree of specific performance is a matter requiring the exercise of judicial discretion, such decree should normally be granted in a land purchase case such as this unless to do so would require a buyer to accept a defective title subject to attack by an adverse interest not before the Court, Alrich v. Wood, 30 Del. Ch. 80, 53 A.2d 439. Here, however, there being no possibility of any adverse claim, according to the record before me, and being satisfied that there is a solid basis in law for sustaining plaintiffs' claim to a fee simple title in the lands here involved in the light of the uncontroverted facts, I am of the opinion that plaintiffs' motion should be granted.

There being a recognized rule of construction permitting "and" to be read as "or" when so to do will carry out the testator's intent in will construction cases such as this, I adopt such rule of construction in the light of the facts in the record before me. The language used by the draftsman of the will namely, ". . . to her and her heirs . . ." adapts readily to the rule which permits such a substitution, and were such rule not to be followed this is a case in which the total testamentary background calls for a finding of intent that a substitutionary gift over to the testator's stepchildren be made in the event of his wife's death prior to his own.

In earlier cases before this Court, such as Equitable Trust Company v. Best, 31 Del. Ch. 247, 70 A.2d 1, and Smith v. Savin, 31 Del. Ch. 347, 73 A.2d 785, the evidence failed to throw any light on the testator's actual intent. Here the evidence sustains a ruling that the will be construed as making a substitutionary devise over to plaintiffs and their sister, persons whom the testator raised as his own, their mother having predeceased the testator.

Plaintiffs' motion for summary judgment is granted.
Order on notice.

In re COOK, 44 N.J. 1, 206 A.2d 865 (1965). By a will drafted by an attorney, testatrix bequeathed her residuary estate "to my sister, Anna J. Wagner, and my step-son, Raymond W. Cook, their heirs and assigns, share and share alike." Raymond predeceased testatrix, leaving a widow Viola surviving. The court held that the residue should be divided equally between Anna and Viola, on the ground that the phrase "their heirs and assigns, share and share alike" evidenced an intent to create a substitutional gift in Raymond's heirs. "While Raymond was not married at that time [the execution of the will] he was then courting Viola whom he later married. Alma and Viola were always friendly and it may fairly be assumed that when Alma decided to make the bequest to Raymond she contemplated not only Raymond but also his wife and family if he should have any. When her attorney drew her will he was clearly alert to the possibility that legatees might predecease the testatrix and undoubtedly intended to make the necessary provisions in this connection throughout the will. Thus, though our law would have taken care of the matter in like fashion . . . , he expressly stipulated in the third and fourth paragraphs that if any of the legatees named there predeceased the testatrix then the legacy shall be cancelled and go to the residue. When he dealt with the residue he did not say anything about cancellation but he did say that it shall go to Anna and Raymond, 'their heirs and assigns, share and share alike.' He presumably understood that this language, which was not necessary to establish a fee simple, was sufficiently substitutionary in nature for if it was not, there would have been, under the law as it then stood, a lapse and an intestacy as to half of the residue; it would appear evident that neither he, nor the testatrix when she read and signed the will, ever intended such a lapse and intestacy."

HOFING v. WILLIS, 31 Ill. 2d 365, 374, 201 N.E.2d 852 (1964): "While there is some support for the proposition that the phrase 'and to their heirs' could be considered as words of purchase by reading the word 'and' as 'or,' (see Kales, Future Interests, pp. 172-175 (2d ed., 1920); cf. Golladay v. Knock, 235 Ill. 412), the presence of the words 'and assigns' makes such a construction unacceptable. If the word 'and' is read 'or', the language creates a substitutionary gift in favor of the 'heirs and assigns' of George's sisters, who would take as purchasers. That a deceased sister's heirs should take as purchasers by way of substitution would be quite reasonable. But it is hardly reasonable to suppose that the grantor would create a substitutionary gift and at the same time designate the assigns of the named takers to take by way of substitution."

2. *Death of a Transferee After Death of Testator and Before Period of Distribution*

SECURITY TRUST CO. v. IRVINE

Court of Chancery of Delaware, New Castle, 1953
33 *Del. Ch.* 375, 93 A.2d 528

Bramhall, Vice Chancellor. In this case this court is asked to determine two issues: (1) whether or not the residuary estate left to brothers and sisters of the testator vested as of the date of his death or at the time of the death of the last life tenant; (2) if it should be decided that the residuary estate vested as of the time of the death of the testator, do the life tenants take as members of the class of brothers and sisters receiving the residuary estate?

Plaintiff is trustee under the last will and testament of James Wilson, deceased, who died on July 29, 1918, leaving a last will and testament dated October 25, 1915. After providing for certain specific bequests, testator gave and devised all his "real and mixed estate" to the Security Trust and Safe Deposit Company, — now the Security Trust Company, — to two sisters, Martha B. Wilson and Mary E. Wilson, during their joint lives and during the lifetime of the survivor of them. Testator further provided that in the event that his sister, Margaret W. Irvine, should be left a widow, she should share equally with the two sisters above named in the benefits of the trust so provided. As to the remainder, testator provided as follows:

> Upon the death of two sisters, Martha B. Wilson and Mary E. Wilson, and the survivor of them, then it is my will that all of my real and mixed estate and any proceeds that may have arisen from the sale of any part thereof, together with any unexpended income there may be, shall be equally divided among my brothers and sisters, share and share alike, their heirs and assigns forever, the issue of any deceased brother or sister to take his or her parent's share.

Testator was survived by his five brothers and sisters: Samuel H. Wilson, Margaret W. Irvine, Martha B. Wilson, Mary E. Wilson, and Henry Wilson. At the time of the execution of the will the ages of the brothers and sisters ranged from 39 to 52 years. Martha B. Wilson and Mary E. Wilson, the two life tenants, died respectively on June 9, 1928, and August 18, 1951, unmarried and without issue, the trust therefore terminating on the latter date. The other devisees all predeceased Mary E. Wilson, the surviving life tenant. Samuel H. Wilson died on October 26, 1926, leaving to survive him three children, Frazer Wilson, Jeannette A. Wilson, and Samuel H. Wilson, Jr., and Grace Wilson Gearhart, daughter of a deceased son, Francis Paul Wilson. Samuel H. Wilson, Jr. died in 1924, unmarried and without issue.

Samuel Irvine, one of the defendants, is the sole residuary legatee under the will of Margaret W. Irvine, deceased. Martha B. Wilson died testate on June 9,

1928, leaving her residuary estate to her two nieces, Margaret Gregg Wilson, now Margaret W. Hanby, and Mary Hope Wilson, each an undivided one-half interest therein.

Mary E. Wilson died testate on August 18, 1951, leaving her entire residuary estate to Margaret W. Hanby, after providing for the payment of her debts and a legacy to Mary Hope Wilson in the sum of $100.

The estate of Martha B. Wilson has been closed, the final account having been passed on February 9, 1935; the estate of Mary E. Wilson has also been closed, the final account in that estate having been passed on September 15, 1952.

I must first determine whether or not the remainder interest of the testator became vested at the time of his death or at the time of the death of the last life tenant, Mary E. Wilson, on August 18, 1951. In order to resolve this question the intention of the testator at the time of the drafting of the will must first be ascertained. If it should be clear that testator intended this provision of the will to take effect at some future date, then the intention of the testator, so far as it may be legally carried out, will prevail. However, in reaching my conclusion, I must accept certain well recognized rules of construction.

The law favors the early vesting of devised estates and will presume that words of survivorship relate to the death of the testator, if fairly capable of that construction. In the absence of a clear and unambiguous indication of an intention to the contrary, the heirs will be determined as of the date of the death of the testator and not at some future date. When the language employed by the testator annexes futurity, clearly indicating his intention to limit his estate to take effect upon a dubious and uncertain event, the vesting is suspended until the time of the occurrence of the event. See Delaware Trust Company v. Delaware Trust Company, Del. Ch., 91 A.2d 44, and cases therein cited.

The assertion that it is indicated in the will that the testator intended the residuary estate to be vested as of the date of the death of the last life tenant is based upon the contentions: (1) the fact that testator left a life estate to two of his sisters and then gave the residuary estate to his brothers and sisters indicates that testator did not intend the two sisters to share in his residuary estate and therefore the residuary estate did not vest until the date of the death of the last life tenant; (2) the use of the words "upon the death of two sisters" and the provision in the will of testator that his estate "should be equally divided among my brothers and sisters" indicates an intention that testator intended a future vesting of his residuary estate.

Whatever may be the law in other states it is well settled in this state that the fact that a life tenant is a member of a class, in the absence of any clear indication in the will to the contrary, does not prevent the life tenant from participating in the remainder of testator's estate as a part of the class. . . .

As to the use of the word "upon", it is equally clear under the decisions in this state and elsewhere, that this word and other words of this nature refer only to the time of payment and not to the substance of the devise. Cann v. Van Sant, 24 Del. Ch. 300, 11 A.2d 388; In re Nelson's Estate, 9 Del. Ch. 1, 74 A. 851. Other Delaware cases are to the same effect. In any event, the use of this word, and the provision for dividing its remainder, under the circumstances of this case would not alone be sufficient to overcome the presumption of immediate vesting.

It is contended on behalf of certain defendants that even though it should be determined that the gift to the brothers and sisters vested as of the date of the death of testator, the life tenants should be excluded from membership in the class of brothers and sisters. They base their contention upon the fact that testator in another item of his will gave them a life interest in his residuary estate.

In endeavoring to ascertain the intention of testator, it is uniformly held that such a provision is not of itself sufficient to prevent the life tenant from participating in the remainder as part of the class. See cases cited in 13 A.L.R. 620. It is not sufficient to show the absence of an intention to include the life tenants; there must be some indication of a clear and unambiguous nature to exclude them. Dillman v. Dillman, 409 Ill. 494, 499, 100 N.E.2d 567; Carver v. Wright, 119 Me. 185, 109 A. 896. I can find no incongruity in the mere fact that testator provided a life estate for his two sisters and later gave the remainder to his brothers and sisters, of which the two sisters were part of the class. They were unmarried. They were no longer young. It seems to be clear from the several provisions in the will of the testator that it was his purpose to provide for them. Such provision does not indicate to me that testator did not intend that they should participate further in his estate. Certainly there is no legal inconsistency in life tenants participating in the remainder. The theory that the testator particularly desired to see that his sisters were provided for is at least as strong as the supposition that he intended to exclude them from participating in the remainder.

I conclude that the life tenants should participate in the remainder devised by testator to his brothers and sisters.

Having determined that the life tenants should participate in the provision for the brothers and sisters, I must next consider the effect of the provision that the "issue of any deceased brothers or sisters to take his or her parent's share".

As to the brothers and sisters who died leaving issue, it was specifically provided that such issue should take the interest of such brother or sister leaving issue. Their interest was thereby divested, their issue being substituted in their place. In such case, the brother or sister dying leaving issue would have no power of disposition of his or her interest in the estate. In re Nelson's Estate, supra.

The will of testator is silent as to any provision relative to any of the brothers and sisters dying without leaving issue. Martha B. Wilson, Mary E. Wilson and Margaret W. Irvine, three sisters of testator, left no issue at the time of their death. Was their interest divested by their death, even though they left no issue, or did their estates receive an absolute interest, free and clear of any conditions subsequent?

Under the will of testator, the death of the life tenants leaving issue caused their interest to be divested. I have determined that the brothers and sisters received an absolute estate, subject to the provision that the interest of any brother or sister dying prior to the death of the life tenant should go by substitution to the issue of such brother or sister. However, this provision of the will does not apply where there is no issue, since there would then be no limitation upon their estate. The decisions in this state are silent as to what would happen under such circumstances. However, the weight of authority in other states is to the effect that in the event of the death of the devisees leaving no issue, the interest of such devisees is not divested by their death. McArthur v. Scott, 113 U.S. 340, 5 S. Ct. 652, 28 L. Ed. 1015; Plitt v. Plitt, 167 Md. 252, 173 A. 35, 109 A.L.R. 1; Jacobs v. Whitney, 205 Mass. 477, 91 N.E. 1009; Rutledge v. Fishburne, 66 S.C. 155, 44 S.E. 564; Gardner v. Vanlandingham, 334 Mo. 1054, 69 S.W.2d 947. Since the estates created were absolute except for the condition subsequent, and since the subsequent condition has been removed, the estates of the sisters dying without issue would have an absolute interest unrestricted by any condition.

I believe that such a determination would be in accord with the plain intention of the testator. He apparently desired to provide for his own brothers and sisters and their issue. If he had desired to provide that the interest of any brother or sister dying without issue should go to the surviving brothers or sisters or had intended to make some other similar provision, it would have been easy for him to do so. The fact that he did not, indicates that he had no such intention. I conclude that the interests of Martha B. Wilson, Mary E. Wilson and Margaret W. Irvine, were not divested by their death without issue and that their interests in the estate of the testator under the residuary clause of the will should go to their respective estates.

The estates of Martha B. Wilson and Mary E. Wilson have been closed. In accordance with the opinion of this court in Cooling v. Security Trust Co., 29 Del. Ch. 286, 76 A.2d 1, their shares may be distributed by the trustee directly to the persons entitled to receive the same, the trustees first seeing that any taxes which may be due or any costs which may be incurred by reason thereof are paid.

NOTES

1. The rule favoring vested interests is analyzed by Rabin, The Law Favors the Vesting of Estates. Why? 65 Colum. L. Rev. 467 (1965). Professor Rabin believes that the rule is useful in protecting the issue of a remainderman who dies before his interest becomes possessory. He thinks that the rule can function somewhat like a modern anti-lapse statute which substitutes the beneficiary's issue for the beneficiary who predeceases the testator; if the rule would protect the beneficiary's issue when the beneficiary predeceases the life tenant, Professor Rabin would apply it. For disadvantages of the rule, the most important of which being that transmissible remainders are subject to estate taxes, see Schuyler, Drafting, Tax, and Other Consequences of the Rule of Early Vesting, 46 Ill. L. Rev. 407 (1951).

In Estate of Houston, 414 Pa. 579, 201 A.2d 592 (1964), testator died in 1895. His will established a trust to pay the income to his issue from time to time living per stirpes and "on the death of my last surviving child I direct that the whole of the principal of the trust estate shall be distributed in equal portions to and among my grand-children, the children of any deceased grandchild taking their deceased parents' share." Testator's last surviving child died in 1961. There were twelve grandchildren born. Eight were alive in 1961; three had died in 1918, 1918, and 1934 intestate and unmarried, leaving their parents as their heirs; and one had died before 1961 leaving issue surviving. The trust was allegedly worth $145,000,000 in 1961. If the remainder were contingent upon the grandchildren and great-grandchildren surviving until 1961, the opinion of the court notes, there would have been "a colossal tax saving." The court held, however, that the remainder to each grandchild was vested subject to being divested only in the event the grandchild left children. See Comment, Consideration of Tax Consequences in Construction of Ambiguous Wills, 113 U. Pa. L. Rev. 472 (1965).

The ruling of the court in the Irvine case directing the trustee to bypass closed estates and distribute the property directly to persons entitled to receive it (thereby saving administrative costs) makes good sense but is unusual. See Will of Woodcock, 19 Misc. 2d 268, 186 N.Y.S.2d 452 (Sur. Ct. 1959), rejecting such a suggestion. In Estate of Houston, supra, the dissent stated that tax savings were not relevant in ascertaining the intention of a nineteenth-century testator, but that "the pyramiding of estate administration costs and expenses and the resulting diminution of assets occasioned by early and almost immediate successive administrations constitute a proper indication of testator's intention." 201 A.2d 600, 603.

2. Suppose the will of James Wilson had devised the remainder to "my brothers and sisters *or* their issue." This is not a *supplanting* limitation, as in the Irvine case, but an *alternative* limitation. Restatement of Property §252 says the alternative form creates a condition precedent that requires the brothers and sisters to survive the preceding life tenants, and many cases so hold.[16] Does the average person intend different consequences to flow from "brothers and sisters or their issue" than flow from "brothers and sisters, the issue of any deceased brother or sister to take his or her share"? If not, should these two limitations create a requirement of survival or no requirement of survival? Halbach, Future Interests: Express and Implied Conditions of Survival: Part II, 49 Cal. L. Rev. 431, 460 (1961).

3. Suppose testator devises property "to A for life, then to my children and the issue of those of my children who may be dead leaving children." Is the gift over to the issue of the children a supplanting or an alternative limitation? 2 Powell, Real Property ¶330 (1970).

4. Suppose testator devises property to "A for life, then to A's issue." A has a son B and a daughter C. B predeceases A, leaving a will devising his entire estate to his wife D. B is survived by a son E. On A's death, who takes the property? Restatement of Property §249, Comment i, says that "issue" connotes a survival requirement; therefore E, not D, would succeed to B's share. Why should survival of A be required where the remainder is to "A's issue" or to "A's heirs" and not when the remainder is to "A's children" or to "A's brothers and sisters"? Halbach, Future Interests: Express and Implied Conditions of Survival: Part I, 49 Cal. L. Rev. 297, 312 (1961); Trautman, Class Gifts of Future Interests: When is Survival Required? 20 Vand. L. Rev. 1 (1966); 5 American Law of Property §21.13 (Casner ed..1952).

[16] See Simes & Smith, The Law of Future Interests §581 (2d ed. 1956).

5. Suppose testator devises property "to my wife for life, then to my surviving children." Testator is survived by two children, A and B. A dies before the wife, survived by a child C. Testator's wife dies. Is C entitled to share in the property? Does the preference for early vesting require that "surviving" means "surviving testator"? 2 Powell, Real Property ¶328 (1970); Simes & Smith, The Law of Future Interests §577 (2d ed. 1956).

6. T bequeaths a fund in trust "to pay the income to A for life, and upon A's death to divide the corpus and pay it over to the children of A." At T's death A has three children, B, C, and D. D predeceases A. Is D's estate entitled to a share of the trust fund at A's death? Note that there is no language of gift to the children of A, only a direction to the trustee to divide and pay over the corpus to them. Some older cases held that where the only words of gift are in a direction to the trustee to divide and pay over, the remaindermen must survive to the date of division and distribution. These cases have been widely criticized and the divide-and-pay-over rule has now been repudiated almost everywhere. 5 American Law of Property §21.21 (Casner ed. 1952); 2 Powell, Real Property ¶333 (1970).

7. It will be apparent to you that the draftsman of the will in Security Trust Co. v. Irvine overlooked a number of questions that might arise. In addition to the two issues stated in the first paragraph of the opinion, here are others:

(a) Do the issue of a brother or sister take per stirpes or per capita?

(b) If a brother or sister dies before testator, would his or her issue share in the remainder?

(c) If a brother or sister dies before the life estates terminate, must his or her issue then living survive the life tenants in order to take?

(d) If a brother or sister dies before the life estates terminate, leaving a grandchild (child of a predeceased child) surviving who survives the life tenants, is such child entitled to share in the remainder? (Note the will says "*parent's* share.")

In the Irvine case the lawsuit was brought some thirty years after the will was probated, and the statute of limitations for negligence of the draftsman had long since run. However, assume that a lawsuit is brought within the statutory period and Samuel, Margaret, and Henry are still alive. Should the draftsman of this will be liable for negligence? If Samuel, Margaret, and Henry survive the life tenants there will be no litigation over the above issues, although there may be litigation over whether Martha and Mary are entitled to share in the remainder. If you conclude that the draftsman was negligent, what will be the measure of damages?

LAWSON v. LAWSON

Supreme Court of North Carolina, 1966

267 N.C. 643, 148 S.E.2d 546

Petition for partition. Petitioners, J. Roscoe Lawson, Ina Rose Lawson Denning, J. Alva Lawson, and Sadie Lawson Long allege that each of them owns a one-fourth undivided interest in the land described in the petition and that respondents have no interest in it. Respondent William Lawson alleges that he owns a one-sixth undivided interest in the property; respondents Leo Harold Lawson, Kenneth Bryan Lawson, Bonnie Jewel Lawson and Barbara Ann Lawson West allege that together they own a one-sixth undivided interest. The facts are admitted in the pleadings.

J. Rad Lawson, the father of petitioners and the grandfather of respondents, died testate in March 1950. He devised the land in suit to his daughter, Opal Lawson Long, with the following provision:

> To be hers for and during the term of her natural life, and at her death to her children, if any, in fee simple; if none, to the whole brothers and sisters of my daughter, Opal Lawson Long, in fee simple. Should my daughter, Opal Lawson Long predecease me, then the lands herein devised shall go to her children, if any, in fee simple; if none, to the whole brothers and sisters of my said daughter, in fee simple.

Opal Lawson Long died in November 1965. She left no children or descendants of children. The whole brothers and sisters who survived her are the petitioners named above. Respondent William Lawson is the only child and descendant of Earl Lawson, a whole brother who died in 1950. The other respondents are the only children and descendants of Leo Lawson, a whole brother who died in 1953.

Upon these facts, Judge Johnson entered judgment decreeing that petitioners own the described property in fee simple and that respondents have no interests in the land. He ordered that it be sold for partition among petitioners. Respondents excepted to this judgment and appealed.

SHARP, Justice. Respondents contend that at the death of the testator, J. Rad Lawson, the six whole brothers and sisters of the life tenant, all of whom were then living, took a vested remainder in the land, and that they, as children of the two whole brothers who predeceased Opal Lawson Long, inherited their interest. The law, however, is otherwise.

This case presents a typical example of a contingent remainder.

> "A devises to B for life, remainder to his children but if he dies without leaving children remainder over, both the remainders are contingent; but if B afterwards marries and has a child, the remainder becomes vested in that child, subject to open and let in unborn children, and the remainders over are gone forever. The remainder becomes a vested remainder in fee in the child as soon as the child is born, and does not wait for the parent's death, and if the child dies in the lifetime of the parent, the vested estate in remainder descends to his heirs." 4 Kent's Commentaries, p. 284 quoted in Blanchard v. Ward, 244 N.C. 142, 146, 92 S.E.2d 776, 779.

In Watson v. Smith, 110 N.C. 6, 14 S.E. 649, testator devised land to J for life, and at J's death to such child or children of his that might then be living, but should he die without issue, then to G, W, H, and O in fee. The Court held that the limitation to G, W, H, and O, was a contingent remainder. "Alternative remainders limited upon a single precedent estate are always contingent. Such remainders are created by a limitation to one for life, with remainder in fee to his children, issue, or heirs, and, in default of such children, issue, or heirs, to another or others. . . ." 33 Am. Jur., Life Estates, Remainders, etc. §148 (1941), citing Watson v. Smith, supra.

Clearly the interests of the whole brothers and sisters was [*sic*] contingent and could not vest before the death of the life tenant, for not until then could it be determined that she would leave no issue surviving. Priddy & Co. v. Sanderford, 221 N.C. 422, 20 S.E.2d 341. "Where those who are to take in remainder cannot be determined until the happening of a stated event, the remainder is contingent. Only those who can answer the roll immediately upon the happening of the event acquire any estate in the properties granted." Strickland v. Jackson, 259 N.C. 81, 84, 130 S.E.2d 22, 25. Respondents' parents, having predeceased the life tenant, could not answer the roll call at her death.

The judgment of the court below is
Affirmed.[17]

NOTE

In accord with Lawson v. Lawson is Schau v. Cecil, 136 N.W.2d 515 (Iowa, 1965), noted 65 Mich. L. Rev. 203 (1966). The majority rule, which is contrary to Lawson v. Lawson, is stated with approval in 5 American Law of Property §21.25 (Casner ed. 1952); Simes and Smith, The Law of Future Interests §594 (2d ed. 1956).

In Drury v. Drury, 271 Ill. 336, 111 N.E. 140 (1915), the court laid down a rule that a gift to a *class* of a future interest contingent on an event unrelated to survivorship is also contingent on survivorship. The rule was disapproved in Hofing v. Willis, 31 Ill. 2d 365, 201 N.E.2d 852 (1964).

CLOBBERIE'S CASE

Court of Chancery, 1677
2 Vent. 342, 86 Eng. Rep. 476

In one Clobberie's case it was held, that where one bequeathed a sum of money to a woman, at her age of twenty-one years, or day of marriage, to be paid unto her with interest, and she died before either, that the money should go to her executor; and was so decreed by my Lord Chancellor Finch [later Lord Nottingham].

But he said, if money were bequeathed to one at his age of twenty-one years, if he dies before that age, the money is lost.

[17] Noted 45 N.C.L. Rev. 264. — Eds.

On the other side, if money be given to one, to be paid at the age of twenty-one years; there, if the party dies before, it shall go to the executors.

NOTES

1. The rules in Clobberie's Case are discussed at 5 American Law of Property §§21.17, 21.18, and 21.20 (Casner ed. 1952), and criticized by Halbach, Future Interests: Express and Implied Conditions of Survival: Part I, 49 Calif. L. Rev. 297, 301 (1961).

2. T bequeaths property "to A until B reaches twenty-one, and when B is twenty-one to B in fee." B dies at age nineteen. Does B's estate have any interest in the property?

3. In 1970 T bequeaths the residue of his estate "to A's children when the youngest reaches 21." At T's death A has three children: B, aged twelve; C, aged seventeen; and D, aged twenty-three. Who is entitled to the income from the residuary estate? 5 American Law of Property §21.36 (Casner ed. 1952). In 1971 C and D die. When B reaches twenty-one will the estates of C and D share in the property? In 1972 E is born to A. In 1973 B dies. When will the residue be distributed? Id. 21.18.

4. T bequeaths a fund "to the children of A, payable to each at twenty-one, and in the meantime they are to receive the income." At T's death A has three children, B, C, and D. B, the eldest, is seventeen. One year later B dies. Is B's administrator entitled to demand immediate distribution of B's share?

McDOUGAL, FUTURE INTERESTS RESTATED: TRADITION VERSUS CLARIFICATION AND REFORM

55 Harv. L. Rev. 1077, 1093-1096 (1942)

Let us now return to the specific practical problem, requirement of survival, which gives name to this chapter. Here a court's job is to determine, in the absence of a clear statement of intent by the donor, whether, if a potential taker dies before a stated distribution date, the estate of such potential taker or some other claimant or set of claimants is to get the property. So far no principle of policy has been announced which would preclude a draftsman who thinks of the problem from stating exactly what the donor intends; the cases come up because the draftsman did not anticipate the problem and a court must make a choice which the donor failed to make for himself. It is, in other words, a task of creating a "judicially ascertained intent," of "painfully pricking out" a nonexistent donative intent, or of creating a reference to person and event for the donor's language when objective observers can find no direction in such language. For judicial guidance in the handling of this problem, the [American Law] Institute, though it boldly stamps out at least one well-known quibble, the so-called "divide-and-pay-over" rule ([3 Restatement of Property] §260), shapes other rules which succumb completely to traditional verbalisms. Such, for example, is the distinction made between the words "or" and "and." Thus, if a remainder or executory interest be limited to "B or his children" or "B or his issue" or "B or his descendants" or by "other language of similar import," the "alternative form" is said to tend to establish a requirement ("condition precedent") that B survive "all preceding interests" (§252). . . .

. . . Is it really credible that a competent draftsman who thinks of the problem of survivorship would rely upon such a slight distinction in verbal form, a distinction which has caused so much litigation, to express his intent?

The attaching of different legal consequences to formulae which specify the same factual reference, or factual references of insubstantial difference, is even more obvious in certain further distinctions. Limitations such as "I give to A, payable when he becomes 21" or "I give to A, to be had by him at 21" are said not to import a condition precedent of survivorship; both "the present identification of an existing person as the intended taker" and "language of present gift" tend to establish the absence of such a condition (§§256, 257). But, in contrast, if in a limitation "otherwise like those described" above, the phrasing happens to be "to B at 21" or "to B when 21" or "to B if he attains 21" "under *crystallized* rules of construction, survival to the stated age is a condition precedent of such interests" (§257, comment *e*) (italics supplied); such limitations are not "couched in 'language of present gift' within the meaning" of the relevant rules. Certain gifts of income may, however, tend to establish that even the interests created by the latter limitations are "free from the condition precedent of survival" (§258).

Not only does the Institute bow to all of these traditional, insubstantial distinctions; but, what is even more regrettable, it makes no sustained effort to delineate any consistent policy norms which the courts may, unavowedly, have been following in splitting such barren verbalisms now one way and now another. Even appellate records, meager as they are, might offer "factual data" enough for the formulation of rules of greater predictive value than can be found in these mare's nests of the orthodox vernacular. Simes, in his study of the meaning of the word "heirs," has made a suggestive demonstration of what might be done.[18] Framed for experimental purposes, his norms were, roughly, in terms of "alienability," "keeping the property in the family," "equality of distribution," "natural objects of the testator's bounty," and "probable intent." As difficult as it may be to frame such norms in terms that are meaningful and relevant, and as laborious as may be the task of uncovering the data necessary for confirmation or disconfirmation, anything, however small, which the Institute might have been able to accomplish in such a direction would have been progress. It is possible that decisions about whether or not a requirement of survival "exists" have so little effect on our economy and on the distribution of values generally that it makes no difference how or by what ritual such cases are

[18] Simes, Knouff, and Leonard, The Meaning of "Heirs" in Wills — A Suggestion in Legal Method (1933), 31 Mich. L. Rev. 356.

decided;[19] but the facts which would confirm or disconfirm even this "common-sense" hunch are still out and the Institute has done nothing to bring them in.

SECTION C. Class Gifts: Class Closing Rules

A class is either open or closed, one or the other. When a class is open, persons not yet born may come into the class. When a class is closed, no more members can be added to the class. Note well that this is all we mean when we say a class is closed: *no person born after this date can share in this property.*[20] The fact that a class is closed does not mean that all members of the class will necessarily share in the property. No one can come in, but present members can drop out. For example, take a bequest of $10,000 to the children of A who reach twenty-one. A predeceases testator. At testator's death there are three children of A alive, ages nine, twelve, and fourteen. The class is then closed, but there is no guarantee that any child will share in the gift. They might all die under the age of twenty-one.

A class can close in two ways: (1) physiologically or (2) by the rule of convenience. A class of children closes physiologically when the parent dies. A class may close earlier by application of the rule of convenience. The rule of convenience is this: *a class will close whenever any member of the class can demand possession and enjoyment of his share.* The justification of this rule can possibly be found in a

[19] Students seldom get excited about whether a widow of some deceased potential taker or a second cousin, once removed, of the donor is to get the property. The fact is that none of the norms occasionally mentioned for controlling distribution in these "requirement of survival" cases is very persuasive. Distribution to "blood relations" makes the questionable assumption that ability and public interest run in the blood of the donor. "Quality [Equality?] of distribution" makes a very inadequate step toward redistribution of wealth or provision for "social security." Promoting "alienability" is based on the assumption, which is false today, that future interests frequently tie up a specific resource. The cases do not frequently come up in a way that courts can "prevent tax avoidance." Both "presumption against intestacy" and "free enterprise" go back for whatever meaning they may have to the mythical intent of the donor. It is, nevertheless, not completely inconceivable that the cumulative effect of hundreds of these decisions may have some effect on the general distribution of values in our society.

One curious justification appears in the introductory chapter of the volume under review. "To whatever extent these modes of resolving an ambiguity frustrate an unexpressed subjective intent of the conveyor," states §243, comment *b*, "the conveyor is responsible for his own frustration because of his failure to foresee the problems implicit in his disposition and to manifest unequivocally his intent relative thereto." Why does not this "blame" rationale, when no persuasive policy norm can be stated for choice between undesignated claimants, point to escheat? A milder proposal might be to run a lottery between the contestants and give a state a certain percentage.

[20] More accurately, we would say that no person conceived after this date can share, for here as elsewhere in property law a child is treated as in being from the time of conception, if he is later born alive. We speak of birth, but we mean conception.

Even more accurately, when children are adopted, the time of adoption, not birth, is controlling. In re Silberman's Will, 23 N.Y.2d 98, 242 N.E.2d 736 (1968). The adopted child must be adopted at the time the class closes. A child in being when the class closes, but subsequently adopted, does not share. Do you see the reason for this? See Fetters, The Determination of Maximum Membership in Class Gifts in Relation to Adopted Children: In Re Silberman's Will Examined, 21 Syracuse L. Rev. 1 (1969).

presumed intent that donors desire early distribution. Another reason sometimes advanced is that unless the class is closed when one member can demand payment, we do not know what his minimum share will be and cannot pay him anything. However, as you read further, you should ask why a class should be closed to the terrible inconvenience of after-born members.

The rule of convenience can best be understood by a series of illustrative cases. In all these cases where we have gifts to the children of B, it is assumed that B is alive at testator's death. Otherwise the class would be physiologically closed.

Immediate gifts. Where there is an immediate gift to a class, the class closes as soon as any member can demand possession, either at testator's death or later. Thus:

> *Case 1.* T bequeaths $10,000 to the children of B. B is alive and has two children, X and Y. X and Y can demand immediate possession of their shares. The class closes. $5000 is paid to X, and $5000 to Y. A year later Z is born to B. Z does not share in the bequest.

There is an exception to this rule if there are no members of the class alive at testator's death. In that case all members can share whenever born. If we closed the class at testator's death the gift would be ineffective. Since we assume testator wanted to make an effective gift, and knew there were no children alive at his death, we assume he intended all children whenever born to share. Hence we close the class at the death of the parent. In *Case 1* if B had no children at testator's death, the class would not close until the death of B.

> *Case 2.* T bequeaths $10,000 to the children of B who reach twenty-one. The class will close when a child of B reaches twenty-one.

> *Case 3.* T bequeaths $10,000 to the children of B, to be paid to them when they reach twenty-one. The class will close when a child of B reaches twenty-one or, if he dies under that age, when he would have reached twenty-one had he lived.

Postponed gifts. If the gift is postponed in possession after a life estate, the class will not close under the rule of convenience until the time comes for taking possession. Thus a gift to a class of remaindermen will not close until the life tenant is dead, and it will not then close unless one remainderman is entitled to possession.

> *Case 4.* T bequeaths $10,000 to A for life, then to the children of B. The class will not close by the rule of convenience until the death of A. If any child of B has been born before that time, he or his administrator can demand payment at A's death and close the class.

Suppose in *Case 4* at the death of A, B has not yet had any children born to him. Will the class be left open, as in the case of an immediate gift to a class, until the death of B? Upon the ground of testator's intent, the case is not so strong for keeping the class open when the gift is postponed as it is when the gift is immediate. Yet there are dicta saying that all children whenever born will share when no child has come into existence before the life estate ends.[21]

Case 5. T bequeaths $10,000 to A for life, then to the children of B who reach twenty-one. The class will not close by the rule of convenience until A dies *and* one child of B has reached twenty-one. Until that time, no child of B is entitled to payment.

Case 6. T bequeaths $10,000 to A for life, then to the children of B to be paid at twenty-one. The class will not close by the rule of convenience until A dies *and* one child of B has reached twenty-one or, if he dies under twenty-one, would have reached twenty-one if he had lived.

Note that the rule of convenience applies only to gifts of principal, not to gifts of income. Suppose there is a trust to pay income to A for life, then to pay income to the children of B. There is no need to close the class at the death of A. The class closes for the gift of income periodically as the income is accrued.

What are the alternatives to closing the class when one member is entitled to demand his share? Should the class closing rule apply to real property? See Cole v. Cole, 259 N.C. 757, 51 S.E.2d 491 (1949). On class closing rules see 5 American Law of Property §§22.39 to 22.46 (Casner ed. 1952).

PROBLEMS

1. T bequeaths $100,000 to the children of A, payable at their respective ages of twenty-one. T dies in 1962. At that time A has three children: C-1 is sixteen, C-2 is fourteen, C-3 is twelve.

(a) C-1 reaches twenty-one in 1967. C-2 dies at the age of twenty in 1968. C-3 reaches twenty-one in 1971. C-4 is born in 1964. C-5 is born in 1970. C-6, who was born to K in 1965, is adopted by A in 1972.

(1) Does C-1 share in the gift?
(2) Does the estate of C-2 share in the gift?
(3) Does C-3 share in the gift?
(4) Does C-4 share in the gift if he reaches twenty-one?
(5) Does the estate of C-4 share in the gift if C-4 dies under twenty-one?
(6) Does C-5 share in the gift if he reaches twenty-one?
(7) Does the estate of C-5 share in the gift if C-5 dies under twenty-one?
(8) Does C-6 share in the gift if he reaches twenty-one?

(b) C-1 dies at the age of nineteen in 1965. C-2 dies at the age of twenty in 1968. C-3 reaches twenty-one in 1971. C-4 is born in 1964. C-5 is born in 1970. C-6 is born in 1972. C-4, C-5, and C-6 all reach twenty-one.

(1) Does C-4 share in the gift?

[21] Re Bleckly, [1951] Ch. 740, per Evershed, M.R., at 749; per Jenkins, L.J., at 755; Simes, Future Interests 209 (2d ed. 1966).

(2) Does C-5 share in the gift?
(3) Does C-6 share in the gift?

2. Compare the following bequests:

(a) T bequeaths $100,000 in trust to distribute it to such children of A as reach twenty-one, and until the trust is terminated to pay the income equally among such of A's children as are from time to time living and are eligible to share in the principal but have not yet received his or her share of the principal.

(b) T devises Blackacre to the children of A, and if any child of A dies under the age of twenty-one, his share shall go to A's other children who reach twenty-one.

At T's death A has two children, B and C. One year later D is born to A. B reaches twenty-one, then C reaches twenty-one. Will D be able to share in either the bequest or devise if he reaches twenty-one?

Per Capita Gifts

The rule of convenience applies only to an aggregate sum to be divided among members of a class, e.g. $10,000 to the children of A. It does not apply where there is a fixed sum given to each member of a class, commonly called a per capita gift. Where the gift is per capita the class closes at the death of the testator. Thus:

Case 7. T bequeaths £500 apiece to each child of A. A has no children living at T's death. The class closes at T's death, and no child of A ever takes anything. Rogers v. Mutch, 10 Ch. Div. 25 (1878).

Wife looked rosy to A as he sat
By the crepe-draped casket of T.
Five hundred pounds for each child he begat
Would soon make him wealthy mused he.
So he married at once, and began procreating
At five hundred per, he supposed;
But you know and I know (what hardly needs stating)
That the class had already closed.
Mistakes of this sort are bound to arise
When a client takes actions like these
Without seeing his lawyer as soon as T dies,
And paying the usual fees.

— Frank L. Dewey[22]

What is the reason for closing the class at the death of the testator?

The class closing rules are rules of construction. They will yield to an expression of intention by the testator that the class stay open until it closes physiologically. In

[22] Reproduced from Leach, Langdell Lyrics of 1938 (1938).

Earle's Estate, 369 Pa. 52, 85 A.2d 90 (1951), George H. Earle, Jr.'s will provided that if his estate exceeded $5 million (as it did), "I give and bequeath to my trustees in Trust for the benefit of each and every male child of my sons who shall by birth inherit and bear the name of Earle, the sum of One Hundred Thousand ($100,000) Dollars for each one of such male children." Anthony Wayne Earle was born to a son of testator twenty-one years after testator's death. The court found that testator intended to give $100,000 in trust for each after-born grandson as well as for grandsons in being at his death. It further found that the testator's residuary trust for members of his family was still intact and that there would be no practical difficulty in paying a $100,000 legacy. Hence the court held Anthony Wayne Earle was entitled to have a $100,000 trust set up for his benefit.

SECTION D. Gifts to Children and Issue

1. *The Meaning of "Children" and "Issue"*

In re VILLALONGA'S WILL
Court of Appeals of New York, 1959
6 N.Y.2d 477, 160 N.E.2d 850

Conway, Chief Judge. The testatrix, Margaret E. Villalonga, drew a will in December, 1923, two years prior to her death. Her will is brief, and provides as follows:

"Second: I give and bequeath One Thousand Dollars ($1000.) in cash to my great-niece and namesake, Margaret Russell Graves.

"Third: I give and bequeath my opal and diamond ring to my niece, Matille Graves.

"Fourth: I give and bequeath my cluster diamond ring to my niece, Leah Peoples.

"Fifth: I give and bequeath my solitaire diamond ring, and my watch and chain to my granddaughter, Amy Villalonga.

"Sixth: All the rest of my jewelry I direct to be divided as equally as possible between my two granddaughters, Jane C. Villalonga and Amy Villalonga.

"Seventh: I give, devise and bequeath all the rest, residue and remainder of my property, both real and personal, wheresoever the same may be found, to my executors, hereinafter named, in trust, however, to keep the same invested, and pay over the income thereof to my son John L. Villalonga, during his life and upon his death the income to go to his wife, Constance C. Villalonga, and upon the death of both my son, John L. Villalonga, and his wife, I direct the principal to be paid over to any *children* surviving them, but in case no children survive him, or his wife, I will and direct that the said property be distributed between the children of my nephew, R. F. Graves." (Emphasis added.)

The life beneficiaries had two daughters, Amy and Jane C. Jane C. did not survive the life tenants, but left a daughter, Jane T., who now claims that she is entitled to share equally in the remainder with Amy, her aunt. Amy contends that, as the sole surviving immediate offspring of the life tenants, she alone is entitled to the remainder given to the surviving "children" of the life tenants. Jane T., however, argues that she also is included in the word "children" as the sole surviving child of Jane C. The resolution of this controversy depends upon the intention of the testatrix. When she gave the remainder to the surviving "children" of the life tenants, did she contemplate only surviving *immediate offspring,* or did she intend that surviving immediate offspring should share the remainder with children of predeceased immediate offspring?

In the leading case of Matter of Schaufele's Will, 252 N.Y. 65, 168 N.E. 831, we stated the rule thus: ". . . grandchildren are never interpreted as children, unless the will as a whole shows that *unmistakable intent.* The term can be so interpreted only when reason demands it [citing cases]. Before such a construction is justifiable, other expressions or clauses in the will must be found tending to contradict the use of a word which denotes immediate offspring, and to reveal a design to include descendants of a later generation." 252 N.Y. at pages 67-68, 168 N.E. at page 831, emphasis added. The same rule of law is expressed in numerous other cases. . . . Under these cases it is clear that we must reverse the orders below and hold that Amy Villalonga Whittemore is alone entitled to the remainder of the estate of Margaret E. Villalonga.

This will is a simple one, cast in ordinary language and not afflicted with the weakness of ambiguity. In the two instances where the testatrix refers to the primary remainderman, she describes that class as surviving "children" only. There is no interchangeable use made of the terms "children" and "issue." Nor does the general distributive scheme disclose a testamentary purpose to benefit children of predeceased immediate offspring together with surviving immediate offspring of the life tenants. Moreover, the use by the testatrix of the terms "granddaughter" and "granddaughters" in paragraphs Fifth and Sixth denies force to the claim that when she said "children" she also meant to include certain grandchildren. There is nothing in this will to support the position of the respondent Jane T. Mann unless, as she strenuously argues, the presence of the gift over to collaterals in the event of a total failure of "children" is a sufficient indication of an intention to enlarge upon the primary meaning of the word "children."

The testatrix provided that "in case no children survive him, or his wife [the life beneficiaries], I will and direct that the said property be distributed between the children of my nephew, R. F. Graves." This provision, contends the respondent, is sufficient indication that the testatrix intended to give the word "children" a broader meaning than immediate offspring. The argument is made that if the testatrix intended "children" to mean only immediate offspring then, in the event of a total failure thereof, the whole of the remainder would go to collaterals to the exclusion of direct descendants of the testatrix. We are told that this could not have been the intent of the testatrix, and that, therefore, the word "children" must be held to include Jane T., the daughter of a deceased immediate child of the life tenants. Great reliance is placed upon the presumption against disinheritance of descendants in favor of collaterals, particularly as expressed in the case of Prowitt v. Rodman, 37 N.Y. 42. However, we are not persuaded either by respondent Jane T. Mann's reasoning or by the authority cited in support thereof. It is of no moment what the intent of the testatrix would have been, or what would have been presumed concerning it, in the event there were no surviving immediate offspring. The controlling fact is that the life tenants *were* survived by an immediate child, the appellant. That the testatrix might have intended to prefer great-grandchildren over collaterals does not at all lead to the conclusion that she intended to benefit a great-grandchild equally with her grandchild. The gift over to collaterals here is inoperative, and, therefore, the presumption against disinheritance is not called into effect. Moreover, the presumption against disinheritance is a mere rule of construction and, as is true of all such rules, may not properly be invoked or applied except where some ambiguity or lack of clarity requires its application for the purpose of resolving a doubt otherwise introduced by the terms of the will. . . . There is nothing unclear or ambiguous here as to who is entitled to take the remainder. The testatrix has given it to the surviving "children" of the life beneficiaries, and both under the law and the terms of this will "children" means immediate offspring.

The case of Prowitt v. Rodman, supra, does not dictate a different result. In that case this court said: "In the case of a contingent future gift to the children of the first taker, followed by a limitation over, for want of such, the presumption is in favor of the first taker's posterity to his remoter descendants in preference to the donee over." 37 N.Y. at page 58. However, in Prowitt there were no surviving immediate offspring of the first taker and the question was whether the property would go to remoter descendants of the life tenant or to her collaterals. Furthermore, in the Prowitt case the words "children" and "issue" were used interchangeably to refer to the same class, thereby resulting in a definite ambiguity as to the make-up of that class. Thus, in that case it was the uncertainty as to the class which required the application of a rule of construction, and the presumption against disinheritance was referred to because the question presented was whether collaterals should take pursuant to the substitutionary gift in preference to remote direct descendants. There was no suggestion whatever in the Prowitt case that the presence of a limitation over to collaterals per se warrants a broader construction of the word "children" than immediate offspring where there is otherwise no doubt that such is its significance. Soper v. Brown, 136 N.Y. 244, 32 N.E. 768, also relied upon heavily by respondent Jane T. Mann, is concerned only with the meaning of the word "issue" and is not relevant here.

It may well be that in some cases the presence of a limitation over to collaterals may be a "factor" tending to indicate a testamentary intent to broaden the meaning of "children". (Restatement, Property, §285, comment f.) However, it is clear that the mere presence of such a provision does not in and of itself establish an "unmistakable" intent so to do in a case such as this where there is otherwise not a fragment of a doubt; where there is a person in existence who answers the primary meaning and the gift over is inoperative; where other portions of the will support the primary meaning of the word; and where there is nothing so unreasonable or unjust about the disposition so as to create grave doubt that such was the intention of the testatrix.

The fact that the disposition made in this will may not be in complete accord with individual notions of equitable distribution is not sufficient to warrant the interference of the courts. It is well settled that "Language should not be strained, nor words given an unusual meaning, in order to work out a result favorable to the issue of a deceased child. . . ." (Matter of Truslow, 140 N.Y. 599, 605, 35 N.E. 955, 956). Of course, if the language employed "is equally susceptible of one or another interpretation, we should, on every principle of right, and within the spirit of all the authorities, give it that which is most equitable and consonant with the dictates of justice." Matter of Paton, 111 N.Y. 480, 486, 18 N.E. 625, 626. However, as already mentioned, there is no ambiguity in this will which would allow a different interpretation from that which we have given it. The word "children" is not, in itself, ambiguous. Indeed, it has a very common and definite meaning upon which attorneys and their clients are entitled to [rely?] when drafting wills. "Children" means immediate offspring, and we reiterate the rule of the Schaufele case (supra, 252 N.Y. at page 67, 168 N.E. at page 831) that it will never be held to include grandchildren "unless the will as a whole shows that unmistakable intent." Only by so holding will there be the stability and consistency so essential to the law of wills if it is to accomplish its function.

The order should be reversed, with costs to all parties appearing and filing briefs, payable out of the estate.

DESMOND, Judge (dissenting). I would affirm here so as to conform this decision to the rule which is ancient in England and in America.

In Prowitt v. Rodman, 37 N.Y. 42 this court nearly a century ago reviewed the already numerous authorities on the question of interpreting the word "children" to include grandchildren and made the statements, many times thereafter repeated in the New York cases, that the word "children" is a "very flexible expression" (at page 55) and (at page 54, quoting Chancellor Kent) that "Children as well as issue may stand in a collective sense for grandchildren, where the justice or reason of the case requires it." . . .

. . .

It seems to me that "reason and justice" dictate that this Villalonga will be construed to mean that if either of the two grandchildren of testatrix should be dead when their second parent dies, the children of the deceased grandchild or grandchildren of testatrix should take. If this be not the meaning, then the testatrix was making a very unusual disposition in that, if one grandchild of hers should survive, that grandchild would get the whole estate to the exclusion of her sister's children, and, if both her grandchildren should fail to survive their parents, their children would get nothing and the estate would go to grandnieces and grandnephews.

Of course, New York cases can be cited on either side of this question but the great majority of them apply the broader meaning. Quite a recent illustration is Matter of Blodgett's Will, 286 N.Y. 602, 35 N.E.2d 940 where we affirmed the determination of the lower courts that "children" included grandchildren.

I suggest that from all these cases taken together there emerge these rules or guides:

(1) That if it is in any way possible the courts, to achieve a reasonable result, construe "children" as including grandchildren. I realize that Matter of Schaufele's Will, 252 N.Y. 65, 67, 168 N.E. 831 says that there must be an "unmistakable intent" to include grandchildren but no other important case agrees to that, and even the Schaufele opinion itself (252 N.Y. at page 67, 168 N.E. at page 831) quotes with approval the ancient Prowitt rule (supra) that grandchildren should be included "when reason demands it";

(2) That while the word "children" is to be taken literally when the testator appears to be referring to his own living children as named individuals (see Matter of Barnes' Will, 2 N.Y.2d 787, 158 N.Y.S.2d 331, 139 N.E.2d 428) the other construction is more appropriate when the "children" are children of his descendants so that he may be considered to be referring rather to a class or group than to individuals;

(3) That, since this is a construction question to be resolved according to reason and probable intent, we ordinarily affirm a not unreasonable construction adopted by the two courts below.

The order should be affirmed.

Fuld, Froessel, Van Voorhis and Burke, JJ., concur with Conway, C.J.

Desmond, J., dissents in an opinion in which Dye, J., concurs.

Note on Per Stirpes and Per Capita

Where there is a gift "to the issue of A" the question arises whether the issue take per capita or per stirpes. If the issue take per capita, all issue who are born before the period of distribution take an equal share. Descendants with living parents share equally with their parents. Thus if A has three children and one of these children has two children, the property is divided into five shares. If the issue take per stirpes, the children of a child of the designated ancestor can take nothing if their parent is alive, and if the parent is dead the children usually take only what the parent would have taken if he were living. Thus if A has three children and one of these three predeceases A, leaving two children surviving A, the property is divided into three shares and the children of the predeceased child divide his one-third. Where there is no claimant who is of the first generation of descendants, Restatement of Property §303 takes the view that the property is distributed among A's issue in such shares as they would have received under the applicable law of intestate succession had A died intestate at the moment of ascertainment of the class membership and owning the property. The effect of this view varies, of course, under the different intestacy statutes. Many intestacy statutes provide that if all issue are related in equal degree to the decedent they share equally. Others provide that the initial division into shares shall be among the oldest generation of which there is at least one living member at the time of distribution, and descendants of this generation will take the shares by representation.[23]

The English courts distributed gifts to the issue of A per capita, on the ground that the word "issue" meant all descendants however remote. This wooden construction, which ignores the average testator's intention, has had some following in the United States — particularly in New York[24] and New Jersey[25] — but in most states a gift to the issue of A is distributed per stirpes.

In drafting a gift to A's issue, words directing distribution "in equal shares" or "share and share alike" should be avoided as these may result in an unwanted per capita distribution. If a per capita distribution is desired, direct it specifically. If a per stirpes distribution is desired, it should also be expressly stated. "To A's issue then surviving per stirpes" will remove doubt about whether survivorship is required (see Problem 1 below), but it will cut out the widow of a child of A who dies without issue before distribution, and the testator may wish to provide for her.

PROBLEMS

1. T devises property "to A for life, then to A's issue per stirpes." At T's death, A has two children, B and C. B dies before A without issue. C survives A. At A's death how is the property distributed? 5 American Law of Property §21.13 (Casner ed. 1952).

2. Samuel devised property to David in trust "for Rose for life, then the property is to be divided among Samuel's three children, David, Sylvia, and Dorothy, one share each, if living; and if any one of them should be then dead, the share of the deceased child shall go to his or her children then living by right of representation." David, son and trustee, misappropriated $40,000 from the trust. After resigning as trustee and executing an agreement acknowledging his indebtedness to the trust estate, David died, leaving two sons, Arthur and Norman. At Rose's death the trust assets are worth $52,000. Sylvia and Dorothy bring suit claiming that the share claimed by Arthur and Norman was forfeited as a result of the misappropriation of trust funds by their father. What result? Would the result be different if the words "if living" were not in the will? Gordon v. Feldman, — Mass. —, 267 N.E.2d 895 (1971). Is an analogy to the law of advancements, page 160, supra, appropriate?

[23] See the problems at page 137, supra.

[24] N.Y. Estates, Powers & Trusts Law §§1-2.11 through 1.2-14 (1967), enacted in 1921, changed the presumption from per capita to per stirpes as to wills which spoke after 1921. Even as to pre-1921 wills, however, New York courts distribute per stirpes if they can find a "faint glimpse" that the testator so intended. 3 Powell, Real Property ¶370 (1970).

[25] A per capita distribution giving A's children and grandchildren equal shares was ordered by a unanimous court in Stickel v. Douglass, 7 N.J. 274, 81 A.2d 362 (1951). In 1952 the New Jersey statutes were amended to provide that, with respect to any will or trust taking effect after 1952, a gift to issue would be distributed per stirpes unless a contrary intent was expressed. N.J. Stat. Ann. §§3A:3A-1 and 3A:3A-2 (1953).

3. Wills draftsmen often define words used in order to avoid ambiguity. The Sisyphus Prize for Heroic Attempts must go to a prominent Detroit law firm which drafted the will of Clyde H. Giltner, late of Tecumseh, Michigan. The will reads:

> (1) The word "descendant" shall mean and include a child, grandchild, great grandchild, great-great grandchild, great-great-great grandchild, and great-great-great-great grandchild, whether by blood, by adoption, or otherwise, of the person whose descendant is referred to, and also any adopted child of any child, grandchild, great grandchild, great-great grandchild or great-great-great grandchild of such person.
>
> (2) The words "child" and "children" shall mean and include, respectively, any child and any children of the person whose child or children is or are referred to by blood, by adoption, or otherwise.
>
> (3) The words "grandchild," "great grandchild," "great-great grandchild," "great-great-great grandchild," or "great-great-great-great grandchild" shall mean and include, respectively, a grandchild, great grandchild, great-great grandchild, great-great-great grandchild, and great-great-great-great grandchild of the person whose grandchild, great grandchild, great-great grandchild, great-great-great grandchild or great-great-great-great grandchild is referred to, whether by blood, by adoption, or otherwise, and also any adopted child of any child, any adopted child of any child of any child, any adopted child of any child of any child of any child and any adopted child of any child of any child of any child of such person.

Suppose Mr. Giltner bequeaths property "to A for life, then to A's children." (1) A has an illegitimate child, B. (2) A adopts his wife, C. (3) A's wife has a baby D during marriage; D is surrendered for adoption and is adopted by Mr. and Mrs. X. (4) A's wife had a previous husband, and their divorce is invalid; A has child E by his wife. (5) A's wife has a child F by artificial insemination by a third-party donor. (6) A gives his brother Y one of his testicles for transplantation (Y's testicles were removed earlier because of cancer); ten months later Y's wife gives birth to G. (7) A takes into his home his niece, H, aged 2, when her parents are killed in an auto wreck; H is reared by A and treated as A's child, but never formally adopted. On A's death do B, C, D, E, F, G, and H share in the bequest of Mr. Giltner? See Thies, A Look to the Future: Property Rights and the Posthumously Conceived Child, 110 Trusts & Estates 922 (1971). For the perpetuities questions that can arise from scientific advances in procreation see page 977, infra.

2. *Adopted Children*

MINARY v. CITIZENS FIDELITY BANK & TRUST CO.
Court of Appeals of Kentucky, 1967
419 S.W.2d 340

OSBORNE, Judge. This is an action for the construction of the will of Amelia S. Minary. The will was executed on the fourth day of April, 1932. After making several bequests of cash to various beneficiaries to pass immediately, the will creates a trust, the income of which is directed to be paid to Thomas J. Minary, husband of Amelia Minary and to her three sons, James S. Minary, Thomas Helm Minary, and Alfred D. Minary. The proceeds of the trust are to be paid in the "absolute and uncontrolled discretion" of the trustees. The trust terminates upon the death of the last surviving beneficiary, and upon termination, the corpus is to be distributed as follows:

> After the Trust terminates, the remaining portion of the Trust Fund shall be distributed to *my* then surviving heirs, according to the laws of descent and distribution then in force in Kentucky, and, if no such heirs, then to the First Christian Church, Louisville, Kentucky.

The testatrix died in 1932 and her husband died in 1935. Left surviving Thomas were two children, Thomas H. Minary, Jr., and Amelia Minary Gant. James and Alfred, the other two sons, died without issue. After testatrix's death, Alfred married Myra Galvin Minary in 1934 and, prior to his death in 1959, he adopted her as his child. The adoption resulted in litigation before this court. See Minary v. Minary, Ky., 395 S.W.2d 588.

The question herein presented is, "Did Alfred's adoption of his wife Myra make her eligible to inherit under the provisions of his mother's will?" More specifically, the question is, "Is Myra included in the term 'my then surviving heirs according to the laws of descent and distribution in force in Kentucky?' "

This has revived a lively question in the jurisprudence of this state and presents two rather difficult legal problems. The first being under what conditions, if any, should an adopted child inherit from or through its adoptive parent? We have encountered little difficulty with the problem of inheriting from an adoptive parent but the question of when will an adoptive child inherit through an adoptive parent has given us considerable trouble. As late as 1945 in Copeland et al. v. State Bank and Trust Company et al., 300 Ky. 432, 188 S.W.2d 1017, we held without hesitation or equivocation that the words "heirs" and "issue" as well as "children" and all other words of similar import as used in a will referred only to the natural blood relations and did not include an adopted child.

In 1950, in Isaacs v. Manning et al., 312 Ky. 326, 227 S.W.2d 418, we adopted the contrary position and held that an adopted child was included in the phrase "heirs at law" wherein a will devised property to designated children and then upon their death to their heirs at law. In the course of the opinion, we said, "where no language [shows] a contrary intent . . . an adopted daughter clearly falls within the class designated." In this case we distinguish the Copeland case, supra.

In 1953, in Major v. Kammer et al., Ky., 258 S.W.2d 506, we again held that an adopted child was included in the term "heirs at law," basing our decision upon the legislative changes made in the adoption laws and overruling Copeland v. State Bank and Trust Company, supra. In Edmands v. Tice, Ky., 324 S.W.2d 491, which was decided in 1959, we held that where testator used the word children, an adopted child could inherit through an adopted parent the same as if heirs at law or issue had been used.

At this point in the evolution of the question in our court we seem to have accomplished a complete 180° turn from the position which we held in 1945 in Copeland v. State Bank and Trust Company, supra. However, our agonies did not cease here, for in 1965 in the case of Wilson v. Johnson, Ky., 389 S.W.2d 634, we overruled Edmands v. Tice, supra, holding that where the word "children" was used in a will the testator uses it in its natural sense or "he is thinking of and [intending] to use the word in its commonly accepted meaning," and thereby restricts the class to those persons who are actually born of the parent or if adopted, were adopted as children.[26]

From the foregoing we conclude that when Amelia S. Minary used the phrase, "my then surviving heirs according to the laws of descent and distribution then in force in Kentucky," she included the adoptive children of her sons. This leaves us with the extremely bothersome question of: "Does the fact that Myra Minary was an adult and the wife of Alfred at the time she was adopted affect her status as an 'heir' under the will?" KRS 405.390 provides: "An adult person . . . may be adopted in the same manner as provided by law for the adoption of a child and with the same legal effect. . . ."

KRS 199.520 provides:

> From and after the date of the judgment the child shall be deemed the child of petitioners and shall be considered for purposes of inheritance and succession and for all other legal considerations, the natural, legitimate child of the parents adopting it the same as if born of their bodies.

It would appear from examination of the authorities that the adoption of an adult for the purpose of making him an heir has been an accepted practice in our law for many years. However, here it should be pointed out that the practice in its ancient form made the person so adopted the legal heir of the adopting party only. This court has dealt with the problem of adopting adults for the purpose of making them heirs on several occasions. . . .

In 1957, in Bedinger v. Graybill's Executors, Ky., 302 S.W.2d 594, we had before us a case almost identical to the one here under consideration. In that case Mrs. Lulu Graybill, in 1914, set up a trust for her son Robert by will. She then provided after the death of the son that the trust "be paid over and distributed by the Trustee to the heirs at law of my said son according to the laws of descent and distribution in force in Kentucky at the time of his death." There was a devise over to others in the event that Robert died without heirs. Robert having no issue adopted his wife long after his mother's death. We held that the wife should inherit the same as an adopted child, there being no public policy against the adoption of a wife. However, it will be noted that in the course of the opinion it is carefully pointed out that the will directed the estate be paid to the "heirs at law of Robert" and did not provide that the estate should go to "my heirs," "his children" or to

[26] Here the adopted parties were step children, both adults at the time of adoption.

"his issue," indicating by this language that if the phrase had been one of the others set out the results might have been different.

In Wilson v. Johnson, Ky., 389 S.W.2d 634, a mother devised her estate to a son Leslie and directed that at the termination of the trust the principal should be divided "equally between the children of Leslie living at that time." Leslie had no issue. He adopted two children of his wife, by a former marriage, who were both adults at the time of the adoption. In holding that the adopted parties could not inherit under the provisions of the trust, we pointed out that the intent of the testator when using the word "children" was to exclude all but children. However, in the course of the opinion we acknowledge that an adult may be adopted in the same manner as a child but stated, unequivocally, that by virtue of that fact "he does not ipso facto become a child." In this case there is no doubt but what the adopted parties were excluded because they were adults at the time of the adoption.

In Pennington v. Citizens Fidelity Bank and Trust Company (Ky. 1965) 390 S.W.2d 671, the appellant was adopted by his wife, Annie, when he was 74 years of age. After her death, he asserted a claim to the estate of her mother, whose will devised the remainder to the "child, or children of my daughter, Annie." Here, we again held that the adopted spouse could not claim under the status of child or children and cited Wilson v. Johnson, supra.

This case could properly be distinguished from Bedinger v. Graybill's Executors, supra, on the basis of the difference in language used in the two wills[;] however, no useful purpose could be served by so distinguishing them. The time has come to face again this problem which has persistently perplexed the court when an adult is adopted for the sole purpose of making him or her an heir and claimant to the estate of an ancestor under the terms of a testamentary instrument known and in existence at the time of the adoption. Even though the statute permits such adoption and even though it expressly provides that it shall be "with the same legal effect as the adoption of a child," we, nevertheless, are constrained to view this practice to be an act of subterfuge which in effect thwarts the intent of the ancestor whose property is being distributed and cheats the rightful heirs. We are faced with a situation wherein we must choose between carrying out the intent of deceased testators or giving a strict and rigid construction to a statute which thwarts that intent. In the Bedinger case there is no doubt but what the intent of the testatrix, as to the disposition of her property, was circumvented. It is our opinion that by giving a strict and literal construction to the adoption statutes, we thwarted the efforts of the deceased to dispose of her property as she saw fit.

When one rule of law does violence to another it becomes inevitable that one must then give way to the other. It is of paramount importance that man be permitted to pass on his property at his death to those who represent the natural objects of his bounty. This is an ancient and precious right running from the dawn of civilization in an unbroken line down to the present day. Our adoption statutes are humanitarian in nature and of great importance to the welfare of the public. However, these statutes should not be given a construction that does violence to the above rule and to the extent that they violate the rule and prevent one from passing on his property in accord with his wishes, they must give way. Adoption of an adult for the purpose of bringing that person under the provisions of a preexisting testamentary instrument when he clearly was not intended to be so covered should not be permitted and we do not view this as doing any great violence to the intent and purpose of our adoption laws.

For the foregoing reasons the action of the trial court in declaring Myra Galvin Minary an heir of Amelia S. Minary is reversed.

The judgment is reversed.

All concur.[27]

NOTES

1. In Ex Parte Libertini, 244 Md. 542, 224 A.2d 443, 21 A.L.R.3d 1008 (1966), an unmarried 56-year-old sergeant in the Women's Army Corps petitioned to adopt a 35-year-old captain in the W.A.C. The chancellor dismissed the petition on the ground that "to declare a person a legal child of an unmarried woman is to declare her to be illegitimate." The Maryland Court of Appeals reversed, pointing out that Maryland statutes permit *any* person, married or unmarried, to adopt any other person. Said the court further: "The effect of the adoption of an adult is the same as that of the adoption of a minor, except as to guardianship. . . . That is, the adopted person is treated as an heir, issue, or an equivalent, in a deed, grant, will, or other written instrument, unless it plainly appears to the contrary by the terms thereof."

A case note in 18 Ala. L. Rev. 178 (1965) states that adoption statutes in thirty-five states and the District of Columbia permit adoption of an adult. See also Wadlington, Adoption of Adults: A Family Law Anomaly, 54 Cornell L. Rev. 566 (1969).

2. No coast-to-coast statement is possible as to whether a child adopted by A is entitled to share in a gift by T to the "children," "issue," "descendants," or "heirs" of A. Adoption was unknown to the common law and "children" and "issue" necessarily connoted a blood relationship. When adoption laws were enacted in the second half of the 19th century, courts were faced with the question of whether an adopted child took under the will of a person who was not the adoptive parent. The early cases were heavily influenced by the inherited reverence for blood relationships; they held an adopted child could not take. These cases gave rise to the stranger-to-the-adoption rule: the adopted child is presumptively barred, whatever generic word is used, except when the donor is the adoptive parent. As adoption became more common and more socially acceptable, courts began to carve exceptions in the stranger-to-the-adoption rule. For example, an adopted child might be permitted to take if he had been adopted before, and not after, the

[27] Discussed in Note, The Dilemma of Adoptees in the Class Gift Structure — The Kentucky Approach: A Rule Without Reason, 59 Ky. L.J. 921 (1971). — Eds.

testator's death. Some courts also drew distinctions between a gift to "A's children" and a gift to "A's issue" or "the heirs of A's body." Unlike the latter terms which were thought to have a biological connotation, a gift to "A's children" presumptively included A's adopted children. Where judicial decisions were found unsatisfactory, legislatures began to intervene in favor of the adopted child. The legislation was seldom retroactive and was sometimes ambiguous. Today in most states adopted children are presumptively included in gifts by T to the "children," "issue," "descendants," and "heirs" of A. But the law of many of these states is likely to have been developed by changing judicial decisions and statutes over the last half century, and whether the adopted child is included may depend on what the law was at testator's death in, say, 1945. The stranger-to-the-adoption concept was not finally abandoned in New York, for instance, until Matter of Park, 15 N.Y.2d 413, 260 N.Y.S.2d 169, 207 N.E.2d 859 (1965), and Matter of Silberman, 23 N.Y.2d 98, 295 N.Y.S.2d 478, 242 N.E.2d 736 (1968). For the development of the law of New Jersey, Rhode Island, and Massachusetts, see In re Thompson, 53 N.J. 276, 250 A.2d 393 (1969).

In Boston Safe Deposit and Trust Company v. Fleming, — Mass. —, 279 N.E.2d 342 (1972), James C. Whitmore died in 1901 devising property in trust for his wife for life; then to his daughter, Grace, for life; then to Grace's issue if any; and if none, to six charitable organizations. In 1901 Mass. Pub. Stats. c. 148, §8, declared that "when the . . . testator is not himself the adopting parent, the child by adoption shall not have, under such an instrument, the rights of a child born in lawful wedlock to the adopting parent, unless it plainly appears to have been the intention of the . . . testator to include an adopted child." In 1958 the Massachusetts statutes were amended to include adopted children within gifts to a "child," "grandchild," "issue," "heir" or "heir-at-law" of a person, but the amendment was confined to instruments executed after its effective date. Grace had no natural-born children, but in 1917 and 1924 she and her husband adopted a boy and a girl. In 1938 Whitmore's widow died; in 1969 Grace died. Grace's adopted children contended that the statute in force in 1901 (and the cases interpreting it) applied only when the contest was between blood issue and adopted issue and not when the contest was between adopted children and a charity. On first hearing before five members of the court, the justices ruled unanimously for the adopted children. On rehearing by the full court, the justices ruled 4 to 3 that the law in force in 1901 prevented the adopted children from taking any interest in the trust. Justice Braucher filed a sharp dissent, accusing the majority of "perverse literalism."

On the rights of adopted children generally to take under the will of someone other than the adoptive parent, see Halbach, The Rights of Adopted Children Under Class Gifts, 50 Iowa L. Rev. 971 (1965); Note, 86 A.L.R.2d 12 (1962).

3. T bequeaths a fund in trust for A for life, then to A's children. After T's death A gives birth to a child B, who is surrendered to, and adopted by, C. On A's death does B share in the fund? Estate of Russell, 17 Cal. App. 3d 758, 93 Cal. Rptr. 824 (1971).

UNIFORM PROBATE CODE

Section 2-611. [*Construction of Generic Terms to Accord with Relationships as Defined for Interstate Succession.*]

Halfbloods, adopted persons and persons born out of wedlock are included in class gift terminology and terms of relationship in accordance with rules for determining relationships for purposes of intestate succession, but a person born out of wedlock is not treated as the child of the father unless the person is openly and notoriously so treated by the father.

3. *"To A and His Children": The Rule in Wild's Case*

The Rule in Wild's Case states two propositions. They are:

(1) If T *devises*[28] *land* to A and his children (or to A and his issue) and A has no children (or issue) at the time of the devise, A takes a fee tail.

(2) If a person transfers property to A and his children (or A and his issue) and A has children (or issue) at the time of transfer, A and his children (or issue) take the fee equally as tenants in common (or as joint tenants if the common law preference for joint tenancy still holds).

This statement is somewhat different from the original statement of the resolutions in Wild's Case (1599), but it is as good a statement of the modern Rule as we can concoct.[29] Both these rules are rules of construction and not rules of law.

First, about the first resolution. The resolution may have been justified originally on the grounds that it carried out the testator's intent. It created a fee tail which would descend to A's children. Then also, the phrase "to A and his children" is very close to standard words creating a fee tail, "to A and the heirs of his body." Today, however, in practically all states the fee tail has been abolished. One would suppose that in these states, at least, the first resolution in Wild's Case would be repudiated, since it does not make sense to have a presumption that a transferor in, say, 1972 would intend to create an estate abolished by the legislature a hundred years ago. But no, the courts did not all adopt any such simple solution. Some did repudiate the first resolution, but others substituted for the fee tail given by the first resolution the estate or estates which the local statute substituted for the abolished fee tail.[30] Where the substituted estate is a fee simple, a new reason — early alienability of land — arises to support the first resolution. Restatement of Property §283 repudiates the result of the first resolution in Wild's Case and adopts the life estate and remainder construction.

Today the second resolution is more justifiable than the first from the view of the transferor's intent. It is more widely followed than the first resolution. It applies

[28] Although the first resolution of Wild's Case, as originally worded, applied only to devises of land, some modern courts have applied it to deeds. See the next case, Ewing v. Ewing.

[29] The Rule in Wild's Case is thoroughly explored by Professor Casner in 5 American Law of Property §§22.16 to 22.28 (Casner ed. 1952).

[30] See page 687, supra.

alike to inter vivos and testamentary transfers and to real and personal property. The effect of this rule is to make A and his children concurrent rather than successive owners.

Where there is a transfer to "A and his children" what are the possible constructions? The construction of "fee simple in A, subject to an executory interest in A's children to take effect upon A's death," seems to have been largely overlooked by the courts. Is this construction preferable to a life estate in A, remainder to A's children?

EWING v. EWING

Supreme Court of Mississippi, 1945

198 Miss. 304, 22 So. 2d 225

ROBERDS, J., delivered the opinion of the court. The question for decision herein is the construction of a deed executed by Mrs. Mollie Waits and her husband E. F. Waits to their daughter Katherine Waits, dated June 20, 1918, and which deed, in the part essential here, reads as follows: "For and in consideration of the sum of One Dollar in hand paid, and for the further consideration of the natural love and affection we have for our daughter, Katherine Waits, we hereby grant, bargain, sell, convey and warrant to her and the children of her body . . . ," the real property described in the deed, reserving to Mrs. Mollie Waits, the then owner, the use thereof during her natural life.

Katherine Waits was an only child of the grantors and when the deed was executed she was sixteen years of age, unmarried, without children. Six years thereafter, and on January 24, 1924, she married Mr. Albert Ewing, Jr., since which time their home has been, and they have resided, in Nashville, Tennessee. Two children have been born of this marriage — Ernest LeRoy Ewing and Albert Ewing III, ages twenty and fifteen years, respectively. Mrs. Mollie Waits departed this life March 24, 1933, and Mr. Waits died November 6, 1938, and Mrs. Katherine Waits Ewing has been in possession of the property since the death of her mother. The property is a lot near the business center of the City of Corinth, Mississippi, upon which is located a two-story frame building.

This bill for construction was filed by the two minor children, through their father as next friend, on behalf of themselves and any and all children who may yet be born to Mrs. Ewing, the mother being respondent to the bill. Complainants assert that they, together with any after-born children of Mrs. Ewing, are either tenants in common with their mother, or that the mother has a life estate and such children the remainder in fee, of said property. The chancellor held that this deed created a fee tail estate, and that Sec. 838, Code 1942, reading "Estates in fee tail are prohibited; and every estate which, but for this statute, would be an estate in fee tail, shall be an estate in fee simple . . . ," converted it into a fee-simple estate in Katherine Waits (Ewing), and dismissed the bill.

As to the contention that appellants are, and that after-born children, if any, will be, tenants in common with their mother and with each other, it will be noted that the grant is immediate and purports to vest title at once, and since there were no children in being on the effective date of the grant, it could not vest in these children the title as tenants in common or as joint tenants. If such children have an interest, it is based upon a life estate in their mother, remainder in fee to them upon her death. The authorities are divided as to whether, in the situation here, there is an implied creation of a life estate in Katherine Waits, remainder to the children of her body at her death, or whether she is granted a fee-simple title absolute. The cases supporting both propositions are too numerous for us to cite, but they will be found and discussed in annotations in 12 L.R.A.(N.S.), page 307; L.R.A. 1917B, page 49; 114 A.L.R., page 618. . . .

In behalf of the life estate–remainder rule it is reasoned that grantors, by mentioning children, evidently intended that the children should take and that it is the duty of the court to give effect to such intent, if that can be done by a reasonable construction of the language used as applied to the facts of each case, and that since the words import an immediate vesting of title, not only to the grantee in being but those not in being, and it is impossible for such vesting to take place as to those not in esse, the only consistent and rational construction is that the testator intended that the named grantee in being should take a life estate and the children, if there should be children, the remainder.

Advocates of the holding that the named living grantee takes an estate in fee go back to the rule in Wild's case, 1599, 6 Coke 16b, 77 Eng. Reprint 277, promulgated, it is reported, by all the judges of England, and known as the "First Resolution in Wild's case," which not only states the rule but some of the reasons therefor, and which is ". . . [if] one deviseth lands to another and to his children or issue, and he hath not any issue at the time of the devise, the same is an estate tail; for the intent of the devisor is manifest and certain that the children or issue should take; and, as immediate devisees, they cannot take because they are not in rerum natura, and by way of remainder they cannot take for that was not his intent, for the gift is immediate; therefore, such words shall be taken as words of limitation." The later cases fix the effective date of a will at the death of the testator and not the date of the will. . . .

On the other hand, Restatement of the Law, and other authorities, accept the life estate and remainder rule. However, it is noted that in many of these cases words are used conveying a different meaning from that conveyed by the words here, or a trust was created, as was the situation in Turner v. Ivy, 5 Heisk. (Tenn.) 222, largely relied upon by appellants.

This court has not passed upon this exact question, although it has adopted the principle announced by the Second Resolution in Wild's case to the effect that where there is a grant or devise to a person and his children or issue, and such person has issue in being at the effective date of such grant or devise, the named grantee and such existing children take an immediate estate as tenants in common. Reddoch v. Williams, 129 Miss. 706, 92 So. 831, 832; Section 834, Code 1942. In that case the devise was to Mrs. Cowan "and her children now living or hereafter born." Mrs. Cowan never had but two children, both living at the date of the codicil and when testator died. Mrs. Cowan had also died; therefore, there was no possibility of other children. It was contended by appellee that the foregoing provision devised a life estate to Mrs. Cowan, remainder to her two children. The Court held that this vested a fee-simple title in Mrs. Cowan and her two living children as tenants in common, the policy of our law preferring estates in common to joint estates. Section 834, Code 1942. The court used this language, "While there is a minority view to the effect that, where a devise includes unborn children, the contention of the appellee is correct, yet the vast majority of the courts hold, and in our judgment the sound view is, that the fee is devised to them as tenants in common."

We think the sounder view, and the one which best accords with the law and public policy of this state is, that where a grant or devise is made to one and his children, or issue, or the children or issue of his body, or equivalent words, and the named person has no child at the effective date of the instrument, that the named person takes a fee-simple title to the property conveyed or devised, unless the instrument by express words or necessary implication, shows a clear intent to create a life estate in the named person, remainder to after-born children or issue. . . .

The relation of life tenant and remainderman is not favored under our land title and economic system. It is common knowledge, as is also shown by the reported cases of this Court, that such relation very frequently engenders disputes, contests, litigation and bitterness between the parties; that it greatly restricts and hampers the use and handling of the property and reduces the income therefrom, and to a large extent takes the property out of the channels of sale and commerce. Some of these disadvantages are illustrated by the case at bar. It is shown that since Katherine Waits has had possession of the property the income therefrom has barely paid the taxes, insurance and repairs thereon. In other words, it has produced no net income. It is further shown that, under the unusual conditions now existing, there is an opportunity to sell it at nine thousand dollars. Now, other children may be born to Mrs. Ewing. If such possible issue has a vested interest in this property, this sale cannot be effectuated, because, of course, it cannot now be known whether there will be future issue, when they will be born, or the number, nor what estate Mrs. Ewing and her two living children now have, or what interest they and the after-born children may have in the property. This means the property can never be sold and title conveyed until the death of Mrs. Ewing, or at least, until such time as it is impossible for issue to be born to her. The net result of that situation is the property, judging by past experience, is practically worthless. This does not mean, of course, that our law prohibits the creation of the relation of life tenant and remainderman. It does mean, however, that we should not strive for a construction to bring about such relation. If one wishes to create the relation, he can do so by apt words, or by necessary implication from those used. We are dealing with words which do not do that, but, on the contrary, by their common, ordinary meaning, convey and vest, directly and immediately, an estate in common.

. . .

Affirmed.[31]

[31] Noted 46 Colum. L. Rev. 306; 17 Miss. L.J. 428. — Eds.

NOTE

A court of equity may direct or approve a sale of property where infants or unborn persons have interests therein and a sale is reasonably necessary for the protection of the estate or the needs of the beneficiaries. Where the land is unproductive and a full and adequate price can be obtained, as the Mississippi court found was true in Ewing v. Ewing, such necessity has been found. Why did not the court order sale on these grounds? This procedure is permitted in Mississippi. Kelly v. Neville, 136 Miss. 429, 101 So. 565 (1924).

SECTION E. Gifts to Heirs

1. *Gifts to Heirs of the Testator*

In re LATIMER'S WILL
Supreme Court of Wisconsin, 1954
266 Wis. 158, 63 N.W.2d 65

Petition by Laurence H. Williams, trustee of the trust created by the last will and testament of Mary L. Latimer, deceased, in the alternative for construction of either the last will of said deceased, or of the final decree entered in the probate proceedings of said will on July 18, 1924.

The will of Mary L. Latimer was executed at Delavan, Wisconsin, on February 11, 1920. At that time testatrix was eighty-three years of age and owned property in the approximate amount of $240,000. Her husband had died in 1904, and her only daughter had died in 1898. The only heir at law and next of kin of the deceased was Mary Widney, a granddaughter, being a child of the deceased daughter. This granddaughter was twenty-one years of age at the time of the making of the will and at that time had been married for about two years but had no children. Testatrix, in her will, bequeathed seven money legacies aggregating $18,000, and the residue of the estate was bequeathed in trust to two named trustees. The material portion of such residuary clause provided as follows:

> Said Trustees shall pay the net annual income arising from said trust estate to my granddaughter, Mary Widney, for and during her natural life; said Trustees shall also pay to my said granddaughter the sum of Five Thousand ($5,000.00) Dollars of the principal of said trust estate five years after the date of my death, and shall also pay to the said Mary Widney the sum of Five Thousand ($5,000.00) Dollars of the principal each fifth year thereafter during the natural life of my said granddaughter.
>
> In case my said granddaughter shall die leaving issue her surviving, I hereby direct that the income from said trust estate be paid in equal parts to such issue,

share and share alike, until they respectively arrive at the age of twenty-one years, and then the rest, residue and remainder of my trust estate shall be turned over, delivered and paid to them in equal parts, share and share alike, as they each reach twenty-one years of age, as their absolute property forever.

If any such issue die before reaching the age of twenty-one years, then the share of said income belonging to such issue so dying shall be paid to the heirs of the body of such issue, and when such issue if living would have reached the age of twenty-one years, the share in said rest, residue and remainder of said estate of such issue shall be turned over, delivered and paid to the said heirs.

If any such issue die without heir of the body before reaching the age of twenty-one years, then the share of said income and said rest, residue and remainder of said estate belonging to such issue shall be paid, turned over and delivered to the survivor or survivors thereof, but *if there be no survivor, or if my said granddaughter die without issue, or heirs of the body thereof, then I give, devise and bequeath the rest, residue and remainder of my estate to my heirs and the heirs of my late husband, James F. Latimer, one-half to my heirs and one-half to the heirs of said James F. Latimer*. (Emphasis supplied.)

Testatrix died August 7, 1923; her will was duly admitted to probate. . . .

The granddaughter, Mary Widney, died on October 8, 1952, without ever having had any issue born to her.

Testatrix originally had five sisters and one brother, all of whom predeceased her, except one sister, who was seventy-eight years of age at the time of making the will. In addition to such sister, she was survived by fourteen nephews and nieces, who were children of her deceased sisters and brother.

There were no brothers or sisters of James F. Latimer living at the time of the death of testatrix, but there were fifteen nephews and nieces, being the children of deceased brothers and sisters of James F. Latimer. Only one of such nephews and nieces, Alice Latimer, also known as Alice Jane Latimer, who was forty years older than Mary Widney, survived the death of Mary Widney on October 8, 1952. Alice Latimer died testate on February 20, 1953, and David B. Latimer, executor of her estate, is the appellant herein.

A hearing was held on the petition by the trustee for construction. In addition to the aforementioned petition by the trustee for construction in the alternative of the will or final decree, Alice Latimer also petitioned the court for an order directing the trustee to transfer one-half of the trust property held in his hands as of the date of the death of Mary Widney to Alice Latimer, alleging that she was the sole heir at law of James F. Latimer, as of the date of the death of the life tenant. A hearing was held upon both petitions and judgment was entered therein under date of July 8, 1953, the material portion of which is as follows:

It is further ordered and adjudged, that the residue and of the trust estate as of October 5, 1952, plus accrued income since said date be and hereby is assigned and the trustee is hereby directed to distribute said estate in accordance with the terms of the Last Will and Testament of Mary L. Latimer, deceased, one-half to the heirs of Mary L. Latimer and one-half to the heirs of her husband, James F. Latimer, said groups to be determined in accordance with the Wisconsin Statutes of Descent and Distribution as of the date of the death of Mary L. Latimer on August 7, 1923.

No appeal was taken as to that part of said judgment which assigned one-half of the trust residue to the heirs of Mary L. Latimer, but the executor of the estate of Alice Latimer has appealed from that portion of the judgment assigning the remaining one-half of such trust residue to the heirs of James F. Latimer, and denying the petition of Alice Latimer.

CURRIE, Justice. The sole question presented upon this appeal is whether the heirs of James F. Latimer (the deceased husband of testatrix), who were to take one-half of the trust residue upon the death of Mary Widney (the life beneficiary), are to be determined as of the date of the death of the testatrix or as of the date of the death of the life beneficiary.

The general rule is that when a will provides for a limitation over to the "heirs" of the testator or of some other person already deceased, to be determined by a statute governing the intestate succession of property, following the expiration of a life estate, the determination of the class of persons who qualify as such heirs is to be made as of the date of the death of the testator *unless an intent of the testator to have such determination made as of the death of the life tenant "is found from additional language or circumstances."* 3 Restatement, Property, p. 1706, sec. 308.

We, therefore, must turn our inquiry to resolving the issue of whether there is additional language in the will or other circumstances present in the instant case which would establish an intent on the part of the testatrix that the heirs of her deceased husband should be determined as of the death of the granddaughter, Mary Widney. In the absence of any such additional language or circumstances so establishing such an intent, the general rule would apply that such heirship must be determined as of the date of testatrix's own death, which latter result was the one reached by the learned trial court.

Counsel for the appellant rely on several provisions in the will and other circumstances as establishing an intent on the part of testatrix that the persons, who are to take as heirs of her deceased husband, were to be determined as of the death of the life beneficiary. However, we find it necessary to consider only two of such points so advanced, they being:

(1) Mary Widney, the life beneficiary, was the sole heir at law of James F. Latimer, deceased husband of testatrix, as of the date of the death of testatrix; and

(2) The remainders provided for by the testatrix, after the death of the granddaughter, Mary Widney, to the children of Mary Widney, or to the issue of such great-grandchildren, or upon said great-grandchildren failing to reach age twenty-one to their issue, and for the gift over upon failure of issue of Mary Widney to the heirs of testatrix and her deceased husband, are alternative remainders and thus necessarily contingent remainders.

Inasmuch as Mary Widney was the sole heir at law of her grandfather, James F. Latimer, at the time of the death of testatrix, Mary L. Latimer, in 1923, there would be an incongruity if the will were to be construed as requiring the heirs of James F. Latimer to be determined as of the date of the death of testatrix instead of at the date of death of Mary Widney. If such heirship were determined as of date of death of testatrix, the only person who would qualify as being an heir of James F. Latimer under our statutes governing the descent and distribution of intestate property was Mary Widney, the life beneficiary. Respondents contend that such incongruity is avoided if the words of the will "*heirs of said James F. Latimer*" be construed as "*heirs of said James F. Latimer excluding Mary Widney*". However, to reach such result a reformation of the language of the will is necessary. Furthermore, such construction attempts to make persons heirs at law of James F. Latimer who never were such heirs.

On the other hand, if the will should be construed as requiring the determination of the class of persons, who are to take as heirs at law of James F. Latimer, to be made as of the date of the death of the life beneficiary, there is no incongruity present and therefore no necessity of reforming the language of the will.

This aspect of the case is one of first impression in this court. The courts of other jurisdictions are divided on the question, and from the decisions of these other courts we are provided with ample precedent for deciding the issue either way. However, the Restatement has adopted the rule that an incongruity is present, if the gift over to heirs following a life estate to the sole heir at law is to be construed as requiring the heirship to be determined as of date of death of the testator. 3 Restatement, Property, p. 1715, sec. 308, comment k., states:

> If a person to whom a prior interest in the subject matter of the conveyance has been given is the sole heir of the designated ancestor at the death of such ancestor, there is some incongruity in also giving such person all the interest under the limitation to "heirs" or "next of kin". The incongruity is especially great when a will conveys property "to B and his heirs but if B dies without issue to my heirs" and B is the sole heir of A. The incongruity is almost as great when A, by will, conveys property "to B for life then to my heirs" and B is the sole heir of A. *Thus, the fact that in such cases, B is the sole heir of A at the death of A tends to establish that A intended his heirs to be ascertained as of the death of B*, so that B is prevented from sharing in the limitation to the heirs of A. (Emphasis supplied.)

. . .

We take cognizance of the fact that the framers of the Restatement on Property were specialists in this field of the law and were selected for such task because of their recognized ability as the leading authorities in the nation on this particular subject. Undoubtedly they fully considered the existing conflict in the decisions and framed comment k., sec. 308, 3 Restatement, Property, in the light of that which they thought the correct rule ought to be. We, therefore, adopt such principle enunciated by the Restatement, and hold that it is directly applicable to the fact situation of the case at bar.

Respondents cite the decisions in Brown v. Higgins, 1923, 180 Wis. 253, 193 N.W. 84, and In re Cowley's Will, 1904, 120 Wis. 263, 97 N.W. 930, 98 N.W. 28, as requiring that the class of persons who take as heirs of James F. Latimer be determined as of the death of testatrix rather than upon the death of the life beneficiary. A study of the facts in such two cases, however, discloses that they are readily distinguishable from those of the instant case. In neither case were the life beneficiaries the sole heirs at law of the testator. In the first mentioned case testator was survived by a wife and seven children, and one son was the life beneficiary, while in the second case testator was survived by a wife and eight children, and two daughters were the life beneficiaries. Therefore, by determining heirship as of the date of the death of testator in those two cases there was not present the incongruity of the remaindermen not being heirs at law of the testator as of the date of testator's death. In commenting on this fact situation, 3 Restatement, Property, p. 1717, sec. 308, comment k., states:

> When the taker of a prior interest is one of several heirs of the designated ancestor at the ancestor's death, no constructional tendency is sufficiently definite to be capable of statement.

In 2 Simes, Law of Future Interests, p. 234, sec. 422, the author states, "While the cases are not in harmony, most courts refuse to determine the testator's heirs as of the death of the sole heir [life beneficiary] in the absence of some additional indication of an intent to that effect." . . .

However, there is another circumstance present in the instant case, in addition to the fact that Mary Widney, the life beneficiary, was the sole heir at law, which tends to establish that the heirship of James F. Latimer was intended by testator to be determined as of the date of the death of Mary Widney rather than that of testatrix. Such circumstance lies in the alternative remainders provided in the will.

. . .

The New York courts in numerous cases have held that, where there are alternative remainders of this kind created by will so that the ultimate gift over to heirs or next of kin is contingent upon the beneficiary of a prior estate not being survived by issue, the determination of those who take as heirs or next of kin is to be determined as of the time of the ending of the life estate which results in the gift over to heirs or next of kin becoming operative, and not as of the date of the death of the testator. Salter v. Drowne, 1912, 205 N.Y. 204, 98 N.E. 401; Matter of Brewster's Estate, 1936, 246 App. Div. 192, 283 N.Y.S. 707, affirmed without opinion 271 N.Y. 599, 3 N.E.2d 204; In re Fishel's Estate, 1938, 167 Misc. 145, 3 N.Y.S.2d 669, affirmed without opinion 256 App. Div. 915, 10 N.Y.S.2d 859, leave to appeal denied 280 N.Y. 851, 20 N.E.2d 397.

. . .

While we are not prepared to lay down a hard and fast general rule that, where a will provides for an alternative remainder to heirs contingent upon whether or not the life beneficiary is survived by issue, such heirs are always to be determined as of the death of the life beneficiary, we do conclude that such circumstance may well indicate an intent to postpone determination of the class of persons who are to take as heirs until the happening of the contingency which converts such a contingent remainder into a vested one. This would seem to be particularly true in those cases where the occurrence of the contingency would be likely to occur a long time in the future, with the further likelihood that the contingency might never occur. In such cases there obviously would be no intent on the part of the testator that any persons alive at the death of testator would benefit from the contingent gift over.

Turning to the facts of the instant case, we have a situation that when testatrix made her will in 1920 her granddaughter, Mary Widney, was but twenty-one years old and recently married. Her life expectancy according to the American Experience Table of Mortality was forty-one and one-half years, and, in addition to that factor, there was every likelihood that she would have children and be survived by them or their issue. There was only a remote possibility that the gift over to her heirs and those of her husband would ever occur. Furthermore, if such a contingency did occur it was unlikely that the nephews and nieces of her husband living at the time of the making of the will, who were then of middle age or beyond would survive such event. For example, his niece, Alice Latimer, was then sixty-two years of age. Any intent to benefit heirs then living of her husband or herself would seem to be entirely lacking. On the contrary, the clause providing for the remainder over to heirs was most likely inserted with the intent that in the event of the happening of such contingency the undistributed balance of the trust should go to those persons who then constituted the heirs of her husband and herself. The court in its opinion in the New York case of Matter of Brewster's Estate, supra, emphasized somewhat the same argument based upon the young ages of the two daughters who by the will in that case were named as life beneficiaries.

In those cases in which a vesting of a contingent remainder to heirs is likely to take place many years after the death of testator, and after the death of testator's living collateral relatives, there are great practical difficulties if heirship is to be determined as of the date of testator's death, instead of the date of the happening of such uncertain future contingency. For example, the estates of at least four of the nephews and nieces of James F. Latimer were probated in Walworth county subsequent to the death of testatrix, and no interest in the trust estate was inventoried in those estates or assigned in the final decrees. If the heirs of James F. Latimer who are now to take a half of the residue were to be determined as of the date of the death of testatrix, all of these estates would have to be opened up. If a testator or testatrix were to give any thought to these possibilities occurring, would he or she not seek to avoid this by having the class of persons who are to take as heirs determined as of the date of the occurrence of such contingency?

. . .

To summarize, the fact that the life beneficiary, Mary Widney, was the sole heir at law of James F. Latimer, both at the time testatrix made her will, and at the time she died, would cause an incongruity if the determination of the class, who were to take as the heirs of James F. Latimer, were to be made as of the death of testatrix, which result would be avoided by determining such heirship as of the death of Mary Widney. Added to this, we have the additional circumstance of the alternative remainders, the particular one under which the heirs of James F. Latimer were to take being contingent upon whether the life beneficiary, a young married woman of an age when the birth of children to her was to be expected, was survived by issue. Under the authorities cited these circumstances are such as to manifest an intent on the part of testatrix that the heirs of James F. Latimer who were to take under the will be determined as of the death of Mary Widney. We, therefore, are constrained to conclude that the will should be so construed.

Counsel for respondents contend that this result will work an injustice in the instant case because one-half of the residue will be distributed in accordance with the will of Alice Latimer, she being the only heir at law of James F. Latimer living at the time of the death of Mary Widney, so that the descendants of the other nephews and nieces of James F. Latimer will take nothing because of the provisions of section 237.01(4), Stats.[32] There are several obvious answers to this contention. One is that this is an unexpected result which it is unlikely testatrix could have contemplated because the respective ages of Mary Widney and Alice Latimer were such that the former would have normally outlived the latter by many years, Mary Widney having been born in 1898, while Alice Latimer was born in 1858, and was ninety-four years old when she died. Another is that if testatrix had given any thought at the time of making her will as to which of the two dates the heirs of James F. Latimer should take would bring about the most equitable result (which we doubt that she did) it might well have occurred to her that the better result might well be obtained by having the class of heirs determined as of the date of the occurrence of the contingency that would enable them to take. This is so because, if such determination of heirs were made as of her own death, persons who were no blood relatives of James F. Latimer might be the ones to ultimately come into enjoyment of part of the estate, by reason of the possibility of husbands of nieces of James F. Latimer inheriting from their wives. Lastly, the best answer is that the intent of testatrix must be construed from the language of the will as of the time it was drafted in the light of the then surrounding circumstances, and not in the light of what developed many years later.

That part of the judgment appealed from is reversed and cause remanded for further proceedings consistent with this opinion.

NOTES

1. In Continental Illinois Nat'l Bank & Trust Co. of Chicago v. Eliel, 17 Ill. 2d 332, 161 N.E.2d 107 (1959), the court held that heirs were to be ascertained at the

[32] Wis. Stat. Ann. §237.01 (1957) provides for the following intestate distribution:

"(3) If the intestate leave no lawful issue nor widow nor widower nor father nor mother the estate shall descend in equal shares to the intestate's brothers and sisters and to the lineal descendants of any deceased brother or sister by right of representation.

"(4) If the intestate leave no lawful issue, widow, widower, father, mother, brother nor sister the estate shall descend to the intestate's next of kin in equal degree, except that when there are two or more collateral kindred in equal degree, but claiming through different ancestors, those who claim through the nearest ancestor shall be preferred to those claiming through an ancestor more remote." — Eds.

death of the ancestor, but such persons must survive to the time of distribution in order to take. Consider the effect of this decision on the following facts: T devises property "to A for life, then to A's issue, and if A dies without issue to T's heirs." At T's death A, B, and C are his heirs. B dies before A, leaving a child D. At A's death without issue, C takes all.

2. Is the following clause adequate to cover the problems raised where there is an end-limitation to testator's heirs? "Any of the trust estate not disposed of under the foregoing provisions shall go and be distributed to my legal heirs, their identity and their respective shares to be determined in all respects as though my demise had occurred immediately following the happening of the event requiring such distribution, and according to the laws of succession of the State of Wisconsin then in force."

3. For an illuminating study of the factors, other than the language of the instrument, which move decision in cases involving the meaning of "heirs," see Simes, Knouff, & Leonard, The Meaning of "Heirs" in Wills — A Suggestion in Legal Method, 31 Mich. L. Rev. 356 (1933). Factors involved included increasing alienability, keeping the property in the family of the testator, equality of distribution, favoring natural objects of testator's bounty, and effecting testator's probable intent.

MASSACHUSETTS GENERAL LAWS C. 184, §6A (1964): "In a limitation of real or personal property to a class described as the 'heirs' or 'next of kin' of a person, or described by words of similar import, to take effect in enjoyment upon the happening of an event within the period of the rule against perpetuities, the class shall, unless a contrary intention appears by the instrument creating such limitation, be determined as if such person died at the time of the happening of such event."

2. *Gifts to Heirs of the Grantor: Herein of The Doctrine of Worthier Title*

HATCH v. RIGGS NATIONAL BANK

United States Court of Appeals, District of Columbia Circuit, 1966

361 F.2d 559

Leventhal, Circuit Judge. Appellant seeks in this action to obtain modification of a trust she created in 1923. The income terms of the trust instrument are of a spendthrift character, directing the trustees to pay to the settlor for life all the income from the trust estate "for her own use and benefit, without the power to her to anticipate, alienate or charge the same . . . ." Upon the death of the settlor-life tenant, the trustees are to pay over the corpus as the settlor may appoint by will; if she fails to exercise this testamentary power of appointment, the corpus is to go to "such of her next of kin . . . as by the law in force in the District of Columbia at the death of the . . . [settlor] shall be provided for in the distribution of an intestate's personal property therein." No power to appoint the corpus by deed, nor any power to revoke, alter, amend or modify the trust, was expressly retained by appellant, and the instrument states that she conveys the property to the trustees "irrevocably."

Appellant does not claim that the declaration of trust itself authorizes her to revoke or modify the trust. In effect she invokes the doctrine of worthier title, which teaches that a grant of trust corpus to the heirs of the settlor creates a reversion in the settlor rather than a remainder in his heirs. She claims that since she is the sole beneficiary of the trust under this doctrine, and is also the settlor, she may revoke or modify under accepted principles of trust law.

The District Court, while sympathizing with appellant's desire to obtain an additional stipend of $5000 a year, out of corpus, "to accommodate recently incurred expenses, and to live more nearly in accordance with her refined but yet modest tastes," [33] felt that denial of the requested relief was required by this court's decision in Liberty National Bank v. Hicks, 84 U.S. App. D.C. 198, 173 F.2d 631, 9 A.L.R.2d 1355 (1948). Summary judgment was granted for appellees. We affirm.

I

The Hicks case involved a spendthrift trust created by Hicks in which all income was reserved to the settlor for life; at his death, half of the corpus was to go, by detailed provisions not relevant here, to his children or their issue, and the other half according to his will or, lacking a will, to his heirs at law according to the statutes of descent of the District of Columbia. The trust, by the terms of the trust agreement, was irrevocable. Hicks subsequently executed an instrument revoking the trust and demanded that the trustees turn over the corpus to him. The bank refused, and Hicks brought an action to have the trust declared void as a spendthrift trust against public policy. The court, noting that any rules against spendthrift provisions were for the protection of creditors, held that the settlor could not invoke the invalidity of his own trust to revoke it. It further held that revocation was not effected because, with [respect?] to both halves of the trust, Hicks had not obtained the consent of all beneficiaries.[34] With respect to the second half of Hicks' trust, analogous to the one set up by appellant in the case at bar, the court stated (84 U.S. App. D.C. at 202, 173 F.2d at 635):

> . . . Hicks reserved no right of disposition except by last will, in the absence of (failing) which it is to pass to his heirs-at-law. This provision of the trust shows,

[33] In her complaint, appellant also sought an additional $50,000 from corpus to purchase a residence, but dropped this request at the hearing. The District Court found that there was "no suggestion of extravagance" in appellant's way of life or in her request for additional funds. She now lives in a one-bedroom apartment in a modest residential section of Long Beach, California, and has no assets except limited jewelry, furniture, personal effects, and a medium-priced automobile.

[34] "[A] trust once validly constituted may not thereafter be terminated without the consent of all the cestuis que trust. This includes not only those specially named but those then unborn who may take on the expiration of the trust according to the terms." 84 U.S. App. D.C. at 201, 173 F.2d at 634. The court relied on an earlier opinion to the same effect in Hurt v. Gilmer, 59 App. D.C. 282, 40 F.2d 794 (1930).

> we think, that as to it Hicks intended to and did reserve only the right to dispose of it by testamentary appointment. This right continues, but, except as it provides, Hicks in creating this trust retained no control or estate, save his life interest in the income. His present effort, contrary to the terms of the trust, to alter and amend its limitations, must, therefore, be held for naught. This is the rule applied by the Maryland Court of Appeals in Allen v. Safe Deposit & Trust Co., 177 Md. 26, 7 A.2d 180, which we adopt and approve.

In neither the Hicks case nor the Allen case which it followed did the court address itself to the doctrine of worthier title. The abbreviated discussion in Hicks may be taken as an implied rejection of that doctrine, though it was not discussed, for if the doctrine of worthier title were applicable, then the gift over to heirs-at-law would not be effective to create a remainder interest making their consent, as beneficiaries, a condition to revocation of the trust. This appeal squarely raises the question, and we deem it appropriate that we rely not on the aura of Hicks, but on an express consideration of the applicability of the doctrine of worthier title.

The doctrine of worthier title had its origins in the feudal system which to a large extent molded the English common law which we inherited. In its common law form, the doctrine provided that a conveyance of land by a grantor with a limitation over to his own heirs resulted in a reversion in the grantor rather than creating a remainder interest in the heirs. It was a rule of law distinct from, though motivated largely by the same policies as, the Rule in Shelley's Case. Apparently the feudal overlord was entitled to certain valuable incidents when property held by one of his feoffees passed by "descent" to an heir rather than by "purchase" to a transferee. The doctrine of worthier title — whereby descent is deemed "worthier" than purchase — remained ensconced in English law, notwithstanding the passing of the feudal system until abrogated by statute in 1833.

The doctrine has survived in many American jurisdictions, with respect to inter vivos conveyances of both land and personalty, as a common law "rule of construction" rather than a "rule of law." In Doctor v. Hughes, 225 N.Y. 305, 122 N.E. 221 (1919), Judge Cardozo's landmark opinion reviewed the common-law history of the doctrine and concluded that its modern relevance was as a rule of construction, a rebuttable presumption that the grantor's likely intent, in referring to his own heirs, was to reserve a reversion in his estate rather than create a remainder interest in the heirs. Evidence might be introduced to show that the grantor really meant what he said when he spoke of creating a remainder in his heirs. "Even at common law," wrote Cardozo, "a distinction was taken between grants to the heirs as such, and grants where the reference to heirs was a mere descriptio personarum." But to overcome the presumption that a reversion rather than a remainder was intended, "the intention to work the transformation must be clearly expressed." 122 N.E. at 222.

In the decades that followed, the worthier title doctrine as a rule of construction with respect to inter vivos transfers won widespread acceptance.[35] The "modern" rationale for the rule is well stated in an opinion of the Supreme Court of California:

[35] See Restatement, Property, §314(1) (1940); Restatement (Second), Trusts, §127 Comment b (1959); Annot., 16 A.L.R.2d 691 (1951).

> It is said that where a person creates a life estate in himself with a gift over to his heirs he ordinarily intends the same thing as if he had given the property to his estate; that he does not intend to make a gift to any particular person but indicates only that upon his death the residue of the trust property shall be distributed according to the general laws governing succession; and that he does not intend to create in any persons an interest which would prevent him from exercising control over the beneficial interest. . . . Moreover, this rule of construction is in accord with the general policy in favor of the free alienability of property, since its operation tends to make property more readily transferable.[36]

While the weight of authority, as just indicated, supports the retention of the doctrine of worthier title (unlike its common-law brother, the Rule in Shelley's Case) as a rule of construction, there has been substantial and increasing opposition to the doctrine.[37]

The views of the critics of the doctrine, which we find persuasive against its adoption, and borne out by the experience of the New York courts in the series of cases which have followed Doctor v. Hughes, supra, may be summarized as follows. The common-law reasons for the doctrine are as obsolete as those behind the Rule in Shelley's Case.[38] Retention of the doctrine as a rule of construction is pernicious in several respects.

First, it is questionable whether it accords with the intent of the average settlor. It is perhaps tempting to say that the settlor intended to create no beneficial interest in his heirs when he said "to myself for life, remainder to my heirs" when the question is revocation of the trust, or whether creditors of the settlor's heirs should be able to reach their interest. But the same result is far from appealing if the settlor-life beneficiary dies without revoking the trust and leaves a will which makes no provision for his heirs-at-law (whom he supposed to be taken care of by the trust). In short, while the dominant intent of most such trusts may well be to benefit the life tenant during his life, a subsidiary but nevertheless significant purpose of many such trusts may be to satisfy a natural desire to benefit one's heirs or next of kin. In the normal case an adult has a pretty good idea who his heirs will be at death, and probably means exactly what he says when he states in the trust instrument, "remainder to my heirs."

It is said that the cases in which such is the grantor's intent can be discerned by an examination into his intent; the presumption that a gift over to one's heirs creates a reversion can thereby be rebutted in appropriate cases. But the only repository of the settlor's intent, in most cases, will be the trust instrument itself. Nor would it

[36] Bixby v. California Trust Co., 33 Cal. 2d 495, 202 P.2d 1018, 1019 (1949). See also McKenna v. Seattle-First Nat. Bank, 35 Wash. 2d 662, 214 P.2d 664, 16 A.L.R.2d 679 (1950).

[37] See, e.g., Simes, Fifty Years of Future Interests, 50 Harv. L. Rev. 749, 756 (1937); Note, 48 Yale L.J. 874 (1939); Note, 39 Colum. L. Rev. 628, 656 (1939); Comment, 34 Ill. L. Rev. 835, 850-51 (1940). A recent study of the subject by Professor Verrall of the University of California, under the auspices of the California Law Revision Commission, resulted in a strong condemnation of the doctrine. Verrall, The Doctrine of Worthier Title: A Questionable Rule of Construction, 6 U.C.L.A.L. Rev. 371 (1959).

[38] The Rule in Shelley's Case (1 Coke Rep. 104) has been abolished by statute in the District of Columbia. D.C. Code §45-203 (1961 ed.).

be fruitful or conducive to orderly and prompt resolution of litigation to engage in searches for other sources of intent. In the typical case of this genre — a stark, unqualified "to myself for life, remainder to my heirs" — the instrument will send forth no signals of contrary intent to overcome the presumption that only a reversion was intended. Yet this is precisely the class of cases in which settlors are likely to have intended to create beneficial interests in their heirs.

A lengthier document may send forth more signals, but they may well be murky. Where other indicia of intent can be discovered in the trust instrument, with the aid of ingenious counsel, the result, as the New York cases have demonstrated, is a shower of strained decisions difficult to reconcile with one another and generative of considerable confusion in the law.[39] After three decades of observing the New York courts administer the rule of construction announced in Doctor v. Hughes, supra, Professor Powell of Columbia observed that "there were literally scores of cases, many of which reached the Appellate Division, and no case involving a substantial sum could be fairly regarded as closed until its language and circumstances had been passed upon by the Court of Appeals. . . . This state of uncertainty was the product of changing an inflexible rule of law into a rule of construction." [40]

An excellent example of this confusion is the effect to be given the fact that, as in the case at bar, the settlor has reserved the power to defeat the heirs' interest by appointing the taker of the remainder by will. One might well think that the reservation of a power of appointment was an index of intent which buttressed the presumption of a reversion by demonstrating that the settlor did not wish to create firm interests or expectations among his heirs, but intended to retain control over the property. Most courts, including the New York Court of Appeals in its most recent pronouncement on the subject, have disagreed, albeit over the voice of dissent.[41] They have reasoned that the retention of the testamentary power of appointment confirms the intent to create a remainder in the heirs, since the settlor would not have retained the power had he not thought he was creating a remainder interest in the heirs.

We see no reason to plunge the District of Columbia into the ranks of those jurisdictions bogged in the morass of exploring, under the modern doctrine of worthier title, "the almost ephemeral qualities which go to prove the necessary intent." [42] The alleged benefit of effectuating intent must be balanced against the resulting volume of litigation and the diversity and difficulty of decision.[43] We are not persuaded that the policy of upholding the intention of creators of trusts is best effectuated by such a rule of construction, with its accompanying uncertainty.

[39] The New York cases are admirably summarized and discussed in Verrall, op. cit. supra note [37], at 374-387.

[40] Powell, Cases on Future Interests 88 n.14 (3d ed. 1961).

[41] In re Burchell's Estate, 299 N.Y. 351, 361, 87 N.E.2d 293, 297 (1949); see Comment, 34 Ill. L. Rev. 834, 844-45 (1940).

[42] In re Burchell's Estate, supra, 299 N.Y. at 361, 87 N.E.2d at 297 (1949).

[43] These results led Judge Fuld to call for "clarifying legislation." Dissent in In re Burchell's Estate, supra.

The rule we adopt, which treats the settlor's heirs like any other remaindermen, although possibly defeating the intention of some settlors, is overall, we think, an intent-effectuating rule. It contributes to certainty of written expression and conceptual integrity in the law of trusts. It allows heirs to take as remaindermen when so named, and promises less litigation, greater predictability, and easier drafting. These considerations are no small element of justice.

We hold, then, that the doctrine of worthier title is no part of the law of trusts in the District of Columbia, either as a rule of law or as a rule of construction. Any act or words of the settlor of a trust which would validly create a remainder interest in a named third party may create a valid remainder interest in the settlor's heirs. It follows that the District Court was correct in granting summary judgment for appellees in this case, since appellant's action is based on the theory that she was the sole beneficiary and hence could revoke the "irrevocable" trust she had created.

II

Appellant's invocation of worthier title was premised in part on the injustice alleged to result in many cases from holding such a trust irrevocable. The irrevocability was supposed to be riveted into the trust by the impossibility of obtaining consent to revocation from all the beneficiaries, since some of them are still unborn. Appellant's argument reflects a misunderstanding of the consequence of the judgment of the District Court.

It is hornbook law that any trust, no matter how "irrevocable" by its terms, may be revoked with the consent of the settlor and all beneficiaries.[44]

The beneficiaries of the trust created by appellant are herself, as life tenant, and her heirs, as remaindermen. Her heirs, if determined as of the present time, are her two sisters. There is no assurance that they will in fact be the heirs who take the remainder under the trust; appellant might survive one or both. Yet their consent is necessary, we think, to revocation, since they are at least the persons who would be beneficiaries if the settlor died today.[45]

In addition, it is necessary to protect the interests of those additional persons, both living and unborn, who may, depending on circumstances, be members of the class of heirs at the time the corpus is distributed. We think that upon an adequate showing, by the party petitioning to revoke or modify the trust, that those who are, so to speak, the heirs as of the present time consent to the modification, and that there is a reasonable possibility that the modification that has been proposed adequately protects the interests of those other persons who might be heirs at the time the corpus is to be distributed, the District Court may appoint a guardian ad litem to represent the interests of those additional persons.

Although the question has not been previously discussed by this court we think basic principles of trust law are in accord with appointment of a guardian ad litem

[44] Restatement (Second), Trusts §338(1) (1959); Scott, Trusts §338 (2d ed. 1956).

[45] One of the sisters is not sui juris. In referring to her consent, we do not mean to exclude consent by her guardian ad litem.

to represent interests of unborn or unascertained beneficiaries, for purposes of consent to modification or revocation of a trust. This use of a guardian ad litem is not uncommon in other jurisdictions. In a number of states authority for such appointments is provided by statute.[46] These statutes reflect a broad sentiment of the approaches that are consistent with the Anglo-American system of law and adopted to promote the objective of justice. Where it is at least debatable whether rulings must await express legislative authorization, this court must take into account the fact that the legislature for the District of Columbia is primarily concerned with awesome questions of national policy, and we should be more ready to accept our obligation as a court to refine and adapt the corpus of law without waiting for a legislative go-ahead. Here we are certainly in a field where it is not inappropriate for courts to act without statutory foundation, as appears from the well-considered authority cited in the margin.[47] "Courts of justice as an incident of their jurisdiction have inherent power to appoint guardians ad litem." [48] The efficacy of a guardian ad litem appointed to protect the interests of unborn persons is no different whether he be appointed pursuant to statute or the court's inherent power. Given such protection, the equitable doctrine of representation embraces the flexibility, born of convenience and necessity, to act upon the interests of unborn contingent remaindermen to the same effect as if they had been sui juris and parties.

The use of guardians ad litem to represent interests of unborn and/or otherwise unascertainable beneficiaries of a trust seems to us wholly appropriate. Though the persons whose interests the guardian ad litem represents would be unascertainable as individuals, they are identifiable as a class and their interest, as such, recognizable.

The settlor seeking to revoke or modify the trust may supplement his appeal to equity with a quid pro quo offered to the heirs for their consent. In many cases it

[46] E.g., Cal. Code Civ. Proc. §373.5; Ill. Rev. Stat. ch. 22, §6 (1959); Restatement, Property §182, Comment e (1936). The leading case upholding such appointments is Gunnell v. Palmer, 370 Ill. 206, 18 N.E.2d 202, 120 A.L.R. 871 (1938), noted in 34 Ill. L. Rev. 101 (1939), where the court viewed the statute as providing the same protections to unborn persons as traditional doctrines of equitable representation. See also Wogman v. Wells Fargo Bank & Union Trust Co., 123 Cal. App. 2d 657, 267 P.2d 423, 429 (1954); Reynolds v. Remick, 327 Mass. 465, 99 N.E.2d 279 (1951). Compare Mullane v. Central Hanover Bank & Trust Co., 339 U.S. 306, 317-318, 70 S. Ct. 652, 94 L. Ed. 865 (1950).

[47] Peoples Nat. Bank v. Barlow, 235 S.C. 488, 112 S.E.2d 396, 398-399 (1960). A few courts have held, to the contrary, that no guardian ad litem for the interests of unborn beneficiaries may be appointed in the absence of express statutory authorization. E.g., Moxley v. Title Ins. & Trust Co., 154 P.2d 417 (Cal. Dist. Ct. App. 1945), decided before the California statute, supra note [46], was passed. That decision, it should be noted, was affirmed by the California Supreme Court, 27 Cal. 2d 457, 165 P.2d 15, 163 A.L.R. 838 (1946), with no discussion of this point; Justice Traynor, dissenting, relied on an earlier California holding that appointment of a guardian ad litem for unborn beneficiaries was proper. 165 P.2d at 26. The Restatement expressly takes no position as to whether the general power of equity, apart from statute, includes the power to appoint such a guardian. Restatement, Property, §182, Comment e (1936).

[48] Mabry v. Scott, 51 Cal. App. 2d 245, 124 P.2d 659, 665, cert. denied sub nom. Title Ins. & Trust Co. v. Mabry, 317 U.S. 670, 63 S. Ct. 75, 87 L. Ed. 538 (1942). See also Smith v. Lamb, 103 Ga. App. 157, 118 S.E.2d 924, 927 (1961) (power to appoint guardian ad litem an "incident of courts"); 27 Am. Jur., Infants §120, pp. 840-41 ("The power to appoint a guardian ad litem is inherent in every court of justice."). Compare Rule 17(c), Fed. R. Civ. P.

may well be consistent with or even in furtherance of the interest of the heirs to grant such consent. The case at bar provides a good example. Here the interest of all heirs is contingent, since appellant can defeat their remainder by exercising her testamentary power of appointment. If the modification agreed upon not only increased the annual income of the life tenant but also transferred assets in trust for the benefit of the heirs, without any power of alteration in the settlor, the heirs' remainder interest would be secure, and accordingly more valuable than it is now. The pattern of such a modification is clearly available where the remaindermen of a trust are specific named persons, and, we think, should also be available where the remaindermen are recognizable as a class even though the members of the class are not now individually ascertainable.

Appellant, proceeding on a different theory, has not taken steps to obtain the consent of heirs. We think it important to make clear that, in rejecting the doctrine of worthier title, we do not mean to put settlors and life tenants of trusts in which the remaindermen are the settlor's heirs at an unwarranted disadvantage with respect to legitimate efforts to modify trust arrangements concluded largely for their own benefit. Our affirmance of the judgment for appellees is without prejudice to a future submission by appellant on such a basis.

Affirmed.[49]

NOTE, TRUSTS: MODIFICATION OF IRREVOCABLE TRUSTS THROUGH APPOINTMENT OF A GUARDIAN FOR UNBORN HEIRS — REPUDIATION OF WORTHIER TITLE DOCTRINE

66 Colum. L. Rev. 1552, 1554-1560 (1966)

Originating in feudal custom, the doctrine of worthier title[50] has achieved surprising longevity in the United States. Under the rule in its classic formulation, a trust which creates a life estate in the settlor or another, with the corpus to pass at his death to the settlor's heirs, establishes a reversion in the settlor rather than a remainder in his heirs. Although the doctrine is no longer an invariable rule of law,

[49] Noted 16 Am. U.L. Rev. 345; 33 Brooklyn L. Rev. 583; 16 Catholic U.L. Rev. 239; 66 Colum. L. Rev. 1552; 42 Notre Dame Law. 542; 41 N.Y.U.L. Rev. 1228; 28 Ohio St. L.J. 166; 42 Wash. L. Rev. 919. — Eds.

[50] The doctrine has been defined as follows:

If a person makes an inter vivos conveyance with an ultimate end limitation to his own heirs or next of kin, the end limitation is void in the sense that it designates purchasers, and the grantor retains a reversionary interest.

Morris, The Inter Vivos Branch of the Worthier Title Doctrine, 2 Okla. L. Rev. 133, 134 (1949).

Under the feudal system the overlord was entitled to the valuable incidents of relief when an heir inherited land. . . . These incidents were preserved if, in an inter vivos conveyance by A "to my heirs," the limitation to the heirs of A was deemed a nullity.

Restatement, Property §314, comment a (1936).

it subsists as a rebuttable rule of construction in many jurisdictions.[51] The finding of a reversion rather than a remainder entails significant consequences. Upon this determination may hinge the inclusion of the property within the estate of the settlor for tax purposes, the ability of creditors to reach the trust property, and the settlor's power to dispose of the property. More importantly, the finding of a reversion affects the settlor's power to revoke or modify the trust. As holder of the reversion and the life estate, the settlor is the sole beneficiary and hence is able to alter the trust to accommodate unforeseen exigencies. In a recent case, the Court of Appeals for the District of Columbia Circuit repudiated the doctrine of worthier title, yet salvaged a method for securing modification of the trust.

I. THE INSTANT CASE

[The opinion in Hatch v. Riggs National Bank, 361 F.2d 559 (D.C. Cir. 1966), the last principal case, is summarized.]

II. EPITAPH FOR THE DOCTRINE

The history of the worthier title doctrine reflects the conflict of two principles: the desire to effectuate the intent of the particular settlor, and the need for a rule which is clear and predictable in its application. The classic version of the rule was unambiguous; under its terms property left to the heirs of the settlor was to revert to his estate. But this approach often led to the frustration of the settlor's purpose, for he might well have intended to vest — at the time of the creation of the trust — an interest in those who would become his heirs when he died. The rule was subsequently modified to permit recognition of settlor's intent; while a grant to the heirs of the settlor was presumed to create a reversion, that presumption could be rebutted by evidence clearly establishing a contrary intent. By contrast, the instant case represents a return to a rigid model which is not dependent upon a showing of the particular settlor's desires. Under the rule set forth in this case, a remainder apparently is created in the heirs irrespective of the actual purpose of the settlor.

The court's conclusion that, in this context, the interest in certainty outweighs the benefits achieved through inquiry into actual intent seems well justified. Assessment of the particular settlor's purpose in using the words "to my heirs" is a precarious and often futile task. The evidence of actual intent is often sparse or ambiguous. As a result, an examination of such evidence will rarely avoid the frustration of actual intent — and even then only at the cost of grave impairment of the rule's certainty. Since the formation of trusts is usually a well-counselled act — more so than most other legal actions — a high premium should be placed on clarity and

[51] Restatement, Property §314, comment a (1936); 2 Scott, Trusts §127.1 (1956). Doctor v. Hughes, 225 N.Y. 305, 122 N.E. 221 (1919), a Cardozo decision, helped provoke the change from a rule of law to one of construction, rebuttable by a clear expression of the settlor's intent to create a remainder interest in his heirs.

predictability. In this context, the best guarantee of the fulfillment of settlor's intent is the lawyer's awareness that the use of a particular term will, with relative certainty, have defined legal consequences.

. . .

III. A GUARDIAN AD LITEM FOR THE INTERESTS OF THE UNBORN

Trusts purporting to be irrevocable ordinarily may be modified or revoked if the consent of all beneficiaries is obtained. Yet a valid remainder interest in the settlor's heirs establishes a class of beneficiaries whose members cannot be ascertained until the settlor's death. The court in the instant case felt that while the individual beneficiaries might not yet be identifiable their interest as a class was cognizable. It therefore suggested the appointment of a guardian ad litem to represent these unborn interests.

The court's contention that the appointment of a guardian for this purpose falls within the inherent power of a court of equity is based on less than overwhelming authority. Many sources, speaking with reference to infants and other incompetents, have asserted the broad proposition that judicial power to appoint guardians inheres in equitable jurisdiction.[52] But the cases cited in the instant decision which broach the specific issue of representation for unborn heirs do not unequivocally affirm the proposition. Peoples Nat'l Bank v. Barlow,[53] for example, holds only that a guardian may be appointed to contest the issue of whether unborn heirs have any legal right under the will there in question. The case supports the instant decision only in dictum.[54] As a general rule, courts have been reluctant to appoint guardians to represent the unborn in the absence of specific legislative authorization. Nonetheless, the exercise of such authority is both reasonable and consonant with equitable principles. Determination of the rights of living persons should not be held in abeyance because of tenuous and contingent future interests, especially when ade-

[52] Woerner's treatise on guardianship flatly states that the power is inherent in every court, including those of justices of the peace. Woerner, Guardianship of Minors and Persons of Unsound Mind §21, at 64 (1897). Mr. Justice Field considered "the general authority of courts of equity over the persons and estates of infants" unquestioned. Insurance Co. v. Bangs, 103 U.S. 435, 438 (1881) (dictum).

[53] 235 S.C. 488, 112 S.E.2d 396 (1960).

[54] See id. at 495, 112 S.E.2d at 399. The Barlow case at one point implies a distinction between proceedings to determine whether unborn heirs possess any legal interests and proceedings to affect their recognized interests. However, the court does not state that the distinction is determinative, or that an appointment of a guardian in the latter situation would be invalid. Ibid. Mabry v. Scott, 51 Cal. App. 2d 245, 124 P.2d 659 (Dist. Ct. App.), certiorari denied, 317 U.S. 670 (1942), another case cited in the instant decision, sanctions the appointment of guardians to represent the unborn, but this approval is given in cursory fashion and as an alternative ground of decision. See also Gertman v. Burdick, 123 F.2d 924 (D.C. Cir. 1941), where, in a suit seeking construction of a will, a guardian ad litem was appointed to represent infants and their unborn issue. The case resembles Barlow in that the effort was made to determine whether the unborn issue had any interest at all, not to affect an established interest; at the same time, the case was appropriate for use of the doctrine of virtual representation and a guardian was not strictly necessary for the unborn issue.

quate safeguards may be erected for these future interests. Appointment of a guardian may be viewed as a constructive aspect of the necessary exercise of jurisdiction over trusts and other property. Thus the court's decision, though lacking in authoritative support, represents a proper extension of prior theory.

A similar device — the doctrine of equitable or virtual representation — has been employed to determine and affect the interests of unborn heirs.[55] Under that doctrine, the unascertainable unborn interests are represented by living heirs.[56] The primary prerequisite to such representation is a relationship sufficiently close to guarantee an identity of interest between the living and unborn; as applied to the class of heirs at law, the doctrine assumes the existence of a nexus between living heirs and unborn potential heirs sufficient to justify representation. The appointment of a guardian ad litem should afford more substantial protection for the interests of the unborn than reliance upon representation by living heirs. While the actions of both a virtual representative and a guardian may be subject to the court's scrutiny, the guardian — as an officer of the court — acts in a formal fiduciary capacity. Moreover, unlike the virtual representative, he is responsible for negligent representation and may be the object of a criminal prosecution. Finally, in the case of modification, the guardian should be less susceptible to collusion than the virtual representative, who is more intimately concerned with the disposition of the trust property.

IV. ADEQUATE PROTECTION FOR THE UNBORN HEIRS

While the court sought to preserve an avenue of modification for trusts creating a remainder interest in heirs, it was also concerned with the protection of unborn or unascertainable interests. The opinion indicates that before any guardian ad litem will be appointed, the party seeking modification must demonstrate a "reasonable possibility" that the proposed modification will "adequately protect" the undeterminable future heirs. The precise meaning of adequate protection is not revealed, but it can be inferred that the court intended a fair exchange for value to be a prerequisite to modification. The decision states that a settlor seeking modification may offer a quid pro quo to the representatives of future interests. This comment is not merely a suggestion, however, for a guardian's consent to modification without securing some benefit would probably not fulfill his fiduciary obligations.

In the absence of decisions under the new standard, the practical effect which these safeguards will have upon the process of modification is difficult to calculate. Certainly, abrogation of the doctrine of worthier title itself impairs the ease of modification. The finding of a reversion greatly facilitates modification, for the settlor, as holder of the residual beneficial interest, may consent to modification for virtually

[55] See, e.g., Mabry v. Scott, 51 Cal. App. 2d 245, 124 P.2d 659 (Dist. Ct. App.), certiorari denied, 317 U.S. 670 (1942). Although virtual representation is usually applied to secure an effective judgment involving title to land, no obstacle prevents its extension to the field of trusts; indeed, the Restatement of Property specifically countenances such an application. Restatement, Property §180, comment b (1936).

[56] See Restatement, Property §183 (1936).

any reason. Social policy may favor alterability in the face of changed circumstances, irrespective of the actual intent of the settlor on this issue.[57] The finding of a remainder interest in the heirs necessarily complicates the process, for then approval of modification will not always be forthcoming as a matter of course.

The primary question, however, is whether the safeguards for the unborn interests outlined in the instant case will excessively impede modification. The protective requirement of a fair exchange for value will not necessarily impose an unwarranted burden. Often, as in the instant case, consideration may be found in a solidification of the heirs' position; that is, the settlor might renounce a previously reserved testamentary power of appointment. Even where no such power has been retained by the settlor, a basis for exchange may be available. Thus, the settlor may transfer other assets to the corpus in exchange for modification of the income provisions.[58] Or the settlor might agree to leave additional property to his heirs, so that they might receive at his death a substantial benefit beyond the corpus of the existing trust.[59] Similarly, a settlor might agree to purchase and transfer to the trust particular assets — for example, a house — with the funds obtained by modification; upon his death, the house as well as its furnishings would go to the heirs.

Significant problems are encountered, however, where the settlor has parted with all substantial assets and needs increased income merely to subsist. If the trust limitation were in favor of specific heirs, an appeal to familial devotion might suffice to secure consent to modification. Recourse to this emotional appeal would apparently be precluded by the scheme outlined in the instant case, for the responsibilities of guardianship ostensibly exclude such factors from consideration. Nor is it clear that the doctrine of virtual representation countenances modification on the basis of emotional factors. Consent to any significant diminution in the heirs' interest would seem to disqualify living representatives from binding the unborn.[60] If it could be presumed that distant and collateral unborn heirs are moved by considerations of familial devotion, the problem would be resolved; but such a presumption would not accurately reflect reality.[61] Moreover, this rationale evaporates where the

[57] Historically, one basis for retention of the doctrine of worthier title has been its utility in allowing modification where the settlor's circumstances have changed. In many of the cases which provoked the resurrection of the doctrine in the 30's, the prior economic disaster of the Depression had left the parties seeking modification in dire straits. See 23 U. Pitt. L. Rev. 1030, 1031 (1962).

[58] This device might be especially useful where the only substantial asset the settlor possessed was the stock of a closely held corporation for which there was no immediate market.

[59] A settlor might arrange this same result by agreeing not to write a will.

[60] See Restatement, Property §185, comment d (1936). The Restatement result may be unduly harsh, for instance, in the case in which there was small likelihood of unascertainable heirs ever materializing. For example, if the owner of the life estate — the settlor — was an aged person with a substantial number of elderly children who themselves were childless, there would be virtually no possibility of anyone but the living children taking the remainder interest. Preventing modification — in the face of the children's approval — on the basis of improbable unborn interests, would produce an extremely unfair result. Perhaps the court in the instant case was aware of such possibilities when it chose to phrase its suggestion of a quid pro quo in less than mandatory terms — using the words "may" and "many" rather than "must" and "all." Permitting a court to adapt the requirements of consideration according to such probabilities would be consonant with both justice and practicality.

[61] The more contingent the nature of these unborn interests, the more appealing creation of

settlor seeks modification in behalf of a life beneficiary who is not a member of the same family as the settlor and the heirs. It will be incumbent upon the courts, then, to weigh the role to be accorded considerations of familial devotion in subsequent cases arising under either guardianship or virtual representation.

CONCLUSION

Repudiation of the doctrine of worthier title represents a forthright effort to rid the law of a concept which has bred confusion and uncertainty. In the process, however, this reform has created serious obstacles to the modification of trust agreements. These difficulties will not be entirely obviated through the warning to drafters provided by the new rule; the fact that a settlor should foresee the legal implications of creating an irrevocable trust, and the possibility of new exigencies, will not prevent settlors from ignoring such possibilities or the courts from mitigating harsh results. Experience will demonstrate, therefore, whether the scheme for modification outlined in the instant case is a viable one. If the results of the new procedure do not prove satisfactory, they will at least be helpful in precipitating ameliorative legislation.[62]

NEW YORK ESTATES, POWERS & TRUSTS LAW (1967)

§6-5.9. Where a remainder is limited to the heirs or distributees of the creator of an estate in property, such heirs or distributees take as purchasers. [Effective Sept. 1, 1967]

§7-1.9(b). For the purposes of this section [revocation of trusts], a disposition in a trust created on or after September first, nineteen hundred fifty-one, in favor of a class of persons described only as the heirs, next of kin or distributees (or by any term of like import[63]) of the creator of the trust does not create a beneficial interest in such persons. [Effective Sept. 1, 1951]

On the doctrine of worthier title see generally Johanson, Reversions, Remainders, and the Doctrine of Worthier Title, 45 Texas L. Rev. 1 (1966).

---

such a presumption would be. However, it is clear that the attribution of any feeling to unborn heirs is fictional, and probably over-speculative.

62 After the Hatch case was decided, a guardian ad litem was appointed to represent the settlor's potential heirs in that case. Agreement was reached among the existing heirs, the guardian ad litem of the unborn heirs, and the settlor to modify the trust. The trustee objected on the grounds that the court did not have the authority to appoint a guardian ad litem for unborn persons without explicit statutory authority. In Hatch v. Riggs National Bank, 284 F. Supp. 396 (D.D.C. 1968), the court held that it did have such authority without statutory authorization, and approved the modification of the trust. — Eds.

63 In In re Dodge's Trust, 25 N.Y.2d 273, 250 N.E.2d 849 (1969), it was held that "surviving lawful representative issue" is not a term of like import with "heirs" — even though the settlor had five children and his surviving issue would very likely be his heirs. — Eds.

3. *Gifts to Heirs of a Transferee: Herein of The Rule in Shelley's Case*

A simplified statement of the Rule is:

If (1) one instrument
(2) creates a life estate in land in A, and
(3) purports to create a remainder in A's heirs, and
(4) the estates are both legal or both equitable,

the remainder becomes a remainder in fee simple in A.[64] The doctrine of merger may then come into play and cause the life estate to merge into the remainder, giving A a fee simple. The rule as traditionally stated applies only to remainders and not to executory interests.[65] Unlike other rules in this chapter, which are rules of construction, the Rule in Shelley's Case is a rule of law and applies regardless of the intent of the transferor.

PROBLEMS

State the effect of the Rule in Shelley's Case upon each of the following transfers of land:

1. To A for life, then to A's heirs if A survives B.
2. To A for ninety-nine years if he so long live, then to A's heirs.
3. Deed of land from O to A for life. O then devises the land to A's heirs.
4. To X in trust for the benefit of A and on A's death to convey to A's heirs.

McRORIE v. CRESWELL
Supreme Court of North Carolina, 1968
273 N.C. 615, 160 S.E.2d 681

Plaintiffs instituted this action to determine the title to a 60-acre tract of land in Cabarrus County known as the southern half of lot No. 1 of the George M. Misenheimer estate. This property is described by metes and bounds in paragraph 2 of the complaint. The allegations of the complaint, which are admitted by the answer plus additional averments in defendant's further answer, established these facts.

Plaintiffs Grace Taylor McRorie and Elizabeth Taylor Burgess are the only children and heirs of Rosanna Misenheimer Taylor, who died intestate in Cabarrus

[64] An elaborate statement of the rule, with all the fanciful distinctions courts have drawn to prevent its operation, may be found in Note, 29 L.R.A. (n.s.) 965 (1911). See also 3 Powell, Real Property ¶¶378-379 (1970); Simes & Smith, The Law of Future Interests §§1541-1572 (2d ed. 1956).

[65] But see Dukeminier, Contingent Remainders and Executory Interests: A Requiem for the Distinction, 43 Minn. L. Rev. 13, 20 (1958).

County on 26 December 1965. Rosanna Misenheimer Taylor was the daughter of George M. Misenheimer, deceased, whose holographic will was probated in Cabarrus County in January 1907. Pertinent portions of the will, which devised the property in suit, are these:

"I want enough of land sold to pay my debts.

"I bequeath and give the balance of my land and other property, except my mill property, to my beloved wife, Sarah, and & [*sic*] daughter Rosanna Misenheimer — their lifetime. Provided Rosanna has no heirs, Then it shall go to C. W. Misenheimer my son, his life time and then to go to his heirs at his death.

"My interest in the mill property with what he owes me goes to C. W. Misenheimer."

On 29 January 1936, Rosanna Misenheimer Taylor and husband, George Taylor, by a deed which contained no covenants of warranty, conveyed her interest in the property in suit to Harry A. Martin. On 28 March 1936, Harry A. Martin and wife quitclaimed the property to Oza Mae Creswell. From that date until her death in 1951 Mrs. Creswell exercised exclusive dominion over the land. Defendant Billy Ray Cresswell, her son and heir, claims the property by inheritance from her. He went into possession of the land at her death and adds his possession to hers.

When the case came on for trial, plaintiffs moved for judgment on the pleadings. The court, being of the opinion that all material facts were established by the pleadings and that the controversy involved only a question of law, entered judgment "that the superior title and right to possession" of the property described in the complaint, as against defendant, ought to be, and the same is hereby decreed to plaintiffs, Grace Taylor McRorie and Elizabeth Taylor Burgess. Defendant excepted to the judgment and appealed.

SHARP, Justice. The controversy between the parties to this action involves the interpretation of the will of George M. Misenheimer (testator). The pleadings raise no issue of fact on any material proposition. Thus, the rights of the parties must be determined as a matter of law on the undisputed facts contained therein. Phillips v. Gilbert, 248 N.C. 183, 102 S.E.2d 771. It follows, therefore, that the trial court was empowered to render its judgment upon the pleadings. 3 Strong, N.C. Index, Pleadings §30 (1960).

The trial court based its decision upon the following rationale: Testator devised to Rosanna Misenheimer (Taylor) a life estate in the land in suit and, by implication, he devised the remainder in fee to her children, the plaintiffs. Rosanna's deed to Martin, therefore, conveyed to him only her life estate in the property. Consequently, his quitclaim deed to Mrs. Creswell gave her only an estate per autre vie, and it was this estate which her son, defendant, inherited. Upon the death of Rosanna on 25 December 1965, plaintiffs' estate vested and defendant's terminated.

Defendant's contention is that under the Rule in Shelley's Case Rosanna acquired a fee defeasible upon her death without children. This same contention was made and held to be feckless in Taylor v. Honeycutt, 240 N.C. 105, 81 S.E.2d 203. In that case, a controversy without action, Rosanna Misenheimer (Taylor), the mother of plaintiffs herein, and her husband sought to secure specific performance of their contract to convey to the defendant Honeycutt a fee simple title to the lands in suit here. Honeycutt declined to accept the plaintiff's tendered deed upon the ground that the title offered was only a life estate. Rosanna contended: (1) that testator devised the land to her for life with remainder (by implication) to her heirs; (2) that the word "heirs" was used in its technical sense; and (3) that this language vested the fee simple title in her under the Rule in Shelley's Case.

One of the prerequisites for the application of the Rule in Shelley's Case is that the words "heirs" and "heirs of the body" be used in their technical sense and not descriptio personarum denoting children, issue, a particular class, or individual persons. Tynch v. Briggs, 230 N.C. 603, 54 S.E.2d 918; Hampton v. Griggs, 184 N.C. 13, 113 S.E. 501, 34 A.L.R. 952; 4 Strong, N.C. Index, Wills §32 (1961). In Taylor v. Honeycutt, supra, the trial court rejected Rosanna's contention that the Rule in Shelley's Case operated to give her a fee. It ruled that by his use of the word "heirs" in the phrase "Provided Rosanna has no heirs," testator meant issue. In affirming the judgment for the defendant, this Court said: "When the testator, after devising a life estate to the feme plaintiff, added, 'provided Rosanna has no heirs,' the land was to go to his son, C. W. Misenheimer, for life, etc., the word 'heirs' referred plainly to children or issue of the feme plaintiff. . . . Rosanna could not die without heirs in a general sense as long as C. W. Misenheimer, her brother, or any of his lineal descendants, lived.

"Our decision is that the feme plaintiff (Rosanna) acquired and now owns a life estate in the land and that the judgment of the trial court must be affirmed." Id., 240 N.C. at 109, 81 S.E.2d at 206.

The Court pointedly refrained from further interpretation of the will because none of Rosanna's children (plaintiffs herein) or grandchildren and none of the children or grandchildren of C. W. Misenheimer, were parties to the case agreed, nor was there any representation of unborns who might have acquired an interest in the property upon the death of Rosanna. The judgment and decision in that case is binding only on the parties and those in privity. Notwithstanding the difference in parties, the well established legal principles which dictated the decision in Taylor v. Honeycutt, supra, control here. Rosanna's interest in the property was clearly a life estate, and when she died her two children (plaintiffs) took the remainder in fee by clear implication.

"[T]he doctrine of devise or bequest by implication is well established in our law." Finch v. Honeycutt, 246 N.C. 91, 98, 97 S.E.2d 478, 484. The rule with us is succinctly stated in 3 Restatement of Property §272 (1940) as follows: "When property is limited by an otherwise effective conveyance 'to B for life, and if B dies without issue, then to C' or by other words of similar import, then, unless a contrary intent of the conveyor is found from additional language or circumstances, an inference is required that the conveyor has limited an interest in favor of the issue of B, in the event that B dies survived by issue." Accord, 1 Mordecai, Law Lectures pp. 494-495 (1916); 28 Am. Jur. 2d Estates §202 (1966). See Annot., "Gift to issue, children, wife, etc., as implied from a provision over in default of such persons," 22 A.L.R.2d 177 (1952).

In Hauser v. Craft, 134 N.C. 319, 46 S.E. 756, the testator devised and bequeathed certain personal property to his granddaughter, Katherine, "to be hers during her natural life only; and should the said Katherine Scott die without leaving any child or children, then the property which I have given to her to be divided among the rest of my heirs." The surviving children of Katherine claimed that they took the remainder in fee upon her death. The defendants claimed that Katherine took a fee defeasible upon her death without children. They asserted that since children survived her, she had an absolute fee and (as here) claimed title by mesne conveyances from her. The Court, reasoning as follows, held that Katherine's children, by implication, took the remainder at her death:

"It will be observed that Katherine had only a life estate, and therefore at her death all of her interest ceased and determined. The heirs of the testator could not take unless she died without children, because it expressly provided by the will that they should take only upon the contingency of her dying without leaving children, and the fact that she died leaving children completely divested the testator's heirs of all right or title in the land. . . . If the estate of Katherine expired at her death, and the heirs cannot take because she left children, who then can take unless it be the children? . . . The implication is not only necessary, but irresistible, that in the situation of the parties as now presented to us, and giving to the will of the testator a natural and reasonable construction, it was intended by him that the plaintiffs should be the objects of his bounty and should take the property in remainder after the death of their mother." Id. at 327-328, 46 S.E. at 759-760. Cf. Whitfield v. Garris, 134 N.C. 24, 45 S.E. 904.

To the same effect is West v. Murphy, 197 N.C. 488, 149 S.E. 731, where the testator devised land to his granddaughter, Bertie Hill, "so long as she should live, and if no children, then to her brother, Frank Hill." Bertie Hill died leaving her surviving a child. This Court held that the child took a remainder in the land by implication upon the termination of his mother's estate.

An examination of testator's holographic will leaves it uncertain whether he placed a comma or a period after the phrase "Provided Rosanna has no heirs." Defendant's contention that "a period would seem to be the proper punctuation mark," and that the phrase should be disregarded as surplusage is untenable.

"That a will is couched in ungrammatical language and is incorrectly punctuated are facts of little importance in construing it. Commas may be inserted for periods, or vice versa, in order to accomplish the paramount object, which is the ascertainment of the testator's will or meaning." Hauser v. Craft, supra, 134 N.C. at 323-324, 46 S.E. at 758. As Parker, J. (now C.J.), said in Clayton v. Burch, 239 N.C. 386, 389, 80 S.E.2d 29, 31. "When necessary to accomplish the testator's intent as ascertained from the context of the will, the court may disregard improper use of capital letters, punctuation, misspelling and grammatical inaccuracies, especially where the will is written by an unlearned person."

We have noted that the pleadings in this case do not disclose whether Sarah Misenheimer, the wife of testator, is still alive. Although it was stipulated in Taylor v. Honeycutt, supra, 240 N.C. at 107, 81 S.E.2d at 204, that she died prior to 1954, we cannot consider that fact as admitted in this case. Her existence, however, is immaterial to decision here. The judgment entered in the court below adjudicated plaintiffs' rights only as against defendant.

The judgment of the trial court is

Affirmed.

ORME v. NORTHERN TRUST CO., 29 Ill. App. 2d 75, 172 N.E.2d 413 (1961). Testatrix bequeathed her estate in trust to pay the income to her three granddaughters for life, and on the death of her three grandchildren to divide the corpus equally among the "children or heirs" of the grandchildren, "one-third to the child or children, heir or heirs" of each grandchild. The court held that "children or heirs" meant issue, and not heirs in the technical sense, and therefore the Rule in Shelley's Case did not apply. For their work on this case the court allowed attorneys fees of $221,901.33 or 14 percent of the estate. If this will had been litigated immediately after the death of testatrix, so that the statute of limitations would not bar liability, should the draftsman of this will be required to pay $221,901.33 to the estate?

The Modern Status of the Rule in Shelley's Case

The Rule in Shelley's Case has been abolished in thirty-nine states and the District of Columbia, as well as in England. In only five states — Arkansas, Delaware, Indiana, North Carolina, and Washington — is it reasonably certain the rule still lives.[66] In some states, however, the abolition by statute is fairly recent and does not apply retroactively.[67]

SECTION F. Gifts Over on Death Without Issue

BROWN v. ROBBINS

Court of Chancery of New Jersey, 1948

142 N.J. Eq. 169, 59 A.2d 378

Kays, Vice-Chancellor. The bill of complaint is filed to obtain the construction of the will of William T. Brown who died May 7, 1916. The will was admitted to probate by the Surrogate of Essex County on June 1, 1916.

The will was drawn by the testator who was not a lawyer and without the aid of counsel. The testator provided for his wife as follows:

"I hereby will and bequeath unto my beloved wife, Mary Spalding Brown, the entire income from my estate, real and personal, during her life time.

[66] See 3 Powell, Real Property ¶380 (1970); Simes & Smith, The Law of Future Interests §1563 (2d ed. 1956); Note, 99 A.L.R.2d 1161 (1965).

[67] See, e.g., Tex. Rev. Civ. Stat. Ann. art. 1291a (1962, Supp. 1971), abolishing the Rule in Shelley's Case as to transfers taking effect on or after January 1, 1964.

"In case of my death it is my wish that my said wife, Mary Spalding Brown, and my daughter, Harriet Irene Brown, be appointed executors for the settling of my estate, and after the estate is settled that they act as trustees of the estate."

The will contained no clear and definite statement as to when the trust should terminate. However, it contains the following provisions:

"Should any one of my children die without issue, the portion of such deceased child shall be divided equally among the remaining chidren [*sic*].

"Should any of my children die after having children in lawful marriage, it is my desire that the child or children of such deceased child shall have the use of the said parent's portion in other words the use and income from my estate, after my death and that of my wife, is to be divided into four parts, each child to share and share alike, and each child's children, in the case of the death of said child, shall have the use of the said parent's portion."

The testator was survived by his wife and four children. A daughter, Harriet Irene Brown, died July 28, 1934 unmarried and without issue. Her portion of the estate thereupon passed to the testator's other three children. Mary Spalding Brown, the wife of the testator, died July 15, 1940.

The complainants are the three children of the testator and the grandchildren of the testator who have obtained their majority. The defendant is a grandchild of the testator, a minor under the age of fourteen years, and appears by his guardian ad litem. There are no issue of the testator other than the complainants and the minor defendant.

Complainants pray for the determination of the following questions:

(1) Did the trust created by the will terminate upon the death of the testator's wife on July 15, 1940, and should the complainants, trustees, distribute the assets of the trust to the testator's surviving children, or does the trust continue and shall the trustees continue to administer it;

(2) If the trust did not terminate upon the death of the testator's wife, the question is, how long does it continue:

(a) Is the entire estate to be held in trust until the death of the last survivor of the testator's children, or

(b) Is there a trust for each of the testator's children which terminates and becomes distributable as each such child dies?

Complainants take the position that the trust terminated upon the death of the testator's wife on July 15, 1940. The defendant, on the other hand, after filing a brief contending that the trust did not terminate upon the death of the wife and that the entire estate is to be held in trust until the death of the last survivor of the testator's children, or, in the alternative, that there is a trust for each of the testator's children which terminates and becomes distributable as each child dies, now recedes from that position and concedes that it is untenable in the light of previous adjudications of the courts in this state.

The testator, as stated, does not expressly dispose of the corpus of his estate upon the termination of the life estate to his wife which is provided for in his will. He did, however, employ the words "use" and "use and income" without limitation as to time in the paragraph of his will where he provides for the contingency of the death of a child after having children.

It is well established in this state that a gift of the use and income of property if for an unlimited time is a gift of the property itself, if there be no expression of a contrary intent. . . . True, the rule stated is merely a rule of construction and not a rule of law. It raises a presumption for the court's guidance where the intent of the testator is not otherwise determinable. National Newark, &c., Co. v. Arthur, &c., Blind Babies, 113 N.J. Eq. 313, 315, 166 A. 635. This rule of construction is so well established that the testator must be presumed to have drawn his will with reference to it. . . .

Testator's will provided for two different contingencies: (a) the death of a child without issue, and (b) the death of a child after having children.

The question to be determined is whether these expressions mean death whenever such event may occur or death during the continuance of the life estate created for testator's wife. In Barrell v. Barrell, 38 N.J. Eq. 60, 62, affirmed 39 N.J. Eq. 603, Chancellor Runyon said: "That clause provides that in case of the death of any one or more of the testator's children without leaving lawful issue, the share or shares of the one or more so dying shall go to the survivors or survivor of his children, but that if any of his children shall die leaving lawful issue living, such issue shall take the share his, her or their parent would have taken if living, share and share alike. It will be seen that here is a gift, absolute in terms, followed by alternative limitations over, which collectively provide for the event of the death of the donee under all possible circumstances — death either with or without issue. In such case the words of contingency are read as applying exclusively to the happening of the event in the testator's lifetime in order to avoid repugnancy, inasmuch as the alternative limitations over, if not so qualified and restricted, would reduce the prior devise from a fee to a life estate. 3 Jarm. on Wills (R. & T. Ed.) 643. The obvious reason is that it is to be presumed that the testator, if he had intended to give only a life estate, would have said so in the first instance, in the terms of the gift itself. Mr. Hawkins says that where a gift of the absolute interest in property to one person is followed by a gift of it to another, in a particular event, the disposition of the courts is to put such a construction on the gift over as will interfere as little as possible with the prior gift, and that when in such case death is spoken of as a contingent event, a gift over in the event of death may well be considered to mean not death at any time but death before a particular period — for example, the period of distribution — and thus the gift over may be read as a gift by way of substitution and not of remainder, and that it is consequently a rule of construction that where there is a bequest to one person, and 'in case of his death' to another, the gift over is construed to take effect only in the event of the death of the prior legatee before the period of payment or distribution, unless an intention appear to the contrary. Hawk. on Wills 254."

In Davis v. Scharf, 99 N.J. Eq. 88, 89, 133 A. 197, 198, Vice Chancellor Backes said: "The accepted rule of construction of wills in this state is, where a limitation over upon failure of issue at the death of the devisee is incident to a devise of a remainder upon the determination of a life estate, to refer the limitation clause to the event of the death of the devisee before the death of the life tenant, unless there are indications in the will of a contrary intent. The inclination of our decisions is to combine absolute ownership with the right of possession and enjoyment and to lay hold of other events than the death of the devisee at any time to affect that end, unless it be inconsistent with the expressed intention of the testator."

In view of the foregoing, it is my opinion that the testator's intent was to provide that his children should have the "use and income" from his estate (heretofore construed to mean his estate) absolutely, if they should be alive at the time of distribution to take it; that is, upon the death of the widow, and if any of the children should then be dead, their children should take in their stead, or, if they left no issue, the testator's remaining children should take by way of substitution. The estate vested in the testator's children immediately upon his death subject to be divested by the death of a child or children of the testator prior to the time of distribution; namely, the death of testator's wife, Mary Spalding Brown.

The gift to the testator's children was a remainder upon the termination of a life estate and the limitation over, in case of the death of any of the children, refers to death before the expiration of the life estate.

I conclude, therefore, that the trust terminated upon the death of the testator's widow, Mary Spalding Brown, and the three surviving children of the testator are entitled to have distribution of the estate made to them.

I will advise a decree in accordance with the views herein expressed.

Note on Death Without Issue

"Die without issue" is one of the most ambiguous phrases around. In England the standard construction was *indefinite* failure of issue, that is, when the bloodline ran out. Thus where there was a devise to "A and his heirs, but if A die without issue to B and his heirs," the courts assumed that testator wanted B to take the property whenever A had no descendants alive on the face of the earth. This construction proved not congenial to the American mind, which had little use for the fee tail from which this construction originated. By statute in over half the states and by judicial decision in many others, the indefinite failure construction was abandoned, and today it exists only in a tiny handful of states as a preferred construction.[68] In most American jurisdictions the preferred construction is *definite* failure of issue, which means failure of issue at some specific date, usually at the death of the named ancestor. The standard drafting language to provide for definite failure is "if A die without issue him surviving." If this language were in the devise above, B will take the property only if *at A's death* A leaves no issue. If A leaves issue at his death, B is completely cut out.

However, the insertion of the words "him surviving" does not cure all the ambiguities in the phrase "die without issue." Suppose T devises property "to A, but if A die without issue him surviving to B." The question arises: does this mean

[68] See page 686, supra.

B is to take only if A dies *before testator* without issue him surviving, or does it mean B is to take if A dies *before or after* testator's death without issue him surviving? Put in legal language, does testator intend a *substitutional* or *successive* construction? A substitutional construction means testator wants either A *or* B to enjoy the property, but not A *and* possibly B in succession. Applying a substitutional construction to the above devise, the devise reads "but if A die before testator without issue surviving A to B." If A survives T, or if A predeceases T leaving issue, B never takes possession. Applying a successive construction to this devise, it reads "but if A die without issue him surviving, whenever that may occur, to B." Under the successive construction, we do not know whether B will take until A dies. If A dies without issue him surviving, then B succeeds to possession and ownership of the property. What are the pros and cons of the substitutional and successive constructions applied to the above devise? The majority view favors the successive construction where the first estate created is a fee simple. 5 American Law of Property §§21.51, 21.52 (Casner ed. 1952); 3 Powell, Real Property ¶337 (1970).

When the devise is "to A for life, remainder to B, but if B die without issue him surviving to C," the question again arises whether the substitutional or successive construction will be applied. Here the first estate created is a life estate rather than a fee. Substitutional in this case would mean either (a) if B dies before testator without issue or (b) if B dies before A without issue. Successive would of course mean if B dies without issue at any time, whenever it might occur. The last principal case, Brown v. Robbins, supports substitutional construction (b), which is also the view taken by Restatement of Property §264. But there are many cases which apply the successive construction here. 5 American Law of Property §21.53 (Casner ed. 1952).

Another construction of death without issue now rarely used is "death without ever having had issue." Applying this construction to a devise "to A for life, then to B, but if B dies without issue to C," if B ever has a child born to him, C is cut out and B has an indefeasibly vested remainder. It does not matter if that child then predeceases B, and B dies without issue him surviving. The birth of the child cuts C out. 5 American Law of Property §21.55 (Casner ed. 1952).

The numerous cases on the meaning of death without issue are collected in Note, 26 A.L.R.3d 407 (1969).

PROBLEMS

1. T devises property "to A for life, then to A's issue, and if A dies without issue to B." A dies survived by no legitimate children, but by an illegitimate child. Does B take? 3 Powell, Real Property ¶339 (1970).

2. T devises property "to A, and if he dies, to B." What is the state of the title? 5 American Law of Property §21.58 (Casner ed. 1952).

SECTION G. Gifts by Implication

ESTATE OF ROBINSON

California Court of Appeal, Fifth District, 1968
262 Cal. App. 2d 32, 68 Cal. Rptr. 420

Gargano, Associate Justice. Appellant Evelyn Haug is a surviving daughter of testators Fred G. Robinson and May N. Robinson. Appellants Lola M. Robinson Padgett and Dorene Robinson Hoyt are the children of testators' deceased son, Fred G. Robinson, Jr., and the grandchildren of the testators. Appellants all appeal from a judgment of the Superior Court of Merced County determining interests in the testators' estates. However, since they present opposed points of view, we shall refer to testators' daughter as appellant Haug, and to the grandchildren as appellants Padgett and Hoyt. Moreover, since the trial court's decision was based solely on the terms of the testators' will the issues presented herein are issues of law, and we shall make our own independent determination (Estate of Platt, 21 Cal. 2d 343, 131 P.2d 825; First Trust & Sav. Bank of Pasadena v. Costa, 83 Cal. App. 2d 368, 188 P.2d 778).

Decedents made their joint and mutual will on June 28, 1949. At the time testators' seven children, two sons and five daughters, were all living. The pertinent provisions of this will are as follows. It establishes a spendthrift trust to contain the bulk of testators' seizeable [sizeable?] estates. 17½ per cent of the trust income is to be distributed to each of testators' two sons, 12 per cent to each of testators' five daughters, and 5 per cent for an emergency fund to be distributed to testators' children in the event of need. The will, however, is silent as to what should be done with a trust beneficiary's income during the period between his death and the death of testators' last surviving child. It simply provides that the trust shall terminate upon the death of testators' last surviving child and that the corpus shall be distributed equally among testators' grandchildren and great grandchildren then living, or in the alternative, if none is living, to the University of California.

On June 26, 1959, testators made a codicil to their joint and mutual will. At the time testators' son, Fred G. Robinson, Jr., had died. Thus, testators directed their trustee to distribute his 17½ per cent share of the trust income in equal parts to their other son and five daughters. At the same time they limited the amount to be accumulated in the emergency fund to not more than 10 per cent of the entire trust estate.

While the estates were still in administration, testators' daughters petitioned the probate court to determine interests and for declaratory relief. They asserted that upon the death of their parents each income gift vested in the income beneficiary and this vested interest passes to the beneficiary's estate upon death. Appellants Padgett and Hoyt then filed a statement of interest in opposition to the petition. They alleged that upon the death of an income beneficiary his or her interest terminates and must be added to the principal of the trust to be distributed to testators' grandchildren and great grandchildren when the trust terminates. However, the court rejected both contentions and implied cross-remainders; the court held that on the death of each income beneficiary his or her share of the income must be distributed equally to the testators' surviving children.

All appellants apparently agree that the probate court correctly interpreted the testators' intent to distribute the trust income. This view seems appropriate since the will does not contain any express provision for the accumulation of excess income and for its eventual addition to the trust fund (see Union Nat. Bank of Pasadena v. Hunter, 93 Cal. App. 2d 669, 673, 209 P.2d 621). Moreover, the testators indicated that they wanted the income distributed, not accumulated, when they limited the amount of the emergency fund to 10 per cent of the entire trust estate. Appellant Haug, however, still asserts that the income gifts to the income beneficiaries are vested interests. On the other hand, appellants Padgett and Hoyt presently maintain that the trust income payable to a deceased beneficiary must be treated as intestate property of the testators to be distributed under the laws of succession. . . .

Implied Remainders

It is uniformly acknowledged by the cases that implied cross-remainders are not favored and that this rule of interpretation is only invoked to effectuate a clear intention of the testator to achieve that result. As the court succinctly stated in Union Nat. Bank of Pasadena v. Hunter, 93 Cal. App. 2d 669, 674, 209 P.2d 621, 623:

> Where the possession and use of the property, as distinct from the mere income thereof, is the subject of conveyance, some courts have implied a cross-remainder in order to carry out the intention of the trustor to transfer the entire undiminished corpus as a unit to the remaindermen upon the termination of the trust. See Dow v. Doyle, 103 Mass. 489; Glover v. Stillson, 56 Conn. 316, 15 A. 752; Jones v. Cable, 114 Pa. 586, 7 A. 791. Others have reached the same result where income is given to the beneficiaries as a class and not individually, see In re Boyer's Estate, 115 Pa. Super. 501, 175 A. 728; Clarke v. Rathbone, 221 Mass. 574, 109 N.E. 651, or where the language of the trust instrument justifies an inference that the income is to be shared equally among such of the named beneficiaries as are living, until the termination of the trust. See Loring v. Coolidge, 99 Mass. 191; New Jersey Title Guarantee & Trust Co. v. Elsworth, 108 N.J. Eq. 229, 154 A. 602; Kramer v. Sangamon Loan & Trust Co., 293 Ill. 553, 127 N.E. 877. The cases uniformly acknowledge that the rule of interpretation favoring cross-remainders by implication is only invoked in order to effectuate a manifested intention of the trustor to achieve that result. See also Rhode Island Hospital Trust Co. v. Proprietors of Swan Point Cemetery, 62 R.I. 83, 3 A.2d 236, 243; In re Grothe's Estate, 229 Pa. 186, 78 A. 88, 90; 33 Am. Jur. sec. 83, p. 540.

Manifestly, we are here concerned with disposition of income and not with the possession and use of the corpus. Moreover, in the instant case the testators did not expressly will the trust income to their children as a class to be shared equally between them nor does the language of the will justify such an inference. Significantly, the only expression which the testators made in this respect forecloses this conclusion. When the testators made their codicil after the death of their deceased son, Fred G. Robinson, Jr., they directed their trustee to distribute his share of the trust income in equal parts to their other children. Thus, they obviously believed that the express direction was necessary in order to accomplish the result. However, they gave no similar directions for the distribution of the trust income upon the death of any of their other children.

According to the trial judge's memorandum of decision, when he implied cross-remainders he relied mainly on the rationale of Union Nat. Bank v. Hunter, supra, 93 Cal. App. 2d 669, 209 P.2d 621. However, this case is contrary to, not supportive of, the trial court's decision. Although the Hunter court recognized the possibility of implying cross-remainders, it held against such an implication for lack of support in the trust instrument. Significantly, the will in the Hunter case gave each beneficiary a set amount (one-half each) of the income and nowhere expressed an intent that any beneficiary should ever get more. Similarly in the instant case, the will and the codicil defined only a set percentage of the trust income for each beneficiary.

Vested Interests

Appellant Haug argues that since her deceased parents did not leave the trust income to their children as a class or in joint tenancy, and since they did not expressly limit the duration of the gifts to the lives of the beneficiaries, the income gifts are pur autre vie; they are all measured by the life of the last surviving child. Thus, appellant concludes that each income beneficiary has a vested interest in his own gift which continues to exist after his death and which passes to his own heirs so long as any child of the testators lives.

There is of course substantial authority for the proposition that if a testator intended an income beneficiary to receive the income during the entire lifetime of someone else, the gift is pur autre vie and passes to the beneficiary's heirs upon his death.

However, when we read the testators' will as a whole and consider its general scheme, we conclude it is reasonably clear the testators could not have intended the result advocated by this appellant.

First, the corpus of the trust is not willed to a surviving child. It is willed in equal shares to the grandchildren and great grandchildren of the testators who are living when the trust terminates. Thus, the testators manifested an intention to treat all grandchildren and great grandchildren alike. However, if an income gift to a deceased beneficiary passes to his estate it could also be distributed to his children. This in turn would favor some of the decedents' grandchildren over others.

Second, when the testators made their codicil after the death of their son, Fred

G. Robinson, Jr., they directed their trustee to distribute his share of the income in equal parts to their six remaining children even though the deceased son was survived by two daughters. Thus, to urge that the testators intended their other children to have vested interests which passed to each deceased child's estate until the death of the last surviving child is to urge that the testators intentionally discriminated against their deceased son's heirs. Manifestly, such flagrant discrimination should not be imputed to the testators in the absence of clear and unequivocal language to justify it.

Third, the words that the testators used simply indicate that they intended each of their children to receive a specified percentage of the trust income during his or her lifetime. The will expressly shows that the testators were trying to give each of their children enough income to provide for their needs. The will authorizes the trustee to use the emergency fund if he determines the income distribution is insufficient "to provide for the reasonable support, care and comfort of such beneficiary." Also, the testators' will establishes a spendthrift trust which provides that the beneficiaries' interests shall not be subject to claims of creditors, legal process or voluntary or involuntary alienation. This testamentary scheme will be effectively thwarted if an income gift passes to a deceased child's executors or administrators.

We note with interest the decision of the Supreme Court of Illinois in Routt v. Newman, 253 Ill. 185, 97 N.E. 208, in which the court considered an almost identical question. In that case the testatrix set up a spendthrift trust with one-fourth of the income to go to each of her four sons. The trust was to continue until all four sons died. It also provided that upon the death of a son his one-quarter share of the income was to go to his children, subject to the spendthrift provision. One son died, leaving a surviving child. This child also died before the trust had terminated. The deceased grandson's mother then claimed a share of the income as a vested interest which passed to his estate. The court, after pointing to the spendthrift provision of the trust, stated:

> The continued existence of the recipient of the fund was necessary to a compliance with this requirement. The portion of testatrix's property included in the trust was manifestly intended to be placed beyond the reach of creditors of the beneficiaries, and that object was an important part of her scheme. She gave other property to her sons in fee simple, but the control of this portion she intended should be so restricted that neither the land itself nor the income could be reached by any creditors during the lifetime of any of her sons. The language quoted is first used in regard to the sons and is then repeated as applying to their children, and in our judgment limits the time during which a share of the net income shall be paid to any child of a son, in his lifetime. (97 N.E. 210.)

Intestacy

We now turn to the claim of appellants Padgett and Hoyt. Succinctly, they assert that since the testators' true intent cannot be ascertained without engaging in sheer speculation, the income gift to each beneficiary lapses upon the death of the beneficiary and must be treated as the testators' intestate property to be distributed accordingly.

Appellants' contention is also without substantial merit. The will, when considered as a whole, clearly demonstrates that the testators intended to make a complete disposition of their property. In fact, the third paragraph states:

"It is the intention of each and of both of us to dispose of by this instrument all of said property."

Moreover, these appellants are the very grandchildren that the testators ignored when they made their codicil after the death of appellants' father. From that fact they have persuasively argued that the theory advocated by appellant Haug is contrary to the testamentary scheme since it does not treat the grandchildren and great grandchildren equally. However, they subtly seek to accomplish the same result in their favor through intestacy; by right of representation a deceased beneficiary's children (including appellants) could receive a share of any trust property distributed from Mr. and Mrs. Robinson's estates according to the laws of intestate succession (Prob. Code, §222).

Conclusion

We conclude that since there are no clear directions for the distribution of the trust income upon the death of the income beneficiaries (with the exception of decedent's deceased son, Fred G. Robinson, Jr.), and the will contains no valid direction for the accumulation of this income, such income, upon the death of each beneficiary becomes undisposed of trust income to be distributed equally to the testators' grandchildren and great grandchildren as the persons presumptively entitled to the next eventual interest (the corpus) pursuant to the provisions of Civil Code, section 733. This section provides:

> When, in consequence of a valid limitation of a future interest, there is a suspension of the power of alienation or of the ownership during the continuation of which the income is undisposed of, and no valid direction for its accumulation is given, such income belongs to the persons *presumptively* entitled to the next eventual interest. (Emphasis added.)

It is of course true that only the grandchildren and great grandchildren living when the trust terminates are entitled to share in the corpus of the trust. However, even so, the grandchildren and great grandchildren living at the death of a beneficiary are the presumptive takers of the corpus and section 733 refers to presumptive, not actual, takers. In fact, a similar solution was adopted by the Supreme Court in Estate of Lefranc, 38 Cal. 2d 289, 299-301, 239 P.2d 617. There a testamentary trust was to last for the life of one niece with the corpus to be distributed to her *children* or, if none, to a second niece. The first niece lost her interest by violating a no contest clause in the will. At the time she had no children. Thus, the trust instrument no longer disposed of the income during the first taker's life. Applying section

733, the court held that the trust continued in existence during the life of the first niece with the income paid to the second niece, as the *presumptive* taker of the next estate until such time as the former should have a child. . . .

We point out that the distribution of the excess trust income pursuant to section 733 not only fairly resolves the dilemma which was created by the testators' omission but reasonably conforms with the testators' intention as gathered from their testamentary scheme when this scheme is viewed in its entirety. It enables each of the testators' children to have his or her share of the trust income in the percentage specified by the will during his or her entire lifetime as the testators have expressly specified. It allows the trustee to distribute all of the excess trust income at a time when it may be needed by the ultimate beneficiaries, instead of accumulating it in an estate which is already quite sizeable. And most important, it treats all of the grandchildren and great grandchildren equally as the testators undoubtedly intended.

The judgment is reversed with directions to the superior court to modify its orders and decrees to determine interests in the estates of Fred G. Robinson and May N. Robinson to conform with the views expressed herein.

The attempted appeals from the findings of fact and conclusions of law are dismissed.

NOTES

1. Where there is a gift "to A, B, and C for life and at *their* death to D in fee," a large majority of cases imply cross-remainders between the life tenants. Thus on A's death, B and C divide the income, and on the death of the second to die, the survivor takes all the income. This is the position taken by the Restatement of Property §115 (1936). A court could also come to the conclusion that the survivors split the income by declaring A, B, and C to be joint tenants for life, with a right of survivorship among themselves. See 2 Powell, Real Property ¶324 (1970).

For perpetuities problems that can arise from implication of cross-remainders see page 1038, infra.

2. T devises property "to A for life, and if he die without issue to B." A dies leaving issue. Who owns the property? 5 American Law of Property §21.34 (Casner ed. 1952).

3. H and W executed a joint and mutual will giving "all our estates and effects unto the survivor of either of us. . . . In the event that we both die, simultaneously or in the same catastrophe, . . . [we give everything to] our dear beloved nieces," Christine and Gloria. W died. Two years later H died. From the gift in case of a common disaster the court implied a gift to Christine and Gloria where there was no common disaster. In re D'Alessandro, 55 Misc. 2d 909, 286 N.Y.S.2d 914 (Sur. Ct. 1968).

SECTION H. Change in Testator's Property Between Execution of Will and Death: Ademption, Satisfaction, and Increase

The gift by will of a piece of real estate or a particular chattel can be revoked by being given away during lifetime. This is known as *ademption by extinction*.[69] To illustrate, suppose T executes a will devising Blackacre to A. After executing the will, but prior to death, T conveys Blackacre to B. T dies without changing his will. The gift to A is adeemed, and A takes nothing.

Revocation by ademption applies only to *specific* devises and bequests. It does not apply to *general* legacies or *demonstrative* legacies. These three categories respond roughly to three different states of mind testator might have. A legacy is "specific" when a particular object, distinct from all other objects, is given by will. Gifts of Blackacre or "my 3-carat diamond ring given to me by my Great-Aunt Jane" are examples of gifts normally deemed specific. A legacy is "general" when testator intends to confer a general benefit, and not a particular asset. A common example is a pecuniary legacy of, say, $1000 to A. If testator does not have $1000 in cash at death, other items will have to be sold to produce the $1000 for payment to A. Another example of a general legacy is "a 3-carat diamond ring" when testator never had a diamond ring. A "demonstrative" legacy is a hybrid: a general legacy payable first from particular property and out of the estate if that property is insufficient. An example of a demonstrative legacy would be: "I give $1000 to A, and I direct that ten shares of General Motors stock be sold and the proceeds used to pay this legacy."

In most states ademption of specific devises and legacies occurs when the property is not part of testator's estate at death. If testator owns the property, the gift is good; if testator does not own the property, the gift is adeemed, unless testator provides otherwise in his will. This is the English rule. It was laid down by Lord Thurlow in Ashburner v. MacGuire.[70] In jurisdictions following this rule, courts have developed several techniques to avoid ademption. (1) *Classify the legacy as general or demonstrative rather than specific*. If testator bequeaths "100 shares of Telegoose Corporation" to B and he owns no shares of Telegoose at death, the court will probably declare this to be a general legacy if Telegoose Corporation has widely held stock traded on a major exchange. Some courts have declared legacies of a precise number of shares of stock to be general even though testator owned exactly that number of shares at the time of execution.[71] On the other hand, if testator had said "*my* 100 shares of Telegoose," the court will likely hold it a specific legacy, and adeemed to the extent the shares are missing at death. A gift that looks specific might also be declared to be demonstrative and not adeemed. Thus a be-

[69] See Atkinson, Wills 433-436, 741-748 (2d ed. 1953); 2 Page, Wills §§21.66 to 21.85, 6 id. §§54.3 to 54.20 (Bowe-Parker Rev. 1960).

[70] 2 Bro. C.C. 108, 29 Eng. Rep. 62 (Ch. 1786).

[71] Paulus, Special and General Legacies of Securities — Whither Testator's Intent, 43 Iowa L. Rev. 467 (1958).

quest "of $10,000, more or less, entered on my bank book" has been held demonstrative.[72] (2) *Classify the inter vivos disposition as a change in form, not substance.* Suppose that after testator executes his will giving "my 100 shares of Telegoose Corporation" to B, Telegoose Corporation (a) exchanges the stock for preferred stock, or (b) exchanges the stock for stock in Radio Corporation of America which merges with Telegoose. Does B take the new stock? The answer depends upon whether the change is in form rather than in substance. There is usually a disposition to avoid ademption, but on most fact situations one can find cases going both ways.[73] (3) *Construe the meaning of the will as of the time of death rather than as of the time of execution.* By this technique a bequest of "that certain Hudson automobile now owned by me" passed a 1948 Hudson owned by testator at his death, though at the time the will was executed testator owned only a 1941 model Hudson.[74] (4) *Create exceptions.* If the testator dies in an accident which also destroys the bequeathed item (a "common disaster"), or if the guardian of an incompetent or insane person transfers the item, cases have held the legacy not adeemed,[75] although here as elsewhere in ademption problems, there are contrary cases.[76]

All these doors in and out have led some to believe that the rules need revision. "The irrelevance of specific description to the testator's intention with respect to whether he would wish a legatee to receive an economic equivalent leads to the conclusion that it should not be considered in ademption cases. If the courts are truly trying to approximate what the testator would desire when a legacy is missing — and there seems to be no other proper aim — they should return to the case-by-case determination which preceded Lord Thurlow's ruling in Ashburner v. MacGuire. In such a quest it should first be determined whether an economic benefit was intended by the original bequest and was unchanged by a subsequent gift. An affirmative finding should, to the extent that the residue cannot provide a monetary equivalent, lead the court to allow the legatee to share proportionately with legatees of primarily economic legacies." [77]

[72] Kenaday v. Sinnott, 179 U.S. 606 (1900).

[73] E.g., a bequest of "all my money on deposit at X bank," later transferred to another bank, was held not to fail in Willis v. Barrow, 218 Ala. 549, 119 So. 678 (1929), but was held to fail in Estate of Rubenstein, 169 Misc. 273, 7 N.Y.S.2d 311 (Sur. Ct. 1938).

[74] In re Cooper's Estate, 107 Cal. App. 2d 592, 237 P.2d 699 (1951). But see Estate of Morris, 11 Misc. 2d 457, 169 N.Y.S.2d 881 (Sur. Ct. 1957), where the legacy failed when testatrix sold a diamond-studded watch referred to in the will and bought another diamond-studded watch worth approximately five times as much.

[75] Estate of MacDonald, 133 Cal. App. 2d 43, 283 P.2d 271 (1955) (common disaster); Walsh v. Gillespie, 338 Mass. 278, 154 N.E.2d 906 (1959) (incompetency). Similar exceptions are provided in Uniform Probate Code §2-608. In some states sales by the guardian to support the ward result in pro tanto ademption.

[76] In re Barry's Estate, 208 Okla. 8, 252 P.2d 437 (1952) (common disaster); Stake v. Cole, 257 Iowa 594, 133 N.W.2d 714 (1965) (incompetency).

[77] Note, Ademption and the Testator's Intent, 74 Harv. L. Rev. 741, 751 (1961). See also Paulus, Ademption by Extinction: Smiting Lord Thurlow's Ghost, 2 Texas Tech. L. Rev. 195 (1971).

PROBLEMS

1. Is the legatee of an insured diamond ring, missing at the time of testator's death, entitled to the insurance proceeds paid the executors on account of the ring? Matter of Wright, 7 N.Y.2d 365, 165 N.E.2d 561 (1960); N.Y. Estates, Powers & Trusts Law §3-4.5 (1967); Uniform Probate Code §2-608(b)(3).

2. T executes a will directing her executor to sell Blackacre and distribute the proceeds to A. After executing the will T enters into a contract with B for the sale of Blackacre for $65,000; the sale price is payable in installments. At T's death $37,000 is owed on the contract. C is T's residuary legatee. Is A or C entitled to the $37,000? Would your answer be different if T had sold Blackacre and taken back a note and mortgage or if T had exchanged Blackacre for Whiteacre? Newbury v. McCammant, 182 N.W.2d 147 (Iowa, 1970).

UNIFORM PROBATE CODE

Section 2-608. [*Nonademption of Specific Devises in Certain Cases; Sale by Conservator; Unpaid Proceeds of Sale, Condemnation or Insurance.*]

(a) If specifically devised property is sold by a conservator, or if a condemnation award or insurance proceeds are paid to a conservator as a result of condemnation, fire, or casualty, the specific devisee has the right to a general pecuniary devise equal to the net sale price, the condemnation award, or the insurance proceeds. This subsection does not apply if subsequent to the sale, condemnation, or casualty, it is adjudicated that the disability of the testator has ceased and the testator survives the adjudication by one year. The right of the specific devisee under this subsection is reduced by any right he has under subsection (b).

(b) A specific devisee has the right to the remaining specifically devised property and:

(1) any balance of the purchase price (together with any security interest) owing from a purchaser to the testator at death by reason of sale of the property;

(2) any amount of a condemnation award for the taking of the property unpaid at death;

(3) any proceeds unpaid at death on fire or casualty insurance on the property; and

(4) property owned by testator at his death as a result of foreclosure, or obtained in lieu of foreclosure, of the security for a specifically devised obligation.

The doctrine of *satisfaction* (sometimes known as ademption by satisfaction) applies where the testator makes a transfer to a *beneficiary* after executing the will. The doctrine applies to general pecuniary bequests, not to specific bequests. When specific property is given to the beneficiary during testator's life, there is ademption by extinction, not satisfaction. Satisfaction may also apply to residuary gifts and to demonstrative gifts, but the cases are not uniform in their holdings. Under the majority view satisfaction does not apply to devises of land; this is a relic from the early days when all devises were thought to be necessarily specific. In all states satisfaction depends upon the intention of the testator.

If the testator is the parent of the beneficiary (or stands in loco parentis) and after the execution of the will transfers to the beneficiary property of a similar nature to that given the beneficiary by the will, there is a rebuttable presumption that the gift is in satisfaction of the gift under the will. Thus:

> *Case* 8. T bequeaths $50,000 to his son, S, residue to his daughter, D. After executing the will T gives S $30,000. There is a presumption that this gift is in satisfaction of the bequest, so that S will take only $20,000 at T's death.

Because the intent of testator is frequently so difficult to ascertain, some states require that the intention of a testator to adeem by satisfaction be shown in writing. Under such a statute, of course, there is no presumption of satisfaction by a gift to a child.

UNIFORM PROBATE CODE

Section 2-612. [*Ademption by Satisfaction.*]

Property which a testator gave in his lifetime to a person is treated as a satisfaction of a devise to that person in whole or in part, only if the will provides for deduction of the lifetime gift, or the testator declares in a contemporaneous writing that the gift is to be deducted from the devise or is in satisfaction of the devise, or the devisee acknowledges in writing that the gift is in satisfaction. For purpose of partial satisfaction, property given during lifetime is valued as of the time the devisee came into possession or enjoyment of the property or as of the time of death of the testator, whichever occurs first.

NOTE, RIGHTS TO STOCK ACCRETIONS WHICH OCCUR PRIOR TO TESTATOR'S DEATH

36 Albany L. Rev. 182, 182-192 (1971)

The determination of testamentary purpose in wills containing legacies of stock has provided the courts with a perplexing constructional problem. Specifically, the dilemma involves the rights to stock accretions resulting from splits and dividends which occur between the execution of the will and the testator's death.

Increasing participation and interest of the general public in stock market transactions has produced numerous bequests of stock, and has given rise to considerable judicial concern over the question of the testator's intent. Unfortunately, this is an area of the law that has failed to keep pace with the realities of the modern business world. In the absence of legislative enactments and in the midst of confusing and contradictory case law, many courts persist in mechanically applying anachronistic rules of construction that more often frustrate than achieve the intent of the testator.

Stock Splits

The stock split issue focuses on the question of whether a legatee is entitled to the additional shares produced by a split, or only to the number of shares expressly bequeathed in the will. Since the realization of the testamentary plan as gathered from the entire will is the cardinal rule of construction, the courts attempt to resolve the controversy by determining what the testator intended. Two distinct lines of cases have developed in arriving at the testator's design; the formalistic approach which utilizes the specific or general nature of the legacy to ascertain intent, and more recently, a line of authority that disregards the distinction between specific and general legacies and relies on other indicators.

By the traditional test only a specific legatee is entitled to the fruits of a stock split. The reason for this rule is undoubtedly rooted in section 24 of the English Wills Act of 1837,[78] and in American legislation and case law which have adopted the essence of that statute. In substance, the principle commands that in the absence of a contrary intent appearing in the will, the instrument will be interpreted as if it had been executed immediately prior to the testator's death. For the disposition to refer to the time of its making and escape the force of the general rule, the property in question must be sufficiently distinguished from all other property of the same kind so that it is clear the testator is referring to that particular item as it existed when the will was drawn. In other words, a general legacy speaks at the time of death while a specific legacy speaks at the time of execution.

Suppose, for example, the testator bequeaths 100 shares of stock which split two for one prior to his death. His total ownership in the corporation remains constant but is now evidenced by 200 shares. For the total value of the original 100 share legacy to remain the same, 200 shares must now pass to the legatee. But if the court decides the legacy is general the legatee will be awarded only 100 shares, since absent evidence of a contrary intent the will must be interpreted to mean 100 shares

[78] The statute states, "Every will shall be construed, with reference to the real estate and personal estate comprised in it, to speak and take effect as if it had been executed immediately before the death of the testator unless a contrary intention shall appear by the will."

at the date of the testator's death, not 100 shares as they existed when the will was executed. However, if the original 100 shares are described as "my shares" or if other such indicators of contrary intent are present to demonstrate that a specific legacy was intended, the disposition will be construed to mean 100 shares as of the date of execution, thus entitling the legatee to the equivalent of the first 100 shares or 200 split shares. . . .

In other jurisdictions the contemporary trend has clearly been away from the specific-general formula. Today, the courts rely on a myriad of factors to reveal the testator's intent. In 1970 the Supreme Court of New Hampshire wrote:

> We consider that the issues presented are not to be decided merely by applying the rubric of specific or general to the . . . legacies and by attaching consequences thought to follow automatically from that determination. . . . The situation of the testator, the surrounding circumstances, his family and his relatives, the devisees and the legatees, the nature, amount, and situation of his property, facts tending to place the court in the position of the testator, constitute evidence competent for our consideration upon the issue of what he meant by the words used.[79]

A number of other states have adopted a similar attitude.[80] The direction taken by these courts is commendable. To argue that a testator consciously evidences his intent by carefully constructing either specific or general legacies is to indulge in a fantasy and put the individual at the mercy of the draftsman. . . .

A number of proposals have been offered as solutions to the stock split problem. It has been suggested that the answer lies in careful draftsmanship, and particularly in the use of percentages and fractions in the bequest of property. While this is no doubt true, it is equally true that we will always be plagued with poorly drawn wills. A statutory solution was advanced by the New York Temporary Commission On Estates. By this proposal, all legacies of stock would be held specific and the legatee would receive the additional shares if no contrary intent was found in the will. Consequently, if the securities were not in the estate at the death of the testator the legacy would adeem. Finally, some recent cases have recommended that share accretions be awarded to the legatee, specific or general, unless the will expressly provides otherwise.[81] The specific-general test would be retained, however,

[79] In re Doonan Estate, — N.H. — , — , 262 A.2d 281, 284, 283 (1970).

[80] California — Estate of Helfman, 193 Cal. App. 2d 652, 14 Cal. Rptr. 482 (1961); Colorado — Heinneman v. Colorado College, 150 Col. 515, 374 P.2d 695; Florida — In re Estate of Parker, 110 So. 2d 498 (Fla. App.), cert. denied, 114 So. 2d 3 (Fla. 1959); Illinois — Allen v. National Bank of Austin, 9 Ill. App. 2d 149, 153 N.E.2d 260 (1953); New Hampshire — In re Doonan Estate, — N.H. — , 262 A.2d 281 (1970); New York — Matter of Fitch, 281 App. Div. 65, 118 N.Y.S.2d 234 (3d Dep't 1952); Matter of the Estate of Julia Roob, 59 Misc. 2d 619, 300 N.Y.S.2d 9 (Surr. Ct. Nassau County 1969); Pennsylvania — In re McFerren's Estate, 365 Pa. 490, 76 A.2d 759 (1950); In re Estate of Marks, 235 Pa. 155, 255 A.2d 512 (1969); Rhode Island — Egavian v. Egavian, 102 R.I. 740, 232 A.2d 789 (1967); Virginia — Warner v. Baylor, 204 Va. 867, 134 S.E.2d 263 (1964); Vermont — In re Estate of Barslow, — Vt. — , 260 A.2d 374 (1969).

[81] In re Estate of Barslow, — Vt. — , 260 A.2d 374 (1969); Egavian v. Egavian, 102 R.I. 740, 232 A.2d 789 (1967); Allen v. National Bank of Austin, 9 Ill. App. 2d 149, 153 N.E.2d 260 (1953).

to decide other issues that may be present such as ademption or abatement. Potentially, this approach offers the legatee the most protection. Since the specific-general test would be retained in regard to ademption and abatement questions, the courts could still construe legacies as specific to avoid ademption. The Commission's recommendation does not allow this flexibility since all legacies would automatically be held specific and subject to ademption.

Stock Dividends

Although quite similar to the stock split issue, the stock dividend controversy has experienced a distinct case law development. Lack of an applicable statute, and disagreement over the nature and consequences of a stock dividend has produced a division of authority. Some difficulty still exists in distinguishing between stock splits and share dividends,[82] but most New York courts appear to have acepted the definitions found in Matter of Fosdick.[83]

> The term "dividend" signifies a distribution of profits or earnings to shareholders. In its most obvious form it consists of a distribution of cash. It may also be in shares of the corporation. When in this form it is accomplished by segregating that part of the earnings it represents. The segregation is accomplished by capitalization. Therein lies the distinction, as found in the cases, between a mere stock split and a share dividend. The stock dividend evidences that the company's accumulated profits have been capitalized, instead of distributed to the shareholders or retained as surplus available for distribution in money or kind should the opportunity offer (Eisner v. Macomber, 252 U.S. 189, 211). A stock split, on the other hand, results from the simple increase in the number of shares without altering surplus or segregating earnings.[84]

Absent clear intent to the contrary most courts deny the benefit of stock dividend accretions to the legatee,[85] while a minority of jurisdictions follow the stock split rule and award the additional shares to a specific legatee.[86] The majority

[82] Note, Trusts and Estates: Corporations: Share Distributions: Allocation Between Income Beneficiaries and Remaindermen: Construction of Legacies, 49 Cornell L.Q. 363, 364-68 (1964).

[83] 4 N.Y.2d 646, 152 N.E.2d 228, 176 N.Y.S.2d 966 (1958).

[84] Id. at 653, 152 N.E.2d at 232, 176 N.Y.S.2d at 971 (1958).

[85] Connecticut — Griffith v. Adams, 106 Conn. 19, 137 A. 20 (1926); Kentucky — Harlan National Bank v. Brown, 317 S.W.2d 903 (Ky. 1958); Maryland — Hicks v. Kerr, 132 Md. 693, 104 A. 426, 10 A.L.R. 1323 (1918); Massachusetts — First National Bank v. Union Hospital, 281 Mass. 64, 183 N.E. 247, 89 A.L.R. 1125 (1932); Missouri — McGregory v. Gaskill, 296 S.W. 833 (Mo. App. 1927); New York — Matter of Howe, 12 N.Y.2d 870, 187 N.E.2d 794, 237 N.Y.S.2d 343 (1962); Matter of Brann, 219 N.Y. 263, 114 N.E. 404 (1916); Brundage v. Brundage, 60 N.Y. 544 (1875); Ohio — Central National Bank of Cleveland v. Cottier, 163 N.E.2d 709 (Ohio P. Ct. 1958); Oregon — Fisher v. Paine, 210 Ore. 429, 311 P.2d 438 (1957); Rhode Island — Sherman v. Riley, 43 R.I. 202, 110 A. 629 (1920).

[86] Florida — In re Vail's Estate, 67 So. 2d 665 (Fla. 1953); Louisiana — Succession of Quintero, 209 La. 279, 24 So. 2d 589 (1945); Maine — Butler v. Dobbins, 142 Me. 383, 53 A.2d 270 (1947); New Jersey — Chase National Bank v. Deichmiller, 107 N.J. Eq. 370, 152 A.

rule is based on the well settled principle that a legatee is not entitled to cash dividends prior to the testator's death. Drawing no significant difference between cash and share dividends, most jurisdictions conclude that a legatee cannot logically be awarded the former when he is denied the latter. . . .

On the other hand, the minority position clearly distinguishes cash and share dividends. These courts point out that the term "stock dividend" is really a misnomer and that the dividend rule should not apply.[87] When a cash dividend is paid assets flow from the corporation to the shareholder, while a stock dividend involves no separation of assets, but a simple bookkeeping transfer from surplus to capital showing that the profits are being plowed back into the company. Arguing that the only real difference between a stock split and a share dividend is the capitalization of surplus in the latter, these courts apply the same rule to both. . . .

Allocation of all share dividends to the legatee absent expression of a contrary intent is clearly the preferable rule. New York and other majority jurisdictions proceed on a faulty premise when they fail to recognize the difference between share and cash dividends. In the landmark case of Eisner v. Macomber[88] the United States Supreme Court was confronted with the issue of whether a share dividend constituted taxable income. Clearly distinguishing between cash and share dividends, the court held that the latter could not be taxed as part of a stockholder's income. While this case involves the question of taxability, the court's discussion of the differences between the two types of dividends is applicable to refute the majority position. The court explained that only when a dividend is paid in cash "does the stockholder realize a profit or gain which becomes his separate property, and thus derive income from the capital that he or his predecessor has invested." [89] Conversely, the court argued that a share dividend is:

> [I]n essence not a dividend but rather the opposite; no part of the assets of the company is separated from the common fund. . . . We are clear that not only does a stock dividend really take nothing from the property of the corporation and add nothing to that of the shareholder, but that the antecedent accumulation of profits evidenced thereby, while indicating that the shareholder is the richer because of an increase of his capital, at the same time shows he has not realized or received any income in the transaction.[90]

Actually, a share dividend has the same practical effect as a stock split and there is no reason why the same principles should not govern both. Furthermore, denying share dividends to the legatee results in a partial ademption of the legacy since

---

697 (1930); New York — In re Watkins, 51 N.Y.S.2d 46 (Surr. Ct. Monroe County 1944); Matter of Good, 145 Misc. 431, 260 N.Y.S. 292 (Surr. Ct. N.Y. County 1932); Matter of Adams, 90 Misc. 254, 152 N.Y.S. 727 (Surr. Ct. N.Y. County 1915); Ohio — Clegg v. Lippold, 123 N.E.2d 549 (Ohio P. Ct. Montgomery County 1951).

[87] Note, Effect of Stock Split or Share Dividend on Bequests of Stock, 50 Calif. L. Rev. 160, 164 (1962).

[88] 252 U.S. 189 (1920).

[89] Id. at 209.

[90] Id. at 210, 212.

the issuance of the dividend diminishes the value of the shares bequeathed. Thus the dividends must pass to the legatee if the substance of the original legacy is to remain the same.

. . .

It is submitted that much of the confusion in the area of share accretions, from both splits and dividends, might be avoided if the legacies were viewed as leaving interests in corporations, and not as the paper certificate representing the interest. Most testators probably never consider the possibility of splits and dividends altering their bequests. Thus changes in form should not be allowed to diminish the substance and value of the property originally bequeathed unless the testator has provided otherwise. Share accumulations should pass to the legatee as part of the interest in the corporation conveyed by the legacy.

13. Building Flexibility into the Estate Plan: Powers of Appointment

SECTION A. Introduction

Suppose Adam Smith decides to set up a life insurance trust in which the income is to be paid to Mrs. Smith for life, and on her death the trust corpus is to be distributed to the Smith children. In Chapter 11 we have already considered the undesirability of simply providing for an outright distribution of the remainder interest "to my children in equal shares." This might produce a distribution to minor children, with the attendant problems of a guardianship administration. Even if all the Smith children have reached legal age at the time of Mrs. Smith's death, they may not have attained a level of maturity at which an outright distribution of a substantial sum would be desirable. Further problems would be raised if one or more of the Smith children were to predecease Mrs. Smith, perhaps survived by a spouse and children, perhaps not.

While these contingencies could be provided for in drafting the remainder interest, there would still be shortcomings in the resulting dispositive plan. Looking first at the remainder interest, Mr. and Mrs. Smith may feel that the distribution among the children should be in equal shares, unless there are unusual circumstances. Prior to the death of Mr. and Mrs. Smith, a number of events might occur to make an equal distribution of the remainder interest undesirable. One of the Smith children may do better financially than the others; one child may be unlucky in marriage; one child (or his child) may incur a serious medical problem; another may have little capacity for managing his property, and so on. Circumstances may, in short, warrant something other than an equal split among the Smith children with outright distribution to each. It is obviously desirable to postpone a final decision on disposition of the remainder interest for so long as is possible, to permit taking into account the actual needs of the Smith children as they may develop in the future. This can be accomplished by giving Mrs. Smith a special power to appoint a portion of the assets among the issue, and spouses of the issue, of Mr. and Mrs. Smith in such shares and upon such terms as she sees fit.[1]

It may be desirable also to give Mrs. Smith a general power of appointment over some of the assets. If the Smiths reside in a common law jurisdiction, Smith will likely want to qualify his estate for the maximum allowable marital deduction under the federal estate tax. If Mrs. Smith is given a life income interest and also a general power of appointment over trust principal, a marital deduction is allowable for that portion of the principal over which she has the general power.[2]

In addition to employing a special power to achieve flexibility and a general power to effect tax savings, Smith may want to insure that Mrs. Smith will have funds sufficient to maintain herself and to educate the Smith children. The income from the trust may prove to be inadequate for these purposes. Furthermore, emergency needs, perhaps for medical or educational expenses, are likely to arise, and there should be some means by which the principal of the trust can be reached for these necessary expenditures. These objectives can be met by giving the trustee discretionary powers over the trust principal or by giving the beneficiary a power to invade principal under specified circumstances.

Because of the elasticity and tax savings which can be secured through the use of powers of appointment, it is a rare trust that is drafted today without the inclusion of one or more powers. But it was not always thus. Powers of appointment first developed in Chancery prior to 1540 as part of a scheme to get around the common law prohibition of wills of land: O transferred his land by feoffment to the use of himself for life and thereafter to the use of such persons as O should designate. The Statute of Wills in 1540 made this evasive scheme unnecessary, but new uses were found for the power of appointment. "In the succeeding centuries powers of appointment gained constantly increasing frequency because of their helpfulness in evading the burdens of feudal tenure, in keeping lands free from the claims of dower and curtesy, in providing property controllable by married women, and, generally, in injecting a desired elasticity into the property settlements of England." [3] There developed a highly refined and complex body of law governing the creation, classification, and exercise of powers of appointment. The conservatism of the judges dictated that — as with the law of future interests — the law of powers progress by spinning finer and finer distinctions. In reading Sugden's classic work on

[1] "Plainly no human foresight is adequate to frame in advance dispositions which will meet the exigencies [that may occur]. . . . [A]ll these are factors whose unpredictability indicates the folly of rigid predetermined future limitations and the desirability of gifts containing a substantial element of flexibility. The power of appointment, particularly the special power, is the most efficient device yet contrived by which an owner may obtain such flexibility while still controlling the general purposes to which his property shall be devoted." 3 Restatement of Property c. 25, Introductory Note (1940).

[2] See page 245, supra.

[3] 3 Powell, Real Property ¶385 (1970).

powers,[4] one sees that Lord Bacon's metaphor truly is no exaggeration: These were men who could spin their brains into cobwebs.

On this side of the Atlantic, however, general and special powers of appointment were rarely created before 1900, and even in 1940 the Restatement of Property could state that "the American case authority on powers of appointment is distinctly thin in quantity." [5] Not being laden with the English precedents, American jurisdictions may be able to escape the anomalies of history in developing and expanding the law of powers.

As with wills, trusts, and future interests, the law of powers of appointment has its own special terminology. The person who creates the power of appointment is the *donor* of the power; the person to whom the power is given is the *donee*. The persons in whose favor the power may be exercised are the *objects* or *beneficiaries* of the power. When a power is exercised in favor of a person, such person becomes an *appointee*. The instrument creating the power may provide for *takers in default of appointment* if the donee fails to exercise his power.

All powers can be divided into general powers and special powers. A *general power* is, in the language of the Internal Revenue Code, "a power which is exercisable in favor of the decedent [donee], his estate, his creditors, or the creditors of his estate." [6] Under the federal estate and gift tax laws, any power that is not a general power is classified as a special power. Thus a *special power* is a power not exercisable in favor of the donee, his estate, his creditors, or the creditors of his estate.[7] Prevail-

[4] Sugden, Powers (1808), was written when Sugden was twenty-seven years old. The treatise went through eight English and three American editions — the last English edition appearing in 1861. Sugden was raised to the peerage as Baron St. Leonards, and served as Lord Chancellor for nine months in 1852. The mysterious disappearance of his will, which he had made some years before his death, occasioned a lawsuit which established the admissibility, as evidence of contents, of the testator's declarations whensoever made. The will was proven on the testimony of one interested witness. Sugden v. Lord St. Leonards, 34 L.T.R. (n.s.) 369 (Ct. of App. 1876).

[5] 3 Restatement of Property c. 25, Introductory Note (1940). However, prior to 1940 there were many cases relating to powers to consume principal, which are dealt with in Section D of this chapter.

[6] Int. Rev. Code of 1954, §2041(b)(1). The Code goes on to exclude from the definition powers limited by "an ascertainable standard relating to the health, education, support, or maintenance" of the donee, powers held with an adverse party, and certain powers created prior to 1942. See pages 231-233, supra.

[7] The Restatement's definition of a special power is narrower in scope. A power is special if "it can be exercised only in favor of persons, not including the donee, who constitute a group not unreasonably large." 3 Restatement of Property §320(2)(a) (1940). Thus a power to appoint "to any person other than the donee, his estate, his creditors, or the creditors of his estate" would qualify as a special power for federal tax purposes, but would be too broad to qualify as a special power under the Restatement definition because it is a power to appoint among an unreasonably large group. Under the Restatement definitions this power is neither a general nor a special power; it is a "hybrid" power. Id. §320, Comment a.

If different rules are applicable to general and special powers, it is not clear how such a hybrid power would be classified outside the field of taxation. Possibly the courts will broaden the definition of special powers to make it congruent with the federal tax statutes, as was done by the New York legislature when it revised its laws on powers of appointment in 1965. N.Y. Estates, Powers & Trusts Law §10-3.2 (1967). It is entirely conceivable, though, that a power could be classified as general for one purpose and special for another. See Comment, Powers of Appointment — The New York Revision, 65 Colum. L. Rev. 1289, 1292 (1965), which criticizes the New York statute for following the federal definition as adversely affecting creditors' claims if an

ing professional usage of these terms is in accord with the definitions contained in the tax laws.

Powers of appointment may be capable of being exercised by deed alone,[8] by will alone, or by either deed or will. When exercisable only by will, the power is called a *testamentary* power. The donor of a testamentary power usually intends to protect the donee from his own indiscretions. A life estate coupled with a general testamentary power is similar to a spendthrift trust insofar as both have the purpose of protecting the donee. A special testamentary power has as one of its purposes keeping the donee free to exercise discretion up until the moment of death. Consider these two examples:

> *Case 1.* O transfers property to X in trust to pay the income to O's daughter A for life or until such time as A appoints, and to pay the principal to such person or persons as A shall appoint either by deed during her lifetime or by will; if A does not exercise the power of appointment, at A's death X is to pay the principal to B. O is the donor. A is the donee of a general power of appointment [9] exercisable by deed or will. B is the taker in default of appointment.
>
> *Case 2.* O transfers property to X in trust to pay the income to O's daughter A for life, and on A's death to pay the principal to such one or more of A's issue or spouses of issue as A shall appoint by will; if A does not exercise the power of appointment, at A's death X is to pay the principal to A's then living issue, such issue to take per stirpes.

"all the world but the donee" power is classified as a special power.

Mich. Stat. Ann. §26.155(102)(h) (1957, Supp. 1971) and Wis. Stat. Ann. §232.01(4) (1957, Supp. 1971), as well as the New York statute noted in the preceding paragraph, adopt the federal definition of a general power without the exceptions excluding powers limited by an ascertainable standard and powers held with an adverse party referred to in note 6 supra. See Effland, Powers of Appointment — The New Wisconsin Law, 1967 Wis. L. Rev. 583. Cal. Civ. Code §1381.2 (1954, Supp. 1971) enacts the federal definition of a general power and, like the Internal Revenue Code, excludes from that definition powers limited by an ascertainable standard and powers held with an adverse party.

[8] Powers exercisable only by deed are rarely created, and often they can be exercised by will unless this is expressly forbidden. N.Y. Estates, Powers & Trusts Law §10-6.2 (1967) provides: "Where the donor has made the power exercisable only by deed, it is exercisable by a written will unless exercise by will is expressly excluded." Similar provisions are found in Cal. Civ. Code §1385.1 (1954, Supp. 1971) and Mich. Stat. Ann. §26.155(105)(2) (1957, Supp. 1971). See also 3 Restatement of Property §347, Comment b (1940); United States v. Bank of Clarksdale, 346 F.2d 638 (5th Cir. 1965) (holding donor intended unlimited power to consume principal to be exercisable only during the donee's life).

[9] Except in Maryland. Under that state's law, a power of appointment is not exercisable in favor of the donee or his estate unless the power in terms authorizes such an appointment. In Estate of Pierpont v. Commissioner, 336 F.2d 277 (4th Cir. 1964), a trust created by H's will was held not to qualify for the marital deduction where W was given a power of appointment similar to that in *Case 1*: Under local law, W's power of appointment was not a general power. But in Guiney v. United States, 425 F.2d 145 (4th Cir. 1970), the testator, after giving his wife a testamentary power, added: "I want to make it clear that I am giving my wife a general power of appointment over this trust in order that one-half of my estate may qualify for the marital deduction . . . as it is fully my intention to take advantage of the marital deduction. . . ." The court held that this language gave the wife a general testamentary power of appointment, and that the trust qualified for the marital deduction.

There is a profound difference between the general power in *Case 1* and the special power in *Case 2*. In *Case 1*, A is very close to being absolute owner of the property since the only thing that stands between A and absolute ownership is a piece of paper A can sign at any time; she merely has to write, "I hereby appoint to myself." (However, because of the common law dogma that the donee is acting as agent for the donor and does not "own" the property subject to a general power, this piece of paper may be an effective shield against A's creditors, her spouse, and other persons seeking to reach the property.) In *Case 2*, A occupies a position similar to that of O's agent or that of a fiduciary. A can exercise the power to benefit her issue, but she cannot appoint the property in such a way as to benefit herself or her estate.[10]

SECTION B. General Powers of Appointment

1. *General Powers to Appoint by Deed or Will*

Historically the courts viewed the donee of a power of appointment as the agent of the donor, and not as the owner of the appointive property. When the power is general, this view is myopic, and particularly so when the general power is presently exercisable by deed. In this century American legislatures and courts increasingly have come to treat the donee of a general power as the owner of the property.

Suppose T bequeaths property to X in trust to pay the income to A for life or until A appoints the property, and to pay the principal as A appoints by deed or will, and in default of appointment to pay the principal to A's issue living at his death per stirpes. By exercising his general power, A at any time can terminate the trust and appoint the principal to himself free of trust. In order to possess the property he has but to reach for it.[11] Why is a general power exercisable by deed or will not treated as the legal equivalent of a fee simple? For some purposes A is treated as the owner. Under the federal tax laws, A is treated as the owner for income, estate, and gift tax purposes.[12] Under the federal bankruptcy act, a general

[10] The existence of the power can, of course, benefit A by assuring filial devotion. "It doubtless occurred to the testator that by restraining a disposition of his property except by will, which is in its nature revocable, [his widow] would, to the end of her life, retain the influence over, and secure the respect of, the several objects of his bounty, which he intended her to have — a result less likely to be accomplished if power were given her to dispose of the property by deed or other irrevocable act to take effect in her lifetime." Hood v. Haden, 82 Va. 588, 591 (1886). As someone once said, a special power over a hundred thousand dollars never hurt an old lady. On the other hand, "as she grows older, the mother will have decreasing capacity of decision, and she may fall under the domination of one of her children who might not be the most deserving member of the family." Bolich, The Power of Appointment: Tool of Estate Planning and Drafting, 1964 Duke L.J. 32, 41.

[11] Yet it has been said that "the power of a person to appoint an estate to himself is no more property than his power to write a book or sing a song." In re Armstrong, 17 Q.B.D. 521, 531 (1886).

[12] Int. Rev. Code of 1954, §§678, 2041, 2514.

power that is exercisable by deed passes to the donee's trustee in bankruptcy.[13] The donee can make an effective contract to appoint the property in a particular way.[14] He can appoint in further trust, create new powers, mortgage the property, and, in general, appoint in any way he pleases.[15] Under the Rule against Perpetuities the donee of a general power presently exercisable is treated as owner of the property.[16]

For other purposes, however, the donee of a general power to appoint by deed or will is not treated as owner of the appointive property. A's wife has no dower in the appointive property if it is land. The appointive property is not in A's probate estate and is not subject to any statutory forced share given A's widow.[17] In several states no death taxes are levied on the death of the donee.[18]

In the absence of statute, in most states the creditors of the donee of a general power of appointment can reach the appointive property only if the donee *exercises* the power.[19] There is no satisfactory explanation of this rule. "Having once taken the position that the donee of such a power is not the owner of the appointive property and that the existence of the power does not, of itself, subject the property to the claims of the donee's creditors, there is no logical reason for distinguishing the situations in which the donee has exercised the power from those in which he has not. To say that a court of equity is stopping the appointed property in transitu and thus making it available to the donee's creditors is merely to state the result in terms of a fiction which is itself contrary to the common law dogma that title to appointed property does not pass through the donee. It also has been said that the reason for the rule lies in the argument that if an insolvent donee should appoint to himself and then give the property to a favored person it would be a fraudulent conveyance and that the donee's creditors should have an equal right where the donee appoints directly to such a person. This rationalization is similar to that offered by the Restatement and by some of the cases to the effect that the donee, in making the appointment, is exercising a dominion which is practically identical to that exercised by him over owned property and so, by analogy, he will not be permitted to direct the property away from his creditors. Both of these rationalizations depend fundamentally on an asserted identity between the interest of the donee of a general power and ownership, which identity has not been accepted, as a generalization, where creditors' rights are concerned. Finally it has been said that the rule is anomalous, that it is simply a unique remedy provided by courts of equity, and that it is perhaps justified by the proposition that general powers of appointment might better have been regarded as interests in property anyway." 5 American Law of Property §23.16 (Casner ed. 1952). In a number of states statutes have been en-

13 Bankruptcy Act §70a, c. 541, 30 Stat. 565 (1898), as amended 11 U.S.C.A. §110a (1958).
14 5 American Law of Property §23.34 (Casner ed. 1952).
15 Id. §§23.48-23.49.
16 See page 1041, infra.
17 Simes & Smith, The Law of Future Interests §947 (2d ed. 1956).
18 5 American Law of Property §23.24 (Casner ed. 1952).
19 Exception: If the donee is also the donor of the general power, creditors can reach the appointive assets. Id. §23.18. The creditors of the donee of a special power cannot reach the appointive property even if the power is exercised, since the power was not intended to benefit the donee. Id. §23.15.

acted enabling creditors of a donee of a general power to reach the appointive property, usually with the qualification that the creditors must first exhaust the donee's own assets before resorting to the appointive property.[20]

Unlike the owner of a fee simple in land, who must find a transferee if he wishes to rid himself of the fee, the owner of a general power of appointment can release his power. The owner of a special power can likewise usually release his power unless the donor manifests a contrary intent or the power is in trust or is an imperative power.[21] Also, unlike a fee simple, powers are personal and cannot be assigned and, if unexercised, die with the donee.

The reason usually asserted for these results — "a power of appointment is not property" — is question begging. If the general inter vivos power functions to avoid the duties and liabilities of ownership while enjoying the benefits, should public policy dictate that a person who holds a general power to appoint by deed or will be treated for all purposes as the owner of the appointive property? What exceptions to such a rule might be justified? [22]

PROBLEMS

1. H bequeaths a fund in trust for W for life, remainder as W appoints by deed or will. W executes a will appointing the fund to her brother B. B dies before W, leaving four children. At W's death, who takes the trust fund? 5 American Law of Property §23.47 (Casner ed. 1952).

2. T bequeaths a fund in trust for A for life, remainder as A appoints by deed or will, and in default of appointment to A's children. A executes a will that appoints the fund to his son B. Subsequently a daughter C is born to A. No mention of C is made in A's will, and C is pretermitted. Upon A's death does C share in the trust fund? Commonwealth v. Fidelity & Columbia Trust Co., 285 Ky. 1, 146 S.W.2d 3 (1940); In re Shoch's Estate, 271 Pa. 158, 114 A. 502 (1921); Rhode Island Hospital Trust Co. v. Anthony, 49 R.I. 339, 142 A. 531 (1928).

2. *General Testamentary Powers*

With a few exceptions, general testamentary powers are treated similarly to general inter vivos powers. A trustee in bankruptcy cannot exercise the donee's testamentary power, and the donee is not treated as owner of the property for purposes of applying the Rule against Perpetuities. Nor can the donee of a general testamentary power contract to exercise it in some specific way.

[20] See Cal. Civ. Code §1390.3 (1954, Supp. 1971); Mich. Stat. Ann. §26.155(113) (1957, Supp. 1971); Minn. Stat. Ann. §502.70 (1947, Supp. 1971); N.Y. Estates, Powers & Trusts Law §10-7.4 (1967).

[21] 3 Powell, Real Property ¶¶393, 394 (1970).

[22] See Berger, The General Power of Appointment as an Interest in Property, 40 Neb. L. Rev. 104 (1960).

SIMES & SMITH, THE LAW OF FUTURE INTERESTS (*2d ed. 1956*)

§1013. *Contracts to Execute Testamentary Powers*

If A has a power to appoint by will only, there are serious objections to the enforcement of a contract to execute it. The reason is not the same as in the case of the special power presently exercisable. There a contract to appoint which benefits the donee or any other non-object is a breach of a quasi-fiduciary relationship. The donee of a general power to appoint by will, however, is not a fiduciary in any sense of the word; the power is for his benefit. The difficulty is that, if a binding contract to exercise such a power can be made inter vivos, then to the extent that the contract is enforceable, the donee has, in effect, exercised the power inter vivos. It may be argued that, if A owns property, he may make a binding contract to devise it, and this contract is enforceable as against his heir, if A fails to make a will, or against his devisees, if A makes a will in violation of his promise. But as owner of the property, A could have disposed of it inter vivos. Whereas, if A has only a testamentary power, he cannot appoint the property inter vivos. Hence, we must conclude that, if a contract to exercise a power to appoint by will only were specifically enforceable, then the donor's intent would be defeated, since he intended the donee to withhold the final exercise of his choice until the moment of his death.

Following this line of reasoning, the English courts have held that a contract to exercise a general power to appoint by will only is not specifically enforceable, but that damages at law may be recovered for its breach. The American courts hold, however, that the contract is wholly void, and that neither damages nor specific performance can be secured. This would seem to be the better view. Even though the contract is not specifically enforceable, the threat of an action for damages would in all probability induce the donee to perform his contract. Thus, the will of the donor would be defeated in that the donee would not withhold his final decision until the moment of his death.

Suppose, however, the donee of a general testamentary power contracts with the donor to exercise it in a particular way. Here it would appear that the contract is valid, since it cannot be said that the donor's wishes would be defeated by failing to leave the donee free to exercise the power up to the moment of the latter's death.

PROBLEM

H bequeaths $400,000 in trust for W for life, remainder as W appoints by will and in default of appointment to the children of H and W equally. W would like to reach $30,000 of the principal to buy a mink coat and a diamond bracelet and take a trip around the world. There are three children of H and W. What would you advise W to do? 5 American Law of Property §23.30 (Casner ed. 1952). Suppose the gift in default were to "the issue of H and W living at W's death per stirpes"; would your advice be the same? Suppose the following statute were in effect. Cal. Civ. Code §1388.2(b) (1954, Supp. 1971): "Any releasable power may be released with respect to the whole or any part of the appointive property and may also be released in such manner as to reduce or limit the permissible appointees. No partial release of a power shall be deemed to make imperative the remaining power that was not imperative before such release unless the instrument of release expressly so provides. No release of a power is permissible when the result of a release is the present exercise of a power that is not presently exercisable."

3. *Exercise of the Power*

FIDUCIARY TRUST CO. v.
FIRST NATIONAL BANK OF COLORADO SPRINGS
Supreme Judicial Court of Massachusetts, 1962
344 Mass. 1, 181 N.E.2d 6

Kirk, J. The petitioner is successor trustee of property held by it under an inter vivos trust created on May 6, 1930, by Alice H. Ware, late of this Commonwealth. The petitioner seeks the instructions of the court as to whether a testamentary power of appointment given in the Alice H. Ware Trust (the Trust) to Francis C. Ware (Francis) late of Colorado Springs, Colorado, was duly exercised by the residuary clause in the will of said Francis. . . .

Under the terms of the Trust, as amended, the trustee was to pay certain income to Alice (the creator of the Trust and the donor of the power) during her lifetime, and, on her death, to pay certain income to her son Stephen if he survived her, during his lifetime, and the balance of the income in equal shares to Alice's other surviving children, or to the widow or issue of deceased children. Paragraph 3 of Article I of the Trust, as amended, required the trustee on the death of Stephen to divide the property "into equal shares, one being set apart for each child of the Donor . . . then living, and one such share being set apart in the case of each child of the Donor (including said Stephen) who is then deceased leaving a widow or issue then living or who is then deceased having died after the Donor and not more than two years prior to the said division into shares."

Paragraph 6 of Article I of the Trust, as amended, provides in part: "Each share set apart in the case of a deceased child of the Donor at the time when the trust is divided into shares as hereinabove provided shall be disposed of as such child shall by will direct to or for the benefit of such child's widow or his issue then or thereafter living or any one or more of such widow and issue, and in default of such direction shall be paid to such child's widow then living. . . ."

Paragraph 7 of Article I of the Trust, as amended, provides in summary that "any unappointed principal payable under paragraph 6 to the widow of a deceased child of the Donor shall be retained in trust for her and her issue, instead of being distributed to her outright."

Alice H. Ware died April 1, 1937. Her son Francis died April 7, 1951, in Colorado Springs, Colorado. Her son Stephen died December 11, 1959. Division of the trust property was not made until Stephen's death. Surviving Francis were his widow and two sons, Francis, Jr., who is married and has two minor children, and Loring who is unmarried.

Francis's will, drawn by a Colorado attorney, was executed by him March 13, 1951, during his last illness while a patient in a Colorado Springs hospital. There is no specific reference in Francis's will to any power of appointment nor to any property over which he had a power of appointment. There are two dispositive clauses in the will. By the first clause Francis left certain personal effects to his son Francis, Jr. The second clause provides: "I give, devise and bequeath the entire remainder of my estate of whatever kind or nature and wheresoever the same may be situated" to The First National Bank of Colorado Springs, Colorado, in trust to pay $100 per year from the income to his friends Hurley Begun and Jeannette Begun, or to the survivor of them, such payments to continue for a period of ten years, to pay the balance of the income to the use of his widow and his two sons for their joint lives and the life of the survivor and, on the death of the last survivor of his widow and sons, to distribute the principal to the then living issue of his son Francis, Jr., and, in default of such issue, to distribute the principal among his (i.e. Francis, the testator) brothers and their wives and issue.

The trust established by Francis in the residuary clause of his will had an inventory value of $88,033.06 and a market value on December 31, 1960, of $109,960.

The final decree entered in the Probate Court declared that the second (residuary) clause of Francis's will "was a valid and effective exercise by the said Francis C. Ware of the power of appointment given him under paragraph 6 of Article I of the Alice H. Ware Trust, as amended, insofar as the trust thereby created is for the benefit of his widow, . . . Harriet Eleanor Ware, his sons, . . . Francis C. Ware, Jr., and Loring Ware, and the issue of his said son, Francis C. Ware, Jr."

From this decree the appeal was taken. . . .

Referring to a general power of appointment, Chief Justice Gray in Sewall v. Wilmer, 132 Mass. 131, 134, citing earlier cases, said "it has been adjudged that the mere facts that the will relied on as an execution of the power does not refer to the power, nor designate the property subject to it, and that the donee of the power has other property of his own upon which his will may operate, are not conclusive against the validity of the execution of the power; but that the question is in every case a question of the intention of the donee of the power, taking into consideration not only the terms of his will, but the circumstances surrounding him at the time of its execution, such as the source of the power, the terms of the instrument creating it, and the extent of his present or past interest in the property subject to it. . . ." The Sewall case is but one of a long line of cases starting with Amory v. Meredith, 7 Allen, 397 (which cites and discusses earlier authorities) holding that, in deciding whether a general testamentary power of appointment has been exercised, the overriding consideration is whether an intention to exercise the power can be ascertained from an interpretation of the donee's will. Worcester Bank & Trust Co. v.

Sibley, 287 Mass. 594, 598-599. Gorey v. Guarente, 303 Mass. 569, 575. Frye v. Loring, 330 Mass. 389, 394. From the inception, as an aid in deciding this question where an intent to exercise the power does not clearly appear from the terms of the will, there has developed a rule of construction, dealing with the exercise of a general testamentary power of appointment, which has been repeatedly affirmed. "Since the decision in Amory v. Meredith, 7 Allen, 397, it has been a settled canon of construction that a general residuary clause will operate as an execution of a general testamentary power unless a contrary intent is shown by the will. . . ." Second Bank–State St. Trust Co. v. Yale Univ. Alumni Fund, 338 Mass. 520, 524. New England Trust Co. v. Faxon, 343 Mass. 273, 279.

The power of appointment given to Francis under the Trust, however, was not a general testamentary power but a special or limited testamentary power of appointment. By the terms of the power, Francis could not appoint to his estate or for the benefit of his creditors. He could, in fact, appoint only to his widow and his issue. . . . We are, therefore, faced with the question whether the canon of construction applied to general testamentary powers is also applicable to special powers of appointment. In other words, are we now to say that a general residuary clause in a will operates as an execution of the special testamentary power unless a contrary intent is shown by the will?

Heretofore it has been unnecessary for us to answer the question . . . although there was a rather strong intimation in Stone v. Forbes, 189 Mass. 163, 168-169, that the answer should be in the affirmative. The question was left open when most recently referred to. See Frye v. Loring, 330 Mass. 389, 395. Now, however, being squarely confronted with the question, we must decide it. Having had the benefit of argument by counsel and having given full consideration to the reasoning which underlies the canon applied to general testamentary powers we hold that the canon should not apply to cases involving special testamentary powers of appointment.

As was said in Boston Safe Deposit & Trust Co. v. Painter, 322 Mass. 362, at 366-367, "This canon of construction is a recognition of the fact that a general power of appointment which may be exercised in favor of the donee or his estate is a close approximation to a property interest (Garfield v. State Street Trust Co. 320 Mass. 646, 656) and can well have been intended to be comprehended within words adapted to the passing of a property interest." Similar observations on the nature of such a power were made in Old Colony Trust Co. v. Allen, 307 Mass. 40, 42, and in Fiduciary Trust Co. v. Mishou, 321 Mass. 615, 625. Moreover, the distinction between a general power and a special power has resulted in the application of different principles to each, respectively, in several different situations.

For example, it is settled that, where a donee of a general testamentary power of appointment exercises it, the appointed property can be reached by the donee's creditors if the other assets of the donee are insufficient to pay the creditors' claims. Clapp v. Ingraham, 126 Mass. 200, 202. . . . Creditors of the donee of a special power, on the other hand, cannot reach the appointive property whether or not the power has been exercised.[23] Prescott v. Wordell, 319 Mass. 118, 120. Restatement: Property, §326.

Again, "It is a recognized principle in the law of property that where the donee of a general power attempts to make an appointment that fails, but where, nevertheless, the donee has manifested an intent wholly to withdraw the appointive property from the operation of the instrument creating the power for all purposes and not merely for the purposes of the invalid appointment, the attempted appointment will commonly be effective to the extent of causing the appointive property to be taken out of the original instrument and to become in effect part of the estate of the donee of the power." Fiduciary Trust Co. v. Mishou, 321 Mass. 615, 624, and cases cited. This so called principle of "capture" (Amerige v. Attorney Gen. 324 Mass. 648, 656) which, "like some other principles applicable to general powers of appointment, owes its origin to the conception that the grant of a general power is in itself almost tantamount to a grant of ownership" (Old Colony Trust Co. v. Allen, 307 Mass. 40, 42) has no application in cases of special powers, where the ineffectively appointed property passes to takers in default of appointment . . . or, in some cases, to the objects of the power where there are no takers in default provided. . . .

Moreover, the extent to which the donee of a power of appointment may, in the exercise of the power, create new powers in the appointees has been held to depend on whether the original power is general or special. . . .

Reference may also appropriately be made to the distinction observed, in cases involving the rule against perpetuities, between appointments made under a general power exercisable inter vivos (period of the "rule" measured from the date of the exercise of the power; . . .) and a special power (period of the "rule" measured from the date of the creation of the power;[24] . . .).

The situations referred to above by no means constitute an exhaustive enumeration of the instances wherein the difference between a general and a special power has been recognized. "The fundamental nature of the distinction between powers of these two types is apparent upon even a casual consideration; and it is significant at almost every point in the law of powers." Am. Law of Property, §23.4. See also id. §23.5.

[23] Other considerations arise if the donee of the special power was formerly the owner of the appointive property and had transferred it in fraud of his creditors, retaining only the special power of appointment. Any right of the creditors to reach the appointive property in such a case, however, would be based on the fraudulent conveyance and not on the fact that the debtor had retained a special power of appointment in the property transferred. Restatement: Property, §326, esp. comment b. See Prescott v. Wordell, 319 Mass. 118, 120.

[24] In the case of a general (or special) power which is exercisable only by will and which, therefore, cannot be practically equated with ownership to the same degree as a general power exercisable inter vivos, we have held that, as in the case of [a] special power, the period of the "rule" is measured from the date of the creation of the power. Minot v. Paine, 230 Mass. 514, 523. Fiduciary Trust Co. v. Mishou, 321 Mass. 615, 622. Amerige v. Attorney Gen. 324 Mass. 648, 656. For the applicability of the so called "second look" doctrine to the "rule," see Sears v. Coolidge, 329 Mass. 340, 345-346.

The "fundamental nature of the distinction between powers of these two types" consists in the difference in the extent of dispositive power over the appointive property. From this root difference have stemmed the distinctions drawn in the cited situations. It is the presence of the virtually unlimited power of disposition in general testamentary powers which is the genesis of the canon of construction applied to such powers. It is the absence of the virtually unlimited power of disposition in special powers which leads us to the conclusion that the canon should not apply to special powers. We think that, unlike a general power, a special power is not "a close approximation to a property interest . . . [which] can well have been intended to be comprehended within words adapted to the passing of a property interest." Boston Safe Deposit & Trust Co. v. Painter, 322 Mass. 362, 366-367. It is our opinion that the traditional common law distinction between "property" and "powers" (National Shawmut Bank v. Joy, 315 Mass. 457, 472-473, and cases cited), which with regard to general powers has in effect been overridden in the cases cited above, persists with undiminished validity in the case of special powers and would alone serve as a sufficiently sound rationale for the nonapplicability of the canon in question to special powers.

There are, however, other considerations, less involved in the niceties of property law, which indicate the same result. The donee of a general testamentary power can appoint the property to anyone, including his own estate. It well may be that a layman with such extensive power of disposition over property is not to be expected to distinguish between such property and that in which he has, in addition to such power of disposal, what the law calls "title" or a "property interest" and that he can reasonably be presumed to regard this appointive property as his own. The donee of a special testamentary power, however, can, by definition, appoint only to a limited class of persons exclusive of his estate. It would in our opinion be unreasonable to presume that a layman with such a limited power of disposal over property would regard such appointive property as his own. He would more likely consider himself to be, as the donor of the power intended, merely the person chosen by the donor to decide who of the possible appointees should share in the property (if the power is exclusive), and the respective shares of the appointees. . . .

In Frye v. Loring, 330 Mass. 389, 394-395, it was said in passing: "In the present cases there was a special testamentary power, yet it might well be contended that the same canon of construction should apply where the recipients under the residuary clause are objects of the power." Again, we think that coincidence between the objects of a special testamentary power and the recipient under a residuary clause is a relevant circumstance on the issue of the donee's intent to exercise the power by his residuary clause. We do not think, however, that it is sufficient to raise a presumption which would be embodied in the canon of construction under consideration. In the first place, the probative value of such a circumstance would depend on a multitude of variables, e.g., the degree of coincidence between the potential appointees and the recipients under the residuary clause, whether the special power is exclusive or non-exclusive (see Frye v. Loring, 330 Mass. 389, 396-397) and whether the objects of the special power would, in any event, be natural objects of the donee's bounty. Secondly, if coincidence of potential appointees and recipients under the residuary clause were sufficient to raise the presumption of intent to exercise the power, it would be because of the coincidence alone and not because of the peculiar nature of a residuary clause. From such a rule it would follow, for example, that, if the appointive property consisted of money and the donee by will left a cash legacy to the objects of the special power, we would be obliged, in the absence of evidence in the will to the contrary, to hold that the coincidence of the objects of the power with the beneficiaries of the legacy operated to make the legacy an exercise of the special power of appointment. Yet we think such a rule would certainly be a misconception of the rationale underlying the canon in question and the role of a residuary clause in this rationale. See Boston Safe Deposit & Trust Co. v. Painter, 322 Mass. 362, 367.

We, therefore, hold that the canon of construction applicable to general testamentary powers of appointment does not apply to special testamentary powers of appointment. It follows that in the case of a special power, as here, our inquiry is not "whether the will shows affirmatively an intention not to exercise the power" (Boston Safe Deposit & Trust Co. v. Painter, supra). Rather the question is, as we stated at the outset, whether we can discover in the will, read in the light of conditions surrounding its execution, a sufficiently declared intention on the part of Francis to exercise the power, having in mind that the " 'province of the court is not to conjecture what the testator's intention was and then read it into the will, but to ascertain his intention by construing the words which he used as the declaration of it.' Sanger v. Bourke, 209 Mass. 481, 486, 487, and cases cited." Gorey v. Guarente, 303 Mass. 569, 575.

We hold that on the record before us the intention of Francis to exercise the power is in fact left to conjecture and, consequently, the property subject to the power passes under paragraphs 6 and 7 of Article I of the Trust, as amended, to the takers in default of appointment. As mentioned previously, there is no reference in Francis's will to a power of appointment, nor is there reference to property which is the subject of a power of appointment. There were sufficient assets in the personal estate of Francis to carry out the provisions of his residuary clause.

The trustee under Francis's will places stress on the fact that apart from the annuity to Francis's two friends and the contingent remainder interests to Francis's brothers and their families, the recipients under the residuary clause were objects of the power. Wholly aside from the fact that some of the recipients under the residuary clause were not objects of the power, we think that the coincidence relied upon is of little significance. In the normal course of events, we would expect that Francis's widow and issue, as natural objects of his bounty, would be provided for in Francis's will. The trust set up by Francis in the residuary clause is the sole provision made for them. In such a case the inference that the residuary clause was also intended to exercise the power is hardly compelling. Moreover, the Trust provides that, in default of appointment by Francis, his widow and issue are to share the unappointed principal (although not in the same manner as if the principal were appointed under the residuary clause). From this fact, in the absence of any reference to the power in the will, it is at least equally inferable that Francis was content to allow the property to pass under the takers-in-default provision of the Alice H. Ware Trust.[25]

In the last analysis we are left only with the introductory terms of the residuary clause where Francis disposed of "the entire remainder of my estate of whatever kind or nature and wheresoever the same may be situated. . . ." We have in mind that "It is the general rule that the intent of a testator is not to be thwarted by refinements and distinctions resting upon subtlety and ingenuity or by lack of technical accuracy in the use of words or by unduly stressing the literal meaning of a few words or by attaching to them a hard and fast meaning which is not in consonance with the setting in which they are employed." Beals v. Magenis, 307 Mass. 547, 552, and cases cited. We think, however, that it would be unreasonable to construe the introductory language of the residuary clause as a manifestation of an intent by Francis to include in such clause not only property owned by him beneficially but also property over which he had merely a limited power of disposition. Compare Frye v. Loring, 330 Mass. 389, 393, 395 (where the preamble of the will declared that the will was to dispose of not only property owned by the testator but also property "over which I may have any power of testamentary disposition at the time of my decease"). See Pitman v. Pitman, 314 Mass. 465, 474, 475 (where the testator's will "contained a residuary clause devising and bequeathing his own property and that over which he had a power of appointment"); Restatement: Property, §341. To construe the introductory language of the residuary clause in such a manner would be the equivalent of adopting the canon of construction which we have decided is not applicable.

The final decree of the Probate Court must be reversed and a decree entered declaring that the power of appointment given to Francis under paragraph 6 of Article I of the Trust was not exercised by Francis's will and that the appointive property should be retained by the petitioner under the in-default-of-appointment provisions of the Trust.[26]

NOTES

1. The rule followed in a majority of states is that a devise of all property or a residuary clause does not, of itself, exercise a general power of appointment.[27] The Massachusetts rule has been adopted by statute in a substantial minority of states.[28]

[25] It appears that Francis's will was drawn by a Colorado attorney. There is, in our opinion, special force in the argument made by the guardian ad litem that the failure of the attorney to include in the will any reference to a power of appointment indicates that his client, Francis, did not intend to exercise the power by his will because the residuary clause in Francis's will would not of itself have exercised the power under the law of Colorado. See Johnson v. Shriver, 121 Colo. 397, 406-407 (decided March 20, 1950, and brought to the attention of the court under G.L. c. 233, §70).

[26] Noted 43 B.U.L. Rev. 338; 47 Minn. L. Rev. 473. — Eds.

[27] 5 American Law of Property §23.40 (Casner ed. 1952); Note, 15 A.L.R.3d 346 (1967).

[28] See, e.g., Cal. Civ. Code §1386.2 (1960, Supp. 1970); N.Y. Estates, Powers & Trusts Law

However, even in those states purporting to follow the majority rule there is a growing tendency to find an intent to exercise a general power even when the evidence consists of not much more than the existence of a residuary clause.[29] In many of the states having statutes adopting the Massachusetts rule, a residuary clause will exercise a special power if the residuary legatees are objects of the power.[30]

2. In order to prevent an unintentional exercise of a power of appointment, should the creating instrument provide that the power can be exercised only by an instrument, executed after the date of the creating instrument, which refers specifically to the power? California Continuing Education of the Bar, California Will Drafting §13.14 (1965); Rabin, Blind Exercises of Powers of Appointment, 51 Cornell L.Q. 1 (1965). What effect would the following statute have on such a provision? Va. Code Ann. §64.1-50 (1968): "No appointment made by will, in exercise of any power, shall be valid unless the same be so executed that it would be valid for the disposition of the property to which the power applies, if it belonged to the testator; and every will so executed shall be a valid execution of a power of appointment by will, notwithstanding the instrument creating the power expressly require that a will made in execution of such power shall be executed with some additional or other form of execution or solemnity." To overcome any doubt as to the validity of a specific reference formality, several states have enacted statutes similar to N.Y. Estates, Powers & Trusts Law §10-6.1(b) (1967): "If the donor has expressly directed that no instrument shall be effective to exercise the power unless it contains a specific reference to the power, an instrument not containing such reference does not validly exercise the power."

3. An attorney should ascertain, when drafting a client's will, whether the client is the donee of any powers of appointment. The will should explicitly provide whether or not the client intends to exercise each power of appointment. In addition to possibly not carrying out the client's wishes, an inadvertent exercise of a power of appointment can have some undesirable consequences.

(a) In most states property subject to a general power of appointment can be reached by the donee's creditors if the power is exercised.

(b) If a person has a general power of appointment created on or before October 21, 1942, the value of the appointive assets will not be includible in his gross estate for federal estate tax purposes if he does not exercise the power. If he exercises the power, the value of the appointive assets will be included in his federal gross estate. Int. Rev. Code of 1954, §2041(a)(1).

(c) In a few states death taxes are imposed if the donee exercises a power of appointment, but not if he does not exercise it. This test for death taxation of

---

§10-6.1(a) (1967). Wis. Stat. Ann. §232.03(2) (1957, Supp. 1971) provides that a residuary clause presumptively exercises a general power of appointment unless the donor provides for takers in default.

[29] See Bank of New York v. Black, 26 N.J. 276, 139 A.2d 393 (1958); Northern Trust Co. v. Moscatelli, 54 Ill. App. 2d 316, 203 N.E.2d 447 (1964).

[30] MacLean v. Citizens Fidelity Bank & Trust Co., 437 S.W.2d 766 (Ky. 1969); In re Biddle's Estate, 333 Pa. 316, 5 A.2d 158 (1939); In re Sheedy's Estate, 20 Misc. 2d 900, 192 N.Y.S.2d 220 (Sur. Ct. 1959); Note, 16 A.L.R.3d 911 (1967).

powers was abandoned by the federal government in 1942, but not all states have followed suit. Rabin, Blind Exercises of Powers of Appointment, 51 Cornell L.Q. 1, 4-7 (1965).

(d) Under the Rule against Perpetuities, the appointment by the donee of a general testamentary power or a special power is read back into the creating instrument, and the measuring lives must be in existence at the date of the creating instrument.[31] Suppose T dies in 1970, leaving a will that bequeaths a fund in trust for A for life, remainder as A appoints by will, and in default of appointment remainder to X charity. In 1971 A marries, and subsequently a child B is born to A. In 1975 A dies. A's residuary clause bequeaths all his property in trust for B for life, remainder to B's children who survive B. If by state law A's residuary clause exercises the power of appointment, the gift to B's children is void because it will not vest, if at all, until the death of B, who was not in being in 1970. A lawsuit will be required to determine whether the invalid remainder was captured and goes to A's heirs or goes in default of appointment to X charity.[32]

4. Is it advisable to include in a will a blanket clause that exercises any power that is acquired after the will's execution? See generally Use and Drafting of Powers of Appointment, 1 Real Prop., Prob. & Trust J. 307 (1966).

4. *Ineffective Exercise*

Here we meet two important doctrines that may be invoked when the donee makes an ineffective appointment. The first of these is capture; the second is marshaling (sometimes known as selective allocation). The doctrine of capture applies only to general powers because the result of its application is to capture the property for the donee's estate. The donor of a special power does not intend for the donee to be able to appoint to his estate.

SIMES & SMITH, THE LAW OF FUTURE INTERESTS
(2d ed. 1956)

§974. *Implied Execution Where Express Appointment Fails — The Capture Doctrine*

When the donee of a general power of appointment attempts to exercise it by will, his appointment may be ineffective for a variety of reasons. Thus, it may be void under the rule against perpetuities; or the appointee may die before the donee, causing the appointment to lapse. Normally, in such situations, the property goes to the taker in default, for the phrase "in default of appointment" in the instrument creating the power is construed to mean "in default of effective appointment."

Sometimes, however, the language of the instrument containing the ineffective

[31] See page 1042, infra.
[32] See Amerige v. Attorney General, 324 Mass. 648, 88 N.E.2d 126 (1949), page 1045, infra.

appointment has been construed to contain an implied appointment to the donee's own estate for all purposes. This has sometimes been referred to in the United States as the doctrine of capture. The principle is well stated in the case of In re De Lusi's Trusts [3 L.R. Ir. 232 (1879)] as follows:

> "The question in all cases of the class of that now before me is one of intention — namely, whether the donee of the power meant by the exercise of it to take the property dealt with out of the instrument containing the power for all purposes, or only for the limited purpose of giving effect to the particular dispositions expressed. . . . This intention may, of course, be gathered from the whole instrument, and if it appears therefrom that the donee meant thereby in the first place to make the fund for all purposes his own, and in the next place to dispose of it in a particular way which fails to take effect, the general intention will still be carried out, and the fund will be held to go to those persons who take the property of the donee either by general disposition or as next-of-kin."

It should clearly be understood that the doctrine here considered is not a legal remedy for the failure of an appointment. It is a doctrine of implied alternative appointment. The instrument is construed as if it said: "I make an express appointment as here indicated, but whether this is valid or not, I appoint the property to my own estate." . . .

A more satisfactory basis for concluding that the donee has appointed to his estate for all purposes is the existence of a blending clause. If the donee in his will states that he disposes of all owned and appointed property as a unit and makes no distinction between these two classes of property, it is fair to assume that he is appointing the property to his own estate whether the express provisions are valid are not. This is because the will indicates that he is thinking of the appointed property as his own property. This view is supported by the Restatement of Property and by Massachusetts and Illinois authorities, besides English authority. Not only would this result be reached if there is an express blending of owned and appointed property by the language of the will, but it should also be reached by the operation of a residuary clause in jurisdictions where the language of such a provision is regarded, either by statute or judicial decision, as exercising general powers.

PROBLEM

T bequeaths a fund in trust to pay the income to A for life, then to pay the principal as A appoints by will, and in default of effective appointment to pay the principal to M. A year after T's death, a son B is born to A. A then dies. The residuary clause of A's will provides: "I give, devise, and bequeath all the rest of my property (including the property over which I was given a power of appointment by the will of T) to the Security Bank in trust in its absolute discretion to pay the income to my son B or to accumulate the income and add it to principal. On the death of B the principal is to be distributed to B's issue then living per stirpes." The residuary gift of A's own property is valid; the appointment of the T trust fund violates the Rule against Perpetuities and is void. If A is held to have captured the trust fund, it is distributed to A's heirs. (Do you see why it cannot be distributed under A's residuary clause?) If A did not capture the trust fund, it goes in default of appointment to M; if there were no default clause, the fund would go back to the donor's estate.

If the court holds that A captured the trust fund, is the fund part of A's probate estate upon which executor's commissions and attorney's fees must be paid? Is it subject to A's widow's statutory forced share? See generally Jones, Consequences of an Ineffective Appointment — Capture, 18 Ala. L. Rev. 229 (1966).

Marshaling can apply to an appointment under either a general or a special power. Assets subject to a special power cannot, of course, be allocated to non-objects of the power, but they can be allocated to objects of the power. Marshaling is particularly useful in saving appointments violating the Rule against Perpetuities.

The doctrine of marshaling is best illustrated by a hypothetical case.

> *Case* 3. T bequeaths $100,000 to X in trust to pay the income to A during his life, remainder to such of A's children as A shall appoint, and in default of appointment to A's children equally. A dies, survived by his widow W and three children, B, C, and D. The residuary clause of A's will bequeaths all his own property (valued at $125,000) and the T trust fund in equal shares to his wife, W, and C. W is not an object of A's special power and cannot take any of the trust fund. If A had had proper legal advice, he would have expressly appointed the entire trust fund and devised $12,500 of his own assets to C, and devised $112,500 of his own assets to W. That would have avoided an ineffective appointment. Can A's executor save A's disposition by marshaling the assets in such a way as to give maximum effect to A's wishes? If he can, he will allocate the entire trust fund to C and of A's own assets allocate $12,500 to C and $112,500 to W. A's dispositive plan is thus entirely saved.

Marshaling applies when the donee blends both the appointive property and his own property and attempts to dispose of both as a single fund. The requisite blending typically occurs when the donee's will states at the beginning that it disposes of both the donee's own assets and the appointive property. Blending may also occur when a residuary clause expressly disposes of both types of property as one fund, but the cases do not reach uniform results in this situation.[33]

[33] See 5 American Law of Property §§23.59, 23.60 (Casner ed. 1952); Simes & Smith, The Law of Future Interests §975 (2d ed. 1956); Hoffman, Powers of Appointment and Selective Allocation, 46 Cornell L.Q. 416 (1961).

5. *Conflict of Laws*

BOLICH, THE POWER OF APPOINTMENT: TOOL OF ESTATE PLANNING AND DRAFTING
1964 Duke L.J. 32, 64-68

The increasingly peripatetic habits of Americans and the multistate contacts of property ownership underscore the necessity for the estate planner and draftsman to be alert to certain conflict of laws problems lest his client's estate plan and its disposition be frustrated by the application of arbitrary conflicts rules which might have been averted by proper foresight and drafting. While the hazard of attempting to suggest reliable guidelines in this area of law is recognized, at least some general observations seem to be called for in a discussion of this kind. In the solution of typical conflicts problems involving trusts, there are three sets of variables in the applicable rules, depending upon (1) whether the res consists of movables or immovables, (2) whether the trust is inter vivos or testamentary, and (3) the type of problem at issue, i.e., validity, such as capacity of parties or compliance with local property law; construction, such as the meaning of terms like "children" or the closing of a class; and administration, such as the trustee's powers or allocation of dividends.

In their decisions the courts are making an effort to keep the law measurably abreast of social conditions. This effort is manifested by a growing tendency in judicial choice of law situations involving trusts and estates for courts to modify traditional conflicts concepts so that undue disruption of an expressed dispositive plan may be avoided by the selection of the most favorable law. As to inter vivos trusts of movables, and possibly as to such testamentary trusts, the settlor or testator is permitted to specify in the deed or will the state law which shall govern the transaction, provided it does not violate settled public policy of the situs state and has some reasonable connection with the transaction. If the instrument contains no such express designation of a governing law and the settlor's intent is not otherwise made clear, the state law applied is generally that of the jurisdiction having closest contact or connection with the trust. Such contacts include the place where the trust is to be administered, the situs of the trust res, the trustee's place of business, the domicile of the parties, and the place of execution of the trust instrument. Subject to the doctrine of equitable conversion, as to inter vivos or testamentary trusts of immovables, the settlor's intent gets less consideration, and situs law is generally applied. The privilege of specifying in the dispositive instrument the state law which is to govern not only prevents conflicts problems, but it should also avoid litigation by enabling a lawyer to draft in accordance with a state law on which he is expert and perhaps to select a favorable jurisdiction. Testamentary and inter vivos trusts are normally drafted in accordance with the law of the settlor's domicile at the time of execution; and with regard to their validity, construction, and administration, that law should usually be the specified governing law, unless it is preferred to rely upon the court and conflicts rules.

As to powers of appointment, conflicts problems arise when the donor and donee are not domiciled in the same jurisdiction or when the appointive assets have a situs in a state where neither the donor nor the donee is domiciled. Even if all contacts are with a single state when the power is created, this may not continue. Quite often today, a person is domiciled in one jurisdiction when he makes his will, in another at the time of his death, and a third state is the situs of both movables and immovables owned by him. By traditional rules his testamentary disposal of movables is governed by the law of his domicile at death and his immovables by the law of the situs. Thus, it is always wise to be certain that every will or deed meets the required formalities of all states having a present or prospective contact with the transaction. In addition to the privilege of specifying the applicable state law, some of the more important construction problems may be avoided by cognizance of them and the insertion of provisions to control in either the creation or exercise of the power. For example, problems which are decided on the basis of the intention of the donor or the donee may be explicitly provided for and litigation prevented. Who are the objects of the power is a matter of the donor's intent, and if the objects of the power are "children" or "issue" or "heirs" of a named person, a definitional clause settling the matter may be inserted by the draftsman of the power. Whether a power is exercised is a matter of the intention of the donee, and a clear intent properly manifested to exercise or not to exercise a power will eliminate this question. Choice of law problems which involve not questions of the intention of the donor or of the donee but rather policy questions such as restraints on alienation or the Rule Against Perpetuities are not so easily handled by specific provision.

Such is the state of uncertainty in the conflicts rules regarding powers of appointment that useful generalization is difficult. For the estate planner and draftsman, principal legal focuses as to powers of appointment concern their creation and exercise. They are usually created as part of a single conveyance, inter vivos or testamentary, which often involves successive estates, legal or equitable, and the same law usually governs the whole transaction, which, as above stated as to movables, may be specified by the transferor-donor. As to immovables, situs law controls the validity of creation of a power by deed or will. As to movables, the same is true for inter vivos creation, but the law of the donor's domicile appears to control testamentary creation. As to exercise, situs normally governs the formal validity of an attempted inter vivos appointment of personalty, and the same is true for either a deed or a will exercising a power of appointment over land. Regarding the validity of a testamentary appointment of personalty, it is the general rule that if the will provision is valid under the law of either the domicile of the donee at his death or that of the donor when he executed the instrument creating the power, the appointment is valid. The basic common law theory of relation back is of much importance in the solution of a conflicts problem when creation and exercise of the power occur in different jurisdictions, and the donee's will exercising a power must generally meet the legal formalities of the donor's state on the theory that the property passes from the donor to the appointee.

Complete and careful drafting of the dispositive instrument which creates the power should usually specify which state law the donor wishes to govern its validity and perhaps should empower the donee to select the state law to govern its exercise by him. Such provisions will likely prevail in the absence of real conflict with local policy, and frequently even in policy matters.

SECTION C. Special Powers of Appointment

1. *Characteristic Problems of Special Powers*

Under a general power of appointment, the donee has the absolute right to create whatever interests he wishes and in whatever persons. This is so because the donee of a general power could appoint to himself or to his estate, and then by a second instrument or second clause in his will transfer the property to whomever and upon whatever terms he pleased. Unlike certain other areas of property law where the transferor must use two pieces of paper rather than one to carry out his intention, here the law is very sensible.

With a special power, on the other hand, the donee's authority is circumscribed. Unless expressly prohibited, the donee of a special power can appoint outright or in further trust, create life estates and future interests, and create new conditions and powers of appointment so long as no benefits accrue to nonobjects of the power. There has been considerable litigation, however, over whether the donee of a special power can create a new power of appointment which can benefit nonobjects of the original power. For example, suppose T gives A a power to appoint among A's children. Can A exercise his power by creating in his son B either a general power[34] or a special power to appoint among B's children? The answer clearly should be yes; since A could appoint outright to B, there is no rational basis for refusing to permit A to appoint to B something less than absolute ownership. Yet the cases are divided on this point.[35]

There are a number of other problems concerning the scope of special powers. The most important restriction involves the persons to whom the donee can appoint. The designation of the objects is usually by a class description, such as "children," "issue," or "heirs." Any appointment to a nonobject of the power is void.[36]

[34] For tax reasons A should *never* exercise his *special* power by creating a *general power to appoint by deed or will.* If a special power of appointment is exercised by creating "another power of appointment which under the applicable local law can be validly exercised so as to postpone the vesting of any estate . . . for a period ascertainable without regard to the date of the creation of the first power [i.e., in most states, a general power to appoint by deed or will]" the appointive property will be included in A's federal gross estate. For an explanation of this tax trap, see page 1044, infra.

[35] 3 Powell, Real Property ¶398 (1970).

[36] A donee may not appoint to an object upon the condition that some benefit be conferred

In determining who comes within the class designation, the law of powers relies heavily on the law of class gifts. It may be wise for the draftsman of the creating instrument to include a clause defining the intended class.

A special power can be exclusive or nonexclusive. If it is exclusive, the donee may exclude entirely one or more objects of the power. The donee may appoint all the property to one member of the class of permissible appointees, excluding the rest. If the power is nonexclusive, the donee must appoint some amount to each permissible object. Thus:

> *Case 4.* T bequeaths a fund in trust for A for life, remainder as A shall appoint by will among his children. A has 3 children, B, C, and D. If the power is exclusive, A can appoint all the property to C. If the power is nonexclusive, A must give some amount each to B, C, and D if he exercises the power.

You must readily see the great difficulty with nonexclusive powers: How much must the donee give each member of the class? Can A appoint $1 each to B and D, and the remainder of the fund to C? In some states the amount cannot be too small because of the "illusory appointment" rule requiring that each permissible appointee receive a "substantial" sum, but in other states the illusory appointment rule has been repudiated.[37]

Whether a power is exclusive or nonexclusive depends upon the intention of the donor as revealed by the creating instrument. Such words as a power to appoint to "any one or more of A's issue in such amount or amounts and for such estates and interests and upon such conditions and limitations as A shall designate" would create an exclusive power. If the creating instrument does not reveal the donor's intent, classification will turn upon the presumption adhered to in the jurisdiction.[38] The Restatement of Property asserts that, in the absence of a contrary intent of the donor, special powers of appointment are presumptively exclusive.[39] As an abstract proposition, this position seems to have the support of most courts. However, there are cases holding that a contrary intent is shown by language creating a power to appoint "*among* A's children as A shall by will appoint." (Compare this with the words, "among *such of* A's children as A shall by will appoint," which would create an exclusive power.) The problem can and should be avoided by proper draftsmanship.[40]

---

upon a nonobject, or upon consideration of a promise by the object to confer a benefit upon a nonobject. Evidence is admissible to show an extrinsic agreement by an appointee to benefit a nonobject. Matter of Carroll, 274 N.Y. 288, 8 N.E.2d 864 (1937).

When an appointment is shown to benefit a nonobject, the whole appointment fails where the evidence shows that the appointment would not have been made but for the intended benefit to the nonobject. Where the appointment probably would have been made anyway, the appointment is cut back only by the part designated to go to the nonobject.

[37] Simes & Smith, The Law of Future Interests §982 (2d ed. 1956); Note, Exclusive and Nonexclusive Powers and the Doctrine of Illusory Appointments, 51 Mich. L. Rev. 936 (1953).

[38] 5 American Law of Property §23.57 (Casner ed. 1952).

[39] 3 Restatement of Property §360 (1940).

[40] See 3 Powell, Real Property ¶398 n. 44 (1970).

PROBLEMS

1. Appraise the following three special power of appointment forms:

(a) T bequeaths a fund in trust for his wife for life, "and upon my wife's death, the trustee shall distribute the corpus of the trust among my children in such shares as my wife shall appoint by will, and in default of appointment to my children in equal shares."

(b) "On the death of the settlor's said daughter, the then remaining principal and undistributed income shall be paid to, or held for the benefit of, such one or more of the group consisting of the spouse of the settlor's said daughter, the issue of settlor living at the death of the settlor's said daughter or born thereafter, and spouses of the settlor's issue, including spouses of issue who predecease the settlor's said daughter as well as spouses of issue who are born after the death of the settlor's said daughter, as the settlor's said daughter shall appoint by a will, executed after the date of this instrument, which refers specifically to this power. The exercise of this power by the settlor's said daughter, however, shall not apply to the proceeds of any life insurance on the life of the settlor's said daughter payable to this trust. Subject to the above restrictions, in the exercise of this power of appointment the settlor's said daughter may appoint outright or in trust; she may select the trustee or trustees if she appoints in trust; she may create new powers of appointment in a trustee or trustees or in any other appointee; she may, if she appoints in trust, establish such administrative powers for the trustee as she deems appropriate; she may create life interests or other limited interests in an appointee with future interests in favor of other appointees; she may impose lawful conditions on an appointment; she may appoint by her will different types of interests to selected appointees; she may impose lawful spendthrift provisions; and generally she may appoint by her will in any manner, provided always, however, that no appointment shall benefit directly or indirectly persons other than members of the restricted group who are the objects of this power, and that nothing herein shall be construed as authorizing the settlor's said daughter to appoint to herself, her creditors, her estate or creditors of her estate." [41]

(c) T bequeaths a fund in trust to pay the income to his son A for life or until A appoints the principal, and "to pay the principal to such person or persons as A by deed or will appoints except that A may not exercise this power by appointing to himself, his creditors, his estate or the creditors of his estate."

2. Why, in form (b), does Professor Casner include this sentence: "The exercise of this power by the settlor's said daughter, however, shall not apply to the proceeds of any life insurance on the life of the settlor's said daughter payable to this trust"?

3. Note that in form (b) the special power can be exercised only by a will "executed after the date of this instrument." If this provision were omitted, could the power be exercised by a will executed prior to the date of the trust instrument

[41] 2 Casner, Estate Planning 1200 (3d ed. 1961).

and containing this clause: "I hereby appoint all property over which I may have a power of appointment at death to my son James"? 5 American Law of Property §23.41 (Casner ed. 1952).

4. In form (c) suppose that A appoints sums from the principal from time to time to pay the educational expenses of his minor child B. At A's death is the property subject to the power includible in A's federal gross estate? Halbach, The Use of Powers of Appointment in Estate Planning, 45 Iowa L. Rev. 691, 696 n. 28 (1960).

5. Suppose J is given the life income of a trust and has an exclusive special power to appoint the trust principal by deed or will to such of J's issue as he wishes. J has an illegitimate daughter, K, who is not known to be illegitimate outside of the immediate families but whom J has recognized in writing as his child. J contracts with his son L to appoint the property to L in consideration of L's promise to give one-third of the trust assets to K. At J's death L is aged twenty-eight, K is aged eleven. J's will appoints the trust property to L. L refuses to give K one-third. What are K's rights? Simes & Smith, The Law of Future Interests §1011 (2d ed. 1956); Coffin v. Cooper, 2 Drew. & S. 365, 62 Eng. Rep. 660 (V.C. 1865).

6. T bequeaths a fund in trust for A for life, then to such of A's children as A shall appoint, and in default of appointment to A's children equally. An anti-lapse statute in the jurisdiction provides: "If a devise or legacy is made to a child or other relation of the testator, who dies before the testator, but leaves issue surviving the testator, such issue shall, unless a different disposition is made or required by the will, take the same estate which the person whose issue they are would have taken if he had survived the testator." B, a child of A, dies in the lifetime of T. C, another child of A, survives T but dies in the lifetime of A. D, a third child of A, survives A. Both B and C leave issue who survive A.

(a) If A makes no appointment, who takes?
(b) Can A appoint to the issue of B?
(c) Can A appoint to the issue of C?
(d) Can A appoint to B or C?

See 3 Restatement of Property §350, caveat, Comment d (1940); Halbach, The Use of Powers of Appointment in Estate Planning, 45 Iowa L. Rev. 691, 721 (1960).

7. T's will contains the following clause: "I bequeath to Eliza V. Seay during her life that portion of the old home tract and household furniture etc., which lies between the Trousdale Ferry turnpike road and the creek of Round Lick and Jennings Fork, and, at her death I desire it to go to one of my nephews and I leave it with her to decide which one it shall be. . . . It is my desire that the above described tract shall remain in the hands of the family as long as possible, for here sleeps my wife, my father and mother." At T's death he had four nephews: W. S., John C., W. R., and Richard. Richard died before the life tenant, Eliza, leaving two children, Elizabeth and Carr. Eliza dies, without exercising her power of appointment. Who owns the old home tract? Bridgewater v. Turner, 161 Tenn. 111, 29 S.W.2d 659 (1930); N.Y. Estates, Powers & Trusts Law §10-6.8(b)(1) (1967).

2. *Tax Reasons for Using Special Powers*

Under the federal estate tax laws the donee of a general power of appointment is treated as the owner of the property that is subject to the power.[42] The appointive property is includible in the donee's gross estate. The donee of a special power of appointment is not, however, treated as the owner of the appointive property for tax purposes. This benevolent tax treatment accorded special powers has caused an increasing use of special powers of appointment in wills and trust instruments. On the other hand, because of their tax treatment, general powers are rarely found in a well-drafted instrument except where the donor intends the gift to qualify for the marital deduction.

The tax savings that can be achieved over several generations through the use of special powers of appointment are considerable. Suppose O has one son A, and the amount of O's property that will reach A's hands after death taxes are paid is $400,000. Let us compare two methods of passing this $400,000 through three generations to O's great-grandson. For purposes of illustration we shall assume the value of the property remains the same and ignore certain other factors, including the marital deduction, which might change the tax picture. O wishes to give his son A as complete ownership as it is possible to do, while at the same time saving taxes.

(1) The *first method* is a series of absolute bequests from generation to generation. O bequeaths the property absolutely to A. After taxes A receives $400,000. Then A bequeaths the property, worth $400,000, in fee simple to his son B. At A's death a federal estate tax of $81,700 must be paid (assuming a $60,000 exemption and debts and expenses of 10 percent). This reduces the principal amount to $318,300. Then B bequeaths the property to his son C. At B's death a federal estate tax of $58,641 must be paid. Thus the property originally worth $400,000 has been reduced in amount to, in round figures, $260,000 when it reaches O's great-grandchild — a loss of $140,000. The successive federal estate taxes alone have resulted in a depletion of 35 percent; the state death taxes will result in further depletion.

(2) The *second method* is a trust with A as trustee and with special powers of appointment in A as beneficiary. Instead of giving A a fee simple, we want to give A as much power over the property as is possible without causing A to be treated as owner for tax purposes. We do this by breaking up the fee simple into various parts and by giving to A as many of those parts as the Internal Revenue Code permits without taxing the property to the holder's estate.

(a) First, O by will transfers the legal title to the property to A in trust. As trustee A has the powers of management. He can decide when to sell and in what to reinvest. If the powers are broadly drafted, A can manage the property almost as if he owned it himself.

[42] Int. Rev. Code of 1954, §2041. See page 231, supra.

(b) Second, O's will gives to A, *not as trustee but as a beneficiary*, the following rights and powers:

(i) the right to receive all the income;

(ii) a special power of appointment exercisable by deed to appoint the trust property to anyone A pleases except himself, his creditors, his estate, and the creditors of his estate;

(iii) a power to consume the trust property measured "by an ascertainable standard relating to the health, education, support or maintenance" [43] of A;

(iv) a power to withdraw each year $5000 or 5 percent of the corpus, whichever is greater;[44]

(v) a special power of appointment exercisable by will to appoint the trust property to anyone A pleases except himself, his creditors, his estate, and the creditors of his estate.

(c) Third, if O desires to make sure that A will always be able to use the entire property if he needs it, O can appoint an independent co-trustee and give this co-trustee the power to pay A the entire principal or to terminate the trust.

Note that none of the above powers given A, individually or collectively, causes A to be treated as owner of the trust fund under the federal estate tax. Yet A has such broad control over the trust fund that in most instances he can do exactly with the trust funds what he could do if he had been bequeathed the property outright.

The trust instrument will further provide that in default of appointment the trust property passes on A's death to A's son B in trust for B for life; B is given all the powers A had, and in default of appointment by B the trust property is to pass on B's death to his son C.[45] Hence, if A and B do not exercise any of these powers, the $400,000 bequeathed by O can pass intact to O's great-grandson C. For purposes of illustration we stop the wealth transmission process by bequeathing absolute ownership to C. However, it need not necessarily stop there. A trust could be set up wherein O gives to successive generations the powers given to A above. This trust could last for the period permitted by the Rule against Perpetuities. If ten healthy babies are selected as measuring lives, in addition to all of O's issue alive at the effective date of the trust, the trust could run on for 100 years or so, and no estate taxes would be paid during this period.

Whether such a transfer, commonly called a generation-skipping transfer, should continue to receive this favorable tax treatment has been hotly debated in recent years. The culmination of a five-year study of the federal estate and gift tax

[43] See page 232, supra.

[44] Ibid.

[45] In reality the gift in default would be more complicated, since the draftsman would direct that on the death of A the trust fund be divided into as many shares as there are children of A then living and children of A who predeceased A leaving issue surviving A. Over each share the child or the issue of a predeceased child would be given powers similar to those given A. For an example of careful draftsmanship covering this problem, see 2 Casner, Estate Planning 1291-1293 (3d ed. 1961).

laws by the American Law Institute was a recommendation of wholesale revision of the federal transfer tax laws, including a proposal that an additional tax, to be paid either by the transferor or by the beneficiary, be imposed on generation-skipping trusts. American Law Institute, Federal Estate and Gift Tax Project (1968). For an explanation of the ALI proposals written by the project's Reporter, see Casner, American Law Institute Federal Estate and Gift Tax Project, 22 Tax L. Rev. 515 (1967). The ALI recommendations were the basis for reform proposals submitted to Congress by the Treasury Department in 1969. Busy with income tax reforms that resulted in the Tax Reform Act of 1969, Congress took no action on the estate and gift tax proposals. Possibly Congress will act on these proposals some time in the 1970s. See page 211, note 9 supra.

PROBLEM

A is the beneficiary of Trust X with a corpus of $150,000. He has a power to withdraw $5000 from principal each year. A is also the beneficiary of Trust Y with a corpus of $200,000, and he has the power to withdraw 5 percent of the value of the trust fund each year.

(a) If A lets his powers lapse in one year, is he protected by §2041(b)(2)? Would he be protected if Trust X had a corpus of $50,000? To the extent that there is a lapse of the donee's power to invade which exceeds $5000 or 5 percent, the donee is deemed to have transferred such excess retaining a life estate therein. The excess is thus included in the donee's gross estate under Int. Rev. Code of 1954, §2036. See page 233, supra; 1 Casner, Estate Planning 717, n. 57a (3d ed. 1961, Supp. 1970).

(b) In Trust Y can A withdraw any amount until the end of the calendar year? Is A entitled to withdraw 5 percent of the specific assets of the trust or only 5 percent of the value of the assets? If the former, does the trust realize capital gain if A withdraws 5 percent of appreciated assets? Covey, Use of Long Term Trusts in Estate Planning, 4 Real Prop., Prob. & Trust J. 489 (1969).

SECTION D. Powers to Invade Principal

1. *Legal Fee Simple with Power to Dispose of the Property*

FOX v. SNOW
Supreme Court of New Jersey, 1950
6 N.J. 12, 76 A.2d 877

Per Curiam. This cause is here on our own certification.

The case involves the construction of a paragraph of the will of Rosa E. Green, deceased, of the Borough of Haledon. The paragraph provided as follows:

> "Third: I give and bequeath unto my husband, William L. Green all of the money which I have on deposit at the Paterson Savings and Trust Company, Paterson, New Jersey, however, any money which is in the said account at the time of my said husband's death, the said sum shall be held by my niece, Catherine King Fox, absolutely and forever."

The will was admitted to probate on April 25, 1949. The husband, William L. Green, died intestate on May 30, 1949. The legacy bequeathed under the paragraph in question is still on deposit in the Paterson Savings and Trust Company.

The question presented is whether William L. Green became the absolute owner of the money on deposit, the gift over to the plaintiff, Catherine King Fox, being void, or whether the husband took a life estate only and the fee vested in the niece.

The bequest to the husband was in general terms with an absolute power of disposal. Under such circumstances the gift over of the part not disposed of is void. As determined by Judge Grimshaw below, the husband, William L. Green, took an absolute ownership, an estate in fee, of the bank account. Downey v. Borden, 36 N.J.L. 460 (E. & A. 1872); Tuerk v. Schueler, 71 N.J.L. 331 (E. & A. 1904); Gaston v. Ford, 99 N.J. Eq. 592 (Ch. 1926); Briggs v. Faulkner, 120 N.J. Eq. 1 (Ch. 1936); Trafton v. Bainbridge, 125 N.J. Eq. 474 (E. & A. 1939).

Appellants ask this Court to explicitly and expressly overrule the long established law of this State. This we decline to do. Such action would be fraught with great danger in this type of case where titles to property, held by bequests and devises, are involved. A change of the established law by judicial decision is retrospective. It makes the law at the time of prior decisions as it is declared in the last decision, as to all transactions that can be reached by it. On the other hand a change in the settled law by statute is prospective only. Stockton v. Dundee Manufacturing Co., 22 N.J. Eq. 56 (Ch. 1871).

The judgment of the Superior Court is affirmed.

VANDERBILT, C.J. (dissenting). I am constrained to dissent from the views of the majority of the court, first, because they apply to the case a technical rule of law to defeat the plain intent of the testatrix without serving any public policy whatever in so doing and, secondly — and this seems to me to be even more important — because their opinion involves a view of the judicial process, which, if it had been followed consistently in the past, would have checked irrevocably centuries ago the growth of the common law to meet changing conditions and which, if pursued now, will spell the ultimate ossification and death of the common law by depriving it of one of its most essential attributes — its inherent capacity constantly to renew its vitality and usefulness by adapting itself gradually and piecemeal to meeting the demonstrated needs of the times.

I. . . . Not only is the meaning of this bequest entirely clear to any mind not encumbered with the involved and technical feudal lore of estates in fee simple, estates in fee tail and estates for life and the medieval doctrines of seisin and possession, but it is consonant with her entire testamentary plan. . . .

By the words in the third paragraph, "any money which is in said account at the time of my said husband's death, the said sum shall be held by my niece, Catherine King Fox, absolutely and forever," the testatrix beyond any doubt intended that her husband could use up the bank account but that if he did not, the plaintiff should take what was left of it on his death. To hold otherwise is to proceed on the untenable assumption that the quoted words are meaningless and to ignore the elementary principle that the provisions of a will are not to be construed as meaningless except on the failure of every attempt to render them effective. . . . This principle is an integral part of the most fundamental rule of testamentary construction, i.e., the duty of the court is to ascertain what the intent of the testator was and, then, having ascertained it, to give it effect. . . .

Instead of following this obviously sound method of testamentary construction our courts have been misled by the complex and artificial rules of the old common law of real property into accepting a technical rule of testamentary construction which gained seeming but altogether undeserved immortality from the opinion of Chancellor Kent in Jackson v. Robins, 16 Johns. 537 (N.Y. Ct. App. 1819), wherein he categorically stated at p. 588:

> . . . we may lay it down as an incontrovertible rule, that where an estate is given to a person generally, or indefinitely, with a power of disposition, it carries a fee; and the only exception to the rule is, where the testator gives to the first taker an estate for life only, by certain and express words, and annexes to it a power of disposal. In that particular and special case, the devisee for life will not take an estate in fee, notwithstanding the distinct and naked gift of a power of disposition of the reversion.

The rule was later set down by Chancellor Kent in his Commentaries as settled law, 4 Commentaries on American Law *270 and *535, and has been followed by the New Jersey courts in a long line of decisions. . . . It has likewise been subscribed to by courts in other jurisdictions, though significantly not without dissent, 75 A.L.R. 71-111.

. . . Because of the fact that in the instant case the clearly expressed intent of the testatrix has been thwarted by this obviously arbitrary and technical rule that owes its continuance to the magic of the name of Chancellor Kent, it is incumbent upon us to inquire closely into its nature in order to determine whether it is a rule necessitated by principles of public policy and founded upon good reason before which testamentary intent should rightly bow, or whether it is merely a rule remarkable only by its ancestry. Gray has stated the alleged reasons for the rule and their complete lack of validity with his customary incisiveness in his Restraints on the Alienation of Property (2d Ed. 1895), supra:

> What are the reasons given? They are, *First*, that the gift over is repugnant; *Second*, that the passage of a fee simple on death of the tenant intestate to the heirs is a necessary incident of the estate; *Third*, that an executory devise contingent upon a circumstance which it is in the power of the first taker to prevent happening

is void. The first is the reason originally given [see Ide v. Ide, 5 Mass. 500 (1809)]; the second is the reason given by Fry, J., in Shaw v. Ford [7 Ch. D. 669 (1877)]; the third is Chancellor Kent's. But these are only words. They merely mean that the courts have set up a certain rule, and that the proposed provision is inconsistent with it; but why that rule should be set up, what interests are forwarded by it, how it helps the well-being, moral or material, of the community, the courts never show, and, to do them justice, never attempt to show. In the hundreds of pages in the reports on this subject, there is no suggestion that this rule tends to promote any good object. (P. 67.)

Stating that the rule is not a rule of construction to carry out the intention of the parties but that its aim and object is to defeat that intention, he observes:

> The courts always recognize this fact; and that no considerations of public policy are involved is shown by its being perfectly easy to carry out the desired result by a slight change of phrase. If you give a man a fee simple, you cannot provide that if he does not sell or devise it it shall go to T., but if you give him a life estate with power to appoint by deed or will, and in default of appointment to T., the gift to T. is perfectly good. In both cases the intention is clear and undisputed; when you defeat the intention in one case, you are defeating exactly the intention that is preserved in the other. (P. 67).

These observations apply equally to the whole line of decisions in New Jersey which follow Chancellor Kent's rule. One may search them from the case of Dutch Church at Freehold v. Smock, et al., . . . 1 N.J. Eq. 148 (Ch. 1830), to Trafton v. Bainbridge, . . . 125 N.J. Eq. 474 (E. & A. 1939), without finding any good reason given for this technical rule.

That the rule is arbitrary and serves no public policy is perhaps best demonstrated by a few illustrations from our own decisions.[46] In the instant case there was a devise to A generally or indefinitely, with absolute power of disposition, and on A's death a gift over to B. By the operation of Chancellor Kent's rule A gets a fee and the gift over is void. . . . A would not have taken a fee, however, and the gift over to B would have been valid, if the devise had been to A for life, instead of generally and indefinitely; . . . or if A's power of disposition had been limited instead of absolute; . . . or even if the devise had been to A absolutely, or forever, or the like, but with only a power of testamentary disposition; . . . or to A absolutely, or forever, or the like, without any mention of a power of disposition. . . . It is thus obvious that the plaintiff herein is denied her due, not because what the testatrix intended was illegal or impossible, but solely because the verbal formula used to express that intent ran afoul of this idiosyncrasy of the law.

II. The opinion of the majority of the court, like every other decision in this State on the subject, makes no attempt to justify the rule it perpetuates either in reason or on grounds of public policy. Despite the deleterious effects of the rule and the lack of any sound principle to support it, the majority maintains that it should not be overthrown, because it has been the long established law of this State and

[46] Seventeen case citations in this paragraph are omitted. — Eds.

because overruling it "would be fraught with great danger in this type of case where titles to property, held by bequests and devises, are involved" by reason of the retroactive effect of all judicial decisions. This view, if it had been consistently applied in the past, would have prevented any change whatever in property law by judicial decisions. There would have been, e.g., no rule against perpetuities, no restraints on the alienation of property, no right to redeem mortgaged premises, no foreclosure of the equity of redemption, and so on endlessly. Every change in the law by judicial decision necessarily creates rights in one party to the litigation and imposes corresponding duties on the other party. This is the process by which the law grows and adjusts itself to the changing needs of the times.

The process is necessarily used not only to create new rights and corresponding duties but, where necessary, to strike down old ones. Cessante ratione legis, cessat et ipsa lex (the reason for a law ceasing, the law itself ceases) is one of the most ancient maxims known to our law and it is constantly followed by our courts. . . . "It is revolting," says Mr. Justice Holmes, "to have no better reason for a rule of law than that so it was laid down in the time of Henry IV. It is still more revolting if the grounds upon which it was laid down have vanished long since, and the rule simply persists from blind imitation of the past," and "To rest upon a formula is a slumber that, prolonged, means death." Collected Legal Papers (1920) 187, 306. . . .

Particularly in the realm of testamentary construction should the courts feel free to depart from precedent when the dictates of justice and reason demand it. Even Chancellor Kent was of this opinion: "Though we are not to disregard the authority of decisions, even as to the interpretation of wills, yet it is certain that the construction of them is so much governed by the language, arrangement, and circumstances of each particular instrument, which is usually very unskillfully and very incoherently drawn, that adjudged cases become of less authority, and are of more hazardous applications, than decisions upon any other branch of the law." 4 Commentaries on American Law *535. . . .

Even in England where the doctrine of the judicial infallibility of the House of Lords has prevailed for a century,[47] we find Lord Chancellor Simon declaring in the case of Perrin v. Morgan (1943), 1 All E.R. 187, 194, when an ancient and well established rule of testamentary construction was urged upon the court:

> The present question is not, in my opinion, one in which this House is required on the ground of public interest to maintain a rule which has been constantly applied but which it is convinced is erroneous. It is far more important to promote the correct construction of future wills in this respect than to preserve consistency in misinterpretation.

The dangers that the majority fear, it is submitted, are more apparent than real. The doctrine of stare decisis tends to produce certainty in our law, but it is important to realize that certainty per se is but a means to an end, and not an end in

[47] But now discarded. See Leach, Revisionism in the House of Lords: The Bastion of Rigid Stare Decisis Falls, 80 Harv. L. Rev. 797 (1967). — Eds.

itself. Certainty is desirable only insofar as it operates to produce the maximum good and the minimum harm and thereby to advance justice. The courts have been reluctant to overthrow established rules when property rights are involved for the simple reason that persons in arranging their affairs have relied upon the rules as established, though outmoded or erroneous, and so to abandon them would result sometimes in greater harm than to observe them. The question whether the doctrine of stare decisis should be adhered to in such cases is always a choice between relative evils. When it appears that the evil resulting from a continuation of the accepted rule must be productive of greater mischief to the community than can possibly ensue from disregarding the previous adjudication on the subject, courts have frequently and wisely departed from precedent, 14 Am. Jur., Courts, §126.

What then, are the relatively evils in the instant case? First, we should consider the evils that will result from a perpetuation of the rule here involved. It has already been demonstrated that the rule, in each and every instance in which it is applied, results in a complete frustration of the legitimate intention of the testator. It can only operate to take property from one to whom the testator intended to give it and to bestow it upon another. There is a further evil, moreover, resulting from the very existence of the rule. As Professor Gray has put it in his Restraints on the Alienation of Property (2d ed. 1895) 68, supra:

> It is often a question of the greatest difficulty to determine whether a testator has given a devisee a life estate with general power of appointment, or whether he has given him a fee with an executory devise over in case the first taker shall not dispose of his interest. If it were not for this rule, that question would almost never become material. But now that a testator's intention, if expressed in one form, cannot be carried out, while it can be, if expressed in another, the question becomes of vital importance, and consequently this arbitrary rule is responsible for an enormous amount of litigation.

Bearing out this observation, an annotation in 75 A.L.R. 71-111, entitled "Devise or bequest which does not state character or duration of estate but purports to dispose of what remains at death of devisee or legatee, as creating a fee or life estate," cites 386 cases of which 28 are from New Jersey, and we cannot even hazard a guess as to the number of additional cases, reported and unreported, in which the rule was involved. That a rule has been so productive of unnecessary litigation is in itself strong proof of its undesirability.

Having considered the evils flowing from continuing to follow the rule, let us now inquire into the evils, if any, which might result from its rejection. It is pertinent at this point to recall the words of Mr. Justice Cardozo minimizing the effect of overruling a decision: "The picture of the bewildered litigant lured into a course of action by the false light of a decision, only to meet ruin when the light is extinguished and the decision is overruled, is for the most part a figment of excited brains." The Nature of the Judicial Process (1921) 122. The rule in question by its very nature is never relied upon by those who are seeking to make a testamentary disposition of their property, for if the rule were known to a person at the time of the drawing of his will, its operation would and could be guarded against by the choice of words appropriate to accomplish the result desired. This rule is truly subversive of the testator's intent. It is relied upon only after the testator's decease by those who seek, solely on the basis of its technical and arbitrary requirements, to profit from the testator's ignorance and to take his property contrary to his expressed desires. Certainly it is not unjust or inequitable to deny such persons resort to this rule. There are three possible factual situations to be considered in weighing the retroactive effect of overturning this rule. First, where a will has already been the subject of legal proceedings, property rights determined by a judgment entered therein are beyond the reach of any change in the law. Such a judgment is res judicata. Second, where a will has been executed, but the testator is still living, or if dead, the clause similar to the one in question has not yet been construed by the courts, the "evil" caused by the overthrow of the rule will be to carry out the testator's intent. No existing will need be changed by a decision doing away with the old rule, since its overturning merely permits the expressed intent of the testator to be given effect. Third, where persons have not now, but may in the future execute wills, no harm can result from overthrowing the rule, for they have neither to forget an old rule nor to learn a new one in order to insure the carrying out of their testamentary plan. In the absence of the rule their intentions, as naturally though perhaps inexpertly expressed, will govern.

Thus it would appear that the dangers envisioned from overthrowing this rule are not present here and that the evils resulting from its continuation are great. This being so, should there be hesitation in rejecting this rule merely because it is old? To recognize a rule solely because it has long been the law "would be to deny every quality of the law but its age, and to render it incapable of progress or improvement. It would be to stamp upon our jurisprudence the unchangeableness attributed to the laws of the Medes and the Persians." Hurtado v. California, 110 U.S. 516, 529 (1883). We should not permit the dead hand of the past to weigh so heavily upon the law that it perpetuates rules of law without reason. Unless rules of law are created, revised, or rejected as conditions change and as past errors become apparent, the common law will soon become antiquated and ineffective in an age of rapid economic and social change. It will be on its way to the grave. In the instant case the rule applied by the court below should be rejected and effect should be given to the testator's intention that the plaintiff have the bank account in question.

For affirmance — Justices Case, Heher, Oliphant, Wachenfeld, Burling and Ackerson — 6.

For reversal — Chief Justice Vanderbilt — 1.[48]

NOTES

1. Why did Chancellor Kent lay down a rule that an executory interest limited after a fee was void if the owner of a fee were given the absolute power to dispose of the property? Apparently he misconceived the common law notion that an executory interest was indestructible. At common law an executory interest was inde-

[48] Noted 5 Rutgers L. Rev. 571. — Eds.

structible *by a gap in seisin or by a common recovery.* An executory interest was indestructible by a gap in seisin by definition, and Pells v. Brown, Cro. Jac. 590, 79 Eng. Rep. 504 (K.B. 1620), held an executory interest could not be defeated by a common recovery and the testator's intent thus frustrated. However, an executory interest could be destroyed (the technical word is "fail") if the event upon which it was limited did not happen. For example, suppose a gift to B and his heirs, but if B dies without issue surviving him, to C and his heirs. The executory interest in C will be destroyed (fail) if B leaves issue surviving him. The testator so intends. Paying no mind either to what was meant by the holding in Pells v. Brown that an executory interest was "indestructible" or to its policy basis (carrying out testator's intent), Chancellor Kent concluded that an executory interest could not exist if it could be destroyed by the fee owner alienating the property. Following Kent's reasoning, would you conclude that vested remainders subject to divestment by exercise of a power of appointment are void? They too were indestructible by a common recovery.[49]

Today the most frequently heard rationalization is that an executory interest which prevents passage of title to the fee owner's heirs if he dies intestate is repugnant to the fee. As Vanderbilt, C.J., points out — quoting Gray — the repugnancy argument begs the question. Moreover, *all* executory interests that cut short fees are conceptually repugnant to the fee, which by definition has an infinite duration. Fees subject to being divested by executory interests are self-contradictory and are thus like Mahaffy's famous Irish bulls, "always pregnant." But by the genius of the common law they have been recognized since the Statute of Uses in 1536.

Fox v. Snow led to the enactment of the following statute in New Jersey in 1951. Even though Chancellor Kent's rule is no longer the law in New Jersey, we include Fox v. Snow because the reasoning of Chief Justice Vanderbilt's magnificent dissent might (and we think should) be followed elsewhere — and, indeed, applied to other antiquarian rules of property law that have nothing going for them but their age.

New Jersey Statutes Annotated §3A:3-16 (1953): "In any devise or bequest of real or personal property set forth in the will of a testator dying after January 1, 1952, the giving to one person of an indeterminate or other interest in the property or an estate in fee therein or absolute ownership thereof, together with a power, absolute or otherwise, to dispose of the property, shall not be construed to render void a limitation over of the property to another person which is to take effect in the event that the first named devisee or legatee shall not have disposed of the property during his lifetime. In all such cases, the testator's intent shall be given effect."

2. With the increasing inclination of courts to carry out the testator's intent, it is not surprising that they have developed a number of constructional devices to avoid the rule. The usual gambit is to construe the interest in the first taker as a life estate.[50] If the first taker gets a fee, under Chancellor Kent's rule the gift over is

[49] See Simes & Smith, The Law of Future Interests §1485 (2d ed. 1956).

[50] Hanks v. McDanell, 307 Ky. 243, 210 S.W.2d 784 (1948). In Slowey v. Jenkins, 408 S.W.2d 452 (Ky. 1966), the Kentucky court read Hanks v. McDanell as discarding Chancellor

void. But if the first taker gets a life estate, the gift over is valid. An express power to dispose in the first taker has been said to be evidence a life estate was intended, since if a fee were intended, the power is superfluous.[51] On the other hand, absence of an express power to dispose may indicate no more than a life estate was intended.[52] Heads, plaintiff wins; tails, defendant loses. Other indications of a life estate may be: (a) there was a gift over; (b) the gift over was in a codicil or subsequent clause; (c) a gift of "what remains" means a gift of a "remainder" and a remainder must follow a life estate.

To strike down the gift over, there is also a requirement that the first taker be given the *absolute* power of disposition. Courts have held the power is not absolute (a) when it is limited to a specific purpose such as supporting and maintaining the first taker; (b) when it is exercisable only during life; or (c) when, although it is exercisable inter vivos or by will, it does not allow devolution to the first taker's heirs by intestacy. Even though on each of these points there are cases to the contrary, they indicate that no astute court can really be forced either way by Chancellor Kent's rule.[53]

What we have here is a bad rule and a profusion of verbal devices to avoid it, many of which only a casuist could follow. The problem is usually stated as simply one of construction. What did the testator intend the first taker to have, fee simple or life estate? The language of the testator — looked at through these darkling devices — frequently leads only to a bad case of eyestrain. Consider two West Virginia cases only two years apart. In Weiss v. Soto, 142 W. Va. 783, 98 S.E.2d 727 (1957), the Supreme Court of Appeals of West Virginia had before it this instrument:

> I, devise and bequeath unto my beloved *wife* Lena Schwertfeger, all of the rest and residue of my real and personal property wherever the same my be situated, *absolutely in fee simple*, and *after the death of my said Dear wife*, the rest and residue of my real property and personal property shall be *devided between* my said three daughters *share and share a like*. [Emphasis added; wording as in original will.]

The court unanimously held that the widow took a life estate and the daughters a remainder. Two years later in Wooddell v. Frye, 144 W. Va. 755, 110 S.E.2d 916 (1959), the same court was called upon to rule on this devise:

> I give and bequeath all my property of both personal and real to my *wife* Sadie Sue Wooddell, to be hers *absolutely* and the *use* of all all the of which I may die seized and possessed for and *during her natural life*; and it is my will that *after her death* my real estate shall *dscend* to any in my children if there be any living *share and share alike*. [Emphasis added; wording as in original will.]

Kent's rule entirely, instead of merely laying down a new rule of construction. The court then classified the estates as a valid fee simple subject to divestment by an executory interest.

[51] DeWolf v. Frazier, 80 Ohio App. 150, 73 N.E.2d 212 (1947).

[52] Keiser v. Jensen, 373 Ill. 184, 25 N.E.2d 819 (1940).

[53] See Simes & Smith, The Law of Future Interests §§1486-1490 (2d ed. 1956). Note, 17 A.L.R.2d 7 (1951), is a 220-page compilation of cases on this subject that attempts to sort the cases by these transient verbal distinctions.

How do you think the court classified the interests? As the lawyer for the claimants under Sadie Sue's will, how would you evaluate your chances of success? If you think your chances are very bright indeed, either you are a fool or you have that mysterious sense of divination that marks a great lawyer, especially in the family wealth field. The court held, 5 to 1, that Sadie Sue took a fee simple absolute.

In spite of solemn statements by the courts that testator's language is controlling, it is pardonable to suspect that other factors are also at work, including the following: (a) the type of property (family heirloom, consumable chattels, money, or residuary personalty difficult to trace), (b) the value of the property, (c) the relationship of the first taker to the testator, (d) the need of the first taker, (e) the relationship of the second takers to the testator (children, collateral relatives, charity), (f) the parties to the lawsuit (is it a quarrel between the first taker and second takers, or between the heirs or legatees of the first taker and the second takers?), (g) the remedy sought. There is no absolute proof, of course, that such factors alone, in combination, or in variation have any influence on decisions. Lawyers and judges are accustomed to traditional explanations in terms of the dispositive language of the instrument. But classification by resort to the dispositive language alone will not explain these cases.

A morass indeed it is — and all because Chancellor Kent did not understand what "indestructible" meant.

3. How would you classify the dispositive language in Fox v. Snow so as to best carry out the testatrix's intent? Consider the following:

(a) fee simple absolute in William

(b) fee simple in William, subject to an executory interest in Catherine to take effect if William owns any of the property at death

(c) life estate in William, coupled with a general inter vivos power to appoint the property, remainder in fee simple in Catherine

(d) life estate in William, coupled with a general inter vivos and testamentary power to appoint the property, remainder in fee simple in Catherine

(e) life estate in William, with a power to consume principal if necessary to support him, remainder in fee simple in Catherine

What different consequences follow from these different classifications? Sparks, A Decade of Transition in Future Interests, 45 Va. L. Rev. 339, 374-378 (1959).

2. *Legal Life Estate with Power to Consume Principal*

COLBURN v. BURLINGAME

Supreme Court of California, 1923

190 Cal. 697, 214 Pac. 226

Kerrigan, J. — This action was brought for the purpose of requiring defendant, Leora W. Burlingame, to render an account of property which had come into her possession under the will of her deceased husband, it being alleged in the complaint (indirectly, it is true) that her interest therein is a life estate limited to certain purposes, and that certain expenditures being made by her are not within those purposes. The relief asked also included an injunction to restrain said defendant permanently from selling, disposing of, or encumbering any of the corpus of said estate, which consists entirely of personal property, and a bond to protect the interest of the plaintiffs as remaindermen.

A demurrer, both general and special, having been interposed to the complaint, it was sustained without leave to amend, the plaintiffs declaring that they did not desire such leave. The plaintiffs other than Dora W. Macauley appeal from the judgment in favor of said defendant entered following such order.

It appears from the allegations of the complaint that the defendant is the widow of Leslie H. Colburn, having remarried since his decease, and the plaintiffs are his brothers and sister-in-law. Leslie H. Colburn was a resident of Pennsylvania and died in that state. He left a will, which was there admitted to probate, and in due course the entire estate was distributed to said defendant, without bond for the protection of the interest of any other person.

The controversy between the parties arises upon the construction of certain provisions of this will, namely, the second and fourth paragraphs thereof, but principally the former.

Said paragraph 2 reads as follows:

"I Give, Devise and Bequeath to My beloved Wife Leora I. Colburn the entire handling and control of any and all of my real estate and any and all my personal property of any and every name nature or kind — wheresoever situate — To have and to hold, occupy or use the whole or any part thereof in such Manner as may in her judgment seem best for her own individual benefit and support without any hindrance on the part of any person or persons wholly confiding in and believing my beloved wife will not allow said property to depreciate or go to waste."

The third paragraph then gives the estate to the mother of the deceased and the mother of the defendant in the event of the latter's death. She, however, has survived them, which brings into operation the fourth paragraph of the will, which is as follows:

> It is my wish and will and I do so direct that in case of the decease of my mother Mrs. Eliza A. Colburn and the mother of my beloved wife Mrs. P. M. Westbrook and my beloved wife Leora I. Colburn shall yet be living, then and in such case I Give, Devise and Bequeath any and all my real estate and any and all personal property of any and every name nature or kind wheresoever situate at the time of the decease of my beloved wife Leora I. Colburn. To my Brothers then living and to my beloved wife's sister Mrs. Dora L. Nehrbass jointly and severally the remainder of my estate Share and Share alike.

As we have seen, the brothers and sister-in-law so mentioned are the plaintiffs in the case.

The appellants' first contention is that the will of the deceased, reading paragraphs 2 and 4 together, gives to the widow a life estate only, with remainder to the persons mentioned in said fourth paragraph, including themselves. . . . That the provision made for the defendant by said will constituted a life estate, although with power to consume the principal of the estate, we have no doubt. By paragraph 2 the entire estate is given over to her to be used for her individual benefit and support, and at her death the remainder, that is, the part of the estate unconsumed by her, is, by paragraph 4, given to the testator's brothers and sister-in-law. The rule of construction here applicable is that stated in Hardy v. Mayhew, 158 Cal. 95 [139 Am. St. Rep. 73, 110 Pac. 113], where it is said: "It appears to be settled by the overwhelming weight of authority that the mere fact that the first taker is invested with the power to dispose of or consume the whole of the property for certain purposes does not invest him with the absolute ownership thereof and render the gift over void where, taking the whole instrument together, it is concluded that the intent was to give only an estate for life with limited power of disposal or consumption," and the rule thus announced was followed in Luscomb v. Fintzelberg, 162 Cal. 433, 440 [123 Pac. 247].

This is also the construction given to bequests and devises by the courts of Pennsylvania, where the will here under consideration was executed and the testator's estate distributed.

. . .

It does not follow, however, that the plaintiffs are entitled to the relief here sought. As already noted, they seek to enjoin the defendant from disposing of the corpus of the estate, and ask that she shall be compelled to furnish a bond to protect their rights as remaindermen. The averments of the complaint upon which they ground this demand are the following:

> IX. That plaintiffs and each of them are informed and believe, and therefore allege, that Merton S. Burlingame, husband of said defendant, shortly after his marriage to her in the year 1920, gave up his employment in Chicago and has not since been employed, and that since their marriage said Merton S. Burlingame and Leora W. Burlingame have been living together in Chicago and California, and that the said Merton S. Burlingame had and has no means of his own to support himself and/or his wife, and that during the period said Merton S. Burlingame gave up his employment and married said defendant, said defendant Leora W. Burlingame has and is contributing to the support and maintenance of said husband from the property of the said estate contrary to the last will and testament of Leslie H. Colburn, deceased, and to the detriment of the plaintiffs herein; that by so contributing to the support of her said husband, Merton S. Burlingame, said defendant is diverting the said life estate to a purpose other than that authorized and directed by the said will of Leslie H. Colburn, to the irreparable injury and damage of the remaindermen under said will, to wit, the plaintiffs herein.
>
> XXI. That the plaintiffs are informed and believe that the defendant has threatened to, or intends to continue to divert the property of her life estate to uses other than those contemplated by the said will.
>
> XXIII. That the defendant is selling off portions of said stock and using the same for purposes not contemplated by the will, and therefore is reducing the corpus

of the life estate, to the irreparable injury and damage of the plaintiffs as remaindermen.

It is apparent that the last two paragraphs state demurrable conclusions of the pleader as to what uses or purposes are contemplated by the will, and that the point of the demurrer under this phase of it is directed to said paragraph IX, namely, that the defendant is contributing to the support of her husband. It is the appellants' contention that she cannot lawfully use the property of the estate for this purpose, and it is based upon plaintiffs' construction of paragraph II of the will hereinbefore set out, as there is not elsewhere in said will (which is set out in haec verba in the complaint), any restriction upon defendant's use of the property.

We are of the opinion that in view of the very broad language in which the bequest to the defendant is couched this contention is untenable.

The life estate of the defendant is in the whole of the property of the estate, "to have and to hold, occupy or use the *whole or any part thereof in such manner as may in her judgment* seem best for her own individual benefit and support *without any hindrance on the part of any person or persons, wholly confiding in and believing my beloved wife will not allow said property to depreciate or go to waste*."

It is seen that the right of the defendant to use the property is not confined to that necessary for her support; she may use it for her *benefit* — a term much broader than support; and she is made the judge of what is for her benefit; and she is to exercise that judgment *without any hindrance on the part of any person or persons* — a plain warning to these plaintiffs to keep hands off. For the preservation of the property the testator wholly confides in his wife. The defendant, it appears, has remarried, and for a time lived with her husband in Chicago. Having ample means — the value of the estate amounting to some ninety thousand dollars — the not unnatural desire arises in her to remove to California, or at least to live there during a part of the year. Should she leave her husband toiling and moiling in Chicago? Presumably she gave this question full consideration and concluded that it would be for her benefit that he should accompany her west. We can readily perceive that it might be much to her advantage that he should do so; and if in her opinion her life is made pleasanter or more to her liking by the freedom of her husband from the irksome demands of business we perceive no reason why, under the wide discretion she enjoys as to what expenditures are for her benefit, the expense of their common life may not be included under this head.

We can imagine expenditures which would be neither for her support nor benefit, the indulgence in which would give to the remaindermen a right to protection by appropriate legal remedy; but until the defendant uses the funds of the estate for a purpose much more remotely connected with her individual benefit than contributing to the support of her husband the plaintiffs must be content to leave the defendant in the undisturbed enjoyment of the estate bequeathed to her by the testator. . . .

It appearing from the complaint in this case, as we have seen, that the life estate given to the defendant is coupled with power to consume the whole thereof for the purposes indicated; that the expenditures being made by the defendant from the funds of the estate have not so far transgressed those purposes, and that the testator has directed that the estate should be placed in the control of the defendant, without requiring any bond or security, the plaintiffs have not stated a case entitling them to the relief sought or any relief. The trial court, therefore, properly sustained the demurrer.

The judgment is affirmed.

Lennon, J., Seawell, J., Myers, J., Lawlor, J., Wilbur, C.J., and Waste, J., concurred.

NOTES

1. The problem involved in Colburn v. Burlingame is delightfully illustrated by Noel Coward's bagatelle, "In a Bar on the Piccola Marina," reproduced on Columbia Masterworks record ML 5063, "Noel Coward in Las Vegas." Coward's song is about a respectable British matron who, recently widowed, discovered in the nick of time that life was for living — on the island of Capri.

2. Where the property involved is a tangible chattel, ordinarily security will not be required by a court unless danger of dissipation is shown. Where the property is money, negotiable securities, or the like (as in Colburn v. Burlingame), the possessory owner can dispose of the property quickly and easily and usually free of the claim of the owner of the future interest. Hence, unless the testator indicates a contrary intent, many courts require the possessory owner to give security before taking possession of this type of property. No showing of danger is necessary.

Does it make any difference whether W has a life estate with power to consume, followed by a remainder in A, *or* W has a fee simple subject to an executory interest in A if W does not dispose of the property? It has been stated that if W has a *fee*, rather than a life estate, the type of property is unimportant. Security will not be required — even for money, negotiable securities, or the like — unless danger of dissipation is shown.[54] The basis for this distinction is that the transferor intends the possessory owner to have greater control over the property when he gives him a fee simple subject to defeasance than he does when he gives him a life estate with power to consume. The difficulty with a distinction based on labels is obvious: The labels "fee" and "life estate" do not distinguish between kinds of events and their probabilities of happening; they ignore important factors that a rational solution requires taking into account.[55] What Simes and Smith say about remedies for waste ought to be applicable to problems of security as well:

> The right to protection against injury should depend, not so much upon the historical classification of the particular interest involved, but rather upon (a) the

[54] 1 American Law of Property §4.110 (Casner ed. 1952); Simes & Smith, The Law of Future Interests §1717 (2d ed. 1956).

[55] See Dukeminier, Contingent Remainders and Executory Interests: A Requiem for the Distinction, 43 Minn. L. Rev. 13, 46-51 (1958).

> kind of remedy sought; (b) the character of the act complained of; (c) the duration of the possessory interest; (d) the probability of the future interest becoming possessory; (e) the time within which the future interest will become possessory; (f) the probable duration of the future interest; and (g) the degree of control which the possessory owner has over the future interest. These are criteria from which the court can fashion rational and flexible judgments to meet the requirements of particular cases. It is believed that . . . the suggested criteria are more likely to be controlling in determining the remedies available than mere variations in the types of future interests.[56]

3. A draftsman should make it as clear as possible exactly what rights to the principal, if any, the life tenant is to have. The litigation over ambiguous language on this subject is extensive. See Annotations, Implication of Right of Life Tenant to Entrench Upon or Dispose of Corpus from Language Contemplating Possible Diminution or Elimination of Gift Over, 31 A.L.R.3d 6 (1970) (158 pages); Implication of Right of Life Tenant to Entrench Upon or Dispose of Corpus from Language Relating to the Extent of His Dominion Over the Corpus, or the Beneficial Purpose of the Provision for the Life Tenant, id. 169 (129 pages); Language of Will or Other Trust Instruments as Implying Right to Invade Principal on Behalf of Life Beneficiary, id. 309 (61 pages).

Which Is Preferable: Legal Life Estate or Trust?

In Colburn v. Burlingame, Leora was given a *legal* life estate in personal property with a power to consume corpus. Assume real property also was involved. What problems might arise during Leora's life that the draftsman should take care of in Leslie's will?

1. *Sale.* No legal life estate should be created without providing a mechanism for sale of the property should circumstances warrant it. (Exception: There may be no need for a power of sale if testator wants to pass grandfather's portrait, or some other item of family sentiment, from generation to generation.) Who is going to have the power of sale? The draftsman could put it in the life tenant, the remainderman, both of them jointly, or some person having no interest in the property.

2. *Reinvestment of proceeds of sale.* Assume the life tenant is given the power of sale. What is to be done with the proceeds? If they are given to the life tenant, the power of sale is in effect a general power of appointment — which means the property must be included in the life tenant's gross estate. This may defeat the purpose of the life estate — to avoid death taxes on the life tenant's death. Instead of giving the proceeds outright to the life tenant, the proceeds could be put in trust, with the life tenant as trustee, to pay the income to the life tenant for life, then the proceeds to go to the remainderman. However, the draftsman must spell out the terms of this trust in the will.

3. *Borrowing money.* During the lifetime of the life tenant, as a practical matter the real estate cannot be mortgaged by the life tenant. No banker is crazy

[56] Simes & Smith, The Law of Future Interests §1652 (2d ed. 1956).

enough to take a life estate as security. It may not be possible to get all the remaindermen and reversioners to sign the mortgage. Only when the remaindermen have an indefeasibly vested remainder is it ordinarily possible to secure a loan with a mortgage on the property, and indefeasibly vested remainders should almost never be created. (Why not? Because if the remainderman dies before the life tenant, any indefeasibly vested remainder will be included in the remainderman's gross estate, and also will be subject to administration costs. These expenses can be avoided by making the remainder contingent upon survival to the time the remainder becomes possessory.) The draftsman should expressly give someone the power to mortgage real estate. Without such a power the life tenant and remainderman may be stuck with property that cannot be improved because it cannot be mortgaged.

4. *Leasing.* If rental property is involved, someone should be given the power to lease the property for a period extending beyond the life tenant's death. Otherwise it may be impossible to rent the premises. If the life tenant is given this power, and can accept a lump-sum payment in advance for the rent, the life tenant has the power to appropriate part of the remainder to himself. To the extent he can appoint the remainder to himself the life tenant has a general power of appointment.

5. *Waste.* Suppose the life tenant wants to take oil out of the land or take down a still usable building. Either action is committing waste, and the remaindermen may be entitled to an injunction or damages.[57] If the life tenant is given the power to drill for oil, open mines, or commit waste with impunity, he may be held to have a general power of appointment for tax purposes.

6. *Expenses.*[58] If land is involved, who is to pay the taxes and the repair bills? The Restatement of Property §129 (1936) provides that the life tenant has a duty to pay taxes and keep the property in repair, but only to the extent the income from the property is adequate to cover those charges. The life tenant also has a duty to pay interest on, but not the principal of, the mortgage. However, the life tenant is under no duty to insure buildings on the land. If the life tenant does insure buildings, and the buildings are destroyed by fire, the life tenant has been held entitled to the whole proceeds and the remainderman nothing. Should the life tenant be required by testator to insure the full value of the property or forfeit his life estate? If the property is destroyed, what is to be done with the insurance proceeds? If, as in the case of a sale, the proceeds are to be held by the life tenant in trust, the trust must be spelled out in the testator's will. Suppose the life tenant wants to use the proceeds to rebuild the premises? The will should say whether this is permissible.

7. *Creditors.* If the life tenant gets into debt, the creditor can seize the life estate and sell it. Of course, very little may be realized upon sale. Likely the creditor himself will buy it for a small amount, and if the life tenant lives a long time he reaps a windfall. A forfeiture restraint against involuntary alienation could be put on the life estate, but its validity is questionable. If the debtor is the remainderman,

[57] For the law of waste see id. §§1651-1667.

[58] On liability of the life tenant for taxes, insurance, mortgages, and current charges, see id. §§1691-1700.

the creditor may be able to seize the remainder and sell it.[59] As with the life estate, the remainder may sell for very little, and the creditor himself will usually be the purchaser.[60]

8. *Miscellaneous*. There are many other problems that may arise. Trespassers may damage the property, the government may exercise eminent domain, a third party may injure himself on the premises. The respective rights of the life tenant and the remainderman must be covered in testator's will unless the law is clear and certain and satisfactory. (It isn't.[61]) If all these foreseeable problems are not covered in testator's will, they may end up being decided in expensive court proceedings.

When we consider all the problems that can arise in the future, we find that a trust is in almost all cases[62] preferable to a legal life estate, even if the life tenant is trustee. Most of the problems above are administrative problems, and the law of trust administration is well established and extensive. If the trustee's powers are not spelled out in the trust instrument, the law will supply him with a charter of administration. Trust administration law is for the most part quite rational; in any case it is simpler and far more rational than the law respecting legal life estates and remainders. Look at the problems above. (1) Standard administrative provisions from any form book almost always give the trustee a power of sale. The draftsman is unlikely to overlook this matter for it is natural to think of the trustee as a manager, whereas the life tenant may be thought of not as a manager but as a user. If the draftsman overlooks a power of sale, the courts are far more ready to find that a power of sale is conferred upon a trustee than upon a legal life tenant.[63] (2) If the property is sold

[59] See Halbach, Creditors' Rights in Future Interests, 43 Minn. L. Rev. 217 (1958); page 722, supra.

[60] In Mayone v. Municipal Court, 335 Mass. 717, 142 N.E.2d 383 (1957), the creditor purchased a remainder interest for $100 at a creditor's sale. Five years later the life tenant died, and the remainder was worth $400,000.

Here is the story from Leach & Logan, Cases and Text on Future Interests and Estate Planning 153 (1961): "The Michael P. Murphy Estate owned a building in Boston; the building was being managed by Miss Helen S. Murphy, a daughter of the deceased. Frank J. Mayone was tenant of a store on the first floor where he sold fish and chips. Two broken electric fans disappeared under circumstances which were in dispute. Miss Murphy accused Mr. Mayone of purloining the fans, filed a complaint, had him arrested, and pressed prosecution. Mayone was acquitted, sued Miss Murphy for malicious prosecution, and recovered a judgment of $1240.40, including costs, in October 1948." When Miss Murphy failed to pay the Mayone judgment, Mayone brought a creditor's action and sold her remainder interest in her father's estate at auction. Mayone was the sole bidder and bought the interest for $100. Five years later when the remainder interest became possessory, Miss Murphy hired a lawyer to retrieve "her" $400,000. The lawyer was successful, but Miss Murphy and he could not agree on the amount of his fee. He sued and won a judgment against her for $55,000 for legal services. Leach and Logan appropriately title the story: Two Very Expensive Broken Electric Fans.

[61] See 1 American Law of Property §§2.16, 2.17, 4.107, 4.112 (Casner ed. 1952).

[62] Almost, not all. If the family residence is placed in trust and the widow wants to sell it and buy another, any capital gain realized on sale may be taxable. Int. Rev. Code of 1954, §1034, which permits postponement of recognition of capital gain where a residence is sold and the proceeds reinvested within a year, does not apply to residences held in trust unless the beneficiary is treated as owner of the trust corpus under Int. Rev. Code of 1954, §§672-678. Rev. Rul. 54-583, 1954-2 Cum. Bull. 158; Rev. Rul. 66-159, 1966-1 Cum. Bull. 162.

[63] 3 Scott, Trusts §190 (3d ed. 1967).

by a legal life tenant and the proceeds are to be put in trust, a trust must be created for the proceeds. This trust should be spelled out in the will, so the careful draftsman will not be saving words by creating a legal life estate. Why not have a trust from the beginning? (3, 4, 5, and 6) As powers of sale are routinely put in any trust instrument, so are powers to mortgage, to lease, to give oil leases, and to pay taxes, insurance, and current charges. Where these powers are omitted in the trust instrument, the law normally gives the trustee these powers.[64] (7) A major difference between legal estates and equitable estates is that the latter can be put out of the reach of creditors. In most states a spendthrift trust, which disables creditors from reaching a beneficiary's interest, is permissible.

A trustee is required to keep the trust property separate from his own property. This requirement, plus the necessity for a separate tax return, tends to keep the bookkeeping accurate and up to date and to eliminate litigation over identification. If a person is trustee and mingles trust funds with his own, the burden is on him to show how much of the mingled fund is his own. If he cannot do this the beneficiary may be entitled to the whole mingled fund.[65]

By the English Law of Property Act of 1925 the legal life estate was abolished. Since that date only two kinds of legal estates can exist in England: the fee simple absolute in possession and the lease. Apart from leases, all life estates and future interests of every kind (remainders, executory interests, reversions, possibilities of reverter, rights of entry) are equitable interests. The holder of the fee simple absolute in possession holds the property in trust for the other interested parties. The purpose of this legislation was to make land marketable by ensuring that a fee simple absolute owner was always available to sell the land. The result was to turn all family settlements into trusts.[66]

In Pennsylvania, since 1948, legal future interests cannot be created in personal property. All legal future interests in personal property are converted into equitable future interests, and the life tenant or owner of the present interest is deemed to be a trustee (without compensation) of the property. 20 Pa. Stat. Ann. §301.13 (Purdon 1950); Estate of Gramm, 420 Pa. 510, 218 A.2d 342 (1966). Would it be desirable to extend this legislation to real property?

3. *Trust with Discretionary Power to Distribute Income or Invade Principal*

OLD COLONY TRUST CO. v. RODD

Supreme Judicial Court of Massachusetts, 1970

356 Mass. 584, 254 N.E.2d 886

Before SPALDING, CUTTER, KIRK and REARDON, JJ.

KIRK, Justice. The respondent, a life beneficiary of a trust created by the will of George A. Sanderson, filed specifications of objection to the allowance of the forti-

64 Id. §§188, 189, 191.

65 See Bell v. Killian, 266 Ala. 12, 93 So. 2d 769 (1957).

66 See Megarry & Wade, Real Property 138-155 (3d ed. 1966).

eth and forty-first accounts of the petitioner as trustee under the will. After a hearing, the probate judge entered two decrees allowing the accounts. The respondent appeals, challenging the adequacy of the amounts paid to her by the trustee, the reasonableness of the trustee's accounting procedure, and the amount of its fees. Her attorney appeals from the denial of his petition to be allowed counsel fees from the trust assets.

Item 8 of Sanderson's will directed the trustee to pay over during the lives of designated beneficiaries "such part of the income or principal as may be necessary in its judgment for the comfortable support of any one or more of said persons, provided that in the judgment of said trustee any one or more of said persons shall need assistance and shall be worthy of the same, it being my intention hereby to carry out as far as possible the wishes of my wife's father . . . as expressed to me on many occasions, namely, that he wished to see to the comfortable support and maintenance of his descendants." The life beneficiaries of the fund were named persons (descendants of the testator's wife's father) "and the children or grandchildren of any of the above named persons who may be living at the time of my decease and born prior to my decease" with one named exception, not here material. Item 8 further directed the trustee, at the death of the last survivor of the life beneficiaries, to transfer free of all trusts whatever remained of the fund "in such proportions as said trustee will decide will accomplish the most good, unto such charities in said Boston, said Berlin . . . [in Massachusetts] and Kingston . . . [in Rhode Island] as said trustee shall select."

We summarize the report of material facts made by the judge. The periods covered by the contested accounts are from November, 1963, through November, 1965. The book value of the trust, comprised of securities, is approximately $220,-000, plus $30,000 in accumulated income to which a further accumulation of $3,500 in unexpended income was added during the accounting periods under consideration. The market value of the securities is approximately $423,000. During the accounting periods there were fifteen potential beneficiaries of the trust, three of whom were over eighty years of age, two between seventy-five and eighty, five between sixty and seventy-five, and the remaining five between forty and sixty. The trustee each year sent a questionnaire to each potential beneficiary in order to determine which if any of them required assistance. In instances where answers to the questionnaire were incomplete, the trustee made no further inquiry of the applicant in order to make an accurate determination of his net worth. The total paid to ten beneficiaries who requested assistance was $7,836 for the fortieth accounting period and $10,850 for the next period. One of the beneficiaries, who died during the accounting periods, who owned a home without a mortgage and had no other assets, was paid $100 a month, and $1,100 for hospital and medical expenses. Two other elderly beneficiaries, with incomes of $2,540 and $3,000, received monthly payments of from $35 to $50. Another elderly beneficiary, with an annual income of $1,985, received $50 a month plus $752.70 for the payment of medical bills. Two other beneficiaries had medical and dental bills paid. An army colonel, fifty years of age, married, and stationed in Europe, with an annual salary of $13,800, exclusive of allowances, received two payments of $500 toward the educational expenses of one of his two daughters. A married woman, age forty-six, whose husband's salary was $10,000 a year, received $500 and $1,500, in the fortieth and forty-first accounting periods, respectively, toward the educational expenses of her two children, seventeen and eighteen years of age. Another married woman, age forty-five, whose husband, a college professor, earned an annual salary of $16,500, received $500 and $1,250 in the fortieth and forty-first accounting periods, respectively, for educational expenses of her two children sixteen and eighteen years of age.

The respondent, age forty-seven, is single, with no dependents. She has no resources other than her salary. During the fortieth accounting period she was employed full time, and earned a gross salary of $4,625. The trustee paid her Federal income taxes, various personal bills, and an allowance of $65 a month, for a total of $2,074. In the forty-first accounting period she earned $5,292. The trustee again paid her Federal income taxes and various personal bills. For the last seven months of the period, her allowance was raised to $115 a month; the total disbursement to her for the year was $2,131.

The trustee charged a fee of five per cent of the income of the trust, and three-tenths of one per cent of the principal.

1. The judge found no facts to support the respondent's objections to the trustee's accounting procedure, investment practice, or the amount of its fees. We agree. The trustee was not obliged to adhere strictly to the accounting form supplied by the Probate Court. General Laws c. 206, §2, requires only a reasonable and orderly statement of the account, and does not require rigid adherence to any method of accounting. Hutchinson v. King, 339 Mass. 41, 157 N.E.2d 525. The respondent also argues that the trustee's filing of the two accounts at the same time, some five months after the close of the forty-first accounting period, violated G.L. c. 206, §1. That section provides that a trustee "shall render an account . . . at least once a year . . . until his trust is fulfilled; but the court may at his request excuse him from rendering an account in any year, if satisfied that it is not necessary or expedient that it should be rendered." In allowing the accounts, the probate judge impliedly found that it was not "necessary or expedient" for the accounts to be filed separately each year. At the most, the failure to file timely was a "mere technical breach" (Attorney Gen. v. Olson, 346 Mass. 190, 195, 191 N.E.2d 132) and done without objection at the time by any beneficiary. See Newhall, Settlement of Estates (4th ed.) §435. Finally, the fees allowed the trustee cannot be said to be unreasonable merely because they are apportioned between income and principal. Such apportionment is expressly permitted by G.L. c. 206, §16. See Old Colony Trust Co. v. Townsend, 324 Mass. 298, 85 N.E.2d 784.

2. The judge found that the "method employed by the trustee in determining the amount of assistance required in each case to attain 'comfortable support and maintenance' was superficial. And having in mind the intent of the settlor, the amounts allocated not only to the respondent but to others of the beneficiaries were parsimonious." With these observations we emphatically agree. The ultimate conclusion of the judge was, "However, the trustee was here given broad discretion and I do not quite find that it has been abused."

This court recently said that in exercising a power of this sort a trustee is "unquestionably under an obligation to give serious and responsible consideration both as to the propriety of the amounts and as to their consistency with the terms and purposes of the trust." Holyoke Natl. Bank v. Wilson, 350 Mass. 223, 227, 214 N.E.2d 42, 45. A court of equity may control a trustee in the exercise of a fiduciary discretion if it fails to observe standards of judgment apparent from the applicable instrument. Copp v. Worcester County Natl. Bank, 347 Mass. 548, 551, 199 N.E.2d 200. Old Colony Trust Co. v. Silliman, 352 Mass. 6, 223 N.E.2d 504. It is our view that, whether due to misuse of discretion or to misconception of the purpose of the trust on the part of the trustee, several of the intended primary beneficiaries of the trust are not receiving that which the settlor intended they should receive and which the trustee has the means to provide: "comfortable support and maintenance." The settlor by will expressed his intention in terms that imported a deep sense of personal obligation to fulfill the wishes of another. By providing for access to principal he provided means "to carry out as far as possible" those wishes. It is inferable that the persons who could be benefited have long since been identified and that with the passing years their number has diminished and henceforth will diminish rapidly. At the same time it is obvious that the corpus of the trust has grown. Inevitably the remainder will go to charities unspecified and unknown to anyone, except, possibly, the trustee. It is clear from the will that the gift of the remainder was of minor significance. And yet it would appear that the trustee regards the disposition of the remainder as the dominant purpose of the trust. The trustee has not only kept the principal inviolate but has accumulated and retained over $30,000 in income. The trustee justifies this course as reasonable and prudent in light of rising medical costs and the advancing age of the beneficiaries. However that may be, the fact remains that the book value of the trust is $220,000 and the market value, at the time of the judge's findings, double that amount. The prospect of illness in old age does not warrant a persistent policy of niggardliness toward individuals for whose comfortable support in life the trust has been established. The payments made to the respondent and several other beneficiaries, viewed in light of their assets and needs, when measured against the assets of the trust show that little consideration has been given to the "comfortable support" of the beneficiaries. Compare Holyoke Natl. Bank v. Wilson, 350 Mass. 223, 214 N.E.2d 42.

Another manifestation of the trustee's indifference to its "obligation to give serious and responsible consideration both as to the propriety of the amounts and as to their consistency with the terms and purposes of the trust" is the payment, noted above, of sums to beneficiaries to assist in the education of their children. In each of the three cases the family income was in excess of $10,000. In each case, laudable though the purpose may have been, the contribution, strictly speaking, was not for "comfortable support" nor was the actual beneficiary a designated beneficiary. Homans v. Foster, 232 Mass. 4, 6, 121 N.E. 417; Parker v. Lloyd, 321 Mass. 126, 134, 71 N.E.2d 889. See Boston Safe Deposit & Trust Co. v. Stebbins, 309 Mass. 282, 287, 34 N.E.2d 616, 148 A.L.R. 1036. In two of the three cases referred to, the amounts given for the education of nonbeneficiaries was greater than one half of the amount granted to the respondent for "comfortable support." The respondent asked that the payments made to her as noted in the fortieth and forty-first accounts be increased by at least fifteen per cent. We think that the request is a modest one.

3. We do not reverse the decrees. Comfort cannot be retroactively given. Our order is that all accounts of the trustee, subsequent to the forty-first account under Item 8 of the will of George A. Sanderson, be so prepared or, if already prepared, be so modified to reflect a trusteeship that is neither superficial in its administration nor parsimonious in its spirit.

4. We think that the probate judge, upon further proceedings, might with complete propriety allow reasonable counsel fees for the respondent's attorney payable from the trust principal. We leave the matter entirely to his discretion.

5. The decrees are affirmed. The case is remanded to the Probate Court for further proceedings consistent with this opinion.

So ordered.

NOTES

1. *Briggs v. Crowley, 352 Mass. 194, 224 N.E.2d 417 (1967)*. In 1938 Ada Langley Briggs executed a deed of trust to herself, Wallace E. Crowley, and Harold W. Martin as trustees to pay the income to certain named beneficiaries. Crowley and Martin were named as remaindermen. The trust instrument provided: "The principal purpose of this trust is to provide for the necessaries and comfort of the persons named herein and in order to accomplish this purpose it is intended to give said trustees the fullest authority and discretion without limit and every other unlimited power to do all things. Said trustees may, if they find this intention and purpose is not being accomplished, withhold any money or otherwise or they may buy materials, provisions or do otherwise as the convenience or necessities of any one or more beneficiaries may be described; also said trustees, at their discretion, may permanently withhold all money, materials, provisions, benefits, or otherwise of every name and nature from any one or more of the beneficiaries."

The trust also provided that the trustees "shall not be called upon to account to anyone or file any accounts or disclose any payments to beneficiaries or who the beneficiaries are or otherwise except to the donor" and that the "discretion of the trustees hereunder shall not be questioned by any beneficiary . . . and the executors, administrators or the heirs or assigns of any beneficiary herein named shall not be entitled to any accounting."

After the settlor's death, when one of the beneficiaries asked for more income, the trustees stopped payments to her altogether. The beneficiary sued for an accounting and an order that the trustees pay the beneficiary "reasonable amounts for her necessaries and comfort." The trustees demurred. The Massachusetts court held that the clauses in the trust instrument purporting to relieve the trustees of the duty imposed by law to account were invalid as against public policy insofar as they purported to deprive a court of jurisdiction and the petitioner of standing to require the trustees to show that they had faithfully performed their duties. The court further held that the trustee's discretion must be exercised in accordance with the standard "necessaries and comfort" — stated in the trust instrument.

2. Suppose the trustee is authorized to pay to the income beneficiary of a trust so much of the principal as is necessary for her health, education, and support. The beneficiary tells the trustee that she needs $3000 because her adenoids are bothering her and she feels that she should spend the winter in Arizona. Should the trustee give the beneficiary $3000? See Halbach, Problems of Discretion in Discretionary Trusts, 61 Colum. L. Rev. 1425 (1961).

3. Covey, Use of Long Term Trusts in Estate Planning, 4 Real Prop., Prob. & Trust J. 489, 492 (1969): "The final point I would like to make is in connection with powers to invade principal. It seems to me that when you put a standard on a power to invade principal, it does nothing more than complicate life for the trustee. These provisions always present interpretative problems; therefore, is it not better to give the trustee a broad power to pay principal and have no standard whatsoever on the exercise? I mean, do not refer to maintenance, support, education and comfort; merely say the trustee may pay to the beneficiary so much or all of the principal as the trustee shall in his discretion determine. Such a power is flexible and much easier to apply. The trustee can make a judgment as to what should be done based on the facts of the particular case, uninhibited by language. In short, put your faith in the trustee and trust his judgment."

Matter of FLYER

Court of Appeals of New York, 1969

23 N.Y.2d 579, 245 N.E.2d 718, 297 N.Y.S.2d 956

Chief Judge FULD. In this proceeding to construe a will, we are presented with the question whether a trustee, vested with sole and absolute discretion to invade the principal of the trust for the support of the life beneficiary, may take the latter's private resources into account before deciding to effect an invasion.

The testator, Jacob Flyer, died in August of 1964. He was survived by three daughters of a deceased first wife and by a second spouse, Elsie, whom he had married in 1945. In 1960, the latter suffered a severe stroke which left her a hopeless and incurable invalid. Soon thereafter, the testator executed his will giving two thirds of his estate outright — or his entire estate if his wife predeceased him — to his three children in equal shares. Out of the last third, "or the sum of $20,000, whichever is greater," he created a trust for his widow, with the remainder to be equally divided at her death among the three daughters. The estate was valued at over $50,000.

The particular clause which prompted the present construction proceeding, after reciting that one third of the testator's estate was to be given in trust to one of his daughters as trustee "to pay to [his] wife Elsie or her representative, or to use for [her] benefit . . . the income thereof for [her] life," went on to provide that,

> if such income be insufficient for the support and maintenance of Elsie, my Trustee shall so pay or use from principal sufficient moneys to provide for Elsie's support and maintenance, in the sole, absolute and uncontrolled discretion of the Trustee. If, in the sole, absolute and uncontrolled discretion of the Trustee, any part of the net income thereof need not be used for the support and maintenance of my said wife, such part of the income shall be added to and become part of the principal of the trust estate.[67]

The testator's wife spent virtually the entire four-year period, between the execution of the will by her husband and his death, in hospitals and nursing homes and was finally confined to Pilgrim State Hospital after she had attempted suicide. She has a sister — who was appointed her committee in 1965 — and a daughter by a previous marriage. Her assets, in addition to the trust set up for her benefit, consist of cash and personal property, worth about $10,000, and income from social security payments amounting to about $1,800 a year.

There is due and unpaid a hospital bill of more than $10,000. The petitioner in this construction proceeding — the incompetent's sister who, as noted, is her committee — contends that the testator "intended" an absolute gift of both income and principal to his widow, without regard to her independent resources, and that, accordingly, the trustee should be required to pay that bill as well as any others which may be incurred. The trustee, one on the testator's daughters, finds no such requirement in the will. It is her position that her father, though desiring to provide for his widow's maintenance out of principal in case of necessity, intended her private income to be used and, in support of this claim, calls attention to the fact that the testator had actually used his wife's social security moneys in paying her hospital bills during his lifetime.

The Surrogate agreed with the petitioner, concluding that the trustee was required to pay all amounts necessary for the widow's support and maintenance out of both principal and income "without regard to [her] private resources." A closely divided Appellate Division affirmed. The minority took the view that it was clear from the will, as well as from the circumstances existing between the time of its execution and the testator's death, that he intended his widow's independent income to be applied toward her support. If the result be otherwise, Justice McGivern pointed out in his dissenting opinion,

> The corpus will be eroded — for as it decreases, its yield will correspondingly diminish, to the point of destruction, if the widow lives long enough. And an injury is wrought to the children of the testator. All the while, the social security payments of the widow here will batten and pointlessly accumulate. Social security was devised to allay the fears and mitigate the privations of old age, not to multiply for some one else, other than the subject, to enjoy. (29 A.D.2d 8, 11.)

[67] If any daughter died before the widow, the testator provided, that daughter's share was to be held in trust for her children until they reached the age of 21 and, again, the trustee was given "sole, uncontrolled and absolute discretion" to invade the principal for their benefit or to add to it any income which remained unused.

We agree with the dissenting justices of the Appellate Division that the present case falls within the decisions holding that a trustee is privileged to consider the beneficiary's independent income before effecting an invasion of principal.

Although the decisions in this area of the law place emphasis on the precise verbiage found in the provision creating the trust, close analysis reveals that they take into consideration more than such verbiage alone in seeking to ascertain the testator's intent. The language may not, of course, be entirely disregarded but, as in every case in which a will is ambiguous or silent with respect to a controverted matter, it is the testator's intent which must control, and we educe his design not only from the language employed but from a "sympathetic reading of the will as an entirety and in view of the facts and circumstances under which [its] provisions . . . were framed." (Matter of Fabbri, 2 N.Y.2d 236, 240; see, also, Matter of Clark, 280 N.Y. 155, 160.)

The principle which emerges from the cases may be briefly stated. A trustee, particularly when given uncontrolled discretion to invade principal (see, e.g., Matter of Bisconti, 306 N.Y. 442, 446; Matter of Messer, 34 Misc. 2d 416, 420), may, before deciding to effect an invasion, take into account the beneficiary's independent resources where there is no "absolute" gift of principal, the prime gift being that of income, and the testator *intended* that the "invasion of the principal . . . [be] dependent upon the needs or requirements of the beneficiary." (Matter of Martin, 269 N.Y. 305, 312; see, also, Matter of Garrett, 9 A.D.2d 545, affd. 8 N.Y.2d 725; Matter of Hogeboom, 219 App. Div. 131; Matter of Messer, 34 Misc. 2d 416, supra.) The rule is, however, different — that is, the trustee may not consider the beneficiary's income — where the testator attached no condition of need and *intended* that "The gift of principal [be] as broad as the gift of interest" and the first inseparable from the other. (Matter of Martin, 269 N.Y. 305, 310, supra; see, also, Matter of Clark, 280 N.Y. 155 supra; Rezzemini v. Brooks, 236 N.Y. 184; Holden v. Strong, 116 N.Y. 471.)

In the case before us, as already noted, the trustee was given an absolute discretion to invade principal if the income were "insufficient" for the wife's support. Silent though the will itself is as to whether her own income was to be considered, study of the testament as a whole, in the light of the attendant circumstances, makes it plain beyond doubt that, although the testator wished to provide for his wife during her lifetime, his paramount concern was for his daughters and their children and his desire was to preserve his estate for them.

Turning, first, to the testator's will, it is instinct with his affection and concern for his descendants. He left his total estate to his three daughters in equal shares if his wife predeceased him. Any income from the trust which she did not need for her support was to be added to the principal which they were to inherit. In the event of a daughter's predeceasing his wife, he made elaborate provision for gifts over to his grandchildren. Inclusion of the latter provision goes far toward establishing that he did not envisage a possible exhaustion of the trust corpus — a result which might ensue if the principal is to be invaded without regard to his wife's own income.

As for the situation existing at the time he made his will — which continued until his death — the testator's wife was incurably ill. The trust which he created for her benefit was designed to assure her an income which would take care of her probable needs if, and only if, her social security payments were also applied to her support. In point of fact, he had actually used those payments for that purpose while he was alive, and there is no reason to believe that he wished that practice to be discontinued after he died. He certainly did not intend the social security payments of his hopelessly ill and incompetent wife to accumulate for her heirs and permit the trust principal, which he wished to preserve for his own issue, to be diminished and, perhaps, consumed.

As already appears from our treatment of the cases, the decisions relied upon by the petitioner (see Matter of Clark, 280 N.Y. 155, supra; Rezzemini v. Brooks, 236 N.Y. 184, supra; Holden v. Strong, 116 N.Y. 471, supra) are inapposite. The court in those cases concluded, not on the basis of the trust language alone, but on the strength of the will as a whole and other relevant factors, that a gift of principal was intended and that the testator's almost exclusive interest was in the beneficiary, the remaindermen occupying a completely subsidiary position. On the other hand, as we have seen, the present testator made it quite plain that his children were his primary concern and any provision for his wife from trust principal, as opposed to income, was clearly secondary.

It follows from what we have said that in the present case the trustee was privileged to take the beneficiary's independent income into account before invading principal.

The order appealed from should be reversed and the matter remitted to the Surrogate's Court for further proceedings in accordance with this opinion, with costs to all parties appearing separately and filing separate briefs payable out of the estate.

Scileppi, J. (dissenting). I dissent and vote to affirm.

In my view, the result reached by the majority is not only contrary to well-settled law, but completely disregards the plain language of the will.

It is axiomatic that the courts do not have the power — nor is it their function — to remake the will of a testator. Thus, if the language used in the will is clear, precise and unambiguous, there is no problem of construction; rather, there is an obligation of enforcement. . . .

The clause in question on this appeal is clear and unequivocal. It establishes a trust, the income of which is to be paid for life to the testator's incompetent widow, and then provides that, "if such income be insufficient for the support and maintenance of [my wife], my Trustee shall so pay or use from principal sufficient moneys to provide for [my wife's] support and maintenance, in the sole, absolute and uncontrolled discretion of the Trustee."

This language clearly makes the gift of principal as broad as the gift of interest. The gift of principal is not conditioned upon the particular needs of the widow but rather upon the insufficiency of the income to provide support and maintenance. In such a situation, the private income of the beneficiary cannot be considered. The applicable rule was succinctly stated by this court in Matter of Martin (269 N.Y. 305, 312): "The primary question in this class of cases always is, does the will constitute an absolute gift of support and maintenance which it makes a charge upon the income from the estate and upon principal? If so, then the private income of the beneficiary cannot be considered. If, however, the gift is of income coupled with a provision that the principal may be invaded in case of need, the private income of the beneficiary must be considered in determining whether such need exists."

In Martin, the court held that the private income of the beneficiary was to be considered in determining whether to invade principal. But, there, unlike the present case, the will provided for the invasion of principal "as [the beneficiary] may require for her care, support and comfort, during her natural life."

In almost every case where the will in question provided for the invasion of principal, if the income from the trust was *insufficient* or in cases where the trust provided for the use of income and so much of principal "as may be necessary" with no limitation of the amount of principal which may be invaded, the courts of this State have uniformly found that such language constituted an absolute gift of support and maintenance without regard to the private income of the beneficiary.

Contrary to the assertion of the majority herein, the case of Rezzemini v. Brooks (236 N.Y. 184) is directly in point. In that case, as in this one, the committee of an adjudged incompetent alleged that it was the duty of the trustee to pay for the support and maintenance of the incompetent out of the income and principal of the trust which had been created by the will of the incompetent's mother. At the time that the testatrix executed her will she was aware that her son owned certain valuable property and was in receipt of an income from the estate of his father. As in the instant case, the trustee in Rezzemini represented the vested remaindermen and claimed that the incompetent's income from all other sources must be exhausted before any invasion of principal was warranted.

In construing the clause in question, which reads as follows: "If the income from my estate shall be insufficient for the proper support of my said son, then in that event, I authorize and empower my said trustee to expend so much of the principal thereof as may be necessary for that purpose," this court held: "Our decision in the case of Holden v. Strong [116 N.Y. 471] involved the construction of a will wherein the testator gave to a trustee 'full power and authority to use so much of the trust fund, either interest or principal, as shall, in his judgment and discretion, be necessary for the proper care, comfort and maintenance' of the plaintiff so long as he should live. We held that the plaintiff there was entitled to support and maintenance even though he was able to support himself and had accumulated a fund which he had on deposit in a bank. The reasoning and principle laid down in that case we regard as controlling the case under consideration." (Rezzemini v. Brooks, supra, p. 193.)

In other words, since the language of the clause — which is almost identical to language of the clause now before us — clearly conditioned the gift from principal solely upon the insufficiency of the income to provide for care and support and not upon the necessity of the beneficiary, it was held that the private income of the beneficiary could not be considered. . . .

It would appear from a review of the cases in this area that the language used in the instant will has acquired through judicial decision a definite and established significance. And, as the author of the majority opinion herein observed in his dissent in Matter of Gulbenkian (9 N.Y.2d 363, 372-373): "when a will contains language which has acquired, through judicial decision, a definite and established significance, the testator is taken to have employed the language in that sense and with that meaning in mind. (See Matter of Kroos, 302 N.Y. 424, 428.)"

I agree with the courts below that the testator's primary intention was to bequeath the income and principal of the trust for the support and maintenance of his widow without regard to her personal income. While it is obvious that testator was concerned with the welfare of his children and grandchildren, it is equally obvious, especially since testator was aware of his wife's permanent incapacity and of her private resources, that her maintenance and support was his primary consideration. If he had intended the result reached by the majority, he could easily have made provision for his wife based upon need. This, however, he did not do. Having provided that if income would be insufficient to provide for the wife, that the trust be invaded, this court should not now remake the will, even though the result may be the depletion of the contingent estate of the children and of the infant contingent remaindermen.

Accordingly, I would affirm.

Judges Burke, Bergan, Keating and Jasen concur with Chief Judge Fuld; Judge Scileppi dissents and votes to affirm in a separate opinion in which Judge Breitel concurs.

Order reversed, etc.

NOTES

1. Restatement (Second) of Trusts §128, Comment e: "By the terms of the trust it may be provided that the trustee shall pay or apply only so much of the income and principal or either as is necessary for the education or support of a beneficiary. In such a case the beneficiary cannot compel the trustee to pay to him or to apply for his benefit more than the trustee in the exercise of a sound discretion deems necessary for his education or support.

"It is a question of interpretation whether the beneficiary is entitled to support out of the trust fund even though he has other resources. The inference is that he is so entitled. It is a question of interpretation whether the trustee is authorized to pay the funeral expenses of the beneficiary. The inference is that he is so authorized."

2. The Connecticut courts have followed a general rule that the trustee must consider the beneficiary's other resources before exercising its discretion to support the beneficiary. Guaranty Trust Co. v. New York City Cancer Committee, 145 Conn. 542, 144 A.2d 535 (1958). The rule is rebuttable by showing a contrary

intent of the settlor, but the Connecticut cases indicate that it is not easy to infer a contrary intent without express language.

Petition of WOLCOTT

Supreme Court of New Hampshire, 1948

95 N.H. 23, 56 A.2d 641, 1 A.L.R.2d 1323

Petition for instructions brought by trustees under the will of Francis E. Getty, late of North Conway, seeking authority to make payments out of principal to the life beneficiary of a trust established under the will. Certain facts were found by the Court (Grimes, J.), who transferred without ruling the question of law presented by the petition.

The testator died on September 23, 1944. By his will made in 1932, he bequeathed to his widow, Ada C. Getty, the sum of $2,500, and all of his personal and household goods, supplies and furniture, of every kind and nature. To each of his two sons, he bequeathed the sum of $5,000. The residue of his estate, he devised and bequeathed to the trustees "to pay over the net income thereof to my wife so long as she lives," and upon her death to pay the principal and any accumulated income "to my then living issue in equal shares by right of representation, and, in default of such issue, to the persons to whom and in the proportions in which the same would be distributable if I had then died intestate and owning such property absolutely." In the event of the wife's decease prior to the testator's, the residue was disposed of by provisions identical with those disposing of the remainder after the life estate.

The will conferred upon the trustees broad powers with respect to investments and management of the trust, including the right to determine what receipts should be "credited to income and what to principal, notwithstanding any determination by the courts," and the power "generally to do all things in relation to the trust fund which the testator could have done if living."

According to the allegations of the petition, the annual income from the trust fund is now slightly in excess of $2,300, and the principal approximates $107,000. The Court has found that the widow is eighty-two years of age, and that she "is ill and infirm and the income of the trust is insufficient to afford her adequate subsistence." It is alleged that her "reasonable and necessary expenses" including those of constant attendance of a nurse and frequent visits of her physician, exceed $5,800. The trustees accordingly ask that they may be authorized and instructed to invade the principal of the fund for the purpose of providing her with reasonable support, the invasion not to exceed $4,000 a year.

In this petition the trustees are joined by the testator's sons, both of whom survived him, and by the eighteen year old son of one of them. The latter is represented by a guardian ad litem, also appointed to represent the possible interests of persons as yet unborn. Because of provisions against alienation by anticipation, the sons may not utilize their interests to benefit their mother; but by joining with the trustees in their petition, they seek to bring to realization their expressed belief that "it could not have been their father's intention that their mother should be deprived of proper support in order that remote future interests might be protected."

DUNCAN, Justice. Although not expressly stated, the testator's purpose that during her life, his wife should have the beneficial use of his entire estate, except for $10,000 bequeathed to his sons, is readily apparent. Apart from these legatees, the only others who might share in the estate are designated not by name, but as members of a class, or as heirs or next of kin, and would take only in the event that the widow survived one or both of the sons. The residue, at the widow's death, is to be distributed among the testator's "then living issue in equal shares by right of representation," a phrase plainly descriptive of the testator's lineal descendants. Kimball v. Penhallow, 60 N.H. 448. See R.L., c. 7, 20. The widow's death before that of her sons would result in a division between them. The only other living issue, whose interest is purely contingent, is the grandson petitioner.

Despite broad discretionary powers conferred upon the trustees, the will contains no provision for the use of principal for the benefit of the widow. On the other hand, such use is not specifically forbidden. It may fairly be assumed that the beneficiary's need of the principal was not anticipated because of a failure to foresee changes which have occurred since the testator's death, including shrinkage in investment returns, decline in purchasing power, and the expense occasioned by the widow's extreme infirmity. The powers conferred upon the trustees as to investments and the allocation of receipts to income are indicative of a purpose to provide the widow with a liberal income, unrestricted by technical rules. No purpose to transmit any specific residuary amount to the sons or to any other issue is disclosed. Fairly construed, the will evidences as its primary purpose "ample and certain provision" for the testator's wife. Cf. Smith v. Fellows, 131 Mass. 20, 22; Trust Co. v. Glunz, 119 N.J. Eq. 73, 77, 181 A. 27.

What is sought by the petition is not construction of any particular provision of the will but rather authority to deviate from the provisions by which principal would be retained intact during the widow's lifetime. No reliance is placed by the trustees upon their general power "to do all things in relation to the trust which the testator could have done if living." The power is at best obscure in meaning, and if construed independently of other provisions, would have doubtful validity. Clark v. Campbell, 82 N.H. 281, 133 A. 166, 45 A.L.R. 1433. Because of the emergency confronting the life beneficiary, the trustees seek authority to do what the testator presumably would have authorized had he foreseen the emergency.

Where a remainder succeeding a life estate may ultimately vest in persons as yet undetermined and perhaps unborn, courts of equity have at times hesitated or refused to sanction an invasion of principal for the benefit of the life tenant. See Annotations, 39 A.L.R. 40; 46 L.R.A., N.S., 43, and cases cited. In one view, permission is sought to appropriate to the use of one beneficiary the property of others without the consent of all. See In re Van Deusen's Estate, Cal. Sup., 182 P.2d 565; Marshall v. Holloway, 2 Swanst. 432; Errat v. Barlow, 14 Ves. Jr. 202. But this view, in our opinion, may be deemed applicable only to the extent that the testator's disclosed intention affords it a foundation. Strictly applied, it may prevent accomplishment of the testator's primary purpose. As is said in 2 Scott, Trusts, §168, p. 855: "As a matter of strict logic it may be necessary to permit a child to suffer in order to protect the possible children which he may ultimately have, but it is difficult to believe that the settlor would ever desire such a result." Where the testator's desire may be gathered from the will, "strict logic" need not to be controlling.

Traditionally, the courts of this jurisdiction have shown a signal regard for the intent of the testator (see Clark v. Campbell, supra), at times at the expense of other recognized principles deemed less cogent in their application. Cf. Edgerly v. Barker, 66 N.H. 434, 31 A. 900, 28 L.R.A. 328. In order to prevent impairment of a testator's primary purpose, authority to deviate from the express terms of a gift has been granted in cases of emergency unforeseen by him, even though contingent remainder interests were incidentally affected.

In Brown v. Berry, 71 N.H. 241, 52 A. 870, 872, trustees under a will sought advice as to whether, when income proved insufficient, principal might be used for the support of the testator's children, and the support and education of his grandchildren. The will directed payment "out of the net income" of sums sufficient for the purposes named, and bequeathed the residue to the grandchildren when the youngest should reach a specified age. In advising the trustees that principal might be used, this court said, "the reading of the testator's will . . . leaves no room for doubt that his primary and controlling purpose was to provide for the proper and reasonable support of his children and grandchildren. . . . For these objects he designated the net income of his large estate as the source of payment, and doubtless supposed, as he reasonably might, that it would be amply sufficient. . . . That this purpose cannot be executed in the particular manner he intended affords no valid reason why it should not be executed at all." In McGill v. Young, 75 N.H. 133, 71 A. 637, the use of principal for the support of the testator's son was authorized, although the will directed the trustee "to pay out of and from said net income . . . the money . . . necessary" for his support. (Demeritt v. Young, 72 N.H. 202, 203, 55 A. 1047, 1048.) The court considered it "highly improbable it was intended to limit the trustee to that fund and to forbid him to use the principal if at any time the income should be insufficient for the purpose. . . ." [75 N.H. 133, 71 A. 637.]

In the will before us, the testator's purpose to furnish reasonable support for his wife is not expressed in words, but it is nevertheless implicit in the disposition made of his estate. His direction that his wife should have the income was a means of executing his purpose, and is "properly to be read as subordinate to (his) paramount intention." In re Walker, (1901) 1 Ch. 879, 885. His intent to provide reasonable support to the widow being evident from the will, those whose interests are secondary to hers take subject to the execution of that intent. The remaindermen are deprived of no rights so long as rights which the life tenant was intended to have are not exceeded.

Because of circumstances not provided for by the will and obviously not anticipated by the testator, an emergency threatens accomplishment of his purpose by the means which he provided. Those whose interests are most immediate consent to the authorization sought by the trustees, and there is no objection by the guardian ad litem. If the consent or acquiescence of the parties is not binding upon unborn contingent remaindermen, still they are sufficiently represented by those having like interests to be bound by a decree. 3 Simes, Future Interests, §676; 33 Am. Jur. 650, §§182, 183. Cf. Longworth v. Duff, 297 Ill. 479, 130 N.E. 690. In this situation a court of equity need not hesitate to exercise its undoubted power to permit a deviation from the literal provisions of the will. A means of accomplishing the testator's purpose is thereby furnished, which it may reasonably be inferred that he himself would have provided, had he been able to foresee the exigency. Trust Co. v. Glunz, supra; Pennington v. Metropolitan Museum of Art, 65 N.J. Eq. 11, 55 A. 468; Curtiss v. Brown, 29 Ill. 201. Cf. Citizens' Nat. Bank v. Morgan, 94 N.H. 284, 51 A.2d 841, and cases cited. This conclusion is in harmony with our own decisions and not without support in other authorities. Longwith v. Riggs, 123 Ill. 258, 14 N.E. 840; McAfee v. Thomas, 121 Or. 351, 255 P. 333.

The trustees are advised that principal not in excess of $4,000 a year may be used to supplement the income of the trust, for the purpose of providing the widow with reasonable support, if the trial court shall find in accordance with the uncontroverted allegations of the petition, and it shall appear that the widow has no other income. In view of the discretion vested in the trustees by the testator, there is no reason why they may not safely be left to determine the amount of principal necessary within the limit specified, due regard being given to considerations of what is prudent and reasonable, and best calculated to accomplish the testator's purposes as a whole. Woodward v. Jolbert, 94 N.H. 324, 52 A.2d 641.

If the requisite findings are made, a decree in accordance with this opinion may be entered by the Superior Court.

Case discharged.

All concurred.[68]

NOTES

1. Where a destitute income beneficiary petitions for power to invade principal for support, and all the beneficiaries do not consent, relief is ordinarily denied unless the trust instrument is construed to contain a power to invade, express or implied. 2 Scott, Trusts §168 (3d ed. 1967). There is, however, a good deal of unhappiness with the state of the law. See comprehensive discussion of the problem in Haskell, Justifying the Principle of Distributive Deviation in the Law of Trusts, 18 Hastings L.J. 267 (1967); Modification of Terms Regarding Amount or Time of Payments to Income Beneficiaries, 4 Real Prop., Prob. & Trust J. 359 (1969); Note, Deviation from the Distributive Terms of the Trust, 53 Nw. U.L. Rev. 268 (1958).

2. New York Estates, Powers and Trusts Law §7-1.6 (1967, Supp. 1971): "Application of principal to income beneficiary.

[68] Noted 28 B.U.L. Rev. 387; 47 Mich. L. Rev. 422. — Eds.

"(a) . . .

"(b) Notwithstanding any contrary provision of law, the court having jurisdiction of an express trust, hereafter created or declared, to receive income from property and apply it to the use of or pay it to any person, unless otherwise provided in the disposing instrument, may in its discretion make an allowance from principal to any income beneficiary whose support or education is not sufficiently provided for, whether or not such person is entitled to the principal of the trust or any part thereof; provided that the court, after a hearing on notice to all those beneficially interested in the trust in such manner as the court may direct, is satisfied that the original purpose of the creator of the trust cannot be carried out and that such allowance effectuates the intention of the creator.

"(c) In the event that an income beneficiary to whom an allowance is made, as provided in this section, is or becomes entitled to a share of the principal of the trust, such allowance, without interest thereon, shall be a charge upon such share.

"(d) The provisions of this section do not apply to any trust by which a future estate is indefeasibly vested in . . . the United States or political subdivision for exclusively public purposes; . . . [a charitable corporation; a charitable trust; a fraternal order; or a veteran's organization]."

SECTION E. Can a Trust Invalid for Want of Definite Beneficiaries Be Treated as a Power?

In re ESTATE OF KRADWELL

Supreme Court of Wisconsin, 1969

44 Wis. 2d 40, 170 N.W.2d 773

This proceeding is for the construction of the will of Pearl A. Kradwell, deceased.

Pearl A. Kradwell, a widow aged seventy-six years, died on April 14, 1967, leaving a will that was executed April 12, 1967. The will was filed for probate April 19, 1967, and admitted to probate February 15, 1968.

Objections to the probate of the will were filed in May of 1967 by the respondent, Janet Nelson Ross, but withdrawn in November of 1967. Mrs. Ross is a daughter of a deceased brother of the testatrix.

On February 12, 1968, Mrs. Ross filed a petition for construction of the residuary clause of the will.

On September 6, 1968, the court entered an order wherein the residuary clause of the will was held to be void and of no effect and the residue ordered to be distributed under the laws of descent.

Akabe Gulbankian, the named executrix of the will, appeals.

Additional facts will be set forth in the opinion.

BEILFUSS, Justice. The will of the testatrix was drafted by Attorney Vartak Gulbankian, witnessed by her and by her sister Rose Gulbankian, and named a third sister, Akabe Gulbankian, as executrix. The will directed the executrix to employ G. B. Gulbankian or Vartak Gulbankian as attorneys to probate the will. The will admitted to probate was the fifth and final will in a series drafted for testatrix by these attorneys between July 6, 1962, and April 12, 1967.

The residuary clause challenged by Mrs. Ross provides:

> *Sixteenth:* All the rest and residue and remainder of my estate I give, devise, and bequeath to my executrix hereinafter named, to distribute the same to and among my heirs, named legatees, and such other persons she may deem deserving and for benevolent objects, and to such of them and in such proportion as she shall deem just and proper, and her decision upon such matters shall be final, conclusive and binding upon all parties.

The will also makes various specific bequests to relatives and friends of the decedent, excluding the contestant, Janet Nelson Ross. Included within the specific bequests is a grant of $10,000 to Akabe Gulbankian individually and not as executrix.

The will further provided that if any legatee files objection or commences any suit to contest the will, then all legacies given to such person "shall cease, and their share of my estate shall become part of the residuary of my estate."

No testimony was taken at the hearing on the petition to construe the residuary clause but Mr. G. B. Gulbankian, attorney for the executrix Akabe Gulbankian, conceded the residuary clause did not make a gift personally to the executrix but rather created a trust for the beneficiaries named in the residuary clause.

The trial court concluded the residuary clause created a trust with the executrix named as trustee and that the trust failed because "[t]here are no named beneficiaries to enforce the trust."

The appellant-executrix does not dispute the trial court's conclusion that the residuary clause created a trust (rather than a gift personally to the executrix) with the executrix to hold the property in a fiduciary capacity. The appellant contends that the residuary clause does identify the beneficiaries of the trust with sufficient certainty to be enforceable.

We agree with the trial court that this case is controlled by our opinion in Estate of Liginger (1961), 14 Wis. 2d 577, 111 N.W.2d 407, 3 A.L.R.3d 1376, that the residuary clause created a trust and the trust fails for want of beneficiaries who can enforce the trust.

The opinion in the Liginger Case provides, in part, at pages 578, 579, 580, 581, 111 N.W.2d at page 408, as follows:

> The first 10 divisions of the will bequeathed 10 specific legacies.
>
> The eleventh division or paragraph of the testatrix's last will and testament contains the following residuary clause:
>
> "Eleventh: I give and bequeath to my executor and trustee hereinafter named, $250 for the purpose of securing Masses for the repose of my soul and that of my dear husband.

"After having paid the inheritance and transfer tax in connection with the above bequests I give, devise, and bequeath the rest, residue and remainder of my estate to my executor.

"My executor shall pay the sums in his hands in his sole discretion to the person or persons which I have previously indicated to him.

"I nominate and appoint as executor of this my last will and testament, John C. McBride, and I direct that no bond be required of him.

"My executor is authorized to do and perform any act deemed by him to be for the best interests of the estate without any limitation whatsoever. I give my executor and trustee the broadest powers . . ."

If all the language of paragraph Eleventh of the will, relating to the disposition of the residue, is read together, it indicates a trust; the executor to be a conduit through which the residue is to flow to the person or persons previously indicated to the executor by the testatrix. That indication, according to the testimony, was oral. Testimony to establish what that indication was cannot be admitted, since there would be little security in the right to transfer property by testamentary devise or bequest if the meaning of the will could be changed by the parole declarations of the testator to scriveners or witnesses. Estate of Pierce (1922), 177 Wis. 104, 188 N.W. 78, and Will of Tousey (1951), 260 Wis. 150, 50 N.W.2d 454, 27 A.L.R.2d 1228. The trust then fails for lack of a beneficiary. . . .

The law does not favor the vesting of bequests of property to the executor in his official capacity where it will result in a partial intestacy. This does not overcome the weightier reasoning that unless the will clearly expresses an intention for the bequest to vest in the executor personally such a bequest is a nullity. Anno. 104 A.L.R. 114, 118, citing Thomas v. Anderson (8th Cir. 1917), 245 F. 642. It therefore necessarily follows that after the distribution of the respective legacies under the provisions of the will, the residue descends intestate.

In this case the appellant contends the beneficiaries are (1) the heirs, and (2) the named legatees, and that to "such other persons" refers only to the heirs and named legatees.

We do not read the will with this limitation. The will directs the executrix ". . . to distribute the same to and among my heirs, named legatees, and such other persons she may deem deserving and for benevolent objects, and to such of them and in such proportion as she shall deem just and proper, and her decision upon such matters shall be final. . . ."

The use of the word "other" in the phrase "such other persons" directly following "heirs" and "legatees" clearly refers to a different or separate class of unknown persons. "[A]nd for benevolent objects" creates still another unknown class of beneficiaries. The terms of the clause, to wit — "and to such of them and in such proportion as she shall deem proper" will allow a distribution that would completely disregard the heirs and named legatees. As such, the beneficiaries are uncertain and no one is in a position to enforce the trust. Under the Liginger Case, supra, the trust fails, the residuary clause is void and unenforceable, and the residue of the estate descends intestate.

Order affirmed.

NOTES

In Morice v. Bishop of Durham, 10 Ves. 522, 32 Eng. Rep. 947 (Ch. 1805), Ann Crackerode gave her residuary estate to the Bishop of Durham, in trust, to dispose of "to such objects of benevolence and liberality as the Bishop of Durham in his own discretion shall most approve of." She appointed the Bishop of Durham her sole executor. The Bishop disclaimed any beneficial interest in himself personally, but he urged that he be permitted to carry out the terms of the gift, subject to being called to account by the court. The court ruled that a private noncharitable trust was intended and that it failed for lack of definite and ascertainable beneficiaries to enforce it.

Up until recent years the Bishop of Durham's case was followed in the United States. For example, in Clark v. Campbell, 82 N.H. 281, 133 A. 166 (1926), testator bequeathed his tangible personal property to his trustees to distribute "to such of my friends as they, my trustees, shall select." The court held that the trust failed for want of definite and ascertainable beneficiaries. There was, however, some authority to the contrary. In In re Lidston's Estate, 32 Wash. 2d 408, 202 P.2d 259 (1949), a testator's will gave legacies to eight persons and then provided, "I further direct my executor to dispose of any balance after the aforementioned gifts have been paid according to his wise discretion." The court held that this gave the executor a general power of appointment.

The Restatement (First) of Trusts §§122, 123, followed the rule of Morice v. Bishop of Durham, although the reporter, Professor Scott, argued that the bequest should be treated as a power, not as a trust. The Restatement (Second) of Trusts §§122, 123, repudiated the rule and adopted Professor Scott's position:

> §122. Except as stated in §121 [which says that a trust for the relatives of X is valid], where the owner of property transfers it in trust for the members of an indefinite class of persons, no enforceable trust is created; but if the transferee is authorized or directed to convey the property to such members of the class as he may select, he has power so to convey, unless the selection is authorized or directed to be made at a time beyond the period of the rule against perpetuities, or the class is so indefinite that it cannot be ascertained whether any person falls within it.
>
> §123. Where the owner of property transfers it in trust for indefinite or general purposes, not limited to charitable purposes, no enforceable trust is created, . . . but if the transferee is authorized or directed to apply the property for such purposes, he has power so to apply it, unless the application is authorized or directed to be made at a time beyond the period of the rule against perpetuities, or the purpose is so indefinite that it cannot be ascertained whether any application falls within it.

For comprehensive treatment of this subject, see Palmer, The Effect of Indefiniteness on the Validity of Trusts and Powers of Appointment, 10 U.C.L.A.L. Rev. 241 (1963). For recent developments in England, which may foreshadow the demise of the above rule in the Bishop of Durham's case, see Hopkins, Certain Uncertainties of Trusts and Powers, 29 Camb. L.J. 68 (1971).

RESTATEMENT (SECOND) OF TRUSTS §419: "(1) Where the owner of property gratuitously transfers it inter vivos for a purpose which is not enforceable because there is no definite or definitely ascertainable beneficiary designated, the transferee can properly apply the property to the designated purpose until his authority to make such application is revoked by the transferor or is terminated by the death or incapacity of the transferor.

"(2) Where the transferor revokes the authority of the transferee, or dies, or is under an incapacity, or the purpose fails, the transferee holds the property, or so much of the property as he has not in the meantime applied to the designated purpose, upon a resulting trust for the transferor or his estate."

PROBLEM

O transfers $100,000 to X in trust for such persons and on such terms as A shall appoint, but A shall have no power to appoint to A. O retains no express power to revoke the trust. Before A appoints the property O dies. A then appoints the property to B. Who takes the property? If X must return the property to O's estate, can you give any reason why this should be valid if it were a testamentary trust but not valid as an inter vivos trust? Palmer, The Effect of Indefiniteness on the Validity of Trusts and Powers of Appointment, 10 U.C.L.A.L. Rev. 241, 285 (1963).

In re SEARIGHT'S ESTATE

Court of Appeals of Ohio, 1950
87 Ohio App. 417, 95 N.E.2d 779

HUNSICKER, Judge. George P. Searight, a resident of Wayne county, Ohio, died testate on November 27, 1948. Item "third" of his will provided:

> I give and bequeath my dog, Trixie, to Florence Hand of Wooster, Ohio, and I direct my executor to deposit in the Peoples Federal Savings and Loan Association, Wooster, Ohio, the sum of $1000.00 to be used by him to pay Florence Hand at the rate of 75 cents per day for the keep and care of my dog as long as it shall live. If my dog shall die before the said $1000.00 and the interest accruing therefrom shall have been used up, I give and bequeath whatever remains of said $1000.00 to be divided equally among those of the following persons who are living at that time, to wit: Bessie Immler, Florence Hand, Reed Searight, Fern Olson and Willis Horn.

At the time of his death, all of the persons, and his dog, Trixie, named in such item third, were living.

Florence Hand accepted the bequest of Trixie, and the executor paid to her from the $1000 fund, 75 cents a day for the keep and care of the dog. The value of Trixie was agreed to be $5.

The Probate Court made a determination of inheritance tax due from the estate of George P. Searight, deceased, the pertinent part of this judgment reading as follows:

> The court further finds that the value of the dog Trixie is taxable as a succession to Florence Hand; that the said dog inherits the sum of $1000.00 with power to consume both the interest and principal at a limited rate; that the state of Ohio, Sec. 5332, levying a tax on successions to property does not levy a tax upon the succession to any property passing to an animal; that the $1000.00 bequest to said dog is therefore not taxable; that the remainder of the $1000.00, if any, remaining after the death of said dog is taxable in the hands of the remaindermen; that there is no certain life expectancy of said dog, and that a tax should therefore be assessed upon the entire bequest to the contingent beneficiaries, subject to the right of refund as provided in Sec. 5343, Ohio General Code, upon final determination of the exact succession to each of the five remaindermen, or the survivor of them.
>
> Wherefore, it is ordered by the court that Florence Hand, as successor to the title of the said dog Trixie, be taxed at the rate prescribed by law on the value of said dog, to wit, $5.00; that Bessie Immler, Florence Hand, Reed Searight, Fern Olson and Willis Horn, as contingent beneficiaries and remaindermen of the said $1000.00, each be taxed on $200.00 at the rate prescribed by law, subject to refund or assessment of any excess as indicated in the findings herein. . . .

The Department of Taxation of Ohio appeals to this court from such judgment. . . .

The questions presented by this appeal on questions of law are:

1. Is the testamentary bequest for the care of Trixie (a dog) valid in Ohio—

(a) as a proper subject of a so-called "honorary trust"?

(b) as not being in violation of the rule against perpetuities?

2. Is the bequest set forth in item third of testator's will subject to the inheritance tax laws of Ohio?

1(a). The creation of a trust for the benefit of specific animals has not been the subject of much litigation in the courts, and our research, and that of able counsel in this case, have failed to disclose any reported case on the subject in Ohio. The few reported cases in this country, in England and in Ireland have been the subject of considerable comment by the writers of text books and by the law reviews of leading law schools.

See: Mitford v. Reynolds, 60 Eng. Rep., 812, 16 Simons, 105 (trust for horses); Pettingall v. Pettingall, 11 L.J. Ch., 176, 8 English and Empire Digest, 264 (trust for horses and hounds); In re Dean, Cooper-Dean v. Stevens, 41 L.R. Ch. D., 552 (trust for horses and hounds); In re Kelly, Clearly v. Dillon, 1932 Irish Rep., 255,

1932 Mews' Annual Digest of English Case Law, 316 (trust for dogs allowed for 21 years); Willett v. Willett, 197 Ky. 663, 247 S.W. 739, 31 A.L.R. 426 (trust for dog allowed on the basis of a statute exempting both trusts for humane purposes and those for charitable purposes from the definite beneficiary requirement); In re Howells' Estate, 145 Misc. 557, 260 N.Y.S. 598 (trust for 5 household pets and one human being declared invalid as violating the New York statute forbidding the suspension of the absolute ownership of personal property for a period longer than two lives in being); In re Renner Estate, 358 Pa. 409, 57 A.2d 836 (a gift of residue in trust to maintain a dog and parrott held valid); 5 Harvard Law Review, 389; 10 Michigan Law Review, 31; 17 Minnesota Law Journal, 563; 46 Harvard Law Review, 1036, 42 Yale Law Journal, 1290; 10 Cincinnati Law Review, 116.

We do not have, in the instant case, the question of a trust established for the care of dogs in general or of an indefinite number of dogs, but we are here considering the validity of a testamentary bequest for the benefit of a specific dog. This is not a charitable trust, nor is it a gift of money to the Ohio Humane Society or a county humane society, which societies are vested with broad statutory authority, Section 10062, General Code, for the care of animals.

Text writers on the subject of trusts and many law professors designate a bequest for the care of a specific animal as an "honorary trust"; that is, one binding the conscience of the trustee, since there is no beneficiary capable of enforcing the trust.

The rule in Ohio, that the absence of a beneficiary having a legal standing in court and capable of demanding an accounting of the trustee is fatal and the trust fails, was first announced in Mannix, Assignee v. Purcell, 46 Ohio St. 102, 19 N.E. 572, 2 L.R.A. 753. . . .

In 1 Scott on the Law of Trusts, Section 124, the author says:

> There are certain classes of cases similar to those discussed in the preceding section in that there is no one who as beneficiary can enforce the purpose of the testator, but different in one respect, namely, that the purpose is definite. Such, for example, are bequests for the erection or maintenance of tombstones or monuments or for the care of graves, and bequests for the support of specific animals. It has been held in a number of cases that such bequests as these do not necessarily fail. It is true that the legatee cannot be compelled to carry out the intended purpose, since there is no one to whom he owes a duty to carry out the purpose.
>
> Even though the legatee cannot be compelled to apply the property to the designated purpose, the courts have very generally held that he can properly do so, and that no resulting trust arises so long as he is ready and willing to carry it out. The legatee will not, however, be permitted to retain the property for his own benefit; and if he refuses or neglects to carry out the purpose, a resulting trust will arise in favor of the testator's residuary legatee or next of kin.

. . .

The object and purpose sought to be accomplished by the testator in the instant case is not capricious or illegal. He sought to effect a worthy purpose — the care of his pet dog.

Whether we designate the gift in this case as an "honorary trust" or a gift with a power which is valid when exercised is not important, for we do know that the one to whom the dog was given accepted the gift and indicated her willingness to care for such dog, and the executor proceeded to carry out the wishes of the testator.

> Where the owner of property transfers it upon an intended trust for a specific noncharitable purpose and there is no definite or definitely ascertainable beneficiary designated, no trust is created; but the transferee has power to apply the property to the designated purpose, unless he is authorized by the terms of the intended trust so to apply the property beyond the period of the rule against perpetuities, or the purpose is capricious. I Restatement of the Law of Trusts, Section 124.

To call this bequest for the care of the dog, Trixie, a trust in the accepted sense in which that term is defined is, we know, an unjustified conclusion. The modern authorities, as shown by the cases cited earlier in this discussion, however, uphold the validity of a gift for the purpose designated in the instant case, where the person to whom the power is given is willing to carry out the testator's wishes. Whether called an "honorary trust" or whatever terminology is used, we conclude that the bequest for the care of the dog, Trixie, is not in and of itself unlawful.

In Ohio, by statute, Section 10512-8, General Code, the rule against perpetuities is specifically defined, and such statute further says: "It is the intention by the adoption of this section to make effective in Ohio what is generally known as the common law rule against perpetuities."

It is to be noted, in every situation where the so-called "honorary trust" is established for specific animals, that, unless the instrument creating such trust limits the duration of the trust — that is, the time during which the power is to be exercised — to human lives, we will have "honorary trusts" established for animals of great longevity, such as crocodiles, elephants and sea turtles. . . .[69]

If we then examine item third of testator's will, we discover that, although the bequest for his dog is for "as long as it shall live," the money given for this purpose is $1000 payable at the rate of 75¢ a day. By simple mathematical computation, this sum of money, expended at the rate determined by the testator, will be fully exhausted in three years and 238⅓ days. If we assume that this $1000 is deposited in a bank so that interest at the high rate of 6% per annum were earned thereon, the time needed to consume both principal and interest thereon (based on semi-annual computation of such interest on the average unused balance during such six month period) would be four years, 57½ days.

It is thus very apparent that the testator provided a time limit for the exercise

[69] Morris & Leach, The Rule Against Perpetuities 323 (2d ed. 1962): "In Re Kelly, Meredith, J. said: 'The court does not enter into the question of a dog's expectation of life.'" However, that was the ground on which Danckwerts, J. in Re Haines is reported to have sustained a gift for the maintenance of two cats: he took judicial notice of the shortness of a cat's life. It seems questionable whether courts should indulge in guesses of this sort; nor is there any justification for assuming that cats cannot live for more than twenty-one years." The authors give these figures for longevity of animals: cats, 25 years; horses, 40 years; ponies, 50 years; parrots, 70 years; tortoises, 100, 150, or even 200 years. — EDS.

of the power given his executor, and that such time limit is much less than the maximum period allowed under the rule against perpetuities.

We must indulge the presumption that the testator was cognizant of the rule against perpetuities and the construction placed upon it by the courts, and that he prepared his will possessed of such knowledge. Everhard et al., Trustees v. Brown, 75 Ohio App. 451, at page 459, 62 N.E.2d 901.

We therefore conclude that the bequest in the instant case for the care of the dog, Trixie, does not, by the terms of the creating instrument, violate the rule against perpetuities.

2. We next consider the problem of the inheritance tax, if any, to be levied on the bequest contained in item third of testator's will. . . .

[The court then decided that Ohio levied no inheritance tax on the amount used for the care of Trixie. The statute, Ohio General Code §5332, levied a tax on all property passing to a "person, institution or corporation." In the court's view, a dog was none of these. Moreover, the court decided the honorary trust was not a power of appointment, as such term is used in the inheritance tax statute.]

The judgment of the Probate Court is affirmed.[70]

Honorary Trusts and the Rule against Perpetuities

Although it is clear that any honorary trust to be valid must be limited to lives in being plus twenty-one years, the theory for the result is disputed. Courts have repeatedly said that a trust for a definite but noncharitable purpose *that may last too long* is void as a perpetuity. However, the accepted Rule against Perpetuities is a rule against remote vesting, not a rule controlling the duration of trusts. Some writers have attempted to bring honorary trusts within the accepted Rule by contending that a trust for a specific noncharitable purpose is in reality a special power of appointment, and, by orthodox doctrine, any special power that can be exercised beyond the perpetuity period is void ab initio. This rationalization has never been accepted by any court, however. Morris and Leach suggest there are two different rules: (1) a rule against remote vesting; and (2) a rule against a noncharitable definite purpose trust that may last beyond lives in being plus twenty-one years. Morris & Leach, The Rule Against Perpetuities 324-327 (2d ed. 1962).

GBS's Alphabet Trusts

George Bernard Shaw was long interested in reforming the English alphabet so that letters, singly and in combination, would have only one pronunciation. He pointed out that fish could be spelled "ghoti" if the "gh" were pronounced like the "gh" in "enough," "o" like the "o" in "women," and "ti" like "ti" in "notion." (He did not also note that Shaw could be spelled "pshaw.") GBS devised the residue of his estate (fattened by royalties from "My Fair Lady") to his executor, in trust for twenty-one years, to develop a new alphabet of forty letters and to propagandize for its adoption. Upon the termination of the alphabet trusts "or if and so far as such trusts shall fail through judicial decision," the principal was to be distrib-

[70] See Comment, Trusts for Animals, 17 Syracuse L. Rev. 705 (1966). — Eds.

uted one-third to the British Museum "in acknowledgment of the incalculable value to me of my daily resort to the reading room of that institution at the beginning of my career," one-third to the National Gallery of Ireland, and one-third to the Royal Academy of Dramatic Art. The court held the trust was not for the advancement of education nor beneficial to the community, and therefore it was not a charitable trust. The court further held that the devise could not be treated as a private trust because it was not in favor of an ascertainable beneficiary. The court referred to the Restatement of Trusts §124 (quoted in In re Searight's Estate), which approves treating the gift as a power, and stated that it was "not at liberty to validate this trust by treating it as a power. The result is that the alphabet trusts are, in my judgment, invalid, and must fail. It seems that their begetter suspected as much, hence his jibe about failure by judicial decision. I answer that it is not the fault of the law, but of the testator, who failed almost for the first time in his life to grasp the problem or to make up his mind what he wanted." In re Shaw, [1957] 1 All E.R. 745, 759 (Ch.). What, again, is the problem that Shaw failed to grasp?

The case was appealed, but while the appeal was pending, a compromise was effected by which a sum was set aside to employ a phonetic expert to develop a phonetic alphabet, transliterate Shaw's play "Androcles and the Lion" into the new alphabet, and publish the transliterated play.

In the course of its opinion on Shaw's will, the court remarked: "This document, moreover, was evidently originally the work of a skilled equity draftsman. As such, I doubt not, it was easily to be understood, if not of the vulgar, at any rate by the initiate. Unfortunately the will bears ample internal evidence of being in part the testator's own work. The two styles, as ever, make an unfortunate mixture." Under the principle of Heyer v. Flaig, page 21 supra, would the draftsman be liable for the failure of the alphabet trusts? To whom? How would you have drafted Shaw's will to carry out his desires? See Fratcher, Bequests for Purposes, 56 Iowa L. Rev. 773 (1971).

14. Gifts to Charity

SECTION A. Nature of Charitable Purposes

WILSON v. FLOWERS
Supreme Court of New Jersey, 1971
58 N.J. 250, 277 A.2d 199

PROCTOR, J. This is a will construction case. Plaintiffs, trustees under the will of Joseph L. K. Snyder, filed a complaint in the Chancery Division seeking instructions regarding the validity of Article Sixth (C)(12) of the testator's residuary trust of his will which directs them, inter alia, to contribute 20% of the residue "to such *philanthropic* causes as my Trustees may select" (emphasis added).

Defendants are the next-of-kin of the testator, and the Attorney General of New Jersey. The latter did not participate in the litigation.

After a hearing, Judge Mintz held that the plaintiffs had established the testator's probable intent that the gifts to "philanthropic causes" be solely charitable in nature. Thus, the gifts were not void and did not pass by intestate succession. Judgment directed 1) that the plaintiffs "shall contribute solely to charitable purposes the income to be disposed under Article Sixth (C)(12) of" the will, 2) that "the dispositions . . . do not violate the rule against perpetuities," and 3) that plaintiffs-trustees "in making contributions to philanthropic causes pursuant to Article Sixth (C)(12) of said will are restricted solely to charities which qualify as charities under Section 2055(a)(3) of the Internal Revenue Code[1] and N.J.S.A. 54:34-4(d),[2] as presently amended." . . .

[1] Section 2055(a)(3) of the Internal Revenue Code exempts from Federal estate tax gifts: "to a trustee or trustees, or a fraternal society, order, or association operating under the lodge

The primary issue on this appeal is whether the testator, in using the term "philanthropic causes," intended to limit his bounty to charitable causes or whether he intended the term to have a broader meaning. If the trust is not limited to charitable purposes, it is void either for uncertainty or for a violation of the rule against perpetuities. Kitchen v. Pitney, 94 N.J. Eq. 485, 119 A. 675 (E. & A. 1923); Sheen v. Sheen, 126 N.J. Eq. 132, 140, 8 A.2d 136 (Ch. 1939); Hegeman's Ex'rs v. Roome, 70 N.J. Eq. 562, 62 A. 392 (Ch. 1905). Defendants contend that the trust is void and that it should pass to them by intestate succession.

On February 28, 1965, Joseph L. K. Snyder died leaving a Will dated September 30, 1960. . . . By Articles First through Fifth the testator directed that his taxes, debts and other expenses be paid and that certain modest legacies be given to named individuals. The great bulk of his estate was disposed of by Article Sixth, which deals with the residuary. By this provision he bequeathed his residuary estate in trust, with directions to pay the income therefrom to three individuals for life (no beneficiary to receive income exceeding an average of $25,000 per year over a period of five consecutive years). Under Subsections (1) to (12) of Section (C) of Article Sixth the decedent directed that the balance of principal and accumulated income of the residuary estate be continued "in perpetual trust" and that the net income be distributed to the beneficiaries in the following proportions:

(1) 25% to Franklin and Marshall College for the education of needy and deserving students.
(2) 10% to the Theological Seminary of the Reformed Church of Lancaster, Pennsylvania, to be used for disabled or retired ministers and their widows.
(3) 10% to the same seminary for the education of needy and deserving students.
(4) 5% to the American Cancer Society, Inc.
(5) 2½% to Muhlenberg Hospital of Plainfield, New Jersey.
(6) 2½% to The Community Chest of Plainfield and North Plainfield.

---

system, but only if such contributions or gifts are to be used by such trustee or trustees, or by such fraternal society, order, or association, exclusively for religious, charitable, scientific, literary, or educational purposes, or for the prevention of cruelty to children or animals, no substantial part of the activities of such trustee or trustees, or of such fraternal society, order, or association, is carrying on propaganda, or otherwise attempting, to influence legislation, and such trustee or trustees, or such fraternal society, order, or association, does not participate in, or intervene in (including the publishing or distributing of statements), any political campaign on behalf of any candidate for public office;"

[2] N.J.S.A. 54.34-4(d) exempts from the New Jersey Transfer Inheritance tax:

"That part of the estate of any decedent which passes to, for the use of or in trust for any educational institution, church, hospital, orphan asylum, public library or Bible and tract society or to, for the use of or in trust for any institution or organization organized and operated exclusively for religious, charitable, benevolent, scientific, literary or educational purposes, including any institution instructing the blind in the use of dogs as guides, no part of the net earnings of which inures to the benefit of any private stockholder or other individual or corporation; provided, that this exemption shall not extend to transfers of property to such educational institutions and organizations of other States, the District of Columbia, territories and foreign countries which do not grant an equal, and like exemption of transfers of property for the benefit of such institutions and organizations of this State."

(7) $2\frac{1}{2}\%$ to the Crescent Avenue Presbyterian Church of Plainfield.
(8) $2\frac{1}{2}\%$ to the United Family & Children's Society.
(9) 10% to Emanuel Reformed Church, Export, Pennsylvania, for college scholarships and loans and church expenses.
(10) 5% to The Chemists Club of New York for the maintenance of its public library.
(11) 5% to the American Foundation for the Blind, Inc.

Defendants do not challenge the qualification of the above beneficiaries as charities. Their attack is limited to the language of Subsection (12) by which the remainder of the residue is disposed. That subsection reads in pertinent part:

> (12) To contribute the remaining twenty per cent (20%) thereof, together with income on hand by reason of the defection of any bequest under Subsections (1) through (11) of Section (C) of this Article Sixth, to such philanthropic causes as my Trustees may select, special consideration, however, to be given to charitable, educational and scientific fields, including universities, research laboratories, foundations or organizations formed for the purpose of the combating of and research on degenerative diseases.

It is estimated that the residuary estate will amount to $2,000,000.

Defendants contend that the word "philanthropic" is broader than the word "charitable" both in terms of the testator's intent so far as that intent can be gleaned from the four corners of the will and in terms of its generally accepted meaning.

Turning to the second point first, we have been cited to no New Jersey case construing the word "philanthropic." However, there are many cases construing the word "benevolent" which defendants contend is more restrictive than "philanthropic." The cases follow the English rule that "benevolent" is broader than "charitable" and that a trust for such purposes is therefore void. . . .[3]

Defendants urge that since New Jersey courts follow the English cases that hold "benevolent" is broader than "charitable," they must, a fortiori, follow the English cases that hold that "philanthropic" is broader than "charitable." Eades v.

[3] This result was reached even though it was sometimes recognized that the testator's intent was being thwarted. In Smith v. Pond, 90 N.J. Eq. 445, 107 A. 800 (Ch. 1919), rev'd on other grounds, 92 N.J. Eq. 211, 111 A. 154 (E. & A. 1920), Vice Chancellor Backes regretfully held that a gift for "such benevolent purposes as the trustees" shall direct was void:

"The result that I have reached, upon principle and authority, is not to my satisfaction, for I am of the impression that the testatrix understood benevolent to be synonymous with charitable, and it is regrettable that her wishes should be frustrated by the inadvertent use of an inept term." 90 N.J. Eq. at 451, 107 A. at 803.

See also the remarks of Lord Justice Goddard in Chichester Diocesean Fund v. Simpson [1944] A.C. 341, where he, feeling bound by precedent, nevertheless was disposed to comment that if it had been pointed out to the testator that the result of the insertion of the words "or benevolent" would be that the money would not go to charity, but to his first cousins once removed of whose existence he probably did not even know, there is not the least doubt in the world that he would, provided he was of sound mind and memory and understanding, have said, "cut out the word 'benevolent'."

Eades [1920] 2 Ch. 353; In re Macduff [C.A. 1896] 2 Ch. 451. We cannot accept this argument. It is no longer clear that "philanthropic" by legal connotation is broader than "charitable" in its legal connotation. Bogert has stated:

> At the present time it would seem that the intent of a donor who leaves property to be distributed for "benevolent" or "philanthropic" purposes is in most cases charitable. If the duration of the trust is indefinite or perpetual, a trust to show mere liberality will be void and in addition it will be subject to heavy tax burdens. Few trustors will desire these results. Common usage has made these words synonyms for charity. . . .
>
> The word "philanthropic" would seem, in its liberal sense, to include all acts of friendliness to mankind, whether conducive to improvement of society or merely to enrichment and enjoyment. In some English cases the word has been construed in this sense, and the result has been that a trust for "philanthropic purposes" has been held non-charitable because it would permit the trustee to perform acts of mere friendliness and generosity, having no connection with the need of the recipients of the benefits and no regard for the effect of the bounty upon the "beneficiaries." This is, however, perhaps a rather bookish meaning of the word. Probably in common use it is taken to mean charity, and some tendency to give it that effect is observable, especially where it is linked with the word "charitable" or with admittedly charitable objects. Bogert, Trusts & Trustees, §370, p. 69, 70 (2d ed. 1964).

There are a number of cases which have rejected the English cases and have treated "philanthropic" as synonymous with "charitable." E.g., MacKinnon v. MacKinnon [1909] Sess. Cas. 1041 ("charitable or philanthropic" institutions are charitable institutions); Rotch v. Emerson, 105 Mass. 431 (1870) ("for the promotion of agricultural or horticultural improvements, or other philosophical or philanthropic purposes" are charitable purposes), Thorp v. Lund, 227 Mass. 474, 116 N.E. 946 (1917) ("national and philanthropic purposes" are charitable purposes); Brewer v. McCauley (Matter of Loggie), [1954] S.C.R. 645 ("for such charitable, religious, educational or philanthropic purposes as the trustees shall appoint" are charitable purposes) (noted in 33 Can. B. Rev. 334 (1955); Moore v. Sellers, 201 S.W.2d 248 (Tex. Civ. App. 1947) ("charitable, philanthropic, religious and/or educational institutions, societies, organizations or undertakings" are charitable purposes).[4]

[4] Numerous courts have also adopted the modern rule that "benevolent" and "charitable" are synonymous. E.g., St. Louis Union Trust Co. v. Burnet, 59 F.2d 922 (8 Cir. 1932); In Re Dulles' Estate, 218 Pa. 162, 67 A. 49 (1907); Fox v. Gibbs, 86 Me. 87, 29 A. 940 (1894); Chicago Bank of Commerce v. McPherson, 2 F. Supp. 110 (W.D. Mich. 1931), aff'd 62 F.2d 393 (6 Cir. 1932), cert. denied 289 U.S. 736, 53 S. Ct. 596, 77 L. Ed. 1484 (1933); In re Snell's Will (Robinson v. Hammel), 154 Kan. 654, 121 P.2d 200 (1942); Sands v. Security Trust Company, 143 W. Va. 522, 102 S.E.2d 733 (1958). See also cases cited in 4 Scott, Trusts, §398.1, p. 3068, n. 19 (3d ed. 1967). New Jersey, like many other states, now has a statute which joins the terms "charitable" and "benevolent" in such a manner that it is apparent the terms are to be given like legal effect. See N.J.S.A. 15:14-6; see Smith v. Pond, 92 N.J. Eq. 211, 111 A. 154 (E. & A. 1920). See also N.J.S.A. 54:34-4(d); In re Kuebler, 106 N.J. Super. 13, 21, 254 A.2d 115 (App. Div. 1969). These statutes do not, however, use the word "philanthropic," and thus do not answer the problem at hand.

But defendants contend that even if philanthropic and charitable have come to mean the same thing, the manner in which the word "philanthropic" is used in the present case indicates a contrary intent. Testator's will directs that 20% of the residue of the estate be given, in trust, "to such philanthropic causes as my Trustees may select, special consideration, however, to be given to charitable, educational and scientific fields." Defendants argue that the "special consideration" clause evidences an intent that charitable, educational and scientific uses must merely be some of the philanthropic uses to which the funds may be given. Thus, they contend "philanthropic" is broader than "charitable" as the testator used it.

It is our duty to follow what we find to be the testator's probable intention. The commonly accepted meaning of words and their context is a strong indication of intent, but that is not the end of the matter. There are frequently other manifestations of intent. In the present case, if we were to accept defendants' argument, we would be left with the conclusion that the testator intended to die intestate. Yet as we noted in Fidelity Union Trust Co. v. Robert, 36 N.J. 561, 572, 178 A.2d 185, 191 (1962), there is a strong presumption that testators do not intend to die intestate, particularly where, as here, the gift is made out of the residuary estate. As we noted there, "The idea of anyone deliberately purposing to die testate as to a portion of his estate and intestate as to another portion is so unusual in the history of testamentary disposition as to justify almost any construction to escape it." Id., quoting 2 Redfield on Wills (3d ed. 235). This presumption is reinforced by the testator's mandate that his trust be perpetual. A perpetual trust for noncharitable purposes would be void, and it is unlikely that the testator intended that result. See Moore v. Sellers, supra.

There is another factor which indicates the testator intended "philanthropic" to be synonymous with "charitable." The other parts of his will demonstrate an interest in charitable causes. In sections (C)(1) through (C)(11), the testator disposed of 80% of the residuary to eleven specific admittedly charitable causes. Only (C)(12), the remaining section of his residuary trust, is challenged here. An overall feeling of charity pervades section (C) and that the testator should link 11 specific charitable causes with the term "philanthropic causes" is an indication that he intended his entire residuary estate to be devoted to charitable causes. See Bogert, supra at §370, p. 69, 70.

Of course, these general indications of intent do not answer defendants' argument that the juxtaposition of the language employed shows the testator intended "philanthropic" to be broader than "charitable." But there is direct evidence which answers the argument. At the trial the scrivener of the will testified, over objection, regarding the reason for the language used:

> The only thing I can think of that I used it was not to repeat the word "charitable" which is used in the same sentence. And it was used with the intent by me to interpret — to convey the impression of the testator in the writing used synonymously with the word charities or charitable. There is no question about that.
>
> The Court: In other words, the word "philanthropic" was a word of your choosing?

> The Witness: Of my choosing and used synonymously with the word charitable because I used the word charitable in the same sentence. I have an abhorrence of repeating the same word twice in the same sentence, or thought.

In other words, the reason for the use of the word "philanthropic" was the scrivener's wish to avoid repetition of the word "charitable"; in his view the two words were synonymous.[5] This testimony comports with all of the other evidence presented at the trial. The testator told the scrivener that he "wanted his entire residuary estate devoted and left to charities . . . in a perpetual trust . . . That was one thought that prevailed in all of the wills that I prepared for him. . . ."[6] [H]e wanted his residuary estate to be exempt from state and federal estate taxes.[7]

Also in evidence were two memoranda drafted by the testator. In the first, a nine page memorandum used in preparation of his 1958 will (later revoked), the testator indicated that his purpose was "to set up a trust fund to run into perpetuity, income from which shall be disposed of in several charitable directions." Notes made on this memorandum by the scrivener during conference demonstrate the testator's preoccupation with insuring that his residuary estate be tax exempt. Although this memorandum was drafted in preparation of an earlier will, it is nevertheless significant since the disposition of the residuary estate under that will roughly parallels the disposition under the present will. The second memorandum dated May 25, 1960, also demonstrated the testator's interest in charities. There is no doubt of the testator's intent if this evidence was properly admitted. But defendants contend that all evidence pertaining to the reason for the use of the word "philanthropic" should have been excluded because it went "too far in extending the doctrine of probable intent." They urge that the trial court erred in admitting: 1) testator's previous wills to show that the testator intended "philanthropic" to be synonymous with "charitable"; 2) the testator's memoranda of November 30, 1957 and May 25, 1960, which showed a concern for charitable gifts; 3) the 1957 tax analysis which showed a concern for charitable tax deductions, and 4) the scrivener's testimony for the use of the word "philanthropic."

. . . Extrinsic evidence which furnishes information regarding the circumstances surrounding the testator should be admitted to aid in ascertaining his probable intent under the will. Where the probable intent is thus made manifest by extrinsic evidence, the court may not refuse to effectuate that intent by indulging in a merely literal reading of the instrument.

Accordingly, we see no difficulty whatsoever involving the prior wills and the tax analysis. They were relevant and properly admitted since they furnished infor-

[5] This technique is referred to pejoratively by Fowler as "elegant variation." Fowler, A Dictionary of Modern English Usage, 148-51 (2d ed. 1965). See also Nicholson, A Dictionary of American-English Usage, 147-149 (1957).

[6] In the six wills preceding the probated will of 1960 and its codicil of 1964 the residuary estate was devoted primarily to charity.

[7] Thus, after receiving a tax analysis from a trust officer of his bank in 1957, he amended his gift to the Chemists Club to limit it to the Club's library which is open to the public. This action assured that the gift would qualify as charitable.

mation of the circumstances surrounding the testator. They were not admitted to vary the will, but merely to shed light on the use of the word "philanthropic." As we have already shown, that word is somewhat ambiguous.

The remaining question is whether the scrivener's testimony and the testator's memoranda should have been admitted. The scrivener's testimony included declarations by the testator that he wanted his entire residuary estate to go to charity, and that the scrivener used the word "philanthropic" as a synonym for "charitable." The memoranda demonstrated testator's charitable intentions. In In re Cook, 44 N.J. 1, 206 A.2d 865 (1965), this Court considered the question whether the wife of a stepson was entitled to share in the testatrix's estate or whether the gift should lapse. In construing the will, we noted that the testatrix had said "she felt under obligation to provide for Viola as Raymond's widow and heir and that *she had done so by the will she had executed*" (emphasis added) and that she had told Viola "that [Viola] would share in her estate as Raymond's widow and heir." Id. at 5, 206 A.2d at 867. Thus, we considered a direct statement by the testatrix of her intent because it helped to explain the meaning of a provision of her will. We did so even though the commonly accepted legal definition of that provision was to the contrary.

In subsequent cases, we have looked to the files of the scrivener and the practice of the firm which drew up the will in an effort to learn the testator's probable intent. Chase Manhattan Bank, et al. v. Mitchell, 53 N.J. 415, 417, 251 A.2d 128 (1969); In re Thompson, 53 N.J. 276, 279, 250 A.2d 393 (1969). We have even remanded a cause to permit the taking of testimony from the scrivener for evidence bearing on the intention of the testator. Surina v. Gilbert, 54 N.J. 68, 70, 253 A.2d 465 (1969). . . .

It is true that pre-Cook cases in this state recognized a distinction between "patent" and "latent" ambiguities. . . . We thought it implicit in Cook and the later cases we have cited that direct statements of intention should be admitted no matter what the form of the ambiguity. If our task is to ascertain and follow the testator's probable intent, we cannot fairly exclude evidence of that intent. Naturally, the circumstances surrounding the evidence may affect what weight, if any, it is to be given but it should not be excluded.

Putting these remarks into the context of the present case, it is apparent that the trial court properly admitted the testator's memoranda and the scrivener's testimony regarding the testator's statements to him and the origin of the disputed word "philanthropic." While "philanthropic" may be technically broader than "charitable," we think that it has come to mean the same thing in modern usage. However, even if it has not, it is ambiguous enough to be construed as such. Most words are susceptible of more than one meaning, for as Justice Holmes has remarked: "A word is not a crystal, transparent and unchanged, it is the skin of a living thought and may vary greatly in color and content according to the circumstances and the time in which it is used." Towne v. Eisner, 245 U.S. 418, 425, 38 S. Ct. 158, 159, 62 L. Ed. 372, 376 (1917). . . . We do not, of course, mean to imply that such evidence can be used to vary the terms of the will, but rather that it should be admitted first to show if there is an ambiguity and second, if one exists, to shed light on the testator's actual intent. . . .

The judgment of the Chancery Division is affirmed.

For affirmance: Chief Justice Weintraub and Justices Jacobs, Francis, Proctor, Hall and Schettino — 6

For reversal: None.

NOTES

1. In Hoenig v. Newmark, 306 S.W.2d 838 (Ky. 1957), there was a bequest "to such educational or charitable institutions or to such individual or individuals as, in their sole discretion, [my trustees] may determine to be worthy, with the suggestion on my part that my said Trustees carefully investigate the schools in the backwoods and mountains of Kentucky lending aid to underprivileged children and needy students." The court held the bequest void because benefits could be bestowed on "worthy" individuals as well as on charities.

What policy would be violated by giving effect to a mixed trust (i.e., a discretionary trust for benefit of charities and individuals) so long as the trust is limited to the perpetuity period?

2. If an institution is conducted for private profit, it is not charitable. In Matter of Shattuck's Will, 193 N.Y. 446, 86 N.E. 455 (1908), testator devised his residuary estate to his executor, in trust, to pay the income "to religious, educational or eleemosynary institutions as in his judgment shall seem advisable." The court held the trust failed because the beneficiaries were not necessarily limited to nonprofit institutions. "Educational institutions" might include a dancing school or a business school. Although the case has been criticized, and not followed in subsequent New York cases, it points up a contemporary drafting problem.

Suppose your client wants to benefit what are commonly known as private colleges and universities. How would you draw the gift? Would you define the class of beneficiaries as "privately endowed colleges and universities?" (a) If "privately endowed" means an educational institution whose *original* funds came from private rather than public sources, this would exclude Harvard and many of the oldest American universities, which were founded by grants from colonial governments.[8] (b) If "privately endowed" means an institution that is currently the beneficiary of endowment given by private individuals, this might include proprietary schools and state colleges, many of which have private endowments. Armstrong College in Berkeley, California, a proprietary school, has an endowment fund of $10,000. The University of Michigan has an endowment of $75,000,000. (c) If "privately endowed" means an educational institution that receives a substantial portion of its current income from endowment, less than twenty private universities would qual-

[8] See Blackman, The History of Federal and State Aid to Higher Education in the United States (1890).

ify.[9] Would it be wiser to define the beneficiaries by reference to who controls than to source of income? Having defined the beneficiaries, should you add — in the language of the Internal Revenue Code — "with respect to which no part of the net earnings inures to the benefit of any private shareholder or individual"?

3. A trust for the benefit of a specified individual is not a charitable trust. If the trust is not charitable, and there is no beneficiary to enforce the trust, the trust is invalid. T devises $10,000 to the Archbishop of Boston for masses to be offered for the repose of his soul. Is the gift valid? Curran, Charitable Trusts for Masses 1931-1956, 5 De Paul L. Rev. 246 (1956); O'Brien, Seventy Years of Bequests for Masses in New York Courts, 23 Fordham L. Rev. 147 (1954).

In re ESTATE OF KIDD, 479 P.2d 697 (Ariz. 1971). James Kidd, a bachelor of frugal nature, wrote a holographic will in 1946 leaving his estate for "reserach [*sic*] or some scientific proof of a soul of the human body which leaves at death I think in time their [there?] can be a Photograph of soul leaving the human at death." Shortly thereafter Kidd disappeared without a trace. In 1964 Kidd's will was discovered and offered for probate. His estate amounted to $175,000. More than a hundred claimants stepped forth. Some of the claimants argued that there was no intent to create a charitable trust but an outright bequest to any person who had scientific proof of a soul which leaves the body at death; one of these claimed to have seen her soul leave her body, and another claimed that scientific proof included inductive logical arguments based upon the Bible. The court held, however, that a charitable trust was intended. Upon remand, the trial court awarded the bequest to the American Society for Psychical Research in New York City. 110 Trusts & Estates 1058 (1971). Among other things, the society studies " 'crisis apparitions' (whereby a person receives a 'vision' of another person undergoing a crisis experience, often death, at another place), 'deathbed visions' (whereby a dying person appears to undergo a transformation allowing him to see into another world), 'physical changes in the surroundings' (whereby the death of a person is signaled by the disturbance of a physical object some distance away), and 'out-of-the-body experiences' (whereby a person in a sleeping or comatose state appears to himself to wander forth from his body and take up a station some distance away, purportedly sometimes to be seen there by others)." 479 P.2d at 702.

SHENANDOAH VALLEY NATIONAL BANK v. TAYLOR

Supreme Court of Appeals of Virginia, 1951

192 Va. 135, 63 S.E.2d 786

Miller, J. Charles B. Henry, a resident of Winchester, Virginia, died testate on the 23rd day of April, 1949. His will dated April 21, 1949, was duly admitted to probate and the Shenandoah Valley National Bank of Winchester, the designated executor and trustee, qualified thereunder.

[9] Millett, Financing Higher Education in the United States 308 (1952).

Subject to two inconsequential provisions not material to this litigation, the testator's entire estate valued at $86,000, was left as follows:

> "SECOND: All the rest, residue and remainder of my estate, real, personal, intangible and mixed, of whatsoever kind and wherever situate, . . . , I give, bequeath and devise to the Shenandoah Valley National Bank of Winchester, Virginia, in trust, to be known as the 'Charles B. Henry and Fannie Belle Henry Fund', for the following uses and purposes:
>
> "(a) My Trustee shall invest and reinvest my trust estate, shall collect the income therefrom and shall pay the net income as follows:
>
> "(1) On the last school day of each calendar year before Easter my Trustee shall divide the net income into as many equal parts as there are children in the first, second and third grades of the John Kerr School of the City of Winchester, and shall pay one of such equal parts to each child in such grades, to be used by such child in the furtherance of his or her obtainment of an education.
>
> "(2) On the last school day of each calendar year before Christmas my trustee shall divide the net income into as many equal parts as there are children in the first, second and third grades of the John Kerr School of the City of Winchester, and shall pay one of such equal parts to each child in such grades, to be used by such child in the furtherance of his or her obtainment of an education."

By paragraphs (3) and (4) it is provided that the names of the children in the three grades shall be determined each year from the school records, and payment of the income to them "shall be as nearly equal in amounts as it is practicable" to arrange.

Paragraph (5) provides that if the John Kerr School is ever discontinued for any reason the payments shall be made to the children of the same grades of the school or schools that take its place, and the School Board of Winchester is to determine what school or schools are substituted for it.

Under clause "THIRD" the trustee is given authority, power, and discretion to retain or from time to time sell and invest and reinvest the estate, or any part thereof, as it shall deem to be the best interest of the trust.

The John Kerr School is a public school used by the local school board for primary grades and had an enrollment of 458 boys and girls so there will be that number of pupils or thereabouts who would share in the distribution of the income.

The testator left no children or near relatives. Those who would be his heirs and distributees in case of intestacy were first cousins and others more remotely related. One of these next of kin filed a suit against the executor and trustee, and others challenging the validity of the provisions of the will which undertook to create a charitable trust. . . .

The sole question presented is: does the will create a valid charitable trust?

Construction of the challenged provisions is required and in this undertaking the testator's intent as disclosed by the words used in the will must be ascertained. If his dominant intent as expressed was charitable, the trust should be accorded efficacy and sustained.

But on the other hand, if the testator's intent as expressed is merely benevolent, though the disposition of his property be meritorious and evince traits of generosity, the trust must nevertheless be declared invalid because it violates the rule against perpetuities. . . .

Authoritative definitions of charitable trusts may be found in 4 Pomeroy's Equity Jurisprudence, 5th Ed., sec. 1020, and Restatement of the Law of Trusts, sec. 368, p. 1140. The latter gives a comprehensive classification definition. It is:

> Charitable purposes include:
> (a) the relief of poverty;
> (b) the advancement of education;
> (c) the advancement of religion;
> (d) the promotion of health;
> (e) governmental or municipal purposes; and
> (f) other purposes the accomplishment of which is beneficial to the community.

. . .

In the law of trusts there is a real and fundamental distinction between a charitable trust and one that is devoted to mere benevolence. The former is public in nature and valid; the latter is private and if it offends the rule against perpetuities, it is void.

> It is quite clear that trusts which are devoted to mere benevolence or liberality, or generosity, cannot be upheld as charities. Benevolent objects include acts dictated by mere kindness, good will, or a disposition to do good. . . . Charity in a legal sense must be distinguished from acts of liberality or benevolence. To constitute a charity the use must be public in its nature. Zollman on Charities, sec. 398, p. 268.

We are, however, reminded that charitable trusts are favored creatures of the law enjoying the especial solicitude of courts of equity and a liberal interpretation is employed to uphold them. Zollman on Charities, sec. 570, p. 391; 2 Bogert on Trusts, sec. 369, p. 1129. . . .

Appellant contends that the gift . . . not only meets the requirements of a charitable trust as defined in Restatement of the Law of Trusts, supra, but specifically fits two of those classifications, viz.:

"(b) trusts for the advancement of education;

"(f) other purposes the accomplishment of which is beneficial to the community."

We now turn to the language of the will for from its context the testator's intent is to be derived. Sheridan v. Krause, 161 Va. 873, 172 S.E. 508, 91 A.L.R 1067. Its interpretation must be free from and uninfluenced by the unyielding rule against perpetuities. Yet, when the testator's intent is ascertained, if it is found to be in contravention of the rule, the will, in that particular, must be declared invalid. . . .

In paragraphs (1) and (2), respectively, of clause "SECOND" in clear and definite language the discretion, power and authority of the trustee in its disposition and application of the income are specified and limited. Yearly on the last school day before Easter and Christmas each youthful beneficiary of the testator's generosity is to be paid an equal share of the income. In mandatory language the duty and the duty alone to make cash payments to each individual child just before Easter and Christmas is enjoined upon the trustee by the certain and explicit words that it "shall divide the net income . . . and shall pay one of such equal shares to each child in such grades."

Without more, that language, and the occasions specified for payment of the funds to the children being when their minds and interests would be far removed from studies or other school activities definitely indicate that no educational purpose was in the testator's mind. It is manifest that there was no intent or belief that the funds would be put to any use other than such as youthful impulse and desire might dictate. But in each instance immediately following the above-quoted language the sentence concludes with the words or phrase "to be used by such child in the furtherance of his or her obtainment of an education." It is significant that by this latter phrase the trustee is given no power, control or discretion over the funds so received by the child. Full and complete execution of the mandate and trust imposed upon the trustee accomplishes no educational purpose. Nothing toward the advancement of education is attained by the ultimate performance by the trustee of its full duty. It merely places the income irretrievably and forever beyond the range of the trust.

Appellant says that the latter phrase, "to be used by such child in furtherance of his or her obtainment of an education", evinces the testator's dominant purpose and intent. Yet it is not denied that the preceding provision "shall divide the net income into as many equal parts . . . and shall pay one of each equal parts to such child" is at odds with the phrase it relies upon. The appended qualification, it says, however, discloses a controlling intent that the 450 or more shares are to be used in the furtherance of education, and it was not really intended that a share be paid to each child so that he or she could during the Christmas and Easter holidays, or at any other time, use it "without let or hindrance, encumbrance or care." With that construction we cannot agree. In our opinion, the words of the will import an intent to have the trustee pay to each child his allotted share. If that be true, — and it is directed to be done in no uncertain language — we know that the admonition to the children would be wholly impotent and of no avail.

In construing wills, we may not forget or disregard the experiences of life and the realities of the occasion. Nor may we assume or indulge in the belief that the testator by his injunction to the donees intended or thought that he could change childhood nature and set at naught childhood impulses and desires.

Appellant asserts that literal performance of the duty imposed upon it — pay to each child his share — would be impracticable and should not be done. Its position in that respect is stated thus: "We do not understand that under the law of Virginia a court would pay money for education into the hands of children who are incapable of handling it." It then says that the funds could be administered by a guardian or under sec. 8-751, Code, 1950 (where the amounts are under $500), a court could direct payment to be made to the recipient's parents.

With these statements, we agree. But because the funds could be administered under applicable statutes has no bearing upon nor may that device be resorted to as an aid to prove or establish the testator's intent. We are of opinion that the testator's dominant intent appears from and is expressed in his unequivocal direction to the trustee to divide the income into as many equal parts as there are children beneficiaries and pay one share to each. This expressed purpose and intent is inconsistent with the appended direction to each child as to the use of his respective share and the latter phrase is thus ineffectual to create an educational trust. The testator's purpose and intent were, we think, to bestow upon the children gifts that would bring to them happiness on the two holidays, but that falls short of an educational trust.

If it be determined that the will fails to create a charitable trust for *educational purposes* (and our conclusion is that it is inoperative to create such a trust), it is earnestly insisted that the trust provided for is nevertheless charitable and valid. In this respect it is claimed that the two yearly payments to be made to the children just before Christmas and Easter produce "a desirable social effect" and are "promotive of public convenience and needs, and happiness and contentment" and thus the fund set up in the will constitutes a charitable trust. 2 Bogert on Trusts, sec. 361, p. 1090, and 3 Scott on Trusts, sec. 368, p. 1972. . . .

Numerous cases that deal with and construe specific provisions of wills or other instruments are cited by appellant to uphold the contention that the provisions of this will, without reference to and deleting the phrase "to be used by such child in the furtherance of his or her obtainment of an education" meet the requirements of a charitable trust. . . . [Citations omitted.]

Upon examination of these decisions, it will be found that where a gift results in mere financial enrichment, a trust was sustained only when the court found and concluded from the entire context of the will that the ultimate intended recipients were poor or in necessitous circumstances.

A trust from which the income is to be paid at stated intervals to each member of a designated segment of the public, without regard to whether or not the recipients are poor or in need, is not for the relief of poverty, nor is it a social benefit to the community. It is a mere benevolence — a private trust — and may not be upheld as a charitable trust. Restatement of the Law of Trusts, sec. 374, p. 1156:

> . . . if a large sum of money is given in trust to apply the income each year in paying a certain sum to every inhabitant of a city, whether rich or poor, the trust is not charitable, since although each inhabitant may receive a benefit, the social interest of the community as such is not thereby promoted.

. . .

Of the cases relied upon which the trust was sustained as charitable In re Mellody (Branwood v. Haden), 1918, 1 Ch. 228, 87 L.J. Ch. 185, 118 L.T. 155, and In re Estate of Nilson, 81 Neb. 809, 116 N.W. 971, appear to be as much if not more in point with appellant's contention than any others.

In the Mellody Case income from the trust fund was to be used by the trustee "to provide an annual treat or field day for the schoolchildren of Turton or as many of such children as the same will provide for." It will thus be seen that the trustee had control of and administered the income from the fund and it was devoted to a supervised annual outing for school children as such. Its intended use bore a direct relationship to their schooling and education. The court held that it was a charitable trust because it (1) tended to the advancement of education, and (2) was "for purposes beneficial to a particular section of the community." Speaking of the annual treat or field day provided for, it said:

> It may well be made, and, I doubt not, often is made, the occasion for pointing out to the children those objects of the countryside and nature about which during their school hours they have read in their books, or which they have seen in the pictures displayed upon the walls of their schoolroom. . . .

In the Nilson Case, the testator, a then resident of Nebraska, recited in his will that—

> Sixth. Being a native of the Tjosvold, Harmoen, Kingdom of Norway, where fishing and sailing are the chief industries, and being acquainted with the social and industrial conditions of the poorer classes of Norway, my sympathies go out to industrious and deserving servant girls, and to widows and orphans of deceased fishermen and sailors. Desiring to relieve such servant girls and widows and orphans, I give and bequeath to Akre church congregation (Akre Kirksogn) six thousand dollars, to be invested . . .", and the interest to be distributed on each "christmas to worthy and needy servant girls and the widows and orphans of deceased sailors and fishermen who are not a public charge. (pp. 810, 811 of 81 Neb.)

The pastor of the congregation or parish, the president of the county commissioners, and the county treasurer of Akre Kirksogn, Norway, and their successors in office were designated trustees. They were peculiarly well situated to know and select who were in need of and deserving of the testator's assistance. Though the language used excludes from the class of beneficiaries those who are public charges, the context of the entire will when the trustees selected and their implied powers and discretion are taken into account sufficiently authorizes selection by them of beneficiaries from the designated class who are in need, deserving and worthy of help. . . .

In Goodell v. Union Association of Children, etc., 29 N.J. Eq. 32, a bequest of $1,000 was left to Trinity Church Sunday School with directions that it be safely invested and the interest used to secure Christmas presents for the scholars of that school. There was no indication that the recipients were to be those found to be in necessitous circumstances nor is any implied power or discretion given to limit or apply the income to such individuals. In the following language, the court declared that no charitable trust was created:

> . . . What the gifts are to be does not appear. It does not appear that they are even to be rewards of merit, or to be used as means of inducing attendance on the part of the scholars at the school, or of promoting their good conduct there, or of inciting them to attention to religious instruction given to them there, nor whether they are to be given to all the scholars or part only. The gift is in trust, and it is not a charity in the legal sense. It is void. (29 N.J. Eq. p. 35).

Of similar import is Pleasants v. Attorney General (1923), 39 T.L.R. 675. There property was left in trust with the direction that the trustee, among other things, buy at a certain time each year a pennyworth of sweets for each boy and girl below fourteen years of age residing within a certain parish. It was decided that the trust was non-charitable and void.

Nor do we find any language in this will that permits the trustee to limit the recipients of the donations to the school children in the designated grades who are in necessitous circumstances, and thus bring the trust under the influence of the case styled Appeal of Eliot, 74 Conn. 586, 51 A. 558.

The conclusion there reached was that where a trust is set up and a class is designated as beneficiary which generally contains needy persons, the testator will be presumed to have intended as recipients those members of the class who are in necessitous circumstances.

Payment to the children of their cash bequests on the two occasions specified would bring to them pleasure and happiness and no doubt cause them to remember or think of their benefactor with gratitude and thanksgiving. That was, we think, Charles B. Henry's intent. Laudable, generous and praiseworthy though it may be, it is not for the relief of the poor or needy, nor does it otherwise so benefit or advance the social interest of the community as to justify its continuance in perpetuity as a charitable trust. . . .

[In an omitted portion of the opinion the court held the cy pres statute inapplicable because the trust was not for an "educational, charitable, or eleemosynary purpose."]

No error is found in the decrees appealed from and they are affirmed.

Affirmed.[10]

---

4 SCOTT, TRUSTS §375.1 (3d ed. 1967): "A trust may be a valid charitable trust for the advancement of religion although the persons who are directly to benefit are limited in number. Thus a perpetual trust to pay or to contribute to the payment of the salary of a minister of a particular church is charitable. Although the direct

[10] Noted 23 Miss. L.J. 62; 20 U. Cin. L. Rev. 505; 37 Va. L. Rev. 642; 9 Wash. & Lee L. Rev. 310. — Eds.

beneficiary for the time being is a single person, the incumbent of the office, yet the effect of the trust is to promote religion. Similarly a trust to use the income for the support of the widows and children of former ministers of a particular church is charitable. Thus in Sears v. Attorney General [11] a fund was raised by subscriptions from persons connected with Trinity Church in Boston 'for the benefit of the widows and orphan children that may be left by the future ministers of this church.' Payments were to be made only to such widows and orphans as were in need. It was held that the trust was charitable both because it was for the relief of poverty and because it tended to promote religion. As a trust for the relief of poverty it was charitable although the class to be relieved was at any one time a small one, since it included an indefinite number of persons in future generations. Moreover, the trust tended to benefit religion by increasing the remuneration of ministers of the church by providing for their families. But if the trust had not been limited to needy widows and orphans and if the persons to be benefited had not been connected with a religious vocation, it would seem that the trust would not have been charitable since the class to be benefited would have been too narrow. Thus it would seem that a trust for the benefit of the families of the presidents of a fraternal organization without regard to poverty would not be charitable."

---

4 SCOTT, TRUSTS §375.2 (3d ed. 1967): "*Employees.* A trust to relieve the necessities of persons who are or have been employed in a particular trade or profession is charitable. Such a trust is charitable where the persons to be assisted are of small means although not in actual need. Thus a trust for the benefit of young seamstresses of a city has been upheld as charitable, and a trust has been upheld to supply medical or surgical care to any member of the Customs Service in the Port of New York.

"Where a trust is created for the relief of poverty or the promotion of health, the fact that the benefits are confined to the employees of a particular railroad or industrial organization does not prevent the trust from being a valid charitable trust. Even though the benefits under the trust are to be extended to employees who are not actually poverty-stricken, yet if they are among the underprivileged the trust may be charitable.

"In the English cases, however, the courts have tended to take a stricter view. Thus it has been held that a bequest for the purpose of contributing to the holiday expenses of the employees of a certain company was not charitable, it being shown that the employees were all paid as much as fifteen shillings a week and could not therefore, so said the court, be classified as poor. In another case, where employees of a company through weekly contributions created a benevolent fund to assist

[11] 193 Mass. 551, 79 N.E. 772, 9 Ann. Cas. 1200 (1907).

In In re Clark, [1961] New Zealand L.R. 635, however, where a testatrix created a trust to pay £50 a year to the wife (if any) of the minister from time to time of a designated church, to be used by her for her own private use, it was held that the trust was not charitable and failed.

them when sick or suffering from air raids, it was held that the trust was not a charitable trust and that the doctrine of cy pres could not be applied.

"At length the question of the validity of trusts for employees of a corporation came before the House of Lords. In Oppenheim v. Tobacco Securities Trust Co.[12] a settlor conveyed property to a trustee in trust to apply the income to the education of children of employees of a large tobacco company and its allied companies, which had 110,000 employees. It was held by the House of Lords that the trust was not charitable, since the beneficiaries constituted too limited a class, even though the trust was for their education, and that the trust failed. Lord Simonds hinted that the House of Lords might repudiate the cases upholding trusts for the relief of poverty of members of a limited class of persons, such as relatives. . . .

"As we have seen, a trust to promote the happiness or well-being of members of the community is charitable, although it is not a trust to relieve poverty, advance education, promote religion or protect health. In such a case, however, the trust must be for the benefit of the members of the community generally and not merely for the benefit of a class of persons. . . .

"But a trust unconnected with the relief of poverty or the advancement of education or religion or health in order to be charitable must be for the benefit of a larger class than need be benefited if the trust is connected with such purposes. Thus, although, as we have seen, a trust for the relief of poverty is charitable even if confined to persons following a particular calling or persons in a particular employment, yet a trust for the general benefit of such persons is not charitable. In an English case it was held that a trust 'for the benefit of individuals who have been engaged in the Oporto Red or Port St. Mary's White Sherry Wine Trade' was not charitable. In an Irish case it was held that a bequest made by one O'Laverty to contribute toward the support and education in Ireland of any Roman Catholic boys of the surname of O'Laverty or Laverty or O'Lafferty or Lafferty, between the ages of eleven and twenty-three, was not charitable. The purpose of the trust was not limited to the relief of poor boys of the designated names nor was it limited to education. According to the terms of the trust the money might be used to support wealthy boys of the designated surnames. The court said of this trust: 'Its purposes can hardly be regarded as one of those general purposes beneficial to the community, or to some class of the community, which have been held charitable without any element of the relief of poverty, or advancement of religion or education.'"

[12] [1951] A.C. 297.

In George Drexler Ofrex Foundation Trustees v. Inland Revenue Commissioners, [1965] 3 All E.R. 529, where a trust was created for the advancement of education among employees or former employees of a large corporation or its associated companies, or the families of such persons, it was held that the trust was not for a charitable purpose and was subject to tax.

ESTATE OF ROBBINS

Supreme Court of California, 1962

57 Cal. 2d 718, 371 P.2d 573, 21 Cal. Rptr. 797

TRAYNOR, Justice. In his will the testator divided his estate into Fund A consisting of "cash, securities and money in the bank" and Fund B consisting of "a parcel of real estate situated in Los Angeles, California, and improved with two (2) single family residences, together with furniture, fixtures, personal belongings and library contained therein." He directed that the assets comprising Fund B be sold and the cash distributed to three named trustees in trust. "The income of said trust, or so much of the principal as in the sole discretion of the Trustees may be deemed desirable or advisable, is to be used for the care, comfort, support, medical attention, education, sustenance, maintenance or custody of such minor Negro child or children, whose father or mother, or both, have been incarcerated, imprisoned, detained or committed in any federal, state, county or local prison or penitentiary, as a result of the conviction of a crime or misdemeanor of a political nature." He then set forth illustrative examples of crimes of a political nature for the guidance of the trustees in the exercise of their discretion and stated his reasons for creating the trust.[13]

In this proceeding to determine heirship (Prob. Code, §1080) the disposition

[13] "In order to clarify my intention and make clear to my Trustees what I mean or intend to be meant by crimes or misdemeanor of a political nature, the following examples are offered for the guidance of my Trustees:

"1. The prosecution, conviction and incarceration resulting from a purported violation of any federal, state or local statute, ordinance or regulation seeking to proscribe, limit, abolish, enjoin or regulate the teaching, advising, adopting, advocating or implementing any political, geopolitical, or social-political doctrine, thesis, theory or philosophy, or speaking or writing in support thereof. I cite the Smith Act of the Federal Government [18 U.S.C.A. §§2385, 2387] and the prosecutions resulting thereunder as an example of this paragraph.

"2. The prosecution, conviction and incarceration resulting from any contempt citation arising out of the refusal to answer any question or questions concerning the religious, social, economic or political opinions, beliefs, persuasions or affiliations, past and present, as may be propounded by any federal, state or local committee or sub-committee, or by any legislative committee of any state or municipality or of the Congress of the United States. I cite the appearances before the Un-American Activities Committee or the Internal Securities Committee of the United States Congress and subsequent prosecutions flowing therefrom as appropriate examples of this paragraph.

"3. The prosecution, conviction and incarceration resulting from the refusal to execute any affidavit, certification or other statement, whether under oath, or not under oath, inquiring into the political affiliations, beliefs or associations of the affiant; or the prosecution, conviction or incarceration which may result from the execution of a purported false statement, affidavit or certification as to the past or present political affiliations, beliefs or associations of the affiant. I cite the prosecutions under the non-Communist affidavit of the Taft-Hartley Act [29 U.S.C.A. §141 et seq.], or the prosecutions flowing from the McCarron-Walters Immigration Act [8 U.S.C.A. §1101 et seq.] or the prosecutions and proceedings filed under the so-called Broyle's Bill of the State of Illinois, or prosecutions pursued by the Un-American Activities Committees of the various states as appropriate examples of this paragraph.

"4. The prosecution, conviction and incarceration resulting from any activity in the organization, or assisting in the organization, of any trade union movement; or from the violation of any injunction of any court, restraining, enjoining or limiting in any way the activities of any union

of Fund A is not in dispute, but Lee Mishkin, a grandnephew of the testator, challenges the validity of the Fund B trust. The trial court determined that the trust is invalid. Since the will contained no residuary clause, the court entered an order determining that the property bequeathed to the trustees should pass by the law of intestate succession. The administrator-with-the-will-annexed appeals.

We agree with the contention of the administrator that the testator established a valid charitable trust. The trustees, the beneficiaries, and the trust purpose are all stated.

> A bequest is charitable if: (1) It is made for a charitable purpose; its aims and accomplishments are of religious, educational, political or general social interest to mankind. [Citations.] (2) The ultimate recipients constitute either the community as a whole or an unascertainable and indefinite portion thereof. [Citations.]

(Estate of Henderson, 17 Cal. 2d 853, 857, 112 P.2d 605, 607.) Provision for the "care, comfort, support, medical attention, education, sustenance, maintenance or custody" of minor children who have been deprived of normal home life by the incarceration of one or both of their parents is unquestionably of social value. Any risk that a parent might be induced to commit a crime he otherwise would not commit because of the possibility that his child might become a beneficiary of this trust is far outweighed by the interests of the innocent children involved and society's interest in them. To hold otherwise would, as stated in another context, "incorporate into the law of the land as legal precepts the sayings that the sins of fathers are visited upon their children and that the child's teeth must be set on edge because the father has eaten sour grapes. . . ."

The testator selected a class of beneficiaries constituting an indefinite part of the community and provided adequate standards to guide his trustees in administering the trust. (Estate of Bunn, 33 Cal. 2d 897, 901-904, 206 P.2d 635, and authorities cited.) Like the aged beneficiaries in Estate of Henderson, supra, 17 Cal. 2d

---

of working men and women in the United States, or restricting and limiting the right to collectively bargain or go out on strike.

"The above examples are cited for illustration purposes only, so as to enable and assist my said Trustees to determine what, in their own collective opinion, shall constitute a crime or misdemeanor of a political nature, in accordance with the uses and purposes of this trust. It is my intention, however, and I do by these presents vest in my said Trustees the full and complete power and authority to determine according to their sole and best judgment what is now, or what in the future may constitute, conviction of a crime or misdemeanor of a political nature. I am aware and cognizant that the law is an ambulatory institution and accordingly is subject to constant change. I anticipate that subsequent to the execution of these presents or subsequent to the date of my demise, laws, statutes and regulations, other than those presently in full force and effect, may be adopted by the Congress of the United States or by the respective legislatures of the several states, which will or may be calculated to limit, abolish or circumscribe the field of activity in unorthodox or unpopular political or economic causes or philosophies; and that people will be arrested, convicted and imprisoned as a result therefrom. Accordingly, and with full cognizance of this eventuality, I hereby endow my said Trustees, in their sole discretion and in accordance with their best collective judgment, to determine who shall receive the benefits of this trust estate. My only stipulation to my said Trustees is that the recipients be the minor Negro children of such defendants. . . ."

853, 112 P.2d 605, Fredericka Home For The Aged v. County of San Diego, 35 Cal. 2d 789, 221 P.2d 68, and Estate of Tarrant, 38 Cal. 2d 42, 237 P.2d 505, these children require special care and attention, and it is immaterial that the beneficiaries are not limited to children in financial need. "Relief of poverty is not a condition of charitable assistance. If the benefit conferred has a sufficiently widespread social value, a charitable purpose exists." (Estate of Henderson, supra, 17 Cal. 2d 853, 857, 112 P.2d 605, 607; see also Estate of Tarrant, supra, 38 Cal. 2d 42, 50, 237 P.2d 505.)

> In short, as the word "charity" is commonly understood in modern usage, it does not refer only to aid to the poor and destitute and exclude all humanitarian activities . . . which are maintained to care for the physical and mental well-being of the recipients, and which make it less likely that such recipients will become burdens on society. (Fredericka Home For The Aged v. County of San Diego, supra, 35 Cal. 2d 789, 793, 221 P.2d 68, 71.)

Lee Mishkin contends, however, that the testator's purpose was to encourage the commission of political crimes and that therefore the trust is illegal. The administrator and amicus curiae contend, on the contrary, that the testator's purpose was to encourage constitutionally protected freedom of speech and expression and to protect the right of lawful dissent and that these are valid charitable purposes. They contend that the illustrations the testator set forth in his will, convictions of violating the Smith Act, convictions of contempt of congressional committees, convictions for violating laws dealing with test oaths, convictions for engaging in labor union activities, all involve areas where the lines between constitutionally protected activity and illegal activity are vaguely defined. . . . They assert that the will can reasonably be interpreted as referring only to parents who have been unlawfully convicted for engaging in constitutionally protected activity and that thereby any question of illegality can be avoided.

We need not search for any such limitation in the language of the will to sustain the trust. We may assume that the testator intended to benefit the children of those convicted of even valid laws of which he disapproved and that his motive in part at least was to encourage challenges to such laws by violations of them. It is the purpose for which the property is to be used, however, not the motives of the testator that determines whether a trust is a valid charitable trust. (. . . Restatement, Trusts 2d, §368, comment d; 4 Scott on Trusts [2d ed.], §§348, 368, pp. 2551, 2628; 2A Bogert, Trusts and Trustees, §364, pp. 30-34.)

Assistance to the minor beneficiaries of the trust in this case is a valid charitable purpose. The risk that such assistance may serve to encourage crime is far more remote than that which the Legislature itself may have created by provision for the care of children that extends to those of convicted prisoners. (See Welf. & Inst. Code, §1500.[14]) The benefit to society offered by the testator transcends whatever criticism there may be of his motives, which have died with him.

[14] This section authorizes aid to families with children under eighteen years of age in need

The order is reversed. The appeal from the order denying the motion for new trial is dismissed. . . .

Gibson, C.J., and Peters and Dooling, JJ., concur.

White, Justice. I dissent.

Undoubtedly a valid trust may be created where its purposes are to effect changes in existing laws. (See 4 Scott on Trusts [2d ed.] §374.4, p. 2677; 2A Bogert on Trusts, §378, pp. 168-170.)

. . .

However, recognition cannot be given to a trust as valid where its purpose is illegal. Therein lies the vice of the trust now engaging our attention. It not only encourages but offers an inducement for violation of the criminal law. In the Restatement of Trusts is found the following cogent statement: "A *trust which tends to induce a breach of the criminal law is invalid.* Thus, a trust of property to be applied to the payment of fines of persons convicted of criminal offenses . . . is invalid." (Emphasis added.) And in 4 Scott on Trusts (2d ed.) section 377 at page 2729, it is said:

> A trust cannot be created for a purpose which is illegal. The purpose is illegal if the trust property is to be used for an object which is in violation of the criminal law, or if the trust tends to induce the commission of crime, or if the accomplishment of the purpose is otherwise against public policy. Questions of public policy are not fixed and unchanging, but vary from time to time and from place to place. A trust fails for illegality if the accomplishment of the purposes of the trust is regarded as against public policy in the community in which the trust is created and at the time when it is created. *Where a policy is articulated in a statute making certain conduct a criminal offense, then, of course, a trust is illegal if its performance involves such criminal conduct, or if it tends to encourage such conduct.* Thus, in an early English case a bequest to trustees "to make seats for poor people to beg in by the highway" was held invalid since such begging was a criminal offense.
>
> A trust is illegal, even if it does not involve the performance of an illegal act by the trustees, if the natural result of the performance of the trust would be to induce the commission of crime. Thus a bequest to purchase the release of persons committed to prison for nonpayment of fines under the game laws was held illegal. (Emphasis added.)

In my opinion, it would do violence to reason and challenge credulity to say that the object of the trust with which we are here concerned is to bring about a change in the law by lawful and orderly means. On the contrary the testator, with care and precision, undertook to instruct his trustees that those who would violate certain named existing penal statutes, or commit any crime or misdemeanor which the testator terms "of a political nature," and [are] convicted thereof, were to be rewarded by the furnishing of aid to their children. That the trust property in the case

---

of support because they have been deprived of parental support due to, among other things, incarceration of a parent. — Eds.

at bar was to be used in the performance of the trust to encourage if not induce the commission of crime, to me seems manifest, and therefore, consonant with the foregoing reasoning and authorities, it cannot be held to be a valid charitable trust.

I would affirm the judgment.

Schauer and McComb, JJ., concur.[15]

NOTES

1. If the testator's motive was to encourage challenges of laws establishing political crimes by violations of them, should that motive be considered in determining whether the trust is against public policy? When a settlor sets up a trust with income going to his daughter A (presently married to B) and principal going to A if she divorces B, the settlor's motive determines whether the trust violates public policy. If his motive is to promote divorce, and not merely to give his daughter the principal because she will need it in case of divorce, the trust is against public policy. 1 Scott, Trusts §62.4 (3d ed. 1967).

2. An ardent sportsman establishes a trust to pay the fines of those who violate the game laws. Is the trust valid? Thrupp v. Collett, 26 Beav. 125, 53 Eng. Rep. 844 (Rolls 1858). What about a trust for the benefit of children of persons convicted of violating the selective service laws? Convicted of desertion from the armed forces? Convicted of violating any statute prohibiting some form of sexual activity between consenting adults?

3. Would a trust to promote the success of the Republican party be charitable? The success of the principles of the Ripon Society? Of the John Birch Society? Of Socialism? Note, Charitable Trusts for Political Purposes, 37 Va. L. Rev. 988 (1951). It is generally held that where the object of the trust is political the trust is not charitable, but where the trust is for the improvement of the structure and methods of government it is charitable. Thus it has been held that a legacy to the Socialist-Labor party is not for charitable purposes (Matter of Grossman, 190 Misc. 521, 75 N.Y.S.2d 335 (Sur. Ct. 1947)), but a trust to provide a place where the doctrines of socialism could be taught by example as well as precept is charitable (Peth v. Spear, 63 Wash. 291, 115 Pac. 164 (1911)). Having been given this fine distinction, do you think a trust for the advancement of adult education especially for the purpose of indoctrinating persons in the theories and ambitions of the Labor Party is charitable? Re Hopkinson, [1949] 1 All E.R. 346 (Ch.).

4. Restatement (Second) of Trusts §374, Comment j (1959): "A trust may be charitable although the accomplishment of the purpose for which the trust is created involves a change in the existing law. If the purpose of the trust is to bring about changes in the law by illegal means, such as revolution, bribery, illegal lobbying or bringing improper pressure to bear upon members of the legislature, the purpose is illegal. The mere fact, however, that the purpose is to bring about a change

[15] Noted 50 Calif. L. Rev. 885; 12 De Paul L. Rev. 364; 48 Iowa L. Rev. 1019; 36 S. Cal. L. Rev. 309; 8 Utah L. Rev. 152; 20 Wash. & Lee L. Rev. 85. — Eds.

in the law, whether indirectly through the education of the electors so as to bring about a public sentiment in favor of the change, or through proper influences brought to bear upon the legislators, does not prevent the purpose from being legal and charitable."

The principal American jurisdiction disagreeing with Comment j of the Restatement, so far as it applies to women's rights, is Massachusetts. In Jackson v. Phillips, 96 Mass. (14 Allen) 539 (1867), the court held that a trust "to secure the passage of laws granting women, whether married or unmarried, the right to vote, to hold office, to hold, manage and devise property, and all other civil rights enjoyed by men" could not be sustained because it was directed toward effectuating a change in the laws, and, indeed, in the Constitution itself.[16] Fifty-five years later the son of the testator in Jackson v. Phillips died leaving a will that established a trust for the promotion of women's rights. The trust was held invalid on the authority of that case.[17] Bowditch v. Attorney General, 241 Mass. 168, 134 N.E. 796, 28 A.L.R. 713 (1922). For a case upholding trusts (a) to support candidates for political office who favor women's equal civil rights, (b) to support the Maryland Branch of the National Woman's Party, and (c) to support passage of the Equal Rights Amendment, see Register of Wills v. Cook, 241 Md. 264, 216 A.2d 542, 22 A.L.R.3d 872 (1966).

5. For analysis of the factors that courts should consider in determining what is charitable, see Lynn, The Questionable Testamentary Gift to Charity: A Suggested Approach to Judicial Decision, 30 U. Chi. L. Rev. 450 (1963).

SECTION B. Cy Pres

HOWARD SAVINGS INSTITUTION v. PEEP

Supreme Court of New Jersey, 1961
34 N.J. 494, 170 A.2d 39

Proctor, J. This appeal and cross appeal from a judgment of the Chancery Division primarily involve the question of whether that court properly applied the doctrine of cy pres to the terms of a trust established by the will of C. Edward McKinney, Jr. Mr. McKinney, a resident of the City of East Orange, died on Oc-

[16] The same will involved a trust to secure the abolition of slavery, and this trust the court held charitable, even though its accomplishment required a change in the law.

[17] The cause of equal rights for women has a history of tough sledding in the Massachusetts court. In Commonwealth v. Welosky, 276 Mass. 398, 177 N.E. 656 (1931), the court denied women the right to serve on juries, a right conferred by a statute enacted prior to the Nineteenth Amendment on "a person qualified to vote." Said Rugg, C.J., "The change in the legal status of women wrought by the Nineteenth Amendment was radical, drastic and unprecedented. While it is to be given full effect in its field, it is not to be extended by implication. It is unthinkable that those who first framed and selected the words for the statute now embodied in G.L. c. 234, §1, had any design that it should ever include women within its scope."

In 1949 women were made eligible for jury service in Massachusetts.

tober 21, 1957. His will, admitted to probate by the Surrogate of Essex County on November 6, 1957, designates the plaintiff, the Howard Savings Institution, as executor and provides in part as follows:

> Thirtieth: I give and bequeath the sum of Fifty Thousand Dollars ($50,000) to Amherst College, an institution of learning, situate at Amherst, Massachusetts, to be held in trust to be used as a scholarship loan fund for deserving American born, Protestant, Gentile boys of good moral repute, not given to gambling, smoking, drinking or similar acts. (It being my thought that if a young man has enough funds to allow the waste of smoking, he certainly does not need help.) The money loaned from said fund is to be repaid to the fund at the earliest moment so that others may benefit from its use. . . .
>
> Thirty-third: All the rest, residue and remainder of my estate, real, personal and mixed, of whatsoever kind and wheresoever situate, of which I shall die seized or possessed, I give, devise and bequeath unto Amherst College aforesaid to be held on the same trusts as mentioned in paragraph Thirtieth aforesaid.

The charter of Amherst College provides that "no student shall be refused admission to, or denied any of the privileges, honors, or degrees of said College, on account of the religious opinions he may entertain." On June 7, 1958 the Board of Trustees of Amherst College adopted a resolution stating that it believed acceptance of a trust discriminating among students on religious grounds would contravene the letter and spirit of the charter and the policy of the college. Accordingly, the Board declined to accept the trust funds unless the Protestant-Gentile restriction was eliminated from the terms of the trust. Plaintiff-executor thereupon instituted this action to obtain judicial construction of paragraphs Thirty and Thirty-three of Mr. McKinney's will and conformable instructions. It joined as defendants the Board of Trustees of Amherst, the Attorney General of New Jersey, and the next-of-kin of the testator.

The Chancery Division, applying the doctrine of cy pres, entered a judgment excluding the words "Protestant" and "Gentile" from paragraph Thirty of the will and ordering the executor to turn the trust funds over to Amherst to be administered in accordance with the remaining terms and conditions of the will. 61 N.J. Super. 119, 160 A.2d 177 (1960). We certified the appeal of the executor and the cross appeal of the next-of-kin before argument in the Appellate Division.

. . . [A]ll parties concede that the next-of-kin have standing to cross-appeal.

. . . No one urges on this appeal that the Protestant-Gentile restriction or its enforcement by the court offends public policy or the Fourteenth Amendment to the Federal Constitution. Hence, we have no occasion to express a view as to those issues. See Clark, "Charitable Trusts, the Fourteenth Amendment and the Will of Stephen Girard," 66 Yale L.J. 979 (1957); Miller, "Racial Discrimination and Private Schools," 41 Minn. L. Rev. 145 (1957).

We first consider whether the Chancery Division should have applied the doctrine of cy pres to the terms of the trust. The doctrine of cy pres is a judicial mechanism for the preservation of a charitable trust when accomplishment of the particular purpose of the trust becomes impossible, impracticable or illegal. In such a situation if the settlor manifested an intent to devote the trust to a charitable purpose more general than the frustrated purpose, a court, instead of allowing the trust to fail, will apply the trust funds to a charitable purpose as nearly as possible to the particular purpose of the settlor. Wilber v. Owens, 2 N.J. 167, 177, 65 A.2d 843 (1949); Restatement, Trusts §399 (1935). Three observations about the doctrine may aid analysis of its applicability to the facts of the present case. First, the term "general charitable intent" ordinarily used by courts articulating the doctrine does not require an intention to benefit charity generally. It requires only a charitable purpose which is broader than the particular purpose the effectuation of which is impossible, impracticable or illegal. Sheridan & Delaney, The Cy-Pres Doctrine (1959); Restatement, Trusts §399, comment c, p. 1211 (1935). Second, the inquiry "did the settlor manifest a general charitable intent" is just another way of asking "would he have wanted the trust funds devoted to a like charitable purpose, or would he have wanted them withdrawn from charitable channels." 4 Scott, Trusts §399, p. 2824 (1956). So stated, it can be seen that cy pres is an intent-enforcing doctrine. But it is well to keep in mind that it is a surmise rather than an actual intent which the courts enforce through application of the doctrine. Rarely does a settlor contemplate the possible nonfulfillment of his precise purpose. Therefore, the court must make an educated guess based on the trust instrument and relevant extrinsic evidence as to what he would have intended had he been aware of the contingency which has frustrated the exact effectuation of his expressed intent. 2A Bogert, Trusts & Trustees §436, p. 344 (1953). And third, recognizing the social benefit deriving from the devotion of property to charitable purposes, courts ascertaining a settlor's surmised intent are guided by the policy of preserving charitable trusts whenever possible and by the established presumption against partial intestacy. Mirinda v. King, 11 N.J. Super. 165, 173, 78 A.2d 98 (App. Div. 1951) and cases cited therein. See Comment, "Revaluation of Cy Pres," 49 Yale L.J. 303 (1939).

Similar to, but distinct from, cy pres is the doctrine of deviation from the terms of a trust. Applicable to private as well as charitable trusts, the doctrine of deviation comes into play when compliance with an administrative provision of the trust is impossible, illegal or in conflict with the essential purpose of the trust. Bogert, op. cit. supra, §561 (2d ed. 1960); 2 Scott, op. cit. supra, §167; Restatement, Trusts §167 (1935). In such a situation, a court, pursuant to its general equity power, may allow modification of the provision. The doctrine is commonly applied, for example, to appoint a substituted trustee when the trustee designated by the settlor cannot or will not serve. E.g., Martin v. Haycock, 140 N.J. Eq. 450, 55 A.2d 60 (Ch. 1947). Essential to application of the doctrine of deviation is a finding that the term of the trust to be deviated from is an administrative one — that is, that it is not essential to fulfillment of the settlor's scheme. See Martin v. Haycock, supra. This finding, in turn, depends on an interpretation of the settlor's intent. Ultimately, therefore, applicability of the doctrine of deviation, like the doctrine of cy pres, depends on what the court concludes the settlor would have wanted to happen if he were aware of the contingency which has made the exact effectuation of his expressed intent impossible.

With the above principles in mind, we return to the question of whether the Chancery Division should have disposed of the trust funds in the present case as it did.

We first consider the next-of-kin's contention that the doctrines of cy pres and deviation are inapplicable to the trust established by Mr. McKinney's will and that therefore the Chancery Division should have declared an intestacy. The next-of-kin's initial argument is that the bequest provided for in paragraphs Thirty and Thirty-three is not a charitable trust. . . . [T]hey rely on the rule that to be characterized as charitable, a trust, regardless of its purpose, must encompass a sufficient number of beneficiaries to warrant a community interest. 4 Scott, op. cit. supra, §375. In order to qualify for scholarship loan aid under Mr. McKinney's will, an Amherst student must be an American born Protestant-Gentile, not given to gambling, smoking, drinking or similar conduct. The next-of-kin assert, and ask us to take judicial notice of, the fact that in light of contemporary social conditions and mores, few if any Amherst students could comply with all of the trust requirements. Paragraph Thirty is not so worded that an isolated indulgence in the proscribed activities would result in disqualification. The testator said that the beneficiaries are to be boys "not given to" smoking, drinking, etc. "Given to" is ordinarily defined as meaning "disposed; inclined; addicted; . . . as, given to drink." Webster's New International Dictionary (2d ed. 1959). It implies at least some degree of regular indulgence. This construction is confirmed by the testator's parenthetical observation: "It being my thought that if a young man has enough funds to allow the waste of smoking, he certainly does not need help." It is obvious that the testator had in mind a person who is so committed to the act of smoking that it becomes a financial drain. Presumably, there are and will be at Amherst enough American born Protestant-Gentiles who do not regularly smoke, drink, gamble or engage in similar conduct, and who thus fall within the class of potential beneficiaries to justify categorizing the trust as charitable. We think that there is a sufficiently broad classification combined with Mr. McKinney's worthy purpose to warrant that appellation. See Clark, op. cit. supra, at p. 998. In any event, we have no information which would merit our taking judicial notice to the contrary. Accordingly, we hold that paragraphs Thirty and Thirty-three of Mr. McKinney's will establish a charitable trust.

The next-of-kin also argue that the Chancery Division erred in applying the doctrine of cy pres because the testator had no general charitable intention. He had, they say, a particular, unitary and inseparable purpose of benefiting Protestant students at Amherst; he was equally interested in Protestantism and the college. Therefore, they contend, since the testator's intent cannot be effectuated exactly as expressed, the funds must pass by intestate succession.

As mentioned above, in ascertaining the existence of a general charitable intent the court must determine whether the testator would have wanted the trust funds to remain devoted to a charitable purpose similar to, but not the same as, he provided, or to go to his next-of-kin. . . .

The will in the present case strongly indicates that Mr. McKinney would not have wanted his next-of-kin to receive the trust funds. There is no provision in paragraphs Thirty and Thirty-three for reverter or a gift over if the trust bequest cannot be carried out in its exact terms. By contrast, the testator provided in paragraph Ninth of the will that if a trust bequest to the Town of Wolfeboro established therein could not be carried out in accordance with its exact terms, it should fail. A comparison of the charitable bequests to Amherst and the Town of Wolfeboro suggests a wholly different intent of the testator as to his willingness to accept some modification of their exact terms. If he had been opposed to any modification in the terms of the bequest to Amherst, it is reasonable to assume that he would have said so, just as he did in the Wolfeboro bequest. Additionally, we note that neither the next-of-kin nor other persons are designated as residuary legatees. Indeed, the residuary legatee is Amherst College under paragraph Thirty-three of the will. Moreover, the testator made specific legacies in varying amounts to twenty different persons, and did not include his next-of-kin. It is apparent from these detailed provisions that he executed his will after careful consideration and did not want his next-of-kin to share in his estate.

Evidence extrinsic to the will confirms the foregoing conclusion. The testator had no close relatives. He left no spouse or descendants or parents or brothers or sisters. His surviving kin are two cousins and a cousin of his mother. These persons lived distant from testator's home, and there is no evidence that he had any personal contact with them. Indeed, he expressly said that they were not to share in his estate. In a memorandum of instructions for the use of his scrivener in the preparation of the will the testator states in four separate places: "I have no immediate relatives, and any others omitted are either well-fixed financially or deliberately omitted for reasons very well known to themselves."

The aforementioned facts in and out of the will compel the conclusion that the Chancery Division properly found that the testator had a general charitable intent in the sense that we would have preferred to retain the charitable bequest — though in modified form — rather than leave the money to his cousins.

This brings us to the question of whether the Chancery Division correctly applied the doctrine of cy pres. First, we consider the executor's argument that the testator's intent can be fully effectuated by turning the funds over to another educational institution willing to honor the Protestant-Gentile restriction. This argument is based on the premise that the testator's intent was to benefit needy Protestant students, and that Amherst was designated trustee merely for administrative purposes. We think that the executor's argument is based on a faulty premise.

The very nature of the bequest indicates that the testator was interested in benefiting Amherst as well as the recipients of scholarship loans. A donor interested in benefiting only students presumedly would make funds available to them regardless of what institution they wished to attend. But Mr. McKinney's will envisions as recipients only those students, who, meeting the other qualifications of the trust, are present or prospective members of the Amherst student body. A scholarship loan program, identified with a particular institution, inevitably benefits that institution by making available to it funds to attract and hold outstanding students. Cf. Deubel v. Kervick, 33 N.J. 568, 576, 166 A.2d 561 (1960). It is reasonable to conclude, therefore, that the creator of such a program intended to benefit the college identified therewith. That Mr. McKinney also intended to benefit the unknown student recipients of loans does not diminish at all his purpose of advancing the interests of Amherst. The foregoing shows, we think, that Amherst was designated trustee for more than mere administrative reasons. But this conclusion does not alone answer the executor's argument. Amherst will not accept the trust if it must enforce the Protestant-Gentile restriction. The question therefore is, would Mr. McKinney rather have the trust remain at Amherst with the restriction eliminated, or would he have preferred that the funds be turned over to another institution with the restriction? The facts indicate that Mr. McKinney was more interested in benefiting Amherst and its needy students than he was in Protestantism.

Mr. McKinney was a graduate of Amherst who continuously manifested an interest in the college. According to the records of contributions to the Alumni Fund which begin with the year 1932, the testator contributed to such fund in 1932 and every succeeding year until his death. In addition, he attended the 50th, 55th and 60th reunions of his graduating class in 1946, 1951 and 1956 respectively. (Amherst College has no record of the attendance of members of his class at previous reunions.) On the other hand, there is no evidence in the record that testator was a church-goer or actively interested in any church activities. In his will be made a bequest of $2,000 to the Board of Congregational Missions in memory of his father, who was born in Natal, and gave the Board the books in his home to be used in their Natal Mission. This modest bequest to the mission in memory of his father contrasts markedly with the sum left to Amherst ($50,000) and the designation of Amherst as legatee of the residuary estate (about $150,000). Additionally, the will contains no bequest to any church. Finally, the trust bequest is so worded that the Protestant-Gentile restriction is merely one of a series of qualifications to be met by recipients of scholarship loan aid. Accordingly, we conclude that Mr. McKinney's primary purpose was to advance the interests of Amherst by making available to it funds for needy students as well as to aid such students, and that to award the funds to another educational institution — if one could be found to enforce the Protestant-Gentile restriction — would contravene that purpose.

The executor further argues that Mr. McKinney's intent can be best effectuated by appointing a substituted trustee to administer the scholarship loan fund for Amherst students. We disagree because we find that it would be impracticable in the circumstances of this case to have a substituted trustee administer the trust for Amherst. In response to an inquiry from this court as to whether the college could cooperate with a substituted trustee, the Board of Trustees of Amherst adopted and forwarded to us, without objection from any party to this appeal, a resolution which states in pertinent part:

> the policy of Amherst College would be to avoid any involvement whatsoever in the administration of the trust in question. Specifically, the College would in no

> way participate in identifying, evaluating, or selecting persons who might be beneficiaries of the trust; the College would not use its facilities to publicize the trust or otherwise bring its existence to the attention of present or future students; the College would neither solicit nor serve as a depository of scholarship applications; the College would not refer its students or other persons to the trust administrator; the College would decline to serve as an intermediary between the trust administrator and potential or actual candidates for benefits under the trust; the College would not at the behest of the trust administrator provide information concerning the scholastic achievement, character, or financial status of any student or applicant for admission. Upon a student's direct request, the College would provide information concerning that student, so far as that information may be readily available in the College's records and so far as its disclosure is consistent with general policies bearing upon confidentiality of the records. A person to whom financial aid has been granted by an outside organization, individual, or trustee would be neither advantaged nor disadvantaged in respect of his becoming or remaining a student at Amherst College.

It is clear from the above-cited resolution that Amherst believes it cannot under its charter cooperate in the administration of the trust if its benefits are confined to Protestant-Gentile students.

Without Amherst's cooperation the administration of this trust would be so impracticable as to defeat the general purpose of the testator. The substituted trustee would have to be a qualified educator with experience in the allocation of scholarship funds. Even if such a willing trustee could be found, the practical disadvantages are numerous. There would be no feasible way in which the scholarship fund could be used to aid students who are seeking to enter Amherst. Often, the availability of scholarship aid will affect the decision of a needy student to attend a particular college. It would be most difficult for a substituted trustee to know who was applying or considering applying for entrance to Amherst without the cooperation of the college. Thus a class of students and the college would be denied the benefit of what must have been one of the purposes of the trust. If the funds are made available only to matriculated students, the trustee would still face well-nigh insuperable obstacles. He would have to obtain detailed information about a scholarship applicant. Whether an applicant was being considered for other aid by the college, for example, would obviously be relevant to a decision to award him aid from the McKinney trust. Then, the award of a scholarship loan involves a delicate weighing of the financial needs of the applicant, his scholastic standing, and his development potential. Moreover, in providing a fund to aid "deserving" boys at Amherst, the testator manifested an essential reliance on the personal discretion of Amherst as trustee. For an applicant is "deserving" in a meaningful sense only in relation to the competency and worth of others who seek to enter or remain at the college. Surely Amherst would not violate the trust if it denied aid to a specific applicant or admitted student if it determined another applicant was more "deserving." Mr. McKinney, therefore, must have contemplated that the merits of loan applications be judged according to those relative standards which Amherst itself may establish to further its conception of what individuals are worthy of membership in its student body. We are unable to understand how any trustee without Amherst's cooperation can possibly make the comparative value judgment which Mr. McKinney had in mind. Finally, once an award is made, the trustee must have some policing mechanism to assure that the recipient continues to meet the trust qualifications. Determination of whether he deserved a loan renewal would realistically require access to college records and consultations with college instructors and administrators. The above factors clearly show that without the college's cooperation it would be impracticable, if not impossible, for a substituted trustee to administer the scholarship loan fund for Amherst students.

The executor argues that to apply cy pres because Amherst will not cooperate with a substituted trustee would be to allow the college by its own action to vary the testator's intent. It cites the rule that a trustee cannot by his own act produce changed conditions which frustrate the donor's intention and still claim the gift. But the cases so holding are distinguishable from the present case. Typical, is Connecticut College v. United States, 107 U.S. App. D.C. 245, 276 F.2d 491 (D.C. Cir. 1960). There a testatrix left funds for the construction of a memorial building in a particular location at the United States Military Academy. The Academy declined to erect the building at the proposed site because the location did not accord with its building-expansion program. Instead, it asked to be allowed to use the funds for the construction of a wing on an existing building. The trial judge applied cy pres and awarded the funds to the Academy. On appeal the judgment was reversed on the ground that cy pres cannot be used to vary the terms of a bequest "merely because the variation will meet the desire and suit the convenience of the trustee." The Court of Appeals emphasized that the refusal of the Academy to apply the funds exactly as prescribed by the testator was not due to circumstances beyond the control of the Academy. In the present case, the refusal of Amherst to accept and administer the trust with the Protestant-Gentile restriction was not merely to serve trustee convenience. The refusal was prompted by the college charter which expressly prohibits the college from denying any privileges of the school to a student because of the religious opinion he may entertain. Clearly, scholarship loan aid is one of those privileges. It seems to us therefore that in the sense required for the application of cy pres, it is impossible for Amherst to accept and administer the trust exactly as desired by the testator. It is as equally clear that college cooperation in the administration of the trust by a substituted trustee would be an indirect violation of the college's charter.

In view of the fact that Mr. McKinney had a general charitable intent, we hold that the bequest does not fail and the funds do not pass to the next-of-kin. And, in view of the additional facts that Amherst conceives it to be inconsistent with its charter to administer or assist in the administration of the trust so long as its funds are available only to Protestants, and that it would be impracticable for a substituted trustee properly to administer the trust, we hold that the testator's intent can be effectuated as nearly as possible by striking the Protestant-Gentile restriction and turning the funds over to Amherst to be administered in accordance with the remaining terms and conditions of the trust. Of course, striking the Protestant-Gentile restriction does not mean that Protestant-Gentile students will be excluded as beneficiaries of the trust. Any Amherst students who meet the other qualifications set forth in the will will be eligible for scholarship loan aid. Accordingly, the judgment of the Chancery Division is affirmed.

For affirmance: Chief Justice Weintraub and Justices Jacobs, Francis, Proctor and Hall — 5.

For reversal: Justice Haneman — 1.

HANEMAN, J. (dissenting). I agree that the executor has a standing to prosecute this appeal and that the testator created a trust of charitable nature which should not fail because of the refusal of the designated trustee to accept and carry out his express directions. I as well agree that the purpose of the testator was to provide scholarship loans for students of Amherst College. However, I conceive that the application of the cy pres doctrine to delete so much of testator's expressed objectives as are allegedly repugnant to the charter of the named corporate trustee is not here warranted. Instead, the court should appoint a substituted trustee to administer the trust in strict accordance with the directions of the testator. To that extent I dissent. . . .

The description of the cestuis que trust is so exact that a substituted trustee could easily select persons meeting the qualifications. The element of discretion is reduced to a minimum. There is not exhibited either in the will or in the extrinsic testimony any evidence that such selection should lie wholly and solely in the discretion of Amherst. The testator's primary purpose was to create scholarship loans for a certain class of Amherst students. The appointment of Amherst College as a trustee was not an essential part of that scheme. Scholarship loans to designated Amherst students was of primary importance and the nomination of a trustee to select those students was of secondary importance. The designated trustee was a mere conduit through which the funds should flow to the specially qualified persons. . . .

There is a multitude of possible means for publicizing the existence and availability of this fund for scholarship loans to "deserving American born, Protestant, Gentile boys of good moral repute, not given to gambling, smoking, drinking or similar acts" attending Amherst College. A simple medium to employ would be the insertion of a paid advertisement in the college newspaper. After application by a student, the essential relevant information for qualification for such a loan could be obtained by the applicant from the college. As noted in the majority opinion, Amherst has signified its willingness to cooperate to the extent that "upon a student's direct request, the College would provide information concerning that student, so far as that information may be readily available in the College's records and so far as its disclosure is consistent with general policies bearing upon confidentiality of the records." Admittedly, Amherst could administer the fund with greater ease. This is not to say, however, that administration by a substituted trustee is either impossible or impracticable. For examples of cases in which trusts for the benefit of college students were administered by trustees other than the particular college at which such students were attending, see Harrold v. First National Bank of Fort Worth, 93 F. Supp. 882 (D.C.N.D. Texas 1950); Hoyt v. Bliss, 93 Conn. 344, 105 A. 699 (Sup. Ct. Err. 1919); Sessions v. Skelton, 163 Ohio St. 409, 127 N.E.2d 378 (Sup. Ct. 1955); Speer v. Colbert, 200 U.S. 130, 26 S. Ct. 201, 50 L. Ed. 403, 413 (1906); Barnard v. Adams, 58 F. 313 (C.C.N.D. Iowa 1893); Field v. Drew Theological Seminary, 41 F. 371 (C.C.D. Del. 1890). That scholarship grants and loans can be efficiently administered by trustees other than educational institutions is evidenced by the some 825 pages of descriptive matter contained in Feingold, Scholarships, Fellowships and Loans (1955), which catalogues such grants and loans from funds administered by other than academic trustees.

I would therefore reverse and remand with directions to the trial court to appoint a substituted trustee to administer the trust under the exact terms of the will.[18]

NOTES

1. Suppose McKinney's scholarship fund was for black students, or for Hindus, or for Moslem males from the Near East? Should Amherst refuse to cooperate? If it did refuse, should the court appoint a substitute trustee? Kaplan, Equal Justice in an Unequal World: Equality for the Negro — The Problem of Special Treatment, 61 Nw. U.L. Rev. 363 (1966).

2. Under the ancient English doctrine of prerogative cy pres, charitable gifts were expected to comply with public policy as established by the king. Any deviations were corrected by the king regardless of the testator's intent. For example, in Da Costa v. De Pas, 1 Amb. 228, 27 Eng. Rep. 150 (Ch. 1754), a Jewish testator left money in trust to form an assembly for the purpose of teaching Jewish law and religion. The trust was declared void because it encouraged a religion other than the state religion. Applying prerogative cy pres, the king allotted the money to instruct foundlings in the Christian religion.

Largely as a reaction to abuses of prerogative cy pres, courts in this country were reluctant to adopt judicial cy pres and seldom altered an instrument until the twentieth century. With the huge growth of charitable trusts and increasing change in American society, modern courts have been more receptive to cy pres. The Connecticut College case, referred to in the Peep case, is a modern example of the ancient hostility to varying the terms of a testatrix' will. The court there held that the United States Military Academy would lose the bequest if it did not build on the exact construction site specified by the testatrix. Other courts have held, however, that such specific conditions can be ignored when they are secondary to a general charitable intent and impracticable. Matter of Neher, 279 N.Y. 370, 18 N.E.2d 625 (1939); Bell v. Shannon, 212 Tenn. 28, 367 S.W.2d 761 (1963).

In Coffee v. William Marsh Rice University, 408 S.W.2d 269 (Tex. Civ. App.

[18] Noted 40 N.C.L. Rev. 308; 36 Tul. L. Rev. 176. — Eds.

1966), the trustees of Rice University petitioned the court for permission to accept students without regard to color and to charge tuition. These actions would violate conditions in the trust instrument executed by William Marsh Rice in 1891 establishing the university. The case was submitted to a jury, which found it was impracticable to continue the school all-white and tuition-free. The jury's findings were affirmed by the appellate court on appeal.

DiClerico, Cy Pres: A Proposal for Change, 47 B.U.L. Rev. 153 (1967), argues for an expanded use of judicial cy pres to change charitable trust provisions in order to maximize community benefits as these are dictated by changing community needs. To carry this proposal one step further: Should the state attorney general have the power to authorize deviation from the terms of a charitable trust? In Application of Schlussel, 195 Misc. 1008, 89 N.Y.S.2d 47 (Sup. Ct. 1949), it was held that the New York Attorney General had the power to consent to an amendment or revocation, by the donor, of an irrevocable charitable trust. The trust as originally established failed to qualify for an estate tax charitable deduction.

See generally Note, Cy Pres and the Discriminatory Trust, 23 Hastings L.J. 604 (1972).

3. Stephen Girard died in 1831, leaving $2 million to establish Girard College for "poor male white orphan children." He appointed the City of Philadelphia to be trustee of the college. The trusteeship eventually passed to the Board of Directors of City Trusts, an agency of the city. In 1954 two black applicants requested admission to the college. They were denied admission because of their race. They took their case to the United States Supreme Court, which held that the board, acting as trustee, was a state agency and such discrimination was barred by the Fourteenth Amendment. Pennsylvania v. Board of Directors of City Trusts, 353 U.S. 230 (1957). On remand the Orphans' Court of Philadelphia County removed the Board of Directors of City Trusts as trustee and appointed private individuals as substitute trustees. They continued in force the discriminatory policies prescribed by Stephen Girard's will. Upon appeal from this action the Supreme Court of Pennsylvania held that the Orphans' Court had acted properly and not unconstitutionally. Girard College Trusteeship, 391 Pa. 434, 138 A.2d 844 (1958), appeal dismissed and cert. denied sub nom. Pennsylvania v. Board of Directors of City Trusts, 357 U.S. 570 (1958).

Hope for the black applicants was rekindled by Evans v. Newton, 382 U.S. 296 (1966). In 1911 Senator Bacon devised to the city of Macon, Georgia, a tract of land to be used as "a park and pleasure ground" for white people only. Because the park as a public facility could not constitutionally be segregated, the city resigned as trustee. The lower court accepted the resignation and appointed three individual trustees. The Supreme Court of Georgia affirmed. Evans v. Newton, 220 Ga. 280, 138 S.E.2d 573 (1964). In reversing, the United States Supreme Court, per Douglas, J., appeared to take the position that once the facility is under public control, the substitution of private trustees to avoid the Fourteenth Amendment is not permissible. "We only hold that where the tradition of municipal control had become firmly established, we cannot take judicial notice that the mere substitution of trustees instantly transferred this park from the public to the private sector." Evans v. Newton, 382 U.S. 296, 301 (1966).

In 1966 seven black male orphans, the Commonwealth of Pennsylvania, and the City of Philadelphia joined in an action in federal district court seeking an injunction against the new trustees of Girard College. The plaintiffs alleged three distinct grounds for relief: (1) The enforcement of the restriction was state action forbidden by the Fourteenth Amendment; (2) the court should invoke the equitable doctrine of cy pres; and (3) the restriction violated the Pennsylvania Public Accommodations Act. The federal district court denied a motion to dismiss. Pennsylvania v. Brown, 260 F. Supp. 323 (E.D. Pa. 1966). On appeal, the Third Circuit vacated the decree as to count three and directed the court to proceed with count one. Pennsylvania v. Brown, 373 F.2d 771 (3d Cir. 1967). On remand the district court concluded that from an analysis of all the factors involving the state with the college, the college was "municipal in nature" and the Fourteenth Amendment applied to it. Commonwealth v. Brown, 270 F. Supp. 782 (E.D. Pa. 1967). On appeal, the Third Circuit affirmed on the basis of Evans v. Newton, 382 U.S. 296 (1966), and Shelley v. Kraemer, 334 U.S. 1 (1948). Pennsylvania v. Brown, 392 F.2d 120, 25 A.L.R.3d 724 (3d Cir. 1968), cert. denied, 391 U.S. 921 (1968).[19]

Meanwhile, the Georgia courts were further considering the will of Senator Bacon. The Georgia Supreme Court interpreted Evans v. Newton as requiring the Macon park to be operated on a nondiscriminatory basis. "Under these circumstances we are of the opinion that the sole purpose for which the trust was created has become impossible of accomplishment and has been terminated." Evans v. Newton, 221 Ga. 870, 871, 148 S.E.2d 329, 330 (1966). Upon remand to the Georgia trial court, the black petitioners and the Attorney General of Georgia argued that the trust should be saved by applying the cy pres doctrine to amend the terms of the will by striking the racial restrictions. The trial court refused to apply cy pres. It held that the doctrine was inapplicable because the park's segregated, whites-

[19] On the extensive Girard College litigation, see Clark, Charitable Trusts, the Fourteenth Amendment and the Will of Stephen Girard, 66 Yale L.J. 979 (1957); Mullen, Constitutional Law — Judicial Enforcement of the Racially Discriminatory Charitable Trust, 10 St. Louis L.J. 576 (1966); Commentary, The Girard Trust — Past, Present, and Future, 20 Ala. L. Rev. 308 (1968).

In a proceeding on an application by a trustee for instructions in view of the last Girard College case, the Court of Chancery of Delaware concluded that in administering a charitable trust establishing a series of scholarships, the trustees should consider applications without limitation as to race notwithstanding the will's reference to white youth. The court held that advising the trustees to reject applications from nonwhites would amount to judicially enforced discrimination in violation of the Fourteenth Amendment. Bank of Delaware v. Buckson, 255 A.2d 710 (Del. Ch. 1969). This case was followed in Will of Potter, 275 A.2d 574 (Del. Ch. 1970), which held that the involvement of the court of chancery in the supervision and direction of the administration of a charitable trust for the benefit of "poor white citizens of Kent County" constituted state action, and ordered that the trust be reformed by striking the word white from the description of the beneficiaries of the trust.

In Sweet Briar Institute v. Button, 280 F. Supp. 312 (W.D. Va. 1967), it was held that the state cannot enforce compliance with provisions in the will of the founder restricting college entrants to white girls.

only character was an essential and inseparable part of the testator's plan. Since the sole purpose of the trust was unconstitutional, the trial court ruled that the trust failed and the trust property reverted to the heirs of Senator Bacon. On appeal, the trial court's decision was affirmed by the Georgia Supreme Court, Evans v. Abney, 224 Ga. 826, 165 S.E.2d 160 (1968), and by the United States Supreme Court, Evans v. Abney, 396 U.S. 435 (1970) (6 to 2 vote). Said Mr. Justice Black for the majority: "The construction of wills is essentially a state-law question, Lyeth v. Hoey, 305 U.S. 188 (1938), and in this case the Georgia Supreme Court, as we read its opinion, interpreted Senator Bacon's will as embodying a preference for termination of the park rather than its integration. Given this, the Georgia court had no alternative under its relevant trust laws which are long standing and neutral with regard to race, but to end the Baconsfield trust and return the property to the Senator's heirs. . . .

"Petitioners also advance a number of considerations of public policy in opposition to the conclusion which we have reached. In particular, they regret, as we do, the loss of the Baconsfield trust to the City of Macon, and they are concerned lest we set a precedent under which other charitable trusts will be terminated. It bears repeating that our holding today reaffirms the traditional role of the States in determining whether or not to apply their cy pres doctrines to particular trusts. Nothing we have said here prevents a state court from applying its cy pres rule in a case where the Georgia court, for example, might not apply its rule. More fundamentally, however, the loss of charitable trusts such as Baconsfield is part of the price we pay for permitting deceased persons to exercise a continuing control over assets owned by them at death. This aspect of freedom of testation, like most things, has its advantages and disadvantages. The responsibility of this Court, however, is to construe and enforce the Constitution and laws of the land as they are and not to legislate social policy on the basis of our own personal inclinations." Id. at 444, 447.[20]

SECTION C. Regulation of Charitable Foundations

Since 1940 the amount of private wealth devoted to charitable purposes in the United States has increased spectacularly. This is largely the result of various income and estate tax savings which can be achieved by gifts to charity. Founders of new charitable enterprises can choose to organize either as a corporation or as a trust. About two-thirds of charitable foundations are corporations, about one-third are trusts.

In 1970 there were 5454 charitable foundations with assets of at least $500,000

[20] Evans v. Abney was widely noted in the law reviews, where the constitutional issues are thoroughly discussed. See 84 Harv. L. Rev. 54; 30 Md. L. Rev. 226; 22 Mercer L. Rev. 493; 42 Miss. L.J. 246; 35 Mo. L. Rev. 545; 16 N.Y.L.F. 448; 49 N.C.L. Rev. 148; 46 Notre Dame Law. 399; 32 Ohio St. L.J. 181; 2 Rutgers Camden L.J. 390; 24 Sw. L.J. 717; 21 Syracuse L. Rev. 1313.

or making grants totaling at least $25,000 a year.[21] The amount of assets held by foundations of this size grew from $10.7 billion in 1958 to $25.2 billion in 1970. In addition to these large foundations there were some 20,000 smaller ones. From Internal Revenue Service records it is estimated that in the 1960s, 1800 new charitable foundations were established each year, but only 100 of these were foundations of substantial size. The explosive growth of small foundations was accompanied by many abuses, and the Tax Reform Act of 1969 attempted to correct these. It is probable that under the restrictions of this Act the formation of new foundations will be slowed and many existing smaller foundations terminated. Once the donor and his immediate friends have passed from the scene, it is unlikely that foundations of less than $1 million will be able to find trustees and staff to adequately administer the funds and have much left over for charitable grants. The problem of administering small perpetual foundations will become more severe in future years and either remedial legislation or a broad use of judicial cy pres will be required.[22]

In 1970 the twelve largest charitable foundations were:

	(millions)
Ford Foundation	$2,902
Lilly Endowment	778
Rockefeller Foundation	757
Duke Endowment	510
Kresge Foundation	433
Kellogg (W. K.) Foundation	393
Mott (Charles Stewart) Foundation	371
Pew Memorial Trust	367
Sloan (Alfred P.) Foundation	303
Carnegie Corporation of New York	283
Hartford (John A.) Foundation	277
Mellon (Andrew W.) Foundation	234

[21] The information in this and the succeeding paragraph is taken from The Foundation Directory, Edition 4 (1971).

[22] See Foundations, Private Giving, and Public Policy: Report and Recommendations of the Commission on Foundations and Private Philanthropy (1971).

The memory of the abuses in England of the prerogative power of cy pres may hinder judicial flexibility, however. For example, in New Hampshire towns are authorized by statute to hold gifts in trust for the care of cemeteries and burial lots in accordance with the terms of the trust. The legislature proposed to amend the statute by adding a provision that the income accumulation of a burial lot trust fund might be used for the general care of the cemetery where the lot is located, if the terms of the trust do not otherwise provide, and if the surplus income is not required for the care of the particular lot. In Opinion of the Justices, 101 N.H. 531, 133 A.2d 792 (1957), the court held the proposed amendment unconstitutional as an invasion of the established equitable powers of the courts. In an earlier decision the same court refused to exercise the power of cy pres to authorize the expenditure for the general care of the cemetery of a fund held in trust for one lot. Town of Boscawen v. Attorney General, 93 N.H. 444, 43 A.2d 780 (1945). To do so, said the court, would be tantamount to exercising a legislative power of cy pres with respect to all cemetery trusts having surplus income. The justices were of the opinion that the cy pres power could be exercised through the courts only by applying the established principles of cy pres to the circumstances of each particular trust.

Most of the charitable foundations are heavily concentrated in the industrial East and particularly in New York, which accounts for over 40 percent of the total foundation assets. The twelve states having the greatest amount of large foundation assets in 1970 were:

	Number	*Assets (millions)*	*Grants (millions)*
New York	1409	$10,158	$729
Pennsylvania	327	1,976	87
Michigan	206	1,746	86
Texas	248	1,359	56
California	380	1,180	57
Ohio	364	1,100	75
Indiana	78	928	21
Illinois	389	756	78
Minnesota	142	643	32
Georgia	107	633	23
Massachusetts	244	554	28
Delaware	56	513	18

From 1961 through 1970 grants of $10,000 or more by large foundations went for the following purposes:

	(millions)	*(percent)*
Education	$1,824	32
International Activities	850	15
Health	814	14
Welfare	710	13
Sciences	708	12
Humanities	485	9
Religion	269	5
	$5,660	100

The government has two basic interests in the administration of charitable foundations: (1) preventing the abuse of tax privileges granted by the state, and (2) as representative of the public, which is the ultimate beneficiary of these funds, assuring their proper administration. The federal government has the primary responsibility of protecting the first interest, and the state governments — through their respective attorneys general — have authority to supervise charitable foundations.

The common law conveyed power on the attorney general to enforce charitable trusts. It denied standing to the general public and to the donor. Other than the attorney general, the only person who can enforce a charitable trust is a person with a special interest as a beneficiary. The person must show that he is entitled to receive a benefit under the trust that is not available to the public at large or to a large class of persons. Thus, for example, the temporary incumbent of an endowed professorial chair is entitled to enforce the trust.[23]

Leaving the enforcement of charitable trusts almost exclusively to the attorney general has resulted in sporadic enforcement. In the case of inter vivos trusts there is ordinarily no contact with the state. Even with testamentary trusts, which are created by the probate court, the duty to render periodic accounts is rarely enforced. Without knowledge of the trustees' actions, or even of the existence of trusts which he is charged with supervising, the attorney general cannot be expected to perform his assigned role as guardian of the public interest. Awareness of the inadequacies of this situation led to the promulgation in 1954 of the Uniform Act for Supervision of Trustees for Charitable Purposes. This act supplements the enforcement duties of the attorney general with supervisory powers. Under the Act trustees of charitable trusts[24] are required to register with the attorney general and submit annual financial reports. In addition the attorney general is given investigatory powers. The Uniform Act has not, however, been widely adopted. As of 1969, the Act or a similar statute had been adopted by only eleven states.[25]

The failure of the states to increase their supervision over charitable foundations in the face of evidence of abuses,[26] particularly in private family foundations, was one of the reasons for the Tax Reform Act of 1969. One of the major abuses was self-dealing. Although trustees and directors of charitable foundations are prohibited under state law from any self-dealing,[27] prior to 1969 the foundations lost their tax-exempt status only if the trustees and directors engaged in certain limited self-dealing transactions.[28] Not being subject to close state audit, the fiduciaries felt they were governed by the more lenient standards of the Internal Revenue Code. Thus a charitable foundation could be established whereby the donor himself was able to borrow back his contributions.

The Tax Reform Act classified organizations that do not depend on public support as "private foundations,"[29] and assesses against them an annual tax of

[23] Ordinarily the attorney general is a necessary party to a suit to enforce a charitable trust by a person with a special interest and, representing the community, he may be entitled to control the litigation. 4 Scott, Trusts §391 (3d ed. 1967).

[24] One of the defects of the Uniform Act as originally drafted was that it was applicable only to trusts, and not to charitable corporations. Most states that adopted the Act have modified it to apply to charitable corporations as well. For detailed description of the statutes and their operation, see Fremont-Smith, Foundations and Government: State and Federal Law and Supervision 272-351 (1965).

[25] The states are California, Illinois, Massachusetts, Michigan, New Hampshire, New York, Ohio, Oregon, Rhode Island, South Carolina, and Washington. See Fremont-Smith, Regulating Charitable Trusts, 103 Trusts & Estates 845 (1964); Fremont-Smith, Impact of the Tax Reform Act of 1969 on State Supervision of Charities, 8 Harv. J. Legis. 537, 564 (1971).

[26] Tax Exempt Foundations and Charitable Trusts: Their Impact on Our Economy (The Patman Report), Select House Committee on Small Business, 87th Cong., 2d Sess. (1962); U.S. Treasury Department, Report on Private Foundations, 89th Cong., 1st Sess. (1965); Andrews, Foundation Reports to the I.R.S., 11 Foundation News 125 (1970).

[27] 2 Scott, Trusts §170 (3d ed. 1967).

[28] Int. Rev. Code of 1954, §503(g).

[29] Id. §509.

4 percent of their net income. It also created a series of substantive rules governing their operation.

> For private foundations, the new prohibitions against self-dealing are more stringent than under state law. In addition to prohibitions on accumulation, these organizations must invade and expend principal in any year that their investment income is less than a federally defined minimum investment return. State laws defining permissible investments have now been superseded by a rule that prevents private foundations, together with their "disqualified persons" from holding more than 20 percent of the voting stock of a single corporation or of the financial interest in a business entity. A new federal "prudent man" rule has been enacted to determine when a manager has acted so as to jeopardize the fulfillment of the trust's exempt purposes. Congress has also prohibited certain types of charitable activities heretofore considered proper (and still not subject to circumscription under state law). This section prohibits expenditures for lobbying, influencing elections, and making certain grants to individuals and other foundations. Violation of any of these substantive provisions can lead to imposition of excise taxes on the foundation and, in some instances, its fiduciaries, principal donors, the families of both groups, and business and financial interests they control. Loss of tax-exempt status will now result in taxation at individual or corporate rates and perhaps imposition of what is, in effect, a confiscatory tax on the foundation's net assets, Severe penalties will also be imposed on the foundation and its managers for failure to make proper and timely reports.[30]

Section 508(e) of the Internal Revenue Code of 1954, as amended, provides that a private foundation shall not be exempt from income taxation unless its governing instrument includes provisions requiring it to act in such a manner as not to incur taxation. A temporary regulation provides that this section will be considered satisfied if a valid state law is enacted that either (1) imposes on foundations the restrictions required by §508(e) to be included in their governing instruments or (2) treats these restrictions as contained in their governing instruments. Section 508(e) applies to existing private foundations.[31]

The Tax Reform Act of 1969 also provides that notice shall be given to the state attorney general of all charitable organizations (not merely private foundations) that have been refused a tax-exempt status or have had their tax-exemption revoked. It also permits state authorities to inspect the tax returns of charitable organizations. These provisions are especially important to effective state regulation of foundations.

[30] Fremont-Smith, Impact of the Tax Reform Act of 1969 on State Supervision of Charities, 8 Harv. J. Legis. 537, 539 (1971). Lehrfeld, The Private Family Foundation: Causa Mortis, 12 B.C. Ind. & Com. L. Rev. 431 (1971), criticizes the Tax Reform Act as too restrictive and predicts that it will result in fewer grants for unusual and experimental projects. See also Private Foundations under the Tax Reform Act of 1969, 7 Colum. J. of Law & Soc. Probs. 240 (1971).

[31] The U.S. Treasury Department believes there are approximately 22,000 private foundations whose assets approximate $20 billion. Hearings on H.R. 13270 Before the Senate Committee on Finance, 91st Cong., 1st Sess., pt. 1, at 709 (1969).

15. The Duration of Family Settlements: The Rule Against Perpetuities and Related Rules

SECTION A. The Rule Against Perpetuities

1. *Introduction*

a. The Development of the Rule

The classic statement of the Rule against Perpetuities, formulated with Delphic simplicity by John Chipman Gray, reads:

> No interest [in real or personal property] is good unless it must vest, if at all, not later than twenty-one years after some life in being at the creation of the interest.

Although Gray put the Rule in this one sentence, to explain what it meant took Gray more than four hundred scrupulously detailed pages in the first edition of his great work, The Rule against Perpetuities (1886).[1] By virtue of his erudition, his rigorous logic, his dogmatic style, and his position as a celebrated teacher of property law at Harvard, Gray became established as not just a leading authority

[1] In Gray's book the Rule is capitalized "Rule against Perpetuities," a style followed by the Harvard Blue (now White) Book until 1955. In that year, for reasons unknown, perhaps a printer's error, the Blue Book decreed that the Rule should be capitalized "Rule Against Perpetuities." See Dukeminier, Perpetuities: Contagious Capitalization, 20 J. Legal Ed. 341 (1968). We prefer the style of Gray.

on the Rule but as *the* authority. As Holdsworth said, "Of the merits of his work, both as a history and as a statement of modern law, it is hardly necessary to speak. It is sufficient to say that his book shares with Professor Dicey's book on the Conflict of Laws, the fame of being as nearly a book of authority in our courts as any modern book is ever allowed to be; and that it is one of the few American law books which have attained this distinction. Hence my statement [of the Rule] . . . must be largely a summary of Professor Gray's results." [2]

Because of the deference paid to Gray's work by the courts, the Rule has sometimes been treated as if it were laid down at one time by this one man. In fact the Rule had a long and involved evolution. The Rule against Perpetuities is judicial legislation par excellence, and the case-by-case development of the Rule by the courts took several centuries. The origins of the Rule against Perpetuities are somewhat obscure because of the ambiguous nature of the concept "perpetuity." The political and social evils attending on perpetual entails, permitted by the Statute de Donis (1285), led judges to become jealous of allowing any limitation tying up land in perpetuity. They defeated the Statute de Donis in 1472 by approving the common recovery, a bogus lawsuit which left the fee tail tenant with a fee simple. When lawyers for landowners tried new devices for keeping land within the family — principally by clauses restraining alienation and by creating executory interests in long terms of years which were indestructible by common recovery — the judges began to throw up new obstacles to limitations "tending to a perpetuity."

From the sixteenth until the nineteenth century judges struggled against perpetuities, without ever defining exactly what a perpetuity was. There were several unrefined notions and doctrines that might be called rules against perpetuities: the early rule against any indestructible contingent interest, the rule against remote vesting, the rule against a gift to the issue of an unborn life tenant, the rule against suspension of the power of alienation, and the rule against double possibilities.[3] Morris and Leach's description of the origin of the rule against double possibilities is fairly illustrative of the judicial process of the period. "This rule," they say, "was a conceit invented by Popham, C.J., fostered to some extent by Lord Coke, repudiated in no uncertain terms by Lord Nottingham in the Duke of Norfolk's Case, and regarded by all modern commentators as sheer fantasy." [4] Nonetheless, at least one of these judicial inventions — the principle of forbidding interests that vest too remotely — brought upon its creator, Lord Nottingham,[5] the praise of history.

The Rule against Perpetuities as we know it began with the Duke of Norfolk's Case, 3 Ch. Cas. 1, 22 Eng. Rep. 931 (Ch. 1682). The Earl of Arundel had eight sons. Thomas, the eldest son and heir apparent, was non compos mentis, weak in

[2] 7 Holdsworth, History of English Law 215 (1925).

[3] The history is recounted in 7 id. 193-238 (1925). See also Simes & Smith, The Law of Future Interests §1211 (2d ed. 1956).

[4] Morris & Leach, The Rule Against Perpetuities 258 (2d ed. 1962).

[5] Lord Nottingham, born Heneage Finch, was one of the greatest of English Chancellors, called the "Father of Equity" by Mr. Justice Story. He was equally devoted to the law and to his family. When he lost his wife, mother of his fourteen children, he comforted himself by taking the Great Seal to bed with him. 4 Campbell, Lives of the Lord Chancellors 273 (1857).

body, and not expected to have children. Thus the Earl assumed that after his own death and the death of Thomas, the earldom and the estates accompanying it would likely descend to his second son, Henry, and his issue. If Henry did inherit the earldom, the Earl wanted the barony of Grostock, which he planned to give initially to Henry, to shift to his fourth son, Charles.[6] The Earl went to an experienced estate planner (known as a conveyancer in those days when land was the chief form of wealth), Sir Orlando Bridgman. This outstanding member of the bar, who later became Lord Keeper, drew up a set of highly complicated documents. They cannot be easily summarized inasmuch as they require an understanding of some very complex doctrines involving terms of years.[7] It is enough to say that the limitation that brought on the Duke of Norfolk's Case boiled down to this: The barony of Grostock was given to Henry, but an executory limitation was created which provided that if the eldest son, Thomas, should die without issue in the lifetime of Henry, then the barony would go to Charles.

In 1652 the Earl of Arundel died and the earldom descended to the mentally defective son, Thomas. Henry then moved into action. He assumed full control of the properties accompanying the title, and he took Thomas to Padua where he was incarcerated until his death. Henry also engineered the restoration of the title, "Duke of Norfolk," to the family. In 1572 Queen Elizabeth I had beheaded the fourth Duke for intrigues involving Mary, Queen of Scots, and by attainder all his honors were forfeited.[8] In 1660 Parliament, with the consent of Charles II, restored the dukedom of Norfolk, and the incompetent Thomas became the premier duke of England. When Thomas died without issue in 1677 Henry became the sixth Duke of Norfolk.

After succeeding to the dukedom and its properties, Henry did not want to give up the barony of Grostock and, in the Duke of Norfolk's Case, he alleged the interest of Charles was void for perpetuity. Lord Nottingham ruled for Charles. He held that the time at which future interests will vest is the sole matter of concern, and that if a future interest must vest, if at all, during or after a life in being (Henry

[6] The Earl's third son, Philip, went into the clergy and eventually became a cardinal, lord almoner to Catherine, queen-consort of Charles II. Burke's Peerage 738 (10th ed. 1848). For further background information on this interesting family see Barry, The Duke of Norfolk's Case, 23 Va. L. Rev. 538 (1937).

[7] If you really want to get into the details of the Duke of Norfolk's Case, Gulliver, Cases on Future Interests 362-390 (1959), contains an excellent and thorough explanation.

[8] The turbulence of the times is reflected in the history of the title of Duke of Norfolk. First conferred by Richard III on Sir John Howard in 1483, it was forfeited two years later when Richard's rival, Henry VII, ascended the throne. The first Duke's son regained royal favor, and in 1514 Henry VIII restored the title. The niece of the third Duke, Catherine Howard, was the fifth wife of Henry VIII, and was beheaded for infidelity. The third Duke subsequently fell from grace, was stripped of his title, and was ordered to be executed. Fortunately for him, Henry died during the night before the morning set for the execution. The Duke was spared, and Queen Mary restored the title to him seven years later. The Duke of Norfolk is the Earl Marshall of England and the premier duke, ranking just below the blood royal.

The Sixth Duke of Norfolk
by Gerard Soest, ca. 1677
Tate Gallery, London

in this case), it is good. The judges (Pemberton and North, C. JJ., and Montague, C.B.), whom Nottingham had called in to advise him, all disagreed with him, as they believed that an executory interest to take effect upon death without issue, even within a life in being, was a mischievous perpetuity. Being Lord Chancellor, Nottingham prevailed. Within a year he died, and Lord Chief Justice North succeeded him as Lord Keeper. On a bill of review North reversed the decision by Nottingham. 3 Ch. Cas. 53. The case was then appealed to the House of Lords, and in 1685, after two days of argument in a crowded house with King James II present, the Lords voted almost unanimously to reverse North and affirm Nottingham. 3 Ch. Cas. 54. At that time the lay lords could vote. They could hardly have understood the legal issues in Norfolk's Case, but the primary supporter of Nottingham's decree was "Bloody" Jeffreys, a bitter antagonist of Lord North. Jeffreys made the case the occasion for a great personal attack on North. Campbell described it thus:

> Lord Chief Justice Jeffreys, by means of some encouragement he had met with, took upon him the part of slighting and insulting his Lordship on all occasions that proffered. And here he had a rare opportunity; for, in his rude way of talking, and others of a party after him, he battered the poor decree; not without the most indecent affronts to his Lordship that in such an assembly ever were heard. The . . . poor Lord Keeper was assailed by the coarsest vituperation, and the most cutting ridicule. . . . He was not roused into retaliation or resistance; and he contented himself with a dry legal argument. The decree was reversed; and when he announced that the *contents had it*, he must have felt as if he had been sounding his own death-knell. The lay lords who voted could have known nothing of the merits of such a nice question; and must have been guided by favour or enmity to the Lord Keeper or the Lord Chief Justice.[9]

In the Duke of Norfolk's Case Lord Nottingham indicated the direction the Rule against Perpetuities should take but he wisely did not attempt a definitive statement. When asked, "Where will you stop?", he replied, "I will tell you where I will stop: I will stop wherever any visible Inconvenience doth appear." From this beginning it took 150 years for the courts to fix the period of the Rule at lives in being plus twenty-one years. In Scatterwood v. Edge, 1 Salk. 229, 91 Eng. Rep. 203 (K.B. 1699), it was held that it was sufficient if an interest would vest within a considerable number of lives in being, not merely one or two, "For let the lives be never so many, there must be a survivor, and so it is but the length of that life; for Twisden used to say, the candles were all lighted at once." [10] In Thellusson v.

[9] 4 Campbell, Lives of the Lord Chancellors 329 (1857).

[10] Twisden's remark was made in Love v. Wyndham, 1 Mod. 50, 54, 86 Eng. 724, 726 (K.B. 1681).

Do You Rule Your Perpetuity?

Lives plus one-and-twenty years,
  The learned fathers thought,
Should be the time for vesting
  Or the gift would come to naught;

As many lives as are ascertained
  Without undue delay,

Woodford, 11 Ves. 112, 32 Eng. Rep. 1030 (Ch. 1805), it was held that any number of lives reasonably capable of being traced could be used.[11] Concurrently with the expansion of lives in being from one or two to a considerable number the courts were adding, first, a minority period and, subsequently, a period of twenty-one years in gross. The first step in this direction was taken in Lloyd v. Carew, Shower 137, 1 Eng. Rep. 93 (H.L. 1698), which held valid a future interest that would vest, if at all, within twelve months of lives in being. Then in Stephens v. Stephens, Cas. t. Talb. 228, 25 Eng. Rep. 751 (Ch. 1736), it was held that the permissible period could be lives in being plus an actual minority of the taker. Finally, in Cadell v. Palmer, 1 Cl. & Fin. 372, 6 Eng. Rep. 956 (H.L. 1832, 1833), the period of the Rule was settled: any reasonable number of lives in being plus twenty-one years thereafter plus any actual periods of gestation. Thus the period was arrived at by accidents and pragmatics, not by any logical extension.

While the judges were marking out the perpetuities period they were at the same time clarifying the principle or principles by which interests would be judged good or bad. Before 1800 writers and judges wrote of *rules* against perpetuities (in the plural). Several doctrines came within that class. The remoteness of vesting test articulated by Lord Nottingham was not the only doctrine thought of as a rule against perpetuities. Not until the nineteenth century did the idea develop that there was *one* rule against perpetuities. What that one rule was, however, was disputed. John Chipman Gray set out to settle the dispute. His book was written "to show how the law of future interests has been thus simplified and reduced to the Rule against Perpetuities" [12] and to prove that the rule against remote vesting was the Rule against Perpetuities. Gray's energies were fired by an élan to understand multiplicity in terms of a few basic ideas (vest being the most important), and to synthesize the cases by a few compendious theorems. This method was sharply criticized by Charles Sweet, an English authority on property law:

For you light the candles all at once,
As Twisden used to say.

This was to keep the land well oiled
And free to come and go,
For a dead man's hand must idle be
And his mind works awful slow.

— Anonymous student at Harvard Law School 1932. (Reprinted from Leach, Langdell Lyrics of 1938 (1938)).

[11] The court in Re Villar, [1929] 1 Ch. 243, sustained a provision postponing vesting until twenty years after the death of the survivor of all descendants of Queen Victoria living at testator's death. There were about 120 known descendants of Queen Victoria then living. The grand-duchess Anastasia, youngest daughter of the last Czar of Russia, was such a descendant, but it was not known whether she escaped the firing squad of the Bolsheviks.

In Warren's Will Trusts, 105 Sol. J. 511 (1961), testatrix postponed vesting until the expiration of twenty years after the death of descendants of Queen Victoria living at testatrix' death (as in Re Villar). There were 194 legitimate issue of the good Queen then alive. The gift was held valid.

In re Moore, [1901] 1 Ch. 936, held void a trust for maintenance of a tomb for "the period of twenty-one years from the death of the last survivor of all persons who shall be living at my death."

[12] Gray, Rule against Perpetuities iv (1st ed. 1886).

> [I]n their systematic treatises on the English law of real property, American lawyers seem to treat it as if it were a collection of rules drawn up by one legislator at one time, and therefore capable of being classified under leading principles. In the attempt to subject the law of real property to this painful process, "something has to break" (to use one of Gray's Americanisms), and any anomalies which suffer fracture are thrown away as useless. This brutal way of treating the English law of real property commends itself to our modern judges, for it saves a good deal of trouble, but it would have scandalized the conveyancers of the last generation.[13]

In spite of Sweet's protests, Gray's claim that the rule against remote vesting was the only Rule against Perpetuities was accepted in England and — despite the later lamentations of Professor Richard Powell — in America.[14]

Although Gray's book is the authority in the field, it is much too detailed and recondite for the student beginning his study of the Rule. From the 400-odd pages of the first edition it has been expanded to more than 800 in the fourth edition by Roland Gray, the son of John Chipman Gray. (Professor Leach, himself a noted authority on the Rule, once asked, "Did anyone ever read Gray through?") Since your time is not unlimited it is essential that you get a competent grasp on the basics of the Rule elsewhere than in Gray. The classic introduction to the Rule for students is Leach's deservedly famous article, Perpetuities in a Nutshell, 51 Harv. L. Rev. 638 (1938), brought up to date by Leach in Perpetuities: The Nutshell Revisited, 78 Harv. L. Rev. 973 (1965). This lucid article, written in a lively, piquant style, for two generations now has introduced students into the magic garden of perpetuities. Other useful short treatments of the Rule can be found in Simes, Future Interests §121 (2d ed. 1966); Schwartz, Future Interests and Estate Planning c. 6 (1965); and Lynn, A Practical Guide to the Rule Against Perpetuities, 1964 Duke. L.J. 207.

b. Policies Basing the Rule

SIMES, PUBLIC POLICY AND THE DEAD HAND
36, 40, 56-60 (1955)

The essence of these statements [by Gray and earlier writers concerning the purposes of the Rule] amounts to this: The Rule against Perpetuities furthers alienability; if it were not for this Rule, property would be unproductive and society would have less income.

But why should a future interest make property inalienable; and why does in-

13 Sweet, John Chipman Gray, 31 L.Q. Rev. 338, 339 (1915).

14 Because "vested" as used in some other contexts is an inaccurate word to describe what interests are valid under the Rule, and because the word "vested" conceals the important social policy underlying the Rule, Professor Powell believes the Rule should be formulated as a rule against specific fetterings of property found socially inconvenient. His position is cogently stated at 5 Powell, Real Property ¶767 (1970), and is adopted by 4 Restatement of Property §§370-382 (1944).

alienability make property unproductive? In answering these questions we must recall that the Rule against Perpetuities developed as a rule restricting future interests in specific land. Viewed thus, the rationale of the rule is not difficult to perceive. In order to make a profit from land, one must have a type of ownership which insures enjoyment forever or for a fixed and determinable period of time. People who purchase land, whether for profit or for their own use and enjoyment, are not likely to buy unless they can secure either a fee simple absolute or a lease for a fixed term of years. . . .

Now, if the policy of the Rule against Perpetuities is to make property productive, just how far is this policy advanced in the application of the Rule today? Is property still taken out of commerce by remote contingent future interests? I believe it is no exaggeration to say that, at the present time, due to changes in both the nature of capital investments and in the law, the proposition that contingent future interests make property unproductive is rarely true in the United States and almost never true in England. I should like to discuss at some length my reasons for this belief. . . . [Professor Simes points out that contingent future interests are nearly always created in trust and that the trustee has the power, express or implied, to sell trust assets and make them productive. He also states that even if legal contingent future interests are created in land a court can order the sale of the land where it is unproductive.]

. . . I should like to propose an answer to the following question: If alienability for purposes of productivity is not the justification of the modern Rule against Perpetuities, then what is the public policy which justifies it?

Before suggesting what I believe to be the true answer, I should like to take a moment to mention two other explanations of the Rule which are sometimes made. First, it is said that the Rule is designed to prevent an undue concentration of wealth in the hands of a few. Professor Leach has indicated that the Rule is intended to remove the "threat to the public welfare from family dynasties built either on great landed estates or on great capital wealth." But, as he points out, that threat is rather effectively removed by our income and estate taxes. I am disposed to agree with him. Indeed, I feel that undue concentration of wealth is an evil which can best be combatted by tax legislation, rather than by perpetuity rules.

A second reason for the Rule, which is sometimes given, is as follows: It is socially undesirable for some members of society to have assured incomes and be protected from the economic struggle for existence; the principle of survival of the fittest should apply, so that those who are unable to maintain themselves in the economic struggle should not survive. . . . Several answers may be made to this argument. The Rule against Perpetuities does permit economic provision for the unfit for one generation, indeed for one generation and during the minority of the next. It would seem almost as bad to permit this sort of thing for the first generation as for succeeding generations. If it be answered that there is a social objection to the continuation of a line of weaklings, the answer is that a restriction on the tying up of property does not eliminate that objection. Modern society, with its elaborate welfare machinery, is not organized on a theory of survival of the fittest, but of survival of the weak. Moreover, if human experience means anything, we may well conclude that the progeny of weaklings are likely to be more numerous in a state of poverty than in a state of wealth.

Thus I believe that neither of these explanations for the Rule is adequate. There are, in my opinion, however, two other bases for the social policy of the Rule, the force of which can scarcely be denied.

First, the Rule against Perpetuities strikes a fair balance between the desires of members of the present generation, and similar desires of succeeding generations, to do what they wish with the property which they enjoy. . . . In a sense this is a policy of alienability, but it is not alienability for productivity. It is alienability to enable people to do what they please at death with the property which they enjoy in life. . . .

But, in my opinion, a second and even more important reason for the Rule is this. It is socially desirable that the wealth of the world be controlled by its living members and not by the dead. I know of no better statement of that doctrine than the language of Thomas Jefferson, contained in a letter to James Madison, when he said: "The earth belongs always to the living generation. They may manage it then, and what proceeds from it, as they please during their usufruct." Sidgwick, in his Elements of Politics, also discusses the problem in the following words: ". . . it rather follows from the fundamental assumption of individualism, that any such posthumous restraint on the use of bequeathed wealth will tend to make it less useful to the living, as it will interfere with their freedom in dealing with it. Individualism, in short, is in a dilemma. . . . Of this difficulty, there is, I think, no general theoretical solution: it can only be reduced by some practical compromise."

We saw in an earlier chapter how the life estate is accorded favorable tax treatment under the federal estate tax laws. A transferor can create a trust giving his child an income interest for life, and nothing will be taxed in the child's estate at his death. The child's interest terminates on death, at which time its value is zero. The transferor can also give his child limited "ascertainable standard" and "$5000 or 5 percent" invasion powers, and the trustee an unlimited power to distribute corpus to the child, with little or no estate tax cost to the beneficiary. Finally, the transferor can give his child the power to control devolution of the property at his death through a power of appointment, provided that the power is "special" rather than "general." In short, the beneficiary can be given most of the sticks in the ownership "bundle of rights" without being taxed as the owner at death.

What is to prevent the attainment of these tax benefits over a number of generations? The transferor, after providing for his child, might further provide that on the child's death (if he does not exercise the special power of appointment) the trust is to continue for the benefit of his children for their lives, then for *their* children for their lives, and so on down the generations. Since each set of successive beneficiaries has only a life estate, the entire donative arrangement incurs only one transfer tax: the estate or gift tax paid at the time the initial transfer was made. Can the assets be thus immunized from tax liability over several generations? The answer is yes — within the limits of the Rule against Perpetuities. The Rule limits the number of life estates that can be successively created by requiring that all interests must vest within lives in being and twenty-one years, with the consequence that the assets must pass into outright ownership a few generations down the line. The assets will then be taxed in that owner's estate, or during his lifetime if he makes an irrevocable inter vivos transfer. (Through the careful selection of measuring lives, however, these tax benefits can be obtained through two, three, and possibly even four generations.)

Developed as a rule of property law, the Rule against Perpetuities also serves as an important rule of tax policy whereby family wealth must be subject to transfer taxation at least once every several generations. If the Rule were to be abolished, doubtless Congress would substitute equally perplexing tax legislation to achieve this objective.

2. *Elements of the Rule*

a. A Preliminary Statement

The Rule against Perpetuities is in a sense a rule of proof. A claimant of an interest in property is required to prove that there is no possibility that his interest may vest more than twenty-one years after the expiration of some life in being at the creation of the interest. If someone can prove that his interest *might* vest too remotely, the interest is void. The Rule is concerned with possible events that might happen after the interest is created, not with actual events. The relevant date for determining the validity of an interest — the date when the measuring lives must be in being — is the testator's death, if the instrument is a will; or the date of effective delivery, if the instrument is a deed. Events that actually occur after this date are irrelevant and are ignored.

> *Case 1.* In 1970 T devises Blackacre to A for life, then to A's oldest child who survives A for life, then to such child's oldest child in fee. At T's death, A and his son, S, and S's son, G, are alive. The life estate to A's oldest surviving child is good because it vests in possession at A's death, and A was alive in 1970 (the relevant date for determining validity). The remainder in fee is void because it may not vest until the death of a child of A who was not alive in 1970. Take this possible sequence of events: In 1972 A has a daughter, D, born to him. In 1973 S, G, and A die, in that order. D is then entitled to the secondary life estate. In the year 2000 D marries, has a child M, and dies in childbirth. M claims Blackacre. This is more than twenty-one years after the death of A, S, and G.
>
> Suppose this devise were litigated upon A's death in 1975, and that A had died without ever having had any children other than S. A is survived by S and G. In 1975 we know that the remainder in fee has in fact vested in interest at A's death. Still the remainder is void; the actual events occurring after 1970 are irrelevant.

Who can qualify as the measuring life or lives? This is usually one of the first questions students ask when they meet the Rule. The answer is: the law allows any lives to be used to prove validity of an interest, but no lives are of the slightest use in proving validity unless they are in some way connected with the vesting of the interest so that the vesting cannot happen more than twenty-one years after the death of such persons. The measuring lives need not be given any beneficial interest in the property nor be referred to in the instrument, but there must be a connection which insures vesting or failure of the interest within the period. This requirement of a connection to vesting immediately restricts the range of lives that one need consider. Suppose there is a devise "to A for life, then to S for life, then to such of S's children as reach twenty-one." We need not consider all the babies in Michigan because, even if they could be ascertained and were a reasonable number, all of them might be wiped out by a virus epidemic at any time, but this would have no effect upon the vesting or failure of the interests. What one is looking for is some life in existence at the creation of the interest by which one can prove that the interest will vest in time; all others are rejected as irrelevant. In the above devise the measuring lives should be obvious. A's life estate vests in possession at T's death; S's life estate vests in interest at T's death. When will the remainder vest, if at all? No later than twenty-one years after S's death, for all of S's children will reach twenty-one within twenty-one years of his death. Hence S is the measuring life. (Yes, S may die leaving his wife two months pregnant, and this posthumous child will not reach twenty-one until twenty-one years and seven months after S's death. But property law has always been generous to the child in the womb. Actual periods of gestation are included within the perpetuity period.)

The measuring lives need not be given any beneficial interest in the property nor be referred to in the instrument. Thus:

Case 2. Professor X gives $10,000 to all members of his Wills class who are admitted to the bar. The members of the class are the measuring lives. All members either will have been admitted to the bar or will have died unadmitted (and hence never share in the gift) at the death of the last survivor of the class. As Twisden used to say, the candles were all lighted at once.

Case 3. T devises property to W for life, then to T's grandchildren. T leaves children but no grandchildren surviving him. The measuring lives are T's children, who are given no interest in the property. T's grandchildren can prove that their interest will vest, if at all, no later than the death of the survivor of T's children.

Sometimes draftsmen find it useful to use extraneous persons as measuring lives. Thus:

Case 4. T bequeaths a sum in trust to pay the income to T's issue per stirpes from time to time living until twenty-one years after the death of the survivor of A, B, C, D, E, F, G, H, I, J, K, and L (who are twelve healthy babies born during the month preceding the execution of the will), at which time the principal is to vest in T's issue then living per stirpes. A, B, C, D, E, F, G, H, I, J, K, and L are the measuring lives. Twenty-one years after the death of the survivor the remainder will vest, or, if there are no issue of T alive at that time, the remainder will fail. Do you see why the gift of income is necessarily also valid in this case?

English lawyers have long been addicted to using a "royal lives" clause to control the duration of a trust. To wean them away, the English Perpetuities and Accumulations Act 1964, §1, enables a settlor or testator to specify a period of years not exceeding eighty as the perpetuity period instead of the normal one of lives in being plus twenty-one years. Similarly, California Civil Code §715.6 provides for an alternative perpetuity period of sixty years.

The twenty-one year period can follow, but it cannot precede, the measuring lives. The measuring lives must be in being at the effective date of the instrument, not twenty-one years later. Where there are no measuring lives, an interest is valid if it must vest, if at all, within twenty-one years of the creation of the interest.

The Rule against Perpetuities is not a rule directly prohibiting over-long trusts. The Rule is concerned only with the vesting of the *interests* in the trust. A trust can last longer than the perpetuity period, so long as all interests in the trust vest or fail within that period. Thus:

> *Case* 5. T bequeaths a fund in trust for A for life, then to A's children for their lives, then to the children of B in fee. The secondary life estate in A's children vests, if at all, at A's death. The remainder to the children of B will vest in interest (or, if there are no such children born, fail) no later than the death of B. B is the measuring life for the gift to his children. A may have children after T's death, and the trust may last longer than lives in being plus twenty-one years (if, for example, one of A's after-born children survives A and B by more than twenty-one years), but no interest in the trust is invalid.

However, it is never wise to create a trust that can exceed the perpetuities period. If in *Case* 5 the trustee had been given a discretionary power to pay the income to A's children or to accumulate it and add it to principal, the power would be void because it can be exercised beyond the perpetuity period. As almost any trust will contain some discretionary powers, the draftsman is wise to require termination of the trust within the perpetuity period.

Note that Gray's statement of the Rule contains the words, "must vest, *if at all*." These last three words are very important. Without them, all contingent interests would be void, because there is no certainty that any contingent interest will ever vest. To illustrate this take the following three devises:

(1) to A for life, remainder to B if B survives A.

(2) to A in fee, but if B marries, to B.

(3) to B for life if all the redwoods in California fall.

The above devises are all perfectly valid. B's interest will vest *or fail* within his own life or at his death. But if the words, "if at all," were omitted from the Rule, B's interest would be void. The Model Rule against Perpetuities Act omits the words, "if at all." The act has been enacted in Wyoming.[15]

Finally, in this preliminary statement, we come to the meaning of "vest." You will find later that this is one of the most unruly of words. But the following definitions will do for a start.

[15] Wyo. Stat. §34-40 (1959, Supp. 1969).

(1) If the interest is created in an *individual* and is a remainder or an executory interest capable of changing into a vested remainder, the interest becomes vested when it either *vests in interest* or *vests in possession.* Such an interest is vested in interest if it is owned by an ascertained person and is not subject to a condition precedent.

(2) If the interest is created in a *class* and is a remainder or an executory interest capable of changing into a vested remainder, the interest becomes vested when (a) *the class closes* and (b) all conditions precedent for *every* member of the class are satisfied.

(3) An executory interest following a defeasible fee simple cannot vest in interest before it becomes possessory.

(4) Reversions, possibilities of reverter, and rights of entry are vested upon creation. They are not subject to the Rule.

PROBLEMS

1. T devises Blackacre to A for life, then to A's oldest child who survives A for life, then to the first child of that child for life, then to B and his heirs. A, B, and A's son, S, survive T. What interests, if any, violate the Rule against Perpetuities?

2. T devises Blackacre to A for life, then to A's first-born child for life, then in fee to the oldest son of that child who survives that child. A and A's son, S, survive T. What interests, if any, violate the Rule against Perpetuities?

3. T obtained a fifty-year lease on Blackacre in 1940. In 1970 T died devising his interest in Blackacre to A for life, then to A's oldest child who survives A for life, then to the children of that child who survive him. A and A's son, S, survive T. What interests, if any, violate the Rule against Perpetuities?

b. The Remote Possibilities Test

GRAY, THE RULE AGAINST PERPETUITIES §629 (4th ed. 1942): "The Rule against Perpetuities is not a rule of construction, but a peremptory command of law. It is not, like a rule of construction, a test, more or less artificial, to determine intention. Its object is to defeat intention. Therefore every provision in a will or settlement is to be construed as if the Rule did not exist, and then to the provision so construed the Rule is to be remorselessly applied."

JEE v. AUDLEY

Court of Chancery, 1787

1 Cox 324, 29 Eng. Rep. 1186

Edward Audley, by his will, bequeathed as follows, "Also my will is that £1000 shall be placed out at interest during the life of my wife, which interest I give her during her life, and at her death I give the said £1000 unto my niece Mary Hall and the issue of her body lawfully begotten,[16] and to be begotten, and in default of such issue I give the said £1000 to be equally divided between the daughters then living of my kinsman John Jee and his wife Elizabeth Jee."

It appeared that John Jee and Elizabeth Jee were living at the time of the death of the testator, had four daughters and no son, and were of a very advanced age. Mary Hall was unmarried and of the age of about 40; the wife was dead. The present bill was filed by the four daughters of John and Elizabeth Jee to have the £1000 secured for their benefit upon the event of the said Mary Hall dying without leaving children. And the question was, whether the limitation to the daughters of John and Elizabeth Jee was not void as being too remote; and to prove it so, it was said that this was to take effect on a general failure of issue of Mary Hall;[17] and though it was to the daughters of John and Elizabeth Jee, yet it was not confined to the daughters living at the death of the testator, and consequently it might extend to after-born daughters, in which case it would not be within the limit of a life or lives in being and 21 years afterwards, beyond which time an executory devise is void.

On the other side it was said, that though the late cases had decided that on a gift to children generally, such children as should be living at the time of the distribution of the fund should be let in, yet it would be very hard to adhere to such a rule of construction so rigidly, as to defeat the evident intention of the testator in this case, especially as there was no real possibility of John and Elizabeth Jee having children after the testator's death, they being then 70 years old; that if there were two ways of construing words, that should be adopted which would give effect to the disposition made by the testator; that the cases, which had decided that after-born children should take, proceeded on the implied intention of the testator, and never meant to give an effect to words which would totally defeat such intention. . . .

MASTER OF THE ROLLS [SIR LLOYD KENYON]. Several cases . . . have settled that children born after the death of the testator shall take a share in these cases; the difference is, where there is an immediate devise, and where there is an interest in remainder; in the former case the children living at the testator's death only shall take; in the latter those who are living at the time the interest vests in possession; and this being now a settled principle, I shall not strain to serve an intention at the expense of removing the landmarks of the law; it is of infinite importance to abide by decided cases, and perhaps more so on this subject than any other. The general principles which apply to this case are not disputed: the limitations of personal estate are void, unless they necessarily vest, if at all, within a life or lives in being and 21 years or 9 or 10 months afterwards. This has been sanctioned by the opinion of judges of all times, from the time of the Duke of Norfolk's Case to the present:

16 A fee tail estate could not be created in personal property. "Unto Mary Hall and the issue of her body" gives Mary the equivalent of a fee simple. — EDS.

17 The court here assumes indefinite failure of issue (i.e. the running out of Mary's line of issue at her death or at any time thereafter). — EDS.

it is grown reverend by age, and is not now to be broken in upon; I am desired to do in this case something which I do not feel myself at liberty to do, namely to suppose it impossible for persons in so advanced an age as John and Elizabeth Jee to have children; but if this can be done in one case it may in another, and it is a very dangerous experiment, and introductive of the greatest inconvenience to give a latitude to such sort of conjecture. Another thing pressed upon me, is to decide on the events which have happened; but I cannot do this without overturning very many cases. The single question before me is, not whether the limitation is good in the events which have happened, but whether it was good in its creation; and if it were not, I cannot make it so. Then must this limitation, if at all, necessarily take place within the limits prescribed by law? The words are "in default of such issue I give the said £1000 to be equally divided between the daughters then living of John Jee and Elizabeth his wife." If it had been to "daughters now living," or "who should be living at the time of my death," it would have been very good; but as it stands, this limitation may take in after-born daughters; this point is clearly settled by Ellison v. Airey, [1 Ves. 111], and the effect of law on such limitation cannot make any difference in construing such intention. If then this will extended to after-born daughters, is it within the rules of law? Most certainly not, because John and Elizabeth Jee might have children born ten years after the testator's death, and then Mary Hall might die without issue 50 years afterwards; in which case it would evidently transgress the rules prescribed. I am of opinion therefore, though the testator might possibly mean to restrain the limitation to the children who should be living at the time of the death, I cannot, consistently with decided cases, construe it in such restrained sense, but must intend it to take in after-born children. This therefore not being within the rules of law, and as I cannot judge upon subsequent events, I think the limitation void. Therefore dismiss the bill, but without costs.

NOTES

1. In Jee v. Audley the Jee daughters brought a suit against Mary Hall "to have the £1000 secured for their benefit." When future interests are created in personal property, without any trust, there is obviously a danger that the possessory owner will dispose of the property so that there is nothing left at her death. The court may, in its discretion, compel the possessory owner to execute a bond. Simes & Smith, The Law of Future Interests §1717 (2d ed. 1956). Mary Hall's defense is that the Jee daughters have no interest to be protected because their interest violates the Rule against Perpetuities and is void.

2. The standard English construction of "if B die without issue" was an indefinite failure construction. If this phrase were used in introducing a gift over after a fee tail, an indefinite failure construction made sense. "If B die without issue" simply referred to the termination of the preceding fee tail estate and meant "when B's bloodline runs out." [18] Where it was not possible to create a fee tail, as in per-

[18] Generally, all limitations after a fee tail are valid because the tenant in tail can at any

sonal property, the preference for an indefinite failure construction is rather hard to justify. But the English courts liked to give fixed meanings to phrases and adhere to them unless the words of the instrument very clearly indicated some other meaning.

If the gift over to the daughters of John and Elizabeth Jee had been construed to be on definite failure of issue of Mary Hall, the gift would have been valid. Definite failure means here "if Mary Hall die without issue living at her death." What arguments can you make, from the *language of the instrument,* that Edward Audley intended a definite failure construction? From the *extrinsic evidence?*

3. Assuming an indefinite failure of issue construction, the gift over to "the daughters then living of John and Elizabeth Jee" is valid if the class of daughters closes at the testator's death. What arguments can you make, from the language of the instrument, that the testator intended to close the class at his death? From the extrinsic evidence?

4. Note that Lord Kenyon rejected all the arguments made to save the gift. The opinion also states that the court was urged "to decide on the events which have happened" between the testator's death and the lawsuit, without specifying what they were. Perhaps John or Elizabeth Jee had died or perhaps Mary Hall had died without issue. The court refused to take into account actual events. In recent years several states have adopted the wait-and-see doctrine, under which the validity of interests is judged by actual events happening after the date the instrument became effective, but the position of Lord Kenyon remains the orthodox one.

5. The possibility that the gift to the living Jee daughters could be adjudged separately from the gift to the after-born daughters was not considered by the court. It was assumed that if the interest of one class member can vest too remotely, the entire class gift must fail. "[T]his tacit assumption is the authority which impelled the English courts to adopt their most destructive application of the Rule against Perpetuities." Leach, The Rule against Perpetuities and Gifts to Classes, 51 Harv. L. Rev. 1329, 1341 (1938).

6. Although the indefinite failure of issue construction has been abolished in almost all states and is of very little modern importance, the principles involved in Jee v. Audley are still fundamental. "Indefinite failure of issue" is the equivalent of any remote event that may happen more than twenty-one years after the death of all living persons. With the gift in Jee v. Audley, compare the following bequests. Which would be valid?

(a) To Mary Hall in fee, but if all the redwoods in California die, to John Jee in fee.

(b) To Mary Hall in fee, but if all the redwoods in California die, to the daughters of John and Elizabeth Jee now living in fee. (Note the dictum of Lord Kenyon on this question.)

(c) To Mary Hall in fee, but if all the redwoods in California die, to the daughters of John and Elizabeth Jee now living and then living in fee.

---

time bar the entail and so destroy the subsequent limitations. Morris & Leach, The Rule Against Perpetuities 195 (2d ed. 1962).

(d) To Mary Hall in fee, but if all the redwoods in California die, to John Jee for life, then to Elizabeth Jee for life, then to the daughters of John and Elizabeth Jee now living for life, then in fee to the issue of John and Elizabeth Jee now living and then living per stirpes.

7. T devises Blackacre "to my good friend, A, for life, then in fee to such of A's nephews and nieces as live to attain the age of twenty-one." At the time of T's death A is living and has two brothers (B and C) and four nephews and nieces, all of whom are under the age of twenty-one. Is the interest given to A's nephews and nieces valid under the Rule against Perpetuities? (A clue: The answer is, "It depends.")

NOTES ON THE PRESUMPTION OF FERTILITY

Myriads of minute metronomes
Baton the Ballet of Chromosomes;
The solo-dancing of unmated genes
Conjures up visions of the might-have-beens.

— Myra Buttle, The Sweeniad 4 (1957)

1. Morris & Leach, The Rule Against Perpetuities 82 n. 20 (2d ed. 1962): "In the United States, statistics covering 20 million births during the 10 years from 1923 to 1932 showed that no children were born to women over 55, and only 0.0001 percent of children to women over 50. In England, statistics covering 83,000 births during 1946 showed that no children were born to women over 55 and only two children to women over 50 (Registrar-General's Statistical Review, 1949, p. 106). A recent survey of the statistics and medical literature concludes that 'parturition in a woman over 52 years of age has not been proved and that, therefore, were it surely to occur in a woman, say, of 55, it must be considered a gross aberration of reproductive physiology': Newell and Rock, 'Upper Age Limit of Parturition,' in (1952) 63 American Journal of Obstetrics and Gynecology 875."

2. What should the law say here about the case of Christine Jorgensen, who started life with male sexual equipment and had it removed? Christine Jorgensen was the first publicized case of a transsexual man who underwent conversion surgery in Denmark in the early 1950s. Since the pioneering operation on Christine Jorgensen, there have been several hundred sexual conversion operations.[19] It is not entirely clear whether a man legally becomes a woman by such an operation.[20] But for purposes of the Rule against Perpetuities it makes no difference. If a man, he is

[19] See Transsexualism and Sex Reassignment (Greene & Money eds. 1969).

[20] Corbett v. Corbett, [1970] 2 All E.R. 33, held that the legal sex of a person could not be changed by a sex change operation and that a marriage between a man and a transsexual who had undergone conversion surgery and had assumed a female name and role was a nullity. Cf. Anonymous v. Weiner, 50 Misc. 2d 380, 270 N.Y.S.2d 319 (Sup. Ct. 1966). See Meyers, Problems of Sex Determination and Alteration, 36 Medico-Legal J. 174 (1968); Comment, Transsexuals in Limbo: The Search for a Legal Definition of Sex, 31 Md. L. Rev. 236 (1971).

castrated. If a woman, she has no ova, no womb, no uterus. There is no present possibility that he or she can have a child, although there is no telling what possibilities future advances in medicine hold in store.

Should the law admit evidence of a conversion operation to show that the person cannot have a child? If so, must evidence likewise be admitted to show a woman has had a hysterectomy? It seems impossible to distinguish the case of a sexual conversion operation from the case of a complete hysterectomy. And so, since evidence of a hysterectomy has traditionally been rejected, must learned judges say that the law conclusively presumes Christine Jorgensen can have a child?

3. T bequeaths a fund in trust for A for life, remainder to A's children. At age sixty A and her then living children petition for the termination of the trust, claiming that they are all the parties interested in the trust. It has been held in such trust termination cases that proof can be offered to show that the life tenant cannot have any more children. In re Ransom's Estate, 89 N.J. Super. 224, 214 A.2d 521 (1965); In re Bassett's Estate, 104 N.H. 504, 190 A.2d 415, 98 A.L.R.2d 1281 (1963).

4. Several jurisdictions have passed legislation to deal with the conclusive presumption of fertility. New York Estates, Powers, and Trusts Law §9-1.3(e), enacted in 1966, provides:

> (1) Where the validity of a disposition depends upon the ability of a person to have a child at some future time, it shall be presumed, subject to subparagraph (2), that a male can have a child at fourteen years of age or over, but not under that age, and that a female can have a child at twelve years of age or over, but not under that age or over the age of fifty-five years.
>
> (2) In the case of a living person, evidence may be given to establish whether he or she is able to have a child at the time in question.

Similar statutes have been adopted in England, New Zealand, Western Australia, and Ontario. See also Ill. Stat. Ann. title 30, §194(c)(3) (1969, Supp. 1971).

Tennessee Code §24-516, enacted in 1965, provides:

> The present absolute common law presumption which prevails in Tennessee that men and women are presumed capable of having children as long as they live shall be only a prima facie presumption and rebuttable by competent evidence.

5. A person at any age can adopt a child. The judicial trend is to construe gifts to the "children of A" to include children adopted by A. If the conclusive presumption of fertility is discarded, how should the possibility of an adopted child be dealt with? Or the possibility of a person of advanced age legitimating a child? The English Perpetuities and Accumulations Act 1964, §2(4), provides that the stated presumptions about the capacity to have children (identical with N.Y. Estates, Powers & Trusts Law §9-1.3(e)(1) reproduced above) apply to adoptions and legitimations; the provision authorizing the admission of evidence relevant to the issue of capacity does not apply. The Ontario Perpetuities Act of 1966, §7(4), provides that

the possibility that a person may have a child by adoption or legitimation shall not be considered in determining the validity of an interest, and that the subsequent adoption or legitimation of a child shall not invalidate an otherwise valid gift; if a person does subsequently have a child by such means the court may make such order as it sees fit to protect the right of such child in the gift. The Illinois statute, which is otherwise comparable to the New York statute quoted above, states: "[T]he possibility of having a child or more remote descendant by adoption shall be disregarded." Ill. Rev. Stat. c. 30, §194(c)(3) (1969, Supp. 1971).

Re GAITE'S WILL TRUSTS
Chancery Division, 1949
[1949] 1 All E.R. 459

[Testatrix bequeathed property in trust to pay the income to Mrs. Hagar Gaite for life, remainder in fee to "such of her grandchildren living at my death or born within five years therefrom who shall attain the age of twenty-one." Testatrix made her will in 1947 and died in the same year. At that time Mrs. Hagar Gaite was a widow, sixty-seven years old. She had two children living and one grandchild, aged eight. The question was whether the remainder to grandchildren violated the Rule.]

ROXBURGH, J. . . . I must assume that Mrs. Hagar Gaite, who was alive at the date of the death of the testatrix, might have had a child within five years after the death of the testatrix. What is impossible is that that child of Mrs. Hagar Gaite, ex hypothesi born after the death of the testatrix, could itself have had a child within that period of five years, and that is essential to qualify for membership of the class. I do not base my judgment on physical impossibility. I leave all questions of that sort open for consideration when they arise because the matter is, in my judgment, concluded — and counsel for the second defendant admitted it was concluded — by the Age of Marriage Act, 1929, s. 1(1), which provides: "A marriage between persons either of whom is under the age of sixteen shall be void." Ex hypothesi, the child of Mrs. Hagar Gaite born after the death of the testatrix must be under the age of 16 years at the expiration of five years from the death of the testatrix, and, therefore, that child could not lawfully be married and have lawful children. In construing the rule, I must have regard to the statute law of England, and, therefore, I hold that the rule is not infringed.

NOTES

1. The reasoning of the court has been criticized on the ground that a valid marriage might take place at an earlier age in a foreign country where the parties were domiciled. Morris & Leach, The Rule against Perpetuities 84-86 (2d ed. 1962). The Family Law Reform Act, 1969, §15(1), provides that thereafter it will be pre-

sumed, in dispositions of property, that references to children and other relatives of a person include illegitimate children.

2. The court's reasoning aside, the gift to grandchildren is void if it is assumed that, all in the space of five years, Mrs. Hagar Gaite could have a child (X) and that child in turn could have a child (Y) who could take as a beneficiary. The youngest mother on record is Lina Medina of Lima, Peru. On May 14, 1939, at the age of five, she was delivered of a $6\frac{1}{2}$-pound boy by caesarian section. An investigation revealed that she had been raped by a mentally retarded teen-age stepbrother. In a story in the New York Times, April 3, 1963, p. 70, one of Lina's obstetricians, Dr. Rolando Colareta, recalled that he and his colleagues were astounded to discover that "although Lina had every aspect of a five-year-old infant, her sexual development corresponded to that of a young lady over 15 years old. . . . Surprising though it seems, we confirmed that Lina had menstrual periods since she was one-month old." Dr. Colareta went on to point out that cases of twelve- and thirteen-year-old mothers were commonplace in the Andes, where Lina came from. "As a matter of fact," he said, "I delivered a child to a 9-year-old girl here last week and it didn't even make the newspapers." The New York Times reported that Lina, then twenty-eight and still unmarried, was working as a secretary. Her son Gerardo, then twenty-three, was living with Lina's parents and studying accounting.

The Statistical Abstract of the United States 48 (1970) reported that for the years 1940 to 1968, approximately one birth in every thousand was to a woman aged ten to fourteen.

3. If the provision, "or born within five years therefrom," had been omitted, would the gift have been valid?

If the provision, "who shall attain the age of twenty-one," had been omitted, would the gift have been valid?

4. T devises property "to A for life, remainder to such of A's children as shall reach their respective twenty-first birthdays." Since a person reaches twenty-one at the first moment of the day before his birthday,[21] it is arguable that this gift exceeds by one day the Rule against Perpetuities. Leach, The Careful Draftsman: Watch Out! 47 A.B.A.J. 259 (1961).

Sperm and Ova Banks and the Fertile Decedent

Medical science has made it possible for a person to become a genetic father or mother after death. For many years, sperm banks have been established for artificial insemination. Having a supply of semen available in a sperm bank permits a man who has undergone a vasectomy to become a father by artificial insemination. Other reasons for deposits in the bank include preservation of semen of men who may be rendered involuntarily sterile by life-saving medical procedures or who may become astronauts and fear the effect of radioactivity in space upon their genes. See Leach,

[21] Erwin v. Benton, 120 Ky. 536, 87 S.W. 291 (1905); Annot. 5 A.L.R.2d 1143 (1949). Twenty-one was fixed by the common law as "full age" because it was believed that males of that age could bear the heavy armor of a knight and thus could be tenants by knight's service.

Perpetuities in the Atomic Age: The Sperm Bank and the Fertile Decedent, 48 A.B.A.J. 942 (1962). Human ova banks comparable to sperm banks are in the offing. Follicular eggs from a woman may be frozen, then some time later fertilized in vitro by the sperm of a sterile woman's husband, then transplanted into the sterile wife's uterus. The child born as a result of such process would not of course bear any genetic resemblance to the foster mother that gave birth to him.[22]

We have already met the Fertile Octogenarian and the Precocious Toddler. Sperm and ova banks may result in a new character, the Fertile Decedent, coming to inhabit the Rule. Suppose that T bequeaths his residuary estate in trust to pay the income to his son (and sole heir) A for life, remainder to A's children who reach twenty-one. The gift to A's children has been assumed to be valid under the Rule against Perpetuities because all of A's children will be born before his death (or within a period of gestation thereafter) and they will all reach twenty-one within twenty-one years thereafter. A is the measuring life in being. Is such a gift now to fail because medical science has made it possible for A to become a parent[23] of a child conceived after he is dead, who may reach twenty-one more than twenty-one years after his death?

In the article first raising the question, cited above, Professor Leach suggested that the duration of a male life in being be treated as "including any post-mortem period during which his sperm remains fertile." Professor Casner has suggested two other possible solutions to the problem: (1) a judicial wait-and-see rule under which, in the example given above, a determination would be made at A's death as to whether A's sperm had in fact been preserved (if it had not, then no child of A could be conceived after his death); (2) a rule of construction that would exclude from the class gift to A's children any child of A born after A's death by the process of artificial insemination.[24] Do you foresee any obstacles to any of these solutions?

The Unborn Widow

1. T bequeaths a fund in trust to pay the income "to my son for life, then to my son's widow, if any, for life, then to pay the principal to my son's issue then living per stirpes." Is the gift to the son's issue valid? Chenowith v. Bullitt, 224 Ky. 698, 6 S.W.2d 1061 (1928).

2. T bequeaths a fund in trust to pay the income "to my son for life, then to my son's widow, if any, for life; then to pay the principal to my son's children, but if no child of my son is alive at the death of the survivor of my son and his widow, then to pay the principal to the American Red Cross." Is any gift invalid? Morris & Leach, The Rule Against Perpetuities 44 (2d ed. 1962).

22 Professor Schuyler has suggested that it may be possible for a person to become a genetic father after his death by a transplantation of his testicles. Schuyler, The New Biology and The Rule Against Perpetuities, 15 U.C.L.A.L. Rev. 420, 433 (1968).

23 The issue is bound to arise over who is the father of a sperm-bank child and who is the mother of an ova-bank child. The legal relationships created by artificial insemination have been the subject of much controversy and are not settled. See Smith, Through a Test Tube Darkly: Artificial Insemination and the Law, 67 Mich. L. Rev. 127 (1968).

24 Casner, Estate Planning, 1969 Supp. 770 (3d ed. 1961).

3. T bequeaths a fund in trust to pay the income "to my son for life, then to my son's widow, if any, for life, then to pay one-half of the principal to the American Red Cross and the other one-half to my heirs then living." Is any gift invalid? Easton v. Hall, 323 Ill. 397, 154 N.E. 216 (1926).

4. California Civil Code §715.7 (West 1970) provides: "In determining the validity of a future interest in real or personal property . . . [under the Rule against Perpetuities], an individual described as a spouse of a person in being at the commencement of a perpetuities period shall be deemed a 'life in being' at such time whether or not the individual so described was then in being." Similar provisions, but varying in detail, have been adopted in England, New Zealand, Ontario, Western Australia, New York, and Illinois.

Other Traps for the Draftsman

BROWNELL v. EDMUNDS

United States Court of Appeals, Fourth Circuit, 1953

209 F.2d 349

PARKER, Chief Judge. This is an appeal in an action commenced by the Attorney General in the court below pursuant to section 17 of the Trading with the Enemy Act, as amended, 50 U.S.C.A. Appendix, §17, to recover a bequest in favor of certain German legatees under the will of Mrs. Shirley M. Suhling, who died a resident of Lynchburg, Virginia, in April 1945. After the termination of the war by the Joint Resolution of Congress of October 19, 1951, the present action was commenced by the Attorney General to collect the bequest. The District Judge in granting a motion of defendants for summary judgment held that no interest in the bequest vested in the legatees until the termination of the war and that the bequest was void because in contravention of the rule against perpetuities, 110 F. Supp. 828. From this judgment in favor of the defendants the Attorney General has appealed.

The will of Mrs. Suhling, which was executed July 11, 1944, contained a number of bequests, one of which was intended to make some provision for the relatives of her deceased husband upon the termination of the war then in progress. That bequest, which is the only one of importance here, is as follows: "I also want my husband's family in Bremen, Germany, the Stellohs and Kleintitschens, to share in my estate (should they survive this war) to the extent of $20,000.00".

Mrs. Suhling's deceased husband was a German who had been naturalized in this country and who had relatives, consisting of a sister and her children and grandchildren, living in Bremen. Mrs. Suhling knew the difficulty of making gifts to residents of enemy countries in time of war because of the experience of her deceased husband, who had attempted to set aside money for a relative in Germany during World War One and had had it confiscated. . . .

Mrs. Suhling was not in touch with her husband's family in Bremen during the war and did not so much as know that the husband's sister had died in 1943. She evidently intended by the bequest, not to make provision for such of the members of the family as might be living at her death, and whose shares would be forfeited if the war was still in progress, but for such as might be living at the end of the war and who would be in need of help at that time. Since it was not certain that the war would end within the period prescribed by the rule against perpetuities, we think, as did the District Judge, that the bequest must fail and the property go under the residuary clause of the will. 1 Minor on Real Property 2d ed. §§809, 811, 824. This being true, there was no vesting of any estate in an alien enemy which would render it subject to seizure under the statute here relied on.

It is argued that, because of the rule favoring the early vesting of estates, the class of persons who are to take the bequest under the will of Mrs. Suhling must be determined as of the date of her death and that the interest thus taken would be subject to the provisions of the statute. We think, however, for the reasons heretofore stated, that the clear intent of the testatrix here was that the class entitled to take under the bequest was to be determined at the end of the war and not at her death. The early vesting rule is to be applied in the absence of any expression of a contrary intent and not to defeat such intent, where, as here, it is clearly expressed.

. . .

The words of the testatrix in the will in this case are, to my husband's family "should they survive this war." Clearly the words of survivorship here relate to the period of distribution, when the war ends, and the gift is contingent with no member of the family having a vested interest. Since the gift is postponed until the happening of a designated contingency, the determination of the membership of the class, "my husband's family," would not be ascertainable until the happening of the contingency and would include all members of the class then in being including those born after the death of the testator. The gift is therefore void under the rule against perpetuities since it might not vest during lives in being plus the 21 year and 10 month period. To come within the requirement of the rule it is not sufficient that the event upon which the estate is to vest, when viewed prospectively, may occur within the crucial period. It is necessary that, when so viewed, it must occur within the period. . . .

Even if the rule against perpetuities be disregarded, we think it clear that the bequest was not subject to seizure under the statute and regulations relied on. The pertinent provision of the Trading with the Enemy Act, Section 7(c), 50 U.S.C.A. Appendix, §7(c), subjects to seizure only property "belonging to or held for, by, on account of, or on behalf of, or for the benefit of, an enemy". . . .

Under the bequest here under consideration, none of the Stellohs or Kleintitschens was to take anything until the end of the war, when the country of which they were nationals would cease to be an enemy country. As they were to take no interest in the property covered by the bequest unless they survived the war, no property vested in them or was held for their benefit by reason of the bequest so long as the war was going on. . . .

Affirmed.

PRIME v. HYNE

California Court of Appeal, Second District, 1968
260 Cal. App. 2d 397, 67 Cal. Rptr. 170

Shinn, J. Appeal by plaintiff from a summary judgment in favor of defendant in an action for a declaration of rights and duties of the parties under a lease and a separate contract for the purchase by plaintiff of prospective interests of defendant devisees in real property now in probate, which may be distributed to them.

By the pleadings and the declarations which were before the court upon the hearing of the motion for summary judgment the following facts were established: July 21, 1961, Estelle Williams owned a parcel of real property on Sunset Boulevard in Los Angeles, which was under lease to plaintiff Pearl Prime and was used as a nursery school. There was then in existence a will of Mrs. Williams by the terms of which she devised her estate to John W. Williams, Jr., Barbara Vickers, Thomas Williams and Marilyn Hodges, hereinafter for convenience referred to as "heirs." July 21, 1961, the heirs and Miss Prime entered into an agreement by which Miss Prime agreed to buy and the heirs agreed to sell whatever interests in the property they might receive through a distribution of the estate of Mrs. Williams. The agreed purchase price was $70,000 payable part in cash and part on time. It was provided that if all the respective interests were not so distributed those that were distributed would be sold for a proportionate part of the total purchase price.

Certain provisions of the agreement were the following: "(a) Second Parties do not now have any right, title, claim or interest in or to said real property, and merely expect to inherit said real property upon the death of Estelle Williams, provided they survive her;

"(b) That Estelle Williams by a last will might devise said real property to others than Second Parties or any of them;

"(c) That it is legally possible that said real property might be sold or hypothecated during the life of Estelle Williams in which event the Second Parties could not deliver title to First Party;

"(d) That if Second Parties or any of them failed to survive Estelle Williams that said real property would in all probability be distributed to minor heirs who would in no way be bound by the within agreement; . . . ."

The agreement also provided that immediately after the parties of the second part (the heirs) received legal title to said property by decree of distribution of Mrs. Williams' estate they would enter into an escrow to carry out the terms of the agreement.

On July 21, 1961, Mrs. Williams and Miss Prime entered into a lease of the property to the latter at a monthly rental of $400 for a term ending "60 days after distribution of this property from Estelle P. Williams' estate." The lease was executed on behalf of Mrs. Williams by John W. Williams, Jr., as her attorney in fact. For no apparent reason the heirs were named with Mrs. Williams as lessors and they also signed the lease.

Mrs. Williams died June 5, 1964, her will was probated, John W. Williams, Jr. was appointed executor but "removed himself" and James Hyne was appointed in his stead.

As far as shown by the record the estate consisted of the real property and shares of stock of an insurance company, of unstated value. By the will the executor was authorized to sell the property of the estate; James Hyne elected to sell the real property; he caused a "for sale" sign to be placed on the property, where it remained for several hours.

Miss Prime instituted the present action for declaratory relief, an injunction against sale of the property by the estate and damages. . . .

Defendants made a motion for summary judgment upon several independent grounds, one of which was that the agreement of sale was void as in violation of the rule against perpetuities as declared in section 715.2 of the Civil Code. The court rendered judgment declaring the agreement to be void and that plaintiff has no right, title, interest or claim in or to the property, and dismissing the action only as to the second cause of action. Plaintiff appeals.

It is apparent from the record and the briefs that the basis of the judgment was the court's conclusion that the agreement was void in its inception for the reason that it was not certain that the title to the interests of the heirs in the property would vest in Miss Prime under the contract within 21 years after the death of Mrs. Williams.

It is well settled that the requirement of the rule against perpetuities as stated in section 715.2 that title *must* vest within the prescribed period means that there must be absolute certainty at the time of the contract that title will vest within that period.

An essential and indispensable condition of the contract was that the interests of the heirs be distributed to them from Mrs. Williams' estate. If this event was not bound to occur within the limited time title to the property could not become vested in plaintiff so as to avoid the effect of the rule against perpetuities.

It has been held in several cases that there is no absolute certainty that the estate of a person living at the time of the creation of some right to an interest in his estate will be distributed within 21 years after his death.

Distribution of the estate of a decedent is subject to many possible delays. Numerous of these are listed in the opinion in Estate of Campbell, 28 Cal. App. 2d 102, 82 P.2d 22, such as delay in the institution of probate proceedings, neglect and inattention, protracted litigation; "[a]ll of these possibilities, not to mention others, might become realities in a particular case, causing a delay beyond the time limited." (P. 106.) The court also said: "While it can be said that the reasonable probabilities were in favor of a distribution of this estate well within the time required, to hold that such a result, with the consequent vesting of interest, was certain to occur and would inevitably take place would be to disregard the statute by accepting a high degree of probability as a certainty." (See also Estate of Johnston, 47 Cal. 2d 265, 270, 303 P.2d 1.)[25]

[25] The will of Campbell left the residue of his estate to officers of a lodge who would be in

Without noticing these cases, which were cited by respondents, appellant contends that the estate should have been distributed within a reasonable time and that a reasonable time would have been less than 21 years; therefore the rule against perpetuities does not apply. For this proposition appellant cites Wong v. DiGrazia, 60 Cal. 2d 525, 35 Cal. Rptr. 241, 386 P.2d 817. In this case the court considered a contract for a lease which was to commence upon completion of a building on the premises. The contract provided that the lessor would forthwith commence construction of the building in accordance with plans and specifications that had been agreed upon and continue expeditiously until the building was completed. The court held that the lessor had a duty imposed by the contract to complete the building within a reasonable time, which would be less than 21 years, and although the lessee's interest would not vest until the building was completed there was no violation of the rule against perpetuities. The court was considering the special problems which arise out of "on completion" leases, a modern and common class of leases. The reasoning of the opinion is not applicable to an agreement for the sale of a mere expectancy. Contracts for the sale of expectancies of heirs and devisees are in the general class of interests created by wills, deeds or contracts to vest in the future. As to these the rules against restraints of alienation and perpetuities are strictly enforced. (Cases cited supra; Estate of Troy, 214 Cal. 53, 3 P.2d 930.) The trial court applied the rule as it existed in California.

A further contention of appellant is that the defendants should be held estopped from selling the property through probate and from contesting her right to buy the property. The argument upon this point may be stated briefly; it runs as follows: Mrs. Williams was the actual seller of the property; through her agent John W. Williams Jr. she agreed upon the price and terms of a sale, but in order to avoid a capital gain tax liability it was agreed that title would be distributed to the heirs through probate of the will and that they would make the conveyance to appellant and receive the purchase price. In reliance upon this plan of procedure appellant sold property she owned and spent large sums in making repairs and improvements of the property and for taxes and insurance, all to her damage if she fails to obtain the property.

The fact that all the interested parties had such a plan of procedure is proved by the lease and the agreement that were entered into. Whether the purpose was to avoid a tax liability is of no consequence. But if that was the purpose, it would only go to prove that Mrs. Williams did not intend to sell the property but was satisfied to receive the rental of $400 per month and to let the heirs have the $70,000.

It is but just to all the parties to say that they acted in good faith. No doubt

---

office at the time of the distribution of the estate and who would be unknown until that time. This provision of the will was held to be invalid as in violation of sections 715 and 716 of the Civil Code in that it purported to restrain the power of alienation for more than 25 years. It was also held to be violative of the prohibition of perpetuities of section 9, Article XX of the State Constitution. Although the court did not so state, the provision was also in violation of the rule of the common law then in effect in California. (Estate of Sahlender, 89 Cal. App. 2d 329 [201 P.2d 69].) That rule was the one which later became section 715.2 of the Civil Code.

they expected the property would be distributed to the heirs. They believed in 1961 that the property was worth $70,000; they did not anticipate that the value would greatly increase while Mrs. Williams still lived. But in 1964 the taxing authorities valued it at $140,000. As a consequence, as shown by the declaration of Mr. Hyne, property had to be sold to realize approximately an additional $30,000 in order to meet the unexpected obligations of the estate for taxes and expenses of administration. Appellant cannot prevent the sale of the real property.

The complete answer to the foregoing contentions of appellant is that she holds an illegal contract under which the court can grant her no relief. "A party to an illegal contract cannot ratify it, cannot be estopped from relying on the illegality, and cannot waive his right to urge that defense." (City Lincoln-Mercury Co. v. Lindsey, 52 Cal. 2d 267, 274, 339 P.2d 851.) . . .

In Bridge v. Kedon, 163 Cal. 493, 499, 126 P. 149, 43 L.R.A. N.S. 404, the court quoted from 3 Pomeroy's Equity Jurisprudence, section 1271, which states that the assignment of an expectancy, possibility or contingency creates "an equitable ownership of property in abeyance, so to speak, which finally changed into an absolute property upon the happening of the future event." The court said (p. 500): ". . . as soon as the assignment is executed the assignee becomes vested of an equitable right to receive the property ultimately, a right which, by the rules of equity, is sure to become an ordinary vested property right when the event occurs by which the possibility is realized as a certainty. . . . In the case of a loan, according to these principles, there is created by the assignment a present equitable charge on the property, which equity recognizes as vested, although it is neither vested nor valid at law, and which, when the descent is cast at once ripens into a lien upon the property for the security of the money loaned."

Appellant had a vested contract right which, if valid and fair, would be enforceable in equity. She had no ownership of a present or future interest in the property. No claim upon the property in excess of her existing rights could vest in her unless the property should be distributed in whole or in part to the heirs, which might never happen.

The determination of appellant's rights under the contract did not require the decision of any question of fact. The undisputed facts presented a pure question of law. The briefs argue the question whether the contract is fair and enforceable in equity but in view of our conclusion that it is void it is immaterial whether it would be enforceable if it were valid.

The judgment is affirmed.

Ford, P.J., and Cobey, J., concurred.

NOTES

1. The agreement between Pearl Prime and the sellers does not create an interest in property until Estelle Williams dies, and, before Estelle's death, the Rule

against Perpetuities is not applicable.[26] Once Estelle dies the Rule comes into play.[27] The agreement provided that immediately after the sellers received legal title to the property by decree of distribution, they would enter into an escrow to carry out the terms of the agreement. The draftsman was apparently unaware that at Estelle's death the legal fee simple title would vest in the sellers immediately by operation of law.[28] Thus at Estelle's death what the sellers are saying to Pearl is: "We have title to this land, and we hereby legally bind ourselves to transfer title to you as soon as debts, taxes, and expenses have been paid and the court approves all the acts of the executor in a decree of distribution." What kind of interest does this create in Pearl?

If a testator does not postpone the ascertainment of the beneficiaries, but merely their enjoyment of the property, until the distribution of an estate, their gifts are vested with possession postponed. Thus a testamentary gift of $50,000 "to my issue per stirpes living at my death, to be paid at distribution," is valid. How far does this differ from the rights created in Pearl Prime?

2. In Belfield v. Booth, 63 Conn. 299, 27 Atl. 585 (1893), the residuary estate was devised in a trust to continue for fourteen years after "the executor has settled with the judge of probate," and at the expiration of that period the trust principal was to be distributed among a class to be then determined. The Connecticut court held that the devise did not violate the Rule. The court reasoned that settlement of the estate would not be delayed beyond a reasonable period of time and that "this time cannot be delayed so long as seven years from his decease." Although most estates are settled within three years of death, any lawyer with an extensive estate practice knows of estates that have been tied up in litigation for more than seven years and, occasionally, for more than twenty-one years. See Estate of Garrett, page 166, supra (twenty-three years); Haddock v. Boston & Maine Ry., 146 Mass. 155, 15 N.E. 495 (1888) (sixty-three years). And then there is the case of Myra Clark Gaines, who for more than seventy years strove to establish a will of her father. New Orleans v. Gaines' Administrator, 138 U.S. 595 (1891); Harmon, The Famous Case of Myra Clark Gaines (1946). In Caudell v. Scroggings, 120 Ga. App. 286, 170 S.E.2d 343 (1969), a will was found and probated fifteen years after the testatrix' death.

3. In Estate of Taylor, 66 Cal. 2d 855, 428 P.2d 301 (1967), Eva Taylor devised one-third of her residuary estate to Ellen Glasky if she survived distribution of the estate. Eva died September 14, 1963. Ellen died eighteen months later, on March 15, 1965. Looking at the facts involved in Eva's estate, the court found that the estate could have been distributed a year or so after she died, and that the delay was unreasonable. Based on this finding the court decided that vesting cannot be

[26] 6 American Law of Property §24.55 (Casner ed. 1952).

[27] Of course if the transfer of the sellers' expectancy is unenforceable because of an inadequate consideration, the Rule would not become involved.

[28] Cal. Probate Code §300 (West. 1956, Supp. 1971). Would equitable conversion apply if the sellers did not receive legal title until the decree of distribution?

postponed by unreasonable delay in distributing an estate, and that when there is such a delay contingent interests vest at the time distribution should have been made. The court then ordered the one-third share to be paid to Ellen's estate.

Apply the theory of Estate of Taylor to this bequest: "I give my residuary estate to my issue per stirpes living when my estate is distributed." Is this valid? Or is it valid only if, on the facts of the case, it would be unreasonable to delay distribution for more than twenty-one years? How, at the date of testator's death, can we tell whether there will be unreasonable delay in settling testator's estate? See Estate of Germond, 4 Cal. 3d 573, 483 P.2d 769, 94 Cal. Rptr. 153 (1971).

4. Suppose Pearl Prime sues for negligence lawyer Jones, who prepared this agreement (and assume further that Lucas v. Hamm, page 15, does not apply). Lawyer Jones defends on the ground that the court was wrong, the agreement does not violate the Rule against Perpetuities, and Prime v. Hyne cannot be res judicata as to him. Would it be appropriate for another district court of appeal in the same state to decide in the negligence suit that Prime v. Hyne was wrongly decided and that lawyer Jones was not negligent? How can a lawyer protect himself against the inadequacy of another lawyer in litigating instruments the first lawyer drafted?

Suppose the court had held that the agreement in Prime v. Hyne was enforceable. Would the sellers have an action for negligence (not foreseeing the adverse tax consequences which would result from a rising market in land) against the lawyer who advised them to enter into this agreement? If so, when would the statute of limitations begin to run? Yandell v. Baker, 258 Cal. App. 2d 308, 65 Cal. Rptr. 606 (1968).

If Estelle Williams had signed a contract in 1961 providing that she leased the property to Pearl Prime for $400 a month until Mrs. Williams' death and that her personal representative was bound to convey the property at her death to Pearl Prime for $70,000, the property would have been included in Mrs. Williams' federal gross estate at a valuation of $70,000. Treas. Reg. §20.2031-2(h). The capital gain which accrued to Mrs. Williams prior to her death would not be taxed as income in respect of a decedent because, according to the Treasury regulations, the transaction was not "consummated" until after Mrs. Williams' death. Treas. Reg. §1.691(a)-2(b). By this method a person can effectively sell land during his life and avoid paying tax on any capital gain. Are the positions of the Treasury Department consistent? If you had been Pearl Prime's lawyer would you have recommended that she enter into such a contract with Mrs. Williams?

5. A story has gone around that W. C. Fields in his will directed that there be carved on his tombstone, "All things considered, I'd rather be in Philadelphia than here." An inspection of his will revealed the story to be apocryphal. Nonetheless, if memory serves, Fields did say, "Anyone who hates children and dogs can't be all bad." Hence it was rather surprising to find that Fields devised the residue of his estate as follows: "I direct that my executors procure the organization of a membership or other approved corporation under the name of the W. C. FIELDS COLLEGE for orphan white boys and girls, where no religion of any sort is to be preached. Harmony is the purpose of this thought. It is my desire the college will be built in

California in Los Angeles County." Does this violate the Rule against Perpetuities? 4 Scott, Trusts §401.8 (3d ed. 1967).

NEW YORK ESTATES, POWERS & TRUSTS LAW §9-1.3(d) (1967): "Where the duration or vesting of an estate is contingent upon the probate of a will, the appointment of a fiduciary, the location of a distributee, the payment of debts, the sale of assets, the settlement of an estate, the determination of questions relating to an estate or transfer tax or the occurrence of any specified contingency, it shall be presumed that the creator of such estate intended such contingency to occur, if at all, within twenty-one years from the effective date of the instrument creating such estate."

c. The Wait-and-See Doctrine

The first attempt in modern times to change the requirement that there be no possibility that an interest might vest too remotely was a cryptic statute enacted in 1947 in Pennsylvania. Pa. Stat. Ann. tit. 20, §301.4(b) (Purdon 1950):

> Upon the expiration of the period allowed by the common law rule against perpetuities as measured by actual rather than possible events any interest not then vested and any interest in members of a class the membership of which is then subject to increase shall be void.

In 1952 Professor W. Barton Leach began his attack upon the Rule against Perpetuities in its orthodox form. Dubbing the Pennsylvania approach "wait-and-see," Leach strongly approved it in substantially identical articles in the Law Quarterly Review and the Harvard Law Review.[29] The issue was joined when Professor Lewis

[29] Leach, Perpetuities: Staying the Slaughter of the Innocents, 68 L.Q. Rev. 35 (1952); Leach, Perpetuities in Perspective: Ending the Rule's Reign of Terror, 65 Harv. L. Rev. 721 (1952).

Neither Leach's style nor his reform ideas have suffered from a dearth of critics. To Professor Percy Bordwell, Leach "is a man of action, somewhat of a legal Billy Graham, who is not content until he has converted others to his views and seen the law changed in accordance with his ideas." Bordwell, Perpetuities From the Point of View of the Draughtsman, 11 Rutgers L. Rev. 429, 431 (1957). To Professor Philip Mechem,

"Mr. Leach, the great protagonist of wait-and-see, cheers the Pennsylvania legislators as hardy pioneers. 'Oh pioneers' apostrophised Walt Whitman, and Leach goes along. Yet, I suspect that hardy pioneers may not be quite what the doctor ordered in this area; there are reasons to think they acted too hardily and too hastily. . . .

"Mr. Leach is a property teacher; they are, by common repute, a conservative folk. Yet, much as I respect him, I have to say that in his crusading he has employed some rather intemperate language. If a use of the pathetic fallacy may be pardoned, I cannot help enjoying the thought of how the entrails of the venerable Law Quarterly Review must have quivered as it gave birth to an article entitled: 'Staying the Slaughter of the Innocents.' In the less prim Harvard Law Review the article appeared under the name of 'Ending the Rule's Reign of Terror.' . . .

"Pennsylvania has rushed blindly into legislation, to me unsound in theory, certainly wholly alien to the common-law concept, incomprehensible, unpredictable. Very sad. I hope we here may do something about it before it is too late. And you from other states — when some enthusiast starts a great hurrah for this new-fangled legislation, I hope you will at least adjure your brothers

Simes in the Michigan Law Review rose to attack both the policy implications and the workability of the wait-and-see approach.[30] These articles sparked a debate that has raged on to the present day.

MERCHANTS NATIONAL BANK v. CURTIS

Supreme Court of New Hampshire, 1953

98 *N.H.* 225, 97 *A.2d* 207

[Testatrix died in 1902, devising a life estate in realty to her son Edward Harrington and her daughter Delana B. Curtis, remainder "to my Grand Daughter Margaret May Curtis, and her heirs forever." The will further provided:

> Fifth: In the event of either of my children having other heirs of their body, surviving them such heir or heirs shall share equally with Margaret May Curtis, and in that event I give bequeath and devise my estate to them, and their heirs, on the death of my children.
>
> Sixth: If my Grand Daughter Margaret May Curtis or other grand children shall survive both of my children and shall have and leave no heirs of her or their body, then and in that event, I give, bequeath and devise all my estate unto my brothers and sisters then living and to the representatives of those not living, and to my late husbands niece, Almeda S. Goyscan formerly Almeda S. Harrington, in equal shares. . . .

No other grandchildren were born. The life tenants died, survived by Margaret May Curtis. Margaret May died without leaving issue. The gift over to the designated relatives in Clause Sixth was claimed to be void under the Rule against Perpetuities.]

KENISON, C.J.[31] . . . The rule against perpetuities, hereinafter called the rule, prevails in this state (Gale v. Gale, 85 N.H. 358) but it has never been "remorselessly applied" as advocated by Gray in "The Rule against Perpetuities" (4th ed.) s. 629. The genesis of the modified rule in New Hampshire began in 1891 with Ed-

---

to think the matter over most prayerfully. Looking before leaping is much better than waiting and seeing." Mechem, Further Thoughts on the Pennsylvania Perpetuities Legislation, 107 U. Pa. L. Rev. 965, 966, 983 (1959).

For Leach's reply "in a somewhat similar vein," see Leach, Perpetuities Legislation: Hail Pennsylvania! 108 U. Pa. L. Rev. 1124 (1960), in which he brands various critics as "irreconcilable; they were brought up on the Gospel according to Gray and seem determined to die in the true faith, fundamentalists to the end." Further, — but no; all of these articles merit reading in the unexpurgated version.

30 Simes, Is the Rule Against Perpetuities Doomed? The "Wait and See" Doctrine, 52 Mich. L. Rev. 179 (1953).

31 Mr. Justice Kenison is hailed as one of our greatest judges in Schwartz, Mr. Justice Kenison and Creative Continuity in Perpetuities Law, 48 B.U.L. Rev. 207 (1968). In Bassett's Estate, 104 N.H. 504, 190 A.2d 415, 98 A.L.R.2d 1281 (1963), Chief Justice Kenison, writing for the court, rejected the fertile octogenarian rule in a trust termination case and implied that it would be rejected in perpetuities cases as well. — EDS.

gerly v. Barker, 66 N.H. 434, when a gift of a remainder interest to grandchildren reaching forty years of age, which offended the rule, was cut down to a gift to grandchildren reaching twenty-one years of age so as to not offend the rule. This decision was bitterly assailed by Gray in his treatise (appendix G) since he thought it was a dangerous thing to tamper with this ancient English rule "which is concatenated with almost mathematical precision." Gray, supra, s. 871. Nevertheless, Edgerly v. Barker, supra, has been followed in subsequent decisions in this state and continues to remain in good standing here. Wentworth v. Wentworth, 77 N.H. 400; Flanders v. Parker, 80 N.H. 566; Gale v. Gale, supra; Amoskeag Trust Company v. Haskell, 96 N.H. 89, 91. See Quarles, The Cy Pres Doctrine: Its Application to Cases Involving the Rule against Perpetuities and Trusts for Accumulation, 21 N.Y.U.L.Q. Rev. 384 (1946). In England the same result has been achieved by legislation. Laws of Property Act, 1925, 15 Geo. V., c. 20, s. 163.

The rationale of the Barker case was that, wherever possible, a will should be construed to carry out the primary intent to accomplish a legal testamentary disposition even though the will may have inadvertently exposed a secondary intent to accomplish the testamentary disposition in an ineffective manner. That rationale has been applied in many recent will cases that have not involved the rule itself. "Traditionally, the courts of this jurisdiction have shown a signal regard for the intent of the testator . . . at times at the expense of other recognized principles deemed less cogent in their application. Cf. Edgerly v. Barker, 66 N.H. 434." Petition of Wolcott, 95 N.H. 23, 26. The same thought received expression in different language in Burtman v. Butman, 97 N.H. 254, 258: "Probably no jurisdiction has stood more steadfastly for giving effect to the intention of the testator rather than to arbitrary rules of law than New Hampshire." The refusal of this court to apply in unmodified form common law principles which defeat normal and reasonable estate plans has not been limited to wills but applies to conveyances as well. Therrien v. Therrien, 94 N.H. 66.

The rule is a technical one, difficult of application and is often enforced to frustrate testamentary intent although the policy of the rule may not require such enforcement in a particular case. It is not surprising, therefore, that there has been an increasing tendency to avoid the application of the rule by various judicial techniques. There is a constructional preference for considering interests vested rather than contingent. Upton v. White, 92 N.H. 221. "The public interest in keeping *the destructive force of the rule against perpetuities within reasonable limits* is a considerable present factor supporting the public interest in that construction which accomplishes the earlier vesting." 3 Restatement, Property, s. 243, comment i. (Emphasis supplied). If a gift is made upon alternative contingencies, one of which might be remote, while the other is not, the gift is valid where the second contingency actually happens. This doctrine is used to prevent the application of the rule in many cases. Anno. 64 A.L.R. 1077. "Essentially this represents a revulsion against the rule requiring absolute certainty of vesting as viewed from the creation of the interest. . . . Courts have a strong tendency to 'wait and see' wherever possible." 6 American Law of Property (1952) s. 24.54. These techniques have the salutary effect of avoiding the punitive and technical aspects of the rule but at the same time confirming the policy and purpose of the rule within reasonable limits. Wentworth v. Wentworth, 77 N.H. 400.

Clause sixth of the will is capable of at least two possible constructions. The first construction is that clause sixth created two contingencies upon which it would take effect: one to occur, if at all, on the death of Margaret May Curtis; the other to occur, if at all, on the death of unborn grandchildren. Since the first contingency actually occurred and is within the period of perpetuities, the gift may be considered valid. A closely parallel case is Springfield Safe Deposit & Trust Co. v. Ireland, 268 Mass. 62. Under this construction the event occurs at the death of Margaret May Curtis, a life in being, and clause sixth would not be considered violative of the rule.

The second possible construction of this sixth clause is the one urged by the Bean-Quirin interests. They argue that the will gives the brothers and sisters an executory interest upon a single contingency which may occur at the death of as yet unborn grandchildren. While this is not the only construction that the clause is susceptible of, it is not a labored one. There is no doubt that, if there had been another grandchild who died after Margaret May Curtis without leaving heirs of his body, this event would have occurred beyond the period allowed by the rule against perpetuities.

Assuming this second construction to be permissible, we come to the crucial question whether we are justified in deciding the perpetuities issue on the facts which actually occurred rather than on facts that might have happened viewed as of the death of the testator. There is little case authority for deciding upon facts occurring after the testator's death in a case such as the one before us. However, recognized modern commentators present convincing arguments for doing so. Leach, Perpetuities in Perspective: Ending the Rule's Reign of Terror, 65 Harv. L. Rev. 721 (1952); 6 American Law of Property (1952) s. 24.10; and a full study by a Pennsylvania law revision commission resulted in a statute that permits such events to be considered. Pa. Estates Act of 1947, s. 4, Purdon, Pa. Stat. Ann. tit. 20, s. 301.4. There is no precedent in this state that compels us to close our eyes to facts occurring after the death of the testator.

In the present case we are called on to determine the validity of a clause of a will that did not in fact tie up property beyond the permissible limit of lives in being plus twenty-one years. There is no logical justification for deciding the problem as of the date of the death of the testator on facts that might have happened rather than the facts which actually happened. It is difficult to see how the public welfare is threatened by a vesting that might have been postponed beyond the period of perpetuities but actually was not. The recent decision in Sears v. Coolidge (Mass.), 108 N.E. (2d) 563, allows the court to take a "second look" under powers of appointment. While this is not direct authority for doing the same thing with a devise or bequest, it is bottomed on the same proposition that the glacial force of the rule will be avoided where the interests actually vest within the period of perpetuities. 6 American Law of Property, s. 24.35. When a decision is made at a time when the events have happened, the court should not be compelled to consider only what might have been and completely ignore what was. Analogy may be found in cases where the validity of a remainder interest is not considered until the facts existing on the death of the life tenant can be established. See Orr v. Moses, 94 N.H. 309; Durfee Trust Co. v. Taylor, 325 Mass. 201.

At the death of the survivor of the life tenants, Edward Harrington and Delana B. Curtis, both of whom were lives in being at testatrix' death, it became certain that no grandchildren of the testatrix would be born after her death. This in turn made it certain that the gift in clause sixth of the will would in fact vest at the death of Margaret May Curtis Reynolds Vreeland, also a life in being at testatrix' death. Consistent with the principles above stated, the facts existing at the death of the two life tenants are taken into consideration in applying the rule.

We therefore conclude that clause sixth does not violate the rule against perpetuities. . . .

Case discharged.[32]

Alternative Contingencies

In the third paragraph of its opinion the New Hampshire court states one of the three exceptions[33] to the rule that possible, not actual, events are to be considered. When a gift is made upon either of two *expressed* contingencies, one of which must occur, if at all, during the perpetuity period, and the other of which might occur beyond the period, the gift is valid if the first contingency occurs. In such a case the court will wait and see. In order for this doctrine to apply the transferor must expressly split the contingencies himself; the court will not do it for him.

Case 6. T devises property to A for life, then to A's widow for her life, then on the death of A's widow or on the death of A if he leaves no widow, to A's issue then living per stirpes. The gift to the issue is good if A dies leaving no widow. Otherwise it is void.

Case 7. T devises property to A for life, then to A's widow for her life, then to A's issue then living per stirpes. Although the testator means exactly the same thing in this devise as in *Case 6*, he has not expressly split the contingencies. The gift to A's issue is void.

[32] Noted 33 B.U.L. Rev. 528; 53 Colum. L. Rev. 1158; 67 Harv. L. Rev. 355; 52 Mich. L. Rev. 305; 38 Minn. L. Rev. 679. — Eds.

[33] The other two exceptions are the "second look" doctrine applicable to appointments under powers and the same doctrine applicable to gifts in default of appointment. See pages 1044-1057. Another exception exists in those jurisdictions which have not abolished destructibility of contigent remainders. If a remainder will either vest or be destroyed within the perpetuity period it is valid. Thus: T devises land to A for life, remainder to A's grandchildren. A has no grandchild alive at T's death. If a grandchild of A is born during A's life, the remainder is valid; otherwise the remainder is destroyed at A's death. See Simes & Smith, The Law of Future Interests §1230 (2d ed. 1956).

In the Curtis case the court could have saved the gift by splitting the contingencies. Should a court split the contingencies when the transferor has not expressly done so?

SIMES, FUTURE INTERESTS
284-285 (2d ed. 1966)

There is another problem of severability which involves a single condition and which may be stated thus. Can a single condition precedent be re-worded in the form of two conditions so that one of the conditions can be held valid under the rule against perpetuities and the other void?

The classic example is presented by the case of Proctor v. The Bishop of Bath and Wells.[34] The limitations under consideration were substantially as follows: "To the first son of Proctor who should become a clergyman; but if Proctor should have no such son, then to Moore in fee." Proctor died without ever having had a son. The question was whether the limitations could be construed to include two conditions as follows: "If Proctor should die without having had a son, or if, having had a son, such son should die without having become a clergyman." If that could be done, then the first condition would be good; and since that is the one which actually occurred, Moore could take. The court, however, refused so to hold, and determined that the gift over was void. It may be said that this is rather strict in view of the fact that, if the testator had been asked whether these two contingencies expressed his meaning, he would undoubtedly have answered in the affirmative. It must be conceded that this rule is not a rule of construction to determine whether the testator would have desired to split the contingency. It is simply a rule as to the form of the language. If the testator has not stated the condition in the form of two contingencies, the court will not do it for him.

The justification for the rule is much the same as one of the arguments commonly urged against the wait-and-see doctrine. If we were to allow the splitting of contingencies, the validity of the interest would be left in a state of uncertainty until the contingency named in the limitation happened. For the possible contingencies into which a condition precedent might be resolved are well nigh infinite. But until the condition precedent named has occurred, we do not know how to split the contingencies in such a way as to make one of them valid. Thus, if we were to split contingencies in the case just discussed, we could say that one contingency is "If Proctor has no son who becomes a clergyman in Proctor's lifetime"; or "If Proctor has no son who becomes a clergyman in Moore's lifetime"; or "If Proctor has no son who becomes a clergyman on or before the age of twenty-one." But until the contingency named in the instrument happens, we do not know just how the settlor would wish to split it. And although this splitting of contingencies could not have been foreseen by the settlor, yet, after it has occurred, we can say he would have desired it, since the limitation is thus rendered valid. But if we wait until the event

[34] 2 H.Bl. 358, 126 Eng. Rep. 594 (C.P. 1794). — Eds.

happens before deciding how to split the contingencies, we have, in effect, adopted the wait-and-see doctrine. And the validity of interests is rendered uncertain until the named condition occurs, in exactly the same way as under the wait-and-see doctrine.

In any jurisdiction which recognizes the cy pres doctrine, it is, of course, possible to reform a contingency which makes an interest void, and substitute another which makes it good. Invalidity under the rule that prohibits the splitting of contingencies might then have been avoided. But the process need not leave the ownership of interests involved in a state of uncertainty, since the limitations can, and probably will, be reformed shortly after the inception of the instrument.[35]

The New Hampshire court was the first court to adopt the wait-and-see approach.[36] Subsequently wait-and-see statutes were enacted in a number of states. These statutes are of two types: (1) those that determine the validity of future interests by actual events existing upon the termination of any preceding life estates, a limited approach exemplified by the Massachusetts statute, infra; (2) those that apply wait-and-see in all cases, pairing it with a reformation power in the court, as is done in the Kentucky statute, infra. A third kind of wait-and-see statute, enacted in England, New Zealand, Ontario, and several of the Australian states, adopts full-scale wait-and-see but does not couple it with a cy pres power.

The arguments against wait-and-see are, in summary form, two. The first objection is that the inability to determine the validity of an interest while we are waiting-to-see will cause inconvenience and, if the interest in question is a future interest in land, will render the property virtually inalienable for the waiting period. The proponents of wait-and-see have replied that where life estates are created, in some states courts have traditionally refused to rule upon the validity of the remainders until the life estates have expired, and that this practice has led to little inconvenience. They have also suggested that a future interest which may turn out to be void or valid, depending upon events, is just another of the species of contingent interests long recognized by the law.

The second objection to wait-and-see is more telling, and here is the heart of the case against wait-and-see. *Who are the measuring lives?* Under the common law Rule any person can be a measuring life so long as you can prove that some event which will necessarily happen within his life or at his death will insure vesting or failure of the interest within twenty-one years of his death. The certainty of vesting requirement governed the selection of measuring lives. Once the requirement of

[35] Professor Robert L. Fletcher has suggested that the rule in Proctor v. Bishop of Bath and Wells be changed. He proposes to sort out the various dispositions possible under a particular instrument, treat each one as having been separately stated, and then let each stand or fall according to the Rule. Fletcher, A Rule of Discrete Invalidity: Perpetuities Reform Without Waiting, 20 Stan. L. Rev. 459 (1968). — Eds.

[36] In Phelps v. Shropshire, 254 Miss. 777, 183 So. 2d 158, 20 A.L.R.3d 1086 (1966), the Mississippi court adopted wait-and-see. It had earlier adopted cy pres. Carter v. Berry, 243 Miss. 321, 140 So. 2d 843 (1962).

initial certainty is removed and a wait-and-see rule is introduced, there arises the difficult problem of defining the measuring lives.[37] It has even been asserted that under wait-and-see, any person who was alive at testator's death can be a measuring life.[38]

The Massachusetts statute adopted a specific standard to measure the period of waiting: If the interest is limited to take effect upon the termination of one or more life estates given to persons in being, you wait until the termination of such life estates and determine the validity of the interests on the basis of facts then existing. Under this statute there are no problems about who the measuring lives are, but the statute, restricted in scope, in some cases does not change the results regarded as indefensible by the proponents of wait-and-see. For example, the Massachusetts act does not apply to a bequest "to my issue per stirpes living at the time of the distribution of my estate," or "to the first child of A to become a physician."

A later statute in Vermont[39] adopted full-scale wait-and-see and cy pres, but made no attempt to specify the measuring lives. In this respect it was similar to the pioneering Pennsylvania statute, supra. Supporters of the Vermont and Pennsylvania type statutes believe that courts will be able to work out in a few cases the measuring lives and that any resulting uncertainty and inconvenience is a reasonable price to pay for eliminating the harsh results of the common law Rule. In England the Law Reform Committee recommended that a wait-and-see statute be enacted without specifying the measuring lives (the English rejected cy pres). Parliament was unhappy with this, however, and the wait-and-see statute finally enacted contained a catalogue of lives that must be used to measure the perpetuity period.[40] These provisions have been sharply criticized as both unnecessary and formidably complex.[41]

The Kentucky statute adopting wait-and-see and cy pres attempted to strike a middle ground between the Vermont statute and specifying a detailed list of measuring lives for all transfers, as the English subsequently did. The statute requires that the measuring lives must have a "causal relationship" to vesting.[42] What is a

[37] The Western Australia Law Reform (Property, Perpetuities, and Succession) Act of 1962 assumed the measuring lives under wait-and-see could be the same as under the common law. See Allan, The Rule Against Perpetuities Restated, 6 U.W. Austl. L. Rev. 27 (1963); Simes, Reform of the Rule Against Perpetuities in Western Australia, 6 U.W. Austl. L. Rev. 21 (1963).

In a unique statute, Illinois has adopted a wait-and-see approach to interests in trust, and has provided that the beneficiaries of the trust alive when the trust is created are the measuring lives. Ill. Stat. Ann. c. 30, §195 (1969, Supp. 1971). See page 1085, infra.

[38] See Simes & Smith, The Law of Future Interests §1230 (2d ed. 1956).

[39] Vt. Stat. Ann. tit. 27, §501 (1967). Similar statutes are Ohio Rev. Code §2131.08 (Baldwin, 1970) and Wash. Rev. Code Ann. §§11.98.010 to 11.98.050 (1965) (applicable to trusts only). See Lynn, The Ohio Perpetuities Reform Statute, 29 Ohio St. L.J. 1 (1968).

[40] English Perpetuities and Accumulations Act of 1964, §3.

[41] Morris & Wade, Perpetuities Reform at Last, 80 L.Q. Rev. 486 (1964).

[42] A similar provision is contained in the Ontario Perpetuities Act of 1966, §6, which states that a measuring life must be "a relevant factor that limits in some way the period within which the conditions for vesting of the interest may occur." Morris & Wade, Perpetuities Reform at Last, 80 L.Q. Rev. 486 (1964), suggest that this standard was inherent under the common law Rule and so applicable under any full-scale wait-and-see statute. For a contrary opinion, see Allan,

causal relationship? First, you determine what events can affect vesting and, second, you determine what persons can affect those events. Such persons have a causal relationship to vesting. If vesting can be caused by a person selected from a class of persons unreasonably large, such persons cannot be used as measuring lives because the Rule permits only a reasonable number. Perhaps the causal relationship test can best be understood by illustrative cases.

Case 8. T bequeaths $10,000 to the first grandchild of A to marry. A is alive and has no married grandchild. This gift will vest if a grandchild of A (1) is born and (2) marries. Anyone who can cause the birth of a grandchild is causally related to vesting. Hence A, who can beget a child who can beget a child, is causally related; so too are all of A's children living at T's death. All of A's grandchildren living at T's death are also causally related to vesting since any one of them can marry and claim the prize. The common law Rule requires the measuring lives to be reasonable in number; hence all persons in the world who might end up as marriage partners of A or his issue are excluded.

Case 9. T bequeaths a fund in trust for the grandchildren of A who reach twenty-one. A is alive, and no grandchild of A has reached twenty-one at T's death. This gift will vest if a grandchild of A (1) is born and (2) reaches twenty-one, but it cannot vest before (3) the class closes and (4) all members of the class have reached twenty-one. By principles explained in *Case* 8, A and all of A's children living at T's death are measuring lives. So also are A's grandchildren alive at T's death if the class closes when any of such grandchildren reaches twenty-one.

Case 10. T bequeaths the residue of his estate to his issue per stirpes living at the distribution of his estate. The measuring lives are T's issue living at his death. A class gift is not vested until the shares of the members of the class are absolutely fixed. By procreating and by dying such issue can affect the size of each member's share. T's executor, by distributing the estate, can affect vesting, and he can be treated as a measuring life. However, any successor administrator c.t.a.d.b.n. cannot be a measuring life since such person could be appointed from a class of individuals unreasonably large. (For the same reason the initial grantee of an assignable option to purchase can be a measuring life, but an assignee cannot be.[43])

MASSACHUSETTS ANNOTATED LAWS C. 184A, §1 (1969, Supp. 1971): "In applying the rule against perpetuities to an interest in real or personal property limited to take effect at or after the termination of one or more life estates in, or lives of, persons in being when the period of said rule commences to run, the validity of the interest shall be determined on the basis of facts existing at the termination of such one or more life estates or lives. In this section an interest which must

---

Perpetuities: Who Are the Lives in Being, 81 L.Q. Rev. 106 (1965); Maudsley, Measuring Lives Under a System of Wait-and-See, 86 L.Q. Rev. 357 (1970).

Professor Leach recommends that the courts in Pennsylvania, Vermont, and Washington read a "causal relationship" test into their statutes. Leach, Perpetuities Legislation: Hail Pennsylvania! 108 U. Pa. L. Rev. 1124, 1146 (1960).

[43] Mumma v. Hinkle, 20 D. & C. 2d 621 (Pa. C.P. 1958), noted 4 Vill. L. Rev. 144.

terminate not later than the death of one or more persons is a 'life estate' even though it may terminate at an earlier time." [44]

KENTUCKY REVISED STATUTES §381.216 (1962): "In determining whether an interest would violate the rule against perpetuities the period of perpetuities shall be measured by actual rather than possible events; provided, however, the period shall not be measured by any lives whose continuance does not have a causal relationship to the vesting or failure of the interest. Any interest which would violate said rule as thus modified shall be reformed, within the limits of that rule, to approximate most closely the intention of the creator of the interest." [45]

PROBLEMS

How would the Pennsylvania, Massachusetts, and Kentucky acts apply to the limitations in the following transfers?

1. The will in Merchants Nat'l Bank v. Curtis.
2. A conveys Blackacre to Trinity Church, but if it ceases to be used for church purposes, then to B and his heirs. Lynn, The Modern Rule Against Perpetuities 53 (1966).
3. T has two children, S and D. T devises one-half of his estate to S in fee. T devises the other one-half in trust "to pay the income to D for life, then to pay the income to D's children for their lives, then to pay the principal to D's grandchildren." Assume the following three sets of facts may exist at D's death: (a) all of D's surviving children were born before T's death; (b) all of D's surviving children were born after T's death; (c) D leaves four children surviving, two of whom were born before T's death and two afterwards. Lynn, The Modern Rule Against Perpetuities 70-74 (1966).

The debate over the wait-and-see doctrine has produced a spate of articles. The most useful include Browder, Construction, Reformation, and the Rule Against Perpetuities, 62 Mich. L. Rev. 1 (1963); Leach, Perpetuities in Perspective: Ending the Rule's Reign of Terror, 65 Harv. L. Rev. 721 (1952); Leach, Perpetuities Legislation, Massachusetts Style, 67 Harv. L. Rev. 1349 (1954); Leach, Perpetuities Legislation: Hail, Pennsylvania! 108 U. Pa. L. Rev. 1124 (1960); Lynn, Reforming the Common Law Rule Against Perpetuities, 28 U. Chi. L. Rev. 488 (1961); Lynn, Raising the Perpetuities Question: Conception, Adoption, "Wait and See" and Cy Pres, 17 Vand. L. Rev. 1391 (1964); Lynn, Perpetuities Reform: An Analysis of

[44] For an explanation see Leach, Perpetuities Legislation, Massachusetts Style, 67 Harv. L. Rev. 1349 (1954). Almost identical statutes have been enacted by Conn. Gen. Stat. Ann. §45-95 (1960, Supp. 1971); Me. Rev. Stat. tit. 33, §101 (1965, Supp. 1970).

[45] For an explanation see Dukeminier, Perpetuities Law in Action: Kentucky Case Law and the 1960 Reform Act 79-91 (1962).

Developments in England and the United States, 113 U. Pa. L. Rev. 508 (1965); Lynn, Reforming the Rule Against Perpetuities: Choosing the Measuring Lives, 1965 Duke L.J. 720 [Lynn's articles are collected in book form, The Modern Rule Against Perpetuities (1966)]; Mechem, Further Thoughts on the Pennsylvania Perpetuities Legislation, 107 U. Pa. L. Rev. 965 (1959); Morris & Wade, Perpetuities Reform at Last, 80 L.Q. Rev. 486 (1964); Schuyler, Should the Rule against Perpetuities Discard Its Vest? 56 Mich. L. Rev. 683, 887 (1958); Simes, The Policy Against Perpetuities, 103 U. Pa. L. Rev. 707 (1955); Smith, Perpetuities in New Jersey: A Plea for Judicial Supremacy, 24 Rutgers L. Rev. 80 (1969); Sparks, A Decade of Transition in Future Interests, 45 Va. L. Rev. 493 (1959); Tudor, Absolute Certainty of Vesting Under the Rule Against Perpetuities — A Self-Discredited Relic, 34 B.U.L. Rev. 129 (1954); Waterbury, Some Further Thoughts on Perpetuities Reform, 42 Minn. L. Rev. 41 (1957).

In 1958 a Committee on Rules Against Perpetuities was established by the American Bar Association Section of Real Property, Probate and Trust Law, to report on developments in perpetuities law and to suggest, if desirable, model legislation. The membership of the committee has changed from time to time, but the committee has been unable to come to any agreement upon desirable perpetuities legislation. In 1967 the committee, chaired by Professor Olin Browder, issued a Perpetuity Legislation Handbook, which contains a useful summary of legislation in this country and abroad. 2 Real Prop., Prob. & Trust J. 176 (1967).

3. *Consequences of Invalidity*

The general rule is that an invalid limitation is stricken from the instrument, and the prior valid estates take effect just as if the invalid limitation were not in the instrument. If the preceding estates are life estates they remain standing. Striking out an invalid remainder leaves a reversion in the transferor if the instrument is a deed. If the instrument is a will and the invalid interest is created by the residuary clause, there is a reversion in the testator's heirs. If the invalid interest is not created by the residuary clause, the property goes to the residuary legatees upon the expiration of the valid estates, but there is some controversy about the appropriate name of the residuary legatees' interest.[46] Thus:

> *Case 11.* T bequeaths $100,000 in trust for A for life, then to A's children for their lives, and on the death of the survivor to A's grandchildren in fee. T bequeaths the residue of his estate to B. T's heir is H. The life estates in A and A's children are valid and take effect. The invalid remainder to A's grandchildren is stricken out. B has a valid remainder in the trust res, which vests in interest at T's death.

If the preceding valid estate is a defeasible fee, the invalid divesting limitation is stricken out, leaving the fee not subject to divestment. It sometimes happens that an instrument first makes a gift to a person and then modifies the gift in some way

[46] See Problem 4, page 706.

so as to violate the Rule. In that case the modifying clause is stricken out, and the gift stands. Thus:

> *Case 12.* T bequeaths $100,000 in trust for A for life, then to A's children, provided that the share of any daughter of A shall be held in further trust for her life, with income payable to her, and on her death the principal shall be paid to her issue per stirpes. A has no children at T's death, and hence the provision for the issue of A's daughters violates the rule. The modifying clause beginning with "provided that . . ." is stricken out; A's children have a valid remainder in fee simple.

The foregoing general principles are subject to the doctrine of infectious invalidity.[47]

TAYLOR v. DOOLEY
Court of Appeals of Kentucky, 1956
297 S.W.2d 905

MONTGOMERY, Judge. This action was filed by Elizabeth D. Flynn Taylor and Lewis B. Flynn, Jr., against Edwin B. Dooley, seeking a declaration of their rights under the will of Asa Dooley, deceased. From an adverse judgment, appellants, plaintiffs below, have appealed.

The effect of the statute against perpetuities is to be determined.

Asa Dooley, the testator, owned a farm of some 2,400 acres in Clark County, Kentucky. He died in 1941, and was survived by Marian F. Dooley, his widow; Edwin B. Dooley, a son; and Elizabeth D. Flynn (later Taylor), a daughter. The daughter remarried after her father's death. At the time of his death, the daughter was about 43 years of age and had one child, an 18-year-old son, Lewis B. Flynn, Jr. She had no other children when this action was filed, but Lewis B. Flynn, Jr., was the father of three children, the oldest being six years of age. Two children were by his first wife and one by his present wife. The first two children intervened in the action, but the third child was never made a party. These two children were permitted to defend the action for all of the children of Lewis B. Flynn, Jr., both those in being and those who might be born thereafter.

The will and codicil of the testator were probated on October 21, 1941. He gave his home and household goods to his widow by Clause 2 of the will. She also received one-half of all his personal property and a dower interest in his real estate by Clause 3 of the will. By Clause 5, he gave his son, Edwin B. Dooley, one-fourth of all his personal property and one-half of his real estate (other than the home), subject to the widow's dower. His daughter also was given one-fourth of all his personal property and the other one-half of the real estate, subject to the widow's dower, but he restricted her interest in the property set apart for her.

It is this restriction, contained in Clause 4 of the will, which we are called upon to interpret. Clause 4 is as follows:

[47] See 6 American Law of Property §24.48 (Casner ed. 1952).

> I will and devise to my daughter, Elizabeth D. Flynn, one-half interest in my real estate, subject to the dower right of her mother, Marian F. Dooley, and one-fourth interest in all of my personal property, for and during her natural life, with remainder to the heirs of her body for and during their natural lives with remainder in fee to the children of her bodily heirs, and in the event she should die without bodily heirs surviving her, then the share herein devised to her shall pass to and become the property of Edwin B. Dooley in fee simple.

The judgment appealed from held that under Clause 4 of the will "the children of Lewis B. Flynn, Jr., including any that may hereafter be born, are the owners of contingent remainder interests in one-half of the real estate and one-fourth of the surplus personal property owned by Asa Dooley at the time of his death."

Appellants contend that the remainder interest in fee provided for in Clause 4 may not vest "during the continuance of a life or lives in being at the creation of the estate, and twenty-one years and ten months thereafter," as prescribed by KRS 381.220, and that it is void. . . .

Appellees construe Clause 4 to mean that the devise is to the daughter for life, then to her children for life, with remainder in fee to her grandchildren. Appellants say that the devise is to the daughter for life, then to the heirs of her body for their lives, with remainder in fee to the children of the heirs of her body. Under the first interpretation, the great-grandchildren of the testator would take the remainder, while under the second view, it is possible that upon his death the children of Lewis B. Flynn, Jr., the son, could take the second life estate as the heirs of the body of Elizabeth, testator's daughter. Consequently, the grandchildren of Lewis (great-great-grandchildren of the testator) would become the class in whom the remainder in fee would vest. Under either interpretation, the possibility of the ultimate vesting of the estate beyond the prescribed period obviously can be anticipated, and the uncertainty of its vesting is certain.

An ultimate remainder to great-grandchildren of the testator following successive life estates to his child and grandchildren has been held to violate the rule against perpetuities, as provided by KRS 381.220. . . .

The life estate devised to the daughter in this case vested upon the death of the testator. The life estate devised to the bodily heirs of the daughter will vest upon her death at the end of a life in being in a class, all of the members of which can be ascertained immediately. So much of Clause 4 of the will of Asa Dooley, deceased, as attempted to create a remainder estate in favor of his great-grandchildren, that is "with remainder in fee to the children of her bodily heirs", is void as violating KRS 381.220, since this remainder interest cannot finally vest until the death of all of the children of the daughter, which may be long after the death of any measuring life in being at the testator's death, and twenty-one years and ten months thereafter.

Since the provision of Clause 4 giving a remainder in fee to the children of the bodily heirs of the daughter is void, what becomes of the remainder in fee and what is the effect on the remaining provisions of the will?

Appellants contend that the invalid gift in Clause 4 to the daughter and her descendants fails and it is so connected with the part of Clause 5 containing a gift to the son that so much of both clauses as contains gifts to his children must fail because of the testator's intent to treat his descendants equally. Thus, he would die intestate as to those gifts, and the daughter and son would each inherit an equal share. They contend that to hold Clause 4 partially invalid without declaring Clause 5 invalid would result in an unequal distribution of the estate, that is, one-fourth to the daughter and three-fourths to the son, which would thwart the obvious intention of the testator to deal equally with his two children and their descendants. There is no question raised as to gifts being subject to the mother's dower right.

The general rule is that a remainder which is void because in violation of the rule against perpetuities does not necessarily render invalid the prior estate, but that the latter will be sustained notwithstanding the invalidity of the ulterior estate, when the two are not inseparable and dependent parts of a general testamentary scheme, and to uphold the one without the other would not defeat the primary or dominant purpose of the testator. See cases . . . in 28 A.L.R. 382, 75 A.L.R. 124, and 168 A.L.R. 323.

If the invalid limitation over is an essential part of the general testamentary scheme, and to uphold the prior estate without the void remainder would defeat the primary or dominant purpose of the testator, no separation will be made, but the valid part will fall with the invalid. Thus, the antecedent particular estate falls as well as the remainder which is void for remoteness, and the heirs at law are entitled to immediate possession, where the chief purpose of the testator is to tie up the estate and prevent its distribution until a period too remote under the rule against perpetuities. Where striking out limitations over which are void under the rule against perpetuities, and leaving prior gifts to take effect as though the limitation over had not been made, will work an unjust distribution of the estate by giving a portion of the testator's family a larger share of the estate than was intended, all the provisions will be declared void. If portions which are valid can be separated from those that are invalid and given effect, the court will do so. 41 Am. Jur., Perpetuities, Section 61, page 105.

These principles are discussed fully in Restatement of the Law, Property, Division IV, Sections 402 and 403. The effect, if any, of the partially invalid attempted disposition of the estate is determined by judicially ascertaining what would more closely approximate the original scheme of disposition if the testator had been able to consider the possibility of the partial ineffectiveness of his complete plan. When no mode of disposition desired by the testator can be discovered and used, the will is found to be a nullity as to the invalid limitations on the property, and the undisposed property is left to pass by intestacy. . . .

We, therefore, conclude that the testator intended to make equal gifts to his daughter and her descendants and to his son. The gift to the widow can be upheld without creating any injustices and without doing violence to his dispositive intent. Since the gift of the remainder in Clause 4 fails and results in that property passing by intestacy, the upholding of Clause 5 would create an injustice, since the daughter would receive one-fourth and the son one-fourth plus the one-half under Clause 5. This would thwart the obvious intent of the testator. Clauses 4 and 5 of the will are connected and dependent provisions in the dispositive scheme, and the property sought to be passed by those clauses, subject to the dower right of the mother, passes by intestacy in equal shares to the daughter and son.

This result seems to be in accord with the statute whereby a void or lapsed devise passes by intestacy rather than by a residuary clause. KRS 394.500. There is no residuary clause in the will under consideration.

Appellants also contend that Clause 6 of the will, which provides that the property passing to the daughter shall be held in trust, is also invalid for the same reasons as Clauses 4 and 5. It is obvious that the testator, by the provisions contained in Clauses 4 and 6, did not intend that the daughter was to have an unrestricted use of the property given to her. Therefore, we cannot agree that Clause 6 is likewise invalid, as there is no basis for holding that it would defeat the dispositive intent. To hold Clause 6 invalid would further thwart the testator's intent. . . .

Judgment reversed.[48]

PROBLEMS

1. What would be the result on the facts of Taylor v. Dooley if Elizabeth Flynn had given birth to a child subsequent to her father's death, such child had survived Marian, Elizabeth, and Lewis, Jr., by more than twenty-one years, and the Kentucky wait-and-see plus cy pres statute[49] had been applicable? Lynn, The Modern Rule Against Perpetuities 135-136 (1966). If the Pennsylvania or Massachusetts wait-and-see statutes[50] had been applicable? 6 American Law of Property §24.52 (Casner ed. 1952, Supp. 1962).

2. In the context of Taylor v. Dooley, is the result required by the following Pennsylvania statute better than the result at common law? What changes, if any, would you make in the statute?

PENNSYLVANIA ESTATES ACT OF 1947, §301.5

(a) Valid interests following void interests. A valid interest following a void interest in income shall be accelerated to the termination date of the last preceding valid interest.

(b) Void interests on condition subsequent or special limitation. A void interest following a valid interest on condition subsequent or special limitation shall vest in the owner of such valid interest.

(c) Other void interests. Any other void interest shall vest in the person or persons entitled to the income at the expiration of the period described in section 4(b).

[48] One year earlier, in Maher v. Maher, 139 F. Supp. 294 (E.D. Ky. 1956), the court ruled that the invalid interest passed to the takers of the last valid life estate. This rule, applied in Kentucky before 1938, was discarded by the court of appeals in Liggett v. Fidelity & Columbia Trust Co., 274 Ky. 387, 118 S.W.2d 720 (1938). — Eds.

[49] See page 996, supra.

[50] See pages 987 and 995, supra.

ESTATE OF CHUN QUAN YEE HOP
Supreme Court of Hawaii, 1970
52 Hawaii 40, 469 P.2d 183

LEVINSON, J. This case presents the question whether the orthodox common law Rule Against Perpetuities will be strictly applied to nullify a testamentary trust which violates the Rule or whether some part of the trust or all of it will be allowed to take effect. We choose to resolve this issue by applying the doctrine of equitable approximation (also known as the cy pres doctrine) so that the trust will not violate the Rule or its underlying policies and the testator's expressed desires will be satisfied.

The facts have been stipulated by the parties. The testator, Chun Quan Yee Hop, died on August 11, 1954 leaving a will executed on September 28, 1953. His wife, who is still living, his four sons and twelve daughters survived him. When this action was filed in 1967 his issue including children, grandchildren, and great grandchildren numbered 135, of whom not less than 85 were living when the testator died.

The portion of the testator's will in question provided that: "This trust shall cease and determine upon the death of my wife, Chun Lai Shee, or thirty (30) years from the date of my death, whichever shall last occur, ..." At the termination of the trust, the trust estate including principal and accumulated income was to vest in and be transferred to the beneficiaries with three-fourths of the trust estate going to the survivors of the four sons and the lawful issue of any deceased son, and the remaining one-fourth of the trust estate going to the survivors of the twelve daughters and the lawful issue of any deceased daughter.

On the advice of counsel that the trust might be in violation of the Rule Against Perpetuities, the trustees filed a petition in the circuit court asking for instructions. After all interested parties were duly notified and represented and after a hearing, the trial court determined that there was a well-founded doubt upon the following questions of law which were reserved to this court for answer and decision pursuant to HRS §642-1:

> Whether, under the Rule Against Perpetuities,
> (1) the trust is valid in its entirety and all provisions can be carried out in accordance with the language of the will;
> (2) the trust is partially valid and partially invalid, and, if so, in what respect it is valid and in what respect it is invalid, and what the effect is of such partial invalidity on the overall validity of the trust and the responsibilities of the trustees in the administration of the trust; and
> (3) the trust is invalid in its entirety, and, if so, what are the responsibilities of the trustees in the administration of the trust.

In resolving an issue which has bedeviled lawyers and engaged legal scholars since Lord Nottingham began it all in the Duke of Norfolk's Case in 1682,[51] we are

[51] 3 Ch. Cas. 1, 49, 22 Eng. Rep. 931, 960 ([Ch.] 1682).

aided by the very able briefs of counsel and a wealth of law review articles and treatises on the subject.[52] Fortunately, we are not confronted by some of the more chimerical characters and situations dealt with by Professor Leach in his writings. We are simply dealing with a testamentary trust which might ultimately vest in the residuary legatees at a time beyond a specified life in being (the testator's widow) and twenty-one years thereafter. Since the Testator's wife might have died within nine years after his death, there was no assurance at the time of his death that the trust estate would vest within the life of his wife or 21 years thereafter. The will expressly says that the trust is to cease and determine on the death of the testator's wife or thirty years from his death, *whichever shall last occur.* The trust, therefore, violated the orthodox Rule Against Perpetuities.[53]

The Rule Against Perpetuities is said to be part of the English common law and is therefore applicable in Hawaii. Fitchie v. Brown, 18 Haw. 52, 69 (1906), aff'd 211 U.S. 321 (1908) . . . (upholding the validity of a testamentary trust whose duration was measured by 42 lives in being plus 21 years). There is no legislation in Hawaii on the subject except the general provision of HRS §1-1 which states that with exceptions not relevant to this case "[t]he common law of England, as ascertained by English and American decisions, is declared to be the common law of the State of Hawaii in all cases, ..." This "common law" spoken of by the statute does not remain in a somnolent and sedentary state. We have repeatedly maintained that "[t]he genius of the common law, upon which our jurisprudence is based, is its capacity for orderly growth." Lum v. Fullaway, 42 Haw. 500, 502 (1958); Fergerstrom v. Hawaiian Ocean View Estates, 50 Haw. 374, 376, 411 P.2d 141, 143 (1968).

Since the Rule Against Perpetuities is a creature of judicial construction, any growth of the law with respect to it is purely one of judicial wisdom unless the state legislature chooses to act. As a judge-made rule of law, it is not so firmly ensconced in Hawaii that this court cannot deal with it like any other rule of judicial origin which must change with the times.[54]

[52] The leading article contributing to reform of the Rule Against Perpetuities was Professor Leach's famous Perpetuities in a Nutshell, 51 Harv. L. Rev. 638 (1938). The article was updated in Leach, Perpetuities: The Nutshell Revisited, 78 Harv. L. Rev. 973 (1965). A recent and comprehensive book on the subject is R. Lynn, The Modern Rule Against Perpetuities (1966). A comprehensive bibliography concerning perpetuity reform is found in Perpetuity Legislation Handbook 32-34 (3d ed. 1967) prepared by the Committee on Rules Against Perpetuities, ABA Section of Real Property, Probate and Trust Law.

[53] Since we decide the case on the grounds of equitable approximation (cy pres), we do not reach the merits of other forms of validating the trust which were ably presented by counsel. These included (a) holding the alternative contingencies "separable" and striking the invalid thirty year contingency; (b) applying the "wait and see" doctrine; (c) finding the gifts to the children and their respective issue to be separate gifts and treating each gift separately as to the time of vesting; and (d) holding the distribution of trust income to each of the children and their issue to be valid for at least twenty-one years on the basis that the trust provides for annual gifts of income. We do not intend to preclude such arguments and others from being raised in the future.

[54] See Tamashiro v. DeGama, 51 Haw. 74, 450 P.2d 998 (1969) (parent-child tort immunity abolished); Lemle v. Breeden, 51 Haw. 426, 462 P.2d 470 (1969) (implied warranty of habit-

It should be no surprise that this court has held on several occasions that various testamentary trusts have complied with the common law Rule Against Perpetuities using accepted techniques of judicial construction to keep the trust from violating the Rule. Queen's Hospital v. Hite, 38 Haw. 494, 506 (1950) (ambiguity in will resolved in favor of trust's validity); Manufacturer's Life Ins. Co. v. Von Hamm-Young Co., 34 Haw. 288 (1937) (creation of interest under a life insurance trust at death of testator). Yet no case in this jurisdiction has heretofore presented the problem whether a testamentary trust, which clearly violates the Rule Against Perpetuities because of a term of years extending beyond the permissible twenty-one years, is to be judicially salvaged in order to effectuate the testator's intent.

We do not mean to say that the Rule Against Perpetuities has outlived its usefulness. Unlike so many rules of property which were handed down from feudal England, this rule is of continuing vitality. This court said in Manufacturer's Life Ins. Co. v. Von Hamm-Young Co., 34 Haw. 288, 293 (1937) of the Rule Against Perpetuities: "This rule was not of feudal origin but has its support in the practical needs of modern times, and was devised in order to restrain the tying up of property in future estates for an unreasonable period of time."

The policy against tying up of property in future estates has a number of important aspects. One is the freeing of wealth so that it can be channeled into open commerce without subjecting it to the limited discretion of a trustee. Another aspect is that the rule is conducive to giving the ultimate recipient complete power of management and disposition over that which is to be his. He may then sink or swim on his own rather than be subordinated to the paternalistic control of a trustee. The last and most important policy is that of letting the living control the wealth here on earth, rather than allowing those who once owned it and have since passed away to retain some powers over that wealth. These reasons all support the proposition that it is wise policy to loosen the dead hand's grip upon the wealth passed from one generation to the next. Dukeminier, Perpetuities Revision in California: Perpetual Trusts Permitted, 55 Calif. L. Rev. 678, 691 (1967); L. Simes, Public Policy and the Dead Hand 58 (1955).

The policy against the tying up of property in future estates is not inconsistent with the application of the doctrine of equitable approximation of a testamentary trust. Limiting an invalid term of thirty years to the twenty-one year period prescribed by the rule does no violence to any of the above policies or to the testator's general intent. The judicial recognition of a decedent's general testamentary intent has been recognized in an analogous body of law which applies the doctrine of equitable approximation to a charitable trust which would otherwise fail. If it is impossible, impractical or illegal to carry out the specific terms of a charitable trust in which the settlor has indicated a general charitable purpose, many courts will authorize the substitution of another charitable scheme within the testator's general purposes. Restatement (Second) of Trusts §399 (1959). We should also keep in mind the analogies mentioned by Chief Justice Doe in Edgerly v. Barker, 66 N.H.

---

ability in lease agreements); Pickard v. City & County of Honolulu, 51 Haw. 134, 452 P.2d 445 (1969) (licensee-invitee status abrogated).

434, 462, 31 A. 900, 909-10 (1891): "The feudal doctrine of forfeiture for and by a conveyance of a larger interest than the grantor has is no part of our common law. . . . A lease for 40 years, made under a power to lease for 21 years, is good for 21. . . . Under a statute restricting to a term not exceeding 21 years the time for which a tenant for life can be empowered to lease, a testamentary gift to a tenant for life of a power to lease for 63 years is not void. If he makes a lease for more than 21 years, it is void for the excess, and no more." (Citations omitted.)

Our decision should not be influenced by the fact that it was the testator's intent to distribute his estate among his children and their issue according to a plan which may appear to some as lopsidedly favoring his male progeny. This was, of course, his right. The wishes of the testator could have been accomplished exactly as he wished without violating the Rule if the attorney who drafted the will had specified that the trust was to continue until 21 years after the death of the last survivor of his wife and all of his issue living at the time of his death but not to exceed 30 years from the date of his death. Without the last mentioned limitation the trust could have continued for nearly 100 years from the date of his death without violating the Rule.

We are not alone in judicially adopting the doctrine of equitable approximation. The courts of New Hampshire and Mississippi have applied this doctrine in varying degrees and circumstances.[55] The adoption of the rule of equitable approximation is further recommended by an overwhelming number of commentators[56] and, although the doctrine has judicial origins, it has been adopted by a number of state legislatures.[57] We therefore hold that any interest which would violate the Rule Against Perpetuities shall be reformed within the limits of that rule to approximate most closely the intention of the creator of the interest. In the present case, where the testamentary trust violated the rule by providing that the trust "shall cease and determine upon the death of my wife, Chun Lai Shee, or thirty (30) years from the date of my death, whichever shall last occur . . . ," the thirty year period need only be reduced to twenty-one years in order to bring the trust within the rule. In response to the questions reserved to this court we may then answer that the trust is valid in its entirety and all provisions are to be carried out in accordance with the language of the will with the exception that the trust shall cease and determine upon the death of the testator's wife, Chun Lai Shee, or twenty-one years from the date of the testator's death, whichever shall last occur.

[55] Edgerly v. Barker, 66 N.H. 434, 31 A. 900 (1891); Carter v. Berry, 243 Miss. 321, 356, 140 So. 2d 843 (1962).

[56] The cy pres doctrine was advanced by Judge James Quarles in 1946 in The Cy Pres Doctrine: Its Application to Cases Involving the Rule Against Perpetuities and Trusts for Accumulation, 21 N.Y.U.L. Rev. 384 (1946). This was a revision of his earlier article in 1904, The Cy Pres Doctrine with Reference to the Rule Against Perpetuities — An Advocation of Its Adoption in All Jurisdictions, 38 Am. L. Rev. 683 (1904). A current exposition can be found in Professor Browder's article, Construction, Reformation, and the Rule Against Perpetuities, 62 Mich. L. Rev. 1 (1963). See also Fletcher, A Rule of Discrete Invalidity: Perpetuities Reform without Waiting, 20 Stan. L. Rev. 459 (1968).

[57] Cal. Civ. Code §715.5 (1963); Idaho Code Ann. §55-111 (1957); Ky. Rev. Stat. §381.216 (1963); Mo. Stat. Ann. §442.555 (1966); 27 Vt. Stat. Ann. §501 (1959); Wash. Rev. Code §11.98.030 (1965).

It is so ordered.

KOBAYASHI, J. I dissent.

. . .

I choose to enforce the Rule under the facts of the instant case. The majority, in its opinion, has now caused this court to be added to the list of appellate courts effectuating an escape to the "harsh" application of the Rule Against Perpetuities. Our attention has been called to the various doctrines relied upon for said escape: such as the cy pres doctrine or the doctrine of alternative contingencies that are "separable," both of which are premised on giving effect to the alleged intent of the testator.

The contradiction of such thinking and avoidance is obvious: the proponents following either of the above doctrines must violate the testator's original intent. To say that an approximation of the intent of the testator is given effect is simply begging the question. In essence the majority of the court has "exercised" a power that it does not have: making a new will for the testator. The decision of the majority appears to be strongly influenced by the alleged fact that the attorney for the testator could have done a better job in drafting the will. It is amazing, to say the least, that the court would give substance or relevancy to the so-called failure of the attorney.

. . .

The undiluted application of the Rule Against Perpetuities was initially rejected in certain jurisdictions because the application of said Rule would have "shocked the conscience of justice."

One of the chief arguments expressed by one of the proponents of the trust in the instant case is that the testator's sons and the children of the sons of the testator will receive less if the Rule Against Perpetuities is strictly enforced. It is most difficult for this writer to agree that such a reason is sufficient to "shock the conscience of justice." In the instant case greater justice and equity are achieved if the Rule Against Perpetuities is strictly applied.

Justice Abe joins in this dissent.[58]

In Edgerly v. Barker, 66 N.H. 434, 31 A. 900 (1891), the testator gave the principal of a trust to such of his grandchildren as reached age forty. The court, in an opinion by Chief Justice Doe, reduced the age contingency to twenty-one. John Chipman Gray sharply criticized this case and the theory of cy pres.[59]

GRAY, THE RULE AGAINST PERPETUITIES
(4th ed. 1942)

§871. It is a dangerous thing to make such a radical change in a part of the law which is concatenated with almost mathematical precision. . . .

[58] Noted 84 Harv. L. Rev. 738; 46 Wash. L. Rev. 785; 28 Wash. & Lee L. Rev. 184. — EDS.

[59] Cy pres comes from Law French and means "as nearly as possible."

§872. II. *Fallacy Involved.* The doctrine of the New Hampshire Court in this case involves a fallacy. It speaks of a primary intent to give to persons and a secondary intent to give to them at a particular time, and it purports to preserve the primary intent while discarding the secondary intent by substituting another time. This assumes that the persons remain the same, and only the time is changed. But that is precisely what does not occur; with the time, the persons are changed. Take the present case. The testator meant to give to those of his grandchildren who reached forty; the Court gives the property to those of the grandchildren who reach twenty-one. There may be six grandchildren who reach twenty-one, and only one who reaches forty. In such case shares would be given to five persons whom the testator never meant to have it. There may be some answer to this, but it is a real and a very serious objection, and deserves an answer, and it gets none from the New Hampshire Court. The case is dealt with throughout as if the only question were whether the same persons should get the property at forty or at twenty-one. . . .

§886. IV. *Applications.*

A. Take first the present case. Here was a gift to grandchildren when they reached forty, the Court cut it down to grandchildren when they reached twenty-one, but why take that date? Why not give it to the grandchildren at once, without waiting till they reach twenty-one? The only answer would seem to be, "Although we cannot put off the period of distribution as late as the testator wished, we will put it off as long as we can." But that the Court has not done. Why not order the fund to be distributed among those grandchildren who are living at the end of twenty-one years from the death of both children? Or, better still, why not make the time of selection to be twenty-one years after the death of both the testator's children and of all his grandchildren living at his death? Or, again, why not make it twenty-one years after the death of all the students now at Dartmouth College? What can be said of the time selected by the Court, more than for any or all of these?

§888. C. Again (what the devise might easily have been in this case), — to such of the testator's grandchildren when the youngest reaches forty as are then of temperate habits. Would a gift to such of the grandchildren as were not drunkards at twenty-one satisfy the general intent of the testator?

§889. D. A gift to A., for life, after his death to any widow he may leave for life, and on the death of such widow to such of his children as are then living. Is this time to be cut down, and if so, to what period must survivorship be referred? The death of the husband? Twenty-one years after the death of the husband? The death of any wife born in the testator's lifetime? Twenty-one years after the death of any wife born in the testator's lifetime?

§890. E. To a church for a parsonage, but, whenever it is no longer used as a parsonage, then to A. and his heirs. Here is a general intent to have the property go over; under certain circumstances this can be done, under other circumstances it cannot; why not carry out that general intent under the former circumstances, if it cannot be under the latter? Why not allow it if the parsonage is given up within twenty-one years after the testator's death? Or within twenty-one years after the death of all the present members of the First Regiment of New Hampshire Militia?

§891. F. To the person who shall be Chief Justice of New Hampshire fifty years from to-day. Is Chief Justice Doe entitled to that gift? Is the Chief Justice who shall be in office twenty-one years from now entitled? Or shall the Chief Justice who attends the funeral of the last member of the New Hampshire bar now living take it?

BROWDER, CONSTRUCTION, REFORMATION, AND THE RULE AGAINST PERPETUITIES
62 Mich. L. Rev. 1, 19-20, 22 (1963)

Is there a significant difference between filling a gap which the draftsman left and filling one created by the invalidity of a particular dispositive provision? Reformation in perpetuities cases may prove less drastic than . . . [inserting gifts by implication, for] it will often consist of nothing more than the insertion of a saving clause inadvertently omitted. In a large proportion of such cases the insertion of such a clause will not alter in any respect the expressed course of distribution on the facts which in due course develop, but will serve merely to insulate the dispositive scheme against the infection preserved in the dogma about unlikely possibilities.

The doctrine of "infectious invalidity" is not without significance in this regard. When the invalidity of an interest causes other interests to fail because of an inference that the testator's intention would be better served thereby, the result technically is not reformation. But in such cases a court is actually deciding upon alternative courses of devolution which are declared either in the instrument or in the intestate law. The most significant fact in the process of selection is that a court has nothing more specific to go on than the donor's scheme of disposition as revealed by his instrument in the light of the surrounding circumstances. This is the same kind of process which would be followed if the court's authority were enlarged by the duty to reform. The only difference is that the selection process in reformation would not be limited to those alternatives provided by the intestate law. Although the possible alternatives in reformation are undefined, the duty to choose that one which most closely approximates the donor's intention serves in fact to confine the choice as much as under infectious invalidity. But since the possible alternatives in reformation are not predetermined, the prospect of finding that one which best preserves the donor's intention is correspondingly improved. In this view, infectious invalidity is nothing other than a restricted form of cy pres construction.

The established practice of dealing cy pres with charitable trusts which fail constitutes a precedent which should apply a fortiori to perpetuities problems. When a gift to charity fails, resort is had to a general inference of a charitable purpose, which is vindicated by substituting for the gift which failed a gift to some other charity of a like nature. . . .

The analysis of the cy pres principle in Edgerly v. Barker calls to mind an analogy in the law of powers of appointment. When a special power to appoint to a restricted class of persons is invalidly exercised, or even when it is not exercised at all, and there is no express gift in default of appointment, a dominant purpose is declared to benefit that class, which is vindicated by the implication of a gift to the class as a whole. At least where such a result is founded on a theory of an implied gift in default of appointment, such an explanation is nothing less than the cy pres principle as defined in Edgerly v. Barker.

Several states have enacted cy pres statutes.[60] They fall into three categories: (1) those that reduce age contingencies only; (2) those that adopt full scale cy pres; and (3) those that couple wait-and-see with cy pres.

NEW YORK ESTATES, POWERS & TRUSTS LAW §9-1.2 (1967):[61] "Where an estate would, except for this section, be invalid because made to depend, for its vesting or its duration, upon any person attaining or failing to attain an age in excess of twenty-one years, the age contingency shall be reduced to twenty-one years as to any or all persons subject to such age contingency."

TEXAS REVISED CIVIL STATUTES ANNOTATED art. 1291b (1962, Supp. 1970):[62] "Section 1. Any interest in real or personal property that would violate the Rule Against Perpetuities shall be reformed, or construed, within the limits of that Rule, to give effect to the general intent of the creator of that interest whenever that general intent can be ascertained. This provision shall be liberally construed and applied to validate such interest to the fullest extent consistent with such ascertained intent."

OHIO REVISED CODE §2131.08(C) (1968).[63] "Any interest in real or personal property which would violate the rule against perpetuities . . . shall be reformed, within the limits of the rule, to approximate most closely the intention of the creator of the interest. In determining whether an interest would violate the rule and in reforming an interest the period of perpetuities shall be measured by actual rather than possible events."

[60] Cy pres has been adopted judicially in Mississippi (Carter v. Berry, 243 Miss. 321, 140 So. 2d 843 (1962)) and seemingly also in Kansas (Estate of Foster, 190 Kan. 498, 376 P.2d 784, 98 A.L.R.2d 795 (1962)). See Leach, Perpetuities: Cy Pres on the March, 17 Vand. L. Rev. 1381 (1964).

[61] Statutes to the same effect are Conn. Gen. Stat. §45-96 (1960, Supp. 1971); Me. Rev. Stat. tit. 33, §102 (1965, Supp. 1970); Mass. Gen. Laws Ann. c. 184A, §2 (1958, Supp. 1971); Ill. Stat. Ann. c. 30, §194(c)(2) (1969, Supp. 1971).

[62] Similar provisions have been enacted by Cal. Civ. Code §715.5 (West 1970) and Mo. Ann. Stat. §442.555 (1952, Supp. 1970). Idaho possibly has enacted cy pres; the statute is ambiguous. Idaho Code Ann. §55-111 (1957) (applicable to trusts only). See Eckhardt, Perpetuities Reform by Legislation, 31 Mo. L. Rev. 56 (1966).

[63] Similar statutes are Ky. Rev. Stat. §381.216 (1962); Vt. Stat. Ann. tit. 27, §501 (1967); Wash. Rev. Code §11.98.030 (1970) (applicable to trusts only).

PROBLEMS

Apply the New York, Texas, and Ohio statutes to the following transfers:

1. T bequeaths a fund in trust for A for life, then to such children of A as reach twenty-five. At T's death A is childless. Lynn, The Modern Rule Against Perpetuities 34-35 (1966); Morris & Leach, The Rule against Perpetuities 36 (2d ed. 1962). Suppose A has one child, aged five. Should the age contingency for this child be reduced? [64] Pasley, Future Interests, 16 Syracuse L. Rev. 343, 350 (1964).

2. T bequeaths a fund in trust for A for life, then to A's children for their lives, then to A's grandchildren in fee. Lynn, The Modern Rule Against Perpetuities 67-74 (1966) (the Ohio statute).

3. The problems posed by Gray in his attack on Edgerly v. Barker.

4. A trust to provide Christmas and Easter gifts to children of the first three grades of the John Kerr School (held void for perpetuity in Shenandoah Valley National Bank v. Taylor, 192 Va. 135, 63 S.E.2d 786 (1951), page 927, supra). See the reference to Morris & Leach on page 917, supra.

BROWDER, CONSTRUCTION, REFORMATION, AND THE RULE AGAINST PERPETUITIES
62 Mich. L. Rev. 1, 5-7 (1963)

But those cases which wait-and-see would save can also be saved by reformation without waiting. In fact those cases in which there is a reasonable prospect that vesting will occur in due time are also the cases for which the appropriate cy pres remedy is most obvious. These include the cases where the possibility of remote vesting is virtually only theoretical, the famous booby trap cases which produced the original demand for wait-and-see: the "fertile octogenarian" and the rest of the company of improbable possibilities. These cases can readily be disposed of either by construing the remote contingencies out of existence or by an obvious verbal reformation in the form of a saving clause which leaves the intention of the donor intact.

In cases where the improbability of actual remote vesting is not so clear as in the celebrated cases just mentioned, the pattern of cy pres amendment will take a similar form. Anyone who deals with saving clauses at the drafting level will perceive that the greatest utility in such a device is to permit many desired arrangements under which remote vesting is possible but not probable. Suppose a testator wants to provide by trust for his son for life and then for the son's children, with ultimate distribution to be a share of the corpus upon each child's attaining the age of thirty, and with alternative provisions in case of a child's death under thirty. It is not expected that the son will have any more children than he now has, and the

[64] In England age contingencies are reduced only to the age necessary to validate the gift, not necessarily to twenty-one. English Perpetuities and Accumulations Act, 1964, §4.

testator would prefer not to distribute at so young an age as twenty-one. The basic scheme could, therefore, be stated in accordance with the arrangement outlined above, which would provide for the circumstances as they were expected to develop. A saving clause would then be added which would provide for a kind of emergency distribution of all undistributed shares upon the expiration of twenty-one years after the death of the last survivor of all the children and grandchildren of the testator's son who were living at the testator's death. Thus, in the event circumstances were to develop as expected, the dispositive scheme would operate intact and, if properly drafted, no perpetuities problem would be presented. Suppose now the draftsman lays out the initial plan but overlooks the necessary safeguard. If the will is attacked, the course of reformation seems clear. In fact, reformation of this kind may more closely approximate the intention of a testator in the age-contingency cases than a specific rule of reformation which in all cases reduces the stated age to twenty-one.

Even in cases at the other extreme on the scale of vesting probabilities, where it appears very improbable that the interest will vest in due time, the way to approximate the donor's intention as closely as possible within the limits of the Rule may be evident from the face of the instrument. As an example, consider the case of a gift in trust for the benefit of a testator's children and issue per stirpes, with a contingent disposition of corpus on the termination of the trust, which is stated to be "upon the death of all my children and the issue of my children." The testator has four children, some of whom have children. Here the necessary alteration suggests itself: restrict the duration of the trust to the death of all the issue of the testator living at the time of his death (or twenty-one years thereafter). Why should not such a modification be made whenever it is called for? Why wait to see whether vesting will occur in due time when it is extremely improbable that it will, and when the potential benefit of waiting can be built into the instrument as so reformed?

LYNN, THE MODERN RULE AGAINST PERPETUITIES 5 (1966): "It bears emphasis that reforming the Rule Against Perpetuities does not eliminate perpetuities problems. It minimizes them. It is significant that the word 'vest' continues to appear in reform legislation despite the censure which that word justifiably has evoked. 'Vest' has a comfortable ring, and the word dies hard. Lawyers and judges will continue to face difficult questions of construction under the Rule in orthodox, 'wait and see' and 'cy pres' forms. A mastery of the mechanics of the Rule will continue to be a prerequisite to solving a perpetuities question, irrespective of the form that the Rule takes. As outworn niceties of the Rule are discarded, new facets of the Rule appear. There is little evidence that the lot of the property lawyer has ever been an easy one. There is nothing in the perpetuities reform movement to suggest that it is about to become so.

> That I have done all my own sums correctly, I do not venture to hope. There is something in the subject [perpetuities] which seems to facilitate error." [65]

[65] Gray [The Rule against Perpetuities (4th ed. 1942)], xi.

4. *Gifts to Classes*

Under the Rule against Perpetuities a class gift cannot be partially valid and partially void. It must be valid for all members of the class, or it is valid for none. If the interest of any member can possibly vest too remotely, the entire class gift is bad. This rule was definitely established in Leake v. Robinson, 2 Mer. 363, 35 Eng. Rep. 979 (Ch. 1817), though it may have been applied in earlier cases such as Jee v. Audley.

In Leake v. Robinson the testator's will gave a life income interest to his grandson, William Rowe Robinson, with the remainder to such of William's children as should attain the age of twenty-five; and "in case the said William Rowe Robinson shall happen to die without leaving issue, living at the time of his decease, or leaving such, they shall all die before any of them shall attain the age of twenty-five, . . . unto and amongst all and every the brothers and sisters of the said William Rowe Robinson, share and share alike, upon his, her, or their attaining twenty-five." William died eight years after the testator; he was not survived by issue. The executors under testator's will petitioned for instructions as to the validity of the gift over to William's brothers and sisters.

At the time of testator's death, William had five brothers and sisters. Two more were born after testator's death but before William's death, and another was born after William's death. The court concluded that under the rule of convenience the class closed at William's death; hence the two brothers born after testator's death but during William's lifetime were included within the class, but the sister born after William's death was excluded.

> Then, assuming that after-born grandchildren were to be let in, and that the vesting was not to take place till twenty-five, the consequence is, that it might not take place till more than twenty-one years after a life or lives in being at the death of the testator. It was not at all disputed that the bequests must for that reason be wholly void, unless the Court can distinguish between the children born before, and those born after, the testator's death. Upon what ground can that distinction rest? Not upon the intention of the testator; for we have already ascertained that all are included in the description he has given the objects of his bounty. And all who are included in it were equally capable of taking. It is the period of vesting, and not the description of the legatees, that produces the incapacity. . . . He supposed that he could do legally all that he has done; — that is, include after-born grandchildren, and also postpone the vesting till twenty-five. But, if he had been informed that he could not do both, can I say that the alteration he would have made would have been to leave out the after-born grandchildren, rather than abridge the period of vesting? I should think quite the contrary. It is very unlikely that he should have excluded one half of the family of his daughters. . . . I am asked why the existence of incapable children should prevent capable children from taking. But, in Jee v. Audley, the mere possibility that there might have been incapable children was sufficient to exclude those who were capable.

In Leake v. Robinson there actually were after-born children with respect to whom the remainder might vest remotely. Given this fact situation, one explanation of the decision is that it was the product of a result-oriented court concerned about the unevenness of a distribution that included some grandchildren and excluded others. The difficulty, however, is that in the great majority of cases that have since invoked the class gift rule (dubbed the all-or-nothing rule by Professor Leach), the possible after-born child that causes the perpetuities problem is just that: a *possible* child who is the product of a fertile imagination.

The all-or-nothing rule requires that (a) the class must close and (b) all conditions precedent for every member of the class must be satisfied, if at all, within the perpetuity period. *Case 13* illustrates a common class gift that is void according to these principles.

> *Case 13.* T devises property "to A for life, then to A's children for life, remainder to A's grandchildren in fee." The remainder to A's grandchildren is void because every member of the class will not be ascertained until the death of A's children, some of whom might not be in being at T's death. If at T's death A has a grandchild, X, alive, X's gift is vested in interest subject to open up and let in after-born grandchildren, but it is not vested for purposes of the Rule, and it is therefore void. *Repeat: A remainder that is vested subject to open is not vested for purposes of applying the Rule against Perpetuities.* The class must be *closed* before a remainder in a class is vested under the Rule.

Class Closing Rule

Some gifts to a class may be saved through the operation of a rule which closes the class prior to the time it closes physiologically. Under the "rule of convenience" the class will close when any member of the class is entitled to immediate possession and enjoyment.[66] Thus:

> *Case 14.* O deeds land "to my daughter A for life, then to my grandchildren in fee." At the time of the transfer O has one grandchild, G, alive. Under the rule of convenience G or his administrator can demand possession of his share at A's death, closing the class and forcing distribution among the grandchildren then living and the estates of grandchildren then dead. The gift thus would be valid. If O has no grandchild alive at the date of the transfer, the gift to grandchildren is void, unless the old common law rule of destructibility of contingent remainders is still in force. If the creating instrument were a will, rather than a deed, the gift to testator's grandchildren would be valid regardless of whether a grandchild were alive at his death. Do you see why?

It does not necessarily follow from the closing of the class within the perpetuity period that the gift is valid. Every member of the class may be ascertained, but every member may not have satisfied some condition precedent; and this too is required.

[66] See pages 786-790, supra.

In a gift of a fee simple, the ultimate number of takers in the class must be fixed so that it neither increases nor decreases. Thus:

Case 15. T devises property "to A for life, remainder in fee to such of A's children as attain the age of twenty-five." The class will close physiologically at A's death (a life in being), but the exact share each child of A will take cannot be determined until all of A's children have passed twenty-five or have died under that age. Here is what might happen: Suppose, at T's death, A has one child (C-1), aged ten. After T's death A might have another child (C-2). Before C-2 reaches age four, A and C-1 might die. Since it would be more than twenty-one years after any life in being at T's death before C-2 can meet the condition precedent, the remainder fails.

Suppose a child of A is aged twenty-five at T's death. Is the gift good? (If you say yes, you have not mastered the principle illustrated by this case.)

WARD v. VAN DER LOEFF

House of Lords, 1924

[1924] A.C. 653

Viscount Haldane L.C. [Testator died in 1916, survived by his wife but no children, by his father and mother, and by two brothers and two sisters. Each of these brothers and sisters had children living at testator's death. Another child of a brother, Philip Ponsonby Burnyeat, was born after testator's death and after the remarriage of his widow. In 1921 testator's widow married Mr. Van der Loeff, a Dutch subject.

Testator left a will executed in 1915, and a codicil executed in 1916. By the will testator left his estate in trust for his wife for life, with the remainder to his children. In the event that he had no children (which happened), he gave his wife a power to appoint the trust fund among the children of his brothers and sisters, and in default of appointment the trust fund was to go in equal shares to the children of his brothers and sisters.]

About the validity of these trusts no question arises. But it is otherwise with the codicil made by the testator. It was in these terms: "I declare that the life interest given to said wife by my said will shall be terminable on her remarriage unless such remarriage shall be with a natural born British subject. I revoke the power of appointment among the children of my brothers and sisters given to my said wife by my said will. And I declare that after her death my trustees shall stand possessed of the residuary trust funds in trust for all or any the children or child of my brothers and sisters who shall be living at the death of my wife or born at any time afterwards before any one of such children for the time being in existence attains a vested interest and who being a son or sons attain the age of twenty-one, or being a daughter or daughters attain that age or marry if more than one, in equal shares."

On the construction of the will and codicil, two questions arise. The first is, whether the limitation in favour of children, contained in the concluding words of the codicil, is valid, having regard to the rule against perpetuities. The second is whether, if invalid, this new limitation and the wording of the codicil have been at all events efficacious as expressing a revocation of his bequest to children contained in the will. If the limitation to children in the codicil be invalid, and that in the will has not been revoked, then a further question arises, whether the gift in the will operated in favour of any children of the brothers and sisters who were not born until after the testator's death. Philip Ponsonby Burnyeat, who is one of the parties to these appeals, was a son of the testator's brother, Myles Fleming Burnyeat, but was not born until after the testator's death and the remarriage of his widow. It is argued against his claim that the life interest of the widow was effectively determined by the provision in the codicil and that the class of children to take was finally ascertained at that date as the time of distribution. If this be so, Philip Ponsonby Burnyeat is excluded.

P. O. Lawrence J. was the judge before whom this summons came in the first instance. He decided that the gift in the codicil in favour of the children of the testator's brothers and sisters was so framed as to be void for perpetuity. He held further, that the codicil operated to revoke the residuary gift in the will only so far as the substituted provision in the codicil was valid, and that the gift in the will in favour of these children, therefore, took effect, but merely in favour of such of the children as were born before the remarriage of the testator's widow. Philip Ponsonby Burnyeat was thus excluded. A majority of the Court of Appeal, Lord Sterndale M.R. and Warrington L.J., agreed with him in holding that the gift in the codicil in favour of the children of brothers and sisters was void for perpetuity, but held that the codicil revoked the gift in their favour contained in the will, and that there was an intestacy as regarded the residuary estate of the testator as from the remarriage of his widow. Atkin L.J. dissented, holding that the testator must be taken, as matter of construction, to have been referring in his codicil only to the brothers and sisters of the whole blood in existence when he died, just as if he had designated them individually. The provision in the codicil was therefore valid, that in the will having been revoked.

My Lords, the principle to be applied in construing instruments for the purpose of ascertaining whether the direction they contain infringes the rule against perpetuity is a well settled one. It was repeated with emphasis in this House in Pearks v. Moseley [5 App. Cas. 714], where it was laid down that in construing the words the effect of the rule must in the first instance be left out of sight, and then, having in this way defined the intention expressed, the Court had to test its validity by applying the rule to the meaning thus ascertained. It is only therefore if, as matter of construction, the words in the codicil, taken in the natural sense in which the testator used them, do not violate the rule that they can be regarded as giving a valid direction. Looking at the language of the testator here, I am wholly unable to read it as not postponing the ascertainment of possible members of the class beyond the period of a life in being and twenty-one years afterwards. No doubt if we were warranted in interpreting the testator as having referred only to the children of those of his brother and sisters who were alive at his death we might read his language in a way which would satisfy the law. But for so restricting the natural meaning of his words there is no justification in the language used in the context. He speaks of his brothers and sisters generally, and there is no expression which excludes the children of other possible brothers and sisters of the whole or half blood who might in contemplation of law be born. He has nowhere indicated an intention that his words are not to be construed in this, their natural meaning. I think, therefore, that the class to be benefited was not one all the members of which were, as a necessary result of the words used, to be ascertained within the period which the law prescribes, and that the gift in the codicil in favour of children of brothers and sisters is wholly void.

The next question is whether the codicil, although inoperative to this extent, was yet operative to revoke the gift to children of brothers and sisters contained in the will. After consideration, I have come to the conclusion that it was not so operative. There is indeed a revocation expressed in the codicil, but it is confined to the power of appointment given to the wife. It does not extend to what follows. That is, in terms, an attempt at a substantive and independent gift, and, as it is wholly void, I think, differing on this point from the Court of Appeal, that the provision in the will stands undisturbed. There is nothing else in the codicil which purports to affect it. It can make no difference that the class of children is a new and different class if the constitution of the new class is wholly inoperative in law. If it fails, then unless an independent and valid intention to revoke has been independently of it expressed, no revocation can take place. There is no such independent expression of intention here.

The only other point is at what period the class of children of brothers and sisters who took under the will is to be ascertained. I think that according to a well-known rule, the period is that of distribution; in other words, taking the valid alteration in the codicil into account, the remarriage of the widow with a foreign subject. Philip Ponsonby Burnyeat is thus excluded.

The result is that the judgment of P.O. Lawrence J. should be restored. As the difficulty has been entirely caused by the testator himself, I think that the costs here and below should be taxed as between solicitor and client and paid out of the residuary estate.

Lord Dunedin. My Lords, the main question in this case seems to me to be determined by what was said in this House by Lord Cairns in the two cases of Hill v. Crook [L.R. 6 H.L. 265] and Dorin v. Dorin [L.R. 7 H.L. 568]. In the former of these cases that noble and learned Lord laid down that when you wish to vary the meaning of a word denoting a class of relations from what the prima facie meaning of that word is — he actually said it of the words legitimate children, but the application is obviously wider — there are two classes of cases only where the primary signification can be departed from. The one is where it is impossible in the circumstances that any person indicated by the prima facie meaning can take under the bequest.[67] That is not the case here because probably in law, though scarcely in fact,

[67] Mary Jackson left part of her residue to "my nephew Arthur Murphy." Three claimants appeared: (1) a nephew named Arthur Murphy, residing in Australia; (2) a nephew named

the idea of other brothers and sisters to the testator coming into existence could not be excluded, but in any case the half-brother or sister was a real possibility. The second class of cases is where you find something in the will itself, that is, in the expressions used in the will, to exclude the prima facie interpretation. That also seems to me absent. He has used the words "brother and sister" without explanation or glossary, and I am afraid he must take the consequences.[68]

[The concurring opinions of Viscount Cave and Lords Blanesburgh and Phillimore are omitted.]

NOTES

1. Do you see why the class closing rule saves the gift to nephews and nieces in the will and does not save the gift in the codicil? Suppose there had been a nephew aged twenty-two at testator's death. Would the gift to the nephews and nieces in the codicil be good?

2. If you were drafting the codicil in the Ward case, you could avoid the perpetuities question by simply naming the brothers and sisters; i.e. "And I declare that after her death my trustee shall stand possessed of the residuary trust funds in trust for all or any the children or child of my brothers *John and Alexander* and sisters *Mary and Patience* who shall . . . (etc.)." The class of their children will close physiologically at the death of the survivor, and all their children will reach twenty-one within twenty-one years of that date.

Suppose your client wishes to give property to his daughter Sally for life, then to Sally's children for their lives, then to Sally's grandchildren in fee. Can you avoid the perpetuities problem by naming Sally's children instead of giving them a class designation? To wit: ". . . to my daughter Sally for her life, then to Sally's children, Arnold, Betty and Carl, for their lives, and on the death of the last survivor of such children to Sally's grandchildren in fee." The gift to grandchildren is good *if* (1) the doctrine of destructibility of contingent remainders is still in effect, or (2) a certain fact exists. What is the fact?

How should the gift to the grandchildren be drafted in order to avoid *any* perpetuities problem, regardless of the facts? McGovern, Perpetuities Pitfalls and How Best to Avoid Them, 6 Real Prop., Prob. & Trust J. 155, 160-163 (1971).

3. T devises Blackacre "to such of the grandchildren of A as shall attain the age of twenty-five." Unless otherwise stated, assume that no grandchild of A has reached age twenty-five. Is the gift valid

(a) if, at T's death, A is dead?

(b) if, at T's death, A and all of A's children are dead?

Arthur Murphy, residing in Southwaite, and (3) a man named Arthur Murphy who was the illegitimate son of Mary Jackson's sister. The court held that since there were two legitimate nephews who answered the description, extrinsic evidence was admissible to show that she intended the illegitimate nephew to take. If there had been only one legitimate nephew, no evidence as to the existence of the illegitimate nephew would be admissible. In re Jackson, [1933] Ch. 237. — Eds.

[68] *He* must take the consequences?? — Eds.

(c) if, at T's death, A is alive and one grandchild of A is twenty-five?
(d) if, at T's death, A is dead and one grandchild of A is twenty-five?
(e) if, at T's death, A is dead and one grandchild of A is four?

4. T bequeaths a fund in trust "to pay the income to A for life, and then in trust for the grandchildren of B, their shares to be payable at their respective ages of twenty-five." Is the gift valid if T is survived by A and B and

(a) the eldest grandchild of B is aged twenty-five at T's death?
(b) the eldest grandchild of B is aged ten at T's death?
(c) the eldest grandchild of B is aged two at T's death?

Suppose B survives T, but A predeceases T, and the eldest grandchild of B is aged two at T's death. Is the gift valid?

Suppose A survives T, but B predeceases T, and the eldest grandchild of B is aged two at T's death. Is the gift valid?

Gifts to Subclasses

Quite frequently testators attempt to tie up property for two generations with remainder in fee to the third generation, as in *Case* 13 on page 1013. If the will is phrased slightly differently from that set forth in *Case* 13, the devise may be valid at common law. The will must provide that upon the death of each of A's children (rather than upon the death of *all* of A's children), the share of such child dying shall vest in his issue. If it does, the issue of the children in being at testator's death can prove that their interests will vest in absolutely fixed shares at the death of A and of their parent, a life in being. Their interests are valid. The issue of A's yet-unborn children cannot offer such proof, since their parents are not lives in being, and their interests are void. This is known as the doctrine of subclasses or the doctrine of Cattlin v. Brown.[69] Thus:

> *Case* 16. T devises property in trust to pay the income "to A for life, then to A's children for life, and as each child of A dies to distribute the share of corpus on which he had been receiving the income to that child's issue then living per stirpes." A has child B, born before T's death, and child C, conceived after T's death. The gift to B's issue is valid because it must certainly vest in possession in fixed shares within the period. The gift to C's issue is void.

BROWDER, CONSTRUCTION, REFORMATION, AND THE RULE AGAINST PERPETUITIES
62 Mich. L. Rev. 1, 24-26 (1963)

American Security and Trust Co. v. Cramer[70] is mentioned first because of an interesting feature which puts to a test the practicability of selecting measuring

[69] From the English case of Cattlin v. Brown, 11 Hare 372, 68 Eng. Rep. 1319 (V.C. 1853). See 6 American Law of Property §24.29 (Casner ed. 1952); 4 Restatement of Property §389; Simes & Smith, The Law of Future Interests §1267 (2d ed. 1956).

[70] 175 F. Supp. 367 (D.C. Cir. 1959).

lives both under wait-and-see and reformation. A testamentary trust was established for the benefit of the testator's wife for life, then for his daughter Hannah for life. At her death the income was to go to the children of Hannah "then living or the issue of such of them as may then be dead leaving issue surviving" Hannah, and "upon the death of each the share of the one so dying shall go absolutely to the persons who shall then be her or his heirs at law according to the laws of descent now in force in said District of Columbia." Two children of Hannah were living at the testator's death, and two more were born thereafter. At the time of the suit, two of the four had died, and another died while the suit was pending. Mary, one of the children who was living at the testator's death, survived. In prior litigation over the same will the interests of the children were held valid, with a ruling on the ultimate interests reserved. In still another prior suit, the interest of the heirs of a deceased child, Hugh, was held valid, for Hugh was also living at the testator's death. In the instant suit, the interest of Mary's heirs was declared valid (in express recognition of the desirability of such a ruling despite the continuance of Mary's life interest), but the gifts to the heirs of the after-born children of Hannah were held void. Under the authority of *Cattlin v. Brown,* the "sub-class" doctrine of class gifts was applied to justify the separation of the good remainders from the bad.

How would this case fare under the wait-and-see doctrine? At the time of the suit it was evident that all remainders would vest not later than the death of Hannah's daughter, Mary, who was a life in being at the testator's death. Could her life be taken as a measuring life for all the remainder interests? The Massachusetts-type statute does not seem applicable. In Pennsylvania and Vermont no answer could be confidently given until the relevant statutes were construed. The Kentucky statute does not seem to help, for Mary's life does not seem to have a causal relationship to the vesting or failure to vest of any interest other than that given to her own heirs. If I understand Professor Dukeminier's elaboration of this requirement, this case does not meet the specific tests which he states for determining the causal relationship. Unless under the Kentucky statute a different standard may be used for reformation, Mary's life could not be used for that purpose. No difficulty is perceived, however, in applying cy pres in the absence of such a restriction. A saving clause could simply provide that the heirs of all the children of Hannah should be ascertained and the remainder vest in them no later than twenty-one years after the death of the last survivor of such of Hannah's children as were living at the testator's death.

QUESTION

In American Security and Trust Co. v. Cramer, is Mary a measuring life for the gift to the heirs of after-born children under wait-and-see? If Mary died before Hannah without issue surviving Hannah, the shares of the heirs of the after-born children of Hannah would be increased. Since a class gift is not vested until the amount taken by each class member is absolutely fixed, and Mary's death without issue can affect that amount, does Mary bear a causal relationship to vesting?

RYAN v. WARD
Supreme Court of Maryland, 1949
192 Md. 342, 64 A.2d 258

MARBURY, C.J. [In 1928 John R. Ward executed and delivered a deed of certain property to the Baltimore Trust Company to be held in trust. John R. Ward died later in 1928, devising all his property to his son, Frank R. Ward. Frank died in 1945, devising all his property to his wife, Olive. He also left three children, Ruth, David, and John. The trustee petitions for construction of the trust deed.]

The deed of trust gives the trustee full and complete power to manage, sell, reinvest, and otherwise deal with the trust estate, and to collect the dividends and profits and to pay over the entire net income in monthly installments to the grantor, John R. Ward, during the term of his natural life. It is further provided that ". . . during the life of the Grantor he shall have the right by one or more instruments in writing, personally signed by him and delivered to the Trustee, to withdraw from the operation of this Deed of Trust such sum or sums as he may in his absolute discretion see fit, such withdrawals, however, shall not be in excess of the sum of Fifteen Hundred Dollars ($1500.00) per annum during his lifetime, and to the extent of any sum or sums so withdrawn, the principal of the trust hereby created shall be reduced accordingly, or expended entirely." It is further provided by the deed of trust:

"From and after the death of the Grantor, the Trustee shall pay over the net income derived therefrom in monthly instalments unto FRANK R. WARD, son of the Grantor, during his lifetime, and upon the death of the Grantor's said son, FRANK R. WARD, or from and after the Grantor's death in case his said son should predecease him, the Trustee shall pay the net income derived from the trust fund unto the lineal descendants, per stirpes, from time to time living, of the Grantor's said son until the death of the last surviving child of the Grantor's said son, who shall be living at the time of the Grantor's death, and upon the death of the last surviving child of the Grantor's said son, who shall be living at the time of the death of the Grantor, the trust hereby created shall terminate, and the corpus or principal thereof shall be by the Trustee conveyed, delivered and paid over absolutely free, clear and discharged of any further trust, in equal and even shares unto the then living children of the Grantor's said son, and unto the issue then living of each then deceased child of the Grantor's said son, so that each then living child of the Grantor's said son shall take and receive, absolutely, one equal share thereof, and the issue then living of each then deceased child of the Grantor's said son shall take and receive, per stirpes and not per capita, one equal share thereof absolutely." . . .

The question before the court is whether any of the estates attempted to be created by this deed of trust are in violation of the rule against perpetuities. . . .

Where an interest or an estate is created by will, the question is determined by looking forward from the date of the taking effect of the will which is, of course, the death of the testator, and not the date of the will. Gray's The Rule Against Perpetuities, 3rd Ed., Paragraph 231, p. 205; 4th Ed., Paragraph 231, p. 235. Where the interest or estate is created by deed, its effectiveness vel non is determined as of the time "when the deed became operative." Bowerman v. Taylor, 126 Md. 203 at page 212, 94 A. 652, 654. . . .

The appellant Ryan suggests (without any citation of authority) that since there is an element of revocability in the deed, the effective date from which we must consider the succeeding estates is not the date of the execution and delivery of the deed, but the date of the death of the grantor. The element of revocability is the right of withdrawal of the original trust fund, not, however, to be "in excess of the sum of $1500.00 per annum during his lifetime". . . . The terms of the provision authorizing the withdrawal of the original principal do not clearly indicate whether this right is cumulative or not, that is, whether the right must be exercised each year, if at all, or whether the grantor could withdraw at any time, not only the $1500 allowed during that year, but also $1500 for each previous year in which he had not exercised the right. Since, however, the grantor attempted to put a limitation upon his own actions, and did not reserve to himself the right to withdraw any or all of the original principal at any time he saw fit, while reserving that right as to subsequent additions, we hold that the right should be construed as non-cumulative, and lost as to the amount authorized to be withdrawn in any year, if not exercised during that year. We are not advised what was his age at the time he created it. No matter what it was, we cannot assume, viewing it prospectively, that he would not live long enough to withdraw the entire principal. Until the grantor actually died, therefore, he had the possible right to destroy the trust estate by withdrawals, although this destruction could be only partial until the end of twenty-two years.

Professor Gray, in his work "The Rule Against Perpetuities" (3rd Ed., Paragraph 203, p. 175; 4th Ed., Paragraph 203, p. 193), states that ". . . a future interest, if destructible at the mere pleasure of the present owner of the property, is not regarded as an interest at all and the Rule does not concern itself with it." This statement is applied to revocable trusts in Paragraph 524.1 of the 4th Edition beginning on page 510. This paragraph is the work of Roland Gray, son of the original author, who died in 1915. The 4th Edition was prepared in 1942. In paragraph 524.1 a case is suggested where a conveyance is made to A for life, with a power of revocation, A being the settlor, and, in default of exercise, to A's children at 25. If the period of the rule against perpetuities runs from the date of the conveyance, the ultimate limitation is too remote, but the author states that it seems to be correct to take A's death as the critical date, because A is at liberty to destroy the future interest. He cites the prevailing doctrine that the remoteness of limitations under a general power to appoint by deed is to be reckoned from the exercise of the power, as a reason why the same construction, by analogy, should be used in a revocable deed. In that connection he approves the reasoning of the Supreme Court of Hawaii in the case of Manufacturers' Life Insurance Company v. von Hamm-Young Company, 34 Hawaii 288. The case, decided in 1937, involves the application of the rule against perpetuities to a life insurance trust agreement. The settlor reserved the right to revoke the trust agreement or change the beneficiary. If the trust became effective at the time of its execution, there was a possibility that the future interest might not vest within the required period after that date. On the other hand, if the future interest did not come into being until the death of the settlor, no transgression of the rule could occur. The court, on the authority of Gray and of other cases, determined that the effective date from which to view the future interest was the death of the settlor, on the ground that such interest was destructible at his pleasure up until that time. . . .

Restatement, Property, Section 373, states "The period of time during which an interest is destructible, pursuant to the uncontrolled volition, and for the exclusive personal benefit of the person having such a power of destruction is not included in determining whether the limitation is invalid under the rule against perpetuities." Comment d states that the required destructibility exists only when some person possesses a complete power of disposition over the subject matter of the future interests, and can exercise this power of disposition for his own exclusive benefit. The destructibility prerequisite for an application of the rule stated in Section 373 can exist when the power of disposition (or revocation) is not presently exercisable at the time of its creation, provided that the period, during which the exercise of such power is postponed, does not invalidate all interests created by the exercise of such power, and thus, in effect, invalidate the power itself.

These cases and statements from recognized authorities amply sustain the proposition that, where a settlor has power during his lifetime to revoke or destroy the trust estate, the question whether interests, or any of them, created by a deed of trust are void because in violation of the rule against perpetuities, is to be determined as of the date of the settlor's death, and not as of the date when the deed of trust takes effect. It will be observed, however, that the cases cited involve situations where the trust is revocable at will, or could be destroyed by a single act of the settlor such as a change of beneficiary in an insurance policy, or a sale of the trust property and the use of the proceeds. . . .

There is no case, so far as we have been able to find, which deals with a strictly limited power of withdrawal which can be exercised only over a period of years, and which cannot be used to destroy the entire estate until a number of years has elapsed. In the case before us, as we have shown, the estate could not be entirely destroyed during the first twenty-two years of its existence.

. . . That being so, we are unable to say that in a case such as the one before us, the trust estate is destructible, as that word is used in connection with the Rule against Perpetuities. . . .

There is, of course, no question that the beneficial life estate of Frank R. Ward, son of the grantor, was valid. Thereafter, the net income is to be paid *unto the lineal descendants per stirpes from time to time living* of Frank R. Ward until the death of the last surviving child of said Frank R. Ward who shall be living at the time of the death of the grantor. At that time, the trust is to terminate, and the residuary estates are to commence. It is apparent that Frank R. Ward could have had a son born prior to the death of John R. Ward, who could have been living at the death of John R. Ward, and who could have lived more than twenty-one years after the death of Frank R. Ward. The death of such child, if he were the last survivor of the children of Frank R. Ward, would fix the date of the ending of the trust estate and the commencement of the estates in remainder created by the deed of trust. It was quite within the bounds of possibility, at the time of the creation of the trust, that this date might be beyond a life and lives then in being and twenty-one years thereafter, plus the usual period of gestation. Consequently, it is agreed by everyone, and the court so held, that the remainders, after the termination of the trust estate, were void.

The gift of the beneficial estates pur autre vie, after the death of Frank R. Ward which gift, as we have shown, is to the lineal descendants per stirpes, *from time to time living,* of the grantor's son, might vest in one of those lineal descendants who was born more than twenty-one years after the death of Frank R. Ward, but before the death of his last surviving child. This is a class gift. In such a case, it is well recognized that if it "is good as to some members of the class, but is within the rule against perpetuities as to other members, the entire gift must fail. The general rule is that if a gift is void as to any of a class, it is void as to all of the class." Miller, Construction of Wills, Paragraph 328. The reason for this rule is that the courts cannot split into portions the gift to the class, and make these gifts what they were never intended to be by the grantor. . . .

The contention was made in this case, and upheld by the chancellor, that the gifts pur autre vie were not gifts to one class, but were gifts to three classes, since there were two sons and a daughter of Frank R. Ward who survived him and who were living at the time of the execution of the deed of trust. The chancellor said that, therefore, as to each of the classes represented by each of these children, they vested in the living children within the period. This result cannot be reached by considering what actually happened. It must be arrived at, if at all by considering what the grantor intended should happen. . . .

In the case of Turner v. Safe Deposit & Trust Co., 148 Md. 371, 129 A. 294, 295, the remainder of the estate was to be *divided* by the trustee, after the death of the testator's wife, "into as many parts as my brother Barreda shall have children living at the time of the death of my dear wife, the child or children of any deceased child . . . if any then living to be treated as representing his or her parent." After the death of "each of said children" his or her share was to become the absolute property of "his or her children" then living, with a per stirpes provision for children of deceased children. In the absence of children or descendants then living, the share was to go to brothers and sisters and their descendants per stirpes then living. The Court held "The final limitations in legal remainder were to distinct classes of persons who were to take the respective parts of the estate into which it was to be separated" and followed the rule quoted from Gray on Perpetuities, 3rd Ed., sec. 391, that "when, on a gift to a class, the number of the shares is definitely fixed within the time required by the rule against perpetuities, the question of remoteness is to be considered with reference to each share separately." . . .

We are unable to find in the case before us, as did the chancellor, that the deed of trust before us created three classes. Even though it is true that there were only three children of Frank R. Ward living at the time of the execution of the deed of trust, the provision in that deed does not divide the estate into shares as was the situation in the Bowerman case, supra. The words "lineal descendants per stirpes from time to time living" do not create three classes. On the contrary, they create one. There is no gift to named children of Frank or even to children of Frank. The gift is to lineal descendants which includes others than children. In the case of Perkins v. Iglehart, 183 Md. 520, 39 A. 2d 672, we held that a bequest to the children of a son then living and the descendants then living of his deceased children per stirpes created only one class, although a stronger argument to the contrary existed in that case than in the one before us.

As a result of our conclusion, we hold that the gifts pur autrie vie [*sic*] are void and the trust estate has now ended. As John R. Ward, by his will, left all his property to Frank R. Ward, who was his only child, the trust property belongs to the latter's estate.

Decree reversed.[71]

NOTES AND PROBLEMS

1. Why is not the gift of income to Frank's "lineal descendants per stirpes from time to time living" good for twenty-one years after the death of the grantor and Frank, on the theory that this is a gift of a series of separate annual income payments, each to a newly ascertained group? Gray, Rule against Perpetuities §§410.1 to 410.5 (4th ed. 1942); 4 Restatement of Property §383, Comment g, Illustration 5 (1944).

2. Why was it "agreed by everyone, and the court so held, that the remainders, after the termination of the trust estate, were void"? Since the remainders were to be divided into as many stirpes as there were children of Frank or their representatives *alive* on the termination of the trust, the division into stirpes is too remote. The doctrine of subclasses does not apply.

Compare the following devise, which appeared on the spring 1969 California bar examination: "Tibs devised Blackacre to Adam for life, remainder to Adam's children for their lives, remainder in fee simple to the issue of Adam's children by right of representation. Adam had one child, Sonny, when Tibs died, and a second, Yancey, was born a few years later." Can the doctrine of subclasses be applied to this devise? 4 Restatement of Property §389 (1944), Comments c and g; 6 American Law of Property §24.29 (Casner ed. 1952); Second Bank–State Street Trust Co. v. Second Bank–State Street Trust Co., 335 Mass. 407, 140 N.E.2d 201 (1957).

3. Suppose the grantor, John, had retained the power to revoke the trust with the consent of Frank. Would the perpetuity period begin to run at the creation of the trust or at John's death? N.Y. Estates, Powers & Trusts Law §10-8.1(b) (1967) provides that the perpetuity period runs from the grantor's death when he reserves

[71] Noted 47 Mich. L. Rev. 1226; 34 Minn. L. Rev. 152; 10 U. Pitt. L. Rev. 566. — Eds.

to himself "an unqualified power to revoke." To the same effect is Pa. Stat. Ann. tit. 20, §301.4(c) (Purdon 1950).

Per Capita Gifts to Members of a Class

In addition to gifts to subclasses, there is another exception to the all-or-nothing class gift rule where there is a gift of a stated sum to each member of a class. In Storrs v. Benbow, 3 De Gex, M. & G. 390, 43 Eng. Rep. 153 (Ch. 1853), testator bequeathed £500 apiece to each child of his nephews, to be paid at age twenty-one. The testator had two brothers living at his death. The court held that the bequest was valid for all children born to testator's nephews living at his death, and invalid for all children of testator's unborn nephews. The reason for this exception, as given by the Restatement of Property, is that "The amount intended by the conveyor to be received by each member of the class is ascertainable without reference to the number of persons in the class." [72]

PROBLEMS

1. Clause 7 of testator's will (which, according to the court, "was not drawn by a skilled draftsman") declared, "To all of my nieces and nephews, I wish that my Estate would provide a four-year college course to any wishing to accept such." Clause 8 devised the residue of testator's estate to his mother, wife and son in equal shares. Testator was survived by the residuary legatees, by several brothers and sisters, and by several nephews but no nieces. If you were representing the residuary legatees, how would you argue against the validity of the gift in clause 7? If you were representing the nephews, what arguments would you make in favor of sustaining the gift? See Crockett v. Crockett, 332 Mass. 564, 126 N.E.2d 363 (1955); compare Burruss v. Baldwin, 199 Va. 883, 103 S.E.2d 249 (1958).

2. T bequeaths $500 "to each of the grandchildren of A to be paid upon his or her attaining twenty-one, but if any grandchild should die under twenty-one, then his bequest should be paid to the surviving grandchildren." At T's death A is alive and has two children, B and C, alive. He also has two minor grandchildren, B^1 and C^1 alive. Several years after T's death another child, K, is born to A. B, C, and K each has a child conceived and born after T's death, denominated Bx, Cx, and Kx. There are thus five grandchildren of A: B^1, Bx, C^1, Cx, and Kx. Which of the following statements are true?

(a) If it is held that the class of grandchildren must close at T's death in order to distribute the residuary estate, then

(i) if Bx reaches twenty-one, he is entitled to $500.

(ii) if C^1 dies under twenty-one, his $500 gift is divided among such of B^1, Bx, Cx, and Kx as survive C^1.

[72] Restatement of Property §385, Comment a (1944).

(b) If it is held that the class of grandchildren does not close at T's death, but includes grandchildren whenever born, then

- (i) if B^1 reaches twenty-one, he is entitled to $500.
- (ii) if Bx reaches twenty-one, he is entitled to $500.
- (iii) if Kx reaches twenty-one, he is entitled to $500.
- (iv) if C^1 dies under twenty-one, his $500 gift is divided among such of B^1, Bx, Cx, and Kx as survive C^1.

In 1938 Professor Leach attacked the all-or-nothing class gift rule.[73] His arguments are hard to answer, but they have been accepted only by the Supreme Court of Mississippi.[74] They are summarized in the following excerpt.

MORRIS & LEACH, THE RULE AGAINST PERPETUITIES 130-131 (2d ed. 1962): "We submit that the analogy between the situation in Leake v. Robinson and the situation in Storrs v. Benbow is striking. In each case the testator wanted all children to take and thus to be treated equally; in each he describes the children by a group designation and not as individuals; in each the Rule against Perpetuities strikes down the gift to some children; and in each the question is whether the other children can take. Equally striking is the similarity between the situation in Leake v. Robinson and the situation in Cattlin v. Brown. In the latter case the testator intended the families of A's children to share equally; he described the families by a group designation — a class of sub-classes; the Rule against Perpetuities strikes down the gift to one of those families; the question is whether the other family can take nevertheless. And this time the courts answer the question in the affirmative. It is submitted that Storrs v. Benbow and Cattlin v. Brown are right and that there is no sufficient distinction between them and Leake v. Robinson to justify the difference in result. There is, of course, this difference: when the invalid gifts are struck out in the first two cases, the valid gift remains as it would be if all gifts were good, whereas in Leake v. Robinson, the elimination of the invalid gift causes the amount of the valid gift to be increased by eliminating the partial divestment which the testator intended. But as we have previously pointed out, this is no objection. Where property is devised to A in fee, but if the testator's grave falls into disrepair to B in fee, the invalidity of the executory devise to B causes A to get much more than the testator intended; yet it is well settled that A gets it. But in Leake v. Robinson and the cases which have followed it the courts failed, it is submitted, to recognize that they are dealing with a situation in which there is a valid interest subject to partial divestment by an invalid gift.

". . . [T]he All or Nothing rule is basically unsound."

[73] Leach, The Rule against Perpetuities and Gifts to Classes, 51 Harv. L. Rev. 1329 (1938).

[74] Carter v. Berry, 243 Miss. 321, 140 So. 2d 843 (1962). See Lynn & Carpenter, Applying the Rule Against Perpetuities to Class Gifts: The Influence of Leach, 43 Texas L. Rev. 37 (1964).

5. *The Meaning of "Vest"*

— Drawing by Saul Steinberg, © 1970 The New Yorker Magazine, Inc.

In Greek mythology Proteus was able to change his shape with relative ease — from wild boar to lion to dragon to fire and flood. But what he found difficult, and would not do unless seized and chained, was to commit himself to a single form, the form most his own, and carry out his function of prophecy. We can say the same about the word "vest."

Historically courts established a vested-contingent dichotomy to deal with all sorts of different problems: whether the taker of the interest must survive to the time of possession ("survivorship"), whether the interest may be destroyed by a gap in seisin ("destructibility"), whether the interest will accelerate into possession when the prior estate is renounced ("acceleration"), and so on. You met these problems in Chapters 11 and 12. Orthodox doctrine states that all the meanings and constructional rules developed to solve those problems are used by the courts to solve perpetuities problems (with one obvious exception, the vesting of class gifts).[75] An interest vested for one purpose is vested for all purposes. We may be forgiven for being a bit skeptical of the soundness of that proposition, remembering the words of that renowned fallacy-hunter, Walter Wheeler Cook: "The tendency to assume that a word which appears in two or more rules, and so in connection with more than one purpose, has and should have precisely the same scope in all of them runs all through legal discussions. It has all the tenacity of original sin and must constantly be guarded against." [76]

PROBLEMS

1. Apply the rules developed in Edwards v. Hammond, page 714 supra, and Festing v. Allen, page 716 supra, to the following bequests. A survives T. No child of A is twenty-five at T's death. Is the Rule against Perpetuities violated? Morris & Leach, The Rule against Perpetuities 45 (2d ed. 1962).

(a) To A for life, remainder in fee to the children of A if they reach twenty-five, but if no child of A reaches twenty-five, then to B in fee.

(b) To A for life, remainder in fee to the children of A who reach twenty-five, but if no child of A reaches twenty-five, then to B in fee.

2. Apply the rules developed in cases involving survivorship to the following bequests. A survives T. No child of A is twenty-five at T's death. Is the Rule against Perpetuities violated? 6 American Law of Property §24.19 (Casner ed. 1952).

(a) To the children of A who shall reach twenty-five.

(b) To the children of A payable at twenty-five.

(c) To the children of A at their respective ages of twenty-five, and in the meantime the trustee shall pay the income in equal shares to A's children until they respectively reach twenty-five.

Many learned judges and writers have long stated that a remainder given to an *individual* (not to a class) is vested under the Rule against Perpetuities if it is "vested in interest." A remainder is vested in interest if the taker is ascertained and there is no condition precedent attached to the remainder other than the termination of the preceding estates. Thus:

[75] Simes & Smith, The Law of Future Interests §§134, 1232 (2d ed. 1956).
[76] Cook, Logical and Legal Bases of the Conflict of Laws 159 (1942).

Case 17. T devises land to A for life, then to A's children for their lives, then in fee to B. B has a remainder indefeasibly vested in interest, i.e., B or his successor is certain to acquire permanent possession of the property in the future. Of course B will not acquire *possession* until the death of A's children, who may not all be living at T's death. His remainder therefore may vest in possession too remotely. Nonetheless, under orthodox doctrine, it is valid under the Rule against Perpetuities because it is indefeasibly vested in interest at T's death.

LETCHER'S TRUSTEE v. LETCHER

Court of Appeals of Kentucky, 1946

302 Ky. 448, 194 S.W.2d 984

[Dr. James Letcher in 1932 devised his "river bottom farms" to his son Gibney for life, then to Gibney's children in fee; if Gibney died without issue him surviving the farms were devised to a bank in trust to pay one-half the income "to the living children" of his nephew Hugh Helm and one-half to the First Presbyterian Church for the maintenance of the Dora Ford Letcher Church House, and upon the death of all Hugh's children to pay all the income to the First Presbyterian Church for the same purpose; but if the church ceased to maintain the church house as a memorial to Dora Ford Letcher, the farms were to go in fee simple to the Synod of the Presbyterian Church. Hugh Helm survived the testator and died leaving three children, all of whom were born before 1932. Gibney, Dr. Letcher's sole heir, died in 1942 without issue. His will devised his residuary estate to his wife Katherine. Katherine sued to establish her title to the land, claiming that the whole devise over if Gibney died without issue violates the Rule against Perpetuities. Agreeing with her claim, the trial court adjudged Katherine to be the owner of the farms in fee simple absolute. The three children of Hugh Helm, the church, and the Synod appeal.]

Latimer, J. . . . We find no difficulty whatsoever in the first provision of Item 2 of Dr. Letcher's will. Had his son, Gibney Oscar, died leaving issue, the estate then would have vested in fee simple in such issue. But, having died without issue, we must face the provision of the will after that point, and if the devise becomes violative of the rule at all it commences where the testator undertakes to appoint a trustee upon the death of his son without issue and directs that the trustee hold and manage the land until the children of Hugh N. Helm are dead. From that point we meet the real difficulty. Appellee insists that it is here that the violation of the rule against perpetuities commences.

. . .

In testing the validity of the will in the instant case, let us observe it, then, in the light of possibilities. At the time Dr. Letcher died and the will was probated, Hugh N. Helm was 51 years old and living. He had three children born in the years 1907, 1910 and 1917, respectively, all of whom were living at the time of testator's death. The trustee named to hold and manage the land was directed to pay each year one-half of the net proceeds to the children of his nephew, Hugh N. Helm, and the other one-half to the Session of the Church. In the light of that situation, throughout how long a period of time would it be possible for the trustee to be required to pay the one-half of the net proceeds to the children of Helm? . . .

The appellants take the position that the devise was to a particular class, namely, the living children of Helm. Consequently, they insist that those born after the death of the life tenant, if any, would not be permitted to share in the proceeds. They cite a number of authorities in support of their contention. But, it will be noted, that these cited authorities exclude the children, or members of a class, who are born after the time fixed for the distribution of the corpus of the estate. In the instant case there is no distribution of the corpus at all, but only a distribution of the profits, which is to continue until all of the children of Hugh N. Helm are dead. . . .

To take appellants' view would mean the adoption of a rather strained construction in order to avoid the application of the rule. Considering the obviously possible length and remoteness of time the trustee is to control and manage the estate before it passes to the Session of the Church in trust, we are constrained to believe there is a violation of the rule.

We now come to that portion of the will dealing with the estate after the death of all the children of the nephew Helm. Up until that time the trustee merely manages and controls the estate. The will provides "therefore, upon the death of all the children of Hugh N. Helm, I give, devise and bequeath the Ohio River farms to the First Presbyterian Church in trust with the direction that the net income be used first toward the upkeep of the Church House." It will be noted by the above that upon the death of all the children of Helm the devise is to the Session of the Church for the maintenance of some of its own property. . . . This church house mentioned in the will appears to be a residence adjoining the property of, and purchased by, the First Presbyterian Church. It was purchased in 1922. Some lien notes were executed by the church as partial payment for the property, which were afterwards paid by Dr. James H. Letcher. In gratitude to Dr. Letcher, and out of respect to the memory of his deceased wife, the church named the house "Dora Ford Letcher Memorial Church House." Appellants maintain that this church house has never been used as a place of public worship but is used for the meetings of the ladies' circles, for the young people, for the forum of men of the church, Girl Scouts, Men's Bible Class, etc. For all the purposes named above, meeting places are provided in practically all modern churches, and appear to be necessary adjuncts to modern churches. To say that the upkeep of this church house and its maintenance meets the intended meaning of the provisions of KRS 381.260 validating grants for "charitable or humane purpose" would be somewhat of a stretch of the imagination. . . .[77]

To this we have the added difficulty that this estate devised to the Session in trust is to be held as long as the First Presbyterian Church of Henderson may exist,

[77] In a part of the opinion excised by the editors the court held the trust for the Presbyterian Church also violated Ky. Rev. Stat. §273.090, since repealed, which prohibited any church or society of Christians from holding more than fifty acres of land. — EDS.

or until its Session shall decide to surrender its interest in the proceeds of the estate and cease to recognize the memorial. The testator hopes it will continue forever. But, be it 50 years, 100 years, or maybe 1000 years from now, the testator finally rests it in fee simple in the Synod of the Presbyterian Church. This final and ultimate devise . . . postpones the vesting of the title for a remote and indefinite period, violative of the rule against perpetuities. . . .

Appellant further insists that if part of the will is valid and part invalid, the valid part should be allowed to stand. That would be true if there were no disturbance of the entire scheme, or if there were separable parts. Obviously, the only separable part of this will is the first portion which gave a life estate to the son, and in the event he had issue, settling the fee in that issue. The vesting here is subject to no condition preceding it except the termination of the life estate. After the first separable part, the remainder of Item 2 appears to us to be one complete and inseparable scheme. To follow this insistence of appellants would result in a division of the testator's intent into two parts, the first being the intent which is consistent with the rule against perpetuities, and the second that which is inconsistent with, or obnoxious to the rule. By discarding the inconsistent and adopting the consistent, we would in fact be altering, if not destroying, the general intent, and substituting therefor a new or different one. . . .

By way of resume, let us then see what we really have before us — a testator by will undertaking to create an estate, first, a life estate which might become a fee-simple estate if the life tenant should die leaving issue. Upon the death of the life tenant without issue, the estate then moves under the control and management of a trustee for a period of time that can very possibly reach beyond the period set by the rule against perpetuities. Upon the death of all the children of the nephew, then, . . . to the Session of the Presbyterian Church in trust, and finally, after dangling through a number of years, or perhaps centuries, all dependent on the action of the Session of the Church, he settles it in fee in the Synod of the Presbyterian Church. . . . Were we to adopt the appellants' views, then, like the moving finger in Omar Khayyam's Rubaiyat which "writes; and, having writ, moves on," we would have an estate, which having commenced to move, moves on. So, on through years, perhaps centuries, it would go, but when and where it would stop nobody knows. We must, therefore, reject those views.

We conclude that the court below properly adjudicated the matter. Wherefore, the judgment is affirmed.

1 SCOTT, TRUSTS §62.10 (3d ed. 1967): ". . . (2) *Duration of Trusts.* If all the interests under a trust vest within the period of the rule against perpetuities, the fact that the trust may continue beyond the period does not invalidate it. Thus if a testator devises land in trust for his son for life, and on the death of the son in trust for the son's children for their lives, and on the death of any of the children his share is to go to a charitable institution, the trust is valid, since all the interests vest within a life in being at the death of the testator, namely the life

of the son. On the death of the son, his children have vested life estates, and the charitable institution has vested remainders."

SIMES, PUBLIC POLICY AND THE DEAD HAND 80-81 (1955): "And now I wish to make one final suggestion concerning legislative reform of the Rule. I make it with a good deal of doubt and uncertainty, because it involves a rather basic change. It is this. Instead of the requirement that a future interest must vest in interest within the period of the Rule, should we require that it vest in possession or enjoyment within that period? This, of course, would mean nothing less than that the Rule would apply to vested as well as contingent future interests." [78]

LYNN, THE MODERN RULE AGAINST PERPETUITIES 28-31 (1966): "That modern courts in perpetuities cases are abandoning the categories of future interests is to a fair degree demonstrable. That they are assimilating functional equivalents can also be shown. . . . The elusive line between contingent and vested remainders is disappearing altogether. But how judges decide cases in the absence of classification is not at all clear. . . .

"Courts are affected by the *probability* that events will occur in the sequence commonly encountered and by the eminence of the authority gaining their attention. Dissatisfied with the 'vesting' test for validity of contingent future interests under the Rule in orthodox form, they sometimes grope for a 'possessory' test suggested by Simes and endorsed by Schuyler.

". . . The heart of the matter is whether or not the donor has violated the spirit of the Rule Against Perpetuities, and modern courts, like Lord Nottingham in the Duke of Norfolk's Case sense that. A lawyer properly prepared to argue classification of interests is ready to demonstrate that answers to perpetuities questions do not necessarily lie therein."

BURTON v. HICKS

Supreme Court of Georgia, 1964

220 Ga. 29, 136 S.E.2d 759

HEAD, Presiding Justice. Item 4 of the will of Odessa Tritt Lassiter is as follows: "My house and lot 109 Peachtree Hills Avenue, Atlanta, Georgia, to be sold at the market price, also my automobile to be sold if I own one at the time of my death. Also all farming tools and my two diamond rings to be sold. All money from sales with all money on hand and U.S. Government Bonds are to be held in trust by my executor hereinafter named for twenty-five (25) years and then divided one-third to Norris Wilson Tritt, one-third to James Elmer Tritt and one-third to my niece, Dorothy Tritt Burton, in case she is living, if not, to be divided equally between the two nephews, Norris Wilson Tritt and James Elmer Tritt."

[78] For the details of a scheme to redefine vesting to mean possession, see Schuyler, Should The Rule Against Perpetuities Discard Its Vest? 56 Mich. L. Rev. 683, 887 (1958).

Dorothy Tritt Burton brought an action against Claud M. Hicks, as administrator with the will annexed of the estate of Odessa Tritt Lassiter. It was alleged that: the testatrix died on June 1, 1948; the defendant was appointed as administrator on June 7, 1948; he has performed all of the duties imposed upon him by the will except that he has not distributed the fund in his hands under Item 4 of the will to those entitled to receive it; the petitioner, Norris Wilson Tritt, and James Elmer Tritt are all sui juris, and have no intemperate, wasteful, or profligate habits; the petitioner has demanded of the defendant that he account to her and pay her one-third of the fund in his custody, which he has refused to do. It is asserted that Item 4 of the will "is offensive to the law of Georgia forbidding perpetuities and is, for such reason, contrary to law, and fully executed." The petitioner prayed that the will be construed and that "the court order, adjudge, and decree that the trust sought to be created by Item 4 of the last will of Odessa Tritt Lassiter has become fully executed, and that the beneficiaries named therein, to wit, your petitioner and Norris Wilson Tritt and James Elmer Tritt, are entitled to the property of every sort and kind in the hands of the defendant fiduciary, share and share alike, immediately." The trial judge sustained a general demurrer to the petition, and the exception is to this judgment.

Section 85-707 of the Code of 1933, which was in effect at the time of the death of the testatrix, provided as follows: "Limitations of estates may extend through any number of lives in being at the time when the limitations commence, and 21 years, and the usual period of gestation added thereafter. A limitation beyond that period the law terms a perpetuity and forbids its creation. When an attempt is made to create a perpetuity, the law gives effect to the limitations not too remote, declaring the others void, and thereby vests the fee in the last taker under legal limitations."

The two assertions of the petitioner, that Item 4 of the will offends the rule of law forbidding the creation of a perpetuity, and that the trust is fully executed and the funds in the hands of the administrator should be paid to the beneficiaries of the trust, are not consistent. In considering a will which attempted to establish a trust similar to the one in the present case, this court, in Fuller v. Fuller, 217 Ga. 316, 323, 122 S.E.2d 234, held: "There is only one specification of the time for the trust to continue which is 25 years. And this is unrelated to the life of any person therein referred to. The purported trust was in violation of the rule against perpetuities (Code Ann. §85-707), and is therefore void."

Since the trust attempted to be set up in Item 4 of the will in the present case is void, and there is no residuary clause in the will, the funds held by the administrator under this item vested in the heirs at law of the testatrix. Trust Company of Ga. v. Williams, 184 Ga. 706, 192 S.E. 913. The petitioner does not allege that she is an heir at law of the testatrix, and her petition therefore does not show that she has any inheritable interest in the estate of the deceased. The trial judge properly sustained the general demurrer to the petition.

Judgment affirmed.

All the Justices concur.

NOTES

1. In Burton v. Hicks who is entitled to the income from Odessa Lassiter's estate during the existence of the trust? There are three possible solutions. The income may be paid to Odessa's heirs as property not disposed of; it may be accumulated for the persons who ultimately take the principal; or one-third of the income may be paid to Norris, one-third to James, and the other one-third accumulated for the persons who ultimately take this third of the principal. 5 American Law of Property §21.36 (Casner ed. 1952). Do you see how the solution to the problem of who receives the income affects the classification — and possibly the validity — of the future interest?

There is a common law rule against accumulating income for a period longer than the period of perpetuities. This rule would prevent the court from adopting any solution in Burton v. Hicks which would allow accumulation for an excessive period.

2. Which of the following transfers violate the Rule against Perpetuities? (First, classify the interests.)

(a) To A for fifty years, then to B in fee.

(b) To B in fee fifty years from now. Gray, The Rule against Perpetuities §201, n. 3 (4th ed. 1942); 3 Simes & Smith, The Law of Future Interests §1236 (2d ed. 1956); 6 American Law of Property §24.20 (Casner ed. 1952).

(c) To Trinity Church for 1000 years if it so long exists, then to B in fee.

(d) $10,000 to A, to be paid without interest at age thirty-five or whenever he would have reached thirty-five if he dies under that age. A is ten years old at T's death. Simes & Smith, The Law of Future Interests §1236 (2d ed. 1956); Lynn, The Modern Rule Against Perpetuities 26 (1966).

(e) $10,000 to A, to be paid without interest upon the distribution of my estate.[79]

(f) O grants Gas Company an easement for pipelines with the right to lay additional pipelines upon payment of $5 per lineal rod. Simes & Smith, The Law of Future Interests §1248 (2d ed. 1956); Battersby, Easements and the Rule against Perpetuities, 25 Convey. N.S. 415 (1961).

3. T devised the residue of her estate in trust to use the income for the support of her two dogs and one cat, and upon the death of the three animals, the trust shall cease and the principal shall be distributed to the SPCA. The court held that the honorary trust violated the Rule and was void, and that the SPCA had a valid vested remainder which accelerated into possession. In re McNeill's Estate, 230 Cal. App. 2d 449, 41 Cal. Rptr. 139 (1964). Do you agree with the classification of the SPCA's interest as a vested remainder?

LYNN, THE MODERN RULE AGAINST PERPETUITIES 26-27 (1966): "Recent cases cast doubt on the traditional notion that a contingent executory in-

[79] Unless otherwise stated in the will, specific legacies carry all income earned after testator's death, and general legacies bear interest beginning one year after death.

terest to be good under the Rule must be so created that it will become *possessory,* if it takes effect at all, within the perpetuities period. The conventional statement is as follows: 'An executory interest (that is, an interest which cuts off a previous estate rather than follows after it when it has terminated) is not "vested" until the time comes for taking possession.' The difficulty in working with the conventional statement originates in the use of the word 'possession.' To use Gray's example, suppose a bequest to trustees 'for the sole benefit of the first-born son of A, payable on his attaining 25.' A is a bachelor at the testator's death. There being no particular estate to support the gift to the first-born son of A, it is an executory interest, not a remainder. On a son being born to A, the executory interest is transformed into an indefeasibly vested equitable estate. The executory interest is good under the Rule Against Perpetuities even though 'possession' or 'enjoyment' may be withheld from the first-born son of A until such son reaches twenty-five — a remote time under the Rule. A more workable statement than the conventional one is as follows: A contingent executory interest must be so created that it will become possessory, or be transformed into a vested remainder or a vested estate, if at all, not later than twenty-one years after some life in being at the creation of the interest."

GRAY, THE RULE AGAINST PERPETUITIES §782 (4th ed. 1942): "A serious objection to the continuance of the old doctrines of real property in the jurisprudence of to-day is that, while the judges are thoroughly familiar with and move at ease among the general doctrines of contract and equity which govern the ordinary transactions of modern life, it is impossible (or if not impossible at least very unlikely) that they should have at their fingers' ends the fundamental distinctions of a highly artificial system, and they are in danger of being unduly governed by 'the *cantilena* of lawyers' and of losing opportunities for the simplification of the law."

WARNER v. WHITMAN

Supreme Judicial Court of Massachusetts, 1968
353 Mass. 468, 233 N.E.2d 14

SPALDING, Justice. On August 6, 1924, Stephen V. R. Crosby executed an irrevocable indenture of trust. Under it he gave his trustees discretionary power to pay one half of the income to his daughter, Katharine Schuyler Choate, for life, and one half to his son, Henry, for life. Upon the death of Katharine her interest was to "revert to her surviving children, share and share alike." Elsewhere the indenture provided that after the death of all the beneficiaries the principal and accumulated income were to revert to the settlor. By a separate instrument dated September 12, 1949, the settlor assigned to The Children's Hospital all his "present and future beneficial interest . . . in the trust property (whether capital or income) now or hereafter held under the said indenture."

At the time the trust was executed Katharine was the mother of one child born on September 24, 1922, and was expecting a second child who was born on November 6, 1924. A third child, Angelica, was born to her on December 31, 1928. Katharine died on November 29, 1959, survived by her three children, Sylvia C. Whitman, Robert B. Choate, Jr. and Angelica C. Goffman.

The income from the trust was paid in equal shares to the three children until the death of Angelica C. Goffman on April 27, 1964, the only child of Katharine who was not a life in being when the trust was created. From April 27, 1964, until April 7, 1965, the trustees paid the entire net income of the trust to the two surviving children of Katharine, Sylvia C. Whitman and Robert B. Choate, Jr., in equal shares.

The trustees then brought this petition in the Probate Court seeking instructions as to whom the one-third share of income to which Angelica had been entitled should be paid. A decree was entered directing the trustees to pay in their discretion Angelica's share of the income to her surviving brother and sister, Robert B. Choate, Jr., and Sylvia C. Whitman, in equal shares. Allen E. Kline and Wells Fargo Bank, executors of Angelica's will, appealed.

We are of opinion that the judge was right in construing the provisions under consideration as creating a class gift with a right of survivorship to Angelica's share of the income in favor of her brother and sister. While there is some authority to the effect that the words "share and share alike" in the trust instrument suggest a tenancy in common (Shattuck v. Wall, 174 Mass. 167, 54 N.E. 488), the following facts lead to an opposite conclusion: (1) The indenture makes no provision for the issue of Katharine's children in the event any child should die before the termination of the trust. See Old Colony Trust Co. v. Treadwell, 312 Mass. 214, 217, 43 N.E.2d 777. Although not decisive, the failure to provide for such issue is significant when coupled with the fact that the settlor expressly provided for his son's income interest should he die without issue. To deal with this possibility the settlor created a cross limitation in favor of Katharine. (2) None of the children of Katharine is named. In fact it would not have been feasible to name them because when the indenture was executed Katharine had but one child and there was a possibility of others. The children thus would seem to constitute a natural group. See Springfield Safe Deposit & Trust Co. v. Dunn, 243 Mass. 7, 9-10, 136 N.E. 622; Boston Safe Deposit & Trust Co. v. Park, 307 Mass. 255, 262-263, 20 N.E.2d 977. (3) Had Angelica predeceased her mother her estate would have taken nothing under the trust because the instrument makes provision only for "surviving children." There is no indication that Angelica's estate should have greater rights with respect to her surviving brother and sister simply because she survived her mother. See New England Trust Co. v. Berry, 310 Mass. 35, 38, 36 N.E.2d 408.

Contending that no class gift was intended, and that a tenancy in common was created whereby the gift of income vested in the children at their mother's death, the appellants argue that a class gift construction would involve a violation of the rule against perpetuities and that, if possible, a construction which is not repugnant to the rule should be adopted. New England Trust Co. v. Wood, 326 Mass. 239, 244, 93 N.E.2d 547. On August 6, 1924, the effective date of the trust, the settlor's daughter, Katharine, had one child almost two years old and was expecting another. A third child, Angelica, whose share of income is now in question, was born approximately four years later. As the gift to the children was not limited to children of Katharine born or conceived prior to the date of the instrument, a class gift construction could result in income shifting among the members of the class, some of whom might have been born after 1924. If, for example, there were two after-born children, it was possible they would survive all others and that more than twenty-one years after the deaths of all lives in being income would shift between them. Since there was, in fact, only one after-born child (Angelica)[80] the rule against perpetuities could not be violated because even if Angelica had been the survivor, she would have received the other children's income shares at the termination of lives in being. As matters turned out Angelica predeceased her brother and sister and her income interest then shifted to lives in being, her brother and sister.

Had the trust instrument become effective at any time after January 1, 1955, the class gift would clearly have been valid and the settlor's intent fully carried out because of the changes made by G.L. c. 184A, §1, inserted by St. 1954, c. 641, §1. Section 1 provides: "In applying the rule against perpetuities to an interest in real or personal property limited to take effect at or after the termination of one or more life estates in, or lives of, persons in being when the period of said rule commences to run, the validity of the interest shall be determined on the basis of facts existing at the termination of such one or more life estates or lives." Section 2 of c. 641 of St. 1954 provides that the act was to take effect on January 1, 1955, and that it should apply to inter vivos instruments taking effect after January 1, 1955.

The question thus presented is whether the validity of the class gift for purposes of the rule against perpetuities may be determined in the light of facts as they actually existed at the death of Katharine. Although the statute operates prospectively, the Legislature has clearly expressed the policy of the Commonwealth and we feel that this court is justified in applying that policy to the provisions under consideration.

The policy behind the rule against perpetuities is not violated if the trust instrument is given the construction we have placed on it. Property was not in fact tied up beyond the period of the rule. As was said in Merchants Natl. Bank v. Curtis, 98 N.H. 225, 232, 97 A.2d 207, 212, "It is difficult to see how the public welfare is threatened by a vesting that might have been postponed beyond the period of perpetuities but actually was not." See Leach, Perpetuities in Perspective: Ending the Rule's Reign of Terror, 65 Harv. L. Rev. 721; Am. Law of Property, §24.10. See also Sears v. Coolidge, 329 Mass. 340, 343, 108 N.E.2d 563.

The decree is affirmed. Costs and expenses of appeal are to be in the discretion of the Probate Court.

So ordered.

[80] For purposes of the rule against perpetuities Katharine's second child, who was born three months after the trust was executed, is to be regarded as a life in being. Am. Law of Property, §24.15.

NOTES

Stephen Crosby's trust gave income to Katharine for life, then to her surviving children, and upon the death of the last surviving income beneficiary, principal was to revert to the settlor. The settlor assigned his reversion to Children's Hospital.[81] For purposes of analyzing the perpetuities problems raised by secondary life estates, assume the trust had read: to Katharine for life, then to her surviving children *for their lives*, then to Children's Hospital in fee. In reading the following, consider whether the conclusions would be changed because of the actual language in the Crosby trust.

Katharine dies. Angelica dies. What happens to her share of the income? [82] The alternatives are: (1) Angelica's estate receives the income until the death of the survivor of Katharine's children. The theory here is that Angelica was a tenant in common holding a life estate pur autre vie, measured by the life of the surviving life tenant. (2) The remainder in Children's Hospital becomes possessory at this time as to Angelica's former one-third interest. If there had been a gift to Katharine's children for their *respective* lives, or other language indicating the remainder was to take effect in segments as each life tenant dies, a court might find the settlor intended the remainder in Children's Hospital to take effect piecemeal. (3) Stephen Crosby's estate receives the income formerly going to Angelica until the death of the surviving life tenant. The theory here is that the trust instrument does not provide for distribution of this income, and therefore it is held on a resulting trust for the estate of the settlor. (4) The surviving children of Katharine (Sylvia and Robert) divide up the income. This is the most common solution courts have arrived at, but the theory has not always been clear. Three theories are available: joint tenancy, cross-remainders, and class gift. (a) If the children of Katharine hold as joint tenants for their lives and until the death of the survivors, there is no perpetuities problem.[83] Each joint tenant owns pur my et pur tout; on the death of one joint tenant nothing passes to the survivor, but the survivor's interest is now free of the claim of the first to die. (b) If there are implied cross-remainders to the surviving children,[84] the cross-remainders do not violate the Rule because they vest at the

[81] Would the interest of Children's Hospital be valid if the 1924 instrument had provided that the principal was to revert to Children's Hospital rather than to the settlor?

[82] See Simes & Smith, The Law of Future Interests §843 (2d ed. 1956).

[83] Gray, The Rule against Perpetuities §232.1 (4th ed. 1942); Morris & Leach, The Rule Against Perpetuities 98 (2d ed. 1962).

[84] The cross-remainder in Angelica's one-third share would read as follows: to Angelica for life; then as to one-half of this share to Robert for life, then to Sylvia for life, and as to the other one-half of this share to Sylvia for life, then to Robert for life. Similar cross-remainders, mutatis mutandis, would be implied in Robert's share and Sylvia's share. If the court were to imply cross-remainders with unusual terms such as "to Katharine for life, then to Katharine's children for their lives, but if any child dies his share of the income shall go to the other children for their lives," the gift over on the death of a child born after the trust was created would be void. For a court to imply cross-remainders that would violate the Rule, when it can imply valid cross-remainders, makes no sense.

death of the primary life tenant, Katharine.[85] (c) If the children of Katharine take a class gift with a right of survivorship inherent in such construction, the Massachusetts court suggests that the Rule against Perpetuities might be violated because income might shift among members of a class of persons unborn at the creation of the trust.[86]

Should the "class gift rule" — that the gift is not vested until the interests of the members of the class are absolutely fixed — be applied to gifts of *income* as well as to gifts of principal?

Suppose that there is a trust to pay income to A for 20 years, then to pay income to A's surviving children for their lives. The Massachusetts perpetuities reform act (Gen. Law c. 184A) does not apply to such a bequest. Is the life estate in A's children void in Massachusetts?

The court made nothing of the fact that this was a discretionary trust, but any discretionary power of disposition which can be exercised beyond the perpetuity period violates the Rule.

MORRIS & LEACH, THE RULE AGAINST PERPETUITIES, 97-100 (2d ed. 1962): "If a life interest to an unborn person is valid under the principles discussed above, does it become invalid if the life tenant's share of income is liable to fluctuate from year to year? It is clear in the first place that if the trustees have a discretion to distribute the income in such proportions as they think fit among the members of a class, some of whom may be unborn, and the discretion is capable of being exercised beyond the perpetuity period, then the whole discretionary trust is void. Such discretionary trusts are in substance powers of appointment and are discussed in more detail in a later chapter. What is the position if the trustees have no such discretion, but the size of the unborn life tenant's interest is contingent on the happening of future events which may happen after the perpetuity period has expired? On principle, it would seem that his interest would be too remote. It has been held in two cases that if a share of the income of a fund is given to an unborn person for life, with a direction that if his income from the fund in any year falls below a stated amount it shall be made up to the stated amount from the capital of the fund or from other shares of income, the direction is void."

The Formula Marital Deduction Clause

We saw in another chapter how a "marital deduction formula clause" is often used to secure the maximum estate tax marital deduction available to a spouse's

[85] Ashley v. Ashley, 6 Sim. 358, 58 Eng. Rep. 628 (V.C. 1833); Gray, The Rule against Perpetuities §207 (4th ed. 1942).

[86] In Dodge v. Bennett, 215 Mass. 545, 102 N.E. 916 (1913), testator established a trust to pay the income to his widow and adopted daughter and then "to the children of my adopted daughter Florence Evelyn Talbot for their lives or the life of the survivors of such children, and at the decease of the survivor of my wife, daughter and the children of my daughter I give, devise and bequeath the remainder to First Universalist Church of Worcester." The court held the trust entirely valid.

estate. Such a clause devises a fractional share or amount of the estate, with the numerator of the fraction determined by the amount of the maximum allowable marital deduction (i.e., one-half the adjusted gross estate), minus the amount passing to the surviving spouse (under the will or by some other transfer) other than under this clause. The formula clause invariably provides that "in computing the numerator of the fraction, the values as finally determined for federal estate tax purposes shall control."

Observe that there are several variables which may postpone determination of the marital deduction gift. For example, there may be a dispute over valuation of various assets in the estate, and these may not be finally determined within the perpetuities period. Also, the amount of the adjusted gross estate (which determines the amount of the maximum allowable deduction) will depend on the amount of administration expenses; these may not be fixed within the permissible period. Does a formula gift therefore violate the Rule against Perpetuities? Professor Casner says no:[87]

"It should be noted that a formula fractional share, as well as a formula pecuniary amount, might not be definitively determined within the period of the applicable rule against perpetuities because the federal estate tax proceedings might not have been concluded within that period. Will this fact result in a trust being invalid where the amount placed in trust is described as a fractional share of the residue? This fact relates only to the quantum of the estate which is subject to the trust and has nothing to do with the vesting of interests under the trust. If every interest under the trust must vest within the required time, the mere fact that the quantum of the interest might conceivably be ascertained beyond the period of the rule should not cause any violation of the rule. It is conceivable that the quantum of the interest of any taker under a residuary gift in a will might not be definitively ascertained within the period of the rule against perpetuities because the quantum going to such a taker normally depends upon the taxes and debts which are payable. Thus, if the quantum of an interest that vests in time also must be certain to be ascertained within the period of the rule, all residuary gifts under a will would be invalid."

Professor Casner's analogy to a residuary gift is not wholly convincing. The quantum of a residuary gift fluctuates because the law requires payment of debts and taxes, not because of a requirement imposed by the testator. A better reason for exemption of formula marital deduction gifts from the Rule appears to be that such gifts are very useful in estate planning and the probabilities of federal estate tax proceedings dragging on for more than the perpetuity period are practically nil. In short, they offend no social policy.

A Final Word on Fluctuation of Amount

The amount of a gift can fluctuate by reason of persons coming into or dropping out of a class. Sometimes these events are taken to be conditions precedent,

[87] 1 Casner, Estate Planning 796 (3d ed. 1961).

sometimes not. For example, compare a bequest "to A for life, remainder to A's children who reach twenty-five" *with* "to A for life, then to A's children as joint tenants for their lives and until the death of the survivor." In the first bequest the amount of principal any child of A takes will depend upon how many children reach twenty-five. In the second the amount of income any child of A takes depends upon how many children are alive from time to time. Reaching twenty-five is deemed a condition precedent in the first bequest and the remainder is void. Dropping out of the class by dying is not a condition precedent in the second bequest, and the bequest is valid. Why? Is there any policy justification for this? Will the property likely be tied up longer under the first bequest or the second?

> . . . Words strain,
> Crack and sometimes break, under the burden,
> Under the tension, slip, slide, perish,
> Decay with imprecision, will not stay in place,
> Will not stay still.
>
> — Eliot, "Burnt Norton" in Four Quartets

6. *Powers of Appointment*

a. General Powers Presently Exercisable

In applying the Rule against Perpetuities to powers of appointment, it is necessary to separate powers into (a) general powers presently exercisable, and (b) general testamentary powers and all special powers. General powers presently exercisable are treated as absolute ownership for purposes of the Rule. Nothing stands between the donee and absolute ownership except a piece of paper that can be signed at any time; hence the property is not tied up. All that the Rule requires of a general inter vivos power is that it become exercisable within the period. When it becomes exercisable, the property becomes marketable and the policy of the Rule is not offended. Since the donee of a general power presently exercisable is treated as owner, the validity of an interest created by exercise of the power is determined on the same basis as if he owned the property in fee. The perpetuity period runs from the exercise of the power.

An unconditional power to revoke in one person is treated the same as a general power presently exercisable when the holder can exercise the power to revoke for his own exclusive benefit. The period runs from the termination of the power. See Ryan v. Ward, page 1020, supra.

b. General Testamentary Powers and Special Powers

General testamentary powers and all special powers are treated differently from the general power presently exercisable. A person holding one of these powers does not have an absolute and unlimited present right to alienate the property, and consequently he is not treated as owner.[88] In applying the Rule to these powers, two questions arise: (a) Is the power itself valid? (b) Are the interests created by the exercise of the power valid? These questions are discussed below.

c. The Initial Validity of Testamentary or Special Powers

For a general testamentary power or a special power to be valid, it must not be possible for the power to be exercised beyond the perpetuity period. If it can possibly be exercised beyond the period, it is void ab initio. A testamentary or special power cannot be given to an unborn person unless its exercise is limited to the perpetuity period. A discretionary power of distribution in a trustee is the equivalent of a special power of appointment.

Case 18. T bequeaths a fund in trust to pay the income to A for life, then to A's eldest son for life, then to distribute the principal to such persons as the eldest son shall appoint by will; in default of appointment, to the eldest son's children in equal shares. At the time of T's death A has no son. The secondary life estate in the eldest son is valid since it will vest in interest, if at all, upon the birth of a son. However, the general testamentary power and the gift in default of appointment are void.

Case 19. T bequeaths a fund in trust to pay the income to A for life; then in the trustee's discretion to pay the income to A's children during their lives or to accumulate the income and add it to principal; then on the death of each child of A to pay a proportionate part of the principal equal to the number of children of A who survived A as such child shall appoint by will. The discretionary power in the trustee to pay or accumulate income is either partially or totally void.[89] The testamentary powers given to children of A born after T's death are void, but the powers given to children of A in being at T's death are valid.

[88] In England by statute, powers exercisable jointly by two or more persons and powers exercisable with the consent of another person are classified as special powers. Perpetuities and Accumulations Act 1964, §7. The authority on these points in the United States is slim, but what there is follows the English view. In re Morgan's Trust, 203 Misc. 149, 111 N.Y.S.2d 142 (1952), *aff'd,* 281 App. Div. 715, 118 N.Y.S.2d 556 (1952); Cal. Civ. Code §1391.1 (West 1970).

[89] Gray took the position that a discretionary trust did not create one power which was void, but a succession of powers which were exercisable with respect to each year's income. Thus the discretionary power in the trustee could be exercised for twenty-one years after A's death, but no longer. Gray, The Rule against Perpetuities §§410.1 to 410.5 (4th ed. 1942). Support for this position is given by Lyons v. Bradley, 168 Ala. 505, 53 So. 244 (1910), and Woodruff Oil & Fertilizer Co. v. Yarborough's Estate, 144 S.C. 18, 142 S.E. 50 (1928). However, in the few cases in which this issue has been directly before the court, the discretionary power has been held void in its entirety if it is capable of being exercised in favor of persons not in being. Thomas v. Harrison, 24 Ohio Op. 2d 148, 191 N.E.2d 862 (1962); Bundy v. United States Trust Co., 257 Mass. 72, 153 N.E. 337 (1926); Andrews v. Lincoln, 95 Me. 541, 50 A. 898 (1901).

d. The Validity of Interests Created by the Exercise of a General Testamentary or Special Power

In the United States general testamentary powers are treated like special powers in determining the validity of the appointment. The donee of a testamentary power or a special power is regarded as an agent of the donor, not as the beneficial owner of the property. The appointments under testamentary and special powers are read back into the instrument creating the power. The perpetuity period runs from the creation of the power.

Although it is now well settled [90] in most of the states that general testamentary powers are to be treated like special powers under the Rule, the question was the subject of an historic debate between John Chipman Gray and his star pupil, Albert M. Kales. Gray maintained that general testamentary powers should be classified with special powers for purposes of the Rule against Perpetuities. Gray's view was that the donee of a general testamentary power "is not practically the owner; he cannot appoint to himself; he is, indeed, the only person to whom he cannot possibly appoint, for he must die before the transfer of the property can take place." [91] Kales thought general testamentary powers should be classified with general inter vivos powers. He answered Gray thus: "When Mr. Gray says the donee cannot appoint to himself so as to enjoy the property during his life, we must agree with him. . . . But is that the important inquiry? Is it not essential to determine whether *at the moment of exercising* the general power the donee is practically the owner? . . . [W]e determine whether he is practically the owner at the moment of death by asking whether he can do everything with reference to the property subject to the power that he could do if he were the owner. We do not need to ask whether he can enjoy the property personally, because we know that no owner of property can at the moment of death enjoy it personally. . . . What, then, is there that an owner of property can do in the way of disposing of his property at the moment of death which the donee of a general power to appoint by will cannot accomplish? Nothing!" [92]

It is curious that Kales thought asking what the donee could do with the property before his death was irrelevant. The donee of an inter vivos general power can sell the property and use the proceeds for a trip to Acapulco or for a new house. He can exchange the property for consumer goods and services. The quantum of wealth represented by the property is not withdrawn from commercial exchange. Thus, in

[90] Well, fairly well settled. In Industrial National Bank of Rhode Island v. Barrett, 220 A.2d 517 (R.I. 1966), the court held the perpetuity period runs from the date of the appointment under a general testamentary power, not from the date of creation. See Jones, The Rule Against Perpetuities and Powers of Appointment: An Old Controversy Revived, 54 Iowa L. Rev. 456 (1968). This position is also taken by the law of Delaware (Del. Code. Ann. tit. 25, §501 (1953, Supp. 1971)) and apparently of Wisconsin as well (Miller v. Douglas, 192 Wis. 486, 213 N.W. 320 (1927)). It is also the law of England: Perpetuities and Accumulations Act, 1964, §7.

[91] Gray, The Rule against Perpetuities §526.2 (4th ed. 1942).

[92] Kales, General Powers and the Rule Against Perpetuities, 26 Harv. L. Rev. 64, 66-67 (1912).

a very real sense the donee of a general inter vivos power is the owner of the property since he can choose exactly what is to be done with it. The owner of a general testamentary power does not, as a practical matter, have this choice. He cannot sell the property and use the proceeds for consumer goods and services for himself. His practical choice is to leave the property to relatives, friends, or charity. Hence, property subject to a general testamentary power is withdrawn from commerce.

A Note on the "Delaware Tax Trap"

In Delaware a statute provides that all interests created in the exercise of *all* powers, special as well as general, must vest within twenty-one years of the death of some life in being at the time the power is *exercised*, not some life in being at the date of creation of the power.[93] Under this statute it is possible to create a private trust that can last forever. T could set up a trust giving his son A the income for life and a special testamentary power to appoint outright or in further trust among his descendants. A could exercise the power by setting up a trust giving his son B the income for life and a special testamentary power in favor of his descendants. B could exercise the power in favor of his son — and so on down the generations.

Out of concern for estate tax avoidance through the use of Delaware trusts (recall that property subject to a special power is not subject to taxation in the donee's estate), Congress enacted §2041(a)(3) of the Internal Revenue Code. This statute taxes the appointive assets in the donee's estate if he exercises a special power "by creating another power of appointment which under the applicable local law can be validly exercised so as to postpone the vesting of any estate or interest in such property, . . . for a period ascertainable without regard to the date of the creation of the first power." [94]

This provision plugs the tax loophole that would otherwise exist for Delaware trusts — but the general language of the statute creates a tax trap for residents of all states. In any jurisdiction, if a donee by will exercises a special power in such a manner as to create a general inter vivos power, the property subject to the special power will be includible in the donee's gross estate. Reread the quoted statutory provision, and you will see that this is so.

This statute is a clear indication that Congress regards the Rule against Perpetuities as an essential part of the tax structure whereby family wealth must be put through the tax wringer from time to time.

The Second-Look Doctrine

Any interest created by exercise of a testamentary or special power must vest, if at all, within twenty-one years after the death of some life in being at the date the power was created. The exercise of the power is read back into the original instrument, taking into consideration facts existing on the date of exercise. This is known

[93] Del. Code Ann. tit. 25, §501 (1953, Supp. 1971).
[94] Int. Rev. Code of 1954, §2041(a)(3).

as the "second-look doctrine" (a variation of wait-and-see). This means we wait and see how the donee actually appoints the property, and then we determine on the basis of facts existing at the date of the appointment whether the appointive interests will vest within the period (computed from date of creation of the power). Thus:

Case 20. T devises property "to A for life, remainder as A appoints by will, outright or in further trust, among his descendants." A appoints "to my children for life, remainder to my grandchildren in fee." We now read A's appointment into the will that created the power; the disposition is treated as though T's will read "to A for life, then to A's children for life, then to A's grandchildren in fee." However, under the second-look doctrine we are allowed to take into account facts existing at the time of A's appointment. If at A's death the only children surviving him were born in T's lifetime, they can be used as measuring lives and the remainder to the grandchildren is valid. Otherwise the remainder is void.

If a donee makes an invalid appointment, what are the consequences? If the power was a general one, the doctrine of capture may apply where it is found the donee intended to blend the appointive assets with his own assets; the appointive assets then pass to the donee's estate. Otherwise the property passes in default of appointment to the takers in default or, if none, to the donor or his heirs.

AMERIGE v. ATTORNEY GENERAL

Supreme Judicial Court of Massachusetts, 1949
324 Mass. 648, 88 N.E.2d 126

SPALDING, J. This is a petition for instructions by the trustees under the will of Mary Elizabeth Williams, late of Hopkinton. The case was heard in the Probate Court on a statement of agreed facts and was reserved and reported to this court without decision. G.L. (Ter. Ed.) c. 215, §13.

The assets in the hands of the trustees, though treated as one fund, are derived from the following sources: property owned by Mary Elizabeth Williams, property which came to her from her father, James Leeds, and personal property and Massachusetts real estate from the estate of her uncle Timothy C. Leeds over which James Leeds had exercised a general testamentary power of appointment. It is with respect to the appointed property from Timothy Leeds's estate that the principal questions for decision have arisen.

[Timothy Leeds, a resident of New York, died in 1864. Under his will, one-half of his property was placed in a trust that gave his brother James Leeds a life estate and a general testamentary power of appointment. Timothy was survived by his brother James and by James's three children: Herbert C. Leeds, Mary Elizabeth Williams, and Annie F. Boardman. None of Mary Elizabeth's children had been born at the time of Timothy's death.

Timothy's will named his brother James and Samuel Guild, both of Boston, as trustees; the will also named James as executor. Provision was made for appointment of a successor trustee if either trustee resigned or died, "subject however to the approval of the person who shall then hold the office of Judge of Probate for the County of Suffolk" in Massachusetts. After administration of Timothy's personal estate in New York, and an ancillary administration in Massachusetts for realty located in that state, the assets were distributed to the trustees, and subsequent accountings for the trust were made in Massachusetts.

James Leeds, a resident of Massachusetts, died in 1875. He left a will and several codicils that provided in part:

> I direct and appoint that the property which my brother Timothy C. Leeds empowered me by his last will and testament, shall be considered and held, in all respects, as part of my own property, and that, when I have bequeathed or devised a proportion or the residue of my estate, the estate of my brother, over which I have the power of appointment, shall be considered and devised and bequeathed as if they were a part of my estates.

Under a later clause in his will one-third of his estate was placed in a trust that gave his daughter Mary Elizabeth Williams a life estate and a general testamentary power of appointment, "and if she shall die intestate then to hold the said fund to the use of her children and the issue of any deceased children taking by representation." James was survived by his wife, by his three children named above, and by two grandchildren: Edward Shirley Goddard and Mary Elizabeth Goddard, children of Mary Elizabeth Williams.]

> [*Question*: Stop right here and reread the facts. Did James Leeds make an effective appointment under the common law Rule against Perpetuities?]

Mary Elizabeth Williams died a resident of Massachusetts February 10, 1925, leaving no spouse and survived by her children Edward Shirley and Mary Elizabeth Goddard. She left a will, the seventh article of which provides in part as follows: "My said daughter Mary E. Goddard, and my said son Edward Shirley Goddard, were both born prior to the decease of my father, James Leeds late of Boston, Massachusetts, under whose will I have a power of appointment. All the rest, residue and remainder of my property, of every name and nature, real and personal, and any property over which I have the power of appointment by will, or otherwise, I give, devise and bequeath to the trustees . . . [named herein and their successors] but in trust nevertheless, for the following purposes, namely:" to divide the residue into two equal shares and to hold one for each child during his or her life, and then to his or her issue, but in default of such issue, to hold the whole for the life of the survivor, and upon the death of the survivor to his or her issue, but if on the death of the survivor no issue of either be surviving, then to pay over the property discharged of all trusts in equal shares to the following charities: Rotch's Travelling Scholarship, the Massachusetts Society for the Prevention of Cruelty to Animals, and the Animal Rescue League. Under the terms of the seventh article, as modified by a codicil, the trustees were empowered to pay to each child out of principal a sum not in excess of $10,000.

During the lifetime of Mary Elizabeth Goddard the income of her share of the trust created by the seventh article of her mother's will was paid to her and she also received payments out of principal amounting to $7,000. She died a resident of Boston, May 16, 1940, without issue, leaving a will and codicil.[95]

The trustees under the will of Mary Elizabeth Williams paid one half of the income of the trust to Edward Shirley Goddard until the death of Mary Elizabeth Goddard, and thereafter, until September 30, 1947, he received the entire income thereof. Since that date he has received one half of the income and the remaining income has been held by the trustees pending the outcome of the present proceeding. The trustees have paid to Edward, who is still living, sums out of principal amounting to $10,000.

The principal contentions of the parties interested in the disposition of the fund in question may be summarized as follows: The respondent Waters, who would take through a partial intestacy of Timothy, argues that the law of New York governs with respect to that percentage of the fund which is derived from Timothy's personalty, and accordingly the interests therein appointed after Mary Elizabeth Williams's life estate (namely, the Goddard life estates, the life estate to the survivor, the provision for payment of principal, the remainder to the Goddard issue, and the remainder to the charities) are invalid as violating the New York perpetuities statute; that the Massachusetts law applies to the realty, and by that law the interests after the Goddard life estates are invalid; that the doctrine of capture set forth in Fiduciary Trust Co. v. Mishou, 321 Mass. 615, 624-625, does not apply to any of the interests; that the default clause in the will of James Leeds is not effective; and that the invalidly appointed property must be considered intestate property of Timothy. The Boardman group, who claim in part through Annie F. Boardman (a daughter of James Leeds), contend that the property should be distributed as intestate property of James by treating James as the donor of the power with respect to the personalty, to which the New York law applies, and by treating him as the donee as to the realty, to which Massachusetts law, including the doctrine of capture, applies. Edward Shirley Goddard argues that the law of New York applies to the personalty; that Mary Elizabeth Williams captured this property for

[95] Article Second of her will contained a recital to the effect that she understood that her mother, Mary Elizabeth Williams, had "a power and/or powers to dispose of certain property under the will of Timothy C. Leeds . . . and under the will of James Leeds . . . and [had] exercised the same under the Seventh Article of her will"; that it had been stated to her that there was some doubt as to the validity of the gifts over to the charitable corporations named in that article; and that she desired to carry out the provisions of that article as far as she was able after the decease of her brother Edward Shirley Goddard. She then went on to provide that "any and all property comprising the Timothy C. Leeds or James Leeds Funds, so called" which she had the right to appoint or dispose of whether it came to her or she had such right "under the will of Timothy C. Leeds and/or the will of James Leeds and/or the will of . . . [her] mother . . . Mary Elizabeth Williams" was to be held in trust to pay the income to Edward Shirley Goddard during his life and at his death to distribute the fund in equal shares to Rotch's Travelling Scholarship, the Massachusetts Society for the Prevention of Cruelty to Animals, and the Animal Rescue League.

her estate; and that there is a resulting trust to her estate. The executors of Mary Elizabeth Williams and of Mary Elizabeth Goddard urge that Massachusetts law determines the validity of the interests sought to be created with respect to both the rule against perpetuities and the consequences of a partially invalid appointment; and that this property was captured by Mary Elizabeth Williams and will go as a resulting trust to her estate. The executor of Mary Elizabeth Goddard contends in the alternative that the property is to go to the issue of Mary Elizabeth Williams by the default clause in James's will. The position of the charitable remaindermen and the guardian ad litem is that under the doctrine of allocation no percentage of the fund now in the hands of the trustees under the will of Mary Elizabeth Williams can be considered as coming from Timothy Leeds and that the appointment of Mary Elizabeth Williams is completely valid.[96]

1. As stated above, Timothy's property over which James and Mary Elizabeth Williams had powers of appointments comprised real estate situated in Massachusetts, and personal property. Questions relating to the validity and effect of the power contained in his will and questions arising out of the exercise of the power, in so far as they concern real estate, must be determined by the law where the real estate is situated. Restatement: Conflict of Laws, §§234, 235, 236. Beale, Conflict of Laws, §§234.1, 235.1. Sewall v. Wilmer, 132 Mass. 131, 138. Russell v. Joys, 227 Mass. 263, 267. Ligget v. Fidelity & Columbia Trust Co., 274 Ky. 387. Lawrence's Estate, 136 Pa. 354. No contention is made to the contrary. Thus the question whether the exercise of the power created interests in the real estate which are remote under the rule against perpetuities is to be governed by the law of this Commonwealth rather than by the law of Timothy's domicil, New York. Bundy v. United States Trust Co., 257 Mass. 72, 79. By §42 of the real property law of New York (N.Y. Consol. Laws, c. 52) limitations extending beyond two lives in being are remote, whereas in Massachusetts the common law rule prevails.

Under the common law rule the interests which Mary Elizabeth Williams attempted to create after the life estates to her children Edward Shirley and Mary Elizabeth Goddard are remote. It is settled in this Commonwealth that "the remoteness of an appointment, made in the exercise of a power to appoint by will alone, so far as affected by the rule against perpetuities must be measured from the time of the creation and not the exercise of the power." Minot v. Paine, 230 Mass. 514, 523. Fiduciary Trust Co. v. Mishou, 321 Mass. 615, 622. The equitable life estate given to James Leeds and that which he gave by the appointment to his daughter Mary Elizabeth Williams were, of course, valid inasmuch as both were lives in being at Timothy's death. The life estates in the appointed property given by Mary Elizabeth Williams to her children Edward Shirley and Mary Elizabeth Goddard were valid since these vested at their mother's death. But the limitations beyond that, namely, those to the issue of the life tenants, the cross remainders, the gifts to the charities and the provisions with respect to payments of principal, were remote. None of these limitations was certain to take effect within twenty-one years

[96] No contention is made by any of the respondents that any of the limitations in the will of Mary Elizabeth Williams are invalid with respect to property owned outright by James or herself.

from the death of Mary Elizabeth Williams. It is settled that a limitation over which violates the rule against perpetuities "will be considered as stricken out, leaving the prior disposition to operate as if a limitation over had never been made." Greenough v. Osgood, 235 Mass. 235, 242. Lovering v. Worthington, 106 Mass. 86, 88.

We pass now to the question of what disposition is to be made of that percentage of the fund derived from Timothy's real estate which Mary Elizabeth Williams did not properly appoint. The situation is one, we think, where the principle of capture becomes applicable. That principle is that "where the donee of a general power attempts to make an appointment that fails, but where, nevertheless, the donee has manifested an intent wholly to withdraw the appointive property from the operation of the instrument creating the power for all purposes and not merely for the purposes of the invalid appointment, the attempted appointment will commonly be effective to the extent of causing the appointive property to be taken out of the original instrument and to become in effect part of the estate of the donee of the power." Fiduciary Trust Co. v. Mishou, 321 Mass. 615, 624. . . .

. . . And where, as here, the invalid appointments are in trust there will be a resulting trust to the estate of the donee of the power. Fiduciary Trust Co. v. Mishou, 321 Mass. 615, 624. Restatement: Property, §365, and Trusts, §426. Scott on Trusts, §426. The complete blending by Mary Elizabeth Williams in her will of the appointive property with that which she owned outright shows her intent to capture the property for her own estate. Since the remote limitations were in the residuary clause, the property cannot pass under that clause for the reasons which are set forth in Fiduciary Trust Co. v. Mishou, 321 Mass. 615, at pages 626 and 627.

2. With respect to that portion of the fund derived from Timothy's estate which was personal property, questions of considerable difficulty are presented. At the outset it is necessary to decide what law is to govern. Ordinarily in the case of personal property questions as to both form and substance relating to the validity and effect of an instrument exercising a power of appointment created by will are determined by the law of the domicil of the donor of the power. . . . We are concerned here not with the validity of the instrument exercising the power or whether the power was exercised but rather with the nature and extent of the interests resulting from its exercise. Whether the principle just stated is applicable here is of importance not only as to whether the New York or Massachusetts rule against perpetuities is to govern but also as to whether the doctrine of capture, discussed above, is applicable.[97] While we do not doubt that the principle stated above is the one ordinarily to be applied, we are of opinion that it ought not to govern here. It has been said that the basis for the principle is that the property subject to the power is considered as belonging to the donor. See Pitman v. Pitman, 314 Mass. 465, 471. But this is not always decisive. The intention, express or presumed, of the

[97] Whether the doctrine of capture, as applied in this Commonwealth, obtains in New York is not clear. We have found no case decided by the Court of Appeals in which the doctrine has been expressly adopted or repudiated.

donor has also been considered as a factor of importance. Sewall v. Wilmer, 132 Mass. 131, 137. In Russell v. Joys, 227 Mass. 263, the question for decision was whether a power of appointment created by an instrument (an antenuptial agreement) made by a Massachusetts resident, who was also the donee of the power, was validly executed by a will admitted to probate in Wisconsin where the donor-donee was domiciled at her death. In holding that the question was to be determined by the law of Massachusetts the court said, "On all the facts we are of opinion that the settlor manifested an intention to have the trust administered, and the validity of the appointment determined by the law of Massachusetts" (page 267). As bearing on the question of the donor's intent the court took into consideration the facts that the donor was domiciled here when the power was created, that the trustee resided here, and that the property (originally real estate) was situated here. See also Greenough v. Osgood, 235 Mass. 235; Hutchins v. Browne, 253 Mass. 55, 58. We are aware that the powers of appointment in Russell v. Joys and Greenough v. Osgood were contained in trusts created inter vivos and that in such trusts the intent of the settlor has been accorded particular importance in determining the choice of law. Wilmington Trust Co. v. Wilmington Trust Co., 26 Del. Ch. 397. Hutchison v. Ross, 262 N.Y. 381. Land, Trusts in the Conflict of Laws, §§21.1 and 24. But we think intent also of significance where a testator creates powers of appointment by testamentary trust.

In the case at bar there are several factors which shed light on the intent of Timothy, the testator-donor. The trustees both were residents of Massachusetts. One of them, James, was the donee of the power. A substantial portion of the property consisted of real estate situated here. Timothy's will provided that the appointment of successor trustees was to be "subject . . . to the approval of the . . . Judge of Probate for the County of Suffolk" in the Commonwealth of Massachusetts. We think it plain that he intended the trust to be administered here, as in fact it was. See Restatement: Conflict of Laws, §298. The trust, therefore, would be administered according to the law of this Commonwealth. Restatement: Conflict of Laws, §299. See Sewall v. Wilmer, 132 Mass. 131, 137; Codman v. Krell, 152 Mass. 214; Greenough v. Osgood, 235 Mass. 235. It is reasonable to infer that Timothy contemplated that the power given to James would be exercised here. Timothy manifested an intention not only that the trust be administered here and according to our law but also that that law should determine the extent and nature of the interests created by the exercise of the power created by his will.

An analogy furnishing support for the conclusion here reached may be found in cases dealing with testamentary trusts. Ordinarily the validity of a testamentary trust of personal property is determined by the law of the testator's domicil at the time of his death. Fellows v. Miner, 119 Mass. 541. McCurdy v. McCallum, 186 Mass, 464, 468. Restatement: Conflict of Laws, §295. Beale, Conflict of Laws, §295.1. But this principle has not been applied invariably. Thus where testamentary trusts of personal property were to be held and administered in a foreign State and were valid in such State but invalid in the State of the testator's domicil they have been upheld. . . . In Wilmington Trust Co. v. Wilmington Trust Co., 21 Del. Ch.

188, the rationale of the rule was said to rest "on the principle that since such questions of public policy as are embodied in the rule against perpetuities and in the mortmain statutes can be of legitimate interest only as to property intended to be held in the particular State where the public policy prevails, it becomes a matter of no concern to that State if public policy in another jurisdiction permits property to be received and held under more liberal regulations than in the former" (page 196). We see no reason why on principle the reasoning underlying these cases should not apply to a case like the present involving the exercise of a power of appointment. We hold, therefore, that the interests created by the limitations contained in the will of Mary Elizabeth Williams are to be determined by the law of Massachusetts. It follows that the personalty derived from Timothy's estate is to go as a resulting trust to the executor of the will of Mary Elizabeth Williams, to be distributed as intestate property. By applying the principle of capture this result would be reached under either the Massachusetts or the New York rule against perpetuities.

3. The charities, as noted above, advance the argument that none of the property appointed by Mary Elizabeth Williams is derived from property of Timothy. They invoke the principle that where the donee of a general power of appointment disposes of owned and appointive property as a single fund the appointive property is allocated to the various dispositions of such fund in such manner as to give the maximum effect to such dispositions. That principle is recognized by our decisions (Stone v. Forbes, 189 Mass. 163, 170-171; Minot v. Paine, 230 Mass. 514, 525) and by the American Law Institute in §363 of the Restatement: Property. Thus, it is argued, James Leeds dealt with his own and the appointive property as a single fund and to give the maximum effect to his dispositions the debts, expenses, legacies and residuary gifts must be charged against the appointive property and if this is done that property is exhausted and there is no property of Timothy remaining which Mary Elizabeth Williams could appoint. But that principle is not applicable here. In the case at bar there were successive donees of the power created by Timothy, James Leeds and Mary Elizabeth Williams. The appointments which violate the rule against perpetuities were made by Mary Elizabeth Williams, the second donee. None of the appointments made by James is invalid and no contention is made to the contrary. In all of the cases we have seen where the principle of allocation has been applied the valid and invalid dispositions have been made by the same person in the same will. To give the maximum effect to such dispositions under the principle of allocation the law is attempting to carry out the presumed intent of the testator. The doctrine ought not to be applied in the case of successive donees where the dispositions of the first donee are valid and those of the second invalid. It cannot reasonably be said that James contemplated that Mary Elizabeth Williams would exercise the power improperly with the result that he must be presumed to have intended that his dispositions be charged against the appointive property.

4. It becomes necessary to determine what proportion of the fund in question can be considered as having come from Timothy's estate. The respondents are not in agreement on this question. The following is stated in the stipulation of agreed facts: "The correct mathematical computation of the proportion of the funds in the

hands of the trustee . . . [under the will of] Mary E. Williams derived from the various sources, tracing the specific assets specified in the foregoing paragraphs and striking proportions in a general fund at each point indicated above at which funds were mingled, is as follows:

Property of —	
Mary E. Williams	16%
James Leeds	31%
Timothy C. Leeds	
Real Estate	6%
Personal Property	47%
	100%"

. . . Here the fund owned by James and that coming from Timothy's estate were held separately until the accounting period ending in 1911, when they were merged. Applying the principle of the Mishou case to the facts here, we are of opinion that the proportion of the fund attributable to Timothy's estate now held by the trustees of Mary Elizabeth Williams ought to be determined, if possible, on the basis of percentages fixed as of that time. No better method appears to be available. The percentages contained in the stipulation apparently were not established in that manner and on this record we are in no position to make the computation. The case, therefore, should be remanded to the Probate Court in order that the proportions be established by the method just outlined. In determining these proportions the debts, expenses and legacies ought to be chargeable against each fund on a pro rata basis. Fiduciary Trust Co. v. Mishou, 321 Mass. 615, 633. For the reasons set forth in the Mishou case there is no occasion here to apply the principle of exoneration illustrated by Tuell v. Hurley, 206 Mass. 65. The debts, expenses and legacies of Mary Elizabeth Williams ought also to be charged against each fund on a pro rata basis in computing the amount of appointive property in her estate.

5. Finally it has been argued that the payments of principal to Mary Elizabeth and Edward Shirley Goddard amounting in all to $17,000 should be treated as having been paid out of property other than that derived from Timothy's estate under the doctrine of allocation. But we are of opinion that that doctrine is not applicable. It is true, of course, that as to Timothy's property the limitations as to these payments were remote because measured from the creation of Timothy's power they might take effect more than twenty-one years after the death of Mary Elizabeth Williams, the last life in being. But in the view that we take of the case allocation is not necessary to save the payments. Edward Shirley and Mary Elizabeth Goddard became entitled to the appointive property as heirs and next of kin of Mary Elizabeth Williams at her death. Consequently, since they own the entire interest in that property, the payments of principal to them were not improper. Had they not become entitled to the property by reason of the resulting trusts a different question would be presented.

The case is remanded to the Probate Court for further proceedings in conformity with this opinion and the trustees are to be instructed in accordance therewith. Costs and expenses of appeal are to be in the discretion of the Probate Court.

So ordered.[98]

PROBLEM

Do you see how, as lawyer for Mary Elizabeth Williams, you could have almost certainly carried out her wishes by a further appointment using extraneous lives to measure the period?

NEW YORK ESTATES, POWERS & TRUSTS LAW §3-5.1(g) (1967): "[T]he intrinsic validity, effect, revocation or alteration of a testamentary disposition by which a power of appointment over personal property is exercised, and the question of whether such power has been exercised at all, are determined by:

"(1) In the case of a presently exercisable general power of appointment, the law of the jurisdiction in which the donee of such power was domiciled at the time of death.

"(2) In the case of a general power of appointment exercisable by will alone or a special power of appointment:

"(A) If such power was created by will, the law of the jurisdiction in which the donor of the power was domiciled at the time of death.

"(B) If such power was created by inter vivos disposition, the law of the jurisdiction which the donor of the power intended to govern such disposition.

"(C) If the donor is himself the donee of a general power of appointment exercisable by will alone, the law of the jurisdiction in which the donor of the power was domiciled at the time of death."

The second-look doctrine permits facts existing at the date a testamentary or special power is exercised to be taken into account in determining the validity of the *exercise* of the power. But what if the donee does not exercise the power, and the assets pass to the takers in default of appointment? Can the second-look doctrine be invoked to sustain the validity of a gift in default of appointment?

> *Case 21.* T devises property "to A for life, remainder as A shall appoint by will; in default of appointment, to A's children for their lives, remainder to A's grandchildren in fee." A dies without exercising the power. The facts existing at A's death show that A's only children (B and C) were alive at T's death. *If* the second-look doctrine can be invoked, the remainder to A's grandchildren is valid; otherwise it is void.

This question came before the Massachusetts court in Sears v. Coolidge.

[98] Noted 50 Colum. L. Rev. 239; 63 Harv. L. Rev. 699. — EDS.

SEARS v. COOLIDGE

Supreme Judicial Court of Massachusetts, 1952
329 Mass. 340, 108 N.E.2d 563

WILKINS, J. These two petitions under G.L. (Ter. Ed.) c. 231A seek binding declarations as to the validity of the provisions relating to income and to gifts of principal by way of remainder in a deed of trust executed by Thomas Jefferson Coolidge, late of Manchester, under date of February 12, 1913. The settlor died on November 17, 1920. In each case a decree was entered declaring that the life interests are valid; but that the gifts over of principal are invalid and void, and upon the termination of the trust the personal representatives of the settlor's estate are to receive the principal and any unpaid accumulated income. The petitioners, the trustees, and numerous other persons interested in the trust or in the settlor's estate appealed.

The net income of the trust was payable one third semi-annually to "such of the issue of my deceased son as shall be living at the time of each such semi-annual payment," and two thirds, divided into three parts payable semi-annually, one part each to Marian A. Sargent and to Sarah L. Newbold and after their death to their respective issue, and one to the living issue of Eleonora R. Sears, who were the petitioner Eleonora R. Sears and Frederick R. Sears.

The appeals relating to the life interests have been "waived and withdrawn." We are now concerned only with the decrees in so far as they affect the remainder interests. Whenever we refer to the appellants, we shall mean all or some of those who are seeking to establish the validity of the remainder interests. The facts are undisputed and, for the most part, are embodied in a written stipulation in the Probate Court. The evidence is reported.

The fundamental issue is whether the remainder interests violate the rule against perpetuities. Paragraph 5 of the trust instrument provides that the capital of the trust is to be distributed "in equal shares to and among my issue living" at the time of distribution. Distribution is to take place upon "whichever shall first happen" of two events: (1) "the death of the last survivor of those of my children, grandchildren and great grandchildren who shall be living at my death"; or (2) "the attainment of fifty years by the youngest surviving grandchild of mine who shall be living at my death." The second event first happened. William A. Coolidge, the youngest grandchild living at the settlor's death, attained the age of fifty years on October 21, 1951.

Where a trust instrument contains two alternative conditions, of which the first might be too remote and the second, which actually occurs, is not too remote, the rule is not violated. Jackson v. Phillips, 14 Allen, 539, 572-573. Stone v. Bradlee, 183 Mass. 165, 171-172. Gray v. Whittemore, 192 Mass. 367, 372. Springfield Safe Deposit & Trust Co. v. Ireland, 268 Mass. 62, 67-68. Accordingly, the appellants contend that the attainment by the youngest grandchild of the age of fifty years was certain to occur within the period required by the rule, and that as matter of construction the reference in paragraph 5 to "the youngest surviving grandchild of mine who shall be living at my death" must be read as if "grandchild" were qualified by "now living" or similar words. In support are adduced various facts in the settlor's family situation obvious to him when he executed the deed of trust. He was then eighty-one years of age and had been a widower for twelve years. At that time he had two living children, Marian A. Sargent, who was aged fifty-nine and had been a widow for twenty years, and Sarah L. Newbold, who was then fifty-five years of age. During the preceding year there had died two of his children, T. Jefferson Coolidge and Eleonora R. Sears. The settlor then had ten living grandchildren. Four were the minor sons of his deceased son. Two were the children of his deceased daughter, one being the petitioner, Eleonora R. Sears, and the other Frederick R. Sears, the administrator of whose estate is the petitioner Fiduciary Trust Company. One was the child of Marian A. Sargent, and three were the children of Sarah L. Newbold. The oldest grandchild was thirty-five and the youngest was seven. No further grandchildren were born in the settlor's lifetime, but the youngest of the ten died before the settlor.

The appellees argue, on the other hand, that it is not permissible thus to qualify the clause in paragraph 5, and for present purposes we accept their position on this point, and assume that the phrase "the youngest surviving grandchild of mine who shall be living at my death" is not to be interpreted as excluding grandchildren who might be born after the trust instrument was created.

The appellants make the contention that the settlor in the trust deed reserved a power which was at least equivalent to a special power of appointment, and that the validity of the remainders must in any event be determined in the light of the facts existing at his death when it was known that his only grandchildren had been lives in being at the time the trust was created. This has been referred to in the arguments as "a second look."

Paragraph 9 reads: "I reserve to myself power at all times to make any additions to the trust property, to change and alter any or all of the trusts herein set forth and to declare new uses and trusts of the property in any way or manner except such as will vest in myself the trust property or any beneficial interest therein, to name and appoint any other persons than those above specified or hereafter appointed as beneficiaries, whether by way of addition or substitution, and to appoint other trustees instead of or in addition to any or all of those above named. Every such change, alteration, nomination and appointment shall be made by my deed and shall take effect immediately upon the delivery thereof to any person who shall at the time be acting as a trustee under the provisions of these presents."

The point, which, so far as appears, has not been pressed upon an appellate court before, is based upon the analogy of Minot v. Paine, 230 Mass. 514. The theory is that at the settlor's death the expiration of the power to divert the property from the takers in default was the same in effect as an appointment of the remainders by the settlor's will.

The reserved power is, at the very least, akin to a power of appointment. National Shawmut Bank v. Joy, 315 Mass. 457, 474. Restatement: Property, §318, comment i. . . . And, for present purposes, we treat it as having attributes of a special power to appoint by deed.

In Minot v. Paine the power to appoint was, in fact, exercised, and there was presented a question as to the effect of the language used by the donee of the power, who had become, in law, the agent of the donor for the purpose. At page 522, it was said: "The donee in exercising the power is in effect writing the will of the donor respecting the appointed property. . . . The words used by the donee in exercising the power are to be construed and interpreted as to their meaning in the light of the facts as they are at the time the power is exercised. The will of the donor is projected forward to the time of the exercise of the power so as to receive the benefit of the facts which have appeared since his decease. . . . As applied to the exercise of a power of appointment the words of the rule are satisfied if it appears that in the light of facts as to relationship and longevity existent when the appointment is exercised, the estates created in truth will vest and take effect within the period limited by the rule, although this may not have been certain at the death of the donor of the power."

In the present instance, no appointment having been made, there were no words expressed by the holder of the reserved power to be read back into the deed of trust. That fact, however, should not be decisive. In every case where there is a power, whether it be exercised or not, there is the common feature that until the opportunity for its exercise ceases to exist, there will persist uncertainty as to the ultimate disposition of the property. Until then nothing final can be known as to what are the provisions for the vesting of the future interests, and it is with such vesting the policy of the rule is concerned. . . .

Since it is permissible to make use of the circumstances known when a power, which is special or testamentary, is exercised to determine validity under the rule, it seems reasonable to afford the same opportunity in cases where such a power is not exercised. In the case of the trust instrument under consideration until it became too late for the settlor to exercise the reserved power no one could tell what might be the ultimate disposition of the trust property. As long as there remained a right to change, alter, and make new appointments, no instructions to the trustees or declaratory decree would ordinarily have been given as to the validity of the settlor's limitations. See National Shawmut Bank v. Morey, 320 Mass. 492, 497-500; Young v. Jackson, 321 Mass. 1, 7; Burn v. McAllister, 321 Mass. 660, 662. Upon his death it could be learned for the first time what definitely were to be the terms of the trust. It then could be seen for the first time that there was to be no failure to vest within the period limited by the rule. No further grandchildren had been born. In these precise circumstances there is no compelling decision which prevents taking advantage of facts known at the moment when the power ceased to be exercisable. American Law of Property, §24.36. We are unwilling to apply the rule so as to invalidate the trust instrument.

The appellees strongly urge that the doctrine of a "second look" has no place in reading the original limitations in default of appointment, which were capable of examination when created, and which should retain the same meaning throughout.

They argue that its adoption would be a nullification of the rule "that executory limitations are void unless they take effect ex necessitate and in all possible contingencies" within the prescribed period. Hall v. Hall, 123 Mass. 120, 124. But this rule, while recognized, was assuaged as to the exercise of a power of appointment in Minot v. Paine, 230 Mass. 514, 522. It was there deemed wise not to apply unmodified a remorseless technical principle to a case which it did not fit. That principle seems equally inappropriate here.

The decrees are reversed and the causes are remanded to the Probate Court for the entry of decrees in accordance with this opinion. Costs and expenses of appeal are to be in the discretion of the Probate Court.

So ordered.[99]

NOTES

1. For very interesting background information on Sears v. Coolidge, including the behind-the-scenes maneuvering with the tax authorities, see Leach & Logan, Future Interests and Estate Planning 785-807 (1961). The pros and cons of applying the second-look doctrine to gifts in default are discussed in 5 American Law of Property §24.36 (Casner ed. 1952); and Simes & Smith, The Law of Future Interests §1276 (2d ed. 1956).

2. In 1950 T bequeaths a fund in trust for A for life, and then for such of A's issue as he shall appoint, and in default of appointment to A's children who reach twenty-five. In 1953 B is born. In 1955 C is born. In 1960 D is born. B, C, and D are grandchildren of A. A dies in 1968. His will appoints the property to B for life, then to C for life, then to D and his heirs. Which of the following statements are true?

(a) The gift to B is void.
(b) The gift to C is void.
(c) The gift to D is void.

Assume that in some way the appointment violates the Rule against Perpetuities.

(d) If at A's death one child of A is aged twenty-five and another child of A is aged two, the gift in default is void.
(e) If at A's death one child of A is aged two, the gift in default is void.
(f) If A's will provided in the beginning that the will disposed of both A's own property and the appointive property, A's executor can contend, with a fair chance of success, that A captured the property.

PAX VOBISCUM

Rounding and turning and doubling back,
Gray's rule runs — on a limitless track.

[99] Noted 33 B.U.L. Rev. 119; 66 Harv. L. Rev. 937; 22 U. Cin. L. Rev. 266. — Eds.

Vest, ait, ordo tranquilitatis est,
Those lucky Scots[100] are deemed thrice blest.

Ubi nunc, O Domine,
Sunt arbusta Academiae?
Damn, tempus non fugit.

Pax, pax, O benedicta pax:
Veni!

— Largely attributable to a learned student of the law who is now a distinguished teacher of Torts.

7. *Savings Clauses*

It should have been apparent, in reading Ryan v. Ward (page 1020) and Sears v. Coolidge (page 1054), that the trusts in those cases were drafted by able and experienced draftsmen. Furthermore, in each case the draftsman employed a "perpetuities savings clause" that terminated the trust on the death of some person who was alive at the transferor's death. Yet in each case a perpetuities problem was litigated. Why? Because the wrong savings clause was used! Using lives in being at the transferor's death will do the job for revocable trusts and wills, but the Ryan and Sears cases involved irrevocable lifetime transfers, for which the period begins to run from the date of the transfer.

Because of the ease with which even experienced draftsmen can run afoul of the Rule, the draftsman should consider incorporating in the trusts he draws a perpetuities savings clause to take care of any possible violation. This practice is advisable even in jurisdictions that have adopted a cy pres or wait-and-see reform statute. As we have seen, these statutes do not eliminate perpetuities problems; they provide solutions for perpetuities problems that do arise. In a state that has a reform statute, litigation may be necessary (a) to determine whether the will or trust contains a perpetuities problem so as to invoke the operation of the statute, and (b) to determine the remedy that is to be given by the statute.

Here is an example of a savings clause:

> Notwithstanding any other provisions in this instrument, this trust shall terminate, if it has not previously terminated, twenty-one years after the death of the survivor of the beneficiaries of the trust living at the date this instrument becomes effective. In case of such termination the then remaining principal and undistributed income of the trust shall be distributed to the then income beneficiaries in the same proportions as they were, at the time of termination, entitled to receive the income.

Instead of terminating the trust on the death of the survivor of the "beneficiaries" in being when the trust becomes effective, the draftsman can, if he wishes, expressly

100 The Rule against Perpetuities is not in force in Scotland. — Eds.

name the measuring lives. This alternative might be more useful in an inter vivos trust than in a testamentary trust. Note also that the second sentence of the saving clause provides how the trust estate is distributed if the trust is terminated under this clause. This is essential, for it is not enough to "terminate" the trust without giving direction for distribution of the principal. The particular provision will be satisfactory if the trust is mandatory. If the trust is discretionary, however, the sentence would have to be re-worded. It could provide that the trust estate is to be distributed to the settlor's issue then living per stirpes.

Professor Leach and Dean Logan have suggested that every will should contain a savings clause. They have drafted an appropriate clause, covering three pages in the Harvard Law Review, which gives to a disinterested corporate fiduciary a power to appoint the assets subject to the challenged limitation in such manner as will most closely approximate the intention of the testator.[101] Their clause is drafted so as not to be effective in states where the court has a cy pres power to reform perpetuities violations. Messrs. Leach and Logan nonetheless recommend that the clause be included in all wills, for the testator may change his domicile after executing the will. Or he may own real property in another state or may be exercising a power created by an instrument governed by the law of some other state.

8. *Commercial Transactions*

The Rule against Perpetuities is a rule of property, not a rule of the law of contracts. Thus, generally speaking, the Rule does not apply to contracts that call for the future payment of money beyond the perpetuity period. Insurance contracts that call for payment of money at some future date, possibly beyond the perpetuity period, are thus exempt. In 6 American Law of Property §24.58 (Casner ed. 1952) is given this example of an exempt insurance contract:

> A pays $100,000 (or annual premiums appropriate to a $100,000 life insurance policy) to the B Life Insurance Company in consideration of the latter's promise to pay commencing now (or at A's death) $3000 per year among all of A's grandchildren, whether born before or after A's death, until the last of the grandchildren shall die, and then to pay $100,000 in equal shares among A's great-grandchildren then living.

Although this contract in some respects functions like a trust, it is not a trust because no interest in specific property is created. B Life Insurance Company is a debtor, not a trustee. However, in terms of public policy there is little difference between this contract and the usual trust where the trustee has a power of sale and reinvestment. No specific property is tied up, and the insurance company will invest its funds conservatively so as to be able to meet its obligations. Yet it is exempt from

[101] Leach & Logan, Perpetuities: A Standard Saving Clause to Avoid Violation of the Rule, 74 Harv. L. Rev. 1141 (1961). See also McGovern, Perpetuities Pitfalls and How Best to Avoid Them, 6 Real Prop., Prob. & Trust J. 155, 175 (1971).

the Rule because it does not create a proprietary interest. If such insurance contracts were to become common, regulatory legislation would likely follow.

WONG v. DI GRAZIA

Supreme Court of California, 1963
60 Cal. 2d 525, 35 Cal. Rptr. 241, 386 P.2d 817

TOBRINER, J. We hold here that an agreement which provided that the lease of a building to commence "upon completion of said building" does not violate the rule against perpetuities. (Civ. Code, §715.2). The nature of the circumstances of the transaction shows that the contemplated building was to be completed within a reasonable time and that such reasonable time was less than 21 years. Hence the interest would either vest or fail within the statutory period. . . . We therefore affirm the judgment in favor of the lessors except as to a minor matter of damages awarded them, which we remand to the trial court for clarification.

The factual background which produced this action is neither complicated nor disputed. On July 11, 1958, plaintiffs and defendants entered into a written agreement in which defendants agreed to lease to plaintiffs for a period of ten years a building to be constructed by defendants. The contract required defendants to construct only the shell of the building, exclusive of toilet facilities, lighting installations, and other improvements.

Paragraph 27 of the agreement provided: "Lessor [defendants] shall forthwith commence the construction of a building upon the herein demised premises, in accordance with plans and specifications noted thereon, a copy of which is attached hereto and made a part hereof. . . . Said plans and specifications are complete and the Lessor shall not be required to provide or pay for any additional construction. . . . Construction shall commence forthwith upon approval of completed plans and specifications and shall continue expeditiously until said building is completed, subject to material and/or labor shortages, strikes, lockouts, governmental actions and all causes beyond the control of Lessor. Said building shall be completed within ninety (90) days after a building permit has been secured from the City and County of San Francisco of said plans and specifications, subject to the contingencies above mentioned, and Lessee shall not delay or impede said construction by making changes or alterations therein, it being understood that the time consumed in effecting any such changes shall be added to the time for the completion of said building. . . . Upon completion of said building . . . Lessor shall forthwith cause a Notice of Completion to be recorded, and the term of this lease shall commence upon the recording of said Notice of Completion. . . ."

The case raises as its major issue the validity of the agreement under the rule against perpetuities. If the agreement survives this attack, we must determine if the court properly held plaintiffs liable for its breach and correctly fixed damages.

Turning to the first point, we note that in an "on completion" lease, such as the present agreement, the question of the application of the rule arises from the fact that the lease term commences upon completion of the building, an event expected to occur in the near future but subject to delay from various contingencies. If the lease were construed to postpone the "vesting" of the lessee's interest until such commencement of the term, vesting might possibly be delayed longer than 21 years from the execution of the lease, thus purportedly rendering the lease invalid under the rule against perpetuities.

Since "on completion" leases represent a relatively new commercial development, the question of their validity has been raised, so far as we have found, in only five cases. Two cases, Haggerty v. City of Oakland (1958) 161 Cal. App. 2d 407, 326 P.2d 957, and Southern Airways Co. v. De Kalb County (1960) 101 Ga. App. 689, 115 S.E.2d 207, have held such leases to be in violation of the rule against perpetuities; the latter case, however, was reversed upon the ground that the agreement did not constitute a lease but a management contract. (Southern Airways Co. v. De Kalb County (1960) 216 Ga. 358, 116 S.E.2d 602.) Three cases, Isen v. Giant Food, Inc. (D.C. Cir. 1961) 295 F.2d 136, City of Santa Cruz v. MacGregor (1960) 178 Cal. App. 2d 45, 2 Cal. Rptr. 727, and Halifax v. Vaughn Constr. Co. (Sup. Ct. Nova Scotia, 1957) 9 D.L.R.2d 431, rev. on other grounds (Sup. Ct. Nova Scotia, in bank, 1958) 12 D.L.R.2d 159, have upheld such leases but advanced somewhat different reasons for doing so.

The rule has been the subject of great debate among scholars and writers; some have suggested basic changes in its application. The rule has also been subjected in some states to sweeping statutory reform. As we point out infra, it has been corroded by many exceptions. Learned writers have questioned whether the concepts of vested and contingent interests may properly be applied to leases at all. The majority have affirmed the legality of "on completion" leases under the rule.

Many factors militate against a rigid mechanistic operation of the rule in the present case. Thus in drafting the lease the parties themselves did not anticipate the application of the rule; otherwise they would have avoided its impact by formalistic provision.[102] Indeed, the attention of the parties and their attorneys to its possible application was first drawn at the *appellate* level by the District Court of Appeal. A noted authority in this field of law has pointed out that ". . . the esoteric learning of the Rule against Perpetuities is, apart from dim memories from student days, a monopoly of lawyers who deal in trusts and estates. Those members of the bar who specialize in corporate matters, including commercial leases, are not intimately familiar with it or alerted to its caprices." (Leach, Perpetuities: New Absurdity, Judicial and Statutory Correctives (1960) 73 Harv. L. Rev. 1318, 1322.) Even in the subject matter of estates this court has recognized the excusable failure of an attorney to comprehend all of its ramifications.[103]

[102] The parties could simply have provided that the lessee's term would commence on filing of the notice of completion, "but not later than twenty-one years from the date of this agreement." If more time were desired, the parties could specify, for example, "twenty-one years after the death of the survivor of X, Y, and Z," these being healthy infants living at the time of the agreement. See Nelson, Financing Commercial Real Estate, in California Land Security & Development (Cont. Ed. Bar 1960) 513, 532-533.

[103] Lucas v. Hamm (1961), 56 Cal. 2d 583, 592-593, 15 Cal. Rptr. 821, 364 P.2d 685.

Unless the precedents compel a rigid application of the rule to the instant facts, these considerations proscribe its unexpected operation here. To determine if we must apply the rule to the instant lease, we briefly examine the history of the rule, its pertinence to the general field of commercial transactions involving leaseholds and its specific relevance to the facts of this case.

The Rule against Perpetuities originated as a rule of property law during the mercantilistic period of English history. Thus the "celebrated decision which marks the beginning of the modern rule against perpetuities," The Duke of Norfolk's Case, was decided in 1682. (3 Simes & Smith, The Law of Future Interests (2d ed. 1956) §1211 at p. 91.) The social order of 1682 demanded as to its property transactions certainty in title and fixation of ownership; the idea of titles which had not vested or ownership which remained inchoate was necessarily anathema. Indeed, the basic purpose of the rule was to limit family dispositions, and in that context the period of lives in being plus 21 years served as a proper measurement. Only later by an overextension of nineteenth century concepts did the courts apply the rule to commercial transactions. (See Leach, Perpetuities: New Absurdity, Judicial and Statutory Correctives (1960) 73 Harv. L. Rev. at p. 1322.)

Rules which bear such birthmarks assume a different aspect when they are applied to contracts or leases in a modern society whose economic structure rests upon planning for the future and whose life blood is credit. Since the rule against perpetuities was born in a society which extolled the tight ownership of inherited real property, it does not facilely operate as to commercial agreements in today's dynamic economy. "The period of lives in being and 21 years, which works admirably with regard to gift transactions for family purposes, has no significance in the world of commercial affairs." (Leach, Perpetuities in a Nutshell (1938) 51 Harv. L. Rev. 638.)

Certainly our function is not to interpret the rule so as to create commercial anomalies. A lease to commence upon completion of the leased building is a common business arrangement. Such a clause is a standard provision of leases in shopping centers, which have been and are being constructed throughout the country; the parties to such transactions do not suspect that the rule will be extended to invalidate their agreements; even the attorneys who draw the leases may excusably not anticipate such application. Surely the courts do not seek to invalidate bona fide transactions by the imported application of esoteric legalisms. Our task is not to block the business pathway but to clear it, defining it by guideposts that are reasonably to be expected. As was pointed out in (1959) 47 Cal. L. Rev. 197, 200: "[A] strict and literal application of the Rule Against Perpetuities to a lease of this nature can do little to serve the basic purpose behind the rule and can result only in placing an unnecessary burden on the parties to an accepted commercial transaction." We therefore do not propose to apply the rule in the rigid or remorseless manner characterized by some past decisions; instead we shall seek to interpret it reasonably, in the light of its objectives and the economic conditions of modern society.

We turn to the specific relevance of the rule to the facts of this case. We could conceivably construe the instant transaction as one which creates a vested interest in a future term and invoke the principle that agreements which establish vested future interests escape the rule, despite the uncertainty or remoteness of the commencement of the term (see e.g., Francis v. Superior Oil Co. (10th Cir. 1939) 102 F.2d 732; Note (1959) 66 A.L.R.2d 733.) Indeed this technique for saving "on completion" leases was utilized in Isen v. Giant Food, Inc., supra (D.C. Cir. 1961) 295 F.2d 136, and to some extent in City of Santa Cruz v. MacGregor, supra (1960) 178 Cal. App. 2d 45, 54. Yet the parties here drew their agreement without regard to such legal niceties; they surely did not mean to differentiate between a present interest in a lease commencing in the future and a lease which only takes effect in the future. We do not believe that our decision should rest upon such contrived technicality, particularly as the distinction between vested and unvested rights is at best a confused one. We construe the document before us as a lease in which the lessee's interest vests only upon completion of the building.

Four contingencies, we are told, arise in the case of this lease to produce the possibility that the building may not be completed within the 21-year period of the statute: first, the process of construction might consume more than that period; second, the plans for the building might not be approved; third, the exceptions which excuse expeditious performance might delay completion beyond the statutory period; fourth, a building permit might not issue during such period. We examine each possibility in detail in order to demonstrate that such conjectures arise from two incorrect assumptions: (1) that cases involving the rule against perpetuities constitute a special legal preserve in which mechanical results will be condoned, and into which the accepted principle of reasonable construction cannot enter; (2) that even though an agreement by its terms does not transgress the rule against perpetuities, a violation may be predicated on the possibilities that the agreement will be broken and the parties unwilling to enforce their rights.

First. Plaintiffs' argument that the process of construction might be completed more than 21 years after the creation of the interest fails in the face of the requirements of the agreement that defendants begin construction "forthwith" upon approval of the completed plans, and "continue expeditiously" until the building is completed. The use of "forthwith" and "continue expeditiously," and additional clauses, contained in a contract which sets no specific date for completion of construction imposes upon defendants an obligation to complete construction within a reasonable time.

Plaintiffs maintain, however, that the requirement for completion within a reasonable time cannot be applied to avoid a violation of the rule against perpetuities. This position finds support in Haggerty v. City of Oakland (1958) 161 Cal. App. 2d 407, 420, 326 P.2d 957, in which the court rejected a similar argument as "deceptively simple" and "unsound," and asserted that "The courts are not permitted to relax the rule against perpetuities. . . . The rule itself contains no exceptions, and the courts should not create them." . . . Courts and scholars almost unanimously agree that provisions which make vesting contingent upon performance within a reasonable time, or some equivalent phrase, do not violate the rule "if, in the light of the surrounding circumstances, as a matter of construction 'a reasonable time' is necessarily less than twenty-one years." (3 Simes & Smith, Future Interests (2d ed. 1956) §1228 at p. 122.) Many courts, in fact, presume that a "reasonable time" is less than the period of the rule. In any event, a reasonable time in the present transaction, in the light of the circumstances, must necessarily be a period far less than 21 years. We cannot accept that portion of Haggerty v. City of Oakland which expresses a contrary position and, to that extent, it is disapproved.

. . .

Second. The argument that the plans for the building might not be approved within the statutory period can only stand if the lease is void for uncertainty; yet it is clearly valid in this respect. The lease provides that construction shall commence forthwith "upon approval of completed plans and specifications." Apparently "completed plans and specifications" refer to the plans which include the improvements to be added by plaintiffs, and the "approval" refers to approval by both parties. Plaintiffs claim this approval may not be forthcoming.

If plaintiffs' argument were correct, the agreement would be void for uncertainty since either party could withhold his approval of the plans and forestall construction (Kerr Glass Mfg. Corp. v. Elizabeth Arden Sales Corp. (1943) 61 Cal. App. 2d 55, 141 P.2d 938). Yet neither party makes such an attack upon it. Nor could such an attack succeed. Only a very narrow area could conceivably become a ground of possible future uncertainty or disagreement: the plans called for by paragraph 27 are "complete," and the parties' assent to the agreement constitutes an approval of those plans; paragraph 7 obligates plaintiffs to comply with municipal regulations. Hence the only possibility of disapproval lies in defendants' rejection of plans which meet municipal requirements. But defendants cannot unreasonably withhold approval of plans and specifications.

. . .

The fact of the matter is that neither party here claims that the courts cannot construe the agreement to effectuate the reasonable intent of the parties and enforce the agreement. The contention seems rather that although courts may construe agreements to avoid an invalidation for uncertainty they may not similarly construe agreements to avoid violation of the rule against perpetuities. Although the courts, at times, have been relentless in their application of the rule against perpetuities, they have seldom carried relentlessness to such extremes. Both the California cases, and those of a majority of other states, hold that a document should be interpreted if feasible to avoid the conclusion that it violates the rule against perpetuities.

Third. Because the agreement provides that the lessor's obligation to construct the building expeditiously is "subject to material and/or labor shortages, strikes, lockouts, governmental actions and all causes beyond the control of the Lessor," plaintiffs contend that such events might excuse the lessor from performance for a period in excess of 21 years. This clause, however, does not alter the fact that the parties contracted for a building to be completed in a reasonable time, that such reasonable time is far less than 21 years, and that failure to complete construction within the expected time will permit the parties to terminate the agreement. The clause simply alters the legal characterization of a failure to complete construction in the contingencies mentioned from that of a breach of duty, for which the lessor may be held responsible, to that of a commercial frustration, for which neither party may be held responsible.

Fourth. Plaintiffs contend that the building may not be constructed until a building permit is obtained and that such permit may conceivably not issue within the period of the rule. In Isen v. Giant Food, Inc., supra (D.C. Cir. 1961), 295 F.2d 136, a case involving an "on completion lease" in which construction turned upon the issuance of a zoning variance, the court stated, "We think, however, that the agreement required that zoning for commercial purposes, if obtained at all, must be obtained within a reasonable time and that such time, in the circumstances of this case, is certainly within the period of perpetuities." (Pp. 137-138.) (Accord, Francis v. Superior Oil Co., supra.) This analysis, we believe, applies here to the acquisition of a building permit.

We conclude that all rights established by the agreement arise within the 21-year period and that any breach of the agreement would be remediable within such period. Since the interest then does not vest or fail later than 21 years after its creation, the rule against perpetuities does not apply.

. . .

Gibson, C.J., Traynor, J., Schauer, J., McComb, J., and Peek, J., concurred.
Peters, J., dissenting.[104]

ATCHISON v. CITY OF ENGLEWOOD

Supreme Court of Colorado, 1969
170 Colo. 295, 463 P.2d 297

Groves, Justice. The plaintiffs in error, referred to as plaintiffs or by name, brought an action against the City of Englewood and Martin-Marietta Corporation as defendants for a determination with respect to plaintiffs' pre-emptive right to repurchase certain lands. The district court granted defendants' motions for summary judgment on the ground that the documentary provisions granting the rights to the plaintiffs were void as violative of the rule against perpetuities. We affirm.

In 1948 Mr. and Mrs. Atchison were, and for a number of years had been, the owners of approximately 2500 acres of land in Jefferson County, together with water rights belonging thereto. Englewood desired to acquire the water rights, but had no use for the land. However, the City concluded that it should purchase the land with the water in order to be in a possibly more favorable position when it prosecuted proceedings to change the points of diversion of the water and to change its use from irrigation to municipal purposes. A sale and purchase of the land and water from the plaintiffs to Englewood was arranged. The written documents involved gave the right to Mr. and Mrs. Atchison to repurchase the land (but without any

[104] Noted 16 Hastings L.J. 470; 12 U.C.L.A.L. Rev. 246. — Eds.

water transferred therefrom in the meantime) upon the same terms and conditions as Englewood might be willing to sell it to a third person. Later Englewood entered into a lease of most of the land (presumably with few or no water rights) and as a part of the lease granted to Martin-Marietta an option to purchase the demised property. Still later Martin-Marietta exercised the option and purchased the land. Under the record existing as a basis for the summary judgment we treat Mr. and Mrs. Atchison as having no knowledge and not being charged with notice of the option rights granted to Martin-Marietta; and that upon obtaining knowledge or being charged with notice they made timely filing of this action. They evinced a desire to purchase the land upon the same terms as the corporation had purchased it.

While there are some other problems involved of which we will make disposition, under our view the two principal questions presented are: (1) was the pre-emptive right granted Mr. and Mrs. Atchison personal, i.e., would it die with them and therefore not be violative of the rule against perpetuities; and (2), even if the pre-emptive right was not personal and would extend more than 21 years beyond the life of a person in being, should it be proscribed by the rule against perpetuities? We have not experienced too much difficulty in concluding that the right was not personal; but, as to the second question, the scales of decision are so evenly balanced that a little weight on either side would weigh it down. . . .

Under date of December 15, 1948 the plaintiffs and Englewood entered into an agreement of sale and purchase, referred to herein as the December agreement. By the terms of this contract the plaintiffs agreed to sell and Englewood agreed to buy the land and water rights (except one-half the mineral rights to be reserved by the plaintiffs) for a sales and purchase price of $350,000 to be paid by January 3, 1949. Paragraphs 11 and 13 of this agreement provided:

> "11. Concurrently with the delivery of the deed to said property and certificate for forty-five shares of stock of the Nevada Ditch Holding Company by the Atchisons to the City as in this contract provided, the parties hereto shall enter into a further contract under which the City shall give to the Atchisons the exclusive and prior right at the option of the Atchisons to repurchase or to lease said real estate, together with any water rights appurtenant to said lands at the time of such sale or leasing at the same price and upon the same terms and conditions upon which the City is willing to sell or lease said real estate and any water right then appurtenant thereto to any third person; and the City shall not sell or convey or contract to sell or convey or lease said lands or the water rights that may then be appurtenant thereto to any third person unless and until the City, for a period of 60 days, shall first offer in writing to sell or lease such lands with the then appurtenant water rights, if any, to the Atchisons at the same price and upon the same terms and conditions as in the case of such other sale or contract of sale or lease of such property to any third person. . . ."
>
> . . .
>
> "13. The terms and provisions hereof shall inure to the benefit of the heirs, legal representatives and assigns of the Atchisons."

On or about January 3, 1949 the consideration was paid to the plaintiffs, the property was conveyed by them to Englewood, and Englewood and the plaintiffs entered into "a further contract" (referred to as the January agreement) which provided as follows:

. . .

"1. The City hereby gives and grants unto the Atchisons the exclusive and prior right at the option of the Atchisons to repurchase or to lease the lands described in said Warranty Deed of even date herewith to which reference is hereby made for description of said lands; together with any water rights appurtenant to said lands at the time of such sale or leasing at the same price and upon the same terms and conditions upon which the City is willing to sell or lease said real estate and any water rights then appurtenant thereto to any third person; and the City shall not sell or convey or contract to sell or convey or lease said lands or the water rights that may then be appurtenant thereto to any third person unless and until the City, for a period of sixty days, shall first offer in writing to sell or lease such lands with the then appurtenant water rights, if any, to the Atchisons at the same price and upon the same terms and conditions as in the case of such other sale or contract of sale or lease of such property to any third person. . . ."

. . .

"3. The rights of the Atchisons under this agreement shall be deemed not in tenancy in common but in joint tenancy in them and in the survivor of them, their assigns and the heirs and assigns of such survivor."

I. Counsel for plaintiffs argue strenuously that the pre-emption granted to the "Atchisons" in paragraph 11 of the December agreement and in paragraph 1 of the January agreement was a right which was granted to them personally and would die with them. . . . [The court held that the pre-emptive right was not personal and would pass to the heirs and assigns of the Atchisons.]

II. We now approach the question of whether the rule against perpetuities should be applied to pre-emptive rights. At the outset the difference between an ordinary option and a pre-emptive right should be noted. In a typical option the optionee has the absolute right to purchase something for a definite consideration. A pre-emptive right involves the creation of the privilege to purchase only on the formulation of a desire on the part of the owner to sell; and, in the case here, the holder of the right must purchase for the price at which the owner is willing to sell to a third person.

It will be recalled that there is a difference between the rule against perpetuities and the rule against restraints upon alienation. Both rules have the same fundamental purpose, namely, to keep property freely alienable; or, stated differently, each stems from a general policy which frowns upon the withdrawal of property from commerce. The rule against perpetuities invalidates interests which *vest* too remotely. The rule against restraints upon alienation relates to other unreasonable restraints. For example, *A* conveys land to *B* in fee simple with the provision that if *B* during his lifetime shall convey or attempt to convey it the land shall become the property of C in fee simple. This does not violate the rule against perpetuities but is violative of the rule against restraints with the result that *B* obtains a fee simple absolute. An option given to a person, his heirs and assigns, to purchase land for $5,000 with no limiting term is void under the rule against perpetuities. The reason is that, with such an option outstanding the owner dare not place substantial improvements on the land, and the likelihood of anyone purchasing it is remote. The reason for application of the rule against perpetuities to a pre-emptive right to purchase at an offeror's price acceptable to the owner is not supported by the same reasoning as found in the option example, thus making the case for non-application much more arguable. See discussions in 6 American Law of Property commencing on the following pages: 13, 22, 141, 411, and 508.

The application of the rule to ordinary options is firmly established. However, so far as we are advised this is the first time that there has been before this court the question of application of the rule against perpetuities to a pre-emptive right to purchase at an offeror's acceptable price. The Restatement of the Law of Property makes no exception of pre-emptive right under the rule against perpetuities and in the comment following §413 it states, "Preemptive provisions, being analogous to options upon a condition precedent, must comply with the rule against perpetuities in so far as their maximum duration is concerned." IV Restatement of the Law of Property, p. 2444. In 6 American Law of Property §24.1, pages 7 and 8 Messrs. Leach and Tudor criticize the Restatement position and deplore what they state is the rule of the American Law Institute that it follows existing law and not what the law should be.

Other authorities supporting, or tending to support, the view that a pre-emptive right such as involved here is void under the rule against perpetuities are: Neustadt v. Pearce, 145 Conn. 403, 143 A.2d 437; H. J. Lewis Oyster Co. v. West, 93 Conn. 518, 107 A. 138; Saulsberry v. Saulsberry, 290 Ky. 132, 160 S.W.2d 654; Roberts v. Jones, 307 Mass. 504, 30 N.E.2d 392, 132 A.L.R. 663; 162 A.L.R. 604; and 41 Am. Jur. Perpetuities and Restraints on Alienation §41 (Supp. 1969). While statements of the American Law of Property, in citations already given, indicate that the law ought to be that the rule should not apply and that non-application is the modern trend, it nevertheless states, "If the preemptive provision is in the contract form only, the equitable future interest created can be held within the rule on the authority of the option cases." 6 American Law of Property §26.66, p. 510.

The plaintiffs rely upon Weber v. Texas Co., 5 Cir., 83 F.2d 807, cert. denied, 299 U.S. 561, 57 S. Ct. 23, 81 L. Ed. 413, and except as later mentioned it supports their position. There the owners of land leased it to Texas Company's assignor for prospecting and drilling for oil and gas. The lease was for a primary term of five years and as long thereafter as either oil or gas is or could be produced from any well on the land. The owners reserved a one-eighth royalty. The lease provided:

> The lessee is hereby given the option of purchasing all or any part of said royalty rights from the lessor at the best bona fide price offered by responsible third parties when and if offered for sale or transfer by lessor.

Texas Company acquired the lessee's interest and brought in a producing well. Prior to completion of the drilling the owners sold a one-fourth interest of their royalty to Weber for $7,000. As soon as Texas Company learned of this they tendered $7,000 for the interest sold. The tender was refused. Texas Company then sued for specific performance. It was held that the pre-emptive right was valid and enforceable. The court concluded that when an option simply gives an oil and gas lessee the prior right to take the lessor's royalty interest at the same price the lessor could and would secure from another purchaser, there is no restraint of free alienation by the lessor. The option, therefore, according to the court, should not be objectionable as a perpetuity. In Beets v. Tyler, 365 Mo. 895, 290 S.W.2d 76 the court indicates approval of the ruling in Weber. However, this is a dictum as the pre-emptive right before the court was for a term of only 20 years (except if all parties in interest should extend it for a further 20-year term by executing a new written instrument). For an interesting discussion of Weber and other authorities see Reasoner, Preferential Purchase Rights in Oil and Gas Instruments, 46 Texas Law Review 57, reprinted in 5 Rocky Mountain Mineral Law Review No. 2, p. 163.

We have held that before us is an inheritable pre-emptive right without limit as to time. It is in no manner connected with any land owned by Mr. and Mrs. Atchison. While they reserved one-half of the mineral rights, this interest can be sold at any time; and following a sale there will be no land title interest of record to give any clue as to the identity of future successors in interest to the pre-emptive right. We feel that at some point in the infinite time at which Englewood might in the future conclude to sell the land, ascertaining and locating the owners of the pre-emptive right would be an unreasonable task. As a result, there would be a sufficiently unreasonable restraint upon the transferability of the property as to justify imposition of the rule against perpetuities. It may be said that we are stating a rule against alienation and giving it a label of the rule against perpetuities. Be that as it may, the result is the same.[105]

It is to be noted that in Weber v. Texas Company, supra the identity of the owners of the interests involved could be ascertained — or at least with some reasonable investigation discovered — from the record title to the mineral rights and royalties. Our conclusion might be different here if the ownership of the pre-emptive right followed the title to designated real property; or, if it were restricted to a limited term found to be reasonable, albeit longer than a life in being plus 21 years. Be that as it may, we rule merely that a contractual right, granted to A and his heirs and assigns, unlimited as to time, to purchase land upon the same terms as the owner could and would sell to a third person, is void.

. . .

[105] Options to purchase land are not subject to the rule prohibiting direct restraints on alienation; if they were, such options could not exist. 6 American Law of Property §26.66 (Casner ed. 1952). However, courts have sometimes dealt with pre-emptions by applying the rule prohibiting direct restraints as well as the Rule against Perpetuities. A pre-emption limited to a life in being to purchase at a stipulated sum below market price seriously impedes marketability and improvement of land. See id. at §26.67; Boyer & Spiegel, Land Use Control: Preemptions, Perpetuities and Similar Restraints, 20 U. Miami L. Rev. 148 (1965). — Eds.

V. Plaintiffs' reply briefs were filed here on September 16, 1968. In August 1969, over objection of the defendants, we granted a motion of plaintiffs to file a supplemental pleading, with leave granted to the defendants to re-present their objections at the time of oral argument. The supplemental brief subsequently filed by the plaintiffs was built around section 394f in the 1948 supplement to the Restatement of the Law of Real Property which reads as follows:

> "*Effect of invalidity of option to repurchase.* An option to purchase the whole or any part of the interest conveyed is necessarily only one ingredient in the entire transaction between the parties. If this ingredient is so essential a part of the entire agreement that the parties would not have made the agreement if they had known of the option's invalidity, then the failure of the option is a sufficient basis for appropriate proceedings to rescind the entire transaction and to restore each of the parties to the situation in which he was before the transaction was made. The rule stated in this comment is a specific application of the rule stated in Section 402 concerning the effect of partial invalidity upon the balance of the attempted limitation."

Plaintiffs argue that, even if the pre-emptive right is violative of the rule against perpetuities, they are entitled to relief in the form of rescission. The first mention of rescission in the case was in the eleventh ground contained in the motion for new trial. This was to the effect that the court should not have granted summary judgment under the rule against perpetuities when the record disclosed facts warranting relief for specific performance, rescission, reformation, fraud, damage, unjust enrichment and failure of consideration.[106] This was an action for a declaratory judgment as to the validity of the plaintiffs' pre-emptive rights. It was presented to the trial court on that basis and neither this statement in the motion for new trial nor fleeting mention of it in the original brief filed here changed the nature of the case. For all practical purposes, this new theory in form of relief was first argued nearly a year after the case was at issue here. Until then the plaintiffs sought solely to have a determination that their pre-emptive right was enforceable. Considering all the circumstances, we think the presentation of this request for rescission came too late, and we now sustain the defendants' objection to that effect.

Judgment affirmed.

Kelley, J., dissenting.

On Petition for Rehearing, McWilliams, C.J., and Day and Groves JJ., would deny the petition.

Pringle, Hodges and Kelley, JJ., would grant the petition.

Lee, J., did not participate. The Court being equally divided, the Petition for Rehearing is denied.

[106] In Eastman Marble Co. v. Vermont Marble Co., 236 Mass. 138, 128 N.E. 177 (1920), it was held that if specific performance must be denied because the option violates the Rule against Perpetuities, damages cannot be obtained against the option-giver. — Eds.

5 POWELL, REAL PROPERTY (1970)

¶771. Privileged fettering — Application of the rule to options

[1] — *Effect generally on alienability.* The options commonly litigated in connection with the rule against perpetuities either

(1) Confer on a lessee some power in the future (if he chooses) to extend his term, or to alter his obligations, or to acquire ownership of the leased land; or

(2) Create a power in gross to buy, or reserve to the settlor a power to repurchase, specified land; or

(3) Authorize the holder of an easement or profit to use more land upon making stipulated future payments.

Insofar as these options involve a purchase they may be dependent only on the volition of the optionee, or they may give the optionee a power if, but only if, the optionor desires to sell. An option of this latter type is called a "preemptive option." It is apparent that any one of these options decreases the ease with which the affected land becomes marketable, and the question should be squarely faced as to what option, if any, serve [*sic*] business ends sufficiently to outweigh the social policy implemented by the rule against perpetuities.

Option cases, and writings concerning them, are full of specious reasoning by which the validity of the option is found without admitting that the case constitutes an exception to the rule against perpetuities. Chief among these are two: (1) that the option is only a "contract" and hence outside the scope of the rule's applicability;[107] and (2) that the optionee has a "present interest" which involves no problem of the rule.[108] Occasionally, a court erroneously construes the common law to be concerned only with suspensions of the power of alienation, and, on this basis, finds the option valid. A more realistic approach concedes that all options offend the basic policy of the rule, but recognizes that this offense can be properly offset by the utilities of some options and that this offsetting can make their validity important and desirable in a modern law not dominated by concepts. The problem then becomes one of balancing social utilities as to each type of option.

[107] This error is blatantly apparent in Courseview, Inc. v. Phillips Petroleum Co., 258 S.W.2d 391 (Tex. Civ. App. 1953); is insidiously present in the argument for allowing damages for breach of an option denied specific performance, Warren, "Progress of the Law," 34 Harv. L. Rev. 643 (1921): Note, 25 Colum. L. Rev. 77, 82 (1925); and seems to gain new vigor in Berg, "Long Term Options and the Rule Against Perpetuities." 37 Calif. L. Rev. 1, 235, 419 (1949).

[108] Gray, Rule Against Perpetuities §230 (4th ed. 1942), where the author in discussing a lessee's power to renew a lease, discards Jessel's suggestion that this is an "exception" to the rule and says: "[I]t seems hardly necessary to create any exception to meet the case — the covenant to renew is part of the lessee's present interest." Of course the lessee presently has the right to exercise his option in the future. In this same sense every future interest is a present interest, . . . but in no reasonable sense is the power to acquire ownership at a future date a present interest outside the purview of the rule. Mr. Gray's argument on this point was refuted adequately by T. Cyprian Williams, 42 Sol. J. 628 (1898), commenting on this passage in the first edition of the book.

On the approach suggested above, four types of options deserve separate weighing:

(1) Options to renew conferred on lessees;

(2) Options to purchase conferred on lessees;

(3) Options to extend the scope of an easement or profit by future acquisitions; and

(4) Options to purchase created either in gross or by the terms of a conveyance in the conveyee, or reserved to the conveyor.

Before engaging in this process of balancing social utilities, it is desirable to stress that the problem is not raised when the duration of an option cannot exceed the permissible period under the applicable rule against perpetuities.

[2] — *Specific types of options — Applicable rules.* Options to renew leases are generally valid and they need not comply with the rule against perpetuities. Such options to renew conferred upon lessees were sustained as valid, despite the rule against perpetuities as early as 1715. This position has found repeated acceptance in more recent cases. Their validity is accepted in the Restatement of Property and explained as a socially desirable exception to the rule against perpetuities.

Options to purchase conferred upon lessees have been held in England subject to regulation by the rule against perpetuities; but in the United States they have been generally treated as socially desirable exceptions to that rule, for the same reasons as those which apply to a lessee's option to renew or to extend his term.

Options to extend the scope of an easement or profit by future money payments have been generally found to be valid despite the rule against perpetuities, but the reasoning supporting the result has been commonly couched in terms of a "present interest," coupled with deferred payments. It would lessen the confusion in the law if these options were frankly recognized as having social advantages which outweigh the policy basing the rule against perpetuities.

Options to purchase or to repurchase land, unconnected with a lease, commonly denominated options in gross, have generally been held bad under the common-law rule against perpetuities, when not restricted in duration so as to comply with the permissible period under that rule. This result applies the rule against perpetuities, as it should be applied, to any future interest in specific property, where social advantages in permitting the type of interest are not affirmatively proved to outweigh the social policy of the rule favoring alienability.[109]

The English Perpetuities and Accumulations Act, 1964, §9, validates options (other than in a lessee) for twenty-one years. Options in leases are exempt from the Rule. Similar legislation exists in Ontario, Western Australia, and New Zealand.

[109] For an argument that options to purchase land should not be subject to the Rule against Perpetuities, see Morris & Leach, The Rule Against Perpetuities 224-227 (2d ed. 1962). — Eds.

ILLINOIS STATUTES ANNOTATED C. 30
(1969, Supp. 1971)

§194. *Application of the Rule Against Perpetuities*

(a) The rule against perpetuities shall not apply:

. . .

(5) to leases to commence in the future or upon the happening of a future event, but no such lease shall be valid unless the term thereof actually commences in possession within 40 years from the date of execution of the lease;

(6) to commitments (A) by a lessor to enter into a lease with a subtenant or with the holder of a leasehold mortgage or (B) by a lessee or sublessee to enter into a lease with the holder of a mortgage; nor

(7) to options in gross or to preemptive rights in the nature of a right of first refusal, but no option in gross shall be valid for more than 40 years from the date of its creation.

Note: Oil and Gas Conveyancing

The application of the Rule against Perpetuities to oil, gas, and mineral interests is quite complex and requires an understanding of a number of technical concepts used in the oil and gas field. The student who is interested in exploring this area further will find a careful and thorough explanation of the application of the Rule in 2 Williams & Meyers, Oil and Gas Law §§322-326, 335 (1970). Professors Williams and Meyers think that the Rule is generally ill-suited for both private needs and public policies in the oil and gas area.

Artists and Perpetuities

Works of art have greatly appreciated in value in the past several decades. An eighteenth-century Brussels hunting tapestry belonging to Adolph Lewisohn was sold at Parke-Bernet in New York for $275 in 1939. In 1965 a similar, but not so fine, tapestry brought $6500. A Baccarat cruciform bouquet paperweight that sold for $1080 in 1964 fetched $6720 in 1968. And paintings . . . ! The sky's the limit. "Portrait of a Scholar" by Frans Hals sold for $11,000 in 1939, but one would have to pay several hundred thousand dollars for a Hals today. Rembrandt paintings are knocked down at auction houses for over two million dollars. And not only the Old Masters fetch these prices. In 1967 modern paintings, on an average, sold for fifteen times their 1951 value while Old Master paintings had multiplied in price by only five or six times.[110] In a technological civilization with great upward social mobility, one-of-a-kind objects like antiques and art provide instant status as well as things of

[110] The Times-Sotheby Index, The Connoisseur, August 1967, p. 243.

beauty.[111] Everyone can have a motor car and a television set. Only the rich can have a Matisse.

Many artists have cast about for ways to cut themselves in for a share of the profit upon resale.[112] Artist Edward Kienholz is one of these. In 1969 Kienholz offered a number of watercolors for sale. He required each purchaser to sign an agreement that gives Kienholz 15 percent of the gross profit upon resale of the watercolor. Reproduced below is a copy of the agreement, using our old friend, Adam Smith, as the collector. Does this agreement violate the Rule against Perpetuities? [113]

AGREEMENT OF PURCHASE AND SALE

WITH RESERVED INTEREST

THIS AGREEMENT made this 1st day of April, 1969, by and between EDWARD KIENHOLZ (hereinafter "Kienholz") and ADAM SMITH (hereinafter "Collector");

WITNESSETH:

WHEREAS, Kienholz has created that certain work of art, a photograph of which is annexed hereto, commonly known as WATERCOLOR "For $68.00" (hereinafter "The Work"); and

WHEREAS, Collector desires to purchase The Work from Kienholz and Kienholz is willing to sell The Work to Collector subject to a reserved interest therein to Kienholz;

NOW, THEREFORE, in consideration of the foregoing premises and the mutual covenants hereinafter set forth, the parties hereto agree as follows:

Article I.

PURCHASE AND SALE

I.A. Kienholz hereby sells, transfers, sets over and assigns The Work to Collector and Collector hereby buys and accepts The Work, subject to the interest reserved to Kienholz in Article II.

I.B. The purchase price shall be the sum of $68.00 plus 3.40 tax payable in full in lawful money of the United States upon the execution of this Agreement.

Article II.

RESERVED INTEREST

II.A. Kienholz hereby reserves a fifteen percent (15%) interest (hereinafter "the interest") in and to The Work payable out of the gross profits (hereinafter "profits") to be derived or obtained from any and all future sales, transfers, trades or charitable gifts of The Work.

II.B. The sum representing the profits shall be paid in lawful money of the United States to Kienholz, concurrently with any transfer or transfers of The Work, whether by

[111] Reitlinger, The Economics of Taste (1961).

[112] In France and Italy laws give the artist a sum upon resale of his works. Price, Government Policy and Economic Security for Artists: The Case of the Droit de Suite, 77 Yale L.J. 1333 (1968).

[113] See 5 Powell, Real Property ¶¶775, 776 (1970); Simes & Smith, The Law of Future Interests §§1246, 1248 (2d ed. 1956).

sale, trade, or charitable gift made by Collector during the term of the interest; or from insurance proceeds therefor; said sum shall likewise be paid upon each successive transfer of The Work whether by sale, trade or charitable gift during the term of the interest.

II.C. "Profits" throughout this Agreement means:

(1) The excess of the agreed price received by the transferee upon any sale, trade or assignment of The Work over the agreed price parted with by the transferee upon acquisition of The Work, or, in the event the transferee is a non-profit institution or body acquiring The Work by gift, the amount specified in Paragraph II.C.(2).

(2) The excess of the value of The Work in the event of a transfer of The Work to a non-profit institution or body by gift over the agreed price parted with by the transferee upon his acquisition of The Work, it being conclusively presumed by the parties that the value of The Work as reflected in the transferor's federal income tax was and is the value of The Work on the date of such transfer.

II.D. The parties hereto agree that Kienholz shall have a lien upon The Work sold hereunder to Collector to secure payment of any sums due Kienholz under the terms of this Agreement and to secure compliance with each of the covenants contained herein. At any time Kienholz may affix to The Work or the base thereof for the duration of the interest, the following legend which shall not be removed:

> "Edward Kienholz, his heirs, assigns and devisees, own fifteen percent (15%) interest of this work and shall be paid fifteen percent (15%) of the gross profit derived from any sale, lease, or loan of this work and an amount equal to fifteen percent (15%) of any charitable deduction upon a gift of this work to a non-profit institution."

II.E. Collector shall advise Kienholz of any transfer, whether by sale, gift, loan, lease or trade, of The Work and shall furnish such information concerning such transfer as Kienholz may reasonably require.

II.F. Kienholz may assign his interest herein at any time and Collector shall make all payments and reports otherwise forthcoming to Kienholz to such assignee upon receiving notice of such assignment.

II.G. As used throughout this Agreement, "Collector" means Adam Smith, his heirs, assigns, beneficiaries, devisees and successors in interest.

II.H. This Agreement shall inure to the benefit of and be binding upon the parties hereto, together with their respective heirs, assigns, beneficiaries and successors in interest.

/s/ Edward Kienholz

EDWARD KIENHOLZ

/s/ Adam Smith

ADAM SMITH, Collector

SECTION B. Statutory Rules Against Perpetuities

Herein of the rule against suspension of the power of alienation, the New York two-life rule, and recent statutes exempting trusts from the Rule against Perpetuities.

1. *The Rule Against Suspension of the Power of Alienation*

Although since the time of Gray it has been settled that the rule against remote vesting is *the* common law Rule against Perpetuities, it was not clear before Gray whether there was also a common law rule against suspension of the power of alienation. Gray insisted there was not, and his view prevailed. However, in 1830 New York enacted statutes forbidding suspension of the power of alienation for more than a specified period.[114] Several other states copied or were influenced by this New York legislation.[115] After Gray's book was published, establishing that the rule against suspension of the power of alienation was not the common law Rule against Perpetuities, these states were left with the problem of determining whether their statutes were declaratory of the common law, as Gray had later interpreted it, or were additions to or replacements of that law.[116]

The rule prohibiting suspension of the power of alienation is clearly distinguishable from the rule against remote vesting. The rule against remote vesting (the common law Rule against Perpetuities) is directed against contingent interests that may remain contingent beyond lives in being plus twenty-one years. The policy underlying it is that all contingent interests, assignable and nonassignable, impair marketability. The rule prohibiting suspension of the power of alienation proceeds upon a different policy assumption. *The power of alienation is suspended only when there are not persons in being who can convey an absolute fee.* The rule assumes that legally unassignable interests make property unmarketable and should be struck down if they remain unassignable for more than the permitted period. Since all vested and contingent future interests are assignable or releasable if (a) the holders thereof are ascertainable and (b) there is no express restraint upon alienation, the only interests that suspend the power of alienation, absent an express restraint, are

[114] In their present form, they are N.Y. Estates, Powers & Trusts Law §9-1.1 (1967).

[115] See 5 Powell, Real Property ¶¶808-827 (1970); Simes & Smith, The Law of Future Interests §§1411-1439 (2d ed. 1956).

[116] Professor Powell argues that the New York revisers were attempting to restate the common law as it existed at that time. 5 Powell, Real Property, ¶791 [3] (1970). In Matter of Wilcox, 194 N.Y. 288, 87 N.E. 497 (1909), the court held that the rule against remoteness of vesting was also part of the New York law, so that New York has both the remoteness of vesting rule and the suspension rule, which has never been repealed.

Practically all of the other states that enacted a rule prohibiting suspension of the power of alienation have in time either reinstated the common law Rule against Perpetuities by statute or declared the suspension statute to be declaratory of the common law rule against remote vesting. 5 Powell, Real Property, ¶¶808-827 (1970). In Minnesota only the suspension rule, and not the remoteness of vesting test, is applicable to interests in land. Id. ¶819. See Newman, Perpetuities, Restraints on Alienation, and the Duration of Trusts, 16 Vand. L. Rev. 57 (1962).

interests given to unborn or unascertained persons. To put it shortly, the rule against remote vesting applies to all contingent interests; the rule against suspension of the power of alienation applies only to interests that are contingent because the taker is unborn or unascertainable (or to interests where the transfer is restrained expressly or by law).

The rule against remoteness of vesting is the more inclusive. Except for a restrained interest, any interest that will violate the suspension rule will necessarily violate the rule against remoteness, but the converse is not true. Thus:

> *Case* 22. (*Contingent remainder after term of years*) T devises property "to A for ninety-nine years, then in fee to B Church if it is then in existence." The power of alienation is never suspended since A, B Church, and T's heir (the reversioner) may join together and convey a fee simple. Under the suspension rule all interests are valid. However, the gift to B Church is contingent on its being in existence after ninety-nine years, and this violates the rule against remote vesting. (If the gift over had been to A's issue whenever born living ninety-nine years from now, the gift over would be to unascertained persons and would have violated both rules.)

> *Case* 23. (*Shifting executory interest*) O deeds land "to B Church, but if it ceases to use the land for church purposes, then to X." The contingent interest in X may be conveyed, and thus does not suspend the power of alienation. However, it is contingent on an event that may happen too remotely and is void under the rule against remote vesting.

Options to purchase land create no suspension of the power of alienation since the holder of the option and the landowner can together convey a fee simple in the land. Similarly a lease to commence in the future does not suspend the power of alienation since the lessee and lessor can together convey a fee simple.

In addition to enacting a rule prohibiting suspension of the power of alienation for more than a specified period, the New York revisers of 1830 provided that the interest of the beneficiary of a trust "to receive" the rents and profits of real property and "apply them to the use of any person" was inalienable.[117] This provision led the New York courts to conclude that the duration of such a trust was limited to the period specified in the perpetuities legislation. Inasmuch as most trusts are trusts "to receive and apply," most New York trusts which can exceed the perpetuity period in duration are invalid. Herein lies the most important difference today between the common law Rule (which does not restrict the duration of trusts) and the New York statutory rule.[118]

[117] A parallel provision was subsequently added to the Personal Property Law, and these provisions, in their present form, are set forth in N.Y. Estates, Powers & Trusts Law §7-1.5 (1967).

[118] 5 Powell, Real Property ¶793 (1970). In re Morosan's Will, 46 Misc. 2d 284, 259 N.Y.S.2d 445 (1965), held that a trust to last until Romania was no longer under communist domination was void, even though all interests in the trust vested at the testator's death. The case is criticized by Pasley, Future Interests, 17 Syracuse L. Rev. 257, 265 (1965).

2. *The New York Two-Life Rule*

Another major innovation of the 1830 New York revisers was to shorten the perpetuity period by (1) reducing the measuring lives from a reasonable number to *two* lives in being, (2) eliminating the twenty-one-year period in gross permitted by the common law rule, and (3) allowing the use of a minority period after the two lives as part of the permissible period under restricted circumstances. This restrictive legislation caused much difficulty for estate planners and extensive litigation over instruments that would have been perfectly valid in states following the common law Rule. In 1886 John Chipman Gray was moved to say that "in no civilized country is the making of a will so delicate an operation, and so likely to fail of success, as in New York." [119]

In an attempt to salvage reasonable dispositions the New York courts invented a number of unusual constructional rules.[120] Among the most important were the following:

1. Inference that separate trusts were intended. A trust for the three children of testator might be saved by inferring separate trusts for each child, particularly where upon the death of each child the share of the corpus on which he had been receiving the income goes to his children. Or a trust for testator's widow for life, then for his children for their lives, might be saved by inferring separate trusts for each child after the widow's death. On the death of each child the corpus of his trust is distributable.

2. Early closing of classes. A testamentary gift to "A's children who reach twenty-one" would be saved by closing the class at testator's death if there were only two children then alive.

3. Construction of "youngest child" to mean youngest child at the time the conveying instrument speaks. A testamentary gift to "A's children when the youngest child reaches twenty-one" would be construed to give the property to A's children when the youngest child living at testator's death reaches twenty-one. That specific child becomes the measuring life.

4. Implication of "or sooner dies." In the preceding example of a gift to "A's children when the youngest child reaches twenty-one" suppose the youngest child living at testator's death, named D, dies at age ten. To insure that only one measuring life and no period in gross would be used, the court would imply, "or sooner dies," and distribute the property at D's death. Such a salvaging operation could not apply if the draftsman had stipulated to "A's children when the youngest child reaches twenty-one or would have attained that age had he lived."

5. Inferring a "natural term" of a trust. A trust for the benefit of more than two persons to end on the death of the last beneficiary may be saved if the court finds the purpose of the trust will be fully accomplished within a natural (and valid) term of not more than two lives. Judicial reasoning applying this rule was not easy to follow.

[119] Gray, Rule against Perpetuities §750 (1st ed. 1886).
[120] 5 Powell, Real Property ¶804 (1970).

6. Postponing selection of second life. The courts permitted the selection of the second measuring life to be made at the end of the first measuring life, provided that all possible candidates for the second measuring life were in being when the instrument spoke. Thus a trust could endure for the life of testator's widow and the youngest child of testator living at the widow's death.

In 1958 New York repealed the two-life rule, and substituted a reasonable number of measuring lives as the permissible period. Two years later New York repealed the restrictive minority provisions and added a twenty-one-year period in gross. Hence after 130 years of experimenting with a different perpetuity period, which engendered the most complex and unpredictable law of any state, New York returned to the perpetuity period of the common law.[121] The 1958-1960 acts were not retroactive, however, and the old law will continue to be relevant for many years.

FETTERS, FUTURE INTERESTS, 19 Syracuse L. Rev. 419, 427-428 (1967): ". . . But why should New York courts continue to be plagued by the old perpetuities rules? Why should we continue to engage in expensive litigation which requires the application of tortuous reasoning, linguistic legerdemain and doubtful speculations as to testamentary intent, to escape results no longer deemed illegal or unreasonable? The stock answer is that 'retrospective legislation, unless adopted in pursuance of the police power, cannot impair vested rights.' But what vested right would be abridged by legislation which would permit courts to apply present perpetuities law retroactively? Does the following argument raise serious constitutional objections to such reform? 'I have an interest in the testator's property because he goofed; and even though he intended for me to take nothing under his will, nonetheless, he violated the rule against perpetuities and so, in effect, his instrument created in me vested rights in his property which cannot be taken from me without due process of law.' Although stated somewhat facetiously and in the extreme, this basically is the substance of the argument against applying a *less restrictive* perpetuities law retroactively." [122]

3. *Exemption of Interests in Trust from the Rule against Perpetuities*

In recent years Wisconsin and Illinois have enacted statutes exempting interests in trust from the Rule against Perpetuities. The Wisconsin statute is more far-reaching and codifies case law in that state. In 1849 Wisconsin enacted a statute, copied from New York, prohibiting suspension of the power of alienation for more than two lives in being. This statute was subsequently changed to permit suspension of the power of alienation for any reasonable number of lives plus thirty years. This

[121] For the whole story, see id. ¶¶791-807B. Several states copied the New York two-life rule in the nineteenth century, but it has been repealed in all of them except Minnesota (applicable to land). Id. ¶819. Vestiges of the restricted minority period remain in South Dakota. Id. ¶825. See also 6 American Law of Property §§25.36 to 25.58 (Casner ed. 1952).

[122] The Massachusetts court applied the state's wait-and-see statute retroactively, even though the statute expressly stated it was to apply to instruments taking effect after its effective date. Warner v. Whitman, page 1035, supra. — EDS.

is the most liberal perpetuity period in effect in any jurisdiction. In interpreting this statute the Wisconsin court held that, in the case of a trust, the existence of a power of sale in the trustee made the trust property alienable, and that alienability of the trust property was all that was required to satisfy the suspension statute.[123] The court also held that the statute prohibiting suspension of the power of alienation was the only rule against perpetuities in the state; the rule against remote vesting had been superseded by the statute. In 1969 this view was enacted into statutory form.

WISCONSIN STATUTES ANNOTATED C. 334 (1969)

§700.16 *Perpetuities and suspension of power of alienation*

(1) (a) A future interest or trust is void if it suspends the power of alienation for longer than the permissible period. The permissible period is a life or lives in being plus a period of 30 years.

. . .

(2) The power of alienation is suspended when there are no persons in being who, alone or in combination with others, can convey an absolute fee in possession of land, or full ownership of personalty.

(3) There is no suspension of the power of alienation by a trust or by equitable interests under a trust if the trustee has power to sell, either expressed or implied, or if there is an unlimited power to terminate in one or more persons in being.

. . .

(5) The common-law rule against perpetuities is not in force in this state.

COMMITTEE ON RULES AGAINST PERPETUITIES, FURTHER TRENDS IN PERPETUITIES

5 Real Prop., Prob. & Trust J. 333, 334-337 (1970)

The duration of any private trust in Wisconsin now rests in the discretion of the settlor, subject only to three provisions in a new chapter on trusts. One of these permits a court, with the consent of the trustee, to terminate a trust, in whole or in part, "if the court is satisfied that because of any substantial reason existing at the inception of a testamentary trust or, in the case of any trust, arising from a subsequent change in circumstances (including but not limited to the amount of principal in the trust, income produced by the trust and the cost of administering the trust), continuation of the trust, in whole or in part, is impracticable." [124] Another provision reserves "the general equitable power of a court to modify or terminate a trust in whole or in part." [125] A third provision permits a court to make an allowance

[123] Will of Walker, 258 Wis. 65, 45 N.W.2d 94 (1950).
[124] Wis. Stat. Ann. ch. 283, §701-13(3) (Wis. Leg. Serv. Supp. 1969).
[125] Id. §701.13(6).

from principal to an income beneficiary if his support or education is not sufficiently provided for, unless the creating instrument provides to the contrary.[126]

Within these limits, it is now possible in Wisconsin for a settlor to leave substantial wealth in trust for his lineal descendants in perpetuity. Regardless of unforeseeable needs and exigencies, the capital fund constituting such a trust estate remains beyond the reach of present and unborn generations of beneficiaries, except for their right to claim the income which it earns or such relief as the abovementioned provisions of the trust statute may provide.

Suppose as a variant possibility a perpetual or unlimited trust for "A and his heirs." This would not offend traditional perpetuity doctrine. But there is authority that the requirements of the Claflin doctrine cannot be invoked to prevent termination of such a trust at any time, if termination is demanded by the beneficiary.[127] In other words a "perpetuity" in its largest sense implies more than a remote vesting of future interests. A special rule about trust duration where the beneficial interests are vested is ancillary to the common-law Rule Against Perpetuities. Is there anything comparable in Wisconsin? If the only perpetuity doctrine is that relating to the suspension of the power of alienation as defined by the Wisconsin statute, there does not appear to be any limitation upon trust duration other than as specified in the new trust and property statutes.

Traditional equitable powers in courts governing trust termination hardly seem equal to the need for reasonable limits on trust duration, especially for trusts containing spendthrift provisions, or trusts which purport to limit only a succession of income interests through successive generations. It would be possible for the Wisconsin courts to adapt and enlarge their equitable powers so as to evolve a doctrine to relieve against the continuance of trusts which otherwise would continue for unreasonably long periods. Perhaps the new Wisconsin legislation was framed upon the expectation of such a development. But no such doctrine now exists, nor is there any assurance that it will be forthcoming.

Whatever may be the historical justification for so limited a conception of the scope of perpetuity doctrine, is there any policy justification for a doctrine which permits perpetual private trusts? What in fact are the proper policy objectives of a modern perpetuity law? Is it solely an economic policy protecting alienability to secure productivity? If so, since the control of the devolution of family wealth is now so much exerted by means of the trust device, has the Rule Against Perpetuities outlived its usefulness?

In a penetrating analysis of the dead-hand control of property, Professor Simes has identified a further principle of social policy to vindicate in our time the basic thrust of the traditional common-law Rule Against Perpetuities.[128] He has defined this policy as follows:

> ". . . [T]he Rule against Perpetuities strikes a fair balance between the desires of members of the present generation, and similar desires of succeeding generations, to do what they wish with the property which they enjoy. . . .

[126] Id. §701.13(2).
[127] Simes and Smith, Future Interests §1393 (1956); Restatement, Property §381 (1944).
[128] Simes, Public Policy and the Dead Hand 58 (1955).

"But, in my opinion, a second and even more important reason for the Rule is this. It is socially desirable that the wealth of the world be controlled by its living members and not by the dead. I know of no better statement of that doctrine than the language of Thomas Jefferson, contained in a letter to James Madison, when he said, 'The earth belongs to the living generation. They may manage it then, and what proceeds from it, as they please during their usufruct.' "

Even under a narrow view of perpetuity policy as limited to protecting alienability to secure productivity, trusts which assure alienability only by virtue of the trustee's power of sale may fall short of adequate protection for such a policy. It is hardly necessary to labor the point that in practical effect the power of sale in a trustee is very different from the power of alienation in an owner in fee simple. . . .

Are the evils of potentially excessive trust duration only theoretical or imaginary? No one has ever been sure what donors would do if the inhibitions of perpetuity doctrine were removed from their planning. But it is evident even as one works within traditional regimes that one of the greatest current incentives in estate planning is the vision of estates passing from generation to generation without the successive impact of estate taxation. These pressures, more than the egocentric whims of eccentric donors about unborn generations of their offspring, are the basis for concern about the proper dimensions of the law on ownership and alienation.

If the specter of a simple perpetual trust for one's issue is not realistic, the pressures for tax avoidance can produce schemes less offensive to perpetuity policy but which suspend the impact of estate taxes over several generations. Throughout the period of a trust for a donor's issue, for example, the income beneficiaries can be given special powers to appoint shares of the corpus and by this means permit partial or complete termination of the trust. If this or more elaborate kinds of tax-avoiding schemes are resorted to in Wisconsin for periods which are in flagrant disregard of the limits of traditional perpetuity law, it is not likely that the guardians of the Internal Revenue Code will allow the matter to pass without notice. Amendments of that Code, couched in terms of general applicability, but designed to plug gaps produced by peculiar local laws, are difficult to frame without creating traps for unwary draftsmen in other states. It would be a formidable undertaking to frame a federal estate tax so as to take into account a variety of local laws on perpetuities.

SIMES & SMITH, THE LAW OF FUTURE INTERESTS
(*2d ed. 1956*)

§1391. *Trusts as Perpetuities*

Without doubt the very existence of a trust often tends to restrain the alienability of property as a practical matter. Sometimes the trustee is given no power, or only a very limited power, to alienate the subject matter of the trust. Even if his powers of investment and reinvestment are very broad, he does not have the unlimited power of alienation of an owner. He cannot give the property away; he cannot spend it for his own enjoyment. It may also be said that the equitable interest in a trust is alienable by the beneficiary in the absence of anything in the terms of the trust to the contrary. However, an equitable interest in a trust is commonly not as marketable as a legal fee simple; and, whatever may be the powers of the beneficiary to alienate, he is not likely to find many buyers for his interest.

Hence, in spite of the fact that the trust is one of the most useful devices in our legal system, it very commonly constitutes an indirect restraint on alienation. Thus it is only reasonable that the law places some restrictions on trusts, in furtherance of its policy of free alienability of property.

Before discussing restrictions peculiarly applicable to the duration of trusts, a few preliminary observations should be made. The rule against remotely contingent future interests, discussed in the preceding chapter, commonly called the rule against perpetuities, applies to contingent equitable interests in trusts as well as to legal interests in property. On the other hand, according to the common law, a private trust with definite beneficiaries, is not void merely because it may endure longer than lives in being and twenty-one years.

It is only when a trust is indestructible that the law has developed special rules for its restriction. What is meant by an indestructible trust? In a word, it is a trust which the courts will not terminate at the request of, and for the benefit of, the beneficiary or some other ascertained person; or it is a trust which is not terminable because it has no definite beneficiary. The policy of the law with respect to the duration of indestructible trusts would seem to be expressed by the following proposition: A private trust cannot be made indestructible, by its terms, for a longer period than a life or lives in being and twenty-one years beyond. The cases are none too clear as to the precise scope of this policy, but the statement herein made is believed to be an expression of the doctrine toward which the courts are tending. It may be said that this is but a branch of the rule against perpetuities. But the present tendency is to treat it as a separate, but closely related, doctrine.

DOWNING, THE DURATION AND INDESTRUCTIBILITY OF PRIVATE TRUSTS

16 W. Res. L. Rev. 350, 362, 365-366, 368, 370, 390-391 (*1965*)

. . . [I]t is the writer's opinion that the public policies which support the Rule Against Perpetuities and provide the essential framework for a discussion of trust duration and indestructibility must be regarded as being primarily concerned with society's interest in promoting the free circulation and maximum utilization of property, and only secondarily concerned with unfettering the interests of individual property owners as a means for achieving those more fundamental ends. It is also the writer's opinion that, given this view of the objectives of public policy, a rule of trust law which serves only to unfetter the interests of individual beneficiaries and which fails to meet the needs of society itself, is inadequate and unacceptable.

If one shares these opinions, it then becomes necessary to consider whether there is anything in the nature of long-lasting private trusts which may offend the interests which society itself has in the free circulation and maximum utilization of property, and which cannot in all cases be remedied by giving trust beneficiaries the power of termination after the perpetuities period has run its course. This is really the most critical aspect of the whole duration and indestructibility problem, for on it the case for a rule strictly limiting trust duration must either stand or fall. . . .

In the writer's opinion, a justification for such a rule in terms of society's interests does in fact exist, and in a word can be traced to the conservative investment control which corporate trustees exercise over the enormous assets which are held today in private trusts. . . . Corporate trustees, aided by tax laws which encourage the settlement of long-lasting trusts and by the complexities involved in administering wealth in today's society, have become the managers of vast wealth, much of it represented by corporate securities. Yet, at the same time, it is also no secret that, while the assets under the investment control of these trustees have increased by geometric leaps and bounds, the inhibitions (practical if not legal) against their investment of even a small fraction of those assets in truly speculative ventures have in no way diminished. Nor are they likely ever to diminish, even with the continued liberalization of the rules regulating the investment powers of trustees, since gambling with trust assets and the welfare of trust beneficiaries has always been, and is likely to always remain, contrary to the corporate trustee's role as protector and preserver of property.

The inevitable result of all of this is the drying up of the available sources of risk capital. . . .

The conclusion which is to be drawn from this discussion on the objectives of social policy and on the economic problems created by conservative trustee investment control over enormous resources is that a rule limiting the duration of private trusts can be legally and socially justified. Such a rule would serve to protect not only the interests of individual trust beneficiaries (except in those cases where the beneficiaries themselves want their interests to remain in trust after the perpetuities period has elapsed), but also the interests which society has in promoting the free circulation and maximum utilization of wealth. . . .

. . . [A]ny rule limiting trust duration must, to be effective, invalidate at the outset any trust having a capacity for excessive duration. Such a rule, while it might operate harshly on the objectives of the settlor, would at least accomplish its stated social objectives, and would in addition serve as a deterrent to the creation of long-lasting trusts. Furthermore, a rule couched in such terms would fit the pattern which has already been set in cases dealing with the duration of "honorary" trusts and trusts for unincorporated associations. . . .

In an area where there is so little conclusive authority and so much uncertainty, this adoption of the rule against prolonged indestructibility by the Restatement [of Trusts, Second §62] may be expected to have a wide influence upon the future course of the law of trusts. Even though all the features of this new rule have not been settled by the courts or the writers, the basic approach to the problem has now been definitely staked out. And while excessive duration itself may no longer subject a trust to immediate external attack, despite the important social and economic reasons for sustaining such external attacks, it is now quite clear that a well-presented argument on behalf of the beneficiaries may expose a trust to internal attack and termination once the perpetuities period has expired.

ILLINOIS STATUTES ANNOTATED C. 30 (*1969, Supp. 1971*)[129]

§195. *Trusts*

(a) Subject to the provisions of paragraphs (e) and (f) of this Section, a trust containing any limitation which, but for this paragraph (a), would violate the rule against perpetuities (as modified by Section [194]) shall terminate at the expiration of a period of (A) 21 years after the death of the last to die of all of the beneficiaries of the instrument who were living at the date when the period of the rule against perpetuities commenced to run or (B) 21 years after that date if no beneficiary of the instrument was then living, unless events occur which cause an earlier termination in accordance with the terms of the instrument and then the principal shall be distributed as provided by the instrument.

(b) Subject to the provisions of paragraphs (c), (d) and (e) of this Section, when a trust terminates because of the application of paragraph (a) of this Section, the trustee shall distribute the principal to those persons who would be the heirs at law of the maker of the instrument if he died at the expiration of the period specified in paragraph (a) of this Section and in the proportions then specified by statute, unless the trust was created by the exercise of a power of appointment and then the principal shall be distributed to the person who would have received it if the power had not been exercised.

(c) Before any distribution of principal is made pursuant to paragraph (b) of this Section, the trustee shall distribute, out of principal, to each living beneficiary who, but for termination of the trust because of the application of paragraph (a) of this Section, would have been entitled to be paid income after the expiration of the period specified in paragraph (a) of this Section, an amount equal to the present value (determined as provided in paragraph (d) of this Section) of the income which the beneficiary would have been entitled to be paid after the expiration of that period.

(d) In determining the present value of income for purposes of any distribution to a beneficiary pursuant to paragraph (c) of this Section:

(1) When income payments would have been subject in whole or in part to any discretionary power, it shall be assumed (A) that the income which would have been paid to an individual income beneficiary would have been the maximum amount of income which could have been paid to him in the exercise of the power, (B) if the income would or might have been payable to more than one beneficiary,

[129] For an explanation see Schuyler, The Statute Concerning Perpetuities, 65 Nw. U.L. Rev. 3, 47-56 (1970).

that (except as hereinafter provided) each beneficiary would have received an equal share of the income, unless the instrument specifies less than an equal share as the maximum amount or proportion of income which would have been paid to any beneficiary in the exercise of the power, in which event the maximum specified shall control, and (C) if the income would or might have been payable to the descendants of the maker of the instrument or of another person that, unless the instrument provides otherwise, the descendants would have received the income per stirpes;

(2) (A) present value shall be computed on an actuarial basis and there shall be assumed a return of 5%, at simple interest, on the value of the principal from which the beneficiary would have been entitled to receive income, and (B) where the interest in income was to be for the life of the beneficiary or for the life of another, the computation shall be made on the expectancy set forth in the most recently published American Experience Tables of Mortality and no other evidence of duration or expectancy shall be considered;

(3) If the trustee cannot determine the present value of any income interest in accordance with the provisions of the instrument and the foregoing rules concerning income payments, the present value of the interest shall be deemed to be zero.

(e) This Section applies only when a trust would violate the rule against perpetuities as modified by Section [194] and does not apply to any trust which would have been valid apart from this Act.

(f) This Section does not apply when a trust violates the rule against perpetuities because the trust estate may not vest in the trustee within the period of the rule.

SECTION C. The Rule Against Accumulations

1 SCOTT, TRUSTS
(3d ed. 1967)

§62.11. *Accumulations.* In England at common law a provision in the terms of the trust that the trustee should not pay out the income but should accumulate it was valid, at least if the accumulation was not for a period longer than that of the rule against perpetuities, namely lives in being and twenty-one years. In other words, if a gift of the principal vested within the period, a provision that the income was to be added to and distributed with the principal at the termination of the trust was valid.

It was so held in the famous case of Thellusson v. Woodford [4 Ves. 227, 31 Eng. Rep. 117 (Ch. 1798); 11 Ves. 112, 32 Eng. Rep. 1030 (Ch. 1805)]. In that case Peter Thellusson left the residue of his estate in trust to collect the income and invest it in land during the lives of all of his issue who should be living at the time of his death, and on the death of the last survivor of such issue to convey one third to the eldest lineal male descendant then living of each of his three sons in tail male with remainders in tail to the others, and in default of such descendant to the King to be applied to reduce the national debt. The widow and children brought a suit in equity, to have the trusts declared void. The Lord Chancellor, assisted by three of the judges, held that the will was valid; and on appeal the decree was affirmed by the House of Lords. It is to be noted that there was no violation of the rule against perpetuities, since the interests all vested at the expiration of lives in being at the time of the testator's death. Lord Eldon, speaking in the House of Lords, said that "another question arises out of this Will; which is a pure question of equity: whether a testator can direct the rents and profits to be accumulated for that period, during which he may direct, that the title shall not vest, and the property shall remain unalienable; and, that he can do so, is most clear law." Since the estate was large, the residue amounting to something like £600,000, and since Thellusson left at his death nine descendants most of whom were infants, Lord Eldon was somewhat appalled at the possible amount of the accumulation, but he thought that the remedy rested with the legislature. Parliament, after the decision of the Lord Chancellor, and before the decision of the House of Lords, enacted the so-called Thellusson Act, by which it was provided that provisions for accumulation should be void if made for any longer term than the life of the settlor, or for twenty-one years from his death, or during the minorities of beneficiaries or others.

In the United States, in the absence of a statute, it is held that a provision for accumulation for a period not longer than the period of lives in being and twenty-one years is valid.

Where the income which is accumulated is to be paid to one whose interest does not vest within the period of the rule against perpetuities, the whole gift to him fails, of course, including the gift of the accumulated income. Suppose, however, that all interests vest within the period, but that there is a provision for accumulation for a longer period. Suppose, for example, that a testator leaves property in trust for the sole benefit of his son, giving the son an immediate and unconditional beneficial interest, but with a provision that the trustees shall accumulate the income for thirty years, and that at the end of that period they shall pay over the principal and accumulated income to the son, his executors, administrators or assigns. In such a case it seems clear that the disposition does not fail altogether, and that the son has the whole beneficial interest in the property. The only question is whether the provision that the trust shall continue for thirty years and that the income shall be accumulated during that period is invalid. If it is invalid, the son will be entitled immediately to demand the income and perhaps also the principal. In England there is no difficulty, since the sole beneficiary of a trust can terminate it at any time. In the United States, however, the sole beneficiary cannot compel the termination of the trust if such termination is contrary to the intention of the settlor, and if the settlor's intention does not run counter to any rule of law or policy. We have seen that a provision precluding the beneficiary from terminating the trust is valid if it does not extend beyond the life of the beneficiary, but that it may be invalid if it extends beyond the period of the rule against perpetuities. At any rate it seems that a provision for accumulation for a period longer than that of the rule against perpetuities should be invalid, even though all interests are vested within the period.

In the case of charitable trusts, the rule is somewhat different. If the gift for charitable purposes is immediately vested or becomes vested within the period of the rule against perpetuities, the trust is valid even though there is a provision for accumulation of the income. The only question is whether that provision is valid. In England it is held that the direction to accumulate the income for charitable purposes is invalid, and the income should be immediately applied to the charitable purposes. In the United States it is held that the provision for accumulation is valid, provided that it is not to continue for an unreasonably long time, and a time may not be unreasonable even though it is longer than lives in being and twenty-one years. But where the gift for charitable purposes is contingent upon an accumulation of income for a period which may exceed the period of the rule against perpetuities, the gift fails altogether.

In several states there are statutes which provide that plans for employees, such as pension, stock-bonus, disability, death-benefit or profit-sharing plans, shall not be held invalid as violating the rule against perpetuities or against suspension of the power of alienation or against accumulations.

The New York Revised Statutes of 1830 drastically reduced the period of time during which income could be accumulated. A number of states followed New York's lead. With the rise of the federal income tax came tax advantages to a trust where the trustee had the power to pay or accumulate income. These tax advantages resulted in the repeal of almost all state statutes restricting the accumulation of income to a period shorter than the perpetuity period. 5 Powell, Real Property ¶¶833-835 (1970). The Tax Reform Act of 1969 curtailed, but did not totally eliminate, the income tax advantages of an accumulation trust. See Int. Rev. Code of 1954, §§665-669; Casner, Effect of Tax Reform Act of 1969 on Usability of Certain Types of Trusts, 6 Real Prop., Prob. & Trust J. 352 (1971).

SECTION D. Farewell to the Rule

One of the stranger epiphenomena of the Rule against Perpetuities is the appearance of student poetry. To end our study of the Rule we offer one student's bid for immortality.

THE RULE AGAINST PERPETUITIES
(Or, Through a Glass Darkly)

A life in being plus twenty-one —
The worst of rules beneath the sun.

Gray's statement of the Rule, though brief,
  Has caused the most God-awful grief.

The unborn widow laughs aloud —
  Her predecessor lies in shroud
(Whose children gnash their teeth and pray,
  "Avoid the gift to the widow of A.")
Oh, if T had but seen their doom,
  Drawing nigh from another's womb.

The octogenarian suppresses a smile,
  Though lacking issue quite a while.
Medically, 'tis said, his chances are nil —
  Our old boy is over the hill.
But the Rule doth plainly say
  That this old dog may have his day.

A limitation of much mirth:
  To miners digging 'neath the earth.
Who, by the court's own fine decree
  Are given jobs — eternally.
No union contract can omit —
  All hail the Magic Gravel Pit!

A rule that is of doubtful worth;
  Lacks common sense but shows much mirth:
No man, it is absurdly said,
  Can have a brother when he's dead.
Rhymes are made by fools like me,
  But rules like this are hard to see.

"To A and heirs — but from the time
  A hardy soul should dare to climb
And, caring little for his fate,
  Leaps from the top of Empire State."
What gift, you ask, is this bequest?
  A springing future interest!

What can be done to set men free
  From rules against perpetuity?
Clearly we must devise some plan
  To keep our families on the land.
The answer makes a socialist quail —
  We'll re-enact the Old Fee Tail!

— The Nitty Gritties

P.S. To the Professor:

If this rhyme has given you mirth,
   Please take it for what it's worth.
Give us a chance for an 83 —
   Question not on Perpetuitee.

It developed that the poet who called himself The Nitty Gritties[130] was a sensitive lad. He must have watched with dismay as the professor read the poem, smiled — and tucked it away. The day's assigned materials did not allow time for reading the poem aloud to the class. The next day another poem appeared.

THOUGHTS UPON AN UNREAD LYRIC

God's blood! What knavery!
   Censorship, after poetic slavery.

If it be that our work offends,
   What can be done to make amends?

If not, please end our gloom,
   And read aloud to the entire room.

— The Nitty Gritties

P.S. Please change the 83 to a 93.

— T. N. G.

The professor then read both poems to the class, commenting on the merits of the verse. Here is T. N. G.'s reply.

L'ENVOI

You've mocked my verse until I curse,
   You've called my meter rotten.
The question is, in this biz,
   What's easier forgotten?

Is it my rhymes — that passed the times,
   Or your rules, so brilliantly given?

130 Reputed to be Peter D. Preston, University of Texas School of Law, Class of '66, now practicing in Seattle, Washington.

It may not avail if the course I should fail,
  But for immortality I've striven.

So in days yonder when you should ponder
  On those who have taken gas,
Save a kind word, since you have heard
  He who rhymed, but could not pass.

— T. N. G.

Appendix A. Estimate of Adam Smith's Life Insurance Needs

The memorandum that follows summarizes our discussion with Adam Smith on his life insurance needs. The approach taken in gauging Smith's insurance requirements is based on The Consumer Union Report on Life Insurance: A Guide to Planning and Buying the Protection You Need (1967). (For a description of this approach see page 190, supra.)

I asked Smith how much monthly income he thought his family would need if he were to die within the next year or so. He replied by asking me, "What do *you* think?" I told him that Consumer Union consultants estimate it would take 65 to 75 percent of a family's after-tax income to maintain the same general standard of living. Said Smith, "That would be around $9000 a year. Let's say $750 a month. That would be about right when the children were being raised, but after that I guess my wife could get along on less; something around $500 a month."

I charted these amounts (see next page), and also the monthly income Mrs. Smith would receive in social security survivor benefits. By my estimate, as of January 1973, Smith's earnings average for social security purposes would be $6780, and the Smith family would be eligible for monthly benefits of $440. This benefit would continue until the youngest Smith child (born 8/22/70) attained age eighteen. At that point Mrs. Smith would no longer be eligible for widow-with-dependent-children benefits. For the next year, however, there would be two Smith children under age twenty-two and (let us assume) in college. The two children would be eligible for combined benefits of around $360 per month. When the second child attained age twenty-two her benefit would terminate, but the youngest child would be entitled to a benefit of about $180 until she attained age twenty-two. After this there would be no social security benefits until Mrs. Smith attained age sixty.

ESTIMATED FAMILY INCOME NEEDS FOR ADAM SMITH FAMILY

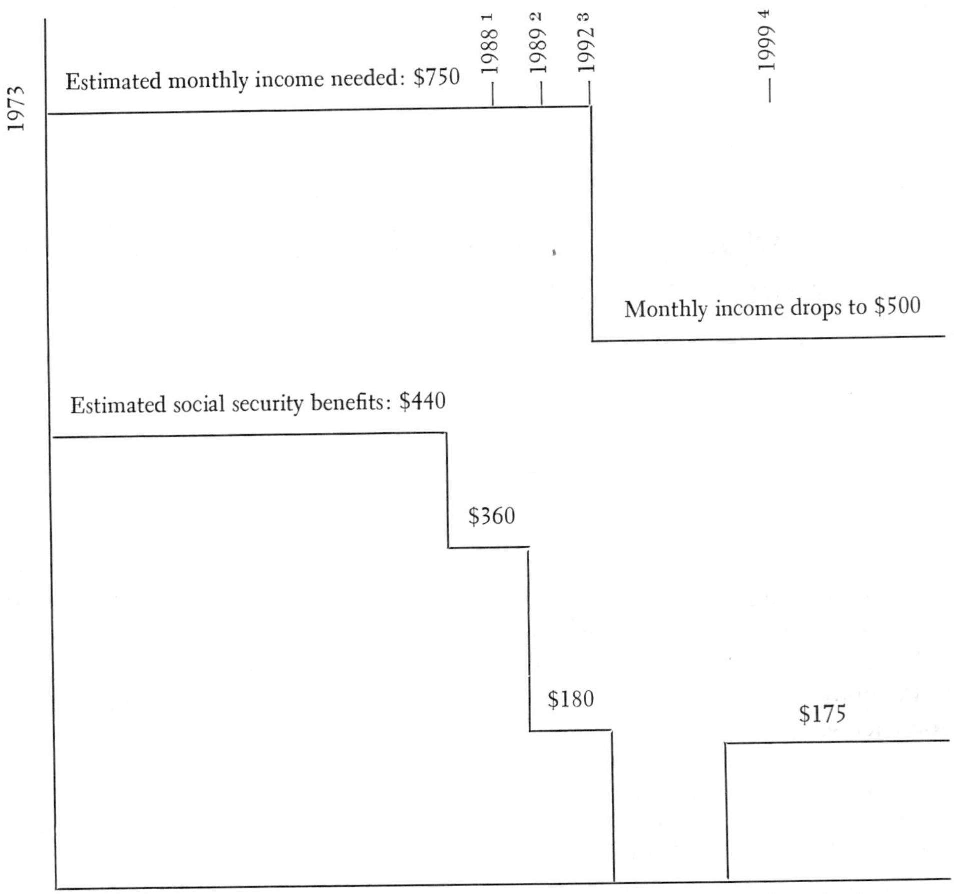

[1] Youngest child (born 8/22/70) attains age 18; social security survivor benefits drop to $360/month.
[2] Second child (born 11/19/67) attains age 22; social security benefits drop to $180/month.
[3] Youngest child attains age 22; social security survivor benefits terminate.
[4] Mrs. Smith (born 6/1/39) attains age 60; eligible for social security benefits of $175/month.

Based on these estimates, if Smith were to die in 1973 his family would need an income, over and above social security, of $310 per month in order to provide the desired income level of $750 per month. This sum would be needed for fifteen years, at which point the social security benefits would decrease and the monthly income required from other sources would increase. The principal amount needed to produce this monthly income for fifteen years would be 141 × $310, or $43,710. (See Table A.) Observe that the Consumer Union table for estimating income requirements uses a net annual interest rate of 3½ percent and contemplates consumption of principal as well as income. In the first year the income earned by a $43,710 fund (at 3½ percent) would be $1530, or around $130 per month. The remaining amount would be taken from principal. Each year the income from the fund would decrease and the amount of principal consumption would increase. In the last month of the fifteenth year the fund would be exhausted.

TABLE A — SURVIVORS' INCOME

After you have determined how much monthly income your survivors would need in addition to social security, and for how long, find the appropriate number of years in the table below. Then apply the adjacent multiplier to the monthly income figure. The resulting amount is the lump sum you need now to provide that monthly income. (This table is constructed on the assumption that the lump sum will be deposited at 3½% net annual interest after income taxes.) Thus, to provide \$100 a month for ten years starting now, you would need \$100 × 102, or \$10,200.

Years of income needed	*Multiplier*	*Years of income needed*	*Multiplier*	*Years of income needed*	*Multiplier*
1	12	16	148	31	229
2	23	17	155	32	233
3	34	18	161	33	237
4	45	19	168	34	241
5	55	20	174	35	245
6	65	21	180	36	248
7	75	22	185	37	252
8	84	23	191	38	255
9	93	24	196	39	258
10	102	25	202	40	261
11	110	26	207	41	264
12	118	27	211	42	267
13	126	28	216	43	270
14	134	29	221	44	272
15	141	30	225	45	275

For the next year social security benefits would drop to \$360 per month; the income from other sources required to produce \$750 per month would increase to \$390. The fund needed to supply this additional monthly income would be 12 × \$390, or \$4680. This fund would not be needed for fifteen years, however. To reflect the interest that would be earned by this fund over a fifteen-year period, this amount should be discounted by 60 percent, to \$2808. (Stated another way, \$2808 deposited at 3½ percent interest compounded annually will grow to \$4680 in fifteen years. See Table B.)

For the next three years social security benefits would drop to \$180 per month; the income required from other sources would increase to \$570 per month. The principal sum would be 34 × \$570, or \$19,380; discounted by sixteen years, \$11,235. For the next seven years there would be no social security benefits; \$500 per month would be required. Principal sum: \$37,500; discounted by nineteen years, \$19,500.

TABLE B — DISCOUNT FACTORS FOR MONEY NEEDED LATER

If your heirs are not to start spending certain insurance funds for a number of years, these funds should be discounted for the interest they can earn in the interim. In the table below, find the number of years before the income will be needed. Then multiply the adjacent discount factor by the lump sum needed. The result is the amount that, when invested at 3½% net, will grow to the lump sum needed in the appropriate number of years. Thus, to provide $8000 for college — but starting 16 years from now — your insurance policy should supply only .58 × $8000, or $4640.

Years before income is needed	*Discount factor*	*Years before income is needed*	*Discount factor*	*Years before income is needed*	*Discount factor*
0	1.00				
1	.97	16	.58	31	.34
2	.93	17	.56	32	.33
3	.90	18	.54	33	.32
4	.87	19	.52	34	.31
5	.84	20	.50	35	.30
6	.81	21	.49	36	.29
7	.79	22	.47	37	.28
8	.76	23	.45	38	.27
9	.73	24	.44	39	.26
10	.71	25	.42	40	.25
11	.69	26	.41	41	.24
12	.66	27	.40	42	.24
13	.64	28	.38	43	.23
14	.62	29	.37	44	.22
15	.60	30	.36	45	.21

Referring once again to the chart on page 1094, I pointed out to Smith that when his wife reached age sixty in 1999, she would be eligible for social security benefits of $175 per month. (At that point Smith gave me an odd look and asked, "Did you say 1999?" I disregarded the question and continued with my explanation.) To bring her monthly income up to $500 per month, $325 would be required from other sources. Using the fifteen-year multiplier, this would require $45,825; discounted by twenty-six years, $18,788.

Hence the amount needed to give the desired income level of $750 per month and later $500 per month, based on these estimates, would be $96,000.

1973 to 1988	$43,710
1988 to 1989	2,808
1989 to 1992	11,235
1992 to 1999	19,500
Retirement income	18,788
	$96,041

Smith commented that despite the seeming precision of the mathematical computations, this was rather more of a guess than a scientific analysis. My reply: "Quite so." He also expressed some astonishment that he would have to provide this large a fund to furnish the desired income level. I then explained that we weren't through yet. Did he want to establish funds for the college education of his three children? "Absolutely. They'd probably need around $2000 per year. I'd like to set up an $8000 fund for each of them." For the eldest Smith child (born 9/25/64) the $8000 fund would be needed in ten years, when he attained age 18. Discounted, the present value of this fund would be $5680. For the second child the required fund (discounted by thirteen years) would be $5120; for the third child (discounted by sixteen years), $4640. Thus the present value of the required college fund would be $15,440.

Finally, I suggested that Smith might want to provide a source of ready funds from which Mrs. Smith could meet the expenses of administering his estate, and medical and other emergency expenses that might arise in the future. Said Smith, "If possible, I'd like to set aside $7500 for this purpose."

Family income fund	$96,000
College fund	15,500
Emergency fund	7,500
	$119,000

I then explained that from this sum we should deduct the amounts that would be available to Mrs. Smith from Smith's present assets. (See Smith family balance sheet, page 77.)

Bank accounts	$5,000
Securities	12,245
Employee death benefit	4,200
Present insurance coverage	47,000
	$68,445

Based on these calculations, estimates and presumptions, Smith would have to acquire an additional $50,500 in insurance coverage in order to provide the desired funds.

PROBLEM

What is your assessment of this method of gauging insurance needs? Specifically, what are its weaknesses? Do any of the factors tend to overstate (or understate) the family's income and other needs, or the funds required to meet those needs? Is it realistic, or even rational, to make the kinds of assumptions upon which the calculations are based?

Appendix B. Will (with Guardianship Provision) for Adam Smith*

LAST WILL OF ADAM SMITH

I, Adam Smith, of 2220 Casino Lane, Arlington, ... County, ..., declare this to be my last Will, and I hereby revoke all wills and codicils heretofore made by me.

ARTICLE I. I give all of my property of whatever kind and wherever located that I may own at the time of my death to my wife, Jane Smith, if she survives me by sixty days. If she does not so survive me, I give the same to my descendants who survive me by sixty days, per stirpes.

I do not intend by this will to exercise any powers of appointment which I possess or may come to possess.

ARTICLE II. I appoint my wife, Jane Smith, as Executrix of this will. If for any reason she is unable or unwilling to serve or continue to serve in that capacity, I appoint my good friend, Einar Paulson, of Arlington, ..., as Executor. If for any reason he, too, is unable or unwilling to serve or continue to serve in that capacity, I appoint the Arlington National Bank, of Arlington, ..., as Executor. My Executrix or Executor shall have the fol-

* *CAVEAT:* The wills and trusts in Appendices B through E are not presented as unimprovable models. With respect to each clause the student should seek to determine its purpose and see if it can be improved upon. The student should also look for problems that may arise and are not solved by clauses in the instruments. The instruments are designed to be used as the basis for classroom discussion.

Many banks with trust departments publish form books that they make available to attorneys and law students. In addition to these form books we have found the following books particularly useful: Casner, Estate Planning (3d ed. 1961, with supplements); Johnson, A Draftsman's Handbook for Wills and Trust Agreements (1961); Shaffer, The Planning and Drafting of Wills and Trusts (1972).

lowing powers and discretions, and any others that may be granted by law, to be exercised without court order:

(a) To retain all property of my estate, regardless of lack of diversification, risk, or nonproductivity;

(b) To sell any real or personal property of my estate, for cash or on credit, at public or private sale, for any purpose; to exchange any such property for other property; to grant options to purchase or acquire any such property; to lease any such property; and to determine the prices and terms of sales, exchanges, options, and leases;

(c) To borrow money and to mortgage or pledge any property of my estate;

(d) To employ attorneys, accountants, and investment advisers, and to act without independent investigation upon their recommendations, and to employ depositaries, proxies, and agents; and to keep any property in the name of an executor or a nominee, with or without disclosure of any fiduciary relationship, or in bearer form;

(e) To collect, pay, contest, compromise, or abandon claims of or against my estate, wherever situated; and to execute contracts, notes, conveyances, and other instruments, including instruments containing covenants and warranties binding upon and creating a charge against my estate, and containing provisions excluding personal liability;

(f) To make any distribution of my estate in cash or in kind or both; and

(g) To allocate different kinds or disproportionate shares of property or undivided interests in property among the beneficiaries, and to determine the value of any such property.

Article III. If my wife does not survive me, or if she dies after my death without having made provision for the custody and care of my minor children, or for the management of such children's estates, I appoint my sister-in-law, Barbara Preston Widman, of San Francisco, California, as Guardian of the persons and estates of my minor children. If for any reason she is unable or unwilling to serve or continue to serve in that capacity, I appoint my brother, Henry M. Smith, of Salem, ..., as Guardian of the persons and estates of my minor children.

The Guardian shall arrange for the welfare and education of my children according to the dictates of her or his conscience, shall have the authority to determine what is in the best interest of my children, and may expend the income and principal from the children's estates as in her or his sole discretion is deemed appropriate for their support, maintenance, and education.

Article IV. I direct that no bond or other security shall be required, in any jurisdiction, of any person named in this will as Executrix, Executor, or Guardian.

Article V. The term "children" as used in this will includes children hereafter born to or adopted by me, as well as the children that I now have. The term "descendants" as used in this will means the immediate and remote lawful, lineal descendants by blood or adoption of the person referred to who are in being at the time they must be ascertained in order to give effect to the reference to them. However, the term "descendants" shall not include persons adopted after they reach the age of twenty-one.

ARTICLE VI. The term "per stirpes" as used in this will means the property shall be distributed to the persons and in the proportions that my personal property would be distributed under the laws of the state of ____________________ in force sixty days after my death if I had died intestate at such time, domiciled in such state, not married and survived by descendants.

ARTICLE VII. My wife and I are at approximately the same time executing wills containing similar dispositive provisions. These wills are not the product of any contract or agreement, and my wife shall be free to dispose of any property (whether acquired under this will or otherwise) either during her lifetime or by will as she sees fit.

I have signed this Will, which is typewritten on three sheets of paper, on this _____ day of ____________________, 19____, and have also written my name on the margin of the first two pages hereof.

____
Adam Smith

On the _____ day of ____________________, 19____, Adam Smith declared to us, the undersigned, that the foregoing instrument was his last Will, and he requested us to act as witnesses to it and to his signature thereon. He then signed the Will in our presence, we being present at the same time. We now, at his request, in his presence, and in the presence of each other, hereunto subscribe our names as witnesses, and each of us declares that in his or her opinion this testator is of sound and disposing mind and memory.

______________________________	______________________________
Name	Address
______________________________	______________________________
Name	Address
______________________________	______________________________
Name	Address

[In executing his will, Adam Smith should follow the procedure recommended at pages 290-292.]

Appendix C. Will (with Contingent Trust Provision) for Adam Smith

LAST WILL OF ADAM SMITH

I, Adam Smith, of 2220 Casino Lane, Arlington, ... County, ..., declare this to be my last Will, and I hereby revoke all wills and codicils heretofore made by me.

ARTICLE I. I give all of my property of whatever kind and wherever located that I own at my death as follows:

1. To my wife, Jane Smith, if she survives me by sixty days.

2. If she does not so survive me but one or more of my children survive me by sixty days, to the Trustee named in Article III, to be held and administered in trust for my children, their spouses, and their descendants pursuant to the terms of the trust there set forth.

3. If neither my wife nor any of my children so survive me, to those persons who would have inherited my personal property were I to have died sixty days after the date of my actual death, not married and domiciled in the State of ...., under the laws of the state of .... in force at that time, the shares and proportions of taking to be determined by said laws.

ARTICLE II. I do not intend by this will to exercise any powers of appointment which I possess or may come to possess.

ARTICLE III. If, pursuant to Article I, property passes to the Trustee for the benefit of my children, the Trustee shall hold and administer the property in trust as follows:

1. So long as there is any living child of mine under the age of twenty-one years, the Trustees may from time to time distribute all or so much of the income

or principal of the trust as the Trustee in her or his discretion deems appropriate for the health, support, maintenance or education of any of my children, their spouses, or their descendants, and any income not so distributed shall be accumulated and added to principal. During the term of the trust the Trustee shall not be obligated to maintain equality among the beneficiaries with respect to distributions either of income or of principal. Distributions of income or principal to or on behalf of the beneficiaries may be made in any one or more of the following ways: (a) directly to the beneficiary; (b) to the Guardian of the person or of the estate of the beneficiary; (c) to a relative of the beneficiary under an agreement to expend it for the benefit of the beneficiary; or (d) by the Trustee expending the income or principal directly for the health, support, maintenance, or education of the beneficiary.

2. As a guide to the Trustee, but without intending to limit or control the Trustee's discretion, I offer the following expressions of intent as to the purposes of this trust. My primary objective is to provide for the support and health needs of my children, their spouses, and their descendants during the term of this trust. A secondary objective is to provide funds for the education of my children. But if any beneficiary has unusual health or medical problems, these shall first be provided for before expenditures for any other purpose. In the absence of competing considerations, the Trustee should make an effort to provide equality of distribution among my children or their families. However, disparate needs may and probably will arise, particularly as to health and medical expenses, and perhaps also as to educational expenses. The Trustee should not hesitate to make unequal distributions if in the Trustee's discretion she or he deems it appropriate.

It is not my primary objective, in establishing this trust, to provide a cash legacy for my children, their spouses, or their descendants living at the termination of the trust. If, after the health or other needs of the beneficiaries have been met during the term of the trust, there is a fund remaining on hand at the trust's termination, well and good. But the Trustee should not be conservative in making interim distributions of principal and income simply to provide lump-sum gifts upon the termination of the trust.

Should this Article III be operative, my minor children will be in the custody and care of the Guardian named elsewhere herein. This is bound to increase the household expenses and cramp the living quarters of the Guardian and her or his family. It is my intent that the Guardian shall not suffer additional expenses and unwarranted inconveniences because of the assumption of this position of responsibility toward my children, and that she or he shall be fully and liberally compensated out of income or principal for all additional expenses occasioned by the guardianship duties. As illustrative of the types of expenditures for which reimbursement should be made, the following are to be deemed for the health, support, and maintenance of my children: (a) The purchase of a larger residence or the remodeling of an existing residence in order to provide appropriate accommodations for my children (the trust should bear the difference between the present value of the existing house and the cost of a new house, if a larger residence is purchased, and the

Guardian should have no obligation to reimburse the children upon their attaining majority or upon termination of the trust); and (b) additional expenses for food, utilities, furniture, and domestic help occasioned by the inclusion of my children in the Guardian's family unit. Although these expenditures may be seen as indirectly benefiting the Guardian, they are seen by me as necessary to provide my children with the style and comforts of life I would have provided them were I living. The decision of the Trustee to make distributions for these purposes shall be conclusive, even though the Trustee makes distribution to herself or himself as Guardian of the person of my children.

3. This trust shall terminate when there are no living children of mine under the age of twenty-one years. Upon termination, the Trustee shall distribute the trust principal and accumulated income as follows:

(a) To my descendants then living, per stirpes. If any of my children dies before termination of the trust, not leaving descendants who are living at the termination of the trust, but leaving a spouse who is living at the termination of the trust, the share that would have passed to the child had he then been living shall instead go to the spouse of that child.

(b) If none of my children, their descendants, or their spouses, is living at the termination of the trust, to those persons who would have inherited my personal property were I to have died intestate on the date of termination of the trust, not married and domiciled in the state of ...., under the laws of the state of .... in force at that time, the shares and proportions of taking to be determined by said laws.

4. No interest under this trust shall be transferable or assignable, or be subject to the claims of any beneficiary's creditors.

5. I appoint my sister-in-law, Barbara Preston Widman, of San Francisco, California, as Trustee. If for any reason she is unable or unwilling to serve or continue to serve in that capacity, I appoint my brother, Henry M. Smith, of Salem, ..., as Trustee. If for any reason he, too, is unable or unwilling to serve or continue to serve in that capacity, I appoint the Arlington National Bank, of Arlington, ..., as Trustee.

6. The Trustee shall have the following powers and discretions, and any others that may be granted by law, to be exercised without court order:

(a) To retain all property devised or transferred to the Trustee, including residential property, regardless of any lack of diversification, risk, or lack of productivity. With respect to any items of tangible personal property that are bequeathed to the Trustee, the Trustee may in her or his discretion hold all or any part of them until termination of the trust, deliver all or any part of them at any time to a beneficiary for his or her use or to any person with whom a beneficiary is residing, without further responsibility, or may sell all or any part of them and add the proceeds to the principal of the trust.

(b) To invest and reinvest the trust estate in any property, including stocks, regardless of class, investment trusts, mutual funds, and common trust funds, without being limited by any statute or rule of law concerning investments by trustees.

(c) To sell any trust property for cash or on credit at public or private sale; to exchange any trust property for other property; to grant options to purchase or acquire any property; to lease any trust property; and to determine the prices and terms of sales, exchanges, options, and leases.

(d) To borrow money and to mortgage or pledge any trust property.

(e) To employ attorneys, accountants, and investment advisers, and to act without independent investigation upon their recommendations, and to employ depositaries, proxies, and agents; and to keep any property in the name of a trustee or a nominee, with or without disclosure of any fiduciary relationship, or in bearer form.

(f) To take any action with respect to conserving or realizing upon the value of any trust property, and with respect to foreclosures, reorganizations, or other changes affecting any trust property; and to collect, pay, contest, compromise, or abandon claims of or against the trust estate.

(g) To make any distribution of trust property in cash or in kind or both; and to allocate different kinds or disproportionate shares of property or undivided interests in property among the beneficiaries, and to determine the value of any such property.

7. No person paying money or delivering any property to the Trustee need see to its application.

8. The approval of the accounts of the Trustee, in an instrument signed by my adult children and by the Guardians of my minor children, shall be a complete discharge and release of the Trustee with respect to the administration of the trust property for the period covered by such accounts, binding on all persons, and no other Trustee shall have any responsibility for such accounts.

9. Any Trustee may resign at any time by a signed instrument filed with the trust records, after giving written notice, specifying the effective date of resignation, to my adult children and to the Guardians of my minor children. Any successor Trustee, whether appointed herein or appointed by a court if all the Trustees named herein are unable to serve or continue to serve, shall have all the title, powers, and discretions of the Trustee succeeded, without conveyance or transfer.

Article IV. I appoint my wife, Jane Smith, as Executrix of this will. If for any reason she is unable or unwilling to serve or continue to serve in that capacity, I appoint my good friend, Einar Paulson, of Arlington, ..., as Executor. If for any reason he, too, is unable or unwilling to serve or continue to serve in that capacity, I appoint the Arlington National Bank, of Arlington, ..., as Executor. My Executrix or Executor shall have all the powers and discretions with respect to my estate during its administration that are enumerated in Article III, clause 6, and any others that may be granted by law, to be exercised without court order.

Article V. If my wife does not survive me, or if she dies after my death without having made provision for the custody and care of my minor children, or for the management of such children's estates, I appoint my sister-in-law, Barbara Preston Widman, of San Francisco, California, as Guardian of the person and

Adam Smith

estates of my minor children. If for any reason she is unable or unwilling to serve or continue to serve in that capacity, I appoint my brother, Henry M. Smith, of Salem, ..., as Guardian of the persons and estates of my minor children.

The guardian shall arrange for the welfare and education of my children according to the dictates of her or his conscience, shall have the authority to determine what is in the best interest of my children, and may expend the income and principal from the children's estates as in her or his sole discretion is deemed appropriate for their support, maintenance, and education.

ARTICLE VI. I direct that no bond or other security shall be required, in any jurisdiction, of any person named in this will as Executrix, Executor, Trustee, or Guardian.

ARTICLE VII. The term "children" as used in this will includes children hereafter born to or adopted by me, as well as the children that I now have. The term "descendants" as used in this will means the immediate and remote lawful, lineal descendants by blood or adoption of the person referred to who are in being at the time they must be ascertained in order to give effect to the reference to them. However, the term "descendants" shall not include persons adopted after they reach the age of twenty-one.

ARTICLE VIII. The term "per stirpes" as used in this will means the property shall be distributed to the persons and in the proportions that my personal property would be distributed under the laws of the state of .... in force sixty days after my death if I had died intestate at such time, domiciled in such state, not married and survived by descendants.

ARTICLE IX. The term "adult" as used in this will means a person over the age of twenty-one. The term "minor" means a person under the age of twenty-one.

ARTICLE X. My wife and I are at approximately the same time executing wills containing similar dispositive provisions. These wills are not the product of any contract or agreement, and my wife shall be free to dispose of any property (whether acquired under this will or otherwise) either during her lifetime or by will as she sees fit.

I have signed this Will, which is typewritten on five sheets of paper, on this _____ day of ____________________, 19____, and have also written my name on the margin of the first four pages hereof.

____

Adam Smith

On the _____ day of ____________________, 19____, Adam Smith declared to us, the undersigned, that the foregoing instrument was his last Will, and he requested us to act as witnesses to it and to his signature thereon. He then signed the Will in our presence, we being present at the same time. We now, at his request, in his presence, and in the presence of each other, hereunto subscribe our names as witnesses, and each of us declares that in his or her opinion this testator is of sound and disposing mind and memory.

Name	Address
____________________	____________________
Name	Address
____________________	____________________
Name	Address

INTEROFFICE MEMORANDUM

The School of Law Date: April 13, 1972

TO: Bill Gibson
FROM: Stanley Johanson
RE: Draft of Will with Contingent Trust Provision for Adam Smith

As I mentioned to you, Adam Smith has decided upon a will that makes outright distribution of his estate to Mrs. Smith if she survives him by sixty days, and establishes a "contingent trust" for the Smith children if she does not. Smith plans to have his life insurance policy proceeds paid outright to Mrs. Smith if she survives him by sixty days; otherwise the proceeds will be paid "to the trustee named in my will" pursuant to the secondary beneficiary designation in his policies.

Attached is the first draft of the will that I have prepared for Smith. I would appreciate your reading it and giving me your observations and suggestions before I present it to him.

/s/ smj

INTEROFFICE MEMORANDUM

The School of Law Date: April 20, 1972

TO: Stanley Johanson
FROM: Bill Gibson
RE: Adam Smith's Will

Here are some observations on the will you have drafted for Adam Smith.

1. The devise to Mrs. Smith is conditioned upon sixty days' survival and, failing such survival, the property is to pass into the contingent trust. The sole condition of the gift to the trust is the failure of Mrs. Smith to survive with the survival of Adam by one or more children. This paragraph's language would cause the property to pass in trust even if all the children were over twenty-one years of age. In the event that all the children were over twenty-one at the time of Adam's death, the trust would probably be considered to have terminated, with the distribution to be made in accordance with its terms. This seems rather awkward; it would seem pref-

erable to place the further condition that the contingent trust would exist only if one or more of the children were under twenty-one or incapacitated in some way. I gather that you had in mind that Adam's children are quite young at this time. But as time passes my observation will become more pertinent. Shouldn't you draft the will to cover this contingency, even though the possibility of this contingency occurring will not arise for a number of years?

PROBLEMS

a. How would you answer Mr. Gibson's question?

b. Redraft Article I to meet Mr. Gibson's objection.

2. It seems to me that you have failed to provide for the possibility that issue of a deceased child may be incapacitated by minority or that a child may be disabled for some other reason at the time the trust is terminated. Wouldn't Smith want the trust to continue if this were the case?

PROBLEM

c. Redraft Article III, paragraph 3, to meet this objection.

3. A question might be raised as to whether the power of appointment given to the trustee is an exclusive or nonexclusive power. While we are told that the trustee does not have to maintain equality, there is nothing suggesting that he can exclude entirely one or more other beneficiaries.

PROBLEM

d. Do you agree that this is a problem? If so, how would you redraft Article III to meet this objection?

4. You have provided that the trustee and the guardian are to be the same person, and you have given the trustee and guardian powers that can be exercised to benefit himself individually. In my opinion, you have given him a general power of appointment under Int. Rev. Code of 1954, §2041. Is this advisable? What size estates do the named trustee-guardians have? In any event the named persons would want to be apprised of this potential tax problem before they qualified.

PROBLEM

e. Is Mr. Gibson correct on this? If so, what should be done?

5. There is perhaps some ambiguity in paragraph 2 of Article III as to whether the reimbursement of the guardian is at the discretion of the trustee or whether it is obligatory. The statement, "It is my intent that the guardian shall not suffer additional expenses and unwarranted inconveniences because of his assumption of this position of responsibility toward my children, and that he shall be fully and liberally compensated out of income or principal for all additional expenses occasioned by his guardianship duties" argues in favor of a mandatory direction. But the next statement, "for which reimbursement should be made," and the last sentence concerning "the decision" argue in favor of discretionary reimbursement. Making a distinction is important both in the situation where the trustee and guardian are

different persons and where they are the same. In the one case a trustee may overemphasize his role as a conservator not wishing to deplete the trust assets, and in the other a conscientious guardian-trustee may resolve all doubts in favor of the trust. If Adam feels strongly about the reimbursement, I would recommend the use of mandatory language.

6. I hope Adam has selected wisely in naming the guardian and trustee, for the fiduciary has certainly been given very liberal and beneficial powers. If Adam's children were in their teens, would he want to create a trust under which the trustee-guardian can benefit himself individually?

7. In paragraph 6 of Article III I am pleased you have enumerated specific trustee powers. Too often a draftsman simply incorporates all powers given a trustee under the state's Trust Act without considering that a transfer agent or other person dealing with the trustee must refer to the Act to see if the trustee has the authority he is trying to exercise.

8. In paragraph 8 of Article III you have provided for approval of the trustee's accounts by an instrument signed by your adult children and guardians of your minor children. I have two questions. First, must at least one adult child sign the instrument or is the instrument effective if all the children are minors and only the guardians sign? Second, if the latter is true, then is this instrument legally effective? Where the trustee and guardian are the same person, as this will provides, I doubt whether the guardian could release the trustee in an instrument binding on the children. If the guardian could, then the guardian-trustee has in effect a fee simple, which is inconsistent with the notion that a trust has been created.

PROBLEMS

f. Redraft paragraph 8 to eliminate the ambiguity pointed out by Mr. Gibson.

g. Where the guardian and trustee are the same person, is the paragraph effective or wise? If not, redraft the paragraph so as to make it effective and to avoid a court accounting.

9. In your memorandum you state that Adam's life insurance proceeds are to be added to the trust under a secondary beneficiary designation of "the trustee named in my will." Will this work in a state that follows Frost v. Frost (page 394), or in a state that has not ruled on the question?

PROBLEM

h. Since the Smith life insurance proceeds are the most important assets in terms of value, how can we integrate their disposition with the testamentary trust provisions?

Subject to these observations, some of which reflect more my own personal preferences in style rather than substantive objections, I think this will provides an effective dispositive plan for the Smiths. I wonder what other law professors and law students will have to say.

/s/ wwg

Appendix D. Unfunded Revocable Life Insurance Trust and Pour-Over Will for Adam Smith (Common Law State)

TRUST AGREEMENT
ADAM SMITH REVOCABLE LIFE INSURANCE TRUST

This trust agreement is made this 25th day of September, 19......, at Arlington, ..., between Adam Smith as Settlor, and the Arlington National Bank, of Arlington, ..., as Trustee.

The Settlor has delivered to the Trustee the life insurance policies described in the attached schedule, and has caused or will cause the Trustee to be designated as beneficiary of them. These policies, and any other policies that may be delivered to the Trustee and of which the Trustee may be designated as beneficiary, the proceeds of all such policies payable to the Trustee, and any other property that may be received by the Trustee, whether from the Settlor during his lifetime or under the Settlor's will, or from any other person or source, shall be held, administered and disposed of as follows:

ARTICLE I

During his lifetime the Settlor may revoke this agreement in whole or in part, and may amend it from time to time in any respect. Revocation or amendment shall be by written instrument signed by the Settlor, and shall be effective upon delivery of the instrument to the Trustee during the Settlor's lifetime. On revocation of this agreement in its entirety, the Trustee shall deliver to the Settlor, or as he directs, all of the trust property.

The Settlor's will may provide for additions to the trust property, and consequently the Settlor's will should be examined in connection with the making of any amendment or revocation of the trust agreement to determine what changes, if any, should be made in the Settlor's will in the light of such amendment or revocation.

Article II

If during the Settlor's lifetime there is any income from the trust property, the Trustee shall pay all of the net income to the Settlor.

Article III

During the Settlor's lifetime the Settlor shall have all rights under the life insurance policies payable to the Trustee, including the right to change the beneficiaries thereunder, the right to assign any of the policies to any lender, the right to use any of the policies as securities for loans made to the Settlor or to any other person, and the right to borrow against the cash surrender values in the policies. The Trustee shall have no responsibility with respect to any policies, for the payment of premiums or otherwise, except to hold for safekeeping any policies that are delivered to the Trustee, and to deliver them upon the Settlor's written request. If any policy is surrendered or if the beneficiary of any policy is changed, this trust shall be revoked with respect to it. However, no revocation of the trust with respect to any policy, whether pursuant to the provisions of the preceding sentence or otherwise, shall be effective unless the surrender or change of beneficiary of the policy is accepted by the insurance company. Upon the death of the Settlor, with respect to any policy held by or known to, and payable to, the Trustee, the Trustee in its discretion either may collect the net proceeds and hold them as part of the principal of the trust estate or may exercise any optional method of settlement available to it. Payment to and the receipt of the Trustee shall be a full discharge of the liability of any life insurance company, which need not take notice of this instrument or see to the application of any payment. The Trustee may compromise, arbitrate, or otherwise adjust claims upon any policy, and may engage in litigation to enforce payment of any policy; provided that if any of the foregoing actions is taken the Trustee shall be indemnified for any resulting expense.

Article IV

Upon the Settlor's death the Trustee shall distribute the trust property to such person or persons, upon such conditions and estates, in trust or otherwise, with such powers, in such manner and at such time or times, as the Settlor appoints by will specifically referring to this power of appointment. If or to the extent that the Settlor does not effectively exercise this power of appointment, after the Settlor's death the Trustee shall hold and dispose of the trust property as follows:

1. If the Settlor's wife, Jane Smith, survives the Settlor, the Trustee shall as of

the date of the Settlor's death divide the trust property (including any property devised to the Trustee by the Settlor, and any proceeds of insurance on the life of the Settlor) into two separate shares. One share, called "Share A," shall consist of the following described fractional share of the trust property (exclusive of property or interests in property, if any, which would not qualify for the federal estate tax marital deduction if left outright to my wife): The numerator of the fraction shall be the maximum estate tax marital deduction (allowable in determining the federal estate tax payable by reason of the Settlor's death) minus the value for federal estate tax purposes of all items in the Settlor's gross estate which qualify for said deduction and which pass or have passed from the Settlor to his wife in a form which qualifies for the estate tax marital deduction (the words "pass or have passed" shall have the same meaning as such words shall have under the provisions of the Internal Revenue Code in effect at the time of the Settlor's death) under provisions of the Settlor's will other than the residuary clause thereof, by right of survivorship with respect to jointly owned property, under settlement arrangements relating to life insurance proceeds, and otherwise than under this fractional share gift of the trust estate (in computing the numerator, the values as finally determined for federal estate tax purposes shall control); and the denominator of the fraction shall be the value of the trust property (in computing the denominator, the value of the trust property shall be on the basis of values as finally determined for federal estate tax purposes). If the numerator of the above-described fraction equals or exceeds the denominator, the entire trust property shall be allocated to Share A.

The other share, called "Share B," shall consist of the fractional share of the trust property that remains after the fractional share allocable to Share A is determined.

The Settlor intends that the value for federal estate tax purposes of the property of Share A shall be available for the marital deduction allowed by the federal estate tax law applicable to his estate, and all questions applicable to this trust agreement shall be resolved accordingly. To this end, the powers and discretions of the trustees with respect to the property in Share A shall not be exercised or exercisable during the lifetime of the Settlor's wife except in a manner consistent with the Settlor's intentions as expressed in the preceding sentence.

2. If the Settlor's wife, Jane Smith, does not survive him, the Trustee shall hold and dispose of the trust property as one trust, called "Share B."

3. For the purposes of this trust agreement, in determining whether the Settlor's wife survives him, if the order of their deaths cannot be established by proof, the Settlor's wife shall be deemed to have survived him. If the Settlor's wife survives the Settlor but does not survive him by six months, the numerator or the above-described fraction used in determining the trust property allocable to Share A shall be reduced by a sum equal to one-half of the amount by which the value of the adjusted gross estate of the Settlor's wife exceeds the value of the items in the Settlor's gross estate (which are also in his wife's gross estate) which qualify for the estate tax marital deduction in determining the Settlor's taxable estate for federal estate tax purposes.

Article V

This Article contains the dispositive terms applicable to Share A.

1. During the lifetime of the Settlor's wife, the Trustee shall pay the net income of Share A to her. Payments shall be in convenient installments at least as often as quarter-annually. In addition, the Trustee shall pay to the Settlor's wife, or as she directs, from the principal of Share A, from time to time, such amount or amounts or all of the principal as the Settlor's wife may specify in an instrument or instruments in writing delivered to the Trustee during her lifetime. In addition, the Trustee may pay to the Settlor's wife, from the principal of Share A, from time to time, such amount or amounts or all of the principal as in its discretion is deemed necessary for her comfortable support, care, and benefit, without regard to her other sources of income.

2. Upon the death of the Settlor's wife, the Trustee shall pay the then remaining principal of Share A, and the income therefrom for the period between the last income distribution date and the date of her death, to, or hold for the benefit of, such person or persons or the estate of the Settlor's wife, upon such conditions and estates, in trust or otherwise, with such powers, in such manner and at such time or times, as the Settlor's wife shall appoint by a will, executed after the Settlor's death, specifically referring to this power of appointment. If or to the extent that she does not effectively exercise this power of appointment, the Trustee shall pay said principal and undistributed income as follows:

(a) If children or other descendants of the Settlor are then living or a widow of a deceased son of the Settlor who has not remarried is then living, the Trustee shall add the same to the principal of Share B.

(b) If none of the persons enumerated in paragraph (a) is then living, the Trustee shall pay the same to those persons who would have inherited the Settlor's personal property were the Settlor to have died intestate the moment after the death of the Settlor's wife, not married and domiciled in the state of ...., under the laws of the state of .... in force at that time, the shares and proportions of taking to be determined by said laws.

Article VI

This Article contains the dispositive terms applicable to Share B.

1. During the lifetime of the Settlor's wife and for so long as she remains unmarried, the Trustee shall pay the net income of Share B to her. Payments shall be in convenient installments at least as often as quarter-annually. In addition, the Trustee may pay to or on behalf of the Settlor's wife, any of the Settlor's descendants, any widow of a deceased son of the Settlor who has not remarried, or any one or more of the foregoing persons, from the principal of Share B, from time to time, such amount or amounts or all of the principal as in its discretion is deemed necessary for the comfortable support, care, and benefit of any such person or per-

sons, taking into account other sources of income that may be available for these purposes. With respect to distributions of principal to the Settlor's wife, the Settlor recommends, but does not require, that the Trustee consider making distributions from the principal of Share A under the discretionary power given the Trustee by paragraph 1 of Article V, before making distributions of principal under the discretionary power given by this paragraph.

2. If the Settlor's wife remarries, during such time as she remains married the Trustee may from time to time pay to or on behalf of the Settlor's wife, any of the Settlor's children or other descendants, any widow of a deceased son of the Settlor who has not remarried, or any one or more of the foregoing persons, such amount or amounts or all of the net income and principal of Share B as in its discretion is deemed necessary for the comfortable support, care, and benefit of any such person or persons, taking into account other sources of income that may be available for these purposes. To the extent that net income is not distributed pursuant to this discretionary power, it shall be added to the principal of Share B.

Should the Settlor's wife, having remarried, again become unmarried because of divorce or the death of her husband, the provisions of paragraph 1 of this Article shall be applicable.

3. Upon the death of the Settlor's wife, the Trustee shall pay the then remaining principal and accumulated income of Share B to, or hold for the benefit of, such one or more of the Settlor's children or other descendants, or any widow of a deceased son of the Settlor who has not remarried, upon such conditions and estates, in trust or otherwise, with such powers, in such manner and at such time or times, as the Settlor's wife shall appoint by a will, executed after the Settlor's death, specifically referring to this power of appointment. If or to the extent that she does not effectively exercise this power of appointment, the Trustee shall pay said principal and accumulated income as follows:

(a) If on the death of the Settlor's wife one or more of the Settlor's children are then living, or an unmarried widow of a deceased son of the Settlor is then living, but no child of the Settlor is under the age of twenty-five years, the Trustee shall pay the same to the Settlor's children or other descendants, per stirpes. If any son of the Settlor dies before termination of the trust under this paragraph (a), not leaving descendants who are living at the termination of the trust, but leaving a widow who is living at the termination of the trust and who has not remarried, the share that would have been paid to the son were he then living shall instead be paid to the son's widow.

(b) If on the death of the Settlor's wife one or more of the Settlor's children are then living but at least one child is under the age of twenty-five years, the Trustee may from time to time pay to or on behalf of any of the Settlor's children or other descendants, any Guardian of a minor child or other descendant of the Settlor, any widow of a deceased son of the Settlor who has not remarried, or any one or more of the foregoing persons, such amount or amounts or all of the net income and principal of Share B as in its discretion is deemed necessary for the comfortable support, care, and benefit of any such person or persons, taking into account other sources of income that may be available for these purposes. To the extent that net income is not distributed pursuant to this discretionary power, it shall be added to the principal of Share B. As a guide to the Trustee, but without intending to limit or control its discretion, the Settlor offers the following expressions of intent as to the purposes of this paragraph (b):

(i) The Settlor's primary objective is to provide for the support and health needs of his children, their descendants, and any unmarried widow of a deceased son of the Settlor. A secondary objective is to provide funds for the education of these persons. But if any beneficiary has unusual health or medical problems, these shall first be provided for before distributions are made for any other purpose. In the absence of competing considerations, the Trustee should make an effort to provide equality of distribution among the Settlor's children and their families. However, disparate needs may and probably will arise, particularly as to health and medical expenses, and perhaps also as to educational expenses. The Trustee should not hesitate to make unequal distributions if in its discretion such unequal distributions are deemed appropriate.

(ii) It is not the Settlor's primary objective, in establishing this trust, to provide a cash distribution to his children, their descendants, or any unmarried widow of a deceased son, living at the termination of the trust. If, after the health or other needs of the beneficiaries have been met during the term of the trust, there is a fund remaining at the trust's termination, well and good. But the Trustee should not be conservative in making interim distributions of principal and income simply to provide lump-sum gifts upon the trust's termination.

(iii) Should this paragraph (b) be operative while any of the Settlor's children or other descendants are minors, such minor beneficiaries will be in the custody and care of a Guardian of their persons. This is bound to increase the household expenses and cramp the living quarters of the Guardian and her or his family. It is the Settlor's intent that the Guardian shall not suffer additional expenses and unwarranted inconveniences because of the assumption of this position of responsibility toward his children, and that the Guardian shall be fully and liberally reimbursed out of the income or principal of Share B for all additional living expenses occasioned by her or his guardianship duties. It is for this reason that the Guardians of any minor children of the Settlor have been named permissible distributees. As illustrative of the types of expenditures for which distribution to the Guardian might be made, the following can be considered by the Trustee as for the comfortable support, care, and benefit of minor beneficiaries: The purchase of a larger residence or the remodeling of an existing residence in order to provide appropriate accommodations for the minor beneficiaries (the trust to bear the difference between the present value of the existing house and the cost of a new house, if a larger residence is purchased), without any obligation to reimburse the trust estate; and additional expenses for food, utilities, furniture and domestic help occasioned by inclusion of the Settlor's children in the Guardian's family unit. Although these expenditures may be seen as indirectly benefiting the Guardian in his individual capacity, they are seen by the Settlor as necessary to provide any minor beneficiaries with the style and comforts of life the Settlor would have provided them if he were living. If the Trustee makes distribution to a Guardian, its decision that the distribution is within the discretionary power given by this paragraph (b) shall be conclusive.

This trust shall terminate when there are no living children of the Settlor under the age of twenty-five years. Upon termination, the Trustee shall pay the trust principal and accumulated income to the Settlor's descendants who are then living, per stirpes. If any son of the Settlor dies before termination of the trust, not leaving descendants who are living at the termination of the trust, but leaving a widow who is living at the termination of the trust and who has not remarried, the share that would have been paid to the son were he then living shall instead be paid to the son's widow. If none of the foregoing persons is living at the termination of the trust, the Trustee shall pay the trust principal and accumulated income to those persons who would have inherited the Settlor's personal property were the Settlor to have died intestate one day after the date of termination of the trust, not married and domiciled in the state of ...., under the laws of the state of .... in force at that time, the shares and proportions of taking to be determined by said laws.

(c) If upon the death of the Settlor's wife no children or other descendants of the Settlor are then living, and no unmarried widow of a deceased son of the Settlor is then living, the Trustee shall pay the same to those persons who would have inherited the Settlor's personal property were the Settlor to have died intestate one day after the date of death of the Settlor's wife, not married and domiciled in the state of ...., under the laws of the state of .... in force at that time, the shares and proportions of taking to be determined by said laws.

Article VII

If under Articles V or VI the Trustee is directed to distribute a share of the trust property to a beneficiary who is under the age of twenty-one years when the distribution is to be made, the share shall vest in interest in the beneficiary indefeasibly, but the Trustee may in its discretion continue to hold the share until the beneficiary reaches age twenty-one, and in the meantime the Trustee may distribute to or apply for his benefit so much of the net income and principal of the share as the Trustee deems necessary for his comfortable support, care, and benefit, without regard to other sources of income that may be available for these purposes, any net income not so distributed to be accumulated.

Article VIII

Notwithstanding anything in this agreement to the contrary, any trust under this instrument shall terminate, if it has not previously terminated, twenty-one years after the death of the last survivor of the Settlor, the Settlor's wife, and the Settlor's children living at the date of this instrument, and the Trustee shall pay the principal and undistributed income to the Settlor's descendants then living, per stirpes. If none of the Settlor's descendants is then living, the Trustee shall pay the same to those persons who would have inherited the Settlor's personal property were the Settlor to have died intestate at such time, not married and domiciled in the state of ...., under the laws of the state of .... in force at that time, the shares and proportions of taking to be determined by said laws.

Article IX

No interest under this agreement shall be transferable or assignable, or be subject during any beneficiary's lifetime to the claims of his creditors.

Article X

The purpose of this Article is to permit the use of assets in Share B as the source of funds for payment of various obligations that arise by reason of the Settlor's death, in the event that the nature or value of the residuary assets in the Settlor's probate estate make it difficult or inadvisable to satisfy these obligations out of the residuary estate. None of the powers granted by this Article shall be exercisable with respect to the interest or principal of Share A.

Upon the Settlor's death the Trustee, using the principal or income from Share B, may in its uncontrolled discretion:

1. Pay all or a portion of: the Settlor's funeral expenses; legally enforceable claims against the Settlor or his estate; reasonable expenses of administration of his estate; any family allowance, cash award in lieu of homestead, or cash award in lieu of exempt personal property, that is ordered by a probate court in the course of administration of the Settlor's estate; and state inheritance and federal and state estate taxes payable by reason of the Settlor's death, together with any interest thereon or additions thereto, other than taxes attributable to the value of assets over which the Settlor held a power of appointment that was granted to the Settlor by someone other than himself. If the Trustee makes such payments he shall not seek reimbursement from the Settlor's executors or administrators or other persons who might otherwise be required to make these payments. These payments may be

made directly to the Settlor's executor or administrator or to the persons entitled or authorized to receive them, upon a certificate from the Settlor's executor or administrator stating the amount due and payable, and the Trustee shall not be bound to inquire into the legality or amount of such payments so certified. Payments made in the bona fide belief that they are pursuant to this Article X shall not be open to question by anyone. Proceeds received by the Trustee under a qualified pension or profit-sharing plan by reason of the Settlor's death shall not be used for the foregoing purposes. Proceeds of insurance on the Settlor's life shall not be used for the foregoing purposes except to the extent that other assets of Share B are insufficient.

2. Purchase and retain as trust property any real or personal property belonging to the estate of the Settlor.

3. Make loans to the Settlor's executor or administrator on such terms as the Trustee deems advisable.

Article XI

The Trustee shall have the following powers and discretions, and any others that may be granted by law, to be exercised without court order:

(a) To retain all property devised or transferred to the Trustee, including residential property, regardless of any lack of diversification, risk, or lack of productivity. With respect to any items of tangible personal property that are devised to the Trustee, the Trustee may in its discretion hold all or any part of them until termination of the trust, deliver all or any part of them at any time to a beneficiary for his use or to any person with whom a beneficiary is residing, without further responsibility, or may sell all or any part of them and add the proceeds to the principal of the trust.

(b) To invest and reinvest the trust estate in any property, including stocks, regardless of class, investment trusts, mutual funds, and common trust funds, without being limited by any statute or rule of law concerning investments by trustees.

(c) To sell any trust property for cash or on credit at public or private sale; to exchange any trust property for other property; to grant options to purchase or acquire any property; to lease any trust property; and to determine the prices and terms of sales, exchanges, options and leases.

(d) To borrow money and to mortgage or pledge any trust property.

(e) To employ attorneys, accountants, and investment advisers, and to act without independent investigation upon their recommendations, and to employ depositaries, proxies, and agents; and to keep any property in the name of a trustee or a nominee, with or without disclosure of any fiduciary relationship, or in bearer form.

(f) To take any action with respect to conserving or realizing upon the value of any trust property, and with respect to foreclosures, reorganizations or other changes affecting any trust property; and to collect, pay, contest, compromise, or abandon claims of or against the trust estate.

(g) To make any distribution of trust property in cash or in kind or both; and to allocate different kinds or disproportionate shares of property or undivided interests in property among the beneficiaries, and to determine the value of any such property.

Article XII

1. This agreement and the dispositions hereunder shall be construed and regulated and their validity and effect shall be determined by the law of ....

2. No person paying money or delivering any property to the Trustee need see to its application.

3. The Trustee shall be entitled to reasonable compensation for services in administering and distributing the trust property, and to reimbursement for expenses.

4. The Trustee may resign at any time by a signed instrument filed with the trust records, after giving written notice, specifying the effective date of resignation, to the Settlor's wife or, if she is not then living, to the Settlor's adult children and to the Guardians of the persons of the Settlor's minor children. If the Trustee resigns or is unable or refuses to act, another corporation, authorized under the laws of the United States or of any state to administer trusts, may be appointed as Trustee in its place by an instrument filed with the trust records and signed by the Settlor's wife or, if she is not then living, signed by a majority of the Settlor's adult children and Guardians of the persons of the Settlor's minor children. Any successor Trustee shall have all the title, powers and discretions of the Trustee succeeded, without conveyance or transfer. Any successor Trustee shall not be accountable for any act or default of, or have any responsibility for the accounts of, any other Trustee.

5. No Trustee shall be required:

a. To give bond.

b. To qualify before or (in the absence of breach of trust) account to any court.

c. To obtain the order or approval of any court in the exercise of any power or discretion hereunder.

d. To be personally liable upon any contract, note, or other instrument executed hereunder or for any indebtedness of the trust estate.

6. After the death of the Settlor, the approval of the accounts of the Trustee, in an instrument signed by the Settlor's wife (or, if she is not then living, by the Settlor's adult children and the Guardians of the persons of the Settlor's minor children) shall be a complete discharge and release of the Trustee with respect to the administration of the trust property for the period covered by such accounts, binding on all persons, provided always, however, that nothing contained in this Article XII shall be deemed to give the Settlor's wife (or the Settlor's children or Guardians of children) acting in conjunction with the Trustee the power to alter, amend, revoke, or terminate the trust or the power to appoint the trust property to

such person, the creditors of such person, such person's estate, or the creditors of such person's estate.

Article XIII

Following are definitions of various terms used in this agreement.

1. The term "children" includes children hereafter born to or adopted by the Settlor, as well as the children of the Settlor living on the date of this agreement. The term "descendants" means the immediate and remote lawful, lineal descendants by blood or adoption of the person referred to who are in being at the time they must be ascertained in order to give effect to the reference to them. However, the term "descendants" shall not include persons adopted after they reach the age of twenty-one.

2. The term "per stirpes" means that property shall be distributed to the persons and in the proportions that the Settlor's personal property would be distributed under the laws of the state of .... in force on the specified date of distribution if the Settlor had died intestate at such time, domiciled in such state, not married and survived by descendants.

3. References in this agreement to the male gender shall include the female and neuter gender, unless otherwise stated or unless the circumstances eliminate such inclusion.

This instrument is signed and sealed on the date first above written.

______________________________ [SEAL]
Adam Smith, Settlor

Arlington National Bank [SEAL]
Trustee

BY ______________________________
Vice President and Trust
Officer, Arlington
National Bank

Attest:

____

____

SCHEDULE

[Here listed are Adam Smith's life insurance policies.]

LAST WILL OF ADAM SMITH

I, Adam Smith, of 2220 Casino Lane, Arlington, ... County, ..., declare this to be my last Will, and I hereby revoke all wills and codicils heretofore made by me.

ARTICLE I. I give all the tangible personal property that I own or have an interest in at the time of my death, and all my interest in the real property at 2220 Casino Lane, Arlington, ... (or if I have no interest in said real property at the time of my death, all interest I may have in any other real property that is my principal residence at that time), as follows:

1. To my wife, Jane Smith, if she survives me by sixty days.

2. If she does not so survive me, the same shall be distributed under Article II as a part of my residuary estate.

ARTICLE II. I give all the rest and residue of my property of whatever kind and wherever located that I own at my death as follows:

1. If my wife survives me by sixty days, to the Arlington National Bank, of Arlington, ..., as Trustee, to be held and disposed of in accordance with a trust agreement made on the 25th day of September, 19____, as such trust agreement is amended on the date of my death.

2. If my wife does not survive me by sixty days, but a child of mine does survive me by sixty days and is at that time under the age of twenty-five years, to the Arlington National Bank, of Arlington, ..., as Trustee, to be held and disposed of in accordance with a trust agreement made on the 25th day of September, 19____, as such trust agreement is amended on the date of my death.

Adam Smith

3. If my wife does not survive me by sixty days, and no child of mine is at that time under the age of twenty-five years, to those persons who would have inherited my personal property were I to have died sixty days after the date of my actual death, not married and domiciled in the state of ...., under the laws of the state of .... in force at that time, the shares and proportions of taking to be determined by said laws, provided that if any of my sons shall be dead at that time, not leaving descendants then living but leaving a widow then living who has not remarried, the share that would have been paid to the son were he then living shall instead be paid to the son's widow.

ARTICLE III. I do not intend by this will to exercise any powers of appointment which I possess or may come to possess.

ARTICLE IV. I appoint my wife, Jane Smith, as Executrix of this will. If for any reason she is unable or unwilling to serve or continue to serve in that capacity, I appoint my good friend, Einar Paulson, of Arlington, ..., as Executor. If for any reason he, too, is unable or unwilling to serve or continue to serve in that capacity, I appoint the Arlington National Bank, of Arlington, ..., as Executor. My Executrix or Executor shall have the following powers and discretions, and any others that may be granted by law, to be exercised without court order:

(a) To retain all property of my estate, regardless of lack of diversification, risk, or nonproductivity;

(b) To sell any real or personal property of my estate, for cash or on credit, at public or private sale, for any purpose; to exchange any such property for other property; to grant options to purchase or acquire any such property; to lease any such property; and to determine the prices and terms of sales, exchanges, options, and leases;

(c) To borrow money and to mortgage or pledge any property of my estate;

(d) To employ attorneys, accountants, and investment advisers, and to act without independent investigation upon their recommendations, and to employ depositaries, proxies, and agents; and to keep any property in the name of an executor or a nominee, with or without disclosure of any fiduciary relationship, or in bearer form;

(e) To collect, pay, contest, compromise, or abandon claims of or against my estate, wherever situated; and to execute contracts, notes, conveyances, and other instruments, including instruments containing covenants and warranties binding upon and creating a charge against my estate, and containing provisions excluding personal liability;

(f) To make any distribution of my estate in cash or in kind or both; and

(g) To allocate different kinds or disproportionate shares of property or undivided interests in property among the beneficiaries, and to determine the value of such property.

ARTICLE V. If my wife does not survive me, or if she dies after my death without having made provision for the custody and care of my minor children, or for the management of such children's estates, I appoint my sister-in-law, Barbara Preston Widman, of San Francisco, California, as Guardian of the persons and estates of my minor children. If for any reason she is unable or unwilling to serve or continue to serve in that capacity, I appoint my brother, Henry M. Smith, of Salem, ..., as Guardian of the persons and estates of my minor children.

Adam Smith

The Guardian shall arrange for the welfare and education of my children according to the dictates of her or his conscience, shall have the authority to determine what is in the best interest of my children, and may expend the income and principal from the children's estates as in her or his sole discretion is deemed appropriate for their support, maintenance, and education.

ARTICLE VI. I direct that no bond or other security shall be required, in any jurisdiction, of any person named in this will as Executrix, Executor, or Guardian.

ARTICLE VII. The term "children" as used in this will includes children hereafter born to or adopted by me, as well as the children that I now have. The term "descendants" as used in this will means the immediate and remote lawful, lineal descendants by blood or adoption of the person referred to who are in being at the time they must be ascertained in order to give effect to the reference to them. However, the term "descendants" shall not include persons adopted after they reach the age of twenty-one.

ARTICLE VIII. My wife and I are at approximately the same time executing wills containing similar dispositive provisions. These wills are not the product of any contract or agreement, and my wife shall be free to dispose of any property (whether acquired under this will or otherwise) either during her lifetime or by will as she sees fit.

I have signed this will, which is typewritten on three sheets of paper, on this _______ day of ______________, 19___, and have also written my name on the margin of the first two pages hereof.

____

Adam Smith

On the _______ day of ______________, 19___, Adam Smith declared to us, the undersigned, that the foregoing instrument was his last will, and he requested us to act as witnesses to it and to his signature thereon. He then signed the will in our presence, we being present at the same time. We now, at his request, in his presence, and in the presence of each other, hereunto subscribe our names as witnesses, and each of us declares that in his or her opinion this testator is of sound and disposing mind and memory.

______________________	______________________
Name	Address
______________________	______________________
Name	Address
______________________	______________________
Name	Address

Appendix E. Unfunded Revocable Life Insurance Trust and Pour-Over Will for Adam Smith (Community Property State)

TRUST AGREEMENT
ADAM SMITH FAMILY TRUST

This trust agreement is made this 25th day of September, 19......, at Arlington, ..., between Adam Smith and his wife, Jane Smith, as Settlors, and the Arlington National Bank, of Arlington, ..., as Trustee.

The Settlors have delivered to the Trustee the life insurance policies described in the attached schedule, and have caused or will cause the Trustee to be designated as beneficiary of them. These policies, which are the community property of the Settlors, and any other policies that may be delivered to the Trustee and of which the Trustee may be designated as beneficiary, the proceeds of all such policies payable to the Trustee, and any other property that may be received by the Trustee, whether from either of the Settlors during his or her lifetime or under the will of either Settlor, or from any other person or source, shall be held, administered, and disposed of as follows:

ARTICLE I

1. This trust shall be known as the Adam Smith Family Trust.

2. It is not the intent of either of the Settlors to alter or in any way affect the ownership of assets placed in this trust, or mutations thereof, during the joint lives of the Settlors. As long as both of the Settlors are living, all interests and powers of the Settlors or either of them with respect to community property placed in this trust shall be held by them as community property.

3. As long as both of the Settlors are living, if there is any income from the trust property the Trustee shall pay all of the net income of the trust to the Settlors or to either of them.

Article II

1. As long as both of the Settlors are living, the Settlors may revoke this agreement in whole or in part, and may amend it from time to time in any respect. (If in the opinion of the Trustee one of the Settlors does not have legal capacity, the other Settlor may revoke this agreement in whole or in part, or may amend it from time to time in any respect.) Revocation or amendment shall be by written instrument signed by both of the Settlors (or by the Settlor having legal capacity), and shall be effective upon delivery of the instrument to the Trustee during the Settlors' lifetime. The Trustee shall deliver to the Settlors, or as the Settlors (or the Settlor having legal capacity) shall direct, the assets removed from the trust by the exercise of this power. Community assets removed from the trust by the exercise of this power shall retain their character as community property.

2. Upon the death of one of the Settlors, the terms of this agreement, insofar as they apply to Share B of the trust (as hereinafter defined), shall be irrevocable and shall not be subject to amendment by the surviving Settlor. Insofar as the terms of this agreement apply to Share A of the trust (as hereinafter defined), the surviving Settlor may revoke the agreement in whole or in part, and may amend it from time to time in any respect. Revocation or amendment shall be by written instrument signed by the surviving Settlor, and shall be effective upon delivery of the instrument to the Trustee during the surviving Settlor's lifetime. The Trustee shall deliver to the surviving Settlor, or as he or she directs, the assets removed from the trust by the exercise of this power.

3. The wills of either Settlor may provide for additions to the trust property, and consequently their wills should be examined in connection with the making of any amendment or revocation of the trust agreement to determine what changes, if any, should be made in their wills in the light of such amendment or revocation.

Article III

As long as both of the Settlors are living, the Settlors shall have all rights under the life insurance policies payable to the Trustee, including the right to change the beneficiaries thereunder, the right to assign any of the policies to any lender, the right to use any of the policies as securities for loans made to the Settlors or to either of them or to any other person, and the right to borrow against the cash surrender values in the policies.

If Jane Smith predeceases Adam Smith, Adam Smith shall have all rights with respect to his proportionate interest (as determined by the laws of the state of ....) in any of the life insurance policies payable to the Trustee, including the right to change the beneficiaries with respect to his interest thereunder, the right to assign his interest in any of the policies to any lender, the right to use his interest in any of the policies as securities for loans made to Adam Smith or to any other person, and the right to borrow against his interest in or his share of the cash surrender values in the policies. Adam Smith shall have no rights with respect to that portion of the life insurance policies, or any interest therein, that represents Jane Smith's community interest therein as determined by said laws.

The Trustee shall have no responsibility with respect to any policies or any portions thereof, for the payment of premiums or otherwise, except to hold for safekeeping any policies that are delivered to the Trustee, and to deliver them upon the Settlors' written request. If any policy is surrendered or if the beneficiary of any policy is changed, this trust shall be revoked with respect to it. However, no revocation of the trust with respect to any policy or portion thereof, whether pursuant to the preceding sentence or otherwise, shall be effective unless the surrender or change of beneficiary of the policy or portion thereof is accepted by the insurance company. Upon the death of Adam Smith, with respect to any policy held by or known to, and payable to, the Trustee, the Trustee in its discretion either may collect the net proceeds and hold them as part of the principal of the trust estate or may exercise any optional method of settlement available to it. Payment to and the receipt of the Trustee shall be a full discharge of the liability of any life insurance company, which need not take notice of this instrument or see to the application of any payment. The Trustee may compromise, arbitrate, or otherwise adjust claims upon any policy, and may engage in litigation to enforce payment of any policy; provided that if any of the foregoing actions is taken the Trustee shall be indemnified for any resulting expense.

Article IV

After the death of the first Settlor to die (hereinafter referred to as the deceased Settlor), the trust property shall be held, administered, and disposed of as two separate shares.

1. One share, called Share A, shall consist of the sum of the following:

    a. The surviving Settlor's share of the community property of the Settlors held in or payable to this trust; and

    b. The surviving Settlor's separate property held in or payable to this trust.

2. One share, called Share B, shall consist of the sum of the following:

    a. The deceased Settlor's share of the community property of the Settlors held in or payable to this trust; and

    b. The deceased Settlor's separate property held in or payable to this trust.

Article V

This Article contains the dispositive terms applicable to Share A.

1. During the lifetime of the surviving Settlor, the Trustee shall pay the net income of Share A to the surviving Settlor. Payments shall be in convenient install-

ments at least as often as quarter-annually. In addition, the Trustee may pay to the surviving Settlor, from the principal of Share A, from time to time, such amount or amounts or all of the principal as in its discretion is deemed necessary for the surviving Settlor's comfortable support, care, and benefit, without regard to his or her other sources of income.

2. Upon the death of the surviving Settlor, the Trustee shall pay the principal of Share A, and the income therefrom for the period between the last income distribution date and the date of his or her death, to, or hold for the benefit of, such person or persons or the estate of the surviving Settlor, upon such conditions and estates, in trust or otherwise, with such powers, in such manner and at such time or times, as the surviving Settlor shall appoint by a will, executed after the deceased Settlor's death, specifically referring to this power of appointment. If or to the extent that the surviving Settlor does not effectively exercise this power of appointment, the Trustee shall pay said principal and undistributed income as follows:

(a) If children or other descendants of the Settlors are then living or a widow of a deceased son of the Settlors who has not remarried is then living, the Trustee shall add the same to the principal of Share B.

(b) If none of the persons enumerated in paragraph (a) is then living, the Trustee shall pay the same as follows: One-half to those persons who would have inherited the surviving Settlor's personal property were he or she to have died intestate the moment after his or her actual death, not married and domiciled in the state of ...., under the laws of the state of .... in force at that time, the shares and proportions of taking to be determined by said laws; and one-half to those persons who would have inherited the deceased Settlor's personal property were he or she to have died intestate the moment after the death of the surviving Settlor, not married and domiciled in the state of ...., under the laws of the state of .... in force at that time, the shares and proportions of taking to be determined by said laws.

Article VI

This Article contains the dispositive terms applicable to Share B.

1. During the lifetime of the surviving Settlor, the Trustee shall pay the net income of Share B to the surviving Settlor. Payments shall be in convenient installments at least as often as quarter-annually. In addition, the Trustee may pay to or on behalf of the surviving Settlor, any of the Settlors' descendants, any widow of a deceased son of the Settlors who has not remarried, or any one or more of the foregoing persons, from the principal of Share B, from time to time, such amount or amounts or all of the principal as in its discretion is deemed necessary for the comfortable support, care, and benefit of any such person or persons, taking into account other sources of income that may be available for these purposes. With respect to distributions of principal to the surviving Settlor, the Settlors recommend, but do not require, that the Trustee consider making distributions from the principal of Share A under the discretionary power given the Trustee by paragraph 1 of

Article V, before making distributions of principal under the discretionary power given by this paragraph.

2. Upon the death of the surviving Settlor, the Trustee shall pay the principal of Share B, and the income therefrom for the period between the last income distribution date and the date of his or her death, to, or hold for the benefit of, such one or more of the Settlor's children or other descendants, or any unmarried widow of a deceased son of the Settlors who has not remarried, upon such conditions and estates, in trust or otherwise, with such powers, in such manner and at such time or times, as the surviving Settlor shall appoint by a will, executed after the deceased Settlor's death, specifically referring to this power of appointment. If or to the extent that the surviving Settlor does not effectively exercise this power of appointment, the Trustee shall pay said principal and undistributed income as follows:

(a) If on the death of the surviving Settlor one or more of the Settlors' children are then living, or an unmarried widow of a deceased son of the Settlors is then living, but no child of the Settlors is under the age of twenty-five years, the Trustee shall pay the same to the Settlors' children or other descendants, per stirpes. If any son of the Settlors dies before termination of the trust under this paragraph (a), not leaving descendants who are living at the termination of the trust, but leaving a widow who is living at the termination of the trust and who has not remarried, the share that would have been paid to the son were he then living shall instead be paid to the son's widow.

(b) If on the death of the surviving Settlor one or more of the Settlors' children are then living but at least one child is under the age of twenty-five years, the Trustee may from time to time pay to or on behalf of any of the Settlors' children or other descendants, any Guardian of a minor child or other descendant of the Settlors, any widow of a deceased son of the Settlors who has not remarried, or any one or more of the foregoing persons, such amount or amounts or all of the net income and principal of Share B as in its discretion is deemed necessary for the comfortable support, care, and benefit of any such person or persons, taking into account other sources of income that may be available for these purposes. To the extent that net income is not distributed pursuant to this discretionary power, it shall be added to the principal of Share B. As a guide to the Trustee, but without intending to limit or control its discretion, the Settlors offer the following expressions of intent as to the purposes of this paragraph (b):

(i) The Settlors' primary objective . . . [see Article VI, paragraph 3(b)(i), page 1114].

(ii) It is not the Settlors' primary objective . . . [see Article VI, paragraph 3(b)(ii), page 1114].

(iii) Should this paragraph (b) be operative while any of the Settlors' children or other descendants are minors, . . . [see Article VI, paragraph 3(b)(iii), page 1114].

This trust shall terminate when there are no living children of the Settlors under the age of twenty-five years. Upon termination, the Trustee shall pay the trust principal and undistributed income to the Settlors' children or other descendants who are then living, per stirpes. If any son of the Settlors dies before termination of the trust, not leaving descendants who are living at the termination of the trust, but leaving a widow who is living at the termination of the trust and who has not remarried, the share that would have been paid to the son were he then living shall instead be paid to the son's widow. If none of the foregoing persons is living at the termination of the trust, the Trustee shall pay the trust principal and undistributed income as follows: One-half to those persons who would have inherited the surviving Settlor's personal property were he or she to have died intestate the moment after his or her actual death, not married and domiciled in the state of ...., under the laws of the state of .... in force at that time, the shares and proportions of taking to be determined by said laws; and one-half to those persons who would have inherited the deceased Settlor's personal property were he or she to have died intestate the moment after the death of the surviving Settlor, not married and domiciled in the state of ...., under the laws of the state of .... in force at that time, the shares and proportions of taking to be determined by said laws.

Article VII

If under Articles V or VI the Trustee is directed to distribute a share of the trust property to a beneficiary who is under the age of twenty-one years when the distribution is to be made, the share shall vest in interest in the beneficiary indefeasibly, but the Trustee may in its discretion continue to hold the share until the beneficiary reaches age twenty-one, and in the meantime the Trustee may distribute to or apply for his benefit so much of the net income and principal of the share as the Trustee deems necessary for his comfortable support, care, and benefit, without regard to other sources of income that may be available for these purposes, any net income not so distributed to be accumulated.

Article VIII

Notwithstanding anything in this agreement to the contrary, any trust under this instrument shall terminate, if it has not previously terminated, twenty-one years after the death of the last survivor of the settlors and the settlors' children living at the date of this instrument, and the Trustee shall pay the same to the Settlors' descendants then living, per stirpes. If none of the Settlors' descendants is then living, the Trustee shall pay the same as follows: One-half to those persons who would have inherited the surviving Settlor's personal property were he or she to have died intestate at that time, not married and domiciled in the state of ...., under the laws of the state of .... in force at that time, the shares and proportions of taking to be determined by said laws; and one-half to those persons who would have inherited the deceased Settlor's personal property were he or she to have died intestate at that time, not married and domiciled in the state of ...., under the laws of the state of

.... in force at that time, the shares and proportions of taking to be determined by said laws.

Article IX

No interest under this agreement shall be transferable or assignable, or be subject during any beneficiary's lifetime to the claims of his creditors.

Article: X-XIII

[See Articles X-XIII on pages 1116-1119. Several of these clauses would have to be reworded to reflect the fact that this trust has two settlors. Also, Article X could be redrafted to provide that the assets of Share A can be used for payment of various obligations that arise by reason of the deceased Settlor's death, and that assets of Share B can be used for payment of obligations that arise by reason of the surviving Settlor's death. The signature block and the schedule of assets for this trust are the same as those for the trust in Appendix D.]

Index